HMH SOCIAL STUDIES

EASTERN WORLD GEOGRAPHY

Printed in the U.S.A.

ISBN 978-0-544-66933-8

5 6 7 8 9 10 0690 26 25 24 23 22 21 20 19

4500787072 D E F G

Educational Advisory Panel

The following educators have provided review during development of HMH programs.

Jose Colon
Berkeley High School
Berkeley, California

Bethany Copeland
Peach County High School
Fort Valley, Georgia

Darrel Dexter
Egyptian Community Unit School
Tamms, Illinois

Charles Dietz
Burnett Middle School
San Jose, California

John Hogan
Brevard High School
Brevard, North Carolina

Jeffrey Kaufman
Aspirations Diploma Plus High School
Brooklyn, New York

Beth E. Kuhlman
Queens Metropolitan High School
Forest Hills, New York

Beatrice Nudelman
Aptakisic Junior High School
Buffalo Grove, Illinois

Kyle Race
Greene High School
Greene, New York

Gretchen Ritter Varela
Northville High School
Northville, Michigan

Sharon Shirley
Branford High School
Branford, Connecticut

Yvette Snopkowski
Davis Junior High School
Sterling Heights, Michigan

La-Shanda West
Cutler Bay Senior High School
Cutler Bay, Florida

Contents

Videos related to each module can be accessed through your digital Student Edition.

HISTORY® Partnership xii
Reading Social Studies H2
Using This Book H6
Explore Online H8

Module 1

A Geographer's World 2

Reading Social Studies Use Prior Knowledge 4

Lesson 1 Studying Geography 5
Lesson 2 The Branches of Geography 10
Lesson 3 Themes of Geography 16
Lesson 4 The Geographer's Tools 20
Lesson 5 Geography Handbook 24

Social Studies Skills Analyze Satellite Images 35
Module Assessment 36

Module 2

The Physical World 38

Reading Social Studies Use Word Parts 40

Lesson 1 Earth and the Sun's Energy 41
Lesson 2 Water on Earth 46
Lesson 3 The Land 52

Case Study The Ring of Fire 60

Lesson 4 Weather and Climate 62
Lesson 5 World Climates 68
Lesson 6 Environments and Biomes 77
Lesson 7 Natural Resources 82

Social Studies Skills Use a Physical Map 89
Module Assessment 90

Module 3

The Human World 92

Reading Social Studies Understand Main Ideas 94

Lesson 1 Elements of Culture 95
Lesson 2 Population 106
Lesson 3 Settlement Patterns 113
Lesson 4 Human-Environment Interaction 118
Social Studies Skills Organize Information 125
Module Assessment 126

Module 4

Government and Citizenship 128

Reading Social Studies Sequence 130

Lesson 1 A World of Nations 131
Lesson 2 World Governments 137
Lesson 3 Citizenship 145
Social Studies Skills Use a Problem-Solving Process 153
Module Assessment 154

Module 5

Economics 156

Reading Social Studies Draw Conclusions 158

Lesson 1 Economic Basics 159
Lesson 2 Economic Systems 164
Lesson 3 Money and Banking 173
Lesson 4 Living in a Global Economy 179
Social Studies Skills Determine the Strength of an Argument 185
Module Assessment 186

Module 6

Early Civilizations of the Fertile Crescent and the Nile Valley 188

Reading Social Studies Paraphrase 190

Lesson 1 Geography and River Valley Civilizations 191
Lesson 2 Sumerian Civilization 196
Lesson 3 Later Peoples of the Fertile Crescent 205
Lesson 4 Geography and Nile Valley Kingdoms 211
Lesson 5 The Middle and New Kingdoms 221
Lesson 6 Kingdoms of Kush 231

Social Studies Skills Analyze Primary and Secondary Sources 239
Module Assessment 240

Module 7

World Religions of Southwest Asia 242

Reading Social Studies Use Context Clues—Synonyms 244

Lesson 1 Origins of Judaism 245
Lesson 2 Origins of Christianity 253
Lesson 3 Origins of Islam 261

Social Studies Skills Interpret a Route Map 269
Module Assessment 270

Module 8

The Arabian Peninsula to Central Asia 272

Reading Social Studies Reread 274

Lesson 1 Physical Geography 275
Lesson 2 The Arabian Peninsula 282

Case Study Oil in Saudi Arabia 286

Lesson 3 Iraq 288
Lesson 4 Iran 293
Lesson 5 Central Asia 298

Social Studies Skills Use and Create Databases 305
Module Assessment 306

Module 9

The Eastern Mediterranean 308

Reading Social Studies Set a Purpose 310

Lesson 1 Physical Geography 311
Lesson 2 Turkey 315
Lesson 3 Israel 319
Lesson 4 Syria, Lebanon, and Jordan 325

Social Studies Skills Create a Cartogram 329

Module Assessment 330

Module 10

North Africa 332

Reading Social Studies Summarize 334

Lesson 1 Physical Geography 335
Lesson 2 Egypt 339
Lesson 3 Libya, Tunisia, Algeria, and Morocco 345

Social Studies Skills Analyze a Diagram 351

Module Assessment 352

Module 11

History of Sub-Saharan Africa 354

Reading Social Studies Understand Cause and Effect 356

Lesson 1 Human Beginnings in Africa 357
Lesson 2 Kingdoms in Africa 364
Lesson 3 Africa in Global Trade 372
Lesson 4 Imperialism and Independence 377

Social Studies Skills Understand Continuity and Change 385

Module Assessment 386

Module 12

West and Central Africa 388

Reading Social Studies Understand Comparison–Contrast........ 390

Lesson 1 Physical Geography 391

Case Study Mapping Central Africa's Forests 396

Lesson 2 West Africa 398

Lesson 3 Central Africa 407

Social Studies Skills Interpret a Population Pyramid 415

Module Assessment 416

Module 13

East and Southern Africa 418

Reading Social Studies Form Generalizations 420

Lesson 1 Physical Geography 421

Lesson 2 East Africa 426

Lesson 3 Southern Africa 433

Social Studies Skills Evaluate a Website 443

Module Assessment 444

Module 14

Indian Early Civilizations, Empires, and World Religions ... 446

Reading Social Studies Understand Fact and Opinion 448

Lesson 1 Early Indian Civilizations 449

Lesson 2 Hinduism 458

Lesson 3 Buddhism 463

Lesson 4 Sikhism 470

Lesson 5 Indian Empires 474

Social Studies Skills Compare Maps 483

Module Assessment 484

Module 15

The Indian Subcontinent 486

Reading Social Studies Visualize 488

Lesson 1 Physical Geography 489

Lesson 2 India 493

Lesson 3 India's Neighbors 503

Social Studies Skills Create a Line Graph 507

Module Assessment 508

Module 16

Early Civilizations of China 510

Reading Social Studies Understand Chronological Order 512

Lesson 1 Early China and the Han Dynasty 513

Lesson 2 The Sui, Tang, and Song Dynasties 521

Lesson 3 The Yuan and Ming Dynasties 528

Social Studies Skills Make Economic Choices 535

Module Assessment 536

Module 17

China, Mongolia, and Taiwan 538

Reading Social Studies Understand Implied Main Ideas 540

Lesson 1 Physical Geography 541

Lesson 2 China 545

Lesson 3 Mongolia and Taiwan 553

Social Studies Skills Identify Point of View 557

Module Assessment 558

HISTORY **Multimedia Connections**
China and the Great Wall 559 MC1

Module 18

Japan and the Koreas 560

Reading Social Studies Identify Bias 562

Lesson 1 Physical Geography 563
Lesson 2 Japan 567
Lesson 3 The Koreas 575

Social Studies Skills Use a Topographic Map 583

Module Assessment 584

HISTORY **Multimedia Connections**
Japan and the Samurai Warrior 585 MC1

Module 19

Southeast Asia 586

Reading Social Studies Use Context Clues—Definitions 588

Lesson 1 Physical Geography 589

Case Study Tsunami! 594
Lesson 2 Mainland Southeast Asia 596
Lesson 3 Island Southeast Asia Today 604

Social Studies Skills Interpret Visuals 609

Module Assessment 610

Module 20

Oceania and Antarctica 612

Reading Social Studies Determine Author's Purpose 614

Lesson 1 Australia and New Zealand 615
Lesson 2 The Pacific Islands 622
Lesson 3 Antarctica 628

Social Studies Skills Make Decisions 633

Module Assessment 634

References

Atlas R2
Regional Atlases and Data Files R22
Gazetteer R60
Writing Workshops R64
English and Spanish Glossary R72
Index R90
Credits and Acknowledgments R111

Available Online

Reading Like a Historian
Biographical Dictionary
Economics Handbook
Geography and Map Skills Handbook
Skillbuilder Handbook

Multimedia Connections

These online lessons feature award-winning content and include short video segments, maps and visual materials, primary source documents, and more.

China and the Great Wall

Japan and the Samurai Warrior

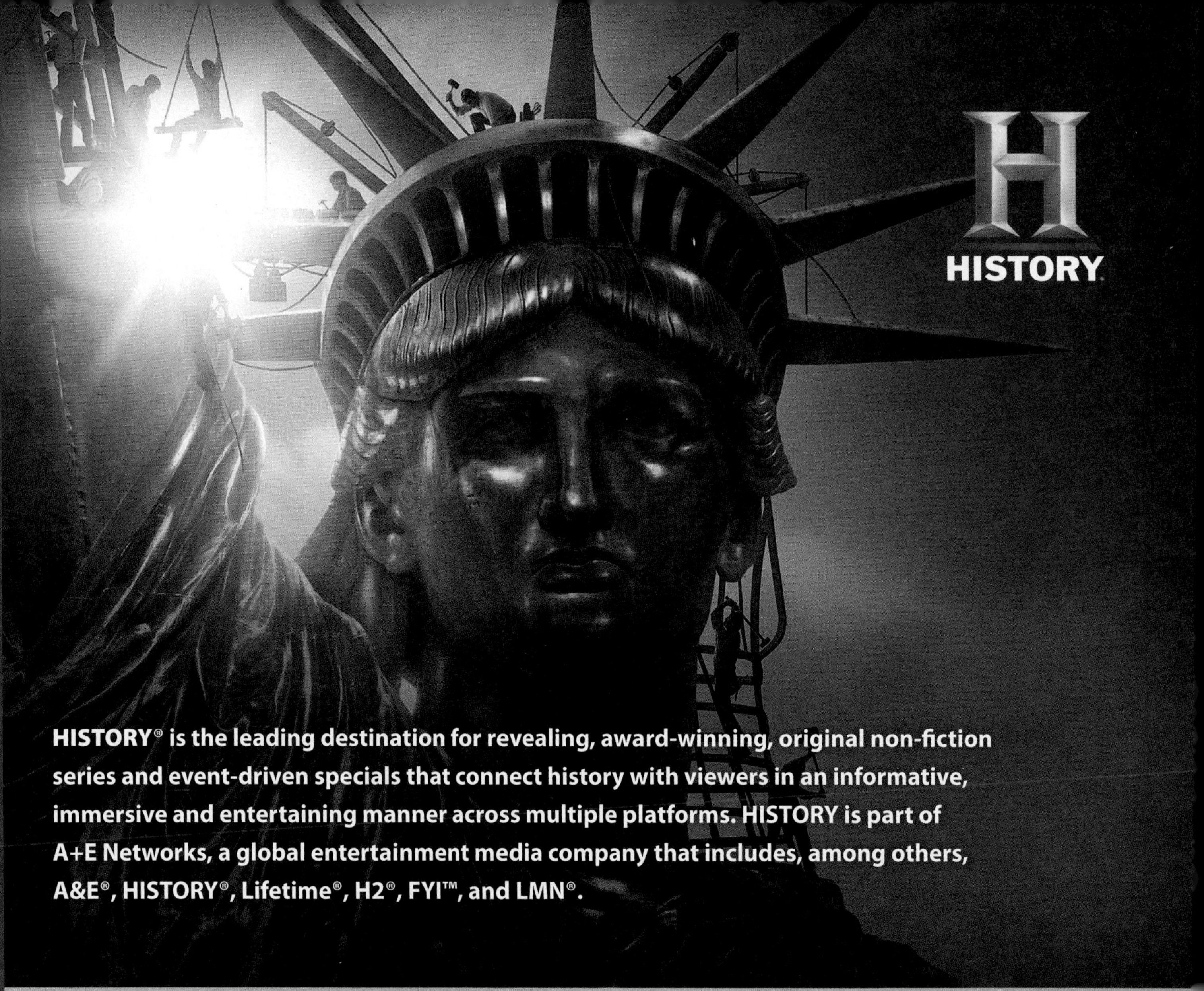

HISTORY

HISTORY® is the leading destination for revealing, award-winning, original non-fiction series and event-driven specials that connect history with viewers in an informative, immersive and entertaining manner across multiple platforms. HISTORY is part of A+E Networks, a global entertainment media company that includes, among others, A&E®, HISTORY®, Lifetime®, H2®, FYI™, and LMN®.

HISTORY programming greatly appeals to educators and young people who are drawn into the visual stories our documentaries tell. Our Education Department has a long-standing record in providing teachers and students with curriculum resources that bring the past to life in the classroom. Our content covers a diverse variety of subjects, including American and world history, government, economics, the natural and applied sciences, arts, literature and the humanities, health and guidance, and even pop culture.

The HISTORY website, located at **www.history.com**, is the definitive historical online source that delivers entertaining and informative content featuring broadband video, interactive timelines, maps, games, podcasts and more.

"We strive to engage, inspire and encourage the love of learning..."

Since its founding in 1995, HISTORY has demonstrated a commitment to providing the highest quality resources for educators. We develop multimedia resources for K–12 schools, two- and four-year colleges, government agencies, and other organizations by drawing on the award-winning documentary programming of A&E Television Networks. We strive to engage, inspire and encourage the love of learning by connecting with students in an informative and compelling manner. To help achieve this goal, we have formed a partnership with Houghton Mifflin Harcourt.

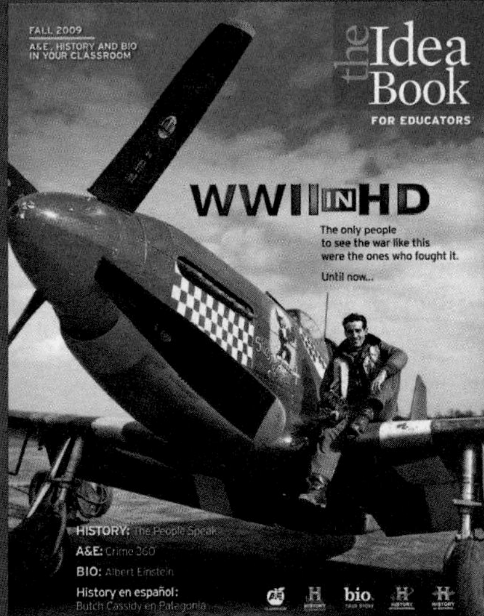

The Idea Book for Educators

Classroom resources that bring the past to life

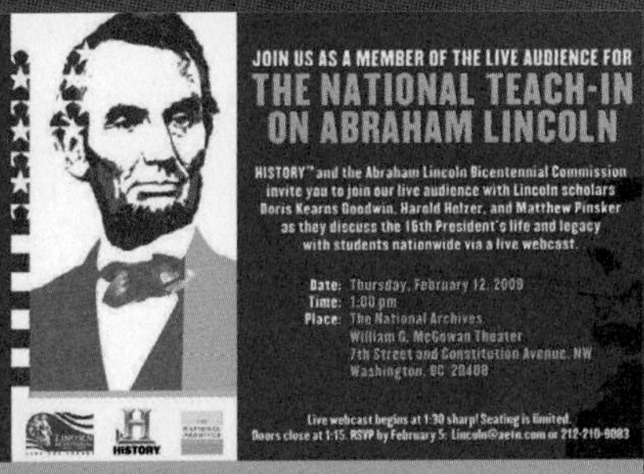

Live webcasts

HISTORY Take a Veteran to School Day

In addition to premium video-based resources, **HISTORY** has extensive offerings for teachers, parents, and students to use in the classroom and in their in-home educational activities, including:

- ***The Idea Book for Educators*** is a biannual teacher's magazine, featuring guides and info on the latest happenings in history education to help keep teachers on the cutting edge.
- **HISTORY Classroom (www.history.com/classroom)** is an interactive website that serves as a portal for history educators nationwide. Streaming videos on topics ranging from the Roman aqueducts to the civil rights movement connect with classroom curricula.
- **HISTORY email newsletters** feature updates and supplements to our award-winning programming relevant to the classroom with links to teaching guides and video clips on a variety of topics, special offers, and more.
- **Live webcasts** are featured each year as schools tune in via streaming video.
- **HISTORY Take a Veteran to School Day** connects veterans with young people in our schools and communities nationwide.

In addition to **Houghton Mifflin Harcourt**, our partners include the *Library of Congress,* the *Smithsonian Institution, National History Day, The Gilder Lehrman Institute of American History,* the Organization of American Historians, and many more. HISTORY video is also featured in museums throughout America and in over 70 other historic sites worldwide.

Reading Social Studies

Did you ever think you would begin reading your social studies book by reading about reading? Actually, it makes better sense than you might think. You would probably make sure you learned soccer skills and strategies before playing in a game. Similarly, you need to learn reading skills and strategies before reading your social studies book. In other words, you need to make sure you know whatever you need to know in order to read this book successfully.

Tip #1

Use the Reading Social Studies Page

Take advantage of the page on reading at the beginning of every module. This page introduces the reading skill you will learn and the reading strategy you will use. Then you will have an opportunity to practice that skill and strategy.

Reading Focus

The Reading Focus describes the reading skill you will learn and explains why it is important to master and use that skill.

Reading Strategy

Good readers use a number of strategies to make sure they understand what they are reading. These strategies are the basic tools you need to read and understand social studies.

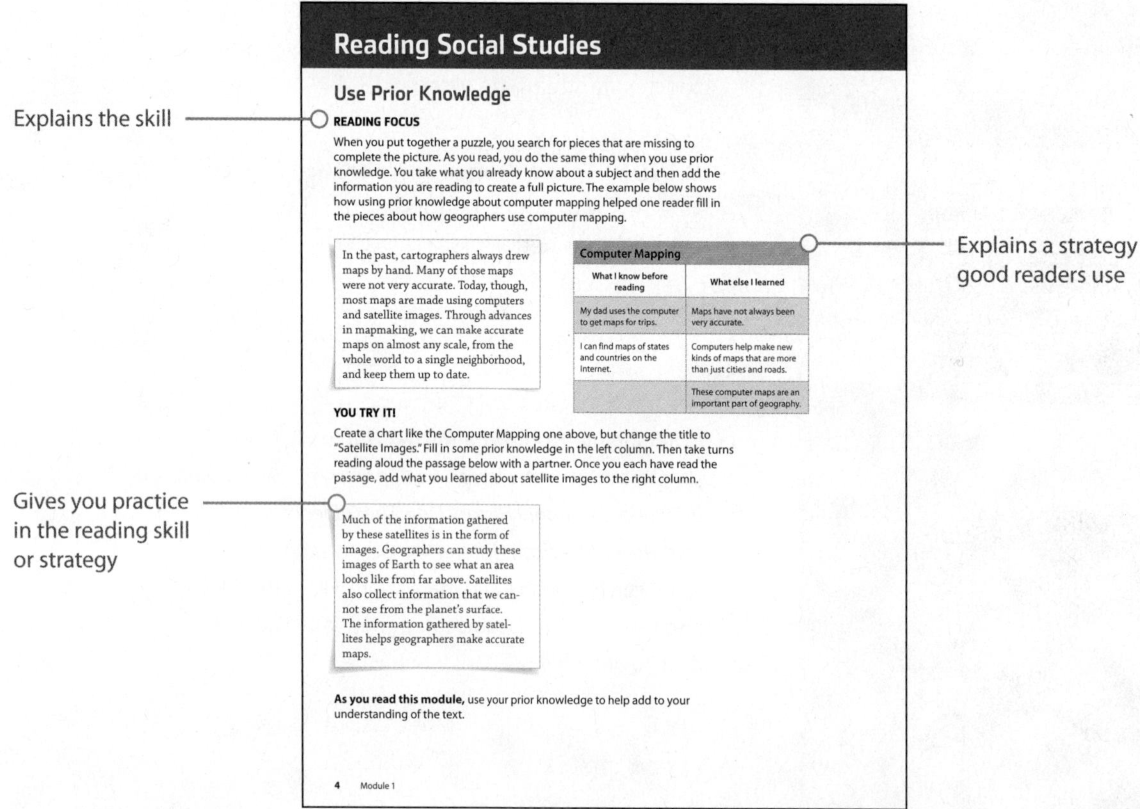

Reading Social Studies

Use Prior Knowledge

READING FOCUS

When you put together a puzzle, you search for pieces that are missing to complete the picture. As you read, you do the same thing when you use prior knowledge. You take what you already know about a subject and then add the information you are reading to create a full picture. The example below shows how using prior knowledge about computer mapping helped one reader fill in the pieces about how geographers use computer mapping.

In the past, cartographers always drew maps by hand. Many of those maps were not very accurate. Today, though, most maps are made using computers and satellite images. Through advances in mapmaking, we can make accurate maps on almost any scale, from the whole world to a single neighborhood, and keep them up to date.

Computer Mapping

What I know before reading	What else I learned
My dad uses the computer to get maps for trips.	Maps have not always been very accurate.
I can find maps of states and countries on the Internet.	Computers help make new kinds of maps that are more than just cities and roads.
	These computer maps are an important part of geography.

YOU TRY IT!

Create a chart like the Computer Mapping one above, but change the title to "Satellite Images." Fill in some prior knowledge in the left column. Then take turns reading aloud the passage below with a partner. Once you each have read the passage, add what you learned about satellite images to the right column.

Much of the information gathered by these satellites is in the form of images. Geographers can study these images of Earth to see what an area looks like from far above. Satellites also collect information that we cannot see from the planet's surface. The information gathered by satellites helps geographers make accurate maps.

As you read this module, use your prior knowledge to help add to your understanding of the text.

4 Module 1

Tip #2

Read like a Skilled Reader

You will never get better at reading your social studies book—or any book for that matter—unless you spend some time thinking about how to be a better reader.

Skilled readers do the following:

- They preview what they are supposed to read before they actually begin reading. They look for vocabulary words, titles of lessons, information in the margin, or maps or charts they should study.
- They divide their notebook paper into two columns. They title one column "Notes from the Lesson" and the other column "Questions or Comments I Have."
- They take notes in both columns as they read.
- They read like **active readers.** The Active Reading list below shows you what that means.
- They use clues in the text to help them figure out where the text is going. The best clues are called signal words.

Chronological Order Signal Words:
first, second, third, before, after, later, next, following that, earlier, finally

Cause and Effect Signal Words:
because of, due to, as a result of, the reason for, therefore, consequently

Comparison/Contrast Signal Words:
likewise, also, as well as, similarly, on the other hand

Active Reading

Successful readers are **active readers.** These readers know that it is up to them to figure out what the text means. Here are some steps you can take to become an active, and successful, reader.

Predict what will happen next based on what has already happened. When your predictions don't match what happens in the text, reread the confusing parts.

Question what is happening as you read. Constantly ask yourself why things have happened, what things mean, and what caused certain events.

Summarize what you are reading frequently. Do not try to summarize the entire module! Read a bit and then summarize it. Then read on.

Connect what is happening in the part you're reading to what you have already read.

Clarify your understanding. Stop occasionally to ask yourself whether you are confused by anything. You may need to reread to clarify, or you may need to read further and collect more information before you can understand.

Visualize what is happening in the text. Try to see the events or places in your mind by drawing maps, making charts, or jotting down notes about what you are reading.

Tip #3

Pay Attention to Vocabulary

It is no fun to read something when you don't know what the words mean, but you can't learn new words if you use or read only the words you already know. In this book, we know we probably have used some words you don't know. But we have followed a pattern as we have used more difficult words.

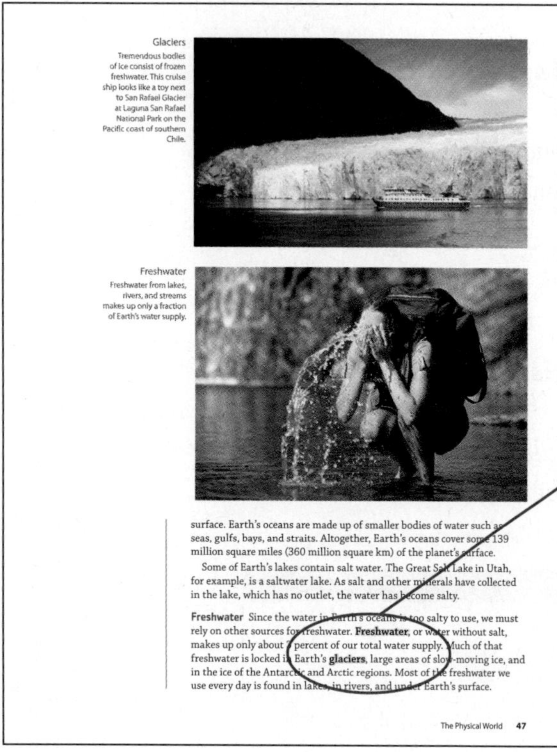

Glaciers
Tremendous bodies of ice consist of frozen freshwater. This cruise ship looks like a toy next to San Rafael Glacier at Laguna San Rafael National Park on the Pacific coast of southern Chile.

Freshwater
Freshwater from lakes, rivers, and streams makes up only a fraction of Earth's water supply.

surface. Earth's oceans are made up of smaller bodies of water such as seas, gulfs, bays, and straits. Altogether, Earth's oceans cover some 139 million square miles (360 million square km) of the planet's surface.

Some of Earth's lakes contain salt water. The Great Salt Lake in Utah, for example, is a saltwater lake. As salt and other minerals have collected in the lake, which has no outlet, the water has become salty.

Freshwater Since the water in Earth's oceans is too salty to use, we must rely on other sources for freshwater. **Freshwater**, or water without salt, makes up only about 3 percent of our total water supply. Much of that freshwater is locked in Earth's **glaciers**, large areas of slow-moving ice, and in the ice of the Antarctic and Arctic regions. Most of the freshwater we use every day is found in lakes, in rivers, and under Earth's surface.

The Physical World 47

Key Terms and Places

At the beginning of each lesson you will find a list of key terms and places that you will need to know. Be on the lookout for those words as you read through the lesson.

...Earth's oceans is t...
...freshwater. **Freshwater**, or wat...
...3 percent of our total water supply. M...
...n Earth's **glaciers**, large areas of slow...
...ic and Arctic regions. Most of th...
...in rivers, and und...

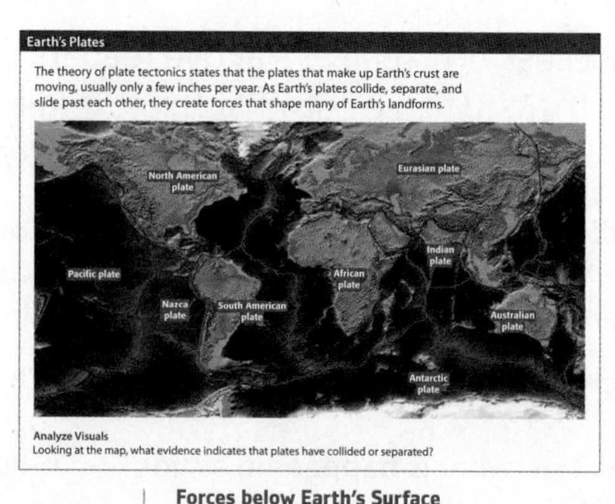

Analyze Visuals
Looking at the map, what evidence indicates that plates have collided or separated?

Academic Vocabulary
structure the way something is set up or organized

Forces below Earth's Surface

Geographers often study how landforms are made. One explanation for how landforms have been shaped involves forces below Earth's surface.

Earth's Plates To understand how these forces work, we must examine Earth's **structure**. The planet is made up of three layers. A solid inner core is surrounded by a liquid layer, or mantle. The solid outer layer of Earth is called the crust. The planet's **continents**, or large landmasses, are part of Earth's crust.

Geographers use the theory of plate tectonics to explain how forces below Earth's surface have shaped our landforms. The theory of **plate tectonics** suggests that Earth's surface is divided into a dozen or so slow-moving plates, or pieces of Earth's crust. As you can see in the image above, some plates, like the Pacific plate, are quite large. Others, like the Nazca plate, are much smaller. These plates cover Earth's entire surface. Some plates are under the ocean. These are known as ocean plates. Other plates, known as continental plates, are under Earth's continents.

Why do these plates move? Energy deep inside the planet puts pressure on Earth's crust. As this pressure builds up, it forces the plates to shift. Earth's tectonic plates all move. However, they move in different directions and at different speeds.

The Physical World 53

Academic Vocabulary

When we use a word that is important in all classes, not just social studies, we define it in the margin under the heading **Academic Vocabulary.** You will run into these academic words in other textbooks, so you should learn what they mean while reading this book.

Academic and Social Studies Words

As you read this social studies textbook, you will be more successful if you know or learn the meanings of the words on this page. Academic words are important in all classes, not just social studies. Social studies words are special to the study of world history and other social studies topics.

Academic Words

abstract expressing a quality or idea without reference to an actual thing

affect to change or influence

agreement a decision reached by two or more people or groups

aspects parts

cause the reason something happens

circumstances conditions that influence an event or activity

concrete specific, real

consequences the effects of a particular event or events

contemporary modern

criteria rules for defining

develop/development 1. to grow or improve; 2. creation

distinct clearly different and separate

distribute to divide among a group of people

effect the result of an action or decision

efficient/efficiency productive and not wasteful

element part

establish to set up or create

execute to perform, carry out

factor cause

features characteristics

function use or purpose

impact effect, result

implement to put in place

implications effects of a decision

incentive something that leads people to follow a certain course of action

influence change or have an effect on

innovation a new idea or way of doing something

method a way of doing something

monumental impressively large, sturdy, and enduring

motive a reason for doing something

neutral unbiased, not favoring either side in a conflict

policy rule, course of action

primary main, most important

procedure a series of steps taken to accomplish a task

process a series of steps by which a task is accomplished

purpose the reason something is done

reaction a response to something

role 1. a part or function; 2. assigned behavior

structure the way something is set up or organized

traditional customary, time-honored

values ideas that people hold dear and try to live by

vary/various 1. to be different; 2. of many types

Social Studies Words

AD refers to dates after the birth of Jesus of Nazareth

BC refers to dates before the birth of Jesus

BCE refers to "Before Common Era," dates before the birth of Jesus

CE refers to "Common Era," dates after the birth of Jesus

century a period of 100 years

civilization the culture of a particular time or place

climate the weather conditions in a certain area over a long period of time

culture the knowledge, beliefs, customs, and values of a group of people

custom a repeated practice, tradition

decade a period of 10 years

democracy governmental rule by the people, usually on a majority rule principle

economy the system in which people make and exchange goods and services

era a period of time

geography the study of Earth's physical and cultural features

monarchy governmental rule by one person, a king or queen

physical features features on the earth's surface, such as mountains and rivers

politics government

region an area with one or more features that make it different from surrounding areas

resources materials found on the earth that people need and value

society a group of people who share common traditions

trade the exchange of goods and service

Using This Book

Studying geography will be easy for you using this textbook. Take a few minutes to become familiar with the easy-to-use structure and special features of your book. See how it will make geography come alive for you!

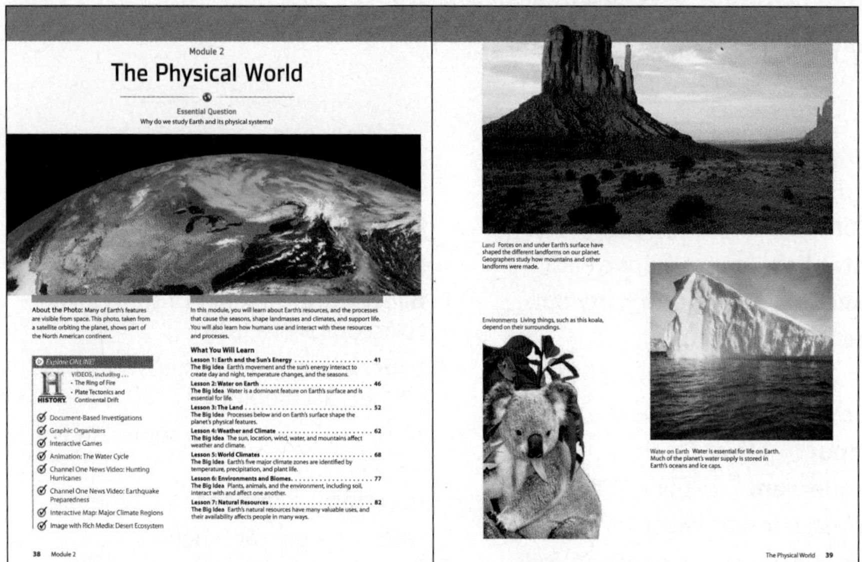

Module 2

The Physical World

Essential Question

Why do we study Earth and its physical systems?

About the Photo: Many of Earth's features are visible from space. This photo, taken from a satellite orbiting the planet, shows part of the North American continent.

Explore ONLINE!

VIDEOS, including . . .
- The Ring of Fire
- Plate Tectonics and Continental Drift

HISTORY

- Document-Based Investigations
- Graphic Organizers
- Interactive Games
- Animation: The Water Cycle
- Channel One News Video: Hunting Hurricanes
- Channel One News Video: Earthquake Preparedness
- Interactive Map: Major Climate Regions
- Image with Rich Media: Desert Ecosystem

In this module, you will learn about Earth's resources, and the processes that cause the seasons, shape landmasses and climates, and support life. You will also learn how humans use and interact with these resources and processes.

What You Will Learn

Lesson 1: Earth and the Sun's Energy 41
The Big Idea Earth's movement and the sun's energy interact to create day and night, temperature changes, and the seasons.

Lesson 2: Water on Earth 46
The Big Idea Water is a dominant feature on Earth's surface and is essential for life.

Lesson 3: The Land 52
The Big Idea Processes below and on Earth's surface shape the planet's physical features.

Lesson 4: Weather and Climate 62
The Big Idea The sun, location, wind, water, and mountains affect weather and climate.

Lesson 5: World Climates 68
The Big Idea Earth's five major climate zones are identified by temperature, precipitation, and plant life.

Lesson 6: Environments and Biomes 77
The Big Idea Plants, animals, and the environment, including soil, interact with and affect one another.

Lesson 7: Natural Resources 82
The Big Idea Earth's natural resources have many valuable uses, and their availability affects people in many ways.

38 Module 2

Land Forces on and under Earth's surface have shaped the different landforms on our planet. Geographers study how mountains and other landforms were made.

Environments Living things, such as this koala, depend on their surroundings.

Water on Earth Water is essential for life on Earth. Much of the planet's water supply is stored in Earth's oceans and ice caps.

The Physical World 39

Module

Each module begins with an Essential Question and a preview of what you will learn and ends with a Module Assessment.

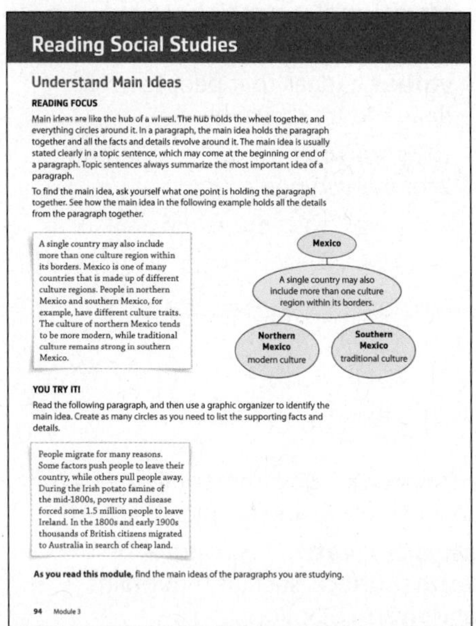

Reading Social Studies

Understand Main Ideas

READING FOCUS

Main ideas are like the hub of a wheel. The hub holds the wheel together, and everything circles around it. In a paragraph, the main idea holds the paragraph together and all the facts and details revolve around it. The main idea is usually stated clearly in a topic sentence, which may come at the beginning or end of a paragraph. Topic sentences always summarize the most important idea of a paragraph.

To find the main idea, ask yourself what one point is holding the paragraph together. See how the main idea in the following example holds all the details from the paragraph together.

A single country may also include more than one culture region within its borders. Mexico is one of many countries that is made up of different culture regions. People in northern Mexico and southern Mexico, for example, have different culture traits. The culture of northern Mexico tends to be more modern, while traditional culture remains strong in southern Mexico.

YOU TRY IT!

Read the following paragraph, and then use a graphic organizer to identify the main idea. Create as many circles as you need to list the supporting facts and details.

People migrate for many reasons. Some factors push people to leave their country, while others pull people away. During the Irish potato famine of the mid-1800s, poverty and disease forced some 1.5 million people to leave Ireland. In the 1800s and early 1900s thousands of British citizens migrated to Australia in search of cheap land.

As you read this module, find the main ideas of the paragraphs you are studying.

94 Module 3

Reading Social Studies

These reading lessons teach you skills and provide opportunities for practice to help you read the textbook more successfully. There are questions in the Module Assessment to make sure you understand the reading skill.

Social Studies Skills

The Social Studies Skills lessons give you an opportunity to learn and use a skill you will most likely use again while in school. You will also be given a chance to make sure you understand each skill by answering related questions in the Module Assessment.

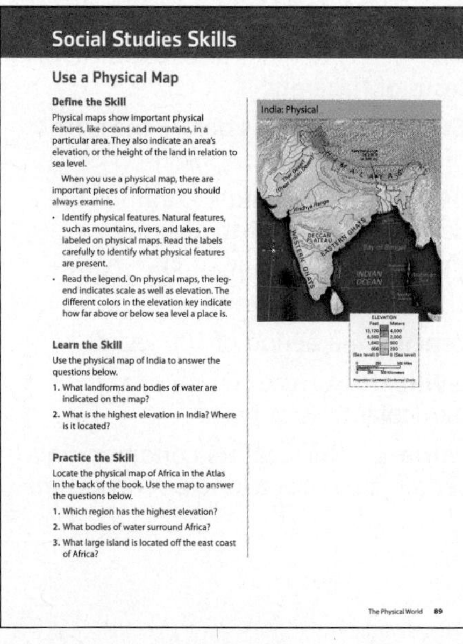

Social Studies Skills

Use a Physical Map

Define the Skill

Physical maps show important physical features, like oceans and mountains, in a particular area. They also indicate an area's elevation, or the height of the land in relation to sea level.

When you use a physical map, there are important pieces of information you should always examine.

- Identify physical features. Natural features, such as mountains, rivers, and lakes, are labeled on physical maps. Read the labels carefully to identify what physical features are present.
- Read the legend. On physical maps, the legend indicates scale as well as elevation. The different colors in the elevation key indicate how far above or below sea level a place is.

Learn the Skill

Use the physical map of India to answer the questions below.

1. What landforms and bodies of water are indicated on the map?
2. What is the highest elevation in India? Where is it located?

Practice the Skill

Locate the physical map of Africa in the Atlas in the back of the book. Use the map to answer the questions below.

1. Which region has the highest elevation?
2. What bodies of water surround Africa?
3. What large island is located off the east coast of Africa?

The Physical World 89

Lesson

The lesson opener includes an overarching Big Idea statement, Main Ideas, and Key Terms and Places.

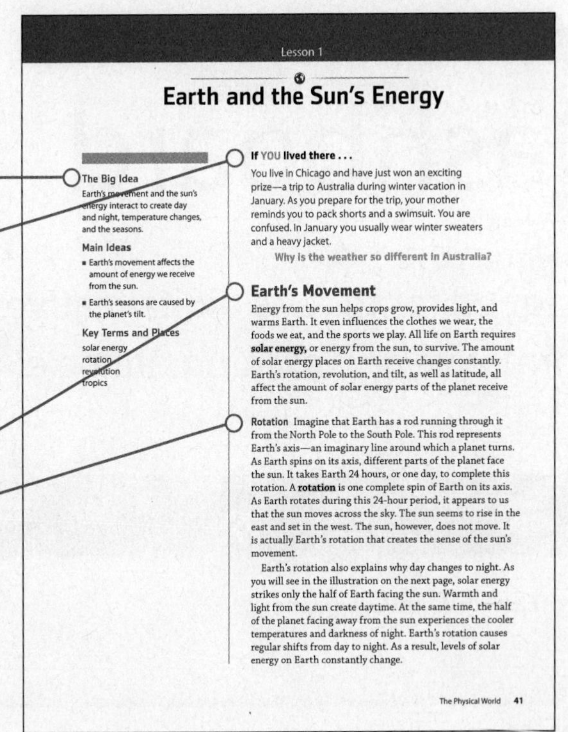

If YOU lived there . . .

introductions begin each lesson with a situation for you to respond to, placing you in a location related to the content you will be studying in the lesson.

Headings and subheadings

organize the information into manageable chunks of text that will help you learn and understand the lesson's main ideas.

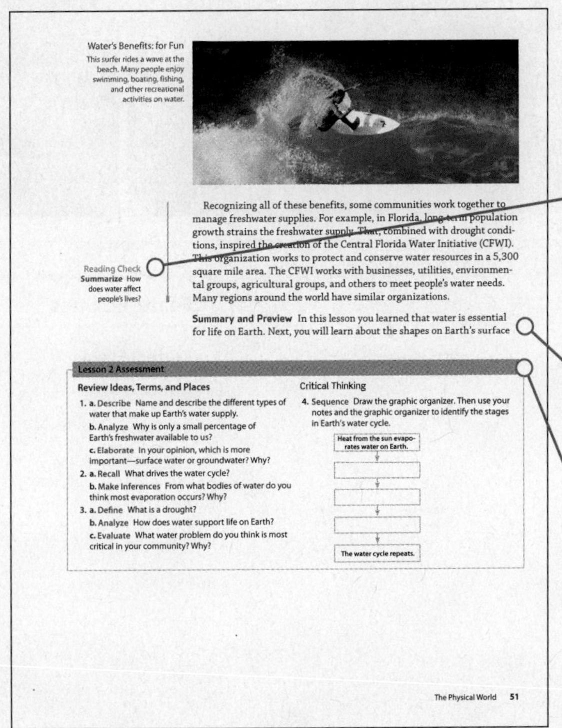

Reading Check

questions are at the end of each main heading so you can test whether or not you understand what you have just studied.

Summary and Preview

statements connect what you have just studied in the lesson to what you will study in the next lesson.

Lesson Assessment

boxes provide an opportunity for you to make sure you understand the main ideas of the lesson.

HMH Social Studies
Dashboard

Designed for today's digital natives, ***HMH® Social Studies*** offers you an informative and exciting online experience.

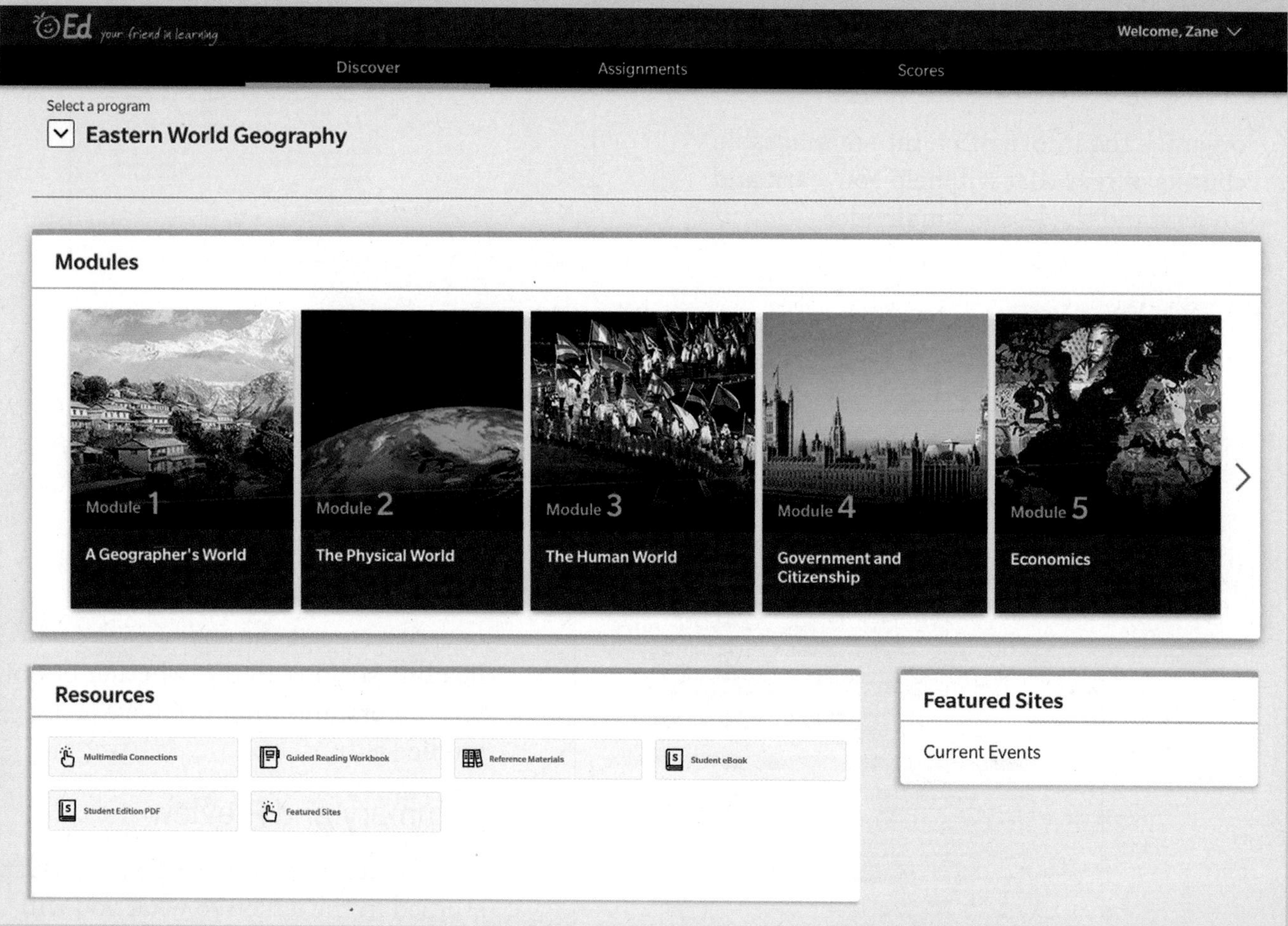

Your personalized Student Dashboard is organized into three main sections:

1. **Discover**—Quickly access content and search program resources
2. **Assignments**—Review your assignments and check your progress on them
3. **Scores**—Monitor your progress in the course

experiences that are energizing, inspiring, and memorable. The following pages highlight some digital tools and instructional support that will help you approach geography through active inquiry, so you can connect to the wider world while becoming active and informed citizens for the future.

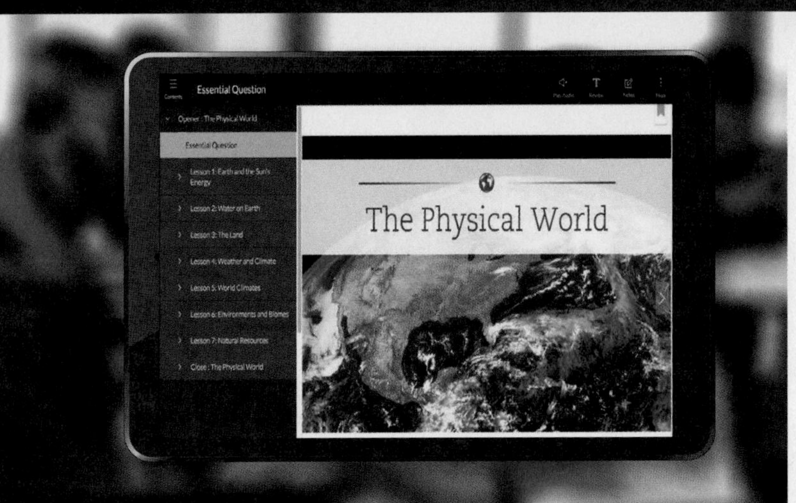

The Student eBook is the primary learning portal.

More than just the digital version of a textbook, the Student eBook serves as the primary learning portal for you. The text is supported by a wealth of multimedia and learning resources to bring geography to life and give you the tools you need to succeed.

Bringing Content to Life

HISTORY® videos and Multimedia Connections bring content to life through primary source footage, dramatic storytelling, and expert testimonials.

In-Depth Understanding

Close Read Screencasts model an analytical conversation about primary sources.

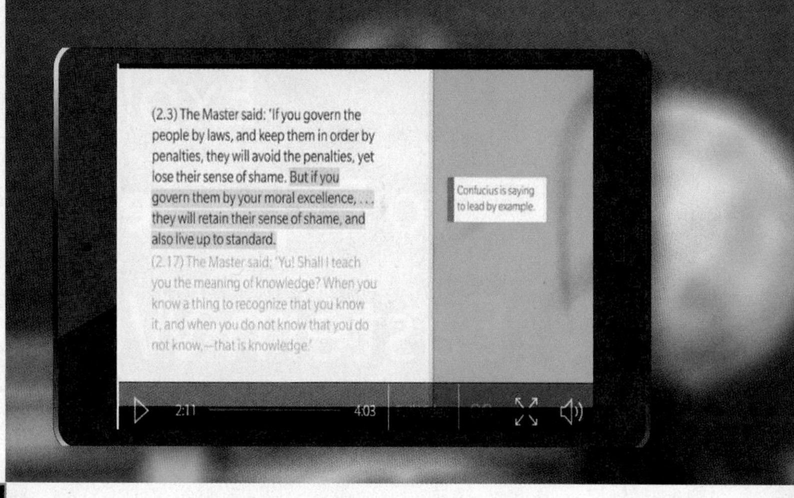

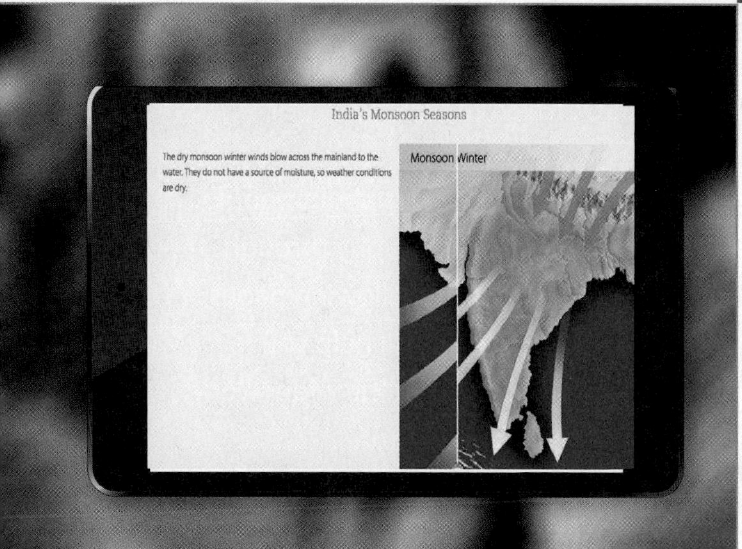

Content in a Fun Way

Interactive Features, Maps, and **Games** provide quick, entertaining activities and assessments that present important content in a fun way.

Focusing on Sources

Document-Based Investigations in lessons build to end-of-module DBI performance tasks so you can examine and assess primary and secondary sources as geographers and historians do.

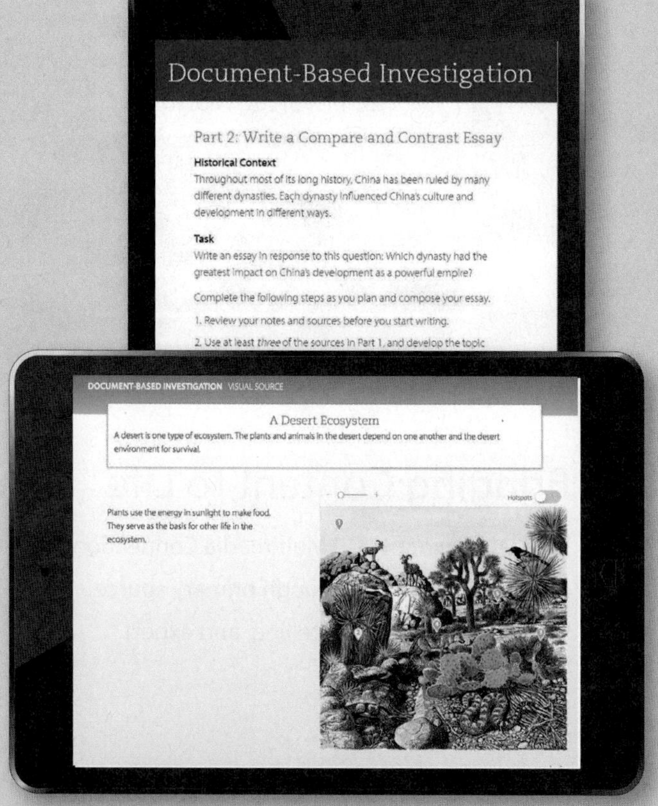

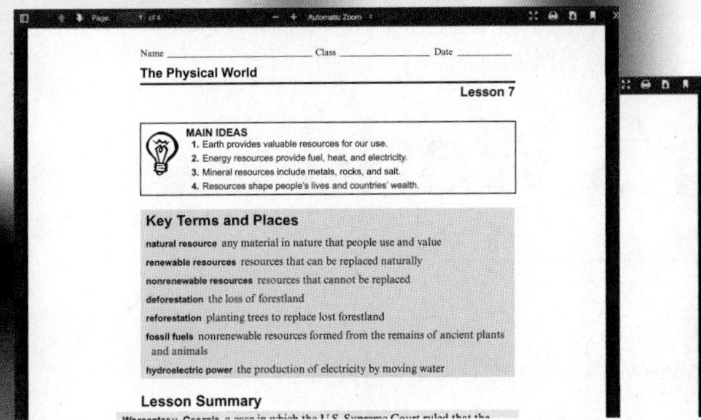

Name ______________ Class ______________ Date ______________

The Physical World

Lesson 7

MAIN IDEAS

1. Earth provides valuable resources for our use.
2. Energy resources provide fuel, heat, and electricity.
3. Mineral resources include metals, rocks, and salt.
4. Resources shape people's lives and countries' wealth.

Key Terms and Places

natural resource any material in nature that people use and value

renewable resources resources that can be replaced naturally

nonrenewable resources resources that cannot be replaced

deforestation the loss of forestland

reforestation planting trees to replace lost forestland

fossil fuels nonrenewable resources formed from the remains of ancient plants and animals

hydroelectric power the production of electricity by moving water

Lesson Summary

The **Guided Reading Workbook** and **Spanish/English Guided Reading Workbook** offer you lesson summaries with vocabulary, reading, and note-taking support.

Current Events features trustworthy articles on today's news that connect what you learn in class to the world around you.

Full-Text Audio Support

You can listen while you read.

Skills Support

Point-of-use support is just a click away, providing instruction on critical reading and social studies skills.

Personalized Annotations

Notes encourages you to take notes while you read and allows you to customize them to your study preferences. You can easily access them to review later as you prepare for exams.

Interactive Lesson Graphic Organizers

Graphic organizers help you process, summarize, and keep track of your learning for end-of-module performance tasks.

No Wi-Fi®? No problem!

HMH Social Studies Eastern World Geography will allow you to connect to content and resources by downloading it when online and accessing it when offline.

Module 1

A Geographer's World

Essential Question

How does the use of geographic tools help us view the world in new ways?

About the Photo: This village is in the country of Nepal. It rests high in the Himalayas, the highest mountains in the world.

Explore ONLINE!

- Document-Based Investigations
- Graphic Organizers
- Interactive Games
- Animation: How Satellites Gather Map Data
- Channel One News Video: Making Art with GPS
- Animation: Map Projections
- Animation: How to Read a Map

In this module, you will learn that geography is the study of the world. You will find out how geographic studies are organized and what tools are used.

What You Will Learn

Lesson 1: Studying Geography 5
The Big Idea The study of geography helps us view the world in new ways.

Lesson 2: The Branches of Geography 10
The Big Idea Geography is divided into two main branches—physical geography and human geography.

Lesson 3: Themes of Geography 16
The Big Idea Geographers have created two different but related systems for organizing geographic studies.

Lesson 4: The Geographer's Tools 20
The Big Idea Geographers use many tools to study the world.

Lesson 5: Geography Handbook 24
The Big Idea Geographers study the world by understanding maps and geographic features of Earth.

Physical Geography Geography is the study of the world's land features, such as this windswept rock formation in Arizona.

Studying the World Exploring the world takes people to exciting and interesting places.

Human Geography Geography is also the study of people. It asks where people live, what they eat, what they wear, and even what kinds of animals they keep.

Reading Social Studies

Use Prior Knowledge

READING FOCUS

When you put together a puzzle, you search for pieces that are missing to complete the picture. As you read, you do the same thing when you use prior knowledge. You take what you already know about a subject and then add the information you are reading to create a full picture. The example below shows how using prior knowledge about computer mapping helped one reader fill in the pieces about how geographers use computer mapping.

In the past, cartographers always drew maps by hand. Many of those maps were not very accurate. Today, though, most maps are made using computers and satellite images. Through advances in mapmaking, we can make accurate maps on almost any scale, from the whole world to a single neighborhood, and keep them up to date.

Computer Mapping

What I know before reading	What else I learned
My dad uses the computer to get maps for trips.	Maps have not always been very accurate.
I can find maps of states and countries on the Internet.	Computers help make new kinds of maps that are more than just cities and roads.
	These computer maps are an important part of geography.

YOU TRY IT!

Create a chart like the Computer Mapping one above, but change the title to "Satellite Images." Fill in some prior knowledge in the left column. Then take turns reading aloud the passage below with a partner. Once you each have read the passage, add what you learned about satellite images to the right column.

Much of the information gathered by these satellites is in the form of images. Geographers can study these images of Earth to see what an area looks like from far above. Satellites also collect information that we cannot see from the planet's surface. The information gathered by satellites helps geographers make accurate maps.

As you read this module, use your prior knowledge to help add to your understanding of the text.

Studying Geography

The Big Idea

The study of geography helps us view the world in new ways.

Main Ideas

- Geography is the study of the world, its people, and the landscapes they create.
- Geographers look at the world in many different ways.

Key Terms and Places

geography
landscape
social science
regions

If YOU lived there . . .

You have just moved to Miami, Florida, from your old home in Pennsylvania. Everything seems very different—from the weather and the trees to the way people dress and talk. Even the streets and buildings look different. One day you get an email from a friend at your old school. "What's it like living there?" your friend asks.

How will you describe your new home?

What Is Geography?

Think about the place where you live. What does the land look like? Are there tall mountains nearby, or is the land so flat that you can see for miles? Is the ground covered with bright green grass and trees, or is the area part of a sandy desert?

Now think about the weather in your area. What is it like? Does it get really hot in the summer? Do you see snow every winter? How much does it rain? Do tornadoes ever strike?

Finally, think about the people who live in your town or city. Do they live mostly in apartments or houses? Do most people own cars or do they get around town on buses or trains? What kinds of jobs do adults in your town have? Were most of the people you know born in your town or did they move there?

The things that you have been thinking about are part of your area's geography. **Geography** is the study of the world, its people, and the landscapes they create. To a geographer, a place's **landscape** is all the human and physical features that make it unique. When they study the world's landscapes, geographers ask questions much like the ones you just asked yourself.

Geography as a Science Many of the questions that geographers ask deal with how the world works. They want to know what causes mountains to form and what creates tornadoes. To answer questions like these, geographers have to think and act like scientists.

As scientists, geographers do field work to gather data, or information, about places. Gathering data can sometimes lead geographers to fascinating places. They might have to crawl deep into caves or climb tall mountains to make observations and take measurements. At other times, geographers study sets of images collected by satellites orbiting high above Earth. These scientists make observations about the places they study. Then they record those observations.

However geographers make observations and gather data, they have to study it carefully. Like other scientists, geographers must examine their findings in great detail before they can learn what all the information means. These scientists interpret and summarize the data gathered. Then they make their conclusions.

Geography as a Social Science Not everything that geographers study can be measured in numbers, however. Some geographers study people and their lives. For example, they may ask why countries change their governments or why people in a place speak a certain language. This kind of information cannot be measured.

Because it deals with people and how they live, geography is sometimes called a **social science.** A social science is a field that studies people and the relationships among them.

The geographers who study people do not dig in caves or climb mountains. Instead, they visit places and talk to the people who live there. That is the field work they do to gather information about people's lives and communities. These geographers may design and conduct surveys to gather information. They also might record oral histories from what people tell them about their communities.

Reading Check
Compare In what ways is geography both a science and a social science?

What Is Geography?

Geography is the study of the world, its people, and the landscapes they create. To study a place's geography, we look at its physical and human features.

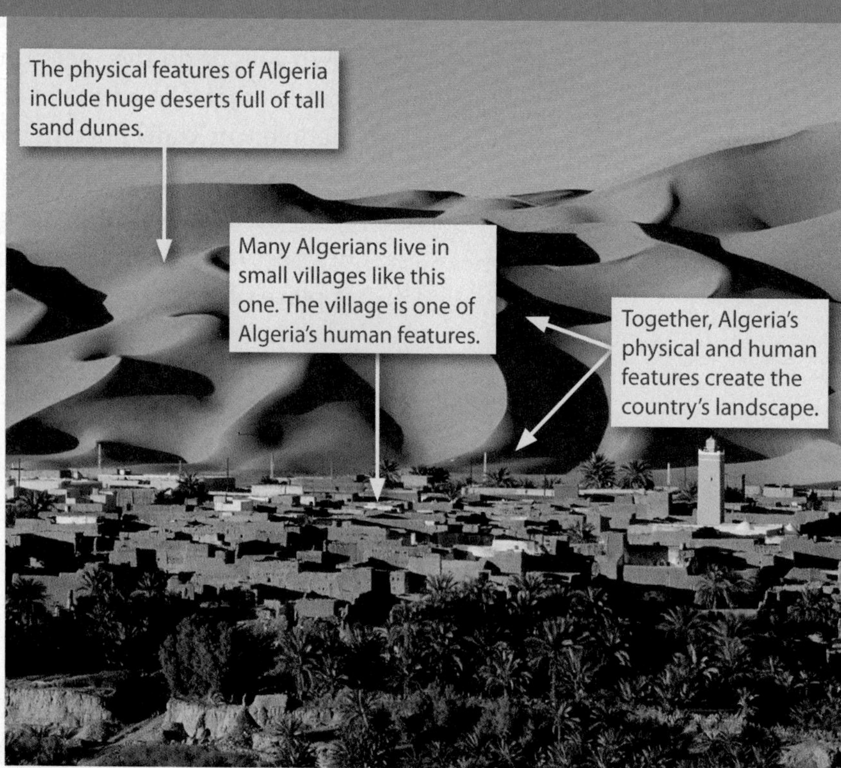

Analyze Visuals
What is the landscape of this part of Algeria like?

Looking at the World

Whether they study volcanoes and storms or people and cities, geographers have to look carefully at the world around them. To fully understand how the world works, geographers often look at places at three different levels.

Local Level Some geographers study issues at a local level. They ask the same types of questions we asked at the beginning of this module: How do people in a town or community live? What is the local government like? How do the people who live there get around? What do they eat?

By asking these questions, geographers can figure out why people live and work the way they do. They can also help people improve their lives. For example, they can help town leaders figure out the best place to build new schools, shopping centers, or sports complexes. They can also help the people who live in the city or town plan for future changes.

Regional Level Sometimes, though, geographers want to study a bigger chunk of the world. To do this, they divide the world into **regions.** A region is a part of the world that has one or more common features that distinguish it from surrounding areas.

Some regions are defined by physical characteristics such as mountain ranges, climates, or plants native to the area. As a result, these types of regions are often easy to identify. The Rocky Mountains of the western United States, for example, make up a physical region. Another example of this kind of region is the Sahara, a huge desert in northern Africa.

Other regions may not be so easy to define, however. These regions are based on the human characteristics of a place, such as language, religion, or history. A place in which most people share these kinds of characteristics can also be seen as a region. For example, most people in Scandinavia, a region in northern Europe, speak similar languages and practice the same religion.

Regions come in all shapes and sizes. Some are small, like the neighborhood called Chinatown in San Francisco. Other regions are huge, like the Americas. This huge region includes two continents—North America and South America. The size of the area does not matter, as long as the area shares some characteristics. These shared characteristics define the region.

Geographers divide the world into regions for many reasons. The world is a huge place and home to billions of people. Studying so large an area can be extremely difficult. Dividing the world into regions makes it easier to study. A small area is much easier to examine than a large area.

Other geographers study regions to see how people interact with one another. For example, they may study a city such as London, England, to learn how the city's people govern themselves. Then they can compare what they learn about one region to what they learn about another region. In this way, they can learn more about life and landscapes in both places.

Global Level Sometimes, geographers do not want to study the world just at a regional level. Instead, they want to learn how people interact globally, or around the world. To do so, geographers ask how events and ideas from one region of the world affect people in other regions. In other words, they study the world on a global level.

Geographers who study the world on a global level try to find relationships among people who live far apart. They may, for example, examine the products that a country exports to see how those products are used in other countries.

Looking at the World

Geographers look at the world at many levels. At each level, they ask different questions and discover different types of information. By putting information gathered at different levels together, geographers can better understand a place and its role in the world.

Local Level

This busy neighborhood in London, England, is a local area. A geographer here might study local foods, housing, or clothing.

Regional Level

As a major city, London is also a region. At this level, a geographer might study the city's population or transportation systems.

Global Level

London is one of the world's main financial centers. Here, a geographer might study how London's economy affects the world.

Analyze Visuals

Based on these photos, what are some questions a geographer might ask about London?

Reading Check
Find Main Ideas At what levels do geographers study the world?

In recent decades, worldwide trade and communication have increased. As a result, we need to understand how our actions affect people around the world. Through their studies, geographers provide us with information that helps us figure out how to live in a rapidly changing world.

Summary and Preview Geography is the study of the world, its people, and its landscapes. In the next lesson, you will explore the branches into which the field is divided.

Lesson 1 Assessment

Review Ideas, Terms, and Places

1. a. **Define** What is geography?
   b. **Explain** Why is geography considered a science?
2. a. **Identify** What is a region? Give two examples.
   b. **Elaborate** What global issues do geographers study?

Critical Thinking

3. **Summarize** Draw two ovals like the ones shown here. Use your notes to fill the ovals with information about geography and geographers.

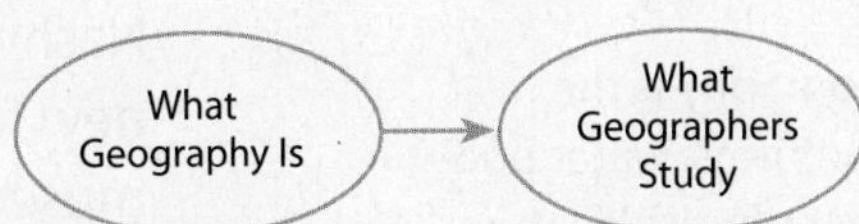

The Branches of Geography

The Big Idea

Geography is divided into two main branches—physical geography and human geography.

Main Ideas

- Physical geography is the study of landforms, water bodies, and other physical features.
- Human geography focuses on people, their cultures, and the landscapes they create.
- Other branches of geography examine specific aspects of the physical or human world.

Key Terms and Places

physical geography
human geography
cartography
meteorology

If YOU lived there . . .

You are talking to two friends about the vacations their families will take this summer. One friend says that his family is going to the Grand Canyon. He is very excited about seeing the spectacular landscapes in and around the canyon. Your other friend's family is going to visit Nashville, Tennessee. She is looking forward to trying new foods at the city's restaurants and touring its museums.

Which vacation sounds more interesting? Why?

Physical Geography

Think about a jigsaw puzzle. Seen as a whole, the puzzle shows a pretty or interesting picture. To see that picture, though, you have to put all the puzzle pieces together. Before you assemble them, the pieces do not give you a clear idea of what the puzzle will look like when it is assembled. After all, each piece contains only a tiny portion of the overall image.

In many ways, geography is like a huge puzzle. It is made up of many branches, or divisions. Each of these branches focuses on a single part of the world. Viewed separately, none of these branches shows us the whole world. Together, however, the many branches of geography improve our understanding of our planet and its people.

Geography's two main branches are physical geography and human geography. Geographers identify and locate major physical and human geographic features of various places and regions in the world. The first branch, **physical geography,** is the study of the world's physical geographic features—its landforms, bodies of water, climates, soils, and plants.

The Physical World What does it mean to say that physical geography is the study of physical geographic features? Physical geographers want to know all about the different features found on our planet. They want to know where mountain ranges are, how rivers flow across the landscape, and why different amounts of rain fall from place to place.

BIOGRAPHY

Eratosthenes (c. 276–c. 194 BC)

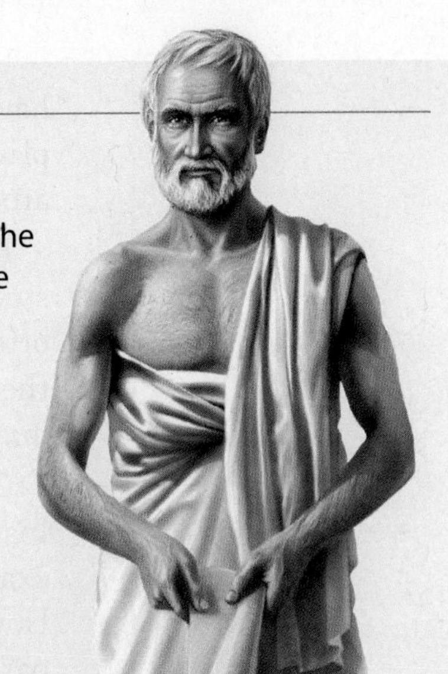

Did you know that geography is over two thousand years old? Actually, the study of the world is even older than that, but the first person ever to use the word *geography* lived then. His name was Eratosthenes (er-uh-TAHS-thuh-neez), and he was a Greek scientist and librarian. With no modern instruments of any kind, Eratosthenes figured out how large Earth is. He also drew a map that showed all of the lands that the Greeks knew about. Because of his many contributions to the field, Eratosthenes has been called the Father of Geography.

Generalize
Why is Eratosthenes called the Father of Geography?

More importantly, however, physical geographers want to know what causes the different shapes on Earth. They want to know why mountain ranges rise up where they do and what causes rivers to flow in certain directions. They also want to know why various parts of the world have very different weather and climate patterns.

To answer these questions, physical geographers take detailed measurements. They study the heights of mountains and the temperatures of places. To track any changes that occur over time, physical geographers keep careful records of all the information they collect.

Uses of Physical Geography Earth is made up of hundreds of types of physical geographic features. Without a complete understanding of what these features are and the effect they have on the world's people and landscapes, we cannot fully understand our world. This is the major reason that geographers study the physical world—to learn how it works.

There are also other, more specific reasons for studying physical geography, though. Studying the changes that take place on our planet can help us prepare to live with those changes. For example, knowing what causes volcanoes to erupt can help us predict eruptions. Knowing what causes terrible storms can help us prepare for them. In this way, the work of physical geographers helps us adjust to the dangers and changes of our world.

Reading Check
Identify Points of View
What are some features in your area that a physical geographer might study?

Human Geography

The physical world is only one part of the puzzle of geography. People are also part of the world. **Human geography** is the study of the world's human geographic features—people, communities, and landscapes. It is the second major branch of geography.

The Human World Put simply, human geographers study the world's people, past and present. They look at where people live and why. They ask why some parts of the world have more people than others, and why some places have almost no people at all.

Human geographers also study what people do. What jobs do people have? What crops do they grow? What makes them move from place to place? These are the types of questions that geographers ask about people around the world.

Because people's lives are so different in different places, no one can study every aspect of human geography. As a result, human geographers often specialize in a smaller area of study. Some may choose to study only the people and landscapes in a certain region. For example, a geographer may study only the lives of people who live in West Africa.

Other geographers choose not to limit their studies to one place. Instead, they may choose to examine only one aspect of people's lives. For example, a geographer could study only economics, politics, or city life. However, that geographer may compare economic patterns in various parts of the world to see how they differ.

Uses of Human Geography Although every culture is different, people around the world have some common needs. All people need food and water. All people need shelter. All people need to deal with other people in order to survive.

Human geographers study how people in various places address their needs. They look at the foods people eat and the types of governments they form. The knowledge they gather can help us better understand people in other cultures. Sometimes, this type of understanding can help people improve their landscapes and situations.

On a smaller scale, human geographers can help people design their cities and towns. By understanding where people go and what they need, geographers can help city planners place roads, shopping malls, and schools. Geographers also study the effect people have on the world. As a result, they often work with private groups and government agencies that want to protect the environment.

Partnering with Archaeology and History Human geography can also help other types of social scientists, such as archaeologists. Archaeologists engage in digs and study artifacts and features in a particular location. They gather evidence about groups of people and how those groups lived at particular times in history. The human geography of a place is part of archaeologists' gathered evidence.

Human geography also contributes to the work of historians. Historians use archaeological, geographical, and other types of evidence to investigate patterns in history. They identify turning points. A turning point can be an event, era, or development in history that brought about social, cultural, ecological, political, or economic change. The geography of places can affect historic turning points.

Reading Check
Summarize
What do human geographers study?

Other Fields of Geography

Physical geography and human geography are the two largest branches of the subject, but they are not the only ones. Many other fields of geography exist, each one devoted to studying one aspect of the world.

Geography

Geography is the study of Earth's physical and human geographic features.

Physical Geography

The study of Earth's physical geographic features, including rivers, mountains, oceans, weather, and other features, such as Victoria Falls in southern Africa

Human Geography

The study of Earth's people, including their ways of life, homes, cities, beliefs, and customs, like those of these children in Malawi, a country in Central Africa

Most of these fields are smaller, more specialized areas of either physical or human geography. For example, economic geography—the study of how people make and spend money—is a branch of human geography. Another specialized branch of human geography is urban geography, the study of cities and how people live in them. Physical geography also includes many fields, such as the study of climates. Other fields of physical geography are the studies of soils and plants.

Cartography One key field of geography is **cartography,** the science of making maps. Without maps, geographers would not be able to study where things are in the world. In addition to locations, maps can display other information about people, places, and environments. Cartographers decide which information to include on a given map and how it is displayed.

In the past, cartographers always drew maps by hand. Many of those maps were not very accurate. Today, though, most maps are made using computers and satellite images. Through advances in mapmaking, we can make accurate maps on almost any scale, from the whole world to a single

Connect to Technology

Computer Mapping

In the past, maps were drawn by hand. Making a map was a slow process. Even the simplest map took a long time to make. Today, however, cartographers have access to tools people in the past—even people who lived just 50 years ago—never imagined. The most important of these tools are computers.

Computers allow us to make maps quickly and easily. In addition, they let us make new types of maps that people could not make in the past.

The map shown here, for example, was drawn on a computer. It shows the number of computer users in the United States who were connected to the Internet on a particular day. Each of the lines that rises off of the map represents a city in which people were using the Internet. The color of the line indicates the number of computer users in that city. As you can see, this data resulted in a very complex map.

Making such a map required cartographers to sort through huge amounts of complex data. Such sorting would not have been possible without computers.

Contrast
How are today's maps different from those created in the past?

neighborhood, and keep them up to date. These maps are not only used by geographers. For example, road maps are used by people who are planning long trips.

Hydrology Another important branch of geography is hydrology, the study of water on Earth. Geographers in this field study the world's river systems and rainfall patterns. They study what causes droughts and floods and how people in cities can get safe drinking water. They also work to measure and protect the world's supply of water.

Meteorology Have you ever seen the weather report on television? If so, you have seen the results of another branch of geography. This branch is called **meteorology,** the study of weather and what causes it. Meteorologists use computers to follow and predict weather.

Meteorologists study weather patterns in a particular area. Then they use the information to predict what the weather will be like in the coming

Reading Check
Find Main Ideas
What are some major branches of geography?

days. Their work helps people plan what to wear and what to do on any given day. At the same time, their work can save lives by predicting the arrival of terrible storms. These predictions are among the most visible ways in which the work of geographers affects our lives every day.

Summary and Preview In this lesson you learned about two main branches of geography—physical and human. Next, you will learn about two systems geographers use to organize their studies.

Lesson 2 Assessment

Review Ideas, Terms, and Places

1. **a. Define** What is physical geography?
   b. Explain Why do we study physical geography?
2. **a. Identify** What are some things that people study as part of human geography?
   b. Summarize What are some ways in which the study of human geography can influence our lives?
   c. Evaluate Which do you think would be more interesting to study: physical geography or human geography? Why?
3. **a. Identify** What are two specialized fields of geography?
   b. Analyze How do cartographers contribute to the work of other geographers?

Critical Thinking

4. **Compare and Contrast** Draw a diagram like the one shown here. In the left circle, list three features of physical geography from your notes. In the right circle, list three features of human geography. Where the circles overlap, list one feature they share.

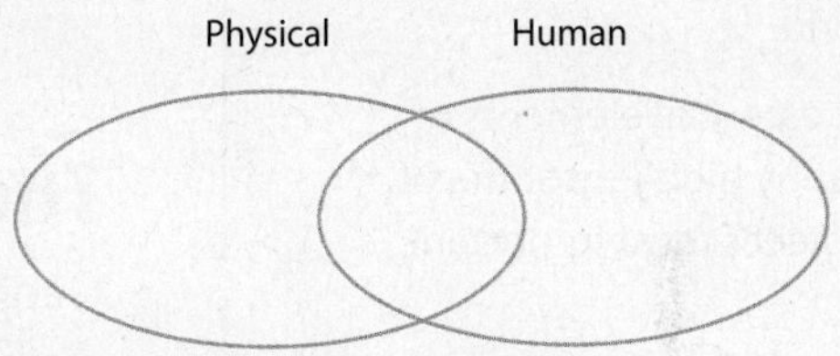

Themes of Geography

The Big Idea

Geographers have created two different but related systems for organizing geographic studies.

Main Ideas

- The five themes of geography help us organize our studies of the world.
- The six essential elements of geography highlight some of the subject's most important ideas.

Key Terms and Places

absolute location
relative location
environment

If YOU lived there . . .

Your older sister has offered to drive you to a friend's house across town, but she doesn't know how to get there. You know your friend's street address and what the apartment building looks like. You know it's near the public library. You also would recognize some landmarks in the neighborhood, such as the gas station and the supermarket.

What might help your sister find the house?

The Five Themes of Geography

Geographers use themes, or ideas, in their work. These geography themes can be applied to nearly everything that geographers study. The five major themes of geography are Location, Place, Human Environment Interaction, Movement, and Regions.

Location Every point on Earth has a location, a description of where it is. This location can be expressed in many ways. Sometimes a site's location is expressed in specific, or absolute, terms, such as an address. For example, the White House is located at 1600 Pennsylvania Avenue in the city of Washington, DC. A specific description like this one is called an **absolute location.** Other times, the site's location is expressed in general terms. For example, Canada is north of the United States. This general description of where a place lies is called its **relative location.**

Place Another theme, Place, is closely related to Location. However, Place does not refer simply to where an area is. It refers to the area's landscape, the features that define the area and make it different from other places. Such features could include land, climate, and people. Together, they give a place its own character.

Human-Environment Interaction In addition to looking at the features of places, geographers examine how those features interact. In particular, they want to understand how people interact with their environment—how people and their physical environment affect each other. An area's **environment** includes its land, water, climate, plants, and animals.

The Five Themes of Geography

Geographers use five major themes to organize and guide their studies: Location, Place, Human-Environment Interaction, Movement, and Regions.

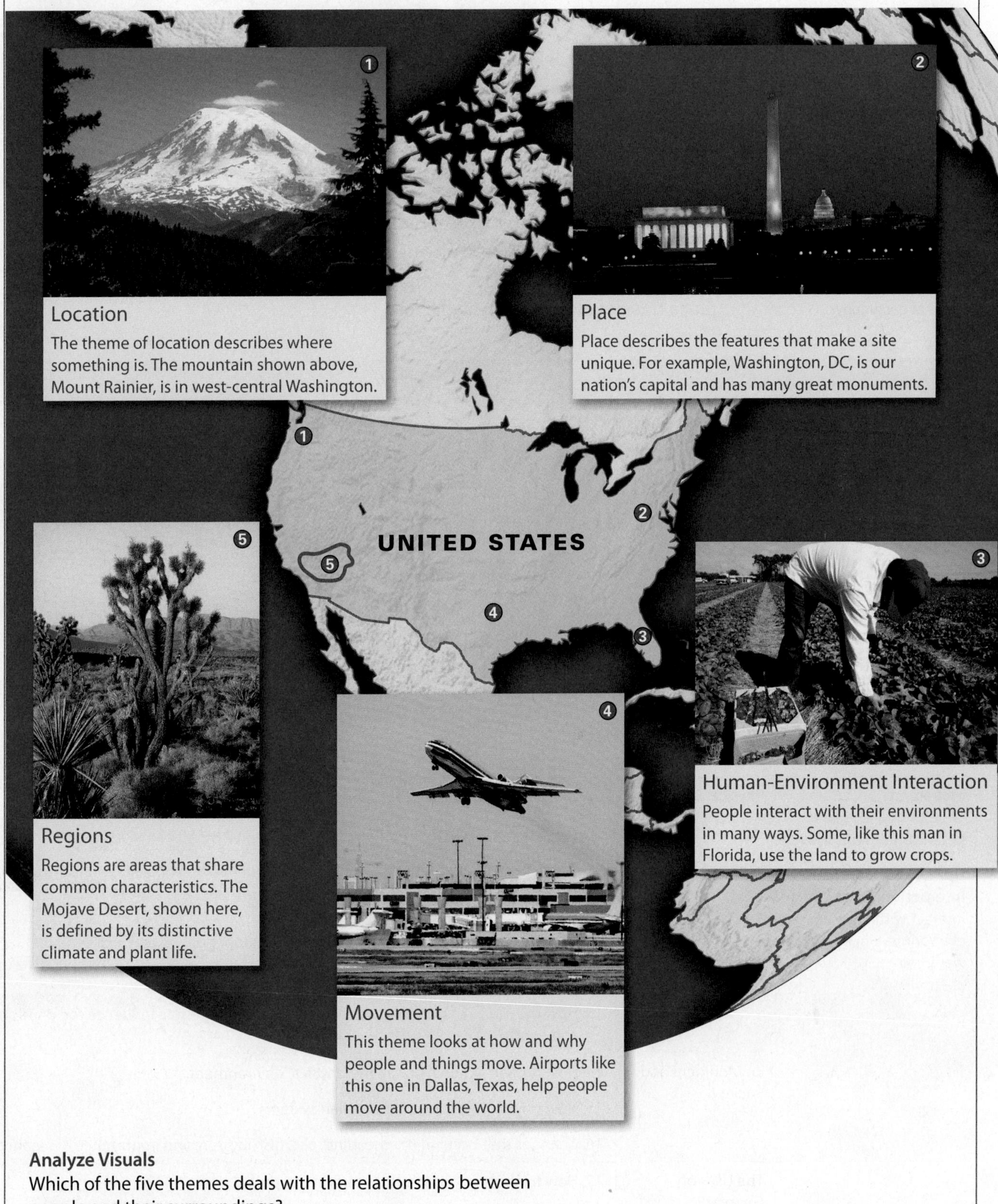

Location
The theme of location describes where something is. The mountain shown above, Mount Rainier, is in west-central Washington.

Place
Place describes the features that make a site unique. For example, Washington, DC, is our nation's capital and has many great monuments.

Regions
Regions are areas that share common characteristics. The Mojave Desert, shown here, is defined by its distinctive climate and plant life.

Human-Environment Interaction
People interact with their environments in many ways. Some, like this man in Florida, use the land to grow crops.

Movement
This theme looks at how and why people and things move. Airports like this one in Dallas, Texas, help people move around the world.

Analyze Visuals
Which of the five themes deals with the relationships between people and their surroundings?

People interact with their environment every day in all sorts of ways. They clear forests to plant crops, level fields to build cities, and dam rivers to prevent floods. At the same time, physical environments affect how people live. People in cold areas, for example, build houses with thick walls and wear heavy clothing to keep warm. People who live near oceans look for ways to protect themselves from storms.

Movement People are constantly moving. They move within cities, between cities, and between countries. Geographers want to know why and how people move. For example, they ask if people are moving to find work or to live in a more pleasant area. Geographers also study the roads and routes that make movement so common.

Regions You have already learned how geographers divide the world into many regions to help the study of geography. Creating regions also makes it easier to compare places. Comparisons help geographers learn why each place has developed the way it has.

Reading Check
Find Main Ideas
What are the five themes of geography?

Geography's Themes, Essential Elements, and Standards

Themes of Geography	Essential Elements	Geography Standards
Location The theme of Location describes where something is.	The World in Spatial Terms	1. How to use maps and other geographic representations, tools, and technologies to acquire, process, and report information from a spatial perspective 2. How to use mental maps to organize information about people, places, and environments in a spatial context 3. How to analyze the spatial organization of people, places, and environments on Earth's surface
Place Place describes the features that make a site unique. **Regions** Regions are areas that share common characteristics.	Places and Regions	4. The physical and human characteristics of places 5. How people create regions to interpret Earth's complexity 6. How culture and experience influence people's perceptions of places and regions
Movement This theme looks at how and why people and things move. **Human-Environment Interaction** People interact with their environment in many ways.	Physical Systems	7. The physical processes that shape the patterns of Earth's surface 8. The characteristics and spatial distribution of ecosystems on Earth's surface
	Human Systems	9. The characteristics, distribution, and migration of human populations on Earth's surface 10. The characteristics, distribution, and complexity of Earth's cultural mosaics 11. The patterns and networks of economic interdependence on Earth's surface 12. The processes, patterns, and functions of human settlement 13. How the forces of cooperation and conflict among people influence the division and control of Earth's surface
	Environment and Society	14. How human actions modify the physical environment 15. How physical systems affect human systems 16. Changes that occur in the meaning, use, distribution, and importance of resources
	The Uses of Geography	17. How to apply geography to interpret the past 18. How to apply geography to interpret the present and plan for the future

The Six Essential Elements

Academic Vocabulary
element part

The five themes of geography are not the only system geographers use to study the world. They also use a system of essential **elements** and national standards. Together, these themes, essential elements, and standards identify the most important ideas in the study of geography. Refer to the chart on the previous page.

The geography standards are 18 basic ideas that are central to the study of geography. The essential elements are based on the geography standards and act as a bridge between the themes and standards. Each element links several standards together. The six essential elements are The World in Spatial Terms, Places and Regions, Physical Systems, Human Systems, Environment and Society, and The Uses of Geography.

Read through that list again. Do you see any similarities between geography's six essential elements and its five themes? You probably do. The two systems are very similar because the six essential elements build on the five themes.

For example, the element Places and Regions combines two of the five themes of geography—Place and Regions. Also, the element called Environment and Society deals with many of the same issues as the theme Human-Environment Interaction.

There are also some basic differences between the essential elements and the themes. For example, the last element, The Uses of Geography, deals with issues not covered in the five themes. This element examines how people can use geography to plan the landscapes in which they live.

Throughout this book, you will notice references to both the themes and the essential elements. As you read, use these themes and elements to help you organize your own study of geography.

Reading Check
Summarize
What are the six essential elements of geography?

Summary and Preview You have just learned about the themes, elements, and standards of geography. In the next lesson, you will learn about the tools geographers use.

Lesson 3 Assessment

Review Ideas, Terms, and Places

1. **a. Contrast** How are the themes of Location and Place different?

   b. Elaborate How does using the five themes help geographers understand the places they study?

2. **a. Identify** Which of the five themes of geography is associated with airports, highways, and the migration of people from one place to another?

   b. Explain How are the geography standards and the six essential elements related?

   c. Compare How are the six essential elements similar to the five themes of geography?

   d. Recall To which essential element does the theme of Location relate?

Critical Thinking

3. **Categorize** Draw a chart like the one below. Use your notes to list the five themes of geography, explain each of the themes, and list one feature of your city or town that relates to each.

Theme					
Explanation					
Feature					

The Geographer's Tools

The Big Idea

Geographers use many tools to study the world.

Main Ideas

- Maps and globes are the most commonly used tools of geographers.
- Many geographers study information gathered by satellites.
- Geographers use many other tools, including graphs, charts, databases, and models, in their work.

Key Terms and Places

map
globe
Global Positioning System (GPS)
Geographic Information System (GIS)

If YOU lived there . . .

Your family's apartment has a leaking pipe under the kitchen sink. The landlord has sent a plumber to your apartment to fix the leak. The plumber arrives carrying a tool chest. You know that plumbers need specific tools to do their jobs correctly.

Can you think of a tool the plumber might use for this job?

Maps and Globes

Like all people with jobs to do, geographers need tools to study the world. The tools that geographers use most often in their work are maps and globes. A **map** is a flat drawing that shows all or part of Earth's surface. A **globe** is a spherical, or ball-shaped, model of the entire planet.

Both maps and globes show what the world looks like. They can show where mountains, deserts, and oceans are. They can also identify and describe the world's countries and major cities.

There are, however, major differences between maps and globes. Because a globe is spherical like Earth, it can show the world as it really is. A map, though, is flat. It is not possible to show a spherical area perfectly on a flat surface. To understand what this means, think about an orange. If you took the peel off of an orange, could you make it lie completely flat? No, you could not, unless you stretched or tore the peel first.

The same principle is true with maps. To draw Earth on a flat surface, people have to distort, or alter, some details. For example, places on a map might look to be farther apart than they really are, or their shapes or sizes might be changed slightly.

Still, maps have many advantages over globes. Flat maps are easier to work with than globes. Also, it is easier to show small areas like cities on maps than on globes. In addition, maps usually show more information than globes. Because globes are more expensive to make, they do not usually show anything more than where places are and what features they have.

Reading Check
Summarize
What are the tools geographers most often use?

Maps, on the other hand, can show all sorts of information. Besides showing land use and cities, maps can include a great deal of information about a place. A map might show what languages people speak or where their ancestors came from. Maps like the one below can even show how many students in an area play soccer.

The Geographer's Tools

Geographers use many tools to study the world. Each tool provides part of the information a geographer needs to learn what a place is like.

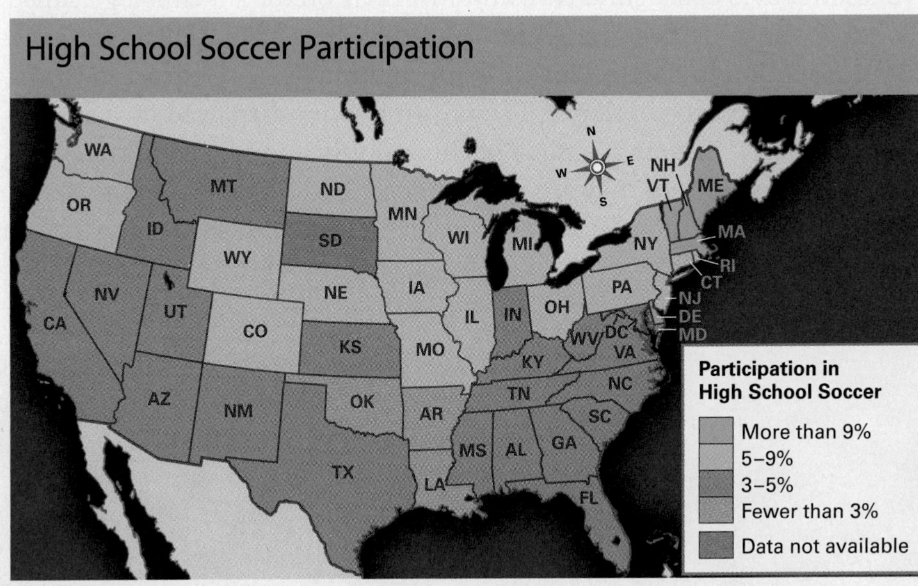

Maps usually give geographers more information about a place than globes do. This map, for example, shows rates of soccer participation in the United States.

A geographer can use a globe to see where a place, such as the United States, is located.

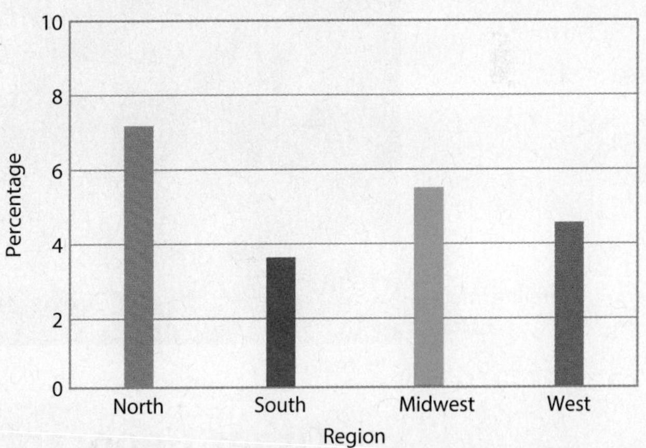

Charts and graphs are also tools geographers can use to study information. They are often used when geographers want to compare numbers, such as the number of students who play soccer in each region of the country.

Analyze Visuals
What information could you learn from each of these tools?

Satellites

Maps and globes are not the only tools that geographers use in their work. As you have already read, many geographers study information gathered by satellites.

Much of the information gathered by these satellites is in the form of images. Geographers can study these images of Earth to see what an area looks like from far above. Satellites also collect information that we cannot see from the planet's surface. The information gathered by satellites helps geographers make accurate maps.

Satellites also collect and transmit information for a technology called **Global Positioning System (GPS).** The system uses 24 satellites to transmit information to Earth. This GPS information gives the exact location of a given object on our planet. The information is displayed on a small receiver. Vehicle drivers are some of the people who use GPS to find out how to get from where they are to other locations. There are many other uses of GPS. These include locating people in need of rescue on boats or in the wilderness. Scientists also use GPS to track and study wildlife.

Reading Check
Summarize
What satellite technology transmits data to people with receivers?

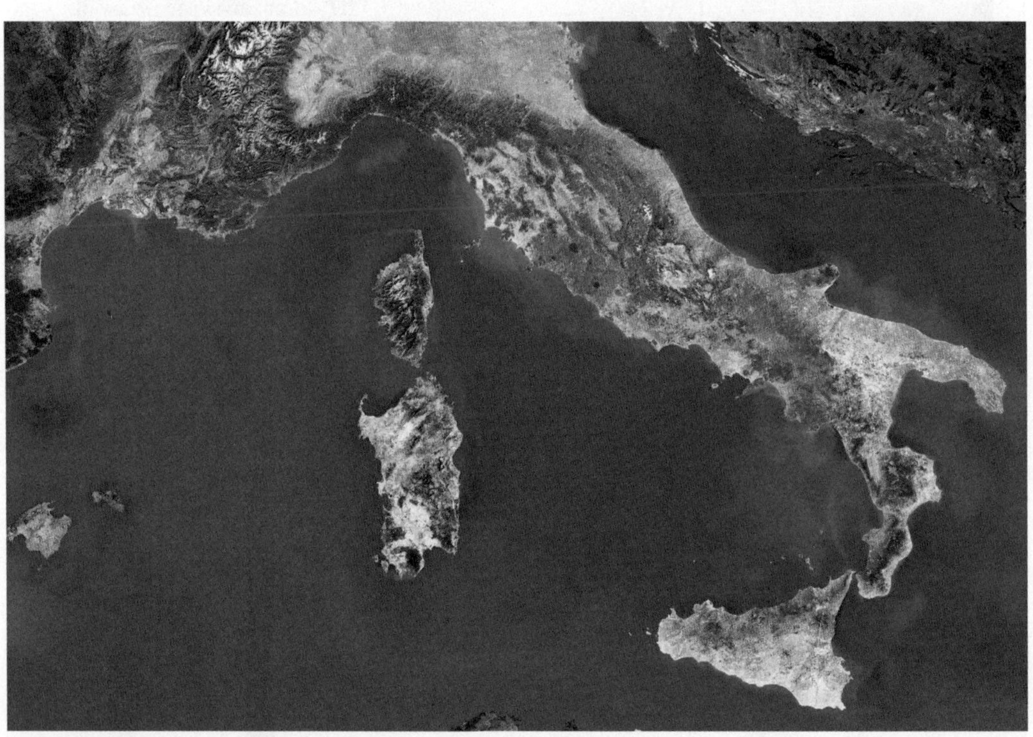

Satellite image of Italy

Other Geographic Tools

Geographers also use many other tools. To depict aspects of various countries and world regions, geographers create graphs, charts, databases, and models. They also use these tools to gather data and compare various world regions.

There is a geography tool that is made up of a group of databases. It is called **Geographic Information System (GIS).** GIS combines and provides information from many different sources. People use GIS by posing questions to the system. For example, a city planner might be looking for the best site near a city to build an airport. To find out, a geographer asks GIS, "What geographic characteristics are important for a good airport site?" GIS pulls together many layers of information, including different types of maps, to answer the question.

Reading Check
Summarize Of what does Geographic Information System (GIS) consist?

In less complex cases, the best tools a geographer can use are a notebook and digital voice recorder to take notes while talking to people. Armed with the proper tools, geographers learn about the world's people and places.

Summary and Preview You have learned that geographers use maps, globes, and other tools to study the world. In the next lesson, you will learn map skills, new geographic terms, and geographic themes and elements.

Lesson 4 Assessment

Review Ideas, Terms, and Places

1. a. **Compare and Contrast** How are maps and globes similar? How are they different?
   b. **Identify** What are the advantages maps have over globes?
2. a. **Describe** How do geographers use satellite images?
   b. **Recall** What are some uses of GPS?
3. a. **Describe** What is GIS?
   b. **Recall** What is the purpose of GIS for geographers?

Critical Thinking

4. **Summarize** Make a chart like the one below that lists some of the geographer's tools.

The Geographer's Tools	

Geography Handbook

The Big Idea

Geographers study the world by understanding maps and geographic features of Earth.

Main Ideas

- When creating maps, cartographers use a pattern of latitude and longitude lines that circle Earth.
- Cartographers have created map projections to show the round surface of Earth on a flat piece of paper.
- Cartographers provide features to help users read maps.
- There are different kinds of maps for different uses.
- There are many kinds of landforms and other features on Earth.

Key Terms and Places

grid
latitude
parallels
equator
degrees
minutes
longitude
meridians
prime meridian
hemispheres
continents
map projections

Latitude and Longitude

As you learned in Lesson 4, a globe is a spherical model of Earth. It is useful for showing the entire Earth or studying large areas of Earth's surface.

To study the world, geographers use a pattern of imaginary lines that circle the globe in east–west and north–south directions. It is called a **grid.** The intersection of these imaginary lines helps us find places on Earth.

The east–west lines in the grid are lines of **latitude.** These lines are called **parallels** because they are always the same distance apart. Lines of latitude measure distance north and south of the **equator.** The equator is an imaginary line that circles the globe halfway between the North and South Poles. It divides the globe into north and south halves. Parallels measure distance from the equator in **degrees.** The symbol for degrees is °. Degrees are further divided into **minutes.** The symbol for minutes is ´. There are 60 minutes in a degree. Parallels north of the equator are labeled with an *N*. Those south of the equator are labeled with an *S*.

The north–south imaginary lines are lines of **longitude.** Lines of longitude are called **meridians.** These imaginary lines pass through the poles. They measure distance east and west of the **prime meridian.** The prime meridian is an imaginary line that divides the globe into east and west halves. It runs through Greenwich, England, and represents 0° longitude.

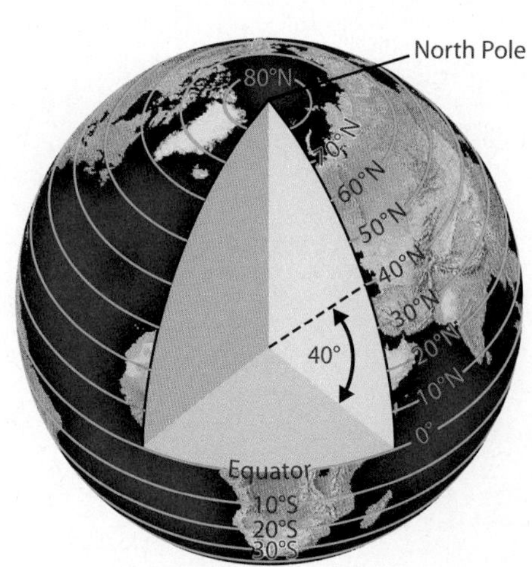

Lines of Latitude

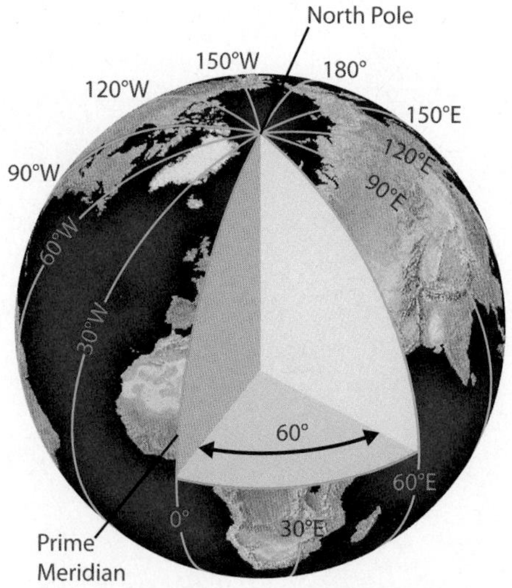

Lines of Longitude

Lines of latitude range from 0°, for locations on the equator, to 90°N or 90°S, for locations at the poles. Lines of longitude range from 0° on the prime meridian to 180° on a meridian in the mid–Pacific Ocean. Meridians west of the prime meridian to 180° are labeled with a *W*. Those east of the prime meridian to 180° are labeled with an *E*. Using latitude and longitude, geographers can identify the exact location of any place on Earth.

The equator divides the globe into two halves, called **hemispheres.** The half north of the equator is the Northern Hemisphere. The southern half is the Southern Hemisphere. The prime meridian and the 180° meridian divide the world into the Eastern and Western Hemispheres.

Earth's land surface is divided into seven large landmasses that are called **continents.** Landmasses smaller than continents and completely surrounded by water are called islands.

Geographers organize Earth's water surface into major regions, too. The largest is the world ocean. Geographers divide the world ocean into the Pacific Ocean, the Atlantic Ocean, the Indian Ocean, the Arctic Ocean, and the Southern Ocean.

Reading Check
Summarize How do geographers use a grid of imaginary lines to study the world?

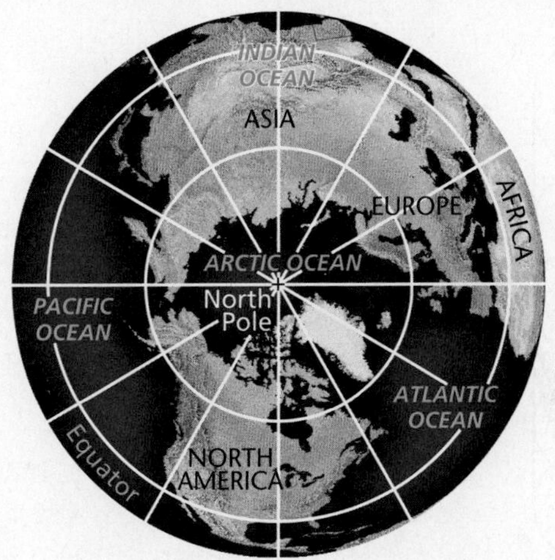

Northern Hemisphere

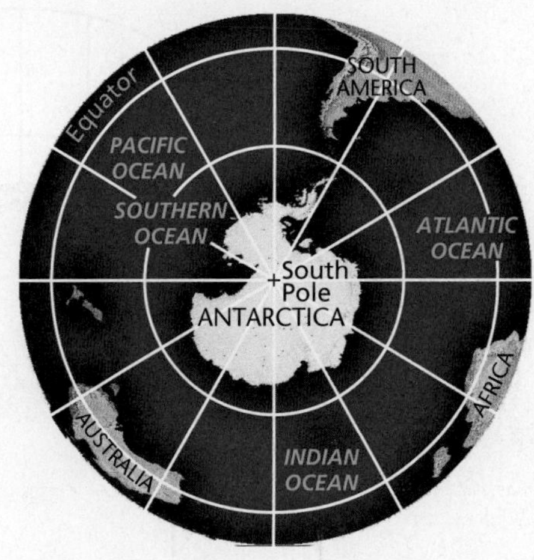

Southern Hemisphere

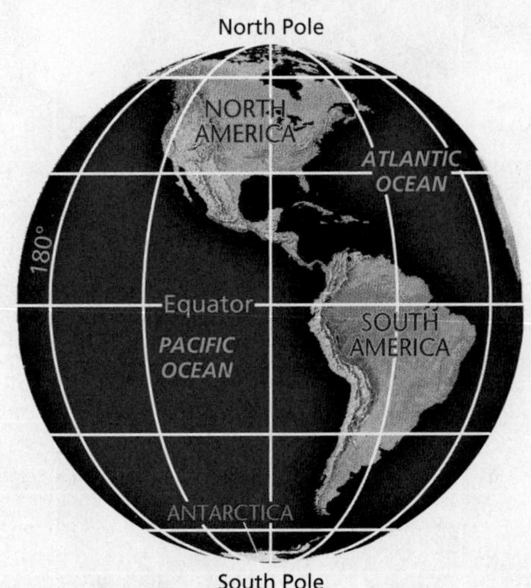

Western Hemisphere

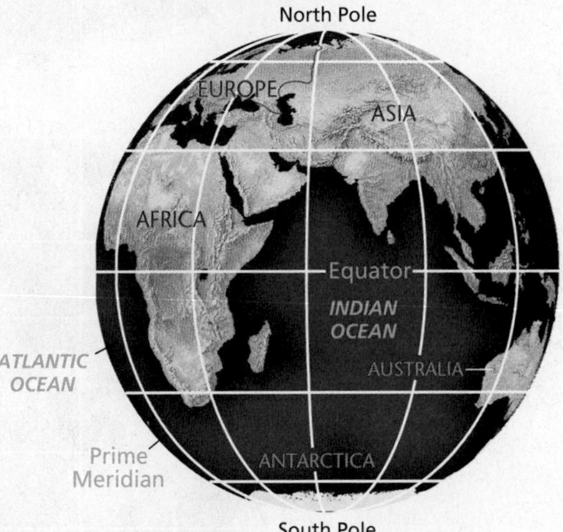

Eastern Hemisphere

Map Projections

A map is a flat diagram of all or part of Earth's surface. Mapmakers have created different ways of showing our round planet on flat maps. These different ways are called **map projections.** Because Earth is round, there is no way to show it accurately on a flat map. All flat maps are distorted in some way. Mapmakers must choose the type of map projection that is best for their purposes. Many map projections are one of three kinds: cylindrical, conic, or flat-plane.

Cylindrical Projections These projections are based on a cylinder wrapped around the globe. See the "Paper cylinder" illustration below. The cylinder touches the globe only at the equator. The meridians are pulled apart and are parallel to each other instead of meeting at the poles. This causes landmasses near the poles to appear larger than they really are.

A Mercator projection is one type of cylindrical projection. The Mercator projection is useful for navigators because it shows true direction and shape. However, it distorts the size of land areas near the poles.

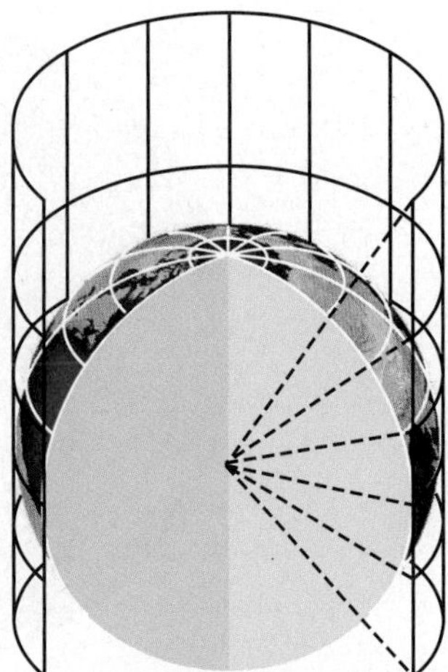

Paper cylinder

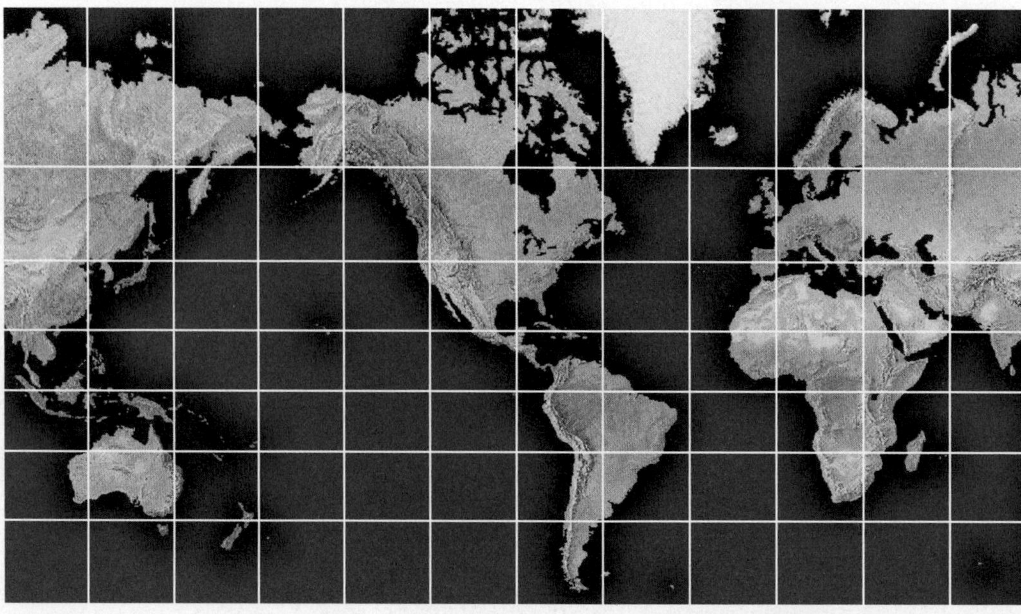

Mercator projection

Conic Projections These projections are based on a cone placed over the globe. See the "Paper cone" illustration below. A conic projection is most accurate along the lines of latitude where it touches the globe. It retains almost true shape and size. Conic projections are most useful for showing areas that have long east–west dimensions, such as the United States.

Reading Check
Identify Problems
Why is it impossible to accurately show large parts of the world on flat maps?

Flat-plane Projections These projections are based on a plane touching the globe at one point, such as at the North Pole or South Pole. See the "Flat plane" illustration below. A flat-plane projection can show true direction to airplane pilots and ship navigators. It also shows true area. However, it distorts the true shapes of landmasses.

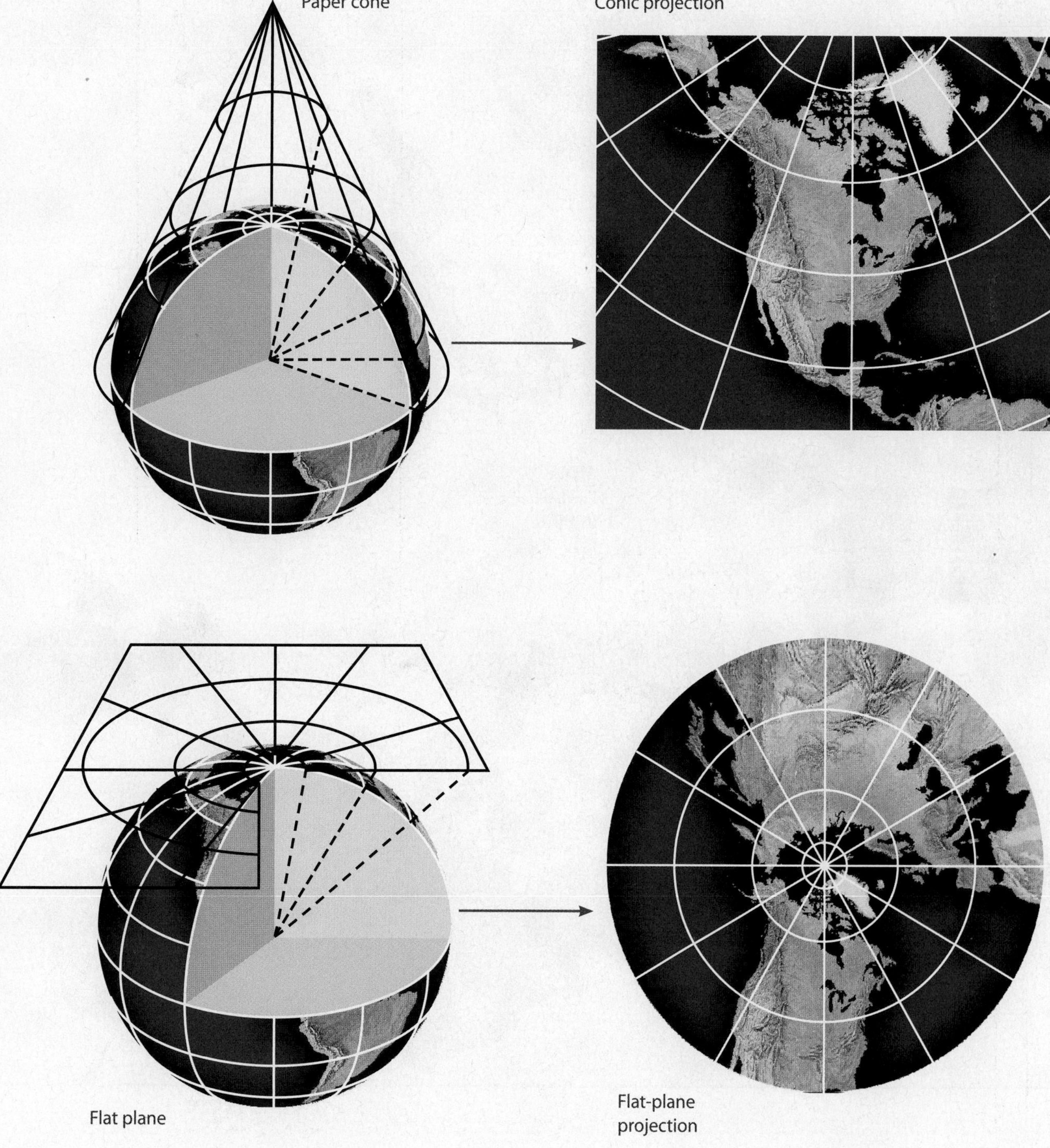

Map Features

Maps are like messages sent out in code. To help us translate the code, mapmakers provide certain features. These features help us understand the message they are presenting about a particular part of the world. Of these features, almost all maps have a title, a compass rose, a scale, and a legend. The map below has these four features plus a fifth—a locator map.

1 Title A map's title shows what the subject of the map is. The map title is usually the first thing you should look at when studying a map, because it tells you what the map is trying to show.

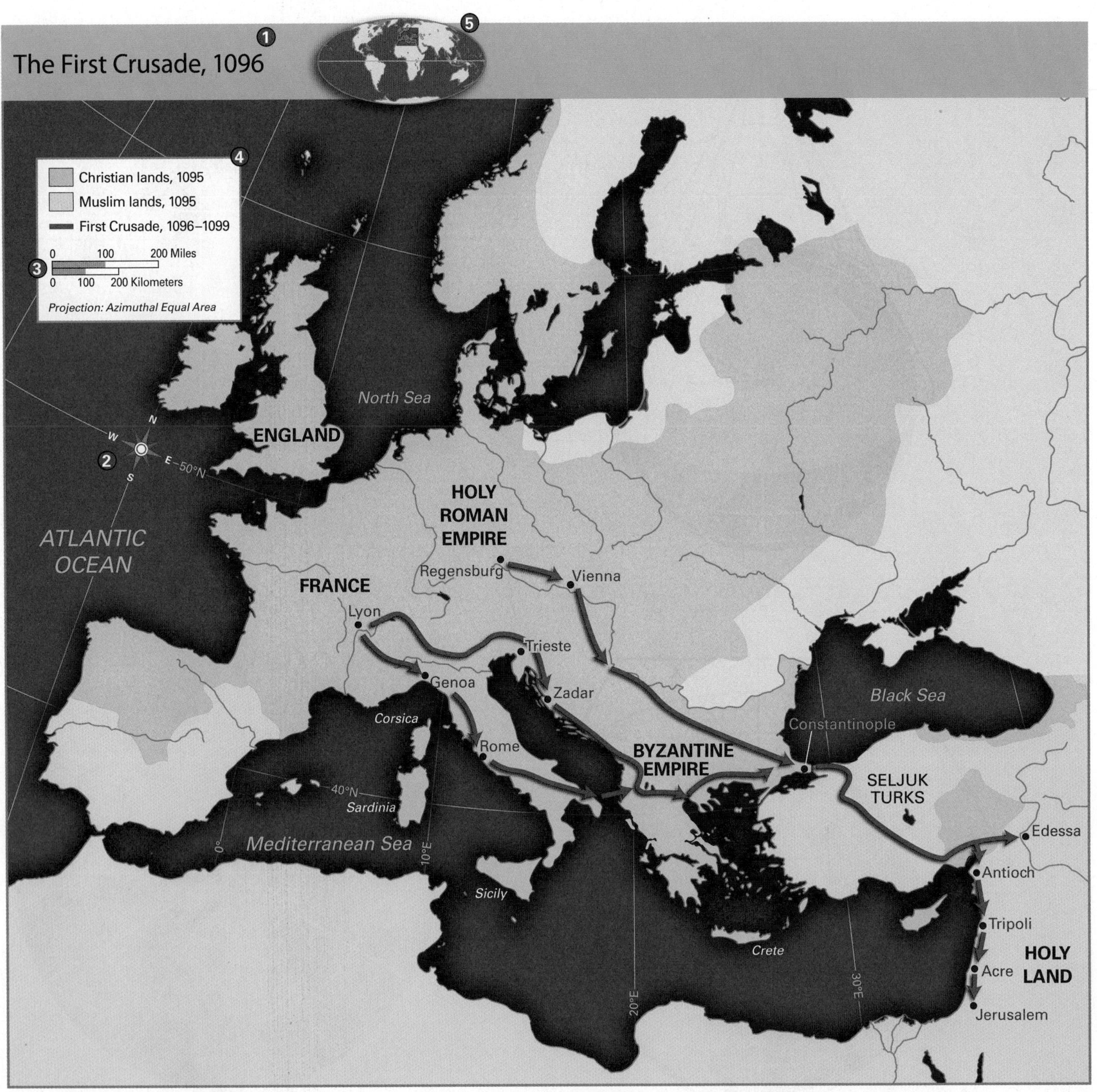

2 Compass Rose A directional indicator shows which way north, south, east, and west lie on the map. Some mapmakers use a "north arrow," which points toward the North Pole. Remember, "north" is not always at the top of a map. The way a map is drawn and the location of directions on that map depend on the perspective of the mapmaker. Most maps indicate direction with a compass rose. A compass rose has arrows that point to all four principal directions, also called cardinal points. The principal directions are north (N), east (E), south (S), and west (W). Some compass roses also show the intermediate directions. These are northeast (NE), southeast (SE), southwest (SW), and northwest (NW).

3 Scale Mapmakers use scales to represent the distances between points on a map. Scales may appear on maps in several different forms. Some maps provide a bar scale. Scales give distances in miles and kilometers.

To find the distance between two points on the map, place a piece of paper so that the edge connects the two points. Mark the location of each point on the paper with a line or dot. Then compare the distance between the two dots with the map's bar scale. The number on the top of the scale gives the distance in miles. The number on the bottom gives the distance in kilometers. Because the distances are given in large intervals, you may have to approximate the actual distance on the scale.

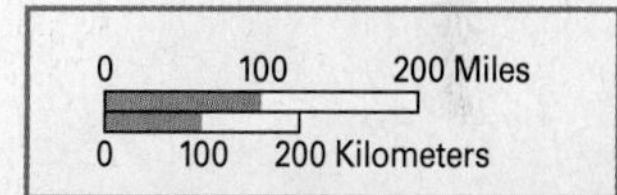

4 Legend The legend, or key, explains what the symbols on the map represent. Point symbols are used to specify the location of things, such as cities, that do not take up much space on the map. Some legends show colors that represent certain features like empires or other regions. Other maps might have legends with symbols or colors that represent features such as roads. Legends can also show economic resources, land use, population density, and climate. Some legends include the map scale as well.

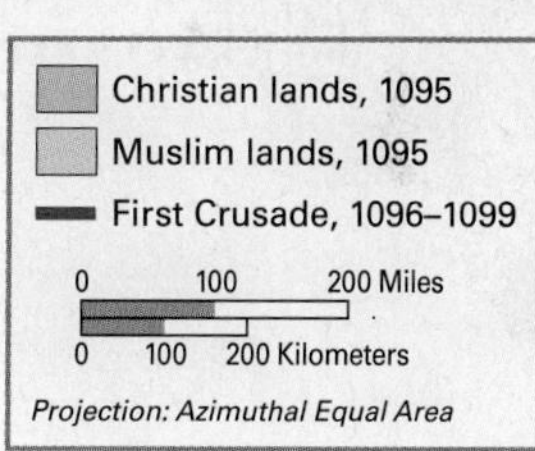

Reading Check
Summarize What four features do most maps have?

5 Locator Map A locator map shows where in the world the area on the map is located. In this example, the area shown on the main map is shown in red on the locator map. The locator map also shows surrounding areas so the reader can see how the information on the map relates to neighboring lands.

Different Kinds of Maps

As you study the world's regions and countries, you will use a variety of maps. Political maps and physical maps are two of the most common types of maps you will study. In addition, you will use thematic maps. These maps might show climate, population, resources, ancient empires, or other topics. By working with these maps, you will see what the physical geography of places is like, where people live, and how the world has changed over time.

Political Maps Political maps show the major political features of a region. These features include country borders, capital cities, and other places. Political maps use different colors to represent countries, and capital cities are often shown with a special star symbol.

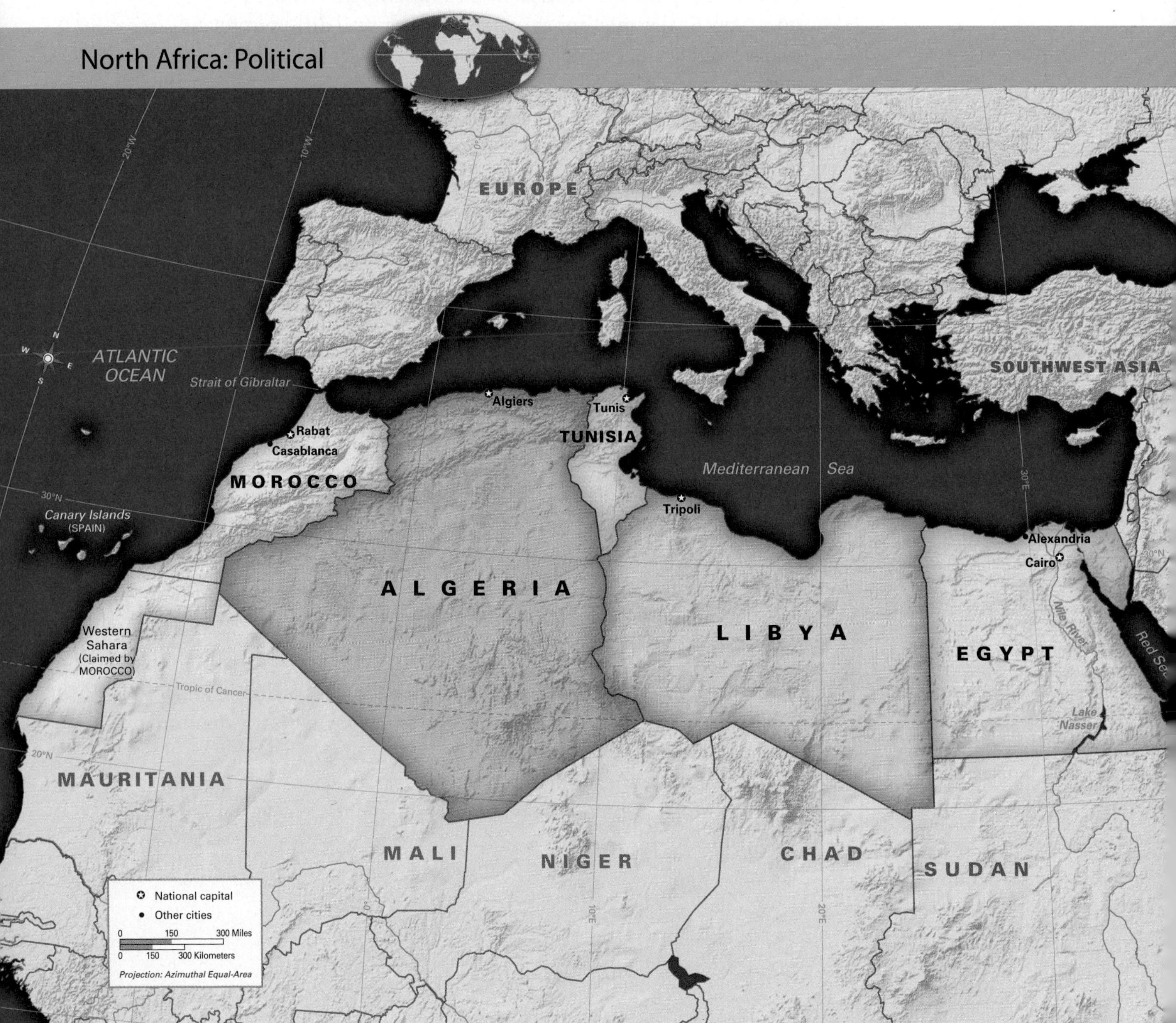

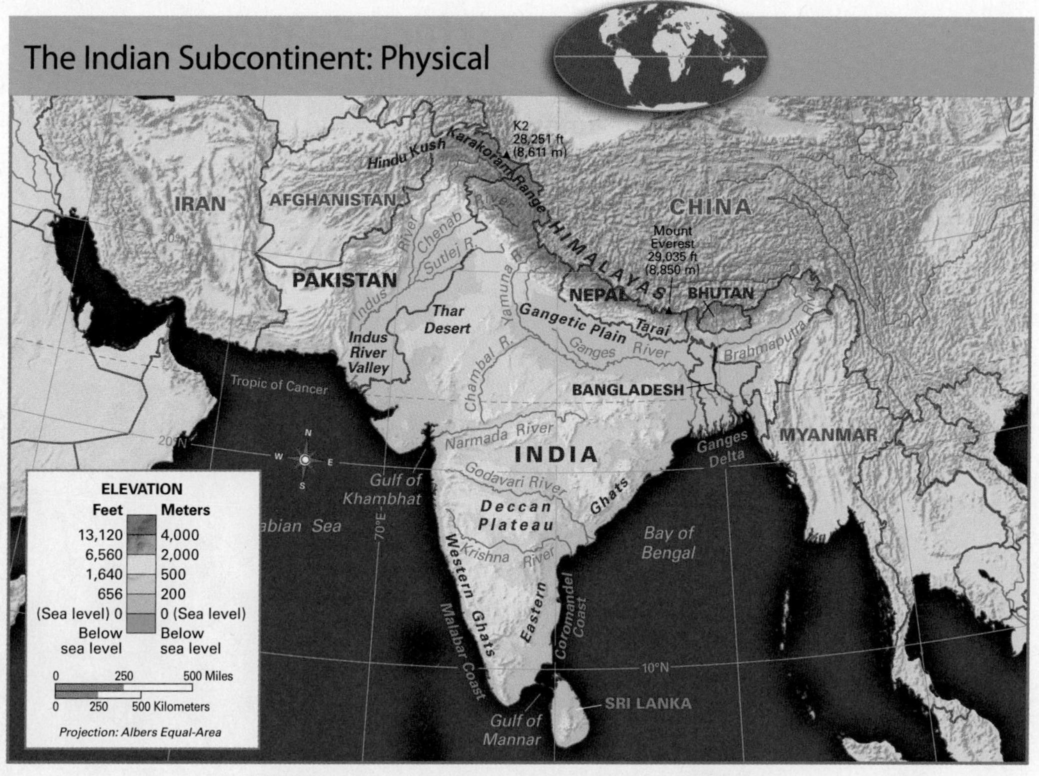

Physical Maps Physical maps show the major physical features of a region. See the map above. These features may include mountain ranges, rivers, oceans, islands, deserts, and plains. Often, these maps use different colors to represent different elevations of land. The reader can easily see which areas are high elevations, such as mountains, and which areas are lower.

Thematic Maps Thematic maps focus on one special topic, such as climate, resources, or population. See the map below. These maps present information on the topic that is particularly important in the region. Depending on the type of thematic map, the information may be shown with different colors, arrows, dots, or other symbols.

Reading Check
Summarize
What are two of the most common kinds of maps used in geography?

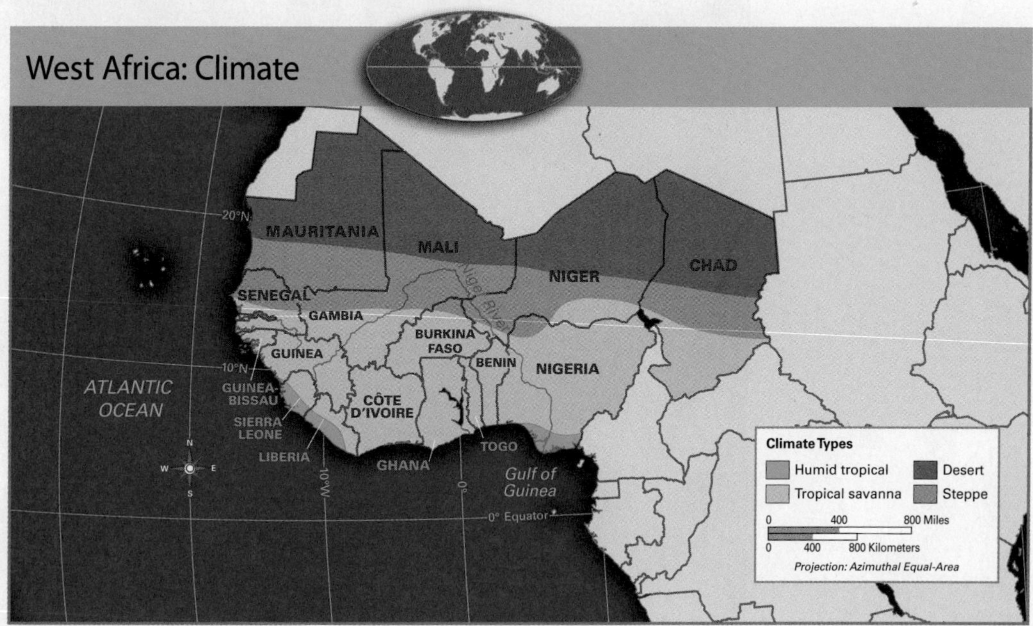

Earth's Surface Features

Reading Check
Summarize What is a landform?

A landform is a naturally formed feature on Earth's surface. There are many kinds of landforms and water features on Earth. Many of these features are shown in this illustration.

Feature Descriptions		
1	**ocean**	large body of water
2	**cape**	point of land that extends into water
3	**coastal plain**	area of flat land along a sea or ocean
4	**coast**	area of land near the ocean
5	**glacier**	large area of slow-moving ice
6	**lake**	inland body of water
7	**plain**	nearly flat area
8	**inlet**	area of water extending into the land from a larger body of water
9	**floodplain**	flat land next to a river formed by silt deposited by floods
10	**timberline**	line on a mountain above which it is too cold for trees to grow
11	**river**	natural flow of water that runs through the land
12	**source of river**	place where a river begins
13	**foothill**	hilly area at the base of a mountain
14	**riverbank**	land along a river
15	**mouth of river**	place where a river empties into another body of water
16	**hill**	rounded, elevated area of land smaller than a mountain
17	**mountain**	area of rugged land that generally rises higher than 2,000 feet
18	**island**	area of land surrounded entirely by water
19	**basin**	bowl-shaped area of land surrounded by higher land
20	**mountain range**	row of mountains
21	**plateau**	large, flat, elevated area of land
22	**bluff**	high, steep face of rock or earth
23	**isthmus**	narrow piece of land connecting two larger land areas
24	**valley**	area of low land between hills or mountains
25	**marsh**	lowland with moist soil and tall grasses
26	**lagoon**	body of shallow water
27	**strait**	narrow body of water connecting two larger bodies of water
28	**canyon**	deep, narrow valley with steep walls
29	**peninsula**	area of land that sticks out into a lake or ocean
30	**volcano**	opening in Earth's crust where lava, ash, and gases erupt
31	**waterfall**	steep drop from a high place to a lower place in a stream or river
32	**delta**	area where a river deposits soil into the ocean
33	**cliff**	high, steep face of rock or earth
34	**reef**	ocean ridge made up of coral, rock, or sand
35	**gulf**	large part of the ocean that extends into land
36	**peak**	top of a mountain
37	**swamp**	area of low, wet land with trees
38	**bay**	part of a large body of water that is smaller than a gulf
39	**dune**	hill of sand shaped by wind
40	**tributary**	stream or river that flows into a larger stream or river
41	**mountain pass**	gap between mountains
42	**sea**	body of salt water smaller than an ocean
43	**desert**	extremely dry area with little water and few plants
44	**oasis**	area in the desert with a water source
45	**mesa**	flat-topped mountain with steep sides
46	**savanna**	area of grassland and scattered trees

Summary As you study geography, one of the main tools you will use is the map—the primary tool of geographers. In this lesson, you learned about some of the basic features of maps. You discovered how maps are made, how to read them, and how they can show the round surface of Earth on a flat piece of paper. You learned about latitude and longitude and map projections. You read about map features, such as titles, compass roses, scales, legends, and locator maps, and different kinds of maps designed for different uses. You've discovered names and descriptions of some of Earth's features. Now use your new knowledge to explore the world from a geographer's perspective.

Lesson 5 Assessment

Review Ideas, Terms, and Places

1. a. **Define** What is the equator?
   b. **Identify** How is the prime meridian used?
2. a. **Define** What is a map projection?
   b. **Explain** Why are cylindrical and flat-plane projections useful for airplane pilots and ship navigators?
3. a. **Describe** Describe a compass rose and the information it contains.
   b. **Identify and Explain** What is a bar scale? How is it used?
4. a. **Analyze** Which kind of map would you use if you wanted to know which part of the mapped area was highest? Why?
   b. **Identify** What characteristic makes a map a thematic map?
5. a. **Define** What is a delta?
   b. **Define** What is a glacier?

Critical Thinking

6. **Compare and Contrast** Create a chart like the one shown that compares and contrasts kinds of map projections.

Map Projections			
	Cylindrical	Conic	Flat-plane
Based on			
Accurately shows			
Distorts			

Social Studies Skills

Analyze Satellite Images

Define the Skill

In addition to maps and globes, satellite images are among the geographer's most valuable tools. Geographers use two basic types of these images. The first type is called true color. These images are like photographs taken from high above Earth's surface. The colors in these images are similar to what you would see from the ground. Vegetation, for example, appears green.

The other type of satellite image is called an infrared image. Infrared images are taken using a special type of light. These images are based on heat patterns, and so the colors on them are not what we might expect. Bodies of water appear black, for example, since they give off little heat.

True-color satellite image of Italy

Learn the Skill

Use the satellite images on this page to answer the following questions.

1. On which image is vegetation red?
2. Which image do you think probably looks more like Italy from the ground?

Infrared satellite image of Italy

Practice the Skill

Search the Internet to find a satellite image of your state or region. Determine whether the image is true color or infrared. Then write three statements that describe what you see on the image.

Module 1 Assessment

Review Vocabulary, Terms, and Places

Match the words in the columns with the correct definitions listed below.

1. geography
2. physical geography
3. human geography
4. element
5. meteorology
6. region
7. cartography
8. map
9. landscape
10. globe

a. a part of the world that has one or more common features that make it different from surrounding areas

b. a flat drawing of part of Earth's surface

c. a part

d. a spherical model of the planet

e. the study of the world's physical features

f. the study of weather and what causes it

g. the study of the world, its people, and the landscapes they create

h. the science of making maps

i. the physical and human features that define an area and make it different from other places

j. the study of people and communities

Comprehension and Critical Thinking

Lesson 1

11. a. **Explain** In what ways do geographers become scientists when working to answer questions?
    b. **Recall** What are three levels at which a geographer might study the world?
    c. **Identify** Which of these levels covers the largest area?

Lesson 2

12. a. **Locate** Choose a country to locate on the political map of the world in this book's atlas. Use latitude and longitude to determine the absolute location of the country.
    b. **Explain** Why did geographers create the five themes and the six essential elements?
    c. **Predict** How might the five themes and six essential elements help you in your study of geography?

Lesson 3

13. a. **Identify** What are the two main branches of geography? What does each include?
    b. **Summarize** How can physical geography help people adjust to the dangers of the world?
    c. **Elaborate** Why do geographers study both physical and human geographic features of places?

Lesson 4

14. a. **Elaborate** How might satellite images and computers help geographers improve their knowledge of the world?
    b. **Define** What is GPS?
    c. **Explain** How might a geographer use a notebook and a digital voice recorder to gather data?

Lesson 5

15. a. **Define** What is a hemisphere of a globe?
    b. **Explain** What features are shown in a political map?
    c. **Identify** What is a peninsula?

Module 1 Assessment, continued

Reading Skills 

16. **Use Prior Knowledge** Use the Reading Social Studies activity in this module to help you create a chart. With a partner, create a three-column chart titled A Geographer's World. In the first column, list what you each knew about geography before you read the module. In the second column, list what you each learned about geography. In the third column, list questions that you each still have about geography.

Social Studies Skills

Analyze Satellite Images *Use the images from the Social Studies Skills activity in this module to answer the questions below.*

17. On which image do forests appear more clearly: the true color or the infrared image?
18. What color do you think represents mountains on the infrared satellite image?
19. Why might geographers use satellite images like these while making maps of Italy?

Map Activity 21st CENTURY

20. **Sketch Map** Look for and read environmental print to help you sketch a map of your school. Environmental print can be found all around you in the form of signs, labels, symbols, words, and numbers that provide information. Your map should include environmental print found in and around classrooms and buildings. Use the basic sketch map shown here as an example.

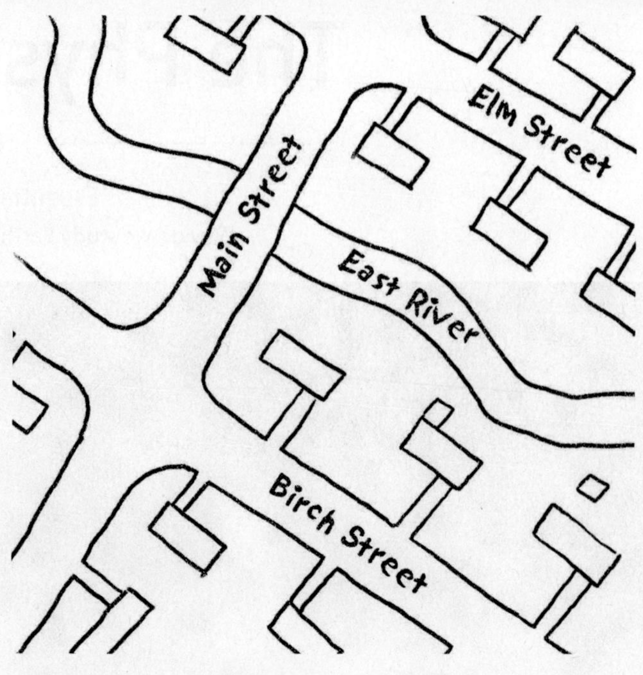

Focus on Writing

21. **Write a Job Description** Review your notes on the different jobs geographers do. Then write a job description of a geographer that could be included in a career planning guide. You should begin your description by explaining why the job is important. Then identify the job's tasks and responsibilities. Finally, tell what kind of person might do well as a geographer.

Module 2

The Physical World

Essential Question

Why do we study Earth and its physical systems?

About the Photo: Many of Earth's features are visible from space. This photo, taken from a satellite orbiting the planet, shows part of the North American continent.

Explore ONLINE!

VIDEOS, including . . .

- The Ring of Fire
- Plate Tectonics and Continental Drift

- Document-Based Investigations
- Graphic Organizers
- Interactive Games
- Animation: The Water Cycle
- Channel One News Video: Hunting Hurricanes
- Channel One News Video: Earthquake Preparedness
- Interactive Map: Major Climate Regions
- Image with Rich Media: Desert Ecosystem

In this module, you will learn about Earth's resources, and the processes that cause the seasons, shape landmasses and climates, and support life. You will also learn how humans use and interact with these resources and processes.

What You Will Learn

Lesson 1: Earth and the Sun's Energy 41
The Big Idea Earth's movement and the sun's energy interact to create day and night, temperature changes, and the seasons.

Lesson 2: Water on Earth 46
The Big Idea Water is a dominant feature on Earth's surface and is essential for life.

Lesson 3: The Land 52
The Big Idea Processes below and on Earth's surface shape the planet's physical features.

Lesson 4: Weather and Climate 62
The Big Idea The sun, location, wind, water, and mountains affect weather and climate.

Lesson 5: World Climates 68
The Big Idea Earth's five major climate zones are identified by temperature, precipitation, and plant life.

Lesson 6: Environments and Biomes. 77
The Big Idea Plants, animals, and the environment, including soil, interact with and affect one another.

Lesson 7: Natural Resources 82
The Big Idea Earth's natural resources have many valuable uses, and their availability affects people in many ways.

Land Forces on and under Earth's surface have shaped the different landforms on our planet. Geographers study how mountains and other landforms were made.

Water on Earth Water is essential for life on Earth. Much of the planet's water supply is stored in Earth's oceans and ice caps.

Environments Living things, such as this koala, depend on their surroundings.

Reading Social Studies

Use Word Parts

READING FOCUS

Many English words are made up of several word parts: roots, prefixes, and suffixes. A root is the base of the word and carries the main meaning. A prefix is a letter or syllable added to the beginning of a root. A suffix is a letter or syllable added to the end to create new words. When you come across a new word, you can sometimes figure out the meaning by looking at its parts. Study the charts of common word parts and their meanings.

Common Prefixes

Prefix	Meaning	Sample Words
geo-	earth	geology
inter-	between, among	interpersonal, intercom
in-	not	ineffective
re-	again	restate, rebuild

Common Roots

Word Root	Meaning	Sample Words
-graph-	write, writing	autograph, biography
-vid-, -vis-	see	videotape, visible

Common Suffixes

Suffix	Meaning	Sample Words
-ible	capable of	visible, responsible
-less	without	penniless, hopeless
-ize	make	equalize
-ment	result, action	commitment
-al	relating to	directional
-tion	the act or condition of	rotation, selection

YOU TRY IT!

Use your knowledge of word parts to understand challenging words such as the ones listed below. Work with a partner to read the words. First separate any prefixes or suffixes and identify the word's root. Use the charts to define the root, the prefix, or the suffix. Then work with your partner to write a definition for each word.

geography regardless reshaping movement invisible seasonal

visualize separation interact

As you read this module, look for words that include these word parts.

Earth and the Sun's Energy

The Big Idea

Earth's movement and the sun's energy interact to create day and night, temperature changes, and the seasons.

Main Ideas

- Earth's movement affects the amount of energy we receive from the sun.
- Earth's seasons are caused by the planet's tilt.

Key Terms and Places

solar energy
rotation
revolution
tropics

If YOU lived there . . .

You live in Chicago and have just won an exciting prize—a trip to Australia during winter vacation in January. As you prepare for the trip, your mother reminds you to pack shorts and a swimsuit. You are confused. In January you usually wear winter sweaters and a heavy jacket.

Why is the weather so different in Australia?

Earth's Movement

Energy from the sun helps crops grow, provides light, and warms Earth. It even influences the clothes we wear, the foods we eat, and the sports we play. All life on Earth requires **solar energy,** or energy from the sun, to survive. The amount of solar energy places on Earth receive changes constantly. Earth's rotation, revolution, and tilt, as well as latitude, all affect the amount of solar energy parts of the planet receive from the sun.

Rotation Imagine that Earth has a rod running through it from the North Pole to the South Pole. This rod represents Earth's axis—an imaginary line around which a planet turns. As Earth spins on its axis, different parts of the planet face the sun. It takes Earth 24 hours, or one day, to complete this rotation. A **rotation** is one complete spin of Earth on its axis. As Earth rotates during this 24-hour period, it appears to us that the sun moves across the sky. The sun seems to rise in the east and set in the west. The sun, however, does not move. It is actually Earth's rotation that creates the sense of the sun's movement.

Earth's rotation also explains why day changes to night. As you will see in the illustration on the next page, solar energy strikes only the half of Earth facing the sun. Warmth and light from the sun create daytime. At the same time, the half of the planet facing away from the sun experiences the cooler temperatures and darkness of night. Earth's rotation causes regular shifts from day to night. As a result, levels of solar energy on Earth constantly change.

Solar Energy

Earth's tilt and rotation cause changes in the amount of energy we receive from the sun. As Earth rotates on its axis, energy from the sun creates periods of day and night. Earth's tilt causes some locations, especially those close to the equator, to receive more direct solar energy than others.

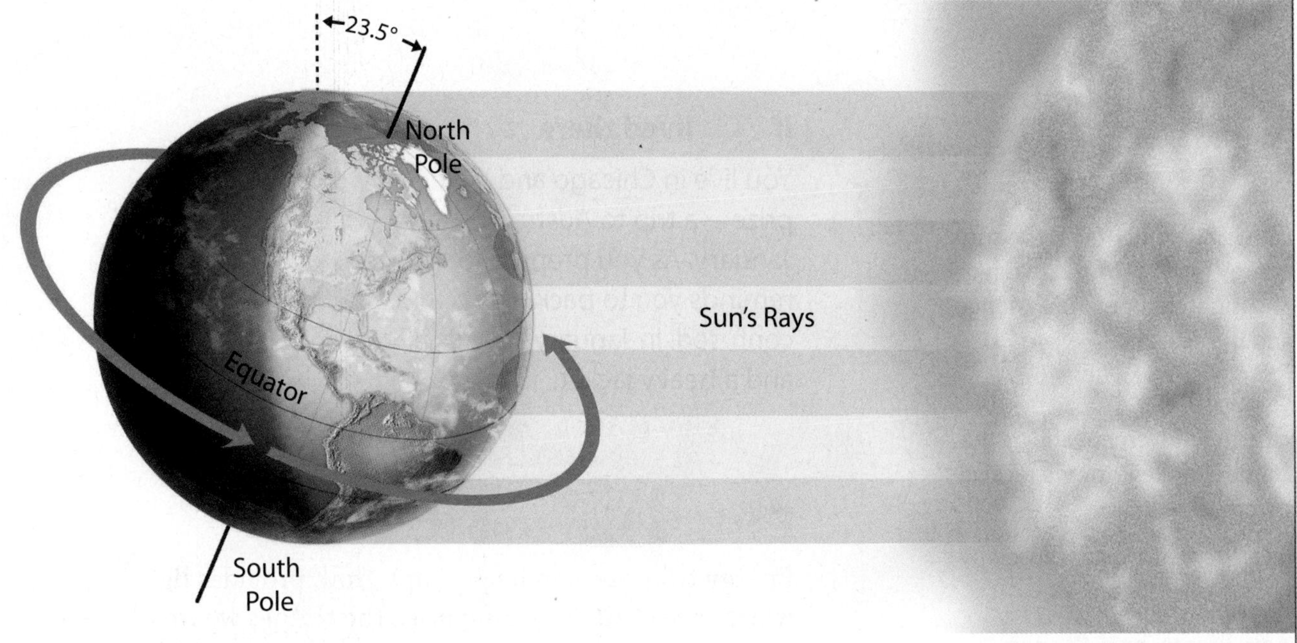

Analyze Visuals
Is the region north or south of the equator receiving more solar energy? How can you tell?

Revolution As Earth spins on its axis, it also follows a path, or orbit, around the sun. Earth's orbit around the sun is not a perfect circle. Sometimes the orbit takes Earth closer to the sun, and at other times the orbit takes it farther away. It takes 365¼ days for Earth to complete one **revolution,** or trip around the sun. We base our calendar year on the time it takes Earth to complete its orbit around the sun. To allow for the fraction of a day, we add an extra day—February 29—to our calendar every four years.

Academic Vocabulary
factor cause

Tilt and Latitude Another **factor** affecting the amount of solar energy we receive is the planet's tilt. As the illustration shows, Earth's axis is not straight up and down. It is actually tilted at an angle of 23.5 degrees from vertical. At any given time of year, some locations on Earth are tilting away from the sun, and others are tilting toward it. Places tilting toward the sun receive more solar energy and experience warmer temperatures. Those tilting away from the sun receive less solar energy and experience cooler temperatures.

A location's latitude, the distance north or south of Earth's equator, also affects the amount of solar energy it receives. Low-latitude areas, those near the equator like Hawaii, receive direct rays from the sun all year. These direct rays are more intense and produce warmer temperatures. Regions with high latitudes, like Antarctica, are farther from the equator. As a result, they receive indirect rays from the sun and have colder temperatures.

Reading Check
Find Main Ideas
What factors affect the solar energy Earth receives?

The Seasons

Does snow in July or high temperatures in January seem odd to you? It might if you live in the Northern Hemisphere, where cold temperatures are common in January, not July. The planet's changing seasons explain why we often connect certain weather with specific times of the year, like snow in January. Seasons are periods during the year that are known for certain types of weather. Many places on Earth experience four seasons—winter, spring, summer, and fall—based on temperature and length of day. In some parts of the world, seasons are based on the amount of rainfall.

Winter and Summer Earth's tilt creates the change in seasons. While one of Earth's poles is tilted away from the sun, the other is tilted toward it. During winter part of Earth tilts away from the sun, causing less direct solar energy, cool temperatures, and less daylight. Summer occurs when part of Earth tilts toward the sun, causing more direct solar energy, warmer temperatures, and longer periods of daylight.

The Seasons: Northern Hemisphere

As Earth orbits the sun, the tilt of its axis toward and away from the sun causes the seasons to change. Seasons in the Northern Hemisphere change at about the same time every year.

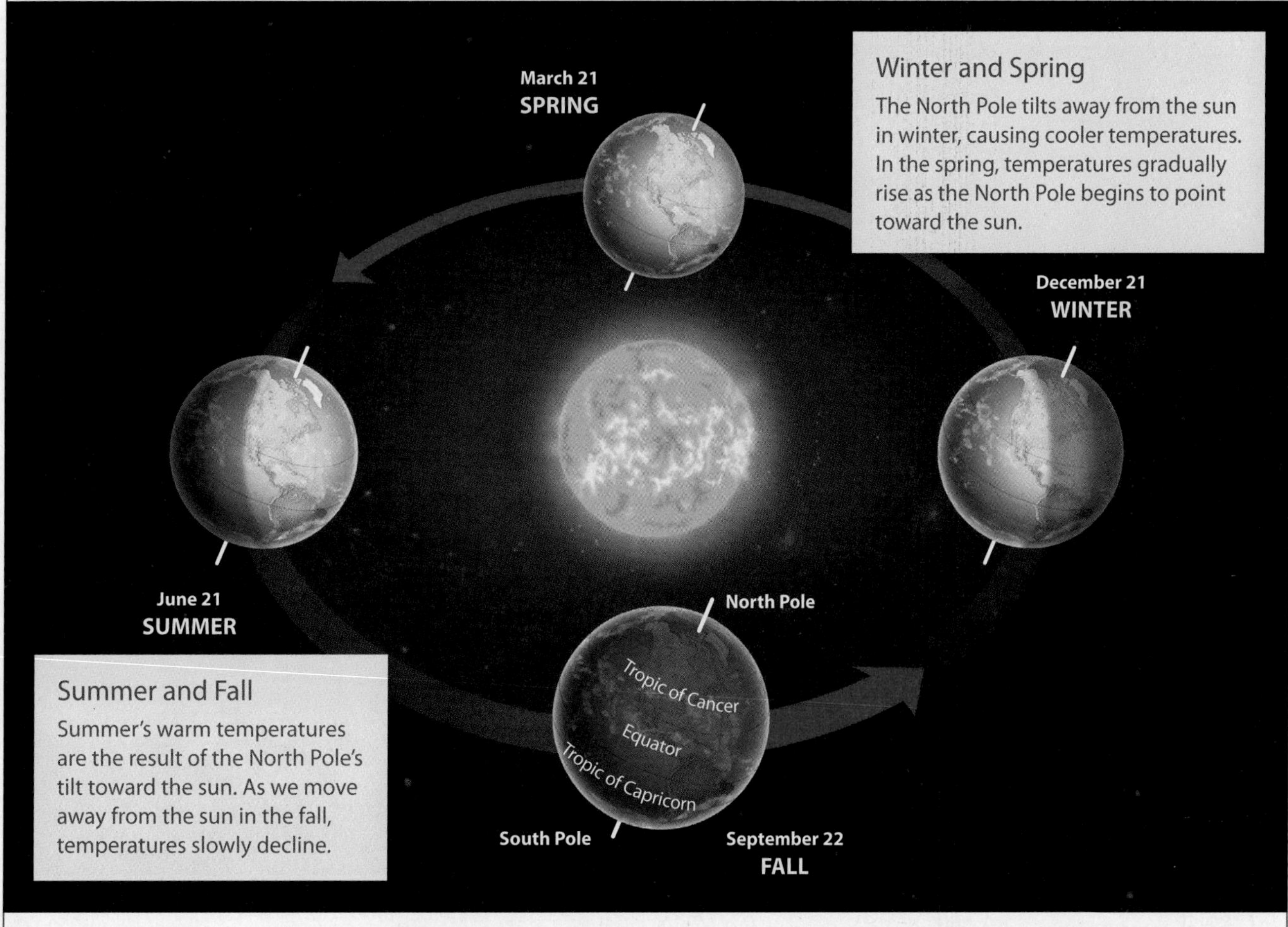

Analyze Visuals
As the Northern Hemisphere experiences winter, what season is it in the Southern Hemisphere?

Because of Earth's tilt, the Northern and Southern Hemispheres experience opposite seasons. As the North Pole tilts toward the sun in summer, the South Pole tilts away from it. As a result, the Southern Hemisphere experiences winter. Likewise, when it is spring in the Northern Hemisphere, it is fall in the Southern Hemisphere.

Spring and Fall As Earth orbits the sun, there are periods when the poles tilt neither toward nor away from the sun. These periods mark spring and fall. During the spring, as part of Earth begins to tilt toward the sun, solar energy increases. Temperatures slowly start to rise, and days grow longer. In the fall the opposite occurs as winter approaches. Solar energy begins to decrease, causing cooler temperatures and shorter days.

Focus on Culture

The Midnight Sun

Can you imagine going to sleep late at night with the sun shining in the sky? People who live near the Arctic and Antarctic Circles experience this every summer, when they can receive up to 24 hours of sunlight a day. The time-lapse photo below shows a typical sunset during this period—except the sun never really sets! This phenomenon is known as the midnight sun. For locations like Tromso, Norway, this means up to two months of constant daylight each summer. People living near Earth's poles often use the long daylight hours to work on outdoor projects in preparation for winter, when they can receive 24 hours of darkness a day.

Predict
How might people's daily lives be affected by the midnight sun?

Reading Check **Identify Cause and Effect** What causes the seasons to change?

Rainfall and Seasons Some regions on Earth have seasons marked by rainfall rather than temperature. This is true in the **tropics,** regions close to the equator. At certain times of year, winds bring either dry or moist air to the tropics, creating wet and dry seasons. In India, for example, seasonal winds called monsoons bring heavy rains from June to October and dry air from November to January.

Summary and Preview Solar energy is crucial for all life on the planet. Earth's position and movements affect the amount of energy we receive from the sun and determine our seasons. The Northern and Southern Hemispheres have opposite seasons. Some regions experience four seasons while others experience only two. In the next lesson you will learn about Earth's water supply and its importance to us.

Lesson 1 Assessment

Review Ideas, Terms, and Places

1. a. **Identify** What is solar energy, and how does it affect Earth?

   b. **Analyze** How do rotation and tilt each affect the amount of solar energy that different parts of Earth receive?

   c. **Predict** What might happen if Earth received less solar energy than it currently does?

2. a. **Describe** Name and describe Earth's seasons.

   b. **Contrast** How are seasons different in the Northern and Southern Hemispheres?

   c. **Elaborate** How might the seasons affect human activities?

Critical Thinking

3. Identify Cause and Effect Use your notes and the chart to identify the causes of seasons.

Water on Earth

The Big Idea

Water is a dominant feature on Earth's surface and is essential for life.

Main Ideas

- Salt water and freshwater make up Earth's water supply.
- In the water cycle, water circulates from Earth's surface to the atmosphere and back again.
- Water plays an important role in people's lives.

Key Terms and Places

freshwater
glaciers
surface water
precipitation
groundwater
water vapor
water cycle

If YOU lived there...

You live in the desert Southwest, where heavy water use and a lack of rainfall have led to water shortages. Your city plans to begin a water conservation program that asks people to limit how much water they use. Many of your neighbors have complained that the program is unnecessary. Others support the plan to save water.

How do you feel about the city's water plan?

Earth's Water Supply

Think of the different uses for water. We use water to cook and clean, we drink it, and we grow crops with it. Water is used for recreation, to generate electricity, and even to travel from place to place. Water is perhaps the most important and abundant resource on Earth. In fact, water covers some two-thirds of the planet. Understanding Earth's water supply and how it affects our lives is an important part of geography.

Salt Water Although water covers much of the planet, we cannot use most of it. About 97 percent of Earth's water is salt water. Because salt water contains high levels of salt and other minerals, it is unsafe to drink.

In general, salt water is found in Earth's oceans. Oceans are vast bodies of water covering some 71 percent of the planet's

Salt Water

Earth's oceans contain some 97 percent of the planet's water supply. Unfortunately, this water is too salty to drink.

Glaciers

Tremendous bodies of ice consist of frozen freshwater. This cruise ship looks like a toy next to San Rafael Glacier at Laguna San Rafael National Park on the Pacific coast of southern Chile.

Freshwater

Freshwater from lakes, rivers, and streams makes up only a fraction of Earth's water supply.

surface. Earth's oceans are made up of smaller bodies of water such as seas, gulfs, bays, and straits. Altogether, Earth's oceans cover some 139 million square miles (360 million square km) of the planet's surface.

Some of Earth's lakes contain salt water. The Great Salt Lake in Utah, for example, is a saltwater lake. As salt and other minerals have collected in the lake, which has no outlet, the water has become salty.

Freshwater Since the water in Earth's oceans is too salty to use, we must rely on other sources for freshwater. **Freshwater**, or water without salt, makes up only about 3 percent of our total water supply. Much of that freshwater is locked in Earth's **glaciers**, large areas of slow-moving ice, and in the ice of the Antarctic and Arctic regions. Most of the freshwater we use every day is found in lakes, in rivers, and under Earth's surface.

One form of freshwater is surface water. **Surface water** is water that is found in Earth's streams, rivers, and lakes. It may seem that there is a great deal of water in our lakes and rivers, but only a tiny amount of Earth's water supply—less than 1 percent—comes from surface water.

Streams and rivers are a common source of surface water. Streams form when precipitation collects in a narrow channel and flows toward the ocean. **Precipitation** is water that falls to Earth's surface as rain, snow, sleet, or hail. In turn, streams join together to form rivers. Any smaller stream or river that flows into a larger stream or river is called a tributary. For example, the Missouri River is the largest tributary of the Mississippi River.

Lakes are another important source of surface water. Some lakes were formed as rivers filled low-lying areas with water. Other lakes, like the Great Lakes along the U.S.-Canada border, were formed when glaciers carved deep holes in Earth's surface and deposited water as they melted.

Most of Earth's available freshwater is stored underground. As precipitation falls to Earth, much of it is absorbed into the ground, filling spaces in the soil and rock.

Water found below Earth's surface is called **groundwater**. In some places on Earth, groundwater naturally bubbles from the ground as a spring. More often, however, people obtain groundwater by digging wells, or deep holes dug into the ground to reach the water.

Reading Check
Contrast Ideas How is salt water different from freshwater?

The Water Cycle

When you think of water, you probably visualize a liquid—a flowing stream, a glass of ice-cold water, or a wave hitting the beach. But did you know that water is the only substance on Earth that occurs naturally as a solid, a liquid, and a gas? We see water as a solid in snow and ice and as a liquid in oceans and rivers. Water also occurs in the air as an invisible gas called **water vapor**.

Water is always moving. As water heats up and cools down, it moves from the planet's surface to the atmosphere, or the mass of air that surrounds Earth. One of the most important processes in nature is the water cycle. The **water cycle** is the movement of water from Earth's surface to the atmosphere and back.

The sun's energy drives the water cycle. As the sun heats water on Earth's surface, some of that water evaporates, or turns from liquid to gas, or water vapor. Water vapor then rises into the air. As the vapor rises, it cools. The cooling causes the water vapor to condense, or change from a vapor into tiny liquid droplets. These droplets join together to form clouds. If the droplets become heavy enough, precipitation occurs—that is, the water falls back to Earth as rain, snow, sleet, or hail.

When that precipitation falls back to Earth's surface, some of the water is absorbed into the soil as groundwater. Excess water, called runoff, flows over land and collects in streams, rivers, and oceans. Because the water cycle is constantly repeating, it allows us to maintain a fairly constant supply of water on Earth.

Reading Check
Find Main Ideas What is the water cycle?

The Water Cycle

Energy from the sun drives the water cycle. Surface water evaporates into Earth's atmosphere, where it condenses, then falls back to Earth as precipitation. This cycle repeats continuously, providing us with a fairly constant water supply.

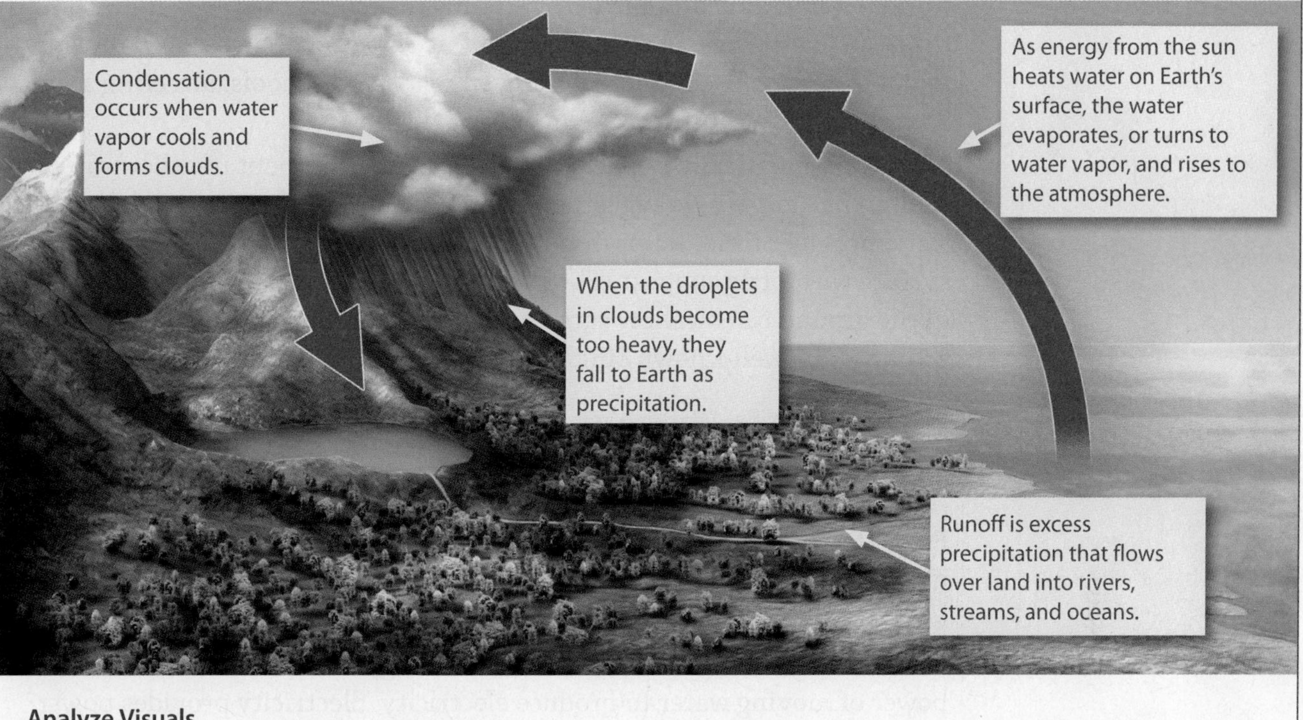

Analyze Visuals
How does evaporation differ from precipitation?

Water and People

How many times a day do you think about water? Many of us rarely give it a second thought, yet water is crucial for survival. Water problems such as the lack of water, polluted water, and flooding are concerns for people all around the world. Water also provides us with countless benefits, such as energy and recreation.

Water Problems One of the greatest water problems people face is a lack of available freshwater. Many places face water shortages as a result of droughts, or long periods of lower-than-normal precipitation. Another cause of water shortages is overuse. In places like the southwestern United States, where the population has grown rapidly, the heavy demand for water has led to shortages.

Water shortages lead to many problems. Crops and livestock die without enough water, leading to food shortages. In many places in Africa, women and girls spend hours every day walking to distant water sources instead of doing other work or going to school.

Water shortages can even lead to or worsen conflict. Because water is necessary for survival, people will fight to control it in an attempt to control other groups.

Even where water is plentiful, it may not be clean enough to use. If chemicals and household wastes make their way into streams and rivers, they can contaminate the water supply. Polluted water can carry diseases. These diseases may harm humans, plants, and animals.

Flooding is another water problem that affects people around the world. Heavy rains often lead to flooding, which can damage property and threaten lives. One example of dangerous flooding occurred in Bangladesh in 2004. Severe floods there destroyed roads and schools, affecting about 25 million people.

Water dramatically impacts the physical environment in other ways as well. In Florida, where limestone is plentiful, sinkholes can arise with little warning. Over time, water dissolves and weakens limestone, leaving the surface with little support. The ground layer collapses. The resulting hole in the ground can swallow cars and houses. The Devil's Millhopper is one example of a well-known sinkhole.

Water's Benefits Water does more than just quench our thirst. It provides us with many benefits, such as food, power, and even recreation.

Water's most important benefit is that it provides us with food to eat. Everything we eat depends on water. For example, fruits and vegetables need water to grow. Animals also need water to live and grow. As a result, we use water to farm and raise animals so that we will have food to eat.

Water is also an important source of energy. Using dams, we harness the power of moving water to produce electricity. Electricity provides power to air-condition or heat our homes, to run our washers and dryers, and to keep our food cold.

Water also provides us with recreation. Rivers, lakes, and oceans make it possible for us to swim, to fish, to surf, or to sail a boat. Although recreation is not critical for our survival, it does make our lives richer and more enjoyable.

Water's Benefits: for Life

Without water, plants won't grow. This modern irrigation system, used for large agricultural projects, ensures that plants get the water they need and humans get the food they need.

Water's Benefits: for Fun

This surfer rides a wave at the beach. Many people enjoy swimming, boating, fishing, and other recreational activities on water.

Recognizing all of these benefits, some communities work together to manage freshwater supplies. For example, in Florida, long-term population growth strains the freshwater supply. That, combined with drought conditions, inspired the creation of the Central Florida Water Initiative (CFWI). This organization works to protect and conserve water resources in a 5,300-square-mile (13,727-sq-km) area. The CFWI works with businesses, utilities, environmental groups, agricultural groups, and others to meet people's water needs. Many regions around the world have similar organizations.

Reading Check
Summarize How does water affect people's lives?

Summary and Preview In this lesson you learned that water is essential for life on Earth. Next, you will learn about the shapes on Earth's surface.

Lesson 2 Assessment

Review Ideas, Terms, and Places

1. a. **Describe** Name and describe the different types of water that make up Earth's water supply.
   b. **Analyze** Why is only a small percentage of Earth's freshwater available to us?
   c. **Elaborate** In your opinion, which is more important—surface water or groundwater? Why?
2. a. **Recall** What drives the water cycle?
   b. **Make Inferences** From what bodies of water do you think most evaporation occurs? Why?
3. a. **Define** What is a drought?
   b. **Analyze** How does water support life on Earth?
   c. **Evaluate** What water problem do you think is most critical in your community? Why?

Critical Thinking

4. **Sequence** Draw the graphic organizer. Then use your notes and the graphic organizer to identify the stages in Earth's water cycle.

Heat from the sun evaporates water on Earth.
↓
[ ]
↓
[ ]
↓
[ ]
↓
The water cycle repeats.

The Land

The Big Idea

Processes below and on Earth's surface shape the planet's physical features.

Main Ideas

- Earth's surface is covered by many different landforms.
- Forces below Earth's surface build up our landforms.
- Forces on the planet's surface shape Earth's landforms.
- Landforms influence people's lives and culture.

Key Terms and Places

landforms
continents
plate tectonics
lava
earthquakes
weathering
erosion
alluvial deposition

If YOU lived there...

You live in the state of Washington. All your life, you have looked out at the beautiful, cone-shaped peaks of nearby mountains. One of them is Mount Saint Helens, an active volcano. You know that in 1980 it erupted violently, blowing a hole in the mountain and throwing ash and rock into the sky. Since then, scientists have watched the mountain carefully.

How do you feel about living near a volcano?

Landforms

Do you know the difference between a valley and a volcano? Can you tell a peninsula from a plateau? If you answered yes, then you are familiar with some of Earth's many landforms. **Landforms** are shapes on the planet's surface, such as hills or mountains. Landforms make up the landscapes that surround us, whether it's the rugged mountains of central Colorado or the flat plains of Oklahoma.

Earth's surface is covered with landforms of many different shapes and sizes. Some important landforms include:

- mountains, land that rises higher than 2,000 feet (610 m)
- valleys, areas of low land located between mountains or hills
- plains, stretches of mostly flat land
- islands, areas of land completely surrounded by water
- peninsulas, land surrounded by water on three sides

Because landforms play an important role in geography, many scientists study how landforms are made and how they affect human activity.

Reading Check
Summarize
What are some common landforms?

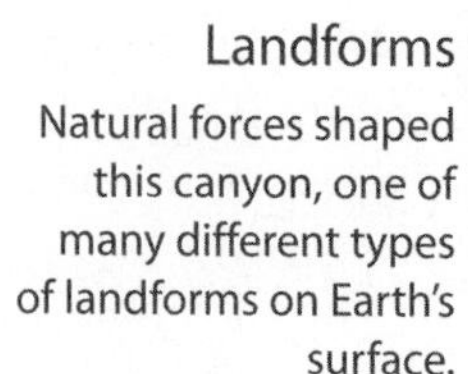

Landforms

Natural forces shaped this canyon, one of many different types of landforms on Earth's surface.

Earth's Plates

The theory of plate tectonics states that the plates that make up Earth's crust are moving, usually only a few inches per year. As Earth's plates collide, separate, and slide past each other, they create forces that shape many of Earth's landforms.

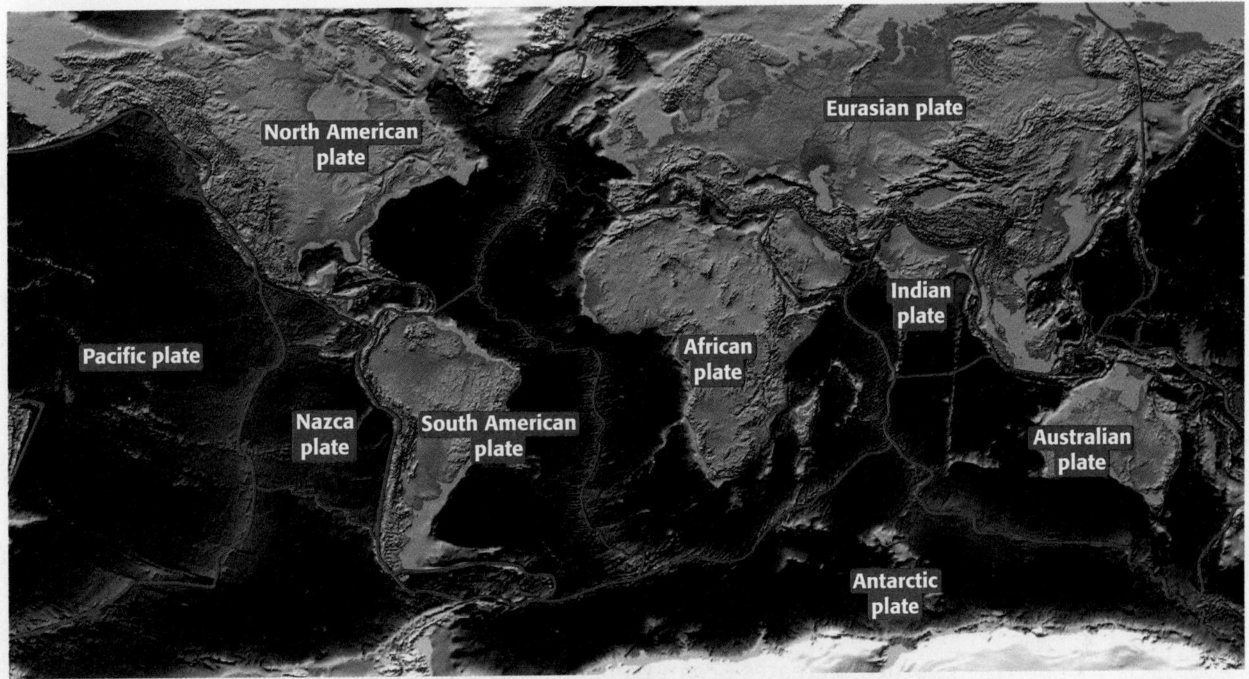

Analyze Visuals
Looking at the map, what evidence indicates that plates have collided or separated?

Forces below Earth's Surface

Geographers often study how landforms are made. One explanation for how landforms have been shaped involves forces below Earth's surface.

Academic Vocabulary
structure the way something is set up or organized

Earth's Plates To understand how these forces work, we must examine Earth's **structure**. The planet is made up of three layers. A solid inner core is surrounded by a liquid layer, or mantle. The solid outer layer of Earth is called the crust. The planet's **continents**, or large landmasses, are part of Earth's crust.

Geographers use the theory of plate tectonics to explain how forces below Earth's surface have shaped our landforms. The theory of **plate tectonics** suggests that Earth's surface is divided into a dozen or so slow-moving plates, or pieces of Earth's crust. As you can see in the image above, some plates, like the Pacific plate, are quite large. Others, like the Nazca plate, are much smaller. These plates cover Earth's entire surface. Some plates are under the ocean. These are known as ocean plates. Other plates, known as continental plates, are under Earth's continents.

Why do these plates move? Energy deep inside the planet puts pressure on Earth's crust. As this pressure builds up, it forces the plates to shift. Earth's tectonic plates all move. However, they move in different directions and at different speeds.

The Movement of Continents Earth's tectonic plates move slowly—up to several inches per year. The continents, which are part of Earth's plates, shift as the plates move. If we could look back some 200 million years, we would see that the continents have traveled great distances. This idea is known as continental drift.

The theory of continental drift, first developed by Alfred Wegener, states that the continents were once united in a single supercontinent. Wegener's inspiration came from the similarity he observed between the western coast of Africa and the eastern coast of South America. According to this theory, Earth's plates shifted over millions of years. As a result, the continents slowly separated and moved to their present positions.

Earth's continents are still moving. Some plates move toward each other and collide. Other plates separate and move apart. Still others slide past one another. Over time, colliding, separating, and sliding plates have shaped Earth's landforms.

Plates Collide As plates collide, the energy created from their collision produces distinct landforms. The collision of different types of plates creates different shapes on Earth's surface. Ocean trenches and mountain ranges are two examples of landforms produced by the collision of tectonic plates.

When two ocean plates collide, one plate pushes under the other. This process creates ocean trenches. Ocean trenches are deep valleys in the ocean floor. Near Japan, for example, the Pacific plate is slowly moving under other plates. This collision has created several deep ocean trenches, including the world's deepest trench, the Mariana Trench.

Mountains Form When Plates Collide

The movement of Earth's tectonic plates has produced many of Earth's landforms. For example, the Himalayas in South Asia resulted from the collision of two massive continental plates.

Analyze Visuals
What type of landform is created by the collision of two continental plates?

Lava Flows When Plates Separate

The separation of Earth's tectonic plates produces landforms, just as the collision of plates does. The separation of plates can allow magma to rise up and create volcanic islands like Surtsey Island, near Iceland.

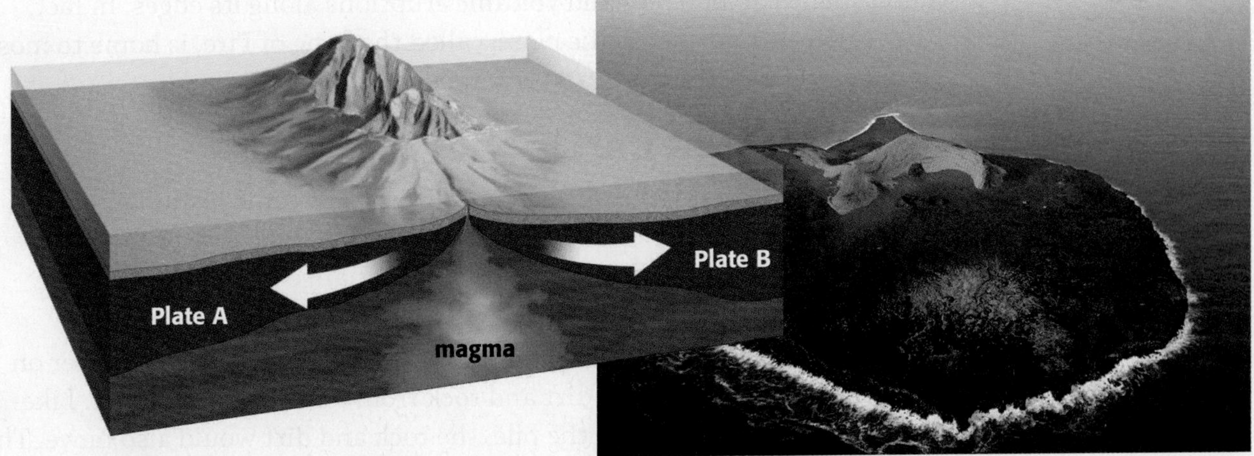

Analyze Visuals
What other landform involves flowing lava?

Ocean plates and continental plates can also collide. When this occurs, the ocean plate drops beneath the continental plate. This action forces the land above to crumple and form a mountain range. The Andes in South America, for example, were formed when the South American and Nazca plates collided.

The collision of two continental plates also results in mountain-building. When continental plates collide, the land pushes up, sometimes to great heights. The world's highest mountain range, the Himalayas, formed when the Indian plate crashed into the Eurasian plate. In fact, the Himalayas are still growing as the two plates continue to crash into each other.

Plates Separate A second type of plate movement causes plates to separate. As plates move apart, gaps between the plates allow magma, a liquid rock from the planet's interior, to rise to Earth's crust. **Lava**, or magma that reaches Earth's surface, emerges from the gap that has formed. As the lava cools, it builds a mid-ocean ridge, or underwater mountain. For example, the separation of the North American and Eurasian plates formed the largest underwater mountain, the Mid-Atlantic Ridge. If these mid-ocean ridges grow high enough, they can rise above the surface of the ocean, forming volcanic islands. Iceland, on the boundary of the Eurasian and North American plates, is an example of such an island.

Plates Slide Tectonic plates also slide past each other. As plates pass by one another, they sometimes grind together. This grinding produces **earthquakes**—sudden, violent movements of Earth's crust. Earthquakes often take place along faults, or breaks in Earth's crust where movement occurs. In California, for example, the Pacific plate is sliding by the edge of the North American plate. This has created the San Andreas Fault zone, an area where earthquakes are quite common.

The San Andreas Fault zone is one of many areas that lie along the boundaries of the Pacific plate. The frequent movement of this plate produces many earthquakes and volcanic eruptions along its edges. In fact, the region around the Pacific plate, called the Ring of Fire, is home to most of the world's earthquakes and volcanoes.

Reading Check
Find Main Ideas
What forces below Earth's surface shape landforms?

Processes on Earth's Surface

For millions of years, the movement of Earth's tectonic plates has been building up landforms on Earth's surface. At the same time, other physical environmental processes are working to change those very same landforms.

Imagine a small pile of dirt and rock on a table. If you poured water on the pile, it would move the dirt and rock from one place to another. Likewise, if you were to blow at the pile, the rock and dirt would also move. The same process happens in nature. Weather, water, and other forces change Earth's landforms by wearing them away or reshaping them.

Weathering One force that wears away landforms is weathering. **Weathering** is the process by which rock is broken down into smaller pieces. Several factors cause rock to break down. In desert areas, daytime heating and nighttime cooling can cause rocks to crack. Water may get into cracks in rocks and freeze. The ice then expands with a force great enough to break the rock. Even the roots of trees can pry rocks apart.

Regardless of which weathering process is at work, rocks eventually break down. These small pieces of rock are known as sediment. Once weathering has taken place, wind, ice, and water often move sediment from one place to another.

Erosion Another force that changes landforms is the process of erosion. **Erosion** is the movement of sediment from one location to another. Erosion can wear away or build up landforms. Wind, ice, and water all cause erosion.

Wind Erosion
Landforms in Utah's Canyonlands National Park have been worn away, mostly by thousands of years of powerful winds.

Powerful winds often cause erosion. Winds lift sediment into the air and carry it across great distances. On beaches and in deserts, wind can deposit large amounts of sand to form dunes. Blowing sand can also wear down rock. The sand acts like sandpaper to polish and wear away at rocks. As you can see in the photo, wind can have a dramatic effect on landforms.

Earth's glaciers also have the power to cause massive erosion. Glaciers, or large, slow-moving sheets of ice, build

Water Erosion

For millions of years, the Colorado River has worn away the rock at Horseshoe Bend in Arizona.

up when winter snows do not melt the following summer. Glaciers can be huge. Glaciers in Greenland and Antarctica, for example, are great sheets of ice up to two miles (3 km) thick. Some glaciers flow slowly downhill like rivers of ice. As they do so, they erode the land by carving large U-shaped valleys and sharp mountain peaks. As the ice flows downhill, it crushes rock into sediment and can move huge rocks long distances.

Water is the most common cause of erosion. Waves in oceans and lakes can wear away the shore, creating jagged coastlines, like those on the coast of Oregon. Rivers also cause erosion. Over many years, the flowing water can cut through rock, forming canyons, or narrow areas with steep walls. Arizona's Horseshoe Bend and Grand Canyon are examples of canyons created in this way.

Flowing water shapes other landforms as well. When water deposits sediment in new locations, it creates new landforms. For example, in a process called **alluvial deposition**, rivers create floodplains when they flood their banks and deposit sediment along the banks. Sediment that is carried by a river all the way out to sea creates a delta. The sediment settles to the bottom, where the river meets the sea. The Nile and Mississippi rivers have created two of the world's largest river deltas.

Reading Check
Compare
How are weathering and erosion similar?

Landforms Influence Life

Why do you live where you do? Perhaps your family moved to the desert to avoid harsh winter weather. Or possibly one of your ancestors settled near a river delta because its fertile soil was ideal for growing crops. Maybe your family wanted to live near the ocean to start a fishing business. As these examples show, landforms exert a strong influence on people's lives. Earth's landforms affect our settlements and our culture. At the same time, we affect the landforms around us.

Earth's landforms can influence where people settle. People sometimes settle near certain landforms and avoid others. For example, many settlements are built near fertile river valleys or deltas. The earliest urban civilization, for example, was built in the valley between the Tigris and Euphrates rivers. Other times, landforms discourage people from settling in a certain place. Tall, rugged mountains, like the Himalayas, and harsh desert climates, like the Sahara, do not usually attract large settlements.

Landforms affect our culture in ways that we may not have noticed. Landforms often influence what jobs are available in a region. For

Living with Landforms

The people of Rio de Janeiro, Brazil, have learned to adapt to the mountains and bays that dominate their landscape.

Analyze Visuals
How have people in Rio de Janeiro adapted to their landscape?

example, rich mineral deposits in the mountains of Colorado led to the development of a mining industry there. Landforms even affect language. On the island of New Guinea in Southeast Asia, rugged mountains have kept the people so isolated that more than 700 languages are spoken on the island today.

People sometimes change landforms to suit their needs. People may choose to modify landforms in order to improve their lives. For example, engineers built the Panama Canal to make travel from the Atlantic Ocean to the Pacific Ocean easier. In Southeast Asia, people who farm on steep hillsides cut terraces into the slope to create more level space to grow their crops. People have even built huge dams along rivers to divert water for use in nearby towns or farms.

Reading Check
Analyze Effects What are some examples of humans adjusting to and changing landforms?

Summary and Preview Landforms are created by actions deep within the planet's surface, and they are changed by forces on Earth's surface, like weathering and erosion. In the next lesson you will learn how other forces, like weather and climate, affect Earth's people.

Lesson 3 Assessment

Review Ideas, Terms, and Places

1. a. **Describe** What are some common landforms?
   b. **Analyze** Why do geographers study landforms?
2. a. **Identify** What is the theory of plate tectonics?
   b. **Compare and Contrast** How are the effects of colliding plates and separating plates similar and different?
   c. **Predict** How might Earth's surface change as tectonic plates continue to move?
3. a. **Recall** What is the process of weathering?
   b. **Elaborate** How does water affect sediment?
4. a. **Recall** How do landforms affect life on Earth?
   b. **Predict** How might people adapt to life in an area with steep mountains?

Critical Thinking

5. **Identify and Describe** Use your notes and a two-column chart to identify and describe different physical environmental processes and their effects on Earth's surface.

Physical Environmental Process	Effect on Earth's Surface

Case Study

The Ring of Fire

Essential Elements

The World in Spatial Terms

Places and Regions

Physical Systems

Human Systems

Environment and Society

The Uses of Geography

Background

"The Ring of Fire" names not a fantasy novel, but a region that circles the Pacific Ocean. Known for its fiery volcanoes and powerful earthquakes, it stretches from the tip of South America to Alaska and from Japan to the islands east of Australia. Along this belt, the Pacific plate moves against several other tectonic plates. Thousands of earthquakes occur there every year, and dozens of volcanoes erupt.

The Eruption of Mount Saint Helens

One of the best-known volcanoes in the Ring of Fire is Mount Saint Helens in Washington State. Mount Saint Helens had been dormant, or quiet, since 1857. Then in March 1980, it released puffs of steam and ash. Officials warned people to leave the area. Scientists brought in equipment to measure the growing bulge in the mountainside.

The Ring of Fire

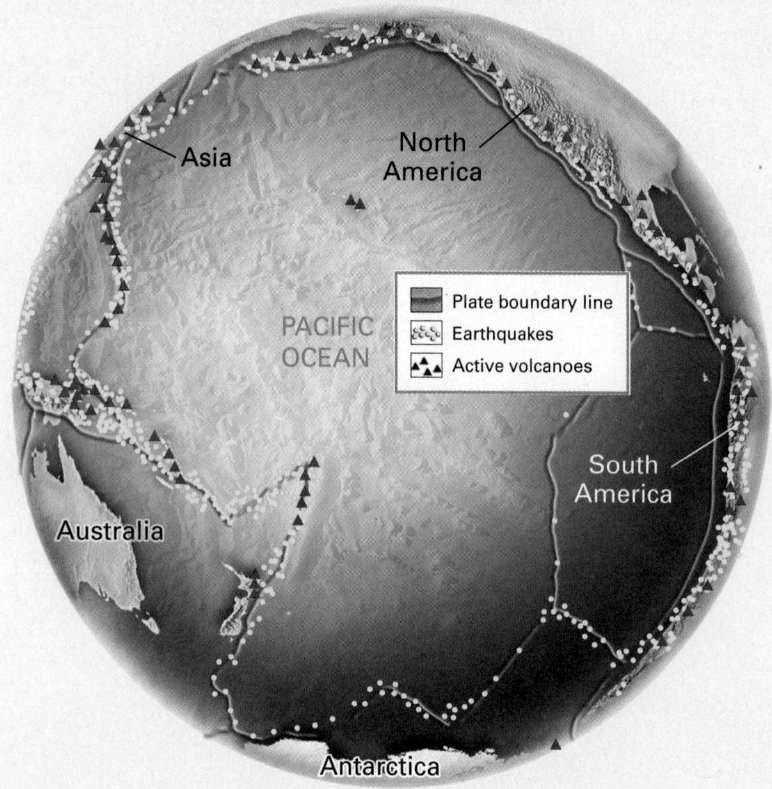

Major Eruptions in the Ring of Fire

Volcano	Year
Tambora, Indonesia	1815
Krakatau, Indonesia	1883
Mount Saint Helens, United States	1980
Nevado del Ruiz, Colombia	1985
Mount Pinatubo, Philippines	1991

Source: *Volcanoes of the World,* Smithsonian Institution.

Mount Saint Helens, 1980 The 1980 eruption of Mount Saint Helens blew ash and hot gases miles into the air. Today, scientists study the volcano to learn more about predicting eruptions.

On May 18, after a sudden earthquake, Mount Saint Helens let loose a massive explosion of rock and lava. Heat from the blast melted snow on the mountain, which mixed with ash to create deadly mudflows. As the mud quickly poured downhill, it flattened forests, swept away cars, and destroyed buildings. Clouds of ash covered the land, killing crops, clogging waterways, and blanketing towns as far as 200 miles (330 km) away. When the volcano finally quieted down, 57 people had died. Damage totaled nearly $1 billion. If it were not for the early evacuation of the area, the destruction could have been much worse.

What It Means

By studying Mount Saint Helens, scientists learned a great deal about stratovolcanoes. These are tall, steep, cone-shaped volcanoes that have violent eruptions. Stratovolcanoes often form in areas where tectonic plates collide.

Because stratovolcanoes often produce deadly eruptions, scientists try to predict when they might erupt. The lessons learned from Mount Saint Helens helped scientists warn people about another stratovolcano, Mount Pinatubo in the Philippines. That eruption in 1991 was the second-largest of the 1900s. It was far from the deadliest, however. Careful observation and timely warnings saved thousands of lives.

The Ring of Fire will always remain a threat. However, the better we understand its volcanoes, the better prepared we'll be when they erupt.

Geography for Life Activity

1. **Summarize** Why do scientists monitor volcanic activity?
2. **Investigate the Effects of Volcanoes** Some volcanic eruptions affect environmental conditions around the world. Research the eruption of either Mount Saint Helens or the Philippines' Mount Pinatubo to find out how its eruption affected the global environment.

Weather and Climate

The Big Idea

The sun, location, wind, water, and mountains affect weather and climate.

Main Ideas

- While weather is short term, climate is a region's average weather over a long period.
- The amount of sun at a given location is affected by Earth's tilt, movement, and shape.
- Wind and water move heat around Earth, affecting how warm or wet a place is.
- Mountains influence temperature and precipitation.

Key Terms and Places

weather
climate
prevailing winds
ocean currents
front

If YOU lived there . . .

You live in Buffalo, New York, at the eastern end of Lake Erie. One evening in January, you are watching the local TV news. The weather forecaster says, "A huge storm is brewing in the Midwest and moving east. As usual, winds from this storm will drop several feet of snow on Buffalo as they blow off Lake Erie."

Why will winds off the lake drop snow on Buffalo?

Understanding Weather and Climate

What is it like outside right now where you live? Is it hot, sunny, wet, cold? Is this what it is usually like outside for this time of year? The first two questions are about **weather,** the short-term changes in the air for a given place and time. The last question is about **climate,** a region's average weather conditions over a long period.

Weather is the temperature and precipitation from hour to hour or day to day. "Today is sunny, but tomorrow it might rain" is a statement about weather. Climate is the expected weather for a place based on data and experience. "Summer here is usually hot and muggy" is a statement about climate. The factors that shape weather and climate include the sun, location on Earth, wind, water, and mountains.

Reading Check **Find Main Ideas** How are weather and climate different from each other?

Stormy Weather Sometimes weather can be extreme. This photo shows a severe thunderstorm. These storms produce heavy rainfall and strong winds.

Global Wind Systems

Prevailing winds blow in circular belts across Earth. These belts occur at about every 30° of latitude.

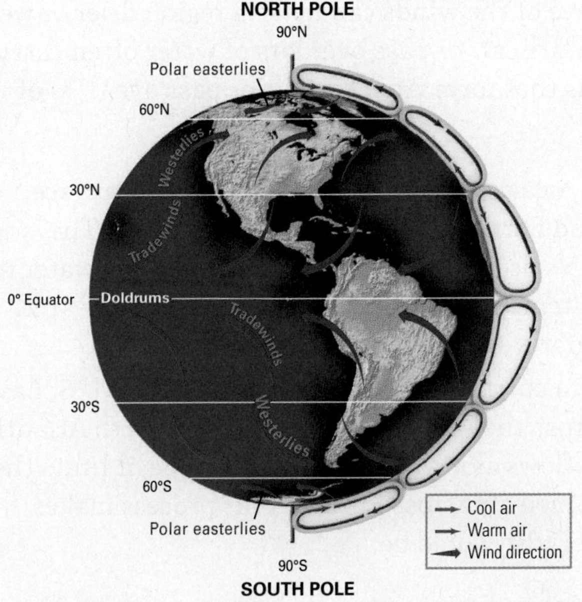

Analyze Visuals
Which direction do the prevailing winds blow across the United States?

Sun and Location

Energy from the sun heats the planet. Different locations receive different amounts of sunlight, though. Thus, some locations are warmer than others. The differences are due to Earth's tilt, movement, and shape.

You have learned that Earth is tilted on its axis. The part of Earth tilted toward the sun receives more solar energy than the part tilted away from the sun. As Earth revolves around the sun, the part of Earth that is tilted toward the sun changes during the year. This process creates the seasons. In general, temperatures in summer are warmer than in winter.

Earth's shape also affects the amount of sunlight different locations receive. Because Earth is a sphere, its surface is rounded. Therefore, solar rays are more direct and concentrated near the equator. Nearer the poles, the sun's rays are less direct and more spread out.

As a result, areas near the equator, called the lower latitudes, are mainly hot year-round. Areas near the poles, called the higher latitudes, are cold year-round. Areas about halfway between the equator and poles have more seasonal change. In general, the farther from the equator, or the higher the latitude, the colder the climate.

Reading Check
Summarize How does Earth's tilt on its axis affect climate?

Wind and Water

Heat from the sun moves across Earth's surface. The reason is that air and water warmed by the sun are constantly on the move. You might have seen a gust of wind or a stream of water carrying dust or dirt. In a similar way, wind and water carry heat from place to place. As a result, they make different areas of Earth warmer or cooler.

Global Winds Wind, or the sideways movement of air, blows in great streams around the planet. **Prevailing winds** are winds that blow in the same direction over large areas of Earth. The illustration under Global Wind Systems shows the patterns of Earth's prevailing winds.

To understand Earth's wind patterns, you need to think about the weight of air. Although you cannot feel it, air has weight. This weight changes with the temperature. Cold air is heavier than warm air. For this reason, when air cools, it gets heavier and sinks. When air warms, it gets lighter and rises. As warm air rises, cooler air moves in to take its place, creating wind.

On a global scale, this rising, sinking, and flowing of air creates Earth's prevailing wind patterns. At the equator, hot air rises and flows toward the poles. At the poles, cold air sinks and flows toward the equator. Meanwhile, Earth is rotating. Earth's rotation causes prevailing winds to curve east or west rather than flowing directly north or south.

Depending on their source, prevailing winds make a region warmer or colder. In addition, the source of the winds can make a region drier or wetter. Winds that form from warm air or pass over lots of water often carry moisture. In contrast, winds that form from cold air or pass over lots of land often are dry.

Ocean Currents Like wind, **ocean currents**—large streams of surface seawater—move heat around Earth. Winds drive these currents. The map below shows how Earth's ocean currents carry warm or cool water to different areas. The water's temperature affects air temperature near it. Warm currents raise temperatures; cold currents lower them.

The Gulf Stream is a warm current that flows north along the U.S. East Coast. It then flows east across the Atlantic, to become the North Atlantic Drift. As the warm current flows along northwestern Europe, it heats the air. Westerlies blow the warmed air across Europe. This process makes Europe warmer than it otherwise would be.

Large Bodies of Water Large bodies of water, such as an ocean or sea, also affect climate. Water heats and cools more slowly than land does. For this reason, large bodies of water make the temperature of the land nearby

Major Ocean Currents

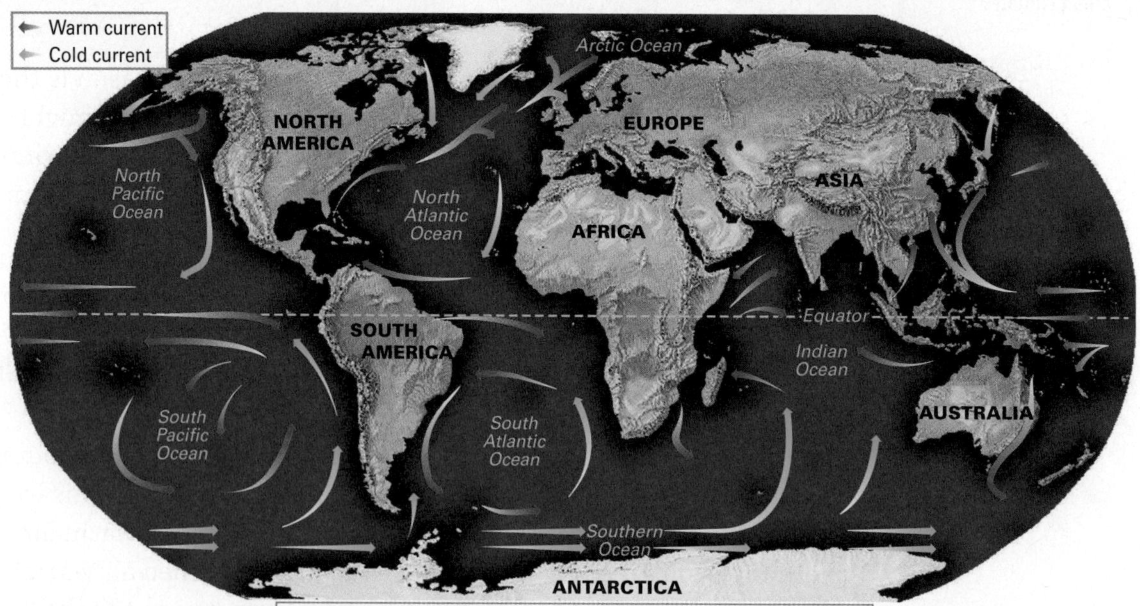

Interpret Maps

1. **Regions** Does a warm or cold ocean current flow along the lower west coast of North America?
2. **Movement** How do ocean currents move heat between warmer and colder areas of Earth?

Extreme Weather

Severe weather is often dangerous and destructive. In the photo to the left, rescuers search for people during a flood in Yardley, Pennsylvania. In the photo to the right, a tornado races across a wheat field in North Dakota.

Analyze Visuals
How might weather like that shown in these photos affect the people living nearby?

milder. Thus, coastal areas, such as the California coast, usually do not have as wide of temperature ranges as inland areas.

As an example, the state of Michigan is largely surrounded by the Great Lakes. The lakes make temperatures in the state milder than other places as far north.

Wind, Water, and Storms If you watch weather reports, you will hear about storms moving across the United States. Tracking storms is important to us because the United States has so many of them. As you will see, some areas of the world have more storms than others do.

Most storms occur when two air masses collide. An air mass is a large body of air. The place where two air masses of different temperatures or moisture content meet is a **front.** Cold air masses from the north and warm air masses from the south frequently collide over the United States, producing dramatic storms.

Fronts can produce rain or snow as well as severe weather such as thunderstorms and icy blizzards. Thunderstorms produce rain, lightning, and thunder. In the United States, they are most common in spring and summer. Blizzards produce strong winds and large amounts of snow and are most common during winter.

Thunderstorms and blizzards can also produce tornadoes, another type of severe storm. A tornado is a small, rapidly twisting funnel of air that touches the ground. Tornadoes usually affect a limited area and last only a

Rain Shadow Effect Most of the moisture in the ocean air falls on the mountainside facing the wind. Little moisture remains to fall on the other side, creating a rain shadow.

few minutes. However, they can be highly destructive, uprooting trees and tossing large vehicles through the air. Tornadoes can be extremely deadly as well. In 1925 a tornado that crossed Missouri, Illinois, and Indiana left 695 people dead. It is the deadliest U.S. tornado on record.

The largest and most destructive storms, however, are hurricanes. These large, rotating storms form over tropical waters in the Atlantic Ocean, usually from late summer to fall. Did you know that hurricanes and typhoons are the same? Typhoons are just hurricanes that form in the Pacific Ocean.

Hurricanes produce drenching rain and strong winds that can reach speeds of 155 miles per hour (250 kph) or more. This is more than twice as fast as most people drive on highways. In addition, hurricanes form tall walls of water called storm surges. When a storm surge smashes into land, it can wipe out an entire coastal area.

Reading Check
Analyze Causes Why do coastal areas have milder climates than inland areas?

Mountains

Mountains can influence an area's climate by affecting both temperature and precipitation. Many high mountains are located in warm areas yet have snow at the top all year. How can this be? The reason is that temperature decreases with elevation, the height on Earth's surface above sea level.

Mountains also create wet and dry areas. Look at the diagram titled Rain Shadow Effect. A mountain forces air blowing against it to rise. As it rises, the air cools and precipitation falls as rain or snow. Thus, the side

Reading Check
Find Main Ideas How does temperature change with elevation?

of the mountain facing the wind is often green and lush. However, little moisture remains for the other side. This effect creates a rain shadow, a dry area on the mountainside facing away from the direction of the wind.

Summary and Preview As you can see, the sun, location on Earth, wind, water, and mountains affect weather and climate. In the next lesson you will learn what the world's different climate regions are like.

Lesson 4 Assessment

Review Ideas, Terms, and Places

1. **a. Recall** What shapes weather and climate?
   b. Contrast How do weather and climate differ?
2. **a. Identify** What parts of Earth receive the most heat from the sun?
   b. Explain Why do the poles receive less solar energy than the equator does?
3. **a. Form Generalizations** Examine the model of Global Wind Systems in this lesson. Pose and answer a question about the geographic patterns of winds shown on the model.
   b. Summarize How do ocean currents and large bodies of water affect climate?
4. **a. Define** What is a rain shadow?
   b. Explain Why might a mountaintop and a nearby valley have widely different temperatures?

Critical Thinking

5. **Identify Cause and Effect** Use your notes and a cause-and-effect chart like the one shown. Use your notes to explain how each factor affects climate.

	Effect on Climate
Sun and Location →	
Wind →	
Water →	
Mountains →	

World Climates

The Big Idea

Earth's five major climate zones are identified by temperature, precipitation, and plant life.

Main Ideas

- Geographers use temperature, precipitation, and plant life to identify climate zones.
- Tropical climates are wet and warm, while dry climates receive little or no rain.
- Temperate climates have the most seasonal change.
- Polar climates are cold and dry, while highland climates change with elevation.

Key Terms and Places

monsoons
savannas
steppes
permafrost

If YOU lived there . . .

You live in Colorado and are on your first serious hike in the Rocky Mountains. Since it is July, it is hot in the campground in the valley. But your guide insists that you bring a heavy fleece jacket. By noon, you have climbed to 11,000 feet (3,353 m). You are surprised to see patches of snow in shady spots. Suddenly, you are very happy that you brought your jacket!

Why does it get colder as you climb higher?

Major Climate Zones

In January, how will you dress for the weekend? In some places, you might get dressed to go skiing. In other places, you might head out in a swimsuit to go to the beach. What the seasons are like where you live depends on climate.

Earth is a patchwork of climates. Geographers identify these climates by looking at temperature, precipitation, and native plant life. Using these items, we can divide Earth into five general climate zones—tropical, temperate, polar, dry, and highland.

The first three climate zones relate to latitude. Tropical climates occur near the equator, in the low latitudes. Temperate climates occur about halfway between the equator and the poles, in the middle latitudes. Polar climates occur near the poles, in the high latitudes. The last two climate zones occur at many different latitudes. In addition, geographers divide some climate zones into more specific climate regions. The map and chart titled World's Climate Regions describe these specific regions. Read the chart and study the map to see if you can identify some climate patterns.

Reading Check
Make Inferences
Why do you think geographers consider native plant life when categorizing climates?

Explore ONLINE!

World Climate Regions

	Climate	Where is it?	What is it like?	Plants
Tropical	HUMID TROPICAL	On and near the equator	Warm with high amounts of rain year-round; in a few places, monsoons create extreme wet seasons	Tropical rain forest
	TROPICAL SAVANNA	Higher latitudes in the tropics	Warm all year; distinct rainy and dry seasons; at least 20 inches (50 cm) of rain during the summer	Tall grasses and scattered trees
Dry	DESERT	Mainly center on 30° latitude; also in middle of continents, on west coasts, or in rain shadows	Sunny and dry; less than 10 inches (25 cm) of rain a year; hot in the tropics; cooler with wide daytime temperature ranges in middle latitudes	A few hardy plants, such as cacti
	STEPPE	Mainly bordering deserts and interiors of large continents	About 10–20 inches (25–50 cm) of precipitation a year; hot summers and cooler winters with wide temperature ranges during the day	Shorter grasses; some trees and shrubs by water
Temperate	MEDITERRANEAN	West coasts in middle latitudes	Dry, sunny, warm summers; mild, wetter winters; rain averages 15–20 inches (30–50 cm) a year	Scrub woodland and grassland
	HUMID SUBTROPICAL	East coasts in middle latitudes	Humid with hot summers and mild winters; rain year-round; in paths of hurricanes and typhoons	Mixed forest
	MARINE WEST COAST	West coasts in the upper-middle latitudes	Cloudy, mild summers and cool, rainy winters; strong ocean influence	Evergreen forests
	HUMID CONTINENTAL	East coasts and interiors of upper-middle latitudes	Four distinct seasons; long, cold winters and short, warm summers; average precipitation varies	Mixed forest
Polar	SUBARCTIC	Higher latitudes of the interior and east coasts of continents	Extremes of temperature; long, cold winters and short, warm summers; little precipitation	Northern evergreen forests
	TUNDRA	Coasts in high latitudes	Cold all year; very long, cold winters and very short, cool summers; little precipitation; permafrost	Moss, lichens, low shrubs
	ICE CAP	Polar regions	Freezing cold; snow and ice; little precipitation	No vegetation
Highland	HIGHLAND	High mountain regions	Wide range of temperatures and precipitation amounts, depending on elevation and location	Ranges from forest to tundra

Interpret Maps

1. Location Which climates are found mainly in the Northern Hemisphere?

2. Region Where are many of the world's driest climates found on Earth?

Tropical and Dry Climates

Are you the type of person who likes to go to extremes? Then tropical and dry climates might be for you. These climates include the wettest, driest, and hottest places on Earth.

Tropical Climates Our tour of Earth's climates starts at the equator, in the heart of the tropics. This region extends from the Tropic of Cancer to the Tropic of Capricorn. Look back at the map to locate this region.

Humid Tropical Climate At the equator, the hot, damp air hangs like a thick, wet blanket. Sweat quickly coats your body. Welcome to the humid tropical climate. This climate is warm, muggy, and rainy year-round. Temperatures average about 80°F (26°C). Showers or storms occur almost daily, and rainfall ranges from 70 to more than 450 inches (180 to 1,140 cm) a year. In comparison, only a few parts of the United States average more than 70 inches (180 cm) of rain a year.

Some places with a humid tropical climate have **monsoons**, seasonal winds that bring either dry or moist air. During one part of the year, a moist ocean wind creates an extreme wet season. The winds then shift direction, and a dry land wind creates a dry season. Monsoons affect several parts of Asia. For example, the town of Mawsynram, India, receives on average more than 450 inches (1,140 cm) of rain a year—all in about six months! That is about 37 feet (11 m) of rain. As you can imagine, flooding during wet seasons is common and can be severe.

The humid tropical climate's warm temperatures and heavy rainfall support tropical rain forests. These lush forests contain more types of plants and animals than anywhere else on Earth. The world's largest rain forest is in the Amazon River basin in South America. There you can find more than 50,000 species, including giant lily pads, poisonous tree frogs, and toucans.

Tropical Climate Known for high temperatures and rainfall, tropical climates may support grasslands or full-blown forests.

Focus on Culture

The Tuareg of the Sahara

In the Sahara, the world's largest desert, temperatures can top 130°F (54°C). Yet the Tuareg (TWAH-reg) of North and West Africa call the Sahara home—and prefer it. The Tuareg have raised camels and other animals in the Sahara for more than 1,000 years. The animals graze on sparse desert plants. When the plants are gone, the Tuareg move on.

In camp, Tuareg families live in tents made from animal skins. Some wealthier Tuareg live in adobe homes. The men traditionally wear blue veils wrapped around their face and head. The veils help protect against windblown desert dust.

Summarize
How have the Tuareg adapted to life in a desert?

Tropical Savanna Climate Moving north and south away from the equator, we find the tropical savanna climate. This climate has a long, hot, dry season followed by short periods of rain. Rainfall is much lower than at the equator but still high. Temperatures are hot in the summer, often as high as 90°F (32°C). Winters are cooler but rarely get cold.

This climate does not receive enough rainfall to support dense forests. Instead, it supports **savannas**—areas of tall grasses and scattered trees and shrubs.

Dry Climates Leaving Earth's wettest places, we head to its driest. These climates are found in a number of locations on the planet.

Desert Climate Picture the sun baking down on a barren wasteland. This is the desert, Earth's hottest and driest climate. Deserts receive less than 10 inches (25 cm) of rain a year. Dry air and clear skies produce high daytime temperatures and rapid cooling at night. In some deserts, highs can top 130°F (54°C)! Under such conditions, only very hardy plants and animals can live. Many plants grow far apart so as not to compete for water. Others, such as cacti, store water in fleshy stems and leaves.

Reading Check
Contrast What are some ways in which tropical and dry climates differ?

Steppe Climate Semidry grasslands or prairies—called **steppes** (STEPS)—often border deserts. Steppes receive slightly more rain than deserts do. Short grasses are the most common plants, but shrubs and trees grow along streams and rivers.

Dry Climate Lots of heat and very little rain characterize dry climates. Any plants or animals living here need to be hardy to survive these extremes.

Temperate Climates

If you enjoy hot, sunny days as much as chilly, rainy ones, then temperate climates are for you. *Temperate* means "moderate" or "mild." These mild climates tend to have four seasons, with warm or hot summers and cool or cold winters.

Temperate climates occur in the middle latitudes, the regions halfway between the equator and the poles. Air masses from the tropics and the poles often meet in these regions, which creates a number of different temperate climates. You very likely live in one, because most Americans do.

Mediterranean Climate Named for the region of the Mediterranean Sea, this sunny, pleasant climate is found in many popular vacation areas. In a Mediterranean climate, summers are hot, dry, and sunny. Winters are mild and somewhat wet. Plant life includes shrubs and short trees with scattered larger trees. The Mediterranean climate occurs mainly in coastal areas. In the United States, much of California has this climate.

Humid Subtropical Climate The southeastern United States is an example of the humid subtropical climate. This climate occurs along east coasts near the tropics. In these areas, warm, moist air blows in from the ocean. Summers are hot and muggy. Winters are mild, with occasional frost and snow. Storms occur year-round. In addition, hurricanes can strike, bringing violent winds, heavy rain, and high seas.

A humid subtropical climate supports mixed forests. These forests include both deciduous trees, which lose their leaves each fall, and coniferous trees, which are green year-round. Coniferous trees are also known as evergreens.

Marine West Coast Climate Parts of North America's Pacific coast and of western Europe have a marine west coast climate. This climate occurs on west coasts where winds carry moisture in from the seas. The moist air keeps temperatures mild year-round. Winters are foggy, cloudy, and rainy, while summers can be warm and sunny. Dense evergreen forests thrive in this climate.

Academic Vocabulary
distinct clearly different and separate

Reading Check
Categorize Which of the temperate climates is too dry to support forests?

Humid Continental Climate Closer to the poles, in the upper-middle latitudes, many inland and east coast areas have a humid continental climate. This climate has four **distinct** seasons. Summers are short and hot. Spring and fall are mild, and winters are long, cold, and, in general, snowy.

This climate's rainfall supports vast grasslands and forests. Grasses can grow very tall, such as in parts of the American Great Plains. Forests contain both deciduous and coniferous trees, with coniferous forests occurring in the colder areas.

Mediterranean Climate

The climate graph shows average temperatures and precipitation for Nice (NEECE), France, which has a Mediterranean climate.

Climate for Nice, France

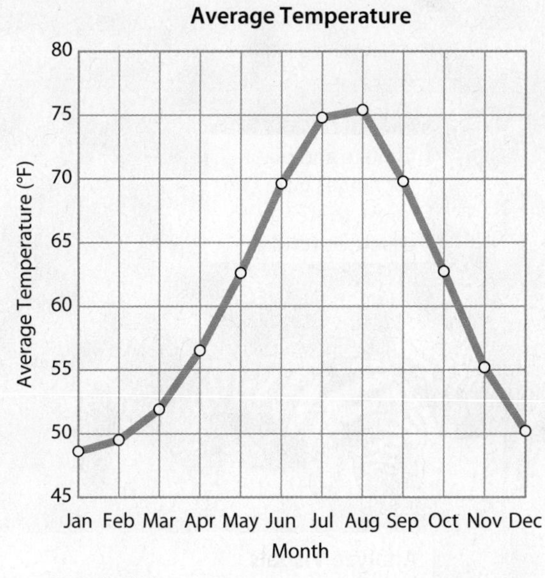

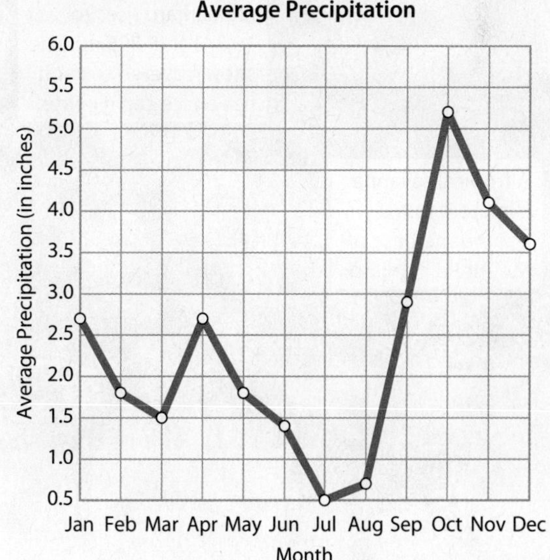

Source: Weatherbase.com.

Analyze Graphs
During which month is precipitation lowest?

Polar and Highland Climates

Get ready to feel the chill as we end our tour in the polar and highland climates. The three polar climates are found in the high latitudes near the poles. The varied highland climate is found on mountains.

Subarctic Climate The subarctic climate and the tundra climate described below occur mainly in the Northern Hemisphere south of the Arctic Ocean. In the subarctic climate, winters are long and bitterly cold. Summers are short and cool. Temperatures stay below freezing for about half the year. The climate's moderate rainfall supports vast evergreen forests, or taiga (TY-guh).

Tundra Climate The tundra climate occurs in coastal areas along the Arctic Ocean. As in the subarctic climate, winters are long and bitterly cold. Temperatures rise above freezing only during the short summer. Rainfall is light, and only plants such as mosses, lichens, and small shrubs grow.

In parts of the tundra, soil layers stay frozen all year. Permanently frozen layers of soil are called **permafrost**. Frozen earth absorbs water poorly, which creates ponds and marshes in summer. This moisture causes plants to burst forth in bloom.

Polar Climate Mountains often sustain polar climates, especially at their peaks. Different kinds of plants and animals may be found at different elevations.

Ice Cap Climate The harshest places on Earth may be the North and South poles. These regions have an ice cap climate. Temperatures are bone-numbingly cold, and lows of more than –120°F (–84°C) have been recorded. Snow and ice remain year-round, but precipitation is light. It is too cold for the water to evaporate into the atmosphere to become precipitation. In fact, the average precipitation is so low that these regions are technically deserts. Not surprisingly, no vegetation grows. However, mammals such as penguins and polar bears thrive. Seals can also live in the ice cap climate, and many birds travel through these cold regions.

Reading Check
Compare How are polar and highland climates similar?

Highland Climates Highland climates are cool to cold climates in mountain areas. They are unique because they contain several climate zones. This is because as you climb to higher elevations on a mountain, the climate changes. Temperatures drop, and plant life grows sparser. Going up a mountain can be like going from the tropics to the poles. On very tall mountains, ice coats the summit year-round.

Summary and Preview As you can see, Earth has many climates, which we identify based on temperature, precipitation, and native plant life. In the next lesson you will read about how nature and all living things are connected.

Lesson 5 Assessment

Review Ideas, Terms, and Places

1. a. **Recall** Which three major climate zones are most closely related to latitude?

   b. **Summarize** How do geographers categorize Earth's different climates?
2. a. **Define** What are monsoons?

   b. **Make Inferences** In which type of dry climate do you think the fewest people live, and why?

   c. **Compare** Look at the photographs in this lesson of a polar climate and a dry climate. What similarities do you notice in the physical characteristics of these regions?
3. a. **Identify** What are the four temperate climates?

   b. **Geographic Questions** Use the climate graph of Nice, France, to pose and answer a question about its climate patterns.
4. a. **Describe** What are some effects of permafrost?

   b. **Explain** How are highland climates unique?

Critical Thinking

5. **Categorize** Create a chart like the one below for each climate region. Then use your notes to describe each climate region's average temperatures, precipitation, and native plant life.

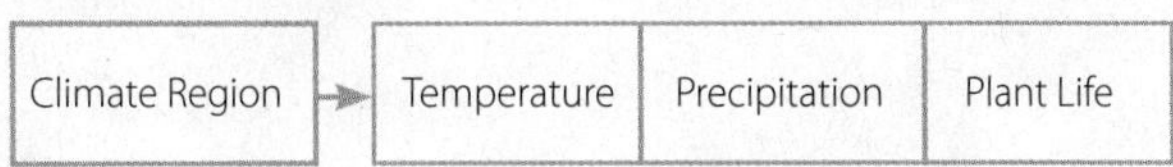

Environments and Biomes

The Big Idea

Plants, animals, and the environment, including soil, interact with and affect one another.

Main Ideas

- The environment and life are interconnected and exist in a fragile balance.
- Soils play an important role in the environment.

Key Terms and Places

environment
ecosystem
biome
habitat
extinct
humus
desertification

If YOU lived there . . .

When your family moved to the city, you were sure you would miss the woods and pond near your old house. Then one of your new friends at school told you there's a large park only a few blocks away. You wondered how interesting a city park could be. But you were surprised at the many plants and animals that live there.

What environments might you see in the park?

The Environment and Life

If you saw a wild polar bear outside your school, you would likely be shocked. In most parts of the United States, polar bears live only in zoos. This is because plants and animals must live where they are suited to the **environment,** or surroundings. Polar bears are suited to very cold places with lots of ice, water, and fish. As you will see, living things and their environments are connected and affect each other in many ways.

Suitable Environment

With thick fur and a layer of fat, this polar bear, wading in shallow water in Svalbard, Norway, is well suited to its cold environment.

Limits on Life The environment limits life. As our tour of the world's climates showed, factors such as temperature, rainfall, and soil conditions limit where plants and animals can live. Palm trees cannot survive at the frigid North Pole. Ferns will quickly wilt and die in deserts, but they thrive in tropical rain forests.

At the same time, all plants and animals are adapted to specific environments. For example, kangaroo rats are adapted to dry desert environments. These small rodents can get all the water they need from food, so they seldom have to drink water.

Connections in Nature The interconnections between living things and the environment form ecosystems. An **ecosystem** is a group of plants and animals that depend on each other and the environment in which they live for survival. Ecosystems can be any size and can occur wherever air, water, and soil support life. A garden pond, a city park, a prairie, and a rain forest are all examples of ecosystems.

In addition to environments and ecosystems, geographers might use the term **biome.** A biome is much larger than an ecosystem. It may be made up of several ecosystems. An entire tropical rain forest can be a biome. Earth itself can be thought of as one big biome.

A Desert Ecosystem

A desert is one type of ecosystem. The plants and animals in the desert depend on one another and the desert environment for survival.

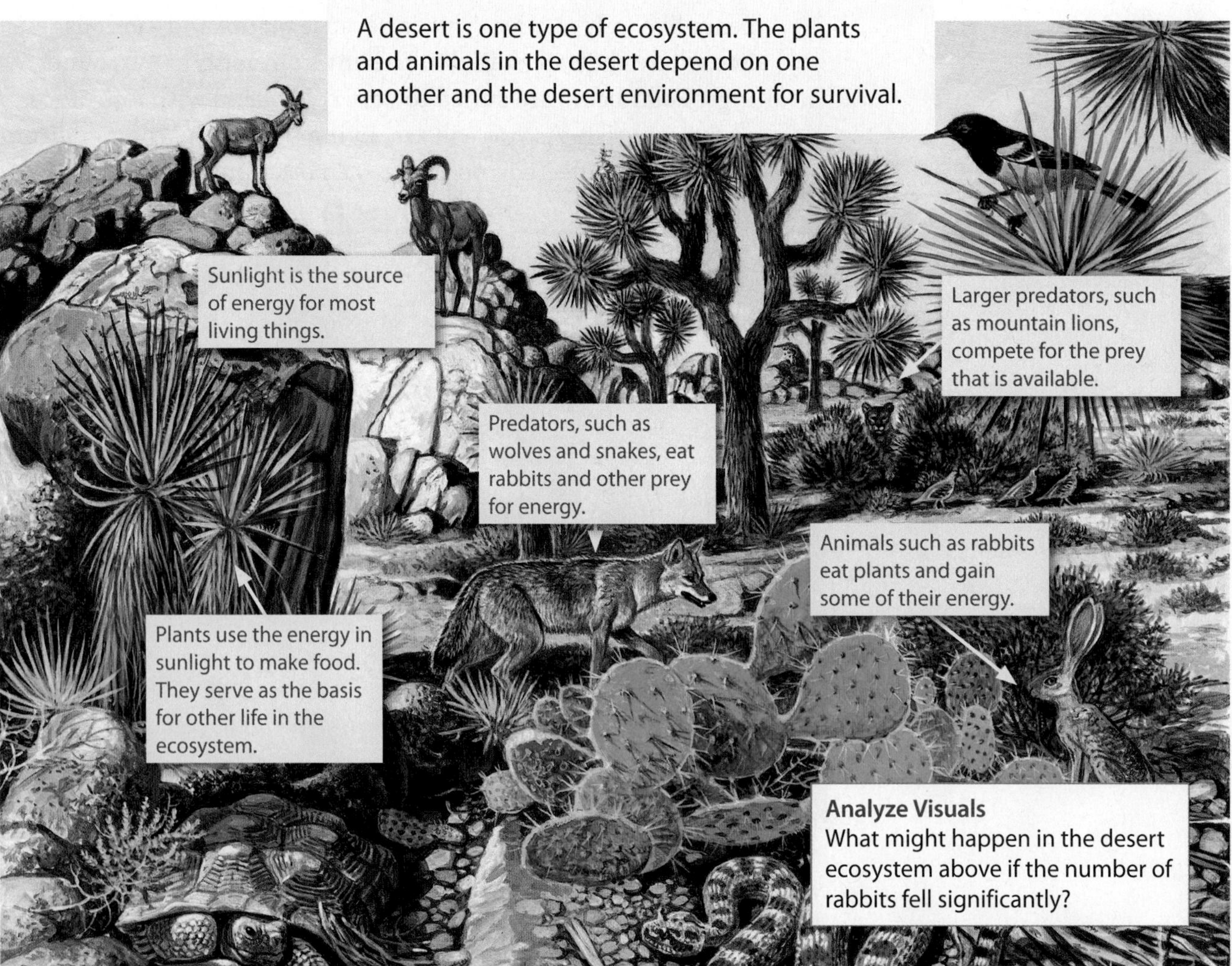

Analyze Visuals
What might happen in the desert ecosystem above if the number of rabbits fell significantly?

The diagram on the previous page shows a desert ecosystem. Each part of this ecosystem fills a certain role. The sun provides energy to the plants, which use the energy to make their own food. The plants then serve as food, either directly or indirectly, for all other life in the desert. When the plants and animals die, their remains break down and provide nutrients for the soil and new plant growth. Thus, the cycle continues.

Changes to Environments The interconnected parts of an ecosystem exist in a fragile balance. For this reason, a small change to one part can affect the whole system. A lack of rain in the forest ecosystem could kill off many of the plants that feed the rabbits. If the rabbits die, there will be less food for the wolves and mountain lions. Then they too may die.

Extinction The dodo is not the only bird to go extinct. The passenger pigeon, shown in this Audubon illustration, went extinct in 1914. Commercial overhunting played a role in its end.

Academic Vocabulary
consequences the effects of a particular event or events

Many actions can affect ecosystems. For example, people need places to live and food to eat, so they clear land for homes and farms. Clearing land has **consequences**, however. It can cause the soil to erode. In addition, the plants and animals that live in the area might be left without food and shelter. Actions such as clearing land and polluting can destroy habitats. A **habitat** is the place where a plant or animal lives. The most diverse habitats on Earth are tropical rain forests. People are clearing Earth's rain forests for farmland, lumber, and other reasons, though. As a result, these diverse habitats are being lost.

Extreme changes in ecosystems can cause species to die out, or become **extinct.** For example, flightless birds called dodos once lived on Mauritius, an island in the Indian Ocean. When people first settled there, they hunted dodos and introduced predators, such as dogs. First seen in 1507, dodos were extinct by 1681.

Recognizing these problems, many countries are working to balance people's needs with the needs of the environment. The United States, for example, has passed many laws to limit pollution, manage forests, and protect valuable ecosystems. These laws rarely please everyone. A law that restricts logging in a forest, for example, may please hikers but frustrate logging companies. A law that bans hunting of threatened species may please wildlife photographers but disappoint hunters.

Reading Check
Make Inferences
How might one change affect an entire ecosystem?

Nevertheless, laws can produce positive results. For example, since the Endangered Species Act of 1973 became law, 47 species have been removed from the endangered species list because their populations have recovered.

Soil and the Environment

As you know, plants are the basis for all food that animals eat. Soils help determine what plants will grow and how well. Because soils support plant life, they play an important role in the environment.

Fertile soils are rich in minerals and **humus** (HYOO - muhs), decayed plant or animal matter. These soils can support abundant plant life. Like air and water, fertile soil is essential for life. Without it, we could not grow much of the food we eat.

Soils can lose fertility in several ways. Erosion from wind or water can sweep topsoil away. Planting the same crops over and over can also rob

Soil Factory

The next time you see a fallen tree in the forest, do not think of it as a dead log. Think of it as a soil factory. A fallen tree is buzzing with the activity of countless insects, bacteria, and other organisms. These organisms invade the fallen log and start to break the wood down.

As the tree decays and crumbles, it turns into humus. Humus is a rich blend of organic material. The humus mixes with the soil and broken rock material. These added nutrients then enrich the soil, making it possible for new trees and plants to grow. Fallen trees provide as much as one-third of the organic material in forest soil.

Summarize
What causes a fallen tree to change into soil?

Soil Layers

The three layers of soil are the topsoil, subsoil, and broken rock. The thickness of each layer depends on the conditions in a specific location. For example, soil can be as much as 100 feet thick in tropical regions.

Analyze Visuals
In which layer of soil are most plant roots and insects found?

Reading Check
Analyze Information What do fertile soils contain, and why are these soils important?

soil of its fertility. When soil becomes worn out, it cannot support as many plants. In fragile, dry environments, this can lead to the spread of desertlike conditions, or **desertification.** The spread of desertlike conditions is a serious problem in many parts of the world.

Summary and Preview Living things and the environment are connected, but changes can easily upset the balance in an ecosystem. Because they support plant life, soils are important parts of ecosystems. In the next lesson you will learn about Earth's many resources.

Lesson 6 Assessment

Review Ideas, Terms, and Places

1. **a. Define** What is an ecosystem, and what are two examples of ecosystems?
   b. Summarize How do nature and people change ecosystems?
   c. Elaborate Why can plants and animals not live everywhere?
   d. Contrast How is a biome different from an ecosystem?
2. **a. Recall** What is humus, and why is it important to soil?
   b. Identify Cause and Effect What actions can cause desertification, and what might be some possible effects?
   c. Elaborate Why is it important for geographers and scientists to study soils?

Critical Thinking

3. Identify Cause and Effect Review your notes. Then draw a two-row, two-column chart. Label one column Causes and the other Effects. Use the chart to identify some of the causes and effects of changes to ecosystems.

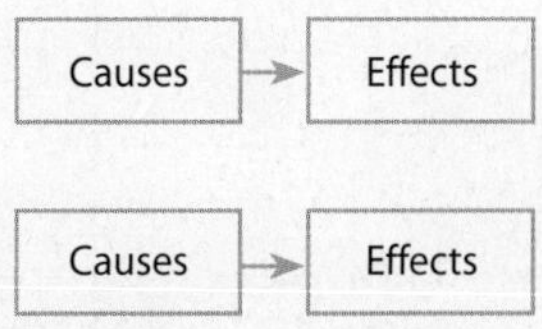

Natural Resources

The Big Idea

Earth's natural resources have many valuable uses, and their availability affects people in many ways.

Main Ideas

- Earth provides valuable resources for our use.
- Energy resources provide fuel, heat, and electricity.
- Mineral resources include metals, rocks, and salt.
- Resources shape people's lives and countries' wealth.

Key Terms and Places

natural resource
renewable resources
nonrenewable resources
deforestation
reforestation
fossil fuels
hydroelectric power

If YOU lived there . . .

You live in Southern California, where the climate is warm and dry. Every week, you water the grass around your house to keep it green. Now the city has declared a "drought emergency" because of a lack of rain. City officials have put limits on watering lawns and on other uses of water.

How can you help conserve scarce water?

Earth's Valuable Resources

Think about the materials in nature that you use. You have learned about the many ways we use sun, water, and land. They are just a start, though. Look at the human-made products around you. They all required the use of natural materials in some way. We use trees to make paper for books. We use petroleum, or oil, to make plastics for cell phones. We use metals to make machines, which we then use to make many items. Without these materials, our lives would change drastically.

Using Natural Resources Trees, oil, and metals are all examples of natural resources. A **natural resource** is any material in nature that people use and value. Earth's most important natural resources include air, water, soils, forests, and minerals.

Understanding how and why people use natural resources is an important part of geography. We use some natural resources just as they are, such as wind. Usually, though, we change natural resources to make something new. For example, we change metals to make products such as bicycles and watches. Thus, most natural resources are raw materials for other products.

Types of Natural Resources We group natural resources into two types: those we can replace and those we cannot. **Renewable resources** are resources Earth replaces naturally. For example, when we cut down a tree, another tree can grow in its place. Renewable resources include water, soil, trees, plants, and animals. These resources can last forever if used wisely.

Reforestation

Members of the Green Belt Movement plant trees in Kenya. Although trees are a renewable resource, some forests are being cut down faster than new trees can replace them. Reforestation helps protect Earth's valuable forestlands.

Analyze Visuals
How does reforestation help the environment?

Other natural resources will run out one day. These **nonrenewable resources** are resources that cannot be replaced. For example, coal formed over millions of years. Once we use the coal up, it is gone.

Managing Natural Resources People need to manage natural resources to protect them for the future. Consider how your life might change if we ran out of forests, for example. Although forests are renewable, we can cut down trees far faster than they can grow. The result is the clearing of trees, or **deforestation.**

By managing resources, we can repair and prevent resource loss. For example, some groups are engaged in **reforestation,** planting trees to replace lost forestland.

Reading Check
Contrast How do renewable and nonrenewable resources differ?

BIOGRAPHY

Wangari Maathai (1940–2011)

Can planting a tree improve people's lives? Wangari Maathai thinks so. Born in Kenya in East Africa, Maathai wanted to help people in her country, many of whom were poor. She asked herself what Kenyans could do to improve their lives. "Planting a tree was the best idea that I had," she says. In 1977 Maathai founded the Green Belt Movement to plant trees and protect forestland. The group has now planted more than 30 million trees across Kenya! These trees provide wood and prevent soil erosion. In 2004 Maathai was awarded the Nobel Peace Prize. She is the first African woman to receive this famous award.

Analyze Effects:
How has Maathai's Green Belt Movement helped Kenya?

Natural Resources
Earth provides many valuable and useful natural resources, such as oil.

Energy Resources

Every day you use plants and animals from the dinosaur age—in the form of energy resources. These resources power vehicles, produce heat, and generate electricity. They are some of our most important and valuable natural resources.

Nonrenewable Energy Resources Most of the energy we use comes from **fossil fuels,** nonrenewable resources that formed from the remains of ancient plants and animals. The most important fossil fuels are coal, petroleum, and natural gas.

Coal has long been a reliable energy source for heat. However, burning coal causes some problems. It pollutes the air and can harm the land. For these reasons, people have used coal less as other fuel options became available.

Today we use coal mainly to create electricity at power plants, not to heat single buildings. Because coal is plentiful, people are looking for cleaner ways to burn it.

Petroleum, or oil, is a dark liquid used to make fuels and other products. When first removed from the ground, petroleum is called crude oil. This oil is shipped or piped to refineries, factories that process the crude oil to make products. Fuels made from oil include gasoline, diesel fuel, and jet fuel. Oil is also used to make petrochemicals, which are processed to make products such as plastics and cosmetics.

As with coal, burning oil–based fuels comes with a tradeoff. Such fuels can pollute the air and land. In addition, oil spills can harm wildlife. International concern over the effect of oil spills inspired the creation of international regulations. These regulations address pollution from oil spills and help ensure a coordinated response. Because we are so dependent on oil for energy, it is an extremely valuable resource.

The cleanest-burning fossil fuel is natural gas. We use it mainly for heating and cooking. For example, your kitchen stove may use natural gas. Some vehicles run on natural gas as well. These vehicles cause less pollution than those that run on gasoline.

Many scientists believe that pollution from burning fossil fuels has caused Earth's temperature to increase. This increase, they argue, is bringing about climate change. The growing scientific agreement on this issue has inspired international action. The Kyoto Protocol to the United Nations Framework Convention on Climate Change was adopted in 1997. The Kyoto Protocol, as it is known, sets internationally binding targets to reduce emissions from burning fossil fuels. More than 190 countries have signed the agreement.

Renewable Energy Resources Unlike fossil fuels, renewable energy resources will not run out. They also are generally better for the environment. On the other hand, they are not available everywhere and can be costly.

The main alternative to fossil fuels is **hydroelectric power**—the production of electricity from water power. We obtain energy from moving water by damming rivers. The dams harness the power of moving water to generate electricity.

Hydroelectric power has both pros and cons. On the positive side, it produces power without polluting and lessens our use of fossil fuels. On the negative side, dams create lakes that replace existing resources, such as farmland, and disrupt wildlife habitats.

Another renewable energy source is wind. People have long used wind to power windmills. Today we use wind to power wind turbines, a type of modern windmill. At wind farms, hundreds of turbines create electricity in windy places.

A third source of renewable energy is heat from the sun and Earth. We can use solar power, or power from the sun, to heat water or homes. Using special solar panels, we turn solar energy into electricity. We can also use geothermal energy, or heat from within Earth. Geothermal power plants use steam and hot water located within Earth to create electricity.

Hydroelectric Power
Glen Canyon Dam, near Page, Arizona, provides roughly 4 billion kilowatt hours per year of hydroelectric power. It also created Lake Powell, which filled to capacity in 1980.

Nuclear Energy A final energy source is nuclear energy. We obtain this energy by splitting atoms, small particles of matter. This process uses the metal uranium, so some people consider nuclear energy a nonrenewable resource. Nuclear power does not pollute the air, but it does produce dangerous wastes. These wastes must be stored for thousands of years before they are safe. In addition, an accident at a nuclear power plant can have terrible effects.

All countries need energy. Yet, energy resources are not evenly spread across Earth. As a result, energy production differs by region. For example, the Middle East has rich oil deposits. For this reason, the Middle East leads the world in oil production.

Reading Check
Make Inferences
Why might people look for alternatives to fossil fuels?

Mineral Resources

Like energy resources, mineral resources can be quite valuable. Whether used locally or traded to distant regions to obtain other valuable goods, mineral resources help an area's economic growth. These resources include metals, salt, rocks, and gemstones.

Minerals fulfill countless needs. Look around you to see a few. Your school building likely includes steel, made from iron. The outer walls might be granite or limestone. The window glass is made from quartz, a mineral in sand. From staples to jewelry to coins, metals are everywhere.

Minerals are nonrenewable, so we need to conserve them. Recycling items such as aluminum cans and personal electronics will make the supply of these valuable resources last longer.

Reading Check
Categorize
What are the major types of mineral resources?

From the Ground to the Air

Humans gather and process minerals before using them. In nature, minerals are often mixed into rock or other solid material, called ore. People mine, or dig in the earth, to extract the ore. Then the ore is processed to get the mineral, which is used to create final products.

Bauxite, a rock, is mined and used to make aluminum.

Aluminum is used in many products, such as jet planes.

Identify
How many other aluminum products can you name?

Products from Petroleum

This Ohio family shows some common products made from petroleum, or oil.

Analyze Visuals
What petroleum-based products can you identify in this photo?

Resources and People

Natural resources vary from place to place. The resources available in a region can shape life and wealth for the people there.

Resources and Daily Life The natural resources available to people affect their lifestyles and needs. In the United States, we have many different kinds of natural resources. We can choose among many different ways to dress, eat, live, travel, and entertain ourselves. People in places with fewer natural resources will likely have fewer choices and different needs than Americans.

For example, people who live in remote rain forests depend on forest resources for most of their needs. These people may craft containers by weaving plant fibers together. They may make canoes by hollowing out tree trunks. Instead of being concerned about money, they might be more concerned about food.

In areas where more than one group wants to use the same resources, conflicts can arise. For example, the Aka people of Central Africa sometimes struggle to find enough resources. Logging companies have been harvesting trees from the forests in which the Aka hunt and gather. The loss of trees has reduced animals' habitats, which makes it harder for the Aka to find food.

Resources and Wealth The availability of natural resources affects countries' economies as well. For example, the many natural resources available in the United States have helped it become one of the world's wealthiest countries. In contrast, countries with few natural resources often have weak economies.

Some countries have one or two valuable resources but few others. For example, Saudi Arabia is rich in oil but lacks water for growing food. As a result, Saudi Arabia must use its oil profits to import food. Indeed, a number of countries in Southwest Asia face similar challenges. In 1960, Iran, Iraq, Kuwait, Saudi Arabia and Venezuela founded the Organization of Petroleum Exporting Countries (OPEC). OPEC works to stabilize the oil markets and ensure a steady income to member states. OPEC has grown to 13 countries.

Reading Check
Identify Cause and Effect
How can having few natural resources affect life and wealth in a region or country?

Summary You can see that Earth's natural resources have many uses. Important natural resources include air, water, soils, forests, fuels, and minerals.

Lesson 7 Assessment

Review Ideas, Terms, and Places

1. a. **Define** What are renewable resources and nonrenewable resources?
   b. **Explain** Why is it important for people to manage Earth's natural resources?
   c. **Identify** What are some things you can do to help manage and conserve natural resources?
2. a. **Define** What are fossil fuels, and why are they significant?
   b. **Summarize** What are three examples of renewable energy resources?
3. a. **Recall** What are the main types of mineral resources?
   b. **Analyze** What are some products that we get from mineral resources?
4. a. **Summarize** How do resources affect people?
   b. **Make Inferences** How might a country with only one valuable resource develop its economy?

Critical Thinking

5. **Categorize** Draw a chart like this one. Use your notes to describe and evaluate each type of energy resource.

Fossil Fuels	Renewable Energy	Nuclear Energy
Pros	Pros	Pros
Cons	Cons	Cons

Social Studies Skills

Use a Physical Map

Define the Skill

Physical maps show important physical features, like oceans and mountains, in a particular area. They also indicate an area's elevation, or the height of the land in relation to sea level.

When you use a physical map, there are important pieces of information you should always examine.

- Identify physical features. Natural features, such as mountains, rivers, and lakes, are labeled on physical maps. Read the labels carefully to identify what physical features are present.
- Read the legend. On physical maps, the legend indicates scale as well as elevation. The different colors in the elevation key indicate how far above or below sea level a place is.

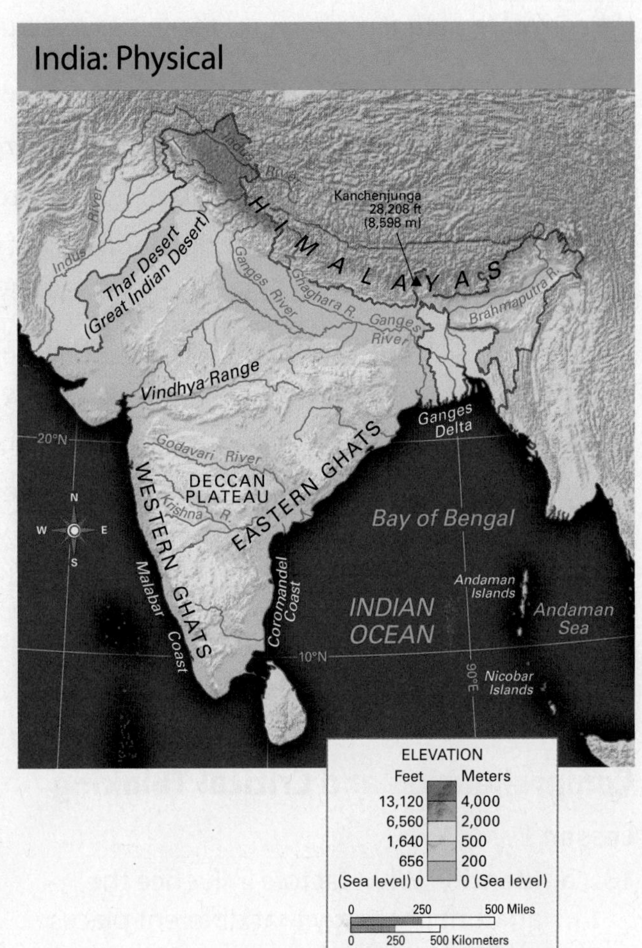

Learn the Skill

Use the physical map of India to answer the questions below.

1. What landforms and bodies of water are indicated on the map?
2. What is the highest elevation in India? Where is it located?

Practice the Skill

Locate the physical map of Africa in the Atlas in the back of the book. Use the map to answer the questions below.

1. Which region has the highest elevation?
2. What bodies of water surround Africa?
3. What large island is located off the east coast of Africa?

Module 2 Assessment

Review Vocabulary, Terms, and Places

For each statement below, write T if it is true and F if it is false. If the statement is false, write the correct term that would make the sentence a true statement.

1. **Weathering** is the movement of sediment from one location to another.
2. Most of our **groundwater** is stored in Earth's streams, rivers, and lakes.
3. It takes 365¼ days for Earth to complete one **rotation** around the sun.
4. Streams are formed when **precipitation** collects in narrow channels.
5. **Earthquakes** cause erosion as they flow downhill, carving valleys and mountain peaks.
6. The planet's tilt affects the amount of **erosion** Earth receives from the sun.
7. When plant or animal matter has decayed, it is called **humus**.
8. Conditions or changes in the air in a certain time and place are called **climate**.
9. **Reforestation** is the act of planting trees where forests once stood.
10. A species is **extinct** when it has completely died out.
11. **Steppes** are areas of tall grasses and scattered shrubs and trees.
12. Winds that change direction with the season and create wet and dry periods are known as **savannas**.

Comprehension and Critical Thinking

Lesson 1

13. a. **Identify** What factors influence the amount of energy that different places on Earth receive from the sun?
    b. **Predict** What might happen to the amount of solar energy we receive if Earth's axis were straight up and down?

Lesson 2

14. a. **Describe** What different sources of water are available on Earth?
    b. **Draw Conclusions** How does the water cycle keep Earth's water supply relatively constant?
    c. **Elaborate** What water problems affect people around the world? What solutions can you think of for one of those problems?

Lesson 3

15. a. **Define** What is a landform? What are some common types of landforms?
    b. **Analyze effects** What are some things that can happen when two tectonic plates interact?
    c. **Elaborate** What physical features dominate the landscape in your community? How do they affect life there?

Lesson 4

16. a. **Identify** What five factors affect climate?
    b. **Analyze** Is average annual precipitation an example of weather or climate?

Lesson 5

17. a. **Recall** What are the five major climate zones?
    b. **Explain** How does latitude relate to climate?

Lesson 6

18. a. **Define** What is an ecosystem, and why does it exist in a fragile balance?
    b. **Explain** Why are plants an important part of the environment?

Module 2 Assessment, continued

Lesson 7

19. a. **Define** What are minerals?
    b. **Contrast** How do nonrenewable resources and renewable resources differ?
    c. **Elaborate** How might a scarcity of natural resources affect life in a region?

Reading Skills

Use Word Parts *Use what you learned about prefixes, suffixes, and word roots to answer the questions.*

20. The prefix *in-* sometimes means "not." What do the words *invisible* and *inactive* mean?
21. The suffix *–ment* means "action" or "process." What does the word *movement* mean?

Social Studies Skills

Use a Physical Map *Use the physical map of the United States in the World Atlas to answer these questions.*

22. What physical feature extends along the Gulf of Mexico?
23. What mountain range in the West lies above 6,560 feet (2,000 m)?

Map Activity

Physical Map *Use the map to answer the questions that follow.*

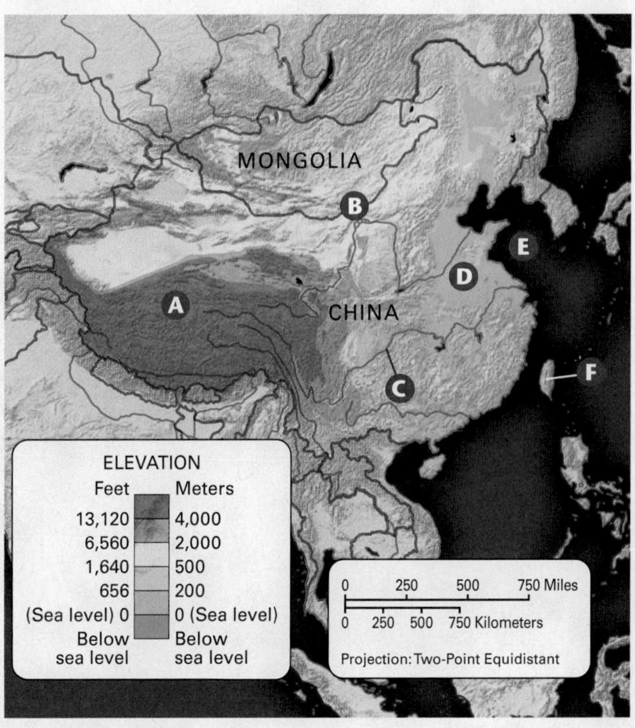

24. Which letter indicates a river?
25. Which letter on the map indicates the highest elevation?
26. The lowest elevation on the map is indicated by which letter?
27. An island is indicated by which letter?
28. Which letter indicates a large body of water?
29. Which letter indicates an area of land between 1,640 feet (500 m) and 6,560 feet (2,000 m) above sea level?

Focus on Reading and Viewing

30. **Present and View a Weather Report** Select a place and a season to write a weather report about. Watch weather reports online or on TV as part of your research. Note interesting vocabulary, and look up words you do not understand. Use what you learn in your research to describe the weather and predict upcoming weather. Include vocabulary from this module. Then present your report to the class. Speak using a professional, friendly tone and a variety of sentence types. Make frequent eye contact with your audience. Listen and take notes as your classmates present their reports. Be prepared to give feedback on the content and their presentation techniques.

Module 3

The Human World

Essential Question

Which geographic concepts are most useful for understanding the world's people?

About the Photo: Many of the world's people come together every four years to compete in the Olympics.

Explore ONLINE!

HISTORY

VIDEOS, including . . .
- Henry Ford's Motor Company
- Computers
- Hoover Dam

- Document-Based Investigations
- Graphic Organizers
- Interactive Games
- Channel One News Video: Young People Keep Mariachi Alive
- Interactive Map: Cultural Diffusion of Baseball
- Interactive Graph: World Population Growth, 1500–2000
- Image with Hotspots: How Fracking Works

In this module, you will learn about geographic concepts that help to explain the human world.

What You Will Learn

Lesson 1: Elements of Culture 95
The Big Idea Culture, a group's shared practices and beliefs, differs from group to group and changes over time while maintaining features common to all societies.

Lesson 2: Population. 106
The Big Idea Population studies are an important part of geography.

Lesson 3: Settlement Patterns. 113
The Big Idea Many factors influence where people settle and how settlements develop.

Lesson 4: Human-Environment Interaction 118
The Big Idea Specific environments present distinct opportunities for people to meet their needs and unique challenges to which they must adapt.

Human-Environment Interaction Farming is one way that humans interact with the environment. These rice farmers in Vietnam utilize the area's rich soil.

Population Geographers study human populations, like this one in India, to learn where and why people live in certain places.

Culture Thousands of different cultures make up our world. Clothing, language, and music are just some parts of culture.

Reading Social Studies

Understand Main Ideas

READING FOCUS

Main ideas are like the hub of a wheel. The hub holds the wheel together, and everything circles around it. In a paragraph, the main idea holds the paragraph together and all the facts and details revolve around it. The main idea is usually stated clearly in a topic sentence, which may come at the beginning or end of a paragraph. Topic sentences always summarize the most important idea of a paragraph.

To find the main idea, ask yourself what one point is holding the paragraph together. See how the main idea in the following example holds all the details from the paragraph together.

A single country may also include more than one culture region within its borders. Mexico is one of many countries that is made up of different culture regions. People in northern Mexico and southern Mexico, for example, have different culture traits. The culture of northern Mexico tends to be more modern, while traditional culture remains strong in southern Mexico.

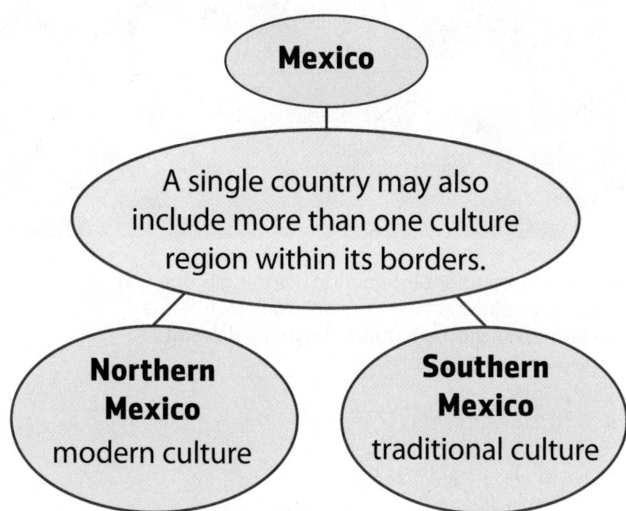

YOU TRY IT!

Read the following paragraph, and then use a graphic organizer to identify the main idea. Create as many circles as you need to list the supporting facts and details.

People migrate for many reasons. Some factors push people to leave their country, while others pull people away. During the Irish potato famine of the mid-1800s, poverty and disease forced some 1.5 million people to leave Ireland. In the 1800s and early 1900s thousands of British citizens migrated to Australia in search of cheap land.

As you read this module, find the main ideas of the paragraphs you are studying.

Elements of Culture

The Big Idea

Culture, a group's shared practices and beliefs, differs from group to group and changes over time while maintaining features common to all societies.

Main Ideas

- Culture is the set of beliefs, goals, and practices that a group of people share.
- The world includes many different culture groups.
- New ideas and events lead to changes in culture.
- The features common to all cultures are called cultural universals.
- All societies have social institutions that help their groups survive.
- Every culture expresses itself creatively in a variety of ways.
- All societies use technology to help shape and control the environment.

Key Terms and Places

culture
culture trait
culture region
ethnic group
multicultural society
cultural diffusion
cultural universals
social institutions
heritage
universal theme
technology

If YOU lived there . . .

You live in New York City, and your young cousin from out of state has come to visit. As you take her on a tour, you point out the different cultural neighborhoods, like Chinatown, Little Italy, Spanish Harlem, and Koreatown. People speak in other languages as they venture to the nearby shops and restaurants that offer a variety of cultural goods. Your cousin can see that shopping and eating special foods are common activities for many cultures. Still, she isn't quite sure what *culture* means or why these neighborhoods are so different from her own.

How can you explain what culture is?

What Is Culture?

If you traveled around the world, you would experience many different sights and sounds. You would probably hear unique music, eat a variety of foods, listen to different languages, see distinctive landscapes, and learn new customs. You would see and take part in the variety of cultures that exist in our world.

A Way of Life What exactly is culture? **Culture** is the set of beliefs, values, and practices that a group of people have in common. Culture includes many aspects of life, such as language and religion, that we may share with people around us. Everything in your day-to-day life is part of your culture—from the clothes you wear to the music you hear to the foods you eat.

On your world travels, you might notice that all societies share certain cultural features. All people have some kind of government, educate their children in some way, and create some type of art or music. However, not all societies practice their culture in the same way. For example, in Japan, the school year begins in the spring and students wear school uniforms. In the United States, however, the school year begins in the late summer and most schools do not require uniforms. Differences like these are what make each culture unique.

Culture Traits

These students in Japan and Kenya have some culture traits in common, like eating lunch at school. Other culture traits are different.

Analyze Visuals
What culture traits do these students share? Which are different?

Culture Traits Cultural features like starting the school year in the spring or wearing uniforms are types of culture traits. A **culture trait** is an activity or behavior in which people often take part. The language you speak and the sports you play are some of your culture traits. Sometimes a culture trait is shared by people around the world. For example, all around the globe, people participate in the game of soccer. In places as different as Germany, Nigeria, and Saudi Arabia, many people enjoy playing and watching soccer.

While some culture traits are shared around the world, others change from place to place. One example of this is how people around the world eat. In China, most people use chopsticks to eat their food. In Europe, however, people use forks and spoons. In Ethiopia, many people use bread or their fingers to scoop their food.

Development of Culture How do cultures develop? Culture traits are often learned or passed down from one generation to the next. Most culture traits develop within families as traditions, foods, or holiday customs are handed down over the years. Laws and moral codes are also passed down within societies. For example, many laws in the United States can be traced back to England in the 1600s and were brought by colonists to America. Among these are the right to a speedy trial, freedom of petition, and due process of law.

Cultures also develop as people learn new culture traits. Immigrants who move to a new country, for example, might learn to speak the language or eat the foods of their adopted country.

Other factors, such as history and the environment, also affect how cultures develop. For example, historical events changed the language and religion of much of Central and South America. In the 1500s, when the Spanish conquered the region, they introduced their language and Roman Catholic faith. The environment in which we live can also shape culture. For example, the desert environment of Africa's Sahara influences the way people who live there earn a living. Rather than grow crops, they herd animals that have adapted to the harsh environment. As you can see, history and the environment affect how cultures develop.

Reading Check
Find Main Ideas
What practices and customs make up culture?

Culture Groups

Earth is home to thousands of different cultures. People who share similar culture traits are members of the same culture group. Culture groups can be based on a variety of factors, such as age, language, or religion. American teenagers, for example, can be said to form a culture group based on location and age. They share similar tastes in music, clothing, and sports.

Culture Regions When we refer to culture groups, we are speaking of people who share a common culture. At other times, however, we need to refer to the area, or region, where the culture group is found. A **culture region** is an area in which people have many shared culture traits.

Arab Culture Region

Culture regions are based on shared culture traits. Southwest Asia and North Africa make up an Arab culture region based on ethnic heritage, a common language, and religion. Most people in this region are Arab, speak and write Arabic, and practice Islam.

Many people share Arab culture traits. An Omani boy, above, and Palestinian girls, at left, share the same language and religion.

Analyze Visuals
What culture traits do you see in the photos?

Sports are played in cultures around the world. These Lenape teens enjoy a game of lacrosse.

In a specific culture region, people share certain culture traits, such as religious beliefs, language, or lifestyle. One well-known culture region is the Arab world. As you can see in the Arab Culture Region feature, this culture region spreads across Southwest Asia and North Africa. In this region, most people write and speak Arabic and are Muslim. They also share other traits, such as foods, music, styles of clothing, and architecture.

Occasionally, a single culture region dominates an entire country. In Japan, for example, one primary culture dominates the country. Nearly everyone in Japan speaks the same language and follows the same practices. Many Japanese bow to their elders as a sign of respect and remove their shoes when they enter a home.

A single country may also include more than one culture region within its borders. Mexico is one of many countries that is made up of different culture regions. People in northern Mexico and southern Mexico, for example, have different culture traits. The culture of northern Mexico tends to be more modern, while traditional culture remains strong in southern Mexico.

A culture region may also stretch across country borders. As you have already learned, an Arab culture region dominates much of Southwest Asia and North Africa. Another example is the Kurdish culture region, home to the Kurds, a people that live throughout Turkey, Iran, and Iraq.

Cultural Diversity As you just learned, countries may contain several culture regions within their borders. Often, these culture regions are based on ethnic groups. An **ethnic group** is a group of people who share a common culture and ancestry. Members of ethnic groups often share certain culture traits such as language and special foods. Religion can also be a shared culture trait within an ethnic group.

People in different ethnic groups can be part of the same religious group. For example, many people around the world practice the religion of Judaism. However, a Jewish person from Hungary would not be in the same ethnic group as a Jewish person from Ethiopia. These two people may share religious beliefs, but they do not have the same ethnic background. In contrast, people can be in the same ethnic group and have different religious beliefs. For example, there are Christian and Muslim Arabs.

Some countries are home to a variety of ethnic groups. For example, more than 100 different ethnic groups live in the East African country of Tanzania. Countries with many ethnic groups are culturally diverse. A **multicultural society** is a society that includes a variety of cultures in the same area. While multiculturalism creates an interesting mix of ideas, behaviors, and practices, it can also lead to conflict.

In some countries, ethnic groups have been in conflict. In Canada, for example, some French Canadians want to separate from the rest of Canada to preserve their language and culture. In the 1990s, ethnic conflict in the African country of Rwanda led to extreme violence and bloodshed.

Although ethnic groups have clashed in some culturally diverse countries, they have cooperated in others. In the United States, for example, many different ethnic groups live side by side. One major reason for this diversity is that people have migrated to the United States from all over the world. Cities and towns often celebrate their ethnic heritage with festivals and parades, like the Saint Patrick's Day Parade in Boston or Philadelphia's Puerto Rican Festival.

Reading Check
Make Inferences Why might multiculturalism cause conflict?

Changes in Culture

You've read books or seen movies set in the time of the Civil War or in the Wild West of the late 1800s. Think about how our culture has changed since then. Clothing, food, music—all have changed drastically. When we study cultural change, we try to find out what factors influence the changes and how those changes spread from place to place.

How Cultures Change Cultures change constantly. Some changes happen rapidly, while others take many years. What causes cultures to change? **Innovation** and contact with other people are two key causes of cultural change.

Academic Vocabulary
innovation a new idea or way of doing something

New ideas often bring about cultural changes. For example, when Alexander Graham Bell invented the telephone, it changed how people communicate with each other. Other innovations, such as motion pictures, changed how people spend their free time. More recently, the creation of the Internet dramatically altered the way people find information, communicate, and shop.

Cultures also change as societies come into contact with each other. For example, when the Spanish arrived in the Americas, they introduced firearms and horses to the region, changing the lifestyle of some Native American groups. At the same time, the Spaniards learned about new foods like potatoes and chocolate. These foods then became an important part of Europeans' diet. The Chinese had a similar influence on Korea and Japan, where they introduced Buddhism and written language.

How Cultural Traits Spread You have probably noticed that a new slang word might spread from teenager to teenager and state to state. In the same way, clothing styles from New York or Paris might become popular all over the world. More serious cultural traits spread as well. Religious beliefs or ideas about government may spread from place to place. The spread of culture traits from one region to another is called **cultural diffusion.**

Cultural diffusion often occurs when individuals move from one place to another. For example, when European immigrants settled in the Americas, they brought their culture along with them. As a result, English, French, Spanish, and Portuguese are all spoken in the Americas. American culture also spread as pioneers moved west, taking with them their form of government, religious beliefs, and customs.

Another factor that leads to cultural diffusion is trade. An example of this developed along the Silk Road of ancient China. The trade route encouraged the exchange of goods and practices between Asia and the

Middle East. Also, the Phoenicians were an early trading civilization that moved Middle Eastern culture throughout the Mediterranean region. They are often called the "carriers of civilization" because of their strong influence on other cultures.

Conflict can also be a reason for cultural diffusion. Recently, millions of Syrians fled their country in a mass migration to escape civil war. Some refugees moved to neighboring countries in the Middle East. Other Syrian people traveled great distances to places such as Europe and North America. This migration contributed to the diversity of each region.

Cultural diffusion also takes place as new ideas spread from place to place. As you can see on the map, the game of baseball first began in New York, then spread throughout the United States. As more and more people learned the game, it spread even faster and farther. Baseball eventually spread to other world societies. Wearing blue jeans became part of our culture in a similar way. Blue jeans originated in the American West in the mid-1800s. They gradually became popular all over the country and the world.

Reading Check
Find Main Ideas
How do cultures change over time?

What Do All Cultures Have in Common?

You may be wondering how cultures can be so different when all people have the same basic needs. All people need food, clothing, and shelter to survive. Geographers and other social scientists believe that some needs

Focus on Culture

Cultural Diffusion of Baseball

Like many other ideas and customs, baseball has spread around the world through the process of cultural diffusion. Since its beginnings in New York in the 1800s, baseball has spread throughout the United States, into Central and South America, and to Asia.

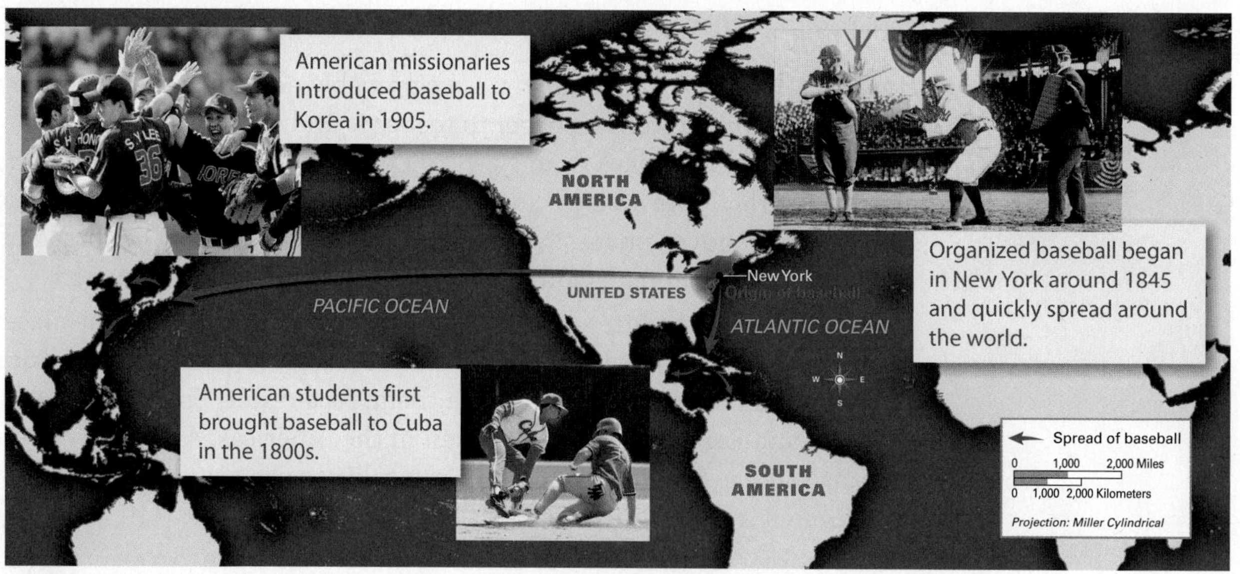

Analyze Visuals
Where did baseball begin, and to what parts of the world did it eventually spread?

Reading Check
Find Main Ideas
What can geographers learn from cultural universals?

are so basic that societies everywhere have developed certain features to meet them. These features, common to all cultures, are called **cultural universals.** In this section, you will learn about three important cultural universals: social institutions, creative expressions, and technology.

Basic Social Institutions

Societies, like people, have basic needs that must be met for a group to survive. **Social institutions** are organized patterns of belief and behavior that focus on meeting these needs. The most basic social institutions are family, education, religion, government, and economy. The core principles and ideals of a society are known as cultural values. They help to shape the group and all of its social institutions. Cultural values and social institutions exist in all societies. However, their specific characteristics and customs, or ways of doing things, vary from culture to culture.

Family Family is the most basic social institution. In all societies, its purpose is the same. The family ensures that children are cared for until old enough to fend for themselves. Families provide emotional and physical support. They also teach the accepted values, traditions, and customs of a culture.

The traditions of a culture hold great significance and get passed along from one generation to the next. One custom in Greece is that people celebrate a "name day" for the saint that bears their name instead of their own birthday. Another tradition is the Battle of Oranges in Northern Italy. Groups of people throw oranges to reenact a famous battle.

Cultural values are also important and often have a long history within a specific culture. For example, the foundation of African cultural values is based on the past and present. This is one reason why elders are so respected there. The elders are to always be acknowledged and served their meals first.

The size of a family can vary from one culture to another. Family members may live together under one roof or they might inhabit an entire village. For example, India's joint family system includes grandparents, parents, uncles, aunts, and all of their children living in one household.

Government To keep order and resolve conflicts, people need a government. A government is a system of leaders and laws that help people live safely together in their community or country. Laws help people live safely with each other because they define standards, protect property and people's rights, and help settle disagreements. Laws can apply to any of a society's social institutions. For example, a country may impose a minimum wage law, which affects the country's economy. Perhaps a government creates new laws for its nation's education system. This may impact what students learn in school.

Economy To support its people, a society must have an economy, or a system of using resources to meet needs. People must be able to make, buy, sell, and trade goods and services to get what they need and want. They must consider the questions of what to produce, for whom to produce, and how to produce. Prosperous nations have strong economic principles in place to guide their business decisions and actions.

Education

In the United States and in Peru, schools teach knowledge, skills, and cultural norms to prepare students for adult roles.

Analyze Visuals
What similarities and differences do you detect between the two classroom environments?

Education Societies rely on education to pass on knowledge to young people. For example, schools across the world teach reading, writing, math, and technical skills that prepare students to take on adult roles. Schools also teach the norms and values that sustain, or support, a society. For instance, one goal of U.S. public schools is to develop informed citizens who contribute to the good of their communities.

Religion The world's religions are incredibly diverse. Still, in all societies, religion helps explain the meanings of life and death and the difference between good and bad behavior. Over time, religion is passed down and supported by traditional practices, literature, sacred texts and stories, and sacred places. All of this makes religion a powerful force. It is often the foundation of a culture's philosophical beliefs and attitudes. Moreover, in all world regions, it has inspired and sustained itself through great works of devotion, including art and **monumental** architecture.

Academic Vocabulary
monumental impressively large, sturdy, and enduring

Reading Check
Summarize
What are the main social institutions?

Creative Expressions

All people are creative. Everyone has the ability to imagine, think, and create. Not surprisingly, all societies express themselves creatively, too. The main types of creative expression are:

- **Performing Arts**—art forms that combine sound and movement for an audience, such as music, theater, and dance
- **Visual Arts**—creative expressions that have both a visual and material form, such as painting, jewelry, sculpture, textiles, and architecture
- **Literary Arts**—art forms rooted in words and language, such as literature, folktales, and stories

Monumental Architecture

Religion inspires creative expressions, including monumental architecture such as France's Notre Dame Cathedral and Shwedagon Pagoda, a Buddhist temple in Myanmar (Burma).

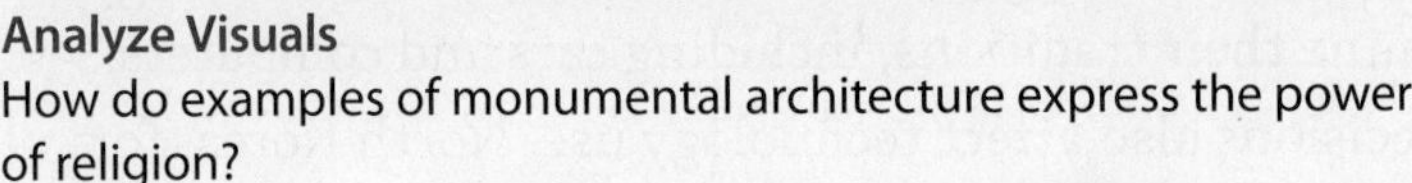

Analyze Visuals
How do examples of monumental architecture express the power of religion?

Creative Forces As you explore creative expressions from all world regions, note how they are influenced by the availability of natural materials and resources. Look, too, for how creative expressions reflect a specific **heritage,** or the wealth of cultural elements that has been passed down over generations.

Creative expressions also express individual choices. People use artistic forms to express individual as well as cultural ideas about what is pleasing, proper, and beautiful. They also use them to address contemporary issues such as politics, war, and social inequality. This is because the arts can inspire us. Creative forms communicate ideas and emotions that stir people to action.

Universal Themes Some creative expressions communicate universal themes. A **universal theme** is a message about life or human nature that is meaningful across time and in all places. Because they express basic human truths, universal themes transcend, or move beyond, the boundaries of a particular society. They speak to people everywhere.

Masterpieces of art have qualities that are meaningful and timeless. Examples include Egyptian hieroglyphics and the sculptures of ancient Greece. The woodblock prints made by the Japanese painter Katsushika Hokusai are also an example of this type of art. They express a love of nature's beauty, simplicity, and power.

Other art forms also gain worldwide appreciation. For example, literature such as *The Lord of the Rings* contains a universal theme of a hero's search for truth, goodness, and honor. Blues music is another example. Derived from African American work songs and spirituals in the American South, blues songs express feelings of sadness and struggle in the face of great challenges.

Reading Check **Describe** What are the main types of cultural expressions?

Science and Technology

All people use technology to shape and control their environments, and they use science to try and understand it. **Technology** refers to the use of knowledge, tools, and skills to solve problems. Science is a way of understanding the world through observation and the testing of ideas.

Factors Shaping Technology Use Historically, the type of technology a culture developed has been strongly tied to environmental factors. Not only were tools and technology made from local resources, they were also designed to solve specific problems posed by nature. For example, farmers might build dams to prevent rivers from flooding and destroying their crops.

Other factors such as belief systems, political decisions, and economic factors can influence technology use, too. Some religious groups, like the Amish people of the United States, selectively use technology. They readily use gas and horse-drawn buggies. However, they reject technology they think will undermine their traditions, including cars and computers.

Government decisions also affect technology use. North Korea, for example, restricts Internet use. To use the Internet, a North Korean must have special permission and may use it for government purposes only. Worldwide, however, the primary barrier between people and technology is economic. New technologies are simply too expensive for many of the world's people to access them.

Impact of Technology Throughout time, advances in science and technology have made life easier. Some discoveries even changed the world.

Consider, for example, the work of French scientist Louis Pasteur. His work revolutionized health and medicine. In 1870 Pasteur discovered that germs caused infections. To prevent the spread of disease, he urged people to wash their hands. He also developed vaccines to prevent deadly diseases and a process for removing bacteria from food. Today, most milk, cheese, and juice on our grocery shelves have been sterilized, or made germ-free, through pasteurization.

Inventors, too, change the world. For example, in 1879, Thomas Edison developed an affordable and practical light bulb. At the time, the invention caused a sensation. People no longer had to burn candles and oil lamps for light at night. Over time, electricity transformed daily life and work for many of the world's people.

Nature's awesome power is a universal theme in the painting of a great wave created by Japanese artist Katsushika Hokusai.

In fact, Thomas Edison had a friend in the auto industry who would greatly benefit from the new technology. In 1913 automaker Henry Ford launched the world's first moving assembly line. This new process allowed workers to decrease construction time on a single vehicle from 12 hours to roughly 90 minutes.

The introduction of computers into the workplace has demanded new skill sets from employees. Consider the work of an auto mechanic from 50 years ago and today. Every car manufactured today contains at least one computer system. Auto mechanics must understand these systems in order to effectively work on a vehicle.

All of these technologies greatly increased the rate of production. People were able to work faster and more efficiently, which resulted in a larger supply of available goods.

Today, scientists and inventors continue to identify and solve problems. They often work in groups to make discoveries or invent new devices or products that will benefit future generations. This involves careful thinking about the future and making predictions about the social, political, economic, cultural, and environmental impact of their work.

Reading Check
Form Generalizations What are the basic purposes of technology and science?

Summary and Preview In this lesson you learned about the role that culture plays in our lives, how our cultures change over time and move around the world, and the features that make cultures similar. Next, you will learn about human populations and how we keep track of Earth's changing population.

Lesson 1 Assessment

Review Ideas, Terms, and Places

1. **a. Define** What is culture?
   b. Analyze What influences the development of culture?
   c. Elaborate How might the world be different if we all shared the same culture?
2. **a. Identify** What are the different types of culture regions?
   b. Analyze How does cultural diversity affect societies?
3. **a. Describe** Identify an example of a cultural trait that has spread. How did that culture trait spread?
   b. Identify Which factors influence cultural change?
   c. Evaluate Do you think that cultural diffusion has a positive or a negative effect? Explain your answer.
4. **a. Identify and Explain** What are five basic social institutions? What purposes do they serve?
   b. Analyze What efforts and activities are most important for a religious institution to last over time? Explain.
5. **a. Describe** What forces influence cultural expressions?
   b. Identify List and explain examples of art, music, and literature with universal themes.
6. **a. Explain** How can factors related to belief systems, government, and economics affect technology use?
   b. Make Inferences How might a resource such as river water affect how farmers use technology?
   c. Explain Give an example of a scientific discovery and an example of a technological innovation that have changed the world. Discuss the role of scientists and inventors in making the discovery and innovation.

Critical Thinking

7. **Find Main Ideas** Using your notes and a chart like the one here, explain the main idea of each aspect of culture in your own words.

Culture Traits	Culture Groups	Cultural Change

Population

The Big Idea

Population studies are an important part of geography.

Main Ideas

- The study of population patterns helps geographers learn about the world.
- Population statistics and trends are important measures of population change.

Key Terms and Places

population
population density
birthrate
migration

If YOU lived there . . .

You live in Mexico City, one of the largest and most crowded cities in the world. You realize just how crowded it is whenever you ride the subway at rush hour! You love the excitement of living in a big city. There is always something interesting to do. At the same time, the city has a lot of crime. Heavy traffic pollutes the air.

What do you like and dislike about living in a large city?

Population Patterns

How many people live in your community? Do you live in a small town, a huge city, or somewhere in between? Your community's **population,** or the total number of people in a given area, determines a great deal about the place in which you live. Population influences the variety of businesses, the types of transportation, and the number of schools in your community.

Because population has a huge impact on our lives, it is an important part of geography. Geographers who study human populations are particularly interested in patterns that emerge over time. They study such information as how many people live in an area, why people live where they do, and how populations change. Population patterns like these can tell us much about our world.

Population Density Some places on Earth are crowded with people. Others are almost empty. One statistic geographers use to examine populations is **population density,** a measure of the number of people living in an area. Population density is expressed as persons per square mile or square kilometer.

Population density provides us with important information about a place. The more people per square mile in a region, the more crowded, or dense, it is. Japan, for example, has a population density of about 897 people per square mile (around 347 per square km). That is a high population density. In many parts of Japan, people are crowded together in large cities and space is very limited. In contrast, Australia has a very low

World Population Density

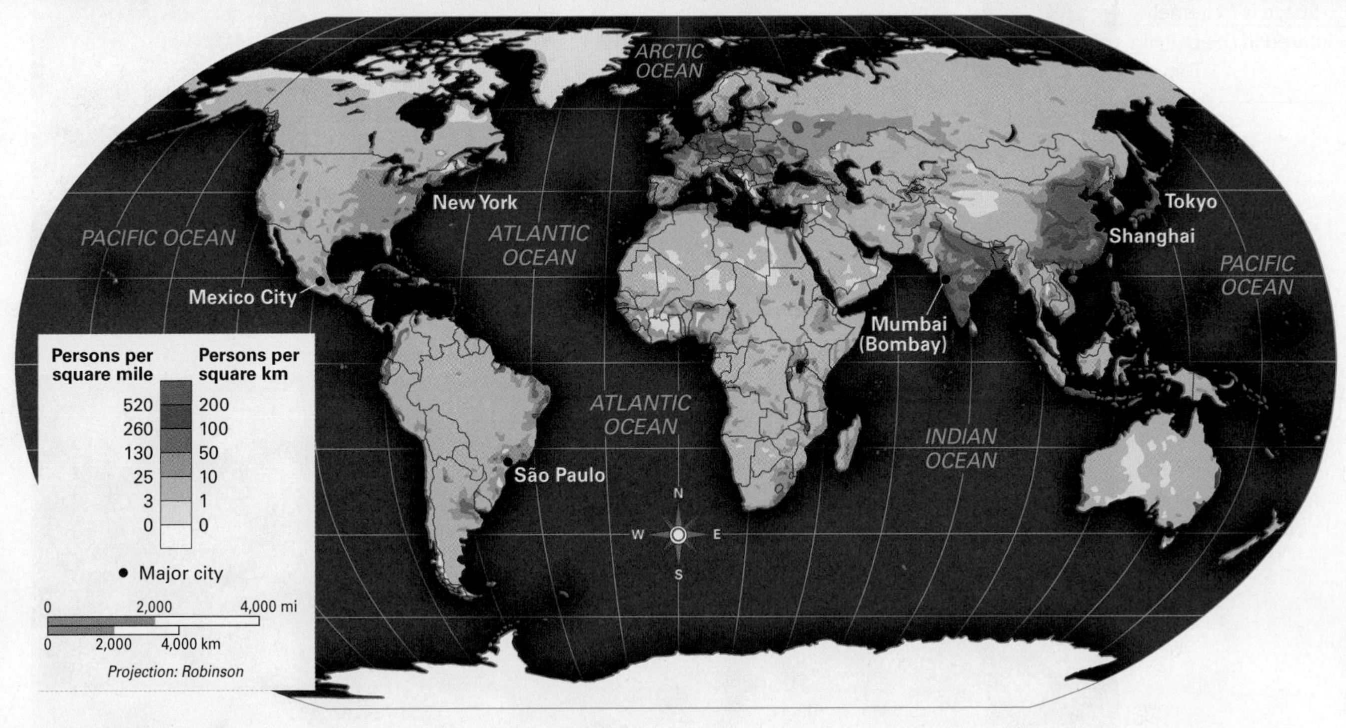

Interpret Maps

1. **Place** Which continent is the most densely populated? Which is the least densely populated?
2. **Region** Why might the population density of far Northern America be so low?

population density. Only around 8 people per square mile (about 3 per square km) live there. Australia has many wide-open spaces with very few people.

How do you think population density affects life in a particular place? In places with high population densities, the land is often expensive, roads are crowded, and buildings tend to be taller. On the other hand, places with low population densities tend to have more open spaces, less traffic, and more available land.

Population density also affects the economic development of a region. These effects can be positive or negative depending on the circumstances. Areas with higher population densities and abundant resources have the potential to create more job opportunities, which can add value to the region. In contrast, a larger population density in regions with limited resources can present many challenges. It may be difficult to provide goods and services to every person when resources are in short supply.

Where People Live Can you tell where most of the world's people live by examining the world population density map above? The reds and purples on the map indicate areas of very high population density, while the light

Many parts of Japan have a high population density. Space is extremely limited in the city of Tokyo.

Australia has a very low population density. There is plenty of space for people living along the Noosa River.

yellow areas indicate sparse populations. When an area is thinly populated, it is often because the land does not provide a very good life. These areas may have rugged mountains or harsh deserts where people cannot grow crops. Some areas may be frozen all year long, making survival there very difficult. For these reasons, very few people live in parts of far North America, Greenland, northern Asia, and Australia.

Notice on the world population density map that some areas have large clusters of population. Such clusters can be found in East and South Asia, Europe, and eastern North America. Fertile soil, plentiful vegetation, reliable sources of water and minerals, and a good agricultural climate make these regions favorable for settlement. For example, the North China Plain in East Asia is one of the most densely populated regions in the world. The area's plentiful agricultural land, many rivers, and mild climate have made it an ideal place to settle. The natural resources in these regions offer job opportunities in farming, mining, and timber production. These industries can provide great economic benefits to the area.

As populations swell in desirable areas, there is a higher demand for resources. These demands can drastically affect the environment. Many developed nations consume resources faster than they can regenerate them. In some areas, population has been growing faster than food supplies. The amount of available farmland is shrinking as regions make room for more people. Coastal ecosystems are being pressured by urban development. The demand for fresh water also increases with population. Some countries may even face shortages in the future.

Reading Check
Form Generalizations What types of information can population density provide?

Connect to Math

Calculate Population Density

Population density measures the number of people living in an area. To calculate population density, divide a place's total population by its area in square miles (or square kilometers). For example, if your city has a population of 100,000 people and an area of 100 square miles, you would divide 100,000 by 100. This would give you a population density of 1,000 people per square mile (100,000 ÷ 100 = 1,000).

City	Population	Total Area (square miles)	Population Density (people per square mile)
Adelaide, Australia	1,255,516	705	1,781
Lima, Peru	9,897,033	1,032	9,590
Nairobi, Kenya	3,914,791	269	14,553

Source: *World Urbanization Prospects*, Population Division, UN Dept. of Economic and Social Affairs

Evaluate
If a city had a population of 615,000 and a total land area of 250 square miles, what would its population density be?

Population Change

The study of population is much more important than you might realize. The number of people living in an area affects all elements of life—the availability of housing and jobs, whether hospitals and schools open or close, even the amount of available food. Geographers track changes in populations by examining important statistics, studying the movement of people, and analyzing population trends.

Tracking Population Changes Geographers examine three key statistics to learn about population changes. These statistics are important for studying a country's population over time.

Three key statistics—birthrate, death rate, and the rate of natural increase—track changes in population. Births add to a population. Deaths subtract from it. The annual number of births per 1,000 people is called the **birthrate.** Similarly, the death rate is the annual number of deaths per 1,000 people. The birthrate minus the death rate equals the percentage of natural increase, or the rate at which a population is changing. For example, Denmark has a rate of natural increase of 0.01 percent. This means it has slightly more births than deaths and a very slight population increase.

Population growth rates differ from one place to another. In some countries, populations are growing very slowly or even shrinking. Many countries in Europe and North America have very low rates of natural increase. In Russia, for example, the birthrate is about 11 and the death rate is around 14. The result is a negative rate of natural increase and a shrinking population.

In most countries around the world, however, populations are growing. Mali, for example, has a rate of natural increase of about 3.1 percent. While that may sound small, it means that Mali's population is expected to double in the next 20 years! High population growth rates can pose

Irish Migration

The failure of Ireland's most important food crop, the potato, caused widespread starvation. Disease and high food prices forced many Irish to flee to America in search of a better life.

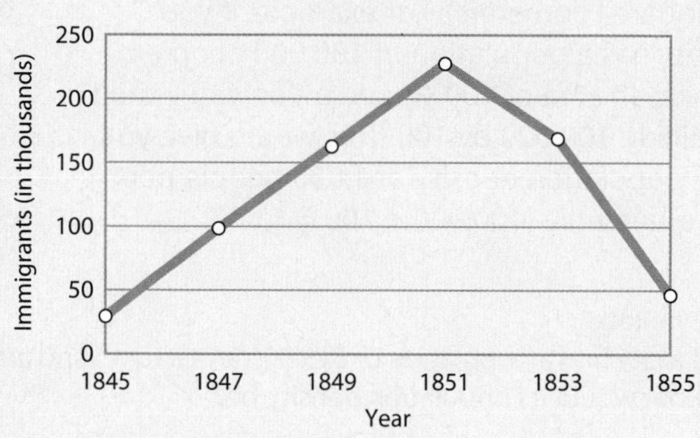

Source: *Historical Statistics of the United States.*

Analyze Graphs
In what year did Irish migration to the United States peak?

Push Factors
- Climate changes, exhausted resources, earthquakes, volcanoes, drought/famine
- Unemployment, slavery
- Religious, ethnic, or political persecution, war

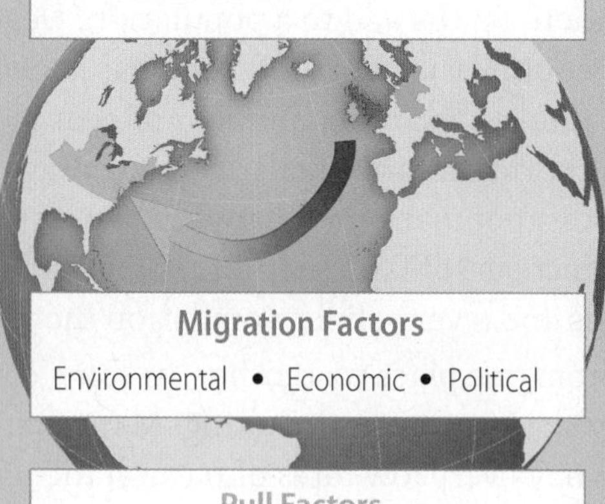

Migration Factors
Environmental • Economic • Political

Pull Factors
- Abundant land, new resources, good climate
- Employment opportunities
- Political and/or religious freedom

some challenges, as governments try to provide enough jobs, education, and medical care for their rapidly growing populations.

Many governments track their regional population patterns and trends. Analyzing current data and making population projections can help leaders address present and future needs of citizens. This might involve enacting new laws that protect the natural resources of an area. A government could also develop policies that provide more economic opportunities for a region. For example, China's most recent Five-Year Plan promotes the use of cleaner energy sources to reduce pollution. The plan also outlines ways that China will strengthen support for farmers, increase agricultural income, and improve rural infrastructure.

Migration A common cause of population change is migration. **Migration** is the process of moving from one place to live in another. As one country loses citizens as a result of migration, its population can decline. At the same time, another country may gain population as people settle there.

People migrate for many reasons. Some factors push people to leave their country, while other factors pull, or attract, people to new countries. Warfare, a lack of jobs, or a lack of good farmland are common push factors. For example, during the Irish potato famine of the mid-1800s, poverty and disease forced some 1.5 million people to leave Ireland. Opportunities for a better life often pull people to new countries. For example, in the 1800s and early 1900s, thousands of British citizens migrated to Australia in search of cheap land.

Political conditions such as freedom or persecution can also cause movement. The political system of apartheid in South Africa imposed a regime of segregation and racial oppression from the mid-1900s until 1994. Thousands of black South Africans were forced to migrate to other parts of Africa. Environmental factors such as climate can also lead to migration. For example, people who live in harsh climates are often attracted to regions with milder climates.

World Population Trends In the last 200 years, Earth's population has exploded. For thousands of years, world population growth was low and relatively steady. About 2,000 years ago, the world had some 300 million people. By 1800 there were almost 1 billion people. Since 1800, better health care and improved food production have supported tremendous population growth. By 2012 the world's population passed 7 billion people.

World Population Growth

Advances in food production and health care have dramatically lowered death rates. As a result, the global population has seen incredible growth over the last 200 years.

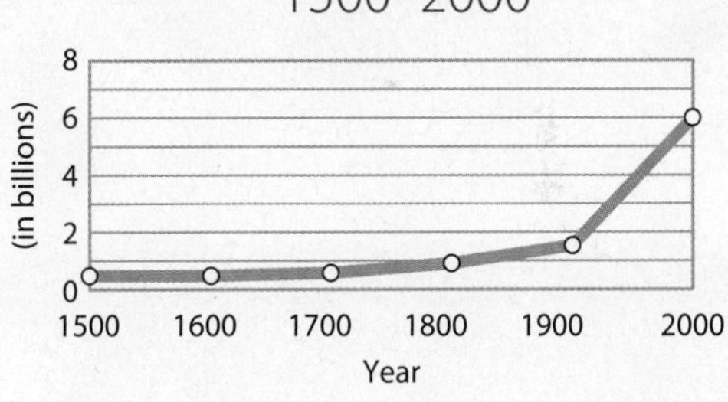

Source: *Atlas of World Population History*

Analyze Graphs
By how much did the world's population increase between 1800 and 2000?

Reading Check
Summarize
What population statistics do geographers study? Why?

Population trends are an important part of the study of the world's people. Two important population trends are clear today. The first trend indicates that the population growth in some of the more industrialized nations has begun to slow. For example, Germany and France have low rates of natural increase. A second trend indicates that less industrialized countries, like Nigeria and Bangladesh, often have high growth rates. These trends affect a country's work force and government aid.

Summary and Preview In this lesson you learned where people live, how crowded places are, and how population changes. Geographers study population patterns and trends to plan for the future. In the next lesson, you will learn about factors that influence the settlement patterns of people.

Lesson 2 Assessment

Review Ideas, Terms, and Places

1. a. **Identify** What regions of the world have the highest levels of population density?
   b. **Draw Conclusions** What information can be learned by studying population density?
   c. **Evaluate** Would you prefer to live in a region with a dense or a sparse population? Why?
2. a. **Describe** What is natural increase? What can it tell us about a country?
   b. **Analyze** What effect does migration have on human populations?
   c. **Predict** What patterns do you think world population might have in the future?

Critical Thinking

3. **Summarize** Draw a chart with two columns. Label one column Population Patterns and the other column Population Change. Use your notes to write a sentence that summarizes each aspect of the study of population.

Population Patterns	Population Change

Settlement Patterns

The Big Idea

Many factors influence where people settle and how settlements develop.

Main Ideas

- Natural resources and trade routes are important factors in determining location for settlements.
- Areas can be defined as urban or rural.
- Spatial patterns describe ways that people build settlements.
- New technology has improved the interaction of regions with nearby and distant places.

Key Terms and Places

settlement
trade route
urban
suburb
metropolitan area
megalopolis
rural
spatial pattern
linear settlements
cluster settlements
grid settlements
commerce

If YOU lived there . . .

You live in Phoenix and your parents tell you that they must relocate for work. The family asks for your opinion on where to move. Do you prefer the city lights and skyscrapers of Chicago or the Smoky Mountains in North Carolina?

How do people decide where to live?

The Importance of Location

A **settlement** is any place where a community is established. Settlements vary in size, ranging anywhere from a heavily populated city to a remote island village. Where people choose to settle depends on many factors. These factors may be economic, political, or related to natural resources.

Natural Resources People have always settled near natural resources. Some of the earliest settlements were started near sources of freshwater or on tracts of land that were good for farming. As people began to use other resources, the places where they settled changed. During the late 1800s, the cities of Pittsburgh, Pennsylvania, and Birmingham, Alabama, grew considerably. This was due to their location near deposits of iron ore and coal. The steel manufacturing industry led to booms in both cities.

Trade Routes Because resources are not distributed evenly, trade routes have always been important to settlements. A **trade route** is a path used by traders for buying and selling goods. Villages, towns, and cities were often started along trade routes, and these places grew as the routes grew. For example,

Birmingham, Alabama, was founded in 1871 at the crossing of two railroad lines, near rich deposits of iron and coal.

Singapore's location along a major shipping route has helped make the tiny island nation rich.

Singapore, in Southeast Asia, grew along a major shipping route. The city of Timbuktu in western Africa was founded at the place where major caravan routes met. The Niger River, an important water trade route, was also located nearby. Timbuktu thrived not only as a trading center but also as a political center because of the different groups that met there to trade.

Reading Check
Find Main Ideas Why are natural resources and trade routes important to a settlement?

Urban and Rural

Geographers often classify patterns of settlement by size. One way they do this is by defining areas as urban or rural.

Urban areas are cities and the surrounding areas. They are heavily populated and very developed. This means that urban areas have many structures such as houses, roads, and commercial buildings. Most people work in jobs not related to agriculture.

Small urban areas might include a city center or a **suburb.** A suburb is an area immediately outside of a city, often a smaller residential community. Large urban areas might include an entire city and nearby suburbs. A city, its suburbs, and surrounding areas form a large urban area called a **metropolitan area.** When several metropolitan areas grow together, they form a **megalopolis.** A megalopolis in the northeastern United States is the tract of cities including Boston, New York, Philadelphia, Baltimore, and Washington, DC.

Rural areas are found outside of cities. They are less densely populated and have fewer structures. The economic activities of rural areas are usually tied to the land. Agriculture, forestry, mining, and recreation are examples of rural economic activities. Settlements in rural areas are often built around these activities.

Reading Check
Contrast What is the difference between rural and urban areas?

Times Square in Manhattan is an urban area.

The economic activities in rural areas are usually tied to the land.

Spatial Patterns

There are many factors that influence settlement design. Within urban and rural areas, settlements are built in certain ways. Geographers use spatial patterns to describe and classify how people build settlements. A **spatial pattern** is the placement of people and objects on Earth and the space between them.

Types of Settlements **Linear settlements** are grouped along the length of a resource, such as a river. They usually form a long and narrow pattern. In the eastern United States, many linear settlements were started along the Fall Line. This is a place where the land drops sharply to the Coastal Plain. This drop causes rivers to form waterfalls and rapids. In the past, people used the fast-moving water along the Fall Line to power factories and machines. Today, this water is used to generate electricity.

Cluster settlements are grouped around or at the center of a resource. Coal became an important resource in Europe in the early 1800s. Settlements were founded on the outskirts of coal deposits, or seams, to support mining operations. The Corn Belt is located in the midwestern United States and includes Iowa, Illinois, and Indiana, as well as parts of Nebraska, Kansas, Minnesota, and Missouri. Since the 1850s, this area has been a leading producer of corn. Settlements in the Corn Belt, like many agricultural areas, are designed to maximize the available land for farming.

Grid settlements are purposefully laid out with a network of transportation routes. Streets form a grid by running at right angles to each other. These settlements are commonly found in urban areas. Transportation networks are commonly made of roads, though some places also have networks of water routes or underground subway and train routes. Washington, DC, is one example of a grid settlement. It was designed using a grid plan that includes diagonal avenues often connected by traffic circles. This layout continued as the capital expanded.

Reading Check
Identify Problems
What is one problem that could occur in a cluster settlement?

Types of Settlement Patterns

Some basic types of settlement patterns include linear, cluster, and grid.

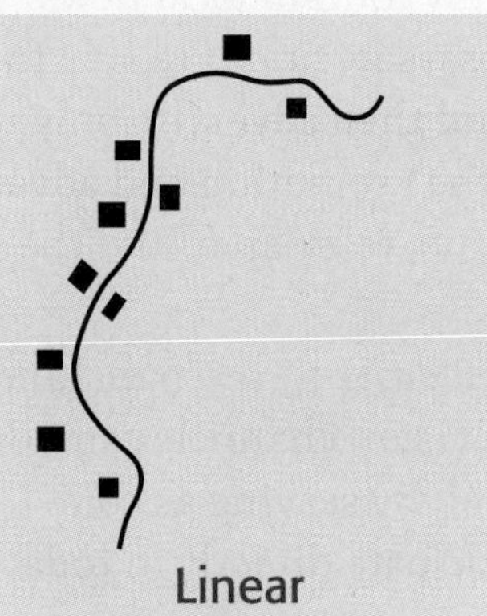
Linear

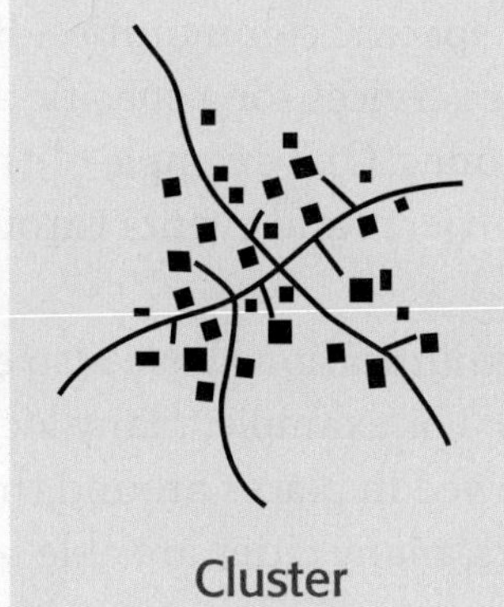
Cluster

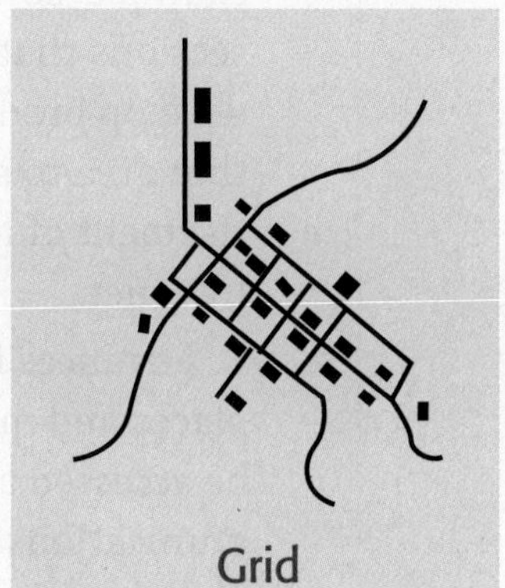
Grid

Analyze Visuals
How would you classify the settlement pattern of your community?

Planned transportation networks, such as this highway system in Los Angeles, California, are a feature of grid settlements.

Regions Interact

People live in or near urban areas because they are centers for commerce and trade. **Commerce** refers to the substantial exchange of goods between cities, states, or countries. Usually, urban areas are also centers of government services for a region. Moreover, cities are often known as hubs for education, communication, transportation, and innovation.

Advances in Technology Starting during the mid-1900s, new inventions including television and satellites greatly improved communications. Later, computers and the Internet also improved communications and changed the ways people collected, stored, shared, and used information.

Technological advances affected cities and the places near them. Cities were able to tailor services and communications to nearby regions. For example, some large metropolitan newspapers now contain local news sections that cover specific communities. Businesses in cities are able to develop products or services for a specific area and then advertise only to that area to save money. One example of this is the promotion and advertisement of local concerts and events through radio, television, and the Internet.

Advances in communications have also enabled cities to reach distant places and markets. For example, many local television channels can now be accessed and viewed in places around the world. By serving as communications centers, many cities are able to participate directly in today's global market.

Advances in transportation have also changed how people and ideas move around the world. Today, people can travel great distances in a

Traders work on the floor of the New York Stock Exchange on Wall Street in New York City. The New York Stock Exchange is one of the world's largest trading marketplaces. Wall Street and New York City have long been hubs of interaction for the financial industry.

shorter amount of time. For example, the 7,500-mile (17,070-km) flight from Los Angeles to Sydney, Australia, takes less than 15 hours. Transportation hubs such as airports, train stations, and subway systems connect major cities across the globe. In a sense, new technology has allowed our enormous world to seem much smaller.

Reading Check
Summarize How has new technology changed interaction between regions?

Summary and Preview In this lesson you learned about the many factors that influence where people settle and how settlements develop. In the next lesson, you will learn about how people interact with their environments.

Lesson 3 Assessment

Review Ideas, Terms, and Places

1. a. **Define** What is a settlement?
   b. **Analyze Effects** How do natural resources and human activities affect settlements?
2. a. **Identify** What terms do geographers use to classify settlement patterns by size?
   b. **Form Opinions** Would you prefer to live in a rural or urban area? Explain your choice.
3. a. **Explain** How do geographers use spatial patterns?
   b. **Synthesize** What pattern would you choose to design a settlement? Provide reasons for your selection.
4. a. **Analyze** How do cities affect nearby and distant places?
   b. **Elaborate** How does technology make the world seem smaller?

Critical Thinking

5. **Summarize** Use a three-column chart to write a sentence that summarizes each type of settlement. Include an example for each.

Linear Settlement	Cluster Settlement	Grid Settlement

Human-Environment Interaction

The Big Idea

Specific environments present distinct opportunities for people to meet their needs and unique challenges to which they must adapt.

Main Ideas

- Geographers examine how environmental conditions shape people's lives.
- Human activity changes specific places, regions, and the world as a whole.

Key Terms and Places

terraced farming
slash-and-burn agriculture
center-pivot irrigation
fracking

If YOU lived there . . .

You live on the beach in Southern California and enjoy daily walks by the water. Lately you have noticed the sand littered with trash and debris. Last week your friend rescued a small turtle that was entangled in a plastic bag. You can't help but wonder why these things are happening to such a beautiful place.

How do people affect the environment?

Responding to the Environment

How does geography shape human behavior? Geographers interested in this question investigate how environmental conditions—such as terrain, climate, vegetation, wildlife, variations in soil, and the availability of water resources—shape people's lives. They also study the human systems, or cultural practices, that people develop in response to environmental conditions. Some human systems, like farming, allow people to benefit from what their environment offers. Other systems develop to protect people from conditions beyond their control, such as natural hazards.

The colorful, traditional clothes worn by the Sami, Norway's original population, help them survive harsh winters.

Types of Farming

Using slash-and-burn agriculture, farmers cut trees, brush, and grasses and burn debris to clear land for farming. The ash produced creates fertile soils for farming.

Terraced farming is an ancient technique for growing crops on hillsides or mountain slopes. Farmers cut steps into hillsides. This creates flat land for growing crops.

Center-pivot irrigation uses a sprinkler unit in the center of a large, circular field. The sprinkler's long arm circles over the field, sprinkling water on the crops.

Analyze Visuals
How does each type of farming help resolve a challenge presented by the environment?

Farming Farming is one of the best examples of human-environment interaction. Over time, people across the globe have developed farming practices to grow food under specific environmental conditions. Most notably, farming is affected by climate, vegetation, and soil conditions.

Moreover, with these practices, people refashion the land, leaving their mark on the environment as they make the most of natural resources. For example, the ancient Inca of Peru created farmland by using a method called **terraced farming.** They carved steps into steep hillsides to create flat land for growing crops. In thickly forested areas, such as the Amazon rain forest, farmers developed **slash-and-burn agriculture.** Using this technique, farmers cut down trees and plants with knives and machetes. Then they burn the fallen trees to clear land for farming. After a few years, when the soil's nutrients have been used up, farmers move to a new area. Today, in dry regions of the United States, farmers use a technique called **center-pivot irrigation,** which uses a sprinkler system in the center of a large, circular field. The long arms of the sprinkler circle over the field to water crops.

Natural Hazards Weather can be harsh and sometimes deadly. People can adapt to their environment by preparing for natural hazards such as fires, tornadoes, earthquakes, and hurricanes. They change what they do to stay safe based on the climate. These preparations may include building storm shelters or having drills to practice what to do in an emergency. Most schools have fire drills to practice leaving the building. Depending on the weather in a location, some schools have tornado drills or earthquake drills. Cities also have building codes for new buildings and structures. These codes are rules that tell what must be done to keep a building safe when people use it.

In the past, people did not have the tools to prepare for natural hazards. One example is the 1815 eruption of Mount Tambora in Indonesia. The eruption scattered tons of ash, dust, and gas into the atmosphere. In the aftermath, there were food shortages and disease outbreaks. This led to a mass migration of people searching for a better place to live.

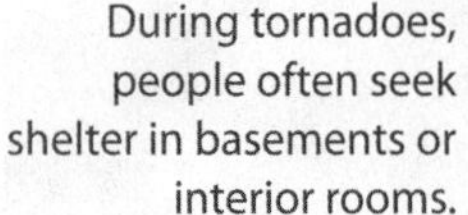
During tornadoes, people often seek shelter in basements or interior rooms.

Reading Check
Summarize How can people prepare for natural hazards?

Although we are more prepared for natural disasters in today's world, the impacts can still be devastating. In 2011 an earthquake in the Tohoku region of Japan caused a tsunami and damaged a nuclear power station. Thousands of people fled the area due to earthquake aftershocks, power outages, a lack of food, and fear of radiation from the nuclear reactors.

Changing the Environment

How do people affect the environment? Geographers interested in this question are particularly concerned with how human activity changes specific places, regions, and the world as a whole. They look at how people use the environment to meet their needs and explore the damaging effects that some human activities have on the environment.

Using Resources People are constantly modifying, or changing, their environment. For example, they build roads and bridges to make it easier to move people and goods. They build dams to create steady water sources and to control floods, and they clear land for farming or for new housing developments. People also dig deep into Earth's surface to obtain natural resources to heat their homes, make clothing, and power their cars and businesses. Human activities that change the environment often improve people's lives. New buildings, roads, and bridges help people live, travel, and work, but they are not always beneficial to the environment.

Dams provide necessary water for communities but also disrupt water flow and surrounding ecosystems.

Water pollution harms our food supplies, drinking water, and environment.

Effects of Human Activity Human activities can have negative effects for people and the environment. For example, when a dam is built, it could disrupt an aquatic ecosystem, or the community of plants and animals that live along the river. Blocking the flow of water could change the amount of water downstream, block migration routes, and even change the water chemistry. These changes could, in turn, affect the survival of many river species.

Human activities can also change environmental conditions in larger regions. An urban heat island occurs in large cities that are densely covered with roads, concrete, and buildings. These human features make an area drier and trap heat, causing parts of the city to be hotter than surrounding, less developed areas.

Geographers are especially concerned with how human activities contribute to global environmental challenges, such as pollution, acid rain, land degradation, ozone depletion, and global warming. Such challenges pose a threat to all people and places. For example, the ozone layer helps protect living things from the sun's harmful rays. Scientists have found that human activities have depleted, or used up, areas of the ozone layer. Specifically, chemicals called chlorofluorocarbons (CFCs) cause ozone depletion. For many years, people released CFCs into the atmosphere when

Most air pollution comes from the production and use of energy.

they made or used products such as spray cans, refrigerators, and Styrofoam cups. CFCs were phased out beginning in 1987, but the ozone layer was already damaged. Scientists think this aggravated problems associated with global warming, such as severe storms and rising sea levels.

People have different perspectives on environmental issues. The argument over hydraulic fracturing offers an example. Also known as **fracking,** this process breaks up rock by injecting large amounts of water and chemicals into cracks. This procedure forces cracks in the rock to widen, which allows oil and gas to flow out. In the United States, those against fracking have concerns that the process will significantly damage the environment or contaminate drinking water. Supporters claim that it will reduce dependence on foreign oil and boost economies with the production of homeland fuel.

Some people believe that government intervention is the best way to prevent businesses and individuals from depleting natural resources. Governments around the world have enacted policies in an effort to protect land, freshwater, air, and ocean resources. For instance, Brazil's government designated more than half of the Brazilian Amazon as national parks or indigenous lands. By establishing these protected areas, rates of deforestation and illegal logging have been drastically reduced.

No matter the viewpoint, environmental issues impact every person on the planet. Deforestation has led to the loss of habitat for many species and increased global warming. The burning of fossil fuels causes high levels of pollution, acid rain, and health issues. Desertification damages soil and vegetation, which can lead to food shortages for a region.

Reading Check
Identify Problems What are some environmental problems caused by humans?

Many countries and organizations are working together to improve environmental quality around the globe. For example, the Environmental Protection Agency (EPA) is working with groups in West Africa to improve drinking water standards. The EPA also helped India introduce technologies to manage air quality and decrease vehicle emissions.

Summary In this lesson you learned that geographers investigate how environmental conditions shape people's lives. You also learned about how people interact with their environments.

Lesson 4 Assessment

Review Ideas, Terms, and Places

1. a. **Define** What is slash-and-burn agriculture?

   b. **Draw Conclusions** What might happen if people did not develop human systems to deal with natural disasters?

2. a. **Explain** How do human activities in one place impact the global environment?

   b. **Form Opinions** Do you support or disagree with fracking? Provide reasons for your opinion.

Critical Thinking

3. **Evaluate** Draw a chart to explain how land is used in your community. Use the chart to help answer the following questions: What changes have been made to the environment to benefit people? How might human activities harm the environment? How can people use resources wisely?

Beneficial Changes	Negative Effects	Conservation Ideas

Social Studies Skills

Organize Information

Define the Skill

Remembering new information is easier if you organize it clearly. As you read and study, try to organize what you are learning. One way to do this is to create a graphic organizer. As you read:

1. Identify the main idea of the text you are reading and write it in a circle.
2. Look for subtopics under the main idea. Write the subtopics in the circles below the main idea.
3. Below each subtopic, draw a big box. Look for facts and supporting details for each subtopic to list in the box.
4. Organizing information is not limited to text. You can organize information found in visuals, too. Take a look at the Irish Migration to the United States, 1845–1855 graph in Lesson 2. You could create a graphic organizer such as a chart showing the changing levels of migration, or you could write a summary that organizes the information.

Learn the Skill

Study the chart about new legal permanent residents in the United States. Then create a graphic organizer or write a summary to organize the information.

Top Five Countries of Birth of New Legal Permanent Residents to the United States (by percent)	
Mexico	13.2
India	7.7
China	7.5
Philippines	4.9
Cuba	4.6
Other	62.1

Source: *U.S. Department of Homeland Security*

Practice the Skill

Turn to Lesson 1 and read the passage titled *Culture Regions.* Draw a graphic organizer and then follow the steps to organize the information you have read. The passage will have two or more subtopics. Add additional circles for each additional subtopic you find.

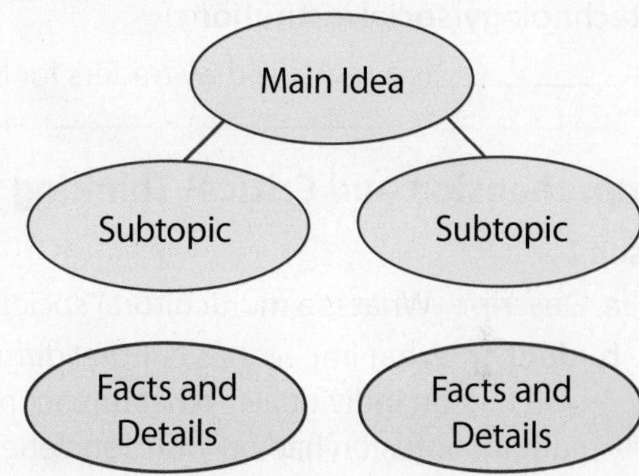

Module 3 Assessment

Review Vocabulary, Terms, and Places

Complete each sentence by filling in the blank with the correct term from the word pair.

1. Members of a/an __________ often share the same religion, traditions, and language. **(ethnic group/population)**
2. Music, art, and literature that transcend the boundaries of one society have __________. **(cultural universals/universal themes)**
3. __________, the process of moving from one place to live in another, is a cause of population change. **(Population density/Migration)**
4. Family, education, religion, government, and economy are all examples of basic __________. **(technology/social institutions)**
5. A __________ is a path used by traders for buying and selling goods. **(settlement/trade route)**

Comprehension and Critical Thinking

Lesson 1

6. a. **Describe** What is a multicultural society?

   b. **Identify** What impact has cultural diffusion had on individuals? What impact has cultural diffusion had on world societies? Define these impacts.

   c. **Elaborate** Describe some of the culture traits practiced by people in your community.

7. a. **Evaluate** Which social institution do you think is most important? Why?

   b. **Explain** What relationship exists between a society and its art, music, literature, and architecture?

   c. **Predict** Make a prediction about a future scientific discovery and a future technological innovation. What problem will each solve? What social, political, economic, cultural, or environmental impacts will each have?

Lesson 2

8. a. **Describe** What does population density tell us about a place?

   b. **Draw Conclusions** Why do certain areas attract large populations?

   c. **Elaborate** Why do you think it is important for geographers to study population trends?

Lesson 3

9. a. **Evaluate** Think about your own city or town. Why did people decide to establish a settlement in that location?

   b. **Make Inferences** Why does a grid settlement design easily support transportation routes?

   c. **Analyze** How can new technology negatively impact interaction between regions?

Lesson 4

10. a. **Form Opinions** Some areas of the world are at a greater risk for certain types of natural disasters such as hurricanes or earthquakes. Would the risk of a natural disaster impact your decision about where to live?

    b. **Identify Problems** Think about one environmental issue that affects your state. What can be done to improve the situation?

    c. **Describe** Give an example of new technology that is environmentally friendly. How does it work to benefit the environment?

Reading Skills

11. **Understand Main Ideas** *Use the Reading Skills taught in this module to answer a question about the reading selection below.*

> The ancient Greeks were the first to practice democracy. Since then many countries have adopted democratic governments. The United Kingdom, South Korea, and Ghana all practice democracy. Democracy is the most widely used type of government in the world today.

What is the main idea of the paragraph?

Social Studies Skills

12. **Organize Information** *Use the Social Studies Skills taught in this module to create a graphic organizer for Lesson 3.*

Use the main ideas on the first page of the lesson for your large circles. Then write the subtopics under each main idea. Finally, identify supporting details for each subtopic.

Map Activity

Population Density *Use the map to answer the questions that follow.*

13. What letter on the map indicates the least crowded area?

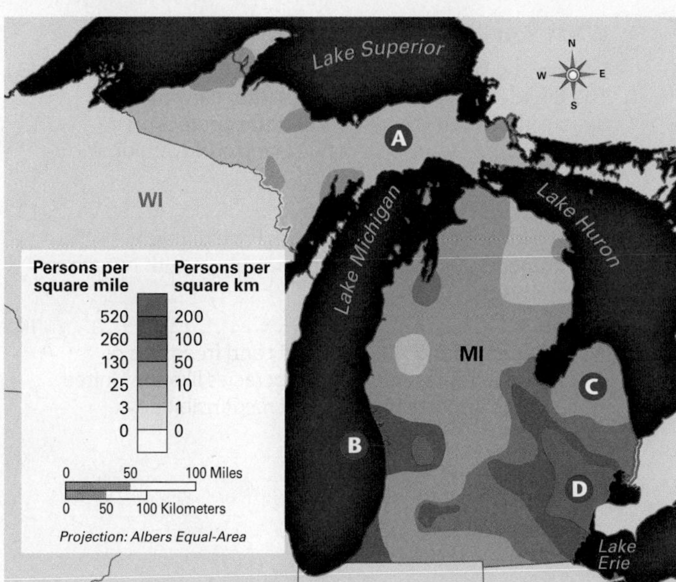

14. What letter on the map indicates the most densely crowded area?

15. Which letter indicates a region with 260–520 people per square mile (100–200 people per square km)?

Focus on Writing

16. **Write a Report** Population changes have a huge effect on the world around us. Countries around the globe must deal with shrinking populations, growing populations, and other population issues. Use Lesson 2 and other primary and secondary sources to explore the issues surrounding world population. Formulate appropriate questions to guide your research. You should use both print and digital sources. Collect information from non-print sources such as maps and graphs. Then imagine you have been asked to report on global population trends to the United Nations. Write a report in which you identify and describe world population trends and their impact on the world today. Be sure to apply key terms acquired from the lesson in your writing. Include at least one graphic that presents information related to the topic. Your report should be focused and organized with a clear introduction, supporting paragraphs, and conclusion. Check your report for spelling, grammar, capitalization, and punctuation.

Module 4

Government and Citizenship

Essential Question

How do systems of government affect the roles of citizens across the globe?

About the Photo: The Palace of Westminster in London is where Parliament meets. Parliament is the United Kingdom's highest legislative authority.

Explore ONLINE!

VIDEOS, including . . .

- Could You Pass the U.S. Citizenship Test?
- Birth of Democracy

- Document-Based Investigations
- Graphic Organizers
- Interactive Games
- Channel One News Video: Students Bring Climate Change Lawsuit
- Image with Hotspots: The DMZ Separates the Koreas
- Interactive Map: Freedom in Governments of the World

In this module, you will learn about how nations across the globe interact and form a world community. You will also learn about the different world governments and how people participate in those governments.

What You Will Learn

Lesson 1: A World of Nations. 131
The Big Idea The world is divided into many different nations that interact together to trade, protect their national interests, resolve conflict, and address global issues.

Lesson 2: World Governments. 137
The Big Idea The world's countries have different governments, and some countries struggle with human rights abuses.

Lesson 3: Citizenship. 145
The Big Idea Along with the rights and freedoms of citizenship in representative democracies like the United States come important duties and responsibilities.

Citizenship Voting is an important responsibility for citizens of India and other free countries.

Global Community The United Nations Headquarters in New York City is where more than 190 member states meet to promote international cooperation.

Government In democratic countries, leaders are elected by the people. Laura Chinchilla was elected president of Costa Rica in 2010.

Reading Social Studies

Sequence

READING FOCUS

Sequence is the order in which events follow one another. To show the order of events or steps in a process, writers use words like *before, after, next, first, then, later,* and *finally.* They also use words and phrases that indicate specific times, such as *the next day* and *on July 4, 1776.* Making a visual such as a sequence chain or a timeline can help you sequence events.

Read the passage below, noting the underlined clue words and dates. Notice how they reveal the order of the events shown in the timeline.

> In 1949 Chinese leader Mao Zedong created an authoritarian Communist system, imprisoning or killing those who spoke out against his policies. He implemented Soviet-style five-year plans for industrial development. Early efforts, begun in 1953, had some success, but widespread food shortages led to the deaths of tens of millions by 1961. In 1966, Mao began the Cultural Revolution, a violent effort to rid China of its pre-Communist customs and beliefs.

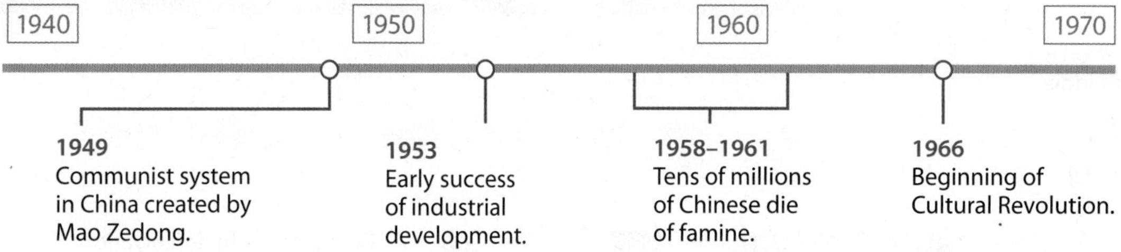

YOU TRY IT!

Read the following passage. Look for dates and clue words to help you figure out the sequence of steps described in it. Then make a sequence chain like the one above to show that order.

> Brazil was a Portuguese colony for 300 years before gaining independence in 1822. The nation became a republic in 1889, but wealthy coffee planters held much of the political power until a series of military-led uprisings began in the 1920s. In 1930 Getúlio Vargas took power in a nonviolent revolution; by 1937 Vargas ruled as a dictator. After alternating attempts at democracy and at military rule, in 1985 the military finally turned over power to a civilian government. Three years later, Brazil enacted a constitution that is still in effect today.

As you read this module, look for clues that show the sequence of events.

A World of Nations

The Big Idea

The world is divided into many different nations that interact together to trade, protect their national interests, resolve conflict, and address global issues.

Main Ideas

- The world is divided into physical and human borders.
- The nations of the world interact through trade and foreign policy.
- The nations of the world form a world community that resolves conflicts and addresses global issues.

Key Terms and Places

borders
sovereign nation
foreign policy
diplomacy
national interest
United Nations
human rights
humanitarian aid

If YOU lived there . . .

You are living through a drought in Sacramento, California. Your teacher splits your class into groups to discuss ways to solve the drought problem. One student thinks using less water is the solution, and another believes people should try to find more water. Your group begins arguing over whose solution is the best. You want everyone to get along, but nobody seems to agree.

How could you help your classmates work together?

Boundaries and Borders

There are about 200 countries in the world today. Each country has political boundaries, or **borders.** Within a country there are also many smaller political units, such as cities, counties, and states, each with its own set of borders. There are two main types of borders used to set political boundaries—physical borders and human borders.

Physical Borders Borders sometimes follow natural boundaries. Mountains, deserts, and oceans make good natural boundaries because they are often difficult to cross and are permanent markers. For example, the Andes Mountains form the eastern border of Chile, while the Pacific Ocean forms Chile's western border. These two physical features give Chile a long, skinny shape.

Rivers and lakes are other natural boundaries used to set borders. For example, the Chattahoochee River forms part of the border between Alabama and Georgia. The Great Lakes form part of the border between the United States and Canada. However, rivers can be troublesome boundaries. Sometimes the flow of a river might shift course, changing the border.

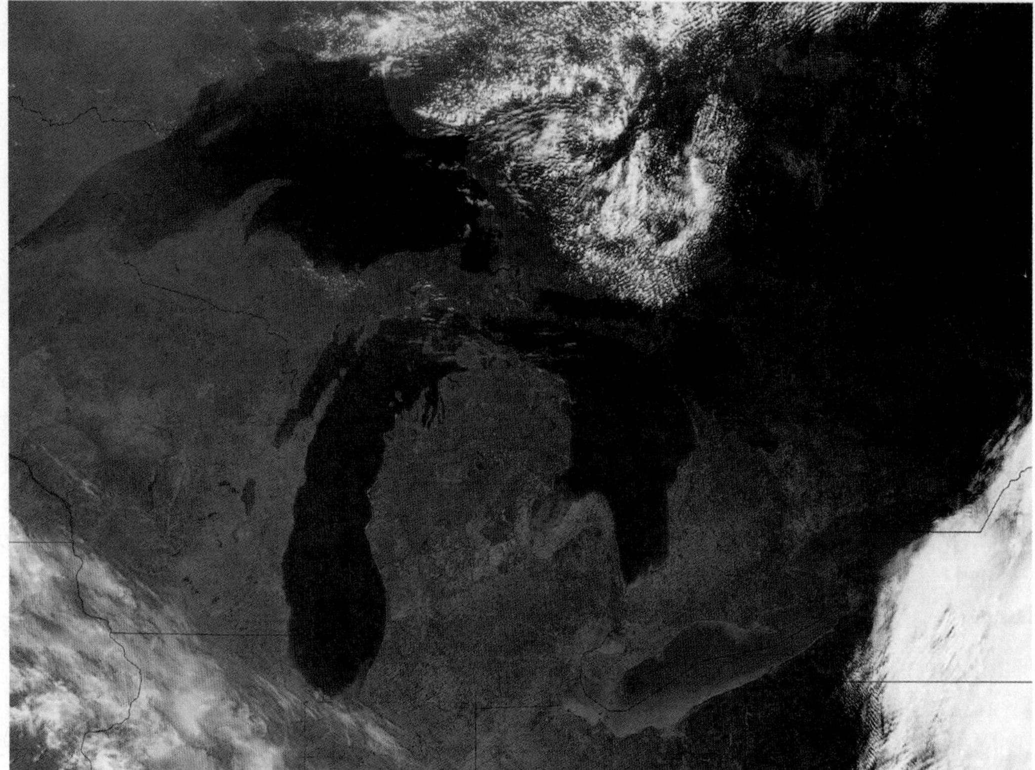

The Great Lakes are a natural boundary between the United States and Canada.

Human Borders Sometimes, borders are determined by humans, with no input from the physical landscape. There are two main types of boundaries used to set human borders: cultural and geometric.

Cultural boundaries are based on cultural traits, such as language or religion. For example, the border between mostly Muslim Pakistan and mostly Hindu India was established largely along religious lines. The border between Portugal and Spain is an example of a cultural boundary based on language.

Geometric boundaries are borders that are not based on natural or cultural patterns. Often, they are straight lines based on lines of latitude or longitude. For example, the border between North Korea and South Korea follows near the 38th parallel, or 38°N latitude. Another example is the part of the border between the United States and Canada that follows 93°N latitude. The borders of many states and counties in the United States are also geometric boundaries.

Reading Check
Identify What natural boundaries are used to form borders?

Nations of the World

Having set borders is one characteristic of a **sovereign nation,** or a government that has complete authority over a geographic area. Sovereign nations rule independently from governments outside their borders. They can make their own laws and enforce them. They can collect taxes, build a military, and make treaties, or written agreements, with other nations. They can also defend themselves against foreign invasion.

Academic Vocabulary
interact to talk or act together

Trade and Foreign Policy Though sovereign nations rule independently, they **interact** with other nations. One way nations interact with each other is through trade. Different nations have different resources, and they also lack different resources. Trade allows nations to exchange the goods that they have or can make for goods that they cannot make.

Another way that nations act together is through **foreign policy,** or a nation's plan for how to act toward other countries. Foreign policy is important because the actions one nation takes affect other nations. For example, when Germany invaded Poland in 1939, Great Britain and France declared war on Germany. This was the start of World War II, a conflict that grew to involve almost every part of the world. Because leaders of the world are concerned with keeping their nations safe, or national security, many leaders try to secure friendly relations with other countries as part of their foreign policy.

The foreign policy work nations do to keep friendly relations with each other is called **diplomacy.** Diplomacy is used to prevent war, solve problems, and open communication between countries. For example, the United States ended diplomatic ties with Cuba in 1961. In late 2014 President Obama announced that the United States and Cuba would have diplomatic relations for the first time in decades. President Obama traveled to Cuba in 2016. An American president had not done that in almost 90 years.

Another important foreign policy tool is foreign aid, or assistance that a country provides to another country. For example, the United States gave large amounts of foreign aid during and after World War II. It sent soldiers to help fight during the war. After the war, the people of Western Europe needed food, clothing, and housing, which the United States helped provide.

The DMZ Separates the Koreas

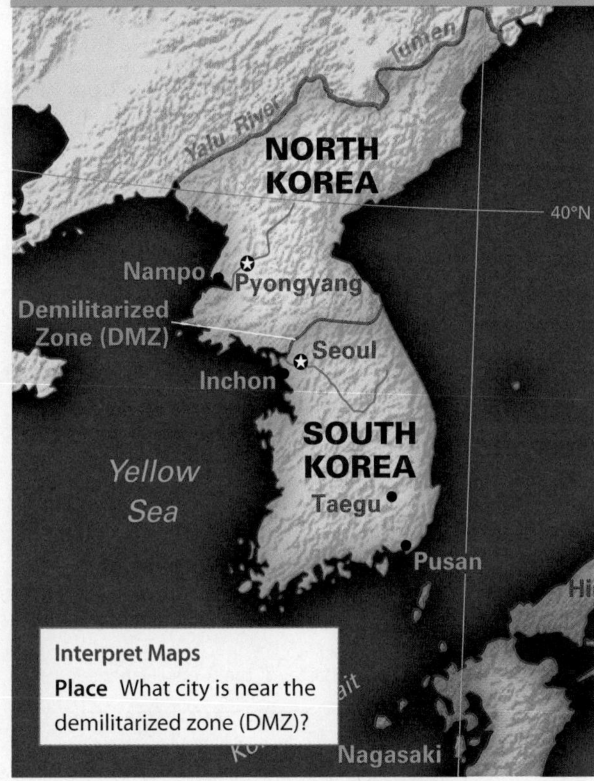

Interpret Maps
Place What city is near the demilitarized zone (DMZ)?

Following World War II, the 38th parallel was used to divide North and South Korea. Above, South Korean soldiers patrol the barbed wire fence along the demilitarized zone (DMZ), which separates the two Koreas today. The DMZ stretches east to west near the old boundary at the 38th parallel.

National Interest Each nation has its own goals to help it succeed. These goals make up a country's **national interest.** Different countries have different national interests. Part of the United States' national interest, for example, is to grow its economy and defend its national security. For New Zealand, protecting its natural resources against climate change is one of its national interests.

When nations have similar national interests, they sometimes become allies, or a group that gives support. For example, in 1949 the United States and 11 other nations formed the North Atlantic Treaty Organization (NATO) to stop a common adversary, or enemy. The Soviet Union was taking over other countries in Eastern Europe and spreading communism. NATO wanted to protect other nations from being invaded and to stop the spread of communism. Today, the Soviet Union no longer exists, but NATO has grown to include 28 nations who share common interests, such as promoting democratic values and peace.

Reading Check
Summarize
How do nations interact with each other?

A World Community

Together, the nations of the world form a world community. Countries are connected to each other through trade and diplomacy. What happens in one part of the world can affect the entire planet. Because of this, the world community works together to promote cooperation among countries in times of conflict and crisis.

Resolving Conflict From time to time, conflicts erupt among the countries of the world. Wars, trade disputes, and political disagreements can threaten the peace. Countries often join together to settle such conflicts. In 1945, for example, 51 nations created the **United Nations** (UN), an organization of the world's countries that promotes peace and security around the globe.

The United Nations now has more than 190 member states. The UN promotes security by calling on quarreling countries to work out a peaceful

Historical Source

The Charter of the United Nations

Created in 1945, the United Nations is an organization of the world's countries that works to solve global problems. The Charter of the United Nations outlines the goals of the UN, some of which are included here.

"We the Peoples of the United Nations Determined . . . to save succeeding generations from the scourge [terror] of war . . . to practice tolerance and live together in peace with one another as good neighbors, and to unite our strength to maintain international peace and security, and to ensure . . . that armed forces shall not be used, save [except] in the common interest, and to employ international machinery [systems] for the promotion of the economic and social advancement of all peoples, Have Resolved to Combine our Efforts to Accomplish these Aims."

—from the Charter of the United Nations

Analyze Sources
What are some of the goals of the United Nations?

Many people believe that health care is a basic human right. Here, a Doctors Without Borders medical team leader examines refugees from Libya.

settlement. It also places sanctions, or penalties, on those who have broken international laws. Sanctions restrict or ban trade, travel, or economic activity with law violators. For example, the United Nations has placed sanctions against the terrorist groups and militant organizations in the Middle East, such as al Qaeda and the Islamic State of Iraq and the Levant (ISIL), as a way to combat terrorism.

The United Nations also works to guarantee **human rights,** or rights that all people deserve. Human rights include political rights, such as the right to vote. Freedom of expression and equality before the law are other examples of human rights. Over the years, the UN has passed several declarations setting standards for such rights.

Nations also form organizations to help out in areas of conflict. These organizations provide **humanitarian aid,** or assistance to people in distress. For example, during the Syrian civil war, the International Committee of the Red Cross (ICRC) brought food, clean water, and essential aid to civilians. Another organization, the United States Agency for International Development (USAID), offers assistance to conflict and poverty-stricken countries all over the world. In Pakistan, USAID has built or rehabilitated 1,040 schools since 2009. Some groups lend aid to refugees, or people who have been forced to flee their homes. Doctors Without Borders, for example, provides medical aid to those fleeing areas of armed conflict, such as South Sudan, Libya, Syria, and Afghanistan.

Organizations are able to help conflict zones because the Geneva Conventions of 1949 protect them. The Geneva Conventions are international agreements that tell countries at war how to treat people. Under the Geneva Conventions, for example, people cannot be held hostage, enslaved, or tortured. The Geneva Conventions protect the human rights of civilians, medics, and aid workers who are not taking part in the fighting. They also protect those who can no longer fight, such as the wounded, the sick, and prisoners of war.

Promoting Cooperation The world community also promotes cooperation in times of crisis. A disaster may leave thousands of people in need. Earthquakes, floods, and droughts can cause crises around the world. Groups from many nations often come together to help out. For example, in 2004 a tsunami, or huge tidal wave, devastated parts of Southeast Asia. Many organizations, like the United Nations Children's Fund (UNICEF) and the International Red Cross, stepped in to provide humanitarian aid to the victims of the tsunami. In addition to providing medical aid in conflict zones, Doctors Without Borders also provides care in places hit by epidemics or natural disasters, such as the Central African Republic and Nepal.

Deadly diseases such as tuberculosis, malaria, and acquired immune deficiency syndrome (AIDS) can spread quickly and devastate entire communities. This is why nations work with health-care initiatives, or organizations that raise money to combat diseases. Examples of global health initiatives include the World Bank's Multi-Country AIDS Programme (MAP), Gavi, the Vaccine Alliance, and the Global Fund to Fight AIDS, Tuberculosis and Malaria (Global Fund). Through their efforts, millions of people in regions such as West and Central Africa have received vaccinations, medications, and disease-prevention education to fight the spread of deadly diseases.

Reading Check
Summarize How do nations promote cooperation?

Summary and Preview In this lesson you learned about borders and how nations work together to solve conflicts and crises. In the next lesson, you will learn about the different ways nations govern themselves.

Lesson 1 Assessment

Review Ideas, Terms, and Places

1. a. **Define** What are borders?

   b. **Identify** What are two types of human boundaries?

2. a. **Describe** What are the characteristics of a sovereign nation?

   b. **Demonstrate** How do nations benefit from interacting with each other?

3. a. **Analyze** How do global organizations help with conflict resolution and cooperation?

   b. **Explain** How do the Geneva Conventions protect individual rights and the common good?

Critical Thinking

4. **Evaluate** Draw a three-column chart to list the global organizations you read about in this lesson. Describe their efforts to combat poverty and promote world peace. If needed, use the Internet for additional research. Then use the chart to help answer this question: Why do you think these organizations are needed to protect human rights?

Organization	Combat Poverty	Promote World Peace

World Governments

The Big Idea

The world's countries have different governments, and some countries struggle with human rights abuses.

Main Ideas

- Limited governments of the world include democracies.
- Unlimited governments of the world include totalitarian governments.
- Most human rights abuses occur under unlimited governments of the world.

Key Terms and Places

limited government
constitution
democracy
direct democracy
representative democracies
common good
unlimited government
totalitarian governments

If YOU lived there . . .

You live in Dallas, Texas. Your class at school is planning a presentation about life in the United States for a group of visitors from Japan. Your teacher wants you to discuss government in the United States. As you prepare for your speech, you wonder what you should say.

How does government affect your life?

Limited Government

Can you imagine what life would be like if there were no rules? Without ways to establish order and ensure justice, life would be chaotic. This explains why societies have governments. Our governments make and enforce laws, regulate business and trade, and provide aid to people. Governments help shape the culture and economy of a country and the daily lives of the people who live there.

One system of government is **limited government.** A limited government has legal limits on its power. These limits are often stated in a **constitution,** or a written plan of government that outlines its purposes, powers, and limitations. A **democracy,** a form of government in which the people elect leaders and rule by majority, is an example of limited government. Many countries—including the United States, Canada, and Mexico—are democracies.

Origins of Democracy Ancient Athens and other Greek city-states were among the first democratic governments. The Athenian government was a **direct democracy,** which means the people made decisions through a process of majority rule. Whatever the majority of voters wanted became law. The citizens met regularly in a popular assembly to discuss issues and vote for leaders. Athenians liked to boast that in their government, everyone had equal say. In truth, Athenian democracy was an elite-based system. Only a small fraction of the male population was eligible to participate in political life. Neither women nor slaves, who formed the majority of the population, could participate.

Modern Democratic Governments Today, most countries have too many people to gather together to make political decisions. That is why most modern democratic governments are indirect democracies, or **representative democracies.** Instead of the citizens making all of the political decisions, they vote for representatives to make and enforce the laws.

Presidential and parliamentary democracies are the two most common democratic systems. In a presidential democracy, the people elect the head of state, called the president. The president heads the executive branch. The president shares power with the legislative branch, which is also elected by the people, and the judicial branch.

In a parliamentary democracy, the voters elect the legislature, or parliament. The parliament chooses the government leader, called the prime minister or chancellor. The head of state in some parliamentary democracies is a constitutional monarch. Constitutional monarchs are often figureheads, or leaders without real power. Instead, the elected parliament holds most of the power. Most of the world's democratic governments are parliamentary democracies.

Modern governments also distribute their powers in different ways. For example, the United Kingdom and Japan are unitary states, in which a central government has all the power and does not share it with its regions or states. The opposite of a unitary state is a confederation. In a confederation, a country's states or regions hold most of the power. Federal governments, on the other hand, divide their power between a central national government and its states. The United States is an example of a federal government.

Characteristics of Limited Governments Because power can be misused, limiting government's reach reduces the chances of abuse and creates freer and fairer societies. Limited governments are governed by rule of law, meaning that no person or government is above the law. This is why many limited governments have a constitution that outlines their laws.

Modern Democracies

Country	Government Power	Type of Democracy	System of Government
United States	Federal	Presidential	Constitutional republic
United Kingdom	Unitary	Parliamentary	Constitutional monarchy
Canada	Federal	Parliamentary	Constitutional monarchy
Japan	Unitary	Parliamentary	Constitutional monarchy
India	Federal	Parliamentary	Constitutional republic

Analyze Information
Which countries are republics with federal governments?

Systems of Government	
Dictatorship **Example: Cuba**	• Single dictator or a small group holds absolute authority and makes all decisions • Violence and force used to maintain rule
Totalitarian Regimes **Example: North Korea**	• Dictator holds ultimate authority • Government tightly controls all aspects of life—political, social, and economic • No formal or informal limits on government
Theocracy **Example: Iran**	• Government by officials regarded to have religious authority • Laws rooted in a particular religion or religious doctrine • Government power is unlimited
Direct Democracy **Example: ancient Greece (Athens)**	• Government by the people; citizens are the ultimate source of government authority • Citizens come together to discuss and pass laws and select leaders • Works best in small communities
Republic/Representative Democracy **Example: ancient Rome, United States**	• Government by the people; citizens are the ultimate source of government authority • Indirect form of democracy; citizens elect representatives to make government decisions and pass laws on their behalf • Representatives elected for set terms

Analyze Information
What is the difference between a direct democracy and a republic?

Nations governed by rule of law protect the rights of individuals. In many limited governments, for example, individuals have the right to a fair trial if they are accused of a crime. Limited governments also balance the welfare of the community, or the **common good,** with individual welfare. For example, individuals might be forced to sell their land to the government so that a new highway or school can be built. This challenges an individual's right to own property. However, a new highway or school benefits the whole community.

Today, nearly half of the almost 200 countries in the world are democratic or partly democratic with a limited system of government. Although the level of freedom in these nations varies, they share some basic characteristics:

- Democratic systems tend to have social welfare policies that seek to improve the quality of their citizens' lives.
- Most democratic governments protect their citizens' rights and freedoms. For this reason, citizens of these countries generally enjoy a high degree of economic and political freedom.
- Strong democratic countries can generally withstand national crises such as war, economic troubles, or civil unrest without major changes to their basic systems or structures.

Compare Limited Governments

Mexico

Government Characteristics

- Presidential, federal system of government
- Three branches of government
- Some legislative seats given to major parties
- President elected directly by the people to a six-year term
- Voting compulsory for people 18 and older

Brazil

Government Characteristics

- Presidential, federal system of government
- Three branches of government
- All legislative seats filled by direct election
- President elected directly by the people to a four-year term
- Voting compulsory for people 18 to 70

The seat of power for Mexico's president is the National Palace in Mexico City.

This map shows the locations of Mexico and Brazil.

Brazil's legislative body meets at the National Congress in Brasília.

Comparing Mexico and Brazil As you know, the United States is a democracy with a limited system of government. Mexico and Brazil are examples of other nations with limited systems. Their governments have much in common with our own.

Mexico's Government Mexico's federal government, like ours, has three branches: legislative, executive, and judicial. In a federal system, powers are divided between central and state governments. Mexico's central government is based in Mexico City, and its 31 states make up its state government.

Mexico's legislative branch has two houses. Three-fifths of the legislators in each house are elected, but the remaining seats are distributed to the major political parties in proportion to the parties' overall share of the popular vote.

The executive branch is led by a president elected directly by the people for a single six-year term. By law, voting is compulsory for people over age 18, although no formal penalty is enforced. Mexico does not have the office of vice-president.

Mexico has an independent judicial branch. Its highest court is the Supreme Court of Justice. Its judges are appointed by the president and must be approved by a single of the houses of the legislature.

Brazil's Government Brazil has a federal system with 26 states and a federal district. In many ways, Brazil's government is similar to that of Mexico and the United States, with three branches and a separation of powers. Brazil's legislature is bicameral and includes a senate and a chamber of deputies. All members are elected.

The executive branch is led by the president. The president and vice-president are elected by a direct vote of the people. Voting is compulsory for literate Brazilians between the ages of 18 and 70, and those who do not vote may be fined.

Brazil's Supreme Court is made up of two courts: the Superior Court of Justice, which deals with nonconstitutional issues, and the Supreme Federal Court, which handles cases involving constitutional interpretation.

Reading Check
Compare and Contrast How are the governments of Mexico and Brazil similar and different?

Unlimited Governments

We categorize governments based on who holds governmental power, as well as by how much power they are allowed to execute. Recall that in a limited government, everyone—including leaders—must obey the law. By contrast, an **unlimited government** is a government in which there are no limits set on a ruler's power. They do not govern by a rule of law that balances individual rights with the common good. Many rulers of unlimited governments view individual rights as a threat to the common good. They define the common good as people doing their part to strengthen the leader, nation, and community.

Totalitarianism Authoritarian governments are unlimited governments, in which power is concentrated in the hands of a single person, such as a dictator, or a small group. Leaders can set laws without input from those they rule. This allows change and decision-making to work more quickly in unlimited governments than in limited governments. Leaders, however, can also break laws without punishment because they answer to no one.

At its most extreme, authoritarian rule becomes totalitarian. **Totalitarian governments** control all aspects of society—the government, the economy, and even people's personal beliefs and actions. The Soviet Union under Joseph Stalin, China under Mao Zedong, and North Korea under Kim Jong-un are examples of totalitarian regimes.

In these societies, citizens have no way to influence or change the government. The government sometimes maintains the appearance of democratic rule. For example, the totalitarian government of North Korea calls itself the Democratic People's Republic of Korea, holds elections, and has a written constitution. But these displays of democracy are nothing more than exhibitions to deceive the nation's people or outside observers.

Characteristics of Unlimited Governments All forms of unlimited government share certain features. In authoritarian and totalitarian systems, ordinary citizens have limited political and economic freedoms. Their rights are rarely recognized or protected, and they may not be able to effectively take part in government or openly express their views.

Totalitarian rulers often use force to put down opposition, such as human rights or pro-democracy movements demanding change. Moreover, because they are not subject to law, totalitarian rulers can change or ignore constitutions or laws intended to restrict their power. For example, before Saddam Hussein of Iraq was overthrown in a 2003 U.S.-led invasion, he used torture and violence against his political opponents, even though torture was officially banned under Iraqi law.

China's Government In 1949 Chinese leader Mao Zedong created an authoritarian Communist system, imprisoning or killing those who spoke out against his policies. He instituted Soviet-style five-year plans for industrial development. Early efforts, begun in 1953, had some success, but widespread food shortages led to the deaths of tens of millions by 1961. In 1966 Mao began the Cultural Revolution, a violent effort to rid China of its pre-Communist customs and beliefs.

Mao's death in 1976 saw a gradual retreat from many of his policies. Deng Xiaoping eventually became China's leader and slowly introduced many economic and a few political reforms. There were limits to what officials would allow, however. In 1989 the government violently crushed a peaceful pro-democracy student demonstration in China's capital, Beijing, in what became known as the Tiananmen Square Massacre.

China's leaders today are balancing authoritarian rule, economic growth, and slow political reform. China continues to limit its citizens' basic freedoms and rights, and the government exercises strict control over the media and the Internet.

Reading Check
Summarize What are the characteristics of unlimited government?

Human Rights Abuses

Though many people and governments support human rights, human rights abuses occur in both limited and unlimited governments. These abuses include torture, slavery, and murder, and are most common in countries that are not free or are partially free. In many countries,

Unlimited Government in China

A 1971 propaganda poster portrays people as happy with China's communist government.

A pro-democracy demonstrator confronts Chinese troops in Tiananmen Square, Beijing, in 1989.

Explore ONLINE!

Freedom in Governments of the World

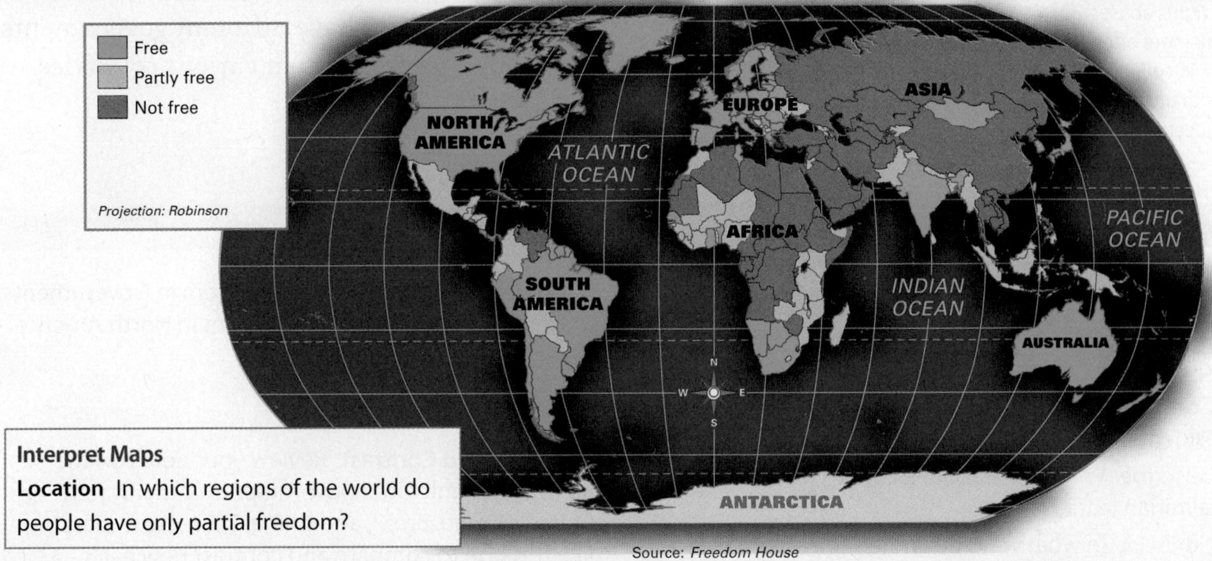

Source: *Freedom House*

Interpret Maps
Location In which regions of the world do people have only partial freedom?

individuals and groups have been arrested or mistreated for political dissent. For example, countries including Iran, Pakistan, Cuba, El Salvador, and the former Soviet Union have persecuted people for their political views.

In unfree or partially free countries, children face the highest risk of becoming victims of human rights abuses. In some countries, such as northern Uganda, fighters have kidnapped thousands of children. These children have been made to fight as soldiers, while other have been enslaved. The United Nations has taken action to try to protect children. For example, the UN Convention on the Rights of the Child was adopted in 1989. The convention focused on trying to keep children free from hunger, neglect, and abuse.

Human rights abuses are also common in countries in the process of establishing democracy. For example, in 2013 the Sudanese government demolished several Christian churches in Sudan as part of an effort to force Christians out of the country. As a result, many Sudanese Christians have fled to South Sudan to avoid persecution.

Abuses in democratic countries are far fewer, but they do occur, often as a result of inaction. For example, the European Union was criticized for not adequately helping asylum seekers fleeing the civil war in Syria in 2013, which left some refugees homeless and without food or water.

As a country with a democratic government, the United States recognizes that respect for human rights promotes peace and deters aggression. To that end, the United States has made promoting human rights a major part of its foreign policy. According to the U.S. Department of State, the United States uses a three-part approach in its work on human rights. Those three parts are learning the truth and stating the facts, taking consistent

Reading Check
Draw Conclusions Why would human rights abuses occur more often in countries with unlimited governments?

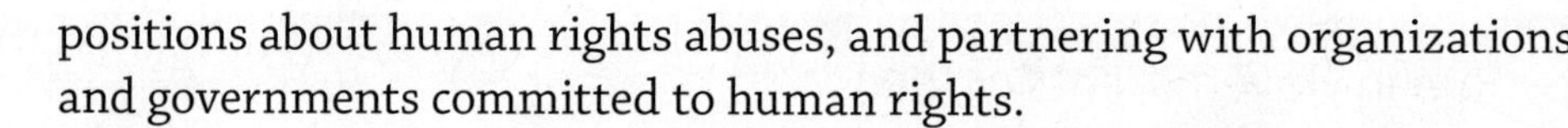

positions about human rights abuses, and partnering with organizations and governments committed to human rights.

Summary and Preview The world's countries have different governments. In the next lesson, you will learn about citizenship in various countries.

Lesson 2 Assessment

Review Ideas, Terms, and Places

1. a. **Define** What is a direct democracy, and what are its origins?
   b. **Contrast** What are the differences between presidential and parliamentary democracies?
2. a. **Describe** What is life like in a country with a totalitarian leader?
   b. **Contrast** In what ways do limited governments differ from unlimited governments?
   c. **Analyze** How does the definition of the common good differ in limited and unlimited governments?
3. a. **Elaborate** How does China's government limit human rights?
   b. **Contrast** Look at the map Freedom in Governments of the World. How does government in North America differ from government in Asia?

Critical Thinking

4. **Compare and Contrast** Review your notes on the limited and unlimited governments of the United States, Mexico, Brazil, and China. Then use a chart like this one to compare and contrast how each government functions and is organized.

United States	Mexico	Brazil	China

Citizenship

The Big Idea

Along with the rights and freedoms of citizenship in representative democracies like the United States come important duties and responsibilities.

Main Ideas

- The duties and roles of citizenship help to make representative government work.
- Good citizens accept their responsibilities for maintaining a strong democracy.
- Citizens influence government through public opinion.
- The type of government in some societies influences the roles of the citizens in those societies.

Key Terms and Places

representative government
draft
jury duty
political parties
interest groups
public opinion
nonrepresentative governments

If YOU lived there . . .

Your older brother and his friends have just turned 18. That means they must register with the Selective Service System. But it also means that they are old enough to vote in national elections. You are interested in the upcoming elections and think it would be exciting to have a real voice in politics. But your brother and his friends don't even plan to register to vote.

How would you persuade your brother that voting is important?

Duties and Roles of Citizenship

The United States has a democratic, **representative government.** In such a system, people are the ultimate source of government authority. Elections are free and fair. Elected representatives closely follow the wishes of the people. Citizens typically enjoy rights and privileges such as freedom of speech and freedom of religion. For a representative government to work well, citizens must participate actively and perform certain duties. Let's look at some duties of U.S. citizens.

Obeying the Law Of course, all Americans must obey the law. Otherwise, our society would collapse. To obey laws, you must know what they are. For example, if you are stopped for speeding, it will not help to claim that you did not know the speed limit. It is your duty to find out what the speed limit is and to obey it.

Attending School You have to go to school, at least until age 16. A democracy cannot function without educated citizens. That is why we have free public schools. People need good reading and thinking skills so they can wisely choose their leaders and understand issues that affect them. Education also provides workforce skills so people can get jobs and help the economy grow.

Cadets from the U.S. Air Force Academy commit to several years of military service.

Paying Taxes If you work or buy things, then you probably have to pay taxes. We might not love paying taxes, but we enjoy the services that result from them, such as police and fire protection, road maintenance, public schools, and countless other services. Tax money also pays the huge costs of national security and defense.

All levels of government rely on a variety of taxes for funding. For example, the federal government relies on income taxes, a tax on personal earnings. These taxes go toward programs such as Social Security, which helps fund your retirement; Medicare, a health insurance program for certain qualifying Americans; and national defense. You are probably familiar with sales taxes, which state and local governments depend on for their revenue. Sales taxes help fund public safety, education, and programs to build and repair roads, buildings, and power plants.

Serving in the Armed Forces Volunteers have fought in every war in U.S. history. When the country's need has exceeded the number of volunteers, however, it sometimes has had to establish a **draft.** Draft laws require men of certain ages and qualifications to serve in the military.

The United States has not had a draft since 1973, during the Vietnam War. However, 18-year-old men must still register their names and addresses with the Selective Service System. If a crisis required that the country quickly expand its armed forces, a draft could be launched and registered citizens could be called up.

Appearing in Court Citizens must report to serve as members of a jury if they are called to do so. This service is called **jury duty.** Jury duty often involves sacrifice. Many citizens must take time off work to serve on a jury, and they are paid very small sums. This sacrifice is necessary because the Constitution guarantees citizens the right to a trial by jury of their peers—that is, their fellow citizens. Citizens must also testify in court if called as witnesses. For our system of justice to function, citizens must fulfill their duty to serve on juries and appear as witnesses.

Reading Check
Summarize
Describe five duties of American citizenship.

Rights and Responsibilities

Civic participation in representative government includes both duties, or the things we *must* do, and responsibilities. Responsibilities are the things we *should* do as citizens. These tasks are not required by law; yet, in the United States, most people accept them as their responsibility. Several of these responsibilities are listed below.

Voting United States government is based on the consent, or the approval, of the governed. Therefore, we must let our legislators know when we approve or disapprove of their actions. One way to do this is by voting for people whose views we support and who we believe to be good, honest candidates. As a citizen of your community, state, and nation, it is your responsibility to vote in local, state, and national elections so that your voice is heard.

There are several different types of elections in the United States. Elections allow citizens to choose leaders for every level of government. Because congressional elections take place every two years, citizens often elect some members of Congress when they vote for the president. State and local elections may also coincide with presidential and congressional elections.

Being Informed To cast your vote wisely, you must be well informed about candidates, current events, and key issues. There are many ways to stay informed. You can go to town meetings to learn about the key issues in your community. To learn about the candidates running for political offices, you can attend debates and forums. You can sit in on legislative sessions to watch public officials decide public policy.

U.S. Elections

Election Type	When Election Occurs	Purpose
Presidential	every 4 years	• vote for the U.S. president/vice-president
Congressional	every 2 years	• elect 1/3 of all U.S. Senate members • elect all 435 members of the U.S. House of Representatives
State	varies by state	• elect state governor • elect state legislators • elect state judges (in some states) • vote on state ballot initiatives
Local	varies by location	• elect various local offices • elect local judges (in some localities) • vote on local ballot initiatives

Analyze Information
Why is it important for citizens to vote in every type of election?

You can also use other tools at your home, school, or library to stay informed. Visiting government websites is a good way to learn about local, state, and national issues and laws. Reading newspapers, watching the news, listening to the radio, and watching televised debates can also keep you up to date on current events and important issues.

Taking Part in Government For a representative government to remain strong, people must participate at all levels. In addition to voting, people can work as public servants, serve in a political office, join a political party, or support other politically active organizations. You can also contact your state representatives and tell them what you think about topics of public concern.

Governments cannot provide services to their citizens without citizen participation. They need people to work as public servants to provide these services. Public servants deliver mail, inspect food and medicines for safety, operate national parks, fight fires, and perform a number of other services.

People are also needed to run for political office and serve wisely if elected. The quality of any democratic government depends on the quality of the people who serve it. Political leaders, for example, take on important roles. They may create laws or decide which programs will receive funding. Some decide the best course of action during local, state, or national emergencies.

Citizens can help shape government by joining **political parties.** Political parties nominate, or select, candidates to run for political office. They also try to convince voters to elect their candidates. Many citizens in the United States have joined one of two political parties—the Democratic Party or the Republican Party. Sometimes, citizens who believe their views are not represented by these parties will form a third party. For example, citizens formed the Green Party to focus on environmental issues.

Responsible Citizenship

Volunteers help citizens sign in to vote at a polling station.

By planting a tree, these volunteers are beautifying their community.

Citizens can also join **interest groups,** or organizations that try to influence government policies and decisions. Members of interest groups share a common goal. Members of the National Association for the Advancement of Colored People (NAACP), for example, work to promote racial equality.

On occasion, you may even need to stand in protest for what you believe. Yet protest, like civic participation in any form, must also be peaceful, respectful of the law, and tolerant of others' rights and liberties.

Helping Your Community Have you ever volunteered to help your community? There are so many ways to help—from giving your time at the public library to participating in a walk for hunger. Citizens should volunteer to improve their communities. The government cannot be aware of every small problem, much less fix them all. Yet solving small problems is something volunteers can do in many ways. Think of how small acts of kindness—such as cheering up a sick person or working in an animal shelter—can make community life better.

Respecting and Protecting Others' Rights In return for performing civic duties and responsibilities, people in the United States enjoy the privileges and rights of citizenship. The lasting success and the strength of the United States depend on the protection of its citizens' rights. You can play an important role in protecting these rights by knowing your own rights as an American citizen and knowing and respecting the rights of the people around you. For example, it is essential that community members respect others' property.

You should also know when people's rights are being violated. All Americans must help defend human rights. As a citizen, you have the responsibility to help make sure that our society works for everyone.

Reading Check
Form Generalizations
How can U.S. citizens contribute to society?

Citizens and the Media

You may not realize it, but you are surrounded by political messages every day. You might see people on the news protesting a government action. You might hear a radio host talk about raising taxes to fund education. Your friends or relatives might share websites or online news articles that support their favorite political candidate. As you have learned, forms of media such as newspapers, magazines, radio, television, film, and books help you stay informed. They also help influence the way you think about political leaders and issues.

Public Opinion The media plays an important role in free societies like the United States. News organizations report on important events and government actions. This allows citizens to stay informed and make their own decisions.

What citizens learn from the media shapes **public opinion,** or the way large groups of citizens think about issues and people. For example, when the media reports the dishonest actions of an elected official, the public may choose not to elect this person again. This puts pressure on political leaders to act honestly and keep their campaign promises.

Sometimes the media, political leaders, and citizens use political symbols to influence others' opinions. Political symbols include images, objects, or music that represent ideas or a political view. For example, a donkey is used as a symbol for the Democratic Party and an elephant is used to represent the Republican Party in the United States.

Have you ever seen a cartoon drawing of an elephant or donkey acting like a politician? Or a cartoon version of the president with exaggerated features? These are political cartoons used in the media to communicate a political view. The creators of these cartoons sometimes use humor as a way to persuade people to side with their political opinion.

Politicians often create political symbols to represent their ideas during campaigns. For example, President Barack Obama's campaign designed a letter *O* that looked like a rising sun. This was to make voters feel hopeful about the future if they voted for him. Citizens also use political symbols to influence public opinion. During the Vietnam War, for example, American citizens used the peace sign to show that they wanted peace. This was a way to gain public support for their protest against the war.

Citizens rely on the media to help them decide how to vote on important issues and how to pick the best candidates. Sometimes, however, the information you receive is inaccurate, misleading, or one-sided. Some sources might be biased, or favor some ideas over others. A newspaper, for example, might give the candidate it agrees with better coverage than another. A part of being a good citizen means you must think critically about what you see, hear, and read.

Reading Check
Analyze Effects How does public opinion help shape government policy and action?

Symbols in Political Cartoons

This cartoon titled "You Can't Have Everything" was created by Herbert Block around 1938. In 1937 President Franklin D. Roosevelt proposed a controversial plan to increase the number of justices on the Supreme Court.

Analyze Visuals
What symbols do you see in this cartoon? What do you think the artist is trying to say?

Citizenship in Other Societies

In other societies with representative governments, citizens' roles and rights are similar to, but not always the same as, those of U.S. citizens. For instance, German citizens are not called to serve on juries, because German courts do not use the jury system. The German constitution guarantees its citizens freedom of the press, but that freedom can be limited in order to protect youth or preserve a person's honor.

There are major differences, however, between the roles and rights of U.S. citizens and those of citizens from societies with **nonrepresentative governments.** In such systems, government power is unlimited and citizens have few, if any, rights. For example, citizens of Iran do not have the right of freedom of speech. Without this freedom, Iranians cannot voice their concerns to their leaders.

Citizens of nonrepresentative governments also have different responsibilities than citizens of representative governments. In autocratic governments, which are ruled by one person who makes all the decisions, citizens do not get to vote. This is the same for citizens of an oligarchy, or a government by a small group of individuals.

Citizens' perception of opportunities to participate in and influence the political process vary among various contemporary societies. For example, in countries where citizens do not trust the people who run their governments, voting turnout is much lower than in countries where citizens tend to trust their governments. Sometimes, distrust leads citizens to revolt against their leaders in an attempt to change governments. The people of Tunisia, for example, led a revolution that ousted their longtime president Zine al-Abidine Ben Ali and established a

Politicians and Political Symbols

Former Vice-President Joe Biden stands in front of the vice-presidential seal of the United States.

Analyze Visuals
What political symbols do you see in the vice-presidential seal? Why do you think those symbols were used?

Reading Check
Contrast How do nonrepresentative governments differ from representative democracies?

democracy in January 2011. Other times, a group of people or the military will overthrow the government and establish their own leader. These attempts are called coups d'état or military coups.

Summary In this lesson, you learned about the rights, duties, and responsibilities of citizenship. Effective citizenship is an important part of representative governments. Without citizens participating in their governments, their governments cannot represent their interests.

Lesson 3 Assessment

Review Ideas, Terms, and Places

1. a. **Define** What is a representative government?
   b. **Predict** What would happen in a representative government if only a small group of people performed their civic duties?
2. a. **Interpret** How are a citizen's duties, rights, and responsibilities connected?
   b. **Summarize** What are the rights and responsibilities of citizens to their community, state, and nation?
3. a. **Summarize** How can citizens influence the political process?
   b. **Compare** How are the methods citizens use to resolve issues in government and society alike?
   c. **Draw Conclusions** How do you think the media helps influence government policy and action?
4. a. **Identify** What is an example of a nonrepresentative government?
   b. **Explain** Why do the levels of civic engagement vary among different contemporary societies?
   c. **Compare** Do you think an election, revolution, or coup is the best way to change governments?

Critical Thinking

5. **Evaluate** **Draw** a two-column chart to list and describe citizens' duties and responsibilities in representative governments. Use the chart to help answer this question: In your opinion, which duty or responsibility expected of citizens is the most important? Explain your answer.

DUTIES	RESPONSIBILITIES

Social Studies Skills

Use a Problem-Solving Process

Define the Skill

Solving problems is a process for finding solutions to difficult situations. Being able to use a problem-solving process is an important skill that will help you identify problems and solve challenges as they appear.

Learn the Skill

Use the following steps to solve problems.

1. Identify the problem. Study the issue to learn about the problem.
2. Gather information. Research and ask questions to learn more about the problem.
3. List options. Identify possible options for solving the problem.
4. Evaluate your options. Consider their advantages and disadvantages.
5. Choose and implement a solution. After comparing your options, choose the one that seems best and apply it to solve your problem.
6. Evaluate the solution. Once the solution has been tried, evaluate how effectively it solved the problem. If the solution does not work, go back to your list of options and start again.

Practice the Skill

With a partner, use the steps of a problem-solving process to address the issue of graffiti in a local park. Express your ideas orally based on your experiences. Also share information that you learn from research. Then, create a graphic organizer like the sample on this page.

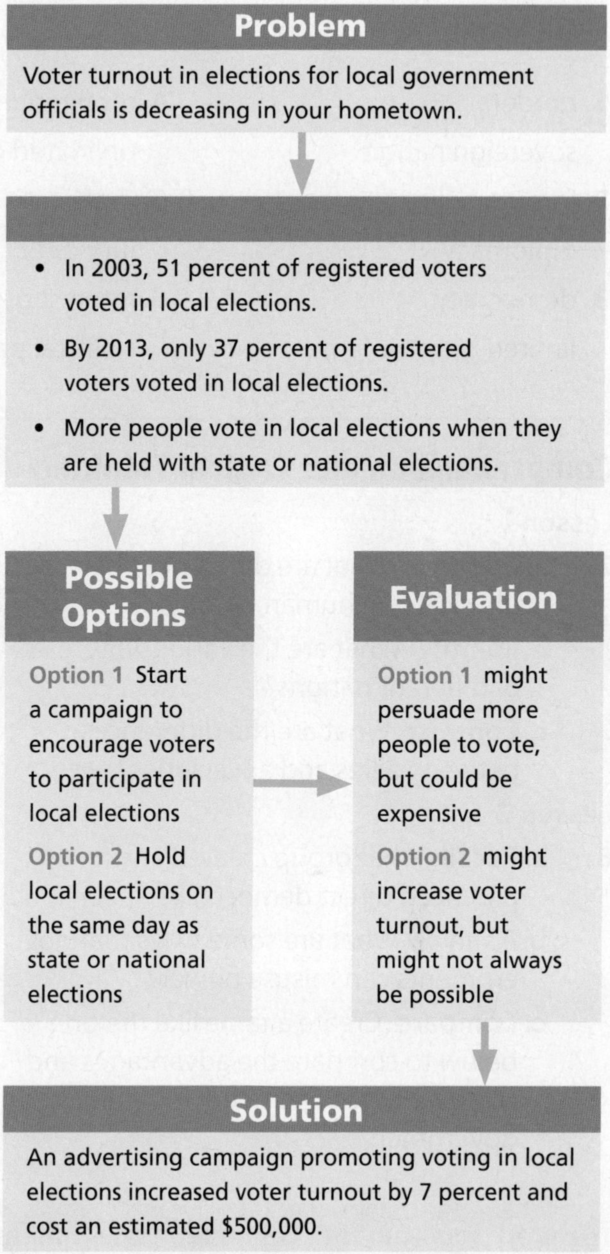

Problem

Voter turnout in elections for local government officials is decreasing in your hometown.

- In 2003, 51 percent of registered voters voted in local elections.
- By 2013, only 37 percent of registered voters voted in local elections.
- More people vote in local elections when they are held with state or national elections.

Possible Options	Evaluation
Option 1 Start a campaign to encourage voters to participate in local elections	Option 1 might persuade more people to vote, but could be expensive
Option 2 Hold local elections on the same day as state or national elections	Option 2 might increase voter turnout, but might not always be possible

Solution

An advertising campaign promoting voting in local elections increased voter turnout by 7 percent and cost an estimated $500,000.

Module 4 Assessment

Review Vocabulary, Terms, and Places

For each pair of terms below, write one or two sentences describing how the terms in the pair are related.

1. borders
sovereign nation

2. foreign policy
diplomacy

3. democracy
limited government

4. totalitarian government
unlimited government

5. draft
jury duty

6. interest group
political party

Comprehension and Critical Thinking

Lesson 1

7. a. **Contrast** What are differences between physical and human borders?
   b. **Identify** What are the various interests of different nations?
   c. **Contrast** What are the differences between allies and adversaries?

Lesson 2

8. a. **Recall** What group created and practiced direct democracy?
   b. **Analyze** What are some ways that governments can misuse power?
   c. **Compare** Create a table like the one below to compare the advantages and disadvantages of limited and unlimited governments.

Limited Government	Unlimited Government
Advantages:	Advantages:
Disadvantages:	Disadvantages:

Lesson 3

9. a. **Explain** Why is public service important in representative governments?
   b. **Analyze** How does volunteering help your community?
   c. **Elaborate** Why would citizens in countries with a nonrepresentative government participate less in civic life?

Reading Skills

10. **Sequence** *Use the Reading Skills taught in this module to sequence the events in the reading section below.*
    After three centuries of control by Spain, in 1810 Mexican revolutionaries rose up against Spanish authority. In 1821 Mexico declared independence. The country's current governmental structure and constitution were established in 1917, after a civil war that began in 1910.

Module 4 Assessment, continued

Social Studies Skills 

11. **Use a Problem-Solving Process** *Use the Social Studies Skills taught in the module to create a problem-solving graphic organizer.* Use the problem-solving process to address the issue of human rights in China. Gather information about the problem, such as the Chinese government's reaction to pro-democracy protests and social media use. Then create a graphic organizer like the one from the Social Studies Skills. List and consider options for solving the problem. Discuss the advantages and disadvantages of each. Express your ideas based on your experiences and research. Be sure to address China's reactions to pro-democracy movements and social media use and evaluate its effect on human rights. Finally, choose what you think is the best solution to improve human rights in China.

Map Activity 

Freedom in Governments of the World *Use the map below to answer the questions.*

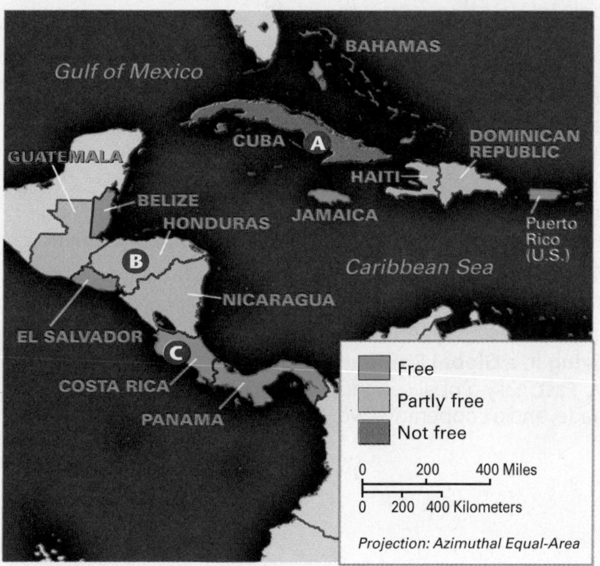

12. Which letter indicates a country whose government does not allow its citizens any rights or freedoms?

13. Which letter indicates a country whose government allows its citizens only partial rights and freedoms?

14. List the countries whose governments allow their citizens rights and freedoms. What system of government do you think is practiced in these countries?

Focus on Writing

15. **Write an Article** Research the direct democracy of ancient Athens and the representative democracy of the United States. Your purpose is to write an article that compares and contrasts the procedures for making decisions in each of these governments. Give your article a headline and write a brief introduction that expresses your main idea. Then write a paragraph comparing and contrasting the procedures each government uses to make decisions. Be sure to describe the roles of citizens in making laws and electing leaders. Then write a paragraph on ways you think you could improve each system's procedures. Write a conclusion that summarizes your main points. Your article should be focused and organized with a clear introduction, supporting paragraphs, and conclusion. Check your article for spelling, grammar, and punctuation.

Module 5

Economics

Essential Question

How does studying economics give us more insight into a country or region?

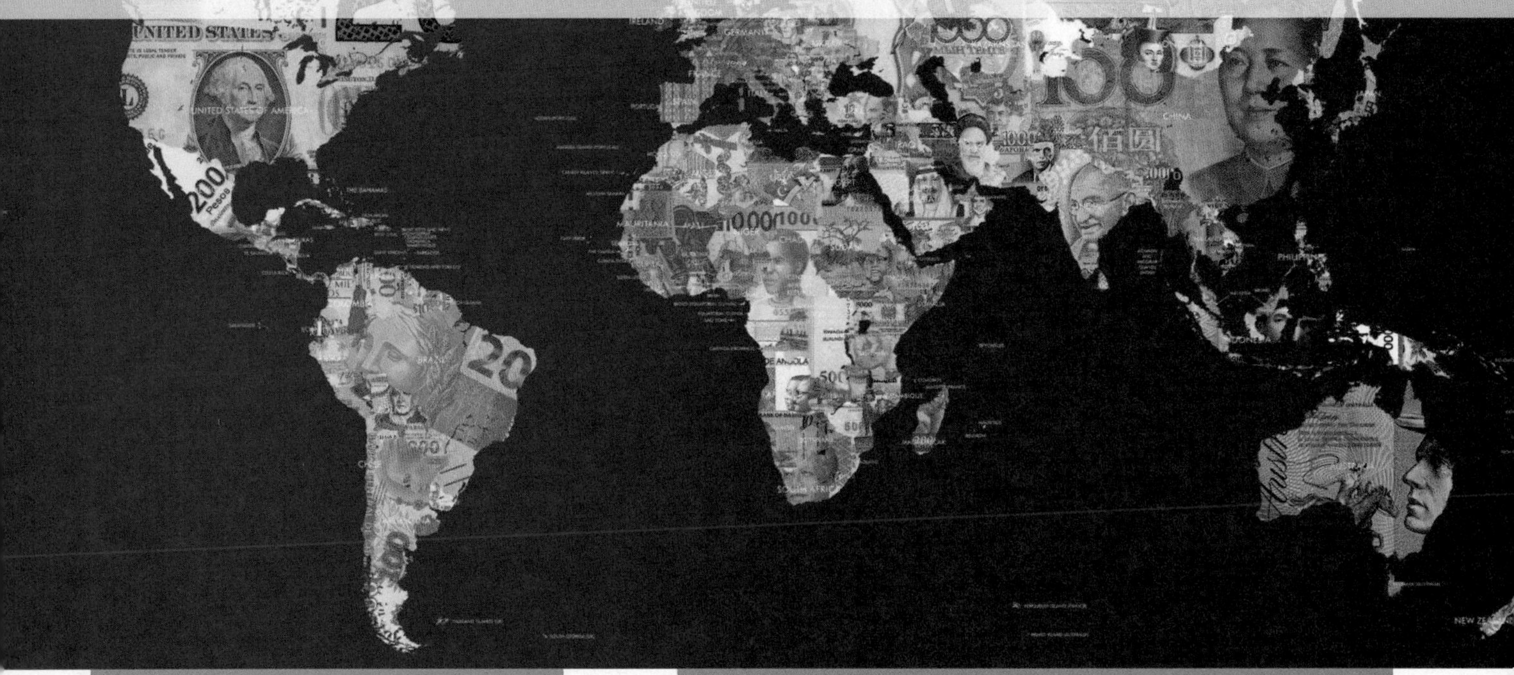

This map collage is made from the currency, or money, that is used around the world.

Explore ONLINE!

- Document-Based Investigations
- Graphic Organizers
- Interactive Games
- Channel One News Video: Generation Money: Teens and Financial Literacy
- Channel One News Video: Millennial Banking
- Channel One News Video: Teen Chef
- Image Carousel: Factors of Production
- Collapsible Table: Compare Economic Systems

In this module, you will learn how economics plays an important role in the way people interact throughout the world.

What You Will Learn

Lesson 1: Economic Basics 159
The Big Idea Economic systems help people buy the goods and services they need.

Lesson 2: Economic Systems 164
The Big Idea Geographers understand world economies by studying factors of production, economic activities, and levels of development.

Lesson 3: Money and Banking 173
The Big Idea People and businesses sell goods and services to earn income, which they can then use to build wealth.

Lesson 4: Living in a Global Economy 179
The Big Idea Fast, easy global connections have made cultural exchange, trade, and a cooperative world community possible.

Global Connections Technology allows people in remote places around the world to communicate.

Economics People buy and sell goods in marketplaces around the world.

Global Trade Around the world, major banking and financial centers such as Wall Street use common currencies for international trade.

Reading Social Studies

Draw Conclusions

READING FOCUS

You have probably heard the phrase, "Put two and two together." When people say that, they don't mean "2 + 2 = 4." They mean, "put the information together." When you put together information you already know with information you have read, you can draw a conclusion. Reach a conclusion by reading the passage carefully. Then think about what you already know about the topic. Put the two together to draw a conclusion.

Read the following text, then add what you know to reach a conclusion.

Today, federal, state, and local governments provide expensive or important services to large groups of people who might otherwise have to do without the service. These government goods and services that the public consumes are called public goods. The government pays for public goods with the taxes they collect.

For example, by establishing schools, government makes it possible for all children to receive a good education. Governments also provide police to protect lives and property, and fire departments to protect homes and businesses.

Information gathered from the passage:
These government goods and services that the public consumes are called public goods. The government pays for public goods with the taxes they collect.

+

What you already know:
Our school band director said we might get new instruments and uniforms next year if the parents approve it.

=

Put the two together to reach your conclusion:
Our parents will probably need to pay more school taxes in order to pay for the new instruments and uniforms.

YOU TRY IT!

Read the following paragraph. Next, think about something you like to do that might be part of our popular culture. Then, put the two together and draw a conclusion.

People around the world are linked through popular culture. Popular culture refers to culture traits that are well known and widely accepted by the general population. Food, sports, music, and movies are all examples of our popular culture. The United States has great influence on global popular culture. At the same time, the United States is influenced by global culture.

As you read this module, look for new facts. Then, add them to what you already know to draw your own conclusions.

Economic Basics

Big Idea

Economic systems help people buy the goods and services they need.

Main Ideas

- The main problem in economics is scarcity.
- Scarcity shapes how societies use factors of production.

Key Terms and Places

economy
scarcity
opportunity cost
profit
factors of production
income
contraction
expansion
economic interdependence

If YOU lived there...

You pour cereal into a bowl for breakfast and discover that you have no milk. How can you get more? Do you have to go to the farm and milk the cows? Of course not. With a quick trip to the store, you can buy a carton of milk.

How are you able to buy what you want or need?

Key Concepts

Every day, people all over the world purchase goods and services from other people. Goods are products that people consume or use, such as food or tools. Services are things that people do. For example, a school nurse provides a service by helping students who are sick or hurt. How people get goods and services is determined by global, national, and local economies. An **economy** is a system of producing, selling, and buying goods and services. The study of economies is called economics.

Scarcity and Choice Economists, who study economics, say that we all face the same basic problem. This problem is scarcity. **Scarcity** is when there are not enough resources to meet people's wants. People's wants are unlimited, but the resources available to satisfy their wants are limited.

When a resource becomes scarce, it is harder for producers to get. So, products made with that resource become more difficult for consumers to find. As a result, the prices for these items usually rise.

Scarcity forces us to make choices. We must decide what things we need and want. Choices always come with costs. For every choice you make, you give up something else. In economics, this choice is called a tradeoff. The value of the thing you give up in the tradeoff is called an **opportunity cost.** For example, suppose you get some money for your birthday. You want to use it to buy a new video game, but your friends invite you to play laser tag. You don't have enough money for both. If you choose the video game, the value of the laser tag games is the opportunity cost. It's the value of the next best choice you gave up in order to get what you wanted more.

Explore ONLINE!

Supply and Demand

Interpret Graphs

Based on this graph, what happens to the demand for a product when the price of the product increases?

If the price of the product changes from $50 to $70, what is likely to happen to the supply?

Supply and Demand Whenever you buy something, you make a choice about the product and the price. Your choice and those of other consumers help determine what sellers will produce and what they will charge for it. The price of a good or service is usually determined by the laws of supply and demand. *Supply* is the amount of a good or service that businesses are willing and able to produce. *Demand* is the desire to have a good or service and the number of people who are ready to buy it at a certain price.

The *law of supply* states that businesses will produce more of a good or service when they can charge a higher price. The *law of demand* states that consumers will want to buy more of a good or service when its price is low. As the price of a good or service rises, consumers will buy less of it.

Incentives Incentives, or benefits, also influence economic activity. **Profit** is a major incentive for both individuals and businesses. Profit is the money an individual or business has left after paying expenses. For example, suppose you help your school sell boxes of popcorn to raise money for your school band. The band's profit is the amount of money that your customers pay, minus the cost that your school actually paid for the popcorn. The profit motive, or the desire to make a profit, is essential in many economies. Without a profit incentive, many people would not start businesses. Then, the consumers in that economy would have no way to get goods and services.

Another type of consumer incentive is saving money. Businesses often offer coupons or advertisements to buy a good or service at a lower price. If enough people use the coupons, the business makes a profit. That's because the business will sell more of the lower-priced or discounted item than other businesses who offer the same thing at a higher price. A third type of incentive is receiving something extra. Has your family ever shopped at a "buy one, get one free" sale? When people buy a particular good or service during these kinds of sales, they also receive a free good or service.

Reading Check
Summarize
What is the connection between scarcity and tradeoffs?

Scarcity and Resource Use

Every day, the interaction between consumers and producers for goods and services happens at the local, state, national, and international levels. In the winter, your family might heat your home with oil that comes from Saudi Arabia or Texas, is refined in Louisiana, is shipped by train to Pittsburgh, and finally is delivered to your home's furnace. How do you think businesses in these diverse places decide what to make or sell?

Factors of Production Scarcity forces businesses to choose which goods and services to provide and how much to charge for them. Individuals, businesses, and societies must answer three basic questions: What will be produced? How will it be produced? For whom will it be produced? To understand how societies answer these questions, economists study **factors of production.** These four main factors are the basic economic resources needed to produce goods and services. They include natural resources, capital, labor, and entrepreneurs. These factors have one thing in common—their supply is limited.

The first factor of production is natural resources, such as oceans, mines, and forests, that provide the raw materials needed to produce goods. Another important natural resource for businesses is land. Every business needs a place to locate. Companies that provide services need to be located near their potential customers. Companies that make goods choose areas with transportation so they can ship their goods.

Factors of Production

Natural Resources

Capital

Labor

Entrepreneurs

The second factor is capital. Businesses need capital. Capital is the goods used to make other goods and services. Capital includes tools, trucks, machines, factories, and office equipment. These items are often called capital goods to distinguish them from financial capital. Financial capital is the money a business uses to buy the tools and equipment, or capital goods that they use in production.

The third factor of production is labor. Labor is the human time, effort, skills, and talent needed to produce goods and services. Workers sell their labor in exchange for payment, called **income.** Many workers earn a form of income called hourly wages. Other workers, such as those who manage companies or have a great deal of responsibility, are paid salaries. Salaries are fixed earnings rather than hourly wages. A salaried person is paid the same amount no matter how many hours he or she works.

Entrepreneurs are the fourth factor of production. An entrepreneur is a person who organizes, manages, and assumes the risk of a business. Entrepreneurs often come up with an idea for a new product or a new way of doing business. They use their own labor or capital and take the risks of failure. In return for the willingness to take risks, an entrepreneur hopes to make a substantial profit.

If a factor of production is in short supply, problems can arise. Suppose a farmer uses skills (labor) and tools (capital) to grow strawberries on a farm (natural resource), and he or she sells them at a market (role of entrepreneur). If a drought destroys farmland, the farmer might produce fewer, if any, crops. The farmer's business would be hurt. Strawberries would be scarce. Consumers would have to buy them at a higher price. This situation would cause what is called a **contraction,** or reduction of the strawberry farmer's business.

On the other hand, if a factor in production is increased, benefits can occur. How might this scenario affect the same farmer? Suppose rain is plentiful, and the farmer has a record crop of strawberries. Although the strawberry prices might be lower, the profits from the greater crop yields could allow the **expansion** of the farmer's business. The farmer could afford to hire more workers, buy more farm equipment, or buy more land to farm.

Availability of Resources

The availability of resources influences economic activity. Rwanda's agricultural economy relies heavily on a large number of workers.

By contrast, the availability of capital resources, such as combine harvesters, helps a small number of U.S. farmers tend large fields.

Resources and Economies The factors of production are not distributed equally. That's why countries decide what to produce based on the resources they have. This situation can create specialization. Specialization occurs when individuals or businesses produce a narrow range of products. For example, South Africa is rich in gold, diamonds, and mineral resources. Developing a mining industry has helped make South Africa one of the richest countries in Africa.

The availability of resources also shapes how a society produces goods and services. For example, Rwanda's economy is based on agriculture. Rwandans are rich in agricultural labor. In fact, nearly 80 percent of Rwandans work in agriculture. Farmers grow crops on small plots of land near their homes. In terms of capital, they have simple farming tools but few tractors and roads. By contrast, only about 2 percent of Americans work in agriculture. U.S. farmers rely heavily on capital. Using machinery and technology, they produce surplus crops on large farms.

Scarcity and Trade When a resource is relatively scarce in one place, people may trade with others to get that resource. This happens within a society as well as between nations. In this way, scarcity contributes to **economic interdependence.** Economic interdependence happens when producers in one nation depend on others to provide goods and services that they don't produce. It is a driving force behind international trade.

For instance, Japan manufactures cars, which require a great deal of steel. However, Japan lacks the iron ore needed to make steel. To obtain iron ore, Japan has formed international trading relationships with Australia and Brazil.

Reading Check
Analyze Effects
How does availability of the factors of production affect a society's economy?

Summary and Preview In this lesson you learned how economic systems help people buy the goods and services they need. In the next lesson, you will learn how geographers categorize various world economies and their peoples.

Lesson 1 Assessment

Review Ideas, Terms, and Places

1. **a. Compare** How do the laws of supply and demand work together?

   b. Summarize In economics, what is scarcity?

2. **a. Describe** What are the factors of production?

   b. Predict What problems might a homebuilder face if one of the factors of production, such as land or labor, was in short supply?

Critical Thinking

3. **Compare** You are supposed to babysit Friday night, but your friend wants you to sleep over and watch a new movie. List the opportunity cost of each tradeoff, then explain what you think is the best action and why.

4. **Identify Problems** Give an example of how the relative scarcity of resources might impact economic interdependence within a country.

5. **Synthesize** Draw a table like the one below. Then list some of the factors of production that were needed to produce a recent meal you had.

Natural Resources	Labor	Capital	Entrepreneurship

Economic Systems

Big Idea

Geographers understand world economies by studying factors of production, economic activities, and levels of development.

Main Ideas

- There are three basic types of economic systems.
- Contemporary societies have mixed economies.
- The United States benefits from a free enterprise system.
- Governments provide public goods.
- Geographers categorize countries based on levels of economic development and range of economic activities.

Key Terms and Places

traditional economy
command economy
market economy
mixed economies
free enterprise system
public goods
agricultural industries
manufacturing industries
wholesale industries
retail industries
service industries
gross domestic product (GDP)
developed countries
developing countries

If YOU lived there . . .

You farm a small plot of land in southern India, and you have a decision to make. You can grow food for your family, or you can grow cassava, a cash crop that can be sold for profit if demand for the crop remains high.

What choice will you make?

Main Types of Economic Systems

An economic system is the way in which a society organizes the production and distribution of goods and services. Economic systems can be divided into three types: traditional, command, and market.

In a **traditional economy,** the work that people do is based on long-established customs. People in these groups hunt, fish, and tend animals and crops. Often, the focus of work is survival. The good of the group is more important than individual desires. The group's leaders decide what to produce and which group members will provide services. Typically, the men hunt and fish and the women tend to crops, animals, and children. In earlier times, all societies had traditional economies.

Today, traditional economies are rare and under pressure to change. Still, you can find this system in many places. For example, the Aymara people of the South American Andes and the Inuit people in northern Canada have traditional economies.

In a **command economy,** the government controls the economy. The government decides what goods and services to produce, how and how much to produce, and how goods and services are distributed. It also sets wages and prices. Some economists refer to command economies as centrally planned economies.

The most common economic system used today is a **market economy.** A market economy is based on private ownership, free trade, and competition. Individuals and businesses are free to buy and sell what they wish, with little interference from government. Prices are determined by the supply of and demand for goods.

Reading Check
Summarize
What are the three basic types of economic systems?

Types of Economic Systems

Traditional
The Inuit of Canada use fishing techniques passed down over many generations.

Command
Food was scarce and expensive in this store in the former Soviet Union, a command economy.

Market
Advertisements, like these billboards in New York City, are a common sight in a market economy.

Modern Economies

Few, if any, pure economic systems exist today. Most countries have **mixed economies,** which combine elements of traditional, market, and command economic systems. The most common types of mixed economies are communist, capitalist, and socialist.

Communist Economies Modern economies tend to emphasize features of one system over others. For example, communist economies are closest to the command model. In a communist economy, the government owns all the factors of production. There is no private ownership of property or resources and little or no political freedom.

How do communist nations decide what, how, and for whom to produce? In countries such as North Korea and Cuba, the government collectivized, or took ownership of, the factors of production. Then government workers, called central planners, make long-term plans. They make all decisions about the production, price, and distribution of goods and services. They may even decide what types of work people are able to do.

Capitalist Economies By contrast, capitalist economies emphasize features of market systems. In capitalist economies, individuals and businesses own the factors of production. They play a major role in answering the basic economic questions, and no central government authority tells them what to do. Consumers buy goods and services that they like best. Their choices push producers to make better products at lower prices.

The economies of the United States, Canada, and Taiwan are capitalist. In these countries, government plays an important but limited role in the economy. For example, in the United States, government agencies enforce health and safety standards. These actions benefit U.S. workers and consumers but affect business planning in complicated ways. Regulations can increase the cost of running a business. On the other hand, the government spends money that it collects in taxes on services that support economic development, such as education, roads, and social welfare programs. Businesses save money by not having to pay for these services themselves.

Socialist Economies The third type of economy falls between communism and capitalism. In socialist economies, the government controls some of the basic factors of production. In most cases, that control is limited to industries and services that are key to a nation's well-being, such as electrical utilities, communications networks, and health care. Other industries are privately controlled.

Today, many nations with elements of a socialist economy, such as Sweden and India, have democratic governments. Still, central planners make decisions about government-owned industries. They also make decisions about other sectors, such as health care, to ensure that everyone has access to services.

Compare Economic Systems

	Communism	Socialism	Free Enterprise
Who owns resources?	Government	Government owns basic resources; the rest are privately owned	Individuals and businesses
Who distributes resources?	Government decides how resources are used	Government regulates basic resources; market allocates privately owned resources	Market allocates resources
What role does government play?	Government makes all economic decisions	Government makes decisions in the basic industries	Government has a limited role, acting mostly to ensure market forces are free to work

Trends Since the Fall of Communism The record of collective, or communist, non-free market economies is poor. From the 1940s until the 1990s, between one-quarter and one-third of the world's people lived under communist regimes. The former Soviet Union and several of its Eastern European neighbors, China and much of Southeast Asia, Cuba, and North Korea all had centrally planned economies.

The failure of these economies is due largely to the shortcomings of communism. Often, central planners had too many decisions to make and too little understanding of local conditions. With wages set, workers had little incentive to work hard. Communism's greatest failing, however, was the suffering that it caused. Shortages of food and goods were common. Millions of people died building huge collective farms in China and the Soviet Union. Millions more were imprisoned for criticizing government policies.

Academic Vocabulary
incentive motivation, or reason to do something

Reading Check
Compare How are socialist economies similar to both communist and capitalist economies?

With the collapse of communism in the early 1990s, most communist countries adopted some form of market economy. Five communist countries are left—China, Cuba, Laos, North Korea, and Vietnam. All allow greater market competition, except for North Korea.

The Free Enterprise System

U.S. capitalism is sometimes called the **free enterprise system.** Under this system, Americans enjoy a number of freedoms. They are free to exchange goods and services and choose careers. They are also free to own and operate enterprises, or businesses, with little government intervention.

The ability to make a profit is one of the chief advantages of the free enterprise system. In this system, profit can reward hard work and innovation. The desire to make a profit also encourages competition, forcing producers to offer higher-quality products at lower prices. Another advantage is that people often have greater freedoms in societies with free enterprise systems. They can own property, make economic decisions, and participate in open elections.

Maintaining a functioning free enterprise system requires people to act in a morally responsible and ethical way. Businesses and individuals must obey laws, be truthful, and avoid behaviors harmful to others.

Unethical behavior can lead to business failure and a loss of trust in the system. For example, if company officials begin to lie about a business's financial condition, then investors can lose thousands, even billions of dollars. Finally, the company itself could go bankrupt.

Reading Check
Summarize How does the ability to make a profit help the economy?

Focus on Economics

Young Entrepreneurs

Let's take a look at one American entrepreneur who took advantage of the free enterprise system. In 2006, eight-year-old Madison Robinson from Galveston, Texas, had an idea to sell light-up flip-flops for kids. With financing from friends and family, she started her own company, Fish Flops. By 2013 Fish Flops had over $1 million in sales, enough profit to cover Robinson's college tuition.

At age eight, Madison Robinson started a business selling flip-flops that she designed.

Government and Public Goods

Today, federal, state, and local governments provide expensive or important services to large groups of people who might otherwise have to do without the service. These government goods and services that the public consumes are called **public goods.** The government pays for public goods with the taxes they collect.

For example, by establishing schools, government makes it possible for all children to receive a good education. Governments also provide police to protect lives and property and fire departments to protect homes and businesses.

This firefighter battles a raging fire to protect public safety.

Because of government, we can travel highways that stretch from border to border. We have a system of money that makes it easy for us to buy and sell things and to know the price of these things. Trash is collected, and health and safety laws are enforced to protect us. We can go to public libraries. By maintaining our infrastructure of bridges, airports, and roads as well as many more services, government helps economic activity.

Government Scarcity Scarcity affects government, too. It has unlimited wants but limited resources. Government collects taxes to pay for the public goods. Some economists believe that if taxes are too high, businesses won't make as much profit. Other economists believe that if taxes are too low, it reduces the public services that protect our quality of life. Therefore, government must determine the opportunity cost of investing in education, national defense, social services, and other programs and try to find a balance.

In addition, federal, state, and local governments use regulations, or a set of rules or laws, to control business behavior. Government regulations must be effective and fairly enforced. These regulations often include protections for public health and safety and the environment. For example, a town in a mountain ski area might determine the opportunity cost of regulations to preserve land versus the rights of property owners to develop it for tourism. Then, it must make tradeoffs.

Reading Check
Find Main Ideas
Why does the government provide public goods?

Economic Activities and Development

Every nation's economy includes a variety of economic activities. Economic activities are the ways in which people make a living. Some people farm, others manufacture goods, and still others provide services. Geographers categorize these economic activities into four levels of industry.

Levels of Industry The first level is called primary industry. People working at this level harvest products from the earth. **Agricultural industries** are primary activities that focus on growing crops and raising livestock. Fishing and mining are also primary activities. Raw materials such as grain, cattle, seafood, and coal are all products of primary activities.

At the next level, secondary industry, people use natural resources and raw materials to make products to sell. In **manufacturing industries,** people and businesses manufacture, or make, finished products from raw materials. For example, a furniture maker could use wood to make a table or a chair.

Economic Activity

Primary Industry

Primary industries use natural resources to make money. This farmer sells milk from dairy cows to earn a living.

Secondary Industry

Secondary economic activities use raw materials to produce or manufacture something new. In this case, the milk from dairy cows is used to make cheese.

Tertiary Industry

Tertiary economic activities provide goods and services to people and businesses. This grocer selling cheese in a market is involved in a tertiary activity.

Quaternary Industry

Quaternary industries process and distribute information. Skilled workers research and gather information. Here, inspectors examine and test the quality of cheese.

In the third level, or tertiary industry, people provide goods and services to customers. Workers at this level may sell goods and products from primary and secondary industries. Some work in **wholesale industries,** businesses that sell to businesses. They help move goods from manufacturer to market. Others work in **retail industries,** businesses that sell directly to final consumers. For example, a furniture wholesaler buys tables from a manufacturer. Then, the wholesaler sells the tables to a retail store, such as a department store, that sells directly to consumers.

Still other tertiary workers, like health-care workers and mechanics, work in **service industries,** businesses that provide services rather than goods. Teachers, store clerks, and doctors are all tertiary workers.

The fourth level of economic activity, quaternary industry, involves the research and distribution of information. People making a living at this level work with information rather than goods and often have specialized knowledge and skills. Architects, librarians, computer programmers, and scientists all work in quaternary industries.

Economic Indicators Economic systems and activities affect a country's economic development, or the level of economic growth and quality of life. Geographers group countries into two basic categories: developed countries and developing countries. To decide if a country is developed or developing, geographers use economic indicators, or measures of a country's wealth.

A Developed and a Developing Country

Australia	Afghanistan
Per Capita GDP (U.S. $): $56,311	Per Capita GDP (U.S. $): $594
Life Expectancy at Birth: 82.2	Life Expectancy at Birth: 51.3
Literacy Rate: 99%	Literacy Rate: 38.2%
Physicians Per 10,000 People: 32.7	Physicians Per 10,000 People: 2.7

Sources: CIA, The World Factbook 2016; World Bank

Contrast
How does the quality of life in Afghanistan differ from that in Australia?

Academic Vocabulary
per capita the average per person

One indicator, **gross domestic product (GDP),** is the value of all goods and services produced within a country in a single year. Another indicator is a country's per capita GDP, or the total GDP divided by the number of people in a country. As you can see in the chart, per capita GDP allows us to compare incomes among countries. Other indicators include literacy and life expectancy and the overall level of industrialization. We also look at the types of industries a country has and at its level of health care and education.

Developed and Developing Countries Many of the world's wealthiest and most powerful nations are **developed countries,** countries with strong economies and a high quality of life. Developed countries like Germany and the United States have a high per capita GDP and high levels of industrialization. Their health care and education systems are among the best in the world.

The world's poorer nations are known as **developing countries.** These countries have less productive economies and a lower quality of life. Almost two-thirds of the world's people live in developing countries. These countries have a lower per capita GDP than developed countries. Most of their citizens work in farming or other primary industries. Although these countries typically have large cities, much of their population still lives in rural areas. People in developing countries usually have less access to health care, education, and technology. Guatemala, Nigeria, and Afghanistan are all developing countries.

Often, a country's economic activities reflect its economic development. In the poorest developing countries, the vast majority of people work in primary industries, such as farming. As a country becomes more

Focus on Culture

Female Literacy

Literacy rates are improving around the world, particularly for women and girls. Still, women lag behind men. Of the 774 million illiterate adults (about 17% of the world's population), two-thirds are women. Religious and cultural beliefs and economic conditions contribute to the problem. Illiteracy severely impacts a country's economic growth, quality of life, and its population's overall health and well-being. At 24.2%, Afghanistan has one of the lowest female literacy rates in the world. In many areas, women and girls are not allowed to attend school or to hold a job.

Reading Check
Contrast How does GDP differ in developed and developing countries?

developed, fewer people work in primary industries. In the mid-1800s about two-thirds of U.S. workers worked in primary activities. Today, 80 percent work in tertiary industries, including wholesale, retail, and service industries. Only 3 percent of Americans work in primary industries.

Summary and Preview In this lesson you learned some of the ways in which geographers categorize world economies and their peoples. In the next lesson, you will learn about how the money and banking systems work.

Lesson 2 Assessment

Review Vocabulary, Terms, and Places

1. **a. Compare** Who makes the economic decisions in a traditional economy? Compare this with market and command economies.
   b. Analyze Effects Why are most modern economies called mixed economies?
2. **a. Identify** What types of industries does a socialist government control?
   b. Evaluate What explains the record of collective, non-free market economies in the world today?
3. **a. Identify** What are the advantages of the free enterprise system?
   b. Analyze Effects How can unethical and immoral behavior hurt the free enterprise system?
4. **a. Define** What are public goods? Give examples, and describe why they are important.
   b. Evaluate What are some of the tradeoffs of government regulations? Include examples in your answer.
5. **a. Define** Describe and give examples of agricultural, wholesale, retail, manufacturing, and service industries.
   b. Explain What are developed and developing countries? Include examples of economic indicators in your answer.

Critical Thinking

6. **Form Generalizations** How might economic factors affect the use of technology in a developing country?
7. **Compare** Use your notes to complete a chart like the one below that compares economic systems. For each system, list how some societies organize the production and distribution of goods and services.

Free Enterprise	Socialist	Communist

Money and Banking

The Big Idea

People and businesses sell goods and services to earn income, which they can then use to build wealth.

Main Ideas

- Money is used as a medium of exchange, a store of value, and a unit of account.
- Banks are places to store money, earn money, and borrow money.
- People can use their earnings to build wealth.

Key Terms and Places

barter
money
medium of exchange
store of value
unit of account
interest rate
assets
savings
investment

If YOU lived there . . .

Sadly, your favorite elderly grandmother has passed away. As a parting gift, she left some money in her will for your college education. Since you are not 18 years old, your parents will manage the money. But, they want you to help them decide the best way to keep it safe and to make it grow.

How would you decide what to do with the money until you are ready for college?

Purposes of Money

Imagine what life would be like if money did not exist. How would people get the goods that they need? One way is to **barter,** or trade a good or service for a good or service provided by someone else. Trading like this is hard because two people who want to barter must at the same time want what the other has to offer. For example, suppose you want to trade two T-shirts for a pair of jeans. One friend may have the jeans but not want your shirts. Another might want your shirts but not have jeans to trade. As a result of these kinds of trading challenges, people created money to use as payment.

The History of Money What do the following things have in common: cattle, corn, salt, copper, gold, silver, seashells, stones, and whale teeth? At different times and in different places, they have all been used as money. **Money** is anything that people will accept as payment for goods and services.

Historians do not know exactly when and where metal coins were first used as money, but most agree that coins were invented in the sixth or seventh century BC. Over time, more and more civilizations began minting, or stamping, their own coins. Eventually, they began producing paper money as well. Today, every country in the world has a currency, or type of money. For example, the United States has the dollar, Mexico has the peso, and many European countries have the euro.

The Functions of Money Money performs three important functions. It serves as a medium of exchange, a store of value, and a unit of account. As you have read, bartering is an

inefficient way for people to meet economic needs. By contrast, money is an efficient **medium of exchange,** or a means through which goods and services can be exchanged. It allows precise, flexible pricing of goods and services.

A **store of value** is something that holds its value over time. People do not have to spend their money all at one time. They can save it and spend it in the future. They know that it will be accepted wherever and whenever they need to use it to make purchases.

Money serves as a good **unit of account,** or yardstick of economic value in exchanges. It allows people to measure the relative costs of goods and services. For example, a $20 T-shirt is worth two $10 gift cards, four $5 burritos, or ten $2 bus rides. In the United States, the economic value of all goods and services can be measured by the dollar, the nation's basic monetary unit.

Reading Check
Draw Conclusions
Why did civilizations begin using coins as money?

Banks and the Economy

Banks offer services that allow them to act like "money stores." Just as stores are places where goods can be bought and sold, banks are places where money can be bought (borrowed) and sold (loaned). Services offered by banks allow customers to store money, earn money, and borrow money. Banks are businesses that earn money by charging interest or fees on these services.

Banks store money and other valuables for their customers in vaults.

Banking Services Although banks can offer many services, they have three main functions. Customers can store money in banks, they can earn money from banks, and they can borrow money from banks. Each of these services is important.

Banks are safe places where people can store money and valuables. Customers deposit money in the bank, and the bank stores the money in vaults. The money stored in banks is insured against theft and other loss. Customers' bank accounts are also insured in case the bank fails.

Customers can earn money when they store their savings in banks. Savings accounts and some checking accounts offer a payment called interest. Interest is a payment that a borrower pays to a lender as a fee for use of the money borrowed. When a person deposits money in a savings account, he or she is loaning money to the bank. In addition to savings accounts, many banks offer types of accounts that have special rules and higher interest rates.

Banks also offer loans to customers. They offer different loans for different reasons. Customers apply for loans, and their applications for each loan must be approved by the bank. In addition, when borrowing money from a bank, the customer must pay interest to the bank. One common loan is a mortgage. A mortgage loan allows a buyer to purchase property such as a house without having all of the money. The lending bank and the borrower agree on a time period for the loan and an interest rate. Then, customers pay the bank a certain amount every month until the loan is paid off.

How Interest Works When customers leave money in a bank, the bank pays the customer for use of that money in the form of interest. The amount of interest paid is determined by the **interest rate,** which is usually a percentage of the total amount of money in the customer's account. The bank doesn't simply store its customers' money, though. It uses the money to make loans to other customers. It charges these borrowing customers a higher interest rate than the rate that it pays on savings accounts. In this way, the bank hopes to make a profit.

Interest rates affect economic activity of businesses and individuals. When interest rates are high, more bank customers will save money so that they can earn more money in interest. When interest rates are low, customers tend to borrow more money to take advantage of the low cost of borrowing. Or, if they have no need to borrow money, they may look for savings products or investments that offer high interest rates so that they can earn more with their money.

Reading Check
Explain What are the effects of high and low interest rates?

Money Management

As you have learned, wants are unlimited and the resources available to meet these wants are limited. For this reason, people and businesses are motivated to save and invest money, which increases their financial resources. Savings and investments are good ways to gain **assets.** An asset is something of economic value that a person or company owns. Some assets, such as houses, are physical and acquired by spending. Other assets, such as savings and investments, are **intangible** but still valuable.

Academic Vocabulary
intangible not perceivable by the senses; not physical

Fastest-Growing Occupations

(projected for 2014–2024)

Occupation	Number of New Jobs in These Occupations	% Change	Average Salary*	Education Needed: High school	Some college or training	College degree
Wind turbine service technicians	4,800	108	$51,050	✓	✓	✓
Web developers	39,500	26.6	$64,970	✓	✓	
Registered nurses	439,300	16.0	$67,490	✓	✓	✓
Home health aides	348,400	38.1	$21,920	✓		
Nurse practitioners	44,700	35.2	$98,190	✓	✓	✓
Retail salespersons	314,200	6.8	$21,780	✓		
Occupational therapy assistants	14,100	42.7	$57,870	✓	✓	

Source: United States Bureau of Labor Statistics, 2017

*Median average salary, 2015

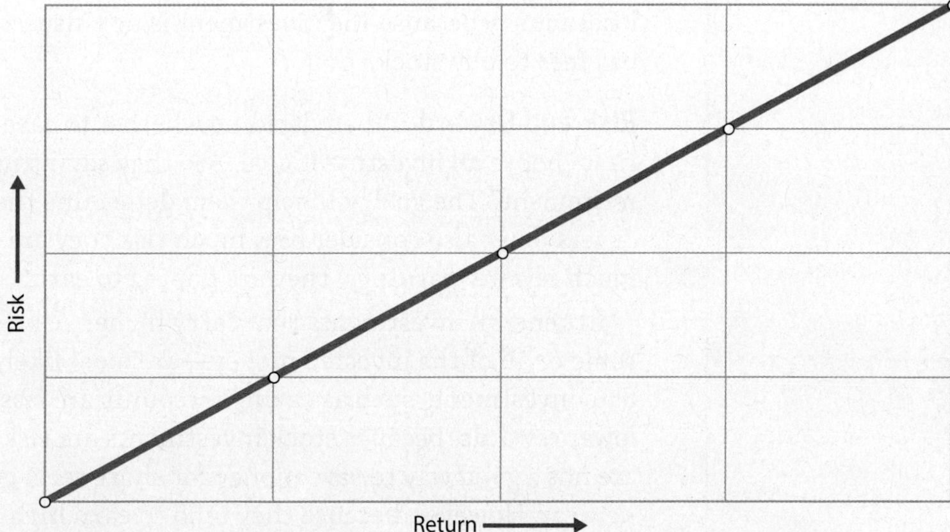

The higher the risk of the investment, the greater the possible return.

Income Every person who has a job that pays a wage earns income. They offer a service (their labor) to a company (their employer) and are paid money in return. Businesses also earn income by selling goods and services. Supply and demand help determine how much businesses and individuals can charge for their goods and services, but a worker can sometimes increase earnings by being especially productive. Why would a business pay a worker more for being productive? It is because the productive worker completes more work in less time than the other workers do.

People can do two things with the money they earn. They can spend it or save it. Much income is spent on basic costs such as housing, food, and utilities. Any money left after these essentials have been covered is called discretionary income. The earner can spend this money on other wants or save it.

Building Wealth **Savings** is income not spent on immediate wants. People have many options for saving money. Common options include savings accounts, certificates of deposit (CDs), and stocks. Savings accounts are good when the money may be needed soon, because these accounts allow customers to withdraw money anytime. However, they pay only a small interest rate. For this reason, savers who do not expect to need their money soon may choose a different way to save.

CDs are offered for a fixed term like six months or a year. Because customers agree to leave the money in the account for a specific time period, banks pay higher interest than they do for savings accounts. In general, the longer the time period of the CD, the higher the interest rate that a bank will pay.

Another option for earners is to invest their money. **Investment** is the use of money today in a way that earns future benefits. One way to invest is to buy stock, or partial ownership, in a company. Savers do this in the hope that the stock price will increase. They could then sell their stock and make a profit. Unlike deposits in savings accounts of banks and credit unions, money invested in stock is not insured. There is always the risk that stock prices could drop instead of rise. In such cases, the investor loses money because the investment is not insured. In addition, investors pay fees to buy stock.

Risk and Reward When deciding whether to save or invest, earners must first choose an investment goal. Are they saving up for a car? a vacation? retirement? The goal will help them determine the best method to save. Savers must also consider how much risk they are able to accept and how much reward (earnings) they are hoping to earn.

In general, investments that carry higher risk—that is, risk of losing some or all of the invested money—are most likely to earn high rewards. Safe investments such as savings accounts are less risky, but they also earn lower rewards. Because stock investments are risky in the short-term, they are not a good way to save money for short-term goals such as vacation or a new car. However, because they tend to earn high returns over many years, they are a good way to save for retirement. Savings accounts and CDs are better savings options for short-term goals.

Inflation is another risk that savers must consider. Because it affects the purchasing power of money, it can affect all types of accounts. Savings accounts may not pay enough interest to keep up with inflation. This means that, over time, the money in the account will buy less and less. For this reason, savers often seek products that can offer a higher rate of return, such as those available from stock investments. Because a higher rate of return comes with a higher risk, savers leave the money in the account for a long time in the hopes that any losses can eventually be regained.

Reading Check
Identify Which types of savings would work best when saving to buy a car?

Summary and Preview In this lesson you learned how our money and banking systems help people spend and save money. In the next lesson, you will learn how world economies interact and trade.

Lesson 3 Assessment

Review Vocabulary, Terms, and Places

1. **a. Summarize** What are the three main functions of money?
   b. Predict Effects What did the invention of coined money likely do for trade?
2. **a. Recall** What are the three main functions of banks?
   b. Explain Why do banks charge more interest to borrowers than they pay to lenders?
3. **a. Elaborate** What are the advantages of savings accounts? their disadvantages?
   b. Identify and Explain Which tool for savers has the potential for the most earnings? What is the downside of this tool?

Critical Thinking

4. **Compare and Contrast** Use your notes to complete a chart like the one below to compare and contrast different savings and investment options. For each option, list the positive and negative aspects.

Savings Account	CDs	Stocks

Living in a Global Economy

Big Idea

Fast, easy global connections have made cultural exchange, trade, and a cooperative world community possible.

Main Ideas

- Globalization links the world's countries together through culture and trade.
- Multinational corporations make global trade easier and allow countries to become more interdependent.
- The world community works together to solve global conflicts and crises.

Key Terms and Places

globalization
popular culture
trade barrier
free trade

If YOU lived there . . .

You live in Louisville, Kentucky, and you have never traveled out of the United States. However, when you got ready for school this morning, you put on a T-shirt made in Guatemala and jeans made in Malaysia. Your shoes came from China. You rode to school on a bus with parts manufactured in Mexico. At school, your class even took part in an online discussion with students who live in Canada.

What makes your global connections possible?

Globalization

In just seconds, an email message sent by a teenager in India beams all the way to a friend in London. A band in Seattle releases a song that becomes popular in China. People from New York to Singapore respond to a crisis in Brazil. These are all examples of **globalization,** the process in which countries are increasingly linked to each other through culture and trade.

What caused globalization? Over the past 100 years, improvements in transportation and communications—like airplanes, telecommunications, and the Internet—have brought the world closer together. As a result, global culture and trade have increased.

Popular Culture What might you have in common with a teenager in Brazil? You probably have more in common than you think. You may use similar technology, wear similar clothes, and watch many of the same movies. You share the same global **popular culture.**

More and more, people around the world are linked through popular culture. *Popular culture* refers to culture traits that are well known and widely accepted by the general population. Food, sports, music, and movies are all examples of our popular culture.

Globalization

The United States has great influence on global popular culture. For example, American soft drinks are sold in almost every country in the world. Many popular American television shows are broadcast internationally. English has become the major global language. One-quarter of the world's people speak English. It has become the main language for international music, business, science, and education.

At the same time, the United States is influenced by global culture. Martial arts movies from Asia attract large audiences in the United States. Radio stations in the United States play music by African, Latin American, and European musicians. We even adopt many foreign words, like *sushi* and *plaza*, into English.

Reading Check
Find Main Ideas
How has globalization affected the world?

Global Trade

Globalization not only links the world's people, it also connects businesses and affects trade. Societies have traded with each other for centuries. Today, global trade takes place at a much faster pace than ever. Cargo ships have grown larger and faster, and specially designed airplanes now move goods at record speeds. Telecommunication, computers, and the Internet have globalized trade and made global buying and selling quick and easy. For example, a shoe retailer in Chicago can order the running shoes she needs on a website from a company in China. The order can be flown to Chicago the next day and sold to customers that afternoon.

Large container ships, such as these in the port of Seattle, are a cost-efficient way to transport goods across the globe.

The expansion of global trade has increased interdependence among the world's countries. Interdependence is a relationship between countries in which they rely on one another for resources, goods, or services. Many companies in one country often rely on goods and services produced in another country. For example, automakers in Europe might purchase auto parts made in the United States or Japan. Consumers also rely on goods produced elsewhere. For example, American shoppers buy bananas from Ecuador and tomatoes from Mexico. Global trade gives us access to goods from around the world.

Multinational Corporations Multinational companies operate in a number of different countries. Examples include Apple, Nike, and Toyota. These companies sell the products and services they offer to places throughout the world. They also have manufacturing plants, offices, and stores in many countries and continents.

To keep costs low, companies often build their manufacturing plants in locations where raw materials or labor is cheapest. They may produce different parts of their products on different continents. Then, the companies ship the various parts to another location to be assembled. The corporations find that if they locate part of their business in a country, local residents are more likely to buy its products and services.

Quick Facts

Arguments For and Against Economic Globalization

For	Against
• promotes peace through trade • raises the standard of living and GDP • creates jobs in developing countries • promotes investment in developing nations' education, technology, and infrastructure • creates a sense of world community	• creates conflict because of an unfair system • benefits developed nations more than developing nations • takes jobs from high-paid laborers in developed countries • may underpay workers in developing nations • hurts local cultures

Reading Check
Analyze Effects
How might the location of multinational companies affect the gross domestic product (GDP) of a developed and developing country?

Many developing nations want multinational corporations to invest in them because they create jobs. Some developing nations offer multinational corporations a promise of low taxes to encourage them to do business there. After all, multinational corporations create jobs and expand the economy of a nation. With additional money coming in because of globalization, developing countries can improve their infrastructure. In this way, governments are better able to meet the needs of their citizens.

Global Economic Issues

Countries trade with each other to obtain resources, goods, and services. However, as you learned, scarcity is not equally divided across nations. While developed nations have found ways to strengthen their economies, developing nations still struggle to gain economic stability. They lack the necessary technologies, well-trained workers, and money for investments.

Economic Aid Organizations Developed nations provide aid to developing nations through the work of international organizations. One of these organizations is the World Bank. The World Bank provides loans for large projects in countries that need them, but might not otherwise be able to pay

Trade Barriers

Type of Trade Barrier	Definition	Example
Tariff	A tax that must be paid on imported items	A country taxes imports of Chinese steel at higher rates to protect steel production within its own country.
Quota	A limit on the amount of product imported or a limit on the amount of product imported at a lower tariff	A country imposes more quotas on goods and materials from developed countries than those from less-developed countries.
Embargo	A restriction or ban of trade with a country for political purposes	The United States restricts trade with Cuba because of concerns about the dictatorship of Raúl Castro.

Analyze Information
Which type of trade barrier do you think is used least often? Why?

for them. These loans often are used to pay for health care, education projects, or infrastructure, such as roads or power plants. Another organization is the International Monetary Fund (IMF). The IMF offers emergency loans to countries in financial trouble. These loans help countries keep a stable money and banking system so people can continue to buy and sell goods and services and their economy can begin to grow and prosper.

While these economic aid organizations can play an important role in development, they also have weaknesses. For example, the World Bank might fund a project that it considers worthy, like the building of a large dam. But, the project may not help the people of a country. Some have criticized the IMF for setting harsh financial conditions for countries receiving loans. For example, the IMF might require a country to cut its government spending drastically, which could affect jobs. Still, developed nations remain interested in helping developing nations. They see developing nations as sources of raw materials and as potential markets for goods. That is why developed nations would like the economies of developing nations to become strong and stable.

U.S. president Donald Trump and Chinese president Xi Jinping shake hands before a G20 (Group of 20) meeting in Hamburg, Germany. G20 meetings bring together the world's 20 leading industrialized and emerging economies for discussions on important issues, such as trade.

The Economics of Free Trade Global trading helps many countries around the world expand their economies. Yet sometimes governments pass laws to try to protect their country's jobs and industries. A **trade barrier** is any law that limits free trade between nations. One type of trade barrier is quotas. Quotas limit the amount of a lower-priced imported product. Another trade barrier is a tariff, or tax on imported goods to protect the price of domestic goods. An embargo is a law that cuts off most or all trade with a specific country. It is often used for political purposes. Since the early 1960s, for example, the United States has had an embargo on trade with communist Cuba. In 2016 President Obama visited Cuba and met with Cuba's president Raúl Castro in an effort to begin to ease relations between the two countries. In 2017 President Trump reversed Obama's policies and created new restrictions on traveling to or doing any business with Cuba.

Trade barriers exist for many reasons. However, some countries look for ways to make it easier for other nations to trade with them. For example, many countries now encourage free trade. **Free trade** removes trade barriers between nations. Since 1995 the World Trade Organization (WTO) has worked with other nations to help trade among nations flow as smoothly and freely as possible. In 2016, there were 164 member countries.

Reading Check
Compare and Contrast
List the differences among the following types of trade barriers: tariffs, quotas, and embargoes.

Summary Economic systems help people around the world buy the goods and services they need. These systems also provide a way for people and businesses to sell goods and services to earn income. Geographers learn more about a country by studying its factors of production, economic activities, and levels of development. Fast and easy global connections have made cultural exchange, trade, and a cooperative world community possible.

Lesson 4 Assessment

Review Ideas, Terms, and Places

1. a. **Describe** What is globalization?
   b. **Make Inferences** How has popular culture influenced countries around the world?
2. a. **Evaluate** Describe the impact of globalization and improved communications technology on cultures.
   b. **Analyze Motives** What benefits do multinational companies receive by locating business in a developing country? What benefits does the government of the developing country receive?
3. a. **Evaluate** In your opinion, has globalization hurt or helped the people of the world? Why?
   b. **Analyze Causes** Why might governments use trade barriers?

Critical Thinking

4. **Identify Cause and Effect** Use your notes and make a graphic organizer like the one below to identify the effects that globalization has on our world.

Globalization		
Effects	Effects	Effects

Social Studies Skills

Determine the Strength of an Argument

Define the Skill

Studying economics and geography often involves learning about different opinions. In order to understand these opinions, it is important to recognize strong arguments. An **argument** is a piece of writing that expresses a particular view. A strong argument presents a position, or claim about a topic, and supports that claim with reasons and evidence. Examples and points should be true and should relate to the argument. It is also important to consider any evidence against the argument.

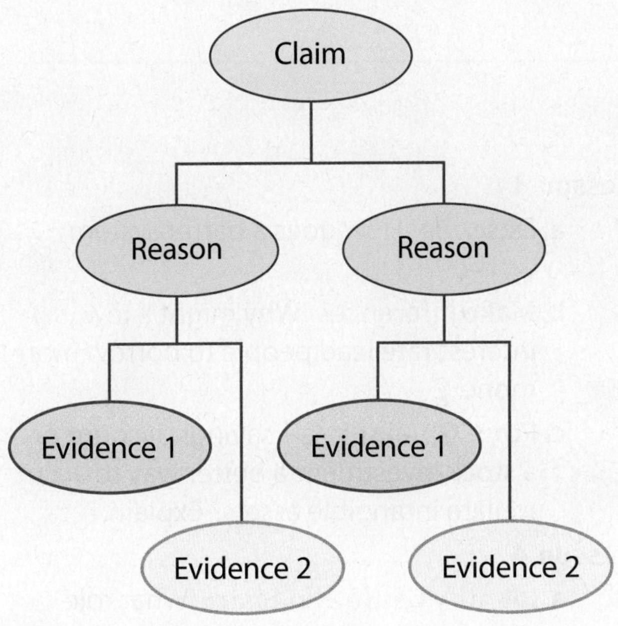

Claim - a writer's position on a problem or issue

Reason - a statement that explains to readers why they should believe your claim

Evidence - proof that supports or backs up each reason, including facts, examples, statistics, and quotations

Although each piece of evidence supports a specific reason, all of the evidence should clearly relate to the writer's position or claim. The evidence must also come from credible, reliable sources.

Learn the Skill

Read the following paragraph. Notice how the claim is supported by a reason and evidence.

> The term literacy means a person's ability to read, write, do basic math, and use technology. Increasing literacy rates is the best way to overcome poverty and disadvantage. People who master these skills are more likely to achieve a higher level of education and get better jobs. Studies have shown that illiterate people earn 30%-42% less than similar literate people. A UNESCO study shows that the income of a person with poor literacy changes very little during his or her working career. However, incomes of people with higher literacy and math skills will increase two to three times more than what they earned at the beginning of their working career.

Claim

Reason

Evidence 1

Evidence 2

Practice the Skill

Use the library or Internet to find an editorial or a reader's letter to the editor in your local newspaper. Print it out or copy it. Then highlight the claim, at least one reason, and one supporting piece of evidence.

Module 5 Assessment

Review Vocabulary, Terms, and Places

For each group of terms below, write one or two sentences to describe how the terms in the group are related.

1. scarcity
   factors of production
2. agricultural industries
   manufacturing industries
   wholesale industries
   retail industries
3. income
   savings
4. developed country
   developing country

Comprehension and Critical Thinking

Lesson 1

5. a. **Describe** What is the relationship between scarcity and international trade?
   b. **Explain** How do the factors of production influence a nation's economy? Give two examples.
   c. **Compare and Contrast** Study the images and text on page 162. How do economic factors affect how U.S. and Rwandan farmers use technology?

Lesson 2

6. a. **Elaborate** Why do you think that market economies are more successful today than command economies are?
   b. **Analyze Effects** In general, how does a country's access to education and technology affect its GDP per capita and standard of living?

Lesson 3

7. a. **Describe** How does a barter system work?
   b. **Make Inferences** Why might a low interest rate lead people to borrow more money?
   c. **Form Opinions** Is a savings account or a stock investment a better way to accumulate intangible assets? Explain.

Lesson 4

8. a. **Identify Cause and Effect** What role does government regulation and taxation play in economic development and business planning?
   b. **Make Inferences** Identify a local business in your community that sells or provides goods or services that were made globally. List two or three examples of the globally produced goods or services, and why you think they are.

Module 5 Assessment, continued

Reading Skills

9. **Draw Conclusions** *Use the Reading Skills taught in this module to answer a question about the reading selection below.*

> The ability to make a profit is one of the chief advantages of the free enterprise system. In this system, profit can reward hard work and innovation.
>
> The desire to make a profit also encourages competition, forcing producers to offer higher-quality products at lower prices.

Think about a popular product. How does the free enterprise system help it to be successful?

Social Studies Skills

10. **Determine the Strength of an Argument** Use the Internet or library to find a magazine or newspaper article. Highlight its claim, at least one reason that backs up the claim, and at least one piece of supporting evidence.

Focus on Writing

11. **Sequence** Describe the sequence of steps for moving goods from maker to consumer Use sequence clue words in your answer.
12. **Write an Online Article** Choose two economic systems, one in a developing country and one in a developed country. Your purpose is to compare the main characteristics of these systems. Write a headline and a brief introduction that expresses your main idea. Then write a paragraph that compares their economic systems. Be sure to describe for each country who decides what to produce, how to produce it, and for whom to produce it. Write a conclusion that summarizes your main points.

Module 6

Early Civilizations of the Fertile Crescent and the Nile Valley

Essential Question

How did the geography of the Fertile Crescent and the Nile Valley lead to the development of advanced civilizations?

About the Photo: During the Old Kingdom, ancient Egyptians built three pyramids in Giza, a plateau on the west bank of the Nile River in Northern Egypt. The Great Pyramid, seen here, was built for the pharaoh Khufu and is the oldest and largest of the three.

Explore ONLINE!

VIDEOS, including . . .
- Seven Wonders of the World
- The Persians
- Secrets of the Mummies

- Document-Based Investigations
- Graphic Organizers
- Interactive Games
- Image Carousel: Civilizations Develop
- Interactive Map: Babylonian and Assyrian Empires
- Image with Hotspots: Temple of Karnak

In this module, you will learn how the world's oldest civilizations developed in the region of the Mesopotamia. You will learn how ancient Egyptian civilization developed along the Nile River and discover the connections between Egypt and Kush.

What You Will Learn

Lesson 1: Geography and River Valley Civilizations 191
The Big Idea The valleys of the Tigris and Euphrates rivers were the site of the world's first civilizations.

Lesson 2: Sumerian Civilization 196
The Big Idea The Sumerians developed the first civilization in Mesopotamia.

Lesson 3: Later Peoples of the Fertile Crescent 205
The Big Idea After the Sumerians, many cultures ruled parts of the Fertile Crescent.

Lesson 4: Geography and the Nile Valley Kingdoms 211
The Big Idea Egyptian civilization developed in the Nile Valley, and Egyptian government and religion were closely connected during the Old Kingdom.

Lesson 5: The Middle and New Kingdoms 221
The Big Idea During the Middle and New Kingdoms, order was restored in Egypt, and Egyptians made lasting achievements in writing, art, and architecture.

Lesson 6: Kingdoms of Kush 231
The Big Idea The kingdoms of Kush, which arose south of Egypt, developed advanced civilizations with large trading networks.

Geography The fertile land along the Nile River drew early people to the region. Cities are still found along the Nile today.

Society The people of Kush often worked as farmers, merchants, and soldiers.

Empires The world's first empires were formed in the Fertile Crescent. Soldiers from these empires wore bronze helmets like this one.

Reading Social Studies

Paraphrase

READING FOCUS

When you paraphrase, you explain someone else's idea in your own words. When you put an idea in your own words, you will understand it better and remember it longer. To paraphrase a passage, first read it carefully. Make sure you understand the main ideas. Then, using your own words, restate what the writer is saying. Keep the ideas in the same order, and focus on using your own, familiar vocabulary. Your sentences may be shorter and simpler, but they should match the ideas in the text. Below is an example of a paraphrased passage.

Original Text	Paraphrase
Priests, people who performed or led religious ceremonies, had great status in Sumer. People relied on them to help gain the gods' favor. Priests interpreted the wishes of the gods and made offerings to them. These offerings were made in temples, special buildings where priests performed their religious ceremonies.	Priests hold the religious services, so people respect them. People want the priests to help them get on the gods' good side. Priests do this by explaining what the gods want and by making offerings. They make offerings in a special building where they lead services.

To paraphrase:
- Understand the ideas.
- Use your own words.
- Keep the same order.
- Make it sound like you.
- Keep it about the same length.

YOU TRY IT!

Read the following passage, and then write a paraphrase using the steps described above.

> Irrigation increased the amount of food farmers were able to grow. In fact, farmers could produce a food surplus, or more than they needed. Farmers also used irrigation to water grazing areas for cattle and sheep. As a result, Mesopotamians ate a variety of foods. Fish, meat, wheat, barley, and dates were plentiful.

As you read this module, practice paraphrasing passages to help you remember the text longer.

Geography and River Valley Civilizations

The Big Idea

The valleys of the Tigris and Euphrates rivers were the site of the world's first civilizations.

Main Ideas

- The rivers of Southwest Asia supported the growth of civilization.
- New farming techniques led to the growth of cities.

Key Terms

Fertile Crescent
silt
civilization
irrigation
canals
surplus
division of labor

If YOU lived there . . .

You are a farmer in Southwest Asia about 6,000 years ago. You live near a slow-moving river that has many shallow lakes and marshes. The river makes the land in the valley rich and fertile, so you can grow wheat and dates. But in the spring, raging floods spill over the riverbanks, destroying your fields. In the hot summers, you are often short of water.

How can you control the waters of the river?

Rivers Support the Growth of Civilization

Early peoples settled where crops would grow. Crops usually grew well near rivers, where water was available and regular floods made the soil rich. One region in Southwest Asia was especially well suited for farming. It lay between two rivers.

The Land between the Rivers The Tigris and Euphrates rivers are the most important physical features of the region sometimes known as Mesopotamia (mes-uh-puh-TAY-mee-uh). *Mesopotamia* means "between the rivers" in Greek.

As you can see on the map, the region called Mesopotamia lies between Asia Minor and the Persian Gulf. The region is part of the **Fertile Crescent,** a large arc of rich, or fertile, farmland. As you can see on the map, the Fertile Crescent extends from the Persian Gulf to the Mediterranean Sea.

In ancient times, Mesopotamia was made of two parts. Northern Mesopotamia was a plateau bordered on the north and the east by mountains. The southern part of Mesopotamia was a flat plain. The Tigris and Euphrates rivers flowed down from the hills into this low-lying plain.

The Rise of Civilization Hunter-gatherer groups first settled in Mesopotamia more than 12,000 years ago. Over time, these people found that they could plant seeds to grow food.

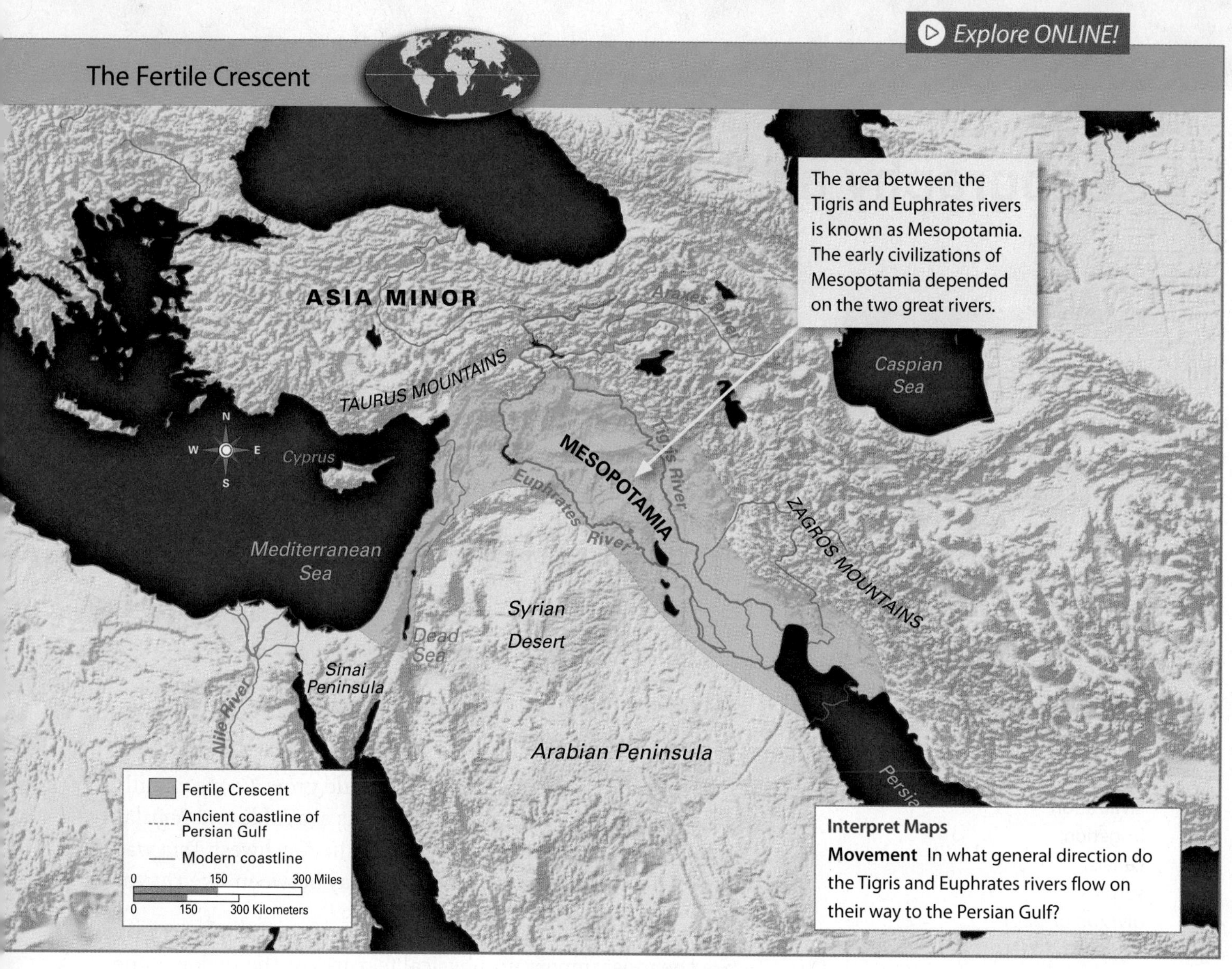

They began forming semi-sedentary settlements. This meant they would settle in one area for part of the year to grow food. The rest of the year they would hunt and gather in other areas.

People eventually became better at growing food. They created tools to help them farm, such as sickles made from flint or clay to harvest crops. Being able to produce food greatly changed how people lived. After a while, people no longer needed to migrate in search of food. They began building permanent settlements so they could raise their crops. This change was so great that historians call the shift from migrating to find food to building settlements to produce food the Neolithic Revolution.

The first farm settlements were formed in Mesopotamia as early as 7000 BC. Every year, floods on the Tigris and Euphrates rivers brought **silt,** a mixture of rich soil and tiny rocks, to the land. The fertile silt made the land ideal for farming. There, farmers grew wheat, barley, and other types of grain. Livestock, birds, and fish were also good sources of food. Plentiful food led to population growth, and villages formed. Eventually, these early villages developed into the world's first civilization.

A **civilization** is an organized society within a specific area. Civilizations often include large cities in which different social classes of people live. Writing, formal education, art, and architecture are features of civilizations. In civilizations, governments are made up of leaders or family groups. The governments make decisions that help the civilization develop. These characteristics improve people's quality of life.

In an established civilization, a government makes economic decisions to help society develop. For example, as populations grow, decisions have to be made about how to effectively produce and distribute food.

Reading Check
Summarize
What made civilization possible in Mesopotamia?

Farming and Cities

Although Mesopotamia had fertile soil, farming wasn't easy there. The region received little rain. This meant that water levels in the Tigris and Euphrates rivers depended on rainfall in eastern Asia Minor where the two rivers began. When a great amount of rain fell, water levels got very high. This flooding destroyed crops, killed livestock, and washed away homes. When water levels were too low, crops dried up. Farmers knew that they needed to develop a way to control the rivers' flow.

Controlling Water To solve their problems, Mesopotamians used **irrigation,** a way of supplying water to an area of land. To irrigate their land, they dug out large storage basins to catch rainwater that fell to the north. Then they dug **canals,** human-made waterways, that connected these basins to a network of ditches. These ditches brought water to the fields. To protect their fields from flooding, farmers built up the rivers' banks. These built-up banks held back floodwaters even when river levels were high.

Historical Source

The First Farmers

Archaeologists use artifacts to learn more about life in ancient Mesopotamia. Bones, metals, and other materials were used to create tools for many different purposes in ancient Mesopotamia. Archaeologists believe that these sickles are from between 4700 BC and 4500 BC. They were found in what is now southern Iraq. These farming tools were made out of clay, an abundant resource in the area.

Analyze Visuals
How do you think these farming tools might have been used?

Irrigation and Civilization

Early farmers faced the challenge of learning how to control the flow of river water to their fields in both rainy and dry seasons.

1. Early settlements in Mesopotamia were located near rivers. Water was not controlled, and flooding was a major problem.

2. Later, people built canals to protect houses from flooding and to move water to their fields.

3. With irrigation, the people of Mesopotamia were able to grow more food.

4. Food surpluses allowed some people to stop farming and concentrate on other jobs, such as making clay pots or tools.

Food Surpluses Irrigation increased the amount of food farmers were able to grow. In fact, farmers could produce a food **surplus,** or more than they needed. Farmers also used irrigation to water grazing areas for cattle and sheep. As a result, Mesopotamians ate a variety of foods. Fish, meat, wheat, barley, and dates were plentiful.

Because irrigation made farmers more productive, fewer people needed to farm. Some people became free to do other jobs. As a result, new occupations developed. For the first time, people became crafters, religious leaders, and government workers. The type of arrangement in which each worker specializes in a particular task or job is called a **division of labor.**

Having people available to work on different jobs meant that society could accomplish more. Large projects, such as raising buildings and digging irrigation systems, required specialized workers, managers, and organization. To complete these types of projects, Mesopotamian society needed to establish order. To do this, the Mesopotamians created structure and rules. These could be provided by laws and government.

Appearance of Cities Over time, Mesopotamian settlements grew both in size and complexity. They gradually developed into cities between 4000 and 3000 BC.

Settlements grew into cities and became the centers of civilizations.

Despite the growth of cities, society in Mesopotamia was still based on agriculture. Most people still worked in farming jobs. However, cities were becoming important places. People traded goods there, and cities provided leaders with power bases. Cities were the political, religious, cultural, and economic centers of civilization.

Reading Check
Analyze Causes Why did the Mesopotamians create irrigation systems?

Summary and Preview Mesopotamia's rich, fertile lands supported productive farming, which led to the development of cities. In the next lesson, you will learn about some of the first city builders.

Lesson 1 Assessment

Review Ideas, Terms, and Places

1. **a. Identify** Where was Mesopotamia?
   b. Explain How did the Fertile Crescent get its name?
   c. Evaluate What was the most important factor in making Mesopotamia's farmland fertile?
2. **a. Describe** Why did farmers need to develop a system to control their water supply?
   b. Explain In what ways did the Neolithic Revolution contribute to the creation of Mesopotamian civilization?
   c. Elaborate How might managing large projects prepare people for running a government?

Critical Thinking

3. **Identify Cause and Effect** Farmers who used the rivers for irrigation were part of a cause-effect chain. Use a chart like this one to show that chain.

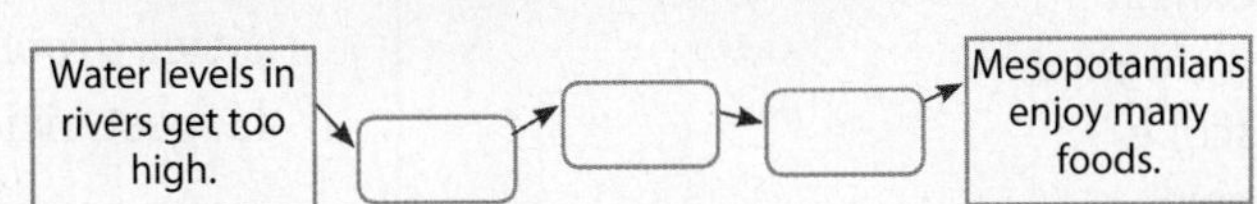

Sumerian Civilization

The Big Idea

The Sumerians developed the first civilization in Mesopotamia.

Main Ideas

- The Sumerians created the world's first advanced society.
- Religion played a major role in Sumerian society.
- The Sumerians invented the world's first writing system.
- Advances and inventions changed Sumerian lives.
- Many types of art developed in Sumer.

Key Terms and Places

Sumer
city-state
empire
polytheism
priests
social hierarchy
cuneiform
pictographs
scribe
epics
architecture
ziggurat

If YOU lived there . . .

You are a crafter living in one of the cities of Sumer. Thick walls surround and protect your city, so you feel safe from the armies of other city-states. But you and your neighbors are fearful of other beings—the many gods and spirits that you have been taught are everywhere. They can bring illness or sandstorms or bad luck.

How might you protect yourself from gods and spirits?

An Advanced Society

In southern Mesopotamia, a people known as the Sumerians (soo-MER-ee-unz) developed the world's first civilization. No one knows where they came from or when they moved into the region. All we know is that by 3000 BC, several hundred thousand Sumerians had settled in Mesopotamia, in a land they called **Sumer** (SOO-muhr). There they built an advanced society.

City-States of Sumer Most people in Sumer were farmers. They lived mainly in rural, or countryside, areas. The centers of Sumerian society, however, were the urban, or city, areas. The first cities in Sumer had about 10,000 residents. Over time, the cities grew. Historians think that by 2000 BC, some of Sumer's largest cities had more than 100,000 residents.

As a result, the basic political unit of Sumer combined the two parts. This unit was the city-state. A **city-state** consisted

Sumerian cities often had crowded marketplaces full of activity. Marketplaces attracted people from throughout the city and surrounding areas.

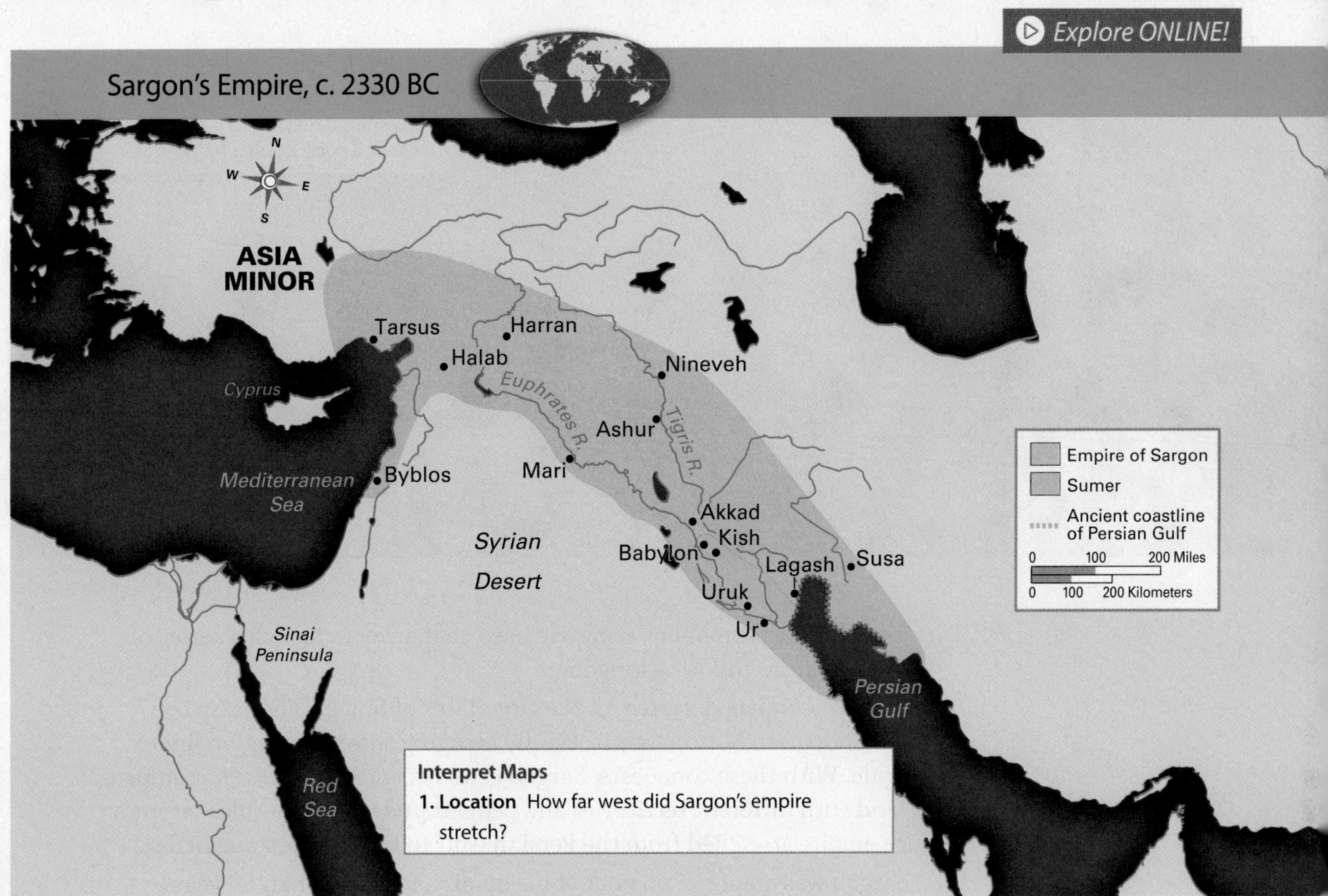

Interpret Maps

1. **Location** How far west did Sargon's empire stretch?

of a central city and all the countryside around it. The amount of farmland controlled by a city-state depended on its military strength. Stronger city-states controlled larger areas.

City-states in Sumer fought each other to gain more farmland. As a result of these conflicts, the city-states built up strong armies. Sumerians also built strong, thick walls around their cities for protection.

Individual city-states gained and lost power over time. By 3500 BC, a city-state known as Kish had become quite powerful. Over the next 1,000 years, the city-states of Uruk and Ur fought for dominance. One of Uruk's kings, known as Gilgamesh, became a legendary figure in Sumerian literature.

Rise of the Akkadian Empire In time, another society developed along the Tigris and Euphrates. This society was built by the Akkadians (uh-KAY-dee-uhns). They lived just north of Sumer, but they were not Sumerians. They even spoke a different language than the Sumerians. In spite of their differences, however, the Akkadians and the Sumerians lived in peace for many years.

That peace was broken in the 2300s BC when Sargon sought to extend Akkadian territory. He built a new capital, Akkad (A-kad), on the Euphrates River, near what is now the city of Baghdad. Sargon was the first

Sargon leads his army into battle. Through conquest, he brought new lands and people under his control.

ruler to have a permanent army. He used that army to launch a series of wars against neighboring kingdoms.

Sargon's soldiers defeated all the city-states of Sumer. They also conquered northern Mesopotamia, finally bringing the entire region under his rule. With these conquests, Sargon established the world's first **empire**, or land with different territories and peoples under a single rule. Sargon's huge empire stretched from the Persian Gulf to the Mediterranean Sea.

Sargon was emperor, or ruler of his empire, for more than 50 years. However, the empire lasted only a century after his death. Later rulers could not keep the empire safe from invaders. Hostile tribes from the east raided and captured Akkad. A century of chaos followed.

Eventually, however, the Sumerian city-state of Ur rebuilt its strength and conquered the rest of Mesopotamia. Political stability was restored. The Sumerians once again became the most powerful civilization in the region.

Reading Check
Summarize How did Sargon build an empire?

BIOGRAPHY

Sargon Ruled 2334–2279 BC

According to legend, a gardener found a baby floating in a basket on a river and raised him as his own child. This baby later became the Akkadian emperor Sargon. As a young man, Sargon served Ur-Zababa, the king of Kish. Sargon later rebelled against the Sumerian ruler, took over his city, and built Akkad into a military power. He was among the first military leaders to use soldiers armed with bows and arrows. Sargon gained loyalty from his soldiers by eating with them every day.

Analyze
Why were Sargon's soldiers loyal to him?

Academic Vocabulary
role a part or function

Religion Shapes Society

Religion was very important in Sumerian society. In fact, it played a **role** in nearly every aspect of life. In many ways, religion was the basis for all of Sumerian society.

Sumerian Religion The Sumerians practiced **polytheism,** the worship of many gods. Among the gods they worshiped were Enlil, lord of the air; Enki, god of wisdom; and Inanna, goddess of love and war. The sun and moon were represented by the gods Utu and Nanna. Each city-state considered one god to be its special protector.

The Sumerians believed that their gods had enormous powers. Gods could bring good harvests or disastrous floods. They could bring illness, or they could bring good health and wealth. The Sumerians believed that success in life depended on pleasing the gods. Every Sumerian had to serve and worship the gods.

Priests, people who performed or led religious ceremonies, had great status in Sumer. People relied on them to help gain the gods' favor. Priests interpreted the wishes of the gods and made offerings to them. These offerings were made in temples, special buildings where priests performed their religious ceremonies.

Sumerian Society

Sumerian society was divided into different groups. This ancient artifact shows Sumerian leaders celebrating a military victory while a musician plays an instrument.

Analyze Visuals
How can you tell from this artifact that Sumerian leaders were important in Sumerian society?

Sumerian Social Order Because of their status, priests occupied a high level in Sumer's **social hierarchy,** the division of society by rank or class. In fact, priests were just below kings. The kings of Sumer claimed that they had been chosen by the gods to rule.

Academic Vocabulary
impact effect, result

Below the priests were Sumer's skilled craftspeople, merchants, and traders. Trade had a great **impact** on Sumerian society. Traders traveled to faraway places and exchanged grain for gold, silver, copper, lumber, and precious stones. Below traders, farmers and laborers made up the large working class. Slaves were at the bottom of the social order.

Men and Women in Sumer In Sumerian society, people needed to own land to have political rights. Men held political power and made laws because property was passed down to male heirs. Women did not have political power. They took care of the home and children. Education was usually reserved for men, but some upper-class women were educated as well.

Some educated women were priestesses in Sumer's temples. They helped shape Sumerian culture. One, Enheduanna, the daughter of Sargon, wrote hymns to the goddess Inanna. Her hymns contain the earliest recorded name of an author of any literary work. She is also the first known female writer in history.

Reading Check
Analyze Effects
How did trade affect Sumerian society?

Invention of Writing

The Sumerians needed a way to keep track of the different types of goods they owned. What they created became one of the greatest cultural advances in history. They developed **cuneiform** (kyoo-NEE-uh-fohrm), the world's first system of writing. The Sumerians did not have pens, pencils, or paper, though. Instead, they used sharp tools called styluses to make wedge-shaped symbols on clay tablets.

Earlier written communication had used **pictographs,** or picture symbols. Each pictograph represented an object, such as a tree or an animal. In cuneiform, symbols could also represent syllables, or basic parts of words. As a result, Sumerian writers could combine multiple symbols to express more **complex** ideas such as "joy" or "powerful."

Academic Vocabulary
complex difficult, not simple

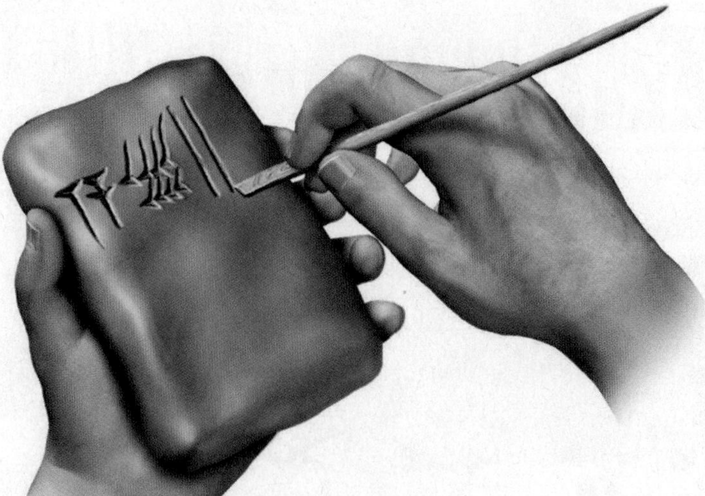

Sumerians wrote on clay tablets with a special tool called a stylus.

Sumerian writing developed from early symbols called pictographs. Writers used clay tablets to record business deals. This tablet describes the number of sheep and goats.

Development of Writing

	3300 BC	2800 BC	2400 BC	1800 BC
Heaven				
Grain				
Fish				
Bird				
Water				

Sumerians first used cuneiform to keep business records. A **scribe,** or writer, would be hired to keep track of the items people traded. Government officials and temples also hired scribes to keep their records. Becoming a scribe was a way to move up in social class.

Sumerian students went to school to learn to read and write. Like today, though, some students did not want to study. A Sumerian story tells of a father who urged his son to do his schoolwork:

> "Go to school, stand before your 'school-father,' recite your assignment, open your schoolbag, write your tablet . . . After you have finished your assignment and reported to your monitor [teacher], come to me, and do not wander about in the street."
>
> —Sumerian essay quoted in *History Begins at Sumer,* by Samuel Noah Kramer

In time, Sumerians put their writing skills to new uses. They wrote works on history, law, grammar, and math. They also created works of literature. Sumerians wrote stories, proverbs, and songs. They wrote poems about the gods and about military victories. Some of these were **epics,** long poems that tell the stories of heroes. Later, people used some of these poems to create *The Epic of Gilgamesh,* the story of a legendary Sumerian king.

Reading Check
Form Generalizations
How was cuneiform first used in Sumer?

Advances and Inventions

Writing was not the only great Sumerian invention. These early people made many other advances and discoveries.

Technical Advances One of the Sumerians' most important developments was the wheel. They were the world's first people to build wheeled vehicles, such as carts. Using the wheel, Sumerians invented a device that spins clay as a craftsperson shapes it into bowls. This device is called a potter's wheel.

The plow was another important Sumerian invention. Pulled by oxen, plows broke through the hard clay soil of Sumer to prepare it for planting. This technique greatly increased farm production. The Sumerians also invented a clock that used falling water to measure time.

Sumerian advances improved daily life. Sumerians built sewers under city streets. They used bronze to make strong tools and weapons. They even produced makeup and glass jewelry.

Math and Science Another area in which Sumerians excelled was math. In fact, they developed a math system based on the number 60. Based on this system, they divided a circle into 360 degrees. Dividing a year into 12 months—a factor of 60—was another Sumerian idea. Sumerians also calculated the areas of rectangles and triangles.

Sumerian scholars studied science, too. They wrote long lists to record their study of the natural world. These tablets included the names of thousands of animals, plants, and minerals.

The Sumerians also made advances in medicine. Using ingredients from animals, plants, and minerals, they produced many healing drugs. Among the items used in these medicines were milk, turtle shells, figs, and salt. The Sumerians catalogued their medical knowledge, listing treatments according to symptoms and body parts.

Reading Check
Categorize What areas of life were improved by Sumerian inventions?

The Arts of Sumer

The Sumerians' skills in the fields of art, metalwork, and **architecture**—the science of building—are well known to us. The ruins of great buildings and fine works of art have provided us with many examples of the Sumerians' creativity.

Architecture Most Sumerian rulers lived in large palaces. Other rich Sumerians had two-story homes with as many as a dozen rooms. However, most people lived in smaller, one-story houses. These homes had six or seven rooms arranged around a small courtyard. Large and small houses stood side by side along the narrow, unpaved streets of the city.

The Sumerians built their homes by using what was in their natural environment. The first Sumerian homes were built using reeds found by rivers. Over time, the Sumerians started using stronger materials. They used clay from the riverbanks to create bricks for building. The Sumerians dried these bricks in the sun and laid them in layers. Brick homes were stronger and lasted longer. This allowed cities to grow larger and become more complex.

City centers were dominated by their temples, the largest and most impressive buildings in Sumer. A **ziggurat,** a pyramid-shaped temple, rose high above each city. Outdoor staircases led to a platform and a shrine at the top. Some temples also had columns to make them more attractive.

The Arts Sumerian sculptors produced many fine works. Among them are the statues of gods created for temples. Sumerian artists also sculpted small objects out of ivory and rare woods. Sumerian pottery is better known for its quantity than its quality. Potters turned out many items, but few were works of beauty.

Jewelry was a popular item in Sumer. The jewelers of the region made many beautiful works out of imported gold, silver, and gems. Earrings and

other items found in the region show that Sumerian jewelers knew rather advanced methods for putting gold pieces together.

Cylinder seals are perhaps Sumer's most famous works of art. These small objects were stone cylinders engraved with designs. When rolled over clay, the designs would leave behind their imprint. Each seal left its own distinct imprint. As a result, a person could show ownership of a container by rolling a cylinder over the container's wet clay surface. People could also use cylinder seals to "sign" documents or to decorate other clay objects.

Some cylinder seals showed battle scenes. Others displayed worship rituals. Some were highly decorative, covered with hundreds of carefully cut gems.

The Sumerians also enjoyed music. Kings and temples hired musicians to play on special occasions. Sumerian musicians played reed pipes, drums,

Sumerian Achievements

The Sumerians' artistic achievements included beautiful works of gold, wood, and stone.

This stringed musical instrument is called a lyre. It features a cow's head and is made of silver decorated with shell and stone.

The Sumerians were the first people in Mesopotamia to build large temples called ziggurats.

The bull's head is made of gold and silver.

Cylinder seals like this one were carved into round stones and then rolled over clay to leave their mark.

Analyze Visuals
The head of a cow or bull is shown in some of these works. Why were cattle important to Sumerians?

Reading Check
Make Inferences
What might historians learn from cylinder seals?

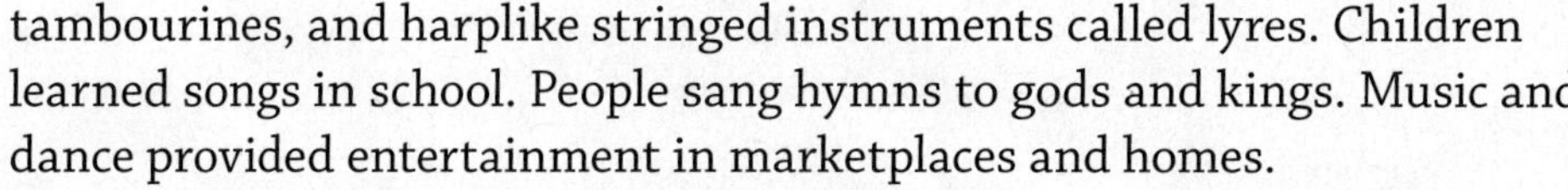

tambourines, and harplike stringed instruments called lyres. Children learned songs in school. People sang hymns to gods and kings. Music and dance provided entertainment in marketplaces and homes.

Summary and Preview In this lesson, you learned about Sumerian city-states, religion, and society. You also learned that the Sumerians greatly enriched their society. Next you will learn about the later people who lived in Mesopotamia.

Lesson 2 Assessment

Review Ideas, Terms, and Places

1. a. **Recall** What was the basic political unit of Sumer?
   b. **Explain** What evidence from the text shows that Sumer was an important part of the region's economy?
   c. **Elaborate** How do you think that Sargon's creation of an empire changed the history of Mesopotamia? Defend your answer.
2. a. **Identify** What is polytheism?
   b. **Draw Conclusions** Why do you think priests were so influential in ancient Sumerian society?
   c. **Elaborate** Why would rulers benefit if they claimed to be chosen by the gods?
3. a. **Identify** What is cuneiform?
   b. **Analyze** Why do you think writing is one of history's most important cultural advances?
   c. **Elaborate** What current leader would you choose to write an epic about, and why?
4. a. **Recall** What were two early uses of the wheel?
   b. **Explain** Why do you think the invention of the plow was so important to the Sumerians?
5. a. **Describe** What was the basic Sumerian building material?
   b. **Make Inferences** Why do you think cylinder seals developed into works of art?

Critical Thinking

6. **Identify Effects** Create a two-column chart. List the advances and achievements of the Sumerians in the first column. Then, identify the effect of each Sumerian advance you listed.

Advance/Achievement	Effect

Later Peoples of the Fertile Crescent

The Big Idea

After the Sumerians, many cultures ruled parts of the Fertile Crescent.

Main Ideas

- The Babylonians conquered Mesopotamia and created a code of law.
- Invasions of Mesopotamia changed the region's culture.
- The Phoenicians built a trading society in the eastern Mediterranean region.

Key Terms and Places

Babylon
Hammurabi's Code
chariot
alphabet

If YOU lived there . . .

You are a noble in ancient Babylon, an adviser to the great king Hammurabi. One of your duties is to collect all the laws of the kingdom. They will be carved on a tall block of black stone and placed in the temple. The king asks your opinion about the punishments for certain crimes. For example, should common people be punished more harshly than nobles?

How will you advise the king?

The Babylonians Conquer Mesopotamia

Although Ur rose to glory after the death of Sargon, repeated foreign attacks drained its strength. By 2000 BC, Ur lay in ruins. With Ur's power gone, several waves of invaders battled to gain control of Mesopotamia.

Rise of Babylon **Babylon** was home to one such group. That city was located on the Euphrates near what is now Baghdad, Iraq. Babylon had once been a Sumerian town. By 1800 BC, however, it was home to a powerful government of its own. In 1792 BC, Hammurabi (ham-uh-RAHB-ee) became Babylon's king. He would become the city's greatest ruler.

Hammurabi's Code Hammurabi was a brilliant war leader. His armies fought many battles to expand his power. Eventually, Hammurabi brought all of Mesopotamia into his empire, called the Babylonian Empire after his capital city.

Hammurabi was not only skilled on the battlefield, though. He was also an able ruler who could govern a huge empire. He used tax money to pay for building and irrigation projects. He also brought wealth through increased trade. Hammurabi is best known, however, for his code of laws.

Hammurabi's Code was a set of 282 laws that dealt with almost every part of daily life. There were laws on everything from trade, loans, and theft to marriage, injury, and murder. It contained some ideas that are still found in laws today.

Under Hammurabi's Code, each crime brought a specific penalty. However, social class did matter. For example, injuring a rich man brought a greater penalty than injuring a poor man.

Historical Source

Hammurabi's Code

The Babylonian ruler Hammurabi is credited with putting together the earliest known written collection of laws. The code set down rules for both criminal and civil law and informed citizens about what was expected of them.

196. *If a man put out the eye of another man, his eye shall be put out.*
197. *If he break another man's bone, his bone shall be broken.*
198. *If he put out the eye of a freed man, or break the bone of a freed man, he shall pay one gold mina.*
199. *If he put out the eye of a man's slave, or break the bone of a man's slave, he shall pay one-half of its value.*
221. *If a physician heal the broken bone or diseased soft part of a man, the patient shall pay the physician five shekels in money.*
222. *If he were a freed man he shall pay three shekels.*
223. *If he were a slave, his owner shall pay the physician two shekels.*

—Hammurabi,
from The *Code of Hammurabi*, translated by L. W. King

Analyze Primary Sources
How does Hammurabi's Code reflect the Babylonians' view of different social classes?

Reading Check
Analyze Effects
What was Hammurabi's most important accomplishment?

Hammurabi's Code was important not only for how thorough it was but also because it was written down for all to see. People all over the empire could read exactly what was against the law.

Hammurabi ruled for 42 years. During his reign, Babylon became the major city in Mesopotamia. However, after his death, Babylonian power declined. The kings who followed faced invasions from the people Hammurabi had conquered. Before long, the Babylonian Empire came to an end.

Invasions of Mesopotamia

Several other civilizations developed in and around the Fertile Crescent. As their armies battled for land, control of the region passed from one empire to another.

Hittites and Kassites A people known as the Hittites built a strong kingdom in Asia Minor, in what is today Turkey. Their success came, in part, from two key military advantages they had over rivals. First, the Hittites were among the first people to master ironworking. This meant they could make stronger weapons than their foes. Second, the Hittite army skillfully used the **chariot,** a wheeled, horse-drawn cart used in battle. Chariots allowed Hittite soldiers to move quickly around a battlefield. Archers riding in the chariots fired arrows at the enemy.

Using these advantages, Hittite forces captured Babylon around 1595 BC. Hittite rule did not last long, however. Soon after taking Babylon, the Hittite king was killed by an assassin. The kingdom plunged into chaos. The Kassites, a people who lived north of Babylon, captured the city and ruled for almost 400 years.

Assyrians Later, in the 1200s BC, a group called the Assyrians (uh-SIR-ee-unz) from northern Mesopotamia briefly gained control of Babylon. However, their empire was soon overrun by invaders. After this defeat, the Assyrians took about 300 years to recover their strength. Then, starting about 900 BC, they began to conquer all of the Fertile Crescent. They even took over parts of Asia Minor and Egypt.

The key to the Assyrians' success was their strong army. Like the Hittites, the Assyrians used iron weapons and chariots. The army was very well organized, and every soldier knew his role.

The Assyrians were fierce in battle. Before attacking, they spread terror by looting villages and burning crops. Anyone who still dared to resist them was killed.

After conquering the Fertile Crescent, the Assyrians ruled from their capital city, Nineveh (NI-nuh-vuh). They demanded heavy taxes from

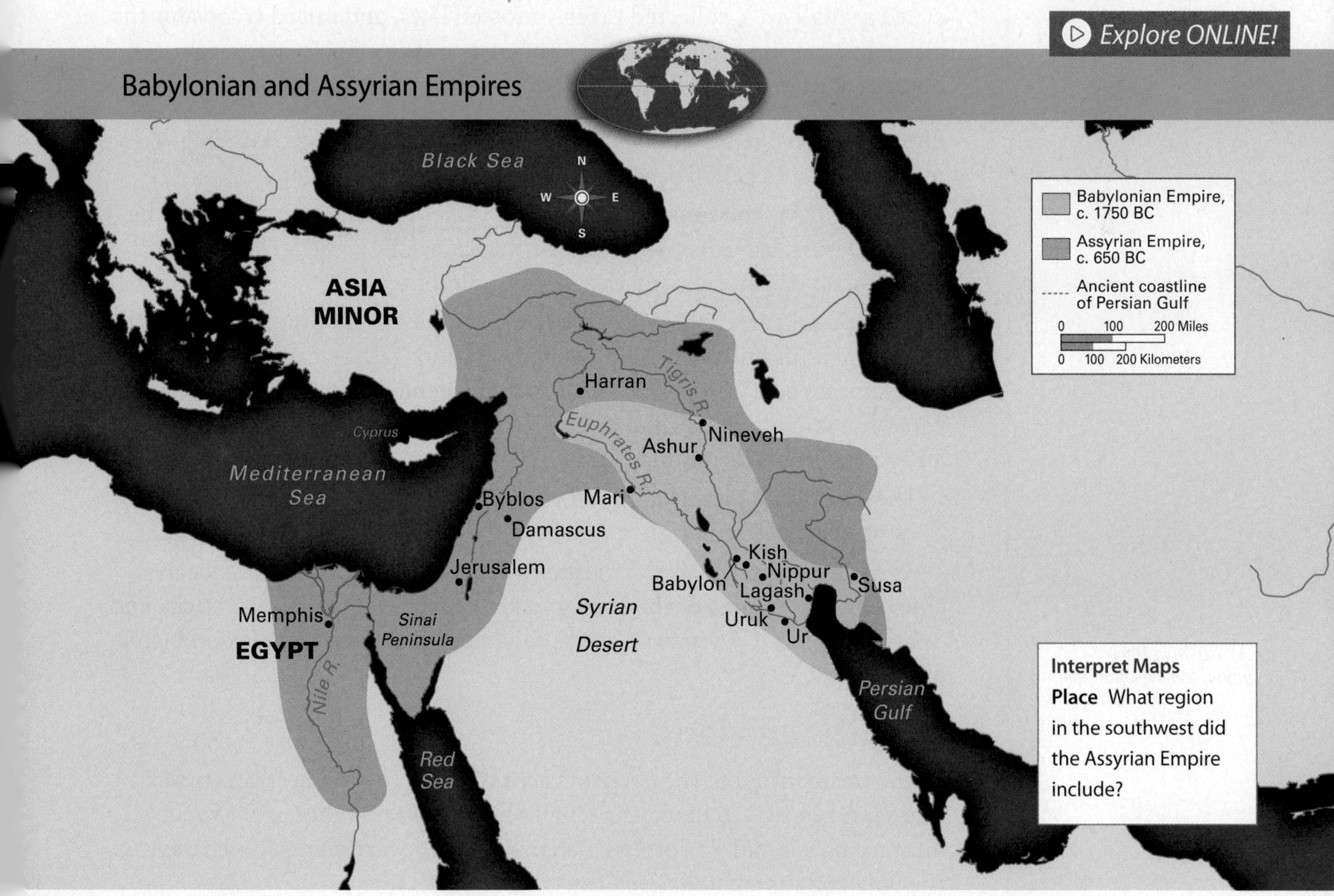

Interpret Maps
Place What region in the southwest did the Assyrian Empire include?

The Assyrian Army

The Assyrian army was the most powerful fighting force the world had ever seen. Large and well organized, it featured iron weapons, war chariots, and giant war machines used to knock down city walls.

Analyze Visuals
What kinds of weapons can you see in this carving?

across the empire. Areas that resisted the Assyrians' demands were harshly punished.

Assyrian kings ruled their large empire through local leaders. Each governed a small area, collected taxes, enforced laws, and raised troops for the army. Roads were built to link distant parts of the empire. Messengers on horseback were sent to deliver orders to faraway officials.

Chaldeans In 652 BC a series of wars broke out in the Assyrian Empire over who should rule. These wars greatly weakened the empire.

Sensing this weakness, the Chaldeans (kal-DEE-unz), a group from the Syrian Desert, led other peoples in an attack on the Assyrians. In 612 BC they destroyed Nineveh and the Assyrian Empire.

In its place, the Chaldeans set up a new empire of their own. Nebuchadnezzar (neb-uh-kuhd-NEZ-uhr), the most famous Chaldean king, rebuilt Babylon into a beautiful city. According to legend, his grand palace featured the famous Hanging Gardens. Trees and flowers grew on its terraces and roofs. From the ground, the gardens seemed to hang in the air.

The Chaldeans greatly admired the ideas and culture of the Sumerians. They studied the Sumerian language and built temples to Sumerian gods.

At the same time, Babylon became a center for astronomy. Chaldeans charted the positions of the stars and kept track of economic, political, and weather events. They also created a calendar and solved complex problems of geometry.

Reading Check
Sequence
List in order the peoples who ruled Mesopotamia.

The Phoenicians

At the western end of the Fertile Crescent, along the Mediterranean Sea, was a land known as Phoenicia (fi-NI-shuh). It was not home to a great military power and was often ruled by foreign governments. Nevertheless, the Phoenicians created a wealthy trading society.

Geography of Phoenicia Today, the nation of Lebanon occupies most of what was Phoenicia. Mountains border the region to the north and east. To the west lies the Mediterranean.

The Phoenicians were largely an urban people. Among their chief cities were Tyre, Sidon, and Byblos. These three cities, like many Phoenician cities, still exist today.

Phoenicia had few resources. One thing it did have, however, was cedar. Cedar trees were prized for their timber, a valuable trade item. But Phoenicia's overland trade routes were blocked by mountains and hostile neighbors. Phoenicians had to look to the sea for a way to trade.

Expansion of Trade Motivated by a desire for trade, the people of Phoenicia became expert sailors. They built one of the world's finest harbors at the city of Tyre. Fleets of fast Phoenician trading ships sailed to ports all around the Mediterranean Sea. Traders traveled to Egypt, Greece, Italy, Sicily, and Spain. They even passed through the Strait of Gibraltar to reach the Atlantic Ocean.

The Phoenicians founded several new colonies along their trade routes. Carthage (KAHR-thij), located on the northern coast of Africa, was the most famous of these. It later became one of the most powerful cities on the Mediterranean.

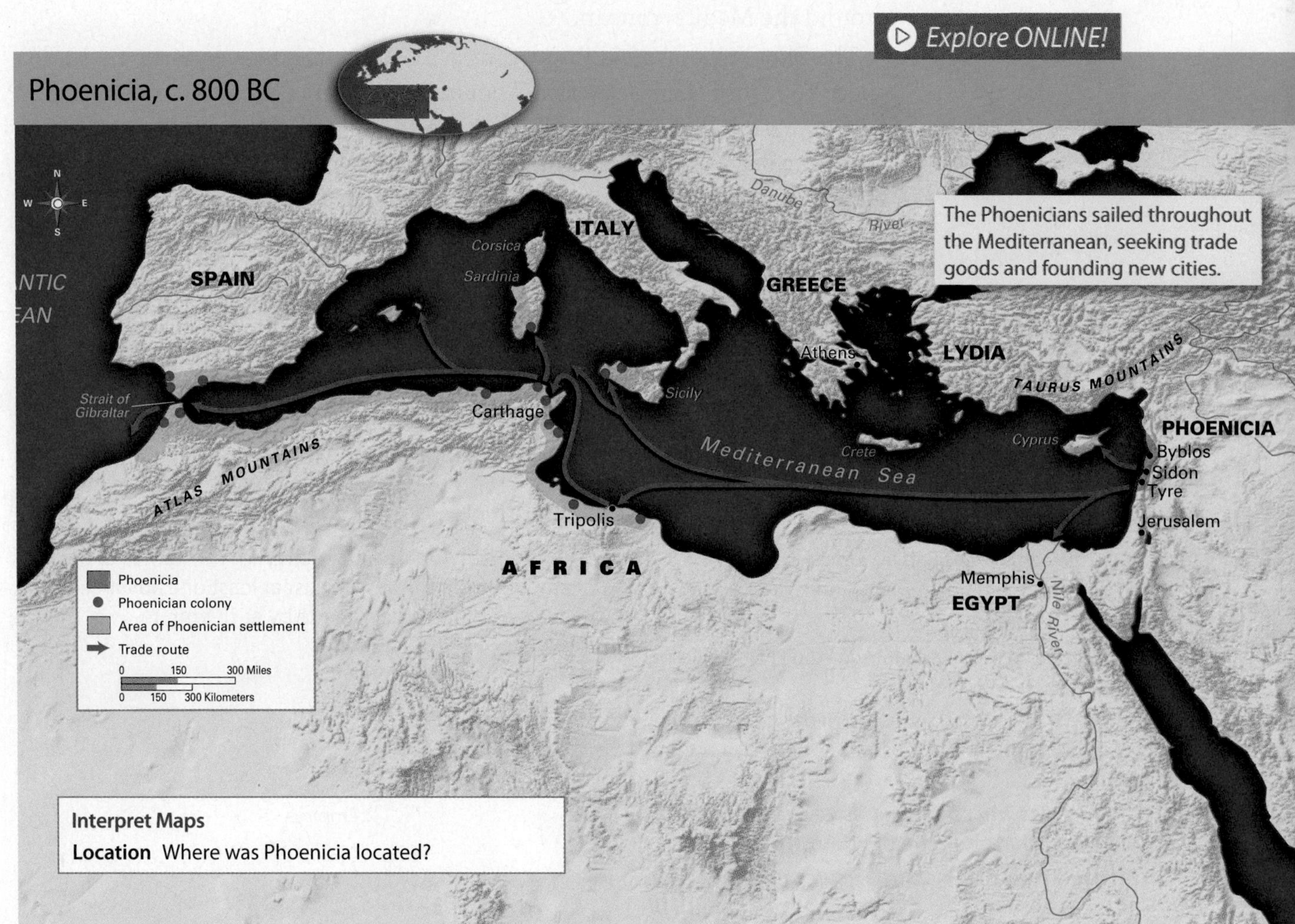

Interpret Maps
Location Where was Phoenicia located?

Phoenician sailors returned home with goods from places as far away as Britain and western Africa. Phoenician port cities, such as Tyre and Sidon, became wealthy centers of trade.

Phoenicia grew wealthy from its trade. Besides lumber, the Phoenicians traded silverwork, ivory carvings, and slaves. They also made and sold beautiful glass items. In addition, the Phoenicians made purple dye from a type of shellfish. They then traded cloth that had been dyed with this purple color. Phoenician purple fabric was very popular with rich people all around the Mediterranean.

The Phoenicians' most important achievement, however, wasn't a trade good. To record their activities, Phoenician traders developed one of the world's first alphabets. An **alphabet** is a set of letters that can be combined to form words. This development made writing much easier. It had a major impact on the ancient world and on our own. In fact, the alphabet we use today is based on the Phoenicians'.

Reading Check
Find Main Ideas
What were the Phoenicians' main achievements?

Summary and Preview Many peoples ruled in the Fertile Crescent after the Sumerians. Some made contributions that are still valued today. Next, you will learn about the development of civilization in the Nile Valley.

Lesson 3 Assessment

Review Ideas, Terms, and Places

1. a. **Identify** Where was Babylon located?
   b. **Analyze** What does Hammurabi's Code reveal about Babylonian society?
2. a. **Describe** What two advantages did Hittite soldiers have over their opponents?
   c. **Rank** Which empire discussed in this section do you feel contributed the most to modern-day society? Why?
3. a. **Identify** For what trade goods were the Phoenicians known? For what else were they known?
   b. **Analyze** How did Phoenicia grow wealthy?

Critical Thinking

4. **Categorize** Create a diagram with the names of the empires from this lesson. List at least one advancement or achievement made by each empire.

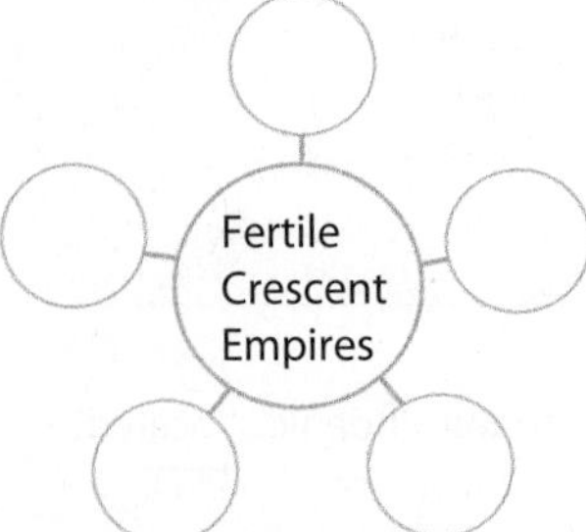

Geography and the Nile Valley Kingdoms

The Big Idea

Egyptian civilization developed in the Nile Valley, and Egyptian government and religion were closely connected during the Old Kingdom.

Main Ideas

- Egypt was called the gift of the Nile because the Nile River was so important.
- Civilization developed after people began farming along the Nile River.
- Strong kings unified all of ancient Egypt.
- Life in the Old Kingdom was influenced by pharaohs, roles in society, and trade.
- Religion shaped Egyptian life.
- The pyramids were built as tombs for Egypt's pharaohs.

Key Terms and Places

Nile River
Upper Egypt
Lower Egypt
cataracts
delta
pharaoh
dynasty
Old Kingdom
theocracy
nobles
afterlife
mummies
pyramids
engineering

If YOU lived there . . .

You are a farmer in ancient Egypt. To you, the pharaoh is the god Horus as well as your ruler. You depend on his strength and wisdom. For part of the year, you are busy planting crops in your fields. But at other times of the year, you work for the pharaoh. You are helping to build a great tomb so that your pharaoh will be comfortable in the afterlife.

How do you feel about working for the pharaoh?

The Gift of the Nile

Geography played a key role in the development of Egyptian civilization. The **Nile River** brought life to Egypt and enabled it to thrive. The river was so important to people in this region that the Greek historian Herodotus (hi-RAHD-uh-tuhs) called Egypt the gift of the Nile.

Location and Physical Features The Nile is the longest river in the world. It begins in central Africa and runs north through Egypt to the Mediterranean Sea, a distance of over 4,000 miles (6,437 km). The civilization of ancient Egypt developed along a 750-mile (1,207-km) stretch of the Nile.

Ancient Egypt included two regions, a southern region and a northern region. The southern region was called **Upper Egypt.** It was so named because it was located upriver in relation to the Nile's flow. **Lower Egypt,** the northern region, was located downriver. The Nile sliced through the desert of Upper Egypt. There, it created a fertile river valley about 13 miles (21 km) wide. On either side of the Nile lay a vast expanse of desert.

The Nile flowed through rocky, hilly land to the south of Egypt. At several points, this rough terrain caused **cataracts,** or rapids, to form. The first cataract was located 720 miles (1,159 km) south of the Mediterranean Sea. This cataract marked the southern border of Upper Egypt. Five more cataracts lay farther south. These cataracts made sailing on that portion of the Nile very difficult.

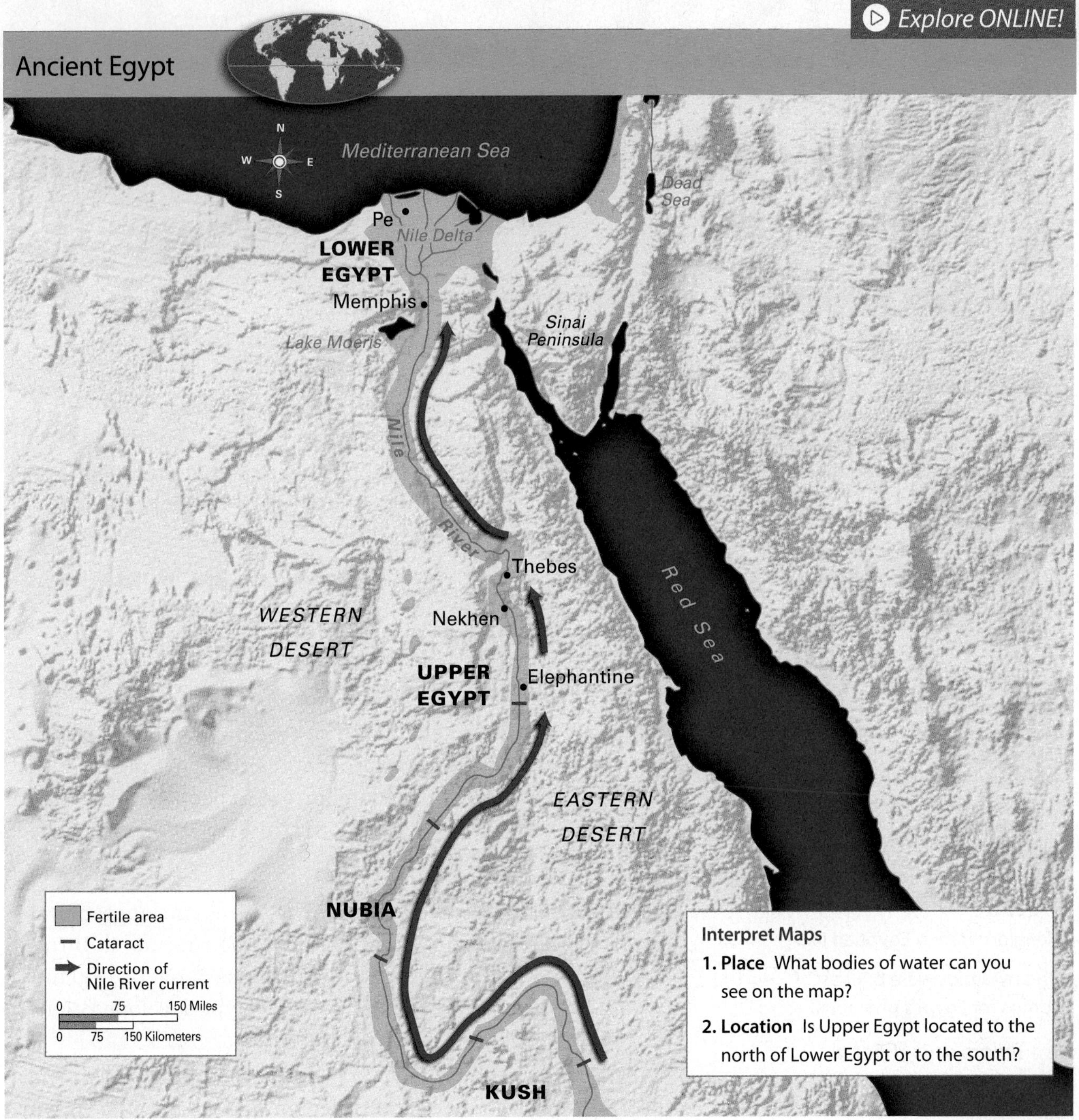

Interpret Maps

1. **Place** What bodies of water can you see on the map?
2. **Location** Is Upper Egypt located to the north of Lower Egypt or to the south?

In Lower Egypt, the Nile divided into several branches that fanned out and flowed into the Mediterranean Sea. These branches formed a **delta,** a triangle-shaped area of land made from soil deposited by a river. At the time of ancient Egypt, swamps and marshes covered much of the Nile Delta. Some two-thirds of Egypt's fertile farmland was located in the Nile Delta.

The Floods of the Nile Because little rain fell in the region, most of Egypt was desert. However, rainfall to the south of Egypt caused the Nile River to flood. Almost every year, the Nile flooded Upper Egypt in midsummer and Lower Egypt in the fall.

The Nile's flooding coated the land around it with a rich silt. This silt made the soil ideal for farming. Each year, Egyptians eagerly awaited the

Reading Check
Find Main Ideas
Why was Egypt called the gift of the Nile?

flooding of the Nile River. For them, the river's floods were a life-giving miracle. Without the Nile's regular flooding, people never could have farmed in Egypt.

Civilization Develops in Egypt

The Nile provided both water and fertile soil for farming. Over time, scattered farms grew into villages and cities. Eventually, an Egyptian civilization developed.

Increased Food Production Hunter-gatherers first moved into the Nile Valley more than 12,000 years ago. They found plants, wild animals, and fish there to eat. In time, these people learned how to farm, and they settled along the Nile. By 4500 BC farmers living in small villages grew wheat and barley.

Just as in Mesopotamia, farmers in Egypt developed an irrigation system. This system consisted of a series of canals that directed the Nile's flow and carried water to the fields.

The Nile provided Egyptian farmers with an abundance of food. Farmers in Egypt grew wheat, barley, fruits, and vegetables. They also raised cattle and sheep. The river provided many types of fish, and hunters trapped wild geese and ducks along its banks. With these many sources of food, the Egyptians enjoyed a varied diet.

Two Kingdoms In addition to a stable food supply, Egypt's location offered another advantage. It had natural barriers, which made it hard to invade Egypt. The desert to the west was too big and harsh to cross. To the north, the Mediterranean Sea kept many enemies away. More desert lands and the Red Sea provided protection to the east. In addition, cataracts in the Nile made it difficult to sail in from the south.

Farming in Egypt

Farmers in ancient Egypt learned how to grow wheat and barley. The tomb painting at left shows a couple harvesting their crop. As the photo below shows, people in Egypt still farm along the Nile.

Analyze Visuals
Based on the photo of the present-day farmer, what methods do Egyptian farmers use today?

Protected from invaders, the villages of Egypt grew. Wealthy farmers emerged as village leaders. In time, strong leaders gained control over several villages. By 3200 BC villages had grown and banded together to create two kingdoms—Lower Egypt and Upper Egypt.

Each kingdom had its own capital city where its ruler was based. The capital city of Lower Egypt was Pe, located in the Nile Delta. There, wearing a red crown, the king of Lower Egypt ruled. The capital city of Upper Egypt was Nekhen, located on the Nile's west bank. In this southern kingdom, the king wore a cone-shaped white crown. For centuries, Egyptians referred to their country as the two lands.

Reading Check
Summarize What attracted early settlers to the Nile Valley?

Kings Unify Egypt

According to tradition, around 3100 BC Menes (MEE-neez) rose to power in Upper Egypt. Some historians think Menes is a myth and that his accomplishments were really those of other ancient kings named Aha, Scorpion, or Narmer.

Menes wanted to unify the kingdoms of Upper and Lower Egypt. He had his armies invade Lower Egypt and take control of it. Menes then married a princess from Lower Egypt to strengthen his control over the newly unified country.

Menes wore both the white crown of Upper Egypt and the red crown of Lower Egypt to symbolize his leadership over the two kingdoms. Later, he combined the two crowns into a double crown.

Many historians consider Menes to be Egypt's first **pharaoh** (FEHR-oh), the title used by the rulers of ancient Egypt. The title pharaoh means "great house." Menes also founded Egypt's first **dynasty,** or series of rulers from the same family.

Menes built a new capital city at the southern tip of the Nile Delta. The city was later named Memphis. It was near where Lower Egypt met Upper Egypt, close to what is now Cairo, Egypt. For centuries, Memphis was

The pharaoh Menes combined the white crown of Upper Egypt and the red crown of Lower Egypt as a symbol of his rule of a united Egypt.

the political and cultural center of Egypt. Many government offices were located there, and the city bustled with artistic activity.

Reading Check
Make Inferences Why do you think Menes wanted to rule over both kingdoms of Egypt?

Egypt's First Dynasty lasted for about 200 years. Over time, Egypt's rulers extended Egyptian territory southward along the Nile River and into Southwest Asia. Eventually, however, rivals arose to challenge Egypt's First Dynasty for power. These challengers took over Egypt and established the Second Dynasty.

The Old Kingdom

The First and Second Dynasties ruled ancient Egypt for about four centuries. Around 2700 BC, though, a new dynasty rose to power in Egypt. Called the Third Dynasty, its rule began a period in Egyptian history known as the Old Kingdom.

Early Pharaohs The **Old Kingdom** was a period in Egyptian history that lasted for about 500 years, from about 2700 to 2200 BC. During this time, the Egyptians continued to develop their political system. The system they developed was based on the belief that Egypt's pharaoh, or ruler, was both a king and a god. It was a **theocracy,** or a government ruled by religious authorities.

The ancient Egyptians believed that Egypt belonged to the gods. The Egyptians believed the pharaoh had come to Earth in order to manage Egypt for the rest of the gods. As a result, he had absolute power over all the land and people in Egypt.

But the pharaoh's status as both king and god came with many responsibilities. People blamed him if crops did not grow well or if disease struck. They also demanded that the pharaoh make trade profitable and prevent wars.

The most famous pharaoh of the Old Kingdom was Khufu (KOO-foo), who ruled in the 2500s BC. Even though he is famous, we know relatively little about Khufu's life. Egyptian legend says that he was cruel, but historical records tell us that the people who worked for him were well fed. Khufu is best known for the monuments that were built to him.

Society and Trade By the end of the Old Kingdom, Egypt had about 2 million people. As the population grew, social classes developed. Egyptians believed that a well-ordered society would keep their kingdom strong. A social structure similar to what was found in Mesopotamia formed.

At the top of Egyptian society was the pharaoh. Just below him were the upper classes, which included priests and key government officials. Many of these priests and officials were **nobles,** or people from rich and powerful families.

Next in society was the middle class. This class included lesser government officials, scribes, and a few rich craftspeople.

The people in Egypt's lower class, more than 80 percent of the population, were mostly farmers. During flood season, when they could not work in the fields, farmers worked on the pharaoh's building projects. Servants and slaves also worked hard.

Quick Facts

Egyptian Society

Pharaoh
The pharaoh ruled Egypt as a god.

Nobles
Officials and priests helped run the government and temples.

Scribes and Craftspeople
Scribes and craftspeople wrote and produced goods.

Farmers, Servants, and Slaves
Most Egyptians were farmers, servants, or slaves.

Analyze Visuals
Which group helped run the government and temples?

Academic Vocabulary
acquire (uh-KWYR) to get

Reading Check
Form Generalizations How was society structured in the Old Kingdom?

As society developed during the Old Kingdom, Egypt traded with some of its neighbors. Traders traveled south along the Nile to Nubia to **acquire** gold, copper, ivory, slaves, and stone for building. Trade with Syria provided Egypt with wood for building and for fire. Egyptian society grew more complex during this time. It continued to be organized, disciplined, and highly religious.

Religion and Egyptian Life

Worshiping the gods was a part of daily life in Egypt. But the Egyptian focus on religion extended beyond people's lives. Many customs focused on what happened after people died.

The Gods of Egypt The Egyptians practiced polytheism. Before the First Dynasty, each village worshiped its own gods. During the Old Kingdom, however, Egyptian officials expected everyone to worship the same gods, though how people worshiped the gods might differ from place to place.

The Egyptians built temples to the gods all over the kingdom. Temples collected payments from both worshipers and the government. These payments enabled the temples to grow more influential.

Over time, certain cities became centers for the worship of certain gods. In the city of Memphis, for example, people prayed to Ptah, the creator of the world.

The Egyptians worshiped many gods besides Ptah. They had gods for nearly everything, including the sun, the sky, and Earth. Many gods blended human and animal forms. For example, Anubis, the god of the dead, had a human body but a jackal's head. Other major gods included

- Re, or Amon-Re, the sun god
- Osiris, the god of the underworld
- Isis, the goddess of magic
- Horus, a sky god; god of the pharaohs
- Thoth, the god of wisdom
- Geb, the Earth god

Egyptian families also worshiped household gods at shrines in their homes.

Emphasis on the Afterlife Much of Egyptian religion focused on the **afterlife,** or life after death. The Egyptians believed that the afterlife was a happy place. Paintings from Egyptian tombs show the afterlife as an ideal world where all the people are young and healthy.

Historical Source

The Afterlife in Ancient Egypt

The ancient Egyptians believed that a person's soul was judged when he or she died. This papyrus shows how that judgment occurred.

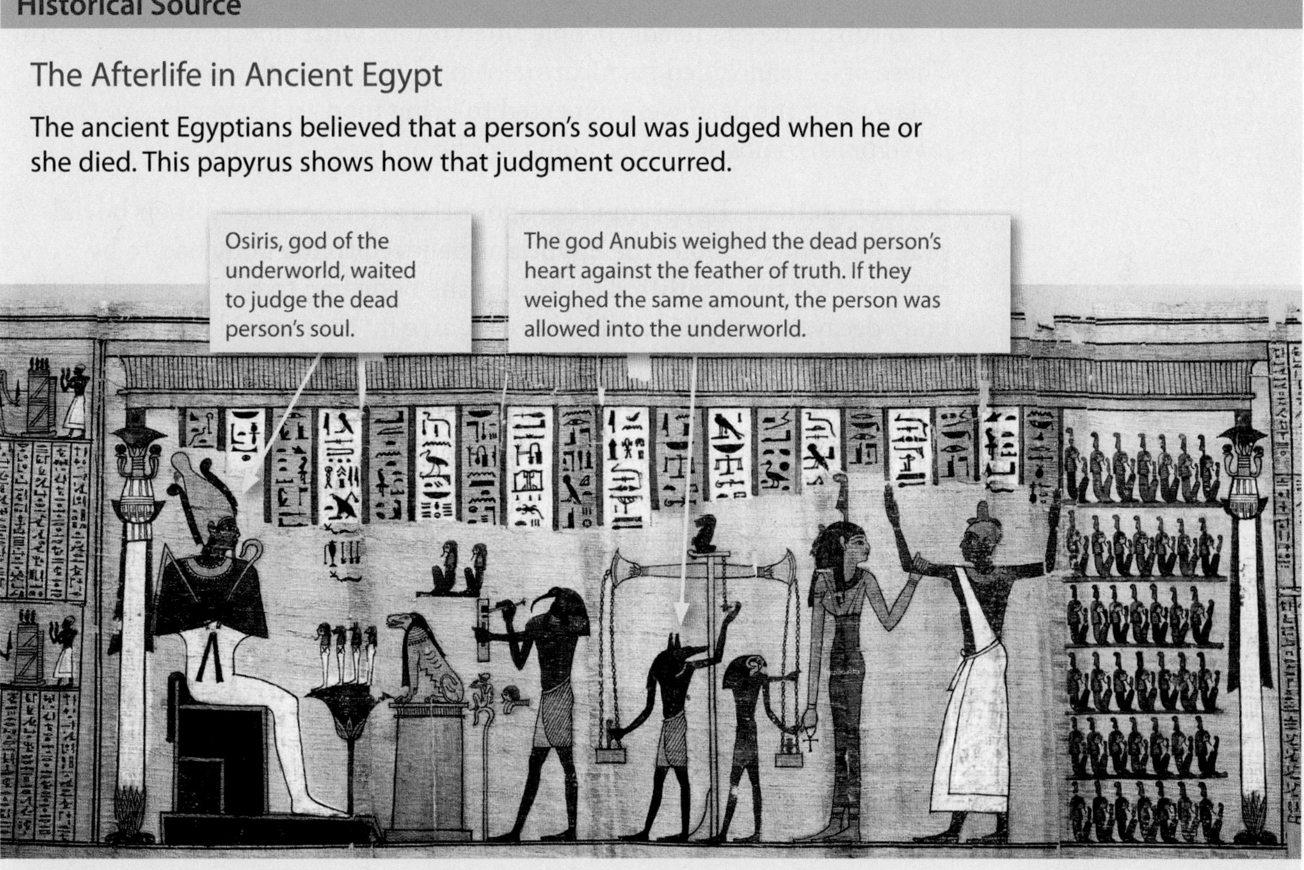

Analyze Historical Sources
Where is Osiris in this drawing? Explain the details that help identify him as the god of the underworld.

Mummies

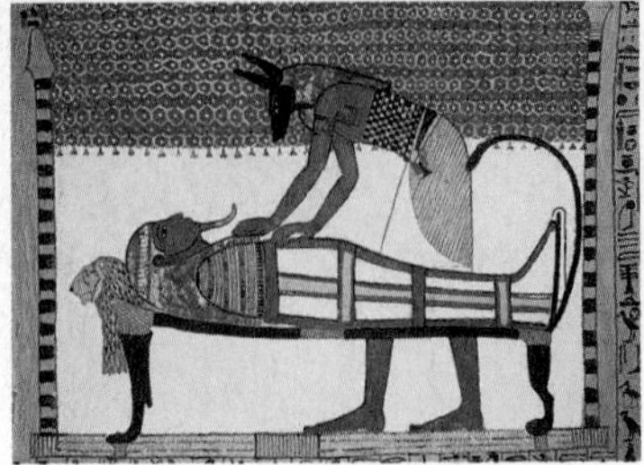

Only the god Anubis was allowed to perform the first steps in preparing a mummy.

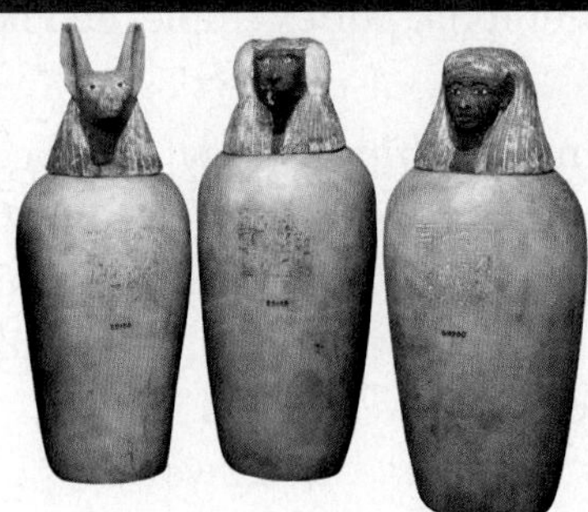

The body's organs were preserved in special jars and kept next to the mummy.

The body was preserved as a mummy and kept in a case called a sarcophagus.

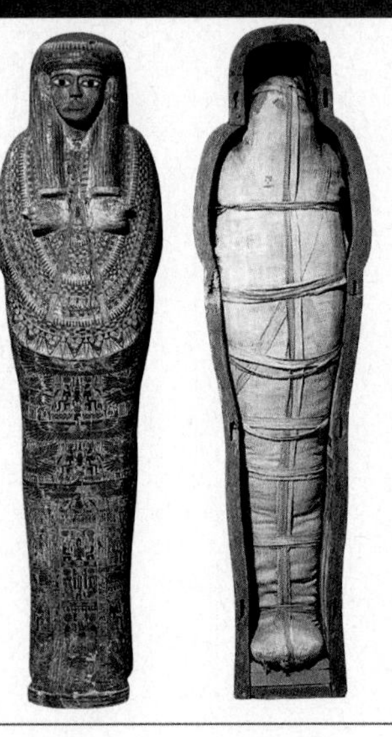

Analyze Visuals
How do these images show the importance of the afterlife to Egyptians?

The Egyptian belief in the afterlife stemmed from their idea of *ka* (KAH), or a person's life force. When a person died, his or her *ka* left the body and became a spirit. The *ka* remained linked to the body and could not leave its burial site. However, it had all the same needs that the person had when he or she was living. It needed to eat, sleep, and be entertained.

To fulfill the *ka's* needs, people filled tombs with objects for the afterlife. These objects included furniture, clothing, tools, jewelry, and weapons. Relatives of the dead were expected to bring food and beverages to their loved ones' tombs so the *ka* would not be hungry or thirsty.

Burial Practices Egyptian ideas about the afterlife shaped their burial practices. For example, the Egyptians believed that a body had to be prepared for the afterlife. This meant the body had to be preserved. If the body decayed, its spirit could not recognize it. That would break the link between the body and spirit. The *ka* would then be unable to receive the food and drink it needed.

Academic Vocabulary
method a way of doing something

To help the *ka*, Egyptians developed a **method** called embalming to preserve bodies. Egyptians preserved bodies as **mummies,** specially treated bodies wrapped in cloth. Embalming preserves a body for many years. A body that was not embalmed decayed far more quickly.

Embalming was a complex process that took several weeks to complete. In the first step, embalmers cut open the body and removed all organs except for the heart. Embalmers stored the removed organs in special jars. Next, the embalmers used a special substance to dry out the body. They later applied some special oils. The embalmers then wrapped the dried-out body with linen cloths and bandages, often placing special charms inside the cloth wrappings. Finally, the mummy was placed in a coffin called a sarcophagus.

Only royalty and other members of Egypt's elite (AY-leet), or people of wealth and power, could afford to have mummies made. Peasant families buried their dead in shallow graves at the edge of the desert. The hot, dry sand preserved the bodies naturally.

Reading Check
Analyze Effects
How did religious beliefs affect Egyptian burial practices?

The Pyramids

Egyptians believed that burial sites, especially royal tombs, were very important. For this reason, they built spectacular monuments in which to bury their rulers. The most spectacular were the **pyramids**—huge, stone tombs with four triangle-shaped sides that met in a point on top. The Egyptians built the first pyramids during the Old Kingdom.

Many Egyptian pyramids are still standing. The largest is the Great Pyramid of Khufu near the town of Giza. It covers more than 13 acres (5.3 hectares) at its base and stands 481 feet (147 m) high. This one pyramid took thousands of workers and more than 2 million limestone blocks to build. The pyramids are amazing examples of Egyptian **engineering**, the application of scientific knowledge for practical purposes.

Building the Pyramids The earliest pyramids did not have the smooth sides we usually imagine when we think of pyramids. The Egyptians began building the smooth-sided pyramids we usually see around 2700 BC. The steps of these pyramids were filled and covered with limestone. The burial chamber was located deep inside the pyramid. After the pharaoh's burial, workers sealed the passages to this room with large blocks.

Historians do not know for certain how the ancient Egyptians built the pyramids. What is certain is that such massive projects required a huge labor force. As many as 20,000 to 30,000 workers may have been needed to build just one pyramid. The government paid the people working on the pyramids. Wages for working on construction projects were paid in goods such as grain instead of money, however.

For years, scholars have debated how the Egyptians moved the massive stones used to build the pyramids. Some scholars think that during the Nile's flooding, builders floated the stones downstream directly to the construction site. Most historians believe that workers used brick ramps and strong wooden sleds to drag the stones up the pyramid once at the building site.

The Great Sphinx of Giza and the Great Pyramid of Khufu are symbols that demonstrate the importance ancient Egyptians placed on the afterlife.

Significance of the Pyramids Burial in a pyramid showed a pharaoh's importance. Both the size and shape of the pyramid were symbolic. Pointing to the sky above, the pyramid symbolized the pharaoh's journey to the afterlife. The Egyptians wanted the pyramids to be spectacular because they believed the pharaoh, as their link to the gods, controlled everyone's afterlife. Making the pharaoh's spirit happy was a way of ensuring happiness in one's own afterlife.

To ensure that the pharaohs remained safe after death, the Egyptians sometimes wrote magical spells and hymns on tombs. Together, these spells and hymns are called Pyramid Texts. The first such text, addressed to Re, the sun god, was carved into the pyramid of King Unas (OO-nuhs). He was a pharaoh of the Old Kingdom.

> "Re, this Unas comes to you, A spirit indestructible . . . Your son comes to you, this Unas . . . May you cross the sky united in the dark, May you rise in lightland, [where] you shine!"
>
> —from Pyramid Text, Utterance 217

Reading Check
Identify Points of View
Why were pyramids important to the ancient Egyptians?

The builders of Unas's pyramid wanted the god Re to look after their leader's spirit. Even after death, the Egyptians' pharaoh was important to them.

Summary and Preview As you have read, during the Old Kingdom, new political and social orders were created in Egypt. Religion was important, and many pyramids were built for pharaohs. In the next lesson, you will learn about Egypt's Middle and New Kingdoms.

Lesson 4 Assessment

Review Ideas, Terms, and Places

1. a. **Identify** Where was the Egyptian kingdom of Lower Egypt located?

   b. **Analyze** Why was the delta of the Nile River well suited for settlement?

   c. **Predict** How might the Nile's cataracts have both helped and hurt Egypt?

2. a. **Describe** What foods did the Egyptians eat?

   b. **Analyze** What role did the Nile play in supplying Egyptians with the foods they ate?

   c. **Elaborate** How did the desert on both sides of the Nile help ancient Egypt?

3. a. **Identify** Who was the first pharaoh of Egypt?

   b. **Draw Conclusions** Why did the pharaohs of the First Dynasty wear a double crown?

4. a. **Define** To what Egyptian period does the phrase *Old Kingdom* refer?

   b. **Analyze** Why did Egyptians never question the pharaoh's authority?

   c. **Elaborate** Why do you think pharaohs might have wanted the support of nobles?

5. a. **Define** What did Egyptians mean by the afterlife?

   b. **Analyze** Why was embalming important to Egyptians?

6. a. **Describe** What is engineering?

   b. **Elaborate** What does the building of the pyramids tell us about Egyptian society?

Critical Thinking

7. **Form Generalizations** Using your notes, complete this graphic organizer by listing three facts about the relationship between government and religion in the Old Kingdom.

Government and Religion
1.
2.
3.

The Middle and New Kingdoms

The Big Idea

During the Middle and New Kingdoms, order was restored in Egypt, and Egyptians made lasting achievements in writing, art, and architecture.

Main Ideas

- The Middle Kingdom was a period of stable government between periods of disorder.
- The New Kingdom was the peak of Egyptian trade and military power, but its greatness did not last.
- Work and daily life differed among Egypt's social classes.
- Egyptian writing used symbols called hieroglyphics.
- Egypt's temples and tombs were lavishly decorated.

Key Terms and Places

Middle Kingdom
New Kingdom
Kush
trade routes
hieroglyphics
papyrus
Rosetta Stone
sphinxes
obelisk

If YOU lived there . . .

You are an artist in ancient Egypt. A powerful noble has hired you to decorate the walls of his family tomb. You are standing inside the new tomb, studying the bare, stone walls that you will decorate. No light reaches this chamber, but your servant holds a lantern high. You've met the noble only briefly but think that he is someone who loves his family, the gods, and Egypt.

What will you include in your painting?

The Middle Kingdom

At the end of the Old Kingdom, the wealth and power of the pharaohs declined. Building and maintaining pyramids cost a lot of money. Pharaohs could not collect enough taxes to keep up with their expenses. At the same time, ambitious nobles used their government positions to take power from pharaohs. By about 2200 BC the Old Kingdom had fallen. For the next 160 years, local nobles ruled much of Egypt. During this period, the kingdom had no central ruler.

Finally, around 2050 BC, a powerful pharaoh defeated his rivals. Once again all of Egypt was united. His rule began the **Middle Kingdom,** a period of order and stability that lasted to about 1750 BC. Toward the end of the Middle Kingdom, however, Egypt began to fall into disorder once again.

Around 1750 BC a group from Southwest Asia called the Hyksos (HIK-sohs) invaded. The Hyksos used horses, chariots, and

Timeline: Periods of Egyptian History

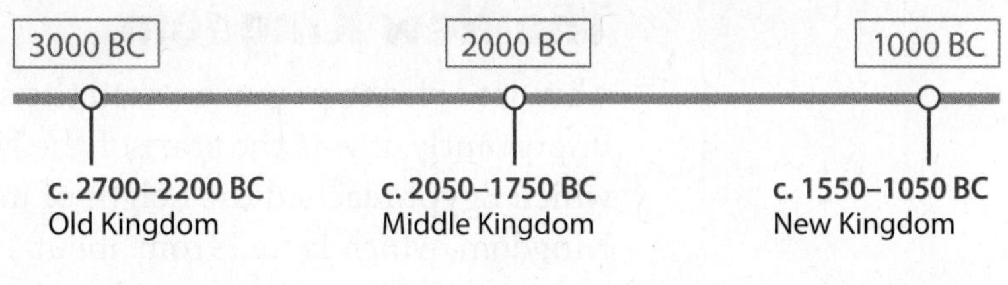

Analyze Timelines
Which kingdom lasted the shortest amount of time?

Explore ONLINE!

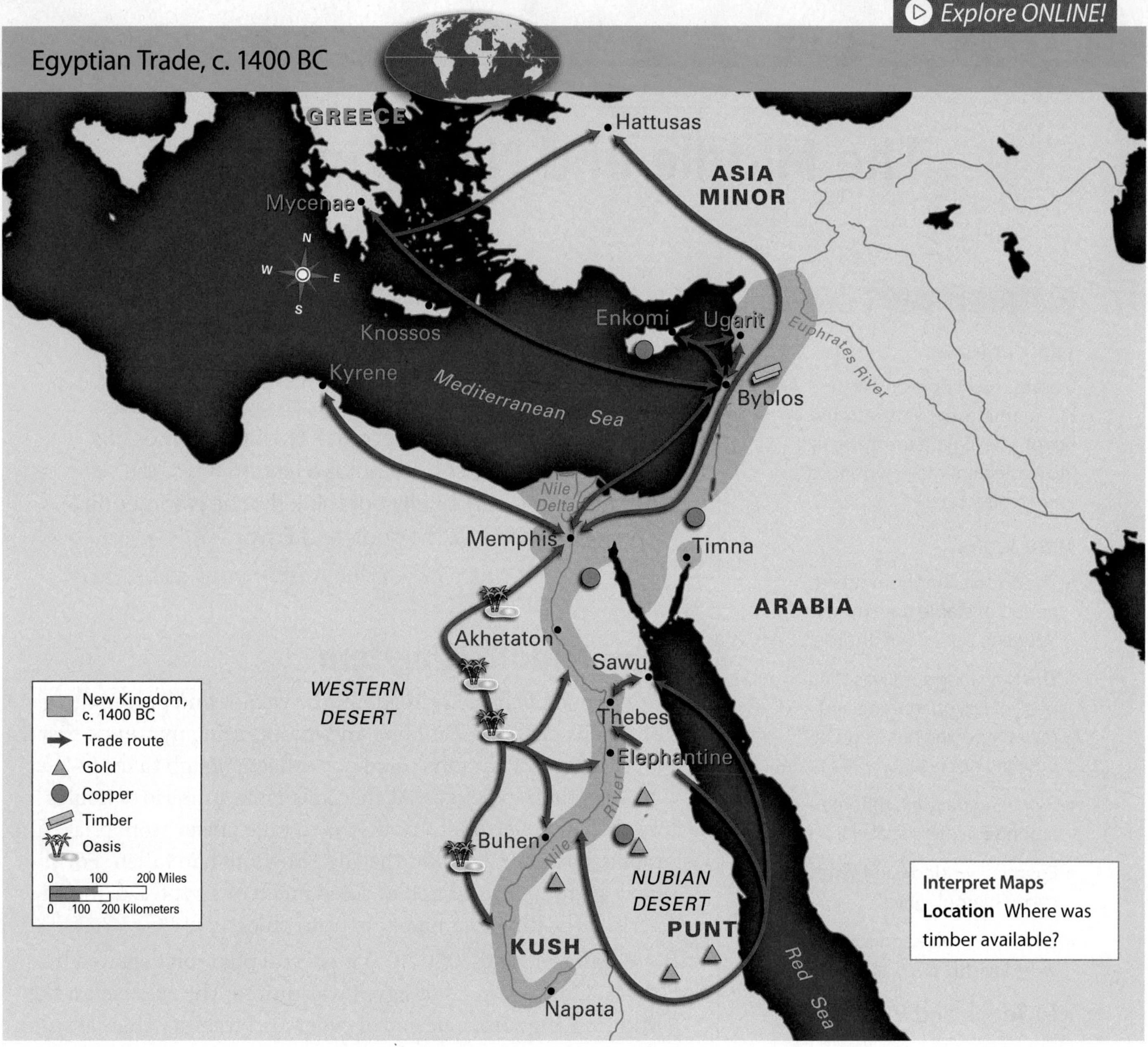

Interpret Maps
Location Where was timber available?

advanced weapons to conquer Lower Egypt. The Hyksos then ruled the region as pharaohs for 200 years.

The Egyptians eventually fought back. In the mid-1500s BC, Ahmose (AMH-ohs) of Thebes declared himself king and drove the Hyksos out of Egypt. Ahmose then ruled all of Egypt.

Reading Check
Summarize What caused the end of the Middle Kingdom?

The New Kingdom

Ahmose's rise to power marked the start of Egypt's 18th dynasty. More importantly, it was the start of the **New Kingdom,** the period during which Egypt reached the height of its power and glory. During the New Kingdom, which lasted from about 1550 to 1050 BC, conquest and trade brought wealth to the pharaohs.

Building an Empire After battling the Hyksos, Egypt's leaders feared future invasions. To prevent such invasions from occurring, they

BIOGRAPHY

Queen Hatshepsut Ruled c. 1503–1482 BC

Hatshepsut was married to the pharaoh Thutmose II, her half-brother. He died young, leaving the throne to Thutmose III, his son by another woman. Because Thutmose III was still very young, Hatshepsut took over power. Many people did not think women should rule, but Hatshepsut dressed as a man and called herself king. After she died, her stepson took back power and vandalized all the monuments she had built.

Identify Cause and Effect
What do you think caused Hatshepsut to dress like a man?

took control of all possible invasion routes into the kingdom. In the process, these leaders turned Egypt into an empire.

Egypt's first target was the homeland of the Hyksos. After taking over that area, the army continued north and conquered Syria. Egypt took over the entire eastern shore of the Mediterranean and the kingdom of **Kush,** south of Egypt. By the 1400s BC Egypt was the leading military power in the region. Its empire extended from the Euphrates River to southern Nubia.

Military conquests made Egypt rich as well as powerful. The kingdoms that Egypt conquered regularly sent gifts and treasure to their Egyptian conquerors. For example, the kingdom of Kush in Nubia sent yearly payments of gold, precious stones, and leopard skins to the pharaohs. In addition, Assyrian, Babylonian, and Hittite kings sent expensive gifts to Egypt in an effort to maintain good relations.

Growth and Effects of Trade As Egypt's empire expanded, so did its trade. Conquest brought Egyptian traders into contact with more distant lands that had valuable resources for trade. Profitable **trade routes,** or paths followed by traders, developed from Egypt to these lands. The Sinai Peninsula, for example, had large supplies of turquoise and copper.

One of Egypt's rulers who worked to increase trade was Queen Hatshepsut. She sent Egyptian traders south to trade with the kingdom of Punt on the Red Sea and north to trade with people in Asia Minor and Greece.

Hatshepsut and later pharaohs used the money they gained from trade to support the arts and architecture. Hatshepsut in particular is remembered for the many impressive monuments and temples built during her reign.

Invasions of Egypt Despite its military might, Egypt still faced threats to its power. In the 1200s BC the pharaoh Ramses (RAM-seez) II, or Ramses the Great, fought the Hittites, who came from Asia Minor. The two powers fought fiercely for years, but neither one could defeat the other. Finally, 15 years after the Battle of Kadesh in 1275 BC, both sides signed the Treaty of Kadesh. Some historians consider this to be the world's first peace treaty.

Historical Source

Ramses the Great

Ramses the Great had a poem praising him carved into the walls of the five temples, including the temple at Karnak. One verse of the poem praises Ramses as a great warrior and defender of Egypt.

> *"Gracious lord and bravest king, savior-guard Of Egypt in the battle, be our ward; Behold we stand along, in the hostile Hittite ring, Save us for the breath of life, Give deliverance from the strife, Oh! Protect us Ramses Miamun! Oh! Save us, mighty king!"*
>
> —Pen-ta-ur, quoted in *The World's Story*, edited by Eva March Tappan

Analyze Sources
According to the poem, from what group did Ramses protect the Egyptians?

Soon after Ramses the Great died, invaders called the Sea Peoples sailed into Southwest Asia. Little is known about these people. Historians are not even sure who they were. All we know is that they were strong warriors who had crushed the Hittites and destroyed cities in Southwest Asia. Only after 50 years of fighting were the Egyptians able to turn them back.

Egypt survived, but its empire in Asia was gone. Shortly after the invasions of the Hittites and the Sea Peoples, the New Kingdom came to an end. Ancient Egypt fell into a period of violence and disorder. Egypt would never regain its power.

Reading Check
Identify Cause and Effect What caused Egypt's growth of trade during the New Kingdom?

Work and Daily Life

Although Egyptian dynasties rose and fell, daily life for Egyptians did not change very much. But as the population grew, Egypt's society became even more complex.

A complex society requires people to take on different jobs. In Egypt, these jobs were often passed on within families. At a young age, boys started to learn their future jobs from their fathers.

Scribes After the priests and government officials, scribes were the most respected people in ancient Egypt. As members of the middle class, scribes worked for the government and the temples. This work involved keeping records and accounts. Scribes also wrote and copied religious and literary texts.

Artisans, Artists, and Architects Another group in society was made up of artisans whose jobs required advanced skills. Among the artisans who worked in Egypt were sculptors, builders, carpenters, jewelers, metalworkers, and leatherworkers. Artisans made items such as statues, furniture, jewelry, pottery, and shoes. Most artisans worked for the government or for temples. Egypt's artisans were admired and often paid fairly well.

Architects and artists were admired in Egypt as well. Architects designed the temples and royal tombs for which Egypt is famous. Talented architects could rise to become high government officials. Artists often worked for the state or for temples. Egyptian artists produced many different types of works. Many artists worked in the deep burial chambers of the pharaohs' tombs painting detailed pictures.

Merchants and Traders Although trade was important to Egypt, only a small group of Egyptians became merchants and traders. Some traveled long distances to buy and sell goods. On their journeys, merchants were usually accompanied by soldiers, scribes, and laborers.

Soldiers After the wars of the Middle Kingdom, Egypt established a professional army. The military offered people a chance to rise in social status. Soldiers received land as payment and could also keep any treasure they captured in war. Soldiers who excelled could be promoted to officer positions.

Farmers and Other Peasants As in the society of the Old Kingdom, Egyptian farmers and other peasants were toward the bottom of Egypt's social scale. These hardworking people made up the vast majority of Egypt's population.

Egyptian farmers grew crops to support their families. These farmers depended on the Nile's regular floods to grow their crops. Farmers used wooden hoes or plows pulled by cows to prepare the land before the flood. After the floodwaters had drained away, farmers planted seeds for crops such as wheat and barley. At the end of the growing season, Egypt's farmers worked together to gather the harvest.

Farmers had to give some of their crops to the pharaoh as taxes. These taxes were intended to pay the pharaoh for use of the land. Under Egyptian law, the pharaoh controlled all land in the kingdom.

All peasants, including farmers, were also subject to special duty. Under Egyptian law, the pharaoh could demand at any time that people work on projects, such as building pyramids, mining gold, or fighting in the army. The government paid the workers in grain.

Most Egyptians spent their days in the fields, plowing and harvesting their crops.

Slaves The few slaves in Egyptian society were considered lower than farmers. Many slaves were convicted criminals or prisoners captured in war. These slaves worked on farms, on building projects, in workshops, and in private households. Unlike most slaves in history, however, slaves in Egypt had some legal rights. Also, in some cases, they could earn their freedom.

Family Life in Egypt Family life was important. Most families lived in their own homes. Sometimes, unmarried female relatives lived with them. Men were expected to marry young so that they could start having children.

Most Egyptian women were devoted to their homes and families. Some women, however, did have jobs outside the home. A few women served as priestesses, and some worked as royal officials, administrators, or artisans. Unlike most women in ancient times, Egyptian women had a number of legal rights. They could own property, make **contracts**, and divorce their husbands. They could even keep their property after a divorce.

Academic Vocabulary
contracts binding legal agreements

Children's lives were not as structured as adults' lives were. Children played with toys such as dolls, tops, and clay animal figurines. Children also played ballgames and hunted. Most children, boys and girls, received some education. At school they learned morals, writing, math, and sports. At age 14, most boys left school to enter their father's profession. At that time, they took their place in Egypt's social structure.

Reading Check
Categorize What types of jobs existed in ancient Egypt?

Egyptian Achievements

If you were reading a book and saw pictures of folded cloth, a leg, a star, a bird, and a man holding a stick, would you know what it meant? You would if you were an ancient Egyptian. In the Egyptian writing system, or **hieroglyphics** (hy-ruh-GLIH-fiks), those five symbols together meant "to teach." Egyptian hieroglyphics were one of the world's first writing systems.

Writing in Ancient Egypt The earliest known examples of Egyptian writing are from around 3300 BC. These early Egyptian writings were carved in stone or on other hard materials. Later, Egyptians learned how to make **papyrus** (puh-PY-ruhs), a long-lasting, paperlike material made from reeds. The Egyptians made papyrus by pressing layers of reeds together and pounding them into sheets. These sheets were tough and durable, yet could be rolled into scrolls. Scribes wrote on papyrus using brushes and ink.

The hieroglyphic writing system used more than 600 symbols, mostly pictures of objects. Each symbol represented one or more sounds in the Egyptian language. For example, a picture of an owl represented the same sound as our letter *M*.

Hieroglyphics could be written either horizontally or vertically. They could be written from right to left or from left to right. These options made hieroglyphics flexible to write but difficult to read. The only way to tell which way a text is written is to look at individual symbols.

The Rosetta Stone Historians and archaeologists have known about hieroglyphics for centuries. For a long time, though, historians did not

Egyptian Writing

Egyptian hieroglyphics used picture symbols to represent sounds.

Symbol	Sound	Meaning
[hieroglyph]	Imn	Amon
[hieroglyph]	Tut	Image
☥	Ankh	Living
Translation—"Living image of Amon"		
[hieroglyph]	Heka	Ruler
[hieroglyph]	Iunu	Heliopolis
[hieroglyph]	Resy	Southern
Translation—"Ruler of Southern Heliopolis"		

Analyze Visuals
What does the symbol for *ruler* look like?

know how to read them. In fact, it was not until 1799 that a lucky discovery by a French soldier gave historians the key they needed to read ancient Egyptian writing.

That key was the **Rosetta Stone,** a huge, stone slab inscribed with hieroglyphics. In addition to the hieroglyphics, the Rosetta Stone had text in Greek and a later form of Egyptian. Because the message in all three languages was the same, scholars who knew Greek were able to figure out what the hieroglyphics said.

Egyptian Texts Because papyrus did not decay in Egypt's dry climate, many ancient Egyptian texts still survive. Historians today can read Egyptian government records, historical records, science texts, and medical manuals. In addition, many literary works have survived. Some of them, such as The Book of the Dead, tell about the afterlife. Others tell stories about gods and kings.

Reading Check
Elaborate Why is the Rosetta Stone an important artifact to world history?

Egyptian Architecture and Art

In addition to their writing system, the ancient Egyptians are famous for their magnificent architecture and art. You have already read about the Egyptians' most famous structures, the pyramids. But the Egyptians also built massive temples. They believed that temples were the homes of the gods. People visited the temples to worship, offer the gods gifts, and ask for favors.

Architecture Many Egyptian temples shared some similar features. Rows of stone **sphinxes**—imaginary creatures with the bodies of lions and the heads of other animals or humans—lined the path leading to the entrance. That entrance itself was a huge, thick gate. On either side of the gate might stand an **obelisk** (AH-buh-lisk), a tall, four-sided pillar that is pointed on top.

Inside, Egyptian temples were lavishly decorated. Huge columns supported the temple's roof. These columns were often covered with paintings and hieroglyphics, as were the temple walls. Statues of gods and pharaohs often stood along the walls as well. The sanctuary, the most sacred part of the building, was at the far end of the temple.

The Temple of Karnak was Egypt's largest temple. Other temples were built by Ramses the Great at Abu Simbel and Luxor. The temple at Abu Simbel is especially known for the huge statues that stand next to its entrance. The statues, which are 66 feet (20 m) tall and are carved out of sandstone cliffs, show Ramses the Great as pharaoh. Nearby are smaller statues of his family.

Paintings One reason Egypt's temples are so popular with tourists is the art they contain. The ancient Egyptians were masterful artists. Many of their greatest works were created to fill temples and the tombs of pharaohs and other nobles.

Egyptian art was filled with lively, colorful scenes. Detailed works covered the walls of temples and tombs. Artists also painted on canvas, papyrus, pottery, plaster, and wood. Most Egyptians never saw these paintings, however. Only kings, priests, and important people could enter temples and tombs, and even they rarely entered the tombs.

The temple at Abu Simbel features seated figures of Ramses the Great. Inside the temple are painted scenes from the Battle of Kadesh.

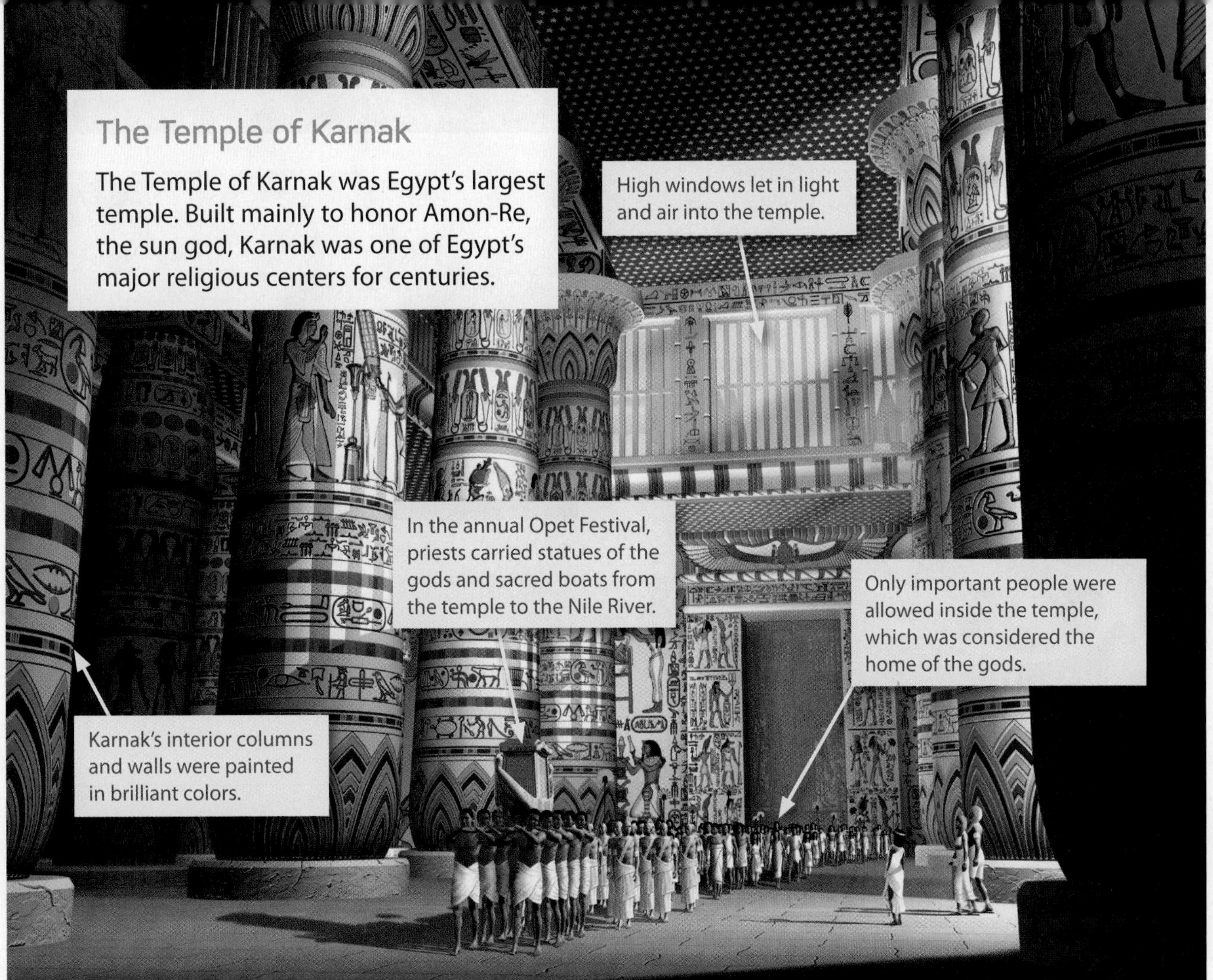

The subjects of Egyptian paintings vary widely. Some of the paintings show important historical events, such as the crowning of a new king or the founding of a temple. Others show major religious rituals. Still other paintings show scenes from everyday life, such as farming or hunting.

Egyptian painting has a distinctive style. People, for example, are drawn in a certain way. In Egyptian paintings, people's heads and legs are always seen from the side, but their upper bodies and shoulders are shown straight on. In addition, people do not all appear the same size. Important figures such as pharaohs appear huge in comparison to others, especially servants or conquered people. In contrast, Egyptian animals were usually drawn realistically.

Carvings and Jewelry Painting was not the only art form Egyptians practiced. The Egyptians were also skilled stoneworkers. Many tombs included huge statues and detailed carvings.

In addition, the Egyptians made lovely objects out of gold and precious stones. They made jewelry for both men and women. This jewelry included necklaces, bracelets, and collars. The Egyptians also used gold to make burial items for their pharaohs.

Over the years, treasure hunters emptied many pharaohs' tombs. At least one tomb, however, was not disturbed. In 1922 some archaeologists

Treasures of King Tut's Tomb

In 1922 the archaeologist Howard Carter discovered the tomb of King Tut. Unlike most Egyptian tombs, it had never been robbed and was still filled with treasures.

King Tut's sarcophagus rests near a wall painting showing his journey through the afterlife.

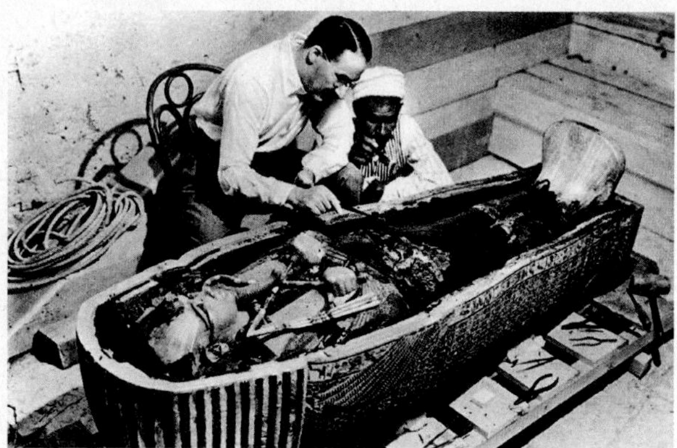

Howard Carter examining King Tut's coffin in 1922

Analyze Visuals
What might archaeologists learn about ancient Egypt from King Tut's tomb?

Reading Check
Summarize What types of artwork were contained in Egyptian tombs?

found the tomb of King Tutankhamen (too-tang-KAHM-uhn), or King Tut. The tomb was filled with many treasures, including boxes of jewelry, robes, a burial mask, and ivory statues. King Tut's treasures have taught us much about Egyptian burial practices and beliefs.

Summary and Preview The Egyptians developed one of the best-known cultures of the ancient world. Next, you will learn about a culture that developed in the shadow of Egypt—Kush.

Lesson 5 Assessment

Review Ideas, Terms, and Places

1. a. **Define** What was the Middle Kingdom?
   b. **Analyze** How did Ahmose manage to become king of all Egypt?
2. a. **Recall** What two things brought wealth to the pharaohs during the New Kingdom?
   b. **Compare** What did Hatshepsut and Ramses the Great do as pharaohs of Egypt?
3. a. **Identify** What job employed the majority of the people in Egypt?
   b. **Analyze** What rights did Egyptian women have?
   c. **Elaborate** Why do you think scribes were so honored in Egyptian society?
4. a. **Define** What are hieroglyphics?
   b. **Contrast** How was hieroglyphic writing different from our writing today?
   c. **Evaluate** Why was the Rosetta Stone important?
5. a. **Describe** What were two ways the Egyptians decorated their temples?
   b. **Evaluate** Why do you think pharaohs like Ramses the Great built huge temples?
   c. **Recall** Why did Egyptians fill tombs with art, jewelry, and other treasures?

Critical Thinking

6. **Categorize** Draw pyramids like the ones shown. Fill in the pyramids with the political and military factors that led to the rise and fall of the Middle and New Kingdoms. Using the chart, answer the following: What common factors led to the rise and fall of these kingdoms?

Rise | Fall — Middle Kingdom
Rise | Fall — New Kingdom

Kingdoms of Kush

The Big Idea

The kingdoms of Kush, which arose south of Egypt, developed advanced civilizations with large trading networks.

Main Ideas

- Geography helped early Kush civilization develop in Nubia.
- Kush and Egypt traded, but they also fought.
- Later, Kush became a trading power with a unique culture.
- Both internal and external factors led to the decline of Kush.

Key Terms and Places

Nubia
ebony
ivory
Meroë
trade network
merchants
exports
imports

If YOU lived there . . .

You live along the Nile River, where it moves quickly through rapids. A few years ago, armies from the powerful kingdom of Egypt took over your country. Some Egyptians have moved to your town. They bring new customs, which many people are beginning to imitate. Now your sister has a new baby and wants to give it an Egyptian name! This upsets many people in your family.

How do you feel about following Egyptian customs?

Geography and Early Kush

South of Egypt along the Nile, a group of people settled in the region we now call Nubia. These Africans established the first large kingdom in the interior of Africa. We know this kingdom by the name the ancient Egyptians gave it—Kush. Development of Kushite civilization was greatly influenced by the geography and resources of the region.

The Land of Nubia **Nubia** is a region in northeast Africa. It lies on the Nile River south of Egypt. Today, desert covers much of Nubia, located in the present-day country of Sudan. In ancient times, however, the region was much more fertile. Heavy rainfall flooded the Nile every year. These floods provided a rich layer of silt to nearby lands. The kingdom of Kush developed in this fertile area.

Ancient Nubia was rich in valuable minerals such as gold, copper, and stone. These natural resources played a major role in the area's history and contributed to its wealth.

Early Civilization in Nubia Like all early civilizations, the people of Nubia depended on agriculture for their food. Fortunately for them, the Nile's floods allowed the Nubians to plant both summer and winter crops. Among the crops they grew were wheat, barley, and other grains. Besides farmland, the banks of the river provided grazing land for cattle and other livestock. As a result, farming villages thrived all along the Nile by about 3500 BC.

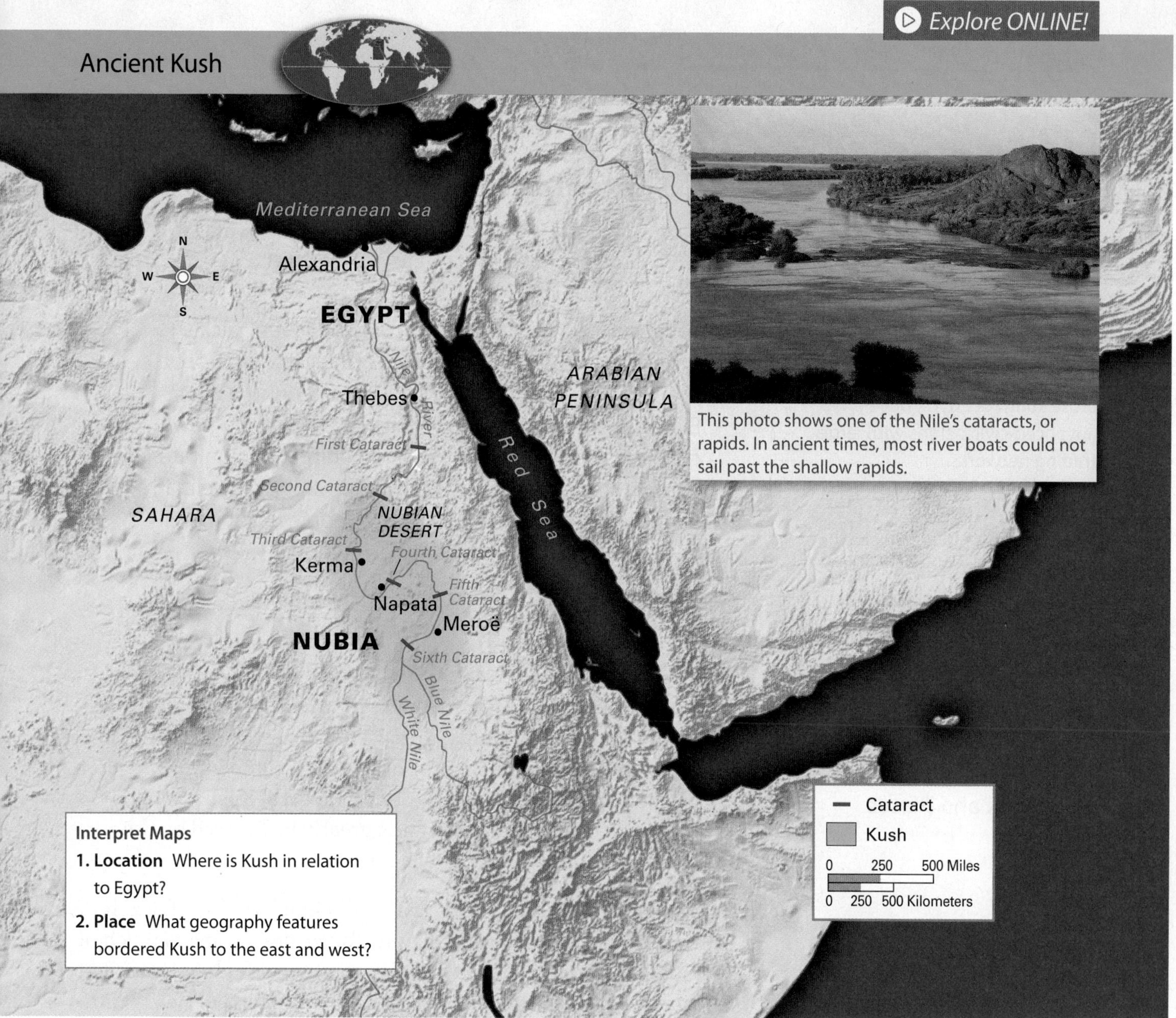

This photo shows one of the Nile's cataracts, or rapids. In ancient times, most river boats could not sail past the shallow rapids.

Interpret Maps

1. **Location** Where is Kush in relation to Egypt?
2. **Place** What geography features bordered Kush to the east and west?

Over time, some farmers became richer and more successful than others. These farmers became village leaders. Sometime around 2000 BC, one of these leaders took control of other villages and made himself king of the region. His new kingdom was called Kush.

The early kings of Kush ruled from their capital at Kerma (KAR-muh). This city was located on the Nile just south of the third cataract. Because the Nile's cataracts made parts of the river hard to pass through, they were natural barriers against invaders. For many years, the cataracts kept Kush safe from the powerful Egyptian kingdom to the north.

As time passed, Kushite society grew more complex. In addition to farmers and herders, some Kushites became priests or artisans. Early Kush was influenced by cultures to the south. Later, Egypt played a greater role in Kush's history.

Reading Check
Find Main Ideas
How did geography help civilization grow in Nubia?

Kush and Egypt

Kush and Egypt were neighbors. At times the neighbors lived in peace with each other and helped each other prosper. For example, Kush became a supplier of slaves and raw materials to Egypt. The Kushites sent materials such as gold, copper, and stone to Egypt. The slaves were forced to be domestic servants and soldiers in pharaoh's army. The Kushites also sent the Egyptians **ebony,** a type of dark, heavy wood, and **ivory,** a white material taken from elephant tusks.

Egypt's Conquest of Kush Relations between Kush and Egypt were not always peaceful. As Kush grew wealthy from trade, its army grew stronger as well. Egypt's rulers soon feared that Kush would grow even stronger. They were afraid that a powerful Kush might attack Egypt.

To prevent such an attack, the pharaoh Thutmose I sent an army to take control of Kush around 1500 BC. The pharaoh's army conquered all of Nubia north of the Fifth Cataract. As a result, the kingdom of Kush became part of Egypt.

After his army's victory, the pharaoh destroyed the Kushite palace at Kerma. Later pharaohs—including Ramses the Great—built huge temples in what had been Kushite territory.

Effects of the Conquest Kush remained an Egyptian territory for about 450 years. During that time, Egypt's influence over Kush grew tremendously. Many Egyptians settled in Kush. Egyptian became the language of the region. Many Kushites used Egyptian names and wore Egyptian-style clothing. They also adopted Egyptian religious practices.

Early in its history, Egypt dominated Kush, forcing Kushites to give tribute to Egypt.

A Change in Power In the mid-1000s BC the New Kingdom in Egypt was ending. As the power of Egypt's pharaohs declined, Kushite leaders regained control of Kush. Kush once again became independent.

We know almost nothing about the history of the Kushites for about 200 years after they regained independence from Egypt. Kush is not mentioned in any historical records until the 700s BC, when armies from Kush swept into Egypt and conquered it.

The Conquest of Egypt By around 850 BC, Kush had regained its strength. It was once again as strong as it had been before it was conquered by Egypt. Because the Egyptians had captured the old capital at Kerma, the kings of Kush ruled from the city of Napata. Napata was located on the Nile, about 100 miles (161 km) southeast of Kerma.

As Kush was growing stronger, Egypt was losing power. A series of weak pharaohs left Egypt open to attack. In the 700s BC a Kushite king, Kashta, took advantage of Egypt's weakness and attacked it. By about 751 BC he had conquered Upper Egypt. He then established relations with Lower Egypt.

After Kashta died, his son Piankhi (PYANG-kee) continued to attack Egypt. The armies of Kush captured many cities, including Egypt's ancient capital. Piankhi fought the Egyptians because he believed that the gods wanted him to rule all of Egypt. By the time he died in about 716 BC, Piankhi had accomplished this task. His kingdom extended north from Napata all the way to the Nile Delta.

The Kushite Dynasty After Piankhi died, his brother Shabaka (SHAB-uh-kuh) took control of the kingdom and declared himself pharaoh. His declaration marked the beginning of Egypt's Twenty-fifth, or Kushite, Dynasty.

Shabaka and later rulers of his dynasty tried to restore many old Egyptian cultural practices. Some of these practices had died out during Egypt's period of weakness. For example, Shabaka was buried in a pyramid. The Egyptians had stopped building pyramids for their rulers centuries earlier.

The Kushite rulers of Egypt built new temples to Egyptian gods and restored old ones. They also worked to preserve many Egyptian writings. As a result, Egyptian culture thrived during the Kushite Dynasty.

The End of Kushite Rule in Egypt The Kushite Dynasty remained strong in Egypt for about 40 years. In the 670s BC, however, the powerful army of the Assyrians from Mesopotamia invaded Egypt. The Assyrians' iron weapons were better than the Kushites' bronze weapons, and the Kushites were slowly pushed out of Egypt. In just ten years, the Assyrians had driven the Kushite forces completely out of Egypt.

Reading Check
Contrast How did Kushite culture differ before and after the Egyptian conquest of Kush?

Later Kush

After they lost control of Egypt, the people of Kush devoted themselves to improving agriculture and trade. They hoped to make their country rich

When the Assyrians invaded Egypt with their iron weapons, they forced Kush's rulers out of Egypt and south into Nubia.

again. Within a few centuries, Kush had indeed become a rich and powerful kingdom once more.

Kush's Iron Industry During this period, the economic center of Kush was **Meroë** (MER-oh-wee), the new Kushite capital. Meroë's location on the east bank of the Nile helped Kush's economy. Gold could be found nearby, as could forests of ebony and other wood. More importantly, the area around Meroë was rich in deposits of iron ore.

In this location, the Kushites developed an iron industry. Because resources such as iron ore and wood for furnaces were easily available, the industry grew quickly.

Expansion of Trade In time, Meroë became the center of a large **trade network,** a system of people in different lands who trade goods. The Kushites sent goods down the Nile to Egypt. From there, Egyptian and Greek **merchants,** or traders, carried goods to ports on the Mediterranean and Red seas and to southern Africa. These goods may have eventually reached India and China.

Kush's **exports**—items sent to other regions for trade—included gold, pottery, iron tools, slaves, and ivory. Merchants from Kush also exported leopard skins, ostrich feathers, and elephants. In return, Kushites received **imports**—goods brought in from other regions—such as jewelry and other luxury items from Egypt, Asia, and lands around the Mediterranean Sea.

Kushite Culture As Kushite trade grew, merchants came into contact with people from many other cultures. As a result, the people of Kush combined customs from other cultures with their own unique culture.

Kush's Trade Network

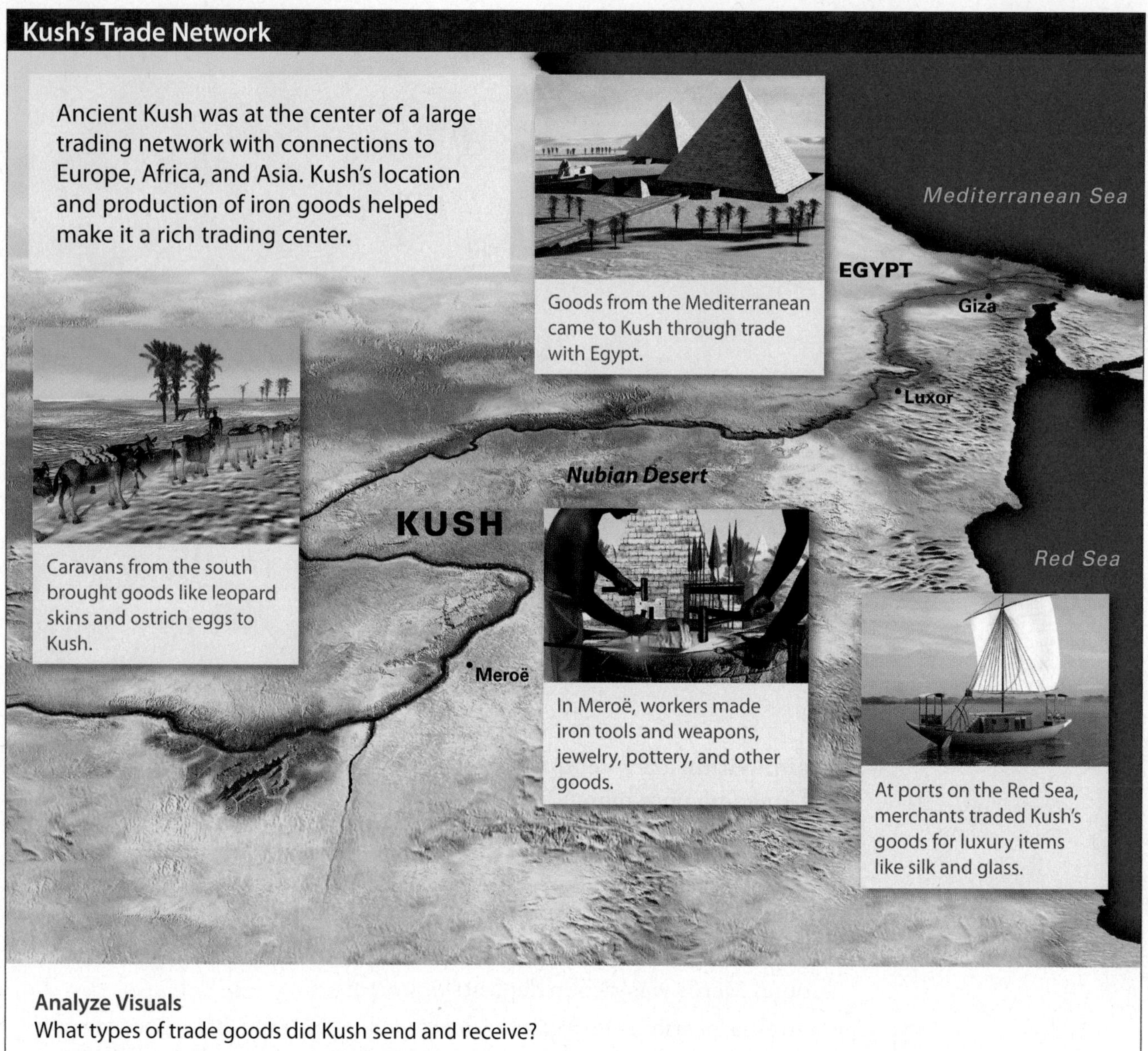

Goods from the Mediterranean came to Kush through trade with Egypt.

Caravans from the south brought goods like leopard skins and ostrich eggs to Kush.

In Meroë, workers made iron tools and weapons, jewelry, pottery, and other goods.

At ports on the Red Sea, merchants traded Kush's goods for luxury items like silk and glass.

Analyze Visuals
What types of trade goods did Kush send and receive?

The most obvious influence on the culture of Kush was Egypt. Many buildings in Meroë, especially temples, resembled those in Egypt. Many people in Kush worshiped Egyptian gods and wore Egyptian clothing. Like Egyptian rulers, Kush's rulers used the title *pharaoh* and were buried in pyramids.

Many elements of Kushite culture were unique and not borrowed from anywhere else. For example, Kushite daily life and houses were different from those in other places. One Greek geographer noted some of these differences.

> "The houses in the cities are formed by interweaving split pieces of palm wood or of bricks . . . They hunt elephants, lions, and panthers. There are also serpents, which encounter elephants, and there are many other kinds of wild animals."
>
> —Strabo, from *Geography*

In addition to Egyptian gods, Kushites worshiped their own gods. For example, their most important god was the lion-headed god Apedemek. The people of Kush also developed their own written language, known today as Meroitic. Unfortunately, historians have not yet been able to interpret the Meroitic language.

Women in Kushite Society Kushite women were expected to be active in their society. Like Kushite men, women worked long hours in the fields. They also raised children, cooked, and performed other household tasks. During times of war, many women fought alongside men.

Academic Vocabulary
authority power or influence

Some Kushite women rose to positions of **authority,** especially religious authority. For example, King Piankhi made his sister a powerful priestess. Later rulers followed his example and made other princesses priestesses as well. Other women from royal families led the ceremonies in which new kings were crowned.

Some Kushite women had even more power. These women served as co-rulers with their husbands or sons. A few Kushite women, such as Queen Shanakhdakheto (shah-nahk-dah-KEE-toh), even ruled the empire alone. Several other queens ruled Kush later, helping increase the strength and wealth of the kingdom.

Reading Check
Contrast In what ways were the society and culture of Kush unique?

Decline and Defeat

The Kushite kingdom centered at Meroë reached its height in the first century BC. Four centuries later, Kush had collapsed. Developments both inside and outside the empire led to its downfall.

Loss of Resources A series of problems within Kush weakened its economic power. One possible problem was that farmers allowed their cattle to overgraze the land. When the cows ate all the grass, there was nothing to hold the soil down. As a result, wind blew the soil away. Without this soil, farmers could not produce enough food for Kush's people.

In addition, ironmakers probably used up the forests near Meroë. As wood became scarce, furnaces shut down. Kush could no longer produce

BIOGRAPHY

Queen Shanakhdakheto Ruled 170–150 BC

Historians believe Queen Shanakhdakheto was the first woman to rule Kush. But because we can't understand Meroitic writing, we know very little about Queen Shanakhdakheto. Most of what we know about her comes from carvings found in her tomb, one of the largest pyramids at Meroë. Based on these carvings, many historians think she probably gained power after her father or husband died.

Draw Inferences What information do you think the carvings in the queen's tomb contained?

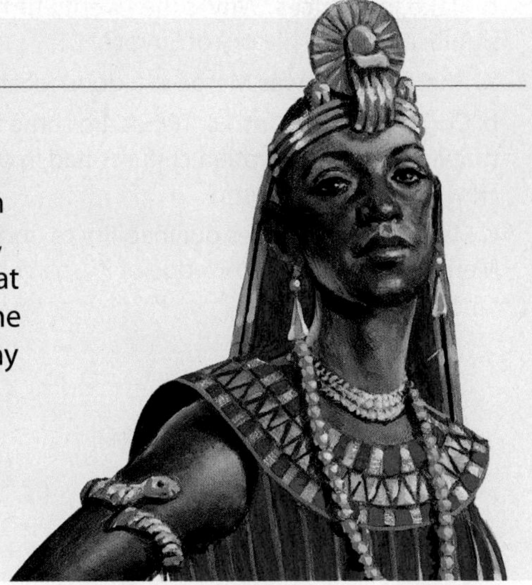

enough weapons or trade goods. As a result, Kush's military and economic power declined.

Trade Rivals Kush was also weakened by a loss of trade. Foreign merchants set up new trade routes that went around Kush. For example, a new trade route bypassed Kush in favor of a nearby kingdom, Aksum (AHK-soom).

Rise of Aksum Aksum was located southeast of Kush on the Red Sea, in present-day Ethiopia and Eritrea. In the first two centuries AD, Aksum grew wealthy from trade. But Aksum's wealth and power came at the expense of Kush. As Kush's power declined, Aksum became the most powerful state in the region.

By the AD 300s, Kush had lost much of its wealth and military might. Seeing that the Kushites were weak, the king of Aksum sent an army to conquer his former trade rival. In about AD 350, the army of Aksum's King Ezana (AY-zah-nah) destroyed Meroë and took over the kingdom of Kush.

In the late 300s, the rulers of Aksum became Christian. Their new religion reshaped culture throughout Nubia, and the last influences of Kush disappeared.

Reading Check
Summarize What internal problems caused Kush's power to decline?

Summary In this lesson, you learned that Kush was conquered by Egypt, but later the Kushites controlled Egypt. You also learned about the rise and fall of a powerful Kushite kingdom centered in Meroë.

Lesson 6 Assessment

Review Ideas, Terms, and Places

1. **a. Identify** On which river did Kush develop?
   b. Analyze How did Nubia's natural resources influence the early history of Kush?
2. **a. Compare** How did trade and conquest have similar effects on the people of Kush and Egypt?
   b. Evaluate Why do you think Thutmose I destroyed the Kushite palace at Kerma?
   c. Make Inferences Why is the Twenty-fifth Dynasty significant in the history of Egypt?
3. **a. Analyze** Why was Meroë in a good location?
   b. Compare and Contrast What are some features that Kushite and Egyptian cultures had in common? How were they different?
   c. Elaborate How does our inability to understand Meroitic affect our knowledge of Kush's culture?
4. **a. Identify** What kingdom conquered Kush in about AD 350?
   b. Summarize What was the impact of new trade routes on Kush?

Critical Thinking

5. **Identify Causes** Review your notes to identify causes of the rise and the fall of the Kushite kingdom centered at Meroë. Use a chart like this one to record the causes.

Causes of rise	Causes of fall

Social Studies Skills

Analyze Primary and Secondary Sources

Define the Skill

Primary sources are materials created by people who lived during the times they describe. Examples include letters, diaries, and photographs. Secondary sources are accounts written later by someone who was not present. They often teach about or discuss a historical topic. This module is an example of a secondary source.

By studying both types, you can get a better picture of a historical period or event. However, not all sources are accurate or reliable. Use these checklists to judge which sources are reliable.

Checklist for Primary Sources

- Who is the author? Is he or she trustworthy?
- Was the author present at the event described in the source? Might the author have based his or her writing on rumor, gossip, or hearsay?
- How soon after the event occurred was the source written? The more time that passed, the greater the chance for error.
- What is the purpose? Authors can have reasons to exaggerate—or even lie—to suit their own purposes. Look for evidence of emotion, opinion, or bias in the source. They can affect the accuracy.
- Can the information in the source be verified in other primary or secondary sources?

Checklist for Secondary Sources

- Who is the author? What are his or her qualifications? Is he or she an authority on the subject?
- Where did the author get his or her information? Good historians always tell you where they got their information.
- Has the author drawn valid conclusions?

Learn the Skill

"The Egyptians quickly extended their military and commercial influence over an extensive [wide] region that included the rich provinces of Syria . . . and the numbers of Egyptian slaves grew swiftly."

—C. Warren Hollister, from *Roots of the Western Tradition*

"Let me tell you how the soldier fares . . . how he goes to Syria, and how he marches over the mountains. His bread and water are borne [carried] upon his shoulders like the load of [a donkey]; . . . and the joints of his back are bowed [bent] . . . When he reaches the enemy, . . . he has no strength in his limbs."

—from *Wings of the Falcon: Life and Thought of Ancient Egypt*, translated by Joseph Kaster

1. Which of the above passages is a primary source, and which is a secondary source?
2. Is there evidence of opinion, emotion, or bias in the second passage? Why or why not?
3. Which passage would be better for learning about what life was like for Egyptian soldiers, and why?

Practice the Skill

Refer to the Ramses the Great Historical Source in this module to answer the following questions.

1. Identify the primary source in the biography.
2. What biases or other issues might affect the reliability or accuracy of this primary source?

Module 6 Assessment

Review Vocabulary, Terms, and Places

Using your own paper, complete the sentences below by providing the correct term for each blank.

1. Mesopotamia is part of the ________________, a large arc of rich farmland.
2. Sumerian society was organized in ______________, which consisted of a city and the surrounding lands.
3. Instead of using pictographs, Sumerians developed a type of writing called ____________.
4. The ____________ is the longest river in the world and brought life to Egypt.
5. The art and science of building is known as _______________.
6. Egypt reached the height of its power during the _______________.
7. The ____________ allowed scholars to translate Egyptian hieroglyphics.
8. Goods were carried to ports by traders called _____________.

Comprehension and Critical Thinking

Lesson 1

9. a. **Analyze** How did irrigation systems allow civilization to develop?

   b. **Elaborate** Do you think a division of labor is necessary for civilization to develop? Why or why not?

Lesson 2

10. a. **Identify** What land did the first empire include?

    b. **Compare and Contrast** How was Sumerian society similar to our society today? How was it different?

Lesson 3

11. a. **Draw Conclusions** Why do you think peoples banded together to fight the Assyrians?

    b. **Evaluate** Do you think Hammurabi was more effective as a ruler or as a military leader? Why?

Lesson 4

12. a. **Identify** Where was most of Egypt's fertile land located?

    b. **Make Inferences** Why did Memphis become a center of Egyptian society?

    c. **Analyze** How were beliefs about the afterlife linked to items placed in tombs?

Lesson 5

13. a. **Analyze** What two factors contributed to Egypt's wealth during the New Kingdom?

    b. **Contrast** How are the symbols in Egyptian hieroglyphics different from the symbols used in our writing system?

Lesson 6

14. a. **Analyze** Why did the relationship between Kush and Egypt change more than once over the centuries?

    b. **Sequence** List in order three steps that led to the development of civilization in the Fertile Crescent and the Nile Valley.

    c. **Synthesize** Create a two column table. Label the columns "Category" and "Similarities." Then add four rows labeled "Geography," "Technology," "Government," and "Economy." List what the Sumerian, Egyptian, and Kush civilizations had in common in each category. Then use your table to explain how those common characteristics shaped early civilizations.

Module 6 Assessment, continued

Reading Skills

Paraphrase *Use the Reading Skills taught in this module to answer the question about the paragraph below.*

Mesopotamia was the home of many ancient civilizations. The first of these civilizations was the Sumerians. They lived in Mesopotamia by 3000 BC. There they built cities, created a system of writing, and invented the wheel.

15. Read the paragraph carefully. Then rewrite the paragraph in your own words, taking care to include all the main ideas.

Social Studies Skills 21st CENTURY

Analyze Primary and Secondary Sources *Use the Social Studies Skills taught in this module to answer the questions.*

Each of the questions below lists two sources that a historian might consult to answer a question about ancient Egypt. For each question, decide which source is likely to be more accurate or reliable and why. Then indicate whether that source is a primary or secondary source.

16. What were Egyptian beliefs about the afterlife?

- **a.** Egyptian tomb inscriptions
- **b.** writings by a priest who visited Egypt in 1934

17. Why did the Nile flood every year?

- **a.** songs of praise to the Nile River written by Egyptian priests
- **b.** a book about the rivers of Africa written by a modern geographer

18. What kind of warrior was Ramses the Great?

- **a.** a poem in praise of Ramses
- **b.** a description of a battle in which Ramses fought, written by an impartial observer

Map Activity

19. Ancient Egypt On a separate sheet of paper, match the letters on the map with their correct labels.

Lower Egypt	Red Sea
Mediterranean Sea	Sinai Peninsula
Nile River	Upper Egypt

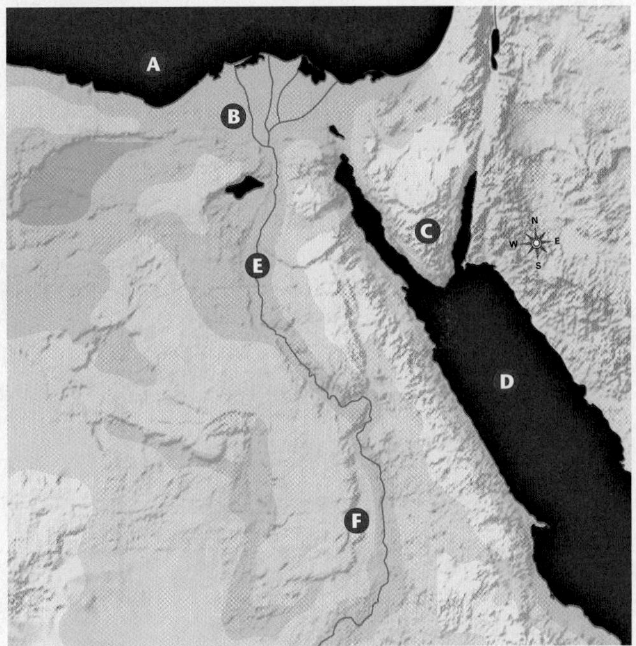

Focus on Writing

20. Write a Research Paper Would you like to travel back in time to ancient Nubia and explore the wonders of that era? Use Lesson 6 and both primary and secondary sources to find out about the people, their customs, and their homes. Then formulate a statement on what was important to the people of ancient Nubia and why. Formulate appropriate questions to guide your research. You should gather relevant information from multiple print and digital sources. Be sure to apply key terms acquired from the lesson in your writing. Your essay should be focused and organized with a clear introduction, supporting paragraphs, and a conclusion. Check your paper for spelling, grammar, capitalization, and punctuation.

Module 7

World Religions of Southwest Asia

Essential Question

How do religious beliefs shape people's lives and behaviors?

About the Photo: Jerusalem is an important place for Jews, Christians, and Muslims. This photo shows the Dome of the Rock (foreground), a holy site for Muslims, and the Christian Church of Mary Magdalene (background, left).

Explore ONLINE!

VIDEOS, including . . .
- Sacred Places: Jerusalem
- The Birth of Christianity

- Document-Based Investigations
- Graphic Organizers
- Interactive Games
- Image Carousel: Jewish Texts
- Interactive Map: Paul's Journeys
- Image with Slider: The Five Pillars of Islam

In this module, you will learn about the origins and spread of three major world religions—Judaism, Christianity, and Islam.

What You Will Learn

Lesson 1: Origins of Judaism. 245
The Big Idea The Israelites formed a great kingdom in Israel and started a religion called Judaism.

Lesson 2: Origins of Christianity 253
The Big Idea Christianity, a religion based on the life and teachings of Jesus of Nazareth, spread throughout the Roman Empire.

Lesson 3: Origins of Islam. 261
The Big Idea Islam, a religion based on the teachings of Muhammad, arose in Arabia and is based on the sacred texts called the Qur'an and the Sunnah.

Islam One of the world's largest religions is practiced by people all around the world. These Muslims, or people who practice Islam, are in India.

Judaism Jews pray at the Western Wall in Jerusalem. The wall is part of the Second Temple, which was built by ancient Hebrews.

Christianity Christianity is based on the life and teachings of Jesus, shown here in his mother's arms.

Use Context Clues—Synonyms

FOCUS ON READING

You have probably discovered that geography is a subject with many new words and terms. What if you don't remember or don't know what a word means? You may be able to use context clues to determine its meaning. Context clues are words near the unfamiliar word that indicate its meaning.

One helpful context clue is the synonym—words or phrases that mean the same as the new word. Look for synonyms in the words and sentences surrounding an unfamiliar term. Synonyms can help you understand the meaning of the new word. They may come in the same sentence or in the sentence following the words they define. Notice how the following passage uses synonyms to define the word *fasting*.

The fourth pillar of Islam is *fasting*. Muslims fast, or go without food or drink, during the holy month of Ramadan (RAH-muh-dahn). The Qur'an says Allah began his revelations to Muhammad in this month. Throughout Ramadan, most Muslims will not eat or drink anything between dawn and sunset.

1. **Look for words or phrases that mean the same thing.**
   The second and fourth sentences describe how Muslims do not eat or drink during certain times.
2. **Substitute the synonym for the new word to confirm its meaning.**
   The fourth pillar of Islam is going without food or drink.

YOU TRY IT!

As you read the following sentences, look for synonyms that mean the same as the italicized words. Then use a graphic organizer like the one shown here to define each italicized word. Make sure to ask your teacher or a classmate for help if you do not understand a word.

Christians further believe that after the *Resurrection*, or rise from the dead, Jesus appeared to some groups of his *disciples* (di-SY-puhls), or followers. Jesus stayed with these disciples for the next 40 days, teaching them and giving them instructions about how to pass on his teachings.

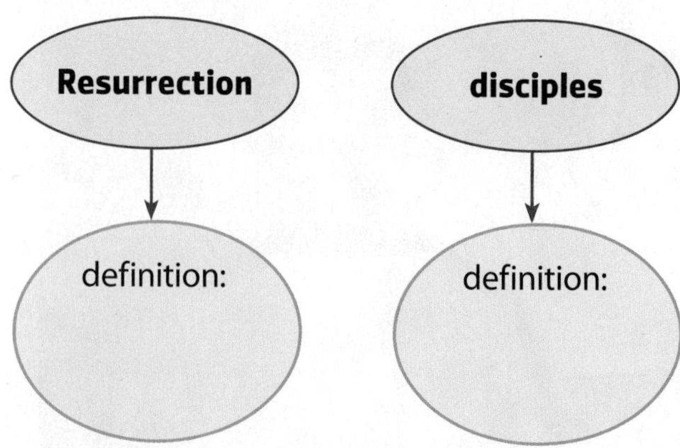

As you read this module, look for context clues that help you to understand unfamiliar words.

Origins of Judaism

The Big Idea

The Israelites formed a great kingdom in Israel and started a religion called Judaism.

Main Ideas

- The Jews' early history began in Canaan and ended when the Romans forced them out of Israel.
- Jewish beliefs in God, justice, and law anchor their society.
- Jewish sacred texts describe the laws and principles of Judaism.
- Traditions and holy days celebrate the history and religion of the Jewish people.

Key Terms and Places

Judaism
Canaan
Exodus
rabbis
monotheism
Torah

If YOU lived there ...

You and your family are herders, looking after large flocks of sheep. Your grandfather is the leader of your tribe. One day your grandfather says that your whole family will be moving to a new country where there is more water and food for your flocks. The trip will be long and difficult.

How do you feel about going to a new land?

Early History

Sometime between 2000 and 1500 BC, a new people appeared in Southwest Asia. They were the Hebrews (HEE-brooz), ancestors of the Israelites and Jews. Much of what is known about their early history comes from the work of archaeologists and from accounts written by Hebrew scribes. These accounts describe their early history and the laws of **Judaism** (JOO-dee-i-zuhm), their religion. In time these accounts became the Hebrew Bible.

Beginnings in Canaan and Egypt The Bible traces the Hebrews back to a man named Abraham. One day, the Bible says, God told Abraham to leave his home in Mesopotamia. He was to take his family on a long journey to the west. God promised to lead Abraham to a new land and make his descendants into a mighty nation.

Abraham left Mesopotamia and settled in **Canaan** (KAY-nuhn) on the Mediterranean Sea. Some of his descendants, the Israelites, lived in Canaan for many years. Later, however, some Hebrews moved to Egypt, perhaps because of famine in Canaan.

The Israelites lived well in Egypt, and their population grew. This growth worried Egypt's ruler, the pharaoh. He feared that the Israelites might soon become too powerful. To stop this from happening, the pharaoh made the Israelites slaves.

The Exodus According to the Hebrew Bible, a leader named Moses appeared among the Israelites in Egypt. In the 1200s BC, God told Moses to lead the Israelites out of Egypt. Moses went to the pharaoh and demanded that he free the Israelites. The pharaoh refused. Soon afterward a series of terrible plagues, or disasters, struck Egypt.

Timeline: Early Hebrew History

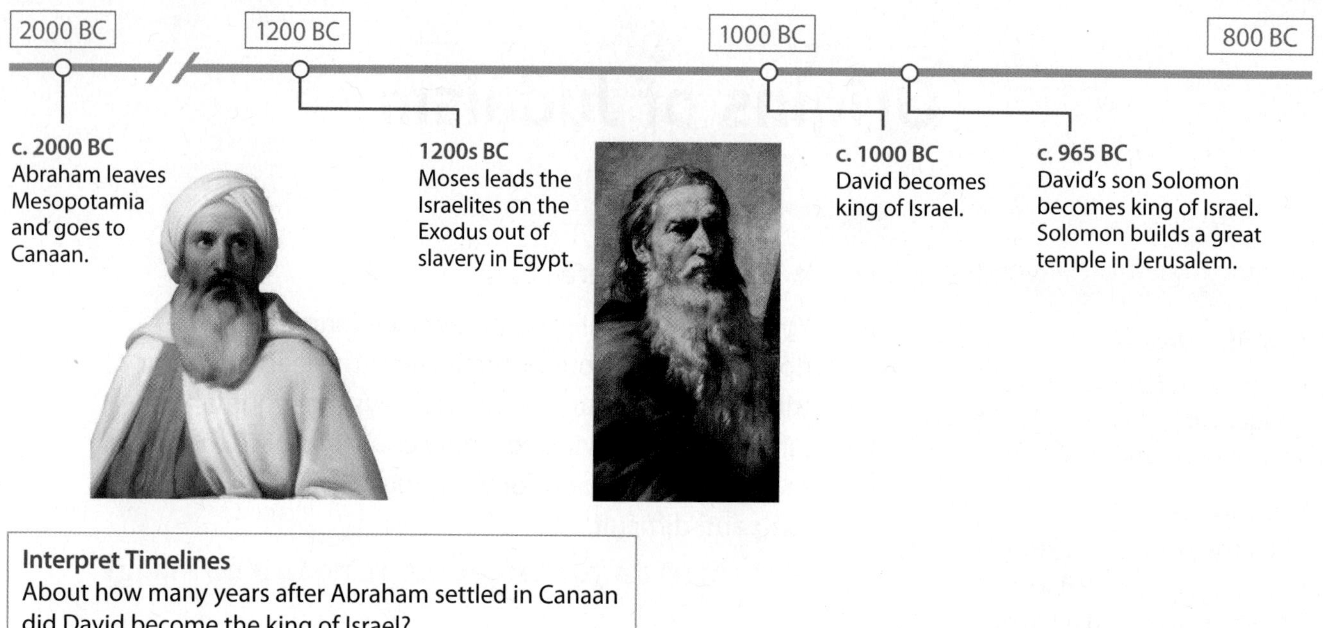

Interpret Timelines
About how many years after Abraham settled in Canaan did David become the king of Israel?

The plagues frightened the pharaoh so much that he agreed to free the Israelites. Overjoyed with the news of their release, Moses led his people out of Egypt in a journey called the **Exodus.** To the Israelites, the release from slavery proved that God was protecting and watching over them.

For years after their release, the Israelites traveled through the desert, trying to return to Canaan. On their journey, they reached a mountain called Sinai. The Hebrew Bible says that while Moses was on the mountain, God gave him two stone tablets. On the tablets was written a code of moral laws known as the Ten Commandments. These laws shaped Jewish society.

Once the Israelites reached Canaan, they had to fight to gain control of the land. After they conquered Canaan and settled down on the land, the Israelites built their own society.

A Series of Invasions The Israelites soon faced more threats to their land. Invaders swept through the region in the mid-1000s BC. For a while, strong kings, like David and Solomon, kept Israel together. Israel even grew rich through trade and expanded its territory. With their riches, the Israelites built a great Temple to God in Jerusalem.

Some years later when one king died, the Israelites could not agree on who would be the next king. This conflict caused Israel to split into two kingdoms, one called Israel and one called Judah (JOO-duh). The people of Judah became known as Jews.

The two new kingdoms lasted for a few centuries. Israel eventually fell to invaders about 722 BC. Judah lasted until 586 BC, when invaders captured Jerusalem and destroyed Solomon's Temple. They sent the Jews out of Jerusalem as slaves. When these invaders were themselves conquered, some Jews returned home. Others moved to other places in Southwest Asia. Scholars call the dispersal of Jews outside of Israel and Judah the Diaspora (dy-AS-pruh).

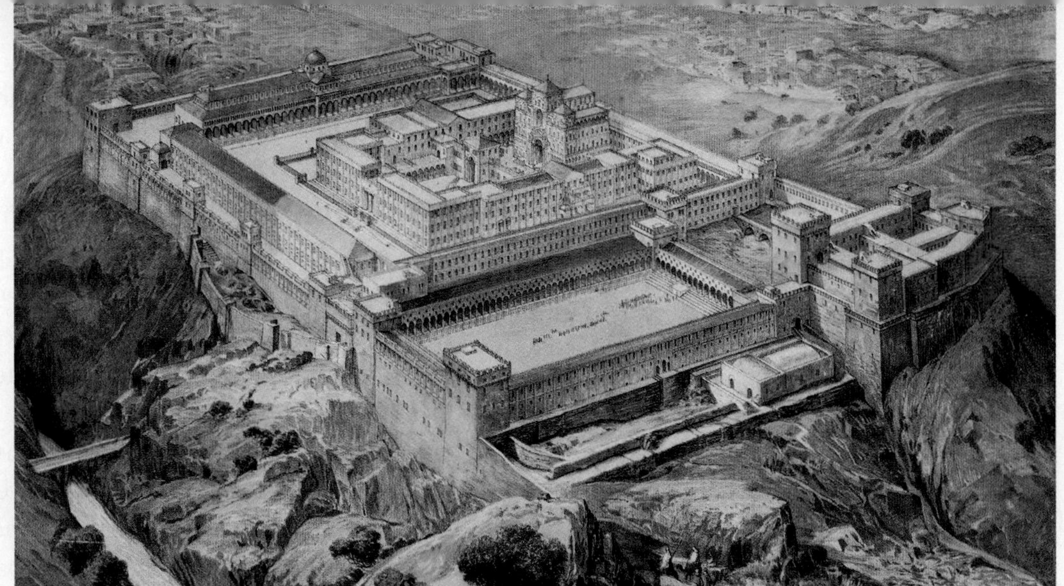

Solomon's Temple in Jerusalem
Solomon built a temple to God in Jerusalem. It was destroyed in 586 BC and rebuilt later. However, it was destroyed again, this time by the Romans in AD 70.

The Jews who returned to Jerusalem ruled themselves for about 100 years. They even rebuilt Solomon's Temple. Eventually, however, they were conquered by the Romans. The Jews revolted against the Romans, but most gave up after the Romans destroyed their Temple. As punishment for the rebellion, the Romans killed or enslaved much of Jerusalem's population. Some Jews stayed in their homeland, but thousands fled Jerusalem. Over the next centuries, Jews moved all around the world. Often they were forced to move by other religious groups who discriminated against them. The shared history and belief system has continued to unite Jews, in spite of being spread out around the world.

Explore ONLINE!

Jewish Migration after AD 70

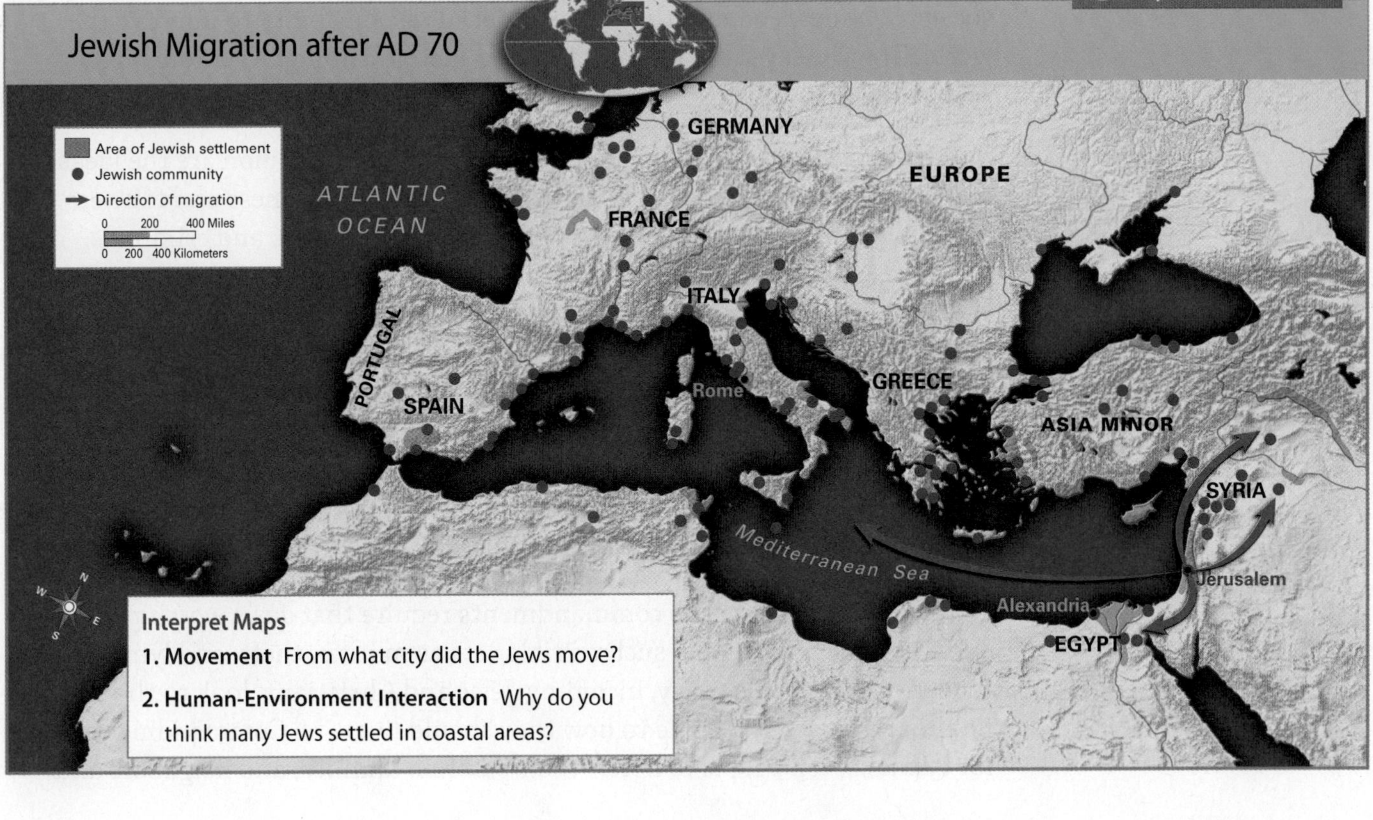

Area of Jewish settlement
Jewish community
Direction of migration
0 200 400 Miles
0 200 400 Kilometers

ATLANTIC OCEAN
GERMANY
EUROPE
FRANCE
ITALY
PORTUGAL
SPAIN
Rome
GREECE
ASIA MINOR
SYRIA
Mediterranean Sea
Jerusalem
Alexandria
EGYPT

Interpret Maps

1. **Movement** From what city did the Jews move?
2. **Human-Environment Interaction** Why do you think many Jews settled in coastal areas?

Israelite Society Roles in society changed after the destruction of the Temple. Before the Temple was destroyed, priesthood was passed from father to son. After the destruction of the Temple, sons still inherited this title from their fathers, but without a Temple at which to make sacrifices, the role of the priest wasn't as central to the religious practice. Instead, as Jews spread out across the world, the role of **rabbis,** or religious teachers, became more important.

Before and after the destruction of the Temple, Israelite government and society were dominated by men, as were most ancient societies. Women and men had different roles. Men made most decisions, and a woman's husband was chosen by her father. However, a daughter could not be forced into marriage. A family's property was inherited by the eldest son, who provided for all children and for women without husbands. Women were not priests or rabbis.

Reading Check
Analyze Effects
How did invasions affect the Jews and Judaism?

Jewish Beliefs

Wherever Jews live around the world, their religion is the foundation upon which they base their whole society. In fact, much of Jewish culture is based directly on Jewish beliefs. The central concepts of Judaism are belief in one God, justice and righteousness, and observance of religious and moral law. These central concepts developed during the times of Abraham and Moses and have remained important to Jews through today.

Belief in One God Most importantly, Jews believe in one God. The belief in one and only one God is called **monotheism.** Many people believe that Judaism was the world's first monotheistic religion.

In the ancient world where most people worshiped many gods, the Jews' worship of only one God set them apart. This worship shaped Jewish society. The Jews believe they have a special responsibility to improve the world. They believe that God guides their history through relationships with Abraham, Moses, and other leaders.

Justice and Righteousness Also central to the Jews' religion are the ideas of justice and righteousness. To Jews, justice means kindness and fairness to other people. Everyone deserves justice, even strangers and criminals. Jews are expected to give aid to those who need it, including the poor, the sick, and orphans. Jews are also expected to be fair in business dealings.

Righteousness refers to doing what is proper. Jews are supposed to behave properly, even if others around them do not. For the Jews, righteous behavior is more important than rituals, or ceremonies.

Observance of Religious and Moral Law Observance of the law is closely related to justice and righteousness. Jews believe that God gave them religious and moral laws to follow. The most important Jewish laws are the Ten Commandments. The commandments require that Jews worship only one God. They also forbid such terrible acts as murder, theft, and lying. Indeed, many people today, including Jews and Christians, look to the Ten Commandments as a guide to how they should live. The Commandments, for example, tell people to honor their parents, families, and neighbors and

Quick Facts

Basic Jewish Beliefs

- Belief in and worship of one and only one God
- Commitment to justice, or dealing with people kindly and fairly
- Commitment to righteousness, or doing what is proper
- Observance of religious and moral law

All Jews share the same basic beliefs, but different Jewish communities around the world have their own cultures. These Jews from Eastern Europe carry a Torah, a practice among Jews everywhere.

not to lie or cheat. In addition, many people observe the directive not to work on weekends in honor of the Sabbath. Although not all these ideas were unique to Judaism, it was through the Jews that they entered Western culture.

The commandments are only one part of Jewish law. Jews believe that Moses recorded a system of laws, now called Mosaic law, that God had set down for them. Mosaic laws guide many areas of Jews' daily lives, such as how people pray and observe holy days.

Among the Mosaic laws are rules about the foods that Jews can eat and rules that must be followed in preparing them. For example, the laws state that Jews cannot eat pork or shellfish, which are thought to be unclean. Today, foods that have been so prepared are called kosher (KOH-shuhr), or fit. There are companies and agencies around the world that certify processed foods as kosher.

Reading Check
Form Generalizations What are the most important beliefs of Judaism?

Jewish Texts

The laws and **principles** of Judaism are described in several sacred texts. Among the main texts are the Torah, the Hebrew Bible, and the commentaries.

Academic Vocabulary
principle basic belief, rule, or law

The Torah The ancient Jews recorded most of their laws in five books. Together, these books are called the Torah. The **Torah** is the most sacred text of Judaism. In addition to laws, it includes a history of the Jewish people until the death of Moses. Jews believe the contents of the Torah were revealed to Moses by God.

Readings from the Torah are central to Jewish religious services today. Nearly every synagogue (SI-nuh-gawg), or Jewish house of worship, has at least one Torah. Out of respect for the Torah, readers do not touch it. They use special pointers to mark their places in the text.

Jewish Texts

The Commentaries

The Talmud is a collection of commentaries and discussions about the Torah and the Hebrew Bible. The Talmud is a rich source of information for discussion and debate. Religious scholars like these young men study the Talmud to learn about Jewish history and laws.

The Torah

Using a special pointer called a *yad*, this girl is reading aloud from the Torah. The Torah is the most sacred of Hebrew texts. It plays a central role in many Jewish ceremonies.

The Hebrew Bible

These beautifully decorated pages are from a Hebrew Bible. Sometimes called the Tanakh, the Hebrew Bible includes the Torah and other ancient writings.

Analyze Visuals
How does the Torah look different from the Hebrew Bible and the commentaries?

The Hebrew Bible The Torah is the first of three parts of a group of writings called the Hebrew Bible, or Tanakh (tah-NAHK). The second part is made up of eight books that describe the messages of Hebrew prophets. Prophets are people who are said to receive messages from God to be taught to others.

The final part of the Hebrew Bible is 11 books of poetry, songs, stories, lessons, and history. Many of these stories are told by Jews to show the power of faith. The Book of Psalms, which is included in this section of the Tanakh, is a collection of songs of praise to God. Some of the psalms are quite short, while others are much longer. Also included in this portion of the Hebrew Bible are the Proverbs, short expressions of Hebrew wisdom. For example, one Proverb says, "A good name is to be chosen rather than great riches." In other words, it is better to be seen as a good person than to be rich and not respected.

The Commentaries For centuries rabbis and scholars have studied the Torah and Jewish laws. Because some laws are hard to understand, scholars write commentaries to explain them. Many explanations can be found in the Talmud (TAHL-moohd), a set of commentaries and lessons for everyday life. The writings of the Talmud were produced between AD 200 and 600. Many Jews consider them second only to the Hebrew Bible in significance to Judaism.

Reading Check
Find Main Ideas
What texts do Jews consider sacred?

Traditions and Holy Days

Jews feel that understanding their history will help them better follow the Jewish teachings. Their traditions and holy days help Jews connect with their past and celebrate their history.

Hanukkah One Jewish tradition is celebrated by Hanukkah, which falls in December. It honors a historical event. The ancient Jews wanted to celebrate a victory that had convinced their rulers to let them keep their religion. According to legend, though, the Jews did not have enough lamp oil to celebrate at the temple. Miraculously, the oil they had—enough for only one day—burned for eight full days.

Today, Jews celebrate this event by lighting candles in a special candleholder called a menorah (muh-NOHR-uh). Its eight branches represent the eight days through which the oil burned. Many Jews also exchange gifts on each of the eight nights.

Passover More important to Jews than Hanukkah, Passover is celebrated in March or April. During Passover, Jews honor the Exodus, the journey of the Israelites out of slavery.

According to Jewish tradition, the Israelites left Egypt so quickly that bakers did not have time to let their bread rise. Therefore, during Passover, Jews eat matzo, a flat, unrisen bread instead. They also celebrate the holiday with ceremonies.

During a special Passover meal called a seder, participants reflect on the events of the Exodus.

High Holy Days The two most sacred of all Jewish holidays are the High Holy Days. They take place in September or October. The first two days of celebration, Rosh Hashanah (rahsh uh-SHAH-nuh), celebrate the start of a new year in the Jewish calendar.

Reading Check
Find Main Ideas
What are the two most important Jewish holidays?

On Yom Kippur (yohm ki-POOHR), which falls soon afterward, Jews ask God to forgive their sins. Jews consider Yom Kippur to be the holiest day of the entire year. Because it is so holy, Jews do not eat or drink anything all day. They also pray, reflect on the past year, and resolve to improve.

Summary and Preview Judaism was the world's first monotheistic religion. Jewish culture and traditions are rooted in the history of the Hebrews and Israelites. Next, you will read about a religion that is related to Judaism—Christianity.

Lesson 1 Assessment

Review Ideas, Terms, and Places

1. a. **Identify** Who first led the Hebrews to Canaan?
   b. **Evaluate** Why was the Exodus a significant event in Jewish history?
2. a. **Define** What is monotheism?
   b. **Explain** What is the Jewish view of justice and righteousness?
   c. **Explain** How have the Ten Commandments continued to be important over time?
3. a. **Identify** What are the main sacred texts of Judaism?
   b. **Elaborate** Why do you think the commentaries are so significant to many Jews?
4. a. **Identify** What event in their history do the Jews celebrate at Passover?
   b. **Elaborate** How do you think celebrating traditions and holy days helps Jews connect to their past?

Critical Thinking

5. **Sequence** Draw a diagram like this one and fill in important events from the history of the Jewish people in the order they occurred. You may add as many boxes as you need for the information.

Origins of Christianity

The Big Idea

Christianity, a religion based on the life and teachings of Jesus of Nazareth, spread throughout the Roman Empire.

Main Ideas

- The life and death of Jesus of Nazareth inspired a new religion called Christianity.
- Christians believe that Jesus' acts and teachings focused on love and salvation.
- Jesus' followers taught others about Jesus' life and teachings.
- Christianity spread throughout the Roman Empire by 400.

Key Terms and Places

Messiah
Christianity
Bible
Bethlehem
Resurrection
disciples
saint

If YOU lived there . . .

You are a fisher in Judea, bringing in the day's catch. As you reach the shore, you see a large crowd. They are listening to a man tell stories. A man in the crowd whispers to you that the speaker is a teacher with some new ideas about religion. You are eager to get your fish to the market, but you are also curious.

What might convince you to stay and listen?

Jesus of Nazareth

Jesus of Nazareth was the man many people believed was the **Messiah**—a great leader the ancient Jews predicted would come to restore the greatness of Israel. Jesus was a great leader and one of the most influential figures in world history. Jesus' life and teachings form the basis of a religion called **Christianity.** However, we know relatively little about his life. Everything we do know is contained in the **Bible,** the holy book of Christianity.

The Christian Bible is made up of two parts. The first part, the Old Testament, is largely the same as the Hebrew Bible. The second part, the New Testament, is an account of the life and teachings of Jesus and of the early history of Christianity.

The Birth of Jesus According to the Bible, Jesus was born in a small town called **Bethlehem** (BETH-li-hem) at the end of the first century BC. Jesus' mother, Mary, was married to a carpenter named Joseph. But Christians believe God, not Joseph, was Jesus' father.

As a young man, Jesus lived in the town of Nazareth and probably studied with Joseph to become a carpenter. Like many young Jewish men of the time, Jesus also studied the laws and teachings of Judaism. By the time he was about 30, Jesus had begun to travel and teach. Stories of his teachings and actions from this time make up the beginning of the New Testament.

The Crucifixion As a teacher, Jesus drew many followers with his ideas. But at the same time, his teachings challenged the authority of political and religious leaders. According to the New Testament, they arrested Jesus while he was in Jerusalem in or around AD 30.

Jesus of Nazareth

The Bible says that Jesus was born in Bethlehem but grew up in Nazareth. Many artists in the past have created paintings, songs, and sculptures influenced by the Bible. In this painting, the famous artist Giotto (1266–1337) painted a scene from Jesus' childhood. Some artists, musicians, and writers today depict Biblical stories and themes in their work. For example, the *Left Behind* series of books and movies was very popular in the 1990s and 2000s and uses ideas presented in the Bible. Some songs by popular artists like U2 and Lenny Kravitz are also about Jesus' life and message.

Analyze Visuals
How does the artist imply that Jesus was important?

Shortly after his arrest, the Romans tried and executed Jesus. He was killed by crucifixion (kroo-suh-FIK-shuhn), a type of execution in which a person was nailed to a cross. In fact, the word *crucifixion* comes from the Latin word for "cross." After he died, Jesus' followers buried him.

The Resurrection According to Christian beliefs, Jesus rose from the dead and vanished from his tomb three days after he was crucified. Now, Christians refer to Jesus' rise from the dead as the **Resurrection** (re-suh-REK-shuhn).

Christians further believe that after the Resurrection, Jesus appeared to some groups of his **disciples** (di-SY-puhls), or followers. Jesus stayed with these disciples for the next 40 days, teaching them and giving them instructions about how to pass on his teachings. Then Jesus rose up into heaven.

Early Christians believed that the Resurrection was a sign that Jesus was the Messiah and the son of God. Some people began to call him Jesus Christ, from the Greek word *Christos*, or "Anointed One." It is from this word that the words *Christian* and *Christianity* eventually developed.

Reading Check
Summarize What do Christians believe happened after Jesus died?

Jesus' Acts and Teachings

During his lifetime, Jesus traveled from village to village spreading his message among the Jewish people. As he traveled, he attracted many followers. These early followers later became the first Christians.

Miracles According to the New Testament, many people became Jesus' followers after they saw him perform miracles. A miracle is an event that cannot normally be performed by a human. For example, the books of the New Testament tell of times when Jesus healed people who were sick or injured. One passage also describes how Jesus once fed an entire crowd with just a few loaves of bread and a few fish. Although there should not have been enough food for everyone, people ate their fill and even had food to spare.

Parables The Bible says that miracles drew followers to Jesus and convinced them that he was the son of God. Once Jesus had attracted followers, he began to teach them. One way he taught was through parables, or stories that teach lessons about how people should live. Parables are similar to fables, but they usually teach religious lessons. The New Testament includes many of Jesus' parables.

Through his parables, Jesus linked his beliefs and teachings to people's everyday lives. The parables explained complicated ideas in ways that most people could understand. For example, in one parable, Jesus compared people who lived sinfully to a son who had left his home and his family. Just as the son's father would joyfully welcome him home, Jesus said God would forgive sinners when they turned away from sin. Other parables he told had other messages.

Jesus' Message Much of Jesus' message was rooted in older Jewish traditions. For example, he emphasized two rules that were also in the Torah: love God and love other people.

Jesus expected his followers to love all people, not just friends and family. He encouraged his followers to be generous to the poor and the sick. He told people that they should even love their enemies. The way people treated others, Jesus said, showed how much they loved God.

Another important theme in Jesus' teachings was salvation, or the rescue of people from sin. Jesus taught that people who were saved from sin would enter the Kingdom of God when they died. Many of his teachings dealt with how people could reach God's kingdom.

Focus on Culture

Christian Holidays

For centuries, Christians have honored key events in Jesus' life. Some of these events inspired holidays that Christians celebrate today.

The most sacred holiday for Christians is Easter, which is celebrated each spring. Easter is a celebration of the Resurrection. On Easter, Christians usually attend church services. Many people also celebrate by dyeing eggs because eggs are seen as a symbol of new life.

Another major Christian holiday is Christmas. It honors Jesus' birth and is celebrated every December 25. Although no one knows on what date Jesus was actually born, Christians have placed Christmas in December since the 200s. Today, people celebrate with church services and the exchange of gifts. Some people reenact scenes of Jesus' birth.

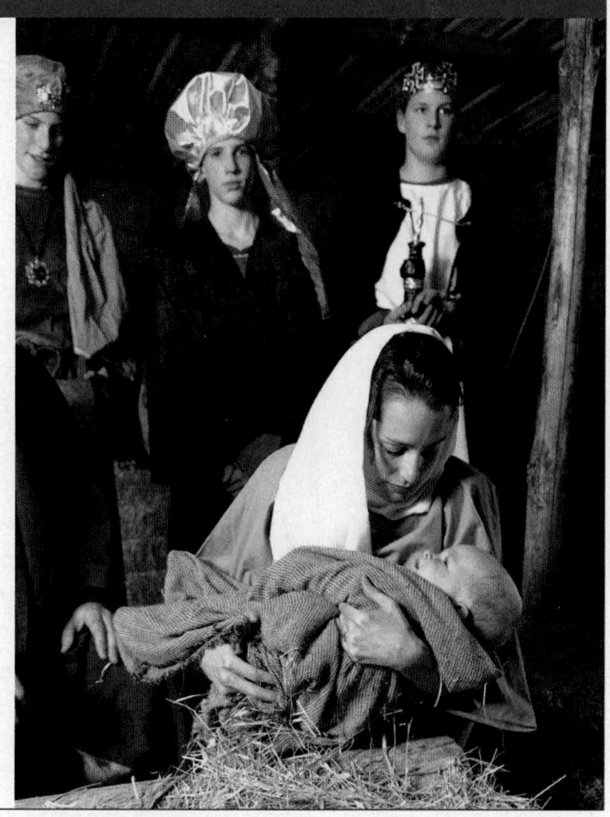

Draw Conclusions
Why do you think people celebrate events in Jesus' life?

Reading Check
Summarize What were the main ideas in Jesus' message?

Over the many centuries since Jesus lived, people have interpreted his teachings in different ways. As a result, many different denominations of Christians have developed. A denomination is a group of people who hold mostly the same beliefs. Despite their differences, however, Christians around the world share many basic beliefs about Jesus.

Jesus' Followers

Shortly after the Resurrection, the Bible says, Jesus' followers traveled throughout the Roman world telling about Jesus and his teachings. Among the people to pass on Jesus' teachings were 12 chosen disciples called Apostles (uh-PAHS-uhlz) and a man called Paul.

The Apostles The Apostles were 12 men whom Jesus chose to receive special teaching. During Jesus' lifetime, they were among his closest followers and knew him very well. Jesus frequently sent the Apostles to spread his teachings. After the Resurrection, the Apostles continued this task.

One of the Apostles, Peter, became the leader of the group after Jesus died. Peter traveled to a few Roman cities and taught about Jesus in the Jewish communities there. Eventually, he went to live in Rome, where he

Historical Source

The Sermon on the Mount

The Bible says that Jesus attracted many followers. One day he led his followers onto a mountainside to give a religious speech. In this speech, called the Sermon on the Mount, Jesus said that people who love God will be blessed. This is an excerpt of this sermon.

Scholars believe this location was the site of Jesus' Sermon on the Mount.

"When Jesus saw the crowds, he went up the mountain; and after he sat down, his disciples came to him. Then he began to speak, and taught them, saying:

'Blessed are the poor in spirit, for theirs is the kingdom of heaven.

'Blessed are those who mourn, for they will be comforted.

'Blessed are the meek, for they will inherit the earth.

'Blessed are those who hunger and thirst for righteousness, for they will be filled.

'Blessed are the merciful, for they will receive mercy.

'Blessed are the pure in heart, for they will see God.

'Blessed are the peacemakers, for they will be called children of God.

'Blessed are those who are persecuted for righteousness' sake, for theirs is the kingdom of heaven.

'Blessed are you when people revile you and persecute you and utter all kinds of evil against you falsely on my account. Rejoice and be glad, for your reward is great in heaven, for in the same way they persecuted the prophets who were before you."

—Matthew 5:1-12, New Revised Standard Version

Analyze Sources
What kinds of qualities does Jesus say will be rewarded?

The Last Supper

This famous painting by Italian artist Leonardo da Vinci shows Jesus and his Apostles sharing their last meal before Jesus was arrested.

Analyze Visuals
What kind of mood do the people appear to be in?

had much authority among Jesus' followers. In later years after the Christian Church was more organized, many people looked back to Peter as its first leader.

The Gospels Some of Jesus' disciples wrote accounts of his life and teachings. These accounts are called the Gospels. Four Gospels are found in the New Testament of the Bible.

The Gospels were written by men known as Matthew, Mark, Luke, and John. All the men's accounts differ slightly from one another, but together they make up the best source we have on Jesus' life. Historians and religious scholars depend on these stories for information about Jesus' life and teachings. The Gospels tell of miracles Jesus performed. They also contain the parables he told.

Paul Probably the most important person in the spread of Christianity after Jesus' death was Paul of Tarsus. Although he had never met Jesus, Paul did more to spread Christian beliefs and **ideals** than anyone else. He had so much influence that many people think of him as another Apostle. After Paul died, he was named a **saint,** a person known and admired for his or her holiness.

Academic Vocabulary
ideals ideas or goals that people try to live up to

Like most of Jesus' early followers, Paul was born Jewish. At first, he strongly opposed the activities of the Christians. For a time, Paul even worked to prevent followers of Jesus from spreading their message.

According to the New Testament, though, something remarkable happened to Paul one day as he traveled on the road to Damascus. He saw a blinding light and heard the voice of Jesus calling out to him. Soon after that event, Paul became a Christian.

After his conversion, Paul traveled widely around the Mediterranean, spreading Christian teachings. As you can see on the map, he visited many of the major cities along the eastern coast of the Mediterranean.

In addition, Paul wrote long letters to communities throughout the Roman world. These letters helped explain and elaborate on Jesus' teachings. In his letters, Paul wrote at length about the Christian belief in the Resurrection and about salvation. He also mentioned the idea of the Trinity. The Trinity is a central Christian belief that God is made up of three persons. They are God the Father, Jesus the Son, and the Holy Spirit. This belief holds that, even though there are three persons, there is still only one God.

Paul's teachings attracted both Jews and non-Jews to Christianity in many areas around the Mediterranean. In time, this growing number of Christians helped the Christian Church break away from its Jewish roots. People began to recognize Christianity as a separate religion.

Reading Check
Find Main Ideas What did Jesus' followers do to help spread Christianity?

The Spread of Christianity

Early Christians like Paul wanted to share their message about Jesus with the world. To do that, Christians began to write down parts of Jesus' message, including the Gospels. They distributed copies of the Gospels and other writings to strengthen people's faith. Because of their efforts, Christianity spread quickly in Roman communities.

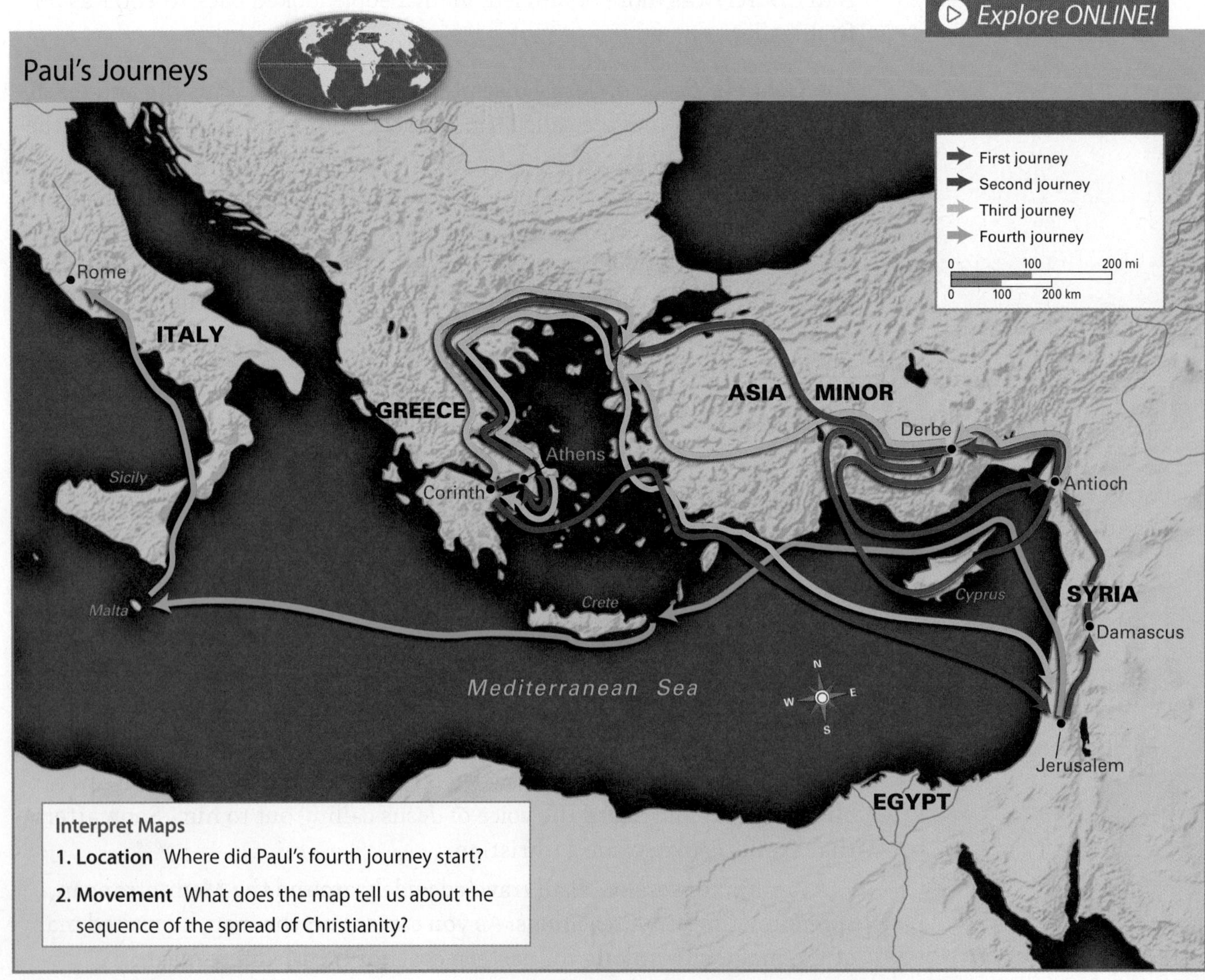

Interpret Maps

1. **Location** Where did Paul's fourth journey start?
2. **Movement** What does the map tell us about the sequence of the spread of Christianity?

Explore ONLINE!

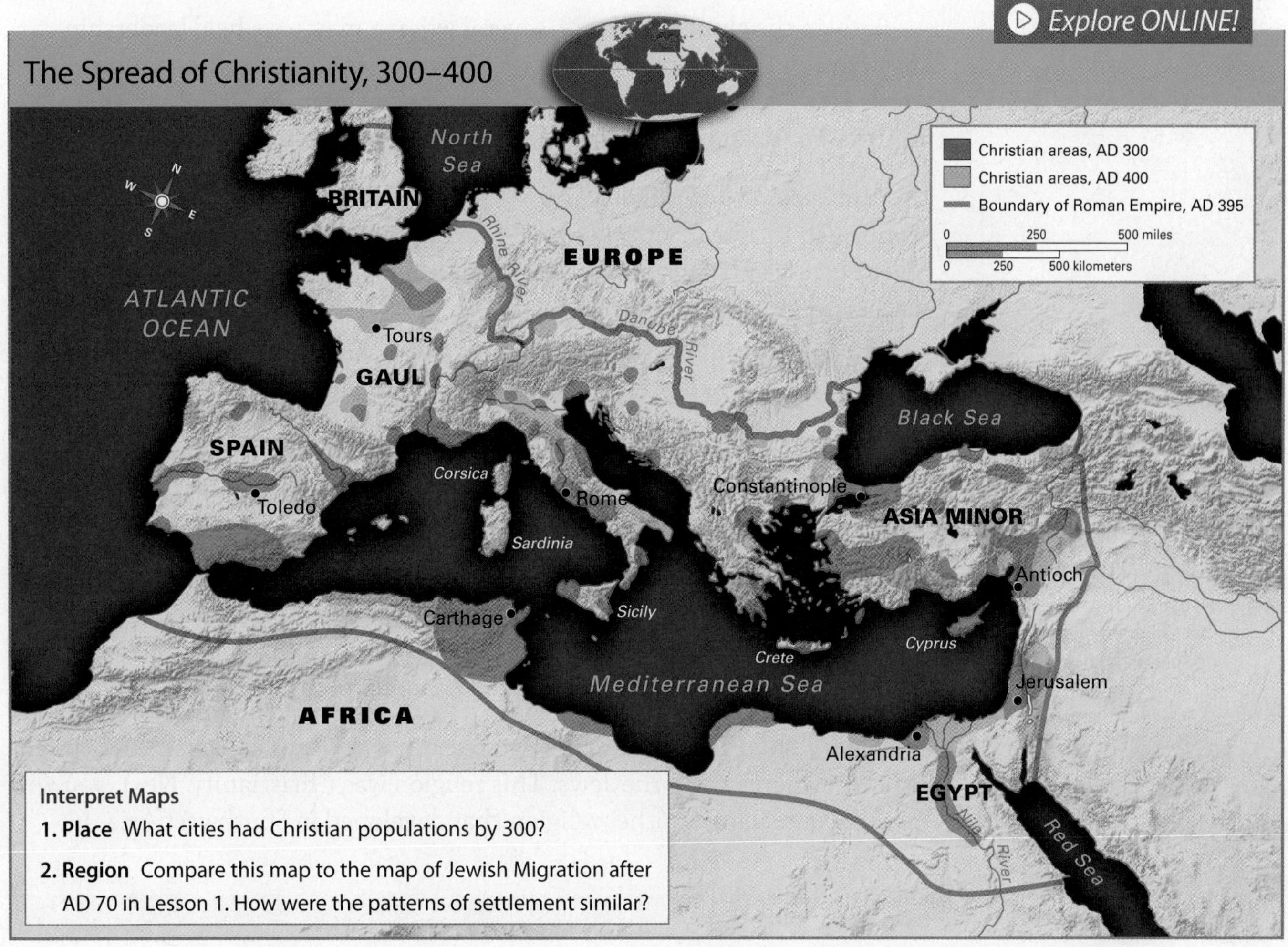

Interpret Maps

1. **Place** What cities had Christian populations by 300?
2. **Region** Compare this map to the map of Jewish Migration after AD 70 in Lesson 1. How were the patterns of settlement similar?

Persecution As Christianity became more popular, some Roman leaders became concerned. They looked for ways to put an end to this new religion. Sometimes, local offícals challenged the Christians trying to spread their beliefs. Some of these officials even arrested and killed Christians who refused to worship the gods of Rome. Many of the leaders of the early Christians, including Peter and Paul, were killed for their efforts in spreading Christian teachings.

Most of Rome's emperors let Christians worship as they pleased. However, a few emperors in the 200s and 300s feared that the Christians could cause unrest in the empire. To prevent such unrest, these emperors banned Christianity. Christians were often forced to meet in secret.

Growth of the Church Because the early church usually had to meet in secret, it did not have any single leader to govern it. Instead, bishops, or local Christian leaders, led each Christian community. Most of these early bishops lived in cities.

By the late 100s, Christians looked to the bishops of large cities for guidance. These bishops had great influence, even over other bishops. The most honored of all was the bishop of Rome, or the pope. Gradually, the pope's influence grew, and many people in the West came to see him as the head of the whole Christian Church. As the church grew, so did the pope's influence.

Early in the church's history, several women may have held leadership positions in Christian communities. However, as Christianity became a more established religion, women lost some of their prominence in the church. For example, they were not allowed to be bishops or popes.

Acceptance of Christianity As the pope's influence grew, Christianity continued to spread throughout Rome even though it was banned. Then an event changed things for Christians in Rome. The emperor himself became a Christian.

The emperor who became a Christian was Constantine (KAHN-stuhn-teen). According to legend, Constantine was preparing for battle against a rival when he saw a cross in the sky. He thought that this vision meant he would win the battle if he converted to Christianity. Constantine did convert, and he won the battle. As a result of his victory, he became the new emperor of Rome.

Reading Check
Identify Problems What difficulties did early Christians face in practicing and spreading their religion?

As emperor, Constantine removed bans against the practice of Christianity. He also called together a council of Christian leaders from around the empire to try to clarify Christian teachings. Almost 60 years after Constantine died, another emperor banned all non-Christian religious practices in the empire. Christianity eventually spread from Rome to all around the world.

Summary and Preview The life and teachings of Jesus of Nazareth inspired a new religion among the Jews. This religion was Christianity. Next, you will learn about Islam, another religion that developed in Southwest Asia.

Lesson 2 Assessment

Review Ideas, Terms, and Places

1. **a. Define** In Christian teachings, what was the Resurrection?
   b. Elaborate Why do you think Christians use the cross as a symbol of their religion?
2. **a. Identify** What did Jesus mean by salvation?
   b. Explain How have differing interpretations of Jesus' teachings affected Christianity?
3. **a. Define** What is a saint?
   b. Summarize How did Paul influence early Christianity?
4. **a. Recall** What was the role of bishops in the early Christian Church?
   b. Explain Why were some Roman leaders worried about the growing popularity of Christianity?
   c. Predict What do you think might have happened to Christianity if Constantine had not become a Christian?

Critical Thinking

5. **Form Generalizations** Review the segment on Jesus' acts and teachings. Then make generalizations about the topics shown in the graphic organizer.

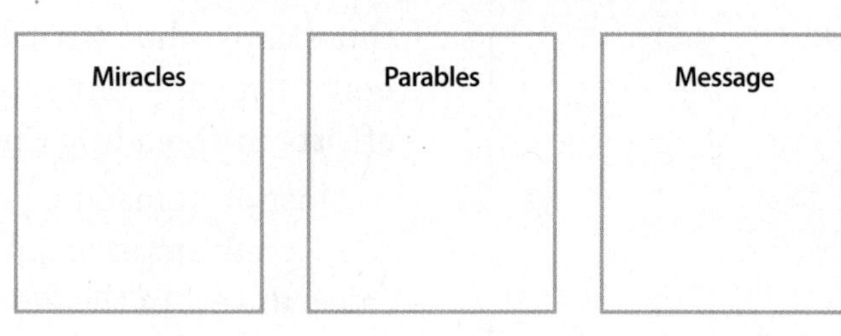

Origins of Islam

The Big Idea

Islam, a religion based on the teachings of Muhammad, arose in Arabia and is based on the sacred texts called the Qur'an and the Sunnah.

Main Ideas

- Arabia is mostly a desert land, where two ways of life, nomadic and sedentary, developed.
- A new religion called Islam, based on the teachings of the prophet Muhammad, spread throughout Arabia in the 600s.
- The Qur'an guides Muslims' lives.
- The Sunnah tells Muslims of important duties expected of them.
- Islamic law is based on the Qur'an and the Sunnah.

Key Terms and Places

oasis
Mecca
Islam
Muslims
Qur'an
Medina
mosque
jihad
Sunnah
Five Pillars of Islam

If YOU lived there . . .

Your family owns an inn in Mecca. Usually business is pretty calm, but this week your inn is packed. Travelers have come from all over the world to visit your city. One morning you leave the inn and are swept up in a huge crowd of these visitors. They speak many different languages, but everyone is wearing the same white robes. They are headed to the mosque.

What might draw so many people to your city?

Life in a Desert Land

The Arabian Peninsula, or Arabia, is located in Southwest Asia. It lies near the intersection of Africa, Europe, and Asia. For thousands of years Arabia's location, physical features, and climate have shaped life in the region.

Physical Features and Climate Arabia lies in a region with hot and dry air. This climate has created a band of deserts across Arabia and northern Africa. Sand dunes, or hills of sand shaped by the wind, can rise to 800 feet (240 m) high and stretch across hundreds of miles!

Arabia's deserts have a very limited amount of water. What water there is exists mainly in scattered oases. An **oasis** is a wet, fertile area in a desert. Oases have long been key stops along Arabia's overland trade routes.

Two Ways of Life To live in Arabia's harsh deserts, people developed two main ways of life. Nomads lived in tents and raised herds of sheep, goats, and camels. Nomads traveled with their herds across the desert in search of food and water for their animals. Among the nomads, water and land belonged to tribes. Membership in a tribe, a group of related people, offered safety from desert dangers.

While nomads moved around, other Arabs lived a more settled life. They made their homes in oases where they could farm. These settlements, particularly the ones along trade routes, became towns.

Reading Check
Categorize What two ways of life were common in Arabia?

Towns became centers of trade. There, nomads traded animal products and herbs for goods like cooking supplies and clothes. Merchants sold spices, gold, leather, and other goods brought by caravans.

A New Religion

In early times, Arabs worshiped many gods. That changed, however, when a man named Muhammad brought a new religion to Arabia. Historians know little about Muhammad. What they do know comes from religious writings.

Muhammad, Prophet of Islam Muhammad was born into an important family in the city of **Mecca** around 570. As a small child, he traveled with his uncle's caravans. Once he was grown, he managed a caravan business owned by a wealthy woman named Khadijah (ka-DEE-jah). At age 25, Muhammad married Khadijah.

The caravan trade made Mecca a rich city, but most of the wealth belonged to just a few people. Traditionally, wealthy people in Mecca had helped the poor. As Muhammad was growing up, though, many rich merchants ignored the needy.

Concerned about these changes, Muhammad often went to the hills to pray and meditate. One day, when he was about 40 years old, he went to meditate in a cave. According to religious writings, an angel spoke to Muhammad, telling him to "Recite! Recite!" Muhammad asked what he should recite. The angel answered:

> "Recite in the name of your Lord who created—created man from clots of blood! Recite! Your Lord is the Most Bountiful One, Who by the pen taught man what he did not know."
>
> —From the *Koran*, translated by N. J. Dawood

The messages that Muhammad received form the basis of the religion called **Islam.** In Arabic, the word *Islam* means "to submit to God."

Muslims, or people who follow Islam, believe that God spoke to Muhammad through the angel and made him a prophet, a person who tells of messages from God. They view Muhammad as God's messenger to the world. Muslims also believe that Muhammad continued to receive messages from God for the rest of his life. Eventually, these messages were collected in the **Qur'an** (kuh-RAN), the holy book of Islam.

Muhammad's Teachings In 613 Muhammad began to talk about his messages. He taught that there was only one God, Allah, which means "the God" in Arabic. Like Judaism and Christianity, Islam is monotheistic, or based on the belief in one God. Although people of all three religions believe in one God, their beliefs about God are not the same.

Muhammad's teachings also dealt with how people should live. He taught that all people who believed in Allah were bound together like members of a family. As a result, he said, people should help those who are less fortunate. For example, he thought that people who had money should use that money to help the poor.

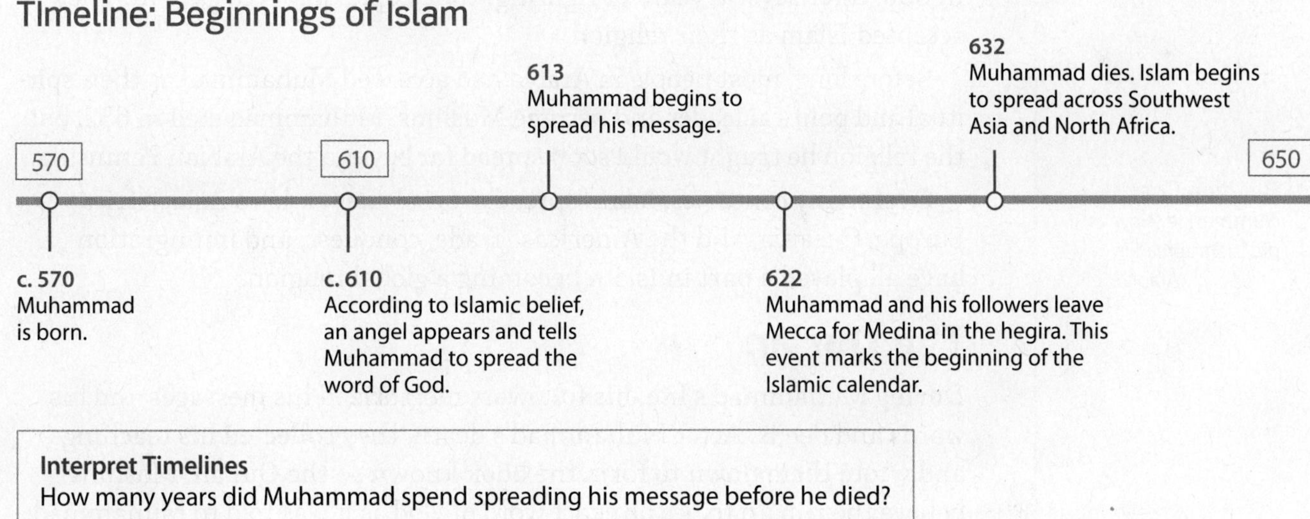

Interpret Timelines
How many years did Muhammad spend spreading his message before he died?

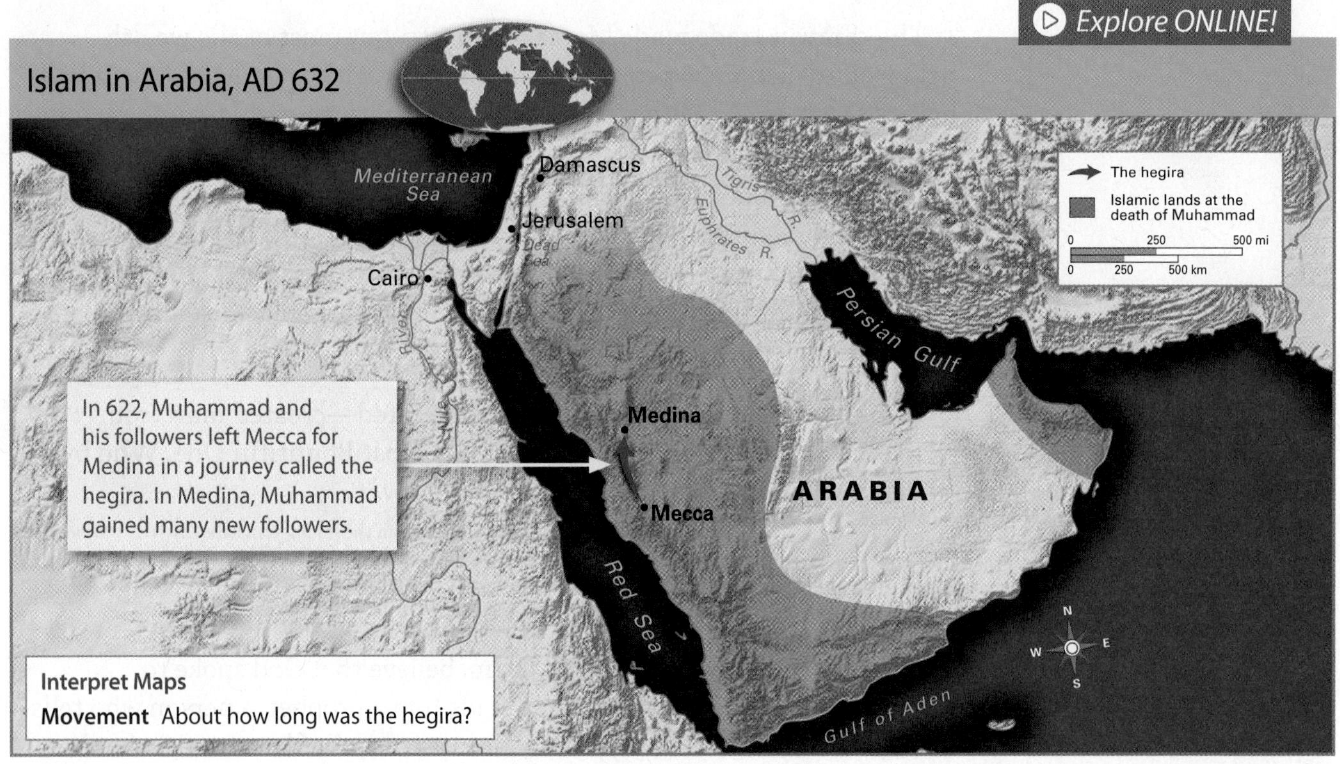

Interpret Maps
Movement About how long was the hegira?

Islam Spreads in Arabia At first Muhammad had few followers. Slowly, more people began to listen to his ideas. As Islam spread, Mecca's rulers grew worried. They threatened Muhammad and even planned to kill him.

A group of people living north of Mecca invited Muhammad to move to their city. So in 622 Muhammad and many of his followers went to **Medina** (muh-DEE-nuh). The name *Medina* means "the Prophet's city" in Arabic. Muhammad's departure from Mecca is called the hegira (hi-JY-ruh), or journey. It is so important a date in the history of Islam that Muslims made 622 the first year of the Islamic calendar.

Muhammad became a spiritual and political leader in Medina. His house became the first **mosque** (MAHSK), or building for Muslim prayer.

As the Muslim community in Medina grew stronger, other Arab tribes began to accept Islam. Conflict with the Meccans, however, increased. In 630, after several years of fighting, the people of Mecca gave in. They accepted Islam as their religion.

Before long, most people in Arabia had accepted Muhammad as their spiritual and political leader and become Muslims. Muhammad died in 632, but the religion he taught would soon spread far beyond the Arabian Peninsula.

Over many centuries, Islam spread around the world to Asia, Africa, Europe, Oceania, and the Americas. Trade, conquest, and immigration have all played a part in Islam becoming a global religion.

Reading Check
Summarize How did Islam spread in Arabia?

The Qur'an

During Muhammad's life, his followers memorized his messages and his words and deeds. After Muhammad's death, they collected his teachings and wrote them down to form the book known as the Qur'an. Muslims believe the Qur'an to be the exact word of God as it was told to Muhammad.

Beliefs The central teaching in the Qur'an is that there is only one God—Allah—and that Muhammad is his prophet. The Qur'an says people must obey Allah's commands. Muslims learned of these commands from Muhammad.

Islam teaches that the world had a definite beginning and will end one day. Muhammad said that on the final day God will judge all people. Those who have obeyed his orders will be granted life in paradise. According to the Qur'an, paradise is a beautiful garden full of fine food and drink. People who have not obeyed God, however, will suffer.

Guidelines for Behavior Like holy books of other religions, the Qur'an describes Muslim acts of worship, guidelines for moral behavior, and rules for social life.

Academic Vocabulary
explicit fully revealed without vagueness

Some of these guidelines for life are stated **explicitly**. For example, the Qur'an clearly describes how a person should prepare for worship. Muslims must wash themselves before praying so they will be pure before Allah. The Qur'an also tells Muslims what they should not eat or drink. Muslims are not allowed to eat pork or drink alcohol.

Academic Vocabulary
implicit understood though not clearly put into words

Other guidelines for behavior are not stated directly but are **implicit** in the Qur'an. Even though they are not written directly, many of these ideas altered early Arabian society. For example, before Muhammad's time, many Arabs owned slaves. The Qur'an does not expressly forbid the practice of slavery, which was common in early Arabia. It does, however, imply that slavery should be abolished. Based on this implication, many Muslim slaveholders chose to free their slaves.

The Qur'an also changed how women were treated. Women in Arabia had few rights. The Qur'an describes rights of women, including rights to own property, earn money, and get an education. However, most Muslim women still had fewer rights than men, just like in other societies of the time.

Studying the Qur'an

The Qur'an plays a central role in the lives of many Muslims. Both children and adults study and memorize verses from the Qur'an at home, at Islamic schools, and in mosques.

Analyze Visuals
Where do you think these children are studying the Qur'an?

Focus on Culture

Muslim Art

Historically, most Muslim art does not show any people or animals. Muslims believe only God can create humans and animals or their images. Art portraying Muhammad is considered very offensive by most Muslims. Instead, Muslim artists created complex geometric patterns. Muslim artists also turned to calligraphy, or decorative writing. They made sayings from the Qur'an into works of art to decorate mosques and other buildings.

Some Muslim artists today, like Sana Naveed and Ali Omar Ermes, continue to use calligraphy in their artwork. The calligraphy here is the statement of faith that Muslims say when they accept Islam and in their daily prayers.

Through history, Muslim art and literature have combined Islamic influences with regional traditions of the places Muslims conquered in history and places where Muslims live now. This mix of Islam with cultures from Asia, Africa, and Europe has given this literature and art a unique style and character.

Analyze Information
How do Muslim beliefs influence Muslim art?

Another important subject in the Qur'an has to do with **jihad** (ji-HAHD), which means "to make an effort, or to struggle." Jihad refers to the inner struggle people go through in their effort to obey God and behave according to Islamic ways. Jihad can also mean the struggle to defend the Muslim community, or, historically, to convert people to Islam. The word has also been translated as "holy war."

Reading Check
Make Inferences
Why is the Qur'an important to Muslims?

The Sunnah

The Qur'an is not the only source for the teachings of Islam. Muslims also study the hadith (huh-DEETH), the written record of Muhammad's words and actions. It is also the basis for the Sunnah. The **Sunnah** (SOOH-nuh) refers to the way Muhammad lived, which models the duties and the way of life expected of Muslims. The Sunnah guides Muslims' behavior.

The Five Pillars of Islam The first duties of a Muslim are known as the **Five Pillars of Islam,** which are five acts of worship required of all Muslims. The first pillar is a statement of faith. At least once in their lives, Muslims must state their faith by saying, "There is no god but God, and Muhammad is his prophet." Muslims say this when they accept Islam. They also say it in their daily prayers.

The second pillar of Islam is daily prayer. Muslims must pray five times a day: before sunrise, at midday, in late afternoon, right after sunset, and before going to bed. At each of these times, a call goes out from a mosque, inviting Muslims to come pray. Muslims try to pray together at a mosque. They believe prayer is proof that someone has accepted Allah.

The third pillar of Islam is a yearly donation to charity. Muslims must pay part of their wealth to a religious official. This money is used to help the poor, build mosques, or pay debts. Helping and caring for others is important in Islam.

The fourth pillar of Islam is fasting—going without food and drink. Muslims fast during the holy month of Ramadan (RAH-muh-dahn). The Qur'an says Allah began his revelations to Muhammad in this month. Throughout Ramadan, most Muslims will not eat or drink anything between dawn and sunset. Muslims believe fasting is a way to show that God is more important than one's own body. Fasting also reminds Muslims of people in the world who struggle to get enough food.

The fifth pillar of Islam is the hajj (HAJ), a pilgrimage to Mecca. All Muslims must travel to Mecca at least once in their lives if they can. The Kaaba, in Mecca, is Islam's most sacred place.

The Sunnah and Daily Life Besides the five pillars, the Sunnah has other examples of Muhammad's actions and teachings. These form the basis for rules about how to treat others. According to Muhammad's example, people should treat guests with generosity.

The Sunnah also provides guidelines for how people should conduct their relations in business and government. For example, one Sunnah rule says that it is bad to owe someone money. Another rule says that people should obey their leaders. Rules about lending money and charging interest have affected the economies of Muslim countries. For example, in Arab countries, fewer families have bank accounts. Historically, traditional banking wasn't common in these societies because of how the prohibition against charging high interest was interpreted. As the economies of countries have globalized, banking has become more common in these countries.

Reading Check
Form Generalizations What do Muslims learn from the Sunnah?

Islamic Law

Together, the Qur'an and the Sunnah are important guides for how Muslims should live. They also form the basis of Islamic law, or Shariah (shuh-REE-uh). Shariah uses both Islamic sources and human reason to judge the rightness of actions a person or community might take. All actions fall on a scale ranging from required to accepted to disapproved to forbidden. Islamic law makes no distinction between religious beliefs and daily life, so Islam affects all aspects of Muslims' lives.

BIOGRAPHY

Ibn Battutah 1304–c.1369

As Islam expanded, Muslim traders and travelers benefited from advances in navigation. One such traveler was Ibn Battutah. He initially began to travel when he went on the hajj, or pilgrimage to Mecca. His travels continued, and he visited Africa, India, China, and Spain between 1325 and 1353. He brought back many stories and eventually these were made into a book. As a result of travels of Ibn Battutah and other explorers, Muslim geographers made more accurate maps than were available before.

Analyze Effects
How did others benefit from Ibn Battutah's travels?

Three Religions of Southwest Asia			
	Judaism	**Christianity**	**Islam**
Place of Origin	Southwest Asia (Israel)	Southwest Asia (Jerusalem)	Southwest Asia (Saudi Arabia)
Age	About 4,000 years	About 2,000 years	About 1,400 years
Holy Book	Torah	Bible	Qur'an
Place of Worship	Synagogue	Church	Mosque
Early Leaders	Abraham, Moses	Jesus, the Disciples, Paul	Muhammad
Basic Beliefs	One God; Messiah yet to come	One God; Jesus is Messiah	One God; Muhammad is prophet

Analyze Information
What are some similarities between these three religions?

Shariah sets rewards for good behavior and punishments for crimes. It also describes limits of authority. It was the basis for law in Muslim countries until modern times. Today, though, most Muslim countries blend Islamic law with legal systems like those in the United States or western Europe.

Islamic law is not found in one book. Instead, it is a set of opinions and writings that have changed over the centuries. As a result, different ideas about Islamic law are found in different Muslim regions.

Reading Check
Find Main Ideas
What is the purpose of Islamic law?

Summary In the early 600s, Islam was introduced to Arabia by Muhammad. The Qur'an, the Sunnah, and Shariah teach Muslims how to live.

Lesson 3 Assessment

Review Ideas, Terms, and Places

1. a. **Define** What is an oasis?
   b. **Form Generalizations** Where did towns develop? Why?
   c. **Predict** Do you think life would have been better for nomads or townspeople in early Arabia? Explain.
2. a. **Identify** What is the Qur'an?
   b. **Explain** According to Islamic belief, what was the source of Islamic teachings?
   c. **Elaborate** Why did Muhammad move from Mecca to Medina? What did he accomplish there?
   d. **Describe** How have Muslim artists created art without showing humans or animals?
3. a. **Recall** What is the central teaching of the Qur'an?
   b. **Explain** How does the Qur'an help Muslims obey God?
4. a. **Recall** What are the Five Pillars of Islam?
   b. **Identify** Who traveled to India, Africa, China, and Spain and contributed his knowledge to the study of geography?
   c. **Form Generalizations** Why do Muslims fast during Ramadan?
5. a. **Identify** What is Islamic law called?
   b. **Make Inferences** How is Islamic law different from law in the United States?
   c. **Elaborate** What is one possible reason that opinions and writings about Islamic law have changed over the centuries?

Critical Thinking

6. **Categorize** Draw a chart like the one shown here. List three key teachings from the Qur'an and three teachings from the Sunnah.

Qur'an	Sunnah

Social Studies Skills

Interpret a Route Map

Define the Skill

A route map shows movement from one place to another. Usually, different routes are shown with different colored arrows. Look at the legend to see what the different arrows represent.

Learn the Skill

Use the map of Possible Routes of the Exodus to answer the following questions.

1. How many possible Exodus routes does the map show?
2. Where did the Exodus begin?
3. Which possible route would have been the longest?
4. Which route would have passed closest to the Mediterranean Sea?

Practice the Skill

Find a map of your city either in an atlas or on the Internet. You will need to draw on the map, so either print it, copy it, or draw a map on your own paper using the information. On the city map, draw the route you take from your home to school. Then draw another route you could take to get to school. Be sure to create a legend to show what your route lines mean. Compare your map to those of your classmates. What trends and patterns do you notice?

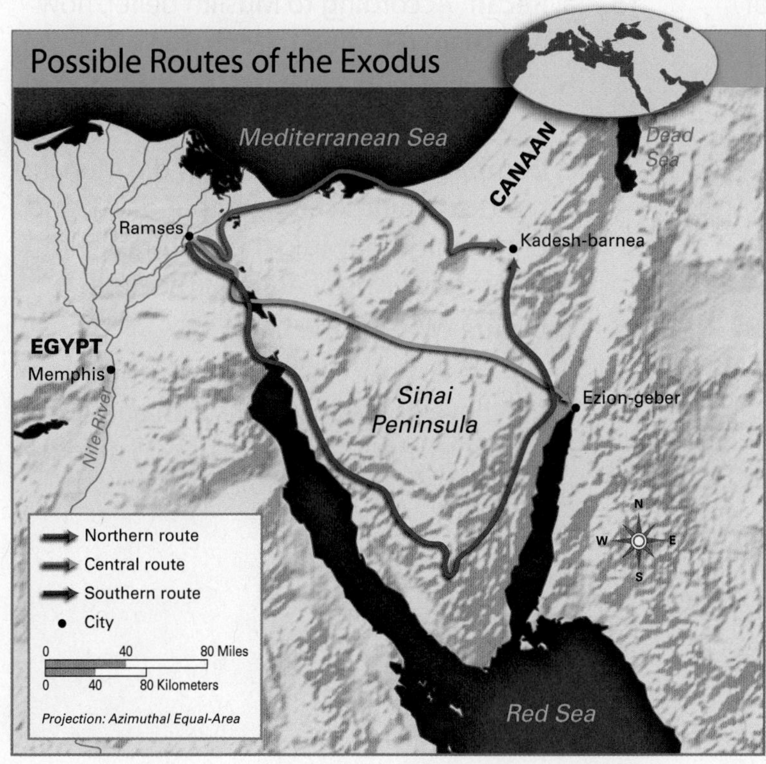

Module 7 Assessment

Review Vocabulary, Terms, and Places

Match each "I" statement with the person, place, or thing that might have made the statement.

1. "I am the town where Jesus of Nazareth was born."
2. "My name means 'the Prophet's city.'"
3. "I am the holy book of Christianity."
4. "I was a promised leader who was to appear among the Jews."
5. "I am a person known and admired for my holiness."
6. "I am the city where Muhammad was born."
7. "I am the most sacred text of Judaism."
8. "I am a follower."
9. "I am the holy book of Islam."
10. "I am a Jewish religious teacher."
11. "I am the belief in only one God."
12. "I am the acts of worship required of all Muslims."

a. Messiah
b. Qur'an
c. Bible
d. saint
e. rabbi
f. Bethlehem
g. Mecca
h. Medina
i. disciple
j. Five Pillars of Islam
k. monotheism
l. Torah

Comprehension and Critical Thinking

Lesson 1

13. **a. Identify** What are the basic beliefs of Judaism?

b. Analyze What do the various sacred Jewish texts contain?

c. Elaborate How are Jewish ideas observed in modern Western society today?

Lesson 2

14. **a. Describe** According to the Bible, what were the crucifixion and Resurrection?

b. Analyze Why do you think Jesus' teachings appealed to many people in the Roman Empire?

c. Evaluate Why do you think Paul is considered one of the most important people in the history of Christianity?

d. Compare With which group did both Jews and Christians come into conflict? How did those conflicts impact Jews and Christians?

e. Explain How did Constantine's victory change Christianity?

Lesson 3

15. **a. Recall** According to Muslim belief, how was Islam revealed to Muhammad?

b. Analyze How did Muhammad encourage people to treat each other?

c. Compare and Contrast How did Muhammad's teachings compare to Judaism and Christianity? How did they contrast with common beliefs of Arabs at the time?

d. Define What is the hajj?

e. Contrast Both the Qur'an and the Sunnah have guided Muslims' behavior for centuries. Apart from discussing different topics, how do these two differ?

Reading Skills

Use Context Clues—Synonyms *Use the Reading Skills taught in this module to answer the question about the reading selection below.*

Muhammad became a spiritual and political leader in Medina. His house became the first *mosque* (MAHSK), or building for Muslim prayer.

16. Based on the context clues in the passage, what does *mosque* mean?

Social Studies Skills

Interpret Route Maps *Use the Social Studies Skills taught in this module to answer the questions about the map of Paul's Journeys in Lesson 2.*

17. How many journeys did Paul take?
18. From where did he start his third journey?
19. On which journeys did Paul visit the cities of Corinth and Athens?
20. What was the last city Paul traveled to?

Map Activity

21. **Religions of Southwest Asia** On a separate sheet of paper, match the letters on the map with their correct labels.

Arabian Sea	Jerusalem	Mecca
Medina	Red Sea	Persian Gulf

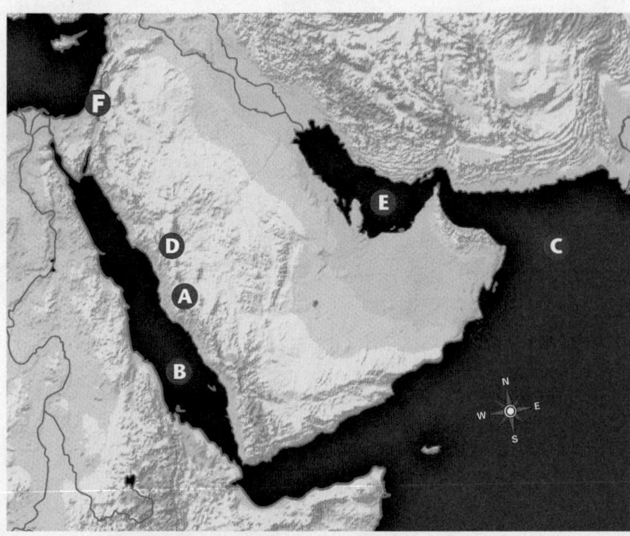

Focus on Writing

22. **Design a Website** You have been asked to design a website about Judaism, Christianity, and Islam for younger students. Create a home page for the site that introduces the website and one webpage for each of these religions. Include the most important information about the history, beliefs, and traditions of each religion. Use details, examples, facts, and definitions. You may design the pages either online or on sheets of paper. Remember that your audience is children, so you should keep the sentences simple, clear, and coherent. Include images or colors to catch the audience's attention and to help students understand the content. When you include new vocabulary from the module, make sure you explain the meaning of the word. Proofread your website for grammar, spelling, and punctuation.

Module 8

The Arabian Peninsula to Central Asia

Essential Question

Can the Arabian Peninsula to Central Asia region achieve stability after a long history of conflict?

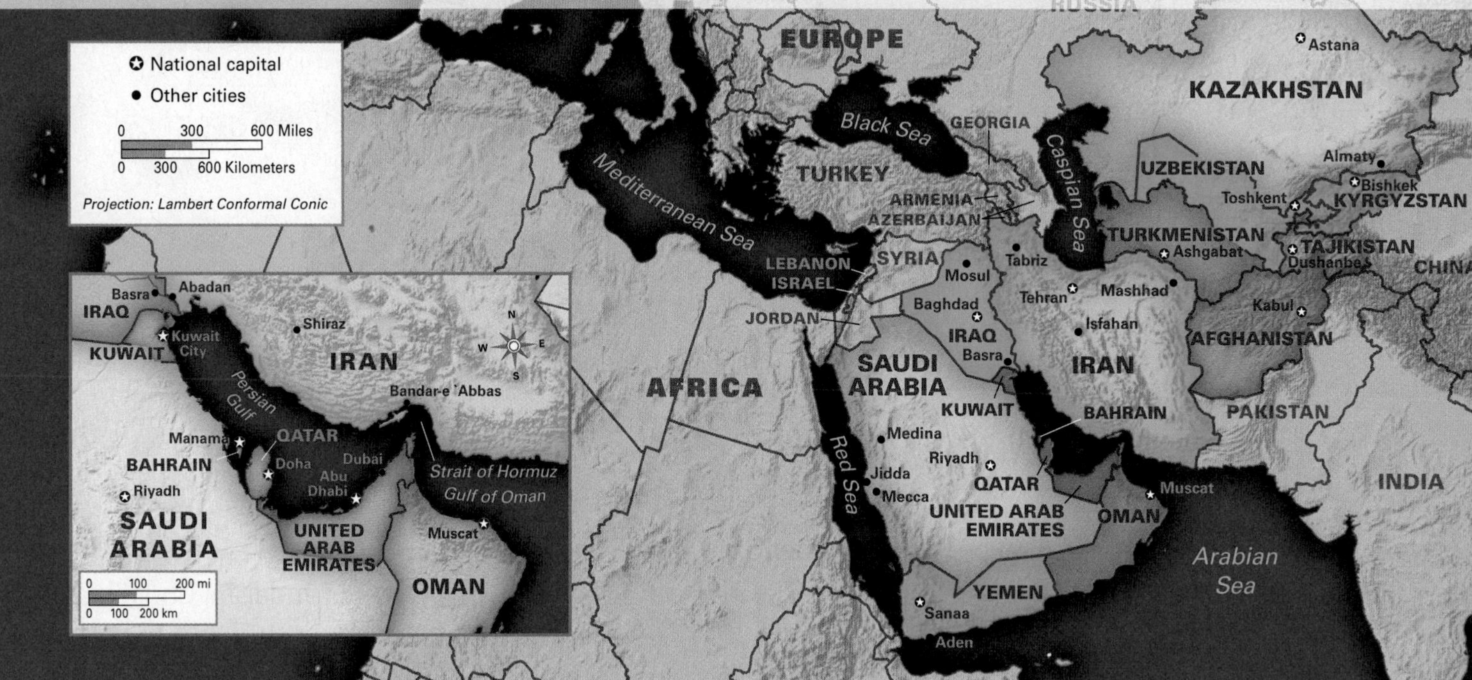

In this module, you will learn about the cultural and geographic characteristics of the Arabian Peninsula to Central Asia. You will also learn how foreign invasion and influence have affected the region.

Explore ONLINE!

VIDEOS, including . . .

- Operation Desert Storm
- The Persians
- The Silk Road

- Document-Based Investigations
- Graphic Organizers
- Interactive Games
- Channel One News Video: Inside Iran, Part 7
- Image with Hotspots: Ancient Irrigation
- Interactive Map: The Safavid Empire
- Compare Images: The Aral Sea

What You Will Learn

Lesson 1: Physical Geography 275
The Big Idea The Arabian Peninsula to Central Asia is an extremely dry region with valuable oil and mineral resources.

Lesson 2: The Arabian Peninsula 282
The Big Idea Most countries of the Arabian Peninsula share three main characteristics: Islamic religion and culture, monarchy as a form of government, and valuable oil resources.

Lesson 3: Iraq 288
The Big Idea Iraq, a country with a rich culture and natural resources, faces the challenge of rebuilding after years of conflict.

Lesson 4: Iran 293
The Big Idea Islam is a huge influence on government and daily life in Iran.

Lesson 5: Central Asia 298
The Big Idea While they share similar histories, traditions, and challenges, different ethnic groups create unique cultures for the countries of Central Asia.

Geography Much of Central Asia's land is rugged. Here, mountains rise behind the city of Almaty, Kazakhstan.

History Stone sculptures of Persians making offerings to their king line the steps of the ancient city of Persepolis in present-day Iran.

Culture Islam is a major part of the culture in every country in the region. These women pray at a mosque in Mecca, Saudi Arabia.

Reading Social Studies

Reread

READING FOCUS

Rereading can help you understand the vocabulary terms, main ideas, and details in a passage. Follow these steps in rereading. First, read the whole passage. Look over the passage and identify the vocabulary terms, main ideas, and details that you need help understanding. Then reread the passage slowly. As you read, make sure you understand new information by summarizing a passage silently. For especially difficult texts, you may wish to take turns reading aloud and checking understanding with a friend. Finally, if necessary, seek help from a teacher to clarify understanding.

The Persian Empire was later conquered by several Muslim empires. Muslims converted the Persians to Islam, but most people retained their Persian culture. They built beautiful mosques with colorful tiles and large domes.

1. **Read the passage.**
2. **Identify the main details to focus on.** Persian Empire, Muslims, culture
3. **Reread and restate the details silently** The Persian Empire was first. Then it was conquered by Muslims. Persian and Muslim cultures blended. Mosques show the region's culture.
4. **Reread with a friend or seek help from a teacher.**

YOU TRY IT!

Read the following passage. Then, following the three steps above, write down the main details to focus on. After you reread the paragraph, write down the information restated in your own words to show that you understood what you read. As needed, seek help from a teacher or friend to clarify meaning.

The Tigris and Euphrates rivers flow across a low, flat plain in Iraq. They join together before they reach the Persian Gulf. The Tigris and Euphrates are what are known as exotic rivers, or rivers that begin in humid regions and then flow through dry areas. The rivers create a narrow fertile area, which in ancient times was called Mesopotamia, or the "land between rivers."

As you read this module, follow the steps for rereading to clarify information and improve understanding.

Physical Geography

The Big Idea

The Arabian Peninsula to Central Asia is an extremely dry region with valuable oil and mineral resources.

Main Ideas

- Major physical features of the Arabian Peninsula, Iraq, and Iran include desert plains and mountains, a dry climate with little vegetation, and valuable oil resources.
- Central Asia is a landlocked region with rugged mountains, a harsh, dry climate with minimal vegetation, and valuable mineral and oil resources.

Key Terms and Places

Arabian Peninsula
Persian Gulf
Tigris River
Euphrates River
oasis
wadis
fossil water
landlocked
Pamirs
Fergana Valley
Aral Sea
Kara-Kum
Kyzyl Kum

If YOU lived there . . .

You are flying in a plane over the Arabian Peninsula to the Central Asia region. As you look down, you see some tents of desert nomads around trees of an oasis. Sometimes you can see a line of camels crossing the dry, rocky terrain. A shiny oil pipeline stretches for miles in the distance. Then the plane flies low over the steep mountains and narrow valleys of Central Asia. Icy glaciers fill some of the valleys. A few silvery rivers flow out of the mountains and across a green plain. This plain is the only green spot you can see in this rugged landscape.

How would these landscapes affect people?

The Arabian Peninsula, Iraq, and Iran

Iran, Iraq, and the countries of the Arabian Peninsula are part of a region sometimes called the "Middle East." This region lies at the intersection of Africa, Asia, and Europe. Much of the region is dry and rugged.

Physical Features Did you know that not all deserts are made of sand? The **Arabian Peninsula** has the largest sand desert in the world. It has huge expanses of desert covered with bare rock or gravel. These wide desert plains are a common landscape in the region that includes the Arabian Peninsula, Iraq, and Iran. Locate the countries of this region on a map. Notice how they appear in a semicircle, with the **Persian Gulf** in the center. The Arabian Peninsula is also bounded by the Strait of Hormuz, the Gulf of Oman, the Arabian Sea, and the Red Sea. The Caspian Sea borders Iran to the north.

The region contains four main landforms: rivers, plains, plateaus, and mountains. The **Tigris** (TY-gruhs) and **Euphrates** (yooh-FRAY-teez) rivers flow across a low, flat plain in Iraq. They join together before they reach the Persian Gulf. The Tigris and Euphrates are what are known as exotic rivers, or rivers that begin in humid regions and then flow through dry areas.

The rivers create a narrow, fertile area, which in ancient times gave rise to the world's first civilization. Many people found it to be an ideal place to settle so they could develop

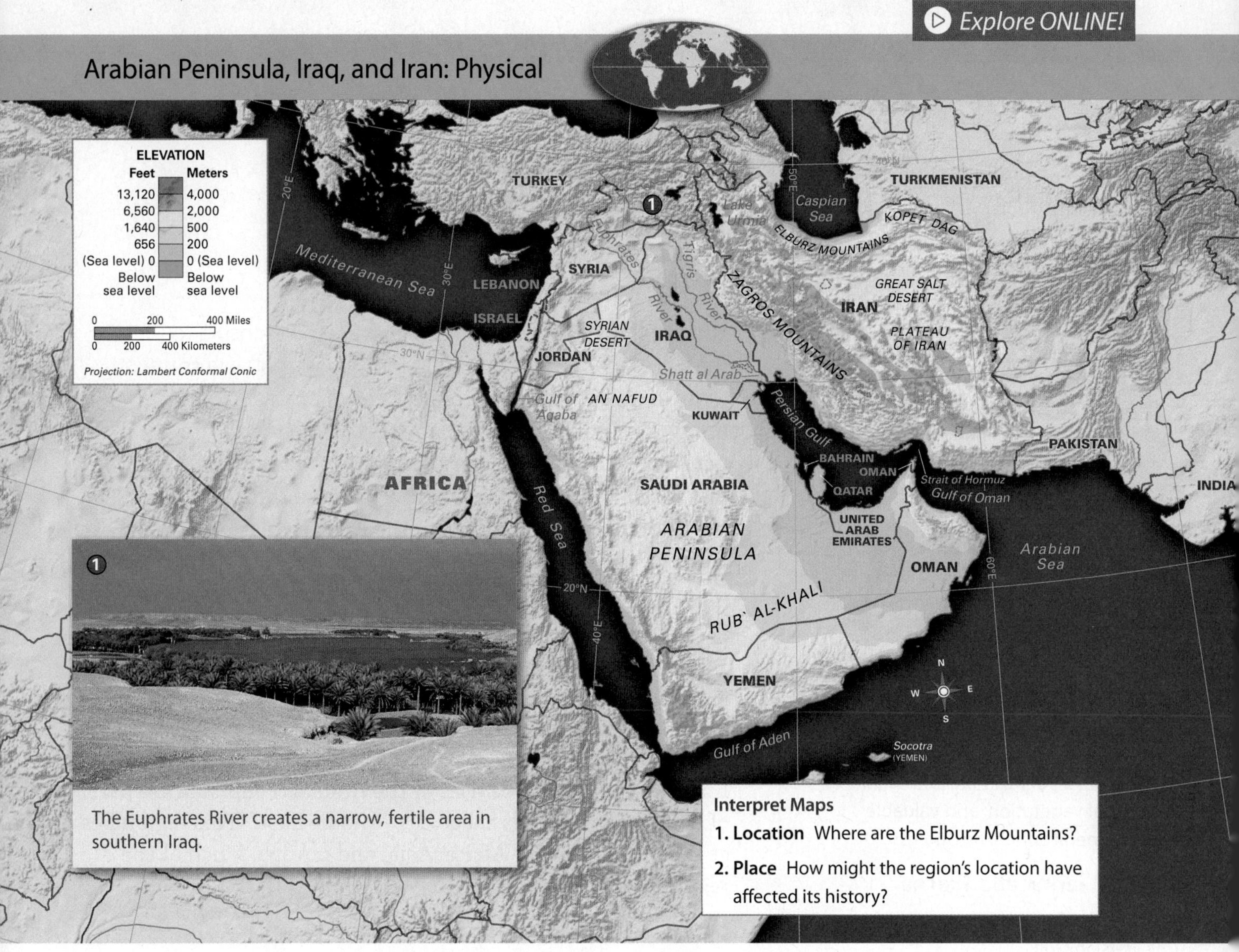

The Euphrates River creates a narrow, fertile area in southern Iraq.

Interpret Maps

1. **Location** Where are the Elburz Mountains?
2. **Place** How might the region's location have affected its history?

farming and domesticate animals. The area is called Mesopotamia, or the "land between the rivers." The Tigris and Euphrates were also important for transportation and trade. Mesopotamia became a crossroads for trade between India, China, Egypt, and people living along the eastern Mediterranean. The rivers helped in water transportation of goods.

The vast, dry expanse of the Arabian Peninsula is covered by plains in the east. The peninsula's desert plains are covered with sand in the south and volcanic rock in the north. As you can see on the map, the surface of the peninsula rises gradually from the Persian Gulf to the Red Sea. Near the Red Sea, the landscape becomes one of plateaus and mountains, with almost no coastal plain. The highest point on the peninsula is in the mountains of Yemen. The Arabian Peninsula has no permanent rivers.

Plateaus and mountains also cover most of Iran. In fact, Iran is one of the world's most mountainous countries. In the west, the land climbs sharply to form the Zagros Mountains. The Elburz Mountains and the Kopet-Dag lie in the north. Historically, the mountains have been a barrier, isolating towns and helping them control their territories.

Climate and Vegetation As you have already read, most of this region has a desert climate. The desert can be both very hot and very cold. In the summer, afternoon temperatures regularly climb to over 100°F (38°C). During the night, however, the temperature may drop quickly. Nighttime temperatures in the winter sometimes dip below freezing.

The world's largest sand desert, the Rub' al-Khali (ROOB ahl-KAH-lee), covers much of southern Saudi Arabia. *Rub' al-Khali* means "Empty Quarter," a name given to the area because there is so little life there. Sand dunes in the desert can rise to 800 feet (244 m) high and stretch for nearly 200 miles (322 km)! In northern Saudi Arabia is the An Nafud (ahn nah-FOOD), another large desert. These deserts are among the driest places in the world. The Rub' al-Khali receives an average of less than 4 inches (10 cm) of rainfall each year.

Some plateau and mountain areas do get winter rains or snow. These higher areas generally have semiarid steppe climates. Some mountain peaks receive more than 50 inches (127 cm) of rain per year.

Rainfall supports vegetation in some parts of the region. Trees are common in mountain regions and in scattered desert oases. An **oasis** is a wet, fertile area in a desert that forms where underground water bubbles to the surface. Most desert plants have adapted to survive without much rain. For example, the shrubs and grasses that grow on the region's dry plains have roots that either grow deep or spread out far to capture as much water as possible. Still, some places in the region are too dry.

People have lived in deserts throughout history. Desert life has many challenges and population density is generally low. The people who inhabit deserts have adapted their lives to this arid land. The Bedouins (BEHD-oo-ihnz) are one example of a desert-dwelling group. These Arab herders have moved from place to place for centuries because of limited farmland.

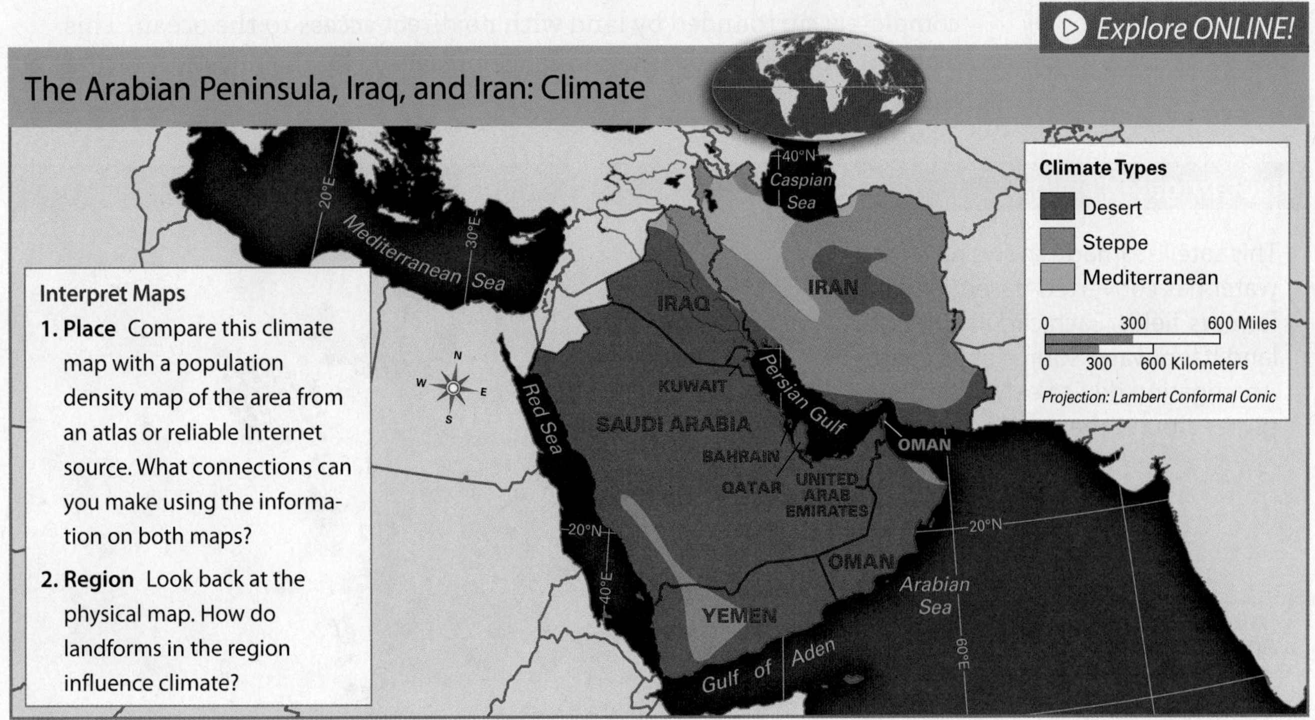

The Arabian Peninsula, Iraq, and Iran: Climate

Interpret Maps

1. **Place** Compare this climate map with a population density map of the area from an atlas or reliable Internet source. What connections can you make using the information on both maps?
2. **Region** Look back at the physical map. How do landforms in the region influence climate?

The Bedouins wear lightweight clothing and headdresses to protect themselves from the harsh environment. They migrate through the desert in search of water and grazing land for their herds. Camels are their main method of transportation because they can survive long periods without water. Today, only a small number of Bedouins continue to live a traditional nomadic lifestyle.

Resources Water is one of the region's two most valuable resources. However, water is very scarce, or limited. The unequal distribution of water impacts irrigation and the availability of drinking water. In some places in the desert, springs provide water. At other places, water comes from wells dug into dry streambeds called **wadis.** Modern wells can reach water deep underground called fossil water. **Fossil water** is water that is not replaced by rainfall. The image shows how farmers modify the environment by using fossil water. Wells that pump fossil water will eventually run dry.

While water is scarce, the region's other important resource, oil, is plentiful. Oil exports bring great wealth to the countries that have oil fields. Most of the oil fields are located near the shores of the Persian Gulf. However, although oil is plentiful now, it cannot be replaced once it is taken from Earth. Too much drilling for oil now may cause problems in the future because most countries of the region are not rich in other resources. Iran is an exception with its many mineral deposits.

Reading Check
Summarize
What are the major physical features of this area?

Central Asia

The physical geography of Central Asia affects the lives of the people who live there. This region has been shaped throughout its history by its isolated location and rugged terrain.

Physical Features As the name suggests, Central Asia lies in the middle of Asia. All of the countries in this region are **landlocked.** Landlocked means completely surrounded by land with no direct access to the ocean. This isolated location is just one challenge presented by the physical features of the region.

Pivot-Irrigated Fields

This satellite image shows how fossil water has converted desert land into farmers' fields. Each circular plot of land has a water source at its center. An irrigation device extends out and pivots around the center.

Irrigated areas

Analyze Visuals
Why are the fields circular?

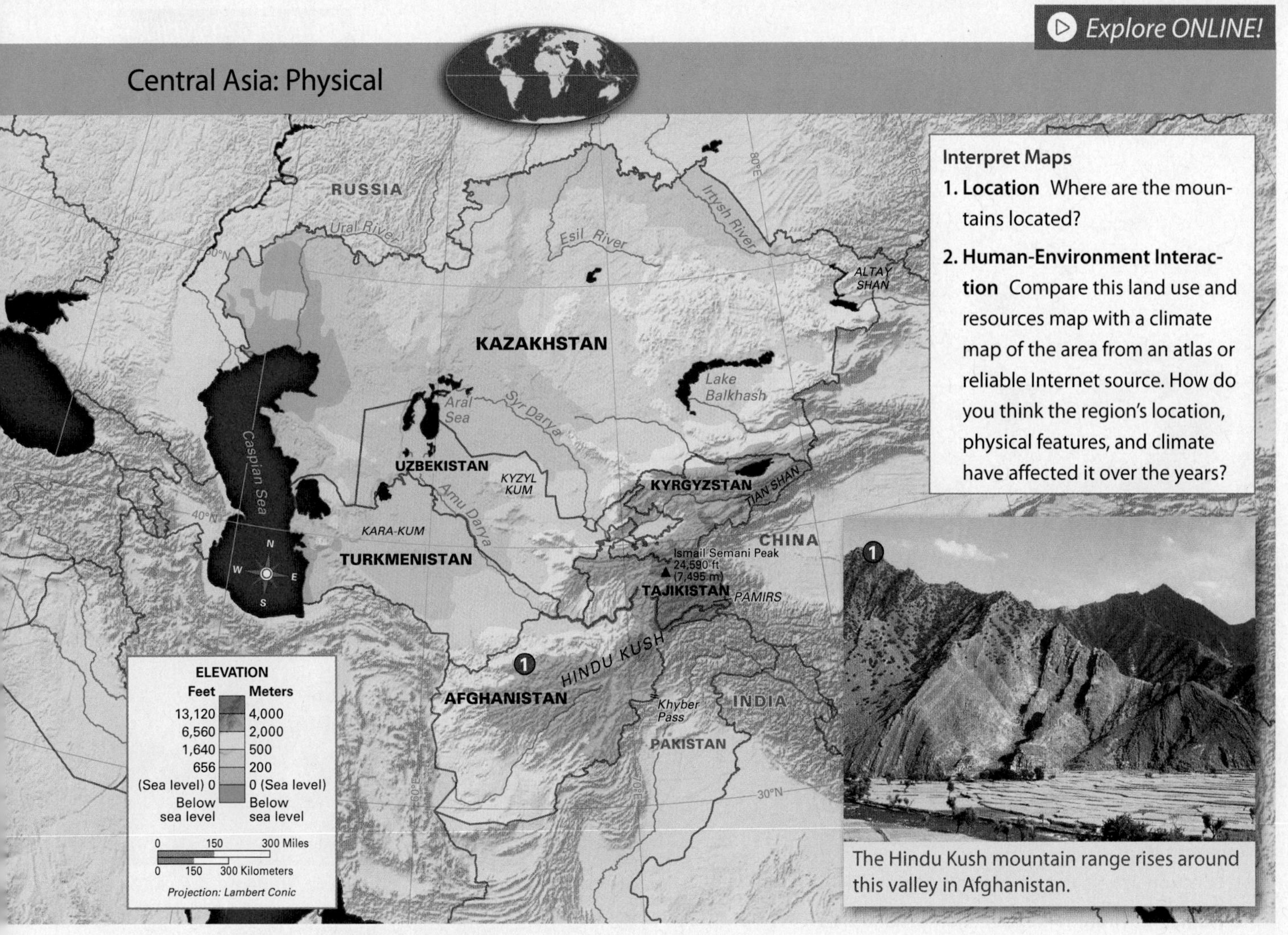

Interpret Maps

1. **Location** Where are the mountains located?
2. **Human-Environment Interaction** Compare this land use and resources map with a climate map of the area from an atlas or reliable Internet source. How do you think the region's location, physical features, and climate have affected it over the years?

The Hindu Kush mountain range rises around this valley in Afghanistan.

Mountains Much of Central Asia has a rugged landscape. In the south, many high mountain ranges, such as the Hindu Kush, stretch through Afghanistan. Tajikistan and Kyrgyzstan are also very mountainous. Large glaciers are common in high mountains such as the **Pamirs.**

Like its landlocked location, Central Asia's rugged terrain presents a challenge for the region. Throughout history, the mountains have made travel and communication difficult and have contributed to the region's isolation. In addition, tectonic activity causes frequent earthquakes there.

Plains and Plateaus From the mountains in the east, the land gradually slopes toward the west. There, near the Caspian Sea, the land is as low as 95 feet (29 m) below sea level. The central part of the region, between the mountains and the Caspian Sea, is covered with plains and low plateaus.

The plains region is the site of the fertile **Fergana Valley.** This large valley has been a major center of farming in the region for thousands of years.

Rivers and Lakes The Fergana Valley is fertile because of two rivers that flow through it—the Syr Darya (sir duhr-YAH) and the Amu Darya (uh-MOO duhr-YAH). These rivers flow from eastern mountains into the **Aral Sea,** which is really a large lake. Another important lake, Lake Balkhash, has freshwater at one end and salty water at the other end.

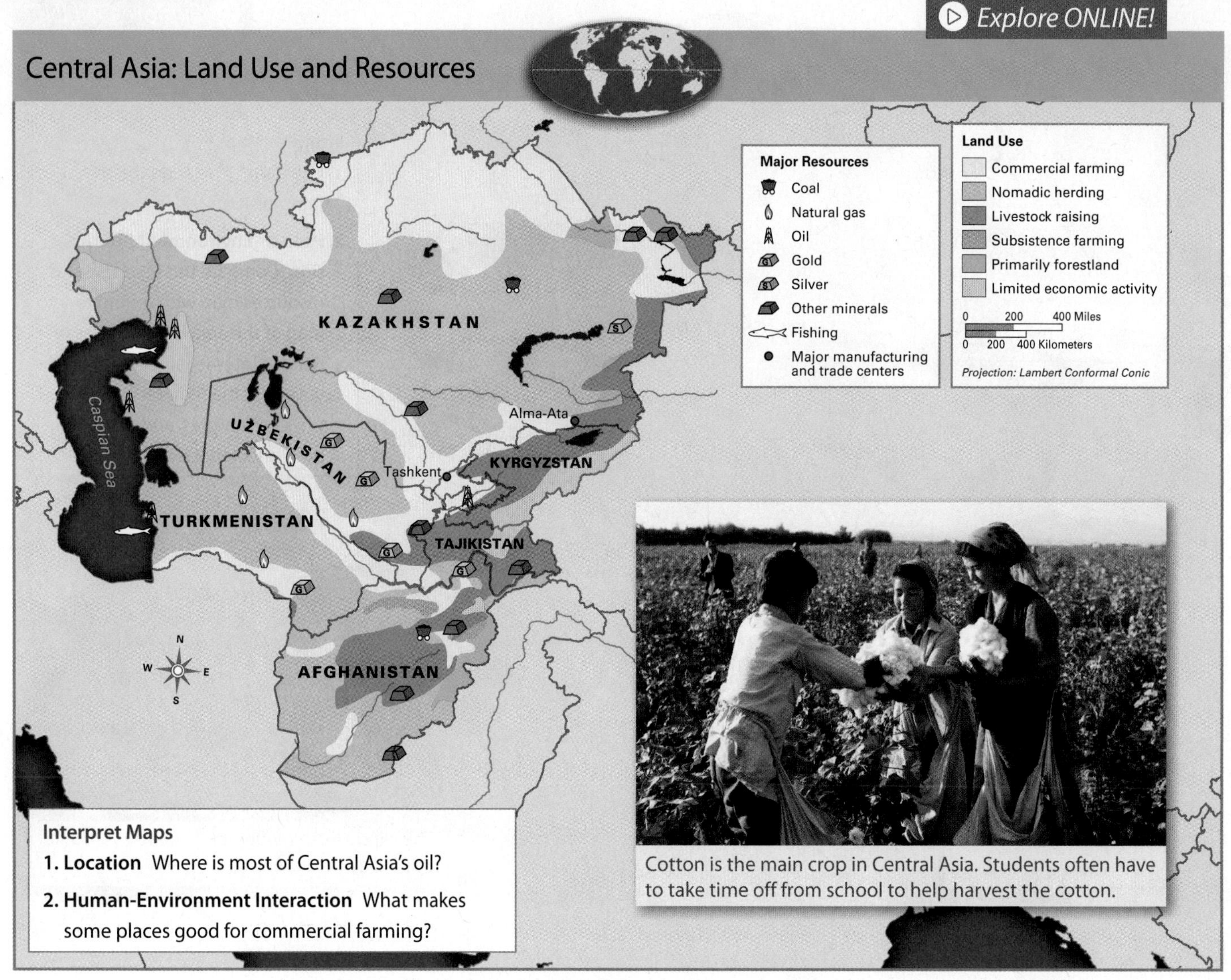

Interpret Maps

1. **Location** Where is most of Central Asia's oil?
2. **Human-Environment Interaction** What makes some places good for commercial farming?

Cotton is the main crop in Central Asia. Students often have to take time off from school to help harvest the cotton.

Climate and Vegetation Most places in Central Asia have harsh, dry climates. Extreme temperature ranges and limited rainfall make it difficult for plants to grow there.

One area with harsh climates in the region is the mountain area in the east. The high peaks in this area are too cold, dry, and windy for vegetation.

West of the mountains and east of the Caspian Sea is another harsh region. Two deserts—the **Kara-Kum** (kahr-uh-KOOM) in Turkmenistan and the **Kyzyl Kum** (ki-ZIL KOOM) in Uzbekistan and Kazakhstan—have extremely high temperatures in the summer. Rainfall is limited, though both deserts contain several settlements. Rivers crossing this dry region make settlements possible because they provide water for irrigation.

The only part of Central Asia with a milder climate is the far north. There, temperature ranges are not so extreme and rainfall is heavy enough for grasses and trees to grow.

Natural Resources In this dry region, water is one of the most valuable resources. Although water is scarce, the countries of Central Asia do have oil and other resources.

Water The main water sources in southern Central Asia are the Syr Darya and Amu Darya rivers. Scarcity has led to different ideas over how to use the water from these rivers, which led to conflict between Uzbekistan and Turkmenistan.

Today, farmers use river water mostly to irrigate cotton fields. Cotton grows well in Central Asia's sunny climate, but it requires a lot of water. Irrigation once took so much water from the rivers that almost no water reached the Aral Sea. The effect of this irrigation was devastating. The Aral Sea lost about 90 percent of its water and large areas of sea floor were exposed. Since then, area governments have built dams to control the water to restore parts of the lake.

In addition to water for irrigation, Central Asia's rivers supply power. Some countries have built large dams on the rivers to generate hydroelectricity.

Oil and Other Resources The resources that present the best economic opportunities for Central Asia are oil and gas. Uzbekistan, Kazakhstan, and Turkmenistan all have huge reserves of these resources. However, these reserves cannot benefit Central Asia unless they can be exported. Since no country in the region has an ocean port, the people are forced to use pipelines. The rugged mountains, along with economic and political turmoil in the area, make building and maintaining pipelines difficult.

In addition to oil and gas, some parts of Central Asia are rich in other minerals. They have deposits of gold, silver, copper, zinc, uranium, and lead. Kazakhstan, in particular, has many mines with these minerals. It also has large amounts of coal.

Reading Check
Form Generalizations Why is it hard for plants to grow in much of Central Asia?

Summary and Preview The Arabian Peninsula, Iraq, and Iran form a desert region with significant oil resources. Central Asia's rugged terrain, dry climate, and limited resources present many challenges for the area. Next you will learn more about the countries of the Arabian Peninsula.

Lesson 1 Assessment

Review Ideas, Terms, and Places

1. **a. Identify and Explain** Where was the world's first civilization located? Why was it there? What was significant about its location?
   b. Explain How have desert plants adapted to their environment?
   c. Define What is fossil water? How do farmers modify, or change, the land to access this water?
   d. Make Inferences How do you think resources in the region influence where people live?
   e. Predict What might happen to the oil-rich countries if their oil was used up or if people found a new energy source to replace oil?
2. **a. Identify** What fertile area has been a center of farming in Central Asia for many years?
   b. Make Inferences How does Central Asia's terrain affect life there?
   c. Describe Where do people find water in the deserts?
   d. Evaluate How has water become a source of conflict in the region?
   e. Elaborate What kinds of situations would make it easier for countries of Central Asia to export oil and gas?

Critical Thinking

3. **Find Main Ideas** Look at your notes from this lesson. Draw a chart and record main idea statements about physical features, climate and vegetation, and natural resources.

	Arabian Peninsula, Iraq, and Iran	Central Asia
Physical Features		
Climate and Vegetation		
Natural Resources		

The Arabian Peninsula

The Big Idea

Most countries of the Arabian Peninsula share three main characteristics: Islamic religion and culture, monarchy as a form of government, and valuable oil resources.

Main Ideas

- Islamic culture and an economy greatly based on oil influence life in Saudi Arabia.
- Most Arabian Peninsula countries other than Iraq and Iran are monarchies influenced by Islamic culture and oil resources.

Key Terms and Places

Islam
Shia
Sunni
OPEC
quota

If YOU lived there . . .

You are a financial adviser to the ruler of Oman. Your country has been making quite a bit of money from oil exports. However, you worry that your economy is too dependent on oil. You think Oman's leaders should consider expanding the economy. Oman is a small country, but it has beautiful beaches, historic palaces and mosques, and colorful markets.

How would you suggest expanding the economy?

Saudi Arabia

Saudi Arabia is by far the largest of the countries of the Arabian Peninsula. It is also a major religious and cultural center and has one of the region's strongest economies.

People and Customs Nearly all Saudis are Arab and speak Arabic. Their culture is strongly influenced by **Islam,** a religion founded around AD 622 in Arabia by Muhammad. It is based on submitting to God (Allah) and on messages Muslims believe Muhammad received from God. These messages are written in the Qur'an, the holy book of Islam.

Nearly all Saudis follow one of two main branches of Islam. **Shia** Muslims believe that true interpretation of Islamic teaching can only come from certain religious and political leaders called imams. **Sunni** Muslims believe in the ability of the majority of the community to interpret Islamic teachings. Approximately 85 to 90 percent of Saudi Muslims are Sunni.

Islam influences Saudi Arabia's culture in many ways. In part because Islam requires modesty, Saudi clothing keeps arms and legs covered. Men wear a long, loose shirt and a cotton headdress held in place with a cord. Saudi women wear a black cloak and veil in public, although some wear Western-style clothing.

Saudi laws and customs limit women's activities. For example, a woman rarely appears in public without her husband or a male relative. However, women can own and run businesses in Saudi Arabia. Only recently, Saudi women gained the rights to drive cars and to attend events in sports stadiums.

Link to Math

Muslim Contributions to Math

During the early centuries of the Middle Ages, European art, literature, and science declined. However, during this same period, Muslim scholars made important advances in literature, art, medicine, and mathematics.

Our familiar system of numerals, which we call Arabic, was first created in India. However, it was Muslim thinkers who introduced that system to Europe. They also developed algebra and made advances in geometry. Muslims used math to advance the study of astronomy and physics. Muslim geographers calculated distances between cities, longitudes and latitudes, and the direction from one city to another. Muslim scientists even defined ratios and used mathematics to explain the appearance of rainbows.

Make Inferences
Why do we need math to study geography?

Government and Economy Saudi Arabia is a monarchy. Members of the Saud family have ruled Saudi Arabia since 1932. Most government officials are relatives of the king. The king may ask members of his family, Islamic scholars, and tribal leaders for advice on decisions.

Local officials are elected. For many years only men were allowed to vote. In 2015 King Abdullah granted Saudi Arabian women the right to vote and run for local offices.

Saudi Arabia's economy and foreign policy is influenced strongly by one geographic factor: oil. Saudi Arabia has almost one-fifth of the entire world's oil reserves, or supplies. It is the world's leading exporter of oil. Because it has so much oil, Saudi Arabia is an influential member of **OPEC,** the Organization of the Petroleum Exporting Countries. OPEC is an international organization whose members work to influence the price of oil on world markets by controlling the supply. The organization places a **quota,** or limit, on each member nation. Quotas provide a number or monetary value to the amount of goods that can be imported or exported over a certain time period. OPEC members are not to exceed their oil production limit.

Oil also shapes the country's domestic policy. In the 1970s, oil industry profits helped Saudi Arabia build roads, schools, hospitals, and universities. Today, Saudi Arabia has a sizable middle class and provides its people with free health care and education.

Despite these gains, Saudi Arabia's oil-based economy faces some challenges. Because oil is a nonrenewable resource, many Saudi Arabians think their nation should develop other industries. Others think that new industries would provide important opportunities for Saudi youth. In 2016, one-quarter of all Saudi workers under 30 was unemployed. To secure its future, Saudi Arabia must create jobs for its young people.

Big, modern cities such as Dubai, UAE, were built with money from oil exports.

Saudi Arabia has created a national reform program that aims to fight unemployment and provide more job opportunities. The Saudi government plans to shut down the bureaucratic system that has hindered economic progress. It wants to increase the number of small businesses and offer more assistance to entrepreneurs. In the past, entrepreneurship was rarely practiced in Saudi Arabia. People did not have the necessary skills or support. With new training programs and better policies, the nation and its citizens will be able to create more opportunities for economic development.

Like many nations in the region, Saudi Arabia is challenged by its lack of renewable water resources. However, nature is not the only reason for this shortage. In the 1970s Saudi Arabia decided to address rising food demands with a self-sufficiency policy. The nation worked to cultivate the desert for wheat, grain, and fruit crops. Over the past 40 years, the Saudis have successfully provided basic food needs for themselves and others in the region. Unfortunately, their progress severely depleted underground water reserves. Policymakers had to examine their management of water resources. Today, great efforts are being made to change old agricultural and water policies.

Reading Check
Find Main Ideas
What religion influences Saudi Arabia's culture?

Other Countries of the Arabian Peninsula

Saudi Arabia shares the Arabian Peninsula with six smaller countries. Like Saudi Arabia, these countries are all influenced by Islam. Also like Saudi Arabia, most have monarchies and economies based on oil.

Kuwait Oil was discovered in Kuwait in the 1930s. Since then, it has made Kuwait very rich. In 1990 Iraq invaded Kuwait to try to control its oil, starting the Persian Gulf War. The United States and other countries defeated Iraq, but the war caused major destruction to Kuwait's oil fields.

Although Kuwait's government is dominated by a royal family, the country did elect a legislature in 1992. Only men from certain families—less than 15 percent of Kuwait's population—had the right to vote in these elections. However, Kuwait gave women the right to vote in 2005.

Bahrain and Qatar Bahrain is a group of islands in the Persian Gulf. It is a monarchy with a legislature. Bahrain is a rich country. Most people there live well in big, modern cities. Oil made Bahrain wealthy, but in the 1990s the country began to run out of oil. Now, banking and tourism are major industries.

Qatar occupies a small peninsula in the Persian Gulf. Like Bahrain, Qatar is ruled by a powerful monarch. In 2003 men and women in Qatar voted to approve a new constitution that would give more power to elected officials. Qatar is a wealthy country. Its economy relies on its oil and natural gas.

Yemen's architecture is an important part of its culture. These buildings are more than 2,000 years old.

The United Arab Emirates The United Arab Emirates, or UAE, consists of seven tiny kingdoms. Profits from oil and natural gas have created a modern, comfortable lifestyle for the people of the UAE. Partly because it is so small, the UAE depends on foreign workers. In fact, it has more foreign workers than citizens.

Oman and Yemen Oman covers most of the southeastern part of the Arabian Peninsula. Oman's economy is also based on oil. However, Oman does not have the great oil wealth of Kuwait or the UAE. Therefore, the government is working to develop new industries such as tourism and manufacturing.

Yemen is located on the southwestern part of the Arabian Peninsula. The country has an elected government, but it has suffered from corruption. Oil was not discovered in Yemen until the 1980s. Oil and coffee generate much of the national income, but Yemen is still the poorest country on the Arabian Peninsula.

In recent years, Yemen has been devastated by a civil war between forces loyal to the government and those supporting a rebel movement. Civilians have felt the greatest impact of the fighting. Restrictions on food and fuel imports have brought Yemen close to famine. Some 2 million people are internally displaced, and thousands of others have fled the country. The United Nations has been working to develop a resolution.

Reading Check
Summarize
How has oil affected the countries of the Arabian Peninsula?

Summary and Preview Islam is a major influence on the people and culture of Saudi Arabia and the other countries of the Arabian Peninsula. The other major influence in the region is oil. Oil has brought wealth to most countries on the peninsula. In the next lesson you will learn about Iraq, a neighboring country with similar influences.

Lesson 2 Assessment

Review Ideas, Terms, and Places

1. a. **Evaluate** What is OPEC and how does its work contribute to the economies of its member nations?
   b. **Compare and Contrast** How are Sunni and Shia Muslims similar, and how are they different from each other?
   c. **Elaborate** What do you think Saudi Arabia would be like if it did not have such huge oil reserves?
2. a. **Identify** Which geographic factor has been most important to the economic development of countries on the Arabian Peninsula?
   b. **Analyze** How does its small size affect the United Arab Emirates?
   c. **Predict Effects** How could oil impact Yemen's economy?

Critical Thinking

3. **Summarize** Look at your notes on the countries of the Arabian Peninsula. Draw a graphic organizer and write a one-sentence summary about the region's culture, government, and economy.

	Summary
Culture	
Government	
Economy	

Case Study

Oil in Saudi Arabia

Essential Elements

The World in Spatial Terms

Places and Regions

Physical Systems

Human Systems

Environment and Society

The Uses of Geography

Background

Try to imagine your life without oil. You would probably walk or ride a horse to school. You would heat your home with coal or wood. You would never fly in a plane, walk in rubber-soled shoes, or even drink out of a plastic cup.

We live in a world that is dependent on oil. In fact, a little over 30 percent of the world's energy comes from crude oil products. However, oil is a nonrenewable resource. This means that supplies are limited, and we may one day run out of oil. How might this affect countries that have economies based on oil production?

Oil Reserves in Saudi Arabia

Saudi Arabia has almost one-fifth of the entire world's oil reserves. This important resource, found naturally in the environment, has had a huge impact on Saudi Arabia's society.

Before the discovery of oil there in the 1930s, Saudi Arabia was a poor country. But income from oil exports has given the government money to invest in improvements such as new communications systems, airports, oil pipelines, and roads. For example, in 1960 Saudi Arabia had only about 1,000 miles (1,600 km) of roads. By 2005 it had over 94,000 miles (151,000 km) of roads. These improvements have helped modernize Saudi Arabia's economy.

Oil exports have also affected Saudi society. Rising incomes have given many people there more money to spend on consumer goods. New stores and restaurants have opened, and new schools have been built

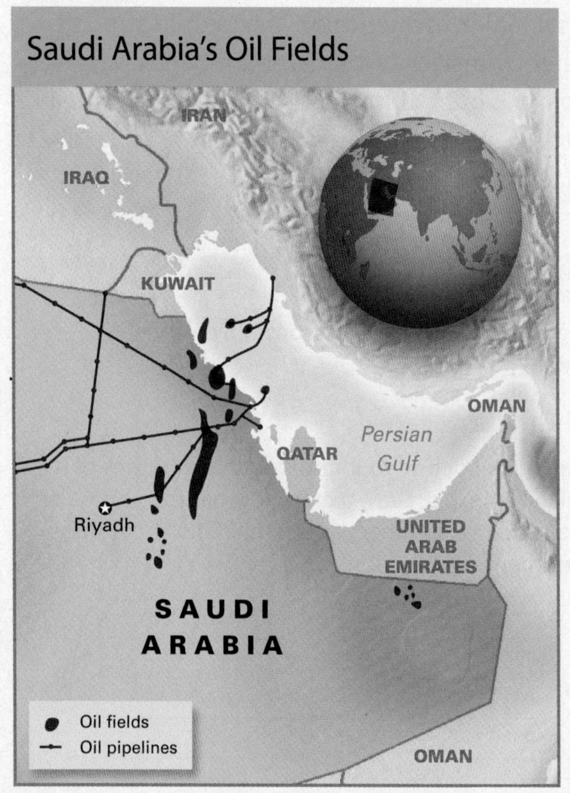

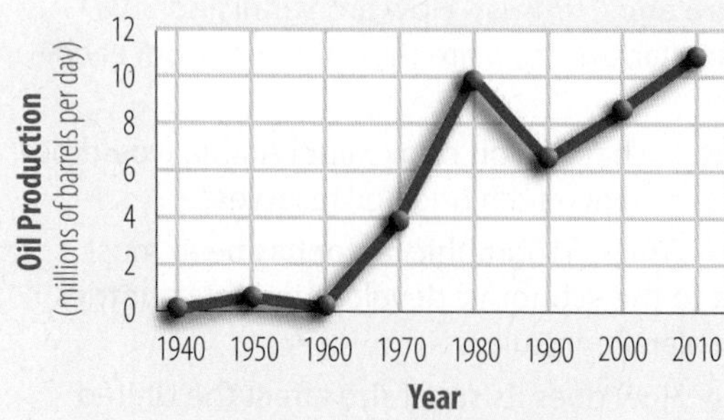

Sources: U.S. Bureau of Mines, *World Oil*, U.S. Energy Information Administration

Saudi Arabia's oil is pumped through pipelines to tankers that ship the oil around the world. The oil industry has made Saudi Arabia a rich country.

throughout the country. Education is now available to all citizens. Increased education means the literacy rate has increased also—from about 3 percent when oil was discovered to about 95 percent today. These factors contribute to an improved standard of living. Health care there has also improved.

The oil industry has also increased Saudi Arabia's importance in the world. Since it is a member of the Organization of the Petroleum Exporting Countries (OPEC), Saudi Arabia influences the price of oil on the world market. Countries around the world want to have good relations with Saudi Arabia because of its vast oil reserves.

What It Means

Today, Saudi Arabia's government has a lot of money. This wealth has come almost entirely from the sale of oil. This is an example of specialization. Saudi Arabia has primarily focused their economy around one product. However, since the world's oil supplies are limited, Saudi Arabia's economy may be at risk in the future. Many countries are beginning to research other types of energy that can be used in place of oil. Until then, the many countries buying oil from Saudi Arabia will continue to pump wealth into Saudi society.

Geography for Life Activity

1. **Analyze Effects** How has oil contributed to the economic development of Saudi Arabia?
2. **Evaluate** What are some advantages and disadvantages for a society that relies on oil?

Iraq

The Big Idea

Iraq, a country with a rich culture and natural resources, faces the challenge of rebuilding after years of conflict.

Main Ideas

- Iraq's history includes rule by many conquerors and cultures. Its recent history includes wars.
- Most of Iraq's people are Arab, and Iraqi culture includes the religion of Islam.
- Iraq today must rebuild its government and economy, which have suffered from years of conflict.

Key Terms and Places

embargo
Baghdad

If YOU lived there . . .

You are a student in a school in Iraq's capital, Baghdad. During the war, your school and its library were badly damaged. Since then, you and your friends have had few books to read. Now your teachers and others are organizing a project to rebuild your library. They want to include books from all countries of the world as well as computers so students can use the Internet.

What topics will you include in the new library's collection to help people learn about Iraq?

History

Did you know that the world's first civilization was located in Iraq? Thousands of years ago, people known as Sumerians settled in Mesopotamia—a region that is part of Iraq today. The country's recent history includes wars and a corrupt leader.

Early Civilization Throughout Mesopotamia's history, different cultures and empires conquered the region. As you can see on the map, the Sumerians settled in southern Mesopotamia. By about 3000 BC the Sumerians built the world's first-known cities there. The Persians then conquered Mesopotamia in the 500s BC. By 331 BC Alexander the Great made it part of his empire. In the AD 600s Arabs conquered Mesopotamia, and the people gradually converted to Islam.

In the 1500s Mesopotamia became part of the Ottoman Empire. During World War I, Great Britain took over the region. The British set up the kingdom of Iraq in 1932 and placed a pro-British ruler in power. In the 1950s a group of Iraqi army officers overthrew this government.

Saddam Takes Power In 1968, after several more changes in Iraq's government, the Ba`ath (bahth) Party took power. In 1979 a Ba`ath leader named Saddam Hussein became Iraq's president. Saddam Hussein was a harsh ruler. He controlled Iraq's media, restricted personal freedoms, and killed an unknown number of political enemies.

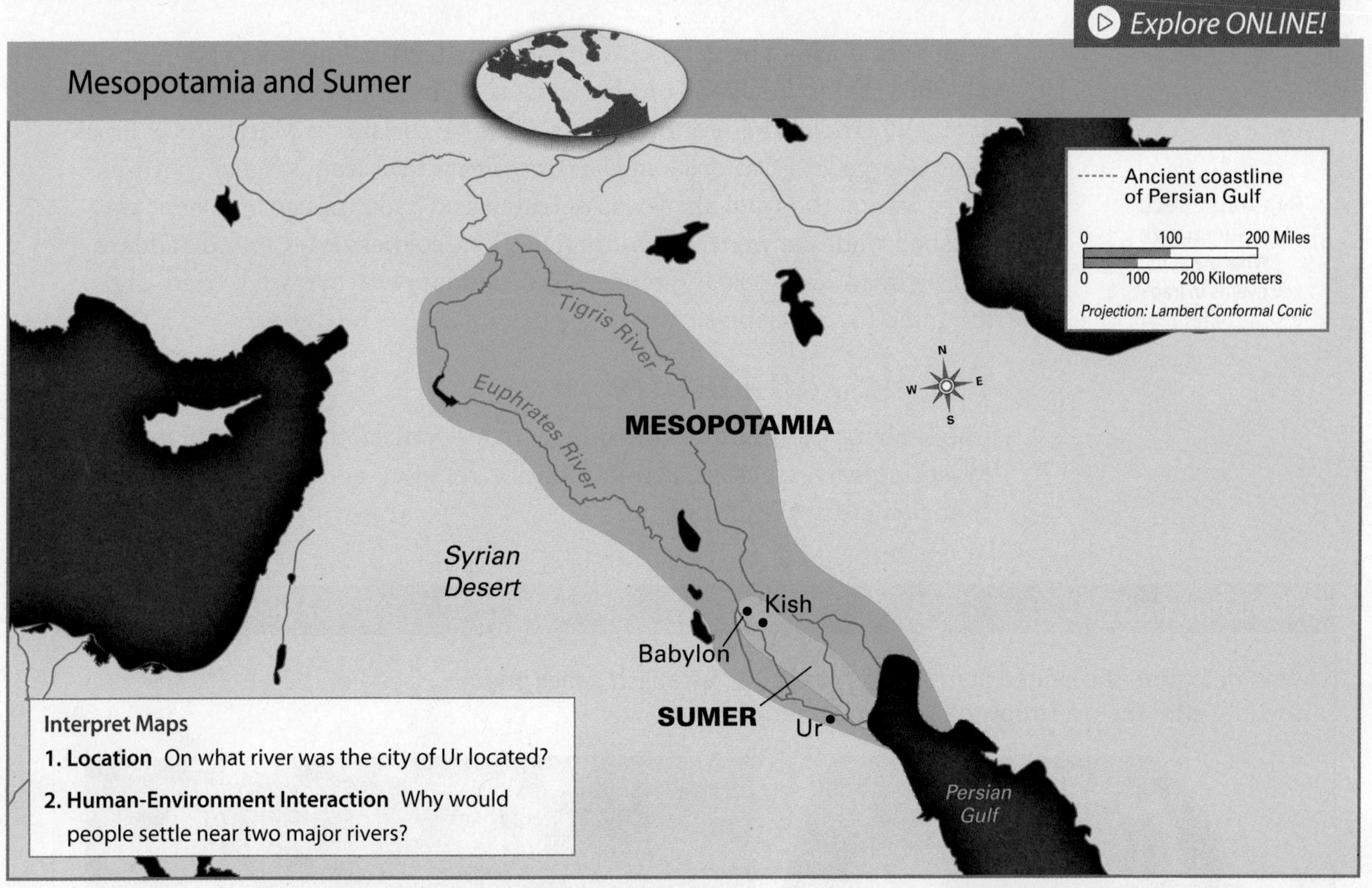

Interpret Maps

1. **Location** On what river was the city of Ur located?
2. **Human-Environment Interaction** Why would people settle near two major rivers?

Invasions of Iran and Kuwait Under Saddam's leadership, Iraq invaded Iran in 1980. The Iranians fought back, and the Iran-Iraq War dragged on until 1988. Both countries' economies were seriously damaged, and many people died.

In 1990 Iraq invaded Kuwait, Iraq's oil-rich neighbor to the south. This event shocked and worried many world leaders. They were concerned that Iraq might gain control of the region's oil. In addition, they worried about Iraq's supply of weapons of mass destruction, including chemical and biological weapons.

War and Its Effects In 1991 an alliance of countries led by the United States forced the Iraqis out of Kuwait. This six-week event was called the Persian Gulf War. Saddam, who remained in power after the war, would not accept all the United Nations' (UN) terms for peace. In response, the UN placed an **embargo,** or limit on trade, on Iraq. As a result, Iraq's economy suffered.

Soon after the fighting ended, Saddam faced two rebellions from Shia Muslims and Kurds. He brutally put down these uprisings. In response, the UN forced Iraq to end all military activity. The UN also required that Iraq allow inspectors into the country. They wanted to make sure that Saddam had destroyed the weapons of mass destruction. Iraq later refused to cooperate completely with the UN.

Ten years after the Persian Gulf War, the terrorist attacks of September 11, 2001, led to new tensions between the United States and Iraq. U.S. government officials believed that Iraq aided terrorists. In March 2003 President George W. Bush ordered U.S. forces to attack Iraqi targets. Within a few weeks, the Iraqi army was defeated and Saddam's government was crushed. Saddam went into hiding, but U.S. soldiers later found Saddam hiding in an underground hole in Iraq. Saddam was arrested, tried, and executed for his crimes.

Reading Check
Summarize
What are some key events in Iraq's history?

People and Culture

Iraq is about the size of California, with a population of about 38 million. Most Iraqis live in cities. Ethnic identity, religion, and food are all important elements of Iraqi culture.

Rebuilding Iraq

With help from the United States, Iraqis worked to establish peace and security after the overthrow of Saddam Hussein.

An Iraqi woman holds up her ink-stained finger in a sign of victory after voting in Iraq's first democratic elections.

U.S. soldiers in Iraq searching for suspected terrorists

A U.S. soldier handing out school supplies to Iraqi schoolchildren

Analyze Visuals
How did the United States support Iraqis in rebuilding their nation?

Ethnic Groups Most of Iraq's people belong to two major ethnic groups—Arabs and Kurds. Arabs are the largest group and make up 75 to 80 percent of Iraq's population. Iraqi Arabs speak the country's official language, Arabic. The smaller group, the Kurds, make up some 15 to 20 percent of the population. The Kurds are mostly farmers and live in a large region of northern Iraq. Most Iraqi Kurds speak Kurdish in addition to Arabic.

Religion Like ethnic identity, religion plays a large role in the lives of most Iraqis. Nearly all Iraqis, both Arab and Kurdish, are Muslim. Within Iraq, the two different branches of Islam—Shia and Sunni—are practiced. About 60 to 65 percent of Iraqis are Shia and live in the south. About 32 to 37 percent of Iraqis are Sunnis and live in the north.

While most Kurdish people identify as Muslim, the Kurds are perhaps the most religiously diverse group in West Asia. They are known to practice a variety of religions including Judaism, Christianity, Yarsan, Yazidism, and Zoroastrianism. The Kurds are widely recognized as one of the few cultures in the region to practice religious tolerance.

Reading Check
Summarize What ethnic groups do most Iraqis belong to?

Iraq Today

Despite years of war, Iraq is slowly rebuilding. However, the country faces many challenges, such as ongoing fighting.

Rebuilding Baghdad Iraq's capital, **Baghdad,** was severely damaged in the overthrow of Saddam's government. For example, the city's 6 million people lost electricity and running water. To help the city's residents, U.S. military and private contractors worked with the Iraqis to restore electricity and water and to rebuild homes, businesses, and schools. However, violence in Baghdad continued, disrupting efforts to rebuild.

Government and Economy In January 2005 Iraqis participated in democracy for the first time. Millions of Iraqis went to the polls to elect members to the National Assembly. One of the Assembly's first tasks was to create a new constitution. Deep divisions among Iraqis led to fierce internal fighting, however, and threatened the new government's stability.

Iraqis also began trying to rebuild their once-strong economy. In the 1970s Iraq was the world's second-largest oil exporter. Time will tell if Iraq can again be a major oil producer.

Oil isn't Iraq's only resource. From earliest times, Iraq's wide plains and fertile soils have produced many food crops. Irrigation from the Tigris and Euphrates rivers allows farmers to grow barley, cotton, and rice.

After years of harsh government and wars, Iraq's future remains uncertain. After the United States military transferred control back to the Iraqis, the country's government faced huge challenges in creating a free and prosperous society. In the past decade, Iraqis have made some progress in building their government. They approved a constitution to replace that of the Saddam Hussein era and have held consecutive elections for parliament and local governments. Even with these advances, governing institutions remain weak, and corruption and poverty are widespread.

A refugee camp serves as a temporary home for these displaced Iraqi children.

Iraq has been devastated in recent years by warfare, separatist movements, a refugee crisis, and the rise and violent spread of a Sunni Muslim militant group called the Islamic State in Iraq and the Levant (ISIL). The goal of ISIL is to create a modern-day Islamic state that supports its extreme form of Islam. ISIL has committed acts of terror across the globe. They have carried out acts of ethnic persecution against various groups. The world's democracies view ISIL as an immediate threat to their basic beliefs of freedom and fair treatment for all.

U.S. military advisers returned to Iraq in 2014 to assist with rising violence and the threat of ISIL. The continued weakness of government and the presence of ISIL create long-term challenges to stability for Iraq and the rest of the world.

Reading Check
Draw Conclusions What happened to Iraq's oil industry?

Summary and Preview In this lesson you have learned about Iraq's ancient history, rich culture, and efforts to rebuild. Next you will learn about Iran, which also has an ancient history but is otherwise quite different from Iraq.

Lesson 3 Assessment

Review Ideas, Terms, and Places

1. a. **Recall** Where was the world's first civilization located?
   b. **Sequence** What events led to the embargo on Iraq by the United Nations?
2. a. **Identify** What are two major ethnic groups in Iraq?
   b. **Contrast** What is one difference between Shia Muslims and Sunni Muslims?
3. a. **Describe** How was Baghdad damaged by war?
   b. **Evaluate** How did democratic reforms impact politics and culture in Iraq?
   c. **Predict** What kind of country do you think Iraq will be in five years?

Critical Thinking

4. **Summarize** Draw a chart, and for each column use your notes to summarize what you have learned about the capital city, government, and economy of Iraq.

Baghdad	Government	Economy

Iran

The Big Idea

Islam is a huge influence on government and daily life in Iran.

Main Ideas

- Iran's history includes great empires and an Islamic republic.
- In Iran today, Islamic religious leaders restrict the rights of most Iranians.

Key Terms and Places

shah
Esfahan
revolution
Tehran
theocracy

If YOU lived there . . .

You are a student in Tehran, the capital of Iran. In school, you are taught that the way of life in the West—countries of Europe and the Americas—is bad. News reports and newspapers are filled with negative propaganda about Western countries. Yet you know that some of your friends secretly listen to Western popular music and watch American television programs that they catch using illegal satellite dishes at home. This makes you very curious about Western countries.

What would you like to know about life in other countries?

History

The early history of the country we now call Iran includes the Persian Empire and a series of Muslim empires. Iran's recent history includes an Islamic revolution. Today, Iran is an Islamic republic, which limits the rights of many Iranians.

Persian Empire Beginning in the 500s BC, the Persian Empire ruled the region around present-day Iran. For centuries, Persia was a great center of art and learning. The Persian Empire was known for its spectacular paintings, carpets, metalwork, and architecture. In the empire's capital, Persepolis, walls and statues throughout the city glittered with gold, silver, and precious jewels.

The Persian Empire was later conquered by several Muslim empires. Muslims converted the Persians to Islam, but most people retained their Persian culture. They built beautiful mosques with colorful tiles and large domes.

The Safavid Empire The great era of Arab Muslim expansion lasted until the 1100s. Afterward, three non-Arab Muslim groups built large, powerful empires that took control of much of Europe, Asia, and Africa. These were the Ottoman, Safavid, and Mughal empires. The Safavids (sah-FAH-vuhds) were gaining power to the east, in the area of present-day Iran. Before long, the Safavids came into conflict with the Ottomans and other Muslims.

The Safavid Empire

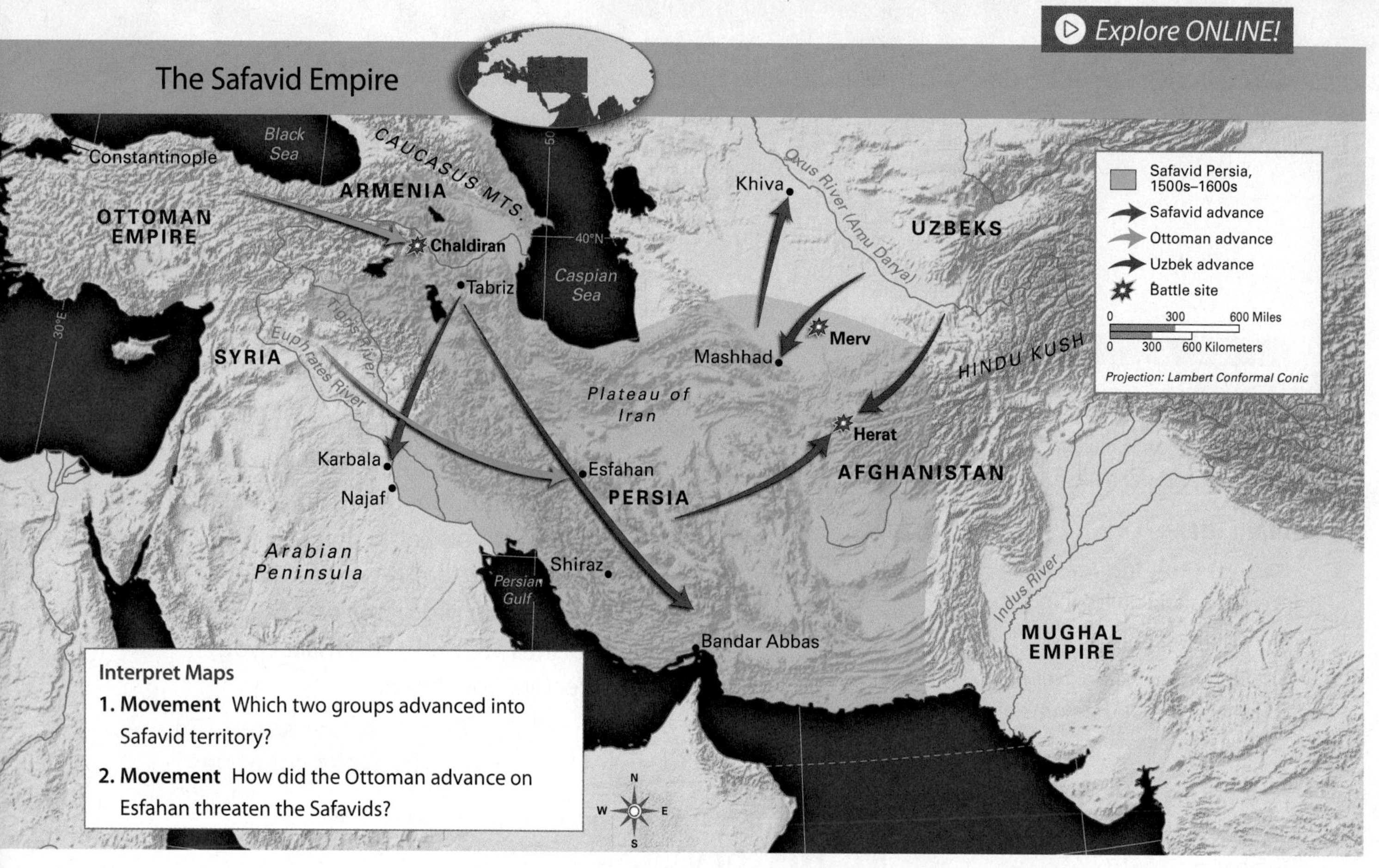

Interpret Maps

1. **Movement** Which two groups advanced into Safavid territory?
2. **Movement** How did the Ottoman advance on Esfahan threaten the Safavids?

The Safavid Empire began in 1501 when a strong Safavid leader named Esma'il (is-mah-EEL) conquered Persia. He took the ancient Persian title of **shah,** or king. Esma'il made Shiism—the beliefs of the Shia—the official religion of the empire. But he wanted to spread Shiism farther. He tried to gain more Muslim lands and convert more Muslims to Shiism. He fought the Uzbek people, but he suffered a major defeat by the Ottomans in 1514.

The Safavids blended many Persian and Muslim traditions. They grew wealthy from trade and built glorious mosques in their capital, **Esfahan** (es-fah-HAHN). The Safavid Empire lasted until the mid-1700s.

The Shah and Islamic Revolution In 1921 an Iranian military officer took power and encouraged change in Iran's government. He claimed the old Persian title of shah. In 1941 the shah's son took control. This shah became an ally of the United States and Great Britain and tried to modernize Iran. His programs were unpopular with many Iranians.

In 1978 Iranians began a **revolution.** A revolution is a drastic change in a country's government and way of life. By 1979 Iranians overthrew the shah and set up an Islamic republic. This type of government follows strict Islamic law.

Soon after Iran's Islamic Revolution began, relations with the United States broke down. A mob of students attacked the U.S. Embassy in Iran's capital, **Tehran.** With the approval of Iran's government, the students took Americans working at the embassy hostage. More than 50 Americans were held by force for over a year.

Reading Check
Draw Conclusions
How did Iran's history lead to the Islamic Revolution?

Iran Today

Iranian culture differs from many other cultures of Southwest Asia. While most of the people in the region are Arabic, more than half of all Iranians are Persian. They speak Farsi, the Persian language.

People and Culture With about 83 million people, Iran has one of the largest populations in Southwest Asia. Iran's population is very young. The average age in Iran is about 29 years old. It is also ethnically diverse. Iranian ethnic groups other than the Persian majority include Azeris, Lurs, Kurds, Arabs, and Turks.

Most Iranians belong to the Shia branch of Islam. Only about 5 to 10 percent are Sunni Muslim. The rest of Iran's people practice Christianity, Judaism, or other religions.

In addition to the Islamic holy days, Iranians celebrate Nowruz—the Persian New Year. Iranians tend to spend this holiday outdoors. As a part of this celebration, they display goldfish in their homes to symbolize life. Iranian culture also includes close-knit families and respect for elders. Most family gatherings in Iran are centered on Persian food, which includes rice, bread, vegetables, fruits, lamb, and tea.

Meat is an important part of Islamic culture. It holds great significance on holidays and within the social structure. Upper-class families eat meat every day. This is viewed as a symbol of wealth by the lower class. Meeting the demand for meat products has sparked concern about the environmental impacts caused by raising animals for food. Animal agriculture contributes to greenhouse gas emissions. In addition, overgrazing is especially harmful in an area where favorable land and water resources are diminishing.

Economy and Government Huge oil reserves make Iran a wealthy country. In addition to oil, the production of beautiful woven carpets contributes to Iran's economy. Agriculture employs only a small portion of the Iranian workforce. Much of Iran's younger population are finding jobs in a growing technology sector. Today, the nation's university system is producing more graduates with degrees in science and engineering. The government identified technological development as a national priority for 2016 to 2021. Entrepreneurs are taking advantage of this opportunity to create new businesses.

When comparing life in Iran to life in the United States, many of the differences are related to forms of government. Today, Iran is led by a **theocracy**—a government ruled by religious leaders. These religious leaders, or *ayatollahs,* control Iran's government. The head of the *ayatollahs,* or supreme leader, has unlimited power. Even though religious leaders control Iran, its government has an elected president and parliament.

The Imam Mosque in Esfahan, Iran, was built during the Safavid Empire.

Life in Iran and the United States	
Iran	**United States**
Daily Life	**Daily Life**
• An Iranian woman has to cover her head and most of her body with clothing in public.	• Americans are free to wear any type of clothing.
• Iranians are forbidden to view most Western websites, and Internet use is monitored by the government.	• Americans are free to surf the Internet and view most websites.
• Boys and girls have separate schools, and they cannot be alone with each other without adult supervision.	• Boys and girls can attend the same school.
Government	**Government**
• Iran is a theocracy.	• The United States is a democracy.
• A supreme religious leader rules Iran.	• A president is the leader of our country.
• Only candidates approved by the government can run for political office.	• Any U.S. citizen can run for political office.
Basic Rights	**Basic Rights**
• Freedom of speech, religion, and the press is limited.	• Freedom of speech, religion, and the press is allowed.

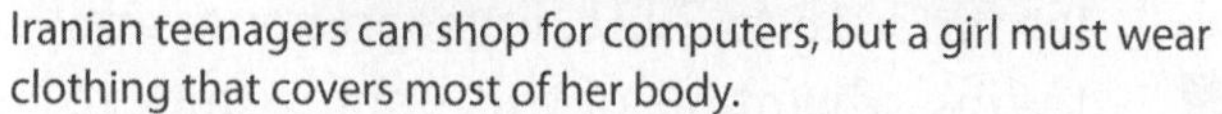

Iranian teenagers can shop for computers, but a girl must wear clothing that covers most of her body.

In the United States, boys and girls can attend the same school.

Interpret Charts
In what ways does Iran's government differ from the U.S. government?

Iran's government has supported many hard-line policies. For example, it has called for the destruction of Israel. It has also supported terrorist groups in other countries. With a newly elected president in 1997, some signs indicated that Iran's government might adopt democratic reforms. This government attempted to improve Iran's economy and rights for women.

However, in 2005 Iranians moved away from democratic reforms by electing Mahmoud Ahmadinejad (mah-MOOD ah-mah-di-nee-ZHAHD)

BIOGRAPHY

Shirin Ebadi 1947–

Iranians hoping for more democratic reforms were encouraged in 2003 when Shirin Ebadi received the Nobel Peace Prize. Ebadi is a lawyer, judge, and author. However, her work attempting to improve human rights in Iran has at times made her unpopular with the country's government leaders. Ebadi's goals include to attain better conditions for women, children, and refugees.

Draw Inferences
Why would Iran's government be opposed to Ebadi's human rights efforts?

president. He wanted Iranians to follow strict Islamic law. After the election, a reporter asked the new president if he had any plans for reforms. He responded, "We did not have a revolution in order to have a democracy." Mahmoud Ahmadinejad was reelected in 2009. The president lost many supporters due to accusations of corruption and mismanagement of the government during his second term. Hassan Rouhani was elected president in 2013.

More recently, international debate arose over Iran's expansion of its nuclear program. The United States and some of its allies feared that Iran was building nuclear weapons, which could threaten world security. Iran claimed it was using nuclear technology to create energy. The United Nations decided to impose sanctions on Iran. In 2016 several countries lifted an economic embargo on Iran after receiving confirmation that the nation had scaled back its nuclear activities.

Reading Check
Analyze
What are Iran's government and people like?

Summary and Preview In this lesson you learned about Iran's history, people, culture, economy, and government. Next you will learn about the unique cultures of Central Asia and the challenges these countries face.

Lesson 4 Assessment

Review Ideas, Terms, and Places

1. **a. Define** What is a revolution?
   b. Explain What was the Persian Empire known for?
   c. Elaborate What changes were made in Iran after the Islamic Revolution?
2. **a. Recall** What kind of leaders have authority over their people in a theocracy?
   b. Compare In what ways does Iran's culture differ from cultures in other countries of Southwest Asia and from culture in the United States?
   c. Identify and Explain What are some examples of conflict that have shaped current conditions in Iran?
   d. Explain What is the relationship between religion, government, and daily life in Iran?

Critical Thinking

3. **Find Main Ideas** Review your notes from the Iran Today segment. Draw a web diagram and fill in the circles with main ideas for Iran's people, culture, economy, and government.

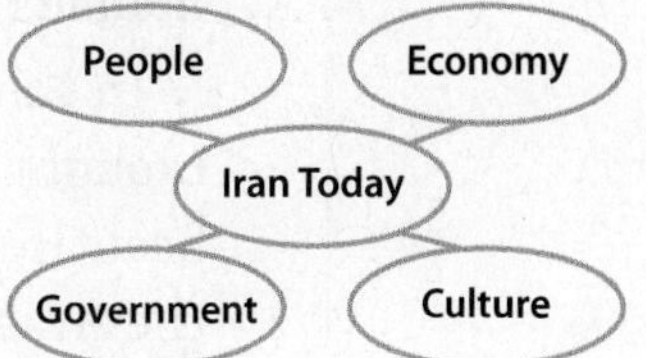

Central Asia

The Big Idea

While they share similar histories, traditions, and challenges, different ethnic groups create unique cultures for the countries of Central Asia.

Main Ideas

- Throughout history, many different groups have conquered Central Asia.
- Many different ethnic groups and their traditions influence culture in Central Asia.
- The countries of Central Asia are working to develop their economies and to improve political stability in the region.
- The countries of Central Asia face issues and challenges related to the environment, the economy, and politics.

Key Terms and Places

Samarqand
nomads
yurt
Taliban
Kabul
dryland farming
arable

If YOU lived there . . .

Your family has always farmed a small plot of land. Most days you go to school and work in the fields. One day you get news that invaders have taken over your country. They don't look like you and they speak a different language, but now they are in charge.

How do you think your life will change under the new rulers?

History

Central Asia has been somewhat of a crossroads for traders and invaders for hundreds of years. As these different peoples have passed through Central Asia, they have each left their own unique and lasting influences on the region.

Trade At one time, the best trade route between Europe and India ran through Afghanistan. The best route between Europe and China ran through the rest of Central Asia. Beginning in about 100 BC, merchants traveled along the China route to trade European gold and wool for Chinese spices and silk. As a result, this route came to be called the Silk Road. Cities along the road, such as **Samarqand** and Bukhara, grew rich from the trade.

By 1500 the situation in Central Asia had changed, however. When Europeans discovered they could sail to East Asia through the Indian Ocean, trade through Central Asia declined. The region became more isolated and poor.

Invasions Because of its location on the Silk Road, cultural diffusion occurred in Central Asia as group after group swarmed into the region. These groups left both positive and negative effects of their culture in the region. Among the first people to establish a lasting influence in the region were Turkic-speaking nomads who came from northern Asia in AD 500.

In the 700s Arab armies took over much of the region. They brought a new religion—Islam—to Central Asia. Many of the beautiful mosques in Central Asian cities date from the time of the Arabs.

Influences on Central Asia

The Arabs, Mongols, and Soviets all had a major influence on Central Asia.

Arab Influence

- The Arabs ruled Central Asia in the 700s and 800s.
- They introduced Islam and built beautiful mosques.
- They influenced styles of art and architecture in the region.

Mongol Influence

- The Mongols ruled from 1220 to the mid-1300s.
- They destroyed cities and irrigation systems.
- Eventually, they supported literature and the arts at Samarqand.

Soviet Influence

- The Soviet Union controlled Central Asia from 1922 to 1991.
- The Soviets separated ethnic groups and banned religious practices.
- They began growing cotton and constructed many useful but stark buildings.

Arabs, followed by other invaders, ruled Central Asia until the 1200s. Then, Mongol armies conquered Central Asia, destroying many cities with their violent attacks. Eventually, their empire crumbled. With the fall of the Mongols, various tribes of peoples, such as the Uzbeks, Kazakhs, and Turkmens moved into parts of the region.

Russian and Soviet Rule In the mid-1800s the Russians became the next major group to conquer Central Asia. Although the Russians built railroads and expanded cotton and oil production, people began to resent their rule.

After the Russian Revolution in 1917, the new Soviet government wanted to weaken resistance to its rule. The new Soviet leaders did this by dividing the land into republics. The Soviets encouraged ethnic Russians to move to these areas and made other people settle on government-owned farms. The Soviets also built huge irrigation projects to improve cotton production.

The Soviet Union collapsed in 1991. As the Soviet government and economy fell apart, it could no longer control its huge territory. The Central Asian republics finally became independent countries.

Reading Check **Form Generalizations** What groups of people influenced Central Asia?

Culture

The people who came through Central Asia influenced culture in the region. They brought new languages, religions, and ways of life that mixed with traditional ways of life in Central Asia.

Traditional Lives For centuries, Central Asians have made a living by raising horses, cattle, sheep, and goats. Many herders live as **nomads,** people who move often from place to place. The nomads move their herds around from one pasture to another. Today, most people in Central Asia live in more permanent settlements, but many others still live as nomads. The nomadic lifestyle is especially common in Kyrgyzstan.

Unique homes, called yurts, make moving with the herds possible. A **yurt** is a movable round house made of wool felt mats hung over a wood frame. Today, the yurt is a symbol of the region's nomadic heritage. Even people who live in cities may put up yurts for special events such as weddings and funerals.

People, Languages, and Religion Most people in Central Asia today belong to one of several ethnic groups that are part of a larger ethnic group called Turkic. Some of these groups are Kazakh (kuh-ZAHK), Kyrgyz (KIR-giz), Turkmen, and Uzbek (OOZ-bek). Another group, ethnic Russians, came to Central Asia when Russia conquered the region. They still live in every Central Asian country.

Each ethnic group speaks its own language. Look at the map to see where a particular language is the primary language. In most countries in the region, more than one language is spoken.

Academic Vocabulary
establish to set up or create

When the Russians conquered Central Asia, they **established** their own language as the official language for business and government. It is still an official language in some Central Asian countries. The Russians also introduced the Cyrillic alphabet, the alphabet used to write the Russian language. Most countries in Central Asia now use the Latin alphabet, however, which is the one used to write English. Afghanistan also has its own alphabet. It is used for writing Pashto, one of that country's official languages.

Just as people in the region are of many ethnic groups and speak different languages, they also practice different religions. Traders and conquerors brought their religious beliefs and practices to the region. Islam, brought by the Arabs, is the main religion in Central Asia. Some people also practice Christianity. Most of the region's Christians belong to the Russian Orthodox Church.

During the Soviet era, the government closed or destroyed more than 35,000 religious buildings and Islamic schools. However, since the end of the Soviet Union in 1991, many are in use once again.

Reading Check
Summarize
How did Russian and Soviet rule influence culture in Central Asia?

Central Asia Today

A history of invasions and foreign rule has made an impact on Central Asia. Because of years of fighting and changes in the region, today many countries of Central Asia face similar issues in building stable governments and strong economies.

Afghanistan The situation in Afghanistan today is in many ways a result of a long war with the Soviet Union in the 1980s. The Soviets left in 1989. However, turmoil continued under an alliance of Afghan groups. In the mid-1990s a radical Muslim group known as the **Taliban** arose. The group's leaders took over most of the country, including the capital, **Kabul.**

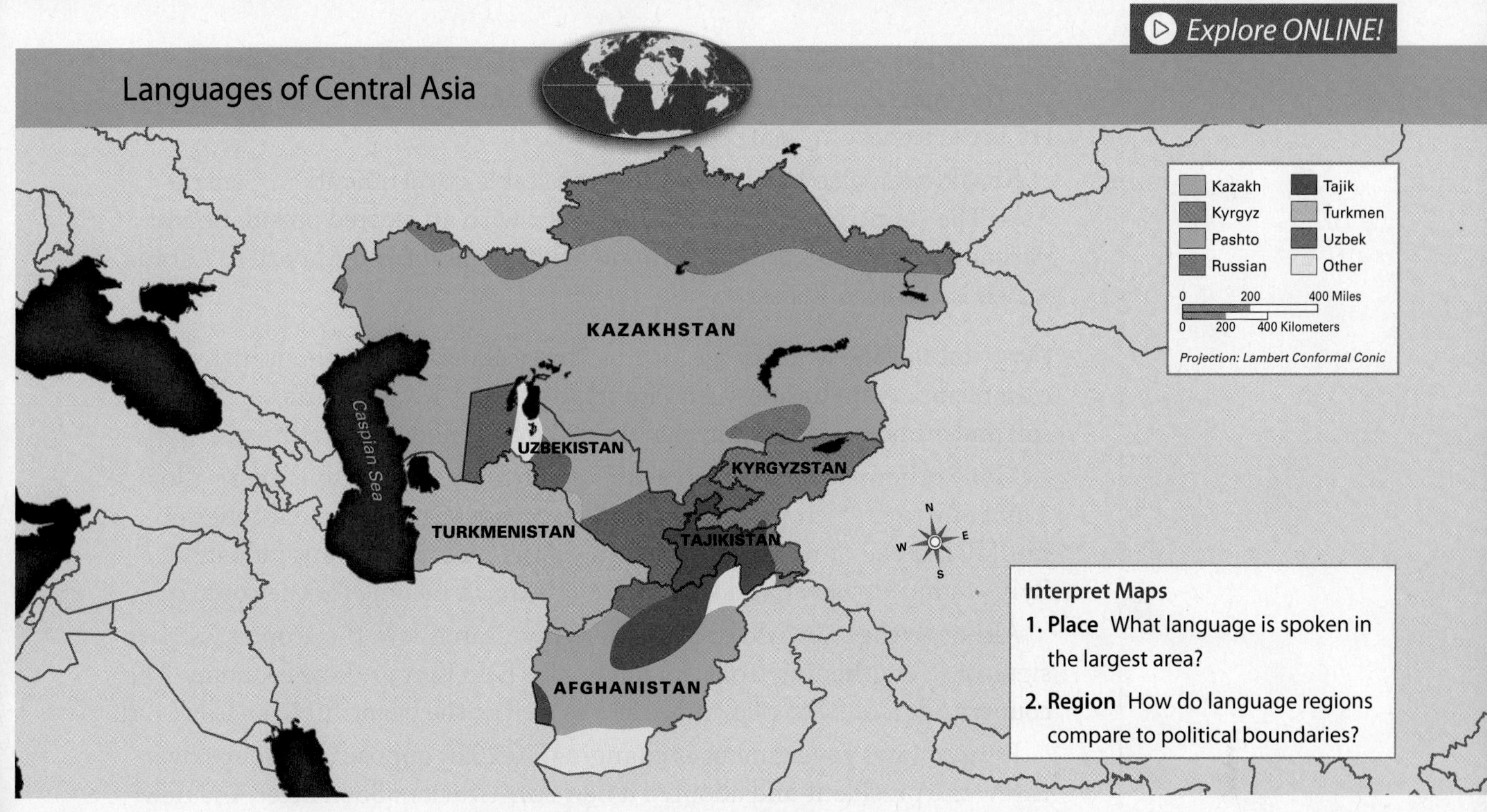

Interpret Maps

1. **Place** What language is spoken in the largest area?
2. **Region** How do language regions compare to political boundaries?

The Taliban used a strict interpretation of Islamic teachings to rule Afghanistan. For example, the Taliban severely limited the role of women in society. They forced women to wear veils and to stop working outside the home. They also banned all music and dancing. Although most Muslims sharply disagreed with the Taliban's policies, the group remained in power for several years.

Eventually, the Taliban came into conflict with the United States. Investigation of the September 11, 2001, terrorist attacks on New York City and Washington, DC, led to terrorist leader Osama bin Laden and his al Qaeda network, based in Afghanistan. U.S. and British forces attacked Taliban and al Qaeda targets and toppled Afghanistan's Taliban government.

Since the fall of the Taliban, Afghanistan's government has changed in many ways. The country has a new constitution. Also, all men and women age 18 and older can vote for the president and for the members of a national assembly. Some members of the assembly are appointed by the president, and the constitution requires that half of these appointees be women.

Many Afghans hope their government will be stable. However, since 2006 Afghans have experienced an organized rebellion, or insurgency, of the Taliban. Afghan leaders are still working today to defeat the insurgents.

Kazakhstan Kazakhstan was the first part of Central Asia to be conquered by Russia. As a result, Russian influence remains strong in that country today. About one-third of Kazakhstan's people are ethnic Russians. Kazakh and Russian are both official languages. Many ethnic Kazakhs grow up speaking Russian at home and have to learn Kazakh in school.

Kazakhstan's economy was once tied to the former Soviet Union's. It was based on manufacturing. When the Soviet Union collapsed, the economy suffered. However, due to its valuable oil reserves and quick adaptation to the free market, Kazakhstan's economy is now growing steadily. The country is the richest in Central Asia.

Kazakhstan also has one of the more stable governments in Central Asia. The country is a democratic republic with an elected president and parliament. In 1998 Kazakhstan moved its capital from Almaty to Astana, which is closer to Russia.

Kyrgyzstan The word *kyrgyz* means "forty clans." Throughout history, clan membership has been an important part of Kyrgyzstan's social, political, and economic life. Many people still follow nomadic traditions.

Many other people in Kyrgyzstan are farmers. Fertile soils there allow a mix of irrigated crops and **dryland farming,** or farming that relies on rainfall instead of irrigation. Farming is the most important industry in Kyrgyzstan. However, it does not provide much income for the country.

Although the standard of living in Kyrgyzstan is low, the economy shows signs of strengthening. Tourism might also help Kyrgyzstan's economy. The country has a Muslim pilgrimage site as well as the beautiful Lake Issyk-Kul.

Kyrgyzstan's government is changing. In 2010 opposition groups overthrew the president and adopted a new constitution. Soon after, the new government held the first-ever elections in Kyrgyzstan.

Tajikistan Like other countries in Central Asia, Tajikistan is struggling to overcome its problems. In the mid-1990s the country's Communist government fought against a group of reformers. Some reformers demanded democracy. Others called for a government that ruled by Islamic law. The groups came together and signed a peace agreement in 1997. As a result, Tajikistan is now a republic with an elected president.

Years of civil war damaged Tajikistan's economy. Both industrial and agricultural production declined. Even with the decline, Tajikistan still relies on cotton farming for much of its income. However, less than 7 percent of the country's land is **arable,** or suitable for growing crops. Lack of arable land makes progress there difficult.

Turkmenistan Turkmenistan's president holds all power in the country. He was voted president for life by the country's parliament. He has used his power to bring about education and health care reforms and to offer free web access at Internet cafes in Ashgabat.

The Turkmen government supports Islam and has ordered schools to teach Islamic principles. However, it also views Islam with caution. It does not want Islam to become a political movement.

Turkmenistan's economy is based on oil, gas, and cotton. Although the country is a desert, about half of it is planted with cotton fields. Farming is possible because Turkmenistan has one of the longest irrigation channels in the world.

Uzbekistan Uzbekistan has the largest population of the Central Asian countries. It also has some of the largest cities in the region. Two cities—Bukhara and Samarqand—are famous for their mosques and monuments.

Reforms in Afghanistan

Some reforms have taken place in Afghanistan since the end of Taliban rule. However, the country still faces many challenges.

Since the End of Taliban Rule . . .

- Afghanistan has a new constitution and an elected president.
- Many people are registered to vote.
- Afghanistan's rules are written and accessible to citizens for the first time.
- New clinics and trained doctors provide more people with access to health care.
- Women can work outside the home.
- Girls can attend school.

Analyze Visuals
What opportunities might education create for this girl?

Reading Check
Make Inferences
How does physical geography affect the economies of Kyrgyzstan and Tajikistan?

As in Turkmenistan, Uzbekistan's elected president holds all the political power. The United States has criticized the government for not allowing political freedom or respecting human rights.

The government also closely controls the economy. For example, they restrict imports by imposing high tariffs in an effort to promote local manufacturing. Uzbekistan's economy, based on oil, gold, and cotton, is fairly stable even though it is growing only very slowly.

Issues and Challenges

As you have read, the countries of Central Asia face similar issues and challenges. Their greatest challenges are in the areas of environment, economy, and politics.

Environment One of the most serious environmental problems is the shrinking of the Aral Sea. Winds swept the dry seafloor and blew dust, salt, and pesticides hundreds of miles. Towns that once relied on fishing were suddenly dozens of miles from the shore. Today new dams are helping to slowly restore the lake.

Another problem is the damage caused by Soviet military practices. The Soviets tested nuclear bombs in Central Asia. Now, people there suffer poor health because of radiation left over from the tests.

Another environmental problem has been caused by the overuse of chemicals to increase crop production. These chemicals have ended up ruining some farmlands. Instead of increasing crop production, the chemicals have hurt the economy.

Economy Many of Central Asia's economic problems are due to reliance on one crop—cotton. Suitable farmland is limited, so employment in the cotton industry is limited. Also, the focus on cotton has not

Protesters show their opposition to the government in Kyrgyzstan.

encouraged countries to develop manufacturing.

Some countries have oil and gas reserves that may someday make them rich. For now, though, outdated equipment, lack of funds, and poor transportation systems slow development in Central Asia.

Politics The other main challenge in Central Asia today is lack of political stability. In some countries, such as Kyrgyzstan, people do not agree on the best kind of government. People who are dissatisfied with their government sometimes turn to violence. These countries today are often faced with terrorist threats from different political groups within their own countries.

Reading Check
Summarize What environmental challenges does Central Asia face?

Summary Many different groups of people have influenced the countries of Central Asia over the years. As a result, the region has a mixture of languages and religions. Central Asia is recovering from a history of foreign rule. The region is struggling to develop sound economies and stable governments.

Lesson 5 Assessment

Review Ideas, Terms, and Places

1. a. **Identify** What people brought Islam to Central Asia?
   b. **Analyze** What impact did the Silk Road have on Central Asia?
   c. **Elaborate** How might Central Asia's history have been different without the influence of the Silk Road?
2. a. **Define** What is a yurt?
   b. **Analyze** What are some of the benefits of nomadic life, and what are some of the challenges of this lifestyle?
   c. **Elaborate** How might the mix of ethnic groups, languages, and religions in Central Asian countries affect life there today?
3. a. **Describe** How did the Taliban affect Afghanistan?
   b. **Contrast** What are some major differences between Afghanistan and Kazakhstan?
   c. **Elaborate** What is one way a country might create more arable land?
4. a. **Identify** What three types of challenges does Central Asia face today?
   b. **Form Generalizations** Why does much of Central Asia face political instability?

Critical Thinking

5. **Categorize** Draw a table and use your notes to categorize information about the government and economy of each Central Asian country.

	Government	Economy
Afghanistan		
Kazakhstan		
Kyrgyzstan		
Tajikistan		
Turkmenistan		
Uzbekistan		

Use and Create Databases

Define the Skill

Geographers use databases to learn about people and places and to identify patterns in various regions. A **database** is a collection of information about a topic that is organized so that it can be easily found. A database could be in print or electronic form, and it could be simple or complex. Almost any kind of information can be stored in electronic databases, including statistics, text, images, audio, and video. The table on this page is a database. So too is your library's electronic catalog. Learning how to read a database will help you learn how to create one.

- Look at the title to identify the topic.
- Read the column and row headings. These keywords tell what kind of data is included.
- Locate specific data where rows and columns intersect by reading across rows and down columns.
- Use critical-thinking skills to organize and interpret data, identify relationships, and note patterns.

Learn the Skill

Use the database to answer the following questions.

1. Which country has the highest total literacy rate?
2. Which country has the largest difference between the literacy rate among men and the literacy rate among women?
3. Organize information from the database into a list that shows the countries in order of highest literacy rate to lowest literacy rate.

Literacy Rates in Southwest Asia

	Literacy Rate (%)		
Country	**Male**	**Female**	**Total**
Iran	91.2	82.5	86.8
Iraq	85.7	73.7	79.7
Oman	93.6	85.6	91.1
Qatar	97.4	96.8	97.3
Saudi Arabia	97	91.1	94.7

Source: *The World Factbook*

Practice the Skill

Using the Internet, an encyclopedia, or an electronic database, locate information on the population density, birthrate, and death rate for each country listed in the table above. Then create a print or electronic database to organize your information.

Module 8 Assessment

Review Vocabulary, Terms, and Places

Match the words in the columns with the correct definitions listed below.

1. arable	**3.** embargo	**5.** fossil water	**7.** shah	**9.** Taliban
2. Kabul	**4.** nomads	**6.** OPEC	**8.** theocracy	**10.** Fergana Valley

a. the Persian title for a king
b. suitable for growing crops
c. fertile region that has been a center of farming for thousands of years
d. people who move often from place to place
e. a radical Muslim group
f. an organization whose members try to influence the price of oil on world markets
g. the capital of Afghanistan
h. a government ruled by religious leaders
i. water that is not being replaced by rainfall
j. a limit on trade

Comprehension and Critical Thinking

Lesson 1

11. a. Identify Through what country do the Tigris and Euphrates rivers flow?

b. Evaluate Do you think oil or water is a more important resource in the region?

c. Make Inferences Look at the physical map of Central Asia and land use and resources map of Central Asia in Lesson 1. What connections can you make between the physical landforms, resources, and economic activities in Central Asia?

Lesson 2

12. a. Describe What kind of government does Saudi Arabia have?

b. Analyze In what ways does religion affect Saudi Arabia's culture and economy?

c. Explain What impact has oil had on Saudi Arabia's economy and foreign and domestic policies?

Lesson 3

13. a. Recall What is Mesopotamia known for?

b. Draw Conclusions Why did Iraq invade Kuwait in 1990?

c. Analyze Which past conflicts are most important to understanding current conditions in Iraq? Explain.

Lesson 4

14. a. Describe What occurred at the U.S. Embassy in Tehran after the Islamic Revolution?

b. Compare and Contrast How is Iran similar to or different from the United States?

c. Predict Do you think Iran's government will ever become more democratic? Why or why not?

Lesson 5

15. a. Describe How did life in Central Asia change under Russian and Soviet rule?

b. Identify How did culture groups influence Central Asia? List at least two positive effects and two negative effects of cultural diffusion in Central Asia.

c. Evaluate How have economic decisions in Central Asia affected the region's environment?

Module 8 Assessment, continued

Reading Skills 21st CENTURY

16. Reread *Use the Reading Skills taught in this module to find main ideas in the reading selection below.*

After you read, write down the main ideas of the passage. Then go back and reread the passage carefully. Identify at least one thing you learned from rereading and add it to your list of main ideas.

> In the mid-1800s the Russians became the next major group to conquer Central Asia. Although the Russians built railroads and expanded cotton and oil production, people began to resent their rule.
>
> After the Russian Revolution in 1917, the new Soviet government wanted to weaken resistance to its rule. The new Soviet leaders did this by dividing the land into republics. The Soviets encouraged ethnic Russians to move to these areas and made other people settle on government-owned farms. The Soviets also built huge irrigation projects to improve cotton production.
>
> The Soviet Union collapsed in 1991. As the Soviet government and economy fell apart, it could no longer control its huge territory. The Central Asian republics finally became independent countries.

Social Studies Skills

17. Create a Database *Use the Social Studies Skills taught in this module to create a database comparing a topic in different world regions.*

First, select one country from each continent that has indigenous human inhabitants. Then, select one of the following topics: population, disease, or economic activities. Use the Internet or an electronic database to locate information about your topic. Then, create a print or digital database to organize your information.

Map Activity

18. The Arabian Peninsula to Central Asia On a separate sheet of paper, match the letters on the map with their correct labels.

Rub' al-Khali	Tehran, Iran
Persian Gulf	Riyadh, Saudi Arabia
Baghdad, Iraq	

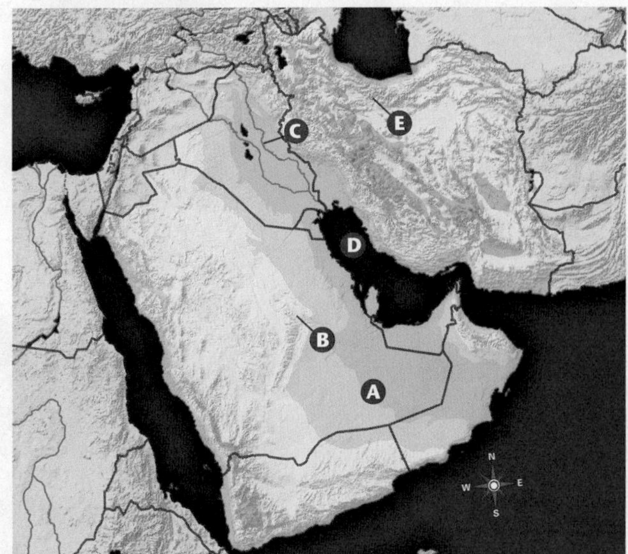

Focus on Writing

19. Give a Travel Presentation Select one country from the region your audience might want to visit. Search the Internet for pictures of at least five locations in that country: buildings, monuments, or other interesting places. Gather relevant information from multiple print and digital sources. As you plan your presentation, develop the topic with well-chosen facts, definitions, and concrete details. Create a short introduction, a brief description of each location and its picture, and a conclusion. Incorporate at least one quotation that supports the content. As you make your presentation, hold up each picture and point out all important features. Speak clearly and keep eye contact with your audience. After you have listened to all of the presentations, choose one to retell to a partner. Make sure to retell the main ideas of the presentation.

Module 9

The Eastern Mediterranean

Essential Question

In what ways has religion been a big influence on the development of Eastern Mediterranean nations?

Explore ONLINE!

VIDEOS, including . . .
- Exile of the Jews
- Israel: Birth of a Nation

- Document-Based Investigations
- Graphic Organizers
- Interactive Games
- Channel One News Video: The Holy Land
- Image Carousel: Eastern Mediterranean Geography
- Interactive Map: Turkey: Population
- Interactive Graphs: Lebanon's People and Religions

In this module, you will learn about the Eastern Mediterranean's climate and resources as well as its land disputes and religious diversity.

What You Will Learn

Lesson 1: Physical Geography **311**
The Big Idea The Eastern Mediterranean, a region with a dry climate and valuable resources, sits in the middle of three continents.

Lesson 2: Turkey **315**
The Big Idea Although Turkey has historically been more Asian than European, its leaders are seeking to develop closer economic ties to Europe.

Lesson 3: Israel **319**
The Big Idea Israel and the Palestinian Territories are home to Jews and Arabs who continue to struggle over the region's land.

Lesson 4: Syria, Lebanon, and Jordan **325**
The Big Idea Syria, Lebanon, and Jordan are Arab nations coping with religious diversity.

Geography The Jordan River valley in Israel provides fertile soil for farming.

Culture In Turkey, a Muslim dervish spins around in a circle during a ritual dance.

History Carved completely out of a sandstone cliff in Jordan, the ancient city of Petra dates back more than 2,000 years.

Reading Social Studies

Set a Purpose

READING FOCUS

When you start on a trip, you have a purpose or a destination in mind. When you read, you should also have a purpose in mind before you start. This purpose keeps you focused and moving toward your goal. To decide on a purpose, look over the headings, pictures, and study tips before you read. Then pose questions that can guide your reading. See how a heading suggested a purpose for the passage below.

Teenagers for Peace

Peace between Israeli Jews and Palestinian Arabs has not been easy in the past. Moreover, some believe peace in the region might be impossible ever to accomplish. But don't tell that to a group of more than 2,000 Jewish and Arab teenagers who are making a difference in Israel. These teens belong to an organization called Seeds of Peace. To learn more about each other's culture and thus understand each other better, these teens meet regularly.

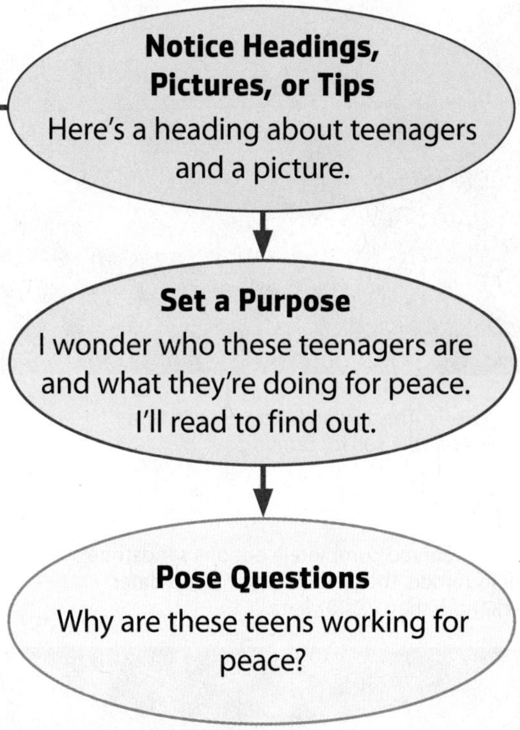

Notice Headings, Pictures, or Tips
Here's a heading about teenagers and a picture.

Set a Purpose
I wonder who these teenagers are and what they're doing for peace. I'll read to find out.

Pose Questions
Why are these teens working for peace?

YOU TRY IT!

Read the following introduction to the section on Israel. Pose questions that can set a purpose for your reading. Following the steps given above, develop a purpose for reading about Israel. State this purpose in one or two sentences.

Do you know that Israel is often referred to as the Holy Land? Some people call Israel the Holy Land because it is home to sacred sites for three of the world's major religions—Judaism, Christianity, and Islam. According to the Bible, many events in Jewish history and in the life of Jesus happened in Israel.

As you read this module, set a purpose for reading to add to your understanding of the text.

Physical Geography

The Big Idea

The Eastern Mediterranean, a region with a dry climate and valuable resources, sits in the middle of three continents.

Main Ideas

- The Eastern Mediterranean's physical features include the Bosporus, the Dead Sea, rivers, mountains, deserts, and plains.
- The region's climate is mostly dry with little vegetation.
- Important natural resources in the Eastern Mediterranean include valuable minerals and the availability of water.

Key Terms and Places

Dardanelles
Bosporus
Sea of Marmara
Jordan River
Dead Sea
Syrian Desert

Mount Ararat's snowcapped peak rises about 17,000 feet (5,182 m) in eastern Turkey.

If YOU lived there . . .

You live in Izmir, Turkey, on the Aegean Sea but are traveling into the far eastern part of the country called eastern Anatolia. At home you are used to a warm, dry Mediterranean climate. You are surprised by the colder and wetter climate you're experiencing. Two mountain ranges come together here, and you notice that the peaks are covered with snow.

How does geography affect climate in these two places?

Physical Features

Locate Israel, Lebanon, Turkey, Cyprus, Syria, and Jordan on the map on the next page. These countries of the Eastern Mediterranean make up part of a larger region called Southwest Asia. This region is sometimes referred to as the Middle East. Europeans first called the region the Middle East to distinguish it from the Far East, which included China and Japan.

A narrow waterway separates Europe from Asia. This waterway is made up of the **Dardanelles** (dahrd-uhn-ELZ), the **Bosporus** (BAHS-puh-ruhs), and the **Sea of Marmara** (MAHR-muh-ruh). Large ships travel through the waterway, which connects the Black Sea to the Mediterranean Sea. The Bosporus also splits the country of Turkey into two parts, a small part lies in Europe and the rest in Asia. The Asian part of Turkey includes the large peninsula called Anatolia (a-nuh-TOH-lee-uh).

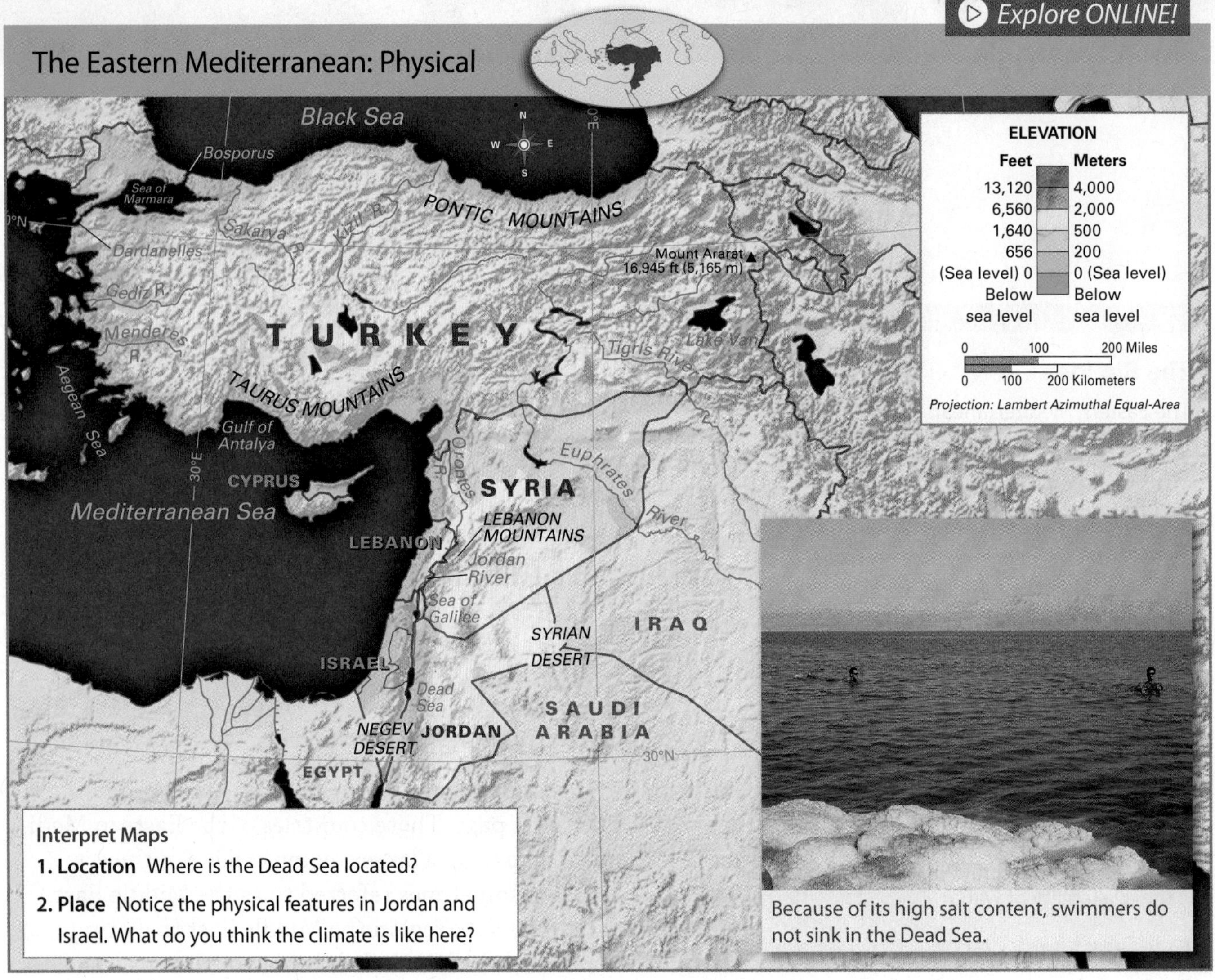

Interpret Maps

1. **Location** Where is the Dead Sea located?
2. **Place** Notice the physical features in Jordan and Israel. What do you think the climate is like here?

Because of its high salt content, swimmers do not sink in the Dead Sea.

Rivers and Lakes The **Jordan River** begins in Syria and flows south through Israel and Jordan. The river finally empties into a large lake called the **Dead Sea.** As its name suggests, the Dead Sea contains little life. Only bacteria live in the lake's extremely salty water. One of the world's saltiest lakes, its surface is about 1,350 feet (411 m) below sea level—the lowest point on any continent.

Mountains and Plains As you can see on the map, two mountain systems stretch across Turkey. The Pontic Mountains run east–west along the northern edge. The Taurus Mountains run east–west along the southern edge.

Heading south from Turkey and into Syria lies a narrow plain. The Euphrates River flows southeast from Turkey through the plains to Syria and beyond.

Farther inland lies plateaus, hills, and valleys. A rift valley that begins in Africa extends northward into Syria. Hills rise on both sides of the rift. Two main mountain ridges run north–south. One runs from southwestern Syria through western Jordan. The other, closer to the coast, runs through Lebanon and Israel.

Reading Check
Summarize What are the region's main physical features?

Istanbul and the Bosporus

Throughout history, geography has almost always determined the location of a city. Istanbul, Turkey, which sits between Europe and Asia, is no exception. In this satellite image, the city of Istanbul appears light brown and white. The body of water that cuts through the city is a strait called the Bosporus. It separates the Sea of Marmara in the south with the Black Sea in the north. Historically, the Bosporus has served as a prized area for empires that have controlled the city. Today, the strait is a major shipping route.

The Bosporus is a strait that divides the city of Istanbul, Turkey.

Draw Conclusions
Why do you think the Bosporus has been seen as a strategic location?

Climate and Vegetation

The Eastern Mediterranean is a mostly dry region. However, there are important variations. As you can see on the map on the next page, Turkey's Black Sea coast and the Mediterranean coast all the way to northern Israel have a Mediterranean climate. Much of interior Turkey experiences a steppe climate. Central Syria and lands farther south have a desert climate. A small area of northeastern Turkey has a humid subtropical climate.

The region's driest areas are its deserts. Much of Syria and Jordan is covered by the **Syrian Desert.** This desert of rock and gravel usually receives less than five inches (12.7 cm) of rainfall a year. Another desert, the Negev (NE-gev), lies in southern Israel. Here the temperatures can reach as high as 114°F (46°C), and annual rainfall totals barely two inches.

In such dry conditions, only shrubs grow scattered throughout the region's deserts. However, in other areas, vegetation is plentiful. In Israel, more than 2,800 species of plants thrive throughout the country's various environments.

Reading Check
Form Generalizations
What are climates like in the Eastern Mediterranean?

Natural Resources

Because the Eastern Mediterranean is so dry, water is a valuable resource. The people of this region are mostly farmers. The region lacks oil resources but does have valuable minerals.

Land and Water In this dry region, the limited availability of water limits how land is used. Commercial farms can only grow crops where rain or irrigation provides enough water.

In drier areas, subsistence farming and livestock herding are common. In the desert areas, available water supports a few nomadic herders but no farming.

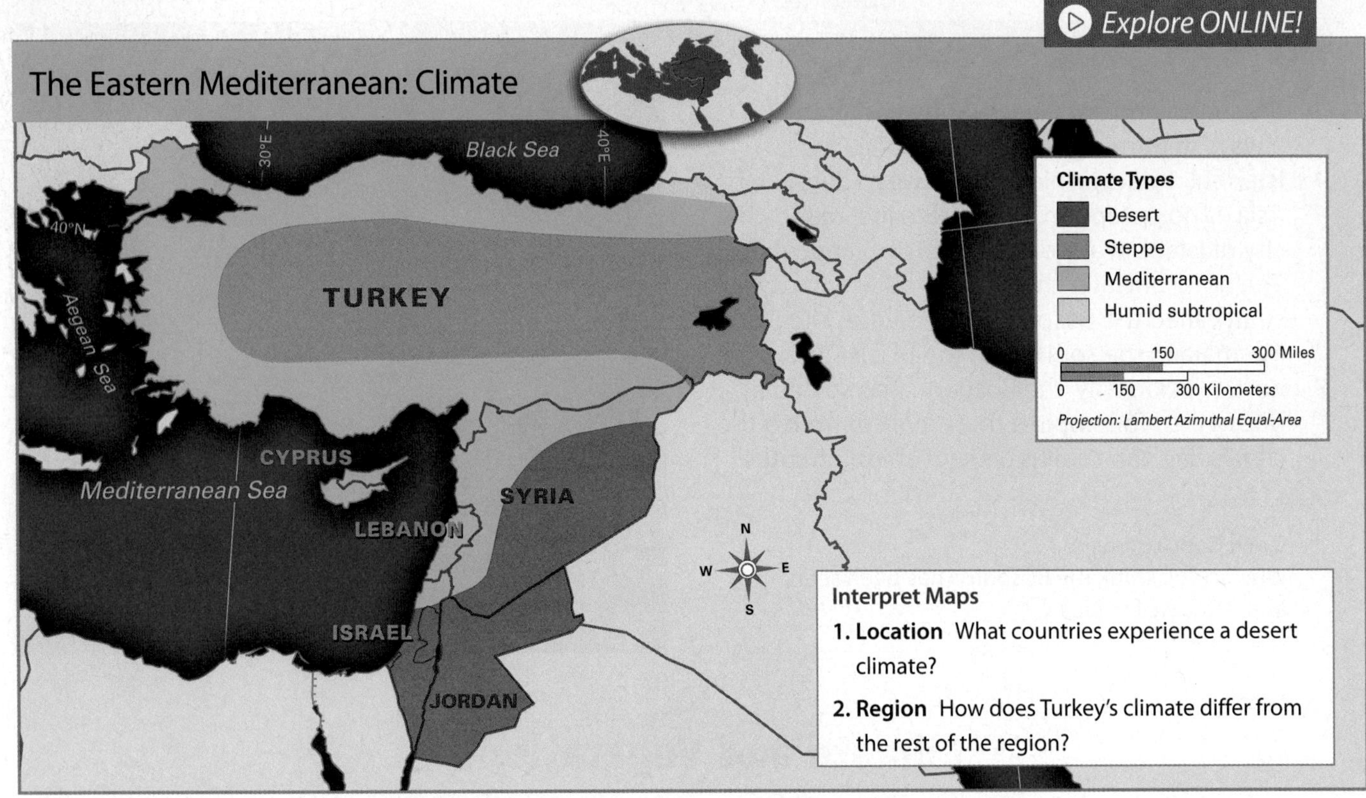

Reading Check
Draw Conclusions How do people use the region's mineral resources?

Mineral Resources The region's resources include many minerals, including sulfur, mercury, and copper. Syria, Jordan, and Israel all produce phosphates—mineral salts that contain the element phosphorus. Phosphates are used to make fertilizers. This region also produces asphalt—the dark tarlike material used to pave streets.

Summary and Preview In this lesson you learned about the physical geography of the Eastern Mediterranean. Next you will learn about Turkey.

Lesson 1 Assessment

Review Ideas, Terms, and Places

1. a. **Describe** What makes the Dead Sea unusual?
   b. **Explain** What physical features separate Europe and Asia?
2. a. **Recall** What desert covers much of Syria and Jordan?
   b. **Form Generalizations** What is the climate of the Eastern Mediterranean like?
3. a. **Identify** What mineral resource is produced by Syria, Jordan, and Israel?
   b. **Draw Conclusions** Why must farmers in the region rely on irrigation?
   c. **Elaborate** Look at the map on this page. Pose and answer a question about climate patterns in the Eastern Mediterranean.

Critical Thinking

4. **Compare** Using your notes, summarize the physical geography of Israel and Turkey. Use this chart to organize your notes.

Physical Features	
Turkey	*Israel*

Turkey

The Big Idea

Although Turkey has historically been more Asian than European, its leaders are seeking to develop closer economic ties to Europe.

Main Ideas

- Turkey's history includes invasion by the Romans, rule by the Ottomans, and a 20th-century democracy.
- Turkey's people are mostly ethnic Turks, and its culture is a mixture of modern and traditional.
- Today, Turkey is a democratic nation seeking economic opportunities and considering European Union membership.

Key Terms and Places

Istanbul
janissaries
Ankara
secular

If YOU lived there . . .

Your cousins from central Turkey are coming to visit your hometown, Istanbul. You think your city is both beautiful and interesting. You like to stroll in the Grand Bazaar and smell the spices for sale. You admire the architecture of the Blue Mosque, whose walls are lined with thousands of tiny tiles. You also like to visit the elegant Topkapi Palace, where sultans once lived.

What sights will you show your cousins?

History

Around 8,000 years ago, the area that is now Turkey was home to one of the world's earliest farming villages. For centuries, invasions from powerful empires shaped the region. By the 1920s Turkey was a democratic nation.

Invasions Byzantium was an ancient Greek city located on the site of present-day **Istanbul.** When the Romans invaded the area, they captured the city of Byzantium and later renamed it Constantinople. Recall how this site is at the crossroads between Europe and Asia. This made Constantinople an important trading port. After the fall of Rome, Constantinople became the capital of the Byzantine Empire.

In the AD 1000s a nomadic people from central Asia called the Seljuk Turks invaded the area. In the mid-1200s Muslim Turkish warriors known as Ottomans began to take territory from the Christian Byzantine Empire. They eventually ruled land from eastern Europe to North Africa and Arabia.

The key to the empire's expansion was the Ottoman army. The Ottomans trained Christian boys from conquered towns to be soldiers. These slave soldiers, called **janissaries,** converted to Islam and became fiercely loyal warriors. The Ottomans also benefited from their use of new weapons, especially gunpowder.

In 1453 Ottomans led by Mehmed II used huge cannons to conquer the city of Constantinople. With the city's capture, Mehmed defeated the Byzantine Empire. He became known as the Conqueror. Mehmed made Constantinople, which the

BIOGRAPHY

Mehmed II (1432–1481)

Mehmed II ruled the Ottoman Empire from 1451 to 1481. During this time, he greatly improved the new capital, Istanbul. He repaired damage caused by fighting and built palaces, mosques, and a huge, covered bazaar. He encouraged people from all over the empire to move to the city.

Summarize
How did Mehmed II improve Istanbul?

Ottomans called Istanbul, his capital. He also turned the Byzantines' great church, Hagia Sophia, into a mosque.

After Mehmed's death, another ruler, or sultan, continued his conquests. This sultan expanded the empire to the east through the rest of Anatolia, another name for Asia Minor. His armies also conquered Syria and Egypt. The holy cities of Mecca and Medina then accepted Ottoman rule.

The Ottoman Empire reached its height under Suleyman I (soo-lay-MAHN), "the Magnificent." During his rule from 1520 to 1566, the Ottomans took control of the eastern Mediterranean and pushed farther into Europe, areas they would control until the early 1800s.

The Ottoman Empire During the 1500s and 1600s the Ottoman Empire continued to be very powerful. The empire controlled territory in northern Africa, southwestern Asia, and southeastern Europe through the 1800s.

During the early 1900s the Ottomans fought on the losing side of World War I. When the war ended, they lost most of their territory. Military officers then took over the government, led by a war hero, Mustafa Kemal.

Kemal later adopted the name Atatürk, which means "Father of Turks." He created the democratic nation of Turkey and moved the capital to **Ankara** from Constantinople, which he officially renamed Istanbul.

Academic Vocabulary
method a way of doing something

Modern Turkey Atatürk believed Turkey needed to modernize and adopt Western **methods** in order to be a strong nation. To achieve this, he focused on making cultural changes. For example, he banned the fez, the traditional hat of Turkish men, and required that they wear

BIOGRAPHY

Kemal Atatürk (1881–1938)

Known as the Father of the Turks, Kemal Atatürk was Turkey's first president. As president, he modernized Turkey, which dramatically changed the Turkish way of life. Atatürk separated all aspects of Islam from Turkey's government. He even closed Islamic schools. Turkey's people were also encouraged to wear Western dress and adopt surnames.

Form Generalizations
How did Atatürk change Turkey's government?

Reading Check
Find Main Ideas How did Atatürk modernize Turkey?

European-style hats. Reforms urged women to stop wearing traditional veils. Women were also encouraged to vote, work, and hold office. Other ways Atatürk modernized Turkey included replacing the Arabic alphabet with the Latin alphabet and adopting the metric system.

People and Culture

Most of Turkey's people are ethnic Turks. Kurds are the largest minority and make up about 20 percent of the population.

Turkey's culture today is a reflection of some of Kemal Atatürk's changes. He created a cultural split between Turkey's urban middle class and rural villagers. The lifestyle and attitudes of middle-class Turks have much in common with those of the European middle class. In contrast, most rural Turks are more traditional. Islam strongly influences their attitudes on matters such as the role of women.

Reading Check
Contrast How are urban Turks different from rural Turks?

Turkish cooking features olives, vegetables, cheese, yogurt, and bread. Kebabs—grilled meats on a skewer—are a favorite Turkish dish.

Turkey Today

Turkey's government meets in the capital of Ankara, but Istanbul is Turkey's largest city. Istanbul's location will serve as an economic bridge to Europe as Turkey plans to join the European Union.

Government Turkey is a parliamentary republic. Its legislature is called the National Assembly. A president and a prime minister share executive power.

Although most of its people are Muslim, Turkey is a secular state. **Secular** means that religion is kept separate from government. For example, the religion of Islam allows a man to have up to four wives. However, by Turkish law, a man is permitted to have just one wife. In recent years, Islamic political parties have attempted to increase Islam's role in Turkish society.

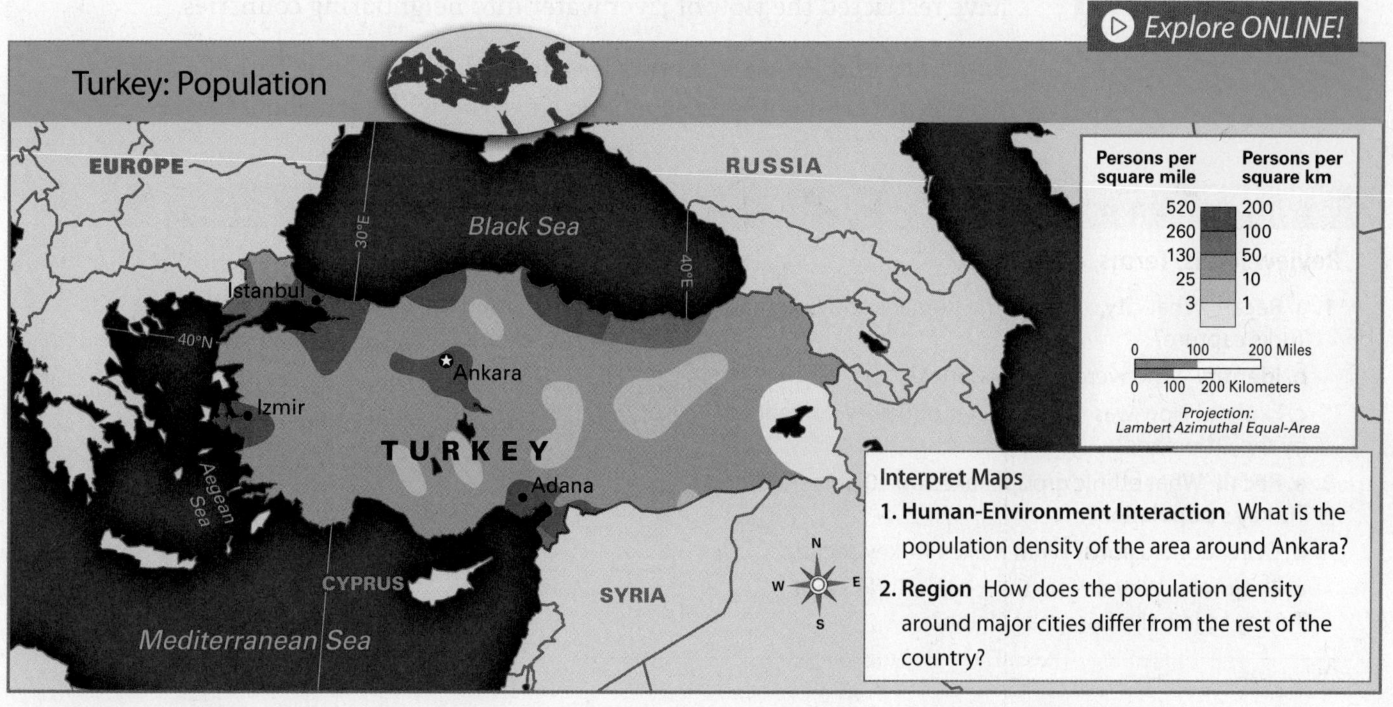

Interpret Maps

1. **Human-Environment Interaction** What is the population density of the area around Ankara?
2. **Region** How does the population density around major cities differ from the rest of the country?

With more than 14 million people, Istanbul is Turkey's largest city.

Economy and Resources Turkey has long sought membership into the European Union. As a member of the European Union, Turkey's economy and people would benefit by increased trade with Europe. Turkey's economy includes modern factories as well as subsistence farming and craft making.

Among the most important industries are textiles and clothing, cement, and electronics. About 25 percent of Turkey's labor force works in agriculture. Grains, cotton, sugar beets, and hazelnuts are major crops.

Turkey is rich in natural resources, which include oil, coal, and iron ore. Water is also a valuable resource in the region. Turkey has spent billions of dollars building dams to increase its water supply. On one hand, these dams provide hydroelectricity. On the other hand, some of these dams have restricted the flow of river water into neighboring countries.

Reading Check **Find Main Ideas** What kind of government does Turkey have?

Summary and Preview In this lesson you learned about Turkey's history, people, government, and economy. Next you will learn about Israel.

Lesson 2 Assessment

Review Ideas, Terms, and Places

1. a. **Recall** What city did both the Romans and Ottoman Turks capture?

   b. **Identify** Who were the janissaries?

   c. **Explain** How was the character of Turkey influenced by the Ottomans?

2. a. **Recall** What ethnic group makes up 20 percent of Turkey's population?

   b. **Draw Conclusions** What makes Turkey secular?

   c. **Elaborate** Why do you think some Turks want Turkey to join the European Union?

Critical Thinking

3. **Summarize** Using the information in your notes, summarize Turkey's history and Turkey today in a chart.

Turkey	
History	Today

Israel

The Big Idea

Israel and the Palestinian Territories are home to Jews and Arabs who continue to struggle over the region's land.

Main Ideas

- Israel's history includes the ancient Israelites and the creation of the State of Israel.
- In Israel today, Jewish culture is a major part of daily life.
- The Palestinian Territories are areas next to Israel—Gaza and the West Bank—controlled partly by Palestinian Arabs.

Key Terms and Places

Judaism
Diaspora
Jerusalem
Zionism
kosher
kibbutz
Gaza
West Bank

If YOU lived there . . .

When you were only six years old, your family moved to Israel from Russia. You are learning Hebrew in school, but your parents and grandparents still speak Russian at home. When you first moved here, your parents worked in an office building, but you now live on a farm where you grow oranges and tomatoes.

What do you like about living in Israel?

History

Israel is often referred to as the Holy Land because it is home to sacred sites for three major religions—Judaism, Christianity, and Islam. **Judaism** is the religion of the Jewish people. It is the world's oldest monotheistic religion. Many events in Jewish history and in the life of Jesus happened in Israel.

The Holy Land The Israelites, the descendants of the Hebrews and ancestors of the Jews, first established the kingdom of Israel about 1000 BC. It covered roughly the same area as the modern State of Israel. In the 60s BC the Roman Empire conquered the region, which was called Judea. After several Jewish revolts, the Romans forced many Jews to leave the region and renamed it Palestine in AD 135. This dispersal of the Jewish population is known as the **Diaspora.**

Muslims conquered Palestine in the mid-600s. However, from the late 1000s to the late 1200s, Christians from Europe launched a series of invasions of Palestine called the Crusades. The Crusaders captured the city of **Jerusalem** in 1099. In time, the Crusaders were pushed out of the area. Palestine then became part of the Ottoman Empire. After World War I, it came under British control.

The city of Jerusalem is sacred to three world religions—Judaism, Christianity, and Islam.

Creation of Israel **Zionism,** a nationalist movement calling for Jews to reestablish a Jewish state in their ancient homeland, began in Europe in the late 1800s. Tens of thousands of Jews and Arabs began moving to the region. Arabs also moved there to counterbalance the number of Jews moving into the region.

In 1947 the United Nations voted to divide the Palestine Mandate, then under British control, into Jewish and Arab states. While Arab countries rejected this plan, the Jews accepted it and a year later created the State of Israel. Five armies from surrounding countries then invaded Israel. Against the odds, the Israelis defeated the Arabs.

After Israel's victory, many Palestinians fled to neighboring Arab countries. Israel and Arab countries have fought each other in several wars since then. Disputes between the two sides continue today.

Reading Check
Summarize What two groups played a large role in Israel's history?

Historical Source

The Dead Sea Scrolls

Written by Jews about 2,000 years ago, the Dead Sea Scrolls include prayers, commentaries, letters, and passages from the Hebrew Bible. Hidden in caves near the Dead Sea, these scrolls were not found until 1947. Here are two passages from a prayer written on one of the scrolls.

"With knowledge shall I sing out my music, only for the glory of God, my harp, my lyre for His holiness established; the flute of my lips will I lift, His law its tuning fork."

"When first I begin campaign or journey, His name shall I bless; when first I set out or turn to come back; when I sit down or rise up, when I spread my bed, then shall I rejoice in Him."

—the Dead Sea Scrolls

Analyze Sources
What does this prayer from the Dead Sea Scrolls reveal about the people who wrote it?

Israel Today

Jews from all over the world, including many who fled from Arab lands, have migrated to Israel hoping to find peace and stability. Yet, they have faced continual conflicts with neighboring countries. Despite these problems, Israelis have built a modern, democratic country.

Government and Economy Israel has a prime minister and a parliament—the Knesset. There are several major political parties and many smaller ones.

Israel's government has built a strong military. At age 18, most Israeli men and women must serve at least one year.

Israel's economy is modern and diverse. Important exports include high-tech equipment and cut diamonds. Israel has increased food production by irrigating farmland. Israel's economy also benefits from the millions of visitors who come to Israel to see the country's historic sites.

Cities, Diversity, and Languages Most of Israel's population live in cities. Jerusalem, the capital, and Tel Aviv are Israel's largest cities.

About 75 percent of Israel's population is Jewish. The rest of the country's people are mostly Arab. About three-fourths of Israeli Arabs are Muslim, but some are Christian. Israel's Jewish population includes Jews from all parts of the world. Many arrive not knowing Hebrew, one of Israel's official languages. To assist these new citizens, the government provides language classes. Israeli Arabs speak Arabic, Israel's other official language.

Israel's Population

Jews from all over the world have settled in Israel. The graph below shows the percentages of Jews who migrated from different places. Non-Jews in Israel include Arabs who are Muslims, Christians, and Druze. This photo shows a Jewish teenager celebrating his bar mitzvah—a ceremony that acknowledges 13-year-old Jewish boys as adults in the community.

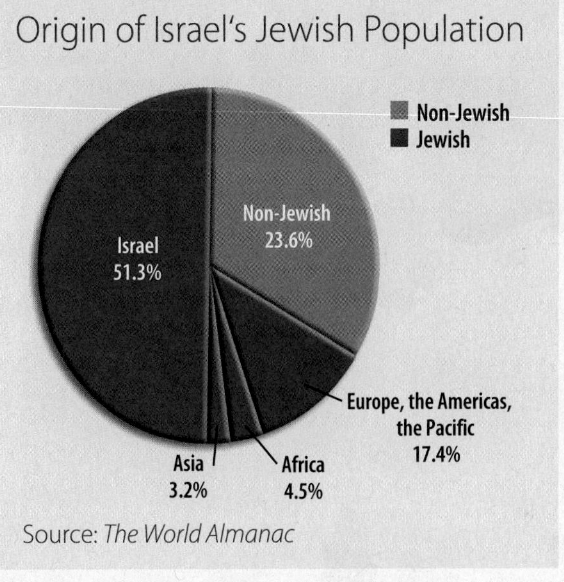

Analyze Visuals
According to the graph, what is the origin of most Israeli Jews?

Culture and Rural Settlements Israeli Jewish culture is rich in holidays and special foods. For Jews, the Sabbath, from sunset Friday until sundown Saturday, is a holy day. Yom Kippur, a very important holiday, is celebrated in the fall. Passover, in the spring, celebrates the Israelites' escape from captivity in ancient Egypt.

Because Judaism is a way of life, religious laws address every aspect of daily life, including what Jews should eat. These laws come from the Hebrew Bible. **Kosher,** which means "fit" in Hebrew, is the term used for food allowed under Jewish dietary laws. Not all Jews in Israel eat a kosher diet, but all government and army kitchens serve kosher food. This enables both religious and secular Jews to participate together in these core institutions.

Some Israeli Jews live in a collective community known as a **kibbutz** (ki-BOOHTS). Traditionally, a kibbutz is a large farm where people shared everything in common. About 100,000 Israeli Jews live in more than 250 diverse kibbutzim.

Reading Check
Form Generalizations
What is Jewish culture in Israel like?

The Palestinian Territories

In 1967, during the Six-Day War, Israel captured areas from Jordan and Egypt inhabited by Palestinian Arabs—Gaza, the West Bank, and East Jerusalem. In the 1990s Israel agreed to turn over parts of these territories to the Palestinians. In return, the Palestine Liberation Organization (PLO) agreed to recognize Israel's right to exist and pledged to renounce terrorism. These territories have continued to be central to ongoing conflicts between Israelis and Arabs.

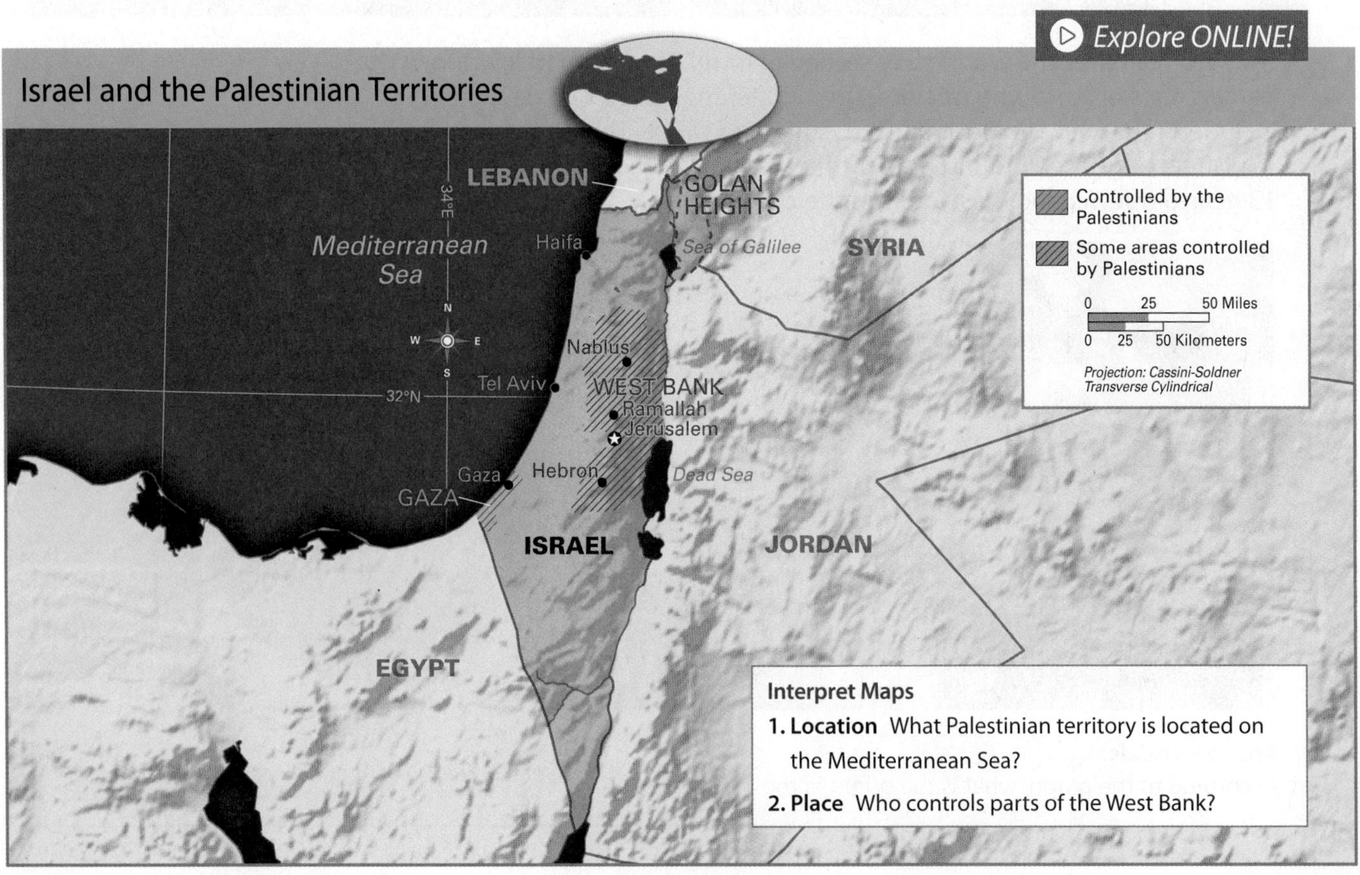

Interpret Maps

1. **Location** What Palestinian territory is located on the Mediterranean Sea?
2. **Place** Who controls parts of the West Bank?

Focus on Culture

Teenagers for Peace

Peace between Israeli Jews and Palestinian Arabs has not been easy in the past. Moreover, some believe peace in the region might be impossible ever to accomplish. But don't tell that to a group of 2,000 Jewish and Arab teenagers who are making a difference in Israel. These teens belong to an organization called Seeds of Peace. To learn more about each other's culture and thus understand each other better, these teens meet regularly.

Seeds of Peace also hosts camps for teenagers from high-conflict regions. Participating students come from across conflict lines. At camp, they live, sleep, and eat with those they have believed are their enemies. They participate in trust activities and learn peace-building and conflict resolution skills. Equipped with new skills and friends, these teens hope they can plant seeds of peace in their home communities.

Draw Conclusions
How are Jewish and Arab teenagers in Israel working toward peace?

Gaza and the West Bank **Gaza** is a small, crowded coastal area where more than a million Palestinians live. The area has few resources. However, citrus fruit is grown in irrigated fields. Unemployment is high for the Palestinians living in Gaza. In 2005 Israel transferred control of Gaza to the Palestinians.

The **West Bank** is much larger than Gaza and has a population of about 2.7 million. It is mostly rural, but the territory has three large cities—Nablus, Hebron, and Ramallah. The West Bank's economy is mostly based on agriculture. Farmers rely on irrigation to grow their crops.

Since Israel gained control of the West Bank in 1967, about 280,000 Israelis have moved there. Israelis and Palestinians dispute the territory. Peace agreements have tried to divide the land fairly. This conflict over land and terrorist attacks against Israel are the greatest sources of tension between Arabs and Israelis.

East Jerusalem Other disputed land includes Israel's capital, Jerusalem. Control of Jerusalem is a difficult and emotional issue for Jews, Muslims, and Christians. The city has sites that are holy to all three religions. Areas of the old city are divided into Jewish, Muslim, and Christian neighborhoods.

After the 1948 war, Israel controlled West Jerusalem and Jordan controlled East Jerusalem. Israel captured East Jerusalem in 1967. Jerusalem is the ancient and modern capital of Israel. Palestinians also claim Jerusalem as their capital.

The Territories Today In 2006 control of the territories was split between two opposing Palestinian political groups. The West Bank was governed by a group called Fatah, and Gaza by the group Hamas. Today, political tensions in the region remain high.

Reading Check
Analyze Causes Why have the Palestinian Territories been a source of tension?

The future of the peace process is uncertain. Some Palestinian groups have continued to commit acts of terrorism, including rocket attacks from Gaza. Israelis fear they would be open to attack if they withdrew from the West Bank.

Summary and Preview In this lesson you learned about Israel's history, people, government and economy, and the future of the Palestinian Territories. In the next lesson you will learn about the history and culture of Israel's neighbors—Syria, Lebanon, and Jordan.

Lesson 3 Assessment

Review Ideas, Terms, and Places

1. a. **Define** What is the Diaspora?
   b. **Explain** How did Zionism help create the nation of Israel?
2. a. **Explain** As a religious observance, what is the significance of a kosher diet?
   b. **Draw Conclusions** Why have Israeli leaders built up a strong military?
   c. **Explain** How has the migration of Jews influenced the character of Israel?
3. a. **Identify** Which territory is fully controlled by Palestinians and which is partly controlled?
   b. **Identify and Explain** Read the Teenagers for Peace feature in this lesson. What conflict are these teens trying to resolve?

Critical Thinking

4. **Categorize** Use the chart below to separate your notes on Israel into categories.

	Israel Today
Government	
Economy	
Diversity and Languages	
Jewish Culture	

Lesson 4

Syria, Lebanon, and Jordan

The Big Idea

Syria, Lebanon, and Jordan are Arab nations coping with religious diversity.

Main Ideas

- Syria is an Arab country that has been ruled by a powerful family and recently torn by civil war.
- Lebanon is recovering from civil war and its people are divided by religion.
- Jordan has few resources and is home to Bedouins and Palestinian refugees.

Key Terms and Places

Damascus
Beirut
Bedouins
Amman

If YOU lived there . . .

You live in Beirut, Lebanon. Your grandparents often tell you about the years before civil wars destroyed the heart of Beirut. The city then had wide boulevards, parks, and elegant shops. It was popular with tourists. Even though much of Beirut has been rebuilt, you find it hard to imagine what the city used to look like.

What hopes do you have for your country?

Look again at the map at the beginning of this module. Notice that Syria, Lebanon, and Jordan all border Israel. These countries, all of which have majority Arab populations, have been involved in conflicts with Israel. In addition, Syria, Lebanon, and Jordan also share a similar history, religion, and culture.

Syria

The capital of Syria, **Damascus,** is believed to be the oldest continuously inhabited city in the world. For centuries, it was a leading regional trade center. Syria became part of the Ottoman Empire in the 1500s. After World War I, France controlled Syria. Syria finally became independent in the 1940s.

In Syria today, ruins of an ancient Roman trading center still stand. The Romans called the city Palmyra, meaning "city of palm trees."

History and Government From 1971 to 2000, the Syrian government was led by a dictator, Hafiz al-Assad. As president, Assad increased the size of Syria's military. He wanted to match Israel's military strength and protect his rule from his political enemies within Syria. After Assad's death in 2000, his son, Bashar, was elected president. One of Bashar al-Assad's main goals was to improve Syria's economy.

In 2011 anti-government protesters challenged Bashar al-Assad's rule. Syria used brutal force—tanks, gunfire, and mass arrests—to crush the protests. By 2012 the protests had grown into an uprising. Syria was divided by a civil war. The war began as a fight between Syria's government and several rebel groups of citizens. The war expanded when the Islamic State of Iraq and the Levant (ISIL) joined the war with the goal of taking territory from Syria. A United States-led coalition of countries gave aid to the rebels and later, to fight ISIL. Russia has also joined to fight ISIL.

Syria's People Nearly 90 percent of Syria's 23 million people are culturally Arab. About 10 percent are Kurd and Armenian. Of Syria's Muslims, about 74 percent are Sunni. About 13 percent are Druze and Alawite, members of small religious groups related to Islam. About 10 percent of Syrians are Christian. There are also small Jewish communities in some cities.

Syria's civil war drastically affected its people. By March 2017 about 368,000 people had died as a result of the fighting, and more than 11 million had lost their homes. About 5 million refugees have left the country.

Reading Check
Analyze Effects How has the recent conflict affected Syria's people?

Lebanon

Lebanon is a small, mountainous country on the Mediterranean coast. It is home to several different groups of people. At times these different groups have fought.

Lebanon's History and People During the Ottoman period, many religious and ethnic minority groups settled in Lebanon. After World War I, France controlled Lebanon and Syria. Lebanon finally gained independence in the 1940s. Even so, some aspects of French culture influenced Lebanese culture. For example, in addition to Arabic, many Lebanese also speak French.

Lebanon's people are overwhelmingly Arab, but they are divided by religion. Most Lebanese are either Muslim or Christian. Each of those groups is divided into several smaller groups. Muslims are divided into Sunni and Shia.

The Maronites are the largest of the Christian groups in the country. Over time, however, Muslims have become Lebanon's majority religious group.

Conflict and Civil War After independence, Christians and Muslims shared power in Lebanon. Certain government positions were held by different religious groups. For example, the president was always a Maronite. However, over time, tensions between Christians and Muslims mounted.

In the 1970s civil war broke out. Lebanon's Muslims, including many Palestinian refugees, fought against Christians. Syria, Israel, and other countries became involved in the conflict. During the fighting, many people died and the capital, **Beirut,** was badly damaged. Warfare lasted until 1990.

Reading Check
Draw Conclusions
What has caused divisions in Lebanese society?

After 1990 Syria continued to maintain a strong influence in Lebanon. In fact, Syrian troops stayed in Lebanon until they were pressured to leave in 2005. In 2006 cross-border attacks by a militant group of Lebanese against Israel led to fighting between the two countries. Today, tensions between Lebanon and Israel threaten renewed violence.

Jordan

Jordan's short history has been full of conflict. The country has few resources and several powerful neighbors.

Jordan's History and Government The borders of what is now Jordan were created after World War I. The British controlled the area as a mandate and named an Arab prince to rule it. In the 1940s Jordan became an independent country.

People of Syria, Lebanon, and Jordan

The people of Syria, Lebanon, and Jordan share many cultural traits. For example, most people living in this region are Arab and practice Islam.

After more than two decades of civil war, Lebanon's people are rebuilding their capital, Beirut. The city's people now enjoy a new public square.

In Syria, drinking tea is an important part of Arab culture. Many Syrians, like this carpet seller, drink tea every day with family and friends.

Jordan's people value education and equal rights for women. Jordanian teenagers, like these girls, are required to attend school until age 15.

Analyze Visuals
What can you see in these photos that tells you about daily life in the region?

At the time of its independence, Jordan's population was small. Most Jordanians lived a nomadic or semi-nomadic life. Hundreds of thousands of Palestinian Arab refugees fled Israel and came to live in Jordan. From 1952 to 1999 Jordan was ruled by King Hussein. The king enacted some democratic reforms in the 1990s.

Jordan's People and Resources Many of Jordan's people are **Bedouins,** or Arabic-speaking nomads who mostly live in the deserts of Southwest Asia. Jordan produces phosphates, cement, and potash. Tourism and banking are becoming important industries. Jordan depends on economic aid from the oil-rich Arab nations and the United States. **Amman,** the capital, is Jordan's largest city. Jordanian farmers grow fruits and vegetables and raise sheep and goats. A shortage of water is a crucial resource issue for Jordan.

Reading Check
Summarize How did King Hussein affect Jordan's history?

Summary In this lesson you learned about the history, government, and people of Syria, Lebanon, and Jordan.

Lesson 4 Assessment

Review Ideas, Terms, and Places

1. a. **Recall** What is the capital of Syria?
   b. **Explain** What does Syria's government own?
   c. **Elaborate** Why did Hafiz al-Assad want to increase the size of Syria's military?
2. a. **Identify** What European country ruled Lebanon after World War I?
   b. **Analyze** How was Beirut damaged?
   c. **Identify and Explain** What is the history of political divisions among religious groups in Lebanon's government? What conflict did this lead to?
3. a. **Define** Who are the Bedouins?
   b. **Explain** Who provides economic aid to Jordan?

Critical Thinking

4. **Compare and Contrast** Use your notes to identify similarities and differences among the people in the three countries.

	Similarities	Differences
Syria		
Lebanon		
Jordan		

Create a Cartogram

Define the Skill

For statistical information like population figures, geographers sometimes create a special map called a cartogram. A cartogram displays information about countries by the size shown for each country. In contrast, a political map like the one on the right reflects countries' actual physical size. Here are some guidelines for reading and analyzing a cartogram.

- Read the title of the map to determine the subject area covered.
- Compare the political map to the cartogram. Notice how some countries are much different in size on the cartogram compared to the map.
- Read the cartogram's legend and think about what the information means.

Learn the Skill

1. Which country has the largest population?
2. How is the size of Saudi Arabia's land area different from the size of its population?
3. Using the cartogram legend, what is the approximate population of Lebanon?

Practice the Skill

Draw your own cartogram using the gross domestic product, or GDP, of each country in Southwest and Central Asia. Use a reference source or the Internet to find these statistics. Then determine the scale for sizing each country by GDP. For example, you might use one square unit of area per $10 billion or $100 billion. Countries with a high GDP should appear larger than countries with a low GDP.

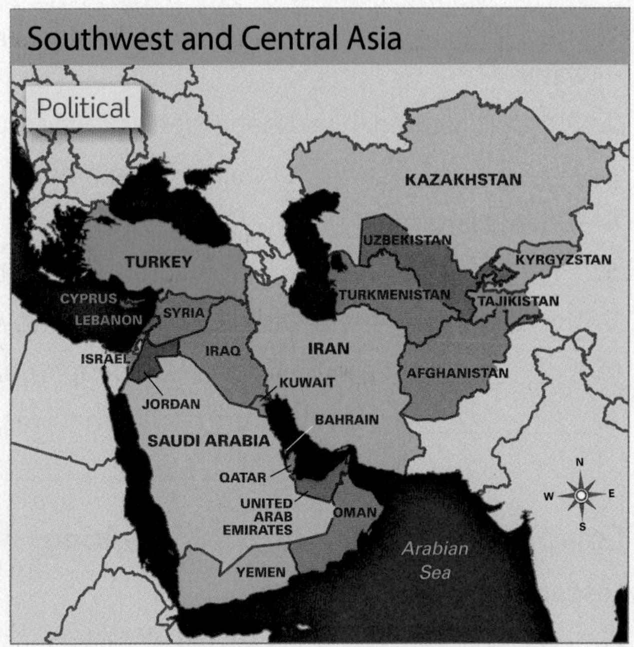

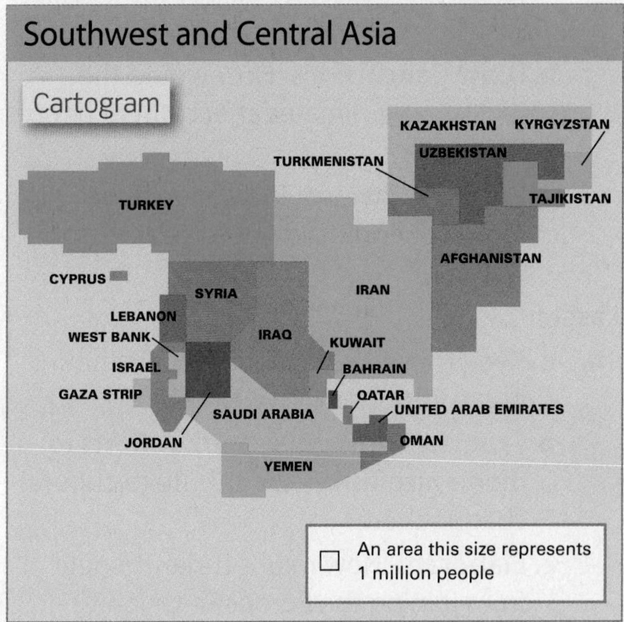

Module 9 Assessment

Review Vocabulary, Terms, and Places

Fill in the blanks with the correct term or place from this module.

1. The __________ is the lowest point on any continent and one of the world's saltiest bodies of water.
2. A desert located in southern Israel is called the __________.
3. A __________ is a way of doing something.
4. Turkey's largest city is __________.
5. ______________ means that religion is kept separate from government.
6. The dispersal of the Jewish population is known as __________.
7. A __________ is a large farm where people share everything in common.
8. ______________ is Lebanon's capital that was badly damaged during the country's civil war.

Comprehension and Critical Thinking

Lesson 1

9. a. **Describe** How is the Eastern Mediterranean considered a part of the Middle East?
   b. **Draw Conclusions** How would the region's dry climates affect where people lived?
   c. **Predict** What would happen if the region's people did not have access to water?

Lesson 2

10. a. **Recall** How was control of Constantinople important?
    b. **Evaluate** How did Atatürk's efforts to modernize Turkey contribute to cultural change there?
    c. **Elaborate** How might Turkey benefit from joining the European Union?

Lesson 3

11. a. **Define** What is Zionism?
    b. **Make Inferences** Why does Israel need a strong military?
    c. **Elaborate** How has Israel's history affected the country today?
    d. **Explain** What is the significance of Passover?

Lesson 4

12. a. **Identify** What is the capital of Syria? Why is it historically significant?
    b. **Identify and Explain** Identify and describe examples of conflict within Syria and Lebanon that led to civil war.
    c. **Evaluate** How do you think Jordan survives with so few resources?

Module 9 Assessment, continued

Reading Skills

Set a Purpose *Use the information in this module to answer the following questions.*

13. How does setting a purpose before you read help you become a better reader?

14. How is your purpose in reading this chapter different from your purpose when you read a newspaper comic strip?

15. How can looking at headings and main idea statements help you set a purpose for reading?

Social Studies Skills

Use the Social Studies Skills taught in this module to complete the following.

16. Create a Cartogram Draw your own cartogram using this life expectancy at birth data for Turkey—72.8, Israel—81.1, Syria—74.9, Lebanon—75.2, Jordan—80.2. Then determine a scale for sizing each country by age. For example, you might use one square unit of area for every 10 years of age. Countries with higher numbers for life expectancy at birth should appear larger than countries with lower life expectancy numbers.

17. Geographic Questions Use your cartogram to pose and answer a question that compares population patterns in Southwest Asia to those in North Africa.

Map Skills

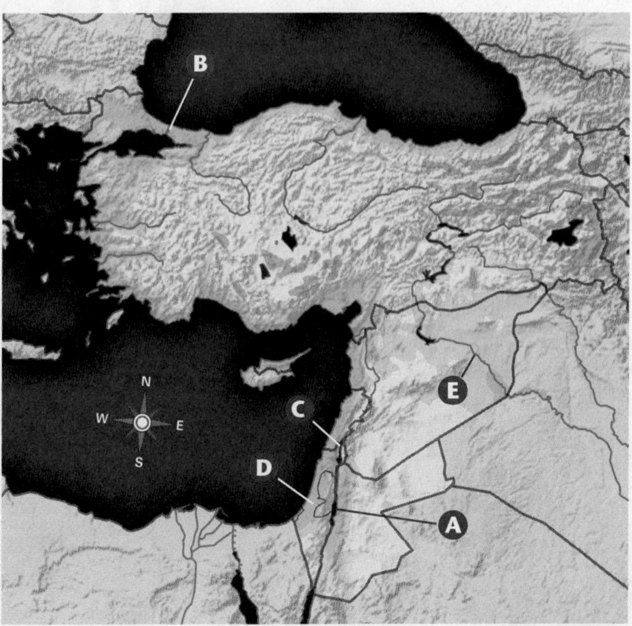

18. The Eastern Mediterranean *On a separate sheet of paper, match the letters on the map with their correct labels.*

Bosporus
Israel
Dead Sea
Negev
Euphrates River

Focus on Writing

19. Write a Description Look over your notes and choose one Eastern Mediterranean country to describe. Organize your notes by topic—physical features, people, culture and government. Then, write a one-to-two-paragraph description of the country. Include information you think would be interesting to someone who knows nothing about the country. Add details that will help your readers picture the country.

Module 10

North Africa

Essential Question

Why has it been hard to establish democracy in North Africa?

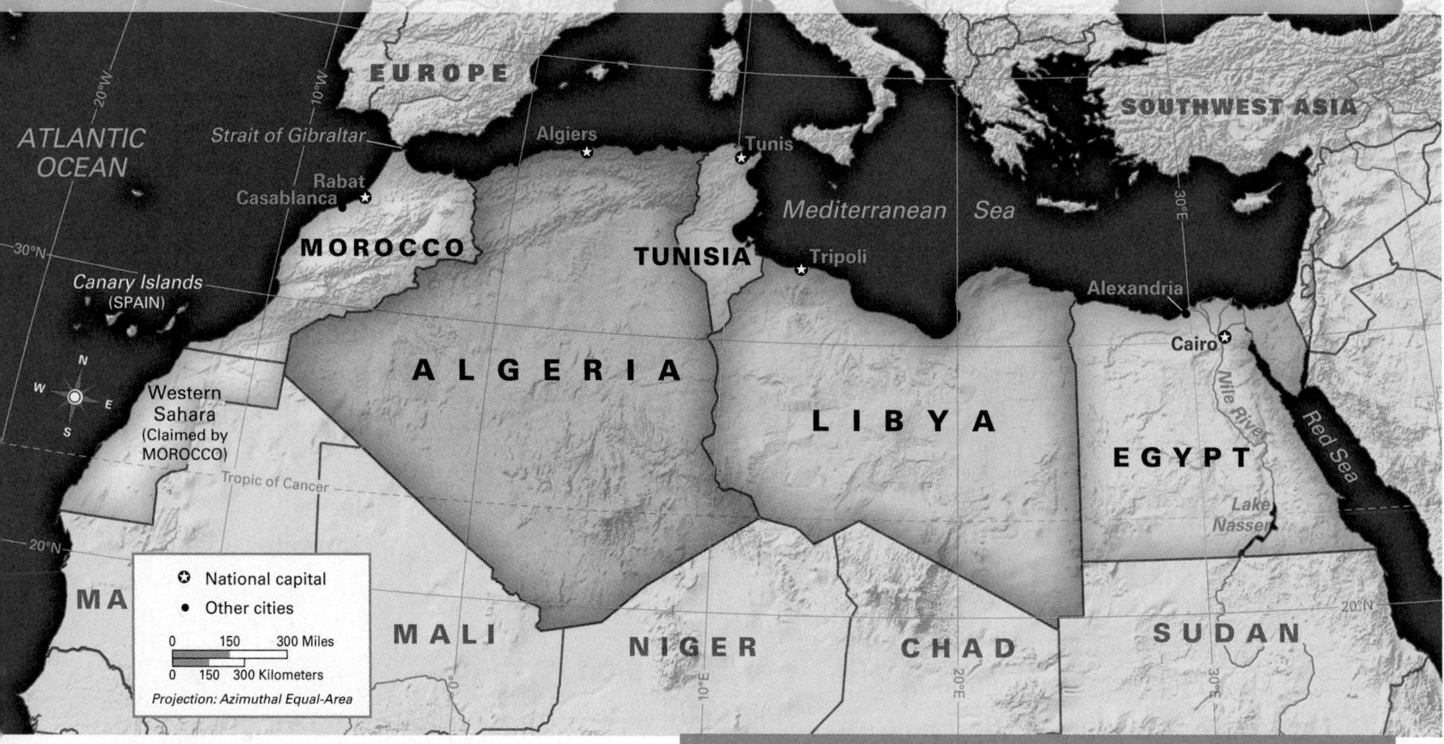

Explore ONLINE!

VIDEOS, including . . .
- The Sahara
- The Sphinx of Egypt
- The Suez Canal

- Document-Based Investigations
- Graphic Organizers
- Interactive Games
- Image with Hotspots: A Sahara Oasis
- Interactive Map: Impact of the Arab Spring
- Interactive Map: Egypt: Population
- Interactive Table: North Africa: Regional Data

In this module, you will learn about the history and culture of North Africa. You will also learn about the special challenges these countries face due to their climate and geography.

What You Will Learn

Lesson 1: Physical Geography 335
The Big Idea North Africa is a dry region with limited water resources.

Lesson 2: Egypt 339
The Big Idea Egyptian civilization has long depended on the Nile River.

Lesson 3: Libya, Tunisia, Algeria, and Morocco 345
The Big Idea Countries in North Africa face great change due to popular protests and political instability.

Geography Most of North Africa is covered by the world's largest desert—the Sahara.

Culture Most North Africans are Muslims and speak Arabic.

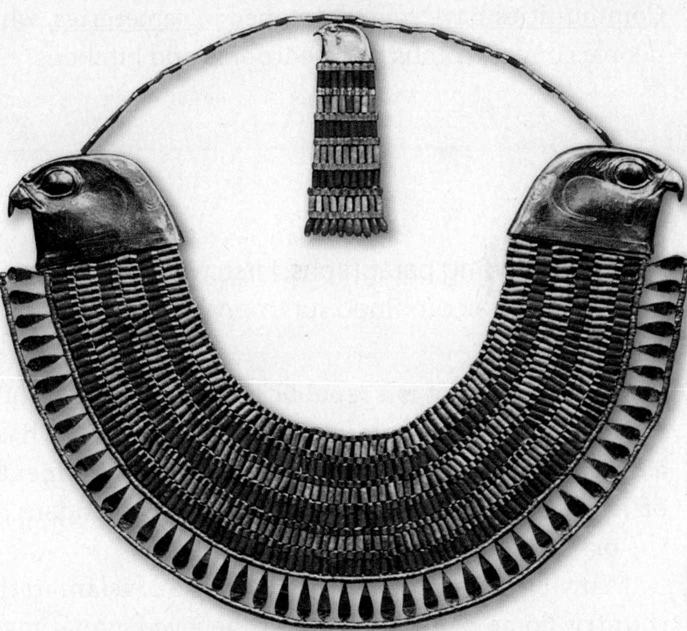

History Artifacts, like this one from King Tutankhamen's tomb, have revealed clues about the daily lives of ancient Egyptians.

Reading Social Studies

Summarize

READING FOCUS

Summarizing is one way to help you handle large amounts of information. A summary is a short restatement of the most important ideas in a text. The example below shows three steps you can use to write a summary. First, underline important details. Then, write a short summary of each paragraph. Finally, combine your summaries into a summary of the whole passage.

With 18.8 million people, Cairo is the largest city in North Africa. The city is crowded, poor, and polluted. Cairo continues to grow as people move into the city from Egypt's rural areas in search of work. For centuries, Cairo's location at the southern end of the Nile delta helped the city grow. The city also lies along old trading routes.

Today, the landscape of Cairo is a mixture of modern buildings, historic mosques, and small, mud-brick houses. However, there is not enough housing in Cairo for its growing population. Many people live in makeshift housing in the slums or boats along the Nile. Communities have even developed in cemeteries, where people convert tombs into bedrooms and kitchens.

From Lesson 3, Libya, Tunisia, Algeria, and Morocco

Summary of Paragraph 1
The crowded city of Cairo is North Africa's largest city and continues to grow.

Summary of Paragraph 2
Without enough housing, people in Cairo live in slums, boats, and cemeteries.

Combined Summary
Cairo is North Africa's largest city, and it is so crowded that people live in makeshift houses, boats, and cemeteries.

YOU TRY IT!

Read the following paragraphs. First, write a summary for each paragraph, and then write a combined summary of the whole passage.

Even though Egypt is a republic, its government is heavily influenced by Islamic law. Egypt's government has a constitution, and Egyptians elect their government officials. Power is shared between Egypt's president and the prime minister.

Many Egyptians debate over the role of Islam in the country. Some Egyptian Muslims believe Egypt's government, laws, and society should be based on Islamic law. However, some Egyptians worry that such a change in government would mean fewer personal freedoms.

As you read this module, look for ways to summarize the paragraphs and passages you are studying.

Physical Geography

The Big Idea

North Africa is a dry region with limited water resources.

Main Ideas

- Major physical features of North Africa include the Nile River, the Sahara, and the Atlas Mountains.
- The climate of North Africa is hot and dry, and water is the region's most important resource.

Key Terms and Places

Sahara
Nile River
silt
Suez Canal
oasis
Atlas Mountains

If YOU lived there . . .

As your airplane flies over Egypt, you look down and see a narrow ribbon of green—the Nile River valley—with deserts on either side. As you fly along North Africa's Mediterranean coast, you see many towns scattered across rugged mountains and green valleys.

What are the challenges of living in a mainly desert region?

Physical Features

The region of North Africa includes Morocco, Algeria, Tunisia, Libya, and Egypt. Locate these countries on the map. From east to west, the region stretches from the Atlantic Ocean to the Red Sea. Off the northern coast is the Mediterranean Sea. In the south lies the **Sahara** (suh-HAR-uh), a vast desert. Both the desert sands and bodies of water have helped shape the cultures of North Africa.

The Nile The **Nile River** is the world's longest river. It is formed by the union of two rivers, the Blue Nile and the White Nile. Flowing northward through the eastern Sahara for about 4,000 miles (6,437 km), the Nile finally empties into the Mediterranean Sea.

For centuries, rain far to the south caused floods along the northern Nile, leaving rich **silt** in surrounding fields. Silt is finely ground fertile soil that is good for growing crops.

The Nile River valley is a fertile area in the midst of the desert. Farmers use water from the Nile to irrigate their fields. The Nile fans out near the Mediterranean Sea, forming a large delta. A delta is a landform at the mouth of a river that is created by the deposit of sediment. The sediment in the Nile delta makes the area extremely fertile.

The Aswan High Dam controls flooding along the Nile. However, the dam also traps silt, preventing it from being carried downriver. Today, some of Egypt's farmers must use fertilizers to enrich the soil.

The Sinai and the Suez Canal East of the Nile is the triangular Sinai Peninsula. Barren, rocky mountains and desert cover the Sinai. The **Suez Canal,** a narrow waterway, connects the Mediterranean Sea with the Red Sea. The French built the canal in the 1860s to make trade and transportation easier. Today, large cargo ships carry oil and other goods through the canal.

Academic Vocabulary
impact effect; result

The Sahara The Sahara, the largest desert in the world, covers most of North Africa. The name *Sahara* comes from the Arabic word for "desert." It has an enormous **impact** on the landscapes of North Africa.

One impact of the very dry Sahara is that few people live there. Small settlements are located near a water source such as an **oasis.** An oasis is a wet, fertile area in a desert where a natural spring or well provides water.

Historically, those traveling through or across the challenging Sahara desert used camels, animals that are well adapted to the dry, sandy conditions. Nowadays, in addition to camels, rugged four-wheel-drive vehicles are used.

In addition to broad, windswept gravel plains, sand dunes cover much of the Sahara. Dry streambeds are also common.

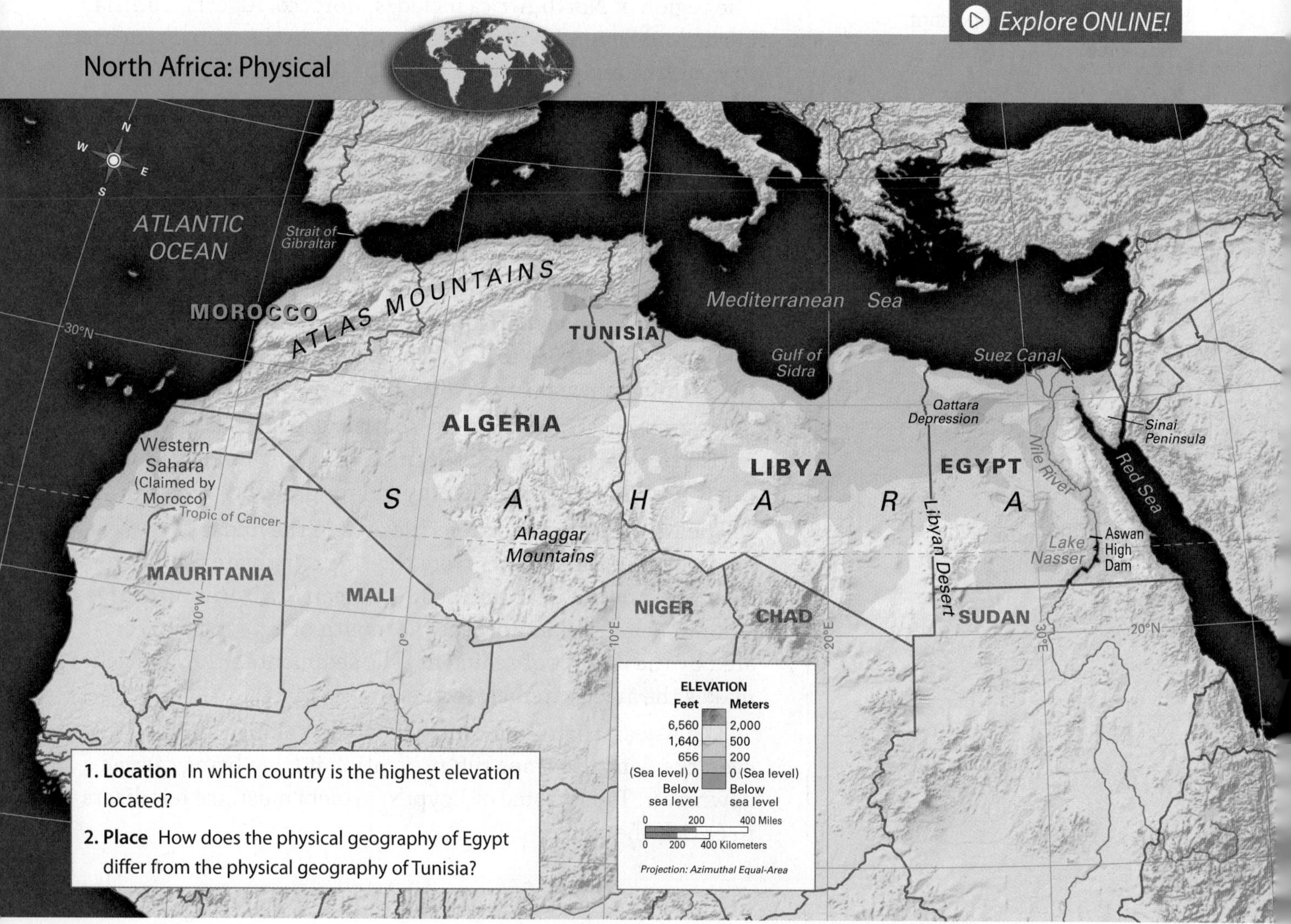

1. **Location** In which country is the highest elevation located?
2. **Place** How does the physical geography of Egypt differ from the physical geography of Tunisia?

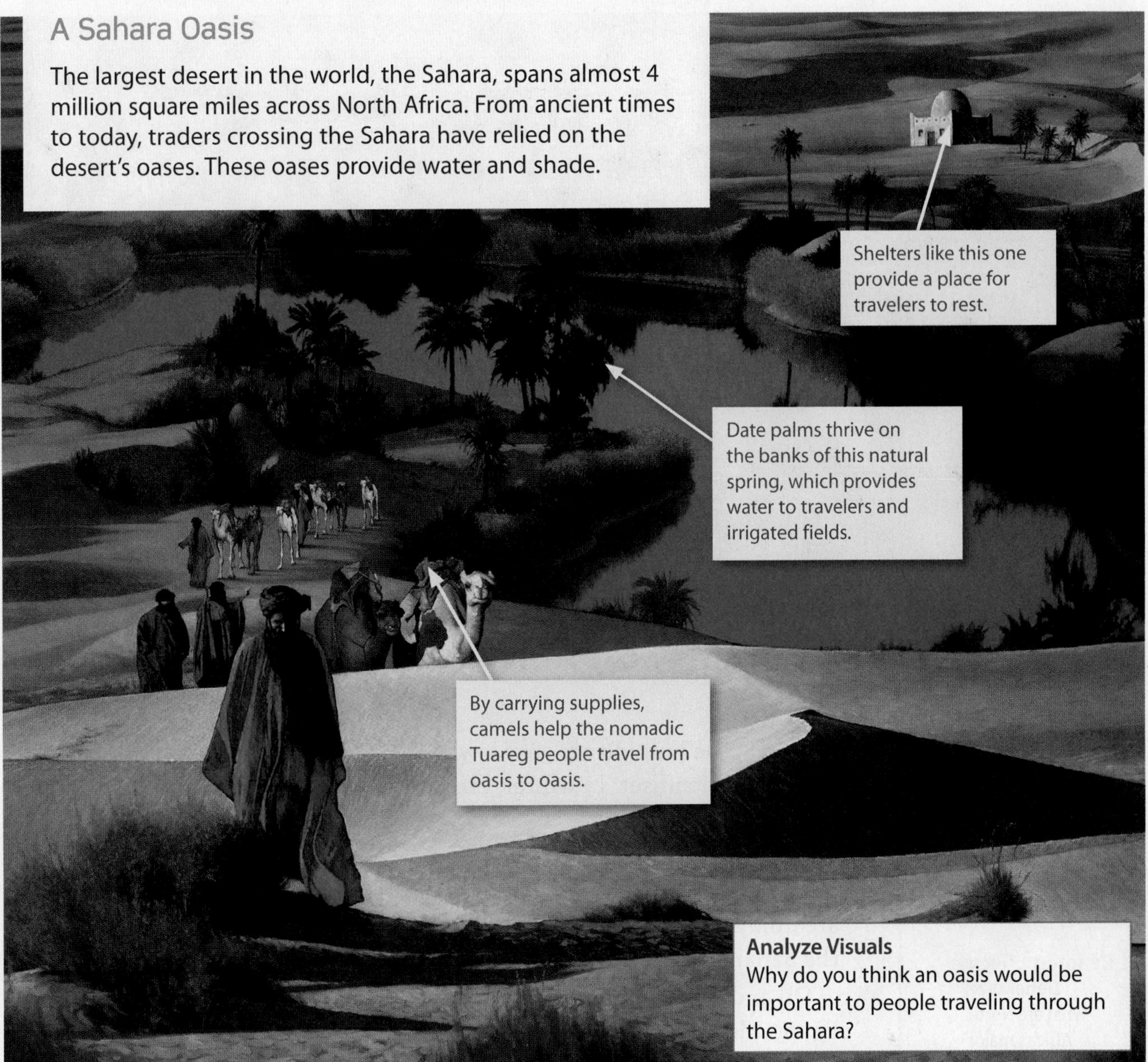

Mountains Do you think of deserts as flat regions? You may be surprised to learn that the Sahara is far from flat. Some sand dunes and ridges rise as high as 1,000 feet (305 m). The Sahara also has spectacular mountain ranges. For example, a mountain range in southern Algeria rises to a height of 9,800 feet (3,000 m). Another range, the **Atlas Mountains** on the northwestern side of the Sahara near the Mediterranean coast, rises even higher, to 13,600 feet (4,145 m).

Reading Check
Summarize
What are the major physical features of North Africa?

Climate and Resources

North Africa is very dry. However, rare storms can cause flooding. In some areas, these floods as well as high winds have carved bare rock surfaces out of the land.

North Africa has three main climates. A desert climate covers most of the region. Temperatures range from mild to very hot. How hot can it get? Temperatures as high as 136°F (58°C) have been recorded in Libya.

Flowing for 4,132 miles, the Nile is the longest river in the world. In addition to providing water for farming and recreation, the river allows easy transportation of goods and resources.

However, the humidity is very low. As a result, temperatures can drop quickly after sunset. In winter, temperatures can fall below freezing at night.

The second climate type in the region is a Mediterranean climate. Much of the northern coast west of Egypt has this type of climate. Winters there are mild and moist. Summers are hot and dry. Areas between the coast and the Sahara have a steppe climate.

Oil and gas are important resources, particularly for Libya, Algeria, and Egypt. Morocco mines iron ore and minerals used to make fertilizers. The Sahara has natural resources such as coal, oil, and natural gas.

Reading Check
Generalize
What are North Africa's major resources?

Summary and Preview In this lesson you learned about the physical geography of North Africa. Next you will learn about the history and cultures of the countries of North Africa, starting with Egypt.

Lesson 1 Assessment

Review Ideas, Terms, and Places

1. a. **Define** What is an oasis?
   b. **Analyze** How did the French modify the Sinai Peninsula? Why?
   c. **Elaborate** Would it be possible to farm in Egypt if the Nile River did not exist? Explain your answer.
2. a. **Recall** What is the climate of most of North Africa?
   b. **Draw Conclusions** What resources of North Africa are the most valuable?

Critical Thinking

3. **Categorize** Draw a diagram like the one shown here. Use your notes to list two facts about each physical feature of North Africa.

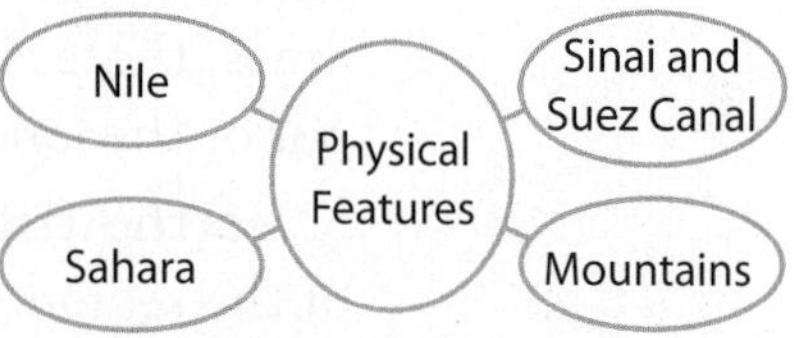

Egypt

The Big Idea

Egypt is rich in history and Islamic culture.

Main Ideas

- Egyptian civilization goes back thousands of years.
- Many of Egypt's people are farmers and live along the Nile River.
- Islam influences Egyptian culture and most people speak Arabic.

Key Terms and Places

Alexandria
Cairo
Arab Spring

If YOU lived there . . .

You live in a village in ancient Egypt in about 800 BC. Your family grows wheat and date palms along the banks of the Nile River, which brings water for your crops. You and your friends like to explore the marshy areas along the banks of the river, where many kinds of birds live in the tall reeds.

How is the Nile River important in your life?

Egypt's Nile River valley was home to some of the world's oldest civilizations. These ancient Egyptians built large monuments, participated in trade, and developed a writing system.

History

Sometime after 3200 BC people along the northern Nile united into one Egyptian kingdom. The ancient Egyptians built large stone monuments and developed a system of writing. Later, Greeks and Arabs, who wanted to expand their empires, invaded North Africa, including Egypt.

The Ancient Egyptians What is the first thing that comes to mind when we think of the ancient Egyptians? Most of us think of the great stone pyramids. The Egyptians built these huge monuments as tombs, or burial places, for pharaohs, or kings.

How did the Egyptians build these huge monuments? Scholars believe thousands of workers cut large blocks of stone far away and rolled them on logs to the Nile. From there, the blocks were moved onto barges. At the building site, the Egyptians finished carving the blocks. They built dirt and brick ramps alongside the pyramids. Then they hauled the blocks up the ramps.

One of the largest pyramids, the Great Pyramid, contains 2.3 million blocks of stone. Each stone averages 2.5 tons (2.27 metric tons) in weight. Building the Great Pyramid probably required from 10,000 to 30,000 workers. They finished the job in about 20 years, and the pyramid still stands thousands of years later.

The Great Sphinx at Giza is one of the many monuments built by the ancient Egyptians.

Egyptian Writing The ancient Egyptians developed a sophisticated writing system, or hieroglyphics (hy-ruh-GLIH-fiks). This writing system used pictures and symbols that stood for ideas or words. Each symbol represented one or more sounds in the Egyptian language. The Egyptians carved hieroglyphics on their temples and stone monuments. Many of these writings recorded the words and achievements of the pharaohs.

Greek and Arab Civilizations Because of Egypt's Mediterranean coastline, the country was open to invaders over the centuries. Those invaders included people from the eastern Mediterranean, Greeks, and Romans. For example, one invader was the Macedonian king Alexander the Great. Alexander founded the city of **Alexandria** in Egypt in 332 BC. Alexandria became an important seaport and trading center. The city was also a great center of learning.

Beginning in the AD 600s, Arab armies from Southwest Asia swept across Egypt. They brought the Arabic language and Islam to the region. Under Muslim rule, Egyptian cities such as **Cairo** became major centers of learning, trade, and craft making.

European Influence In 1798 Napoleon captured Alexandria and Cairo as part of a larger strategy in a war against Britain. Later that year, the Egyptians revolted against French rule. Eventually, in the 1880s, the British controlled Egypt.

Egypt did not regain its independence until decades later. The country gained limited independence in 1922. The British kept military bases there and maintained control of the Suez Canal until 1956. During World War II, Britain's military bases in Egypt supported the war effort. Egypt also suffered invasions from Italy and Germany during the war.

Arab Ties Since independence, Egypt has tried to build stronger ties with other Arab countries, both within and outside of North Africa. Before signing a peace treaty in 1979, Egypt led other Arab countries in several wars against Israel.

Reading Check
Evaluate What was one significant event in Egypt's history?

Egypt Today

With more than 85 million people, Egypt is North Africa's most populous country. Most of Egypt's population lives near the Nile River. Most Egyptians are poor farmers living with political instability and limited resources.

Government and Society In 2011 massive popular protests broke out across Egypt as part of what became known as the **Arab Spring.** This wave of pro-democracy uprisings shook North Africa and Southwest Asia. Poverty, unemployment, rising prices, and political corruption stirred the unrest. Egypt's military forced President Hosni Mubarak from power, ending 30 years of autocratic rule. An autocratic ruler has absolute power. People living under such a regime often do not have the freedom to vote or express what they really think of the government.

After a heated presidential campaign, Egyptians elected Mohamed Morsi in May 2012. Morsi had the support of the Muslim Brotherhood, a multinational activist political organization that believes Egypt's government, laws, and society should be based on Islamic law.

Still, Egyptians were divided and unhappy. They debated the role of Islam in government and society. Many feared losing personal freedoms. Others were concerned by Egypt's weak economy and failing social services.

Hundreds of thousands of protesters gathered in Cairo's Tahrir Square, the center point of pro-democracy protests in Egypt.

In June 2013 massive protests called for Morsi's resignation. Again, Egypt's armed forces intervened. The military removed Morsi from power, banned the Muslim Brotherhood, and suspended Egypt's constitution. Former general Abdel Fattah el-Sisi was elected president in May 2014. Today, Egypt's government and society continue to face many challenges.

Many Egyptians live in poverty, without clean water for cooking or washing. The spread of disease in cities is also a problem. In addition, about 25 percent of Egyptians cannot read or write. Still, Egypt has made progress. Today, Egyptians live longer and are much healthier than they were 50 years ago.

Resources and Economy In addition to political instability, Egypt is challenged by its limited resources. The country's only farmland is in the Nile River valley and delta. To keep the land productive, farmers must use more and more fertilizer. In addition, salt water drifting up the Nile from the Mediterranean has been harmful to crops. These problems and a rapidly growing population force Egypt to import much of its food.

About 29 percent of Egyptians are farmers, but less than 4 percent of the land is used for farming. Most farming is located along the Nile delta, which is extremely fertile. A warm, sunny climate and water for irrigation

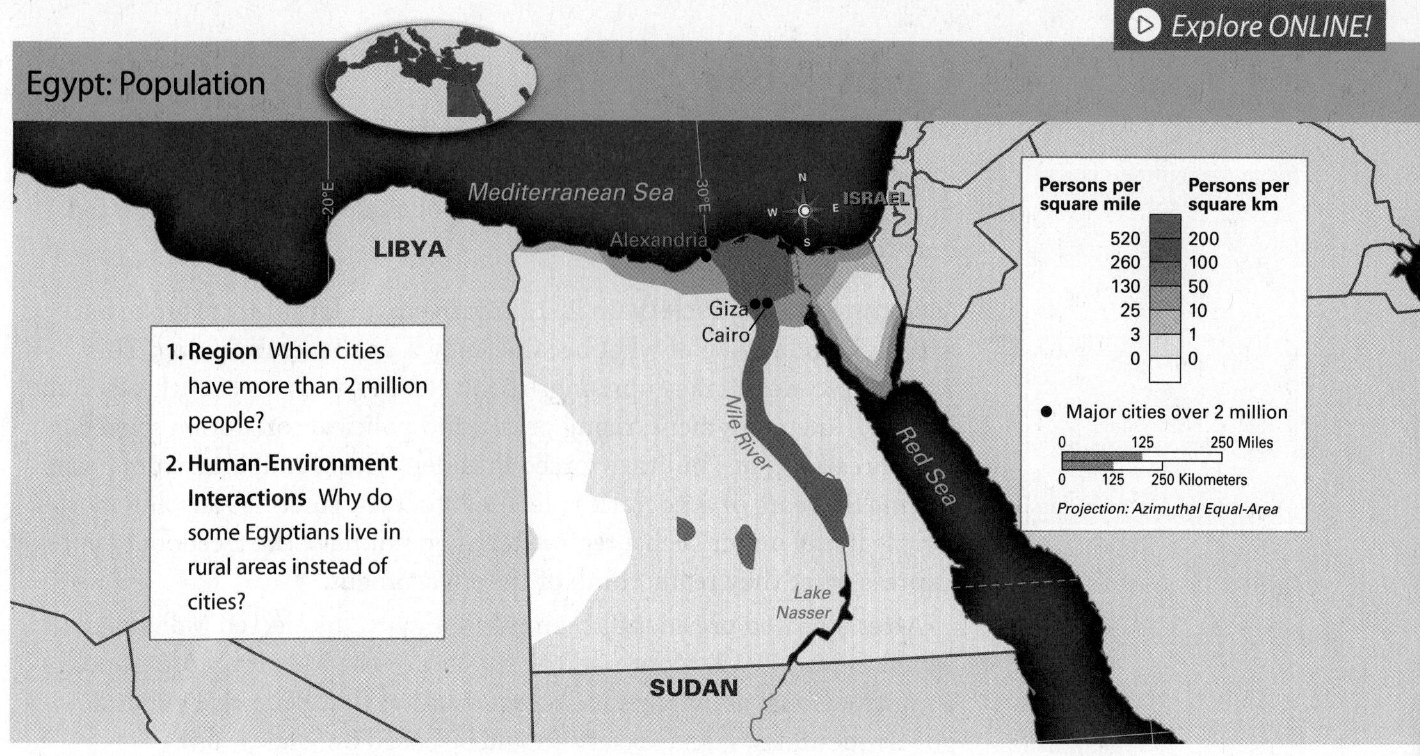

make the delta ideal for growing cotton. Farmlands along the Nile River are used for growing vegetables, grain, and fruit.

The Suez Canal is an important part of Egypt's economy. The canal makes more than $5 billion a year by requiring tolls from ships that pass through the canal. Thousands of ships use the canal each year to avoid making long trips around Southern Africa. This heavy traffic makes the canal one of the world's busiest waterways. In 2015 and 2016 Egypt completed expansion projects on the canal that nearly doubled its capacity.

Due to its limited resources, Egypt is forced to specialize and trade with other countries. It uses the money from this trade to invest in industry and buy what it needs. Egypt's economy depends mostly on agriculture, petroleum exports, and tourism. Unfortunately, in 2011 civil unrest caused a decline in tourism. To provide for its people, Egypt is working to rebuild tourism and expand other industries. Recently, the government has invested in the country's communications and natural gas industries.

Many Egyptians depend on money sent home by family members working in Europe or oil-rich countries in Southwest Asia. Often, Egyptians work abroad because there are not enough jobs in Egypt.

Cities and Rural Life Most North Africans live in cities along the Mediterranean coast or in villages in the foothills of the Atlas Mountains. However, 99 percent of Egyptians live in the Nile valley and delta. Egypt's capital, Cairo, is located in the Nile delta.

With 18.8 million people, Cairo is the largest city in Africa. The city is crowded, poor, and polluted. Cairo continues to grow as people move into the city from Egypt's rural areas in search of work. For centuries, Cairo's location at the southern end of the Nile delta helped the city grow. The city also lies along old trading routes.

Today, the landscape of Cairo is a mixture of modern buildings, historic mosques, and small, mud-brick houses. However, there is not enough housing in Cairo for its growing population. Many people live in make-shift housing in the slums or boats along the Nile. Communities have even developed in cemeteries, where people convert tombs into bedrooms and kitchens.

Alexandria is Egypt's second-largest city. As you learned earlier in this lesson, the city was founded by Alexander the Great. Known in ancient times for its spectacular library, it is now home to a large university and many industries. Its location on the Mediterranean Sea has made it a major seaport. The home of some 5 million people, Alexandria is as poor and crowded as Cairo.

Reading Check
Find Main Ideas
What are some of the challenges Cairo faces today?

More than half of all Egyptians live in small villages and other rural areas. Most rural Egyptians are farmers called fellahin (fel-uh-HEEN). These farmers own very small plots of land along the Nile River. Some fellahin also work large farms owned by powerful families.

Cultures

Egypt shares many aspects of its history and culture with other countries of North Africa. These include its language, religion, foods, holidays, customs, and arts and literature.

People and Language Egyptians, Berbers, and Bedouins make up nearly all of Egypt's population. Bedouins are nomadic herders who travel throughout the deserts of Egypt. The majority of Egyptians, and North Africans, speak Arabic. Some also speak French, Italian, and English.

Religion About 90 percent of Egyptians are Muslims who practice the religion of Islam. Islam plays a major role in Egyptian life. For example, Egyptian Muslims stop to pray five times a day. In addition, Fridays are special days, when Muslims meet in mosques for prayer. About 10 percent of Egyptians are Christians or practice other religions.

The Nile River

From space, the Nile looks like a river of green. The areas that appear green in this satellite image are actually thousands of irrigated fields that line the banks of the river. The river deposits silt along its banks, which makes the land extremely fertile. Farmers also depend on the Nile's waters to irrigate their crops. Without water, they could not farm in the desert.

Notice how the river appears smaller at the bottom of this image. The Aswan High Dam controls the river's flow here, which prevents flooding and provides electricity.

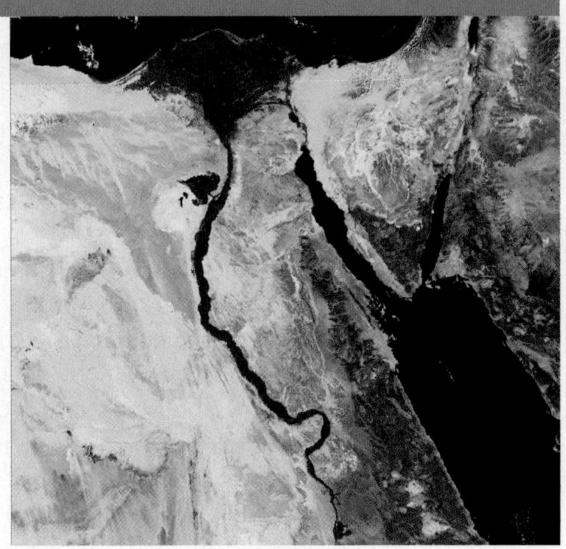

Analyze Visuals
How is the Nile important to Egypt's people?

Many meals in Egypt are vegetarian, such as this stew. Various spices add to the flavor.

Foods Grains, vegetables, fruit, and nuts are common foods in Egypt. Meals here sometimes include a dish called couscous (KOOS-koos). It is made from wheat and looks like small pellets of pasta.

Couscous is usually steamed over boiling water or soup. Often it is served with vegetables or meat, butter, and olive oil.

Egyptians also enjoy a dish called *fuul.* It is made with fava beans mashed with olive oil, salt, pepper, garlic, and lemons. It is often served with hard-boiled eggs and bread. Many Egyptians eat these foods on holidays and at family gatherings.

Holidays Egypt observes two Revolution Day holidays. The one on January 25 celebrates the 2011 revolution, while the one on July 23 celebrates the 1962 revolution, when Egypt gained its independence from Britain.

Egypt also celebrates the birthday of Muhammad, the prophet of Islam. This holiday is marked with lights, parades, and special sweets of honey, nuts, and sugar. During the holy month of Ramadan, Muslims abstain from food and drink during the day.

The Arts and Literature North Africa has a rich and varied tradition in the arts and literature, which Egypt shares. While traditional arts include woodcarving and weaving, Egypt also boasts a growing movie industry. Egyptian films in Arabic have become popular throughout Southwest Asia and North Africa.

Egypt has also produced important writers and artists. For example, Egyptian poetry and other writings date back thousands of years. One of Egypt's most famous writers is Naguib Mahfouz. In 1988 he became the first Arabic writer to win the Nobel Prize in Literature.

Reading Check
Analyze What are some important facts about the people and culture of Egypt?

Summary and Preview In this lesson you learned about the history and culture of Egypt and North Africa. Next you will learn about the North African region today.

Lesson 2 Assessment

Review Ideas, Terms, and Places

1. a. **Define** What are hieroglyphics?
   b. **Make Inferences** What made the city of Alexandria important?
   c. **Evaluate** Why do you think European countries wanted to take over countries in North Africa?
2. a. **Identify and Explain** Which geographic factor is responsible for Egypt's population pattern? Explain.
   b. **Draw Conclusions** Why is housing scarce in Cairo?
   c. **Analyze** How have conflicts associated with the Arab Spring shaped current conditions in Egypt?
3. a. **Recall** What language do most Egyptians speak?
   b. **Summarize** What is one religious holiday or observance followed in Egypt? Why is it significant?

Critical Thinking

4. **Describe** Use your notes to describe the cultural traits that are common in Egypt.

Language	
Religion	
Food	
The Arts	
Literature	

Libya, Tunisia, Algeria, and Morocco

The Big Idea

Countries in North Africa face great change due to popular protests and political instability.

Main Ideas

- In 2011 a pro-democracy movement called the Arab Spring brought change to North Africa.
- The North African countries share a common history and culture, with most people following Islam.
- People in the Maghreb countries of North Africa are mostly pastoral nomads or farmers, and oil is an important resource in the region.

Key Terms and Places

dictator
Maghreb
souks
free port

If YOU lived there . . .

You live in Tunis, Tunisia. The city is known for its architecture, a mix of French and Arab styles. Ordinarily, you could stroll a maze of streets in the city's ancient, walled center, where blacksmiths and leather tanners still work. But today, the streets are filled with protesters demanding change.

What might cause you to join a protest?

The Arab Spring

As you read in the previous lesson, in 2011 a wave of pro-democracy uprisings called the Arab Spring shook North Africa and Southwest Asia. Tired of living under authoritarian regimes, people took to the streets. Some demanded the right to vote and an end to political corruption. Others wanted better living conditions, better jobs, and the freedom to write and say what they wanted.

In different countries, protesters used similar strategies. They held strikes and mostly nonviolent protests. They used the Internet, cell phones, and social media to unite people and promote their cause. Likewise, different governments acted similarly to stop the protests. For example, they used violence against their own people and blocked Internet and mobile network access.

Each country touched by the Arab Spring has had a different outcome. Some protests were successful. Dictators were forced out of power in Tunisia, Egypt, and Libya. A **dictator** is someone who rules a country with complete power. By contrast, Bahrain and Syria used brutal force to stop the protests. Regardless, the Arab Spring gave hope to millions of people in the region. Only time will tell the extent to which these hopes will be met.

Reading Check
Find Main Ideas
What were the Arab Spring protesters seeking?

Shared History and Culture

Like Egypt, North Africa's long Mediterranean coastline opened it to invasion over the centuries from people from the eastern Mediterranean, Greeks, and Romans. The region also

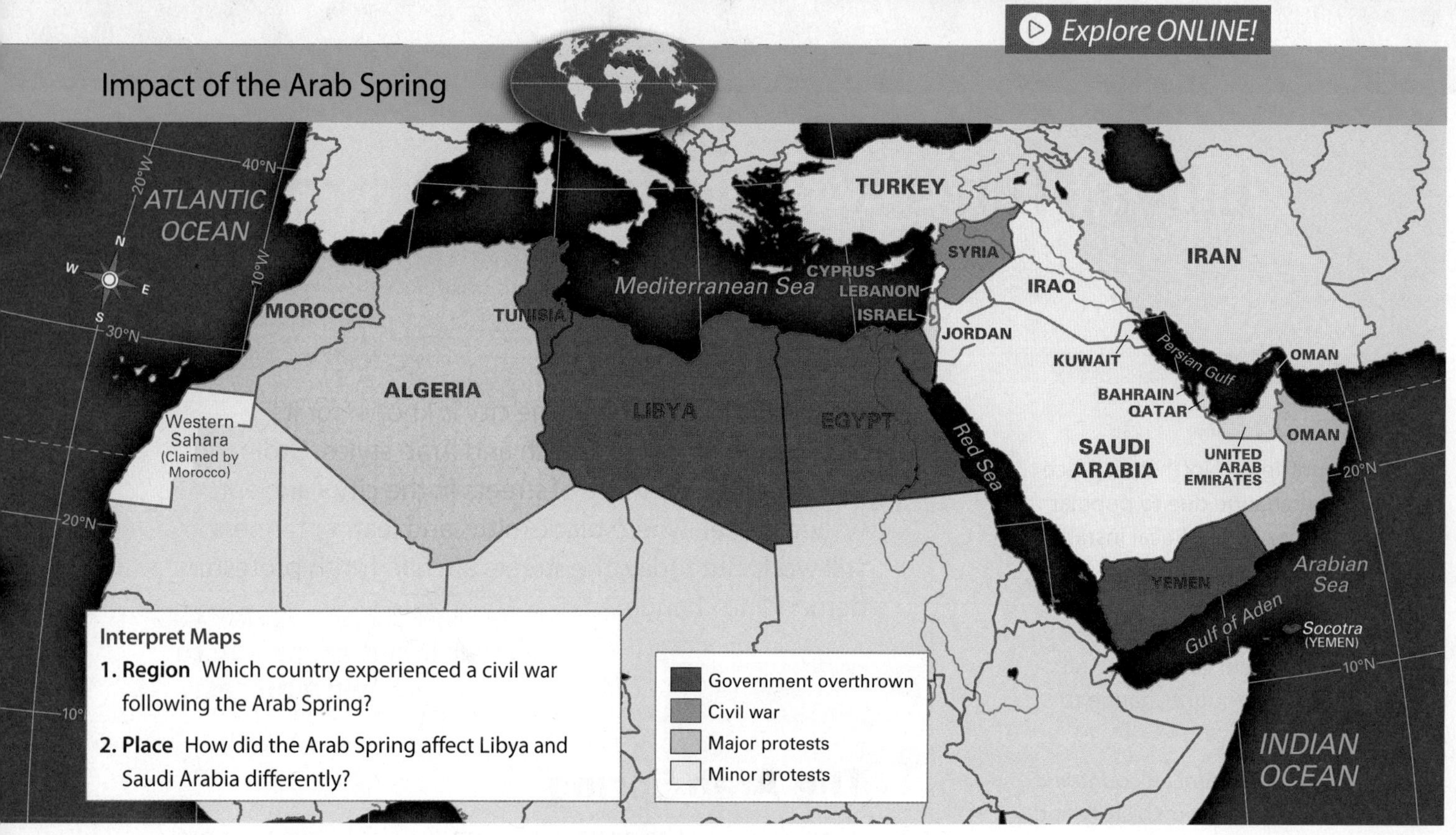

Interpret Maps

1. **Region** Which country experienced a civil war following the Arab Spring?
2. **Place** How did the Arab Spring affect Libya and Saudi Arabia differently?

saw Arab armies invade it from Southwest Asia, and as a result, Islam and the Arabic language took root here. The city of Fès in Morocco, along with other North African cities, became a center for craft making, trade, and learning.

In the 1800s European countries began to take over the region. By 1912 they had authority over all of North Africa. In that year, Italy captured Libya. Spain already controlled northern Morocco. France ruled the rest of Morocco as well as Tunisia and Algeria.

The countries of North Africa gradually gained independence. During World War II, the region was a major battleground. Libya, Morocco, and Tunisia each won independence in the 1950s.

Algeria was the last North African country to win independence. Many French citizens had moved to the country, and they considered Algeria part of France. Algeria finally won independence in 1962. In 1976 Morocco took over the former Spanish colony of Western Sahara.

People and Language Most people in North Africa are of mixed Arab and Berber ancestry. The Berbers are an ethnic group who are native to North Africa and speak Berber languages. As you have previously read, the majority of North Africans speak Arabic, but some also speak French, Italian, and English.

Religion, Holidays, and Customs As in Egypt, most North Africans are Muslims who practice the religion of Islam. This is reflected in their holidays, which include the birthday of Muhammad, the prophet of Islam, as well as the holy month of Ramadan.

Gathering at cafes is a custom practiced by many men in North Africa. The cafes are a place where they go to play chess or dominoes. Most women in North Africa socialize only in their homes.

A certain way of greeting each other on the street is another North African custom. People greet each other by shaking hands and then touching their hand to their heart. If they are family or friends, they will kiss each other on the cheek. The number of kisses varies from country to country.

Many North Africans wear traditional clothes, which are long and loosely fitted. Such styles are ideal for the region's hot climate. Many North African women dress according to Muslim tradition. Their clothing covers all of the body except the face and hands.

The Arts and Literature North Africa is famous for beautiful handwoven carpets. The women who weave these carpets use bright colors to create complex geometric patterns. Beautifully detailed hand-painted tile work is also a major art form in the region.

Many North Africans also enjoy popular music based on singing and poetry. The musical scale there has many more notes than are common in Western music. As a result of this difference, North African tunes seem to wail or waver. Musicians in Morocco often use instruments such as the three-stringed sintir.

Reading Check
Analyze What are some important facts about the people and culture of North Africa?

Countries of North Africa

Western Libya, Tunisia, Algeria, and Morocco are often called the **Maghreb** (MUH-gruhb). This Arabic word means "west" or "the direction of the setting sun." Since most of the Maghreb is covered by the Sahara, cities and farmland are located in narrow bands along the coast.

Focus on Culture

The Berbers

Before the AD 600s, when Arabs settled in North Africa, a people called the Berbers lived in the region. The descendants of these ancient peoples live throughout North Africa today—mostly in Morocco and Algeria. Some Berbers are nomadic and live in goat-hair tents. Other Berbers farm crops that include wheat, barley, fruits, and olives. Some also raise cattle, sheep, or goats.

Berber culture is centered on a community made up of different tribes. Once a year, Berber tribes gather at large festivals. At these gatherings, Berbers trade goods, and many couples get married in elaborate ceremonies.

Draw Conclusions
How have Berbers kept their culture alive?

Government and Economy Major political changes have occurred in the Maghreb since 2011. Following the Arab Spring, Tunisia and Libya experienced revolutions and new governments. Political unrest still challenges the region, as does conflict over the role of Islam in society.

Oil, mining, and tourism are important industries for the countries of North Africa. Oil is the most important resource, particularly in Libya and Algeria. Money from oil pays for schools, health care, food, social programs, and military equipment. The region's countries also have large deposits of natural gas, iron ore, and lead. The largest trade partners of Algeria, Libya, and Morocco are European Union members.

Agriculture is a major economic activity in North Africa. About one in six workers in Libya, Tunisia, and Algeria is a farmer. In Morocco, farmers make up about 40 percent of the labor force. North Africa's farmers grow and export wheat, olives, fruits, and nuts. Tourism is also an important economic activity in the region, especially in Morocco and Tunisia.

Some North African countries have experienced unusual challenges when trading with each other. As far back as 20 years ago, these countries had negotiated favorable trade deals with European, Asian, and American countries. Due to the way they structured their tariffs, however, they did not have favorable deals with each other. Thus, it had become easier, for example, for Morocco to trade with the United States than with Libya.

Cities Many North African cities have large marketplaces, or **souks.** The souks are located in the Casbah, or old district of a city. These souks sell various goods such as spices, carpets, and copper teapots. The Casbah in Algeria's capital, Algiers, is a maze of winding alleys and tall walls.

Tunisia Protests in Tunisia, the birthplace of the Arab Spring uprisings, led to a revolution that ousted a dictator.

Algiers, Algeria
Algeria's capital and major port, Algiers, sits on the Mediterranean Sea.

Libya and Tunisia's cities and most of its population are found in the coastal areas. Libya is the most urbanized country in the region. About 77 percent of Libya's roughly 6 million people live in cities. The largest cities are Benghazi and the capital, Tripoli. Tunisia's capital and largest city, Tunis, lies on the Mediterranean coast.

Morocco's largest city, Casablanca, has about 3.2 million people. Another Moroccan city, Tangier, overlooks the Strait of Gibraltar. This beautiful city was once a Spanish territory. Today, tourists can take a quick ferry ride from Spain across the strait to Tangier, a **free port.** A free port is a city in which almost no taxes are placed on goods sold there.

In addition to sharing similar economies, the countries of North Africa also share similar challenges. Some countries are dealing with violence, while others are strengthening their trading relationships with the United States and Europe.

Libya From 1969 to 2011, Libya was ruled by a dictator, Colonel Muammar Gaddafi. In 2011 pro-democracy protests broke out in Libya. Gaddafi's crackdown on protesters led to a civil war. An international air and naval intervention sealed the dictator's fate. Gaddafi's regime toppled. In 2012 Libya formed a new parliament and elected Ali Zaydan prime minister.

Libya is a member of OPEC. This means that it is normally subject to a quota, or limit, on the amount of oil it is permitted to produce. Because it was so affected by the Arab Spring uprisings, in 2017 OPEC granted it an exemption from an oil production cut in quotas for its members. The idea was that Libya would gradually increase production and revenue to help its economy rebound. The country's economy appears to be on its way to recovery.

Fès, Morocco

At a tannery in the city of Fès, men dye sheepskins in large vats of dyes. The city's craftspeople use yellow-dyed leather to make distinctive leather shoes.

Analyze Visuals
What other colors are the sheepskins dyed?

Algeria Following a series of protests in 2011, Algeria's government made reforms. It lifted a 19-year state of emergency. It also eased restrictions on the media, political parties, and the ability of women to serve in elected office.

Tunisia The protests of the Arab Spring started in Tunisia in December 2010. By January 2011 protesters had forced longtime President Zine al-Abidine Ben Ali from power. Since that time, Tunisians have held democratic elections and struggled with the role of Islam in government and society.

Reading Check
Summarize What are some of the challenges these countries face?

Morocco Morocco is the only North African country with little oil. Today, the country is an important producer and exporter of fertilizer.

Summary In this lesson you learned about North Africa today.

Lesson 3 Assessment

Review Ideas, Terms, and Places

1. **Recall** In which three countries were dictators forced out of power in the Arab Spring?
2. a. **Recall** What countries in North Africa make up the Maghreb?
   b. **Analyze** How do you think the countries of North Africa can improve their economies?
   c. **Evaluate** What do you think are the most important political contributions made by the Arab Spring protesters?

Critical Thinking

3. **Compare** Use your notes to compare Egypt with the other countries of North Africa.

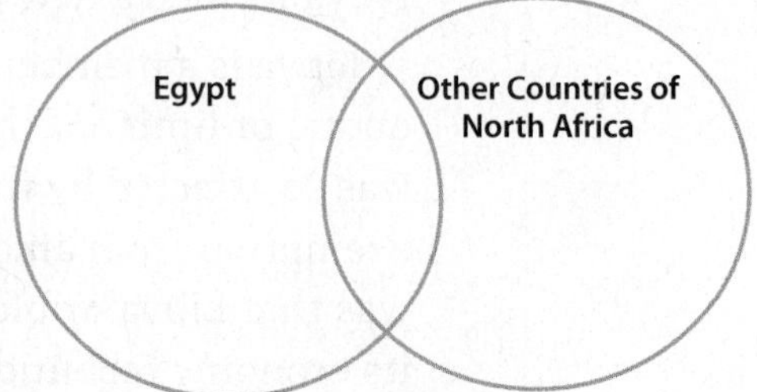

Social Studies Skills

Analyze a Diagram

Define the Skill

Diagrams are drawings that use lines and labels to explain or illustrate something. Pictorial diagrams show an object in simple form, much like it would look if you were viewing it. Cutaway diagrams, like the one of an Egyptian pyramid below, show the "insides" of an object. These diagrams usually have labels that identify important areas of the diagram.

Learn the Skill

Analyze the diagram below, and answer the following questions.

1. What type of diagram is this?
2. What labels in the diagram suggest what this pyramid was used for?
3. Of what materials was the pyramid made?

Practice the Skill

Draw a cutaway diagram of your school. Label classrooms, hallways, the cafeteria, and other areas. Use your diagram to answer the following questions.

1. How many stories are in your school?
2. Where is the closest exit located from the classroom you are sitting in now?
3. What are some of the materials your school is made of?

Module 10 Assessment

Review Vocabulary, Terms, and Places

Unscramble each group of letters below to spell a term or place that matches the given definition.

1. **sasoi**—wet, fertile area in a desert where a spring or well provides water
2. **ashraa**—the largest desert in the world that covers most of North Africa
3. **ipmtac**—effect; result
4. **enli virer**—the world's longest river that empties into the Mediterranean Sea in Egypt
5. **oicar**—a city founded more than 1,000 years ago on the Nile and is the capital of Egypt today
6. **uahtroyti**—power; right to rule
7. **tidrotca**—someone who rules a country with complete power
8. **ksuos**—marketplaces
9. **efer tpro**—a city in which almost no taxes are placed on goods sold there

Comprehension and Critical Thinking

Lesson 1

10. a. **Describe** What is the Nile River valley like? Describe the river and the landscape.
    b. **Elaborate** Why do you think few people live in the Sahara? What role does climate play in where people live? Explain your answer.
    c. **Form Generalizations** Look back at the model of A Sahara Oasis in Lesson 1. Pose and answer a geographic question about how physical features shape patterns of human movement in the Sahara.

Lesson 2

11. a. **Recall** What types of monuments did the ancient Egyptians build?
    b. **Contrast** How did Egypt's experience of the Arab Spring differ from Libya's?
    c. **Elaborate** Why do you think some groups living in North Africa are nomadic people?

Lesson 3

12. a. **Define** What is the Maghreb? What physical feature covers this region?
    b. **Make inferences** Why did European countries want to control most of North Africa?
    c. **Predict** Think about the goals shared by the Arab Spring protesters. Do you think they will achieve these goals? Explain.

Module 10 Assessment, continued

Reading Skills

13. **Summarize** Use the Reading Skills taught in this module to answer a question about the reading selection below.

> For centuries, rain far to the south caused floods along the northern Nile, leaving rich silt in surrounding fields. Silt is finely ground fertile soil that is good for growing crops.
>
> The Nile River valley is a fertile area in the midst of the desert. Farmers use water from the Nile to irrigate their fields. The Nile fans out near the Mediterranean Sea, forming a large delta. A delta is a landform at the mouth of a river that is created by the deposit of sediment. The sediment in the Nile delta makes the area extremely fertile.

Write a summary of the paragraphs above. What are the important details?

Social Studies Skills

14. **Create a Diagram to Compare Regions** The ancient Maya of Mexico also built pyramids. Create a diagram that compares Egyptian and Mayan pyramids. Conduct research, including searching on the Internet, to learn more about both types of pyramids. Be sure to use clear labels on your diagram. Also include maps showing the distribution of pyramids in each region. Use your model to pose and answer a geographic question about the distribution of pyramids in each region. Finally, present your diagram and pose your question to the class.

Map Activity

15. **North Africa** On a separate sheet of paper, match the letters on the map with their correct labels.

Nile River
Atlas Mountains
Cairo
Tripoli
Strait of Gibraltar

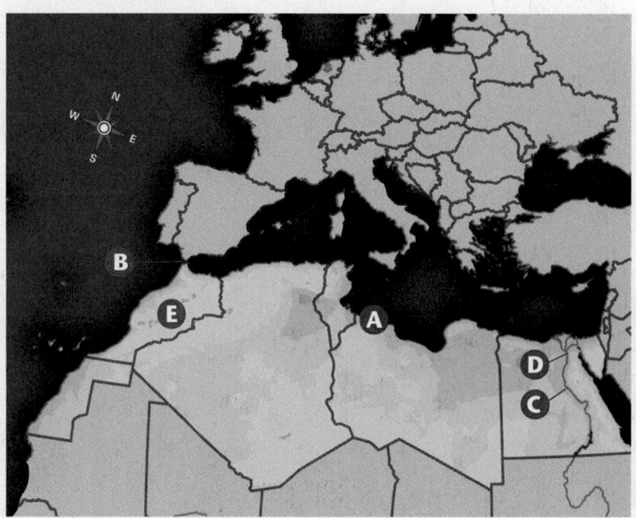

Focus on Writing

16. **Write a Myth** Identify one major physical or human feature in North Africa to be the subject of your myth. Write several paragraphs describing the characteristics of your feature and how you think ancient peoples would find it important. Use your imagination! For example, your myth might explain why it rarely rains in the Sahara, how the Nile brings water to the region, or why pyramids have been built. Research books of myths in the library to get a feel for the kind of language and vocabulary used when telling a myth. Make sure that your myth is clear and coherent, with proper story development and organization, and told in a style that is appropriate to its task, purpose, and audience.

Module 11

History of Sub-Saharan Africa

Essential Question

How is the story of Africa the story of humankind?

About the Photo: After the 700s, Islam spread throughout West Africa's empires. Muslim architects built mud-walled mosques, where people would meet and pray.

Explore ONLINE!

VIDEOS, including . . .

- The Golden Age of Africa
- Trans-Saharan Trade
- African Slave Trade

- Document-Based Investigations
- Graphic Organizers
- Interactive Games
- Interactive Map: Mali Empire, c. 1300
- Compare Images: Imperialism in Africa

In this module, you will learn about the history of sub-Saharan Africa—Africa south of the Sahara—from early humans to great kingdoms. You will read how Africa's mineral wealth attracted the attention of other cultures, with terrible results. You will also learn how European countries divided up Africa into colonies to gain resources and power.

What You Will Learn

Lesson 1: Human Beginnings in Africa 357
The Big Idea During the Stone Age, the early inhabitants of Africa learned to make tools and to adapt to their environments.

Lesson 2: Kingdoms in Africa 364
The Big Idea Between 300 and 1500, the people of Africa formed powerful kingdoms in several parts of the continent.

Lesson 3: Africa in Global Trade 372
The Big Idea Africa's wealth and mineral resources attracted the attention of traders from other parts of the world, whose actions eventually led to the enslavement of millions of Africans.

Lesson 4: Imperialism and Independence 377
The Big Idea In the late 1800s, Europeans once again created colonies in Africa and became involved in African politics and economics.

Trade West Africa's salt mines were a great source of wealth. Camels carried salt from Saharan mines to the south to trade for gold.

Traditions Many African cultures had no written languages. Instead, storytellers, or griots, kept the cultures of West Africa alive with their stories.

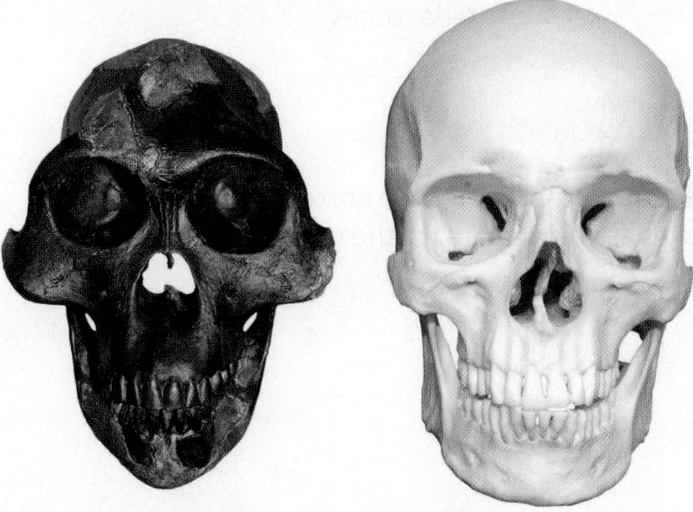

Human Beginnings The oldest hominid remains ever discovered were found in East Africa. Anthropologists believe humans first developed in Africa and spread from there to the rest of the world.

Reading Social Studies

Understand Cause and Effect

READING FOCUS

To understand a country's history, you should look for cause-and-effect chains. A cause makes something happen, and an effect is what happens as a result of a cause. The effect can then become a cause and create another effect. Notice how the events below create a cause-and-effect chain.

As the trade in gold and salt increased, Ghana's rulers gained power. Over time, their military strength grew as well. With their armies, they began to take control of this trade from the merchants who had once controlled it. Merchants from the north and south met to exchange goods in Ghana. As a result of their control of trade routes, the rulers of Ghana became wealthy.

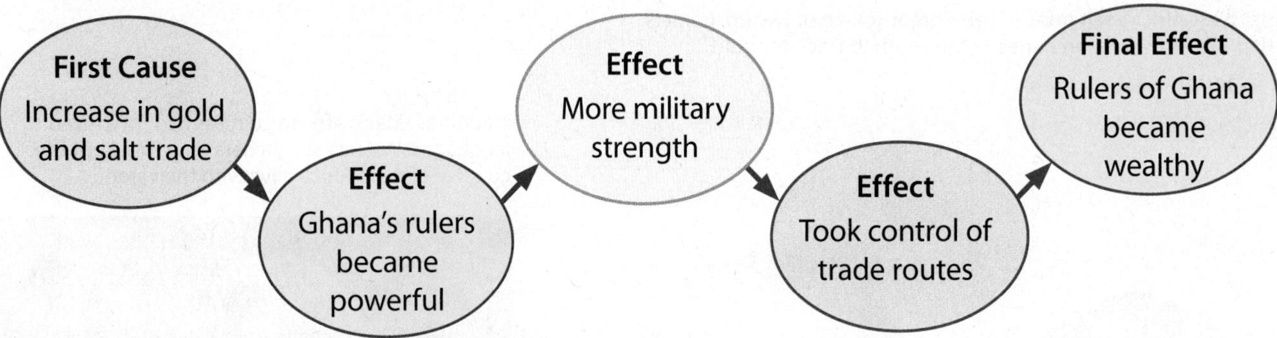

YOU TRY IT!

Read the following sentences. Then, use a graphic organizer like the one above to analyze causes and effects. Create as many boxes as you need to list the causes and effects.

When Mansa Musa died, his son Maghan took the throne. Maghan was a weak ruler. When raiders from the southeast poured into Mali, he couldn't stop them. The raiders set fire to Timbuktu's great schools and mosques. Mali never fully recovered from this terrible blow. The empire continued to weaken and decline.

As you read this module, create cause-and-effect chains to help you understand the relationships between events in African history.

Human Beginnings in Africa

The Big Idea

During the Stone Age, the early inhabitants of Africa learned to make tools and to adapt to their environments.

Main Ideas

- The remains of early humans have been found at sites all around Africa.
- During the Stone and Iron Ages, people learned to make increasingly complex tools and formed Africa's first societies.
- Anthropologists have learned how early Africans adapted to different environments by studying modern cultures.

Key Terms and Places

Olduvai Gorge
hominids
hunter-gatherers
rock art
nomads

If YOU lived there . . .

You live 200,000 years ago, in a time known as the Stone Age. A member of your group has offered to teach you his skill. You watch carefully as he strikes two black rocks together. A small piece flakes off. You try to copy him, but the rocks just break. Finally you learn to strike the rock just right. You have made a sharp stone knife!

How will you use your new skill?

Early Human Sites

The Stone Age was a long period of human development. As the name suggests, people during this period made tools and weapons out of stone—or sometimes bone—because they had not yet learned to shape metals. It is part of the period historians refer to as prehistory, the time before written records.

The Stone Age lasted more than 2.5 million years in some places. Because of how long ago it began, and because of the lack of written records, it is difficult to know what life was like for Stone Age people. However, anthropologists have found hundreds of early human sites that have revealed clues about early societies. The oldest of these sites are all located in Africa.

Olduvai Gorge Perhaps the most famous Stone Age site in Africa is **Olduvai Gorge.** This steep canyon is located on the Serengeti Plain in northern Tanzania. Anthropologists working in the gorge have discovered the fossil remains of more than 60 **hominids,** or early ancestors of humans. Examined together, these remains have given scientists their clearest view of how early humans developed and changed.

The first major discovery at Olduvai Gorge was made by British anthropologist Mary Leakey in 1959. Working with her husband, Louis, she uncovered pieces of a hominid skull more than 1.5 million years old. Leakey's discovery was, at the time, the oldest hominid fossil ever found. It was later found to be an Australopithecus (aw-stray-loh-PI-thuh-kuhs), one of the earliest ancestors of humans. These early hominids walked on two legs but had much smaller brains than modern humans.

Early Hominid Sites

Explore ONLINE!

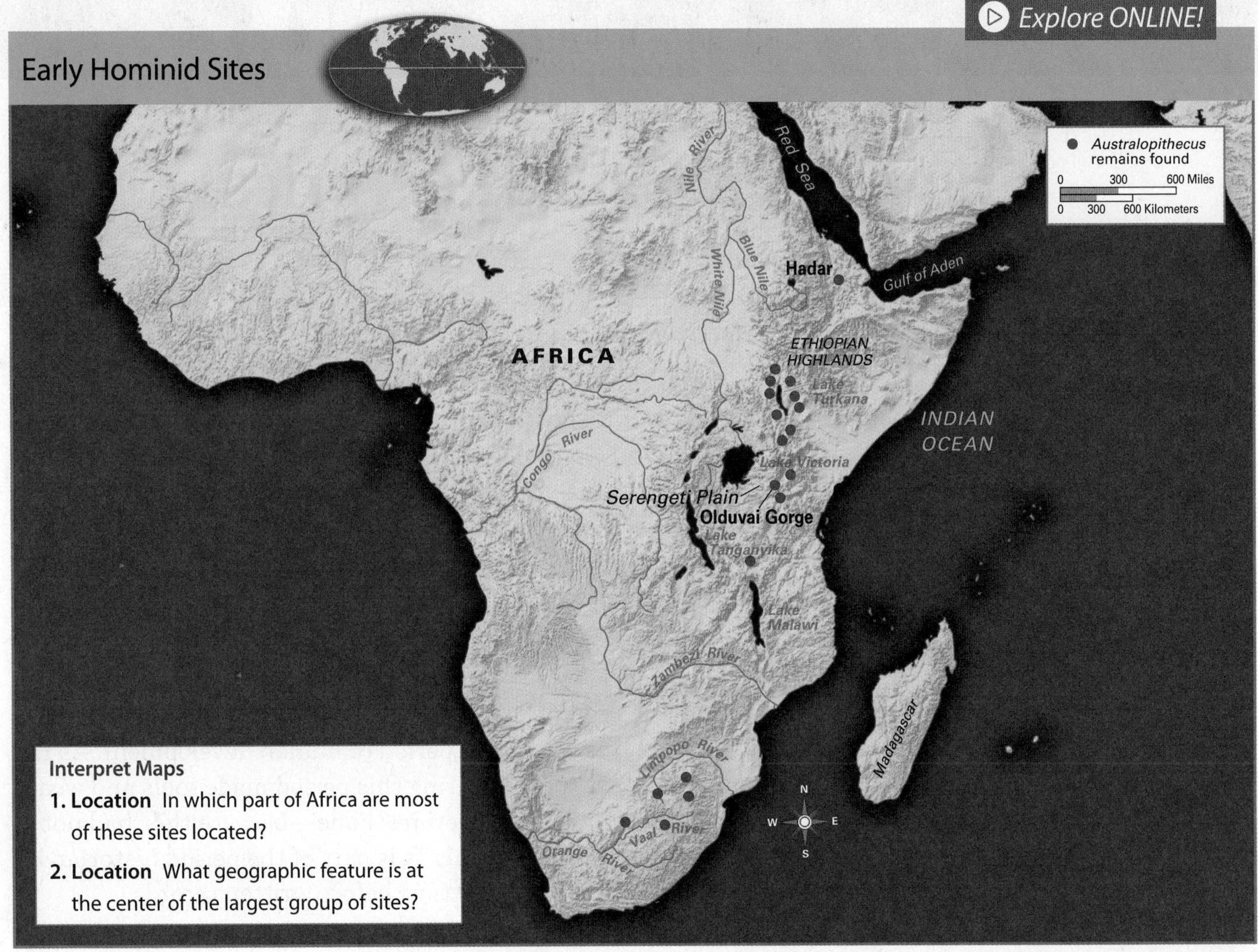

Interpret Maps

1. **Location** In which part of Africa are most of these sites located?
2. **Location** What geographic feature is at the center of the largest group of sites?

About a year later, the Leakeys made another exciting discovery at Olduvai. They found the bones of another hominid. This one, however, was from a more developed species of hominids. Louis Leakey called this new species *Homo habilis*, or "handy man." Leakey and his son Richard believed that *Homo habilis* was more closely related to modern humans than their earlier finds. They also believed it had a larger brain than earlier hominids.

Over the years scientists have found the remains of two more hominid species at Olduvai Gorge. *Homo erectus*, or "upright man," is thought to have appeared in Africa about 1.5 million years ago. Scientists think these people walked completely upright and knew how to control fire. They used fire to cook food, for heat, and as protection against wild animals.

Much later, hominids developed characteristics of modern humans. Scientists are not sure exactly when or where the first modern humans lived. Scientists call these people *Homo sapiens*, or "wise man." Every person alive today belongs to this group.

Other Discovery Sites Since the early discoveries at Olduvai Gorge, anthropologists working all over Africa have found remains that add to our understanding of prehistoric people. In 1974, for example, Donald Johanson (joh-HAN-suhn) was exploring near Hadar, Ethiopia. There he found bones from an Australopithecus he named Lucy. Tests showed that

Quick Facts

Early Hominids

Four major groups of hominids appeared in Africa between 5 million and about 200,000 years ago. Each group was more advanced than the one before it and could use better tools.

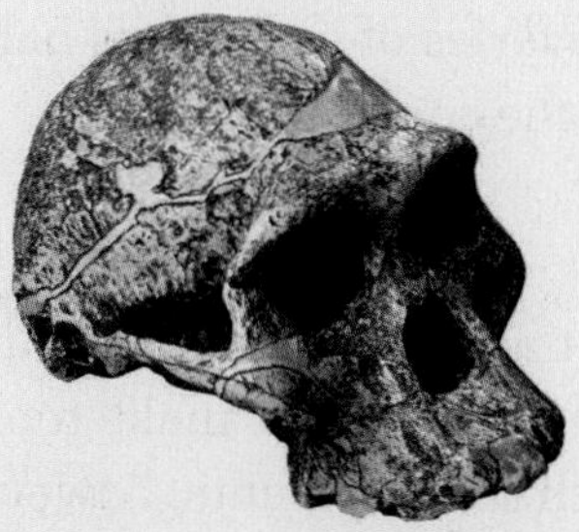

Australopithecus

- Name means "southern ape"
- Appeared in Africa about 4–5 million years ago
- Stood upright and walked on two legs
- Brain was about one-third the size of modern humans

An early Stone Age chopper

Homo habilis

- Name means "handy man"
- Appeared in Africa about 2.4 million years ago
- Used early stone tools for chopping and scraping
- Brain was about half the size of modern humans

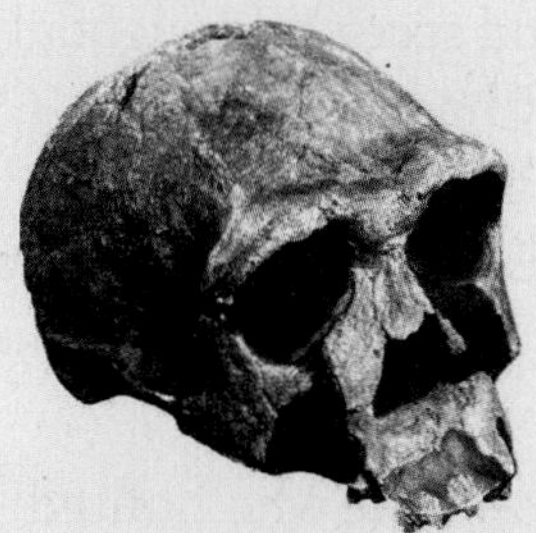

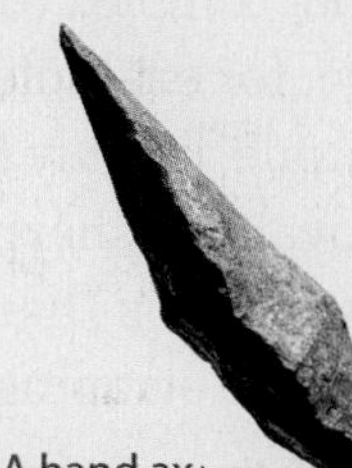

A hand ax

Homo erectus

- Name means "upright man"
- Appeared in Africa about 2–1.5 million years ago
- Used early stone tools like the hand ax
- Learned to control fire
- Migrated out of Africa to Asia and Europe

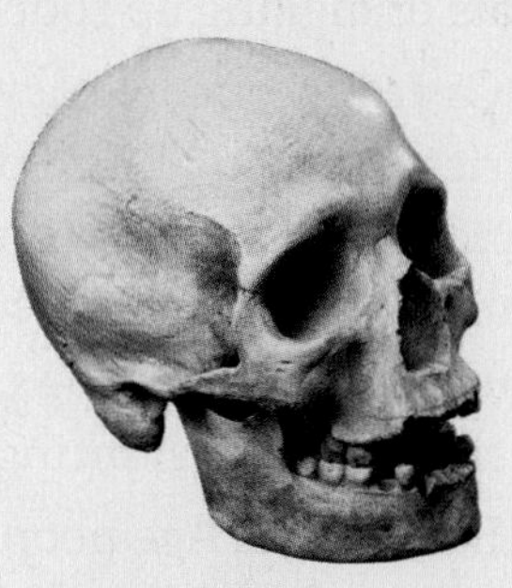

A flint knife

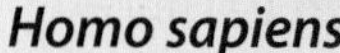

Homo sapiens

- Name means "wise man"
- Appeared in Africa about 200,000 years ago
- Migrated around the world
- Same species as modern human beings
- Learned to create fire and use a wide variety of tools
- Developed language

she lived more than 3 million years ago. Soon afterward, Mary Leakey also found evidence that hominids had lived that long ago. In 1976 she found fossilized hominid footprints near Laetoli, Tanzania. The prints were from a hominid who, like Lucy, walked upright.

Most of the earliest hominid discoveries, including the Leakeys' and Johanson's, have been made in East Africa. Scholars working other parts of Africa, though, have also made significant finds. At Sterkfontein in South Africa, paleontologists found the remains of several Australopithecus specimens, some as old as Lucy.

In addition to these very early sites, anthropologists have discovered the remains of later hominids all around Africa. *Homo habilis* remains have been found in Tanzania, Kenya, and Ethiopia, not too far from the Leakeys' original discovery at Olduvai Gorge. Skeletons from *Homo erectus* and early *Homo sapiens,* though, are more widespread. They have been found all along the rift valleys of East Africa, in southern Africa, and along the Mediterranean in Morocco and Algeria. The discoveries of these sites help scholars trace the spread of early people through the continent.

Reading Check
Form Generalizations In what parts of Africa have major anthropological discoveries been made?

The Stone and Iron Ages

Scientists believe that some of the most important achievements in human history occurred during the Stone Age. Humans learned how to make tools and build fires. They also developed language. Such developments, however, took place over a long time. To help organize their studies, scholars of African anthropology divide the Stone Age into three periods.

The Early Stone Age The first and longest part of the Stone Age is called the Early Stone Age. It began in East Africa as long as 2.5 million years ago when early people first learned to shape stone into rough tools. By striking small rocks against harder surfaces, people created sharp edges. These sharpened rocks could then be used for such tasks as hunting small animals or digging up roots.

Over time, people developed more complex tools and spread throughout Africa. By about 1 million years ago, for example, they had invented the hand ax. This tool was made of a stone, usually flint, that had been shaped into a rough oval. One side of the oval was sharpened. The opposite end was rounded to make the ax easier to hold. This "handle" end made the hand ax easier to use for hunting, skinning, and scraping than earlier tools.

Early Stone Age people were **hunter-gatherers,** or people who hunted animals and gathered plants, seeds, and nuts for food. People most likely lived in small groups that worked together to find and **distribute** food. These groups moved around in pursuit of animal herds. They took shelter in caves for protection from weather and animals. At times, they decorated these caves or nearby rock formations with **rock art,** or drawings and paintings left on stone. Some African rock art shows elaborate scenes of hunting or other activities. Examples of this art can be found throughout Africa. Many of the best preserved are in the deserts of southern Africa. The dry climate there helped protect the art from wind and rain.

Academic Vocabulary
distribute to divide among a group of people

The Middle Stone Age The Early Stone Age ended at different times in different parts of Africa. By about 100,000 years ago, however, most people had advanced to what anthropologists call the Middle Stone Age. They learned how to make smaller, finer tools with sharper edges. They also learned how to attach bone or wooden handles to blades to make simple spears, axes, and other tools. Many of these new tools helped people adapt to new environments. Fishing spears, for example, allowed people to get food from the rivers that ran through deep forests. As a result, people could for the first time move into the rain forests of Central Africa.

Rock Art

Ancient images like this one in the desert of western Libya appear on rock formations around Africa. Anthropologists are not sure what the purpose of the art may have been.

The Later Stone Age By about 20,000 years ago technology in Africa had advanced into the Later Stone Age. During this period, people learned how to make more advanced tools, such as knives and saws. They developed the bow and arrow, which made hunting easier. At the same time, new technologies developed. People learned how to make woven baskets and pottery containers for cooking and storage. Near the coasts and along rivers, boats appeared for the first time.

Across the continent, some people learned how to plant crops and herd animals, allowing them to settle in more permanent communities. Agriculture provided a steady supply of food, which allowed populations to grow in these communities. As people settled, they began to develop distinct ways of life. These lifestyles were shaped in large part by the environments in which each group lived. You will learn more about how people were influenced by their environments later in this lesson.

The Iron Age The Stone Age ended when people learned how to shape metal into tools. This happened at different times in various parts of the continent. In fact, in some places people did not start to work with metal at all until very recently. In some remote parts of southern Africa, people continued to use stone tools well into the 20th century.

Iron was the most common metal used to make tools in Africa. Iron ore can be found in many parts of Africa, and iron tools are both very strong and very sharp. Anthropologists are not sure how people in Africa first learned to shape iron. Some believe that people developed the technology on their own over many years. Others argue that early Africans probably learned about iron from other civilizations with whom they came into contact. However they developed the technology, evidence shows that Africans had begun making iron tools in some places by about 600 BC.

Reading Check
Summarize
What technological advances did people in Africa make during the Later Stone Age?

Africans Adapt to Different Environments

As people moved into and settled various parts of Africa during the Stone Age, they developed distinct cultures. These cultures were heavily influenced by the natural environments in which they were located. Some were agricultural, while others were based on hunting and gathering.

Despite the lack of written records, anthropologists have been able to make some assumptions about early Africa based on cultures that maintained traditional customs into modern times. Although some members of these cultures have adopted new ways of life, others continue to live as their ancestors did. By studying how these people live and work today, they have formed ideas about how people lived thousands of years ago.

Quick Facts

Traditional Cultures in Modern Africa

Bambuti	San	Maasai
• Live in the rain forests of the Democratic Republic of the Congo • Hunter-gatherers • Use wooden tools and weapons to hunt forest animals • Gather fruits, nuts, and other wild plants • Trade with nearby farmers for food and other products	• Live in Botswana, Namibia, and Angola, including in the Kalahari Desert • Hunter-gatherers • Use bows, snares, spears, and other tools to catch desert game • Gather wild vegetables, fruits, nuts, and insects • Have learned to collect water from deep under desert sands	• Live near the Great Rift Valley in southern Kenya and northern Tanzania • Nomadic herders • Keep large herds of cattle and other animals for meat, blood, and milk • Trade with neighboring societies for additional food and supplies • Celebrated as fierce warriors

A Forest Culture Among the African cultures that anthropologists have studied are the Bambuti of Central Africa. They live deep in the tropical rain forests of the Congo Basin and depend on the forest to provide their needs. They use wood from trees to make bows, arrows, and spears. With these tools they hunt hogs, antelope, monkeys, and other game. Men, women, and children often hunt together. Wild yams, fruits, berries, and other plants add variety to their diet. Many Bambuti groups trade game with nearby communities for tools and additional food.

The Bambuti are **nomads,** or people who move from place to place in search of food or other needs. Most Bambuti live in small groups of 10 to 100 people. For shelter, they build temporary homes of sticks and leaves. As they move to new areas, these homes are abandoned. Their frequent movement has affected many areas of Bambuti society. For example, they do not create carvings or paintings, which would have to be carried from place to place. Music, however, is very important in their society.

A Desert Culture Like the Bambuti, the San people have lived for thousands of years as hunter-gatherers. However, their home is in a very different climate. They live in and around the Kalahari Desert in southwest Africa. San hunters today still use tools similar to those made in the region thousands of years ago. These tools, made mostly of wood, bone, reeds, and stone, include snares, throwing sticks, bows, and arrows. They hunt wild game and gather wild vegetables, fruits, nuts, and insects to eat.

Like the Bambuti, the San move frequently in search of food, water, and supplies. However, unlike the Bambuti, they do not build temporary homes in various locations. Instead, the San build portable shelters of branches, twigs, and grass. As they travel, they bring these shelters with them. The San live and travel in bands made up of several families. These bands generally include 25 to 60 people.

The harsh conditions of the Kalahari have been a major factor in San life. Over the centuries, they have developed techniques to adapt to their environment. For example, a major concern of any desert culture is finding water. Only one river runs through the Kalahari, and rainfall is rare. During water shortages, the San use long reeds to pull water up from deep beneath the sand, much like you would use a drinking straw. They store the water they have collected in hollowed-out ostrich eggs for future use.

A Savanna Culture In the savanna of East Africa, the Maasai people developed a very different culture from the Bambuti and the San. Like the other groups, the Maasai are nomads. However, instead of hunting and gathering, the Maasai herd cattle and other animals to survive. Meat, blood, and milk from their animals are the bases of the Maasai diet.

The Maasai generally live and travel in large clans. Decisions are made by the clan elders, advised by the clan's senior members. Traditionally, the Maasai have been known as fierce warriors, and they continue to train young men in their customs. Warriors in training, usually between 14 and 25 years old, are sent to live apart from the clan. During this time, they learn tribal customs and develop strength, courage, and endurance.

Reading Check
Compare and Contrast How are the Bambuti and San cultures alike? How are they different?

Summary and Preview During the Stone Ages, African cultures developed lifestyles largely based on hunting and gathering or herding. In Lesson 2, you will learn how some cultures in West Africa grew more complex and formed the first African empires.

Lesson 1 Assessment

Review Ideas, Terms, and Places

1. a. **Identify** What is a hominid? What hominids lived in early Africa?
   b. **Explain** What evidence suggests that early hominids first appeared in East Africa and moved to other parts of the continent later?
   c. **Synthesize** Olduvai Gorge has been called the "Cradle of Mankind." Why do you think this is so?
2. a. **Recall** Into what periods do anthropologists organize their studies of early Africa?
   b. **Contrast** How were tools in the Middle Stone Age different from tools in the Early Stone Age?
   c. **Draw Conclusions** How do you think the invention of tools like the bow and arrow changed early people's lives?
3. a. **Describe** In what environment do the Bambuti people live? In what environment do the Maasai live?
   b. **Form Generalizations** How have the San adapted to life in a desert environment?
   c. **Make Inferences** What types of challenges do members of hunter-gatherer societies face in their daily lives? What challenges do herding societies face?

Critical Thinking

4. **Sequence** Copy the graphic organizer. Use it to highlight changes in how people lived during Africa's prehistoric period.

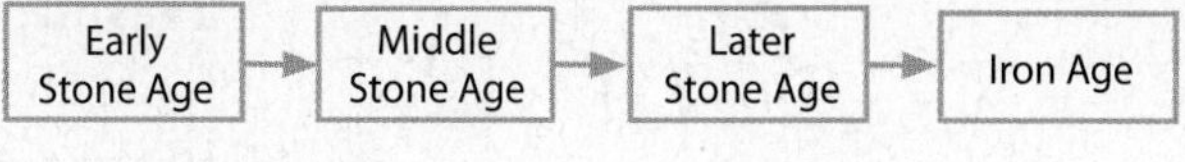

Kingdoms in Africa

The Big Idea

Between 300 and 1500, the people of Africa formed powerful kingdoms in several parts of the continent.

Main Ideas

- Christianity became the major religion in Aksum and Ethiopia.
- Through its control of trade, Ghana built an empire.
- The empire of Mali built upon the foundation laid by Ghana, but the empire fell to invaders in the 1400s.
- Songhai took over West Africa and built a new Islamic empire, conquering many of the lands that were once part of Mali.
- Bantu peoples established several kingdoms as they migrated through Africa.

Key Terms and Places

Coptic Christianity
silent barter
Timbuktu
mosque
Gao
Djenné
Bantu migration

If YOU lived there . . .

You are a trader, traveling in a caravan from the north into West Africa in about 1000. The caravan carries many goods, but the most precious is salt. Salt is so valuable that people trade gold for it! You have never met the mysterious men who trade you the gold. You wish you could talk to them to find out where they get it.

Why do you think the traders are so secretive?

Christian Kingdoms in Africa

As Stone Age people in Africa began to settle in communities, they developed more complex societies. Over time, some of these communities grew more powerful and formed kingdoms.

Aksum One of the new kingdoms that developed was Aksum (AHK-soom), located near the Red Sea in northeast Africa. This location made it easy to transport goods over water, and Aksum became a major trading power as a result. Traders from inland Africa brought goods like gold and ivory to Aksum. From there, the items were shipped to markets as far away as India. In return for their goods, the people of Aksum received cloth, spices, and other products.

Because Aksum was a thriving trade center, people from various cultures gathered there. As these people met to trade goods, they also traded ideas and beliefs. One of the beliefs brought to Aksum by traders was Christianity. Christian teachings quickly took hold in Aksum, and many people converted. In the late 300s, Aksum's most famous ruler, King Ezana (AY-zah-nah), made Christianity the kingdom's official religion.

As a Christian kingdom, Aksum developed ties with other Christian states. For example, it was an ally of the Byzantine Empire. However, contact with these allies was cut off in the 600s and 700s, when Muslim armies from Southwest Asia conquered most of North Africa. Although Aksum itself was never conquered, its major ports were taken by the Muslims. As a result, the kingdom became isolated from other lands. Cut off from their allies and their trade, the people of Aksum retreated to the mountains of northern Ethiopia.

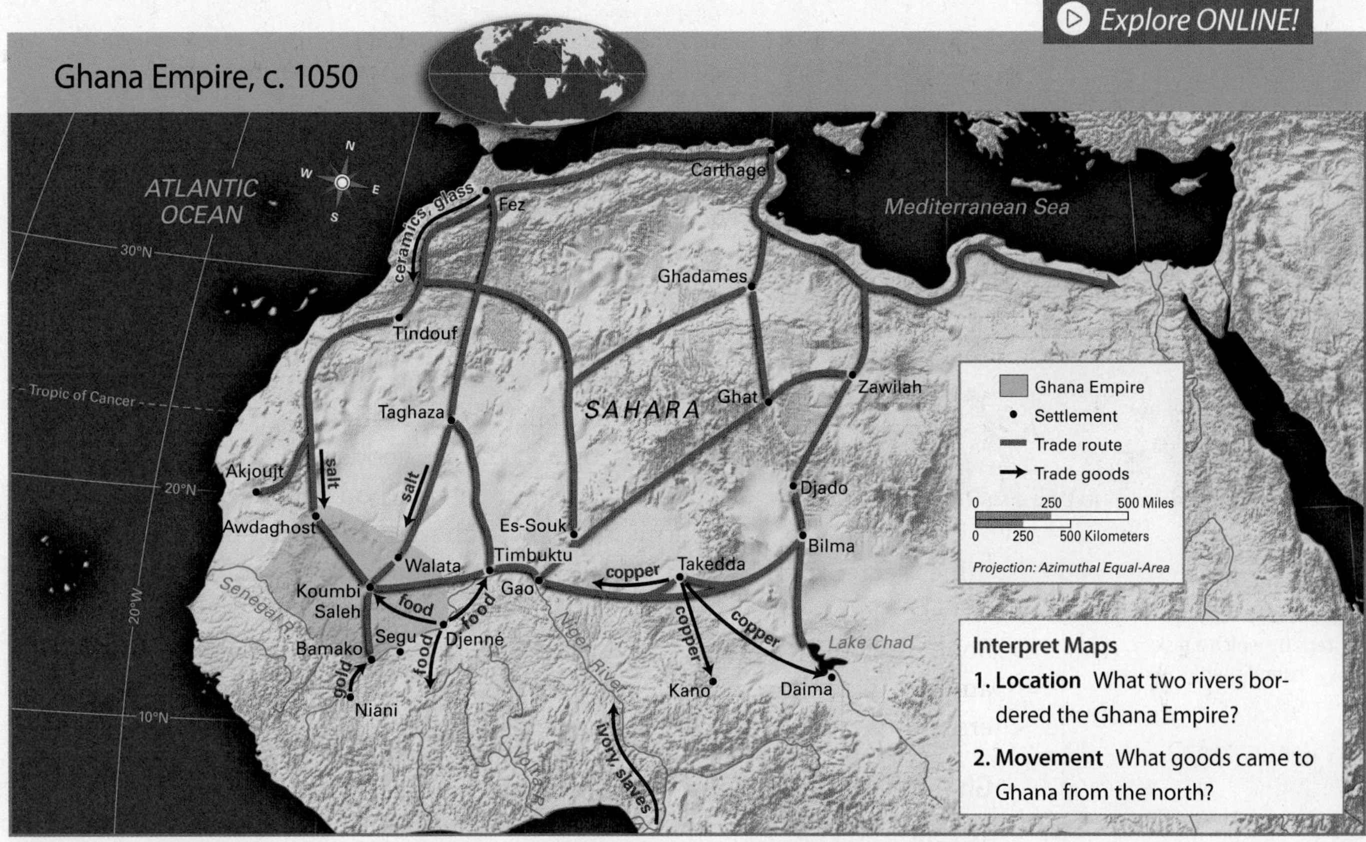

Interpret Maps

1. **Location** What two rivers bordered the Ghana Empire?
2. **Movement** What goods came to Ghana from the north?

Ethiopia In time, the descendants of the people of Aksum formed a new kingdom called Ethiopia. By about 1150 Ethiopia had become a powerful trading state.

Like Aksum, Ethiopia was a Christian kingdom. The most famous of Ethiopia's rulers was King Lalibela, who ruled in the 1200s. He is famous for the 11 churches he built, many of which still stand. The churches of Lalibela were carved into solid rock, many of them set into the ground. Impressive feats of engineering, these churches also show the Ethiopians' devotion to Christianity. Their religion set the Ethiopians apart from their neighbors, most of whom were Muslim.

Shared beliefs helped unify Ethiopians, but their isolation from other Christians led to changes in their religion. Over time, some local African customs blended with Christian teachings. This resulted in a new form of Christianity in Africa called **Coptic Christianity**. The name *Coptic* comes from an Arabic word for "Egyptian." Most Christians who live in North Africa today—including many Ethiopians—belong to Coptic churches.

Reading Check
Sequence How did Christianity take hold in parts of Africa?

Ghana Controls Trade

For hundreds of years, trade routes crisscrossed West Africa. For most of that time, West Africans did not profit much from the Saharan trade because the routes were run by Berbers from northern Africa. Eventually, that situation changed. Ghana (GAH-nuh), an empire in West Africa, gained control of the valuable trade routes. As a result, Ghana became a powerful state.

Ghana's rulers became rich by controlling the trade in salt and gold. Gold, like what this woman is wearing, came from the south.

Trade in Valuable Goods Ghana lay between the vast Sahara and deep forests. In this location, they were in a good position to trade in the region's most valuable resources—gold and salt. Gold came from the south, from mines near the Gulf of Guinea and along the Niger. Salt came from the Sahara in the north.

The exchange of gold and salt sometimes followed a **process** called silent barter. **Silent barter** is a process in which people exchange goods without contacting each other directly. The method kept the business peaceful. It also kept the exact location of the gold mines secret from the salt traders. In the silent barter process, salt traders left slabs of salt near a river, beat a drum, and moved back several miles. Soon afterward, gold miners arrived and left what they considered a fair amount of gold in exchange for the salt. They moved back so the salt traders could return. This process continued until both sides were satisfied.

Academic Vocabulary
process a series of steps by which a task is accomplished

Ghana Builds an Empire By 800 Ghana was firmly in control of West Africa's trade routes. Nearly all trade between northern and southern Africa passed through Ghana. Traders were protected by Ghana's army, which kept trade routes free from bandits. As a result, trade became safer. Knowing they would be protected, traders were not scared to travel to Ghana. Trade increased, and Ghana's influence grew.

With so many traders passing through their lands, Ghana's rulers looked for ways to make money from them. One way they raised money was by forcing traders to pay taxes. All traders who entered Ghana had to pay a special tax on the goods they carried. Then they had to pay another tax on any goods they took with them when they left.

Not all of Ghana's wealth came from taxes. Ghana's rich mines produced huge amounts of gold. Some gold was carried by traders to lands as far away as England, but Ghana's kings kept huge stores of gold for themselves. In fact, all gold produced in Ghana was the property of Ghana's kings.

Expansion of the Empire Ghana's kings used their great wealth to build a powerful army. With this army, the kings of Ghana conquered many of their neighbors. Many of these conquered areas were centers of trade. Taking over these areas made Ghana's kings even richer.

Ghana reached its peak under Tunka Manin (TOOHN-kah MAH-nin). At his capital in Koumbi Saleh, he had a splendid court where he displayed his vast wealth. A Spanish writer noted the court's splendor.

> "The king adorns himself . . . round his neck and his forearms, and he puts on a high cap decorated with gold and wrapped in a turban of fine cotton. Behind the king stand ten pages holding shields and swords decorated with gold."
>
> —al-Bakri, from *The Book of Routes and Kingdoms*

Ghana's Decline In the mid-1000s Ghana was rich and powerful, but by the end of the 1200s the empire had collapsed. Three major factors contributed to its end. The first factor was invasion. A Muslim group called the Almoravids (al-moh-RAH-vidz) attacked Ghana in the 1060s, in an effort to force its leaders to convert to Islam. The invaders cut off many of the empire's major trade routes. Without this trade, Ghana could no longer support its empire.

The second factor in Ghana's decline was an indirect result of the Almoravid conquest. When the Almoravids moved into Ghana, they brought herds of animals with them. These animals ate all the grass in many pastures, leaving the soil exposed to hot desert winds. These winds blew away the soil, leaving the land worthless for farming or herding. Unable to grow crops, many farmers had to leave in search of new homes.

The third factor that helped bring about the decline of Ghana's empire was rebellion. In about 1200 the people of a country that Ghana had conquered rose up against the king. The rebellion weakened Ghana, which was soon attacked and defeated by one of its neighbors. The empire fell apart.

Reading Check
Summarize How did the rulers of Ghana control trade?

Mali Builds on Ghana's Foundation

Rising from the ruins of Ghana, Mali (MAH-lee) took over the trade routes of West Africa and grew into a powerful state. According to legend, Mali's rise to power began under a ruler named Sundiata (soohn-JAHT-ah).

Sundiata Makes Mali an Empire When Sundiata was a boy, a harsh ruler conquered Mali. But as an adult, Sundiata built up an army and won back his country's independence. He then conquered nearby kingdoms, including Ghana, in the 1230s. After Sundiata conquered Ghana, he took over the salt and gold trades. He also worked to improve agriculture in Mali. Sundiata had new farmlands cleared for beans, onions, rice, and other crops. He even introduced a valuable new crop—cotton.

To keep order in his prosperous kingdom, Sundiata took power away from local leaders. Each of these local leaders had the title *mansa* (MAHN-sah), a title Sundiata now took for himself. Mansas had both political and religious roles in society. By taking on the religious authority of the mansas, Sundiata gained even more power in Mali. Later rulers also took the title of mansa. Unlike Sundiata, most of these rulers were Muslims.

Mansa Musa Mali's most famous ruler was a Muslim named Mansa Musa (MAHN-sah moo-SAH). Under his skillful leadership, Mali reached the height of its wealth, power, and fame. Mansa Musa ruled Mali for about 25 years, from 1312 to 1337. During that time, Mali added many important trade cities to its empire, including **Timbuktu** (tim-buhk-TOO). Because of Mansa Musa's power and influence, Islam spread through a large part of West Africa, gaining many new believers.

Religion was very important to Mansa Musa. In 1324 he left Mali on a pilgrimage to Mecca. Making such a journey, or hajj, is a spiritual duty for all Muslims. Through his journey, Mansa Musa introduced his empire to the Islamic world. He spread Mali's fame far and wide.

Geography and Animals

Too many animals grazing in one area can lead to problems, such as the loss of farmland that occurred in West Africa.

Analyze Visuals
How did humans create long-term environmental change in West Africa?

Mansa Musa also supported religious education. He sent many scholars to study in Morocco. These scholars later set up schools in Mali. Mansa Musa stressed the importance of learning to read the Arabic language so that Muslims in his empire could read the Qur'an. To spread Islam in West Africa, Mansa Musa hired Muslim architects to build mosques. A **mosque** (mahsk) is a building for Muslim prayer. Some of the mosques built by Mansa Musa can still be seen in West Africa today.

The Fall of Mali When Mansa Musa died, his son Maghan (MAH-gan) took the throne. Maghan was a weak ruler. When raiders from the southeast poured into Mali, he couldn't stop them. The raiders set fire to Timbuktu's great schools and mosques. Mali never fully recovered from this terrible blow. The empire continued to weaken and decline.

Other invaders also helped weaken the empire. In 1431 the Tuareg (TWAH-reg), nomads from the Sahara, seized Timbuktu. By 1500 nearly all of the lands the empire had once ruled were lost.

Reading Check
Sequence What steps did Sundiata take to turn Mali into an empire?

Songhai Takes Over

Even as the empire of Mali was reaching its height, a rival power was growing in the area. That rival was the Songhai (SAHNG-hy) kingdom. From their capital at **Gao**, the Songhai participated in the same trade that had made Ghana and Mali so rich. The rulers of Songhai were Muslims. So too were many of the North African Berbers who traded in West Africa. Because of this shared religion, the Berbers were willing to trade with the Songhai, who grew richer.

Building an Empire As the Songhai gained in wealth, they expanded their territory and built an empire. Songhai's expansion was led by Sunni Ali (SOOH-nee ah-LEE), who became ruler in 1464. Before he took over, the Songhai state had been disorganized and poorly run. As ruler, Sunni Ali worked to unify and enlarge his empire. He added many lands that had been part of Mali, including the wealthy trade cities Timbuktu and Djenné.

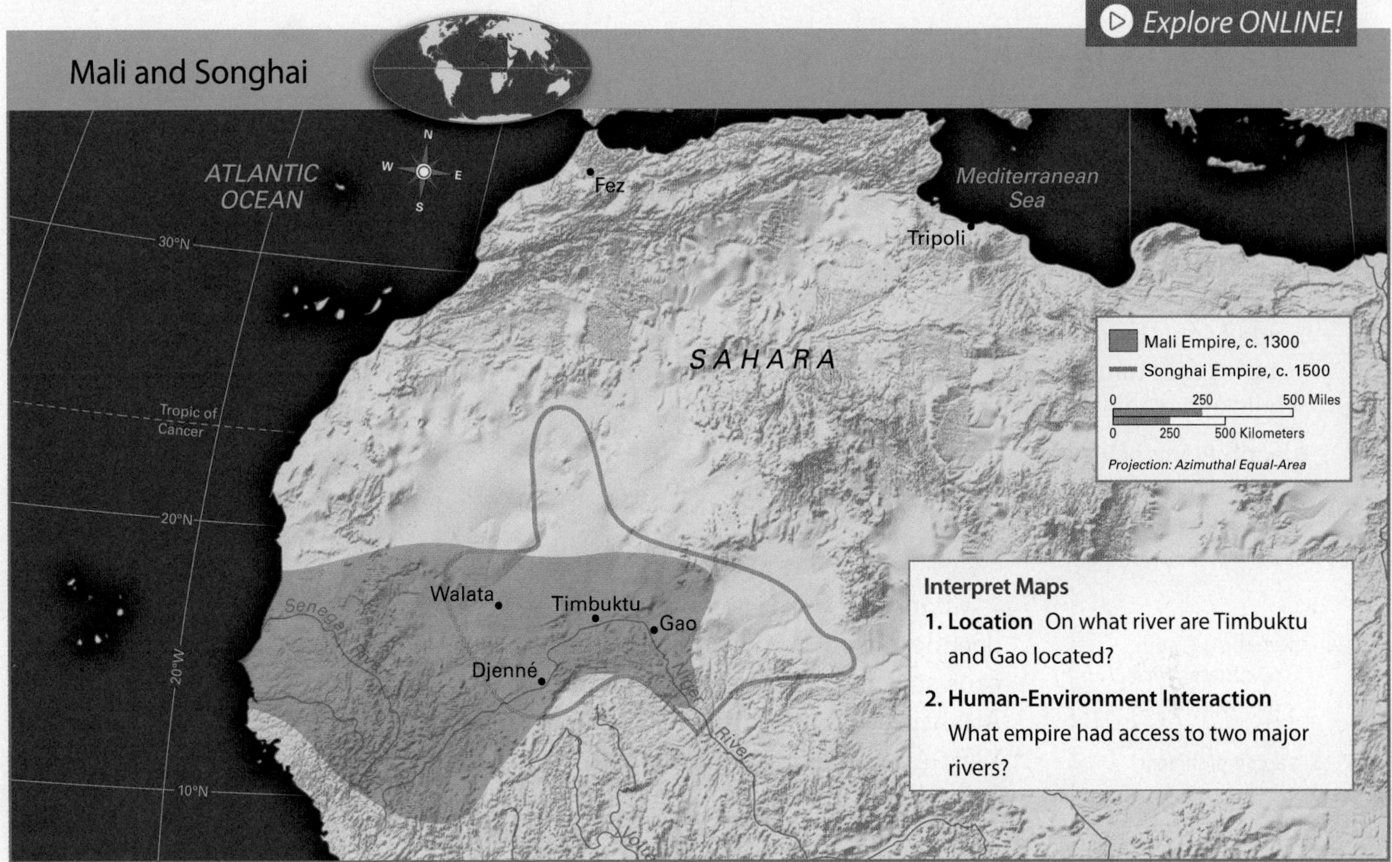

As king, Sunni Ali encouraged everyone in his empire to work together. To build religious harmony, he participated in both Muslim and local religious traditions. As a result, he brought stability to Songhai.

Askia the Great Songhai reached its peak under a ruler called Askia the Great. Askia supported education and learning. Under his rule, Timbuktu flourished, drawing thousands to its universities, schools, libraries, and mosques. The city was especially known for the University of Sankore (san-KOH-rah). People arrived there from North Africa and other places to study math, science, medicine, grammar, and law. **Djenné** (jeh-NAY) was another city that became a center of learning.

Askia, a devout Muslim, encouraged the growth of Islamic influence in his kingdom. Like Mansa Musa, he made a pilgrimage to Mecca. He also made many laws similar to those in other Muslim nations. To help maintain order, Askia set up five provinces within Songhai. He appointed governors who were loyal to him. Askia also created a professional army and specialized departments to oversee tasks.

Songhai Falls to Morocco A northern rival of Songhai, Morocco, wanted to gain control of Songhai's salt mines. So the Moroccan army set out for the heart of Songhai in 1591. Moroccan soldiers carried advanced weapons, including the terrible arquebus (AHR-kwih-buhs). The arquebus was an early form of a gun. The swords, spears, and bows used by Songhai's warriors were no match for the Moroccans' guns and cannons. The invaders destroyed Timbuktu and Gao.

BIOGRAPHY

Mansa Musa c. late 1200s–early 1300s

Mansa Musa, the ruler of Mali, was one of the Muslim kings of West Africa. His pilgrimage to the city of Mecca attracted the attention of the Muslim world and of Europe. He took around 60,000 people with him on his journey, mostly servants and slaves. During his travels, Mansa Musa gave out huge amounts of gold that would be worth more than $100 million today. His spending made people eager to find the source of such wealth. For the first time, other people's eyes turned to West Africa. Within 200 years, European explorers would arrive on the shores of western Africa.

Identify Points of View
How do you think Mansa Musa changed people's views of West Africa?

Reading Check
Evaluate What do you think was Askia's greatest accomplishment?

Changes in trade patterns completed Songhai's fall. Overland trade declined as port cities on the Atlantic coast became more important. Africans south of Songhai and European merchants both preferred trading at Atlantic ports to dealing with Muslim traders. Slowly, the period of great West African empires came to an end.

Bantu Kingdoms

Historians use the name Bantu as a way to identify 400 ethnic groups with origins in West Africa. The word *bantu* means "people" in many of the languages that these groups spoke.

Between 5,000 and 2,000 years ago, Bantu groups began spreading out from West Africa. Historians call this widespread movement of people the **Bantu migration**. No one is certain why the Bantu migrated. Some experts believe people left their homes because the Sahara was drying out and becoming a desert. Others think population growth led people to search for new land. By about AD 300, Bantu peoples had conquered and settled much of Africa south of the Sahara.

Great Zimbabwe As they settled in parts of central and southern Africa, some Bantu groups formed kingdoms. One such kingdom was Great Zimbabwe, founded by the Shona people around the year 1000.

Historians do not know much about the people who lived in Great Zimbabwe or their society. They left no written records behind. However, archeologists have uncovered ruins that tell us something about life in the kingdom. They have found stone walls and buildings. The bricks with which these structures were built were placed with such precision that nothing was needed to hold them in place. Many of the walls are as smooth as modern brick walls. Judging by its size, the city may have had a population of 10,000 to 20,000.

Great Zimbabwe was a trading center. Merchants carried valuable products, especially gold, from other parts of Africa to the city. There they met traders from lands as far away as China. Scholars estimate that traders carried more than 2,000 pounds (907 kg) of gold through the city per year.

In the 1400s, Great Zimbabwe began to decline. Scholars are not sure why, but some believe that drought and environmental issues could have contributed to their fall. Gradually, trade shifted away from Great Zimbabwe to other cities in Africa. By 1500 Great Zimbabwe was abandoned.

The Kongo Kingdom Another powerful Bantu kingdom formed in Central Africa in the 1300s. Located along the Congo River, the Kongo Kingdom became large and powerful. From their capital at Mbanza, Kongo's rulers oversaw the growth of a profitable trade network.

In the 1400s, Portuguese traders arrived in Kongo. At first, relations between the two groups were good. The Kongo traded copper, iron, and ivory in exchange for guns, horses, and manufactured goods. In fact, relations between the two groups were so good that one king of Kongo, Nzinga Mbemba, took a new Portuguese name. He called himself Afonso I and adopted many Portuguese customs. He learned to read and write the Portuguese language and made Roman Catholicism Kongo's official religion. He also changed his government to be more like those in Europe.

Soon, however, the Portuguese became more interested in trading slaves than in these products. As slave traders carried off more people from West Africa, Kongo's rulers became alarmed. They tried to stop the slave trade but had little success. In response, they cut off ties with Portugal. Without this wealthy trade partner, however, Kongo began to decline. The Portuguese later returned and took over the struggling kingdom.

Reading Check
Find Main Ideas
Who are the Bantu peoples?

Summary and Preview Many powerful kingdoms developed in Africa after AD 300. These kingdoms grew rich by controlling trade, especially in gold and other luxury items. Next you will learn how this trade attracted other cultures to Africa and tied the continent into a global trading network. You will also learn how this trade had devastating effects within Africa.

Lesson 2 Assessment

Review Ideas, Terms, and Places

1. a. **Identify** What was the first kingdom in Africa to become Christian?
   b. **Draw Conclusions** What led to the creation of Coptic Christianity in Africa?
2. a. **Identify** What were the two most valuable resources traded in Ghana?
   b. **Generalize** What did Ghana's kings do with the money they raised from taxes?
   c. **Summarize** How did overgrazing help cause the fall of Ghana?
3. a. **Identify** Who was Sundiata?
   b. **Explain** Why did the rulers of Mali want to take control of Ghana's trade?
   c. **Elaborate** What effects did the rule of Mansa Musa have on Mali and West Africa?
4. a. **Identify** Who led the expansion of Songhai?
   b. **Explain** How did Askia the Great's support of education affect Timbuktu?
   c. **Elaborate** What were two reasons why Songhai fell to the Moroccans?
5. a. **Identify** What was the Bantu Migration?
   b. **Explain** How did Great Zimbabwe become rich?

Critical Thinking

6. **Identify Causes** Make a table like the one shown here. Use it to identify factors that caused West African kingdoms to grow and those that caused their decline.

	Growth	Decline
Ghana		
Mali		
Songhai		

Africa in Global Trade

The Big Idea

Africa's wealth and mineral resources attracted the attention of traders from other parts of the world, whose actions eventually led to the enslavement of millions of Africans.

Main Ideas

- Trade led to the spread of Islam in East Africa.
- Europeans arrived in Africa in search of valuable trade goods.
- The slave trade had terrible effects in Africa.
- Many European countries established colonies in Africa.

Key Terms and Places

Swahili
Middle Passage
Gold Coast

If YOU lived there . . .

You are a sailor on a trading ship from Arabia in search of new products to sell back home. After several days at sea, your captain decides to land along the African coast. As you reach the shore, you are greeted by a group of villagers wearing gold and ivory jewelry.

What does this suggest about Africa's resources?

Trade in East Africa

By the 1100s, waves of Bantu-speaking people had made their way to Africa's eastern coast. There they built small villages, where people farmed and fished to survive. The arrival of traders from across the ocean, however, soon changed their lives.

Trade Cities Located on the Indian Ocean, East Africa drew the attention of traders from Asia. Among these traders were Muslims from India, Persia, and Arabia. They came to Africa in search of exotic African goods and new markets for products from their homelands. By selling the visiting merchants such products as ivory, gold, tortoise shells, and animal skins, African villagers became skilled traders themselves.

As trade increased, villages grew into busy seaports. This growth was aided by Persian and Arab merchants, who thought larger cities would make trade easier. They were correct. As they grew, African cities attracted merchants from distant lands. By 1300, East African coastal cities like Mogadishu, Mombasa, Kilwa, and Sofala had become major trade centers.

Merchants from across the Indian Ocean flocked to these cities with goods to exchange. Persian merchants brought manufactured goods from Asia. Arab traders brought porcelain from China and cotton from India. Many East African cities also produced their own goods for sale. Mogadishu and Sofala, for example, became known for their fine cloth. Workers in Mombasa were celebrated for their iron work.

Muslim traders from Arabia and Persia settled down in many of these coastal trading cities. In time, the cities developed large Muslim communities. Africans, Arabs, and Persians lived near each other and worked together.

Modern ships such as this are similar to those used long ago in trading along the East African coast.

One result of this closeness was the spread of Islam through East Africa. People at all levels of society, from workers to rulers, adopted Islam. As a result, mosques appeared in cities throughout the region.

Swahili Culture The contact between cultures also led to other changes in East Africa. Many of the Arab traders who had settled in the area married African women and had families. As a result communities began to reflect the influences of both cultures. For example, the region's architecture changed. People began to build houses that mixed traditional materials, such as coral and mangrove trees, with Arab designs, such as arched windows and carved doors.

As the cultures grew closer, their speech began to reflect their new relationship. Some Africans, who spoke mostly Bantu languages, adopted many Arabic and Persian words. In time, the languages blended into a new language, **Swahili** (swah-HEE-lee). The term Swahili refers to the blended African-Arab culture that had become common in East Africa.

East African Slave Trade Muslim traders were first drawn to Africa by luxury goods such as gold and ivory. Before long, however, they found that they could also make large profits by selling enslaved people. These slaves, usually individuals kidnapped and taken from their families, were shipped across the Indian Ocean to places like Persia and Iraq. Many became servants in the homes of wealthy citizens, while others were sent further to India to become soldiers. A few were even taken as far as China. All together, Muslim traders probably sold about 1,000 slaves per year.

Reading Check
Summarize How did trade lead to major changes in East Africa?

The Arrival of Europeans

In the late 1400s explorers set sail from ports around Europe. Many of these explorers hoped to find new trade routes to places like India and China. There, they could find goods that would sell for high prices in Europe and make them wealthy.

As part of their quest, some Portuguese explorers set out to sail around Africa. During their journeys, many landed at spots along the African coast. Some of these explorers soon found that they could get rich without ever reaching India or China.

Rumors of Gold For centuries, Europeans had heard rumors of golden kingdoms in Africa. Those rumors began in the 1300s when Mansa Musa, the ruler of Mali, set out on his famous hajj, or Muslim pilgrimage, to Mecca. He was accompanied by thousands of attendants and slaves. As they traveled, the pilgrims gave away lavish gifts of gold to the rulers of lands through which they passed.

For years after Mansa Musa's hajj, stories of his wealth passed from Southwest Asia into Europe. However, most Europeans did not believe they could find gold in Africa. When the Portuguese reached the coasts of West Africa, however, they learned that the stories had been true. Africa did have gold, and the Europeans wanted it.

Trade Goods Gold was the first item to bring European attention to Africa, but it was not the only valuable product to be found there. Another was ivory. Europeans used ivory to make furniture, jewelry, statues, piano keys, and other expensive items.

At first, the Portuguese had little interest in products other than gold and ivory. Before long, however, they found that they could make more profit from the sale of slaves.

Reading Check
Explain Why did some Europeans become interested in Africa?

The Atlantic Slave Trade

Slavery was not new to Africa. For centuries, societies within Africa had kept slaves. Most of these slaves were prisoners captured in battle or as the result of raids on rival villages or kingdoms.

Beginnings of the Slave Trade Although slavery had existed for centuries in Africa, the arrival of Europeans in West Africa led to a drastic increase in the demand for slaves. Europeans wanted slaves to put to work on plantations, or large farms, in the Americas. Slave traders made deals with many rulers in West and Central Africa to buy the slaves they captured in battle. These slaves were then put in chains and loaded onto ships. These ships carried the slaves on a grueling trip across the Atlantic called the **Middle Passage.**

Africans captured by slave traders were brought to forts like this one on the West African coast to be sent across the ocean.

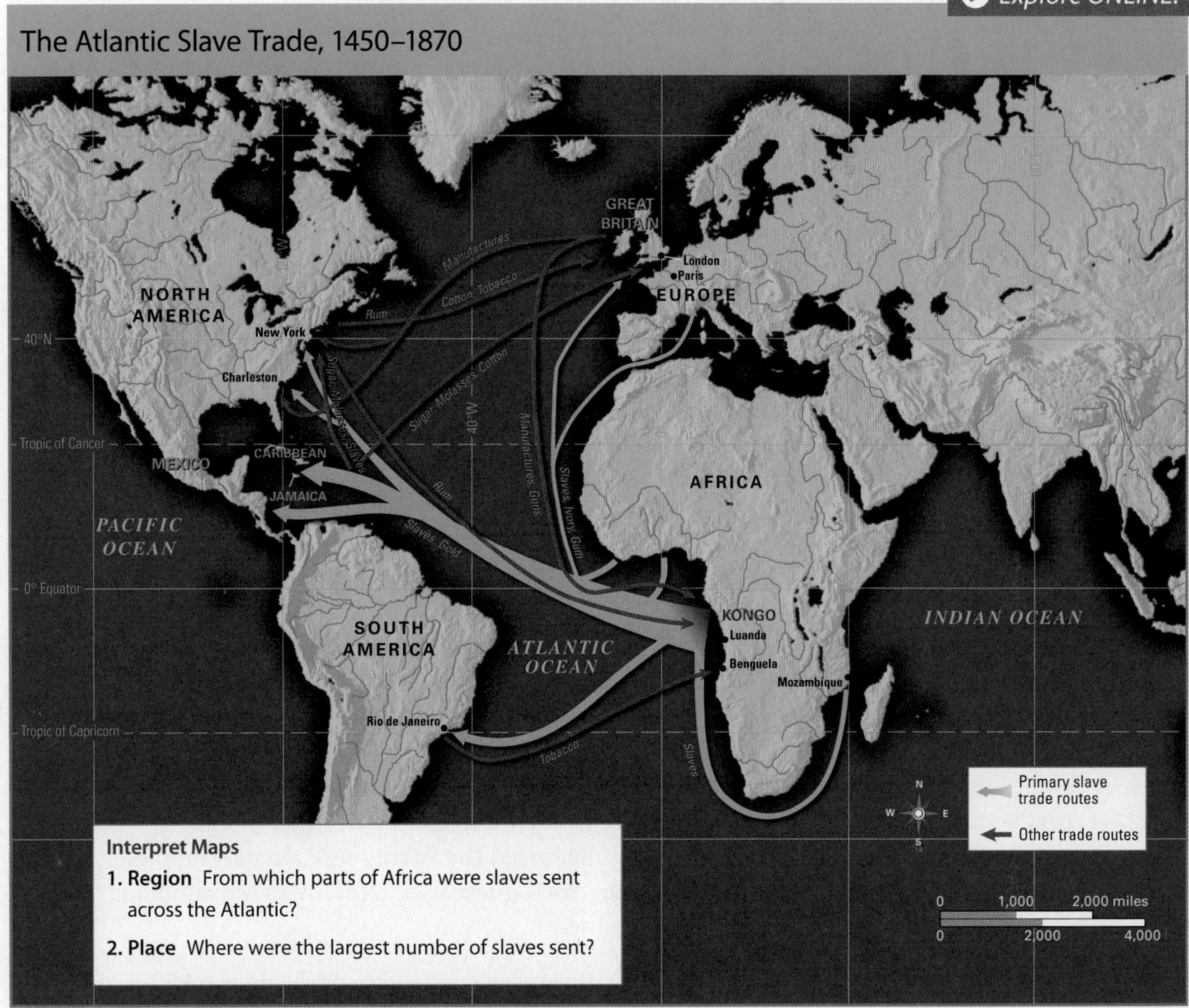

The Atlantic Slave Trade, 1450–1870

Interpret Maps

1. **Region** From which parts of Africa were slaves sent across the Atlantic?
2. **Place** Where were the largest number of slaves sent?

The slave trade continued for more than 300 years. Though some Europeans argued against slavery, calling it an evil institution that should be stopped, slave traders considered the practice too profitable to end. It was not until the 1800s that European governments stepped in and finally banned the trading of slaves.

Effects of the Slave Trade The European slave trade in Africa had devastating consequences. It led to a drastic decrease in Africa's population. Millions of young African men were forced to move away from their homes to lands far away, and thousands of them died. Historians estimate that 15 to 20 million African slaves were shipped to the Americas against their will. Millions more were sent to Europe, Asia, and the Middle East.

The slave trade had terrible effects on those who remained in Africa as well. The efforts of some kingdoms to capture slaves from their rivals led to decades of warfare on the continent. This warfare further reduced Africa's population and weakened many societies. It also caused years of resentment and mistrust between many African peoples.

Reading Check
Analye Effects What were the effects of the slave trade?

European Colonies in Africa

Trade in gold, ivory, and slaves made many Portuguese merchants very rich. Envious, other European countries rushed to grab part of the trade. The result was a struggle among several countries to establish colonies.

Colonies in West Africa The first European colony in West Africa was the **Gold Coast**, established by the Portuguese in 1482. It was located in the area now occupied by the country of Ghana. Most colonies in West Africa were named after the products traded there. In addition to the Gold Coast, the region had colonies called Ivory Coast and Slave Coast. To keep order in their colonies, Europeans built forts along West Africa's coast. These forts served both as trading centers and military outposts.

Over time, the colonies of West Africa merged. For example, the Portuguese gave their colony to the Dutch in the mid-1600s. Eventually, the entire Gold Coast came under the control of the British, who maintained the colony until the 1950s.

The Portuguese in East Africa While several countries had colonies in West Africa, only the Portuguese were interested in East Africa. They knew that trade on the Indian Ocean was very profitable, and they wanted to control that trade. However, the Portuguese knew they could not take over East Africa as long as strong African kingdoms ruled the region. To weaken those kingdoms, they encouraged rulers to go to war with each other. The Portuguese then made alliances with the winners.

However, Portuguese influence in East Africa was weakened when Muslims arrived. The Muslims forced the Portuguese almost completely out of the region. Although the Portuguese kept a colony in Mozambique, their influence was almost gone.

Reading Check
Identify Cause and Effect Why did Europeans establish colonies in Africa?

Summary and Preview Europeans arrived in Africa in the 1500s and built a number of colonies. Next, you will learn about another period of European involvement in Africa during the 1800s and about efforts to break free from European control.

Lesson 3 Assessment

Review Ideas, Terms, and Places

1. **a. Define** To what does Swahili refer?
   b. Predict How might East Africa have developed differently had Muslim traders not traveled there?
2. **a. Identify** What goods brought Europeans to Africa?
   b. Make Generalizations How did Mansa Musa's travels affect European views of Africa?
3. **a. Identify** What was the Middle Passage?
   b. Summarize Why did Europeans want slaves?
4. **a. Explain** Why did Europeans want to form colonies in West Africa?
   b. Make Inferences What do the names of European colonies suggest about European views of Africa?

Critical Thinking

5. **Summarize** Make a chart like this one. Then, use your notes to summarize the effects of each event or issue on the development of Africa.

Event or Issue	Effects
Muslim Trade	
Slavery	
European Colonization	

Imperialism and Independence

The Big Idea

In the late 1800s Europeans once again created colonies in Africa and became involved in African politics and economics.

Main Ideas

- The search for raw materials led to a new wave of European involvement in Africa.
- The Scramble for Africa was a race to form colonies there.
- Some Africans resisted rule by Europeans.
- Nationalism led to independence movements in Africa.

Key Terms and Places

entrepreneurs
imperialism
ethnocentrism
Suez Canal
Berlin Conference
Boers
nationalism

If YOU lived there . . .

You are the chief of an African village in 1890. For many years, your people have been at war with a village in the next valley. One day, however, a warrior from that village delivers a message to you. His chief has been approached by soldiers with strange clothes and weapons. They say that both villages are now part of a colony that belongs to a place called England. The other chief wants to know how you will deal with these strangers.

How will you respond to the other chief?

New Involvement in Africa

When Europeans first arrived in Africa in the 1400s, they hoped to get rich through trade. For centuries, controlling the trade of rare products from distant lands had been the surest road to wealth in Europe. The merchants who brought spices, silks, and other goods from Asia had been among the richest people on the continent.

With the beginning of the Industrial Revolution in the 1700s, however, a new road to riches emerged. Europeans found that they could become rich by building factories and making products that other people wanted, such as cheap cloth, tools, or steel. In order to make products, these business owners needed raw materials. However, Europe did not have sufficient resources to supply all the factories that were opening. Where were these resources to come from?

European explorers and traders journeyed to Africa in search of raw materials, such as ivory.

The Quest for Raw Materials By the 1880s Europeans had decided that the best way to get resources was to create new colonies. They wanted these colonies to be located in places that had abundant resources not easily available in Europe.

One such place was Africa. Since the slave trade had ended in the early 1800s, few Europeans had paid much attention to Africa. Unless they could make a huge fortune in Africa, most people did not care what happened there. As factory owners looked for new sources of raw materials, though, some people took another look at Africa. For the first time, they noticed its huge open spaces and its mineral wealth.

Once again, Europeans rushed to Africa to establish colonies. Most of the new colonists who headed to Africa in the 1800s were **entrepreneurs,** or independent business people. In Africa, they built mines, plantations, and trade routes with the dream of growing rich.

Cultural Interference Though they were in Africa to get rich, the European entrepreneurs who moved there frequently became involved in local affairs. Often, they became involved because they thought their ideas about government and culture were better than native African ways. As a result, they often tried to impose their own ideas on the local people. This sort of attempt to dominate a country's government, trade, or culture is called **imperialism.**

Academic Vocabulary
values ideas that people hold dear and try to live by

European imperialists justified their behavior by claiming that they were improving the lives of Africans. In fact, many Europeans saw it as their duty to introduce their customs and **values** to what they saw as a backward land. This type of thinking is called **ethnocentrism.** It is the belief that one's own group or culture is better or more important than others. Europeans forced Africans to assimilate, or adopt, many elements of European culture. As a result, thousands of Africans became Christian and learned to speak European languages.

Imperialism had other effects on the lives of Africans. During the early 1900s several famines occurred across the continent. Often, these famines began because of a lack of rain. However, the production of cash crops in African colonies made the famines worse. Instead of growing food for Africans, many plantations produced raw materials for Europeans. This led to food shortages. Thousands of Africans died as a result.

One firm believer in imperialism was English business owner Cecil Rhodes. He believed that British culture was superior to all others and that it was his duty to share it with the people of Africa. To that end, he planned to build a long railroad between Britain's colonies in Egypt and South Africa. He thought this railroad would bring what he saw as the benefits of British civilization to all Africans. However, his railroad was never completed.

Government Involvement Though the early imperialists in Africa were entrepreneurs, national governments soon became involved as well. Their involvement was largely the result of rivalries between countries. Each country wanted to control more land and more colonies than its rivals did. As a result, countries tried to create as many colonies as they could and to block others from creating colonies.

For example, France began to form colonies in West Africa in the late 1800s. Seeing this, the British hurried to the area to form colonies of their own. Before long, Germany and Italy also sought to control land in West Africa. They did not want to be seen as less powerful than either France or Britain.

The English government also got involved in Africa for other reasons. The British wanted to protect the **Suez Canal,** a waterway built in Egypt in the 1860s to connect the Mediterranean and Red seas. The building of the

Link to Economics

Diamond Mining

Among the resources that caught the eye of European entrepreneurs in Africa were diamonds. First discovered in South Africa in 1867, diamonds were extremely profitable. South Africa soon became the world's leading diamond producer. Nearly all of that production was done by one company, the De Beers Consolidated Mine Company, owned by English business leader Cecil Rhodes. De Beers mines, like the one shown here at Kimberley, poured the gems into the world market.

South Africa is still one of the world's leading diamond producers, and De Beers is one of the leading companies. By controlling the supply of diamonds available to the public, the company can command higher prices for its gems.

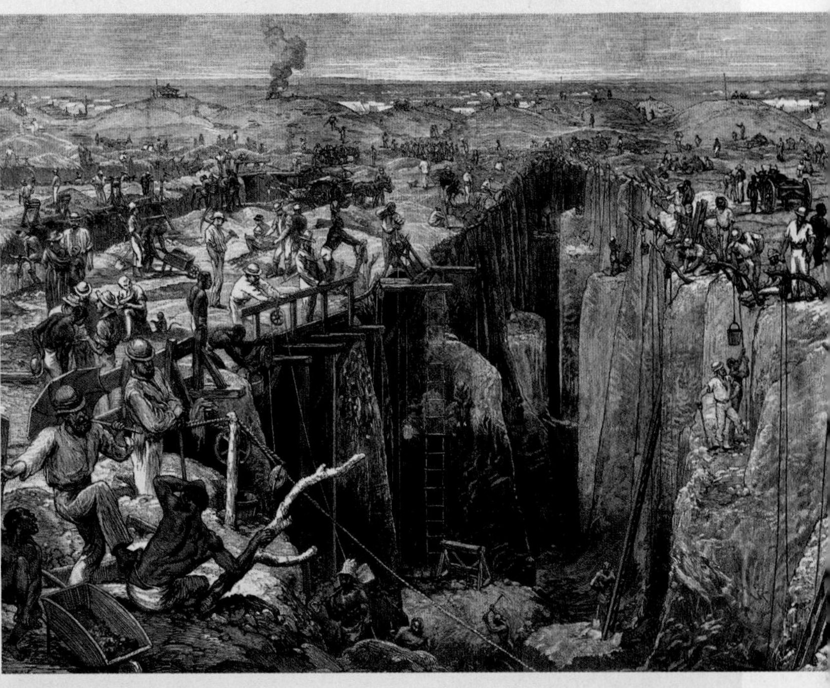

Analyze Information
How can a company control the supply of a product?

canal had been funded by the Suez Canal Company. At first, this company consisted of French and Egyptian investors. Later, the British government became a main investor. The British used the canal as a fast route to their colonies in India. This led to increased trade between Britain and Asia. In the 1880s, however, instability in Egypt's government made the British fear they would lose access to the canal. As a result, the British moved into Egypt and took partial control of the country to protect their shipping routes.

Reading Check
Categorize
What were three reasons Europeans went to Africa?

The Scramble for Africa

Desperate to have more power in Africa than their rivals, several European countries rushed to claim as much land there as they could. Historians refer to this rush to claim land as the Scramble for Africa. The Europeans moved so quickly to snap up land that by 1914 most of Africa had been made into European colonies. Only Ethiopia and Liberia remained independent.

The Berlin Conference For many years Europeans competed aggressively for land in Africa. Conflicts sometimes arose when many countries tried to claim the same area. To prevent these conflicts from developing into wars, Europe's leaders agreed to meet and devise a plan to maintain order in Africa. They hoped this meeting would settle disputes and prevent future conflicts.

The meeting European leaders held was called the **Berlin Conference.** Begun in 1884, it included representatives from 14 countries. Their decisions led to the division of Africa among various European powers. The conference left Africa a patchwork of European colonies.

When they were dividing Africa among themselves, Europe's leaders paid little attention to the people who lived there. As a result, the boundaries they drew for their colonies often divided kingdoms, clans, and families.

Separating people with common backgrounds was bad, but so was forcing people to live together who did not want to. Some European colonies grouped together peoples with different customs, languages, and religions. This forced contact between peoples often led to conflict and war. In time, the Europeans' disregard for Africans led to significant problems for Europeans and Africans alike.

The Boer War The Berlin Conference was intended to prevent conflicts over African territory, but it was not completely successful. In the late 1890s war broke out in South Africa between British and Dutch settlers. Each group had claimed the land and wanted to drive the other out.

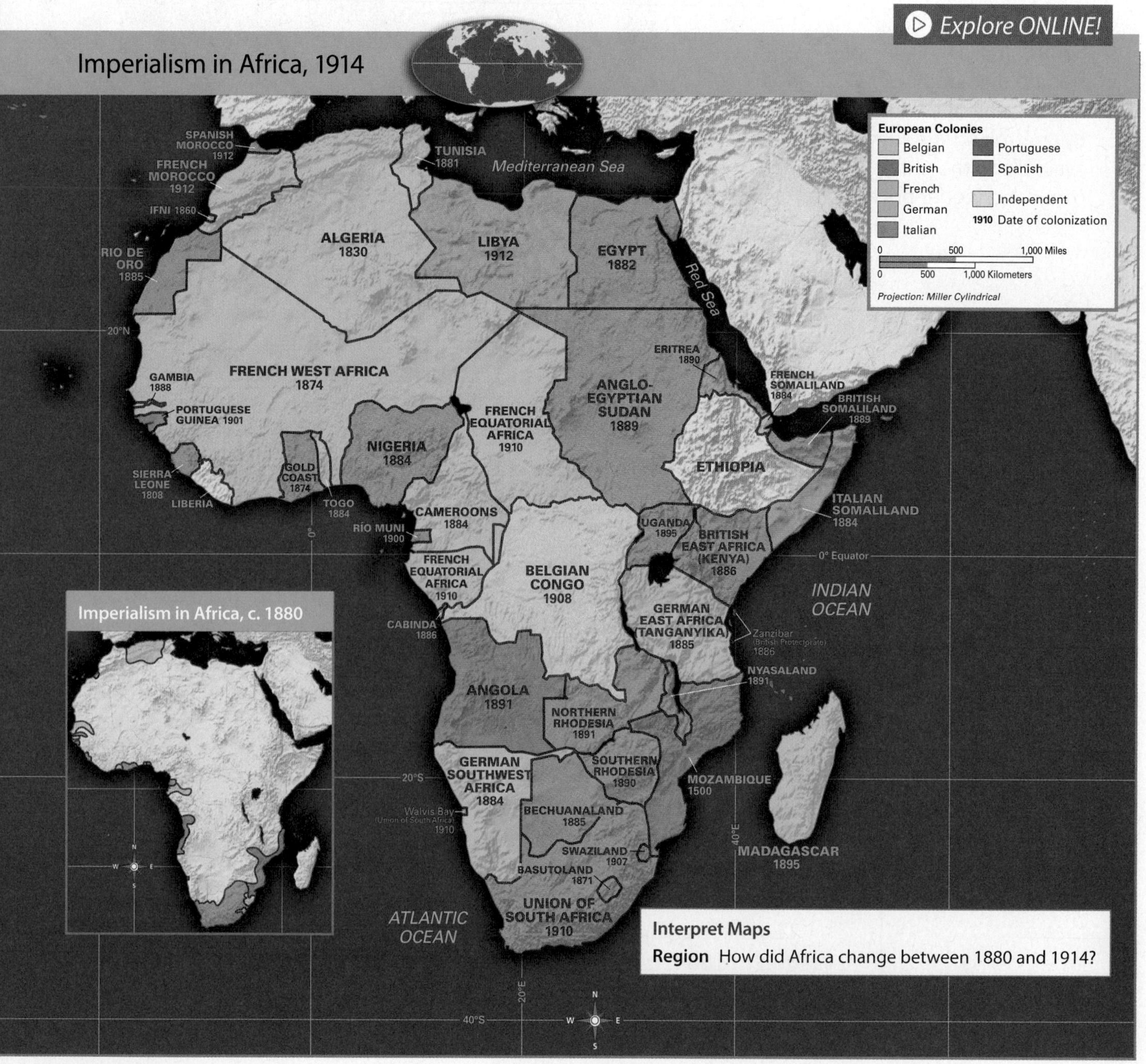

Interpret Maps

Region How did Africa change between 1880 and 1914?

Dutch farmers called **Boers** had arrived in South Africa in the 1600s. There they had established two republics. For about 200 years, the Boers lived mainly as farmers. During that time, they met with little interference from other Europeans. Things changed in the 1800s, though. In 1886 gold was discovered near the Orange River in South Africa. Suddenly, the land on which the Boers had been living became highly desirable.

Among those who wanted to control South Africa after gold was discovered were the British. In 1899 the British tried to make the Boers' land part of the British Empire. The Boers resisted, and war broke out.

The Boers did not think they could defeat the British in a regular war. The British had a much larger army than they did. In addition, the British troops had much better weapons than the Boers had. Instead, the Boers decided to wage a guerrilla war, one based on sneak attacks and ambushes. Through these tactics, the Boers quickly defeated several British forces and gained an advantage in the war.

However, these guerrilla tactics angered the British. To punish the Boers, they began attacking and burning Boer farms. They captured thousands of Boer women and children, imprisoning them in concentration camps. More than 20,000 women and children died in these camps, mostly from disease. In the end, the British defeated the Boers. As a result, South Africa became a British colony.

Reading Check
Analyze Effects
What were the results of the Berlin Conference?

African Resistance

The Europeans thought the Berlin Conference and the Boer War would put an end to conflict in Africa. Once again, however, they had overlooked the African people. For centuries, many Africans had fought against the slave trade. Now they fought against being ruled by Europeans. They refused to peacefully give up their own cultures and adopt European ways.

As a result, the Europeans who entered African territory often met with resistance from local rulers and peoples. Europeans were able to end most of these rebellions quickly with their superior weapons. However, two well-organized peoples, the Zulu and the Ethiopians, caused more problems for the Europeans.

Zulu Resistance One of the most famous groups to resist the Europeans was the Zulu of southern Africa. In the early 1800s a leader named Shaka had brought various Zulu groups together into a single nation. This nation was so strong that the Europeans were hesitant to enter Zulu territory.

After Shaka's death, the Zulu nation began to weaken. Even without Shaka's leadership, the fierce Zulu army successfully fought off the British for more than 50 years. In 1879, however, the British attacked the Zulu in force. Their superior weapons helped the British soundly defeat the Zulu in a few months. The Zulu lands were made into a new British colony.

Cetshwayo, king of the Zulu nation, led his army to resist imperial control. Though Zulu resistance was fierce, the British defeated them in 1879.

This painting of the Battle of Adwa was created years after the battle. The battle kept Ethiopia from becoming an Italian colony and is still celebrated today.

Ethiopian Resistance Although most resistance to European imperialism was ended, one kingdom managed to remain free from European control. That kingdom was Ethiopia. It is the only country in Africa never to have been a European colony. Its success in fighting the Europeans was due largely to the efforts of one man, Emperor Menelik II.

Menelik had seen that the strength of European armies was based on their modern weapons. He therefore decided that he would create an equally powerful army with modern weapons bought from Europeans. As a result, when the Italians invaded Ethiopia in 1895, the Ethiopian army was able to defeat the invaders. This victory in the Battle of Adwa is celebrated as a high point in Ethiopian history.

Reading Check
Draw Conclusions
Why did many Africans resist European imperialism?

Nationalism and Independence

Many Africans were understandably unhappy with European control of their lands. For centuries, they had ruled their own kingdoms. Now they were forced to accept foreign leaders. After several rebellions had been put down, however, many people had resigned themselves to being colonies.

In the 20th century that attitude began to change. Across Africa, people in European colonies began to call for—and eventually gain—their independence. This call was largely the result of increased **nationalism,** or devotion and loyalty to a country. How nationalism was expressed, and how it affected independence, varied from place to place. South Africa, Nigeria, and Kenya, for example, followed very different paths.

South Africa South Africa was one of the first African colonies to gain independence. After the Boer War, the British tried to promote British culture in the colony. This move angered descendants of early Dutch settlers, who were called Afrikaners. The Afrikaners feared, for example, that laws requiring all children to learn English were an attempt to stamp out their language. Afrikaner nationalists complained to the new government.

Explore ONLINE!

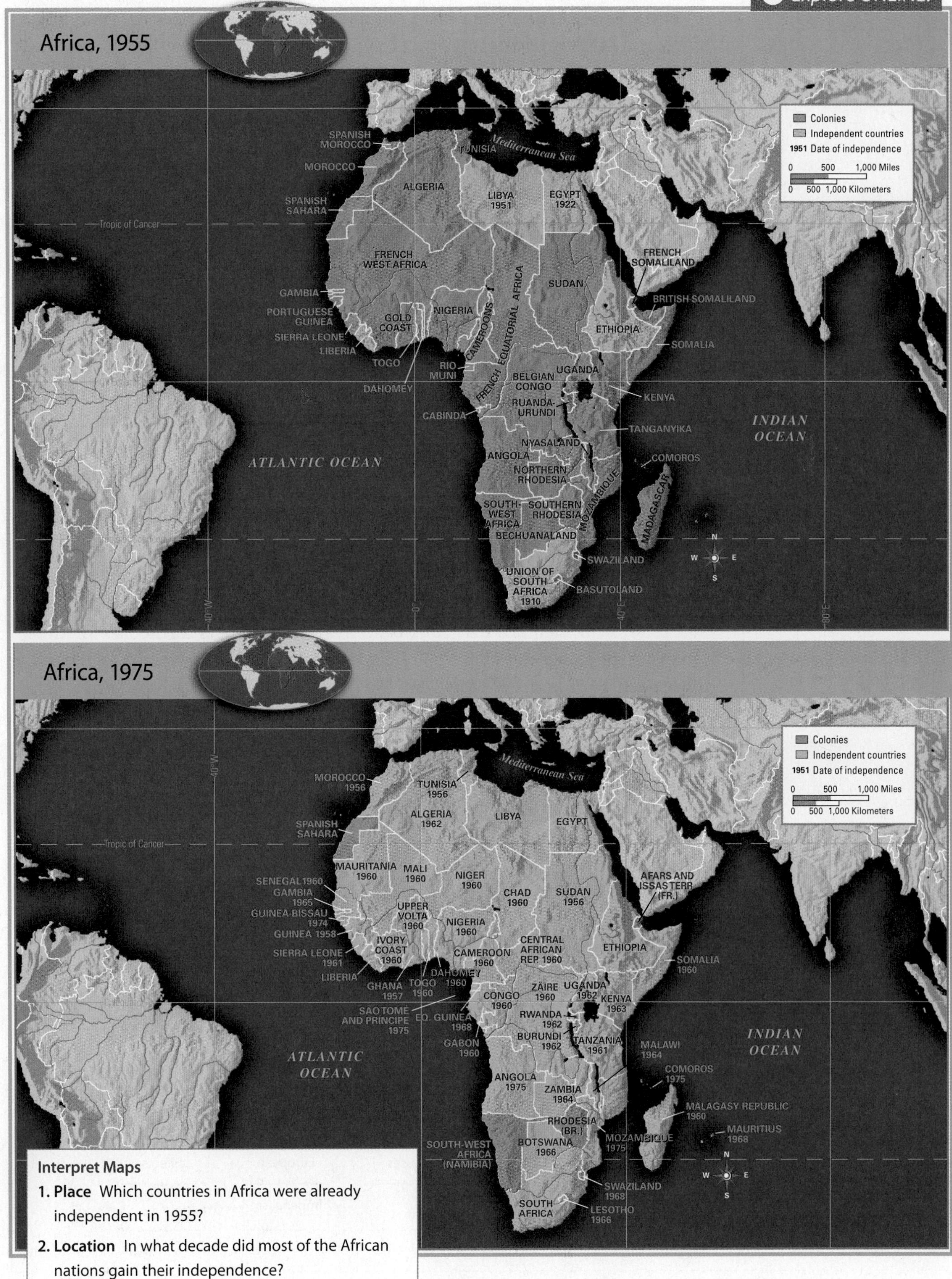

Interpret Maps

1. **Place** Which countries in Africa were already independent in 1955?
2. **Location** In what decade did most of the African nations gain their independence?

Outnumbered by the Afrikaners, the British agreed to compromise. They allowed Afrikaners to run for and hold political offices. In 1908 English and Afrikaner delegates met to write a constitution for South Africa. It granted equal power to English and Afrikaner citizens but banned native Africans from any role in the government. The constitution was approved by Parliament the next year, and South Africa became independent.

Nigeria Like South Africa, Nigeria had been a British colony. By the early 20th century, however, many Nigerians were unhappy with colonial rule. In an effort to keep people happy, the British created assemblies and allowed Nigerian colonists to vote for their representatives. These assemblies had little power, but they were welcomed as a step toward freedom.

Although the people of Nigeria belonged to hundreds of ethnic groups, they banded together in their quest for independence. In the 1920s Nigerian nationalists formed their first political party. Over the next few decades, nationalist politicians ran for and won offices. Soldiers who had fought for Britain in World War I and World War II joined in their call for self-rule. Feeling pressured, the British gradually gave the assemblies more power. Finally, in 1960, the British granted Nigeria full independence.

Kenya Some British colonies did not find the road to independence as smooth as South Africa and Nigeria. For example, Kenya only became independent after a long and violent struggle. The British were determined to hold onto Kenya, where they could grow such valuable crops as coffee.

To reclaim their land, a group of Kenyan nationalists formed a violent movement called the Mau Mau. Its goal was to rid Kenya of white settlers. Between 1952 and 1960 the Mau Mau terrorized the British in Kenya, killing any who opposed them. The British tried to fight back but were unsuccessful. Eventually, they gave in. In 1963 they made Kenya a free country.

Reading Check
Contrast How were the paths taken to independence by Nigeria and Kenya different?

Summary In the 1800s Europeans divided Africa into dozens of colonies. In the 20th century, many African nations achieved independence, though the steps they took to reach that goal varied widely.

Lesson 4 Assessment

Review Ideas, Terms, and Places

1. a. **Define** What role did entrepreneurs play in European imperialism in Africa?
   b. **Explain** Why did European governments want to form colonies in Africa?
2. a. **Summarize** What happened at the Berlin Conference?
   b. **Predict** What problems do you think the Berlin Conference caused in Africa after the Europeans left?
3. a. **Identify** Which African country never became a colony?
   b. **Make Inferences** Why did most African resistance fail?
4. a. **Explain** How did nationalism help bring about independence in South Africa, Nigeria, and Kenya?
   b. **Draw Conclusions** Why do you think the British were determined to keep Kenya a colony?

Critical Thinking

5. **Identify Cause and Effect** Use your notes and the diagram to identify the causes and effects of European imperialism in Africa.

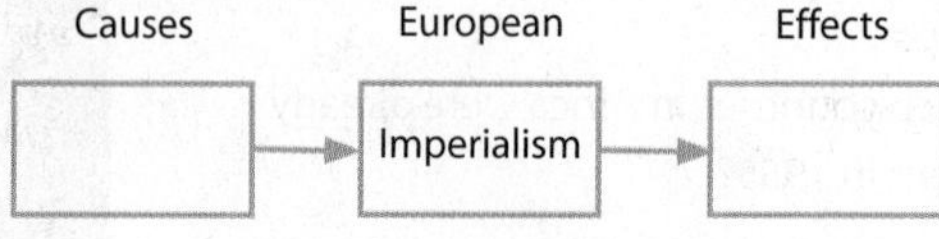

Social Studies Skills

Understand Continuity and Change

Define the Skill

A well-known saying claims that "the more things change, the more they stay the same." Nowhere does this observation apply better than to the study of history. Any examination of the past will show many changes—nations expanding or shrinking, empires rising and falling, changes in leadership, or people on the move, for example.

The reasons for change have not changed, however. The same general forces have driven the actions of people and nations across time. These forces are the threads that run through history and give it continuity, or connectedness. They are the "sameness" in a world of continuous change.

Learn the Skill

You can find the causes of all events of the past in one or more of these major forces or themes that connect all history.

1. **Cooperation and Conflict** Throughout time, people and groups have worked together to achieve goals. They have also opposed others who stood in the way of their goals.
2. **Cultural Invention and Interaction** The values and ideas expressed in art, literature, customs, and religion have enriched the world. But the spread of cultures and their contact with other cultures have produced conflict as well.
3. **Geography and Environment** Physical environments and natural resources have shaped how people live. Efforts to gain, protect, or make good use of land and resources have been major causes of cooperation and conflict in history.
4. **Science and Technology** Technology, or the development and use of tools, has helped humans across time make better use of their environment. Science has also changed their knowledge of the world and their lives.
5. **Economic Development** From hunting and gathering to herding, farming, trade, and manufacturing, people have tried to make the most of their resources. The desire for a better life has also been a major reason people have moved from one place to another.
6. **The Impact of Individuals** Political, religious, military, business, and other types of leaders have shaped history. The actions of many ordinary people have also influenced events.
7. **Nationalism and Imperialism** *Nationalism* is the desire of a people to have their own country. *Imperialism* is the desire of a nation to influence or control other nations. Both have existed across time.
8. **Political and Social Systems** People have always been part of groups—families, villages, nations, or religious groups, for example. The groups to which people belong shape how they relate to others.

Practice the Skill

Check your understanding of continuity and change in history by answering the following questions.

1. What forces of history are illustrated by the events in the module you just studied? Explain with examples.
2. How do the events in this module show continuity between earlier and later periods in African history? Can you compare some themes across time?

Module 11 Assessment

Review Vocabulary, Terms, and Places

Choose the letter of the answer that best completes each statement below.

1. People who move from place to place in search of food are called
   a. nomads. c. traders.
   b. hominids. d. entrepreneurs.
2. The earliest sites where anthropologists found hominids were in
   a. Asia. c. Africa.
   b. Europe. d. North America.
3. The blended culture that formed in East Africa by blending elements of African and Arab culture is called
   a. Coptic. c. Gao.
   b. Swahili. d. Mali.
4. Enslaved Africans were carried to the Americas on a trip called the
   a. hajj. c. Bantu migration.
   b. Gold Coast. d. Middle Passage.
5. The Muslim leader of Mali who spread Islam and made a famous pilgrimage to Mecca was
   a. Emperor Menelik II. c. Mansa Musa.
   b. Askia the Great. d. Shaka.
6. Early Stone Age nomadic peoples who lived off the land were called
   a. farmers. c. traders.
   b. hominids. d. hunter-gatherers.
7. When one country tries to dominate another country's trade, government, or culture, it is called
   a. imperialism. c. entrepreneurs.
   b. ethnocentrism. d. hunter-gatherers.

Comprehension and Critical Thinking

Lesson 1

8. a. **Describe** What kinds of tools did people make in the Stone Age in Africa?
   b. **Analyze Issues** What evidence have anthropologists found to suggest hominids first developed in East Africa and moved to the rest of the continent?
   c. **Make Inferences** Why have anthropologists studied African cultures to learn what life was like in the Stone Age?

Lesson 2

9. a. **Sequence** List the three great kingdoms of West Africa in the order in which they came to power.
   b. **Contrast** How were the religious beliefs of the people of Ethiopia different from those of the people of Songhai?
   c. **Draw Conclusions** What role did gold play in the histories of Africa's major kingdoms?

Lesson 3

10. a. **Analyze Events** What brought Islam to East Africa? What was the result of its arrival?
    b. **Draw Conclusions** Why do you think early European activity in Africa was limited mostly to West Africa?
    c. **Develop** How did the slave trade weaken African society?

Lesson 4

11. a. **Define** What is imperialism, and what led to European imperialism in Africa?
    b. **Sequence** What led to the Boer War?
    c. **Elaborate** Why do you think few groups were successful in resisting European imperialism?

Reading Skills

12. **Understand Cause and Effect** Use the Reading Skills taught in this module to complete the following activity.

> To make trade easy and profitable, traders and African locals built cities all along the coast. Muslim traders from Arabia and Persia settled down in many of these coastal trading cities. In time, the cities developed large Muslim communities. Africans, Arabs, and Persians lived near each other and worked together.
>
> One result of this closeness was the spread of Islam through East Africa. People at all levels of society, from workers to rulers, adopted Islam. As a result, mosques appeared in cities and towns throughout the region.

Make a graphic organizer to analyze causes and effects listed above. Create as many boxes as you need to list the causes and effects.

Social Studies Skills

13. **Understand Continuity and Change** Use the Social Studies Skills taught in this module to complete the following activity. List an example from this module of people or groups who have worked together to achieve goals, and list one example of people or groups who opposed each other.

Map Activity

14. **Africa** On a separate sheet of paper, match the letters on the map with their correct labels.

Ghana Empire | South Africa | Egypt
Kongo Kingdom | Kingdom of Ethiopia

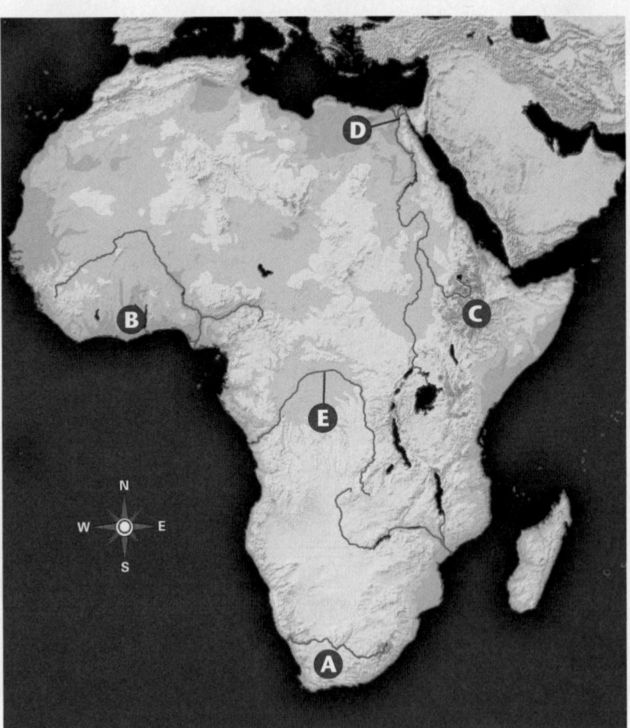

Focus on Writing

15. **Write a Proverb** Does the early bird get the worm? If you go outside at sunrise to check, you missed the fact that this is a proverb that means "The one that gets there first can earn something good." West African storytellers created many proverbs that expressed wisdom or truth. Write three proverbs that might have been said during the time of the West African empires. Make sure your proverbs are written from the point of view of a person living during those centuries.

Module 12

West and Central Africa

Essential Question

How are West and Central Africa shaped by their diverse climates and people groups?

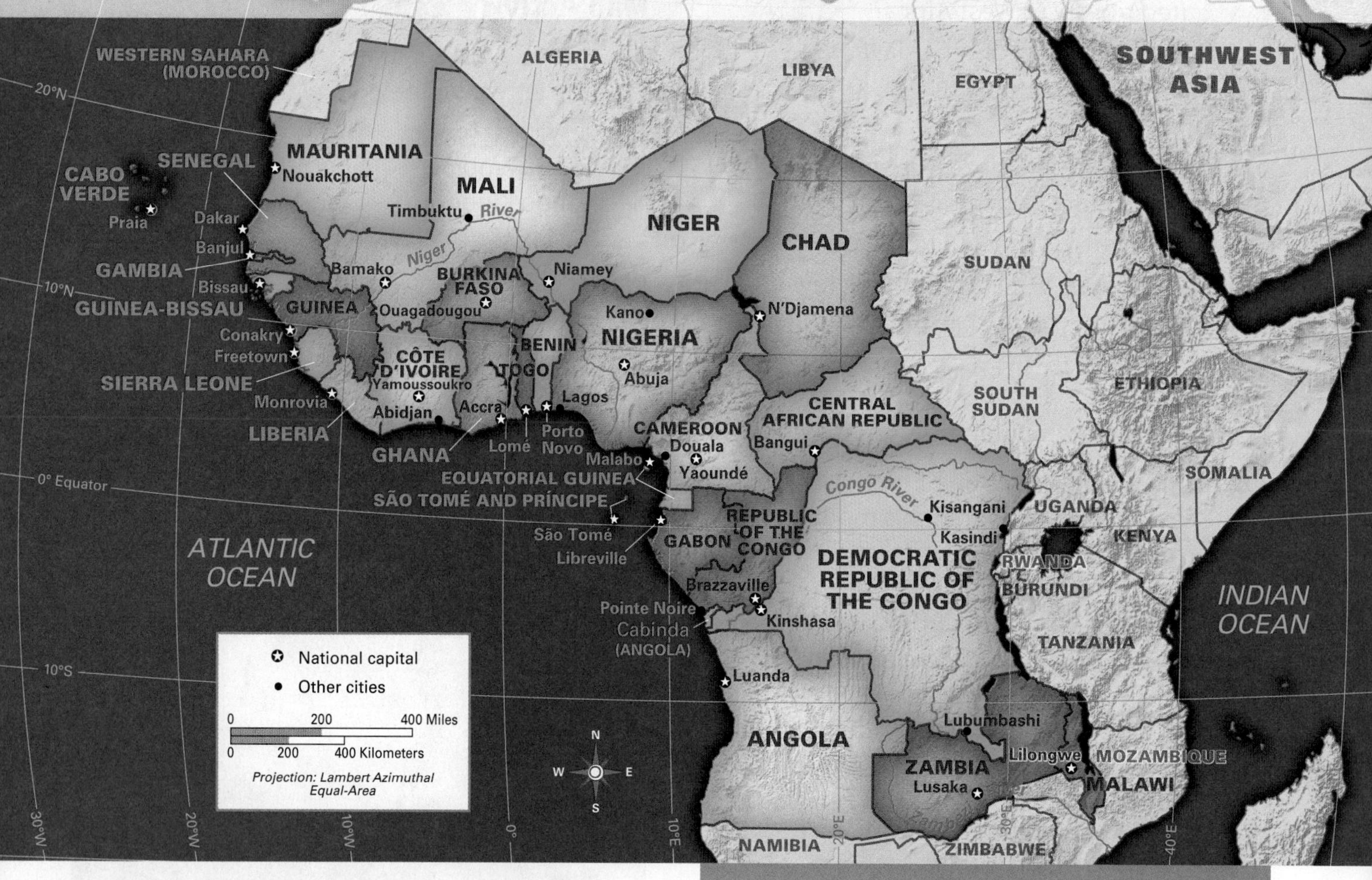

Explore ONLINE!

- Document-Based Investigations
- Graphic Organizers
- Interactive Games
- Channel One News Video: Chocolate Shortage
- Channel One News Video: Ebola Orphans
- Channel One News Video: Stunted Children
- Interactive Map: West Africa: Climate
- Image with Hotspots: Timbuktu

In this module, you will learn about the diversity of West and Central Africa's geography, climate, and peoples as well as the regions' resources and current challenges.

What You Will Learn

Lesson 1: Physical Geography **391**
The Big Idea West Africa is a region mostly of plains, while the Congo River and tropical forests are important features of Central Africa's physical geography.

Lesson 2: West Africa **398**
The Big Idea Powerful early kingdoms, European slave trade and colonization, and traditions from a mix of ethnic groups have all influenced West African culture.

Lesson 3: Central Africa **407**
The Big Idea Central Africa's history and culture have been influenced by native traditions and European colonizers.

Geography Many of West Africa's main cities, such as Dakar, Senegal, are located on the coast.

Culture These men wear kente cloth, a traditional type and pattern of cloth originally from Ghana.

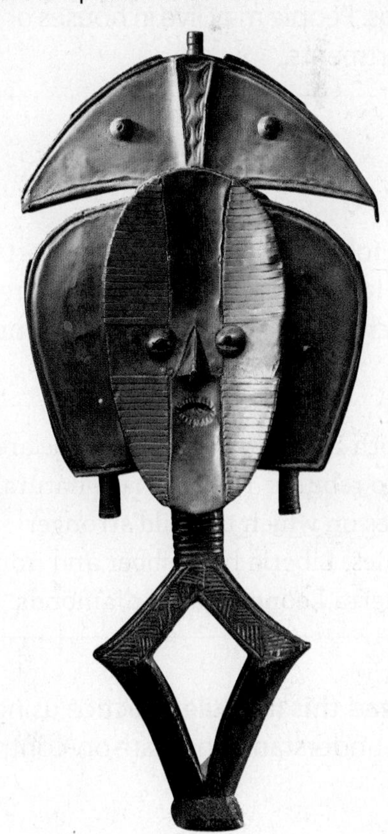

History People in Central Africa have been making copper statues for hundreds of years. This one is meant to represent an ancestor.

Reading Social Studies

Understand Compare-Contrast

READING FOCUS

Geographers comparison and contrast to understand how various world regions and countries are alike and different. They may describe similarities and differences in text or show them in a visual such as a chart. You can understand compare-contrast by learning to recognize clue words and points of comparison. Clue words let you know whether to look for similarities or differences. Points of comparison are the main topics that are being compared or contrasted. Notice how the passage below compares and contrasts life in rural and urban areas.

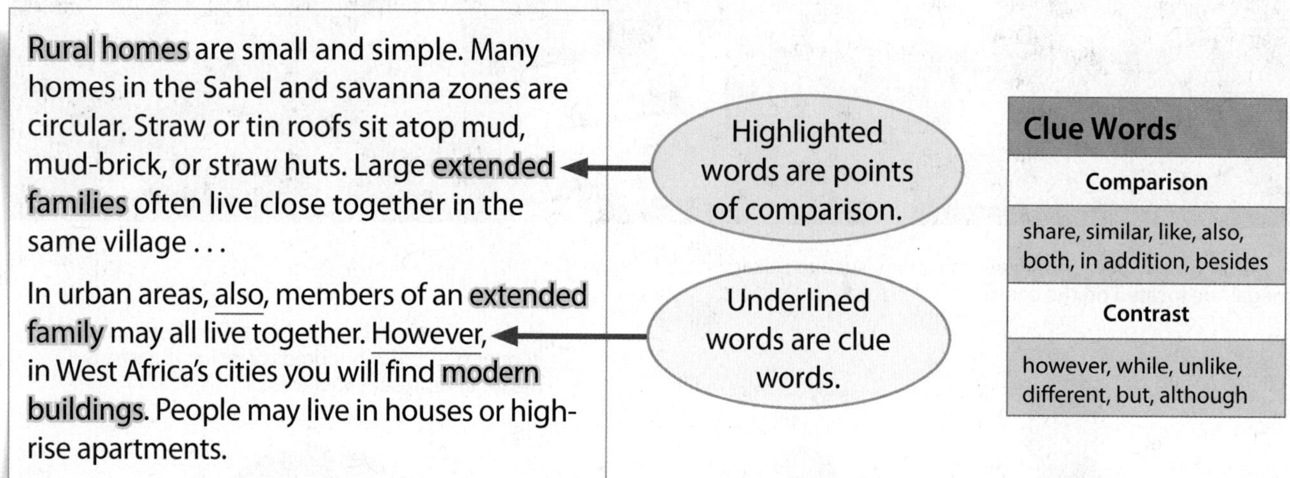

YOU TRY IT!

Read the following passage with a partner. Use your knowledge of clue words to help you identify similarities and differences between Liberia and Sierra Leone. Create a chart like the one here to compare and contrast the two countries.

> Now, both Liberia and Sierra Leone are trying to rebuild. They do have natural resources on which to build stronger economies. Liberia has rubber and iron ore, while Sierra Leone exports diamonds.

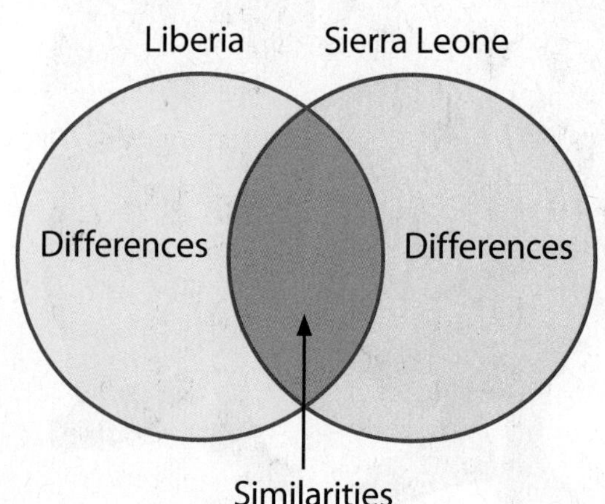

As you read this module, practice using clue words to understand comparison-contrast.

Physical Geography

The Big Idea

West Africa is a region mostly of plains, while the Congo River and tropical forests are important features of Central Africa's physical geography.

Main Ideas

- West Africa's key physical features include plains and the Niger River.
- West Africa has distinct climate and vegetation zones, such as arid and tropical.
- Central Africa's major physical features include the Congo Basin and plateaus surrounding the basin.
- Central Africa has a humid tropical climate and dense forest vegetation.

Key Terms and Places

Niger River
zonal
Sahel
desertification
savanna
Congo Basin
basin
Congo River
Zambezi River

If YOU lived there . . .

You are on a nature hike with a guide through the forests of the Congo Basin. It has been several hours since you have seen any other people. Sometimes your guide has to cut a path through the thick vegetation, but mostly you try not to disturb any plants or animals. Suddenly, you reach a clearing and see a group of men working hard to load huge tree trunks onto big trucks.

How do you feel about what you see?

Physical Features of West Africa

The region we call West Africa stretches from the Sahara in the north to the coasts of the Atlantic Ocean and the Gulf of Guinea in the west and south. While West Africa's climate changes quite a bit from north to south, the region does not have a wide variety of landforms. Its main physical features are plains and rivers.

Plains and Highlands Plains, flat areas of land, cover most of West Africa. The coastal plain is home to most of the region's cities. The interior plains provide land where people can raise a few crops or animals.

West Africa's plains are vast, interrupted only by a few highland areas. One area in the southwest has plateaus and cliffs. People have built houses directly into the sides of these cliffs for many hundreds of years. The region's only high mountains are the Tibesti Mountains in the northeast.

The Niger River As you can see on the map titled West Africa: Physical, many rivers flow across West Africa's plains. The most important river is the Niger (NY-juhr). The **Niger River** starts in some low mountains not too far from the Atlantic Ocean. From there, it flows 2,600 miles (4,184 km) into the interior of the region before emptying into the Gulf of Guinea.

The Niger brings life-giving water to West Africa. Many people farm along its banks or fish in its waters. It is also an important transportation route, especially during the rainy season.

Reading Check
Summarize
Why is the Niger River important to West Africa?

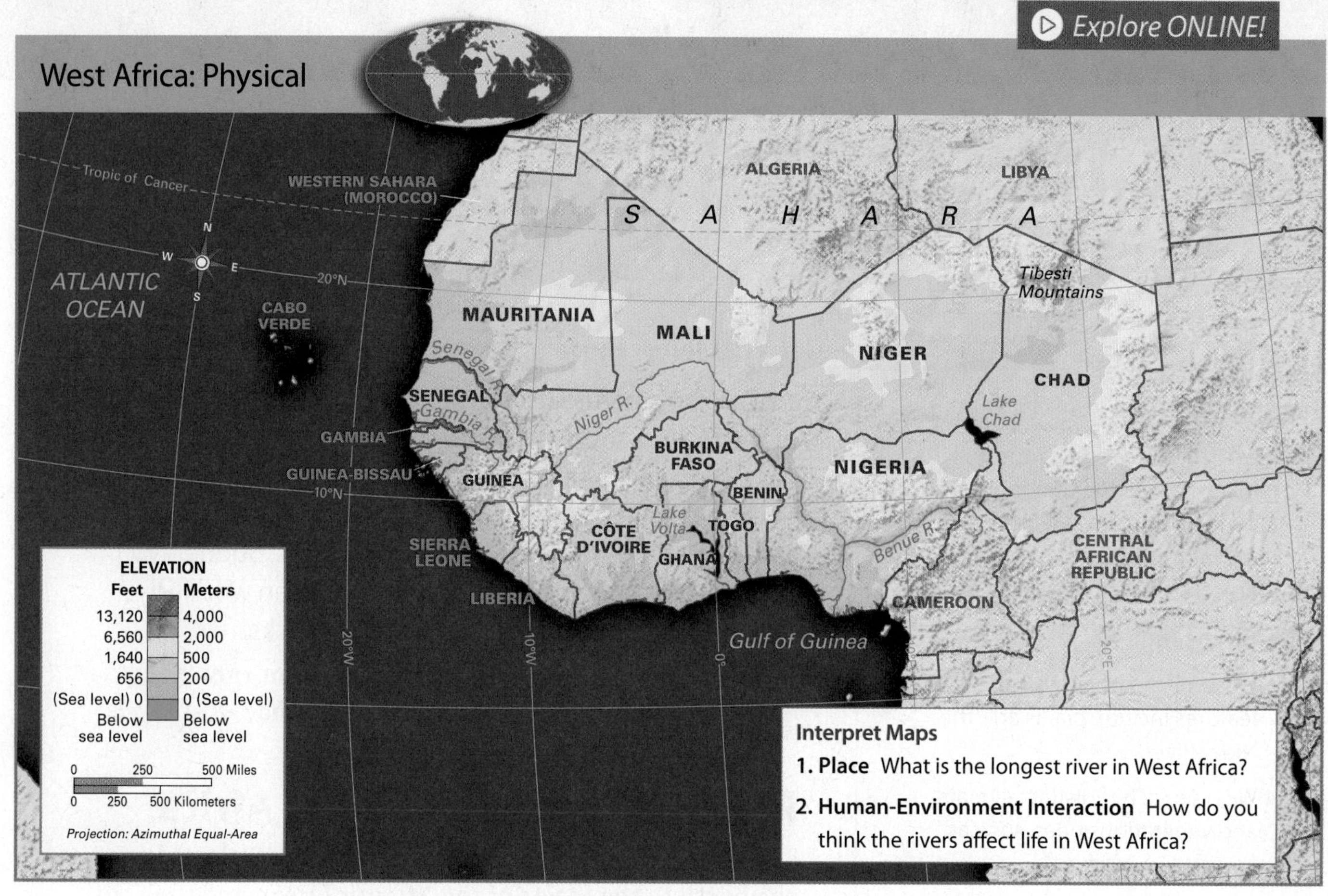

Climate and Vegetation

West Africa has four different climate regions. As you can see on the map, these climate regions stretch from east to west in bands or zones. Because of this, geographers say the region's climates are **zonal,** which means "organized by zone."

The northernmost zone of the region lies within the Sahara, the world's largest desert. Hardly any vegetation grows in the desert, and large areas of this dry climate zone have few or no people.

South of the Sahara is the semiarid **Sahel** (SAH-hel), a strip of land that divides the desert from wetter areas. It has a steppe climate. Rainfall there varies greatly from year to year. In some years, it never rains. Although the Sahel is quite dry, it does have enough vegetation to support hardy grazing animals.

However, the Sahel is becoming more like the Sahara. Animals have overgrazed the land in some areas. Also, people have cut down trees for firewood. Without these plants to anchor the soil, wind blows soil away. These conditions, along with drought, are causing desertification in the Sahel. **Desertification** is the spread of desertlike conditions.

To the south of the Sahel is a savanna zone. A **savanna** is an area of tall grasses and scattered trees and shrubs. When rains fall regularly, farmers can do well in this region of West Africa. The southern countries of the savanna, such as Nigeria, have large populations. This is due to the climate of the savanna, which is milder than other parts of Africa. The soil is also more fertile there than the arid regions of North Africa.

Reading Check
Categorize What are the region's four climate zones?

The fourth climate zone lies along the coasts of the Atlantic and the Gulf of Guinea. This zone has a humid tropical climate. Plentiful rain supports tropical forests. However, many trees have been cut from these forests to make room for the region's growing populations.

Physical Features of Central Africa

Central Africa is bordered by the Atlantic Ocean in the west. In the east, it is bordered by a huge valley called the Western Rift Valley. The land in between has some of the highest mountains and biggest rivers in Africa.

Landforms You can think of the region as a big soup bowl with a wide rim. Near the middle of the bowl is the **Congo Basin.** In geography, a **basin** is a generally flat region surrounded by higher land such as mountains and plateaus.

Plateaus and low hills surround the Congo Basin. The highest mountains in Central Africa lie farther away from the basin, along the Western Rift Valley. Some of these snowcapped mountains rise to more than 16,700 feet (5,090 m). Two lakes also lie along the rift—Lake Nyasa and Lake Tanganyika (tan-guhn-YEE-kuh). Lake Nyasa is also called Lake Malawi.

Rivers The huge **Congo River** is fed by hundreds of smaller rivers. They drain the swampy Congo Basin and flow into the river as it runs toward the Atlantic. Many rapids and waterfalls lie along its route, especially near its mouth. These obstacles make it impossible for ships to travel from the

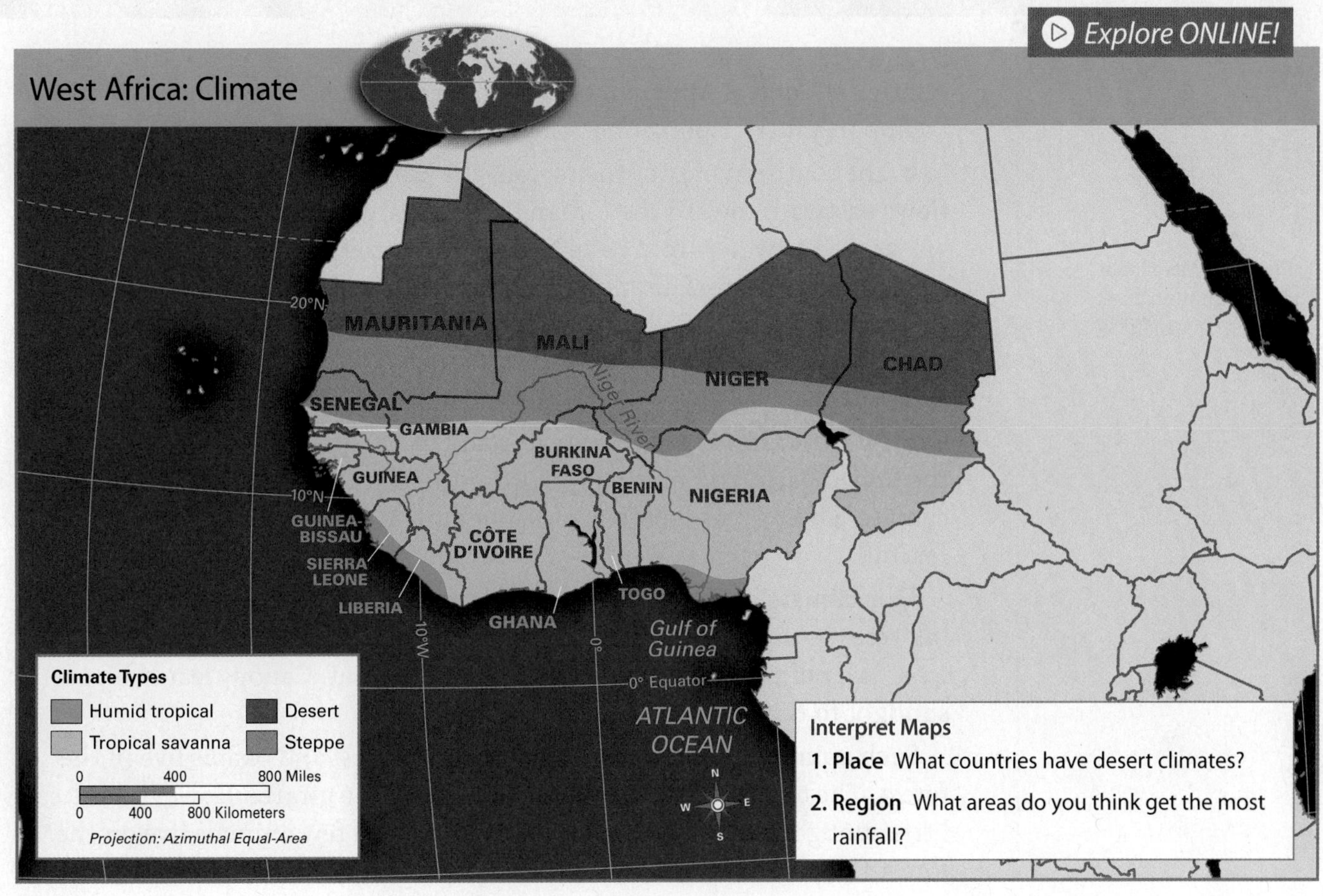

Interpret Maps

1. **Place** What countries have desert climates?
2. **Region** What areas do you think get the most rainfall?

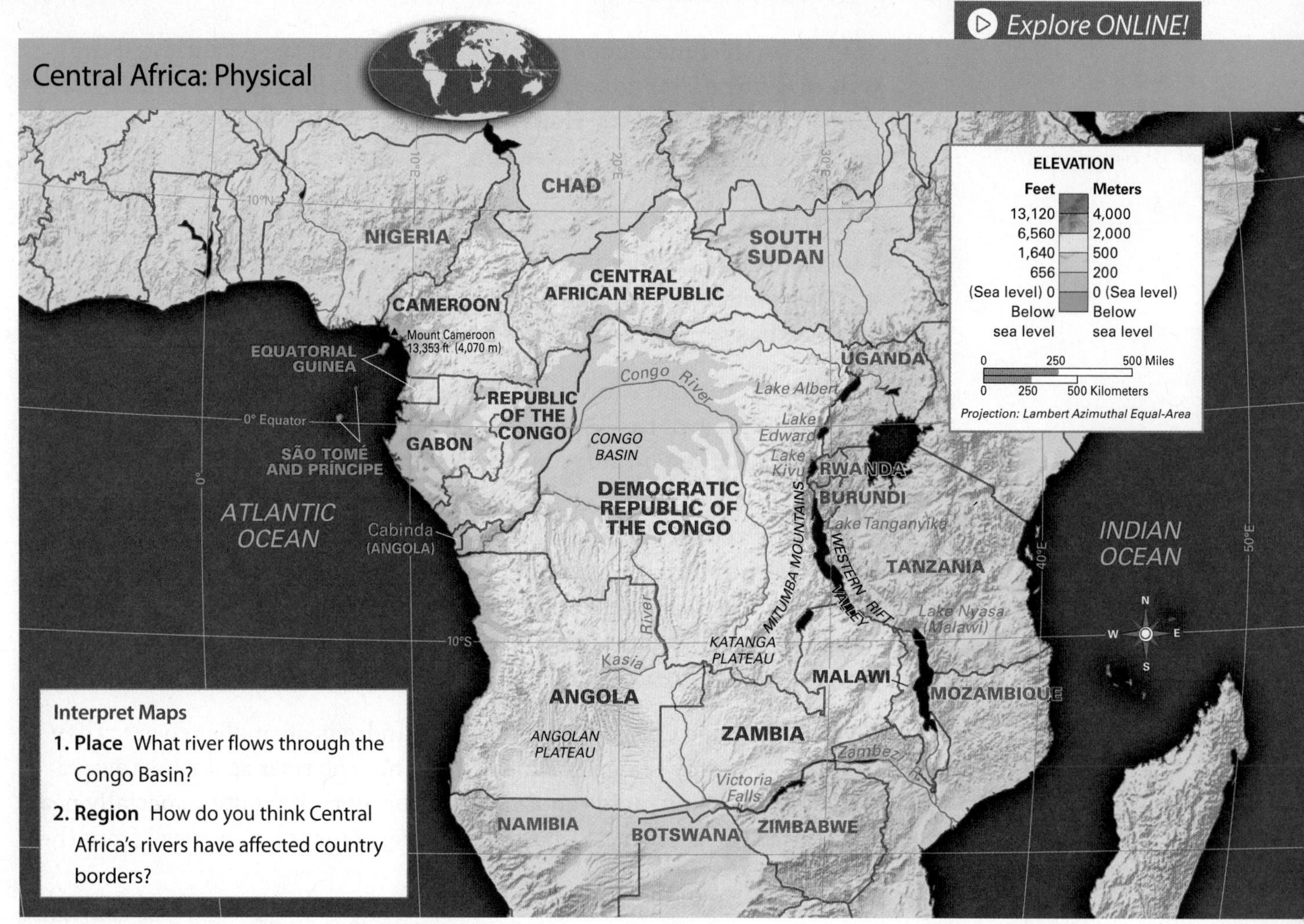

Interpret Maps

1. **Place** What river flows through the Congo Basin?
2. **Region** How do you think Central Africa's rivers have affected country borders?

interior of Central Africa all the way to the Atlantic. The Congo provides an important transportation route in the interior, however.

In the southern part of the region, the **Zambezi** (zam-BEE-zee) **River** flows eastward toward the Indian Ocean. Many rivers in Angola and Zambia, as well as water from Lake Nyasa, flow into the Zambezi. The Zambezi also has many waterfalls along its route, the most famous of which are the spectacular Victoria Falls.

Reading Check
Find Main Ideas
Where is the highest land in Central Africa?

Climate, Vegetation, and Animals

Central Africa lies along the equator and in the low latitudes. Therefore, the Congo Basin and much of the Atlantic coast have a humid tropical climate. These areas have warm temperatures all year and receive a lot of rainfall.

This climate supports a large, dense tropical forest. The many kinds of tall trees in the forest form a complete canopy. The canopy is the uppermost layer of the trees where the limbs spread out. Canopy leaves block sunlight to the ground below.

Such animals as gorillas, elephants, wild boars, and okapis live in the forest. The okapi is a short-necked relative of the giraffe. However, since little sunlight shines through the canopy, only a few animals live on the forest floor. Some animals, such as birds, monkeys, bats, and snakes, live in the trees. Many insects also live in Central Africa's forest. Due to the thick vegetation, the people who live in the tropical forests live in small villages near rivers and streams.

North and south of the Congo Basin are large areas with a tropical savanna climate. Those areas are warm all year, but they have distinct dry and wet seasons. There are grasslands, scattered trees, and shrubs. The high mountains in the east have a highland climate. Dry steppe and even desert climates are found in the far southern part of the region.

Reading Check
Summarize
What are the climate and vegetation like in the Congo Basin?

The natural habitat of the okapi is the Ituri Forest, a rain forest in Central Africa.

Summary and Preview West Africa is mostly covered with plains. Across these plains stretch four different climate zones, most of which are dry. In Central Africa, mighty rivers, tropical forests, and mineral resources characterize its physical geography. Next, you will learn about the history and culture of West Africa.

Lesson 1 Assessment

Review Ideas, Terms, and Places

1. a. **Describe** What is the inland delta on the Niger River like?
   b. **Summarize** What is the physical geography of West Africa like?
   c. **Elaborate** Why do you think most of West Africa's cities are located on the coastal plain?
2. a. **Recall** Why do geographers say West Africa's climates are zonal?
   b. **Compare and Contrast** What is one similarity and one difference between the Sahel and the savanna?
   c. **Evaluate** How do you think desertification affects people's lives in West Africa?
3. a. **Describe** What is the Congo Basin?
   b. **Elaborate** How do you think the Congo River's rapids and waterfalls affect the economy of the region?
4. a. **Recall** What part of Central Africa has a highland climate?
   b. **Make Inferences** Why would the thick vegetation of Central Africa forests cause people to live in small villages?

Critical Thinking

5. **Identify Cause and Effect** Review your notes on climate. Using a graphic organizer like the one here, identify the causes and effects of desertification.

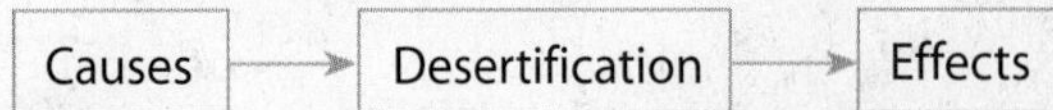

Case Study

Mapping Central Africa's Forests

Essential Elements

The World in Spatial Terms

Places and Regions

Physical Systems

Human Systems

Environment and Society

The Uses of Geography

Background

Imagine taking a walk along a street in your neighborhood. Your purpose is to see the street in spatial terms and gather information to help you make a map. While you walk, you ask the kinds of questions geographers ask. How many houses, apartment buildings, or businesses are on the street? What kinds of animals or trees do you see? Your walk ends, and you organize your data. Now imagine that you are going to gather data on another walk. This walk will be 2,000 miles (3,219 km) long.

A 2,000-Mile Walk

In September 1999 an American scientist named Michael Fay began a 465-day, 2,000-mile walk through Central Africa's forests. He and his team followed elephant trails through thick vegetation. They waded through creeks and mucky swamps.

On the walk, Fay gathered data on the number and kinds of animals he saw. He counted elephant dung, chimpanzee nests, leopard tracks, and gorillas. He counted the types of trees and other plants along his route.

He also counted human settlements and determined the effect of human activities on the environment.

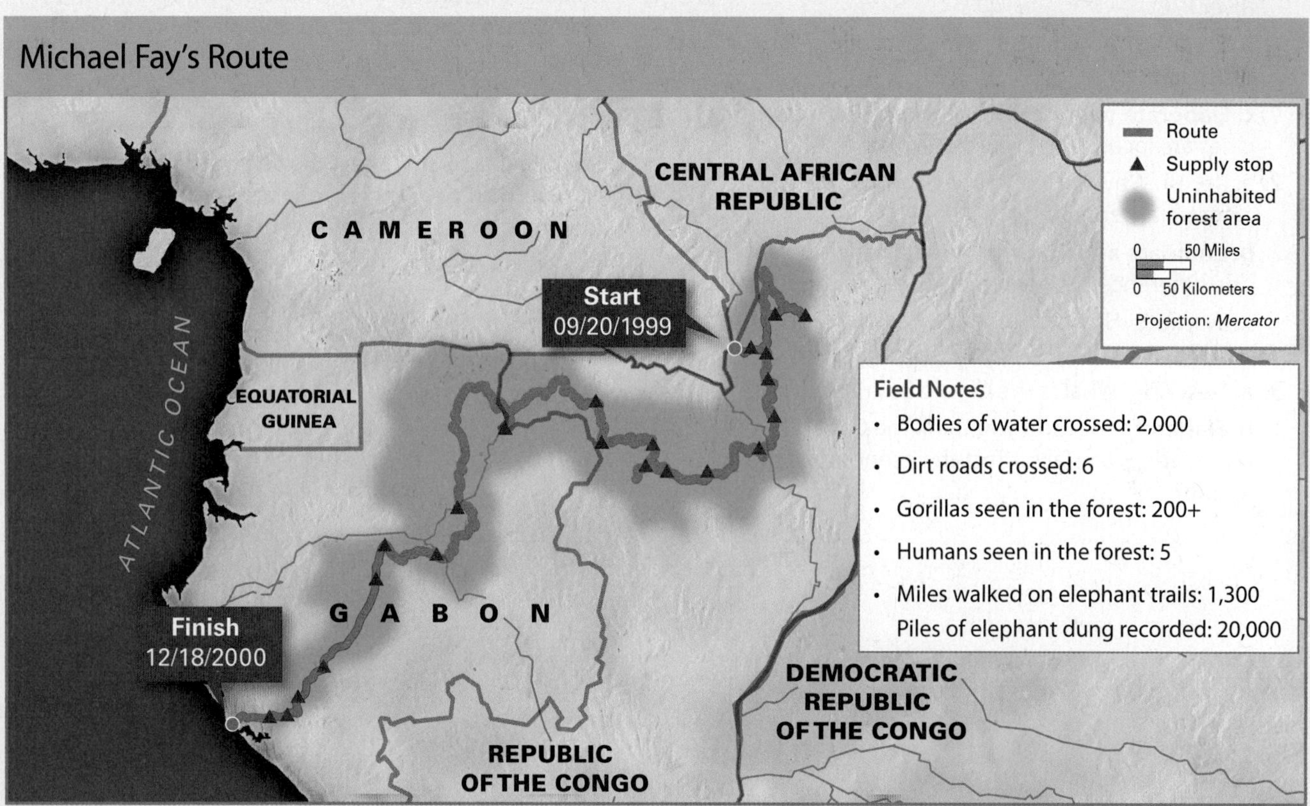

Exploring Central Africa

Michael Fay and his team had to chop their way through thick forest and vegetation.

In a clearing, they spotted this group of elephants.

Fay used a variety of tools to record the data he gathered on his walk. He wrote down what he observed in waterproof notebooks. He shot events and scenes with video and still cameras. To measure the distance he and his team walked each day, he used a tool called a Fieldranger. He also kept track of his exact position in the forest by using a GPS, or global positioning system.

What It Means

Michael Fay explained the purpose of his long walk. "The whole idea behind this is to be able to use the data we've collected as a tool." Other geographers can compare Fay's data with their own. Their comparison may help them create more accurate maps. These maps will show where plants, animals, and humans are located in Central Africa's forests.

Fay's data can also help scientists plan the future use of land or resources in a region. For example, Fay has used his data to convince government officials in Gabon to set aside 10 percent of its land to create 13 national parks. The parks will be protected from future logging and farming. They also will preserve many of the plants and animals that Fay and his team observed on their long walk.

Geography for Life Activity

1. Why did Michael Fay walk 2,000 miles?
2. In what practical way has Michael Fay used his data?
3. **Read More about Fay's Walk** Read the three-part article on Michael Fay's walk in *National Geographic* October 2000, March 2001, and August 2001. After you read the article, explain why Fay called his walk a "megatransect."

West Africa

The Big Idea

Powerful early kingdoms, European slave trade and colonization, and traditions from a mix of ethnic groups have all influenced West African culture.

Main Ideas

- In West Africa's history, trade made great kingdoms rich, but this greatness declined as Europeans began to control trade routes.
- The culture of West Africa includes many different ethnic groups, languages, religions, and housing styles.
- Most coastal countries of West Africa have struggling economies and weak or unstable governments.
- Lack of resources in the Sahel countries is a main challenge to economic development.

Key Terms and Places

Timbuktu
animism
extended family
Lagos
famine

If YOU lived there . . .

You live in the Sahel country of Niger, where your family herds cattle. You travel with your animals to find good grazing land for them. In the past few years, however, the desert has been expanding. It is getting harder and harder to find good grass and water for your cattle. You worry about the coming years.

How does this environment affect your life and your future?

History

Much of what we know about West Africa's early history is based on archaeology. Oral history—a spoken record of past events—offers other clues.

Great Kingdoms Ancient artifacts suggest that early trading centers developed into great kingdoms in West Africa. One of the earliest kingdoms was Ghana (GAH-nuh). By controlling the Sahara trade in gold and salt, Ghana became rich and powerful by about 800.

According to legend, Ghana fell to a mighty warrior from a neighboring kingdom in about 1300. Under this leader, the empire of Mali (MAH-lee) replaced Ghana. Mali gained control of the Sahara trade routes. Mali's most famous king, Mansa Musa, used wealth from trade to support artists and scholars. However, invasions caused the decline of Mali by the 1500s.

As Mali declined, the kingdom of Songhai (SAWNG-hy) came to power. With a university, mosques, and more than 100 schools, the Songhai city of **Timbuktu** was a cultural center. By about 1600, however, invasions had weakened this kingdom.

Merchants from North Africa crossed the Sahara to trade for West African gold and salt.

Historical Source

I Speak of Freedom

As European colonizers left West Africa, some people believed that Africa should not be divided into independent countries. Kwame Nkrumah, a future leader of Ghana, explained in 1961 why he thought Africans should unite.

> *"It is clear that we must find an African solution to our problems, and that this can only be found in African unity. Divided we are weak; united, Africa could become one of the greatest forces for good in the world."*
>
> —Kwame Nkrumah, from *I Speak of Freedom: A Statement of African Ideology*

Analyze Historical Sources
Why did Kwame Nkrumah think Africa would be better off united than divided?

The great West African trade cities also faded when the Sahara trade decreased. Trade decreased partly because Europeans began sailing along the west coast of Africa. They could trade for gold on the coast rather than with the North African traders who carried it through the desert.

The Slave Trade For a while, both Europeans and Africans profited from trade with each other. However, in the 1500s the demand for labor in Europe's American colonies changed this relationship. European traders met the demand for labor by selling enslaved Africans to colonists.

The slave trade was profitable for these traders, but it devastated West Africa. Many families were broken up when members were kidnapped and enslaved. Africans often died on the voyage to the Americas. By the end of the slave trade in the 1800s, millions of Africans had been enslaved.

Colonial Era and Independence Even with the end of the slave trade, Europeans wanted access to West Africa's resources. To ensure that access, France, Britain, Germany, and Portugal all claimed colonies in the region in the 1800s.

Some Europeans moved to West Africa to run the colonies. They built schools, roads, and railroads. However, they also created new and difficult problems for the people of West Africa. For example, many West Africans gave up farming and instead earned only low wages working in the new commercial economy.

After World War II, Africans worked for independence. Most of the colonies became independent during the 1950s and 1960s. All were independent by 1974.

Reading Check
Summarize What impact did Europeans have on West Africa?

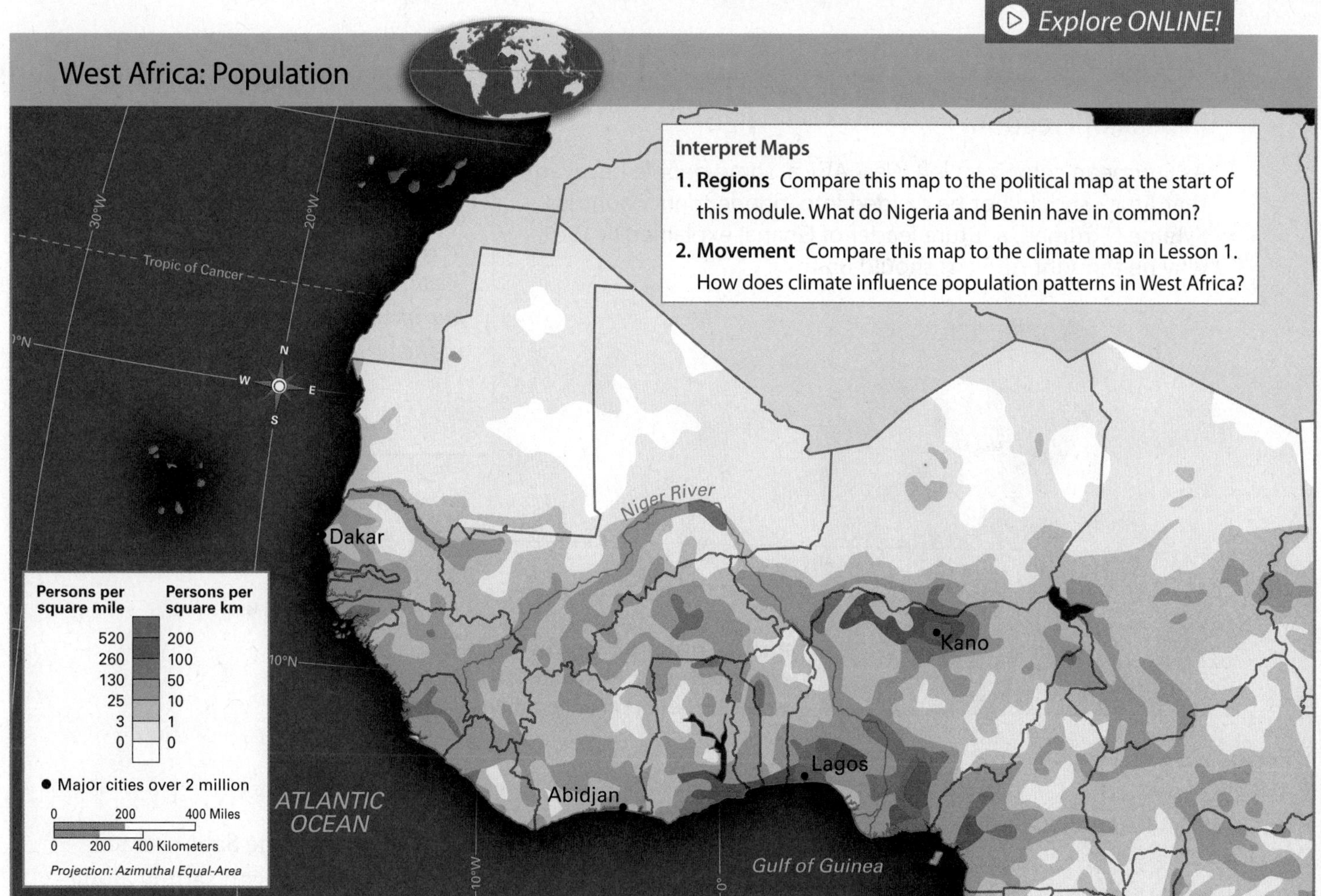

Culture

About 5 percent of the world's population lives in West Africa, making it the world's fastest-growing region. With so many people living in this region, West African societies are very diverse. Their culture reflects three main influences—traditional African cultures, European culture, and Islam.

People and Languages West Africa's people belong to hundreds of different ethnic groups. In fact, Nigeria alone is made up of more than 250 ethnic groups. The biggest ethnic groups there are Hausa and Fulani, Yoruba, and Igbo. The Ashanti are a major ethnic group in Ghana. Members of some ethnic groups in West Africa still live in their traditional villages. Other ethnic groups mix with each other in the region's cities.

Because of the way the European colonizers drew political boundaries, country borders sometimes separated members of the same ethnic group. Other borders grouped together peoples that did not get along. As a result, many West Africans are more loyal to their own ethnic groups than they are to their countries.

Because of the huge number of ethnic groups, hundreds of different languages are spoken in West Africa. In some areas, using the colonial languages of French, English, or Portuguese helps people from different groups communicate with each other. Also, West African languages that many people share, such as Fula and Hausa, help with communication in the region.

Religion Like peoples and languages, many forms of religion exist in West Africa. Traditional religions of West Africa have often been forms of animism. **Animism** is the belief that bodies of water, animals, trees, and other natural objects have spirits. Animists also honor the memories of ancestors.

The two most common religions came from outside the region. They are Islam and Christianity. North African traders brought Islam to West Africa. Europeans introduced Christianity. Today, most West Africans of the Sahel practice Islam. Many towns there have mosques built of mud. Christianity is the most common religion south of the Sahel.

Clothing, Families, and Homes West Africans wear a mix of traditional and modern clothing styles. Some West Africans, particularly in the cities, wear Western-style clothing. Traditional robes, pants, blouses, and skirts are made from colorful cotton fabrics. Women often wear beautiful wrapped headdresses. Because of the warm climate, most clothing is loose.

Rural homes are small and simple. Many homes in the Sahel and savanna zones are circular. Straw or tin roofs sit atop mud, mud-brick, or straw huts. Large extended families often live close together in the same village. An **extended family** includes the father, mother, children, and close relatives in one household.

In urban areas also, members of an extended family may all live together. In the cities, people may live in houses or high-rise apartments.

Reading Check **Form Generalizations** What are some features of West African culture?

Coastal Countries

Several West African countries lie along the Atlantic Ocean and the Gulf of Guinea. Many of these countries have struggling economies and unstable governments. Some countries in this region, including Benin, have literacy rates below 50 percent. This contributes to the challenges faced in this region. Countries with low literacy rates usually have less wealth and a lower standard of living.

Link to the Arts

Masks

Masks are one of the best-known West African arts. They are traditionally carved out of wood only by skilled and respected men. The colors and shape of a mask have specific meanings. For example, the color white represents the spirit world.

Masks are used in ceremonies to call spirits or to prepare boys and girls for adulthood. Ceremony participants often wear a mask as part of a costume that completely hides the body. The wearer is believed to become what the mask represents.

Draw Inferences
Why would someone want to wear a mask?

Quick Facts

A West African Village

- These homes are in Burkina Faso. Trees are scarce in the Sahel and savanna, so there is little wood for construction.
- These homes are made of a mixture of mud, water, and cow dung.
- Women are responsible for painting and decorating the walls of the homes.

Nigeria Nigeria is the second-largest country in West Africa. With more than 186 million people, it has Africa's largest population, sub-Saharan Africa's largest city, and one of the continent's strongest economies.

Like many other former colonies, Nigeria has many different ethnic groups within its borders. Conflicts have often taken place among those ethnic groups. Avoiding conflict was important in choosing a site for a new capital in the 1990s. Leaders chose Abuja (ah-BOO-jah) because it was centrally located in an area of low population density, meaning there were fewer people to cause conflicts. Nigeria's government is now a democracy after years of military rule.

Nigerian Economy Nigeria has some of Africa's richest natural resources. Major oil fields, the country's most important resource, are located in the Niger River delta and just off the coast.

Nigeria specializes in oil trade. Specialization is when a country produces goods it can provide, like oil, to sell to other countries that need those goods. They then use the money earned from this trade to buy goods and services that they cannot produce from other countries. Oil accounts for about 95 percent of Nigeria's export earnings.

Income from oil exports has allowed Nigeria to build good roads and railroads for transporting oil. The oil industry is centered around **Lagos** (LAY-gahs). Also the former capital, Lagos is the most populous city in West Africa.

Although Nigeria is rich in resources, many Nigerians are poor. One cause of the poverty there is a high birthrate. Nigeria cannot produce enough food for its growing population. Another cause of Nigeria's poverty is a history of bad government. Corrupt government officials have used their positions to enrich themselves.

Senegal and the Gambia Senegal wraps around the Gambia. The odd border was created by French and British diplomats during the colonial era. Senegal is larger and richer than the Gambia, but the two countries do have many similarities. For example, peanuts are their major crops. Also, tourism is becoming more important in both countries.

Many people in Senegal and the Gambia speak a language called Wolof (WOH-lawf). Griots (GREE-ohz), or storytellers, are important to the Wolof speakers there and to other West Africans.

Guinea, Guinea-Bissau, and Cabo Verde Guinea and its small neighbor, Guinea-Bissau (GI-nee bi-SOW), are poor countries. Guinea's main natural resource is bauxite, which is used to make aluminum. Guinea-Bissau has undeveloped mineral resources.

Cabo Verde (VUHRD) is a group of volcanic islands in the Atlantic. It is West Africa's only island country. Once a Portuguese colony, Cabo Verde now has one of the most stable democratic governments in Africa. Services such as tourism form the main part of the country's economy.

Liberia and Sierra Leone Liberia is Africa's oldest republic. Americans founded it in the 1820s as a home for freed slaves. The freed slaves who settled in Liberia and their descendants lived in towns on the coast. They often clashed with Africans already living there. Those Africans were usually poorer and lived in rural areas. In the 1980s these conflicts led to a civil war, which ended in 2003.

Sierra Leone (lee-OHN) also experienced violent civil war, from 1991 to 2002. The fighting wrecked the country's economy, killed thousands of people, and forced millions from their homes.

Now, both Liberia and Sierra Leone are trying to rebuild. They do have natural resources on which to build stronger economies. Liberia exports rubber and iron ore, while Sierra Leone exports diamonds.

Crowding in Lagos

Lagos is a busy seaport and industrial center. Most people travel in the city by walking, driving, or taking public transportation. Overcrowding leads to problems common in big cities such as traffic jams and poor housing.

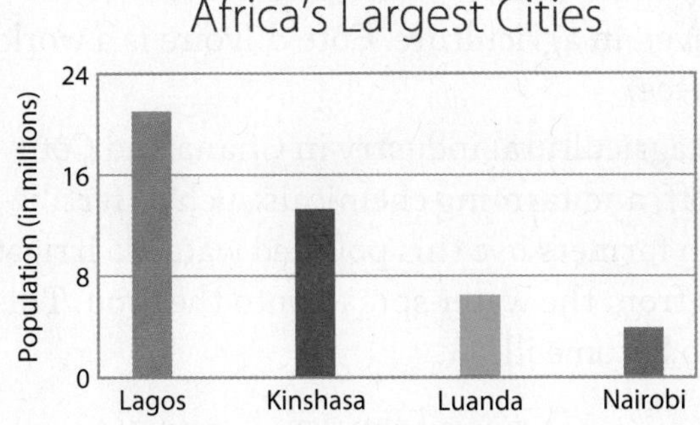

Analyze Graphs
About how much larger is the population of Lagos compared to Nairobi?

West Africa: Land Use and Resources

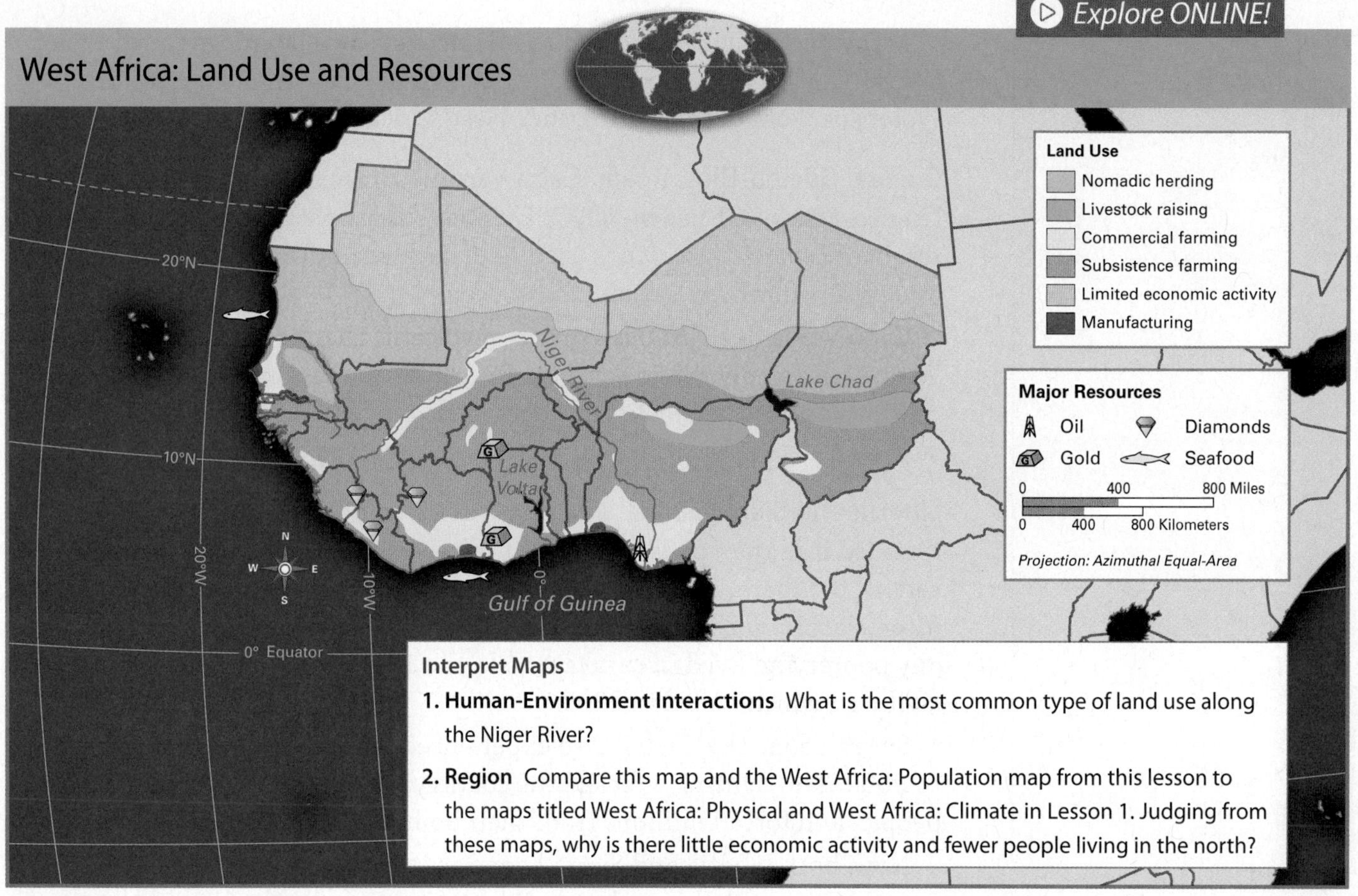

Interpret Maps

1. **Human-Environment Interactions** What is the most common type of land use along the Niger River?
2. **Region** Compare this map and the West Africa: Population map from this lesson to the maps titled West Africa: Physical and West Africa: Climate in Lesson 1. Judging from these maps, why is there little economic activity and fewer people living in the north?

Ghana and Côte d'Ivoire Ghana is named for an ancient kingdom. Côte d'Ivoire (koht-dee-VWAHR) is a former French colony whose name means "Ivory Coast" in English. Côte d'Ivoire boasts Africa's largest Christian church building.

These two countries have rich natural resources. Both Ghana and Côte d'Ivoire also have large agricultural industries. Farming makes up about 20 percent of Ghana's gross domestic product (GDP), and farmers make up close to half of Ghana's workforce. It is a big exporter of cacao (kuh-KOW), rice, cassava, peanuts, shea nuts, and bananas. Almost 70 percent of the Côte d'Ivoire population is involved in agriculture. Côte d'Ivoire is a world leader in export of cacao and coffee.

Water pollution threatens the agricultural industry in Ghana and Côte d'Ivoire. Sewage, industrial runoff, and farming chemicals such as fertilizers contaminate the water. When farmers use this polluted water to irrigate their fields, bacteria and viruses from the water spread onto the food. This causes consumers and farmers to become ill.

Togo and Benin Unstable governments have troubled Togo and Benin (buh-NEEN) since independence. These two countries have experienced periods of military rule. Their fragile economies have contributed to their unstable and sometimes violent politics.

Both Togo and Benin are poor. The people depend on farming and herding for income. Palm products, cacao, and coffee are the main crops in both countries.

Reading Check
Form Generalizations What are the economies of the coastal countries like?

Sahel Countries

The Sahel region of West Africa includes some of the poorest and least developed countries in the world. The lack of water for drinking and growing food creates challenges for the people of the Sahel. Though around 135 million people live in the Sahel, the eastern and southern parts have little water compared to other parts of Africa. This region of the Sahel has about 18 percent of the renewable water resources in Africa, while other parts of West Africa and Central Africa have about 72 percent. Water scarcity and the expanding desert make feeding the people of the Sahel difficult.

Mauritania, Niger, and Chad Most Mauritanians were once nomadic herders. Today, the expanding Sahara has driven more than half of the nomads into cities. Those who kept the nomadic lifestyle, such as the Taureg, travel in family groups of fewer than 100. They walk or ride camels through the Sahara and the Sahel to lead their herds to water and food.

Many people in cities use buses, trains, or cars to travel. But city-dwellers, as well as the rest of the country, are very poor. Only in the far south, near the Senegal River, can people farm. Near the Atlantic Ocean, people fish for a living. Corrupt governments and ethnic tensions between blacks and Arabs add to Mauritania's troubles.

In Niger (nee-ZHER), only about 11 percent of the land is good for farming. The country's only farmland lies along the Niger River and near the Nigerian border. Farmers there grow staple, or main, food crops, such as millet and sorghum.

In 2005 locusts and drought destroyed Niger's crops. The loss of crops caused widespread **famine,** or an extreme shortage of food. International groups provided some aid, but it was impossible to **distribute** food to all who needed it. In 2007 fighting broke out between Tuareg rebels and government forces. In 2009 President Mamadou Tandja used his emergency powers to dissolve the government. He then instituted changes that would allow him to serve a third term as president.

Academic Vocabulary
distribute to divide among a group of people

Chad has more land for farming than Mauritania or Niger, and conditions there are somewhat better than in the other two countries. In addition to farming, Lake Chad once had a healthy fishing industry and

This aerial view shows how, with just a little water, people can farm in the dry Sahel.

Women wearing traditional clothing shop at an open-air market in Mali

supplied water to several countries. However, drought has evaporated much of the lake's water in the past several years. The shrinking of the lake and the lack of water in the region lead to conflicts over control of the remaining water. These conflicts disrupt trade and industry in the region. For example, fishers want farmers to stop using the water for their crops and animals.

The future may hold more promise for Chad. A long civil war finally ended in the 1990s. Also, oil was recently discovered there, and Chad began to export this valuable resource in 2004.

Mali and Burkina Faso The Sahara covers about 40 percent of the land in Mali. The scarce amount of land available for farming makes Mali one of the world's poorest countries. The available farmland lies in the southwest, along the Niger River. Most people in Mali fish or farm in this small area along the river. Cotton and gold are Mali's main exports.

Mali's economy does have some bright spots, however. A fairly stable democratic government has begun economic reforms. Also, the ancient cities of Timbuktu and Gao (GOW) continue to attract tourists.

Burkina Faso is also a poor country. It has thin soil and few mineral resources. Few trees remain in or near the capital, Ouagadougou (wah-gah-DOO-goo), because they have been cut for firewood and building material. Jobs in the city are also scarce. To support their families, many men try to find work in other countries. Thus, when unrest disrupts work opportunities in other countries, Burkina Faso's economy suffers.

Reading Check
Summarize What are the challenges facing Chad and Burkina Faso?

Summary and Preview In this lesson, you learned that great kingdoms and European colonists once ruled West Africa and how these historical influences still affect West Africa's diverse cultures. Next, you will learn how native traditions and European colonizers influenced Central Africa.

Lesson 2 Assessment

Review Ideas, Terms, and Places

1. a. **Identify** What was the significance of Timbuktu?
   b. **Explain** How did the slave trade affect West Africa?
   c. **Evaluate** Do you think West Africans mostly appreciated or disliked the European colonizers? Explain your answer.
2. a. **Recall** What do people who believe in animism think about natural objects?
   b. **Analyze** How did European colonizers affect tension between ethnic groups?
3. a. **Compare** What are some similarities between Togo and Benin?
   b. **Elaborate** Why do you think countries with poor economies often have unstable governments?
4. a. **Describe** What caused famine in Niger?
   b. **Evaluate** What do you think is the biggest problem facing the Sahel countries? Explain.
   c. **Identify and Explain** Which geographic factors best explain the patterns of land use and economic activity shown on the Land Use and Resources map in this lesson?

Critical Thinking

5. **Compare and Contrast** Review your notes on the coastal countries and the Sahel countries. Then create a Venn diagram to compare and contrast the two regions.

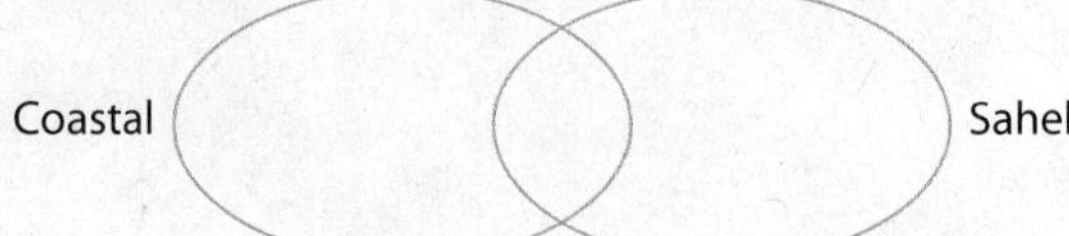

Central Africa

The Big Idea

Central Africa's history and culture have been influenced by native traditions and European colonizers.

Main Ideas

- Great African kingdoms and European colonizers have influenced the history of Central Africa.
- The culture of Central Africa includes many ethnic groups and languages, but it has also been influenced by European colonization.
- The countries of Central Africa are mostly poor, and many are trying to recover from years of civil war.
- Challenges to peace, health, and the environment slow economic development in Central Africa.

Key Terms and Places

Kongo Kingdom
dialects
periodic market
copper belt
Kinshasa
inflation
malaria
malnutrition

If YOU lived there . . .

You are an economic adviser in Zambia. Your country is poor, and most people are farmers. But scientists say Zambia has a lot of copper underground. With a new copper mine, you could sell valuable copper to other countries. However, the mine would destroy a lot of farmland.

Do you support building the mine? Why or why not?

History

Early humans lived in Central Africa many thousands of years ago. Yet, the descendants of these people have had less impact on the region's history than people from the outside. Peoples from West Africa, and later European colonists, brought their customs to the region and changed the way people lived.

Early History About 2,000 years ago, new peoples began to migrate to Central Africa from West Africa. They eventually formed several kingdoms in Central Africa. Among the most important was the **Kongo Kingdom.** Founded in the 1300s, it was located near the mouth of the Congo River.

The Kongo people established trade routes to western and eastern Africa. Their kingdom grew rich from the trade of animal skins, shells, slaves, and ivory. Ivory is a cream-colored material that comes from elephant tusks.

In the late 1400s Europeans came to the region. They wanted the region's forest products and other resources such as ivory. They used ivory for fine furniture, jewelry, statues, and piano keys. Europeans also began to trade with some Central African kingdoms for slaves. Over a span of about 300 years, the Europeans took millions of enslaved Africans to their colonies in the Americas.

Some African kingdoms became richer by trading with Europeans. However, all were gradually changed and weakened by European influence. In the late 1800s European countries divided all of Central Africa into colonies. The colonial powers were France, Belgium, Germany, Spain, the United Kingdom, and Portugal.

Ivory Trade

Ivory traders collected elephant tusks for export to Europe.

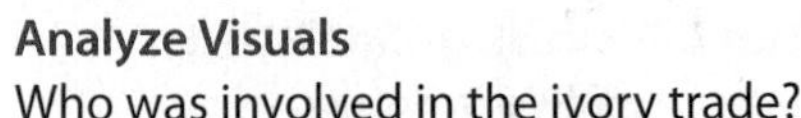

Analyze Visuals
Who was involved in the ivory trade?

Many objects were made from ivory, such as this armlet worn by an African king.

These European powers drew colonial borders that ignored the homelands of different ethnic groups. Many different ethnic groups were lumped together in colonies where they had to interact. These groups spoke different languages and had different customs. Their differences caused conflicts, especially after the colonies won independence.

Modern Central Africa Central African colonies gained their independence from European powers after World War II. Some of the colonies fought bloody wars to win their independence. The last country to become independent was Angola. It won freedom from Portugal in 1975.

Independence did not bring peace to Central Africa, however. Ethnic groups continued to fight one another within the borders of the new countries. Also, the United States and the Soviet Union used Central Africa as a battleground in the Cold War. They supported different allies in small wars throughout Africa. The wars in the region killed many people and caused great damage.

Reading Check
Summarize
What role did Europeans play in Central Africa's history?

Culture

Today, about 173 million people live in Central Africa. These people belong to many different ethnic groups and have different customs.

People and Language The people of Central Africa speak hundreds of different languages. They also speak different **dialects,** regional varieties of a language. For example, although many Central Africans speak Bantu languages, those languages can be quite different from one another.

The main reason for this variety is the number of ethnic groups. Most ethnic groups have their own language or dialect. Most people in the region speak traditional African languages in their daily lives. However, the official languages of the region are European because of the influence of the colonial powers. For example, French is the official language of the Democratic Republic of the Congo. Portuguese is the language of Angola. English is an official language in Zambia and Malawi.

Religion Central Africa's colonial history has also influenced religion. Europeans introduced Christianity to the region. Now many people in the former French, Spanish, and Portuguese colonies are Roman Catholic. Protestant Christianity is most common in former British colonies.

Two other religions came to parts of Central Africa from other regions. Influenced by the Muslim countries of the Sahel, the northern part of Central Africa has many Muslims. Zambia is the home of Muslims as well as Hindus.

The Arts Central Africa's traditional cultures influence the arts of the region. The region is famous for sculpture, carved wooden masks, and beautiful cotton gowns dyed in bright colors.

Central Africa also has popular styles of music. The *likembe*, or thumb piano, was invented in the Congo region. Also, a type of dance music called *makossa* originated in Cameroon and has become popular throughout Africa. It can be played with guitars and electric keyboards.

Reading Check
Form Generalizations What are characteristics of culture in Central Africa?

Resources and Countries of Central Africa

Central Africa has many resources; however, most of the countries in Central Africa are very poor. After years of colonial rule and then civil war, they are struggling to build stable governments and strong economies.

Resources The tropical environment of Central Africa is good for growing crops. Most people in the region are subsistence farmers. However, many farmers are now beginning to grow crops for sale. Common crops are coffee, bananas, and corn. In rural areas, people trade agricultural and other products in periodic markets. A **periodic market** is an open-air trading market that is set up once or twice a week.

Quick Facts

Christianity in Central Africa

Christian missionaries established churches and schools throughout Central Africa. Christianity has grown to become the dominate religion of Central Africa. These students attend a Catholic school in Malawi.

Central Africa is rich in other natural resources as well. The large tropical forest provides timber, while the rivers provide a way to travel and to trade. Dams on the rivers produce hydroelectricity, an important energy resource. Other energy resources in the region include oil, natural gas, and coal.

Central Africa also has many valuable minerals, including copper, uranium, tin, zinc, diamonds, gold, and cobalt. Of these, copper is the most important. Most of Africa's copper is found in an area called the **copper belt.** The copper belt stretches through northern Zambia and southern Democratic Republic of the Congo. However, poor transportation systems and political problems have kept the region's resources from being fully developed.

Democratic Republic of the Congo The Democratic Republic of the Congo was a Belgian colony until 1960. When the country gained independence, many Belgians left. Few teachers, doctors, and other professionals remained in the former colony. In addition, various ethnic groups fought each other for power. These problems were partly to blame for keeping the new country poor.

A military leader named Joseph Mobutu came to power in 1965. He ruled as a dictator. During his rule, the government took over foreign-owned industries. It borrowed money from foreign countries to try to expand industry. However, most farmers suffered, and government and business leaders were corrupt. While the economy collapsed, Mobutu became one of the richest people in the world and used violence against people who challenged him.

In 1997, after a civil war, a new government took over. The new government renamed the country the Democratic Republic of the Congo.

The Democratic Republic of the Congo is a treasure chest of minerals that could bring wealth to the country. The south is part of Central Africa's rich copper belt. The country also has gold, diamonds, and cobalt. In addition, the tropical forest provides wood, food, and rubber. However, civil war, bad government, and crime have scared many foreign businesses away. As a result, the country's resources have helped few of its people.

Kinshasa is the largest city in the Democratic Republic of the Congo and the second-largest city in sub-Saharan Africa.

Most people in the Democratic Republic of the Congo are poor. They usually live in rural areas where they must farm and trade for food. Many people are moving to the capital, **Kinshasa.** This crowded city has some modern buildings, but most of the city consists of poor slums.

Central African Republic and Cameroon North of the Democratic Republic of the Congo is the landlocked country of Central African Republic. Since independence, this country has struggled with military coups, corrupt leaders, and improper elections.

Although the country has diamonds and gold, it does not have railroads or ports needed to transport the resources for export. This makes it difficult to trade with other countries. Central African Republic receives some aid from foreign countries, but this is not enough to meet the needs of its people.

Between Central African Republic and the Atlantic Ocean is Cameroon. Unlike most countries in Central Africa, Cameroon is fairly stable. It is a republic. The president is elected and holds most of the power.

Political stability has made economic growth possible. The country has oil reserves and good conditions for farming. Cacao, cotton, and coffee are valuable export crops. A good system of roads and railways helps people transport these goods for export to other countries.

Because of the steady economy, the people of Cameroon have a high standard of living for the region. For example, more people in Cameroon are enrolled in school than in most places in Africa.

Equatorial Guinea and São Tomé and Príncipe Tiny Equatorial Guinea is divided between the mainland and five islands. The country is a republic. It has held elections, but many have seen the elections as being flawed. These elections have kept the same president ruling the country for more than 25 years. Although the discovery of oil has produced economic growth, living conditions for most people are still poor.

The island country of São Tomé and Príncipe has struggled with political instability. In addition, it is a poor country with few resources. It produces much cacao but has to import food. The recent discovery of oil in its waters may help the economy.

Gabon and Republic of the Congo Gabon has had only one president since 1967. For many years, Gabon held no multiparty elections. Gabon's economy provides the highest standard of living in the region. More than half the country's income comes from oil.

Like Gabon, the Republic of the Congo receives much of its income from oil. It also receives income from forest products. Despite these resources, a civil war in the late 1990s hurt the economy.

The Republic of the Congo is mostly urban and growing more so. Many people are moving from villages to cities. The biggest city is the capital, Brazzaville.

Angola Angola won independence from Portugal in 1975. The country then plunged into a long civil war. Fighting finally ended in 2002, and the country has been more stable since then. Angola is now a republic with an elected president.

Even with peace, Angola's economy is struggling. For about 85 percent of the population, subsistence farming is the only source of income. Even worse, land mines left over from the civil war endanger the farmers. A high rate of **inflation,** the rise in prices that occurs when currency loses its buying power, hurt Angola's economy during the early 2000s. Finally, corrupt officials have taken large amounts of money meant for public projects.

Village Architecture

Although Central Africa has several big cities, many people still live in rural villages. Different groups of people have different styles of architecture for their villages. Building materials vary depending on the resources available in the geographic setting.

An extended family lives together in these adobe homes in the mountains of Cameroon.

The strong tropical sun provides power for this hut in Angola.

A family sits outside their home in Zambia.

Analyze Visuals
How does the construction of the huts help you recognize different climates in Central Africa?

Reading Check
Summarize
What are the economies like in Central African countries?

Zambia and Malawi The southernmost countries in Central Africa are Zambia and Malawi. About 85 percent of Zambia's workers are farmers. Though rich with copper mines, Zambia's economy is growing very slowly. It is hurt by high levels of debt and inflation.

Nearly all of Malawi's people farm for a living. About 83 percent of the people live in villages in rural areas. Aid from foreign countries and religious groups has been important to the economy. However, the country has been slow to build factories and industries. In the future, Malawi will probably have to develop its own industries rather than rely on aid from foreign countries.

Issues and Challenges

As you have read, many of the countries in Central Africa have unstable governments and poor economies. These circumstances have been either the cause or effect of the grave challenges that face the region today.

Ethnic and Regional Conflict A mix of ethnic groups and competing desires for power has led to civil war in many of the region's countries. Millions of people have been killed in these wars, especially in the Democratic Republic of the Congo.

Wars have also contributed to poor economies in the region. The people injured in the fighting can no longer work. In addition, the fighting destroys land and other resources that could be used in more productive ways.

Health Like war, disease kills many people in the region. **Malaria** is a disease spread by mosquitoes that causes fever and pain. Without treatment, it can lead to death. In fact, malaria is by far the most common cause of death in Central Africa. A child there dies from malaria every 45 seconds. On the Malaria in Central Africa map, you can see that this disease is a problem almost everywhere.

Academic Vocabulary
implement to put in place

International health organizations and some national governments have begun to **implement** strategies to control malaria. These strategies include educating people about the disease and passing out nets treated with insecticide. The nets and medicine are expensive, and not everyone can afford them. However, people who sleep under these nets will be protected from mosquitoes and malaria.

While some countries are beginning to control malaria, another disease is spreading rapidly. HIV, the virus that causes AIDS, is very common in Central Africa. Hundreds of thousands of people die of AIDS each year in Central Africa. There is no cure for HIV infection, and medicines to control it are very expensive. International groups are working hard to find a cure for HIV and to slow the spread of the disease.

Partly because so many people die of disease, Central Africa has a very young population. Almost 45 percent of people living in Central Africa are under age 15. For comparison, only about 20 percent of the people in the United States are under age 15. Although many young people in Central Africa work, they do not contribute to the economy as much as older, more experienced workers do.

Resources and Environment One of the challenges facing Central African countries is the ability to develop and manage their natural resources. Agricultural land is one resource that has become challenging to manage. For example, excessive use of fertilizers in agricultural areas has polluted the water people use and drink.

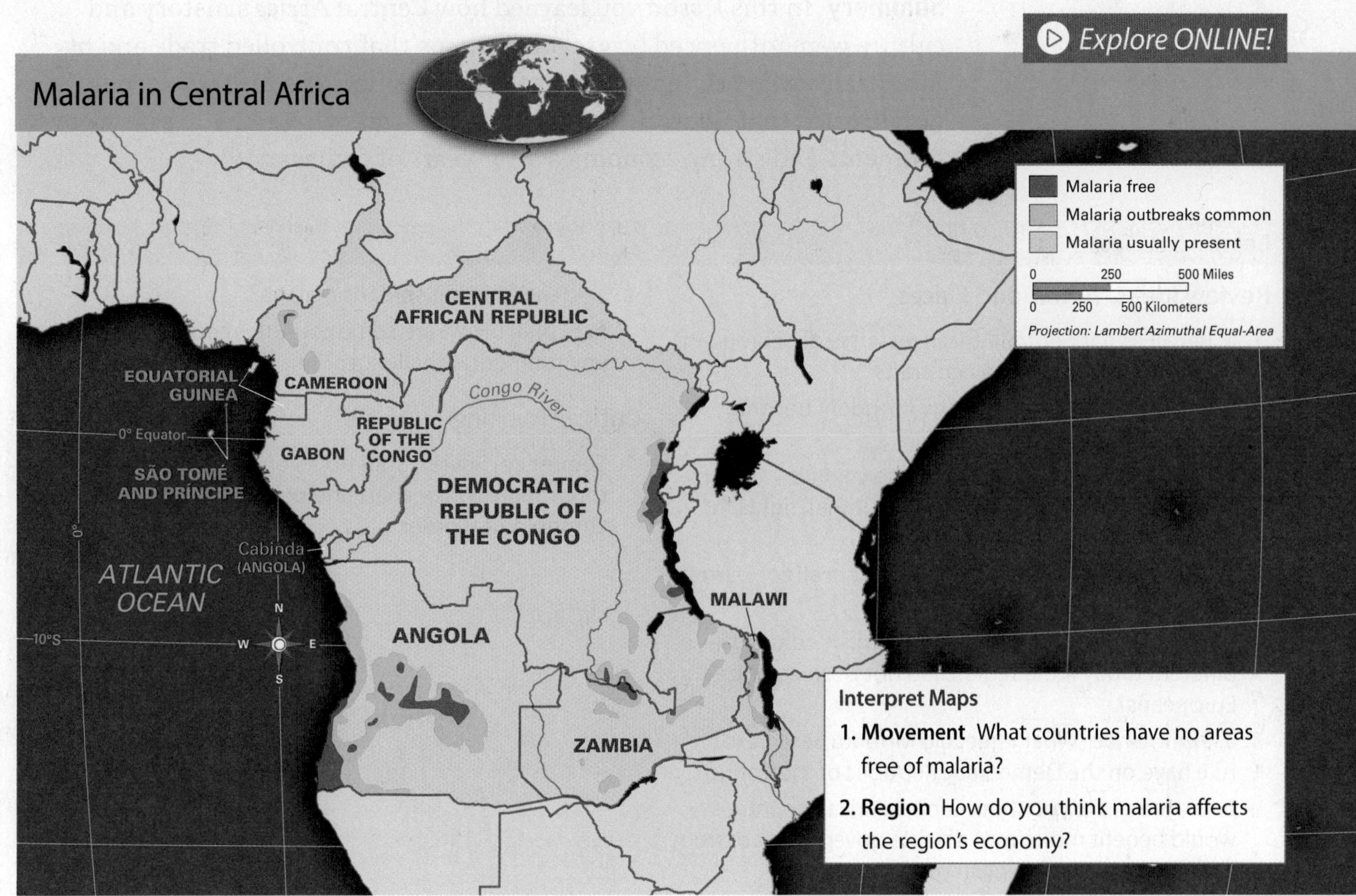

Interpret Maps

1. **Movement** What countries have no areas free of malaria?
2. **Region** How do you think malaria affects the region's economy?

A medical assistant teaches villagers about the prevention of malaria.

In some places, partly because of war, food production has actually declined. Also, food production cannot keep up with the demands of the growing population. The results are food shortages and malnutrition. **Malnutrition** is the condition of not getting enough nutrients from food.

The environment is another important resource that must be managed. Some of Central Africa's most important industries are destroying the environment. Lumber companies cut down trees in the tropical forest, threatening the wildlife that live there. Mining is also harming the environment. Diamonds and copper are mined in huge open pits. This mining process removes large areas of land and destroys the landscape.

Many people in Central Africa and around the world are working hard and spending billions of dollars to improve conditions in the region. National parks have been set up to protect the environment. Projects to provide irrigation and prevent erosion are helping people plant more crops. Central Africa's land and people hold great potential for the future.

Reading Check
Summarize What are some threats to Central Africa's environment?

Summary In this lesson you learned how Central Africa's history and culture were influenced by great kingdoms that controlled trade and by Europeans, who originally came to the region looking for trade goods. You also learned that Central African countries are trying to build stable governments and strong economies after years of civil war.

Lesson 3 Assessment

Review Ideas, Terms, and Places

1. **a. Recall** What Central African resource did Europeans value for making jewelry and crafts?
   b. Explain How did the Kongo Kingdom become important?
   c. Elaborate How do you think the colonial borders affected Central African countries' fights for independence?
2. **a. Summarize** How did the colonial era affect Central Africa's culture?
   b. Elaborate How might Central Africa's culture be different today if the region had not been colonized by Europeans?
3. **a. Summarize** What effect did Mobutu Sese Seko's rule have on the Democratic Republic of the Congo?
   b. Evaluate Do you think Central African countries would benefit more from a stable government or from a strong economy? Explain your answer.
4. **a. Identify** What spreads malaria?
   b. Explain How are some countries coping with environmental challenges?

Critical Thinking

5. **Sequence** Review your notes on Central Africa's history. Create a flow chart and put the major events in chronological order.

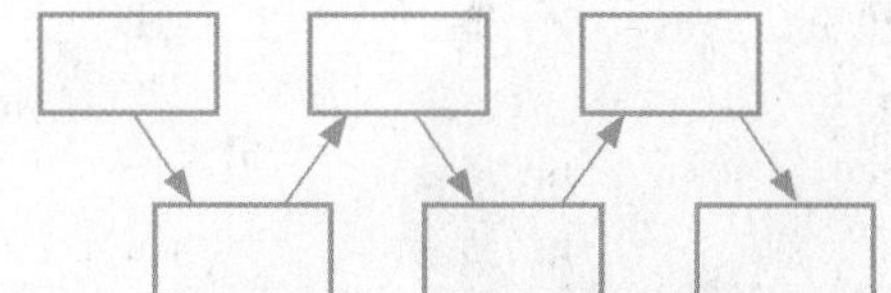

Interpret a Population Pyramid

Define the Skill

A population pyramid is a graph that shows the percentages of males and females by age group in a country's population. The pyramids are split into two sides. Each bar on the left shows the percentage of a country's population that is male and of a certain age. The bars on the right show the same information for females.

Population pyramids help us understand population trends in countries. Countries that have large percentages of young people have populations that are growing rapidly. Countries with more older people are growing slowly or not at all.

Learn the Skill

Interpret information from the population pyramid graph of Angola to answer the following questions.

1. What age group is the largest?
2. What percent of Angola's population is made up of 15- to 19-year-old males?
3. What does this population pyramid tell you about the population trend in Angola?

Practice the Skill

Do research at the library or on the Internet to find age and population data for the United States. Use that information to answer the following questions.

1. What age group is the largest?
2. Are there more males or females over age 80?
3. How would you describe the shape of the population pyramid?

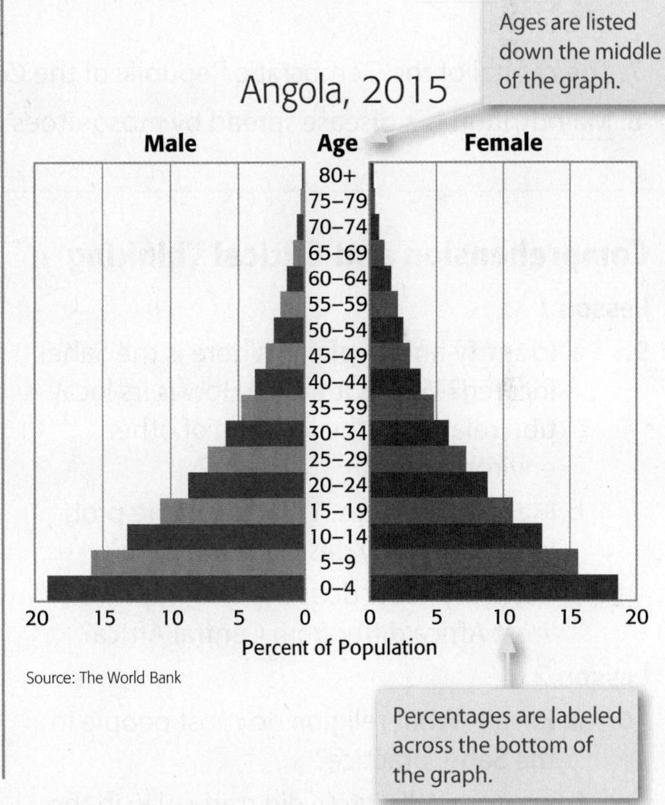

Module 12 Assessment

Review Vocabulary, Terms, and Places

For each statement below, write T if it is true and F if it is false. If the statement is false, write the correct term that would make the sentence a true statement.

1. West Africa's climate is described as savanna because it is organized by zone.
2. Animism, a belief that natural objects have spirits, is a traditional religion in West Africa.
3. An extended family is one that includes a mother, father, children, and close relatives in one household.
4. Loss of crops can cause widespread famine.
5. Timbuktu is the largest city in Nigeria.
6. The Niger River flows through many countries in West Africa and empties into the Gulf of Guinea.
7. The capital of the Democratic Republic of the Congo is Kongo Kingdom.
8. Malnutrition is a disease spread by mosquitoes that causes fever and pain.

Comprehension and Critical Thinking

Lesson 1

9. a. **Identify and Explain** Where is the Sahel located? Why is it there? How is its location related to the location of other environments?
   b. **Make Inferences** What are some problems caused by desertification?
   c. **Contrast** How does the geography of West Africa differ from Central Africa?

Lesson 2

10. a. **Recall** What religion do most people in the Sahel practice?
    b. **Analyze** What role did trade play in the early West African kingdoms and later in West Africa's history?
    c. **Identify** Which country in West Africa has an economy based nearly entirely on oil?

Lesson 3

11. a. **Recall** When did European countries divide Central Africa into colonies?
    b. **Contrast** How do you think the perspectives of the Central Africans and Europeans differed on colonialism? Why do you think they differed?
    c. **Identify** What are the diseases that affect many people in Central Africa?

Reading Skills

Use the Reading Skills taught in this module to complete this activity. Look over your notes and reread Lesson 1. Use the information on climate and vegetation to answer the following questions.

12. How are the Sahara and the Sahel similar?
13. How are the Sahara and the Sahel different?
14. Compare the Sahel and the savanna zone. How are they similar?
15. Contrast the savanna region and the humid tropical region along the coast. How are these areas different?

Social Studies Skills

Interpret a Population Pyramid *Use the graph in the Social Studies Skills of this module to answer the following questions.*

16. **Interpret Graphs** What age group is the smallest?
17. **Evaluate** Use the population pyramid graph to pose and answer a question about population patterns in Angola.
18. **Organize Information** Organize information from the population pyramid graph into a written summary of population trends in Angola.

Map Activity 

19. **West Africa** On a separate sheet of paper, match the letters on the map with their correct labels.

Niger River	Senegal River
Lagos, Nigeria	Mali
Gulf of Guinea	

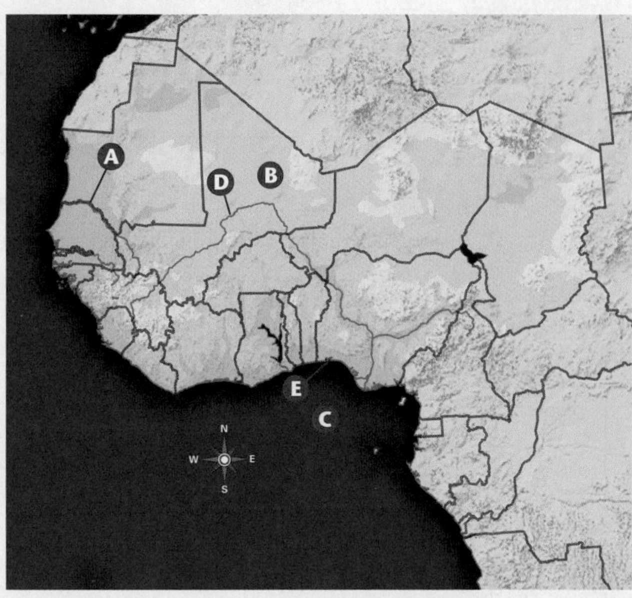

Focus on Writing

20. **Present an Oral Description** Read over your notes. Then prepare a brief oral presentation about a day in the life of someone from West Africa. Tell about the land, climate, and vegetation. Describe the culture, including family life. Tell what this person does for a living. With a partner, practice your presentation. As you present, make eye contact and speak clearly. Plainly state your topic and main ideas. For supporting ideas and details, use descriptive language that will interest your audience. Then listen as your partner presents. Practice active listening and take notes. Ask questions to clarify anything that was unclear or confusing. Review your notes right away to make sure that you understand what was said. Finally, summarize aloud your partner's main points.

Module 13

East and Southern Africa

Essential Question

How has human migration affected the culture and geography of East and Southern Africa?

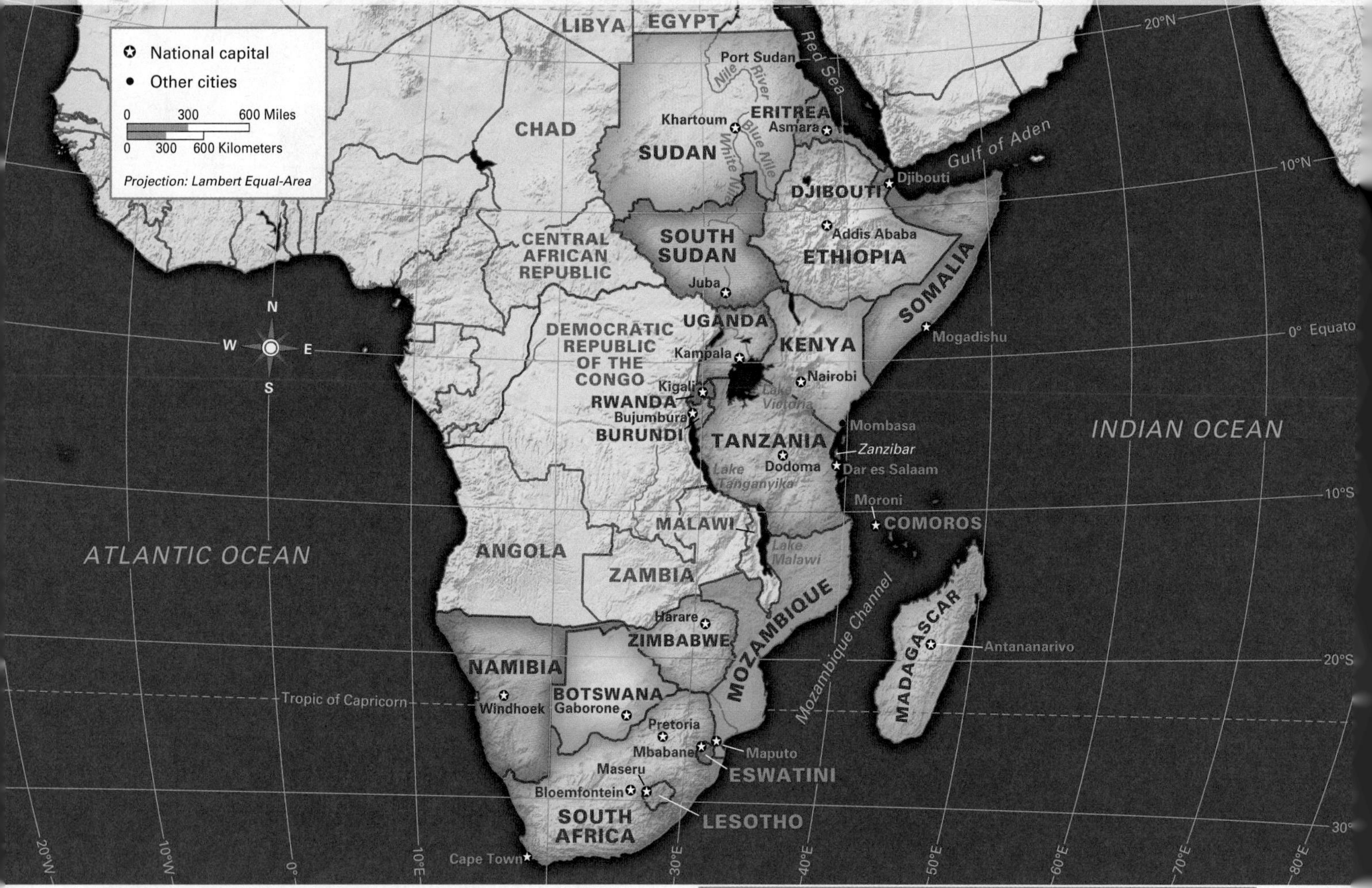

Explore ONLINE!

- Document-Based Investigations
- Graphic Organizers
- Interactive Games
- Channel One News Video: South Africa
- Interactive Chart: Threats to Africa's Wildlife
- Image with Hotspots: Serengeti National Park
- Channel One News Video: Nelson Mandela
- Interactive Table: Southern Africa: Regional Data

In this module, you will learn about the geographic and historical forces that have shaped life in East and Southern Africa.

What You Will Learn

Lesson 1: Physical Geography 421
The Big Idea Rift valleys, plateaus, grassy plains, and diverse climate and vegetation types shape life in East and Southern Africa.

Lesson 2: East Africa 426
The Big Idea East Africa's history and geography have contributed to cultural diversity and ongoing challenges.

Lesson 3: Southern Africa. 433
The Big Idea Since independence, nations in Southern Africa have struggled with inequality and conflict.

Geography The plains surrounding Mount Kilimanjaro are rich in wildlife. Millions of tourists come to visit this part of East Africa each year.

Culture Maasai women in East Africa wear colorful jewelry and traditional clothing.

History Ancient rock art in Southern Africa often shows hunters and animals.

Reading Social Studies

Form Generalizations

READING FOCUS

As you read about different people and cultures, you probably notice many similarities. Seeing those similarities may help you form a generalization. A generalization is a statement that applies to many different situations or people, even though it is based on a few specific situations or people. In the following example, a generalization is formed by combining new information with information from personal experience. Sometimes you might also form a generalization by reading about several new situations, even though you don't have personal experience with the situation.

Several large rivers cross Southern Africa's plains. The Okavango River flows from Angola into a huge basin in Botswana. There, it forms a swampy inland delta that is home to crocodiles, zebras, hippos, and other animals. Many tourists travel to Botswana to see these wild animals in their natural habitat.

1. **What you read:** Tourists will travel to see wild animals.

2. **What you know from personal experience:** My family loves to see wild animals in the zoo.

3. **Generalization:** Many people enjoy seeing wild animals in person.

YOU TRY IT!

Read the following text selections about countries in Southern African. Then, using information from the selections and any prior knowledge that you might have, form a generalization about a country's economy and its political stability.

1. Zimbabwe has gold and copper mines as well as productive agriculture and manufacturing. However, high inflation, debts, and war have hurt the economy.
2. Mozambique is one of the world's poorest countries. The economy has been badly damaged by civil war, but it is improving.
3. Comoros is a country made up of four tiny islands. It suffers from a lack of resources and political instability. The government of Comoros is struggling to improve education and promote tourism.

As you read this module, use what you already know along with new information to form generalizations about East and Southern Africa.

Physical Geography

The Big Idea

Rift valleys, plateaus, grassy plains, and diverse climate and vegetation types shape life in East and Southern Africa.

Main Ideas

- East and Southern Africa's physical features range from rift valleys to sweeping plateaus.
- Location and elevation shape East and Southern Africa's climate and vegetation.
- Water and minerals are vital resources in East and Southern Africa.

Key Terms and Places

rift valley
Great Rift Valley
escarpment
Mount Kilimanjaro
Serengeti Plain
veld
Namib Desert
droughts

If YOU lived there . . .

You and your friends are planning to hike up Mount Kilimanjaro, near the equator in Tanzania. It is hot in your camp at the base of the mountain. You're wearing shorts and a T-shirt, but your guide tells you to pack a fleece jacket and jeans. You start your climb, and soon you understand this advice. The air is much colder, and there's snow on the nearby peaks.

Why is it cold at the top of the mountain?

Physical Features

Geographically, East and Southern Africa are vast regions with spectacularly varied landscapes and wildlife. On a visit to the region, you might see steep mountains, deep gorges, lakes, and a series of plateaus featuring dry grasslands, sandy savannas, and deserts.

Rift Valleys Locate the Great Rift Valley on the physical map of East and Southern Africa. Seen from the air, the Great Rift Valley looks like a giant scar, cutting across Africa from the Red Sea to Mozambique. A **rift valley** is a long narrow valley with flat floors and steep walls. Rift valleys form when Earth's tectonic plates pull away from one another at two parallel fault lines. When the plates pull apart, the land between the faults drops down, forming a valley floor.

The **Great Rift Valley** is the largest rift on Earth. In fact, it extends beyond Africa, northward into Syria, and contains many rifts. In Africa, the Great Rift Valley is made up of two rifts—the eastern rift and the western rift. The steep rift walls form a series of high cliffs. These cliffs rise as much as 6,000 feet (1,829 m). The rifts contain a number of active and dormant volcanoes and are lined by plateaus and mountains.

Plateaus and Mountains East and Southern Africa have many high plateaus. Plateaus are extensive areas of flat upland. Often they are bound by an **escarpment,** a steep slope that separates the plateau from surrounding low-lying land. Some plateaus are bound by mountains.

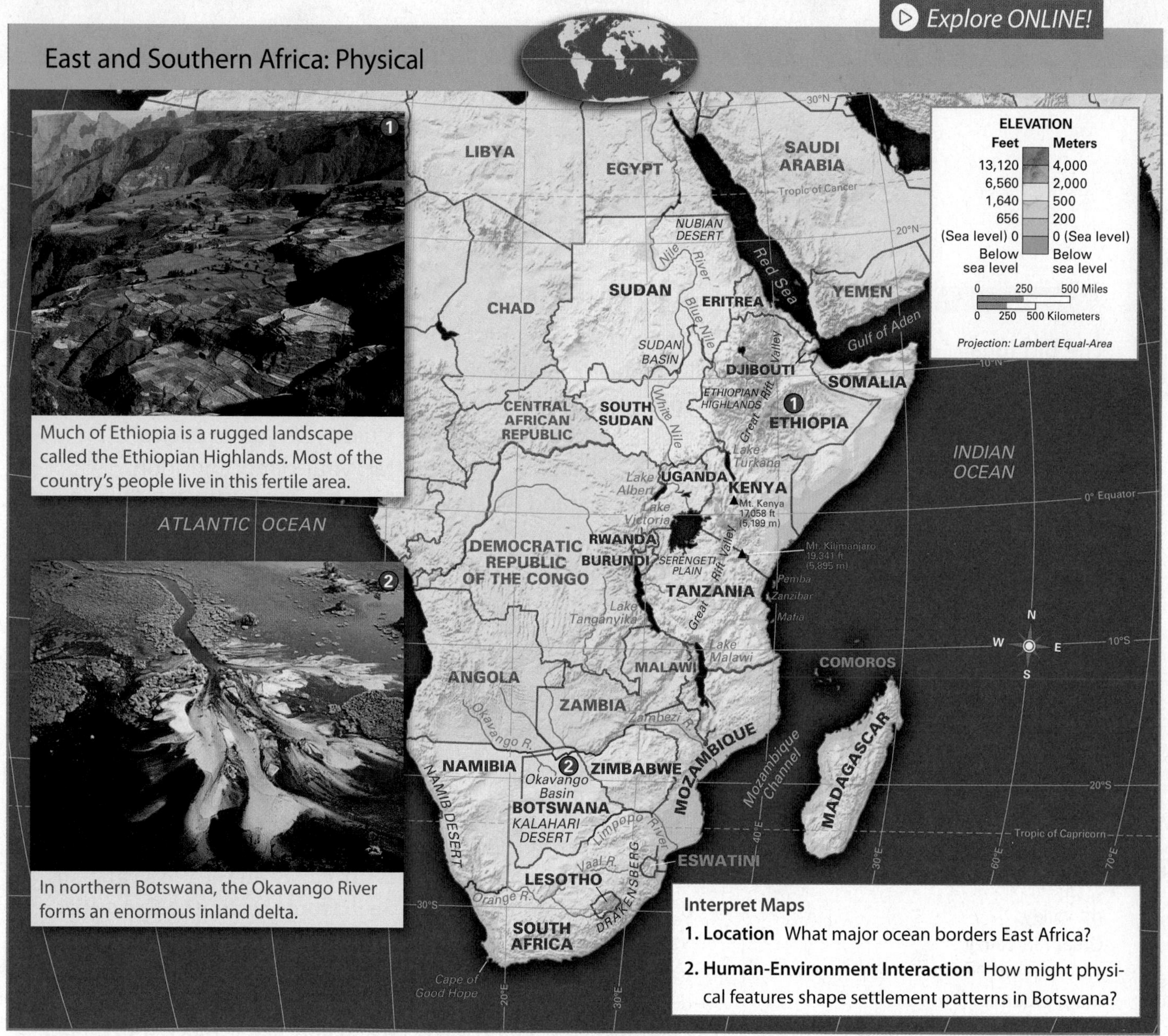

1 Much of Ethiopia is a rugged landscape called the Ethiopian Highlands. Most of the country's people live in this fertile area.

2 In northern Botswana, the Okavango River forms an enormous inland delta.

Interpret Maps

1. **Location** What major ocean borders East Africa?
2. **Human-Environment Interaction** How might physical features shape settlement patterns in Botswana?

Most of Southern Africa lies on a plateau. Parts of this plateau reach more than 4,000 feet (1,219 m) above sea level. The land drops sharply toward coastal areas. In South Africa, the southeastern part of the escarpment is made up of a mountain range called the Drakensberg (DRAH-kuhnz-buhrk). The peaks rise as high as 11,425 feet (3,482 m). Farther north, another mountain range, the Inyanga (in-YANG-guh) Mountains, separates Zimbabwe and Mozambique. Southern Africa also has mountains along its western coast.

The East African Plateau in parts of Kenya, Tanzania, and Uganda is higher than the plateau in Southern Africa. Rift valleys run north and south through this plateau. To the east, high volcanic mountains tower over the plateau. The highest mountain in Africa, **Mount Kilimanjaro** (ki-luh-muhn-JAHR-oh), rises to 19,340 feet (5,895 m). Despite Kilimanjaro's location near the equator, the mountain's peak has long been covered in snow. This much colder climate is caused by Kilimanjaro's high elevation.

Farther north, the Ethiopian Highlands form another significant plateau region. Deep river valleys cut through these mountainous and rugged highlands.

Plains Grassy plains cover wide expanses of the plateaus in East and Southern Africa. For example, plains stretch as far as the eye can see along the eastern rift in Tanzania and Kenya. Wildlife thrives on Tanzania's **Serengeti Plain,** one of the region's largest plains. The plain's grasses, trees, and water provide nutrition for elephants, giraffes, lions, cheetahs, and zebras. To protect its wildlife, Tanzania established a national park.

Southern Africa's narrow coastal area and wide plateaus are also covered with grassy plains. These flat plains are home to animals such as lions, leopards, elephants, baboons, and antelope.

Rivers and Lakes East Africa has a number of rivers and large lakes. The world's longest river, the Nile, begins in East Africa. The Nile is formed by the meeting of the Blue Nile and the White Nile at Khartoum, Sudan. The White Nile flows from Africa's largest lake, Lake Victoria. The Blue Nile forms from waters that run down from Ethiopia's highlands. As the Nile flows north to the Mediterranean Sea, its banks provide a narrow but extremely fertile strip of land beyond which there is only desert.

Several large rivers cross Southern Africa's plains. The Okavango River flows from Angola into a huge basin in Botswana. There, it forms a swampy inland delta that is home to crocodiles, zebras, hippos, and other animals. Many tourists travel to Botswana to see these wild animals in their natural habitat. The Orange River passes through the rocky Augrabies (oh-KRAH-bees) Falls as it flows to the Atlantic Ocean. During the rainy season, the water cascades down 19 separate waterfalls with a thunderous roar. **Features** such as waterfalls block ships from sailing up these rivers. Still, in an otherwise dry area, these rivers provide farmers with a source of water to irrigate farmland.

Academic Vocabulary
features characteristics

Reading Check
Describe What are East and Southern Africa's main physical features?

Climate and Vegetation

When you think of Africa, do you think of a hot or a cold place? Wet or dry? Many people think all of Africa is hot and dry. However, East and Southern Africa are home to a variety of climate and vegetation types, including some that might surprise you.

Highlands Compared to other equatorial regions, East Africa is cool and dry. This is due to high elevations and a rain shadow effect that prevents wet weather from entering into the region from the west.

The plateaus and mountains north of the equator have a cool, highland climate and dense forests. The highlands experience heavier rainfall than the low-lying, drier valleys in the region. This mild climate makes farming possible. As a result, most of the region's population lives in the highlands.

Savanna and Deserts A large savanna region extends south from the equator, covering much of East and Southern Africa. Shrubs and short trees grow on the grassy plains of the savanna. In South Africa, these open

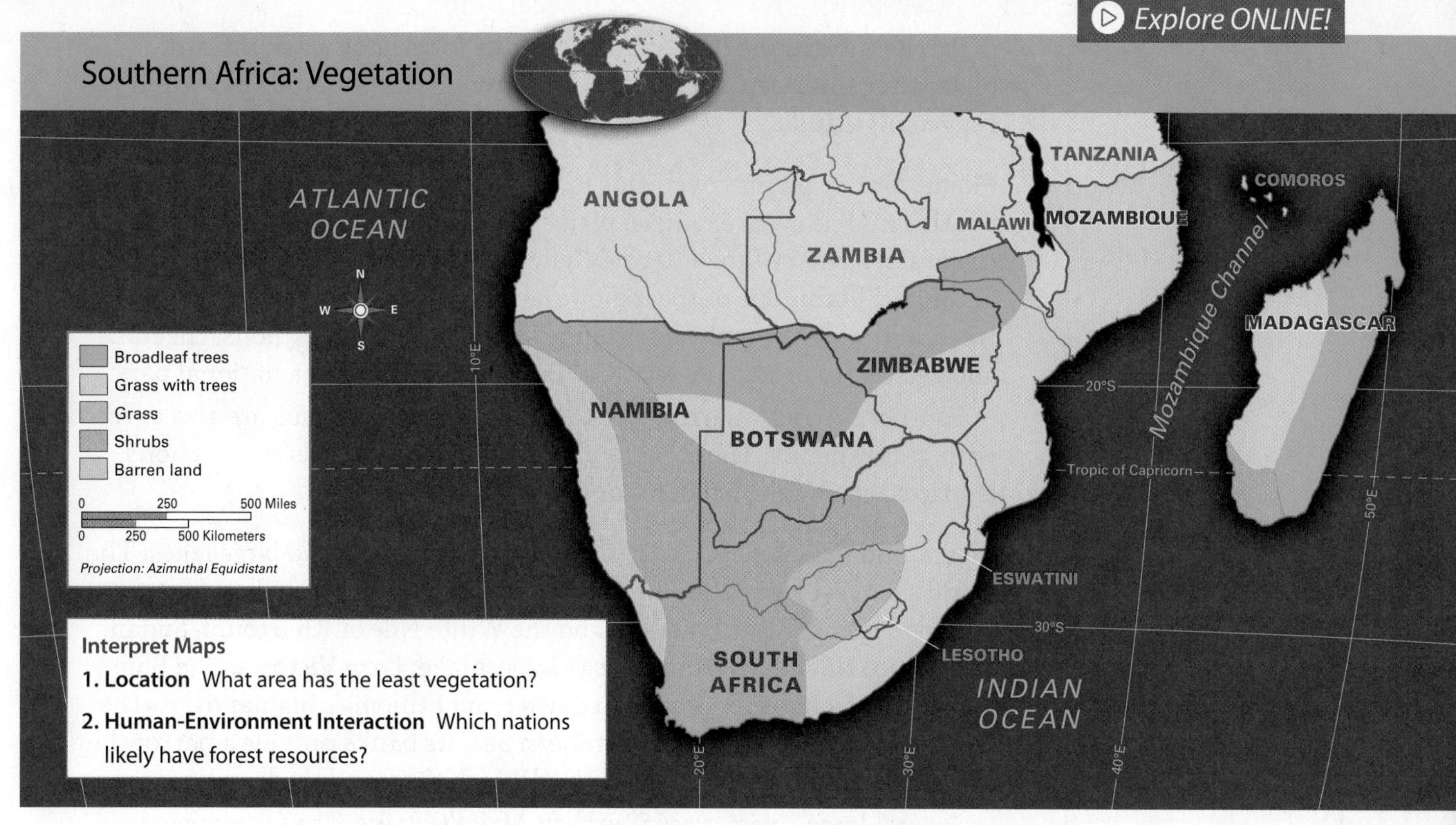

Interpret Maps

1. **Location** What area has the least vegetation?
2. **Human-Environment Interaction** Which nations likely have forest resources?

grassland areas are called the **veld** (VELT). To the veld's west, the savanna gives way to steppe and desert climates. Vegetation is limited to shrubs and hardy grasses that are adapted to water shortages.

Strictly speaking, Southern Africa's Kalahari Desert is not a desert. Rather, it is a huge sandy savanna that covers most of Botswana and parts of South Africa and Namibia. In the north, where it gets enough rain, the Kalahari's sandy plains support grasses and scattered shrubs and trees. In the southwest, the Kalahari merges with the **Namib Desert** on the Atlantic coast of Southern Africa. Some parts of the Namib get as little as a half inch (13 mm) of rainfall per year. In this dry area, plants get water from dew and fog rather than from rain.

Tropical Forests Unlike the mainland, Madagascar has lush vegetation and tropical forests. It also has many animals found nowhere else. For example, some 50 species of lemurs, relatives of apes, live only on this island. However, the destruction of Madagascar's forests has endangered many of the island's animals.

Reading Check
Summarize What is the climate like in East and Southern Africa?

Resources

Water is a vital resource for human health, wildlife, and industry in East and Southern Africa. Rivers supply hydroelectricity and water for irrigation. Where rain is plentiful or irrigation is possible, farmers can grow a wide range of crops.

However, water is not distributed evenly across East and Southern Africa. Eritrea, Somalia, and South Africa have especially low rates of annual rainfall. Moreover, population growth, economic development, and pollution place additional stress on already limited water supplies. As a result, many people living in these countries have little or no access to safe drinking water.

Seasonal droughts are also common in East and Southern Africa. **Droughts** are periods when little rain falls and crops are damaged. During a drought, crops and the grasses for cattle die and people begin to starve. Several times in recent decades, droughts have affected the people of East and Southern Africa.

In recent years, significant discoveries of gas and oil resources have been made in East and Southern Africa. In 2012, one of the world's largest natural gas deposits was discovered in Mozambique. Tanzania, Uganda, and Kenya are also rich in gas and oil resources.

Southern Africa is abundant in other natural resources as well. Madagascar's forests provide timber. The region's most valuable resources, however, are minerals. Mines in South Africa produce most of the world's gold. In addition, South Africa, Botswana, and Namibia have productive diamond mines. Other mineral resources in Southern Africa include coal, platinum, copper, uranium, and iron ore. Although mining is very important to regional economies, the mines and the pollution they produce have damaging effects on surrounding natural environments.

Reading Check
Describe What resources are found in East and Southern Africa?

Summary and Preview In this lesson you learned about the geography, climate, and resources of East and Southern Africa. Next you will learn about East Africa's rich history and culture.

Lesson 1 Assessment

Review Ideas, Terms, and Places

1. **a. Define** What are rift valleys?
   b. Explain Why is there snow on Mount Kilimanjaro?
2. **a. Recall** Where is Southern Africa's driest climate?
   b. Develop How are the climates of some areas of East Africa affected by elevation?
3. **a. Explain** How do you think South Africa's gold and diamond mines affect its economy?
   b. Elaborate How might pollution and the uneven distribution of water affect irrigation, trade, industry, and drinking water in East and Southern Africa?

Critical Thinking

4. **Categorize** Using your notes and this chart, place details about East Africa's physical features into different categories.

Physical Features			
Rift Valleys	Plateaus and Mountains	Plains	Rivers and Lakes

East Africa

The Big Idea

East Africa's history and geography have contributed to cultural diversity and ongoing challenges.

Main Ideas

- Religion, trade, and European imperialism have shaped East Africa's history.
- East Africa is home to a diversity of languages and religions.
- Though resource rich, nations in East Africa have suffered conflicts, poverty, and drought.
- The Horn of Africa is one of the most troubled regions of the world.

Key Terms and Places

Zanzibar
imperialism
safari
geothermal energy
Darfur
genocide
Mogadishu

If YOU lived there . . .

You live on the island of Zanzibar, part of the country of Tanzania. Your hometown has beautiful beaches, grand palaces, and historic sites associated with the East African slave trade. Although you and your friends learn English in school, you speak the African language of Swahili to each other.

How has your country's history affected your life today?

History

Many historical forces have shaped East Africa. Top among these are religion, imperialism, and independence movements.

Religion Christian missionaries from Egypt brought Christianity to East Africa as early as the AD 300s. Over time, Ethiopian Christianity developed its own unique traditions that blended with local African customs. In the early 1200s a powerful Christian emperor named Lalibela ruled Ethiopia. Lalibela is best known for building 11 rock churches, which are still in use today.

By about AD 700, Islam was a major religion in North Africa. Gradually, Muslim Arabs from Egypt spread Islam into northern Sudan. At the same time, Muslim city-states, such as Mogadishu and Mombasa, developed along the East African coast. These coastal cities became Islamic centers and grew wealthy from overseas trade.

Trade and Slavery East Africa's coastal cities linked foreign merchants with goods from Africa's interior. These merchants brought goods such as glassware, porcelain, and silk to Africa. They departed with coconut oil, copper, leopard skins, ivory, and gold. In addition, enslaved Africans captured in the interior were exported through coastal cities to markets in Arabia, Persia, and India. By the early 1500s the Portuguese had built forts and settlements along East Africa's coast to support the slave trade. In the late 1700s the island of **Zanzibar** became an international slave-trading center. Later, Zanzibar's slave population was forced to harvest cloves and other spices on plantations.

The Rock Churches of Lalibela, Ethiopia

In the 1200s highly skilled Ethiopian architects and craftspeople built churches, like this one, from the top down out of a single block of stone.

Workers dug deep trenches to carve out the church.

Craftspeople used special tools to carve windows and doors out of solid rock.

Analyze Visuals
What Christian symbol does the church resemble?

European Imperialism As European countries industrialized, their need for raw materials rose sharply. To meet this demand, they turned to other world regions. In Africa, they claimed lands to gain access to gold, ivory, rubber, and other natural resources. Building an empire by claiming lands, setting up colonies, and controlling those areas is called **imperialism.**

European powers competed with each other to control Africa. The British gained control over much of East Africa. In 1884 European leaders met to divide Africa among themselves. They drew boundaries that split some ethnic groups apart. In other areas, unfriendly groups were lumped together. To maintain power, colonial rulers appointed African deputies. Many deputies were African chiefs, who favored their own peoples. This practice contributed to ethnic rivalries.

After 1945, nationalist movements formed across Africa. They pressed for self-rule. Some efforts turned violent. In the 1950s a militant nationalist group in Kenya called the Mau Mau used violence and terror to resist British rule. The British fought back with brutal force, eventually defeating the Mau Mau. After eight years of conflict, an estimated 11,000 Mau Mau and just 32 white settlers were killed. Still, by the 1960s Kenya, like most other nations in East Africa, gained its independence.

Reading Check
Explain How did nationalist movements impact Kenya?

Culture

East Africa's history has contributed to its present-day cultural diversity. Today, the region is home to a variety of languages and religions.

Language Hundreds of languages are spoken in East Africa. With about 80 million speakers, Swahili is the most widely spoken language. The language developed in East Africa's coastal city-states, where the languages of Africans and Arab traders blended. Even the term *Swahili* comes from an

Explore ONLINE!

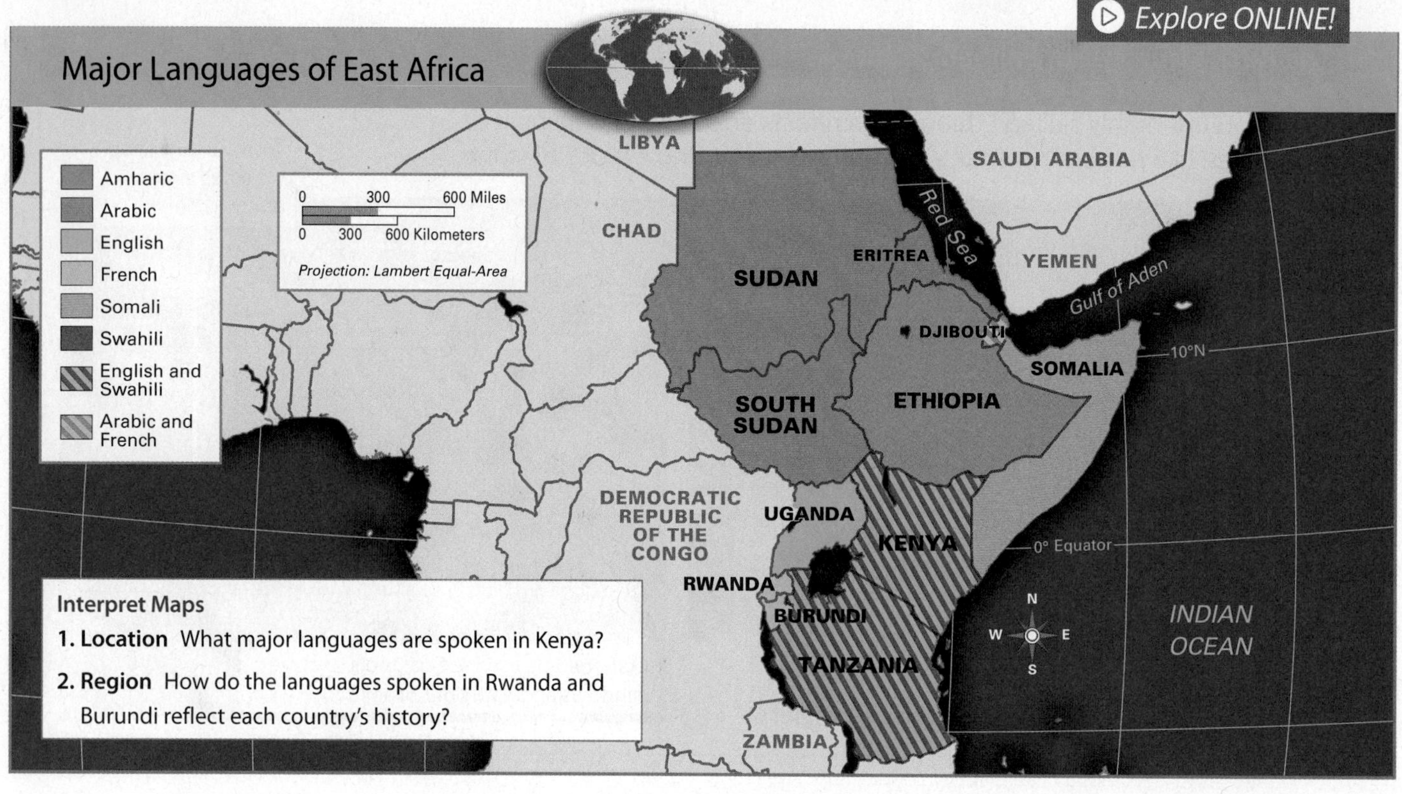

Interpret Maps

1. **Location** What major languages are spoken in Kenya?
2. **Region** How do the languages spoken in Rwanda and Burundi reflect each country's history?

Arabic word meaning "coast." Other African languages include Amharic in Ethiopia and Somali in Somalia. Language use in East Africa has also been influenced by European imperialism. Today, French is an official language in Rwanda, Burundi, and Djibouti. English is the primary language of millions of people in Uganda, Kenya, and Tanzania.

Reading Check
Analyze Causes Why might people in East Africa speak a European language?

Religion East Africa is home to a great diversity of religions. The largest religious groups are Christian and Muslim. Most Ethiopians are Christian, while most Sudanese and Somalis are Muslim. Many East Africans follow animist religions. Animists believe the natural world contains spirits. Some people combine animist worship with religions such as Christianity.

East Africa Today

The nations in East Africa's Great Rift Valley are rich in natural resources—including wildlife—but people disagree about the best way to use them. Droughts can make life here difficult. In addition, political and ethnic conflicts have led to unrest and violence in some areas of the region.

Kenya and Tanzania Though Kenya and Tanzania are among the world's poorest nations, both are popular tourist destinations. With nearly 3 million visitors each year, tourism is a major source of income for both countries. Many tourists visit to go on a **safari,** an overland journey to view African wildlife.

Agriculture dominates Kenya's economy. Kenya's rich volcanic soil sustains crops of coffee, flowers, and tea that are grown for exports. Much of Kenya's land has been set aside as national parks. Though some would like to farm these areas, farming might endanger wildlife and Kenya's tourist economy.

Serengeti National Park

The Serengeti Plain is home to one of the world's greatest concentrations of wildlife. In Tanzania, part of the plain is a national park. About 350,000 people visit the Serengeti National Park each year to view its diverse wildlife.

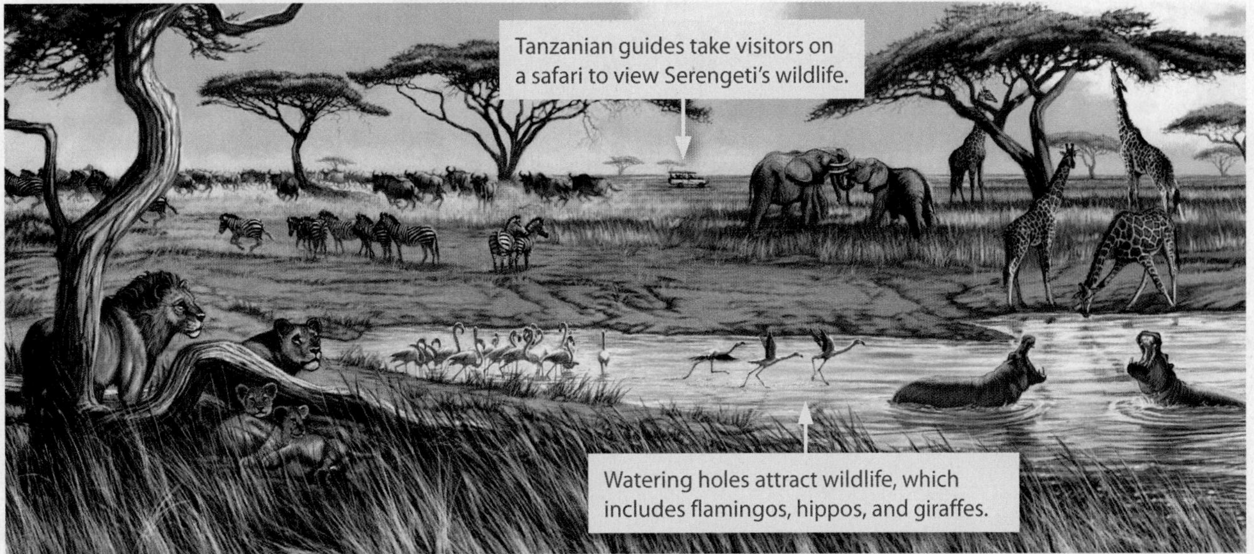

Analyze Visuals
How would you describe the Serengeti landscape?

Kenya's economy also benefits from **geothermal energy,** energy produced from the heat of Earth's interior. This heat—in the form of extremely hot steam—comes up to the surface through cracks in the rift valleys.

Tanzania is particularly rich in gold and diamonds. However, it is still a poor country of mainly subsistence farmers. Poor soils and limited technology have restricted the nation's productivity.

Both Kenya and Tanzania boast vibrant modern cities with colorful outdoor markets, soaring skyscrapers, and beautiful parks. Kenya's capital, Nairobi, also serves as the country's industrial center. Nairobi is well connected to the rest of East Africa by a network of railways. By rail, Kenyans transport tea and other crops to Mombasa, a major port city on Kenya's coast. Tanzania's largest city and business center is Dar es Salaam, a port city on the Indian Ocean with about 5 million people.

Even though Kenya and Tanzania are peaceful countries, Dar es Salaam and Nairobi have both endured terrorist attacks. In 1998 members of the al-Qaeda terrorist group bombed the U.S. embassies in Dar es Salaam and Nairobi. Most of the more than 250 people killed and the thousands injured were Africans.

Sudan and Uganda Sudan is a mix of Arab, Afro-Arab, and African cultures. Its people follow Muslim, animist, and Christian traditions. Sudanese Arabs, Sudan's majority population, hold political power. Sudan's government has abused the human rights of ethnic and religious minorities. It has also

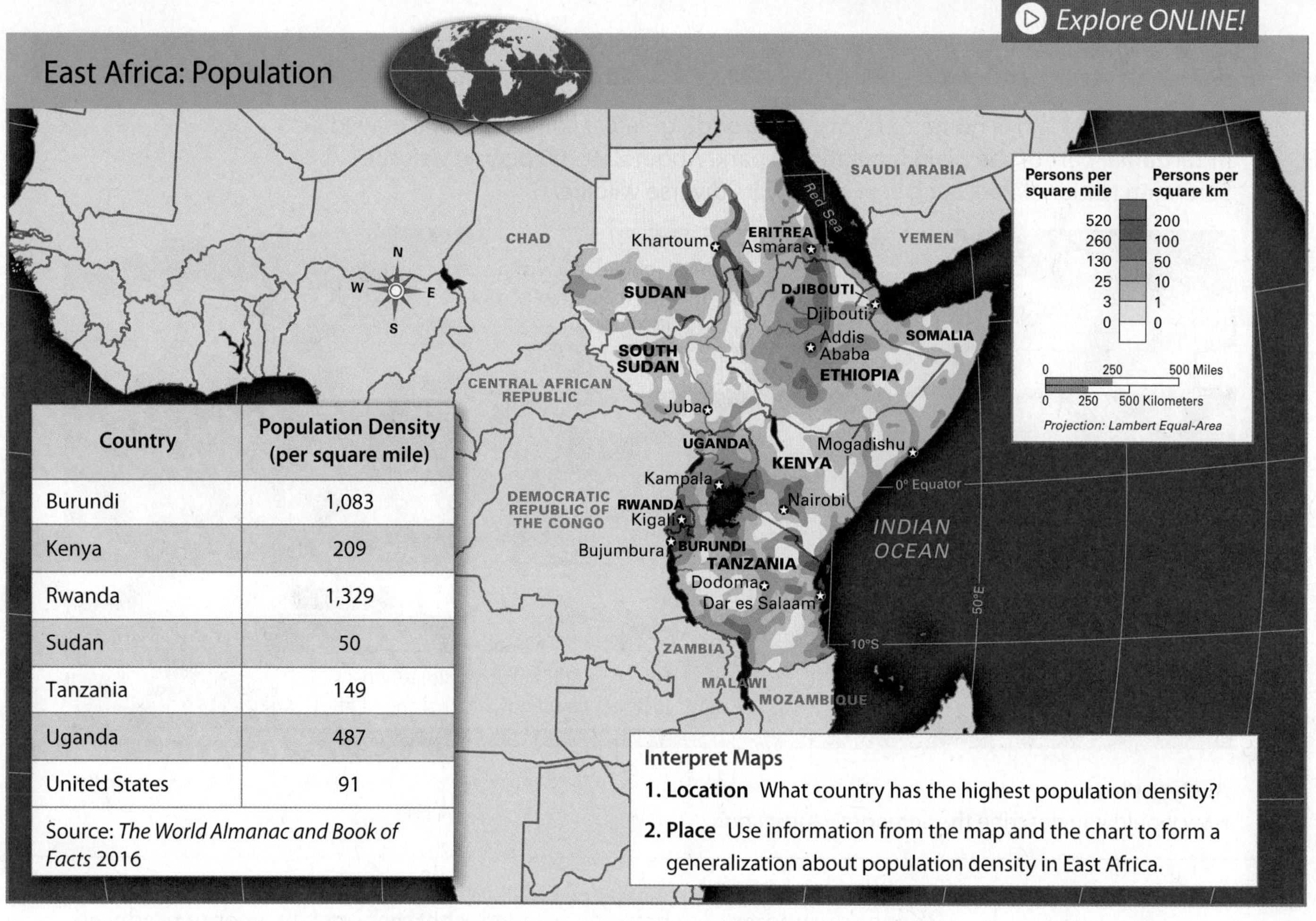

Country	Population Density (per square mile)
Burundi	1,083
Kenya	209
Rwanda	1,329
Sudan	50
Tanzania	149
Uganda	487
United States	91

Source: *The World Almanac and Book of Facts* 2016

Interpret Maps

1. **Location** What country has the highest population density?
2. **Place** Use information from the map and the chart to form a generalization about population density in East Africa.

supported a violent Arab militia, the Janjaweed. Since 1984 the Janjaweed has killed an estimated 1.5 million Christians. From 2003 to 2008 the Janjaweed killed hundreds of thousands of ethnically African Sudanese in a region called **Darfur.** Millions more fled Darfur as refugees.

In 2011 South Sudan gained independence, becoming Africa's newest country. South Sudan's population is mostly African and follows animist or Christian faiths.

Today, Uganda is still recovering from several decades of military dictatorship. Since 1986 Uganda has become more democratic, but economic progress has been slow. About 80 percent of Uganda's workforce is employed in agriculture, with coffee as the country's major export.

Rwanda and Burundi Rwanda and Burundi are two of the most densely populated countries in all of Africa. Both are located in fertile highlands and share a history as German and, later, Belgian colonies. Rwanda and Burundi are populated by two main ethnic groups—the Tutsi and the Hutu. Since gaining independence from Belgium, these nations have experienced ethnic conflict, much of which is rooted in the national borders drawn by Europeans that ignored or split traditional ethnic territories.

In the 1990s hatred between the Hutu and the Tutsi led to **genocide** in Rwanda. A genocide is the intentional destruction of a people. The Hutu tried to completely wipe out the Tutsi. Armed bands of Hutu killed hundreds of thousands of Tutsi.

Reading Check
Analyze What were some of the effects of ethnic conflict in Sudan and Rwanda?

Barriers to Education in East Africa

Children in East Africa face many barriers to education, including poverty, war, gender inequality, and a lack of schools. Sudan has one of the highest out-of-school rates in the region. Nearly 3 million Sudanese children do not attend school, and girls are often specifically excluded. As a result, Sudan's literacy rate is 83 percent for males and 69 percent for females. By contrast, Kenya has made education a priority for all students. Its literacy rate is 81 percent for males and 75 percent for females.

Analyze Visuals
What challenges might students in this Sudanese classroom face?

The Horn of Africa

Four East African countries along the Red Sea and the Indian Ocean are called the Horn of Africa. On a map, these countries—Eritrea, Djibouti, Somalia, and Ethiopia—resemble the horn of a rhinoceros. For many years, the Horn of Africa has been one of the world's most troubled regions.

Eritrea Eritrea's path to independence has been long. A former Italian and British colony, Eritrea was annexed by Ethiopia in the 1960s. In 1992, after 32 years of armed conflict, Eritrea finally gained independence. However, independence did not bring peace. Bloody clashes with Yemen and neighbors Djibouti and Ethiopia have followed.

In recent years, Eritrea has been widely criticized as one the world's most secretive states and for its human rights abuses. In 2015 more than 26,000 Eritrean refugees between the ages of 18 and 34 fled to Europe. Thousands more fled to other countries.

Djibouti Located on a narrow strait connecting the Red Sea and the Indian Ocean, Djibouti (ji-BOO-tee) is a small, desert country. The strait lies along a major shipping route. The country's capital and major port is also called Djibouti. Since Djibouti has few resources, the port is a major source of income.

Though it gained independence from France in 1977, Djibouti continues to receive economic and military support from France. Djibouti is home to two major ethnic groups—the Issa and the Afar. The Issa are closely related to the people of Somalia. The Afar are related to the people of Ethiopia. Members of both groups are Muslim. In the early 1990s a civil war between the Afar and Issa broke out. In 2001 the two groups signed a peace treaty, which ended the fighting.

Somalia Somalia's deserts and dry savannas are not suitable for farming. Still, its economy relies heavily on agriculture. Major crops include bananas, sorghum, and rice. Many Somalis are nomadic herders, and fishing is also important.

In the Ethiopian Highlands, many children, like these boys, spend their days herding animals across miles of rocky terrain.

Most Somalis are Muslim, ethnically Somali, and speak the Somali language. Despite these shared cultural traits, Somalia has been torn apart by chaos and violence. Somalia has no central government of any kind. Different clans fight over grazing rights and control of port cities such as **Mogadishu.**

In the 1990s Somalis experienced widespread starvation caused by a civil war and a severe drought. The United Nations sent aid and troops to the country. Since the civil war, Somali pirates have terrorized the coast, capturing cargo ships and demanding millions of dollars in ransom money.

Ethiopia Landlocked Ethiopia is the only nation in the Horn of Africa to have escaped European colonization. In addition to providing a natural defense, Ethiopia's mountains and highlands have rich, volcanic soil. Agriculture is the nation's chief economic activity. Many people also herd sheep and cattle. Top exports include coffee, vegetables, livestock, and oilseeds.

Long periods of severe drought have affected all of the nations in the Horn of Africa. In 2011 East Africa faced what many called the worst drought in 60 years. The drought killed crops, causing a severe food crisis for about 9.5 million people living in Ethiopia, Somalia, Kenya, and Djibouti.

Reading Check
Form Generalizations
How has the geography of East Africa shaped economic activity?

Summary and Preview In this lesson you learned about East Africa's past and present. Next you will learn about the countries of Southern Africa.

Lesson 2 Assessment

Review Ideas, Terms, and Places

1. a. **Define** What is imperialism?
   b. **Explain** Why do you think Europeans wanted colonies in East Africa?
   c. **Describe** Explain the factors behind and the impact of the cultural diffusion of Christianity and Islam to East Africa.
2. a. **Define** What is geothermal energy?
   b. **Generalize** Why are Kenyans not allowed to farm in national parks?
3. a. **Define** What is genocide?
   b. **Compare and Contrast** How have recent conflicts in Rwanda and Sudan been similar and different?
   c. **Analyze** Why are millions of Sudanese refugees?
4. a. **Recall** What two major world religions are practiced in Ethiopia?
   b. **Analyze** How do you think Djibouti's location has helped its economy?

Critical Thinking

5. **Summarize** Draw a chart like this one. Using your notes, summarize in at least two sentences what you learned about each topic.

History	
Culture	
East Africa	
The Horn of Africa	

Southern Africa

The Big Idea

Since independence, nations in Southern Africa have struggled with inequality and conflict.

Main Ideas

- Southern Africa's history began with hunter-gatherers, followed by great empires and European settlements.
- The cultures of Southern Africa are rich in different languages, religions, customs, and art.
- The countries of Southern Africa are diverse in their resources and governments.
- Today, the people of Southern Africa face economic, environmental, and health challenges.

Key Terms and Places

Great Zimbabwe
Cape of Good Hope
Boers
Afrikaners
apartheid
townships
sanctions
Cape Town
enclave

If YOU lived there . . .

You are an economic adviser in Botswana. In recent years, your country has made progress toward improving people's lives, but you think there is room for improvement. Botswana already has amazing natural landscapes and fascinating animals. One way you plan to help the economy is by promoting tourism.

What could your country do to attract more tourists?

History

Southern Africa's earliest people belonged to a language group called the Khoisan. The Khoisan were hunter-gatherers and herders. About 2,000 years ago, Bantu-speaking people from West and Central Africa joined them. The Bantus' knowledge of farming and iron working helped make them the dominant group in the region. Much later, Europeans arrived and forever changed Southern Africa and its people.

Great Zimbabwe One Bantu group, the Shona, built an empire that peaked in the 1400s. The Shona farmed, raised cattle, and traded gold with other groups on the coast. Their empire included much of what is now Zimbabwe and Mozambique. The Shona are best known for **Great Zimbabwe,** their stone-walled capital. Founded in the late 1000s, Great Zimbabwe was a small trading and herding center. In the 1100s the population grew, as did gold mining and farming. These resources helped the city become the center of a large trading network. At its peak, Great Zimbabwe may have had 10,000 to 20,000 residents.

Archaeologists have found Chinese porcelain and glass beads from India at Great Zimbabwe. Such artifacts suggest the Shona traded with the Swahili, who lived on the East African coast. Through the Swahili, the Shona were connected to an Indian Ocean trade network.

Trade made Great Zimbabwe's rulers wealthy and powerful. However, in the 1400s the gold trade declined. Deprived of its main source of wealth, Great Zimbabwe weakened. By 1500 it was no longer a capital and trading center.

Great Zimbabwe

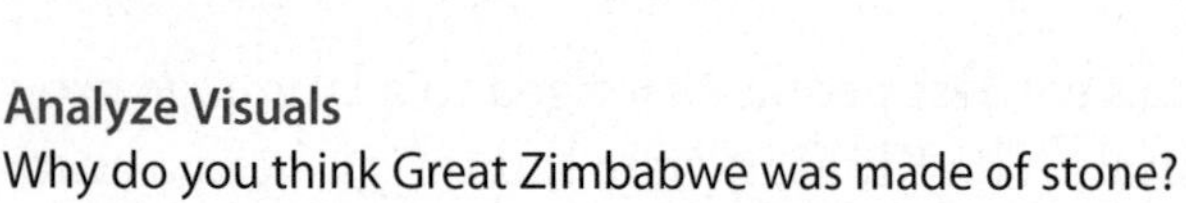

Highly skilled craftspeople built several stone walls that surrounded the Shona capital of Great Zimbabwe. Today, the ruins are a World Heritage Site.

Analyze Visuals
Why do you think Great Zimbabwe was made of stone?

European Colonization In the late 1400s Portuguese traders explored Southern Africa on their way to Asia. The trip was long and difficult, so traders set up bases on the Southern African coast. These bases provided ships with supplies. In 1652 the Dutch East India Company set up a trade station at a natural harbor near the **Cape of Good Hope.** The Cape sits at the tip of Africa. Its mild climate was similar to the climate the Dutch were used to in the Netherlands. The Cape Colony provided supplies for Dutch ships sailing between the East Indies and the Netherlands. In 1657 the company allowed some workers to start their own farms. These farmers became known as **Boers.**

The arrival of Europeans devastated local populations. Many died of diseases, such as small pox. The survivors fought the colonists or became their slaves or servants.

More European settlers—Dutch, French, and German—soon arrived on the Cape. These settlers and their descendants were called **Afrikaners.** Over time, a new language called Afrikaans emerged in the Cape Colony. Afrikaans combined Dutch with Khoisan and Bantu words. German, French, and English also influenced the language's development.

In the early 1800s the British took control of the Cape. They clashed with the Boers. Many Boers packed their belongings into wagons and moved east and north. Those moving north were intruders in Zulu territory. The Zulu were a Bantu-speaking group and the mightiest fighting force in Southern Africa. The Boers and the Zulu fought over land.

This painting by artist Charles Bell (1813–1882) shows the 1652 arrival of Dutch settlers in Table Bay, near the Cape of Good Hope.

Eventually, the British wanted Zulu land, too. The British also set their eyes on the rich deposits of gold and diamonds that Afrikaners in the interior of the country controlled. After a series of battles, the British defeated the Zulu. And, in 1902, after eight years of war, the British defeated the Boers.

Independence After the Zulu and Boer wars, Great Britain granted independence to South Africa in 1910. The new nation united former British and Boer colonies but was under white minority rule. Black South Africans were denied voting rights.

Other Southern African nations began gaining independence in the 1960s. For some, the struggle was long and violent. For example, Africans resisted colonization in Rhodesia. After white colonists declared their own white-dominated republic in 1970, fighting between whites and Africans continued. Finally, in 1980 the Africans won independence and renamed their country Zimbabwe. Despite violent resistance, Namibia continued to be ruled by South Africa until 1990. Mozambique was granted independence in 1975, after ten years of war against Portuguese rule.

Apartheid in South Africa In the early 1900s white South Africans controlled South Africa's government and excluded black South Africans from power. To defend their rights, black South Africans formed the African National Congress (ANC) in 1912.

In the late 1940s racial inequality in South Africa grew worse. The government set up a policy called **apartheid** to separate whites and nonwhites. This policy divided people into four groups: whites, blacks, coloureds, and Asians. Apartheid placed harsh controls on nonwhites, especially blacks. Blacks were denied citizenship, the right to vote, and the ability to hold political offices. Housing, health care, and schools for blacks were poor compared to those for whites. Moreover, blacks were restricted to certain occupations and poor pay.

BIOGRAPHY

Nelson Mandela 1918–2013

Because he protested against apartheid, Nelson Mandela was imprisoned for 27 years. In 1990, however, South Africa's President Frederik Willem de Klerk released Mandela from prison. Mandela and de Klerk shared the Nobel Peace Prize in 1993. One year later, Mandela became South Africa's first black president. He wrote a new constitution and worked to improve the living conditions of black South Africans.

Identify
What did Nelson Mandela accomplish when he was South Africa's president?

Starting in the 1950s, the government created rural "homelands" for different South African peoples. Most of these areas lacked farmland, mines, and other natural resources. In cities, blacks had to live in separate areas called **townships,** crowded clusters of tiny homes. The townships were far from the jobs in the cities and mines.

In South Africa, many groups, including the ANC, opposed apartheid. Internal protests took the form of boycotts, strikes, marches, and occasional violence. Opposition also came from the international community. The United States and other nations applied **sanctions**—economic or political penalties imposed to force a change in policy—on South Africa. Some countries banned trade or refused to invest their money in South Africa. In addition, the Olympics banned South Africa from participation for nearly 30 years.

In the late 1980s the efforts of the ANC and anti-apartheid protesters contributed to social and political change. In 1990 and 1991, South Africa repealed all of its apartheid laws. The country held its first free, multiracial election in 1994, awarding the presidency to ANC leader Nelson Mandela. In 1996 South Africa adopted a new constitution, guaranteeing basic freedoms to all of its citizens.

Reading Check
Form Generalizations
How did European colonization impact independence movements in Southern Africa?

Culture

Over time, many groups created a diverse culture in Southern Africa. Today, the region's culture reflects both African and European influences.

People The people of Southern Africa belong to hundreds of different ethnic groups. Some groups are very large. For example, about 11 million people in South Africa are Zulu. Nearly 1.6 million of Botswana's 2 million people belong to a single ethnic group, the Tswana.

Other ethnic groups are small, and some trace their heritage to other world regions. For example, about 6 percent of Namibia's population is of European descent. The Malagasy people in Madagascar are a mix of 18 small ethnic groups whose ancestors migrated across the Indian Ocean from Indonesia.

Languages People in Southern Africa also belong to many language groups. Most of the African languages spoken in the region are related to one of two language families—Khoisan or Bantu. The earliest people of Southern Africa spoke Khoisan languages. Today, Khoisan speakers are known for the "click" sounds they make when they speak. The majority of Khoisan speakers belong to the San ethnic group and live in remote areas of Botswana and Namibia.

Most people in Southern Africa speak one of the more than 200 Bantu languages. For example, most of South Africa's 11 official languages are Bantu languages.

In countries with a history of European influence, European languages are also spoken. For example, English is the official language of Namibia and Zimbabwe. The official language of Mozambique is Portuguese.

Art The art of Southern Africa reflects its cultural diversity. For example, South African artists make traditional ethnic designs for items such as clothing, lamps, linens, and other products. Artists in Lesotho are famous for their woven tapestries of daily life. In Zimbabwe, artists are known

Ndebele Village

The Ndebele are one of many ethnic groups in South Africa who have kept their traditional culture alive. Many live in villages of brightly painted houses.

Painting houses is traditionally the role of Ndebele women. They paint colorful geometric patterns.

Analyze Visuals
What aspects of Ndebele culture do you see in these two photographs?

for their beautiful stone sculptures of birds and other animals. Traditional crafts of Botswana include ostrich-eggshell beadwork and woven baskets with complex designs. People there also produce colorful wool rugs.

Religion In addition to language, Europeans introduced Christianity to Southern Africa. Today, millions of people in Southern Africa are Christians. In Namibia and South Africa, the majority of the population identify as Christians.

Many other people in Southern Africa practice traditional African religions. Some of these people believe that ancestors and the spirits of the dead have divine powers. In Zimbabwe, traditional beliefs and Christianity have been mixed together. About half of the people in Zimbabwe practice a combination of traditional beliefs and Christianity.

Reading Check
Analyze Causes
Why is there such a diversity of languages in Southern Africa?

Southern Africa Today

Today, Southern Africa consists entirely of independent nations. All have joined the Southern African Development Community (SADC). SADC promotes economic development, peace, and a better life for all peoples in the region. Because trade is key to development, SADC nations do not impose trade barriers, such as tariffs and quotas, on each other's goods. Still, nations in the region have achieved varying degrees of economic success.

South Africa South Africa's government and economy are well positioned to create a better future for the country. South Africa's government is a republic with an elected president. The country's constitution emphasizes equality and human rights. The country's public schools and universities are open to all people, as are hospitals and transportation. However, economic equality has come more slowly. Whites still control most of South Africa's wealth and industries. The government is actively trying to create equal opportunities and jobs for black workers and farmers.

Specialization in resource-based industries continues to create opportunities for trade. For example, South Africa is one of the world's leading producers of several valuable minerals, including gold, platinum, and diamonds. Not surprisingly, gold and diamonds are the nation's top exports. Its top imports—crude and refined petroleum—are resources it has little of.

Major cities also help South Africa's economy. Johannesburg is Africa's largest industrial area and a center for telecommunications. Beautiful coastal cities such as **Cape Town** support shipping and tourism.

Lesotho and Eswatini Both Lesotho and Eswatini are enclaves of South Africa. An **enclave** is a small territory surrounded by foreign territory. In fact, Lesotho is located completely within South Africa. Eswatini shares part of its border with Mozambique. Lesotho and Eswatini are also both kingdoms. Each country has a king as head of state but is governed by an elected prime minister and a parliament.

Lesotho is a small country with few resources and little agricultural land. As a result, it is a poor country. Many of its people work in nearby South Africa. In spite of its poverty, Lesotho has the highest female literacy rate in Africa. Most children, including girls, obtain a primary education in free schools run by Christian churches.

Cape Town

Founded by the Dutch in 1652, Cape Town is a bustling international port city. It lies on the South Atlantic Ocean and is home to about 3.7 million people.

Analyze Visuals
What features in this photograph might appeal to tourists?

Eswatini has some important mineral deposits and industry. Cattle raising and farming are also common there. A good transportation system helps Eswatini to participate in foreign trade.

Namibia Namibia gained its independence from South Africa in 1990. Now it is a republic with an elected president and legislature. Its capital, Windhoek, is located in the central highlands.

Very few people live in Namibia's deserts, but these areas hold some of the richest mineral deposits in Africa. Most of the country's income comes from mining diamonds, copper, uranium, lead, and zinc. Fishing in the Atlantic Ocean and sheep ranching are also important sources of income. In spite of its strong economy, however, most Namibians are still poor.

Botswana Thanks to a stable democracy and mineral resources, Botswana is thriving. Its main economic activities are cattle ranching and diamond mining. Recently, international companies have built factories here and tourism is increasing. Although unemployment is high, the country has had one of the world's highest rates of economic growth since the 1960s.

Link to Economics

Tourism in Southern Africa

Tourism is a rapidly growing industry in a number of countries in Southern Africa. The region's wildlife is its main attraction. People come from all over the world to see lions, elephants, zebras, and giraffes in their natural habitats. Many countries have established huge parks to protect these habitats.

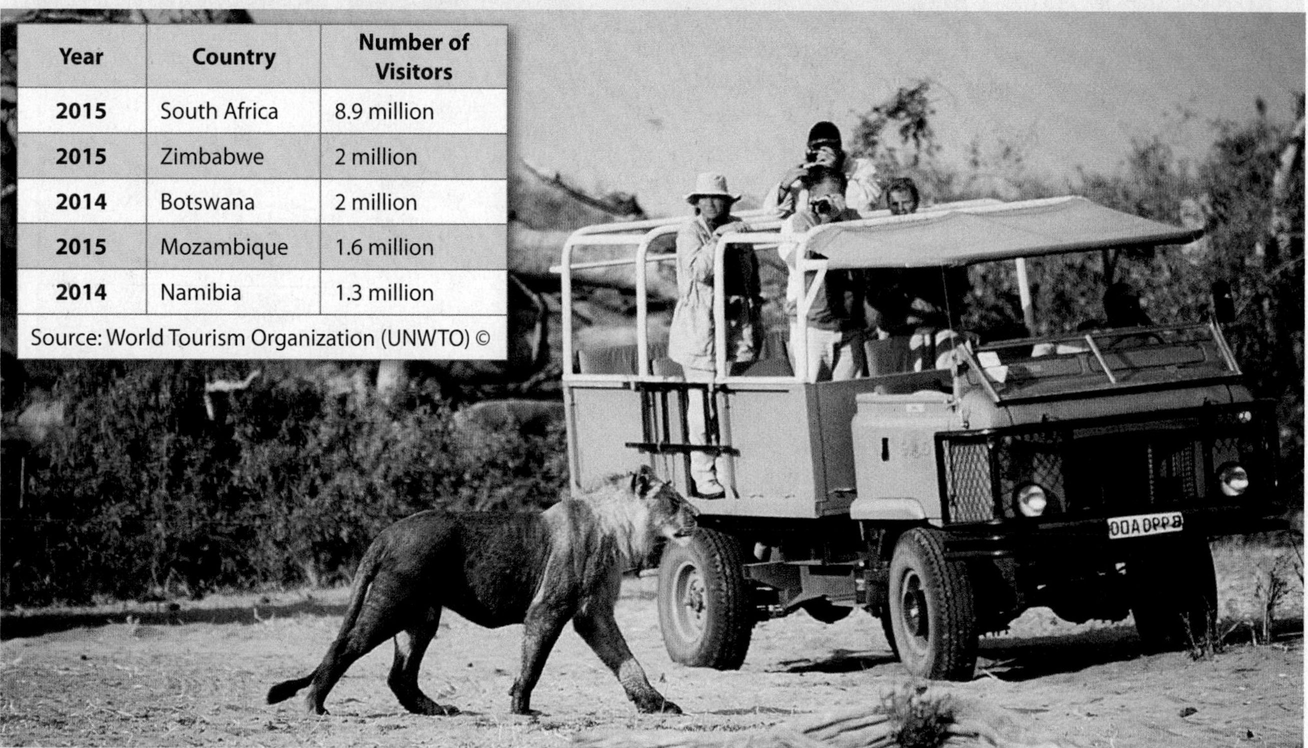

Year	Country	Number of Visitors
2015	South Africa	8.9 million
2015	Zimbabwe	2 million
2014	Botswana	2 million
2015	Mozambique	1.6 million
2014	Namibia	1.3 million

Source: World Tourism Organization (UNWTO) ©

Analyze Tables
Which country had the most visitors in 2015?

Zimbabwe Zimbabwe has suffered from a poor economy, political instability, and inequality. Zimbabwe has gold and copper mines as well as productive agriculture and manufacturing. However, high inflation, debts, and war have hurt the economy. In addition, racial inequality persists.

Although white residents make up less than 1 percent of the population, they own most of the nation's large farms and ranches. In 2000 Robert Mugabe, Zimbabwe's president, began a program to take farmland from whites and give the land to black residents. This program led many white farmers to leave the country and caused food shortages.

Economic collapse, high unemployment, and Mugabe's use of violence to maintain power made Zimbabweans unhappy with their president. In November 2017, after 37 years as leader of the country, Mugabe was forced from office.

Mozambique Mozambique is one of the world's poorest countries. The economy has been badly damaged by civil war, but it is improving. Mozambique's ports ship many products from the interior of Africa. Taxes

Baobab trees line a street in Madagascar.

collected on these shipments are an important source of income. Also, plantations grow cashews, cotton, and sugar for export. The country must import more than it exports, however, and it relies on foreign aid.

Madagascar and Comoros Madagascar was ruled for more than 20 years by a socialist dictator. Today, the elected president is working to improve a struggling national economy. Most of the country's income comes from exports of coffee, vanilla, sugar, and cloves. Madagascar also has some manufacturing, and the country is popular with tourists who come to see the unique plants and animals.

Comoros is a country made up of four tiny islands. It suffers from a lack of resources and political instability. The government of Comoros is struggling to improve education and promote tourism.

Reading Check
Contrast
In what ways are Botswana and Zimbabwe different?

Issues and Challenges

Although conditions in many countries of Southern Africa are better than they are on much of the continent, the region has its own challenges. One of the most serious problems facing Southern Africa is poverty. Terrible droughts often destroy food crops. In addition, many of Southern Africa's people are unemployed.

Poverty contributes to another serious issue—disease. Worldwide, about one-third of all people living with HIV and AIDS live in Southern Africa. Tuberculosis and malaria are also a problem. Because such diseases threaten people's well-being and economic development, governments throughout the region are working to combat them.

Environmental destruction is another challenge. Madagascar has lost about 90 percent of its natural vegetation to deforestation. The devastation has decimated animal habitats and caused erosion. However, there is hope for the future. Madagascar's government and local communities are working with international organizations to reforest the island and protect wildlife. Other nations are also working to protect natural resources. Namibia was the first country in the world to put environmental protection in its constitution. Also, the African Union (AU) promotes cooperation among African countries to protect wildlife resources across the continent.

Reading Check
Describe What main challenges does Southern Africa face?

Summary Southern Africa's early history and later European settlement have greatly influenced the region's culture. Today, some countries have more stable governments and economies than others.

Lesson 3 Assessment

Review Ideas, Terms, and Places

1. a. **Identify** Who were the Khoisan?
   b. **Draw Conclusions** Why did the Shona capital of Great Zimbabwe decline as a trading center?
   c. **Define** What was apartheid?
   d. **Contrast** How did South African independence impact white and black South Africans differently?
2. a. **Recall** What ethnic group in Southern Africa speaks languages that use click sounds?
   b. **Draw Conclusions** How do the religions practiced in Southern Africa reflect the region's history?
3. a. **Recall** Which country's president began a program to take farmland from white farmers?
   b. **Rank** Besides South Africa, which two countries in the region seem to have the strongest economies?
4. a. **Explain** How are people in Southern Africa addressing the challenges in the region?
   b. **Form Generalizations** Use the photograph and chart in the Link to Economics feature along with what you already know to form a generalization about patterns of tourism in Southern Africa.

Critical Thinking

5. **Summarize** Review your notes on Southern Africa. Then using a graphic organizer like this one, describe the factors that shaped the region in each period.

Before Colonization	During Colonization	After Independence

Social Studies Skills

Evaluate a Website

Define the Skill

The Internet can be a powerful research tool. However, not all information found on the Internet is reliable. You must be careful to evaluate a website for the quality of its content.

A good website should be accurate and up-to-date. Before you use a site for research, find out who produced it. The author should be qualified and unbiased. Also, check to see when the site was last updated. If it has not been updated recently, the information it contains may no longer be accurate.

Learn the Skill

Study the page below taken from a website. Then answer the following questions:

1. Who do you think produced this website? How can you tell?
2. What kinds of information can you find on this site? Is the information verifiable or consistent with other credible sources?
3. Do you think this would be a good site for research? Why or why not?

Practice the Skill

Locate a website about one of the countries in East or Southern Africa. Analyze the site and determine whether you think it would be a good site for research. Write a one-paragraph report explaining your decision. Be sure to include the site's URL and the date on which you visited it in your report.

A country's official website is usually a good source for information.

Welcome to the official South
www.gov.za/welcome-official-government-online-site
Republic of South Africa
South African Government
www.gov.za
Together we move South Africa forward
HOME ABOUT NEWSROOM SERVICES DOCUMENTS
YOUTH DAY 2017
The Year of OR Tambo:
Advancing Youth Economic Empowerment
Youth Month 2017
SHING EXT 2, SPORTS GROUND
VENTERSDORP, NORTH WEST
read more...
Latest information
NEWS
SA companies spot business opportunities in Kenya
29 June 2017
Probe underway after Basic Education website hack
29 June 2017
SPEECHES & STATEMENTS
Minister Michael Masutha: Media briefing on status of political offend...
29 June 2017
Minister Joe Maswanganyi: National Youth Road Safety Summit
29 June 2017
IN FOCUS
Life and legacy of
OR TAMBO, CENTENARY
OR TAMBO CENTENARY
South Africa will this year celebrate the centenary of the birth of...
Read More

Notice what type of information is present on the website. Is the site biased or unbalanced?

Check to see how current the articles on the website are. Have they been updated regularly?

Module 13 Assessment

Review Vocabulary, Terms, and Places

Match the words with their definitions.

1. drought
2. Zanzibar
3. safari
4. genocide
5. Boers
6. apartheid
7. sanctions
8. escarpment

a. the steep face at the edge of a plateau or other raised area
b. economic or political penalties imposed by one country on another to force a change in policy
c. an East African island that was a slave-trading center in the 1700s
d. Afrikaner frontier farmers in South Africa
e. period when little rain falls and crops are damaged
f. the intentional destruction of a people
g. South Africa's policy of separation of races
h. an overland journey that is taken to view African wildlife

---

Comprehension and Critical Thinking

Lesson 1

9. a. **Identify** What are the two driest regions of Southern Africa?
   b. **Contrast** How is the geography of East Africa different from Southern Africa?
   c. **Predict** What can individuals, groups, and nations do to reduce the effects of drought and water scarcity?

Lesson 2

10. a. **Identify** In which East African country did an emperor build 11 rock churches?
    b. **Summarize** How did the language of Swahili develop?
    c. **Draw Conclusions** How might a decline in Tanzania's tourist industry affect local communities, wildlife resources, and the national economy?

Lesson 3

11. a. **Define** Who are the Afrikaners? What country do they live in?
    b. **Explain** What was life like for black South Africans under the policy of apartheid?
    c. **Identify Problems** What is the most serious challenge facing Southern Africa? Explain your choice.

Reading Skills 

Form Generalizations *Use the information in this module to answer the following question.*

12. Reread the information about Southern Africa Today in the lesson Southern Africa. Using information from the text, form one generalization about a trend in the country's economy and one about a trend related to its population.

Social Studies Skills

Use the Social Studies Skills taught in this module to complete the following.

13. **Evaluate a Website** Research online to locate two websites about an issue affecting East or Southern Africa. One should be a site that you determine is a good source for research. The other site should represent an unreliable source. Before you research, brainstorm a list of search terms that will help you locate reliable websites. Select your sites, and create a poster that compares them. Be sure to include a title. Use call-out captions to point to and explain the features that helped you determine whether or not each site was a valid source for research.

Map Skills 

14. **Southern Africa** *Match the letters on the map with their correct labels.*

Cape of Good Hope
Okavango Basin
Orange River
Namib Desert
Drakensberg

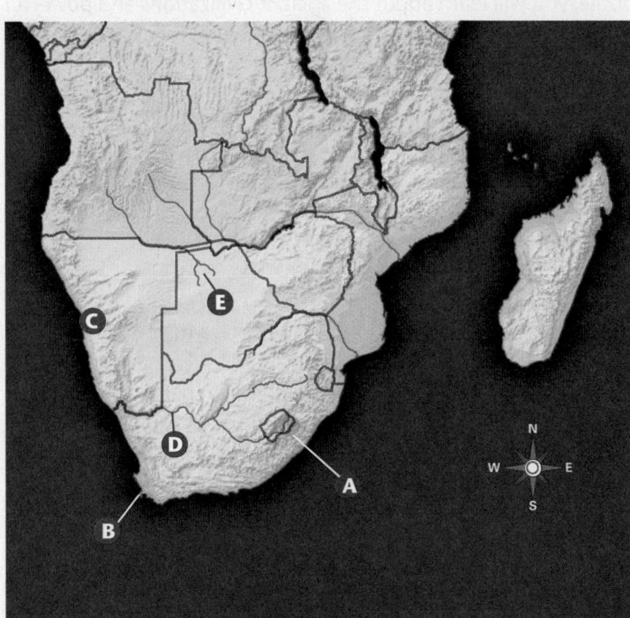

15. **East Africa** Use your textbook and research online to locate a variety of maps of East Africa, including physical, climate, vegetation, population, land use, and natural resources maps. Use the maps to pose and answer at least two questions about how physical features and the scarcity of natural resources impact patterns of human settlement and economic activity.

Focus on Speaking

16. **Present a TV News Report** Imagine that you are a reporter covering economic development in East or Southern Africa. Pick a nation to investigate. Gather data related to employment, unemployment, literacy, inflation, total production, income, and economic growth. Note any trends in the data that reveal how the economy affects different groups, such as urban and rural dwellers or men and women. Also note factors that influence economic development, such as natural resources, population growth, literacy rates, conflict, or public health issues.

    Write a news report summarizing your findings. Think about how images could enhance your story. Include at least one photograph, chart, map, or diagram to help you explain your topic. Present your report to the class, as if you were on the TV news.

Module 14

Indian Early Civilizations, Empires, and World Religions

Essential Question

What role did religion play in the development of Indian civilizations and empires?

About the Photo: The Dalai Lama, a Buddhist leader, walks with representatives of other religions, including Jainism, Hinduism, Islam, and Sikhism.

Explore ONLINE!

VIDEOS, including . . .

- Reincarnation

- Document-Based Investigations
- Graphic Organizers
- Interactive Games
- Channel One News Video: Next Big Thing: Meditation Gyms
- Image with Hotspots: Life in Mohenjo-Daro
- Image Carousel: Hindu Gods
- Interactive Map: Mughal Empire

In this module, you will learn about the ancient civilizations and powerful empires of India, the birthplace of several major world religions including Hinduism, Buddhism, and Sikhism.

What You Will Learn

Lesson 1: Early Indian Civilizations. 449
The Big Idea Indian civilization first developed along the Indus River.

Lesson 2: Hinduism. 458
The Big Idea Hinduism, the largest religion in India, developed out of ancient Indian beliefs and practices.

Lesson 3: Buddhism 463
The Big Idea Buddhism began in India and became a major religion.

Lesson 4: Sikhism. 470
The Big Idea Sikhism originated in the Punjab region of India and has grown to include nearly 25 million followers around the world.

Lesson 5: Indian Empires 474
The Big Idea The Mauryas, the Guptas, and the Mughals built great empires in India and made important contributions to the arts and sciences.

Buddhism India was also the birthplace of another religion, Buddhism. Buddhist temples like this one at Ajanta are found all over India.

Early India The first civilization in India, the Harappans were skilled builders and artists.

Hinduism A major world religion, Hinduism developed in India. In this photo, Hindus bathe in the sacred river Ganges.

Reading Social Studies

Understand Fact and Opinion

READING FOCUS

When you read, it is important to distinguish facts from opinions. A fact is a statement that can be proved or disproved. If a statement is false, it is sometimes called fiction. An opinion is a personal belief or attitude, so it cannot be proved true or false. Words that evaluate, like *best* or *worst*, often signify an opinion. When you are reading a social studies text, you want to read only facts, not the author's opinions. To determine whether a sentence is a fact or an opinion, ask if it can be proved using outside sources. If it can, the sentence is a fact. The following pairs of statements show the difference between facts and opinions.

Fact: Asoka was an emperor of the Mauryan Empire. *(This fact can be proved through research.)*

Opinion: I believe Asoka was the Mauryan Empire's best emperor. *(The word* best *signifies that this is the writer's judgment, or opinion.)*

Fact: There are Buddhist temples at Ajanta and Ellora. *(These locations can be checked for accuracy.)*

Opinion: The temple at Ajanta is the most beautiful Buddhist temple. *(No one can prove the temple is the most beautiful because it is a matter of personal taste.)*

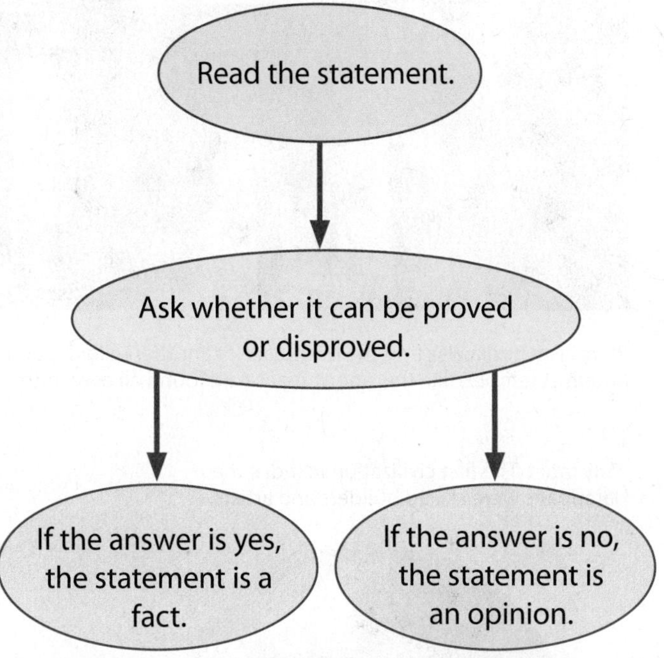

YOU TRY IT!

Read the following sentences and identify each as a fact or an opinion.

1. Babur was a leader of the Mughal Empire.

2. Shah Jahan was another Mughal leader.

3. Shah Jahan built the Taj Mahal for his wife.

4. Everyone should visit the Taj Mahal.

5. The Taj Mahal is the most fascinating place in India.

6. The Taj Mahal was built in the 1600s and still stands today.

As you read this module, be alert for any opinions that you might read.

Early Indian Civilizations

The Big Idea

Indian civilization first developed along the Indus River.

Main Ideas

- Located on the Indus River, the Harappan civilization also had contact with people far from India.
- Harappan achievements included a writing system, city planning, and art.
- The rise of the Aryan tribes changed India's civilization.
- The Vedas were the basis of religion in the Vedic era and moving forward.
- Indian society divided into distinct groups.

Key Terms and Places

Indus River
Harappa
Mohenjo-Daro
Sanskrit
caste system

If YOU lived there . . .

You are a trader in the huge city of Mohenjo-Daro. Your business is booming, as traders come to the city from all over Asia. With your new wealth, you have bought a huge house with a rooftop terrace and even indoor plumbing! This morning, however, you heard that invaders are headed toward the city. People are telling you that you should flee for your safety.

What will you miss most about life in the city?

Harappan Civilization

In the 1920s while digging for artifacts along the **Indus River,** archaeologists found not one but two huge cities. The archaeologists had thought people had lived along the Indus long ago, but they had no idea that an advanced civilization had existed there. These sites and the artifacts found there have been critical to historians' and archaeologists' understanding of ancient Indian civilizations.

India's First Civilization Historians call the civilization that developed along the Indus and Sarasvati rivers the Harappan (huh-RA-puhn) civilization. The name comes from the modern city of Harappa (huh-RA-puh), Pakistan. It was near this city that the ruins of the ancient civilization were first discovered. Archaeologists currently estimate that the civilization thrived between 2600 and 1700 BC. Harappan civilization is considered a civilization because there is evidence of an organized society within a specific area that had writing, art, architecture, and government.

The Harappan civilization controlled large areas on both sides of the Indus River. Settlements were scattered over a huge area. Most of these settlements lay next to rivers. The largest settlements were two cities, **Harappa** and **Mohenjo-Daro** (mo-HEN-joh DAR-oh).

Like most other ancient societies including Sumerian civilization and Egyptian civilization, the Harappan civilization was dependent on river valley agriculture. Farmers in the Indus valley grew a variety of crops—from wheat and barley to dates

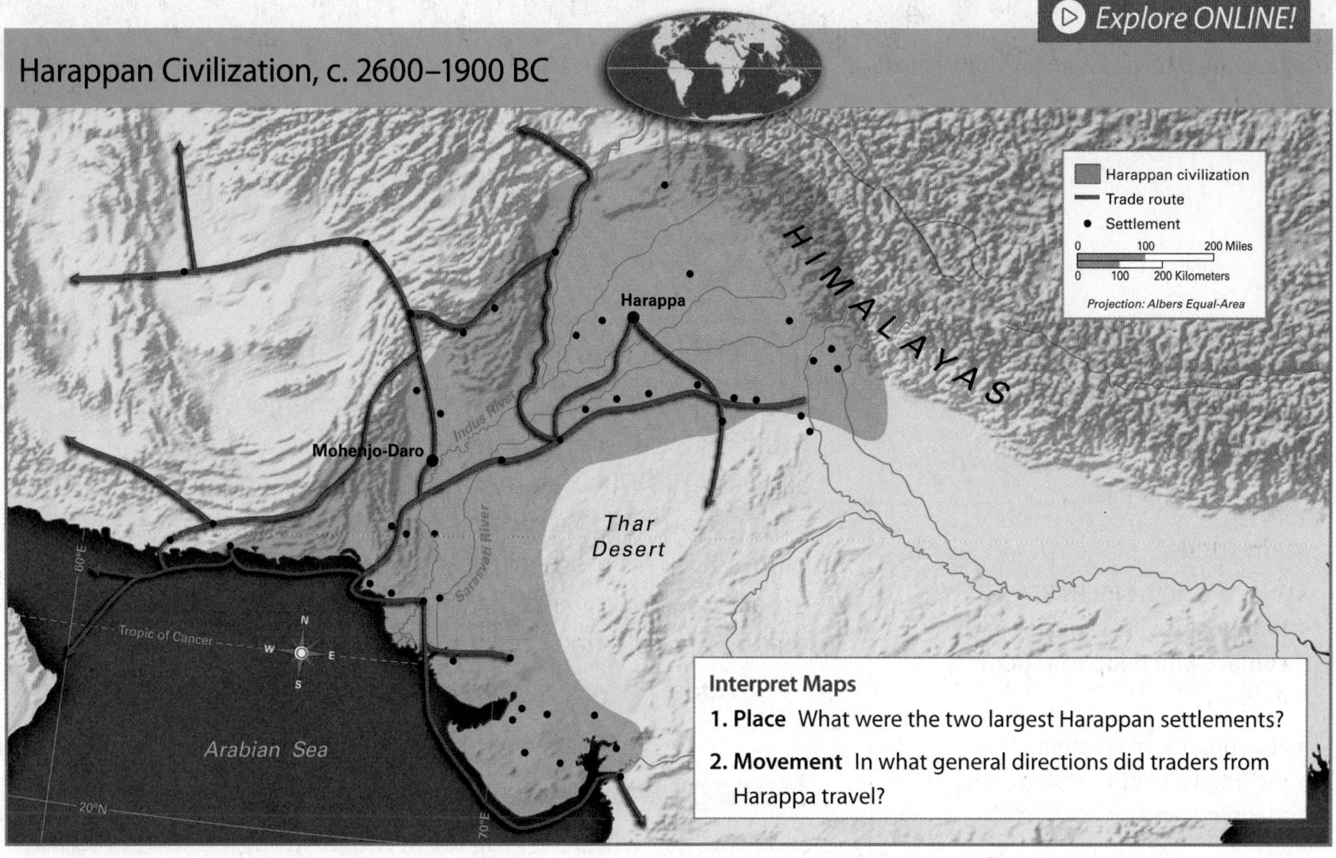

Interpret Maps

1. **Place** What were the two largest Harappan settlements?
2. **Movement** In what general directions did traders from Harappa travel?

and vegetables—to feed both themselves and city dwellers. They also grew cotton for clothing. The fertile land and water from the river allowed them to develop a farming economy. They used irrigation canals to bring water from the Indus and other rivers to their fields to help their crops grow. While they did grow plants and keep animals for food, wild species continued to be important to their civilization and growth.

Contact with Other Cultures Although the Harappan civilization was centered on the Indus, its influence reached far beyond that area. In fact, archaeologists have found evidence that the Harappans had contact with people as far away as southern India and Mesopotamia.

Most of this contact with other cultures was in the form of trade. The Harappans traded to obtain raw materials. They then used these materials to make products such as pottery, stamps and seals, and statues.

Reading Check
Find Main Ideas
Where was the Harappan civilization located?

Harappan Achievements

Historians do not know much about the Harappan civilization. They think the Harappans had kings and strong central governments, but they are not sure. They also know little about Harappan religion.

Although we do not know much about how the Harappans lived, we do know that they made great achievements in many fields. Everything we know about these achievements comes from artifacts.

Writing System The ancient Harappans developed India's first writing system. However, scholars have not yet learned to read this language. Because we cannot read what they wrote, we rely on other clues to study Harappan society.

City Planning Most of what we have learned about the Harappans has come from studying their cities, especially Harappa and Mohenjo-Daro. The two cities lay on the Indus more than 300 miles (483 km) apart, but they appear to have been remarkably similar.

Both Harappa and Mohenjo-Daro were well-planned cities. A close examination of their ruins shows that the Harappans were careful planners and skilled engineers. Each city stood near a towering fortress. From these fortresses, defenders could look down on the cities' carefully laid-out brick streets. These streets crossed at right angles and were lined with storehouses, workshops, market stalls, and houses.

Most of the structures were built of mud brick. Following floods, the mud deposited by the river could be shaped into bricks. These bricks were then fired in a kiln, making them harder than sun-dried bricks. The bricks were uniform in size across Harappan civilization. This suggests that there was a strong, central government in this society.

Using their engineering skills, the Harappans built extensive sewer systems to keep their streets from flooding. They also installed plumbing in many buildings.

Harappan Art

Like other ancient peoples, the Harappans made small stone seals like the ones on the left and in the center that were used to stamp goods. They also used clay pots like the one on the right decorated with a goat. These artifacts were important to Harappan society and give scholars clues about what Harappan life was like.

Analyze Visuals
What natural resources did the Harappan people use to make some of their art?

Artistic Achievements In Harappan cities, archaeologists have found many artifacts that show that the Harappans were skilled artisans. For example, they have found sturdy pottery vessels, jewelry, and ivory objects.

Some of these ancient artifacts have helped historians draw conclusions about Harappan society. For example, they found a statue that shows two animals pulling a cart. Based on this statue, they conclude that the Harappans built and used wheeled vehicles. Likewise, a statue of a man with elaborate clothes and jewelry suggests that Harappan society had an upper class.

Harappan civilization ended by the early 1700s BC, but no one is sure why. Perhaps invaders destroyed the cities or natural disasters, like floods or earthquakes, caused the civilization to collapse.

Reading Check
Analyze Causes Why do we not know much about Harappan civilization?

A New Culture Arises

A new group of tribes arrived in the Indus River valley, probably during the Harappan civilization's peak or decline. They were called the Aryans (AHR-ee-uhnz). Most historians believe they came from Central Asia. Over time, they became the dominant society in India during a time known as the Vedic period or Vedic age.

Origins and Spread Aryan tribes may have first arrived in India in the 2000s BC. Most historians and archaeologists believe that the Aryans crossed into India through mountain passes in the northwest. Others think the Aryans might have been native to the subcontinent. Over many centuries, they spread east and south into central India. From there they moved even farther east into the Ganges River valley. There they established societies that endured for many centuries.

Explore ONLINE!

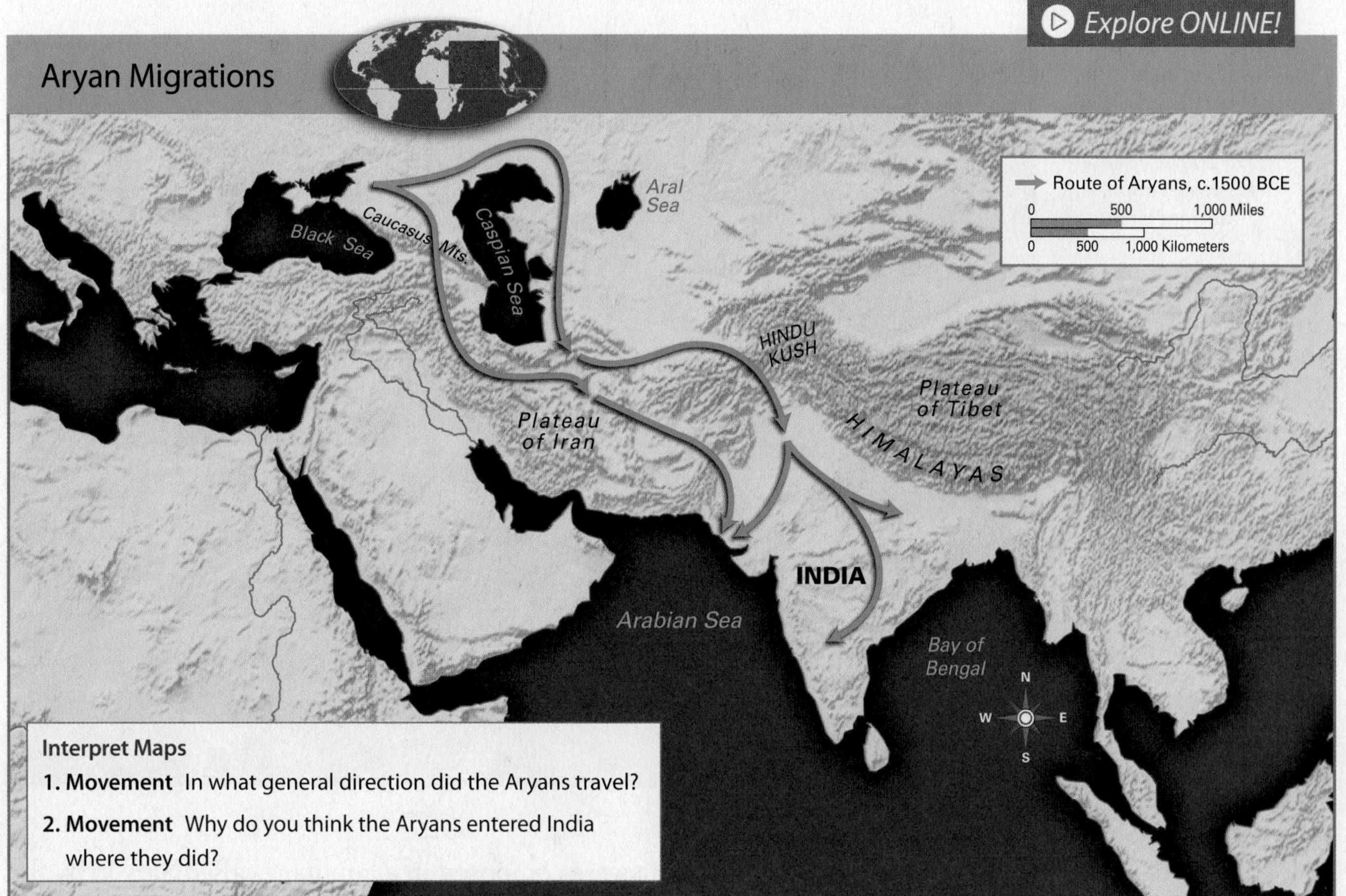

Interpret Maps

1. **Movement** In what general direction did the Aryans travel?
2. **Movement** Why do you think the Aryans entered India where they did?

Much of what we know about Aryan society comes from religious writings known as the Vedas (VAY-duhs). These are collections of poems, hymns, myths, and rituals that were passed down orally and later written down.

Government and Society As nomads, the Aryans took along their herds of animals as they moved. But over time, they settled in villages and began to farm. Unlike the Harappans, they did not build big cities.

The Aryan political system was also different from the Harappan system. The Aryans lived in small communities, based mostly on family ties. No single ruling authority existed. Instead, each group had its own leader, often a skilled warrior.

Aryan villages were governed by rajas (RAH-juhz). A raja was a leader who ruled a village and the land around it. Villagers farmed some of this land for the raja. They used other sections as pastures for their cows, horses, sheep, and goats.

Although many rajas were related, they didn't always get along. Sometimes, rajas joined forces before fighting a common enemy. Other times, however, rajas went to war against each other. In fact, Aryan groups fought each other nearly as often as they fought outsiders.

Language Early Aryans are not known to have had written language. Because of this, they had to memorize the poems and hymns that were important in their culture, such as the Vedas. If people had forgotten these poems and hymns, the works would have been lost forever.

The text carved into this stone is an ancient example of Sanskrit. While it is no longer widely spoken, Sanskrit remains an important ancient language.

Aryan poems and hymns were composed in a language called **Sanskrit,** the most important language of ancient India. At first, Sanskrit was only a spoken language. Eventually, however, people figured out how to write it down so they could keep records and write down scriptures, which are the basis for Hinduism. These Sanskrit records and scriptures are a major source of information about Vedic society. Sanskrit is not widely spoken today, but it is used in Hindu rituals. It is also the root of many modern South Asian languages.

Reading Check
Identify
What source provides much of the information we have about the Aryans?

Vedic Religion and Early Hinduism

Religion was important during the Vedic age. Originally, people's practice of religion was limited to rituals. Over time, religion took on even more meaning and became a part of daily life in ancient India. Many scholars call the early Hinduism of this period Vedic religion or Brahmanism because of the religion's emphasis on the Vedas and the belief in a divine reality known as Brahman.

The Vedas Early Hinduism was based on the Vedas. There are four Vedas, each containing sacred hymns and poems. The oldest of the Vedas, the *Rigveda*, was probably compiled in the second millennium BC. It includes guidance on seeking truth and hymns of praise to many gods. This passage, for example, is the opening of a hymn praising Indra, a god of the sky and war.

> "He who just born chief god of lofty spirit by power and might became the gods' protector, Before whose strength in majesty of valour the two worlds trembled, He, O men, is Indra."
>
> –from *The Hymns of the Rigveda* translated by Ralph T. H. Griffith

The Vedas eventually became the basis of Hinduism. These writings continue to be important to Hindus and Hinduism today, over 3,000 years later.

Later Vedic Texts Over the centuries, the Aryans wrote down poems and hymns in Sanskrit. In time, these were compiled into collections called Vedic texts.

One collection of Vedic texts describes religious rituals. For example, it describes how to perform sacrifices. Priests prepared animals, food, or drinks to be sacrificed in a fire. The Aryans believed that the fire would carry these offerings to the gods.

A second collection of Vedic texts describes secret rituals that only certain people could perform. In fact, the rituals were so secret that they had to be done in the forest, far from other people.

The final group of Vedic texts are the Upanishads (oo-PAHN-ee-shads), most of which were written by about 600 BC. These writings are religious students' and teachers' reflections on the Vedas. The Upanishads had a great impact on later religious expression. Religious texts modeled after the Upanishads were written until about AD 1400. The Upanishads teach that Brahman, which is the force behind everything, is found in the *atman*, the soul or self of an individual. Understanding this connection is still a goal in modern Hinduism.

Later Vedic Society Over the course of the later Vedic period, rulers began to rule over areas instead of families. Some rulers became much more powerful. Powerful chiefs surrounded themselves with advisers and began to collect taxes.

Elaborate religious ceremonies provided more power and status to the chiefs, or kings. Vedic society had a hierarchy of priests. During rituals, sacrifices of wealth would be made from the chief to the priest. During this period, the priests and upper class grew in importance and wealth, leading to greater divisions in ancient Indian society.

Reading Check
Find Main Ideas
What are the Vedic texts?

Indian Society Divides

As Aryan society became more complex, it became divided into groups. These groups were largely organized by people's occupations. Rules developed about how people of different groups could interact. As time passed, these rules became stricter and became central to Indian society.

The *Varnas* According to the Vedas, there were four main *varnas*, or social divisions. These were based on temperaments that vary from person to person. In ancient Indian society, these *varnas* were

- Brahmins (BRAH-muhns), or priests
- Kshatriyas (KSHA-tree-uhs), or rulers and warriors
- Vaisyas (VYSH-yuhs), or farmers, craftspeople, and traders
- Sudras (SOO-drahs), or laborers and servants

The Vedas saw the four roles as equals, but social divisions and rankings grew over time. Later on, as Indian society developed, Brahmins came to be regarded as the highest group.

The Caste System As Indian social order became more complex, another set of groups called *jatis* emerged. Membership in *jatis* was determined by birth. *Jatis* were associated with specific occupations, and they had different rules about how they could interact with each other. Over many centuries, each

Quick Facts

The *Varnas*

Brahmins
Brahmins were India's priests.

Kshatriyas
Kshatriyas were rulers and warriors.

Analyze Visuals
To which *varna* would a chief belong?

of the four *varnas* in Indian society merged with hundreds of *jatis*. These social divisions are now known as castes, which is what Portuguese travelers called them in the 1400s.

Over many centuries, the **caste system** divided Indian society into groups based on a person's birth, wealth, or occupation. Though *varnas* were not based on birth, eventually they merged with birth-based *jatis*. At one time, some 3,000 separate castes existed in India. By about AD 500, a group called the Untouchables emerged. They didn't belong to any caste. Members of this group were later known as Dalits. They were allowed to hold only certain jobs, which were often unpleasant, such as tanning animal hides and disposing dead animals.

Caste Norms In general, the caste to which a person belonged determined his or her place in society. In ancient Indian society, caste roles were by no means permanent. However, social mobility among castes became more limited over the centuries.

As time went by, each caste developed its own norms. Norms are unwritten rules that people in a community know they are required to follow. Caste norms were passed down from generation to generation through social and cultural practices. Caste norms could be exclusive. For example, people would not marry someone from a different caste. People from one caste may also not have eaten meals with people from another. Caste interactions also depended on the villages in which a person lived.

Most Indians identified with the system, so caste also shaped the daily lives of other religious groups in India. The system became formal in the late 1800s when the British began gathering information on caste in the census. This social order continued for over a century. In India, discrimination by caste was officially banned when the independent Indian government was established in 1949, but caste still plays a role in many people's lives.

Vaisyas

Vaisyas were farmers, craftspeople, and traders.

Sudras

Sudras were workers and servants.

Reading Check

Make Inferences How did a person become a member of a caste?

The Role of Women In ancient India, women had most of the same rights as men. They could, for example, own property and receive an education. They could also perform in religious ceremonies. Over time, however, laws were passed to limit these rights.

Summary and Preview The earliest civilizations in India were centered in the Indus valley. In the next section, you will learn about a religion that developed in the Indus valley after the Aryans settled there—Hinduism.

Lesson 1 Assessment

Review Ideas, Terms, and Places

1. a. **Analyze** Why are the archaeological site at Harappa and the artifacts found there important?

   b. **Compare** How was Harappan civilization similar to Sumerian civilization?

   c. **Explain** Why did the Harappans make contact with people far from India?

2. a. **Identify** What was Mohenjo-Daro?

   b. **Analyze** What is one reason that scholars do not completely understand some important parts of Harappan society?

3. a. **Identify** Who were the Aryans?

   b. **Contrast** How was civilization during the Vedic period different from the Harappan civilization?

4. a. **Identify** What texts have remained important to Hinduism for thousands of years?

   b. **Analyze** What role did sacrifice play during the Vedic period?

5. a. **Identify** What is the caste system?

   b. **Explain** How has the caste system changed over time? How has it stayed the same?

Critical Thinking

6. **Summarize** List the major achievements of India's first two civilizations. Record your conclusions in a diagram like this one.

Early Indian Achievements	
Harappan society	Vedic society

Hinduism

The Big Idea

Hinduism, the largest religion in India, developed out of ancient Indian beliefs and practices.

Main Ideas

- Hinduism developed out of Brahmanism and influences from other cultures.
- Jainism is another religion that arose in ancient India.

Key Terms and Places

reincarnation
karma
nonviolence

If YOU lived there . . .

You are a Hindu girl who is about to have a rite of passage, or *samskara*. This rite of passage will celebrate that you are becoming an adult. After this, you will be allowed to light oil lamps and participate more fully in your religion. You will also receive gifts such as jewelry.

Do you look forward to becoming an adult or are you nervous?

Hinduism Develops

The Vedas, the Upanishads, and the other Vedic texts became the basis for Hinduism, the largest religion in India today. Over time, the ideas of these sacred texts began to blend with ideas from other cultures. People from Persia and other kingdoms in Central Asia, for example, brought their ideas to India. Hinduism was also influenced by religious texts written in Tamil and other South Asian languages. Since Hinduism is a blending of ideas, it does not have a single founder. It also does not have one set of teachings that all Hindus agree on. Hinduism is the third-largest religion in the world today, with over a billion followers. Most of the followers are in India. Many consider it to be the world's oldest major religion.

Hindu Beliefs Most Hindus believe in a single universal spirit called Brahman, which can come in many forms. While there are many gods and goddesses in Hinduism, there are three major gods who are commonly part of Hindu texts: Brahma the Creator, Siva the Destroyer, and Vishnu the Preserver. There are other gods and goddesses in both human and animal form, including the goddess Lakshmi, the elephant god Ganesha, and the monkey god Hanuman. They are popularly worshiped by Hindus across the world. However, Hindus believe that each god and goddess is part of Brahman. They believe that Brahman created the world and preserves it. Gods such as Brahma, Siva, and Vishnu represent different aspects of Brahman. In fact, Hindus believe that everything in the world is part of Brahman.

Hindu Gods

Hindus believe in many gods, but they believe that all the gods are aspects of a single universal spirit called Brahman. Three aspects of Brahman are particularly important in Hinduism—Brahma, Siva, and Vishnu.

The god Brahma represents the creator aspect of Brahman. His four faces symbolize the four Vedas.

Siva, the destroyer aspect of Brahman, is usually shown with four arms and three eyes. Here he is shown dancing on the back of a demon he has defeated.

Vishnu is the preserver aspect of Brahman. In his four arms, he carries a conch shell, a mace, and a discus, symbols of his power and greatness.

Analyze Visuals
What symbols are used in these statues?

Life and Rebirth According to Hindu teachings, everyone has a soul, or *atman*. This soul holds the person's personality, those qualities that make a person who he or she is. Many Hindus believe that a person's ultimate goal should be to reunite that soul with Brahman, the universal spirit.

Many Hindus believe that their souls will eventually join Brahman because the world we live in is an illusion. Brahman is the only reality. The Upanishads teach that people must try to see through the illusion of the world. Because it is hard to see through illusions, this can take several lifetimes. That is why Hindus believe that souls are born and reborn many times, each time in a new body. This process of rebirth is called **reincarnation.**

Major Beliefs of Hinduism
• A universal spirit called Brahman created the universe and everything in it. Everything in the world is just a part of Brahman.
• Every person has a soul, or *atman,* that will eventually join with Brahman.
• People's souls are reincarnated many times before they can join with Brahman.
• A person's karma will affect a person's next life after reincarnation.

Hinduism and Society According to the traditional Hindu view of reincarnation, a person who has died is reborn in a new physical form. The type of form depends upon his or her **karma,** the effects that good or bad actions have on a person's soul. Evil actions will build bad karma. People with bad karma will face the consequences of their actions in a future birth.

In contrast, good actions build good karma. People with good karma will see benefits in future births. In time, good karma will bring liberation from life's worries and the cycle of rebirth. This liberation is called *moksha*. The idea of karma encourages people to behave well in society.

Hinduism teaches that each person has a *dharma*, or set of spiritual duties, to fulfill. *Dharma* is seen as Hinduism's guidelines for living a moral life and includes nonviolence, self-restraint, and honesty. Karma and *dharma* promote good behavior and social order. Hindus are not the only group that emphasizes spiritual duty. Buddhists, Jains, and Sikhs all view *dharma* as part of their religions. You will read about these other religions later.

Customs and Traditions Rituals and ceremonies have always been and continue to be important parts of Hinduism. *Samskaras*, which are rites of passage to prepare a person for a certain event or for the next stage in life, are still practiced today. Many rituals revolve around birth. Other *samskaras* occur throughout childhood. There is an initiation in which girls are given the authority to light oil lamps. This signals that a girl is now a full participant in the Hindu faith and worship.

The Sacred Ganges

Summarize
Why is the Ganges a pilgrimage site?

Hindus believe that there are many sacred places in India. Making a pilgrimage to one of these places, they believe, will help improve their karma and increase their chance for salvation. The most sacred of all the pilgrimage sites in India is the Ganges River in the northeast.

Known to Hindus as Mother Ganga, the Ganges flows out of the Himalayas. In traditional Hindu teachings, however, the river flows from the feet of Vishnu and over the head of Siva before it makes its way across the land. Through this contact with the gods, the river's water is made holy. Hindus believe that bathing in the Ganges will purify them and remove some of their bad karma.

Although the entire Ganges is considered sacred, a few cities along its path are seen as especially holy. At these sites, pilgrims gather to bathe and celebrate Hindu festivals. Steps lead down from the cities right to the edge of the water so people can more easily reach the river.

Weddings are also a time for customs and traditions. Wedding ceremonies have special rituals, though they can vary depending on the cultural group and sect of Hinduism. For example, offerings of roasted grain are thrown into a sacrificial fire. The bride and groom must also take seven steps together to symbolize their unity.

Because Hindu beliefs vary so widely, religious practices vary as well. At home, individual worshipers might say special prayers or meditate, or silently reflect upon the world and its nature. To help them meditate, some Hindus also practice a series of integrated physical and mental exercises called yoga. The purpose of yoga is to teach people how to focus their bodies and minds. They believe this will aid their meditation and help them attain *moksha.*

Pilgrimages are important to many Hindus. Pilgrims travel to different shrines and temples, to the Ganges River, and to festivals. These pilgrims can spend significant amounts of money and impact the economy of the areas they visit.

Hinduism and Women Early Hinduism taught that both men and women could gain salvation. However, like in other ancient religions, women were considered inferior to men. Women were generally not allowed to study the Vedas.

The Spread of Hinduism Hinduism spread throughout Southeast Asia during the first few centuries AD. This happened largely through trade and the influence of Hindu kingdoms. As traders exchanged goods, they also learned about different cultures and religions. Later, Hinduism spread through colonization. Hindus were often taken to British and Dutch colonies to work as indentured servants. They brought their religion with them to the West Indies, Fiji, and parts of Africa. Hinduism spread again in the 20th century as Indians migrated to other parts of the world, such as Great Britain, Canada, and the United States. Today, there are more than 2 million Hindus in the United States.

Reading Check
Summarize
What factors determined how a person would be reborn?

Jainism

Although Hinduism was widely followed across the Indian subcontinent, it was not the only religion to influence how Indians lived. Other religious groups emerged in the region over many centuries. One such group was Jains (JYNZ), believers in a religion called Jainism (JY-niz-uhm).

Jainism is an ancient religion that is believed to have existed in India for thousands of years. Some people think that Jainism is older than Hinduism. Others think that it grew out of Hinduism. Jainism spread because of the teachings of a man named Mahavira, who is believed to have been born around 599 BC. Mahavira was an Indian prince who gave up his luxuries to become a monk.

Jains try to live by four principles: injure no life, tell the truth, do not steal, and own no property. In order to not injure anyone or anything, Jains practice **nonviolence,** or the avoidance of violent actions. The Sanskrit word for this nonviolence is *ahimsa* (uh-HIM-sah), which is also an important part of Hindu philosophy.

These Jain women are wearing masks to make sure they don't accidentally inhale and kill insects.

The Jains' emphasis on nonviolence comes from their belief that everything is alive and part of the cycle of rebirth. Jains are very serious about not injuring or killing any creature—humans, animals, insects, or plants. They do not believe in animal sacrifice, unlike many ancient religions. Because they do not want to hurt any living creatures, Jains are vegetarians. They do not eat any food that comes from animals.

Reading Check
Identify Points of View Why do Jains avoid eating meat?

Summary and Preview You have learned about two religions that grew in ancient India—Hinduism and Jainism. In the next lesson you will learn about a third religion that began there—Buddhism.

Lesson 2 Assessment

Review Ideas, Terms, and Places

1. a. **Define** What is karma?
   b. **Sequence** How did Vedic religion develop into Hinduism?
   c. **Elaborate** How does Hinduism reinforce good behavior and social order?
2. a. **Recall** What are the four main teachings of Jainism?
   b. **Predict** How do you think the idea of nonviolence affected the daily lives of Jains in ancient India?

Critical Thinking

3. **Summarize** Use a graphic organizer like the one below to summarize the main beliefs of Hinduism.

Gods	Life and Rebirth	Karma and *Dharma*

Buddhism

The Big Idea

Buddhism began in India and became a major religion.

Main Ideas

- Siddhartha Gautama searched for wisdom in many ways.
- The teachings of Buddhism deal with finding peace.
- Buddhism spread far from where it began in India.

Key Terms and Places

fasting
meditation
nirvana
missionaries

If YOU lived there . . .

You are a trader traveling in northern India in about 520 BC. As you pass through a town, you see a crowd of people sitting silently in the shade of a huge tree. A man sitting at the foot of the tree is speaking about how one ought to live. His words are like nothing you have heard from the Hindu priests.

**Will you stay to listen?
Why or why not?**

Siddhartha's Search for Wisdom

In the late 500s BC a restless young man, dissatisfied with the teachings of Hinduism, began to ask his own questions about life and religious matters. In time, he found answers. These answers attracted many followers, and the young man's ideas became the foundation of a major new religion in India.

The Quest for Answers The restless young man was Siddhartha Gautama (si-DAHR-tuh GAU-tuh-muh). Born around 563 BC in northern India near the Himalayas, Siddhartha was a prince who grew up in luxury. Born a Kshatriya, a member of the warrior class, Siddhartha never had to struggle with the problems that many people of his time faced. However, Siddhartha was not satisfied. He felt something was missing in his life.

Siddhartha looked around him and saw how hard most people had to work and how much they suffered. He saw people grieving for lost loved ones and wondered why there was so much pain in the world. As a result, Siddhartha began to ask questions about the meaning of human life.

Before Siddhartha reached age 30, he left his home and family to look for answers. His journey took him to many regions in India. Wherever he traveled, he had discussions with priests and people known for their wisdom. Yet no one could give convincing answers to Siddhartha's questions.

In this painting, Prince Siddhartha leaves his palace to search for the true meaning of life, an event known as the Great Departure. Special helpers called *ganas* hold his horse's hooves so he won't awaken anyone.

The Buddha Finds Enlightenment Siddhartha did not give up. Instead, he became even more determined to find the answers he was seeking. For several years, he wandered in search of answers.

Siddhartha wanted to free his mind from daily concerns. For a while, he did not even wash himself. He also started **fasting,** or going without food. He devoted much of his time to **meditation,** the focusing of the mind on spiritual ideas.

According to legend, Siddhartha spent six years wandering throughout India. He eventually came to a place near the town of Gaya, close to the Ganges River. There, he sat down under a tree and meditated. After seven weeks of deep meditation, he suddenly had the answers that he had been looking for. He had realized that human suffering comes from three things:

- wanting what we like but do not have,
- wanting to keep what we like and already have, and
- not wanting what we dislike but have.

Siddhartha spent seven more weeks meditating under the tree, which his followers later named the Tree of Wisdom. He then described his new ideas to five of his former companions. His followers later called this talk the First Sermon.

Siddhartha Gautama was about 35 years old when he found enlightenment under the tree near the town that became known as Bodh Gaya. From that point on, he would be called the Buddha (BOO-duh), or the "Enlightened One." The Buddha spent the rest of his life traveling across northern India and teaching people his ideas.

Reading Check
Summarize
What did the Buddha conclude about the cause of suffering?

Teachings of Buddhism

As he traveled, the Buddha gained many followers. Many of these followers were merchants and artisans, but he even taught a few kings. These followers were the first believers in Buddhism, the religion based on the teachings of the Buddha.

The Buddha was raised Hindu, and many of his teachings reflected Hindu ideas. Like Hindus, he believed that people should act morally and treat others well. In one of his sermons, he said

> "Let a man overcome anger by love. Let him overcome the greedy by liberality [giving], the liar by truth."
>
> –The Buddha, quoted in *The History of Nations: India*

The teachings of the Buddha were passed down orally for centuries. The Tipitaka, also known as the Pali canon, Tripitaka, or Triple Basket, records many teachings that Buddhists see as scripture. Some Buddhists also revere other writings.

Four Noble Truths At the heart of the Buddha's teachings were four guiding principles.

These became known as the Four Noble Truths:

1. Suffering and unhappiness are a part of human life. No one can escape sorrow.
2. Suffering comes from our desires for pleasure and material goods. People cause their own misery because they want things they cannot have.
3. People can overcome their desires and ignorance and reach **nirvana,** a state of perfect peace. Reaching nirvana frees a person's soul from suffering and from the need for further reincarnation.
4. People can overcome ignorance and desire by following an Eightfold Path that leads to wisdom, enlightenment, and salvation.

The Buddha believed that the Eightfold Path was a middle way between human desires and denying oneself any pleasure. He said:

> "A life given to pleasures, devoted to pleasures and lusts: this is degrading, sensual, vulgar, ignoble, and profitless; and a life given to mortifications: this is painful, ignoble, and profitless. . . . [It is] the Middle Path which leads to insight, which leads to wisdom, which conduces to calm, to knowledge, to the Sambodhi, to Nirvana."
>
> —The Buddha, quoted in the Mahavagga

The Buddha believed that people should overcome their desire for material goods. They should, however, be reasonable, and not starve their bodies or cause themselves unnecessary pain.

Challenging Traditional Ideas Some of the Buddha's teachings challenged traditional Hindu ideas. For example, the Buddha told people that they did not have to follow the Vedas to achieve enlightenment. The Buddha also challenged the authority of the Hindu priests, the Brahmins. He did not believe that the priests or their rituals were necessary for enlightenment.

Quick Facts

The Eightfold Path

1. Right Thought
   Believe in the nature of existence as suffering and in the Four Noble Truths.

2. Right Intent
   Incline toward goodness and kindness.

3. Right Speech
   Avoid lies and gossip.

4. Right Action
   Don't steal from or harm others.

5. Right Livelihood
   Reject work that hurts others.

6. Right Effort
   Prevent evil and do good.

7. Right Mindfulness
   Control your feelings and thoughts.

8. Right Concentration
   Practice proper meditation.

Instead, he taught that it was the responsibility of each person to work for his or her own liberation. Priests could not help them. However, the Buddha did not reject the Hindu teaching of reincarnation. He taught that people who failed to reach nirvana would have to be reborn until they achieved it.

The Buddha was opposed to people needing to follow social roles to achieve liberation or good karma. He didn't think that people should be confined to a particular place in society. He taught that those who followed the Eightfold Path properly would reach nirvana. It didn't matter what *varna* they had belonged to in life as long as they lived the way they should.

The Buddha's teachings won over many people. Many herders, farmers, and artisans liked hearing that their lack of knowledge of sacred texts would not be a barrier to their enlightenment. Buddhism made them feel that they had the power to change their lives without rituals or priests.

Reading Check
Compare
How did the Buddha's teachings agree with Hinduism?

The Buddha also gained followers among Brahmins and princes, who welcomed his ideas about avoiding extreme behavior while seeking salvation. By the time of his death around 483 BC, the Buddha's influence was spreading rapidly throughout India.

Buddhism Spreads

Buddhism continued to attract followers after the Buddha's death. After spreading through India, the religion began to spread to other areas as well.

Buddhism Spreads in India According to Buddhist tradition, 500 of the Buddha's followers gathered together shortly after he died. They wanted to make sure that the Buddha's teachings were remembered correctly.

In the years after this council, the Buddha's followers spread his teachings throughout India. The ideas spread very quickly, because Buddhist teachings were popular and easy to understand. Within 200 years of the Buddha's death, Buddhism had spread through most of India.

Buddhism Spreads beyond India The spread of Buddhism increased after one of the most powerful kings in India, Asoka, became Buddhist in the 200s BC. Once he converted, he built Buddhist temples and schools throughout India. More importantly, though, he worked to spread Buddhism into areas outside of India. You will learn more about Asoka and his accomplishments in the next lesson.

Asoka sent Buddhist **missionaries,** or people who work to spread their religious beliefs, to other kingdoms in Asia. One group of these missionaries sailed to the island of Sri Lanka around 251 BC. Others followed trade routes east to what is now Myanmar and to other parts of Southeast Asia. Missionaries also went north to areas near the Himalayas.

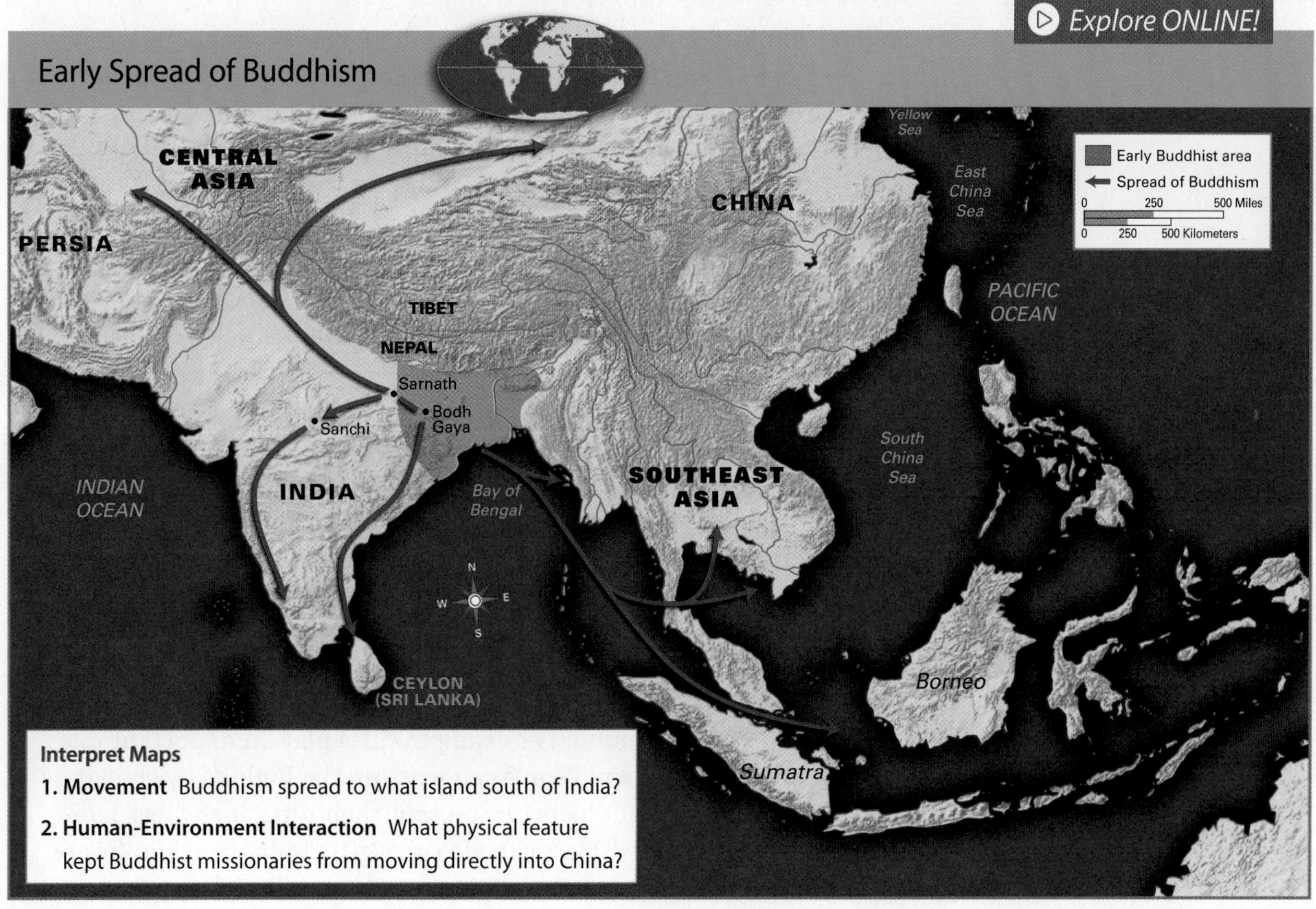

Interpret Maps

1. **Movement** Buddhism spread to what island south of India?
2. **Human-Environment Interaction** What physical feature kept Buddhist missionaries from moving directly into China?

Young Buddhist students carry gifts in Sri Lanka, one of the many places outside of India where Buddhism spread.

Missionaries also introduced Buddhism to lands west of India. They founded Buddhist communities in Central Asia and Persia. They even taught about Buddhism as far away as Syria and Egypt. Buddhism continued to grow over the centuries. Eventually, it spread via the Silk Road into China, then Korea and Japan. Through their work, missionaries taught Buddhism to millions of people.

A Split within Buddhism Even as Buddhism spread through Asia, however, it began to change. Not all Buddhists could agree on their beliefs and practices. Eventually, disagreements between Buddhists led to a split within the religion. Two major branches of Buddhism were created—Theravada and Mahayana.

Members of the Theravada branch tried to follow the Buddha's teachings exactly as he had stated them. Mahayana Buddhists, though, believed that other people could interpret the Buddha's teachings to help people reach nirvana. Both branches have millions of believers today, but Mahayana is by far the larger branch.

As immigrants have moved from Asia around the world, Buddhism has spread globally, including to the United States. As Buddhism has spread, it has continued to influence the arts in India and around the world. Modern cultural products around the world show Buddhism's influence. For example, a television show called *Buddha* was created in India in 2013 and has been broadcast in countries around the world. It depicts the life of Siddhartha Gautama and how he became the Buddha.

Customs and Traditions Both branches of Buddhism have some traditions and customs in common. For example, gifts play an important role in the customs of Buddhism. People can worship the Buddha by showing respect or giving gifts. Buddhists can present their gifts at shrines dedicated to the Buddha. Worshipers can also give gifts to monks. Monks are people who devote themselves to religious study and discipline.

Buddhists observe many holidays. The three main events of the Buddha's life—his birth, enlightenment, and death—are all holidays. The end of *vassa*, the rainy season, is celebrated. All Souls Day, New Year's, and Harvest Festivals are also celebrated. For some holidays, people may wear all white or new clothes to symbolize rebirth and renewal. Or they may visit temples for special sutras, or services. One of the most important rituals in Buddhism is making a pilgrimage. These travels to holy sites are meant to aid in a person's spiritual development.

Reading Check
Sequence
How did the Buddha's teachings spread out of India?

Summary and Preview Buddhism, one of India's major religions, grew more popular once it was adopted by rulers of India's great empires. In the next lesson, you will read about another religion that started in India, Sikhism.

Lesson 3 Assessment

Review Ideas, Terms, and Places

1. **a. Identify** Who was the Buddha, and what does the term *Buddha* mean?
   b. Summarize How did Siddhartha Gautama free his mind and clarify his thinking as he searched for wisdom?
2. **a. Identify** What is nirvana?
   b. Contrast How are Buddhist teachings different from Hindu teachings?
   c. Elaborate Why do Buddhists believe that following the Eightfold Path leads to a better life?
3. **a. Describe** Into what lands did Buddhism spread?
   b. Summarize What role did missionaries play in spreading Buddhism?

Critical Thinking

4. **Find Main Ideas** Draw a diagram like this one. Use it to identify and describe Buddhism's Four Noble Truths. Write a sentence explaining how the truths are central to Buddhism.

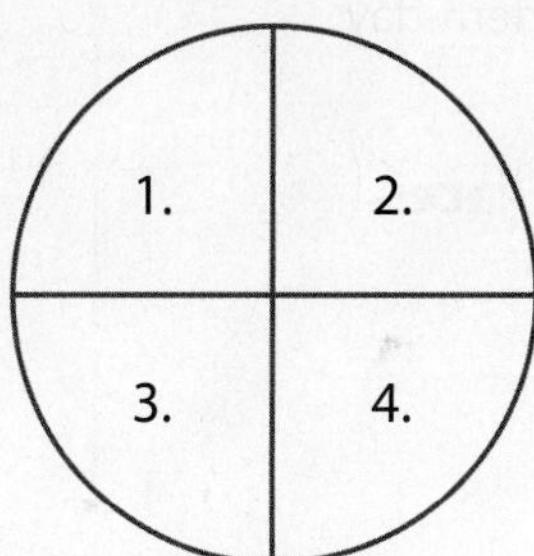

Sikhism

The Big Idea

Sikhism originated in the Punjab region of India and has grown to include nearly 25 million followers around the world.

Main Ideas

- Sikhs believe in equality and generally reject the caste system.
- Sikhs have responded to historical and modern-day challenges.

Key Terms and Places

langar
gurdwaras

If YOU lived there . . .

You hear a guru, or teacher, speaking in public. He is a Sikh, and he believes that all people should be treated equally. He talks about a community of Sikhs near you who embrace this principle.

Are you curious to learn more about Sikhism?

Sikh Religion

Sikhism (SIK-iz-uhm), the world's fifth-largest religion, began in the Punjab in the late 15th century, and people who follow the religion are known as Sikhs (SIKS). Sikhism was started by Guru Nanak. The title *guru* is Sanskrit for "teacher."

The Origin of Sikhism In the Punjabi language, the word *sikh* means "learner." People who joined the Sikh community looked for spiritual guidance. In Punjabi, Sikhism is called Gurmat, which means "the way of the Guru."

Guru Nanak, who lived from 1469 to 1539, was the first guru. Nanak was raised a Hindu. However, he disagreed with some of the Hindu teachings. While traveling, Nanak came into contact with many other religions, including Islam. In reaction to the teachings of Hinduism and Islam, he preached a path that was independent from both. He thought people from different social classes should be treated equally. Many people were attracted to Nanak's ideas about equality. After he died, nine other gurus followed Nanak. The essential beliefs of Sikhism are found in the teachings of all ten of these gurus.

Sikh Beliefs Sikhs believe that each of these gurus was inhabited by a single spirit. Each time a guru died, this spirit, or eternal Guru, transferred itself to the next human guru. The tenth guru, Guru Gobind Singh, died in 1708. Sikhs believe that at that time, the spirit transferred itself to the sacred scripture of the Sikhs. This scripture is called Guru Granth Sahib. It contains the actual words spoken by the Sikh gurus, which Sikhs believe to be the word of Waheguru, or God. It also contains passages from Hindu and Muslim teachers.

In a langar, Sikhs and visitors share a meal sitting on the floor together. This signifies a strong belief in social equality.

Sikhs believe there is only one God and that God does not have a form or gender. They also believe that everyone has equal access to God and that everyone is equal before God, including men and women and people of different classes. Living honestly and caring for others is important to Sikhs. Like Hindus, Sikhs believe that humans cycle through life, death, and reincarnation. They also believe in karma.

Sikh Religious Practices Sikhs do not agree with many aspects of the caste system. They believe in equality between social classes. You can see this equality in the kitchens at their places of worship. In the **langar,** or kitchen, food is served without charge. Everyone sits on the floor together. This practice came about as a protest against the caste system, which forbade eating with other castes. Sitting on the floor together is a symbol of social equality.

However, some aspects of the caste system are still observed in two areas of Sikh society—marriage and some **gurdwaras,** or places of worship. Sikhs are expected to marry someone of their own caste. Some castes have also created gurdwaras for their caste only.

Sikhism is based on a need to understand and experience God. It is a goal to eventually become one with God. To achieve this, Sikh philosophy refers to three duties: to pray, to work, and to give. This means keeping God in mind at all times through prayer and meditation, earning an honest living, and giving to others. One way to keep God in mind is to wear certain articles that signify faith. These articles include uncut hair, a sword, a metal bracelet, and a wooden comb.

Sikhs also believe there are five vices that make people self-centered, which they try to avoid. The five vices are lust, greed, attachment to worldly things, anger, and pride. Sikhs believe that avoiding these vices will help in attaining spiritual liberation.

Sikh Articles of Faith

Kesh	Uncut hair often covered by a distinctive turban, which represents spirituality
Kirpan	A religious sword, which represents readiness to protect the weak and fight against injustice
Kara	A metal bracelet, which represents an eternal connection to Waheguru
Kanga	A wooden comb, which represents cleanliness
Kachera	Cotton undergarments, which represent self-discipline

Interpret Charts
Why do you think many Sikhs wear these articles on a daily basis?

Like other religions, Sikhs celebrate special times in individuals' lives and important holidays for the community. New babies are celebrated with a special naming ceremony at the gurdwara. Formally joining the Sikh community, or Khalsa, as a mature adult is also marked with a sacred ceremony. After this ceremony, Sikhs are expected to wear the five articles of faith and live by the religion's rules. Anniversaries of events in the lives of the ten gurus, called gurpurabs, are celebrated. One of the most important holidays is Vaisakhi, the anniversary of the creation of the Khalsa.

Reading Check
Draw Conclusions What effects has Sikhism's rejection of the caste system had on its society?

Sikh History

Many Sikhs lived in the Punjab region of India. In the 1600s Sikhs occasionally came into conflict with the ruling Mughal Empire. The Mughals controlled much of what is now India. There were uprisings over unfair taxes and other mistreatment. When Sikhs gathered to protest, the Mughals often sent war elephants to stop them. As a result of these harsh policies, violent revolts occurred throughout the region in the 1600s and 1700s.

Sikh Power in the Punjab Region Over time, however, the Mughal Empire began to weaken, and Sikh resistance to Mughal rule intensified. After conflict with the Mughals to the east and the Afghans to the west, Sikhs controlled much of the Punjab in the late 1700s. In 1799 a man named Ranjit Singh declared himself maharaja, or ruler, of the Punjab. This was the beginning of the Sikh Empire.

For the next 50 years, the Sikhs ruled much of what is now northwestern India and eastern Pakistan. It was during this time that a gurdwara in northwestern India was rebuilt using marble and gold. This was a symbol of Sikh power. It became known as the Golden Temple. Ranjit Singh was

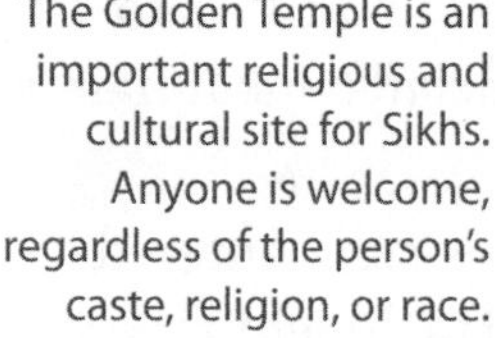

The Golden Temple is an important religious and cultural site for Sikhs. Anyone is welcome, regardless of the person's caste, religion, or race.

a strong ruler, and the Sikh Empire thrived for many years. However, the Sikh Empire began to weaken when he died in 1839. After conflict with the British, the Punjab became a part of British India in 1849.

Sikhism Spreads There are nearly 25 million Sikhs worldwide today. Most live in India. For many years, most migrant Sikhs were traders. They often settled close to the Punjab region, though others went to other parts of the Indian subcontinent. When the British took control of India in 1858, they recruited Sikhs to serve as soldiers. Sikh soldiers were posted in the British colonies of Malaya and Hong Kong. This encouraged Sikh migration to other parts of the world.

Sikh migration expanded in the 20th century to different regions in Asia, Australia, and North America. The west coast of North America provided opportunities for jobs, and the first Sikhs began arriving there in 1903.

Globalization presents both struggles and opportunities to Sikhs living outside India. Because of their distinctive dress, Sikhs remain a visible minority in their adopted homelands. In response to economic challenges, many Sikhs migrated to the United Kingdom and North America after World War II. They arrived in search of educational and employment opportunities. In the United States and Canada, there are now large Sikh communities consisting of thousands of people.

Reading Check
Analyze Motives
Why have many Sikhs left India?

Summary and Preview In this lesson you learned about the beliefs of Sikhism and how the religion began. You also learned about the Sikh Empire and why many Sikhs have migrated from India to other parts of the world. In the next lesson, you will learn about some of India's greatest empires.

Lesson 4 Assessment

Review Ideas, Terms, and Places

1. a. **Summarize** How did Sikhism begin, and how has it been passed down through generations?
   b. **Recall** What are the three duties referred to in Sikh philosophy?
   c. **Summarize** What do the Sikhs believe will happen if they avoid the five vices?
2. a. **Analyze** Why did Sikhs first leave India?
   b. **Summarize** What drew Sikhs to other countries after World War II?

Critical Thinking

3. **Compare and Contrast** In this lesson, you learned about how Sikhism is similar to and different from Hinduism. Create a graphic organizer similar to the one below to note these differences and similarities.

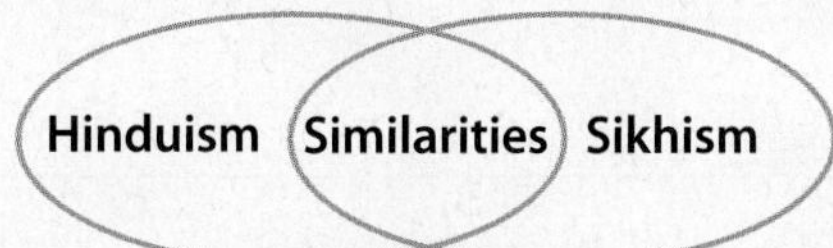

Indian Empires

The Big Idea

The Mauryas, the Guptas, and the Mughals built great empires in India and made important contributions to the arts and sciences.

Main Ideas

- The Mauryan Empire unified most of India.
- Gupta rulers promoted Hinduism in their empire.
- The Mughal Empire reunited much of India during the 16th century.
- The people of ancient India made great contributions to the arts and sciences.

Key Terms and Places

mercenaries
edicts
metallurgy
alloys
inoculation
Hindu-Arabic numerals

If YOU lived there . . .

You are a merchant in India in about 240 BC. You travel from town to town on your donkey, carrying bolts of colorful cloth. In the heat of summer, you are grateful for the banyan trees along the road. They shelter you from the blazing sun. You stop at wells for cool drinks of water and rest houses for a break in your journey. You know these are all the work of your king, Asoka.

How do you feel about your king?

Mauryan Empire Unifies India

In the 320s BC a military leader named Chandragupta Maurya (kuhn-druh-GOOP-tuh MOUR-yuh) rose to power in northern India. Using an army of **mercenaries,** or hired soldiers, he seized control of the entire northern part of India. By doing so, he founded the Mauryan Empire. Mauryan rule lasted for about 150 years.

The Mauryan Empire Chandragupta Maurya ruled his empire with the help of a complex, bureaucratic government. It included a network of spies and a huge army of some 600,000 soldiers. The army also had thousands of war elephants and thousands of chariots. In return for the army's protection, farmers paid a heavy tax to the government.

BIOGRAPHY

Asoka ?–238 BC

Asoka is one of the most respected rulers in Indian history and one of the most important figures in the history of Buddhism. After he became a devout Buddhist, Asoka stopped waging war and worked for years to spread the Buddha's teachings. In addition to sending missionaries around Asia, he had huge columns carved with Buddhist teachings raised all over India. Largely through his efforts, Buddhism became one of Asia's main religions.

Form Generalizations
How did Asoka's life change after he became a Buddhist?

Explore ONLINE!

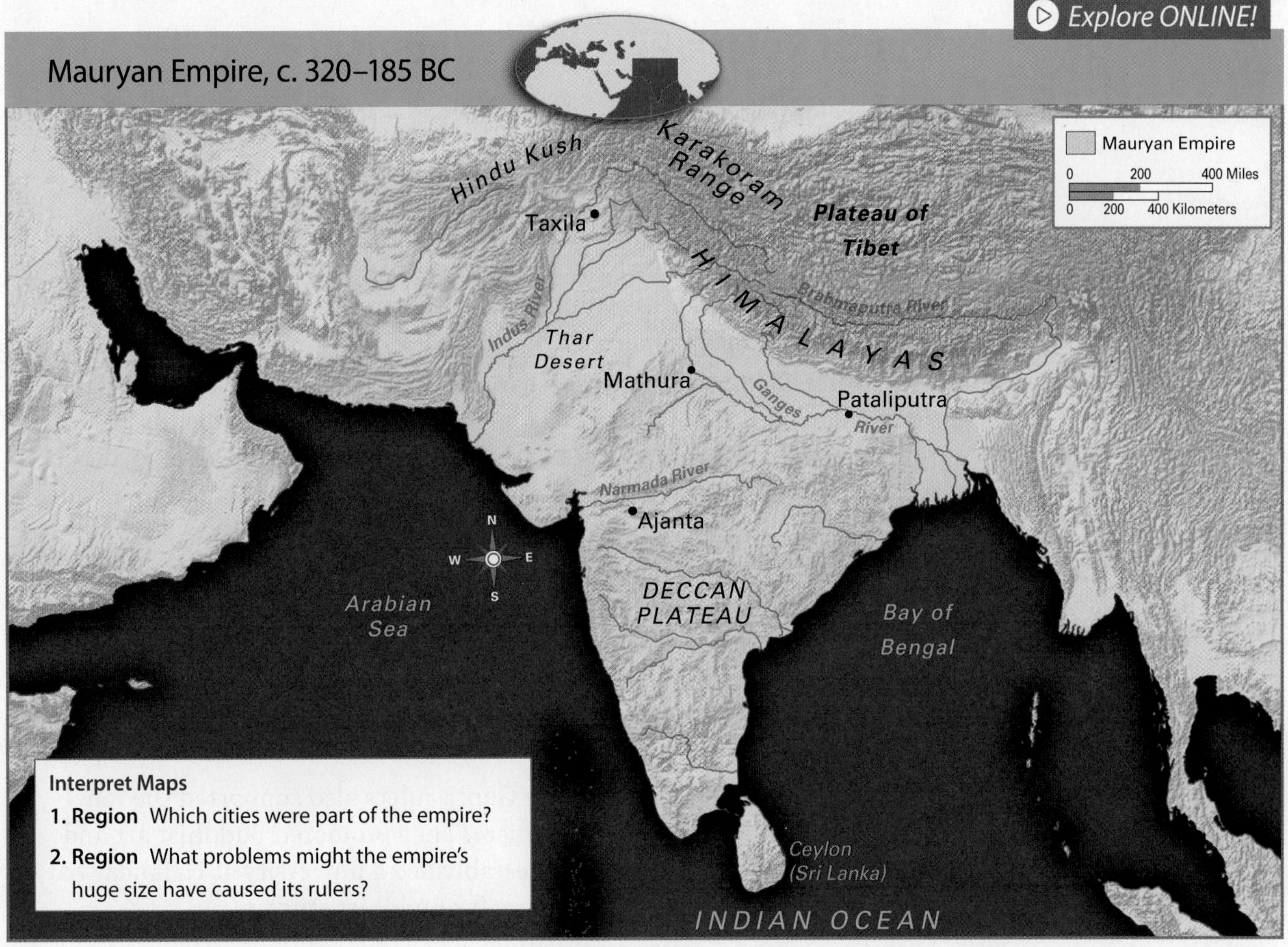

Interpret Maps

1. **Region** Which cities were part of the empire?
2. **Region** What problems might the empire's huge size have caused its rulers?

In 301 BC Chandragupta decided to become a Jainist monk. To do so, he had to give up his throne. He passed the throne to his son, who continued to expand the empire. Before long, the Mauryas ruled all of northern India and much of central India as well.

Asoka Around 270 BC Chandragupta's grandson Asoka (uh-SOH-kuh) became king. Asoka was a strong ruler, the strongest of all the Mauryan emperors. He extended Mauryan rule over most of India. In conquering other kingdoms, Asoka made his own empire both stronger and richer.

For many years, Asoka watched his armies fight bloody battles against other peoples. A few years into his rule, however, Asoka converted to Buddhism. When he did, he swore that he would not launch any more wars of conquest.

After converting to Buddhism, Asoka had the time and resources to improve the lives of his people. He had wells dug and roads built throughout the empire. Along these roads, workers planted shade trees, built rest houses for travelers, and raised large stone pillars carved with Buddhist **edicts,** or laws. Asoka also encouraged the spread of Buddhism in India and the rest of Asia. He sent missionaries to lands all over Asia.

Asoka died in 238 BC, and the empire began to fall apart soon afterward. His sons fought for power, and invaders threatened the empire. In 184 BC the last Mauryan king was killed by one of his generals. India divided into smaller states once again.

Reading Check
Find Main Ideas
How did the Mauryans gain control of most of India?

Gupta Rulers Promote Hinduism

After the collapse of the Mauryan Empire, India remained divided for about 500 years. During that period, Buddhism continued to prosper and spread in India, and so the popularity of Hinduism declined.

Academic Vocabulary
establish to set up or create

A New Hindu Empire Eventually, however, a new dynasty was **established** in India. It was the Gupta (GOOP-tuh) dynasty, which took over India around AD 320. Under the Guptas, India was once again united, and it once again became prosperous.

The first Gupta emperor was Chandra Gupta I. Although their names are similar, he was not related to Chandragupta Maurya. From his base in northern India, Chandra Gupta's armies invaded and conquered neighboring lands. Eventually, he brought much of the northern part of India under his control. The Gupta government was bureaucratic, like the Mauryan government, but gave more power to local entities.

Indian civilization flourished under the Gupta rulers. These rulers were Hindu, so Hinduism became India's dominant religion. Gupta kings built many Hindu temples, some of which became models for later Indian architecture. They also promoted a revival of Hindu writings and worship practices.

Although they were Hindus, the Gupta rulers also supported the religious beliefs of Buddhism and Jainism. They promoted Buddhist art and built Buddhist temples. They also established a university at Nalanda that became one of Asia's greatest centers for Buddhist studies.

Gupta Society In 375 emperor Chandra Gupta II took the throne in India. Gupta society reached its high point during his rule. Under Chandra Gupta II, the empire continued to grow, eventually stretching all the way across northern India. At the same time, the empire's economy strengthened, and so people prospered. They created fine works of art and literature. Outsiders admired the empire's wealth and beauty.

This painting is of a palace scene. It was painted during the Gupta period.

Gupta kings believed the strict social order of the caste system would strengthen their rule. They also thought it would keep the empire stable. As a result, the Guptas considered the caste system an important part of Indian society. *Jatis*, the occupation-based groupings, became more complex during this period.

During this time, women's roles were very limited. A woman's role was to marry and have children. Women couldn't even choose their own husbands. Parents arranged all marriages. Once married, wives had few rights. They were expected to serve their husbands. Widows had an even lower social status than other women.

Gupta rule remained strong in India until the late 400s. At that time the Huns, a group from Central Asia, invaded India from the northwest. Their fierce

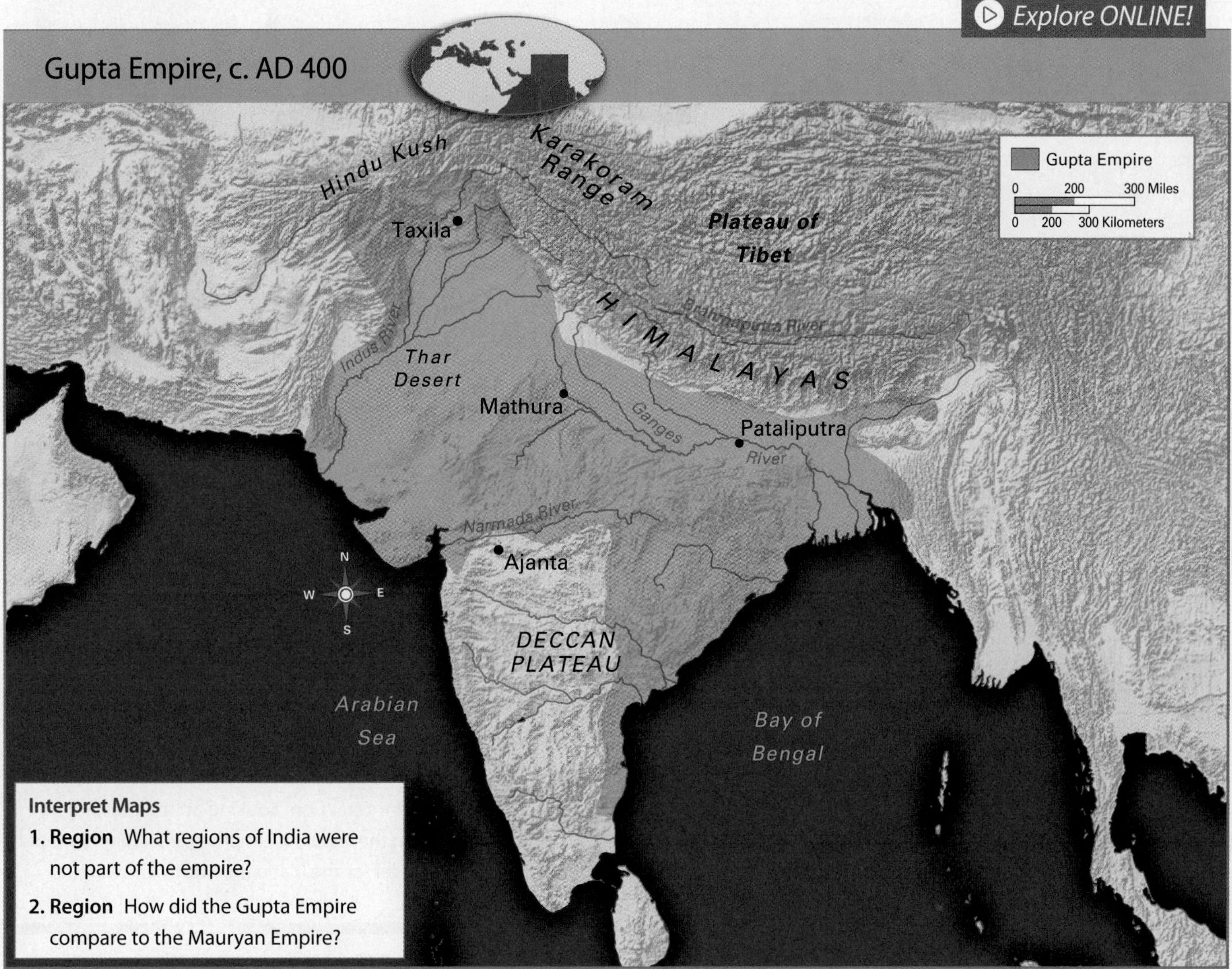

Interpret Maps

1. **Region** What regions of India were not part of the empire?
2. **Region** How did the Gupta Empire compare to the Mauryan Empire?

Reading Check
Summarize
What was the Gupta dynasty's position on religion?

attacks drained the Gupta Empire of its power and wealth. As the Hun armies marched farther into India, the Guptas lost hope. By the middle of the 500s, Gupta rule had ended, and India had divided into small kingdoms yet again.

The Mughal Empire

About 1,000 years later, the Mughal (MOO-guhl) Empire reunited much of India. The Mughals were Turkish Muslims from Central Asia. Their empire was established by a leader named Babur (BAH-boohr), or "tiger." He tried for years to build an empire in Central Asia. When he did not succeed there, he decided to create an empire in northern India instead. The result was the Mughal Empire, created in 1526.

In the mid-1500s an emperor named Akbar conquered many new lands and worked to strengthen the government of the empire. Like the Mauryas and the Guptas, the Mughal government was complex and bureaucratic.

In addition to reforming government, Akbar also instituted a tolerant religious policy. While the Mughals spread Islam through the land they conquered, Akbar believed members of all religions could live and work together.

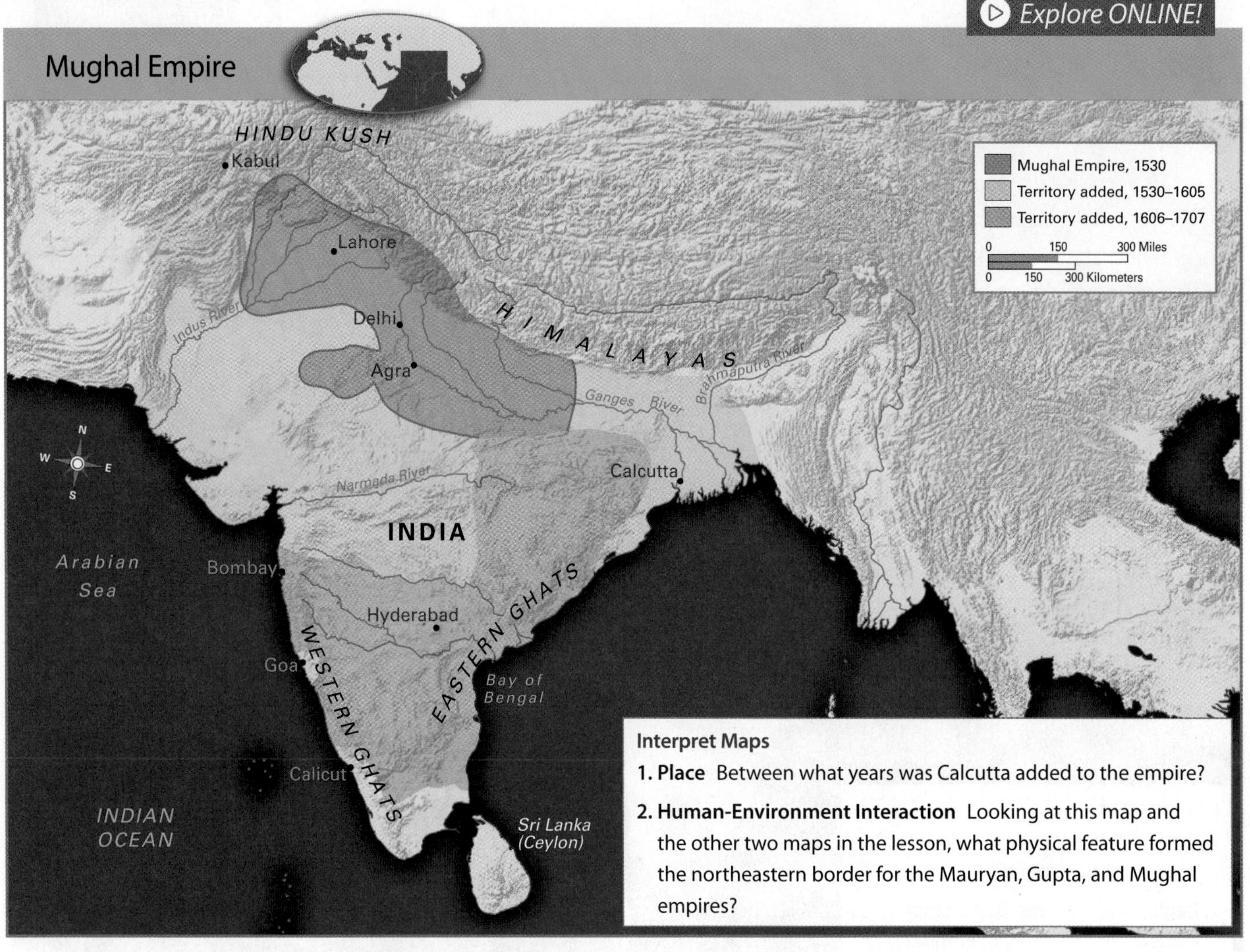

Interpret Maps

1. **Place** Between what years was Calcutta added to the empire?
2. **Human-Environment Interaction** Looking at this map and the other two maps in the lesson, what physical feature formed the northeastern border for the Mauryan, Gupta, and Mughal empires?

Akbar's tolerance allowed Muslims and Hindus in the empire to live in peace. In time, cooperation between the two groups helped create a unique Mughal culture. It blended Persian, Islamic, and Hindu elements. The Mughals became known for their monumental works of architecture. One famous example of this architecture is the Taj Mahal, a tomb built in the 1600s by emperor Shah Jahan for his wife. Its graceful domes and towers are a symbol of India today.

In the late 1600s an emperor named Aurangzeb reversed Akbar's tolerant policies. He destroyed many Hindu temples, and violent revolts broke out. The Mughal Empire fell apart.

Reading Check
Find Main Ideas
How was Akbar able to build a strong empire and government?

Indian Achievements

The Indians of the Mauryan and Gupta periods created great works of architecture, art, and literature, many of them religious. Indian achievements were not limited to the arts. Indian scholars also made important advances in metalworking, math, and science.

Religious Art During the Gupta and Mauryan periods, religion influenced the arts. Many paintings and sculptures illustrated either Hindu or Buddhist teachings. Some of the most elaborate architecture of those periods were Buddhist and Hindu temples.

Early Hindu temples were small, stone structures. They had flat roofs and contained only one or two rooms. In the Gupta period, though, temple architecture became more complex. Gupta temples were topped by huge towers and covered with carvings of the god worshiped there.

Buddhist temples of the Gupta period are also impressive. Some Buddhists carved entire temples out of mountainsides. The most famous such temples are at Ajanta and Ellora. Builders filled the caves there with beautiful paintings and sculpture.

Another type of Buddhist temple was the stupa. Stupas had domed roofs and were built to house sacred items from the life of the Buddha. Many of them were covered with detailed carvings.

The Gupta period also saw the creation of many paintings and statues. Hindu and Buddhist artists found inspiration from their beliefs to create their works. As a result, many of the finest paintings of ancient India are found in temples. Hindu painters drew hundreds of gods on temple walls and entrances. Buddhists covered the walls and ceilings of temples with scenes from the life of the Buddha.

Sculptors made many statues for Buddhist cave temples. In addition to the temples' intricately carved columns, sculptors carved statues of kings and the Buddha. Some of these statues tower over the cave entrances. Hindu temples also featured impressive statues of their gods. In fact, the walls of some temples, especially in southern India, were completely covered with carvings and images.

This Hindu temple is covered with finely detailed carvings and decorations. Many individual sculptures are images of major Hindu gods, like the statue of Vishnu at the right.

Indian Literature Sanskrit was the main language in north India. During the Mauryan and Gupta periods, many works of Sanskrit literature were written down. These works were later translated into many other languages. In southern India, major works were composed in languages such as Tamil.

The greatest of these Sanskrit writings are two religious epics, the *Mahabharata* (muh-HAH-bah-ruh-tuh) and the *Ramayana* (rah-MAH-yuh-nuh). Both of these works are popular across the world. The *Mahabharata* is one of the world's longest literary works. It is a story about a struggle between two families for control of a kingdom. Included within the story are long passages about Hindu beliefs. The most famous is called the *Bhagavad Gita* (BUG-uh-vuhd GEE-tah), which has influenced thinkers such as Henry David Thoreau and leaders including Mohandas Gandhi and Nelson Mandela.

The *Ramayana*, another great epic, tells about a prince named Rama. In truth, the prince was the god Vishnu in human form. He had become human so he could rid the world of demons. He also had to rescue his wife, a princess named Sita. For centuries, characters from the *Ramayana* have been seen as models for how to lead good lives. For example, Rama is seen as the ideal ruler and his relationship with Sita as the ideal marriage. The *Ramayana* is also an important text in Buddhism and Jainism. Many different versions of it have been written over time, including modern versions in print and film. The *Ramayana* is also the national epic of Indonesia, the world's most populous Muslim country.

Writers in the Gupta period also created plays, poetry, and other types of literature. Sometime before 500, Indian writers produced a book of stories called the *Panchatantra* (PUHN-chuh-TAHN-truh). The stories in this collection were intended to teach lessons. They praise people for cleverness and quick thinking. Each story ends with a message about winning friends, losing property, waging war, or some other idea.

Eventually, translations of this popular collection spread throughout the world. It became popular in countries even as far away as Europe.

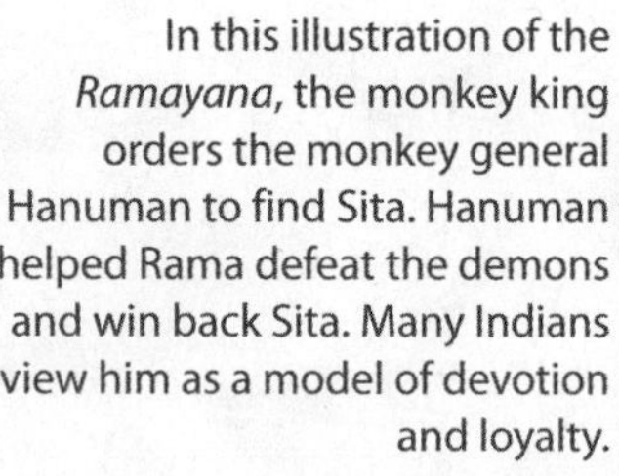

In this illustration of the *Ramayana,* the monkey king orders the monkey general Hanuman to find Sita. Hanuman helped Rama defeat the demons and win back Sita. Many Indians view him as a model of devotion and loyalty.

Indian Science

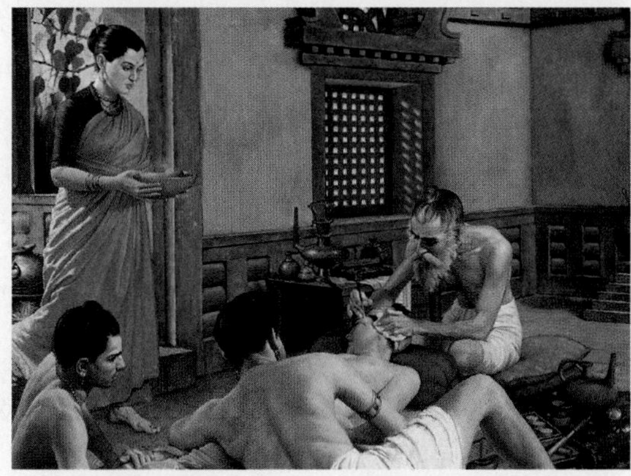

Medicine

In this modern painting, the Indian surgeon Susruta performs surgery on a patient. The ancient Indians had an advanced knowledge of medicine.

Metalworking

The Indians were expert metalworkers. This gold coin shows the emperor Chandra Gupta II.

Mathematics

The Hindu scholar Aryabhata was a mathematician and astronomer. He wrote one of the first books on algebra about AD 500.

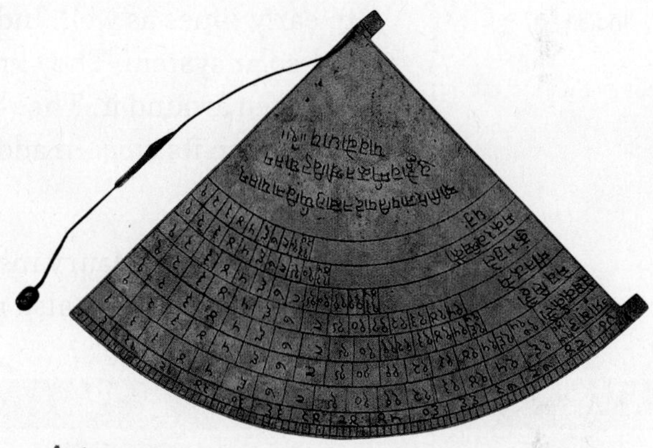

Astronomy

The Guptas made great advances in astronomy, despite their lack of modern devices such as telescopes. They used devices like this one from the 1700s to observe and map the stars.

Analyze Visuals
What are some areas of science that people studied in ancient India?

Academic Vocabulary
process a series of steps by which a task is accomplished

Scientific Advances The ancient Indians were pioneers of **metallurgy** (MET-uhl-uhr-jee), the science of working with metals. Their knowledge allowed them to create high-quality tools and weapons. Indians also knew **processes** for mixing metals to create **alloys,** mixtures of two or more metals. Alloys are sometimes stronger or easier to work with than pure metals.

Metalworkers made their strongest products out of iron. Indian iron was very hard and pure. These features made the iron a valuable trade item. Indian steel has been a valued export for centuries. Even today, India is one of the top steel producers in the world.

The ancient Indians were also very skilled in the medical sciences. As early as the AD 100s, doctors were writing their knowledge down in textbooks. Among the skills these books describe is how to make medicines from plants and minerals.

Besides curing people with medicines, Indian doctors knew how to protect them against diseases. They used **inoculation** (i-nah-kyuh-LAY-shuhn), the practice of injecting a person with a small dose of a virus to help him or her build a defense to a disease. By fighting off this small dose, the body learns to protect itself. People still get inoculations against many diseases.

For people who were injured, Indian doctors could perform surgery. Surgeons repaired broken bones, treated wounds, removed infected tonsils, reconstructed broken noses, and even reattached torn earlobes!

Gupta scholars also made advances in math. They developed many of the elements of our modern math system. The very numbers we use today are called **Hindu-Arabic numerals** because they were created by Indian scholars and brought to Europe by Arabs. The Indians were also the first people to create the zero. Although it may seem like a small thing, modern math and technology wouldn't be possible without the zero.

Reading Check
Summarize
How did religion influence ancient Indian art?

Indian interest in astronomy, the study of stars and planets, dates back to early times as well. Indian astronomers knew of seven of the planets in our solar system. They knew that the sun was a star and that the planets revolved around it. They also knew that Earth was a sphere and that it rotated on its axis. In addition, they could predict eclipses of the sun and the moon.

Summary The Mauryans, Guptas, and Mughals united much of India in their empires. They also made many achievements in the arts and sciences.

Lesson 5 Assessment

Review Ideas, Terms, and Places

1. a. **Identify** Who created the Mauryan Empire?
   b. **Elaborate** Why do you think many people consider Asoka the greatest of all Mauryan rulers?
2. a. **Recall** What religion did most of the Gupta rulers belong to?
   b. **Compare and Contrast** How were the rulers Chandragupta Maurya and Chandra Gupta I alike, and how were they different?
3. a. **Summarize** What role did Akbar play in the blended culture in the Mughal Empire?
   b. **Analyze** Why was the Taj Mahal built?
   c. **Compare** How did Mauryan, Gupta, and Mughal leaders' views on religion impact how their societies developed?
4. a. **Describe** What did Hindu temples of the Gupta period look like?
   b. **Evaluate** Why do you think both Hindu and Buddhist temples contained great works of art?
   c. **Identify** What is the *Bhagavad Gita*?
   d. **Elaborate** Why do you think people are still interested in ancient Sanskrit epics today?
   e. **Explain** Why do we call the numbers we use today Hindu-Arabic numerals?

Critical Thinking

5. **Sequence** Create a timeline of the empires and rulers mentioned in this lesson.
6. **Categorize** Draw a chart like this one. Fill it with facts about India's rulers.

Ruler	Dynasty	Accomplishments

Social Studies Skills

Compare Maps

Define the Skill

Maps are a necessary tool in the study of both history and geography. Sometimes, however, a map does not contain all the information you need. In those cases, you may have to compare two or more maps and combine what is shown on each.

For example, if you look at a physical map of India, you can see what landforms are in a region. You can then look at a population map to see how many people live in that region. From this comparison, you can conclude how the region's landforms affect its population distribution.

Learn the Skill

Compare the two maps on this page to answer the following questions.

1. What was the northeastern boundary of the Gupta Empire? What is the physical landscape like there?
2. What region of India was never part of the Gupta Empire? Based on the physical map, what might have been one reason for this?

Practice the Skill

Choose two maps from this module or two maps from an atlas or reliable Internet source. Study the two maps and then write three questions that someone could answer by comparing them. Remember that the questions should require people to look at both maps to determine the correct answers.

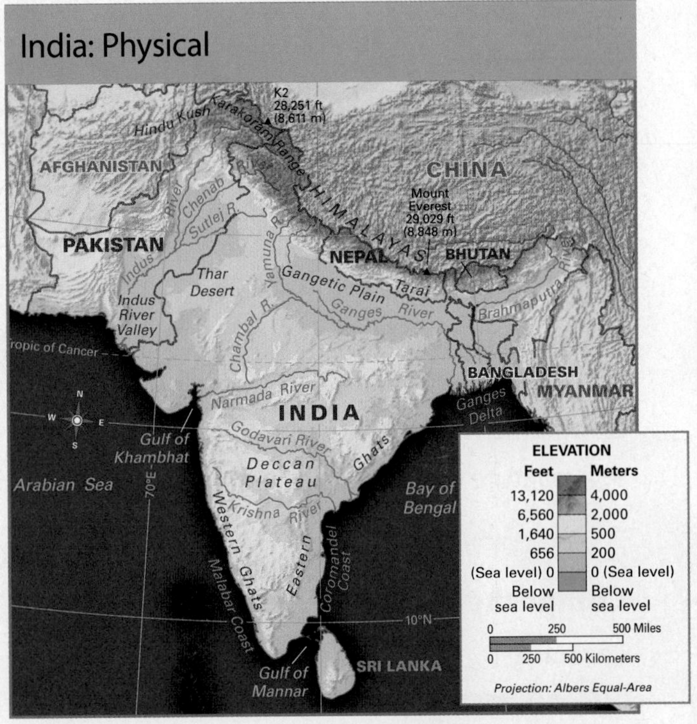

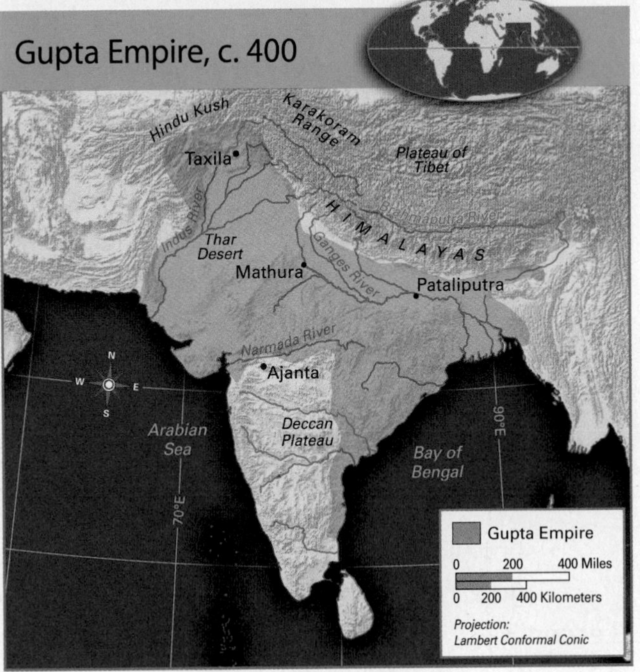

Module 14 Assessment

Review Vocabulary, Terms, and Places

Fill in the blanks with the correct term or name from this module.

1. __________ are hired soldiers.
2. A __________ is a division of people into groups based on birth, wealth, or occupation.
3. Hindus believe in __________, the belief that they will be reborn many times after death.
4. Harappa and __________ were the largest cities of the Harappan civilization.
5. The focusing of the mind on spiritual things is called __________.
6. People who work to spread their religious beliefs are called __________.
7. People who practice __________ use only peaceful ways to achieve change.
8. Indian civilization first developed in the valley of the __________.
9. A mixture of metals is called an __________.

Comprehension and Critical Thinking

Lesson 1

10. a. **Describe** What caused floods on the Indus River, and what was the result of those floods?
    b. **Contrast** How was Aryan culture different from Harappan culture?
    c. **Elaborate** In what ways was Harappan society an advanced civilization?
    d. **Identify** Who were the Brahmins, and what role did they play in Vedic society?

Lesson 2

11. a. **Analyze** How do Hindus believe karma affects reincarnation?
    b. **Elaborate** Hinduism has been called both a polytheistic religion—one that worships many gods—and a monotheistic religion—one that worships only one god. Why do you think this is so?

Lesson 3

12. a. **Describe** What did the Buddha say caused human suffering?
    b. **Analyze** How did Buddhism grow and change after the Buddha died?
    c. **Elaborate** Why did the Buddha's teachings about nirvana appeal to so many people?

Lesson 4

13. a. **Identify** Who was Guru Nanak?
    b. **Explain** Why does Sikhism generally not follow the caste system?
    c. **Analyze** How did the British influence Sikh migration from India?

Lesson 5

14. a. **Compare and Contrast** What was one similarity among the Mauryans, the Guptas, and the Mughals? What was one difference among them?
    b. **Analyze** How did the issue of religious tolerance both help the Mughal Empire to grow and lead to its demise?
    c. **Compare and Contrast** How did Akbar and Asoka affect the social and cultural development of their communities?
    d. **Describe** What kinds of religious art did the ancient Indians create?
    e. **Make Inferences** Why do you think religious discussions are included in the *Mahabharata*?
    f. **Evaluate** Which of the ancient Indians' achievements do you think has had the most lasting impact? Why?

Reading Skills

Understand Fact and Opinion *Use the Reading Skills taught in this module to decide whether each statement below is a fact or opinion.*

15. The Ganges River is an important place in Hinduism.
16. Taking a trip to the Ganges River is the best thing to do when in India.

Social Studies Skills

Compare Maps *Use the Social Studies Skills taught in this module and the physical and population maps of South and East Asia in the atlas to answer the following questions.*

17. Along what river in northeastern India is the population density very high?
18. Why do you think fewer people live in far northwestern India than in the northeast?

Map Activity

19. **Ancient India** On a separate sheet of paper, match the letters on the map with their correct labels.

Mohenjo-Daro
Harappa
Bodh Gaya
Indus River
Ganges River

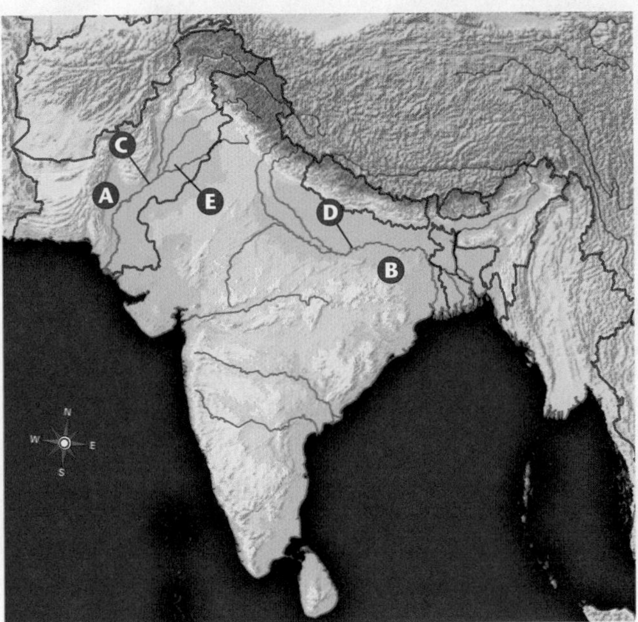

Focus on Writing

20. **Make an Illustrated Poster** Ancient India was a fascinating place with amazing cities and empires. It was also the birthplace of several major religions. Decide how you could illustrate one aspect of ancient Indian culture in a poster. On a large sheet of paper or posterboard, write a title that identifies your subject. Then draw pictures, maps, or diagrams that illustrate it. Next to each picture, write a short caption. Each caption should be two sentences long. The first sentence should identify what the picture, map, or diagram shows. The second sentence should explain why the picture is important to the study of Indian history, geography, or culture.

Module 15

The Indian Subcontinent

Essential Question

What role did geography play in shaping the history and cultures of the Indian Subcontinent?

▷ Explore ONLINE!

VIDEOS, including . . .
- The Mughals of India: Taj Mahal

- Document-Based Investigations
- Graphic Organizers
- Interactive Games
- Channel One News Video: Youngest Female Everest Climber
- Channel One News Video: Malala Yousefzai
- Compare Images: Effects of Monsoons

In this module, you will learn about the history and culture of India and other countries of the Indian Subcontinent, as well as their resources and current challenges.

What You Will Learn

Lesson 1: Physical Geography 489
The Big Idea The physical geography of the Indian Subcontinent includes unique physical features and a variety of climates and resources.

Lesson 2: India 493
The Big Idea Ancient civilizations and powerful empires have shaped the history of India, which today features a blend of modern and traditional cultures.

Lesson 3: India's Neighbors 503
The Big Idea Despite cultural differences, the countries that border India share similar challenges.

Geography The Ganges River flows from the Himalayas to the Bay of Bengal, supplying water and food for tens of millions of Indians.

Culture The people of the subcontinent represent the many cultures and religions of the region.

History India's Taj Mahal was built during the Mughal Empire, one of many empires that ruled the Indian Subcontinent.

Reading Social Studies

Visualize

READING FOCUS

Maybe you have heard the saying "a picture is worth a thousand words." That means a picture can show in a small space what might take many words to describe. Visualizing, or creating mental pictures, can help you see and remember what you read. When you read, try to imagine what a snapshot of the images in the passage might look like. First, form the background or setting in your mind. Then keep adding specific details that can help you picture the rest of the information.

Form the background picture: I see the shape of the Indian Subcontinent.

Add specific details: I see a huge diagonal line near the top left dividing the country into India and Pakistan.

Add more specific details: I see two large crowds of people moving toward the diagonal line and the number 10,000,000.

Add more specific details: I see two large arrows. The arrow pointing left says, "This way to Pakistan for Muslims." The arrow pointing right says, "This way to India for Hindus."

To avoid a civil war, the British government agreed to the partition, or division, of India. In 1947 two countries were formed. India was mostly Hindu. Pakistan, which included the area that is now Bangladesh, was mostly Muslim. As a result, some 10 million people rushed to cross the border. To avoid religious persecution, Muslims and Hindus wanted to live in the country where their religion held a majority.

YOU TRY IT!

Read the following sentences. Then, using the process explained above, describe the images you see.

Flooding is one of Bangladesh's biggest challenges. Many circumstances cause these floods. The country's many streams and rivers flood annually, often damaging farms and homes. Summer monsoons also cause flooding. For example, massive flooding in 2004 left more than 25 million people homeless. It also destroyed schools, farms, and roads throughout the country.

As you read this module, visualize details to help you remember information.

Physical Geography

The Big Idea

The physical geography of the Indian Subcontinent includes unique physical features and a variety of climates and resources.

Main Ideas

- Towering mountains, large rivers, and broad plains are the key physical features of the Indian Subcontinent.
- The Indian Subcontinent has a great variety of climate regions and resources.

Key Terms and Places

subcontinent
Mount Everest
Ganges River
delta
Indus River
monsoons

If YOU lived there . . .

You live in a small farming village in central India. Every year your father talks about the summer monsoons, winds that often bring heavy rains to the region. You know that too much rain could cause floods that may threaten your house and family. Too little rain could cause your crops to fail.

How do you feel about the monsoons?

Physical Features

Locate Asia on a map of the world. Notice that the southernmost portion of Asia creates a triangular wedge of land that dips into the Indian Ocean. The piece of land jutting out from the rest of Asia is the Indian Subcontinent. A **subcontinent** is a large landmass that is smaller than a continent.

Use the map on the next page to locate the nations of the Indian Subcontinent—Bangladesh, Bhutan, India, Maldives, Nepal, Pakistan, and Sri Lanka. This region, also called South Asia, is one of the most diverse geographic regions in the world. Soaring mountains, powerful rivers, and fertile plains are some of the region's dominant features.

Mountains Huge mountain ranges separate the Indian Subcontinent from the rest of Asia. The rugged Hindu Kush mountains in the northwest divide the subcontinent from Central Asia. Historically, they made land travel from Asia and Europe difficult. However, mountain passes in the Hindu Kush have allowed people to enter the subcontinent for thousands of years.

Two smaller mountain ranges stretch down India's coasts. The Eastern and Western Ghats (GAWTS) are low mountains that separate India's east and west coasts from the country's interior.

Perhaps the most impressive physical features in the subcontinent, however, are the Himalayas. These enormous mountains stretch about 1,500 miles (2,414 km) along the northern border of the Indian Subcontinent. Formed by the collision of two massive tectonic plates, the Himalayas are home to the world's highest mountains. On the border between Nepal and

Explore ONLINE!

The Indian Subcontinent: Physical

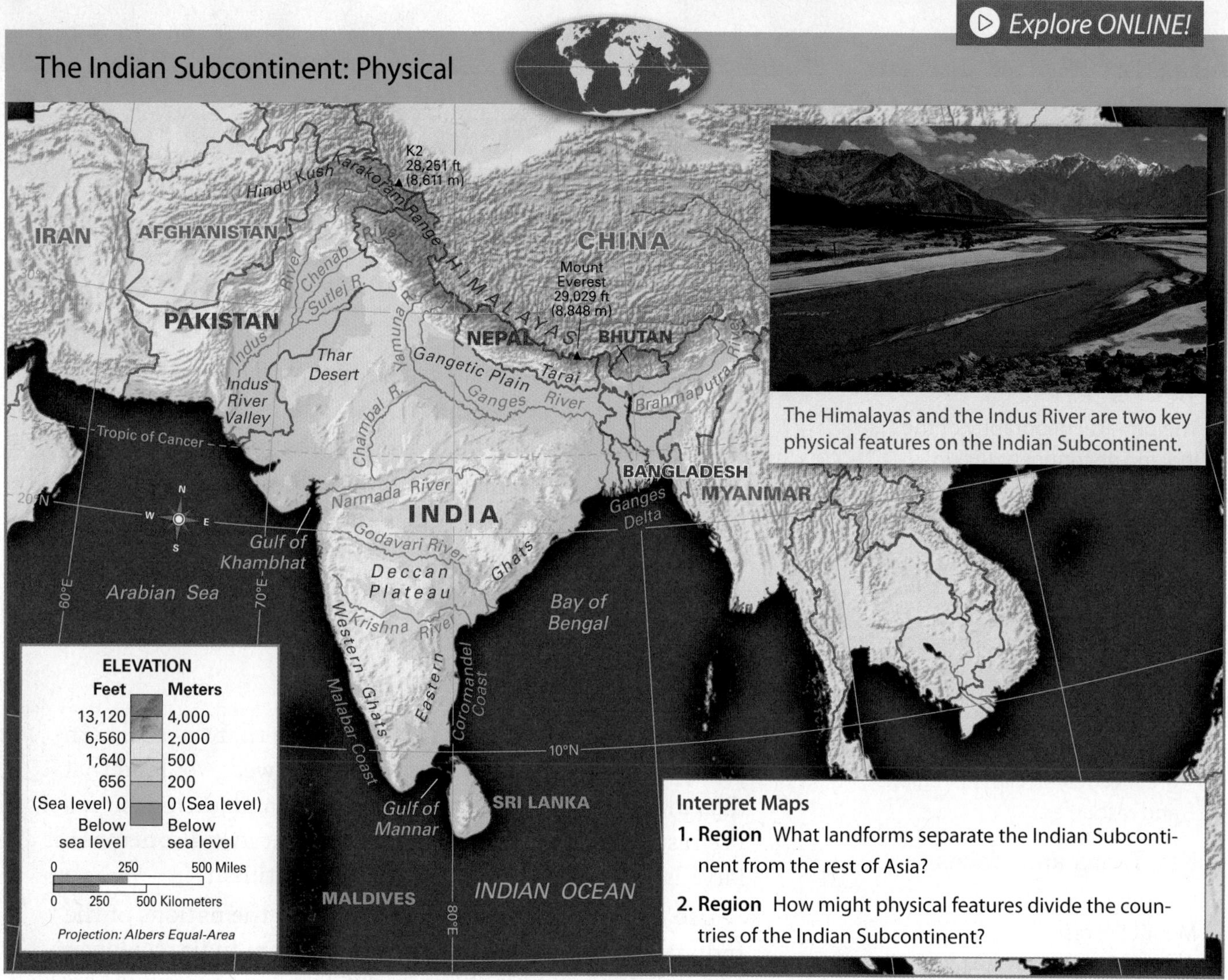

The Himalayas and the Indus River are two key physical features on the Indian Subcontinent.

Interpret Maps

1. **Region** What landforms separate the Indian Subcontinent from the rest of Asia?
2. **Region** How might physical features divide the countries of the Indian Subcontinent?

China is **Mount Everest,** the highest mountain on the planet. It measures some 29,035 feet (8,850 m). K2 in northern Pakistan is the world's second-highest peak.

Rivers and Plains Deep in the Himalayas are the sources of some of Asia's mightiest rivers. Two major river systems—the Ganges (GAN-jeez) and the Indus—originate in the Himalayas. Each carries massive amounts of water from the mountains' melting snow and glaciers. For thousands of years, these rivers have flooded the surrounding land, leaving rich soil deposits and fertile plains.

India's most important river is the Ganges. The **Ganges River** flows across northern India and into Bangladesh. There the Ganges joins with other rivers and creates a huge delta. A **delta** is a landform at the mouth of a river created by sediment deposits. Along the length of the Ganges is a vast area of rich soil and fertile farmland. Known as the Ganges Plain, this region is India's farming heartland. Unfortunately, waste from farms, cities, and factories has caused the Ganges to become highly polluted.

Likewise, Pakistan's **Indus River** also creates a fertile plain known as the Indus River valley. This valley was once home to the earliest Indian civilizations. Today, it is Pakistan's most densely populated region.

Other Features Other geographic features are scattered throughout the subcontinent. South of the Ganges Plain, for example, is a large, hilly plateau called the Deccan. East of the Indus valley is the Thar (TAHR), or Great Indian Desert. Marked by rolling sand dunes, parts of this desert receive as little as 4 inches (102 mm) of rain per year. Still another geographic region is the Tarai (tuh-RY) in southern Nepal. It has fertile farmland and tropical jungles.

Reading Check
Summarize
What are the physical features of the Indian Subcontinent?

Climates and Resources

Just as the physical features of the Indian Subcontinent differ, so do its climates and resources. A variety of climates and natural resources exist throughout the region.

Climate Regions From the Himalayas' snow-covered peaks to the dry Thar Desert, the climates of the Indian Subcontinent differ widely. In the Himalayas, a highland climate brings cool temperatures to much of Nepal and Bhutan. The plains south of the Himalayas have a humid subtropical climate. Hot, humid summers with plenty of rainfall are common in this important farming region.

Explore ONLINE!

The Indian Subcontinent: Precipitation

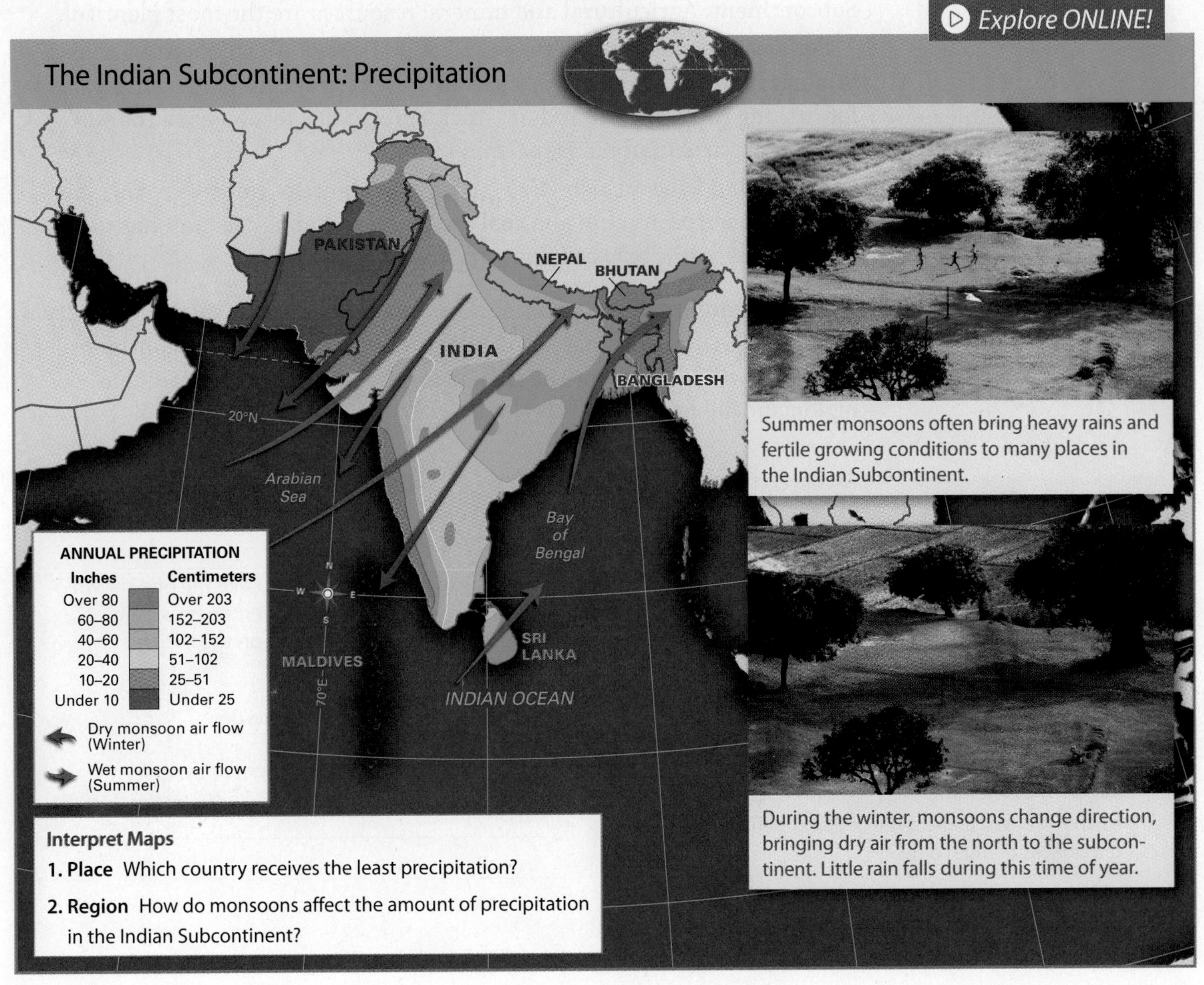

Summer monsoons often bring heavy rains and fertile growing conditions to many places in the Indian Subcontinent.

During the winter, monsoons change direction, bringing dry air from the north to the subcontinent. Little rain falls during this time of year.

Interpret Maps

1. **Place** Which country receives the least precipitation?
2. **Region** How do monsoons affect the amount of precipitation in the Indian Subcontinent?

Tropical climates dominate much of the subcontinent. The tropical savanna climate in central India and Sri Lanka keeps temperatures there warm all year long. This region experiences wet and dry seasons during the year. A humid tropical climate brings warm temperatures and heavy rains to parts of southwest India, Sri Lanka, Maldives, and Bangladesh.

The remainder of the subcontinent has dry climates. Desert and steppe climates extend throughout southern and western India and most of Pakistan.

Monsoons have a huge influence on the weather and climates in the subcontinent. **Monsoons** are seasonal winds that bring either moist or dry air to an area. From June to October, summer monsoons bring moist air up from the Indian Ocean, causing heavy rains. Flooding often accompanies these summer monsoons. In 2005, for example, the city of Mumbai (Bombay), India, received some 37 inches (94 cm) of rain in just 24 hours. The flood shut down the city and killed nearly 1,500 people. However, in winter, the monsoons change direction, bringing dry air from the north. Because of this, little rain falls from November to January.

Natural Resources A wide variety of resources are found on the Indian Subcontinent. Agricultural and mineral resources are the most plentiful.

Perhaps the most important resource is the region's fertile soil. Farms produce many different crops, such as tea, rice, nuts, and jute, a plant used for making rope. Timber and livestock are also key resources in the subcontinent, particularly in Nepal and Bhutan.

The Indian Subcontinent also has an abundance of mineral resources. Large deposits of iron ore and coal are found in India. Pakistan has natural gas reserves, while Sri Lankans mine many gemstones.

Reading Check
Summarize
What climates and resources are located in this region?

Summary and Preview In this section you learned about the wide variety of physical features, climates, and resources in the Indian Subcontinent. Next, you will learn about the rich history and culture of this unique region and about India today.

Lesson 1 Assessment

Review Ideas, Terms, and Places

1. a. **Define** What is a subcontinent?

   b. **Make Inferences** Why do you think the Indus River valley is so heavily populated?

   c. **Form Opinions** Which physical features in the Indian Subcontinent would you most want to visit? Why?

2. a. **Identify** What natural resources are found in the Indian Subcontinent?

   b. **Analyze** What are some of the benefits and drawbacks of monsoons?

Critical Thinking

3. **Draw Conclusions** Draw a chart like the one shown here. Using your notes, write a sentence explaining how each aspect affects life on the Indian Subcontinent.

	Effect on Life
Physical Features	
Climates	
Natural Resources	

India

The Big Idea

Ancient civilizations and powerful empires have shaped the history of India, which today features a blend of modern and traditional cultures.

Main Ideas

- Advanced civilizations and powerful empires shaped the early history of India.
- Powerful empires controlled India for hundreds of years.
- Independence from Great Britain led to the division of India into several countries.
- Indian culture is shaped by many things, including religion and a caste system.
- Daily life in India is centered around cities, villages, and religion.
- Today, India faces many challenges, including a growing population and economic development.

Key Terms and Places

Delhi
colony
partition
Hinduism
Buddhism
Jainism
Sikhism
caste system
Mumbai (Bombay)
Kolkata (Calcutta)
urbanization
green revolution

If YOU lived there . . .

You live in New Delhi, India's capital city. Museums in your city display artifacts from some of India's oldest civilizations. People can visit beautiful buildings built by powerful empires. Statues and parades celebrate your country's independence.

How does your city reflect India's history?

Early Civilizations and Empires

India, the largest country on the Indian Subcontinent, is one of the world's oldest civilizations. Early civilizations and empires greatly influenced the history of the Indian Subcontinent.

Ancient Civilizations The Indus River valley in Pakistan supported one of the world's largest ancient civilizations. It is often called the Harappan civilization, after its first discovered city, Harappa. Harappa was one of at least eight major Harappan cities that flourished between 3000 BC and 1700 BC. All were trade centers located along waterways, which allowed traders to travel easily between them. Archaeologists believe that over 30,000 people may have lived in Mohenjo-Daro, the best-known Indus city.

Archaeologists have uncovered a wealth of Harappan artifacts and ruins. However, the end of Harappan civilization is shrouded in mystery. Some scholars believe the Indus River may have changed its course. This could have caused destructive floods in some cities, and water shortages and transportation problems for others.

There is also little evidence to explain how Sanskrit, an Indo-Aryan language, spread into the region. Some scholars believe that, beginning in about 1500 BC, small groups of Indo-Aryan language speakers began to migrate into the Indus valley from Central Asia. They likely encountered and mixed with the descendants of the Indus valley civilizations. Over time their language, Sanskrit, became the main language in northern India.

Ancient Civilizations	Early Empires
• Around 2300 BC the Harappan civilization begins in the Indus River valley. • Beginning in about 1500 BC, Indo-Aryan language speakers from Central Asia move into the Indus valley, bringing their language, Sanskrit, with them.	• By 233 BC the Mauryan Empire controls most of the Indian Subcontinent. • Emperor Asoka helps spread Buddhism in India. • Indian trade and culture flourish during the Gupta Empire.

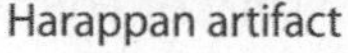

Harappan artifact

Mauryan troops atop a war elephant

Early Empires In about 320 BC a ruler by the name of Chandragupta Maurya united nearly all of northern India, Afghanistan, and parts of Asia into the Mauryan Empire. Under Chandragupta, trade flourished, farming improved, and weights and measures were made standard. Asoka, one of the greatest Mauryan emperors, helped expand the empire and improve trade. Asoka also encouraged the acceptance of other religions. After his death, however, the empire slowly crumbled. Power struggles and invasions destroyed the Mauryan Empire.

Academic Vocabulary
influence the ability to change, or have an effect on

After the fall of the Mauryan Empire, India split into many small kingdoms. Eventually, a strong new empire gained **influence**. In the AD 300s the Gupta Empire united much of northern India. Under Gupta rulers, trade and culture thrived. Scholars made important advances in math, medicine, and astronomy. Indian mathematicians, for example, first introduced the concept of zero.

Gradually, the Gupta Empire also declined. Attacks by invaders, such as the Huns or Hunas from Central Asia, weakened the empire. By about 550, India was once again divided.

Reading Check
Summarize
How did early civilizations and empires influence India?

Powerful Empires

Powerful empires controlled India for much of its history. First the Mughal Empire and then the British Empire ruled India for hundreds of years.

The Mughal Empire In the late 600s Muslim armies began launching raids into India. Some Muslims tried to take over Indian kingdoms.

Turkish Muslims, for example, established a powerful kingdom at **Delhi** in northern India. In the 1500s a new group of Muslim invaders swept into the subcontinent. Led by the great warrior Babur (BAH-boohr), they conquered much of India. In 1526 Babur established the Mughal (MOO-guhl) Empire.

Babur's grandson, Akbar, was one of India's greatest rulers. Under Akbar's rule, trade flourished. Demand for Indian goods such as spices and tea increased. The Mughal Empire grew rich from trade.

Akbar and other Mughal rulers also promoted culture. Although the Mughals were Muslim, most Indians continued to practice Hinduism. Akbar's policy of religious tolerance, or acceptance, encouraged peace throughout his empire. Architecture also thrived in the Mughal Empire. One of India's most spectacular buildings, the Taj Mahal, was built during Mughal rule.

The British Empire The Mughals were not the only powerful empire in India. As early as the 1500s, Europeans had tried to control parts of India. One European country, England, rose to power as the Mughal Empire declined.

The English presence in India began in the 1600s. At the time, European demand for Indian goods, such as cotton and sugar, was very high. Mughal rulers granted the East India Company, a British trading company, valuable trading rights.

The Mughal Empire	The British Empire
• Babur establishes the Mughal Empire in northern India in 1526. • Indian trade, culture, and religion thrive under the rule of Akbar the Great. • By 1700 the Mughal Empire rules almost all of the Indian Subcontinent.	• The East India Company establishes trade in northern India in the early 1600s. • Indian troops trigger a massive revolt against the East India Company. • The British government takes direct control of India in 1858. • India and Pakistan gain independence in 1947.

The first Mughal emperor, Babur

Indian troop in the British army

Historical Source

Gandhi's "Quit India" Speech

On August 8, 1942, Indian independence leader Mohandas Gandhi delivered this speech before the All India Congress Committee. At the time, the committee was considering a resolution demanding that the British "quit," or leave, India.

As you read, look for main ideas and details related to how Gandhi thinks India should achieve independence.

Ours is not a drive for power, but purely a non-violent fight for India's independence. In a violent struggle, a successful general has been often known to effect a military coup[1] and to set up a dictatorship. But under the Congress scheme of things, essentially non-violent as it is, there can be no room for dictatorship. A non-violent soldier of freedom will covet nothing for himself, he fights only for the freedom of his country. . . .
I believe that in the history of the world, there has not been a more genuinely democratic struggle for freedom than ours. I read Carlyle's French Revolution while I was in prison, and Pandit Jawaharlal has told me something about the Russian revolution. But it is my conviction that in as much as these struggles were fought with the weapon of violence they failed to realize the democratic ideal. In the democracy which I have envisaged[2], a democracy established by non-violence, there will be equal freedom for all. Everybody will be his own master. It is to join a struggle for such democracy that I invite you today.

Here, Gandhi refers to two violent revolutions that did not result in a lasting democracy, the French Revolution (1789–1799) and the Russian Revolution (1917).

[1] *military coup* a sudden seizure of political power by a nation's armed forces

[2] *envisaged* imagined

Gandhi's "Quit India" speech helped unite India's people against British rule.

Analyze Historical Sources
Why does Gandhi mention the Russian and French revolutions in his speech?

BIOGRAPHY

Mohandas Gandhi (1869–1948)

Considered by many to be the founder of modern India, Mohandas Gandhi led the struggle for Indian independence. As a leading member of the Indian National Congress, Gandhi introduced a policy of nonviolent resistance to British rule. He led millions in fasts, peaceful protest marches, and boycotts of British goods. His devotion to nonviolence earned him the name *Mahatma*, or "Great Soul." Gandhi's efforts proved successful. In 1947 India won its independence from Britain.

Draw Conclusions
Why did people call Gandhi *Mahatma*?

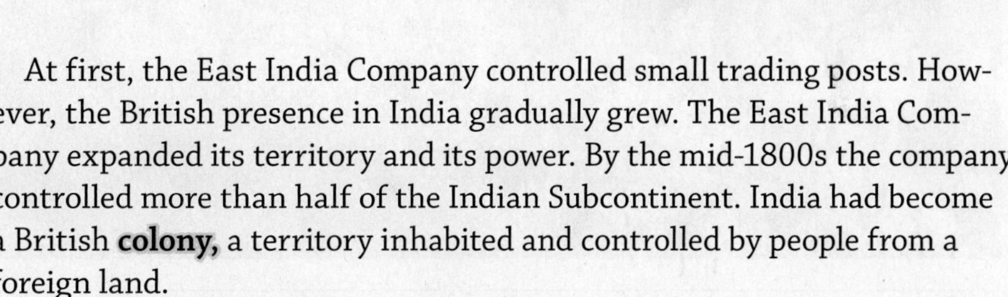

At first, the East India Company controlled small trading posts. However, the British presence in India gradually grew. The East India Company expanded its territory and its power. By the mid-1800s the company controlled more than half of the Indian Subcontinent. India had become a British **colony,** a territory inhabited and controlled by people from a foreign land.

British rule angered and frightened many Indians. The East India Company controlled India with the help of an army made up mostly of Indian troops commanded by British officers. In 1857 Indian troops revolted, triggering violence all across India. The British government crushed the rebellion and took control of India away from the East India Company. With that, the British government began to rule India directly.

Reading Check
Analyze
How did powerful empires affect Indian history?

Independence and Division

By the late 1800s many Indians had begun to question British rule. They were upset about being treated as second-class citizens. This resentment led to the rise of nationalism, or devotion and loyalty to one's country. In 1885 a group of Indians created the Indian National Congress. Their goal was to gain more rights and opportunities.

As more and more Indians became dissatisfied with British rule, they began to demand independence. Mohandas Gandhi was the most important leader of this Indian independence movement. During the 1920s and 1930s, his strategy of nonviolent protest convinced millions of Indians to support independence.

Finally, Great Britain agreed to make India independent. However, tensions between the Hindu and Muslim communities caused a crisis. India's Muslims, fearing they would have little say in the new government, called for a separate nation.

In part to avoid a civil war, the British government agreed to the **partition,** or division, of India. In 1947 two countries were formed. India was mostly Hindu. Pakistan, which included the area that is now Bangladesh,

The Partition of India

Following the partition, riots claimed the lives of as many as 1 million Indians and created a massive refugee crisis. Hindus and Muslims who found themselves on the wrong side of the new border crowded onto trains that would take them to their new homelands in India and Pakistan.

was mostly Muslim. As a result, some 10 million people rushed to cross the border. To avoid religious persecution, Muslims and Hindus wanted to live in the country where their religion held a majority.

Soon after India and Pakistan won their independence, other countries in the region gradually did, too. Sri Lanka and Maldives gained their independence from Great Britain. In 1971, after a bloody civil war that killed almost 1 million people, East Pakistan broke away from Pakistan to form the country of Bangladesh.

Reading Check
Identify Cause and Effect What were the effects of Indian independence from Great Britain?

Indian Culture

India's rich culture has been shaped by many factors. History, geography, language, the arts, and interactions with other cultures have all played a part. So too have religion and a social class system.

Religion Religion has played a very important role in Indian history. In fact, India is the birthplace of several major religions, including Hinduism and Buddhism.

One of the world's oldest religions is **Hinduism,** the dominant religion of India. According to Hindu beliefs, everything in the universe is part of a single spirit called Brahman. Hindus believe that their ultimate goal is to reunite their souls with that spirit. Hinduism teaches that souls are reincarnated, or reborn, many times before they join with Brahman.

Another Indian religion is Buddhism, which began in northern India in the late 500s BC. **Buddhism** is a religion based on the teachings of Siddhartha Gautama—the Buddha. According to the Buddha's teachings, people can rise above their selfish desires and reach nirvana. Nirvana is a state of perfect peace in which suffering and reincarnation end.

An ancient religion, **Jainism** teaches nonviolence as a way of life. Jains are vegetarians who believe in the importance of every living thing. They are also taught not to steal, lie, or own property.

Sikhism (SIK-iz-uhm) is the youngest of India's major religions. A blending of ideas from Hinduism and Islam, **Sikhism** embraces equality for all, belief in one God, service to humanity, and honest labor. The religion developed from the teachings of the Guru Nanak in the 1400s.

Caste System India's class system began to develop in ancient times. Over many centuries, a complex social order emerged. This social order, often called the **caste system,** divided Indian society into hundreds of groups based on a person's birth or occupation. The social classes, or castes, had different rules about how their members could interact with people from other castes. One group, the Dalits, was restricted to jobs that were unpleasant and seen as impure. Although caste discrimination is banned today in India, Dalits still often face obstacles.

Reading Check
Analyze How do religion and the caste system influence Indian culture?

Daily Life in India

About 1.3 billion people live in India today. This huge population represents modern India's many different ethnic groups, religions, and ways of life. Despite these many differences, city life, village life, and religion all help unite the people of India.

Cities Millions of Indians live in large, bustling cities. In fact, India's three largest cities—**Mumbai (Bombay),** Delhi, and **Kolkata (Calcutta)**—are among the world's most populous cities. Many people in Indian cities work in factories and offices. Some cities, like Bangalore and Mumbai, are home to universities, research centers, and high-tech businesses. Most city dwellers, however, struggle to earn a living. Those who live in slums often live in makeshift shacks with no plumbing and little access to clean water.

Villages Most Indians still live in rural areas. Hundreds of thousands of villages are home to more than 70 percent of India's population. Most villagers work as farmers and live with an extended family in simple homes.

Religious Practice Religious celebrations are an important part of life in Indian cities and villages. One of India's most popular holidays is Diwali. Called the "Festival of Lights," Diwali is a New Year celebration marked by gift giving and family gatherings. As part of the festival, Hindus light small oil lamps that symbolize the victory of good over evil.

Vaisakhi is one of the most popular days on the Sikh calendar. The holiday originated as a harvest festival in Punjab. All Punjabis celebrate the day with parades, dancing, and singing. For Sikhs, however, Vaisakhi also has special religious significance. It marks the Sikh New Year and honors the establishment of the *Khalsa*, or the community of initiated Sikhs.

Reading Check
Contrast How does life differ in Indian cities and villages?

Focus on Culture

Diwali: The Festival of Lights

Diwali, or the "Festival of Lights," is one of the most important celebrations in India. A variety of activities on each of the five days of Diwali celebrate Hindu, Sikh, and Jain beliefs.

Beautiful fireworks displays are common during Diwali.

Elaborate chalk designs, called *rangolis*, often decorate floors and walls.

Diwali is a time to spend with friends and family. Cards and small gifts, such as sweets and candles, are often exchanged.

Small oil lamps, or *diyas,* decorate homes inside and out.

Analyze Visuals
What elements of Indian daily life do you see in the illustration?

India's Challenges

India has undergone drastic changes since gaining independence. Today, the country faces several major challenges, such as dealing with a growing population and managing its economic development.

Population With about 1.3 billion people, India is the world's second most populous country. Only China has a larger population. India's population has grown rapidly, more than tripling since 1947. This huge population growth places a strain on India's environment and many of its resources, including food, housing, and schools. A combination of population growth and industrial expansion has led to dangerous levels of air pollution, which kills over a million people in India each year.

India's cities are particularly affected by the growing population. As the country's population has grown, urbanization has taken place. **Urbanization** is the increase in the percentage of people who live in cities. Many millions of people have moved to India's cities in search of jobs.

Government and Economy Since India gained independence, its leaders have strengthened the government and economy. Today, India is the world's largest democracy and one of the strongest nations in Asia.

Explore ONLINE!

India: Population

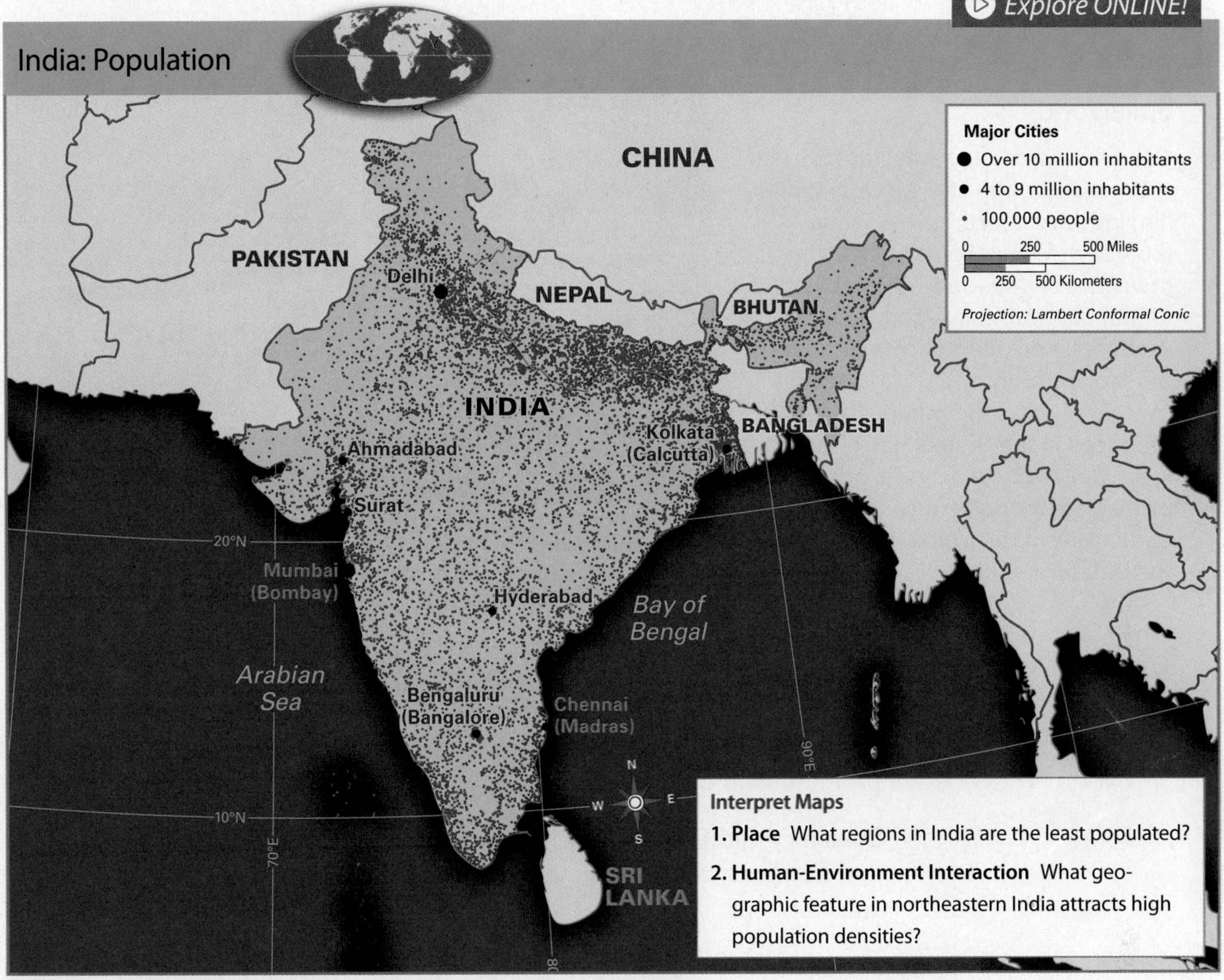

CHINA
PAKISTAN
NEPAL
BHUTAN
INDIA
BANGLADESH
Delhi
Kolkata (Calcutta)
Ahmadabad
Surat
Mumbai (Bombay)
Hyderabad
Bengaluru (Bangalore)
Chennai (Madras)
Arabian Sea
Bay of Bengal
SRI LANKA
20°N
10°N
70°E
80°E
90°E
N
S
E
W

Major Cities
- Over 10 million inhabitants
- 4 to 9 million inhabitants
- 100,000 people

0 250 500 Miles
0 250 500 Kilometers

Projection: Lambert Conformal Conic

Interpret Maps

1. **Place** What regions in India are the least populated?
2. **Human-Environment Interaction** What geographic feature in northeastern India attracts high population densities?

Streets like this one in Delhi are crowded due to India's rapid urbanization.

The greatest challenges facing India's government are providing for a growing population and resolving conflicts with its neighbor, Pakistan. Both India and Pakistan have nuclear weapons.

India's gross domestic product (GDP) places it among the world's top five industrial countries. However, millions of Indians live in poverty. The country's per capita, or per person, GDP is only about $6,100.

India's government has taken steps to reduce poverty. In the 1960s and 1970s the **green revolution,** a program that encouraged farmers to adopt modern agricultural methods, helped farmers produce more food. Recently, the government has succeeded in attracting many information technology (IT) businesses

Connect to Economics

Bollywood

One of India's largest industries is its moviemaking industry. Much of India's film industry is located in Mumbai (Bombay). Many people refer to the industry as Bollywood—a combination of Bombay and Hollywood. Bollywood produces more films each year than any other country. In fact, India produces over three times the number of films produced in the United States. In recent years, Bollywood films have become increasingly popular outside of India—particularly in the United Kingdom and the United States.

Draw Conclusions
How might the film industry affect India's economy?

Reading Check
Find Main Ideas
What are India's government and economy like?

to India. This specialization is now an important part of India's economy. Indian entrepreneurs, or business operators, have built companies that export IT to other countries. Many U.S. companies hire Indian software programmers to work on projects.

Summary and Preview In this lesson you learned about India's history and its society today. Next you will learn about India's neighbors on the subcontinent.

Lesson 2 Assessment

Review Ideas, Terms, and Places

1. a. **Identify** What different peoples ruled India?
   b. **Analyze** How did these early civilizations and empires influence Indian culture?
2. a. **Describe** What were some accomplishments of the Mughal Empire?
   b. **Predict** How might Indian history have been different if the British had not ruled India?
3. a. **Recall** Who was the leader of India's independence movement?
   b. **Explain** What led to the partition of India?
4. a. **Define** What is the caste system?
   b. **Elaborate** Why do you think India is home to some of the world's oldest religions?
5. a. **Explain** What is the significance of Diwali? Vaisakhi?
   b. **Compare and Contrast** In what ways are Indian cities similar to cities in the United States? How are they different from U.S. cities?
   c. **Elaborate** Why do you think that a majority of Indians live in villages?
6. a. **Recall** What is urbanization? What is one cause of urbanization?
   b. **Make Inferences** How did the green revolution affect India's economy?
   c. **Predict** What effects might India's growing population have on its resources and environment in the future?

Critical Thinking

7. **Find Main Ideas** Using your notes and the web diagram, write the main idea for each element of historical and present-day India.

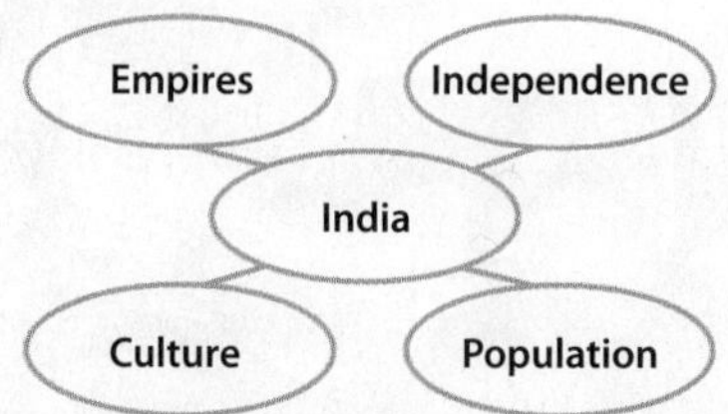

India's Neighbors

The Big Idea

Despite cultural differences, the countries that border India share similar challenges.

Main Ideas

- Many different ethnic groups and religions influence the culture of India's neighbors.
- Rapid population growth, ethnic conflicts, and environmental threats are major challenges to the region today.

Key Terms and Places

Sherpas
Kashmir
Dhaka
Kathmandu

If YOU lived there . . .

You live in the mountainous country of Bhutan. For many years, Bhutan's leaders kept the country isolated from outsiders. Recently, they have begun to allow more tourists to enter the country. Some of your neighbors believe that tourism will greatly benefit the country. Others think it could harm the environment.

How do you feel about tourism in Bhutan?

Culture

Five countries—Pakistan, Bangladesh, Nepal, Bhutan, and Sri Lanka—share the subcontinent with India. Though they are neighbors, these countries have significantly different cultures.

People The cultures of the countries that border India reflect the customs of many ethnic groups. For example, the **Sherpas,** an ethnic group from the mountains of Nepal, often serve as guides through the Himalayas. Members of Bhutan's largest ethnic group originally came from Tibet, a region in southern China. Many of Sri Lanka's Tamil (TA-muhl) people came from India to work the country's huge plantations.

Religion As you can see on the map on the next page, a variety of religions exist on the Indian Subcontinent. Most countries, like India, have one major religion. In Pakistan and Bangladesh, for example, most people practice Islam, and small portions of the population follow Hinduism, Christianity, and tribal religions. In Nepal, the dominant religion is Hinduism, although Buddhism is practiced in some parts of the country. Buddhism dominates both Bhutan and Sri Lanka.

Reading Check
Contrast
In what ways are the cultures of this region different?

The Region Today

Like India, the other nations of the subcontinent face a variety of challenges. Two of the greatest challenges are population growth and poverty.

Pakistan One of the greatest challenges Pakistan faces is the lack of government stability. Since its creation in 1947, Pakistan has suffered from rebellions and assassinations of

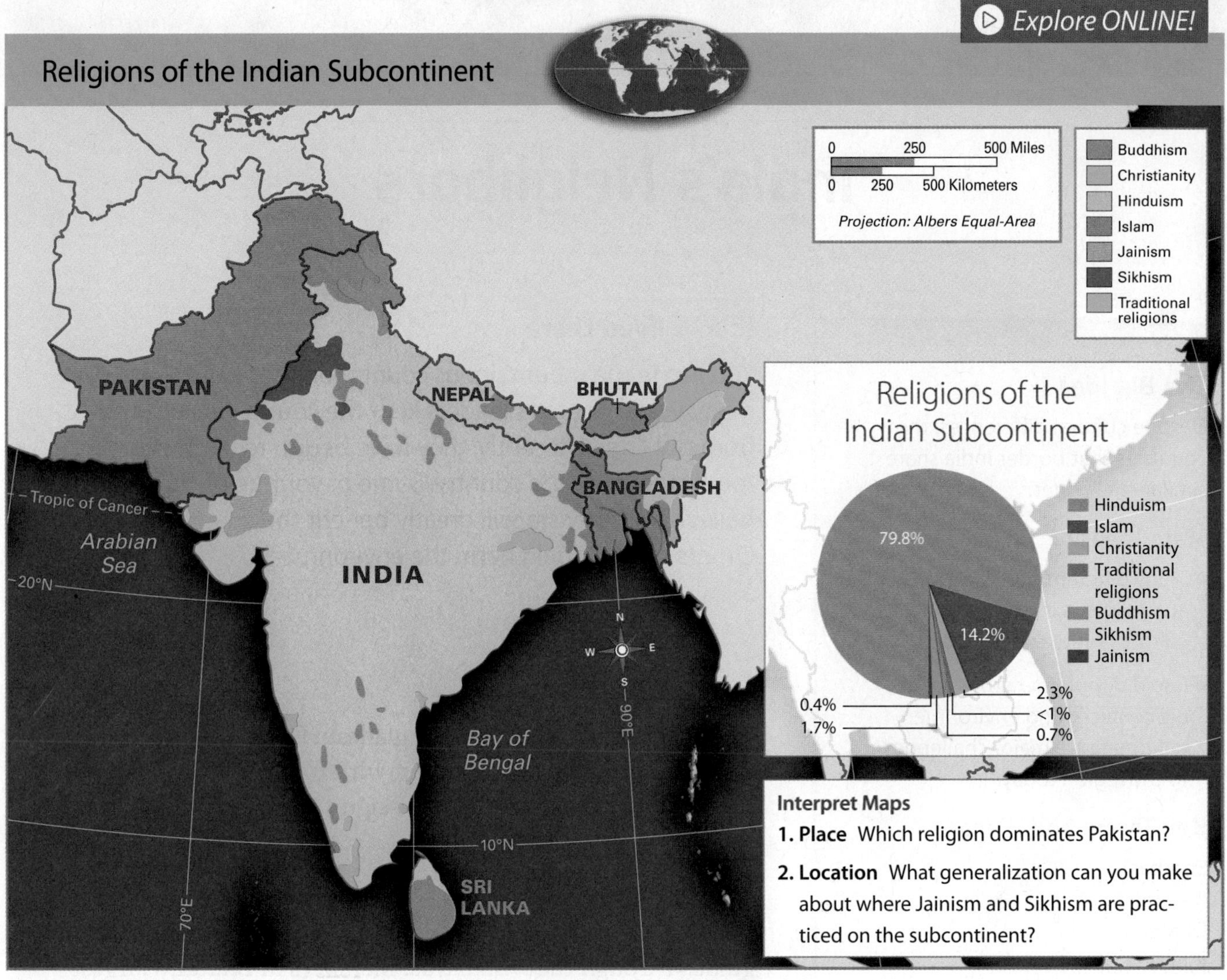

Interpret Maps

1. **Place** Which religion dominates Pakistan?
2. **Location** What generalization can you make about where Jainism and Sikhism are practiced on the subcontinent?

government leaders. In 2001 General Pervez Musharraf came to power in a military coup. Under pressure from protesters calling for democracy, Musharraf resigned in 2008. Pakistanis then elected Asif Ali Zardari as president. He stepped down after five years, becoming the first democratically elected president of Pakistan to complete a full term in office.

Another challenge is Pakistan's rapid population growth. The country's government struggles to manage resources and to reduce poverty.

Relations with India are another important issue in Pakistan today. Since the partition in 1947, the two countries have clashed over the territory of **Kashmir.** Both India and Pakistan claim control of the region. Today, Pakistan controls western Kashmir, while India controls the east. Armed troops from both countries guard a "line of control" that divides Kashmir.

Since 2001 Pakistan has aided the United States in its war on terrorism. Pakistan's military has arrested hundreds of terrorists and provided information about suspected terrorists. Despite this crackdown, however, many people believe that there are still terrorists within Pakistan's borders.

Bangladesh Bangladesh is a small country about the same size as the state of Wisconsin. Despite its small size, Bangladesh's population is almost half the size of the U.S. population. As a result, it is one of the world's most densely populated countries, with some 3,279 people per square mile (1,266 per square km). The capital and largest city, **Dhaka** (DA-kuh), is home to more than 17 million people. Overcrowding is not limited to urban areas, however. Rural areas are also densely populated.

Academic Vocabulary
circumstances conditions that influence an event or activity

Flooding is one of Bangladesh's biggest challenges. Many **circumstances** cause these floods. The country's many streams and rivers flood annually, often damaging farms and homes. Summer monsoons also cause flooding. For example, massive flooding in 2004 left more than 25 million people homeless. It also destroyed schools, farms, and roads throughout the country.

Nepal The small kingdom of Nepal also faces many challenges today. Its population is growing rapidly. In fact, the population has more than doubled in the last 30 years. **Kathmandu** (kat-man-DOO), the nation's capital and largest city, is troubled by overcrowding and poverty. Thousands have moved to Kathmandu in search of jobs and better opportunities. As a result of population growth and poor resources, Nepal is one of the world's least developed nations.

Nepal also faces environmental threats. As the population grows, more and more land is needed to grow enough food. To meet this need, farmers clear forests to create more farmland. This deforestation causes soil erosion and harms the wildlife in the region. Nepal's many tourists add to the problem, as they use valuable resources and leave behind trash.

Bhutan Bhutan is a small mountain kingdom that lies in the Himalayas between India and China. Because of the rugged mountains, Bhutan has been isolated throughout much of its history. This isolation limited outside influences until the 1900s, when Bhutan's king established ties first with Great Britain and later with India. By the mid-1900s Bhutan had ended its long isolation. Efforts to modernize Bhutan resulted in the construction of new roads, schools, and hospitals.

Nepal
Many of Nepal's people live in the rugged Himalayas and earn a living herding animals.

Sri Lanka

These women are picking tea on one of Sri Lanka's many tea plantations.

Today, Bhutan continues to develop economically. Most Bhutanese earn a living as farmers, growing rice, potatoes, and corn. Some raise livestock such as yaks, pigs, and horses. Another important industry is tourism. The government, however, limits the number of visitors to Bhutan to protect Bhutan's environment and way of life.

Sri Lanka Sri Lanka is a large island country located some 20 miles (32 km) off India's southeast coast. Because of its close location, India has greatly influenced Sri Lanka. In fact, Sri Lanka's two largest ethnic groups—the Tamil and the Sinhalese (sin-huh-LEEZ)—are descended from Indian settlers.

Conflicts between the Sinhalese and the Tamil divide Sri Lanka today. The Tamil minority has fought for years to create a separate state. In 2009 government troops declared an end to the fighting after the Tamil leader was killed.

Parts of Sri Lanka were devastated by the 2004 tsunami in the Indian Ocean. Thousands of Sri Lankans were killed, and more than 500,000 people were left homeless. The tsunami also damaged Sri Lanka's fishing and agricultural industries, which are still struggling to rebuild.

Reading Check
Summarize What key issues affect India's neighbors today?

Summary In this lesson you learned about the important challenges that face India's neighbors on the subcontinent.

Lesson 3 Assessment

Review Ideas, Terms, and Places

1. a. **Identify and Explain** Use the map and graph titled "Religions of the Indian Subcontinent" to pose and answer a question about the geographic distribution of religion in the Indian Subcontinent.

   b. **Summarize** What cultural differences exist among India's neighbors?

   c. **Elaborate** Why do you think there are so many different religions in this region?

2. a. **Compare and Contrast** In what ways are the countries of this region similar and different?

   b. **Predict** How might conflict over Kashmir cause problems in the future?

   c. **Analyze** How do summer monsoons affect people living in Bangladesh?

Critical Thinking

3. **Identify Problems** Using your notes and a chart like the one here, identify one challenge facing each of India's neighbors. Then develop a solution for each challenge.

Challenges	Solutions

Create a Line Graph

Define the Skill

Line graphs are drawings that display information in a clear, visual form. People often use line graphs to track changes over time. For example, you may want to see how clothing prices change from year to year. Line graphs also provide an easy way to see patterns, like increases or decreases, that emerge over time. Use the following guidelines to analyze a line graph.

- **Read the title.** The title will tell you about the subject of the line graph.
- **Examine the labels.** Note the type of information in the graph, the time period, and the units of measure.
- **Analyze the information.** Be sure to look for patterns that emerge over time.

Learn the Skill

Examine the line graph carefully, then answer the questions below.

1. What is the subject of this line graph?
2. What units of measure are used? What period of time does the line graph reflect?
3. What pattern does the line graph indicate? How can you tell?

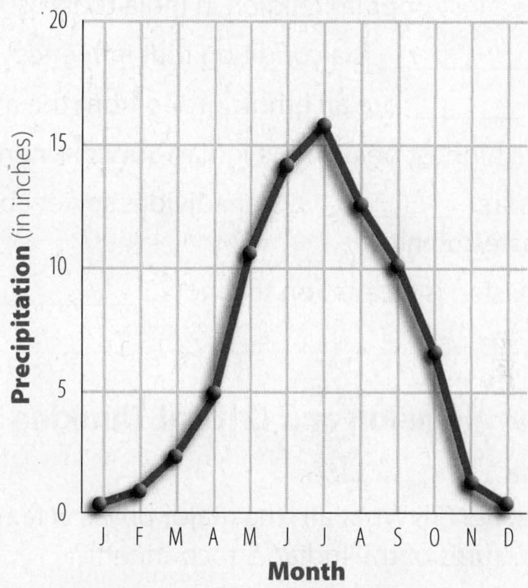

Source: *National Geographic Atlas of the World, Seventh Edition*

Practice the Skill

Create a line graph that tracks your grades in a particular class. Start by organizing your grades by the date of the assignment. Then plot your grades on a line graph. Be sure to use labels and a title to identify the subject and information presented in your line graph. Finally, organize information from the graph into a summary statement that describes any patterns that you see in your grades.

Module 15 Assessment

Review Vocabulary, Terms, and Places

Choose one word from each word pair or group to correctly complete each sentence below.

1. __________ often bring heavy rains to the Indian Subcontinent in summer. **(Monsoons/Ghats)**
2. The most popular religion in India today is __________. **(Buddhism/Hinduism/Islam)**
3. A __________ is a condition that influences an event or activity. **(feature/circumstance)**
4. __________ are an ethnic group from the mountains of Nepal. **(Tamils/Sherpas)**
5. The highest peak in the Indian Subcontinent and the world is __________. **(Mount Everest/K2)**
6. India's __________ system divides society based on a person's birth, wealth, and job. **(caste/colonial)**
7. Pakistan is located on the Indian __________, a large landmass. **(Peninsula/Subcontinent)**

Comprehension and Critical Thinking

Lesson 1

8. a. **Recall** What are the major physical features of the Indian Subcontinent?
   b. **Draw Conclusions** Why are rivers important to the people of the Indian Subcontinent?
   c. **Evaluate** Do you think monsoons have a positive or negative effect on India? Why?

Lesson 2

9. a. **Describe** What was the partition of India? When and why did it take place?
   b. **Compare and Contrast** In what ways were Mughal and British rule of India similar and different?
   c. **Evaluate** In your opinion, was partitioning India a good decision? Why or why not?
   d. **Explain** What is the significance of Vaisakhi?
   e. **Analyze** How has population growth affected India's economy?
   f. **Predict** What steps might India's leaders take to control pollution?

Lesson 3

10. a. **Identify** What countries share the subcontinent with India?
    b. **Analyze** How was Sri Lanka affected by the 2004 tsunami?
    c. **Predict** How might conflict between India and Pakistan lead to problems in the future?

Module 15 Assessment, continued

Reading Skills

11. **Visualize** Read the historical source feature "Gandhi's 'Quit India' Speech." As you read, visualize the scenes that Gandhi describes. Then make a list of words from the passage that help you create a mental image of a nonviolent soldier fighting for freedom. Lastly, draw a rough sketch of your soldier.

Social Studies Skills

Create a Line Graph *Use the information in the chart to complete the tasks below.*

Population Growth in India	
Year	**India's Population**
1951	361,088,000
1961	439,235,000
1971	548,160,000
1981	683,329,000
1991	846,387,888
2001	1,028,737,436
2011	1,210,193,422
Source: *Census of India*	

12. Plot the data from the chart on a line graph. Be sure to use labels and a title to identify the subject and information presented in your line graph. Finally, organize information from your line graph into a brief summary that identifies any patterns that you see in the data.

Map Skills

13. **The Indian Subcontinent** Locate major human and geographic features of this region. On a sheet of paper, match the letters on the map with their correct labels.

Deccan	Mount Everest
Indus River	Himalayas
Mumbai (Bombay)	Sri Lanka
Kashmir	New Delhi

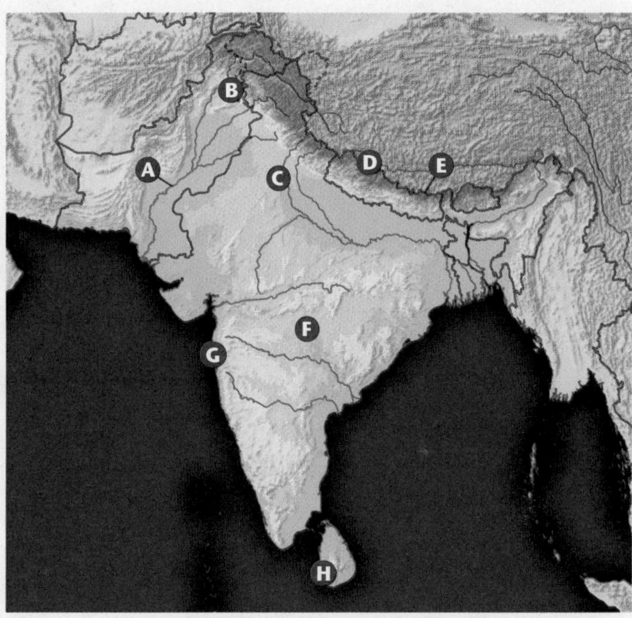

Focus on Speaking

14. **Present a Travelogue** Imagine that you have just traveled through the Indian Subcontinent. Write a short script describing your travels. Gather images to illustrate your descriptions of India and the other nations of the subcontinent. Then present your travelogue to the class.

Module 16

Early Civilizations of China

Essential Question

How did the progression of ruling dynasties shape the culture of ancient China?

About the Photo: The Great Wall of China stretches more than 2,000 miles (3,219 km) across mountains, deserts, and plains. Construction on the wall began more than 2,000 years ago.

Explore ONLINE!

VIDEOS, including . . .
- Confucius: Words of Wisdom
- The First Emperor of China
- Song Dynasty Inventions

- Document-Based Investigations
- Graphic Organizers
- Interactive Games
- Image Carousel: Guardians of Shi Huangdi's Tomb
- Interactive Map: The Silk Road
- Interactive Map: The Voyages of Zheng He

In this module, you will learn about the history and culture of ancient China. China was one of the world's early centers of civilization.

What You Will Learn

Lesson 1: Early China and the Han Dynasty 513
The Big Idea Early Chinese history was shaped by four dynasties—the Shang, the Zhou, the Qin, and the Han.

Lesson 2: The Sui, Tang, and Song Dynasties 521
The Big Idea Later Chinese dynasties were periods of economic, cultural, and technological accomplishments, including Confucian thought.

Lesson 3: The Yuan and Ming Dynasties. 528
The Big Idea The Chinese were ruled by foreigners during the Yuan dynasty, but they threw off Mongol rule and prospered during the Ming dynasty.

Yuan and Ming Dynasties Under the Yuan and Ming dynasties, Beijing became China's largest city and a center of Chinese culture.

Tang and Song Dynasties The Chinese invented many items that we still use today, including fireworks.

Early China The first dynasties to rule China left behind artifacts such as this clay figure of a soldier.

Reading Social Studies

Understand Chronological Order

READING FOCUS

When you read a paragraph in a history text, you can usually use clue words to help you keep track of the order of events. When you read a longer section of text that includes many paragraphs, though, you may need more clues. One of the best clues you can use in this case is dates. Each of the sentences below includes at least one date. Notice how those dates were used to create a timeline that lists events in chronological, or time, order.

- As early as **7000 BC,** people had begun to farm in China.
- After **3000 BC,** people began to use potter's wheels to make many types of pottery.
- The first dynasty for which we have clear evidence is the Shang, which was firmly established by the **1500s BC.**
- Shang emperors ruled in China until the **1100s BC.**

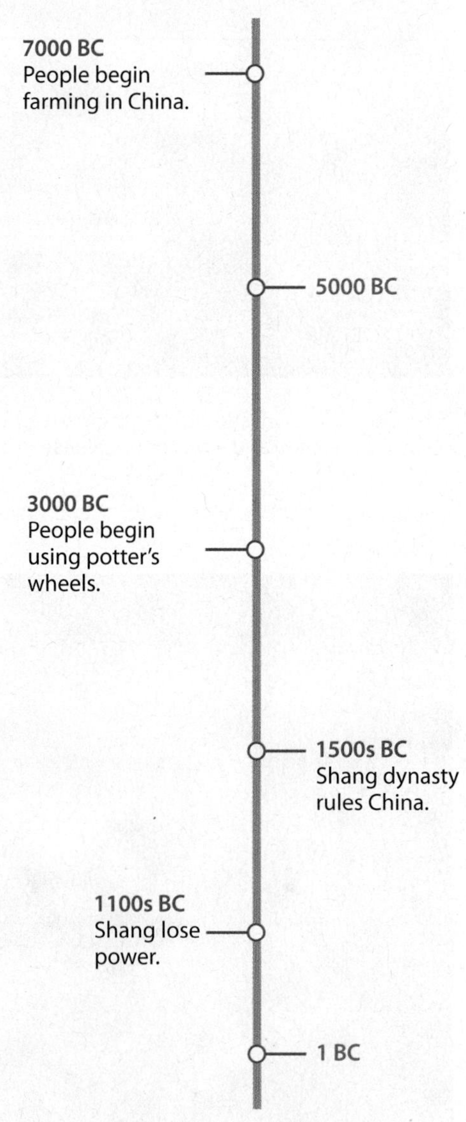

YOU TRY IT!

Read the following sentences. Use the dates in the sentences to create a timeline listing events in chronological order.

- The Ming dynasty ruled China from 1368 to 1644.
- Genghis Khan led his armies into northern China in 1211.
- Between 1405 and 1433, Zheng He led seven grand voyages to places around Asia.
- In the 1300s many Chinese groups rebelled against the Yuan dynasty.

As you read this module, use clue words to help you keep track of the chronological order of historic events.

Early China and the Han Dynasty

The Big Idea

Early Chinese history was shaped by four dynasties—the Shang, the Zhou, the Qin, and the Han.

Main Ideas

- Chinese civilization began along two rivers.
- The Zhou and Qin dynasties changed Chinese society and made great advances.
- Under the Han dynasty, China's government and society were largely based on the ideas of Confucius.
- The Han made many achievements in art, literature, and learning and began trade with distant lands.

Key Terms and Places

Chang Jiang
Huang He
mandate of heaven
Xi'an
Great Wall
sundial
seismograph
acupuncture
Silk Road

If YOU lived there . . .

You are the ruler of China, and hundreds of thousands of people look to you for protection. For many years, your country has lived in peace. Large cities have grown up, and traders travel freely from place to place. Now, however, a new threat looms. Invaders from the north are threatening China's borders. Frightened by the ferocity of these invaders, the people turn to you for help.

What will you do to protect your people?

Chinese Civilization Begins

As early as 7000 BC people had begun to farm in China. They grew rice in the middle of the **Chang Jiang** valley. North, along the **Huang He,** the land was better for growing cereals such as millet and wheat. At the same time, people tamed animals such as pigs and sheep. Supported by these sources of food, China's population grew. Villages appeared along the rivers.

A River Valley Civilization Some villages along the Huang He grew into large towns. Walls surrounded these towns to defend them against floods and hostile neighbors. Villagers built houses out of wood and packed earth. Most of these houses were built facing south. This plan allowed sunlight into the house and blocked cold winds from entering the door.

Over time, Chinese culture became more advanced. As in other river valley civilizations, some people took up activities other than farming. After 3000 BC, for example, some became expert pottery makers. Others learned to weave silk to make clothing, mostly long belted tunics. As time passed, new social orders began to develop within villages. Some people grew wealthy by amassing large amounts of property. Eventually, their wealth gave them influence, and a noble class developed.

The Shang Dynasty As time passed, dynasties, or families, of strong rulers began to take power in China. The first dynasty for which we have clear evidence is the Shang, which was established by the 1500s BC. Strongest in the Huang He valley, the Shang ruled a broad area of northern China. Shang emperors ruled until the 1100s BC.

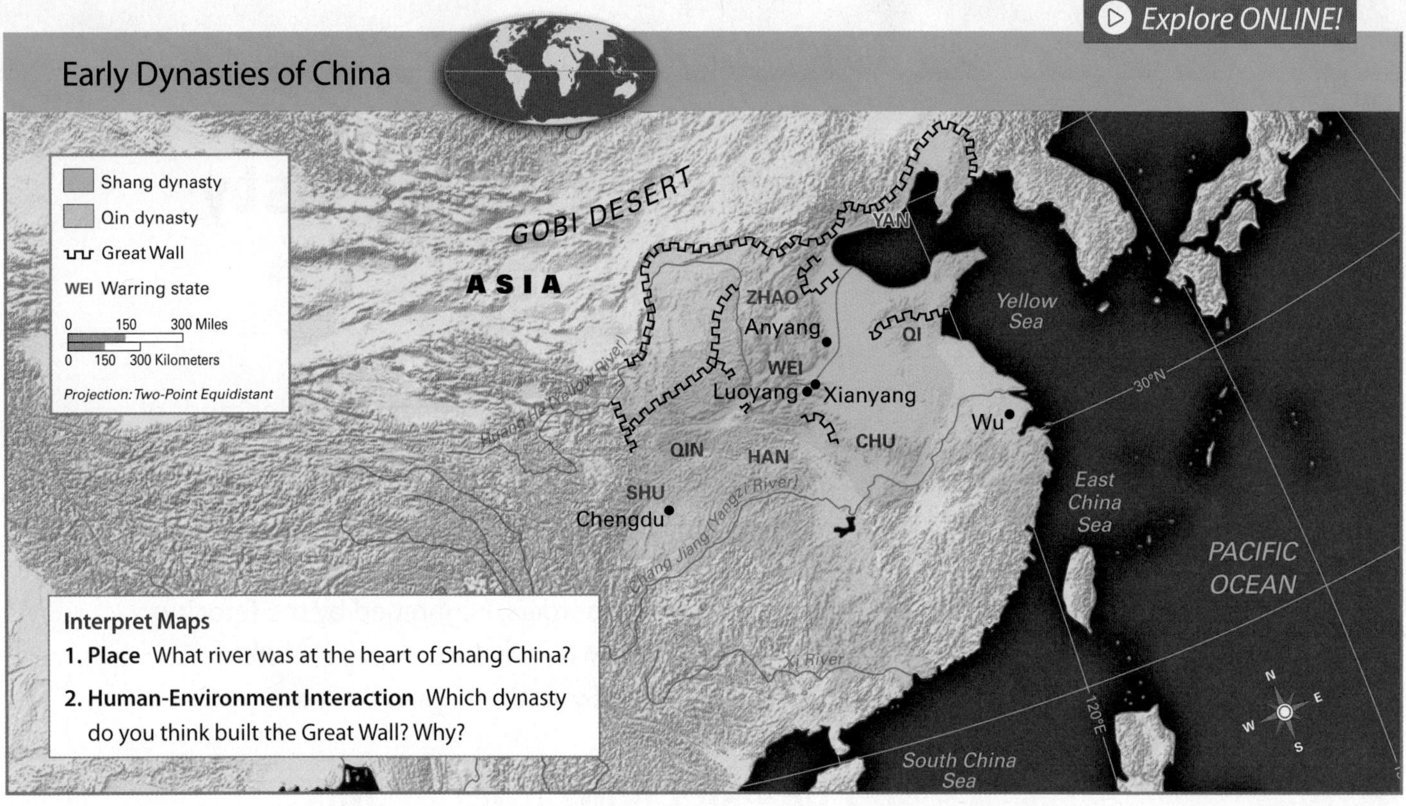

Early Dynasties of China

Interpret Maps

1. **Place** What river was at the heart of Shang China?
2. **Human-Environment Interaction** Which dynasty do you think built the Great Wall? Why?

The Shang made many advances, such as creating China's first writing system. This system used more than 2,000 symbols to express words or ideas. Although the system has gone through changes over the years, the Chinese symbols used today are based on those of the Shang period.

Many examples of Shang writing have been found on cattle bones and turtle shells. Priests had carved questions about the future on these bones or shells, which were then heated, causing them to crack. The priests believed they could "read" these cracks to predict the future. They believed the cracks were shaped by spirits, including the spirits of their ancestors.

In addition to writing, the Shang also made other advances. Artisans made beautiful bronze containers for cooking and religious ceremonies. They also made axes, knives, and ornaments from jade. The Shang also invented a calendar based on the cycles of the moon.

Reading Check
Summarize What were two Shang achievements?

Zhou and Qin Dynasties

The Shang dynasty was only the first of many dynasties described in Chinese records. After the Shang lost power, other dynasties rose up to rule China. Two of those dynasties were the Zhou (JOH) and the Qin (CHIN).

Zhou Dynasty In the 1100s the Shang rulers of China were overthrown in a rebellion. They were replaced by the Zhou dynasty. It lasted longer than any other in Chinese history. Zhou rulers held power until 771 BC.

The Zhou claimed that they had been chosen by heaven to rule China. They believed that no one could rule without heaven's permission. This idea that heaven chose China's ruler was called the **mandate of heaven.** A dynasty would keep the mandate of heaven as long as it was strong. Rulers who grew weak lost the mandate and could be overthrown.

Under the Zhou, a new political order formed in China. The emperor was at the top of society. Everything in China belonged to him, and everyone had to be loyal to him. Emperors gave land to people in exchange for loyalty or military service. Those people who received this land became lords. Below the lords were peasants, or farmers who owned little land. In addition to growing their own food, peasants had to grow food for lords.

New Belief Systems Some of the most influential thinkers in Chinese history are believed to have lived during the Zhou dynasty. One of these thinkers was Laozi (LOWD-zuh). He founded a school of thought known as Daoism (DOW-ih-zum). Daoism stressed living in harmony with the Dao, the guiding force of all reality. It taught that people should not interfere with nature or with each other. Like water, people should flow through life in a natural way.

The other great teacher of the Zhou dynasty was Confucius. His ideas emphasize the importance of ethics and moral values, such as respect for elders and loyalty toward family. Confucius's teachings were collected after his death in a book called *The Analects*.

Confucius felt that China was overrun with rude and dishonest people. He wanted the country to return to ideas and practices from a time when people knew their proper roles in society. He taught that fathers should display moral values to inspire their families. Children should obey and respect their parents. Family members should be loyal to each other.

Confucius's ideas about government were similar to his ideas about family. He thought moral leadership, not laws, would bring order to China. He taught that kings should lead by example, inspiring good behavior in all their subjects. He also believed that the lower classes, like children, would learn by following the example of their superiors.

Both Daoism and Confucianism attracted many followers during the Zhou dynasty. In fact, both have shaped how people act and think in China for centuries. Over the centuries, their influence has also spread into other parts of East Asia, including Japan, Vietnam, and Korea.

BIOGRAPHY

Emperor Shi Huangdi (c. 259–210 BC)

Shi Huangdi was a powerful emperor and a very strict one. He demanded that everyone in China believe the same things he did. To prevent people from having other ideas, he ordered all books that did not agree with his beliefs burned. When a group of scholars protested the burning of these books, Shi Huangdi had them buried alive. These actions led many Chinese to resent the emperor. As a result, they were eager to bring the Qin dynasty to an end.

Draw Conclusions
Why do you think Shi Huangdi tried to ban all opposing points of view in China?

In 1974 archaeologists found the tomb of Emperor Shi Huangdi near Xi'an and made an amazing discovery. Buried close to the emperor was an army of more than 6,000 life-size terra cotta, or clay, soldiers. They were designed to be with Shi Huangdi in the afterlife. In other nearby chambers of the tomb there were another 1,400 clay figures of cavalry and chariots.

Warring States Period The Zhou political system broke down as lords grew less loyal to the emperors. When invaders attacked the capital in 771 BC, many lords would not fight. As a result, the emperor was overthrown. China broke apart into many kingdoms that fought each other for power and influence. This time of disorder in China is called the Warring States period.

Qin Dynasty The Warring States period came to an end when one state became strong enough to defeat all its rivals. That state was called Qin. In 221 BC a king from Qin managed to unify all of China under his control and name himself emperor.

As emperor, the king took a new name. He called himself Shi Huangdi (SHEE hwahng-dee), a name that means "first emperor." Shi Huangdi was a very strict ruler, but he was an effective ruler as well. He expanded the size of China both to the north and to the south.

Shi Huangdi greatly changed Chinese politics. Unlike the Zhou rulers, he refused to share his power with anyone. Lords who had enjoyed many rights before now lost those rights. In addition, he ordered thousands of noble families to move to his capital, now called **Xi'an** (SHEE-AHN). He thought nobles that he kept nearby would be less likely to rebel against him.

The Qin dynasty did not last long. While Shi Huangdi lived, he was strong enough to keep China unified. The rulers who followed him, however, were not as strong. In fact, China began to break apart within a few years of Shi Huangdi's death. Rebellions began all around China, and the country fell into civil war.

Qin Achievements Although the Qin did not rule for long, they saw great advances in China. As emperor, Shi Huangdi worked to make sure that people all over China acted and thought the same way. He created a system of laws that would apply equally to people in all parts of China. He also set up a new system of money. Before, people in each region had used local currencies. He also created a uniform system of writing that eliminated minor differences between regions.

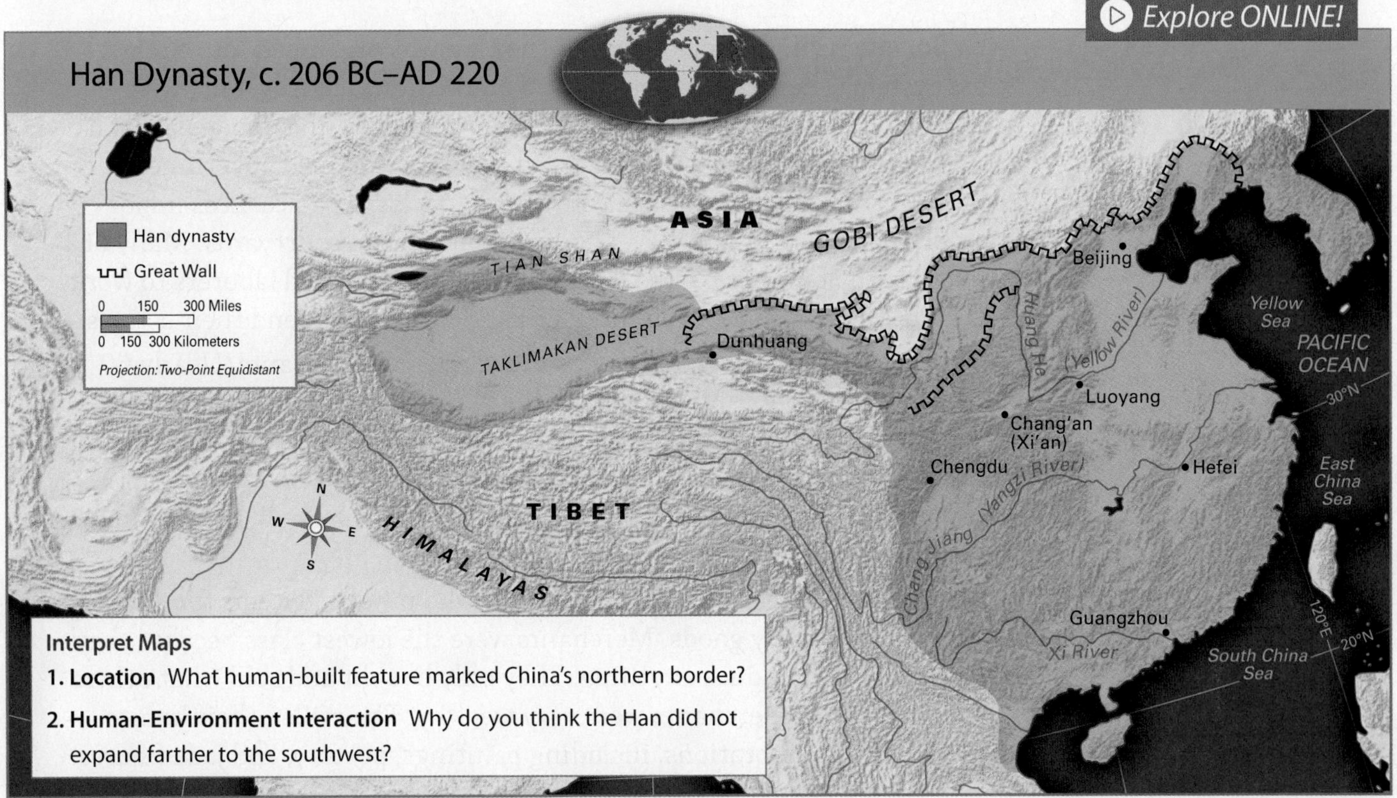

Interpret Maps

1. **Location** What human-built feature marked China's northern border?
2. **Human-Environment Interaction** Why do you think the Han did not expand farther to the southwest?

The Qin's best-known achievements, though, were in building. Under the Qin, the Chinese built a huge network of roads and canals. These roads and canals linked distant parts of the empire to make travel and trade easier.

To protect China from invasion, Shi Huangdi built the **Great Wall,** a barrier that linked earlier walls that stood near China's northern border. Building the wall took years of labor from hundreds of thousands of workers. Later dynasties added to the wall, parts of which still stand today.

Reading Check
Summarize
What happened under the Qin dynasty?

The Han Dynasty

When the Qin dynasty collapsed, many groups fought for power. After years of fighting, an army led by Liu Bang (lee-OO bang) won control. In 206 BC Liu Bang became the first emperor of the Han dynasty, which lasted more than 400 years.

The Rise of a New Dynasty Liu Bang's rule was different from the strict government of the Qin. He wanted to free people from harsh government policies. He lowered taxes for farmers and made punishments less severe. He gave large blocks of land to his supporters. In addition, Liu Bang changed the way government worked. Unlike many earlier rulers, he relied on educated officials to help him rule.

In 140 BC Emperor Wudi (WOO-dee) took the throne. He wanted to create a stronger government. To do that, he took land from the lords, raised taxes, and put the supply of grain under government control. He also made Confucianism China's official government philosophy. Under the Han, government officials were expected to practice Confucianism. Wudi even began a university to teach Confucian ideas.

Han Society Chinese society under the Han was organized into a strict class system. These classes were based on the Confucian system, with strict guidelines that governed each class's behavior. The upper class was made up of the emperor, his court, and scholars who held government positions. The emperor and his court lived in a large palace. Less important officials lived in multilevel houses built around courtyards. Many of these wealthy families owned large estates and employed laborers to work the land. Some families even hired private armies to defend their estates.

The second class, the largest, was made up of the peasants. Nearly 60 million people lived in China during the Han dynasty, and about 90 percent of them were peasants. Although they were respected for their labor, most peasants were poor. They wore plain clothing and ate cooked grains like barley. Most peasants lived in small villages. Their small, wood-framed houses had walls made of mud or stamped earth.

The next social class included artisans, who produced items for daily life and some luxury goods. Merchants were the lowest class because they did not actually produce anything. They only bought and sold what others made. Still, some merchants were very wealthy. They filled their homes with expensive decorations, including paintings, pottery, and jade figures.

The military was not a class in the Confucian system. However, joining the army offered men a chance to rise in social status because the military was considered part of the government.

Reading Check
Analyze Causes
What shaped social structure in China under the Han?

The Revival of the Family Since Confucianism was the government's official philosophy during Wudi's reign, Confucian teachings about the family were also honored. Children were taught from birth to respect their elders. Disobeying one's parents was a crime. Even emperors had a duty to respect their parents. Within the family, the father had absolute power. The Han taught that it was a woman's duty to obey her husband, and children had to obey their father. All members of a family were expected to care for family burial sites and to honor their ancestors with rituals and ceremonies.

Honoring one's family was an important duty in Han China. In this painting, people give thanks before their family shrine.

Han Achievements and Trade

Han rule was a time of great achievements. Art and literature thrived, and inventors developed many useful devices.

Art and Literature The Chinese of the Han period produced many works of art. They became experts at figure painting—a style of painting that includes portraits of people. Portraits often showed religious figures and Confucian scholars. Han artists also painted realistic scenes from everyday life on the walls of palaces and tombs.

In literature, Han China is known for its poetry. Poets developed new styles of verse, including the *fu* style, which was the most popular. *Fu* poets combined prose and poetry to create long literary works. Another style, called *shi*, featured short lines of verse that could be sung. Many Han rulers hired poets known for the beauty of their verse.

Han writers also produced important works of history. A historian named Sima Qian wrote a history of all the dynasties through the early Han. His format and style became the model for later historical writings.

Inventions and Advances The Han Chinese invented one item that we use every day—paper. They made it by grinding plant fibers, such as mulberry bark and hemp, into a paste. Then they let it dry in sheets. Chinese scholars produced books by pasting several pieces of paper together into a long sheet. Then they rolled the sheet into a scroll.

Academic Vocabulary
innovation a new idea, method, or device

The Han also made other **innovations** in science. These included the sundial and the seismograph. A **sundial** is a device that uses the position of shadows cast by the sun to tell the time of day. It was an early type of clock. A **seismograph** is a device that measures the strength of earthquakes. Han emperors were very interested in knowing about the movements of the earth. They believed that earthquakes were signs of future evil events.

Another Han innovation, acupuncture (AK-yoo-punk-cher), improved medicine. **Acupuncture** is the practice of inserting fine needles through the skin at specific points to cure disease or relieve pain. Many Han inventions in science and medicine are still used today.

Han Achievements

During the Han dynasty, the Chinese made many advances in art and learning. Some of these advances are shown here.

Art
This bronze horse is just one example of the beautiful objects made by Chinese artisans.

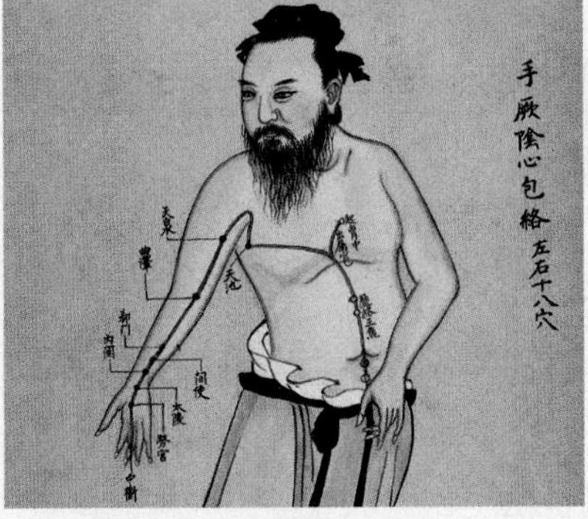

Medicine
Han doctors studied the human body and used acupuncture to heal people.

Science
This is a model of an ancient Chinese seismograph. When an earthquake struck, a lever inside caused a ball to drop from a dragon's mouth into a toad's mouth, indicating the direction from which the earthquake had come.

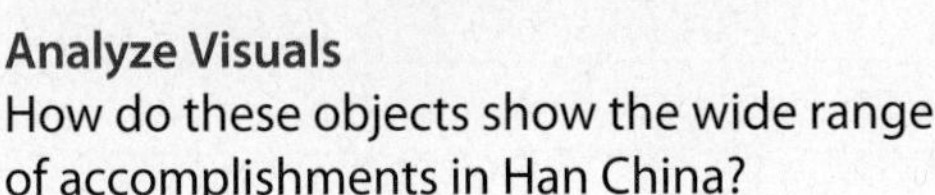

Analyze Visuals
How do these objects show the wide range of accomplishments in Han China?

Trade with Other Lands Under Wudi, the Han dynasty expanded west into Central Asia. There, the Chinese learned that silk, which the Chinese had been making for centuries, was in high demand in lands farther west. China's rulers realized they could make huge profits through trade.

Traders used a series of overland routes to take Chinese goods to distant buyers. The most famous trade route was known as the **Silk Road.** This 4,000-mile-long network of routes stretched westward from China across deserts and mountains, through the Middle East, until it reached the Mediterranean Sea. Chinese traders did not travel the entire Silk Road. Upon reaching Central Asia, they sold their goods to local traders who would take them the rest of the way.

Traveling the Silk Road was difficult. Hundreds of men and camels loaded with valuable goods, including silks and jade, banded together for protection. Armed guards were hired to protect traders from bandits. Weather presented other dangers, including blizzards and sandstorms. Still, the Silk Road was worth its many risks. Silk was so popular in Rome, for example, that China grew wealthy from that trade relationship alone. Traders returned from Rome with silver, gold, precious stones, and horses.

But trade goods and money were not the only things exchanged on the Silk Road. Traders on the route exchanged ideas along with trade goods. For example, traders carried the technique of papermaking from China to Southwest Asia and Europe. At the same time, missionaries carried new religions, including Christianity and Buddhism, to China. Buddhism in particular would play a major role in China in later centuries.

Reading Check
Categorize What advances did the Chinese make during the Han period?

Summary and Preview Early Chinese history was shaped by the Shang, Zhou, Qin, and Han dynasties. In the next lesson, you will learn about two dynasties that also made great advances, the Tang and the Song.

Lesson 1 Assessment

Review Ideas, Terms, and Places

1. **a. Identify** On what rivers did Chinese civilization begin?
   b. Analyze What advances did the early Chinese make before and during the Shang dynasty?
   c. Evaluate What do you think was the Shang dynasty's most important achievement? Why?
2. **a. Define** What is the mandate of heaven?
   b. Form Generalizations How did Shi Huangdi change China?
   c. Make Inferences Why do you think Shi Huangdi called himself the first emperor?
3. **a. Identify** What is Confucianism? How did it affect the government during the Han dynasty?
   b. Explain How did Emperor Wudi create a strong central government?
   c. Summarize How was Han society organized?
4. **a. Identify** What device did the Chinese invent to measure the strength of earthquakes?
   b. Summarize What was the Silk Road? What products were traded along it?
   c. Judge Do you think the trade goods or the ideas carried on the Silk Road were more influential? Why?

Critical Thinking

5. **Analyze** Draw a chart like the one shown here. Using your notes, write details about the achievements and political system of China's early dynasties.

	Achievements	Political System
Shang		
Zhou		
Qin		
Han		

The Sui, Tang, and Song Dynasties

The Big Idea

Later Chinese dynasties were periods of economic, cultural, and technological accomplishments, including Confucian thought.

Main Ideas

- After the Han dynasty, China fell into disorder but was reunified by new dynasties.
- Cities and trade grew during the Tang and Song dynasties.
- The Tang and Song dynasties produced fine arts and inventions.
- Confucianism influenced the Song system of government.
- Scholar-officials ran China's government during the Song dynasty.

Key Terms and Places

Grand Canal
Kaifeng
porcelain
woodblock printing
gunpowder
compass
bureaucracy
civil service
scholar-official

If YOU lived there ...

It is the year 1270. You are a rich merchant in a Chinese city of about a million people. The city around you fills your senses. You see people in colorful clothes among beautiful buildings. Glittering objects lure you into busy shops. You hear people talking—discussing business, gossiping, laughing at jokes. You smell delicious food cooking at a restaurant down the street.

How do you feel about your city?

Disorder and Reunification

When the Han dynasty collapsed, China split into several rival kingdoms, each ruled by military leaders. Historians call the time of disorder that followed the collapse of the Han the Period of Disunion. It lasted from 220 to 589. War was common during the Period of Disunion. The lack of a stable government also made trade difficult. China grew more isolated.

The Spread of Buddhism During the violence and uncertainty of the Period of Disunion, many Chinese people tried to find spiritual comfort. Some looked to Daoism and Confucianism to find out why they had to suffer so much, but they did not find helpful answers. However, Buddhism, which had recently arrived in China from India, did provide the answers people sought. They took comfort in the Buddhist teaching that people can escape suffering and achieve a state of peace. By the end of the Period of Disunion, Buddhism was well established in China. Wealthy people donated land and money to Buddhist temples, which arose across the land.

Sui Dynasty Finally, after centuries of political confusion and cultural change, China was reunified. The man who finally ended the Period of Disunion was a northern ruler named Yang Jian (YANG jee-EN). In 589 he conquered the south, unified China, and created the Sui (SWAY) dynasty.

The Sui dynasty did not last long—only from 589 to 618. During that time, however, its leaders restored order and began the **Grand Canal.** This huge series of canals and waterways linked parts of northern and southern China.

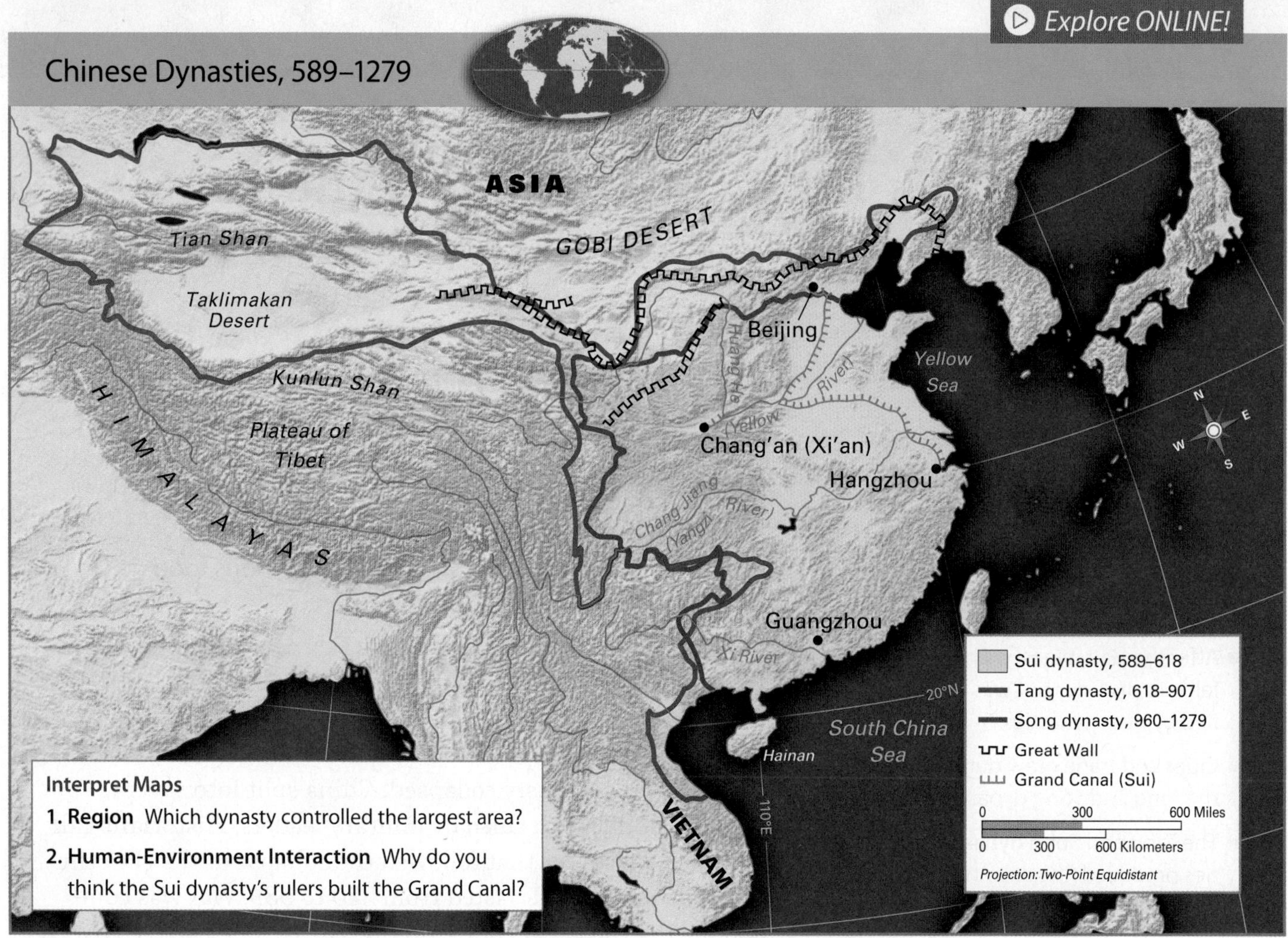

Tang Dynasty The Sui dynasty was followed by the Tang, which would rule for nearly 300 years. As you can see on the map, China grew under the Tang dynasty to include much of eastern and central Asia.

Historians view the Tang dynasty as a golden age in China. Tang rulers conquered many lands, reformed the military, and created law codes. The Tang period also saw great advances in art. Some of China's finest poets, for example, lived during this time.

The Tang dynasty included the only woman to rule China—Empress Wu. Married to a sickly emperor, she took power for herself and ruled from the 650s until 704. Her methods were often vicious, but she was intelligent and talented. She helped bring stability and prosperity to China.

Song Dynasty After the Tang dynasty fell, China entered another period of chaos and disorder, with separate kingdoms competing for power. As a result, this period in China's history is called the Five Dynasties and Ten Kingdoms. The disorder only lasted 53 years, from 907 to 960.

In 960 China was again reunified, this time by the Song dynasty. Like the Tang, the Song ruled for about 300 years, until 1279. Also like the Tang, the Song dynasty was a time of great achievements. The Song greatly strengthened the Chinese economy, making it the strongest in the world at that time. They also oversaw some amazing cultural advances.

Reading Check
Find Main Ideas
What dynasties restored order to China?

Cities and Trade

Throughout the Tang and Song dynasties, much of the food grown on China's farms flowed into the growing cities and towns. China's cities were crowded, busy places. Shopkeepers, government officials, doctors, artisans, entertainers, religious leaders, and artists made them lively places as well.

City Life China's capital and largest city of the Tang dynasty was Chang'an (chahng-AHN), a huge, bustling trade center now called Xi'an. With a population of more than a million, it was by far the largest city in the world. Like other trading cities, Chang'an was home to a mix of people from many cultures—China, Korea, Persia, Arabia, and Europe. It was also known as a religious and philosophical center, not just for Buddhists and Daoists but for Asian Christians as well.

Cities continued to grow under the Song. Several cities, including the Song capital, **Kaifeng** (KY-fuhng), had about a million people. A dozen more cities had populations of close to half a million.

Trade in China and Beyond Trade grew along with Chinese cities. This trade, combined with China's agricultural base, made China richer than ever before.

Much trade took place within China itself. Traders used the country's rivers to ship goods on barges and ships. In addition, the Grand Canal carried a huge amount of trade goods. Construction on the canal had begun during the Sui dynasty. During the Tang dynasty, it was improved and expanded. The Grand Canal allowed the Chinese to move goods and crops from rural areas into cities.

The Grand Canal

China's Grand Canal is the world's longest human-made waterway. It was built largely to transport rice and other foods from the south to feed China's cities and armies in the north.

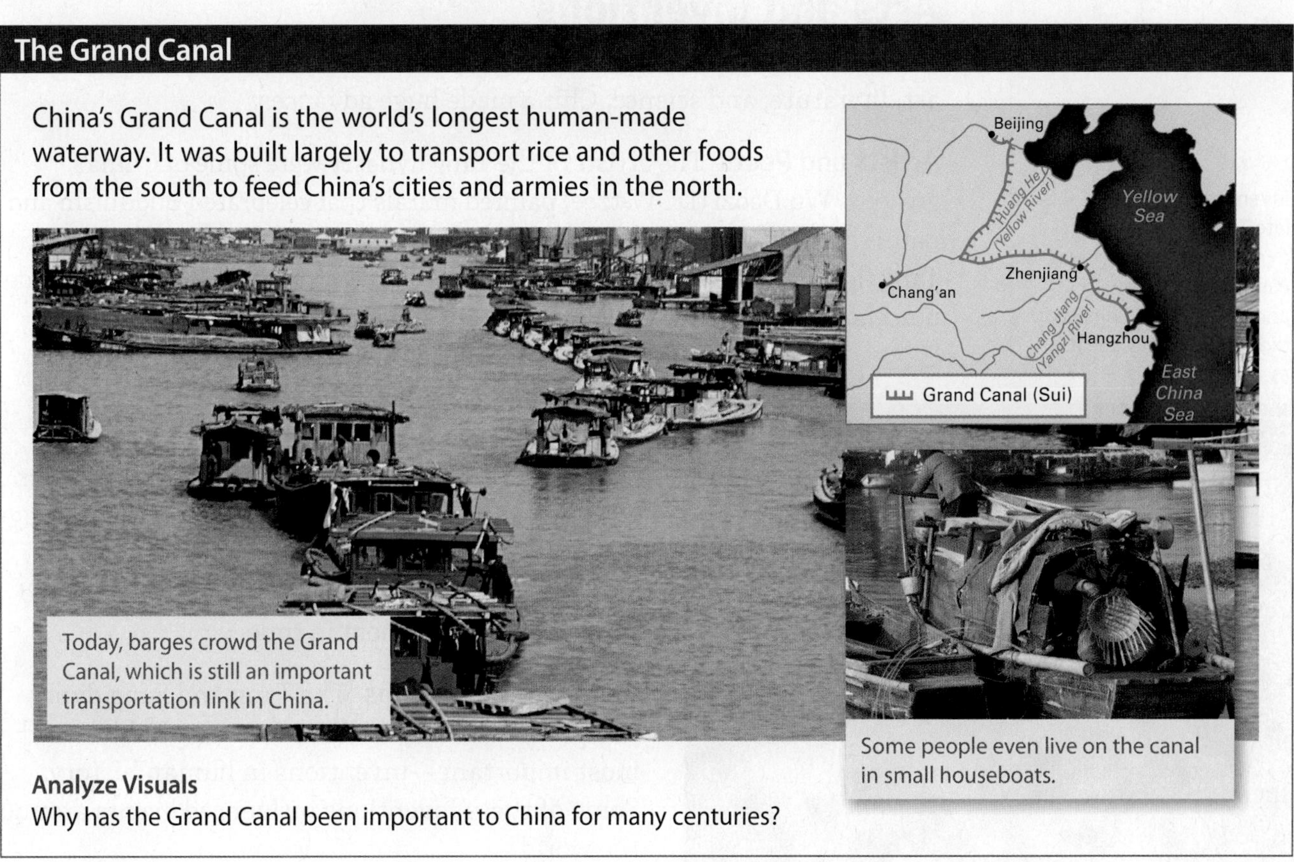

Today, barges crowd the Grand Canal, which is still an important transportation link in China.

Some people even live on the canal in small houseboats.

Analyze Visuals
Why has the Grand Canal been important to China for many centuries?

Porcelain was first made during the Tang dynasty, but it wasn't perfected for many centuries. Chinese artists were famous for their work with this fragile material.

The Chinese also carried on trade with other lands and peoples. During the Tang dynasty, most foreign trade was over land routes leading to India and Southwest Asia, though Chinese traders also went to Korea and Japan in the East. The Chinese exported many goods, including tea, rice, spices, and jade. However, one export was especially important—silk. So valuable was silk that the Chinese kept the method of making it secret. They feared that if other countries learned to make their own silk, they would no longer import it from China. In exchange for their exports, the Chinese imported different foods, plants, wool, glass, and precious metals like gold and silver.

During the Song dynasty, sea trade became more important. China opened its Pacific ports to foreign traders. The sea-trade routes connected China to many other countries. During this time, the Chinese also developed another valuable product—a thin, beautiful type of pottery called **porcelain.** Porcelain became so popular in the West that it became known as "chinaware," or just "china."

All of this trade helped create a strong economy. As a result, merchants became important members of Chinese society during the Song dynasty. Also as a result of the growth of trade and wealth, the Song invented the world's first system of paper money in the 900s.

Reading Check
Summarize
How far did China's trade routes extend?

Arts and Inventions

While China grew rich economically, its cultural riches also increased. In art, literature, and science, China made huge advances.

Artists and Poets The artists of the Tang dynasty were some of China's greatest. Wu Daozi (DOW-tzee) painted murals that celebrated Buddhism and nature. Artists of the Tang and Song dynasties made exquisite objects in clay. Tang figurines of horses clearly show the animals' strength. Song artists made porcelain items covered in a pale green glaze called celadon (SEL-uh-duhn).

Invented during the late Tang or early Song dynasty, gunpowder was used to make fireworks and signals. The Chinese did not generally use it as a weapon.

The Tang and Song dynasties were also noted for their literature. The Tang period, for example, produced two of China's greatest poets, Li Bo and Du Fu, who wrote poems that readers still enjoy for their beauty. The Song dynasty's Li Qingzhao (ching-ZHOW) was perhaps China's greatest female poet. She once said that the purpose of her poetry was to capture a single moment in time.

Important Inventions The Tang and Song dynasties produced some of the most remarkable—and most important—inventions in human history. Some of these inventions influenced events around the world.

According to legend, a man named Cai Lun invented paper in the year 105, during the Han dynasty. A later Tang invention built on this achievement—**woodblock printing,** a form of printing in which an entire page is carved into a block of wood. The printer applies ink to the block and presses paper against the block to create a printed page. Printers could copy drawings or texts quickly, much faster than they could be copied by hand. The world's first known printed book was printed in this way in China in 868.

Another invention of the Tang dynasty was gunpowder. **Gunpowder** is a mixture of powders used in guns and explosives. It was originally used only in fireworks, but it was later used to make small bombs and rockets. Eventually, gunpowder was used to make explosives, firearms, and cannons. Gunpowder dramatically altered how wars were fought and, in doing so, changed the course of human history.

One of the most useful achievements of the Tang dynasty was the perfection of the magnetic **compass.** This instrument, which uses Earth's magnetic field to show direction, revolutionized travel. A compass made it possible to find direction more accurately than ever before. Explorers the world over used compasses to travel vast distances. Both trading ships and warships also came to rely on the compass for their navigation. Thus, the compass has been a key factor in some of the most important sailing voyages in history.

The Song dynasty also produced many important inventions. Under the Song, the Chinese invented movable type. Movable type is a set of letters or characters that are used to print books. Unlike the blocks used in block printing, movable type can be rearranged and reused to create new lines of text and different pages.

The Song dynasty also developed the concept of paper money. People were used to buying goods and services with bulky coins made of metals such as bronze, gold, and silver. Paper money was far lighter and easier to use. As trade increased and many people in China grew rich, paper money became more popular.

Reading Check **Find Main Ideas** What were some important inventions of the Tang and Song dynasties?

Connect to Economics

The Paper Trail

Paper money was printed for the first time in China in the AD 900s. It was in use for about 700 years, through the Ming dynasty, when the bill shown here was printed. However, so much money was printed that it lost value. The Chinese stopped using paper money for centuries.

The use of paper money caught on in Europe, though, and eventually became common. By the late 1700s and early 1800s paper money was in use all around the world. Most countries now use paper money. National governments regulate how much money is in circulation at any time to prevent the same devaluation that occurred in China long ago.

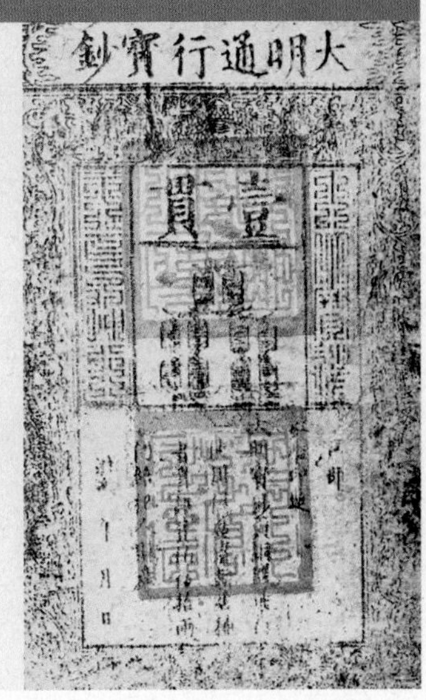

Draw Conclusions
How would life be different today without paper money?

This painting from the 1600s shows civil servants writing essays for China's emperor.

Confucianism

During the Period of Disunion, which followed the Han dynasty, Confucianism was overshadowed by Buddhism as the major tradition in China. Many Chinese people had turned to Buddhism for peace and comfort during those troubled times. In doing so, they largely turned away from Confucian ideas and outlooks.

When the Period of Disunion ended, Buddhism remained popular. It appealed to both the rich and the poor. By AD 200s, Buddhist altars could even be found in the emperor's palace.

During the Sui and early Tang dynasties, Buddhism remained very influential. Unlike Confucianism, which focused on ethical behavior, Buddhism stressed a more spiritual outlook that promised escape from suffering. Late in the Tang dynasty, however, many Chinese historians and scholars once again became interested in the teachings of Confucius. Their interest was sparked by their desire to improve Chinese government and society.

During the Song dynasty, a new philosophy called Neo-Confucianism began to develop. The term *neo* means "new." Based on Confucianism, Neo-Confucianism was similar to the older philosophy in that it taught proper behavior. However, it also emphasized spiritual matters. For example, Neo-Confucian scholars discussed such issues as what made human beings do bad things even if their basic nature was good.

Neo-Confucianism became very influential under the Song. Its influence grew even more later on. In fact, the ideas of Neo-Confucianism became official government teachings in China after the Song dynasty.

Reading Check
Contrast
How did Neo-Confucianism differ from Confucianism?

Scholar-Officials

The Song dynasty took another major step that affected China for centuries. They improved the system by which people went to work for the government. These workers formed a large **bureaucracy,** or a body of unelected government officials. They joined the bureaucracy by passing civil service examinations. **Civil service** means service as a government official.

To become a civil servant, a person had to pass a series of written examinations. The examinations tested students' grasp of Confucianism and related ideas. Difficult exams were designed to make sure that government officials were chosen by ability—not by wealth or family connections. To pass, a student might be required to memorize an entire Confucian text.

Because the tests were so difficult, students spent years preparing for them. To pass the most difficult tests, students might study for more than 20 years! A single exam could last as long as 72 hours. During that time, test-takers were locked in private rooms. Guards kept watch over the examination halls to prevent cheating.

Academic Vocabulary
incentive something that leads people to follow a certain course of action

Because of the extreme difficulty of the tests, only a very small fraction of the people who took the tests would reach the top level and be appointed to a position in the government. However, candidates for the civil service examinations had a strong incentive for studying hard. Passing the tests meant life as a **scholar-official**—an educated member of the government.

Scholar-officials were elite members of society. They performed many important jobs and were widely admired for their knowledge and ethics. Their typical responsibilities might include running government offices; maintaining roads, irrigation systems, and other public works; updating and keeping official records; or collecting taxes.

The jobs performed by scholar-officials were often challenging, but they came with impressive benefits as well. Scholar-officials were granted considerable respect from the Chinese people. They often received reduced penalties for breaking the law. Many also became wealthy from gifts given by people seeking their aid.

Reading Check
Analyze Effects How did the Song dynasty change China's government?

The civil service examination system helped ensure that only talented, intelligent people became scholar-officials. The civil service system was a major factor in the stability of the Song government. Scholar-officials remained important in China for centuries.

Summary and Preview The Tang and Song dynasties were periods of great advancement. Many great artists and writers lived during these periods. Tang and Song inventions also had dramatic effects on world history. During the Song period, Confucian ideas helped shape China's government. In the next lesson, you will read about the next two dynasties: the Yuan and the Ming.

Lesson 2 Assessment

Review Ideas, Terms, and Places

1. **a. Recall** What was the Period of Disunion? What dynasty brought an end to that period?
   b. Explain How did China change during the Tang dynasty?
2. **a. Describe** What were the capital cities of Tang and Song China like?
   b. Draw Conclusions How did geography affect trade in China?
3. **a. Identify** Who was Li Bo?
   b. Draw Conclusions How may the inventions of paper money and woodblock printing have been linked?
   c. Rank Which Tang or Song invention do you think was most important? Defend your answer.
4. **a. Identify** What led to the decline of Confucianism in China after the Han dynasty?
   b. Explain What was Neo-Confucianism?
   c. Elaborate Why do you think Neo-Confucianism appealed to many people?
5. **a. Define** What was a scholar-official?
   b. Explain Why would people want to become scholar-officials?
   c. Evaluate Do you think civil service examinations were a good way to choose government officials? Why or why not?

Critical Thinking

6. **Categorize** Copy the chart below. Use it to organize your notes on the Tang and Song into categories.

	Tang Dynasty	Song Dynasty
Cities		
Trade		
Art		
Inventions		

The Yuan and Ming Dynasties

The Big Idea

The Chinese were ruled by foreigners during the Yuan dynasty, but they threw off Mongol rule and prospered during the Ming dynasty.

Main Ideas

- The Mongol Empire included China, and the Mongols ruled China as the Yuan dynasty.
- The Ming dynasty was a time of stability and prosperity.
- The Ming brought great changes in government and relations with other countries.

Key Terms and Places

Beijing
Forbidden City
isolationism

If YOU lived there . . .

You are a farmer in northern China in 1212. As you pull weeds from a wheat field, you hear a sound like thunder. Looking toward the sound, you see hundreds—no, *thousands*—of warriors on horses on the horizon, riding straight toward you. You are frozen with fear. Only one thought fills your mind—the Mongols are coming.

What can you do to save yourself?

The Mongol Empire

Among the nomadic peoples who attacked the Chinese were the Mongols. For centuries, the Mongols had lived as tribes in the vast plains north of China. Then in 1206, a strong leader, or khan, united them. His name was Temüjin. When he became leader, though, he was given a new title: "Universal Ruler," or Genghis Khan (JENG-guhs KAHN).

The Mongol Conquest Genghis Khan organized the Mongols into a powerful army and led them on bloody expeditions of conquest. The brutality of the Mongol attacks terrorized people throughout much of Asia and Eastern Europe. Genghis Khan and his army killed all of the men, women, and children in countless cities and villages. Within 20 years, he ruled a large part of Asia.

A Mongol warrior

Genghis Khan then turned his attention to China. He first led his armies into northern China in 1211. They fought their way south, wrecking whole towns and ruining farmland. By the time of Genghis Khan's death in 1227, all of northern China was under Mongol control.

The Mongol conquests did not end with Genghis Khan's death, though. His sons and grandsons continued to raid lands all over Asia and Eastern Europe. The destruction the Mongols left behind was terrible, as one Russian chronicler noted:

> "There used to be the city of Riazan in the land of Riazan, but its wealth and glory ceased, and there is nothing to be seen in the city excepting smoke, ashes, and barren earth."
>
> –from "The Tale of the Destruction of Riazan," in *Medieval Russia's Epics, Chronicles, and Tales*, edited by Serge Zenkovsky

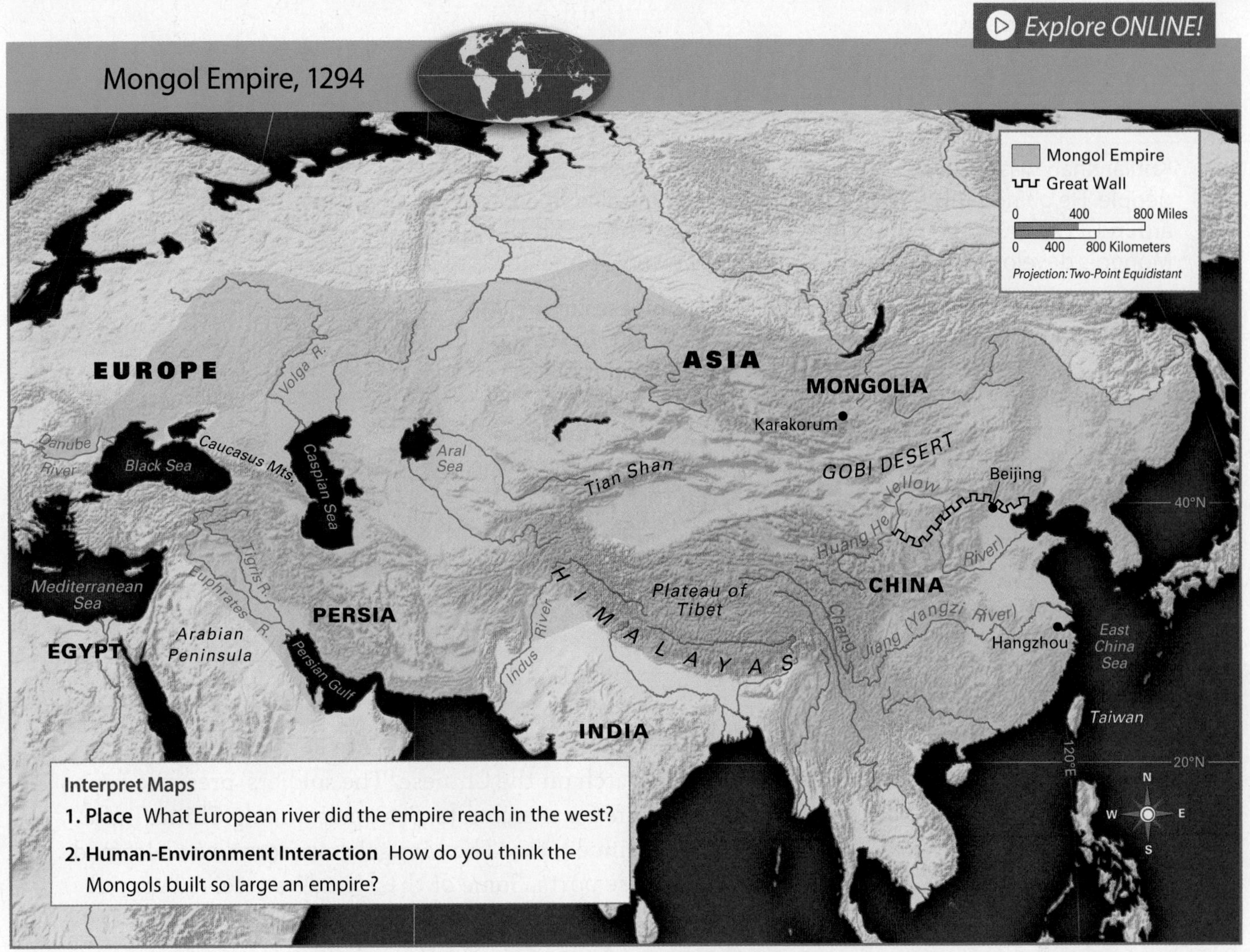

Interpret Maps
1. **Place** What European river did the empire reach in the west?
2. **Human-Environment Interaction** How do you think the Mongols built so large an empire?

In 1260 Genghis Khan's grandson Kublai Khan (KOO-bluh KAHN) became ruler of the Mongol Empire. He completed the conquest of China and in 1279 declared himself emperor of China. This began the Yuan dynasty, a period that some people also call the Mongol Ascendancy. For the first time in its long history, China was ruled by foreigners.

Life in Yuan China Kublai Khan and the Mongols belonged to a different ethnic group than the Chinese did. They spoke a different language, worshiped different gods, and had different customs. The Chinese resented being ruled by these foreigners, whom they saw as rude and uncivilized.

However, Kublai Khan did not force the Chinese to accept Mongol ways of life. Some Mongols even adopted aspects of Chinese culture, such as Confucianism. Still, the Mongols made sure to keep control of the Chinese. They prohibited Confucian scholars from gaining too much power in the government. The Mongols also placed heavy taxes on the Chinese.

Much of the tax money the Mongols collected went to pay for vast public-works projects. These projects required the labor of many Chinese people. The Yuan added to the Grand Canal and built new roads and palaces. Workers also improved the roads used by China's postal system. In addition, the Yuan emperors built a new capital, Dadu, near modern **Beijing.**

BIOGRAPHY

Kublai Khan (1215–1294)

Kublai Khan was known as the "Great Khan," the leader of all Mongol people. He gained this title in 1260 and named himself emperor of China around 1279. During his rule, China opened up to the outside world. The Mongols developed a thriving sea trade and welcomed foreign visitors.

Unlike most Mongols, Kublai was interested in Chinese culture. At the same time, he remained loyal to his Mongol roots. To remind him of home, he planted grass from the northern plains in his palace garden in Beijing. He also honored his ancestors in Mongolian style. Every August he performed a special ritual, scattering horse milk on the ground and calling out the name of his grandfather, Genghis Khan.

Kublai Khan ruled China for 15 years, until his death.

Draw Conclusions
How can you tell that being a Mongol was important to Kublai Khan?

Mongol soldiers were sent throughout China to keep the peace as well as to keep a close watch on the Chinese. The soldiers' presence kept overland trade routes safe for merchants. Sea trade among China, India, and Southeast Asia continued, too. The Mongol emperors also welcomed foreign traders at Chinese ports. Some of these traders received special privileges.

Part of what we know about life in the Yuan dynasty comes from one such trader, an Italian merchant named Marco Polo. Between 1271 and 1295 he traveled in and around China. Polo was highly respected by the Mongols and even served in Kublai Khan's court. When Polo returned to Europe, he wrote of his travels. Polo's descriptions of China fascinated many Europeans. His book sparked much European interest in China. It also resparked interest in trade between Europe and China, which had declined. As a result of his journey, trade once again increased.

The End of the Yuan Dynasty Despite their vast empire, the Mongols were not content with their lands. They decided to invade Japan. A Mongol army sailed to Japan in 1274 and 1281. The campaigns, however, were disastrous. Violent storms and fierce defenders destroyed most of the Mongol force.

The failed campaigns against Japan weakened the Mongol military. The huge, expensive public-works projects had already weakened the economy. These weaknesses, combined with Chinese resentment, made China ripe for rebellion.

In the 1300s many Chinese groups rebelled against the Yuan dynasty. In 1368 a former monk named Zhu Yuanzhang (JOO yoo-ahn-JAHNG) took charge of a rebel army. He led this army in a final victory over the Mongols. China was once again ruled by the Chinese.

Reading Check
Find Main Ideas How did the Mongols come to rule China?

Historical Source

A Chinese City

In this passage, Marco Polo describes his visit to Hangzhou (HAHNG-JOH), a city in southeastern China.

> *"Inside the city there is a Lake . . . and all round it are erected [built] beautiful palaces and mansions, of the richest and most exquisite [finest] structure that you can imagine . . . In the middle of the Lake are two Islands, on each of which stands a rich, beautiful and spacious edifice [building], furnished in such style as to seem fit for the palace of an Emperor. And when any one of the citizens desired to hold a marriage feast, or to give any other entertainment, it used to be done at one of these palaces. And everything would be found there ready to order, such as silver plate, trenchers [platters], and dishes, napkins and table-cloths, and whatever else was needful. The King made this provision for the gratification [enjoyment] of his people, and the place was open to every one who desired to give an entertainment."*
>
> —Marco Polo, from *Description of the World*

Analyze Sources
From this description, what impression might Europeans have of Hangzhou?

The Ming Dynasty

After his army defeated the Mongols, Zhu Yuanzhang became emperor of China. The Ming dynasty that he founded ruled China from 1368 to 1644—nearly 300 years. Ming China proved to be one of the most stable and prosperous times in Chinese history. The Ming expanded China's fame overseas and sponsored incredible building projects across China.

Great Sea Voyages During the Ming dynasty, the Chinese improved their ships and their sailing skills. The greatest sailor of the period was Zheng He (juhng HUH). Between 1405 and 1433, he led seven grand voyages to places around Asia. Zheng He's fleets were huge. One included more than 60 junks, or ships, and 25,000 sailors. Some of the ships were gigantic, perhaps more than 300 feet (91.4 km) long—almost as long as a football field!

In the course of his voyages, Zheng He sailed his fleet throughout the Indian Ocean. He sailed as far west as the Persian Gulf and the easternmost coast of Africa. His stops included what are now Vietnam, Thailand, and India. Everywhere his ships landed, Zheng He presented leaders with beautiful gifts from China. He boasted about his country and encouraged foreign leaders to send gifts to China's emperor. From one voyage, Zheng He returned to China with representatives of some 30 nations, sent by their leaders to honor the emperor. He also brought goods and stories back to China.

Zheng He's voyages rank among the most impressive in the history of seafaring. Although they did not lead to the creation of new trade routes or the exploration of new lands, they served as a clear sign of China's power.

The Voyages of Zheng He

Zheng He's ocean voyages were remarkable. Some of his junks, such as the one shown here, were among the largest in the world at the time.

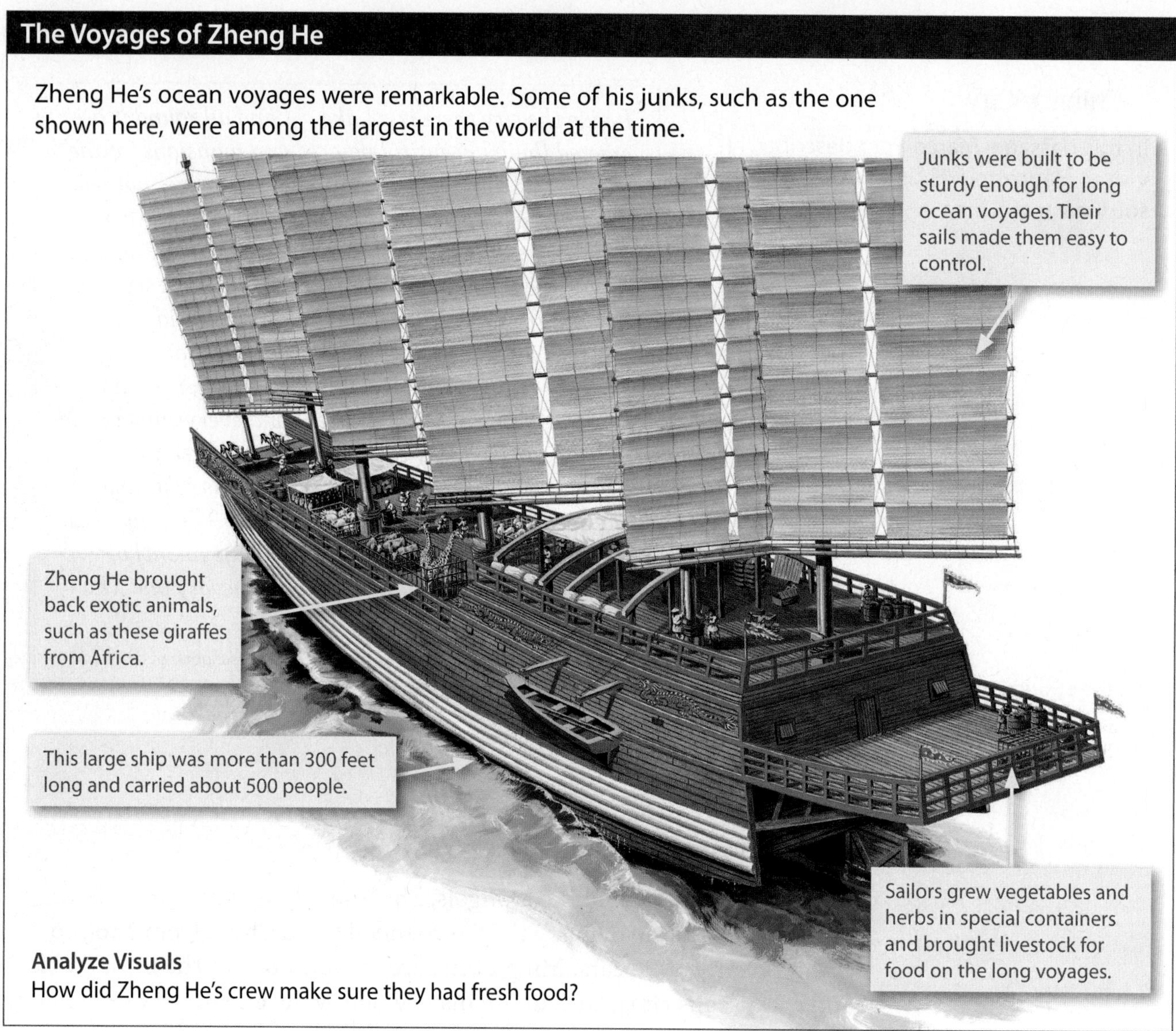

Analyze Visuals
How did Zheng He's crew make sure they had fresh food?

Great Building Projects The Ming were also known for their grand building projects. Many of these projects were designed to impress both the Chinese people and their enemies to the north.

In Beijing, for example, the Ming emperors built the **Forbidden City,** a huge palace complex that included hundreds of imperial residences, temples, and other government buildings. Within them were some 9,000 rooms. The name Forbidden City came from the fact that the common people were not even allowed to enter the complex. For centuries, this city within a city was a symbol of China's glory.

Ming rulers also directed the restoration of the famous Great Wall of China. Large numbers of soldiers and peasants worked to rebuild fallen portions of walls, connect existing walls, and build new ones. The result was a construction feat unmatched in history. The wall was more than 2,000 miles (3,219 km) long. It would reach from San Diego to New York! The wall was about 25 feet (7.6 m) high and, at the top, 12 feet (3.7 m) wide. Protected by the wall—and the soldiers who stood guard along it—the Chinese people felt safe from invasions by the northern tribes.

Reading Check
Form Generalizations
In what ways did the Ming dynasty strengthen China?

The Forbidden City

The Forbidden City is not actually a city. It's a huge complex of almost 1,000 buildings in the heart of China's capital. The Forbidden City was built for the emperor, his family, his court, and his servants, and ordinary people were forbidden from entering.

Analyze Visuals
How did the Forbidden City show the power and importance of the emperor?

China Under the Ming

During the Ming dynasty, Chinese society began to change. This change was largely due to the efforts of the Ming emperors. Having expelled the Mongols, the Ming emperors worked to eliminate all foreign influences from Chinese society. As a result, China's government and relations with other countries changed dramatically.

Government When the Ming took over China, they adopted many government programs that had been created by the Tang and the Song. However, the Ming emperors were much more powerful than Tang and Song rulers had been. They abolished the offices of some powerful officials and took a larger role in running the government themselves. These emperors fiercely protected their power, and they punished anyone whom they saw as challenging their authority.

Despite their personal power, though, the Ming did not disband the civil service system. Because he personally oversaw the entire government, the emperor needed officials to keep his affairs organized.

The Ming also used examinations to appoint censors. These officials were sent all over China to investigate the behavior of local leaders and to judge the quality of schools and other institutions. Their job was to prevent corruption in the government. The censors reported any evidence of wrongdoing to the emperor for further investigation.

Censors had existed for many years in China, but under the Ming their power and influence grew. Access to the emperor gave censors great power, and many people feared crossing them. In fact, many officials stopped proposing new programs for fear of catching the censors' attention.

Relations with Other Countries In the 1430s a new Ming emperor made Zheng He return to China and dismantle his fleet. At the same time, he banned foreign trade. China entered a period of isolationism. **Isolationism** is a policy of avoiding contact with other countries.

Academic Vocabulary
consequences effects of a particular event or events

In the end, this isolationism had great **consequences** for China. By the late 1800s the Western world had made huge leaps in technological progress. Westerners were able to take power in some parts of China. Partly due to its isolation and lack of progress, China was too weak to stop them. Gradually, China's glory faded.

Reading Check
Identify Cause and Effect How did isolationism affect China?

Summary In this module, you have learned about the long history of China and its many ruling dynasties. You have also read about the many cultural achievements that China contributed to the world during those dynasties.

Lesson 3 Assessment

Review Ideas, Terms, and Places

1. **a. Identify** Who was Genghis Khan?
   b. Explain How did the Mongols gain control of China?
   c. Evaluate Judge this statement: "The Mongols should never have tried to invade Japan."
2. **a. Identify** Who was Zheng He, and what did he do?
   b. Analyze What impression do you think the Forbidden City had on the residents of Beijing?
   c. Develop How may the Great Wall have both helped and hurt China?
3. **a. Define** What is isolationism?
   b. Explain How did the Ming change China?
   c. Develop How might a policy of isolationism have both advantages and disadvantages?

Critical Thinking

4. **Compare and Contrast** Draw a diagram like this one. Use your notes to see how the Yuan and Ming dynasties were alike and different.

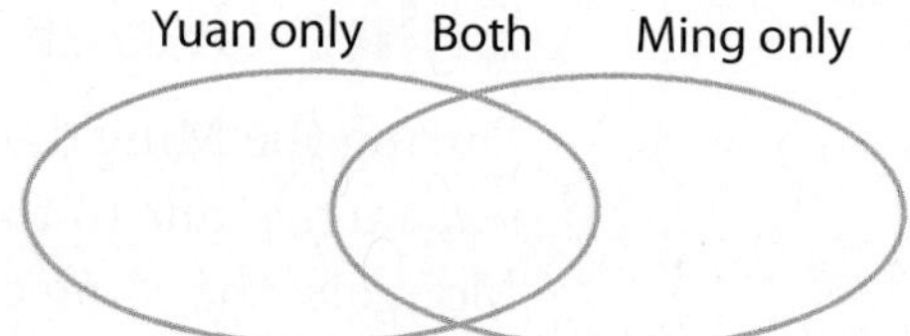

Make Economic Choices

Define the Skill

Economic choices are a part of geography. World leaders must make economic choices every day. For example, a country's president might face a choice about whether to spend government money on improving defense, education, or health care.

You also have to make economic choices in your own life. For example, you might have to decide whether to go to a movie with a friend or buy a new shirt. You cannot afford to do both, so you must make a choice.

Making economic choices involves sacrifices, or tradeoffs. If you choose to spend your money on a movie, the tradeoffs are the other things you want but cannot buy. By considering tradeoffs, you can make better economic choices.

Learn the Skill

Imagine that you are in the school band. The band has enough money to make one major purchase this year. As the diagram below shows, the band can spend the money on new musical instruments, new uniforms, or a band trip. The band decides to buy new instruments.

1. Based on the diagram below, what are the tradeoffs of the band's choice?
2. What would have been the tradeoffs if the band had voted to spend the money on a trip instead?
3. How do you think creating a diagram like the one below might have helped the band make its economic choice?

Practice the Skill

1. Describe an example of an economic choice you might face that has three possible tradeoffs.
2. For each possible economic choice, identify what the tradeoffs are if you make that choice.
3. What final choice will you make? Why?
4. How did considering tradeoffs help you make your choice?

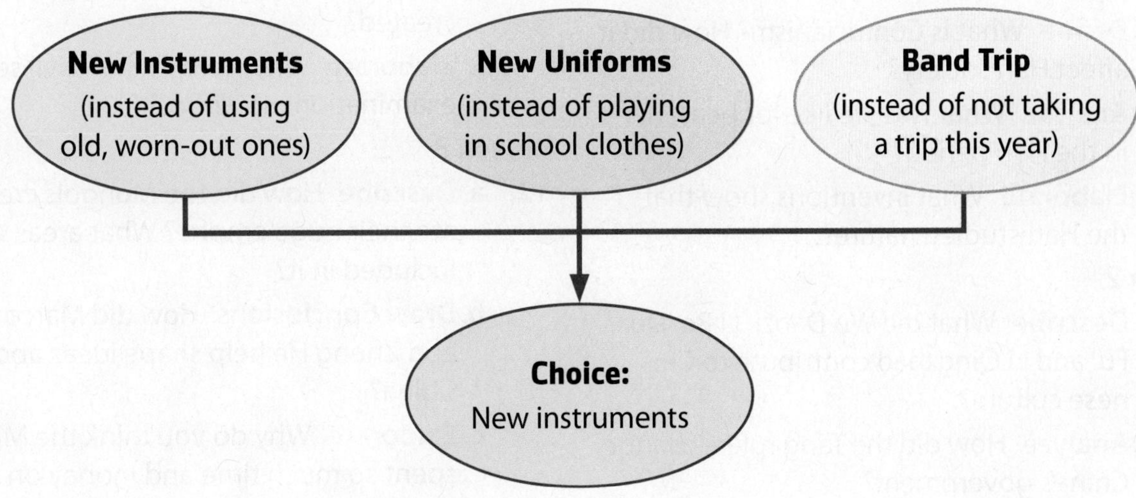

Module 16 Assessment

Review Vocabulary, Terms, and Places

Match the words or names with their definitions or descriptions.

a. gunpowder
b. scholar-official
c. mandate of heaven
d. bureaucracy
e. seismograph
f. porcelain
g. Great Wall
h. isolationism
i. incentive

1. a device to measure the strength of earthquakes
2. something that leads people to follow a certain course of action
3. body of unelected government officials
4. thin, beautiful pottery
5. educated government worker
6. policy of avoiding contact with other countries
7. a barrier along China's northern border
8. a mixture of powders used in explosives
9. the idea that heaven chose who should rule

Comprehension and Critical Thinking

Lesson 1

10. a. **Identify** What was the first known dynasty to rule China? What did it achieve?
    b. **Analyze** Why did the Qin dynasty not last long after Shi Huangdi's death?
    c. **Evaluate** Do you think Shi Huangdi was a good ruler for China? Why or why not?
    d. **Define** What is Confucianism? How did it affect Han society?
    e. **Analyze** What was life like for peasants in the Han period?
    f. **Elaborate** What inventions show that the Han studied nature?

Lesson 2

11. a. **Describe** What did Wu Daozi, Li Bo, Du Fu, and Li Qingzhao contribute to Chinese culture?
    b. **Analyze** How did the Tang rulers change China's government?
    c. **Evaluate** Which Chinese invention has had a greater effect on world history—the magnetic compass or gunpowder? Why do you think so?
    d. **Define** How did Confucianism change in and after the Song dynasty?
    e. **Make Inferences** Why do you think the civil service examination system was created?
    f. **Elaborate** Why were China's civil service examinations so difficult?

Lesson 3

12. a. **Describe** How did the Mongols create their huge empire? What areas were included in it?
    b. **Draw Conclusions** How did Marco Polo and Zheng He help shape ideas about China?
    c. **Elaborate** Why do you think the Ming spent so much time and money on the Great Wall?

Reading Skills

13. **Understand Chronological Order** *Arrange the following list of events in the order in which they happened. Then write a brief paragraph describing the events, using clue words such as* then *and* later *to show proper sequence.*
    - The Han dynasty rules China.
    - The Shang dynasty takes power.
    - Mongol armies invade China.
    - The Ming dynasty takes control.

Social Studies Skills

Make Economic Choices *You have enough money to buy one of the following items: shoes, a movie, or a book.*

14. What are the tradeoffs if you buy the movie?
15. What are the tradeoffs if you buy the book?

Map Skills

16. **Ancient China** On a separate sheet of paper, match the letters on the map with their correct labels.

Beijing	Chang Jiang	Huang He
Kaifeng	Chang'an (Xian)	

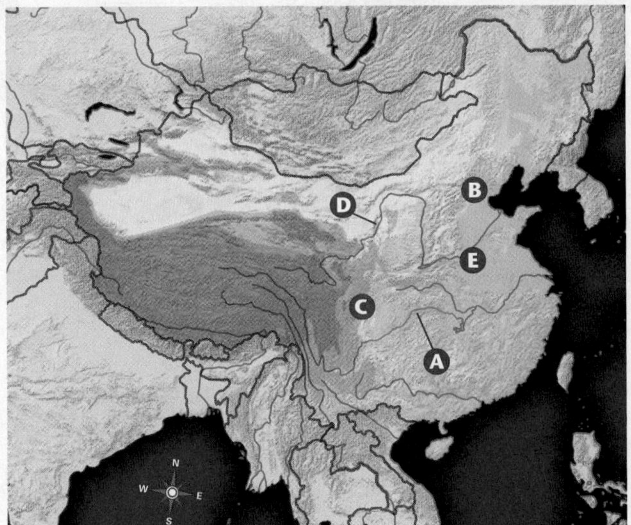

Focus on Writing

17. **Write a Magazine Article** You are a freelance writer who has been asked to write a magazine article about the achievements of the ancient Chinese. Identify the achievements or inventions that you want to write about. Begin writing your article. Open with a sentence that states your main idea. Include a paragraph of two or three sentences about each invention or achievement. Describe each achievement or invention and explain why it was so important. End your article with a sentence or two that summarizes China's importance to the world.

Module 17

China, Mongolia, and Taiwan

Essential Question

How can history and geography help us understand population patterns in China, Mongolia, and Taiwan?

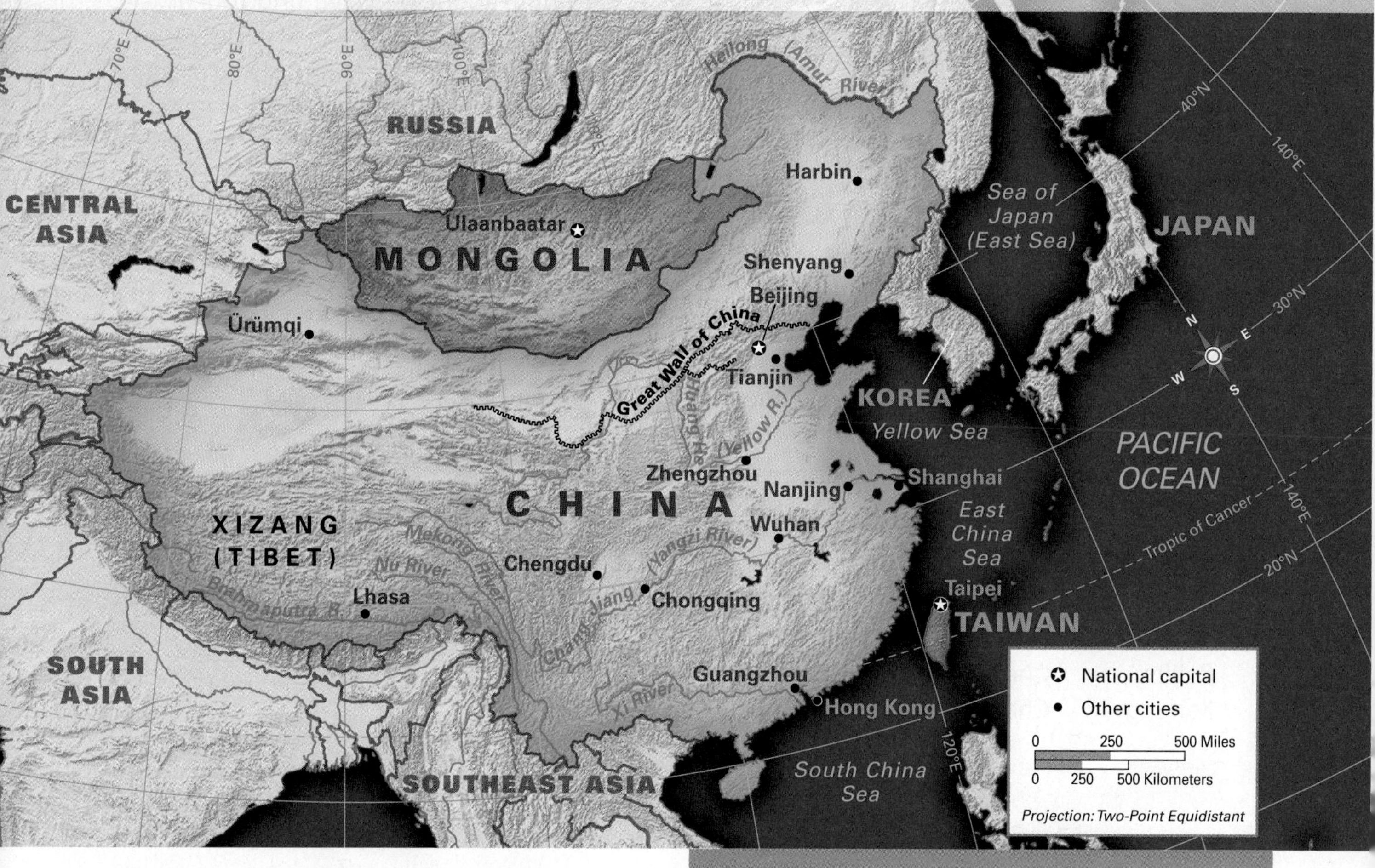

Explore ONLINE!

- Document-Based Investigations
- Graphic Organizers
- Interactive Games
- Channel One News Video: Made in China: Building Boom
- Channel One News Video: People and Politics
- Image with Hotspots: Terraced Rice Fields
- Interactive Graph: China's Projected Urban Population
- Image with Hotspots: Mongols on the Move

In this module, you will learn about the land and people of China, Mongolia, and Taiwan.

What You Will Learn

Lesson 1: Physical Geography **541**

The Big Idea Physical features, climate, and resources vary across China, Monglia, and Taiwan.

Lesson 2: China **545**

The Big Idea China's economy and cities are growing rapidly, but the Chinese have little political freedom and many environmental problems.

Lesson 3: Mongolia and Taiwan **553**

The Big Idea Mongolia is a rugged land with a nomadic way of life and growing cities, while Taiwan is a densely settled and industrialized island.

Geography Horses play an important role in Mongolian life and culture. Many Mongolians are nomads and use horses to travel across the country's large plains.

History China's capital city, Beijing, is over 3,000 years old and home to more than 23 million people.

Culture Chinese opera uses music and symbolism to tell stories. The actors wear bold and colorful makeup that has special meanings.

Reading Social Studies

Understand Implied Main Ideas

READING FOCUS

Main ideas are often stated in a paragraph's topic sentence. When the main idea is not stated directly, you can find it by looking at the details in the paragraph. First, read the text carefully and think about the topic. Next, look at the facts and details and ask yourself what details are repeated. What points do those details make? Then create a statement that sums up the main idea. Examine how this process works for the paragraph below.

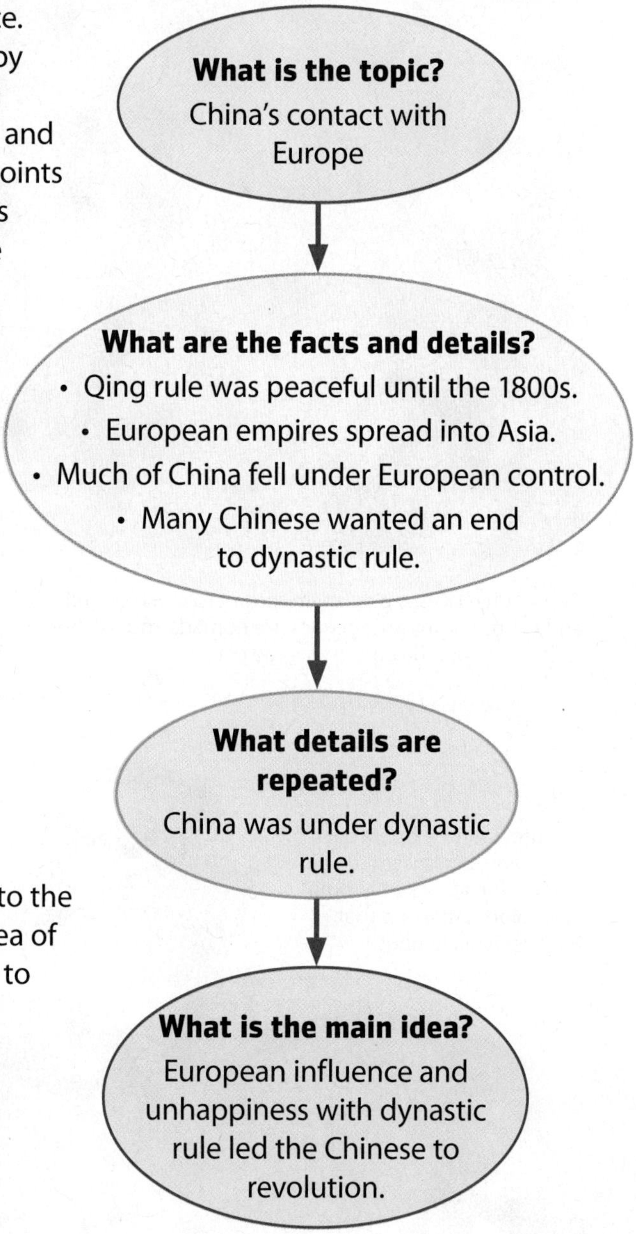

> In 1644 an ethnic group called the Manchu from northeastern Asia took control of China and founded the Qing (CHING) dynasty. Qing rule was peaceful until the 1800s. At that time, European powers began spreading their empires into Asia. Much of China fell under European influence. At the same time, many Chinese wanted to end dynastic rule. This unhappiness sparked a revolution.

What is the topic?
China's contact with Europe

What are the facts and details?
- Qing rule was peaceful until the 1800s.
- European empires spread into Asia.
- Much of China fell under European control.
- Many Chinese wanted an end to dynastic rule.

What details are repeated?
China was under dynastic rule.

What is the main idea?
European influence and unhappiness with dynastic rule led the Chinese to revolution.

YOU TRY IT!

Read the following sentences. Then use the steps listed to the right to develop a statement that expresses the main idea of the paragraph. Exchange your statement with a partner to check your understanding of the implied main idea.

> About 300 million Chinese work in farming. The country is a leading producer of rice, wheat, corn, and potatoes. Only about 11 percent of China's land is good for farming. Most farms are in China's eastern plains and river valleys. So how does China produce so much food? More than a third of Chinese workers are farmers. In addition, farmers cut terraces into hillsides to make the most use of the land.

As you read this module, use the steps in this lesson to help you identify implied main ideas.

Physical Geography

The Big Idea

Physical features, climate, and resources vary across China, Mongolia, and Taiwan.

Main Ideas

- Physical features of China, Mongolia, and Taiwan include mountains, plateaus and basins, plains, and rivers.
- China, Mongolia, and Taiwan have a range of climates and natural resources.

Key Terms and Places

Himalayas
Plateau of Tibet
Gobi
North China Plain
Huang He
loess
Chang Jiang

If YOU lived there . . .

You are a young filmmaker who lives in Guangzhou, a port city in southern China. You are preparing to make a documentary film about the Huang He, one of China's great rivers. To make your film, you will follow the river across northern China. Your journey will take you from the Himalayas to the coast of the Yellow Sea.

What do you expect to see on your travels?

Physical Features

Have you seen the view from the top of the world? At 29,029 feet (8,848 m), Mount Everest in the **Himalayas** is the world's highest mountain. From atop Everest, look east. Through misty clouds, icy peaks stretch out before you, fading to land far below. This is China. About the size of the United States, China has a range of physical features. They include not only the world's tallest peaks but also some of its driest deserts and longest rivers.

Two other areas are closely linked to China. To the north lies Mongolia (mahn-GOHL-yuh). This landlocked country is dry and rugged, with vast grasslands and desert. In contrast, Taiwan (TY-WAHN), off the coast of mainland China, is a green tropical island. Look at the map to see the whole region's landforms.

Mountains Much of this large region, including Taiwan, is mountainous. In southwest China, the Himalayas run along the border. They are Earth's tallest mountain range. Use the physical map of China, Mongolia, and Taiwan in this lesson to locate the region's other ranges. As a tip, the Chinese word *shan* means "mountain."

Other Landforms Many of the mountain ranges are separated by plateaus, basins, and deserts. In southwest China, the **Plateau of Tibet** lies north of the Himalayas. The world's highest plateau, it is called the Roof of the World.

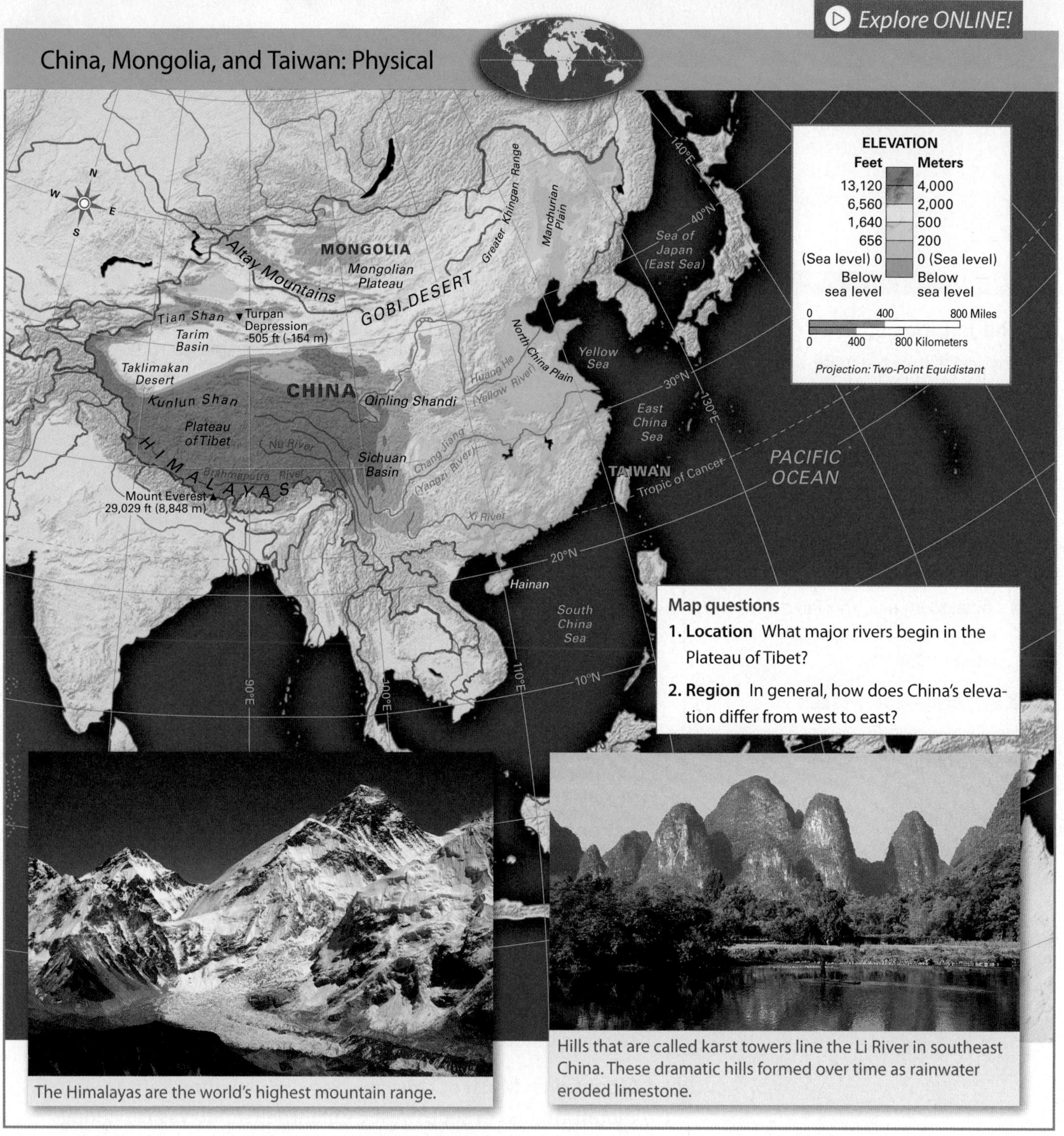

Map questions

1. **Location** What major rivers begin in the Plateau of Tibet?
2. **Region** In general, how does China's elevation differ from west to east?

The Himalayas are the world's highest mountain range.

Hills that are called karst towers line the Li River in southeast China. These dramatic hills formed over time as rainwater eroded limestone.

Moving north, we find a low, dry area. A large part of this area is the Taklimakan (tah-kluh-muh-KAHN) Desert, a barren land of sand dunes and blinding sandstorms. In fact, sandstorms are so common that the desert's Turkish name, Taklimakan, has come to mean "Enter and you will not come out." To the northeast, the Turpan (toohr-PAHN) Depression is China's lowest point, at 505 feet (154 m) below sea level.

Continuing northeast, in Mongolia we find the **Gobi.** This harsh area of gravel and rock is the world's coldest desert. Temperatures can drop to below –40°F (–40°C).

In east China, the land levels out into low plains and river valleys. These fertile plains, such as the **North China Plain,** are China's main population centers and farmlands. On Taiwan, a plain on the west coast is the island's main population center.

Rivers In China, two great rivers run west to east. The **Huang He** (HUANG HEE), or the Yellow River, flows across northern China. Along its course, this river picks up large amounts of **loess** (LES), or fertile, yellowish soil. The soil colors the river and gives it its name.

In summer, the Huang He often floods. The floods spread layers of loess, enriching the soil for farming. However, such floods have killed millions of people. For this reason, the river is called China's Sorrow.

Reading Check
Summarize
What are the main physical features found in this region?

The mighty **Chang (CHAHNG) Jiang,** or the Yangzi (YAHNG-zee) River, flows across central China. It is Asia's longest river and a major transportation route.

Climate and Resources

Climate varies widely across the region. The tropical southeast is warm to hot, and monsoons bring heavy rains in summer. In addition, typhoons can strike the southeast coast in summer and fall. Similar to hurricanes, these violent storms bring high winds and rain. As we move to the northeast, the climate is drier and colder. Winter temperatures can drop below 0°F (–18°C).

Flooding in China

China's rivers and lakes often flood during the summer rainy season. The satellite images here show Lake Dongting Hu in southern China. The lake appears blue, and the land appears red. Soon after the Before image was taken, heavy rains led to flooding. The After image shows the results. Compare the two images to see the extent of the flood, which killed more than 3,000 people and destroyed some 5 million homes.

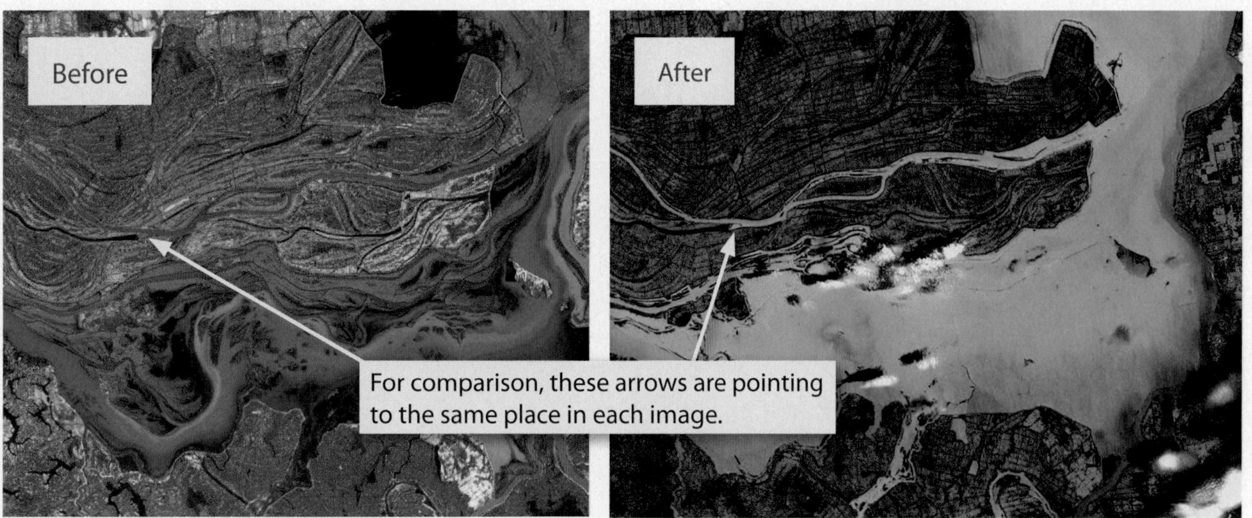

Analyze Visuals
Why might people continue to live in areas that often flood?

In the north and west, the climate is mainly dry. Temperatures vary across the area and can get both very hot and cold.

China has a wealth of natural resources. Like its climate, China's natural resources show tremendous variety. The country is rich in mineral resources and is a leading producer of coal, lead, tin, and tungsten. China produces many other minerals and metals as well. China's forestland and farmland are also valuable resources.

Mongolia's natural resources include minerals such as coal, iron, and tin as well as livestock. Taiwan's major natural resource is its farmland. Important crops include sugarcane, tea, and bananas.

Reading Check
Contrast Which of these three countries has the most natural resources?

Summary and Preview As you have read, China, Mongolia, and Taiwan have a range of physical features, climate, and resources. Next, you will read about the history and culture of China.

Lesson 1 Assessment

Reviewing Ideas, Terms, and Places

1. a. **Identify** What two major rivers run through China?
   b. **Explain** How does the Huang He both benefit and hurt China's people?
   c. **Elaborate** Why do you think many people in China live on the North China Plain?
2. a. **Define** What is a typhoon?
   b. **Contrast** What are some differences between the climates of southeast and northwest China?
   c. **Rate** Based on the different climates in this region, which part of the region would you prefer to live in? Why?

Critical Thinking

3. **Categorize** Use a chart like the one shown here to organize, identify, and describe the main physical features of China, Mongolia, and Taiwan.

Physical Features	Details
plateaus, basins, deserts	
plains and river valleys	
rivers	

China

The Big Idea

China's economy and cities are growing rapidly, but the Chinese have little political freedom and many environmental problems.

Main Ideas

- In China's modern history, revolution and civil war led to a communist government.
- China's booming economy is based on agriculture and manufacturing.
- China has a massive population and its urban areas are growing.
- China's environment faces a number of serious problems.
- China has a rich culture shaped by ancient traditions.

Key Terms and Places

Beijing
Tibet
command economy
Shanghai
Hong Kong
dialect
Daoism
Confucianism
pagodas

If YOU lived there . . .

Long ago, your family owned a small farm in the countryside. But, in the 1950s, China's government took over people's farms to create large government-run farms. For years, your parents grew tea on a government farm. Since the government began allowing private businesses, your parents have been selling tea in the market. Now, they are considering opening a tea shop.

What do you think your parents should do?

Modern History

In 1644 an ethnic group called the Manchu from northeastern Asia took control of China and founded the Qing (CHING) dynasty. Qing rule was peaceful until the 1800s. At that time, European powers began spreading their empires into Asia. Much of China fell under European influence. At the same time, many Chinese wanted to end dynastic rule. This unhappiness sparked a revolution.

Revolution and Civil War In 1911 a revolution ended 2,000 years of rule by emperors. The rebels founded a republic, a political system in which voters elect their leaders. Two rival political groups soon emerged—the Nationalists, led by Chiang Kai-shek (chang ky-SHEK), and the Communists, led by Mao Zedong (MOW ZUH DOOHNG). The Nationalists wanted China to remain a republic based on democracy. The Communists believed that communism was the best political and economic system for China.

The two groups fought a bloody civil war. That war ended in October 1949 with the Communists as victors. They founded a new government, the People's Republic of China. The Nationalists fled to Taiwan, where they founded the Republic of China.

Communist China Mao, the Communists' leader, headed China's new government. In a Communist system, the government owns most businesses and land and controls all areas of life. China's new Communist government began by taking over control of the economy. The government seized all private farms and organized them into large, state-run farms. It also took over all businesses and factories.

National Day

October 1 is National Day in China, a public holiday celebrating the founding of the People's Republic of China. Every five years, Beijing hosts huge parades and festivities in Tiananmen Square, one of the world's largest public gathering places. The parades can include more than 500,000 participants.

A military parade of soldiers, tanks, and other equipment shows China's power.

The Gate of Heavenly Peace displays Mao Zedong's portrait above the entrance.

The Chinese believe dragon dances bring good fortune to important events.

The parades include couples married on National Day, a popular time to wed.

Lion dances are performed to spread blessings to the community.

Analyze Visuals
Why might China's government include so many different groups in the National Day parades?

While some changes improved life, others did not. On one hand, women gained more rights and were able to work. On the other hand, the government limited freedoms and imprisoned people who criticized it. In addition, many economic programs were unsuccessful. Some were outright disasters. In the early 1960s, for example, poor planning and drought led to a famine that killed millions.

China Since Mao After Mao's death in 1976, Deng Xiaoping (DUHNG-SHOW-PING) rose to power. Deng worked to modernize and improve China's economy. He allowed some private businesses and encouraged nations to invest in China. Leaders after Deng continued making economic reforms. They also invested in new technologies and transportation networks, such as roads, shipyards, and railways. These actions made it easier to produce, move, and trade resources and goods. As a result economic interdependence has increased, both regionally and globally.

More economic freedom and growth has not lead to more political freedom in China. The Communist government still tightly controls most areas of life. For example, the government censors newspapers and Internet access, which restricts the flow of information and ideas.

In addition, China harshly punishes people who oppose the government. In 1989 more than 100,000 pro-democracy protestors gathered in Tiananmen Square in **Beijing,** China's capital. The protestors demanded more political rights and freedoms and refused to leave the square. In response, the government deployed troops and tanks to make them leave. Hundreds of protestors were killed. Many more were injured or imprisoned.

China has also taken harsh actions against ethnic rebellions. For example, China controls the Buddhist region of **Tibet,** in southwest China. When the Tibetans rebelled in 1959, the Chinese quickly crushed the revolt. The Dalai Lama (dah-ly LAH-muh), Tibet's Buddhist leader, had to flee to India. China then cracked down on Tibetans' rights.

Because of actions such as these, many countries have accused China of violating human rights. Some countries, including the United States, have considered limiting trade with China until it shows more respect for human rights.

Reading Check: Summarize How did communism change life in China?

Economy

Until the 1970s, China had a **command economy,** an economy in which the government owns all businesses and decides where people work and what industries produce. In the late 1970s, China developed a mixed economy by adopting aspects of a market economy. People were allowed to choose careers, start businesses, and keep the profits they earned. China's economy boomed. Today China has the world's second largest economy.

Farmers near Yunnan, in southern China, use traditional methods to work rice paddies.

About 300 million Chinese work in farming. The country is a leading producer of rice, wheat, corn, and potatoes. Only about 11 percent of China's land is good for farming. Most farms are in China's eastern plains and river valleys. So how does China produce so much food? More than a third of Chinese workers are farmers. In addition, farmers cut terraces into hillsides to make the most use of the land.

Today, China is best known for manufacturing, especially of low-cost goods. China is the world's largest producer and exporter of manufactured goods. The familiar label "Made in China" marks all sorts of products worldwide, from satellites and chemicals to clothing and toys. China is able to produce goods cheaply because of its vast resources and a massive, inexpensive labor force.

The global demand for cheap goods has made manufacturing the most profitable part of China's economy. In turn, economic growth has improved wages and living standards. Almost all homes now have electricity. More and more Chinese can afford goods such as TVs, computers, and cars. Still, in rural China, many remain poor and unemployment is high.

Reading Check Identify Cause and Effect How have changes in China's economic policies affected individuals and businesses?

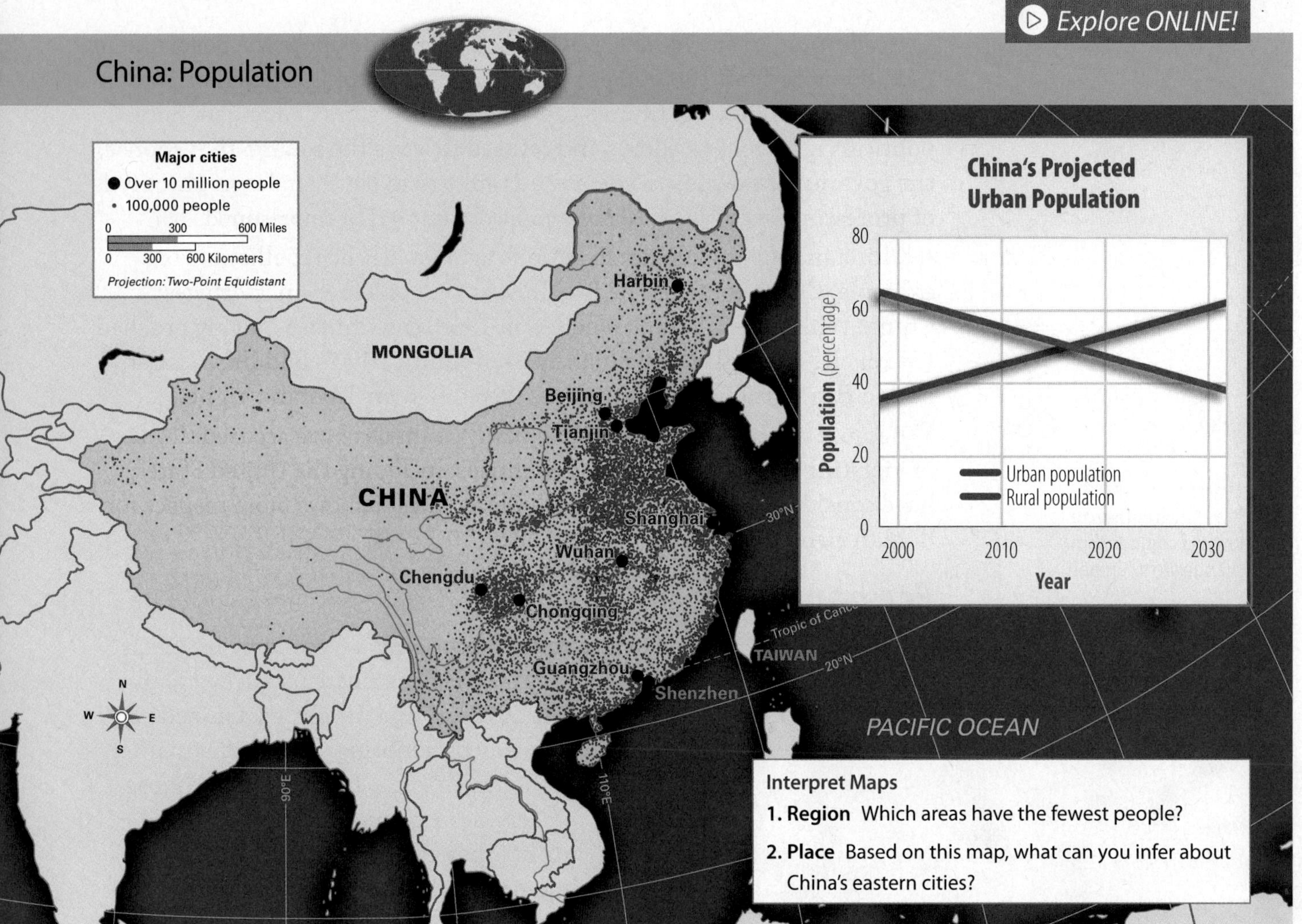

Interpret Maps

1. **Region** Which areas have the fewest people?
2. **Place** Based on this map, what can you infer about China's eastern cities?

Population

With more than 1.3 billion people, China has the world's largest population and it is on the rise. China's population grows by about 6 million each year. To slow this growth, the government implemented a one-child policy from 1978 to 2015. The policy limited couples to one child. These actions have succeeded in slowing China's population growth. As of 2016, Chinese couples have been able to apply to have a second child.

The vast majority of Chinese people are jam-packed in the eastern part of the country. China's east has fertile farmland. For centuries, its rivers and oceans have supported transportation and communication networks. Historically, these factors gave rise to early civilizations. Today they support industrial and urban growth.

Only 10 percent of China's massive population lives the country's west. Covered by mountains and deserts, this region has little farmland. Many highlanders are nomadic herders of horses and grazing animals such as yaks, sheep, and goats. Because vegetation—mostly mosses and short shrubs— is scarce, grazing herds must be kept moving to find new sources of food. In the mountains, yaks are used for milk, meat, fiber, and transportation across rocky terrain. In the harsh Gobi Desert, people have used camels to travel across vast stretches of desert since ancient times.

Many of China's rapidly growing cities are severely crowded, as can be seen in this Shanghai shopping area. Overcrowding is expected to worsen as China's cities continue to grow.

Until 2011, the majority of Chinese people lived in small, rural villages. Today China's massive population is on the move to urban areas. By 2030, approximately 1 billion Chinese are expected to live in cities, which are booming thanks to growing industry and trade.

Most large cities are on the coast or along major rivers. China's largest city, **Shanghai,** is located where the Chang Jiang meets the East China Sea. It is China's leading seaport and an industrial center. China's second-largest city is its capital, Beijing. A mix of old and new, Beijing is China's political and cultural center. In central Beijing, large walls hide the golden-roofed palaces of the Forbidden City, former home of China's emperors. Once off-limits to all but the emperor's household, the city is now a museum open to the public.

Reading Check
Contrast In what ways might rural life differ from city life in China?

In southern China, **Hong Kong** and Macao (muh-KOW) are major port cities. Both cities were European colonies until the late 1990s. The United Kingdom returned Hong Kong to China in 1997, and Portugal returned Macao in 1999.

Environment

Technological hazards caused by urban and industrial growth threaten China's people and environment. Every year, about 25 billion tons of industrial waste and sewage is dumped into the Chang Jiang. The pollution dirties the water, makes it unsafe to drink, and kills fish. Air pollution is another severe problem. Air pollution kills more than 1 million Chinese every year. Burning coal for electricity has the worst effect on China's air quality. Car emissions contribute to the problem. In the past, officials and industry leaders have disagreed over setting emissions standards.

Deforestation is also an issue in China. These children are planting trees to help create new forestland north of Beijing.

Residents of Baotou, in north-central China, wear masks to keep from inhaling harmful particles in the city's polluted air.

▷ Explore ONLINE!

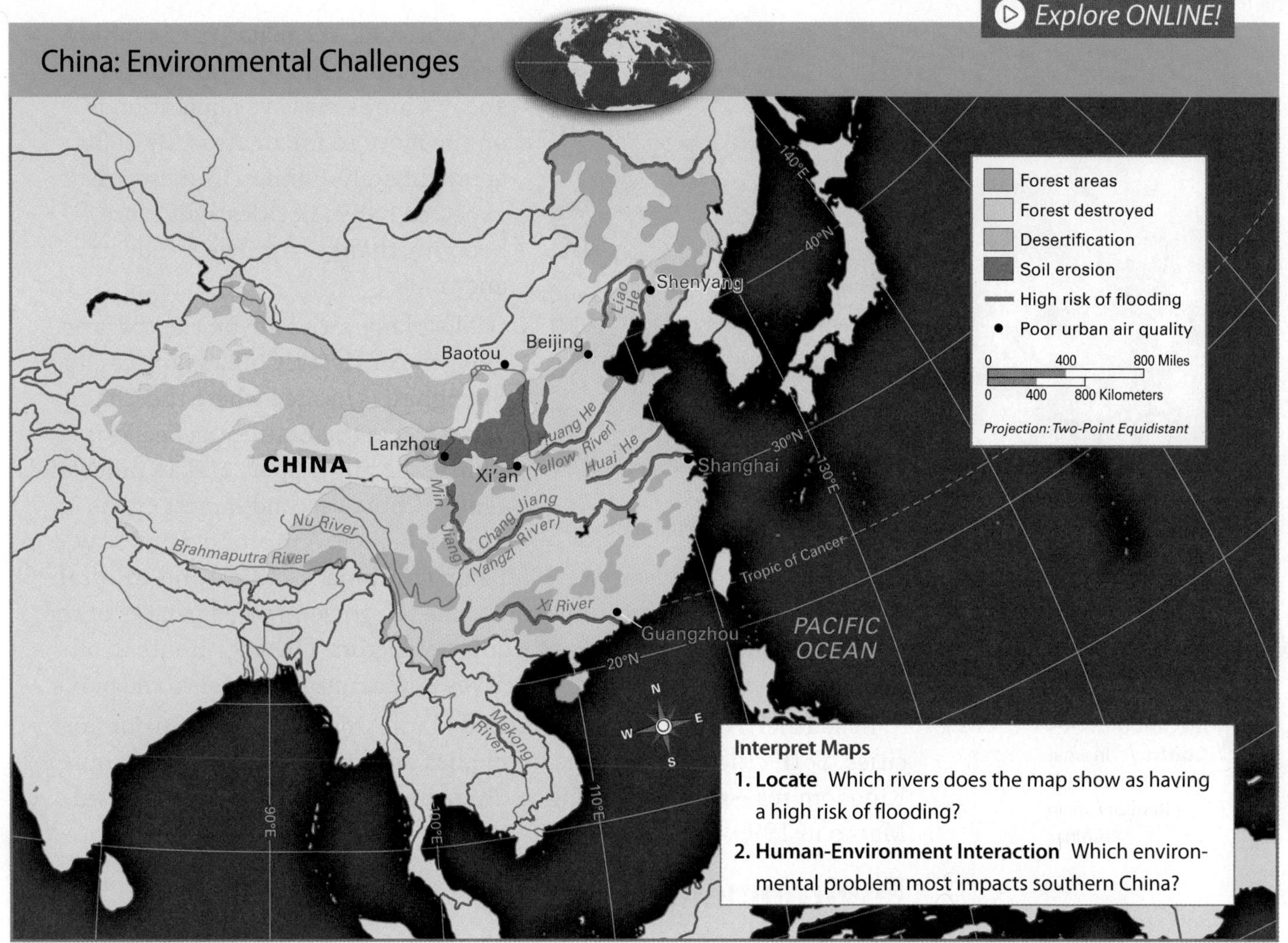

Interpret Maps

1. **Locate** Which rivers does the map show as having a high risk of flooding?
2. **Human-Environment Interaction** Which environmental problem most impacts southern China?

Today China's government is taking steps to combat pollution. In addition to wind and solar power, China is investing in hydroelectric power, electricity produced from dams. China has built the Three Gorges Dam on the Chang Jiang. It is the world's largest dam and generates as much power as 15 coal-burning power plants. However, the water of the dam's reservoir now covers hundreds of towns and huge amounts of farmland. Millions of people have had to move, and plant and animal habitats have been harmed.

Reading Check **Identify Cause and Effect** What are the causes and effects of the pollution of the Chang Jiang?

Culture

Ethnic Groups and Language Of China's millions of people, 92 percent identify their ancestry as Han Chinese. These people share the same culture and traditions. Many Han speak Mandarin, one of China's official languages. Others speak a **dialect,** a regional version of a language.

Some 55 other ethnic groups make up the remaining 8 percent of China's population. Most minority groups live in western and southern China, where they have their own distinct cultures.

Academic Vocabulary
values ideas that people hold dear and try to live by

Religion, Values, and Beliefs Ancient religions, values, and beliefs shape life for China's many people, even though the Communist government

Ethnic Groups

The majority of Chinese are Han. However, China includes 55 other ethnic groups. Most of these people live in western and southern China.

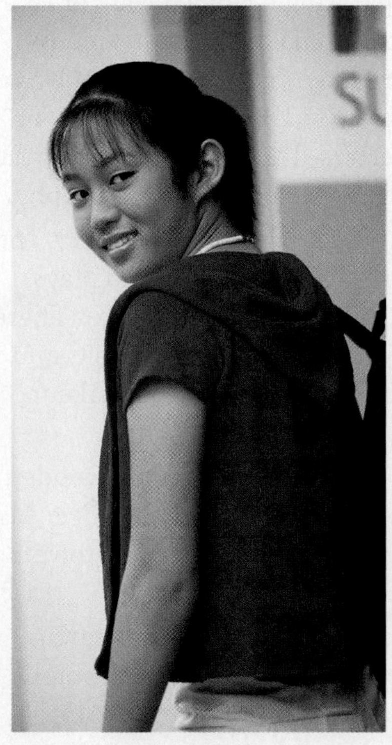

Han
This woman and other Han make up about 92 percent of China's population. They share the same culture and traditions.

Hui
This Hui man is from Gansu province, in central China. Most Hui are Sunni Muslims.

Zhuang
This Zhuang man is from Guizhou, in southern China. The Zhuang are China's largest minority group.

discourages the practice of religion. China's two main belief systems are Daoism (DOW-i-zuhm) and Buddhism. **Daoism** stresses living simply and in harmony with nature. It takes its name from the word *Dao*, which means "the way."

Buddhism came to China from India about AD 100. This religion is based on the teachings of Siddhartha Gautama—the Buddha, who lived from 563 to 483 BC. Buddhists believe moral behavior, kindness, and meditation can lead to peace. Many Chinese blend **elements** of Daoism and Buddhism with **Confucianism,** a philosophy based on the ideas and teachings of Confucius. This philosophy stresses the importance of family, moral values, and respect for one's elders.

Academic Vocabulary
elements parts of a whole

Other major religions in China include Christianity and Islam. Ancestor worship and fortune telling are popular among the Chinese as well.

Art and Popular Culture China has a rich artistic tradition. Traditional Chinese crafts include items made of bronze, jade, ivory, silk, or wood. Chinese porcelain, which the ancient Chinese developed, is highly prized for its quality and beauty.

Starting as early as age 6, many young Chinese memorize up to several hundred martial arts movements. These movements include different kicks, jumps, and punches.

Traditional Chinese painting is done on silk or fine paper and reflects a focus on balance and harmony with nature. Chinese art often includes calligraphy, or decorative writing. Chinese writing uses symbols, or characters, instead of letters. This writing makes beautiful art, and some paintings feature just calligraphy.

In literature, the Chinese are known for poetry, and poems appear on paintings and in novels and plays. In theater, traditional Chinese opera is popular. These operas tell stories through spoken words, music, and dance. Actors wear elaborate costumes and makeup that have special meanings.

Traditional Chinese architecture features wooden buildings on stone bases. Large tiled roofs curve upward at the edge. Also common are **pagodas,** Buddhist temples that have multi-storied towers with an upward curving roof at each floor.

Popular culture includes many activities. Popular sports are martial arts and table tennis. A popular game is mah-jongg, played with small tiles. People also enjoy karaoke clubs, where they sing to music.

Reading Check
Evaluate Which aspect of Chinese culture most interests you? Why?

Summary and Preview China is undergoing great economic and social change. Still its government restricts freedom and faces environmental challenges. In the next lesson you will learn about Mongolia and Taiwan.

Lesson 2 Assessment

Review Ideas, Terms, and Places

1. a. **Recall** How did Mao contribute to the economic and political history of China?
   b. **Evaluate** What is your opinion of China's handling of the 1989 demonstration at Tiananmen Square?
2. a. **Define** What is a command economy?
   b. **Identify Causes** What factors contributed to China's rapid economic development?
3. a. **Analyze** Why did China implement a one-child policy? What were the consequences of the policy?
   b. **Describe** How have China's mountain, desert, and water features affected where people live and work?
4. a. **Explain** Which technological hazards most affect China's people and environment?
   b. **Identify Cause and Effect** What are the causes and effects of air pollution in China?
   c. **Evaluate** Do you think building the Three Gorges Dam was beneficial to China?
5. a. **Identify** What are some popular pastimes in China today?
   b. **Elaborate** What is the relationship between religious and philosophical ideas such as Buddhism, Confucianism, and Daoism and Chinese culture?

Critical Thinking

6. **Categorize** Create a table like the one shown to organize information about life in China today.

China Today	
Modern History	
Economy	
Population	
Environment	
Culture	

Mongolia and Taiwan

The Big Idea

Mongolia is a rugged land with a nomadic way of life and growing cities, while Taiwan is a densely settled and industrialized island.

Main Ideas

- Mongolia is a sparsely populated country where many people live as nomads.
- Taiwan is a small island with a dense population and a highly industrialized economy.

Key Terms and Places

gers
Ulaanbaatar
Taipei
Kao-hsiung

If YOU lived there . . .

Like many Mongolians, you have loved horses since you were a small child. You live in an apartment in the city of Ulaanbaatar, however. Some of your family are talking about leaving the city and becoming nomadic herders like your ancestors were. You think you might like being able to ride horses more. You're not sure you would like living in a tent, though, especially in winter.

Do you want to move back to the land?

Mongolia

A wild and rugged land, Mongolia is home to the Mongol people. They have a proud and fascinating history. This history includes conquests and empires and a culture that prizes horses.

Mongolia's History Today when people discuss the world's leading countries, they do not mention Mongolia. However, 700 years ago Mongolia was perhaps the greatest power in the world. Led by the ruler Genghis Khan, the Mongols conquered much of Asia, including China. Later Mongol leaders continued the conquests. They built the greatest empire the world had seen at the time.

The Mongol Empire reached its height in the late 1200s. During that time, the empire stretched from Europe's Danube River in the west to the Pacific Ocean in the east. As time passed, however, the Mongol Empire declined. In the late 1600s China conquered Mongolia and ruled it for more than 200 years.

With Russia's help, Mongolia declared independence from China in 1911. Soon Communists gained control and in 1924 formed the Mongolian People's Republic. Meanwhile, Russia had become part of the Soviet Union, a large Communist country north of Mongolia. The Soviet Union strongly influenced Mongolia and gave it large amounts of economic aid. This aid ended, however, after the Soviet Union collapsed in 1991. Since then, Mongolians have struggled to build a democratic government and a free-market economy.

Nomadic Life in Mongolia

Some Mongolians are nomads, who live in tents called *gers*. Inside, gers are furnished mainly with rugs. Different areas of the gers are used for specific purposes. For example, the back is used for an altar.

Analyze Visuals
What do you think it is like to live in a ger?

Gers have wooden, painted doors. The doors always face south because the wind usually blows from the northeast.

Mongolia's Culture In spite of years of Communist rule, many Mongolians follow a way of life that is traditional and adapted to the landscape. Nearly half of Mongolia's people live as nomads. They herd livestock across Mongolia's vast grasslands and make their homes in **gers** (GUHRZ). These are large, circular, felt tents that are easy to put up, take down, and move.

Academic Vocabulary
role part or function

Since many Mongols are nomadic, horses play a major **role** in Mongolian life. As a result, Mongolian culture highly prizes horse skills, and Mongolian children often learn to ride when they are quite young.

Mongolia Today Mongolia is sparsely populated. Slightly larger than Alaska, it has about 3 million people. More than a quarter of them live in **Ulaanbaatar** (oo-lahn-BAH-tawr), the capital and only large city. Mongolia's other cities are quite small. However, Mongolia's urban population is slowly growing.

Reading Check
Summarize
Which features of Mongolia's culture have stayed the same across time? Which have changed?

The country's main industries include textiles, carpets, coal, copper, and oil. The city of Ulaanbaatar is the main industrial and commercial center. Mongolia produces little food other than from livestock, however, and faces food and water shortages.

Taiwan

When Portuguese sailors visited the island of Taiwan in the late 1500s, they called it *Ilha Formosa*, or "beautiful island." For many years, Westerners called Taiwan by the name Formosa. Today the loveliness of Taiwan's green mountains and waterfalls competes with its modern, crowded cities.

Taiwan's History The Chinese began settling Taiwan in the 600s. At different times in history, both China and Japan have controlled Taiwan. In 1949, though, the Chinese Nationalists took over Taiwan. Led by Chiang Kai-shek, the Nationalists were fleeing the Communists, who had taken control of China's mainland. The Chinese Nationalist Party ruled Taiwan under martial law, or military rule, for 38 years. Today Taiwan's government is a multiparty democracy.

As the chart below explains, tensions remain between China and Taiwan. The Chinese government claims that Taiwan is a rebel part of China. In contrast, Taiwan's government claims to be the true government of China. For all practical purposes, though, Taiwan functions as an independent country.

Taiwan's Culture Taiwan's history is reflected in its culture. Its population is about 85 percent native Taiwanese. These people are descendants of Chinese people who migrated to Taiwan largely in the 1700s and 1800s. As a result, Chinese ways dominate Taiwan's culture.

Other influences have shaped Taiwan's culture as well. Because Japan once ruled Taiwan, Japanese culture can be seen in some Taiwanese buildings and foods. More recently, European and American practices and customs are becoming noticeable in Taiwan, particularly in larger cities.

Taiwan Today Taiwan is a modern country with a population of about 23 million. These people live on an island about the size of Delaware and Maryland combined. Because much of Taiwan is mountainous, most people live on the island's western coastal plain. This region is home to Taiwan's main cities.

Explore ONLINE!

Tensions between China and Taiwan

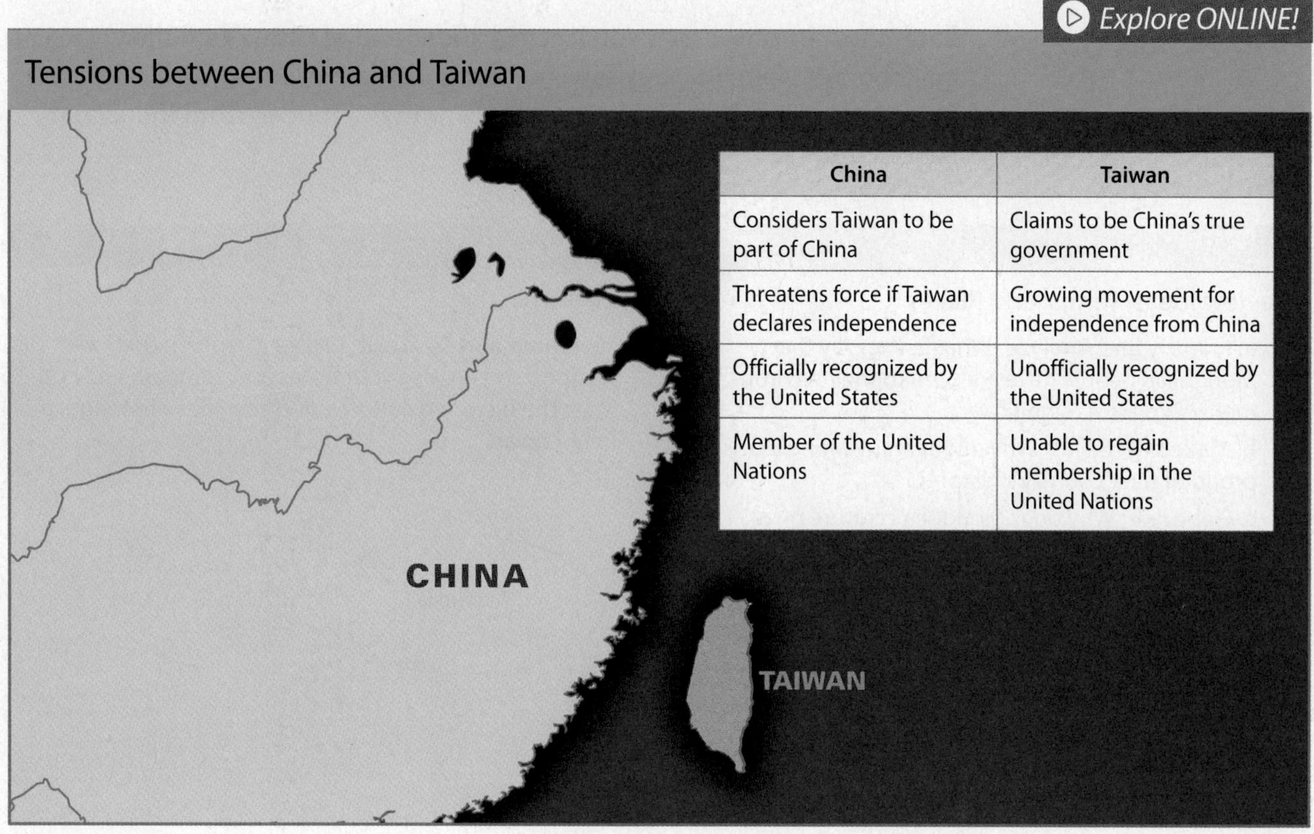

China	Taiwan
Considers Taiwan to be part of China	Claims to be China's true government
Threatens force if Taiwan declares independence	Growing movement for independence from China
Officially recognized by the United States	Unofficially recognized by the United States
Member of the United Nations	Unable to regain membership in the United Nations

Taipei

Taiwan's capital, Taipei, is a bustling city of more than 2 million people. The tall tower in the photo is the Taipei 101, which is 101 stories tall.

The two largest cities are **Taipei** (TY-PAY) and **Kao-hsiung** (KOW SHY-OOHNG). Taipei, the capital, is Taiwan's main financial center. Because it has grown so quickly, it faces serious overcrowding and environmental problems. Kao-hsiung is a center of heavy industry and Taiwan's main seaport.

Reading Check
Contrast
How does Taiwan's economy differ from Mongolia's?

Taiwan is one of Asia's richest and most industrialized countries. It is a leader in the production and export of computers and sports equipment. Taiwan's farmers grow many crops as well, such as sugarcane.

Summary In this lesson you learned about two of China's smaller neighbors—Mongolia and Taiwan. Mongolia is a wild land with a nomadic people who prize horses. In contrast, Taiwan is a modern and industrialized island.

Lesson 3 Assessment

Review Ideas, Terms, and Places

1. a. **Identify and Analyze** What is one way that Mongolia's people have adapted to their environment? Explain its significance.

   b. **Make Inferences** Why might many Mongolians be proud of their country's history?

   c. **Elaborate** Why does Mongolia's culture prize horses?

2. a. **Recall** Why is Taipei an important Taiwanese city, and what problems does the city face?

   b. **Summarize** What is the significance of Chiang Kai-shek in Taiwan's history?

   c. **Evaluate** Would you rather live in Taiwan or Mongolia? Provide information about each place to explain your answer.

Critical Thinking

3. **Compare and Contrast** Create a Venn diagram like the one shown. Use your notes and compare and contrast the histories, cultures, and societies of Mongolia and Taiwan.

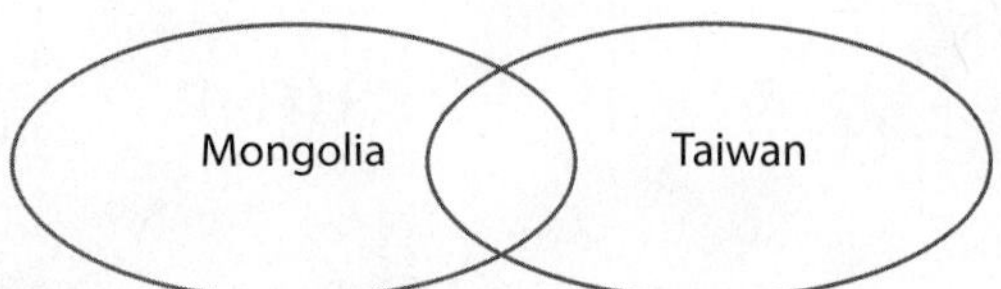

Social Studies Skills

Identify Point of View

Define the Skill

Geographers study issues that affect the world's people and places. To better understand such issues, geographers seek to understand point of view. The way people look at an issue is their point of view. Often, a point of view expresses a person's frame of reference—the elements of a person's background that shapes how he or she sees the world. Sometimes, a point of view may also express a bias, or a one-sided, slanted, or prejudiced view.

To identify point of view, use these tips:

- Consider **frame of reference**. Think about where the person lives, what the person does, and what his or her beliefs and attitudes are.
- Examine the evidence, such as facts and statistics, to see what point of view it supports.
- Look for signs of **bias**. The inclusion or avoidance of particular facts and loaded or emotional language, such as name-calling, can reveal both bias and point of view.
- Put it all together to identify the point of view.

Learn the Skill

Read the passage "New Law Angers Taiwan" about a law forbidding any part of China to declare independence. Then answer the questions that follow.

1. What is China's point of view about Taiwan?
2. What is Taiwan's point of view about China?

Apply the Skill

1. In the passage "New Law Angers Taiwan," how might the elements of each side's frame of reference affect its point of view?
2. Which point of view does the evidence about China's military-spending support?
3. What aspects of the text, such as word choice or the selection of facts, reveal the author's point of view, purpose, or bias? Explain.

New Law Angers Taiwan

Taiwan's government has warned that China's new anti-secession [anti-independence] law . . . will have a "serious impact" on security in the region. . .

Taiwan officials were quick to call the measure a "war bill," coming as China boosts its military spending by 13 percent to $30 billion. . . .

But Chinese Premier Wen Jiabao said the new legislation [law] was not a "war bill" and warned outsiders not to get involved . . . . "It is not targeted at the people of Taiwan, nor is it a war bill," Wen said at a news conference.

Source: *CNN International*, March 14, 2005

Consider frame of reference—China considers Taiwan a rebel province. Taiwan has a growing independence movement.

Look at the evidence—The information about military spending is evidence supporting one point of view.

Check for bias—The phrase "war bill" appeals to the emotions. People have strong feelings about war.

Put it all together to identify each point of view.

Module 17 Assessment

Review Vocabulary, Terms, and Places

Match the words or places below with their definitions or descriptions.

1. command economy
2. North China Plain
3. pagodas
4. gers
5. Tibet
6. Dialect
7. Himalayas
8. Taipei

a. Buddhist region in southwest China
b. world's highest mountain range
c. regional version of a language
d. capital city of Taiwan
e. system in which the government owns most businesses and makes most economic decisions
f. fertile and highly populated region in eastern China
g. circular, felt tents in which Mongol nomads live
h. Buddhist temples with multiple stories

Comprehension and Critical Thinking

Lesson 1

9. a. **Recall** What physical features separate many of the mountain ranges in this region?
   b. **Explain** What is the Huang He called in English, and how did the river get its name?
   c. **Elaborate** What physical features might you see on a trip from the Himalayas to Beijing?

Lesson 2

10. a. **Draw Conclusions** How did China's one-child policy impact individuals and families? How did it affect the nation?
    b. **Summarize** What elements of a market economy has China adopted and how have they affected the economy?
    c. **Explain** Look back at the physical map and the population map of China in this module. What population patterns can you identify for China? Which geographic factors do you think are responsible for these patterns?

11. a. **Describe** How did the size of China's population contribute to its rapid economic growth?
    b. **Explain** After Mao, how did investing in new technologies and transportation networks affect China's economy and economic interdependence?
    c. **Predict** How might the economic decisions made by American consumers influence China's environment and the daily lives of its people?
    d. **Draw Inferences** Look back at the map titled China: Environmental Challenges in this module. What issues affect Shanghai? What laws or policies might develop in Shanghai in response to the issues? How might an industry leader and an environmentalist respond to the issues?

Lesson 3

12 a. **Identify** What is the capital of Mongolia?
   b. **Analyze** How is Taiwan's history reflected in the island's culture today?
   c. **Predict** Do you think China and Taiwan can resolve their disagreements? Why or why not?
   d. **Explain** What is the natural vegetation of Mongolia like and how has it shaped the development cultures in the region?

Module 17 Assessment, continued

Reading Social Studies

13. **Understand Implied Main Ideas** Read the first paragraph under the heading Revolution and Civil War in Lesson 2. What is the implied main idea of this paragraph? What words and phrases help signal the implied main idea?

Social Studies Skills

Identify Point of View *Read the following passage from this chapter. Then answer the questions below.*

> "In 1989 more than 100,000 pro-democracy protestors gathered in Tiananmen Square in Biejing, China's capital. The protestors demanded more political rights and freedoms and refused to leave the square. In response, the government deployed troops and tanks to make them leave. Hundreds of protestors were killed. Many more were injured or imprisoned."

14. What was the point of view of the protestors toward China's government? What elements shaped their frame of reference?

15. What was the point of view of China's government toward the protestors? What elements shaped its frame of reference?

Map Activity

16. Recall that small-scale maps show large regions and large-scale maps show smaller areas. Locate an economic activity map and a political map that show China, Mongolia, and Taiwan. Then find an economic activity map and a political map of China. Use content from the maps to answer these questions: Which scale, small or large, best shows patterns of political connections across the region? Which scale best shows political patterns within a nation? How do patterns of economic activity in China compare to patterns of economic activity in the region as a whole?

17. **China, Mongolia, and Taiwan** Locate major human and geographic features of this region. On a separate sheet of paper, match the letters on the map with their correct labels below.

Beijing, China	Hong Kong, China
Taipei, Taiwan	Chang Jiang
Huang He	Himalayas
Great Wall of China	Ulaanbaatar, Mongolia

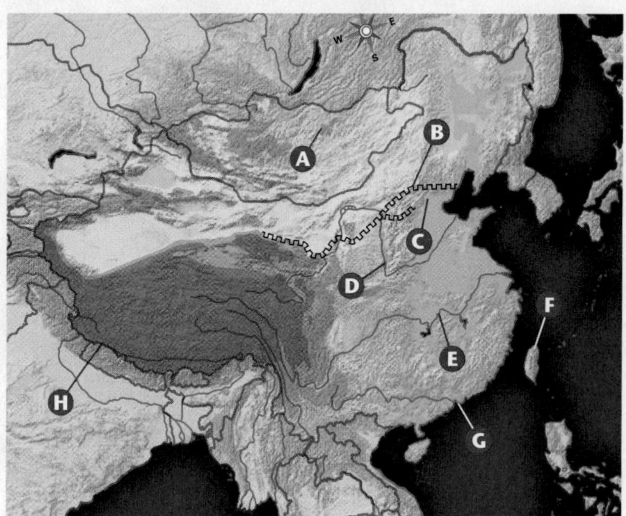

Focus on Writing

18. **Write a Legend** Choose one physical or cultural feature and decide how you will explain its creation. Then review your notes and choose characters, events, and settings for your legend. Your legend should be two to three paragraphs. It should include (a) a beginning; (b) a middle that includes a climax, or high point of the story; and (c) a conclusion, or end. Remember, legends tell about extraordinary events, so you should use your imagination and creativity.

MULTIMEDIA CONNECTIONS

China and the Great Wall

Today, the Great Wall of China is an impressive symbol of the Asian giant's power, genius, and endurance. It wasn't always so. For much of its history, the Chinese people saw the Great Wall as a symbol of cruelty and oppression. This is just one way in which the wall differs from what we think we know. In contrast to popular notions, the wall that draws tourists to Beijing by the millions was not built 2,000 years ago. Nor is the Great Wall a single wall. Instead, it was patched together from walls built over many centuries. And for all its grandeur, the wall failed to keep China safe from invasion.

Explore facts and fictions about the Great Wall online. You can find more information, video clips, primary sources, and activities through your online textbook.

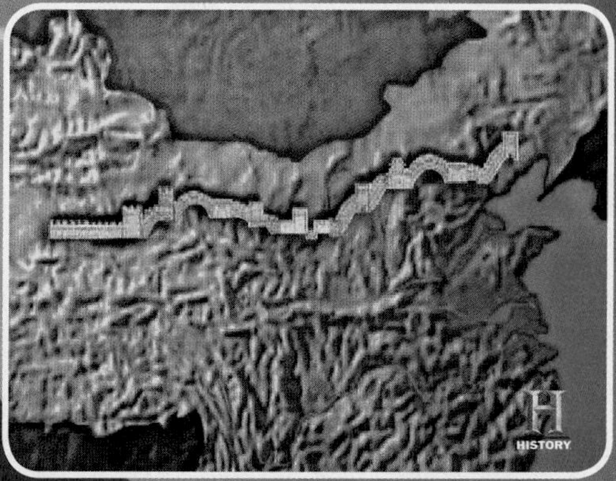

The Great Wall of China

Watch the video to learn the history and significance of the magnificent, mysterious walls that snake across northern China.

A Land of Walls Within Walls

Watch the video to learn how the Great Wall fits within the ancient Chinese tradition of wall-building.

The Human Costs of Building

Watch the video to learn about the miseries that awaited the men who built the wall.

Twentieth-Century China

Watch the video to examine the role that the wall has played in modern Chinese history.

Module 18

Japan and the Koreas

Essential Question

How does geography affect daily life in Japan and the Koreas?

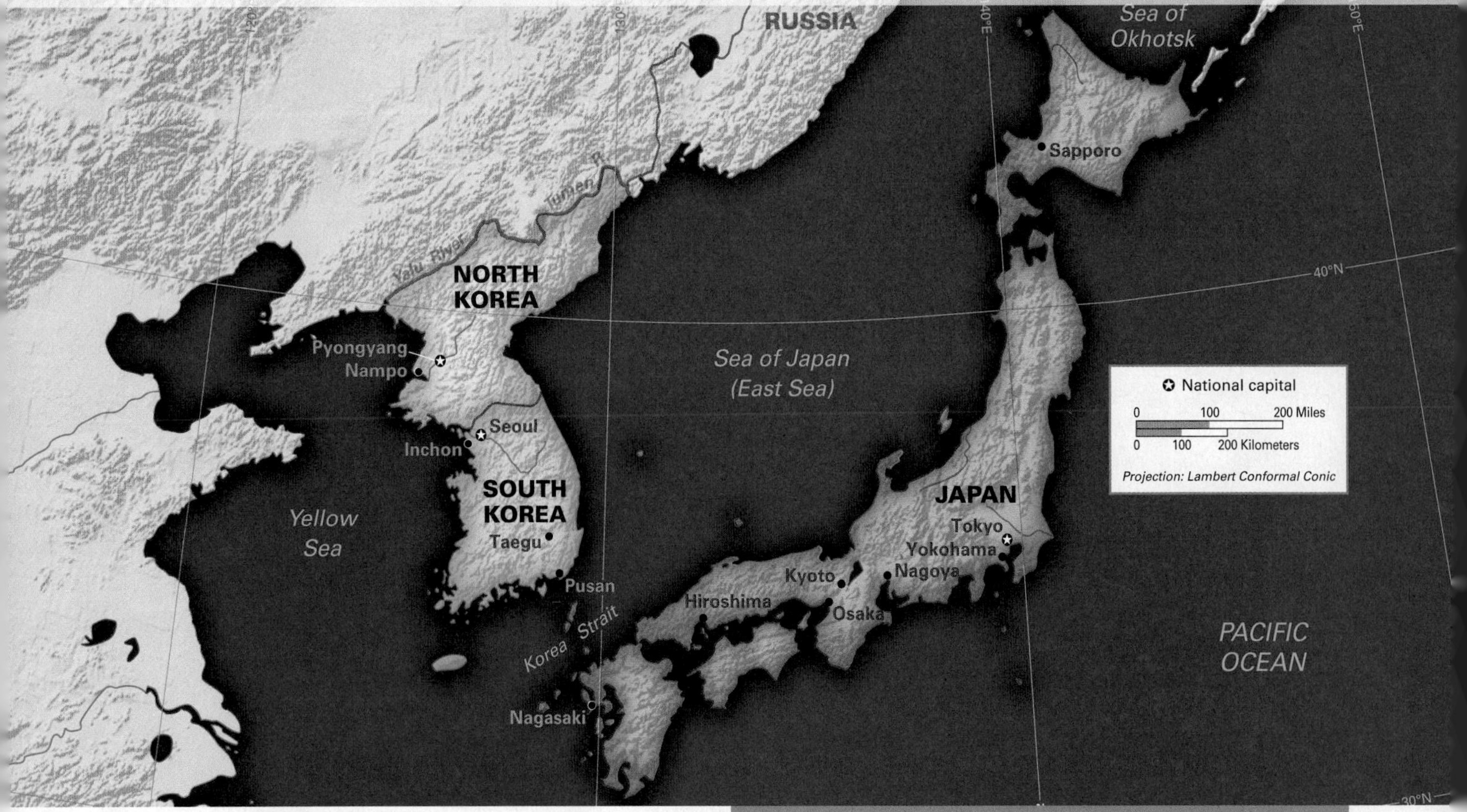

RUSSIA
Sea of Okhotsk
Sapporo
Tumen R.
Yalu River
NORTH KOREA
Pyongyang
Nampo
Sea of Japan (East Sea)
Seoul
Inchon
SOUTH KOREA
Yellow Sea
Taegu
Pusan
Korea Strait
Nagasaki
Hiroshima
Kyoto
Osaka
Nagoya
Yokohama
Tokyo
JAPAN
PACIFIC OCEAN
40°N
30°N
120°E
130°E
140°E
150°E

National capital
0 100 200 Miles
0 100 200 Kilometers
Projection: Lambert Conformal Conic

Explore ONLINE!

VIDEOS, including . . .

- The Rise of the Samurai
- Emperor Hirohito

- Document-Based Investigations
- Graphic Organizers
- Interactive Games
- Channel One News Video: Geo Quiz: Japan
- Channel One News Video: North Korean Refugee
- Interactive Chart: A Military Society
- Image with Hotspots: Life in Tokyo
- Interactive Map: War in Korea, 1950–1953

In this module, you will learn about how geography has shaped Japan and the Koreas' history, culture, and daily life and how these countries developed after major global conflicts.

What You Will Learn

Lesson 1: Physical Geography 563
The Big Idea Japan and the Koreas are rugged, mountainous areas surrounded by water.

Lesson 2: Japan 567
The Big Idea Japan has overcome many challenges to become one of the most highly developed countries in Asia.

Lesson 3: The Koreas 575
The Big Idea Though they share a common history and culture, the two Koreas have very different governments and economies.

Geography Mount Fuji, a common symbol of Japan, is one of the thousands of mountains found in the region.

History The Silla kingdom unified Korea in AD 668.

Politics Under Kim Il Sung, North Korea became a Communist country.

Reading Social Studies

Identify Bias

READING FOCUS

To understand the events and people in history, you have to be able to recognize a speaker's or writer's bias. Bias is the habit of favoring some people or ideas over others. Being biased can affect the accuracy of how someone discusses events and people. Here are some steps you can take to identify bias.

Steps to Recognize Bias

1. **Look at the words and images.** Are they emotionally charged? Do they present only one side or one point of view?
2. **Look at the writer.** What's the writer's background and what does that tell you about the writer's point of view?
3. **Look at the writer's sources.** Where does the writer get his or her information? Does the writer rely on sources who only support one point of view?
4. **Look at the information.** How much is fact and how much is opinion? Remember, facts can be proven. Opinions are personal beliefs—they can easily be biased.

"By their actions in Korea, Communist leaders have demonstrated their contempt for the basic moral principles on which the United Nations is founded. This is a direct challenge to the efforts of the free nations to build the kind of world in which men can live in freedom and peace."

—*Harry S. Truman, Radio and Television Address to the American People on the Situation in Korea, July 19, 1950*

Read from President Harry S. Truman's address to the American people on the Korean War, and study the steps below used to identify Truman's bias.

1. The word *contempt* is emotionally charged.
2. As the leader of a democratic country, he may not like Communist leaders.
3. He cites the United Nations' principles as a source. Principles are beliefs, not facts.
4. Most of his statement is opinion and is based on personal beliefs about freedom and morals.

YOU TRY IT!

U.S. general Douglas MacArthur led the United Nations' forces during part of the Korean War. Examine the statement he made after he met with an ally. Use the steps from this skill to identify bias within the quote.

"His indomitable determination to resist Communist domination arouses my sincere admiration. His determination parallels the common interest and purpose of Americans that all peoples in the Pacific area shall be free—not slave."

—*General Douglas MacArthur, Statement on His Trip to Formosa, August 1, 1950*

As you read this module, practice the steps above to identify bias.

Physical Geography

The Big Idea

Japan and the Koreas are rugged, mountainous areas surrounded by water.

Main Ideas

- The main physical features of Japan and the Koreas are rugged mountains.
- The climates and resources of Japan and the Koreas vary from north to south.

Key Terms and Places

Fuji
Korean Peninsula
tsunamis
fishery

If YOU lived there . . .

You are a passenger on a very fast train zipping its way across the countryside. If you look out the window to your right, you can see the distant sparkle of sunlight on the ocean. If you look to the left, you see rocky, rugged mountains. Suddenly the train leaves the mountains, and you see hundreds of trees covered in delicate pink flowers. Rising above the trees is a single snowcapped volcano.

How does this scenery make you feel?

Physical Features

Japan, North Korea, and South Korea are on the eastern edge of the Asian continent, just east of China. Separated from each other only by a narrow strait, Japan and the Koreas share many common landscape features.

Physical Features of Japan Japan is an island country. It is made up of 4 large islands and more than 3,000 smaller islands. These islands are arranged in a long chain more than 1,500 miles (2,400 km) long. This is about the same length as the eastern coast of the United States, from southern Florida to northern Maine. All together, however, Japan's land area is slightly smaller than the state of California.

About 95 percent of Japan's land area is made up of four large islands. From north to south, these major islands are Hokkaido (hoh-KY-doh), Honshu (HAWN-shoo), Shikoku (shee-KOH-koo), and Kyushu (KYOO-shoo). Together they are called the home islands. Most of Japan's people live there.

Rugged, tree-covered mountains are a common sight in Japan. In fact, mountains cover some 75 percent of the country. For the most part, Japan's mountains are very steep and rocky. As a result, the country's largest mountain range, the Japanese Alps, is popular with climbers and skiers.

Japan's highest mountain, **Fuji,** is not part of the Alps. In fact, it is not part of any mountain range. A volcano, Mount Fuji rises high above a relatively flat area in eastern Honshu.

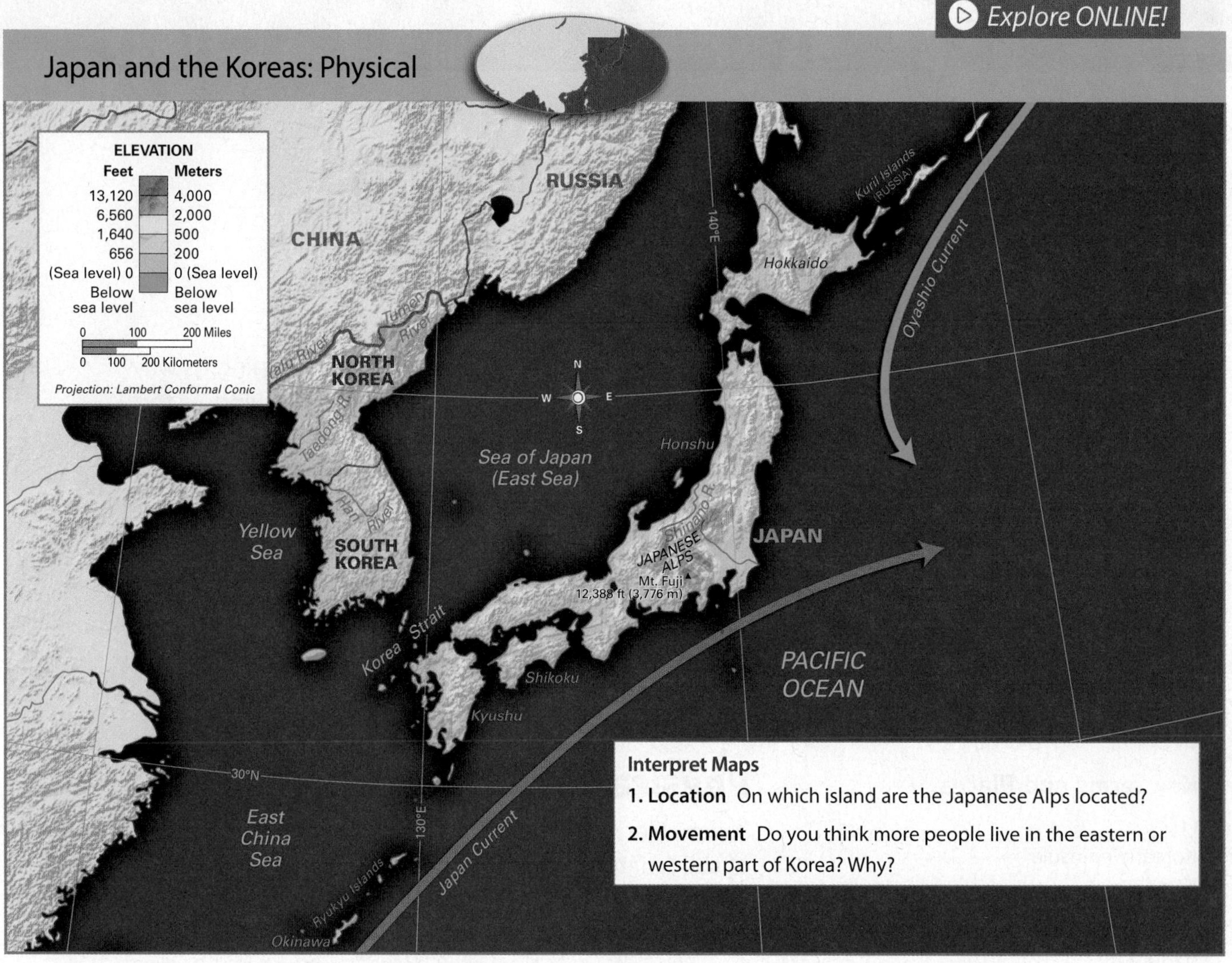

Interpret Maps

1. **Location** On which island are the Japanese Alps located?
2. **Movement** Do you think more people live in the eastern or western part of Korea? Why?

The mountain's cone-shaped peak has become a symbol of Japan. In addition, many Japanese consider Fuji a sacred place. As a result, many shrines have been built at its foot and summit.

Physical Features of Korea Jutting south from the Asian mainland, the **Korean Peninsula** includes both North Korea and South Korea. Like the islands of Japan, much of the peninsula is covered with rugged mountains. These mountains form long ranges that run along Korea's eastern coast. The peninsula's highest mountains are in the north.

Unlike Japan, Korea also has some large plains. These plains are found mainly along the peninsula's western coast and in river valleys. Korea also has more rivers than Japan does. Most of these rivers flow westward across the peninsula and pour into the Yellow Sea.

Natural Disasters Because of its location, Japan is subject to many sorts of natural disasters. Among these disasters are volcanic eruptions and earthquakes. As you can see on the map, these disasters are common in Japan. They can cause huge amounts of damage in the country. In addition, large underwater earthquakes sometimes cause destructive waves called **tsunamis** (sooh-NAH-mees).

Reading Check
Contrast
How are the physical features of Japan and Korea different?

Korea does not have many volcanoes or earthquakes. From time to time, though, huge storms called typhoons sweep over the peninsula from the Pacific. These storms cause great damage in both the Korean Peninsula and Japan.

Climate and Resources

Just as Japan and the Koreas have many similar physical features, they also have similar climates. The resources found in each country, however, differ greatly.

Climate The climates of Japan and the Koreas vary from north to south. The northern parts of the region have a humid continental climate. This means that summers are cool, but winters are long and cold. In addition, the area has a short growing season.

Explore ONLINE!

Japan and the Koreas: Volcanoes and Earthquakes

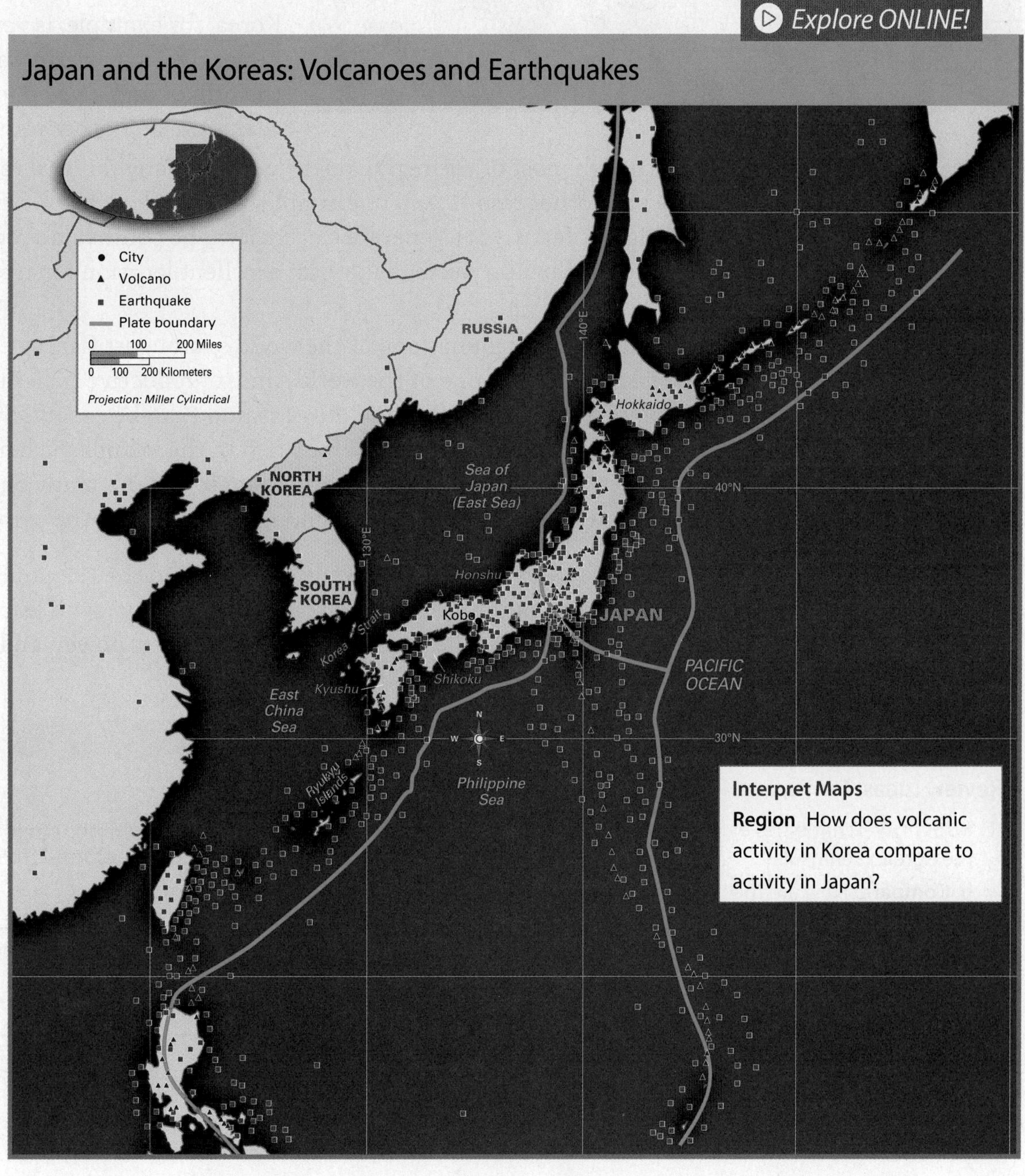

Interpret Maps
Region How does volcanic activity in Korea compare to activity in Japan?

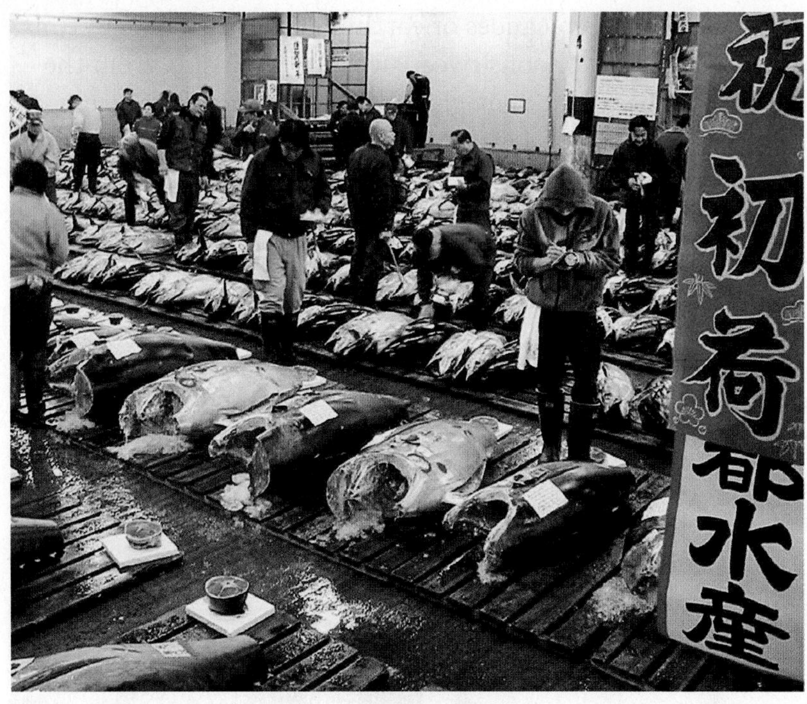

This fish market in Tokyo, Japan, is the busiest in the world. People gather here every morning to buy freshly caught fish.

To the south, the region has a humid subtropical climate with mild winters and hot, humid summers. These areas see heavy rains and typhoons in the summer. Some places receive up to 80 inches (200 cm) of rain each year.

Resources Resources are not evenly distributed among Japan and the Koreas. Neither Japan nor South Korea, for example, is very rich in mineral resources. North Korea, on the other hand, has large deposits of coal, iron, and other minerals.

Although most of the region does not have many mineral resources, it does have other resources. For example, the people of the Koreas have used their land's features to generate electricity. The peninsula's rocky terrain and rapidly flowing rivers make it an excellent location for creating hydroelectric power.

In addition, Japan has one of the world's strongest fishing economies. The islands lie near one of the world's most productive fisheries. A **fishery** is a place where lots of fish and other seafood can be caught. Swift ocean currents near Japan carry numerous fish to the islands. Fishers then use huge nets to catch the fish and bring them to Japan's many bustling fish markets. These fish markets are among the busiest in the world.

Reading Check
Analyze
What are some resources found in Japan and the Koreas?

Summary and Preview The islands of Japan and the Korean Peninsula share many common features. In the next lesson, you will learn about Japan's history and culture, its rise as an economic power, and the current challenges it faces.

Lesson 1 Assessment

Review Ideas, Terms, and Places

1. **a. Identify** What types of landforms cover Japan and the Korean Peninsula?

   b. Compare How are the physical features of Japan and Korea similar?

   c. Predict How do you think natural disasters affect life in Japan and Korea?

2. **a. Describe** What kind of climate is found in the northern parts of the region? What kind of climate is found in the southern parts?

   b. Draw Conclusions Why are fisheries important to Japan's economy?

Critical Thinking

3. **Categorize** Draw a chart like this one. In each row, describe the region's landforms, climate, and resources.

	Japan	Korean Peninsula
Landforms		
Climate		
Resources		

Japan

The Big Idea

Japan has overcome many challenges to become one of the most highly developed countries in Asia.

Main Ideas

- Japan's early government was ruled by emperors and shoguns.
- Japanese culture blends traditional customs with modern innovations.
- Since World War II, Japan has developed a democratic government.
- Japan has become one of the world's strongest economies.
- A shortage of open space shapes daily life in Japan.
- Crowding, competition, and pollution are among Japan's main issues and challenges.

Key Terms and Places

Kyoto
shoguns
samurai
kimonos
Diet
Tokyo
work ethic
trade surplus
tariff
Osaka

If YOU lived there . . .

You and your family live in a small apartment in the crowded city of Tokyo. Every day you and your friends crowd into jammed subway trains to travel to school. Since your work in school is very hard and demanding, you really look forward to weekends. You especially like to visit mountain parks where there are flowering trees, quiet gardens, and ancient shrines.

Do you like your life in Tokyo? Why or why not?

History

Japan has a very long history. Early in its history, Japan was influenced by China. Since Japan lies just across the sea from China, elements of Chinese culture seeped into Japan.

Among the elements of Chinese culture that influenced Japan was Buddhism. Scholars and missionaries first brought Buddhism into Korea. From there, visitors carried it to Japan. Before long, Buddhism was the main religion in both countries.

Emperors, Shoguns, and Samurai The first central government in Japan was based on China's government. For many centuries, emperors ruled in Japan just as they did in China. The imperial capital at Heian, now called **Kyoto,** was a center of art, literature, and learning. At times, some of Japan's emperors were more concerned with art than with running the country. Eventually, their power slipped away.

As the emperors' power faded, Japan fell under the control of military leaders called **shoguns.** Powerful generals, the shoguns ruled Japan in the emperor's name. Only one shogun could hold power at a time.

Serving under the shogun were armies of **samurai,** or highly trained warriors. They were fierce in battle and devoted to their leaders. As a result, the samurai were very respected in Japanese society. With their support, the shoguns continued to rule Japan well into the 1800s.

Buddhism became important to Japanese culture. Artists created statues of Buddha, such as this one.

BIOGRAPHY

Hirohito 1901–1989

Hirohito was Japan's emperor for most of the 1900s. As such, he led the country through periods of great crisis and change. He was emperor when Japan launched wars against China and Russia in the 1930s. He was also in power in 1945 when the United States bombed Hiroshima and Nagasaki. After World War II ended, Hirohito led Japan through changes in its government and economy. Many of these changes affected Hirohito personally. For example, he gave up much of the power he had once held as emperor in favor of a democratic government.

Draw Conclusions
Why might a ruler give up much power?

Later Japan Not everyone was happy with the rule of the shoguns. In 1868 a group of samurai overthrew the shogun and gave power back to the emperor.

When World War II began, Japan allied itself with Germany and Italy. It wanted to build an empire in Southeast Asia and the Pacific. The Japanese drew the United States into the war in 1941 when they bombed the naval base at Pearl Harbor, Hawaii. After many years of fighting, the Americans took drastic measures to end the war. They dropped devastating atomic bombs on two Japanese cities, Hiroshima and Nagasaki. Shocked by these terrible weapons, the Japanese surrendered.

Reading Check
Sequence List in order the groups that ruled Japan from its early history to World War II.

Japanese Culture

Japan's culture reflects the country's long and varied history. For example, some elements of the culture reflect the influence of the Chinese, while others are native to Japan. Since World War II, Western ideas and innovations have also helped shape Japanese life.

Language Nearly everyone in Japan speaks Japanese. The Japanese language is complicated and can be difficult for other people to learn. This difficulty stems in large part from the Japanese writing system. Japanese writing uses two different types of characters. Some characters, called kanji, represent whole words. There are about 2,000 kanji characters in common use today. Other characters, called kana, stand for parts of words. Most texts written in Japanese use both kanji and kana characters.

Religion Religion can also be complicated in Japan. Most people who live there blend elements of two religions—Shinto and Buddhism.

Unlike Buddhism, which was brought to Japan from Korea, Shinto is native to the islands. According to Shinto teachings, nature spirits called *kami* (KAH-mee) live in the world. Shintoists believe everything in nature—the sun, the moon, trees, rocks, waterfalls, and animals—has

Kimonos are the traditional clothing style in Japan. Both men and women wear kimonos for special occasions, such as weddings.

kami. They also believe that some *kami* help people live and keep them from harm. As a result, they build shrines to the *kami* and perform ceremonies to ask for their blessings.

Buddhists have also built shrines and temples all over Japan. Some temples are very old. They date back to the earliest days of Buddhism in Japan. People visit these temples to seek peace and enlightenment. The search for enlightenment is Buddhists' main goal.

Customs and Traditions Japan's history lives on in its customs and traditions. For example, many Japanese wear traditional robes called **kimonos** on special occasions, just as samurai did long ago. Most of the time, though, people in Japan wear Western-style clothing.

Traditional forms of art are also still popular in Japan. Among these art forms are two types of drama, Noh and Kabuki. Noh plays use music and dance to tell a story. Actors do not move much and wear masks, using their gestures to convey their tale. Kabuki actors, on the other hand, are much more active. Kabuki plays tell stories, but they often teach lessons about duty and other **abstract** ideas as well.

Reading Check
Summarize How did Japan's history affect its culture today?

Academic Vocabulary
abstract a quality or idea without reference to an actual thing

Government

Since World War II, Japan's government and economy have changed dramatically. Japan was once an imperial state that was shut off from the rest of the world. Today, Japan is a democracy with one of the world's strongest economies.

Shortly after World War II, Japan's government became a constitutional monarchy headed by an emperor. Although the emperor is officially the head of state, he has little power. His main role is to act as a symbol of Japan and of the Japanese people. In his place, power rests in the people, who elect a legislature called the **Diet.** The Diet chooses the prime minister. From the capital city of **Tokyo,** the Diet and the prime minister make the laws that govern life in Japan today.

Under the constitution, all Japanese citizens 18 years of age or older can vote. It also guarantees that all Japanese citizens are equal under the law. It also protects the personal freedoms of the Japanese people. For example, the constitution promises that the Japanese people have the right to pursue happiness, and it protects freedom of thought.

Reading Check
Find Main Ideas How has Japan's government changed since World War II?

Economy

Do you own any products made by Sony? Have you seen ads for vehicles made by Honda, Toyota, or Mitsubishi? Chances are good that you have. These companies are some of the most successful in the world, and all of them are Japanese.

Today, Japan is an economic powerhouse. However, this was not always the case. Until the 1950s, Japan's economy was not that strong. Within a few decades, though, the economy grew tremendously.

The most successful area of Japan's economy is manufacturing. Japanese companies are known for making high-quality products, especially cars and electronics. Japanese companies are among the world's leading manufacturers of cars, electronic motors, video games and consoles, and video recording equipment. The methods that companies use to make these products are also celebrated. Many Japanese companies are leaders in new technology and ideas.

Reasons for Success Many factors have contributed to Japan's economic success. One factor is the government. It works closely with business leaders to control production and plan for the future.

Japan's workforce also contributed to its success. Japan has well-educated, highly trained workers. As a result, its companies tend to be both efficient and productive. Many workers in Japan also have a strong work ethic. A **work ethic** is the belief that work in itself is worthwhile. People with a strong work ethic work hard and are often loyal to their companies. As a result, the companies are successful.

Trade Japan's economy depends on trade. In fact, many products manufactured in the country are intended to be sold outside of Japan. Japan specializes in manufacturing high-tech items and cars. Many of these goods are sent to China and the United States. The United States is Japan's major trading partner.

Japan's trade has been so successful that it has built up a huge trade surplus. A **trade surplus** exists when a country exports more goods than it imports. Because of this surplus, many Japanese companies have become very wealthy.

Japan is able to export more than it imports in part because of high tariffs. A **tariff** is a fee that a country charges on imports or exports. For many years, Japan's government has placed high tariffs on goods brought into the country. This makes imported goods more expensive, and so people buy Japanese goods rather than imported ones.

Resources Although its economy is based on manufacturing, Japan has few natural resources. As a result, the country must import raw materials. In addition, Japan has little arable land. Farms cannot grow enough food for the country's growing population. Instead, the Japanese have to buy food from other countries, including China and the United States.

Reading Check
Summarize What have the Japanese done to build their economy?

Daily Life

Japan is a densely populated country. Slightly smaller than California, it has nearly three times as many people! Most of these people live in crowded cities such as the capital, Tokyo.

Life in Tokyo Besides serving as the national capital, Tokyo is the center of Japan's banking and communication industries. As a result, the city is busy, noisy, and very crowded. About 13 million people live in a relatively small area. Because Tokyo is so densely populated, land is scarce. As a result, Tokyo's real estate prices are among the highest in the world. Some people save up for years to buy homes in Tokyo. They earn money by putting money in savings accounts or by investing in stocks and bonds.

Because space is so limited in Tokyo, people have found creative ways to adapt. Buildings tend to be fairly tall and narrow so that they take less land area. People also use space underground. For example, shops and restaurants can be found below the streets in subway stations. Another way the Japanese have found to save space is the capsule hotel. Guests in these hotels—mostly traveling businesspeople—crawl into tiny sleeping chambers rather than having rooms with beds.

Many people work in Tokyo but live outside the city. So many people commute to and from Tokyo that trains are very crowded. During peak travel times, commuters are crammed into train cars.

Tokyo is not all about work, though. During their leisure time, people can visit Tokyo's many parks, museums, and stores. They can also take short trips to local amusement parks, baseball stadiums, or other attractions. Among these attractions are a huge indoor beach and a ski resort filled with artificial snow.

Life in Other Cities Most of Japan's other cities, like Tokyo, are crowded and busy. Many of them serve as centers of industry or transportation.

The second-largest city in Japan, **Osaka,** is located in western Honshu. In Osaka—as in Tokyo and other cities—tall, modern skyscrapers stand next to tiny Shinto temples. Another major city is Kyoto. Once Japan's capital, Kyoto is full of historic buildings.

Transportation between Cities To connect cities that lie far apart, the Japanese have built a network of rail lines. Some of these lines carry very fast trains called *Shinkansen*, or bullet trains. They can reach speeds of more than 160 miles per hour (260 kph). Japan's train system is very **efficient**. Trains nearly always leave on time and are almost never late.

Academic Vocabulary
efficient productive and not wasteful

Rural Life Not everyone in Japan lives in cities. Some people live in the country in small villages. The people in these villages own or work on farms.

Relatively little of Japan's land is arable, or suitable for farming. Much of the land is too rocky or steep to grow crops on. As a result, most farms are small. The average Japanese farm is only about 2.5 acres (1 hectare). In contrast, the average farm in the United States is 175 times that size.

Because their farms are so small and Japan imports so much of its food, many farmers cannot make a living from their crops. As a result, many people have left rural areas to find jobs in cities.

Reading Check
Find Main Ideas What are Japanese cities like?

Life in Tokyo

Home to some 13 million people, Tokyo is one of the world's busiest cities. This illustration shows what a typical day in Tokyo is like.

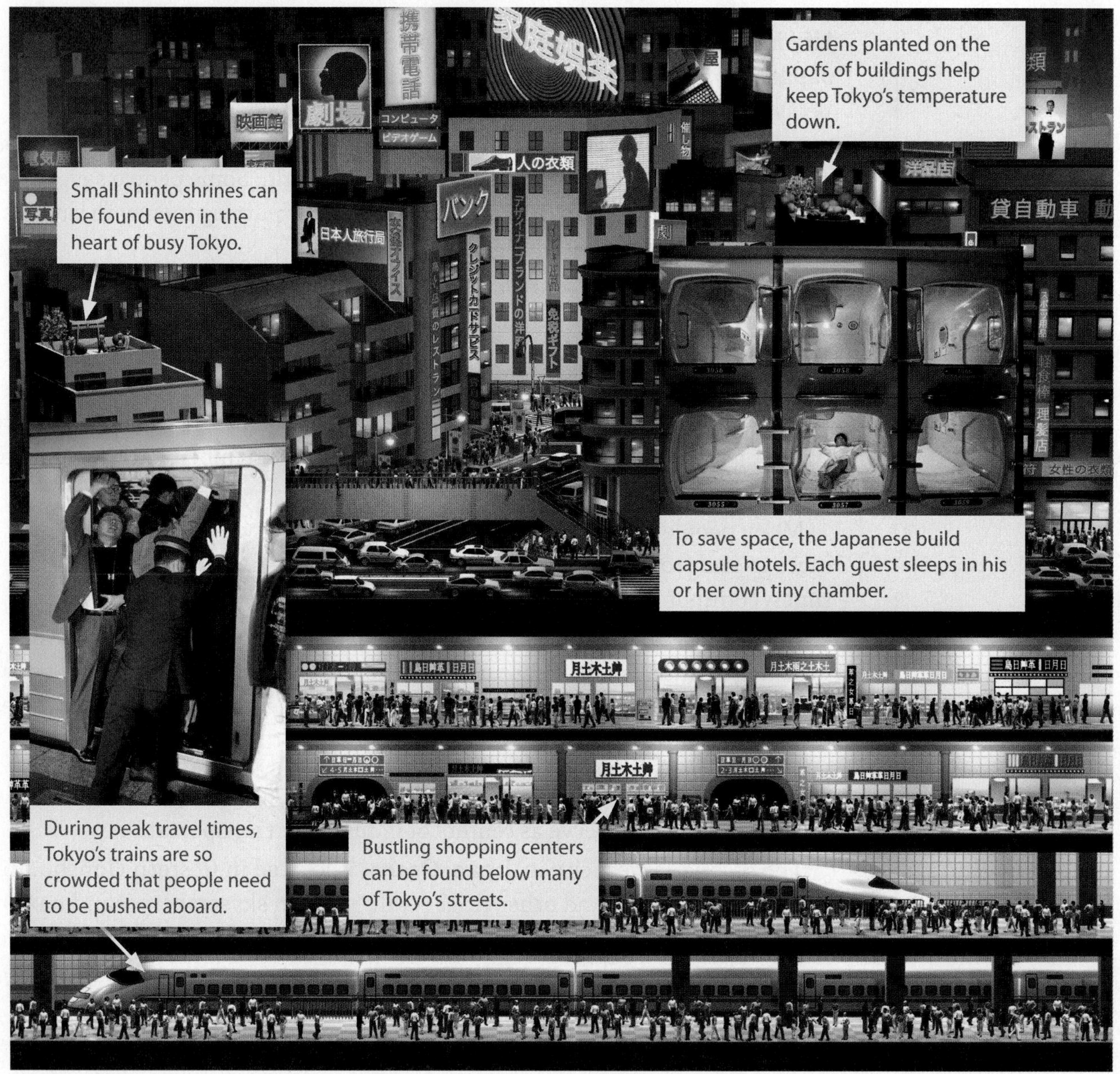

Analyze Visuals
Based on this image, how does life in Tokyo compare to daily life where you live?

Issues and Challenges

Many people consider Japan one of the world's most successful countries. In recent years, however, a few issues have arisen that present challenges for Japan's future.

One of these issues is Japan's lack of space. As cities grow, crowding has become a serious issue. It is not uncommon for a family of four to live in a one-bedroom apartment. To escape overcrowded city life, some move to distant suburbs. Unfortunately, many suburban dwellers must travel back to the city for work. For commuters, two- or three-hour daily trips to and from work are normal.

To make space, some people have begun to construct taller buildings. Such buildings have to be carefully planned, though, to withstand earthquakes.

Japan also faces economic challenges. For many years, it had the only strong economy in East Asia. Recently, however, other countries have challenged Japan's economic dominance. Competition from China and South Korea has begun taking business from some Japanese companies.

Some of the economic challenges Japan faces come from within. Many of its top companies are decades old. Some economists believe that Japan needs new businesses. However, Japan has one of the lowest levels of entrepreneurship, or the setting up of businesses, in the developed world. Though as the economy begins to slow down, there is a greater push for more entrepreneurship.

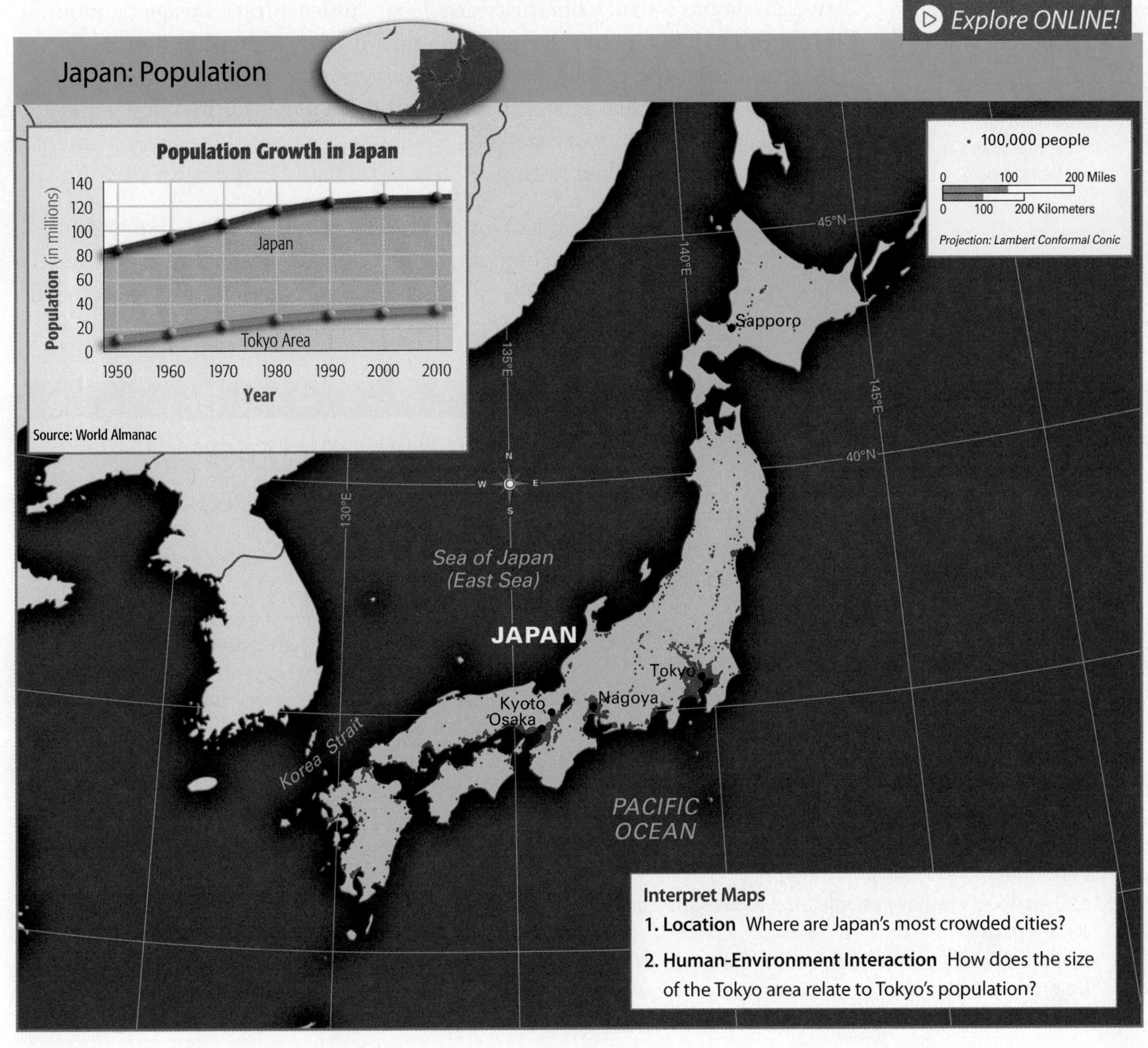

Interpret Maps

1. **Location** Where are Japan's most crowded cities?
2. **Human-Environment Interaction** How does the size of the Tokyo area relate to Tokyo's population?

Parts of northeastern Japan, such as the city of Sendai shown here, were devastated by the tsunami that followed the massive earthquake in 2011.

Pollution has also become a problem in Japan. In 1997 officials from more than 150 countries met in Japan to discuss the pollution problem. They signed the Kyoto Protocol, an agreement to cut down on pollution and improve air quality.

Japan's stability was deeply shaken on March 11, 2011, when a massive earthquake struck northeastern Japan, unleashing a savage tsunami. More than 18,000 people were killed; most died by drowning. To make matters worse, the tsunami caused a cooling system failure at the Fukushima Daiichi Nuclear Power Plant, resulting in a nuclear meltdown and the release of radioactive materials. Today, Japan's people and government continue to rebuild their nation.

Reading Check
Find Main Ideas
What are three issues facing Japan?

Summary and Preview Since World War II, Japan has created a democratic government and a strong, highly technological economy. In the next lesson, you will learn about Korea's history and changes that have occurred in South Korea and North Korea.

Lesson 2 Assessment

Review Ideas, Terms, and Places

1. a. **Define** Who were the shoguns?
   b. **Explain** Why did Japan enter World War II?
2. a. **Elaborate** How did World War II affect life in Japan?
   b. **Elaborate** How does Japan's religion reflect its history?
   c. **Identify** What is one traditional style of clothing in Japan? What do people wear most of the time?
3. a. **Explain** How has Japan's government changed since World War II?
   b. **Summarize** What personal freedoms does Japan's constitution protect?
4. a. **Identify** What are some goods made in Japan?
   b. **Elaborate** Why do you think a work ethic is so important to the Japanese economy?
5. a. **Describe** How have people tried to save space in Japanese cities?
   b. **Identify and Explain** Look back at the model of Daily Life in Tokyo. Use the model to pose and answer a question about population patterns in Japan.
6. a. **Identify** What is one issue that crowding has caused for Japan?
   b. **Analyze** How are other countries presenting challenges to Japan's economy?

Critical Thinking

7. **Analyze** Draw a graphic organizer made of three circles. In one circle, write two sentences about city life in Japan. In another, write two sentences about rural life. In the third, write two sentences about issues facing the Japanese.

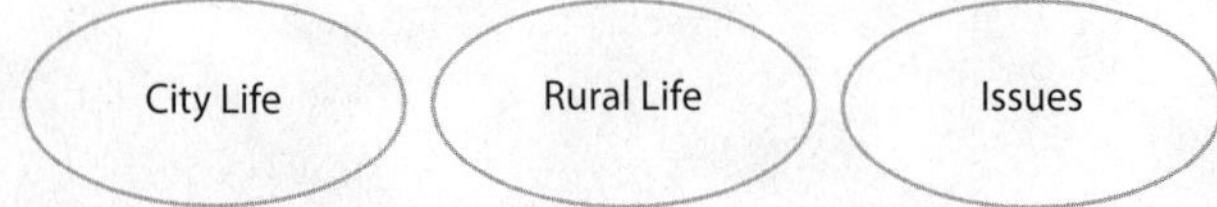

The Koreas

The Big Idea

Though they share a common history and culture, the two Koreas have very different governments and economies.

Main Ideas

- Korea was one state with a shared history until the Korean War.
- Korean culture reflects its long history, and traditions continue into today.
- The people of South Korea today have freedom and economic opportunities.
- The people of North Korea today have little freedom or economic opportunity.
- Some people in both South and North Korea support the idea of Korean reunification.

Key Terms and Places

Silla
kimchi
Seoul
demilitarized zone
Pyongyang

If YOU lived there . . .

You live in Inchon, one of South Korea's largest cities. Sometimes your grandparents tell you about the other family members who still live in North Korea. You have never met them, of course, and your grandparents have not seen them since they were children, more than 50 years ago. After hearing stories about these family members, you are curious about their lives.

Would you like to visit North Korea?

History

Throughout its early history, Korea was ruled by several different kingdoms. The first may have been the Gojoseon kingdom. This kingdom fell to Han China in 108 BC. Later, three powerful kingdoms competed for control of Korea. Eventually the kingdom of **Silla** unified the Three Kingdoms and ruled Korea.

Silla rulers fought against China for many years. During this time, the Silla adapted the Chinese system of governing and embraced Buddhism and Confucianism. The Koryo dynasty succeeded the Silla. The English name *Korea* comes from Koryo. Then, in 1392 the Joseon kingdom took over and became Korea's last dynasty.

The Gyeongbokgung Palace was built during the Joseon dynasty. The palace is located in South Korea's bustling capital, Seoul.

Later, the Japanese invaded the Korean Peninsula. They were harsh rulers, and the Korean people grew to resent the Japanese.

After World War II, Korea was taken away from Japan and once again made independent. Rather than forming one country, though, Korea was divided into two. Aided by the Soviet Union, North Korea created a Communist government. In South Korea, the United States helped build a democratic government.

Reading Check
Analyze
How did the Koreas change after World War II?

In 1950 North Korea invaded South Korea, starting the Korean War. The North Koreans wanted to unify all of Korea under a Communist government. With the aid of many other countries, including the United States, the South Koreans drove the invaders back. The Korean War was costly, and its effects linger in the Koreas today.

Korean Culture

Korea's culture reflects the peninsula's long history. Traditional ways of life influence how people act and think.

Language and Religion People in both North Korea and South Korea speak Korean. Unlike Japanese, Korean is written with an alphabet. People combine letters to form words, rather than using symbols to represent entire words or syllables as in Japanese.

Korea's traditional religion is shamanism, which is the belief that a person called a shaman can communicate with and influence spirits. Shamanism, Buddhism, and Confucianism shaped Korea's culture throughout its history, and their influence is still strong today.

Recently, though, Christianity has become the most widely practiced religion in South Korea. Buddhism is the second-most commonly

These Korean dancers are wearing hanboks, the Korean traditional dress, to perform Buchaechum, a fan dance.

Seoul's Post-war Transformation

South Korea was one of the world's poorest countries after the Korean War. Much of its infrastructure was destroyed during the war. Today, South Korea is a major economic power and has one of the strongest economies in East Asia.

Women and children search for items to burn as fuel in war-torn Seoul, 1950.

Today, South Korea's capital city, Seoul, is a busy metropolis.

Analyze Visuals
How has Seoul changed since 1950?

practiced. Confucianism is also widely practiced, though it is seen as a philosophy rather than a religion. The majority of the population, however, does not identify with a particular faith. North Korea, like many Communist countries, discourages people from practicing any religion.

Customs and Traditions The people of Korea have kept many ancient traditions alive. Many Korean foods, for example, have been part of the Korean diet for centuries.

One example of a long-lasting Korean food is **kimchi,** a dish made from pickled cabbage and various spices. First created in the 1100s, kimchi is still served at many Korean meals. In fact, many people think of it as Korea's national dish.

Traditional art forms have also remained popular in parts of the Koreas. Traditional Korean dance began as shamanistic rituals. A famous example is a fan dance called Buchaechum, in which dancers dance with large painted fans.

Korean traditions are especially important in North Korea. Since World War II, the Communist government of North Korea has encouraged people to retain many of their old customs and traditions. The Communists think that Korean culture is the best in the world and do everything they can to preserve it.

In South Korea, urbanization and the spread of modern lifestyles have led to a decline in some traditional customs. Rural areas are still very traditional, but people in urban areas have adopted new ways of life. Many

Quick Facts

South Korea's Higher Education Boom

South Korea's investment in higher education has fueled dramatic growth in enrollment. It now has one of the highest rates of higher education student enrollment in the world.

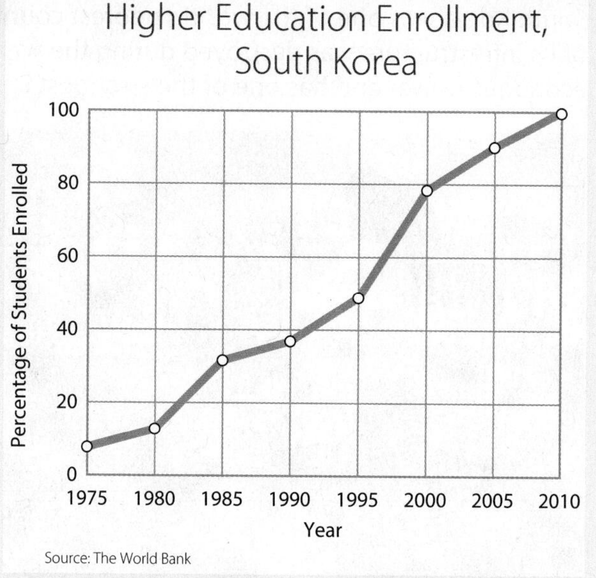

Analyze Graphs
Which year saw the largest growth in student enrollment?

Reading Check
Contrast How are North and South Korea's cultures different?

of these ways are combinations of old and new ideas. For example, Korean art today combines traditional themes such as nature with modern forms, like film.

South Korea Today

Japan's closest neighbor is both a major economic rival and a key trading partner. That neighbor is South Korea. Like Japan, South Korea is a democratic country with a strong economy. Unlike Japan, South Korea shares a border with a hostile neighbor—North Korea.

Government and Economy The official name of South Korea is the Republic of Korea. As the name suggests, South Korea's government is a republic. It is headed by a president and an assembly elected by the people, much like the United States is. In fact, the United States helped create South Korea's government after World War II. It also helped South Korea economically in the years after the war.

During the first half of the 20th century, South Korea was an impoverished nation. Today, South Korea's economy is one of the strongest in East Asia. Korean business leaders and government officials have worked together to ensure that the economy stays strong. In recent years, South Korea has become a major manufacturing country, exporting goods to places all around the world.

Education and Employment Education also played a large role in the dramatic growth of South Korea's economy. Since the 1950s, South Korea experienced an educational revolution. The literacy rate for South Korea in 1945 was about 22 percent. Today, the literacy rate is almost 99 percent. South Korean students are some of the highest performing in the world.

Because of this investment in education, the majority of South Koreans ages 25 to 34 have had higher education, or education beyond high school. However, many South Korean college graduates have trouble finding jobs due to increased competition. At the same time, South Korea needs more skilled workers. To help solve these problems, the South Korean government is beginning to invest more in vocational training, or training for a specific job skill or trade.

Daily Life Like Japan, South Korea is very densely populated. The capital city, **Seoul** (SOHL), is one of the most densely populated cities in the world. It has more than 44,000 people per square mile (17,000 per sq km).

Although parts of South Korea are densely populated, very few people live in the mountainous interior. Most people live near the coast. A coastal plain in western South Korea is the most crowded part of the country.

In South Korea's cities, most people live in small apartments. Because space is scarce, housing is expensive. Also, cities sometimes suffer from pollution from the many factories, cars, and coal-fired heating systems found there. In some cities, industrial waste has also polluted the water.

Outside the cities, many South Koreans still follow traditional ways of life. Most of them are farmers who grow rice, beans, and cabbage they can use to make kimchi. They usually live on small farms.

Issues and Challenges Government policies and international politics have led to some challenges for South Korea. Although South Korea has a successful economy, some people feel that its government is corrupt. For many years, four families have controlled much of the country's industry. As a result, wealth and power became concentrated in the hands of big business.

This led to corruption of government officials. In 2016 then president Park Geun-hye was impeached in connection to a scandal involving bribes

Political Upheaval in South Korea

When news broke of the corruption scandal, many South Koreans held mass protests calling for President Park Geun-hye's resignation. After her removal from office on March 10, 2017, thousands of her supporters began holding demonstrations in Seoul. After months of upheaval, Moon Jae-in was elected president.

Supporters of former president Park Geun-hye set up a camp near City Hall in Seoul to protest her impeachment.

Moon Jae-in was elected as South Korea's 19th president after Park's impeachment.

from several businesses. A new presidential election took place in May 2017, in which the Koreans elected former student activist and human rights lawyer Moon Jae-in.

A bigger challenge to South Korea is its relationship with North Korea. Since the end of the Korean War in the 1950s, the two countries have been separated. Between them is a **demilitarized zone,** an empty buffer zone created to keep the two countries from fighting. Although troops are not allowed in the demilitarized zone, guards patrol both sides.

Reading Check
Summarize
What issues face South Korea today?

North Korea Today

The official name of North Korea is the Democratic People's Republic of Korea. Its name, however, is misleading. North Korea is neither a democracy nor a republic. It is a totalitarian, Communist state.

Government and Economy The government of North Korea was created soon after World War II. Its first leader, Kim Il Sung, ruled from 1948 until his death in 1994. During this time North Korea was a Communist dictatorship, at times under the Soviet Union's sphere of influence.

Kim Il Sung was succeeded by his eldest son, Kim Jong Il. Called "Dear Leader" by the North Korean state, Kim Jong Il was in fact a brutal, secretive, and unpredictable dictator. He tightly controlled life in North Korea. Under his rule, North Koreans suffered human rights abuses, poverty, and widespread hunger. He also developed long-range missiles and nuclear weapons that he used to threaten neighboring countries.

When Kim Jong Il died in December 2011, his son Kim Jong Un took over. The rise of a new leader brought hope that life would improve for

Life in South and North Korea

The differences between life in South Korea and North Korea can be seen in their capitals. Seoul, South Korea (shown on the left), is a busy, modern city and a major commercial center. By contrast, North Korea's capital, Pyongyang (shown on the right), has little traffic or commercial development.

Analyzing Visuals
What do these photos suggest about life in Seoul and Pyongyang?

Academic Vocabulary
policies rules, courses of action

North Koreans. However, Kim Jong Un has followed his father's domestic **policies.** He also continues to develop and test weapons, which has threatened stability in the region.

As a Communist country, North Korea has a command economy. This means that the government plans the economy and decides what is produced. It also owns all land and controls access to jobs.

Unlike Japan and South Korea, North Korea is rich in mineral resources. With these resources, factories in North Korea make machinery and military supplies. However, most factories use out-of-date technology. As a result, North Korea is much poorer than Japan and South Korea.

Because North Korea's land is so rocky, very little of it can be farmed. The farmland that does exist is owned by the government. It is farmed by cooperatives—large groups of farmers who work the land together. These cooperatives are not able to grow enough food for the country. As a result, the government has to import food. This can be a difficult foreign policy task because North Korea's relations with most other countries are strained.

Daily Life Like Japan and South Korea, North Korea is largely an urban society. Most people live in cities. The largest city is the capital, **Pyongyang** (PYUHNG-YAHNG), in the west. Pyongyang is a crowded urban area. About 3 million people live in the city.

Life in Pyongyang is very different from life in Tokyo or Seoul. For example, few people in Pyongyang own private cars. The North Korean government allows only top Communist officials to own cars. Most residents have to use buses or the subway to get around. At night, many streets are dark because of electricity shortages.

North Koreans have fewer rights than the people of Japan or South Korea. For example, the government controls individual speech and the press. Because the government feels that religion conflicts with Communist ideas, it also discourages people from practicing religion.

Issues and Challenges Why does North Korea, which is rich in resources, have shortages of electricity and food? These problems are due in part to North Korea's foreign policies. For years, North Korea had ties with other Communist countries. Since the breakup of the Soviet Union, North Korea has isolated itself from the rest of the world. It has closed its markets to foreign goods, which means that other countries cannot sell their goods there. At the same time, North Korea lacks the technology to take advantage of its resources. As a result, many people suffer and resources go unused.

Many countries worry about North Korea's possession of nuclear weapons. In 2006 North Korea declared that it had successfully conducted its first underground nuclear test. After several more tests, North Korea claimed to have successfully tested a hydrogen bomb in September 2017. These developments concern countries in Asia and around the world.

Reading Check
Form Generalizations
What is North Korea's relationship with the world?

A crowd of people at a political rally express support for reunification. The flag in the background shows a united Korea.

Korean Reunification

For years, many South and North Koreans wanted their country to be reunited. The creation of two Koreas split friends and family. It also divided people who shared a common culture and history. Many believed that reunification would heal families and Korean culture as a whole.

At times, the governments of both South Korea and North Korea have expressed their support for reunification. Leaders from the two countries met in 2000 for the first time since the Korean War. As part of their meeting, they discussed ways to improve relations between the two countries. For example, they agreed to build a road through the demilitarized zone to connect the two Koreas.

The question of government is an obstacle to reunification. South Koreans want democracy, while North Korean leaders insist on communism. Another obstacle is generational. As time passes, fewer young South Koreans support reunification. Some even fear that they will inherit the social and political problems of North Korea.

Reading Check
Summarize
What issues stand in the way of Korean reunification?

Summary In this lesson, you learned about the history, cultures, and people of the Koreas. Both countries shared a long history as one state until the Korean War. Since then, each country developed in drastically different ways, but some Koreans still long for reunification.

Lesson 3 Assessment

Review Ideas, Terms, and Places

1. a. **Identify** Which kingdom unified the Three Kingdoms?
   b. **Identify Cause and Effect** Why did North Korea invade South Korea? What was the result?
2. a. **Identify** What helped shape traditional Korean culture?
   b. **Recall** What is kimchi? Why is it important in Korea?
   c. **Explain** What has led to many of the differences between modern culture in North and South Korea?
3. a. **Summarize** What factors have helped South Korea develop a strong economy?
   b. **Define** What is the demilitarized zone? Why does it exist?
4. a. **Explain** Which geographic factor explains why North Korea must import food? Why is this a difficult foreign policy task?
   b. **Compare** What was the standard of living like for both Japan and South Korea before the 1950s? What was it like afterward?
5. a. **Recall** Why do many Koreans support the idea of reunification?
   b. **Evaluate** If you lived in North or South Korea, do you think you would support the reunification of the countries? Why or why not?

Critical Thinking

6. **Analyze** Draw a diagram to analyze the differences between the societies of South and North Korea. Write three statements about South Korea and three statements about North Korea. In the oval, list one factor that supports reunification and one that hinders it.

South Korea | Reunification | North Korea

Social Studies Skills

Use a Topographic Map

Define the Skill

Topographic maps show elevation, or the height of land above sea level. They do so with contour lines, lines that connect points on the map that have equal elevation. Every point on a contour line has the same elevation. In most cases, everything inside that line has a higher elevation. Everything outside the line is lower. Each contour line is labeled to show the elevation it indicates.

An area that has lots of contour lines is more rugged than an area with few contour lines. The distance between contour lines shows how steep an area is. If the lines are very close together, then the area has a steep slope. If the lines are farther apart, then the area has a much gentler incline. Other symbols on the map show features such as rivers and roads.

Learn the Skill

Use the topographic map on this page to answer the following questions.

1. Is Awaji Island more rugged in the south or the north? How can you tell?
2. Does the land get higher or lower as you travel west from Yura?

Practice the Skill

Search the Internet or look in a local library to find a topographic map of your area. Study the map to find three major landmarks and write down their elevations. Then pose and answer two geographic questions about the landmarks or patterns that you see on the map.

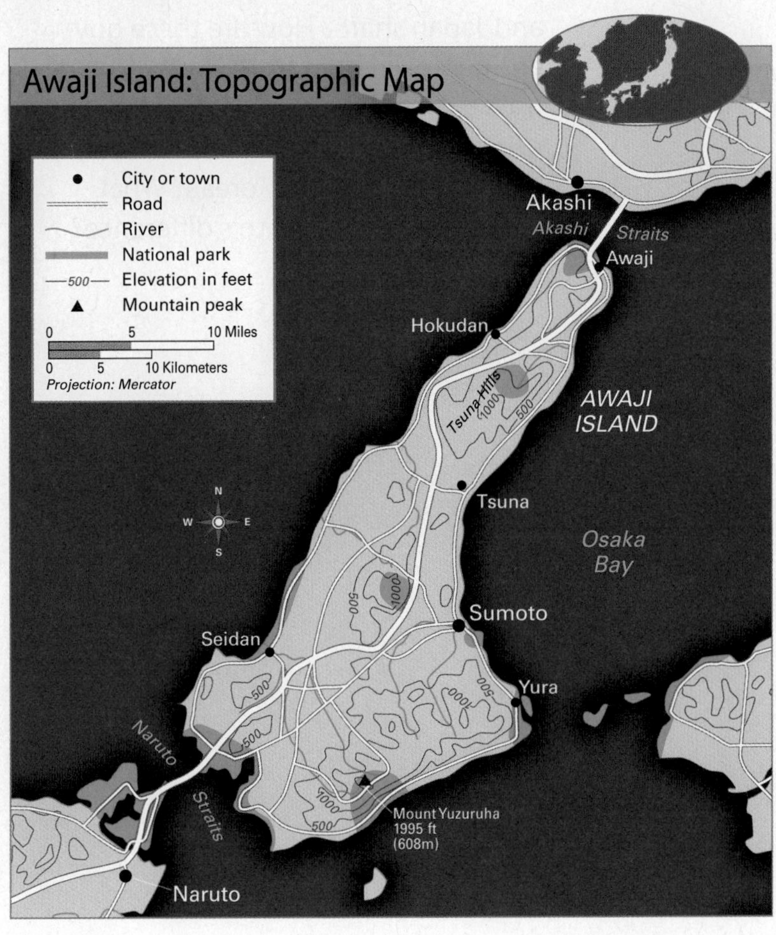

Module 18 Assessment

Review Vocabulary, Terms, and Places

Imagine these terms from the module are correct answers to items in a crossword puzzle. Write the clues for the answers.

1. Tokyo
2. abstract
3. trade surplus
4. tariff
5. kimono
6. efficient
7. work ethic
8. Seoul
9. fishery
10. Pyongyang
11. kimchi
12. policy

Comprehension and Critical Thinking

Lesson 1

13. a. **Identify** What physical feature covers most of Japan and the Korean Peninsula? What is one famous example of this landform?
    b. **Draw Conclusions** Fish and seafood are very important in the Japanese diet. Why do you think this is so?
    c. **Predict** How do you think earthquakes and typhoons would affect your life if you lived in Japan?

Lesson 2

14. a. **Identify** Who were the shoguns? What role did they play in Japanese history?
    b. **Recall** What is the most important aspect of Japan's economy?
    c. **Develop** How might Japan try to address the problem of crowding in its cities?

Lesson 3

15. a. **Elaborate** How have the histories of Japan and the Koreas affected their cultures?
    b. **Compare and Contrast** What similarities do the governments of South Korea and Japan share? How are these governments different from North Korea's government?
    c. **Contrast** How is South Korea's economy different from North Korea's? What events helped create this difference?

Module 18 Assessment, continued

Reading Skills

Use the Reading Skills taught in this module to complete this activity.

16. Examine this quote from President Truman on the Korean War. Use the steps from the Reading Skills to identify four ways this quote shows bias.

> "We have the resources to meet our needs. Far more important, the American people are unified in their belief in democratic freedom. We are united in detesting Communist slavery."
>
> —Harry S. Truman, Radio and Television Address to the American People on the Situation in Korea, July 19, 1950

Social Studies Skills

Using a Topographic Map *Use the topographic map in this module's Social Studies Skills lesson to answer the following questions.*

17. What elevations do the contour lines on this map show?

18. Where are the highest points on Awaji Island located? How can you tell?

19. Is the city of Sumoto located more or less than 500 feet above sea level?

Map Activity

20. Japan and the Koreas On a separate sheet of paper, match the letters on the map with their correct labels.

North Korea	Tokyo, Japan
South Korea	Hokkaido
Korea Strait	Sea of Japan (East Sea)

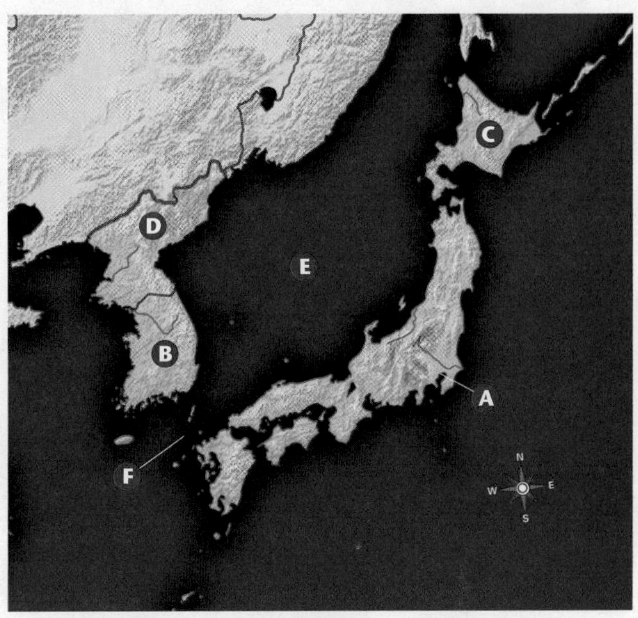

Focus on Writing

Write Your Five-Line Poem *Use your notes and the instructions below to create your poem.*

21. Review your notes and decide on a topic to write about. Remember that your poem should describe one image or picture—an object, a place, etc.—from Japanese or Korean culture.

The first three lines of your poem should describe the object or place you have chosen. The last two should express how it makes you feel. Try to use the traditional Tanka syllable count in your poem: five syllables in lines 1 and 3; seven in lines 2, 4, and 5. Remember that your poem does not have to rhyme.

Japan and the Samurai Warrior

For over a thousand years, the samurai—an elite warrior class—were a powerful force in Japanese society. The way of life of the samurai lords and warriors was, in many ways, like those of the medieval lords and knights of Europe. The great samurai warlords ruled large territories and relied on the fighting skills of their fierce samurai warriors to battle their enemies. But samurai warriors were more than just soldiers. Samurai were expected to embrace beauty and culture, and many were skilled artists. They also had a strict personal code that valued personal honor above all things—even life itself.

Explore the fascinating world of the samurai warrior online. You can find a wealth of information, video clips, primary sources, activities, and more through your online textbook.

HISTORY

Go online to view these and other **HISTORY®** resources.

Rise of the Samurai Class

Watch the video to learn how the samurai developed from armed tax collectors into warlords and armies that ruled Japan.

A New Way of Life in Japan

Watch the video to learn how peace and isolation took hold in Japan and changed the role of the samurai in society.

"I have no eyes;
I make the Flash of Lightning my Eyes.
I have no ears; I make Sensibility my Ears.
I have no limbs;
I make Promptitude my Limbs.
I have no laws;
I make Self-Protection my Laws."

A Code for Samurai Living

Read the document to learn about the strict but lyrical code of the samurai warrior

Death of the Samurai Class

Watch the video to see how the end of Japan's isolation from the outside world signaled the beginning of the end of the samurai class.

Module 19

Southeast Asia

Essential Question

What characteristics unite the diverse nations of Southeast Asia?

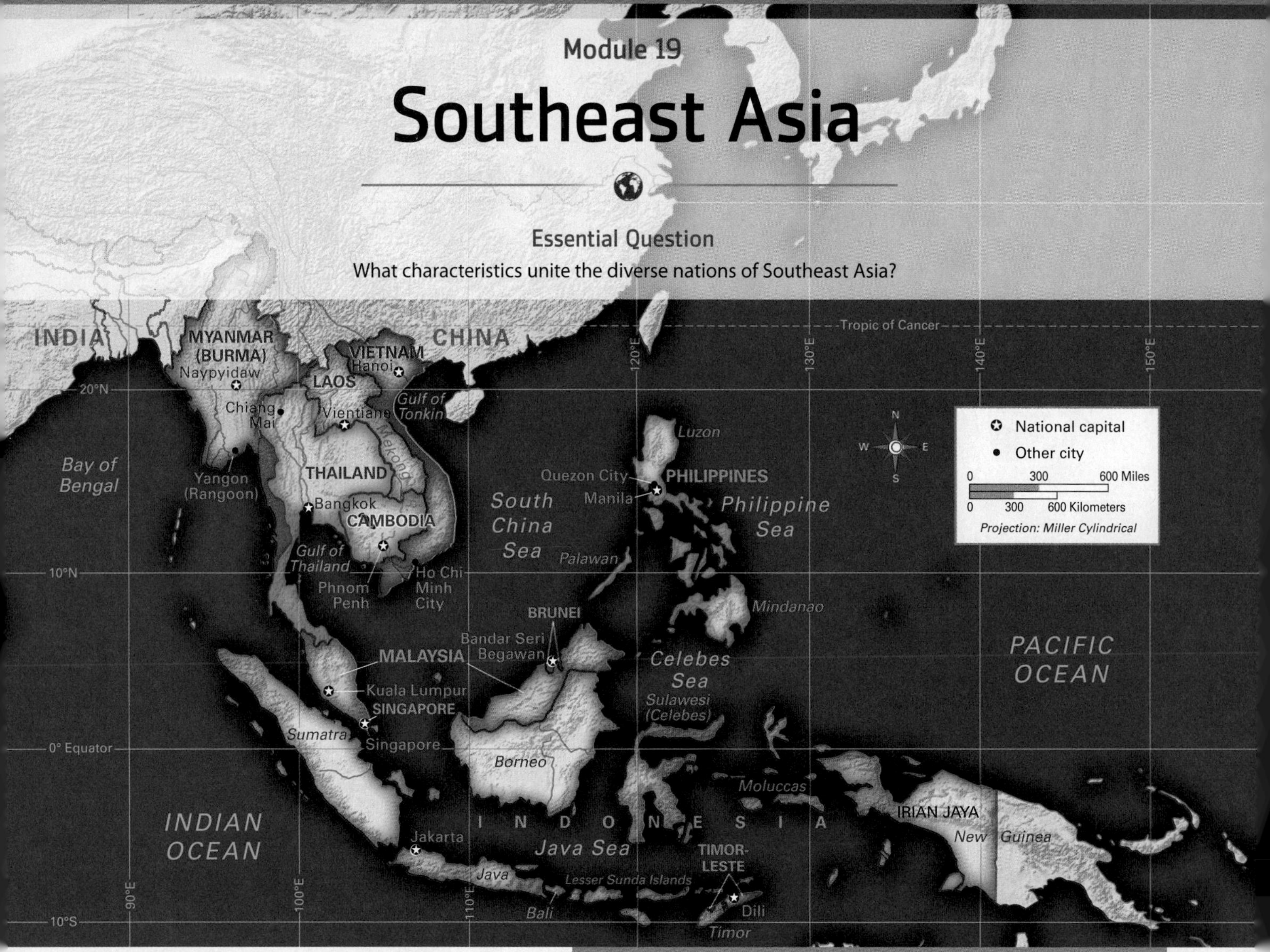

Explore ONLINE!

VIDEOS, including . . .

- Cambodia

- Document-Based Investigations
- Graphic Organizers
- Interactive Games
- Channel One News Video: Tsunami: Ten Years Later
- Channel One News Video: Orangutans
- Interactive Table: Southeast Asia: Regional Data

In this module, you will learn about the geographic and historical forces that have shaped life in Southeast Asia.

What You Will Learn

Lesson 1: Physical Geography 589
The Big Idea Southeast Asia is a tropical region of peninsulas, islands, and waterways with diverse plants, animals, and resources.

Lesson 2: Mainland Southeast Asia 596
The Big Idea People, ideas, and traditions from China, India, Europe, and elsewhere have shaped Southeast Asia's history and culture. Today, many farming areas of Mainland Southeast Asia are poor but working to improve their economies.

Lesson 3: Island Southeast Asia Today 604
The Big Idea The countries of Island Southeast Asia range from wealthy and urban to poor and rural.

Geography Boats lie along the shore of Phi Phi Don Island in Thailand. The island's beauty makes it a popular vacation spot.

Culture Traditional dances remain an important part of the culture of Bali. Barong dancers use their hands, arms, and eyes to tell a traditional story.

History The golden Shwedagon Pagoda is a Buddhist shrine in Yangon, Myanmar. Pagodas have been on this site since the 500s BC.

Reading Social Studies

Use Context Clues—Definitions

READING FOCUS

One way to figure out the meaning of an unfamiliar word or term is by finding clues in its context, the words or sentences surrounding the word or term. A common context clue is a restatement. Restatements are simply a definition of the new word using ordinary words you already know. Notice how the following passage uses a restatement to define *archipelago*. Some context clues are not as complete or obvious. Notice how the following passage provides a description that is a partial definition of *peninsula*.

The region of Southeast Asia is made up of two *peninsulas* and two large island groups. The Indochina *Peninsula* and the Malay (muh-LAY) *Peninsula* extend from the Asian mainland. . . . The two island groups are the Philippines and the Malay Archipelago. An ***archipelago*** (ahr-kuh-PE-luh-goh) is a large group of islands.

Peninsula: land that extends from a mainland out into water

Archipelago: large group of islands

YOU TRY IT!

Read the following passages and identify the meaning of the italicized words by using definitions, or restatements, in context. Seek help from a classmate or a teacher to confirm your understanding.

The many groups that influenced Southeast Asia's history also shaped its culture. This *diverse* culture blends native, Chinese, Indian, and European ways of life.

The economy is based on farming, but good farmland is limited. Most people are *subsistence farmers,* meaning they grow just enough food for their families.

As you read this module, look for words that provide context clues that define, or restate, other words and phrases.

Physical Geography

The Big Idea

Southeast Asia is a tropical region of peninsulas, islands, and waterways with diverse plants, animals, and resources.

Main Ideas

- Southeast Asia's physical features include peninsulas, islands, rivers, and many seas, straits, and gulfs.
- The tropical climate of Southeast Asia supports a wide range of plants and animals.
- Southeast Asia is rich in natural resources such as wood, rubber, and fossil fuels.

Key Terms and Places

Indochina Peninsula
Malay Peninsula
Malay Archipelago
archipelago
New Guinea
Borneo
Mekong River

If YOU lived there . . .

Your family lives on a houseboat on a branch of the great Mekong River in Cambodia. You catch fish in cages under the boat. Your home is part of a floating village of houseboats and houses built on stilts in the water. Boats loaded with fruits and vegetables travel from house to house. Even your school is on a nearby boat.

How does water shape life in your village?

Physical Features

Where can you find a flower that grows up to 3 feet across and smells like rotting garbage? How about a lizard that can grow up to 10 feet long and weigh up to 300 pounds? These amazing sights as well as some of the world's most beautiful tropical paradises are all in Southeast Asia.

The region of Southeast Asia is made up of two peninsulas and two large island groups. The **Indochina Peninsula** and the **Malay** (muh-LAY) **Peninsula** extend from the Asian mainland. We call this part of the region Mainland Southeast Asia. The two island groups are the Philippines and the **Malay Archipelago.** An **archipelago** (ahr-kuh-PE-luh-goh) is a large group of islands. We call this part of the region Island Southeast Asia.

Halong Bay, Vietnam, is filled with limestone karsts, a formation that happens when water dissolves rock. Ships called "junks" are a common sight here. Some serve as homes, while others serve as tour boats showing visitors the natural beauty of the bay.

Landforms In Mainland Southeast Asia, rugged mountains fan out across the countries of Myanmar (MYAHN-mahr), Thailand (TY-land), Laos (LOWS), and Vietnam (vee-et-NAHM). Between these mountains are low plateaus and river floodplains.

Island Southeast Asia consists of more than 20,000 islands, some of them among the world's largest. **New Guinea** is Earth's second-largest island, and **Borneo** its third largest. Many of the area's larger islands have high mountains. A few peaks are high enough to have snow and glaciers.

Island Southeast Asia is a part of the Ring of Fire as well. As a result, earthquakes and volcanic eruptions often rock the area. When such events occur underwater, they can cause tsunamis, or giant series of waves. In 2004 a tsunami in the Indian Ocean killed hundreds of thousands of people, many in Southeast Asia.

Reading Check
Find Main Ideas What are Southeast Asia's major physical features?

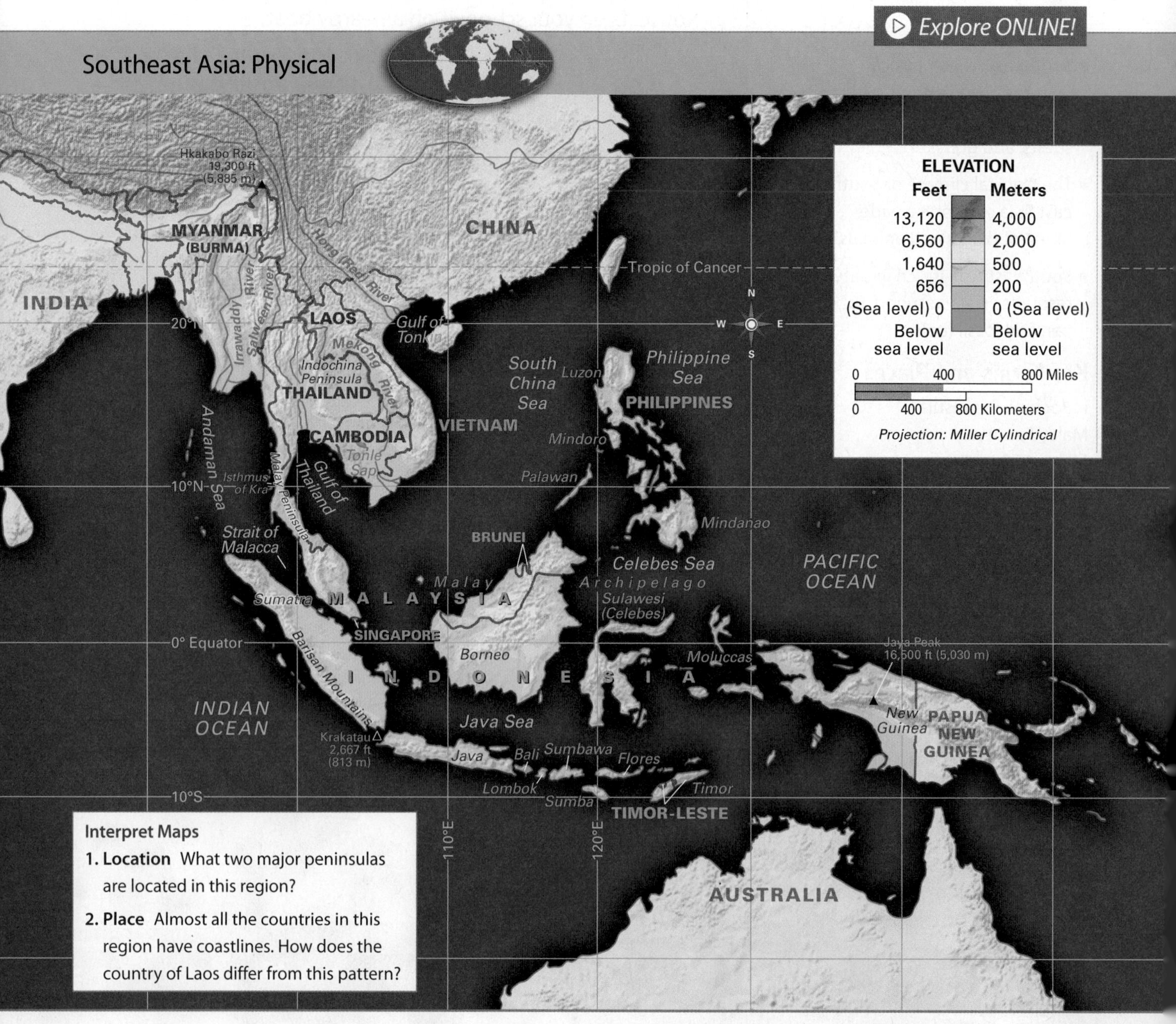

Interpret Maps

1. **Location** What two major peninsulas are located in this region?
2. **Place** Almost all the countries in this region have coastlines. How does the country of Laos differ from this pattern?

Mist hovers over the Mekong River as it flows through the forested mountains of northern Thailand.

Bodies of Water Water is a central part of Southeast Asia. Look at the map to identify the many seas, straits, and gulfs in this region.

In addition, several major rivers drain the mainland's peninsulas. Of these rivers, the mighty **Mekong** (MAY-KAWNG) **River** is the most important. The mainland's fertile river valleys and deltas support farming and are home to many people.

Climate, Plants, and Animals

Southeast Asia lies in the tropics, the area on and around the equator. Temperatures are warm to hot year-round, but become cooler to the north and in the mountains.

Much of the mainland has a tropical savanna climate. Seasonal monsoon winds from the oceans bring heavy rain in summer and drier weather in winter. Severe flooding is common during wet seasons. This climate supports savannas—areas of tall grasses and scattered trees and shrubs.

The islands and the Malay Peninsula mainly have a humid tropical climate. This climate is hot, muggy, and rainy all year. Showers or storms occur almost daily. In addition, huge storms called typhoons can bring heavy rains and powerful winds.

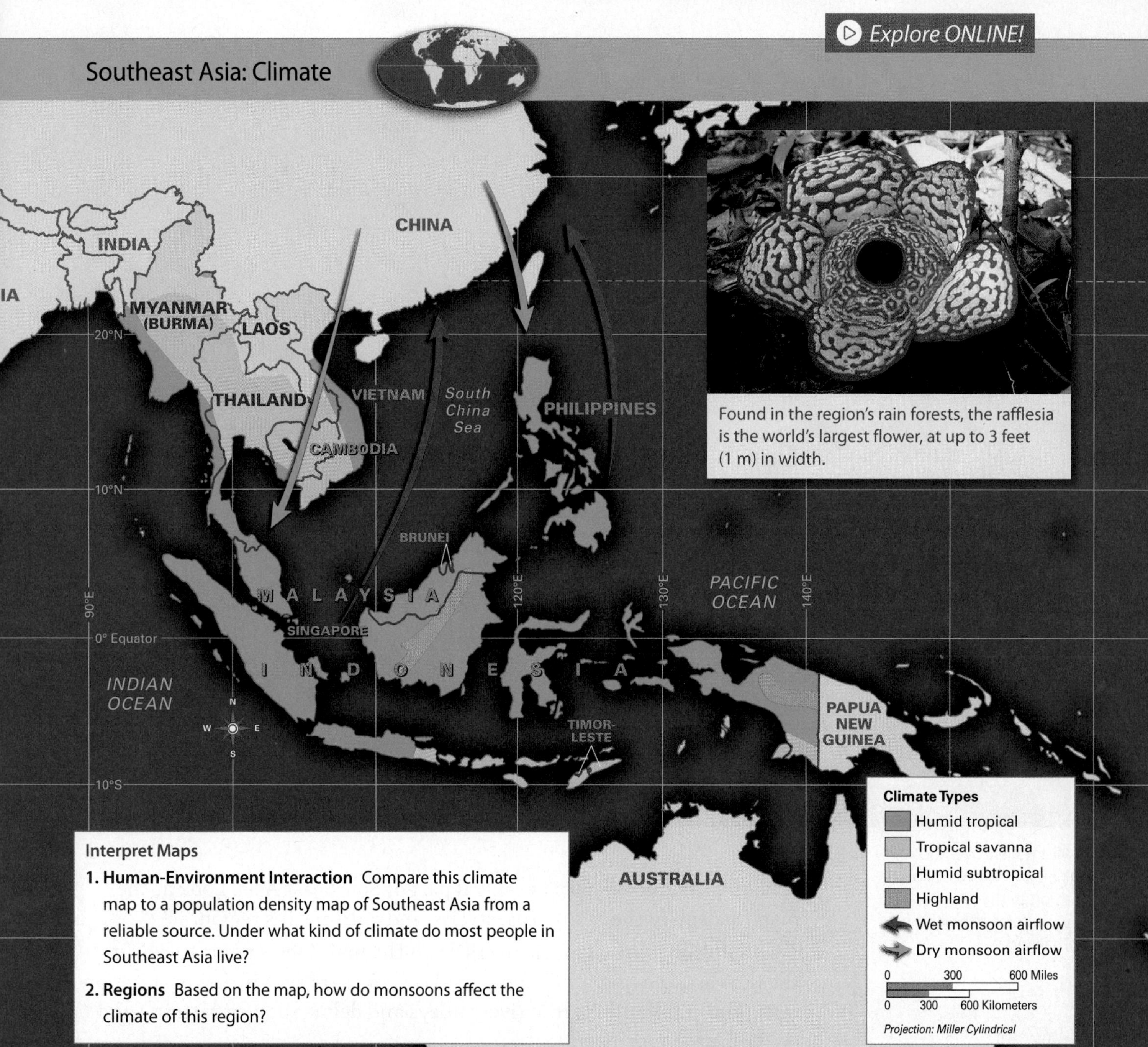

Found in the region's rain forests, the rafflesia is the world's largest flower, at up to 3 feet (1 m) in width.

Interpret Maps

1. **Human-Environment Interaction** Compare this climate map to a population density map of Southeast Asia from a reliable source. Under what kind of climate do most people in Southeast Asia live?
2. **Regions** Based on the map, how do monsoons affect the climate of this region?

The humid tropical climate's heat and heavy rainfall support tropical rain forests. These lush forests are home to a huge number of different plants and animals. About 40,000 kinds of flowering plants grow in Indonesia alone. These plants include the rafflesia, the world's largest flower. Measuring up to 3 feet (1 m) across, this flower produces a horrible, rotting stink.

Rain forest animals include elephants, monkeys, tigers, and many types of birds. Some species are found nowhere else. They include orangutans and Komodo dragons, lizards that can grow 10 feet (3 m) long.

Many of these plants and animals are endangered because of loss of habitat. People are clearing the tropical rain forests for farming, wood, and mining. These actions threaten the area's future diversity.

Reading Check
Analyze Effects
How does climate contribute to the region's diversity of life?

Natural Resources

Southeast Asia has a number of valuable natural resources. The region's hot, wet climate and rich soils make farming highly productive. Rice is a major crop, and others include coconuts, coffee, sugarcane, palm oil, and spices. Some countries, such as Indonesia and Malaysia (muh-LAY-zhuh), also have large rubber tree plantations.

Orangutans live in the rain forests of Borneo and Sumatra. Deforestation has seriously reduced their habitat.

The region's seas provide fish, and its tropical rain forests provide valuable hardwoods and medicines. The region also has many minerals and fossil fuels, including tin, iron ore, natural gas, and oil. For example, the island of Borneo sits atop an oil field.

Reading Check
Summarize What are the region's major natural resources?

Summary and Preview Southeast Asia is a tropical region of peninsulas, islands, and waterways with diverse life and rich resources. Next, you will read about the region's history and culture.

Lesson 1 Assessment

Review Ideas, Terms, and Places

1. a. **Define** What is an archipelago?
   b. **Compare and Contrast** How do the physical features of Mainland Southeast Asia compare and contrast to those of Island Southeast Asia?
   c. **Make Inferences** Look at the climate map in Lesson 1. Use a reliable source to find a population density map of Southeast Asia. Compare the two maps. Given the area's climate, why do you think the population density is so low for much of this region?
2. a. **Recall** What type of forest occurs in the region?
   b. **Summarize** What is the climate like across much of Southeast Asia?
   c. **Predict** What do you think might happen to the region's wildlife if the tropical rain forests continue to be destroyed?
3. a. **Identify** Which countries in the region are major producers of rubber?
   b. **Analyze** How does the region's climate contribute to its natural resources?

Critical Thinking

4. **Summarize** Draw a chart like this one. Use your notes to provide information about the climate, plants, and animals in Southeast Asia. In the left-hand box, also note how climate shapes life in the region.

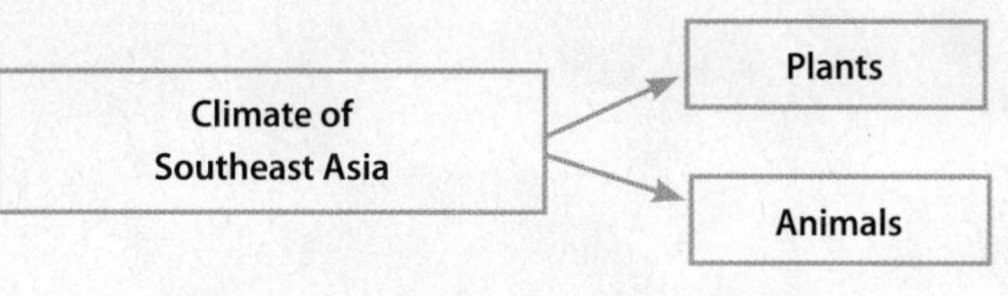

Tsunami!

Essential Elements

- The World in Spatial Terms
- Places and Regions
- Physical Systems
- Human Systems
- Environment and Society
- The Uses of Geography

Background

"Huge Waves Hit Japan." This event is a tsunami (soo-NAH-mee), a series of giant sea waves. Records of deadly tsunamis go back 3,000 years. Some places, such as Japan, have been hit time and again.

Tsunamis occur when an earthquake, volcanic eruption, or other event causes seawater to move in huge waves. The majority of tsunamis occur in the Pacific Ocean because of the region's many earthquakes.

Warning systems help alert people to tsunamis. The Pacific Tsunami Warning Center monitors tsunamis in the Pacific Ocean. Sensors on the ocean floor and buoys on the water's surface help detect earthquakes and measure waves. When a tsunami threatens, radio, TV, and sirens alert the public.

Indian Ocean Catastrophe

On December 26, 2004, a massive earthquake erupted below the Indian Ocean. The earthquake launched a monster tsunami. Within half an hour, walls of water up to 65 feet high came barreling ashore in Indonesia. The water swept away boats, buildings, and people. Meanwhile, the tsunami kept traveling in ever-widening rings across the ocean. The waves eventually wiped out coastal communities in a dozen countries. Some 200,000 people eventually died.

At the time, the Indian Ocean did not have a tsunami warning system. Tsunamis are rare in that part of the world. As a result, many countries there had been unwilling to invest in a warning system.

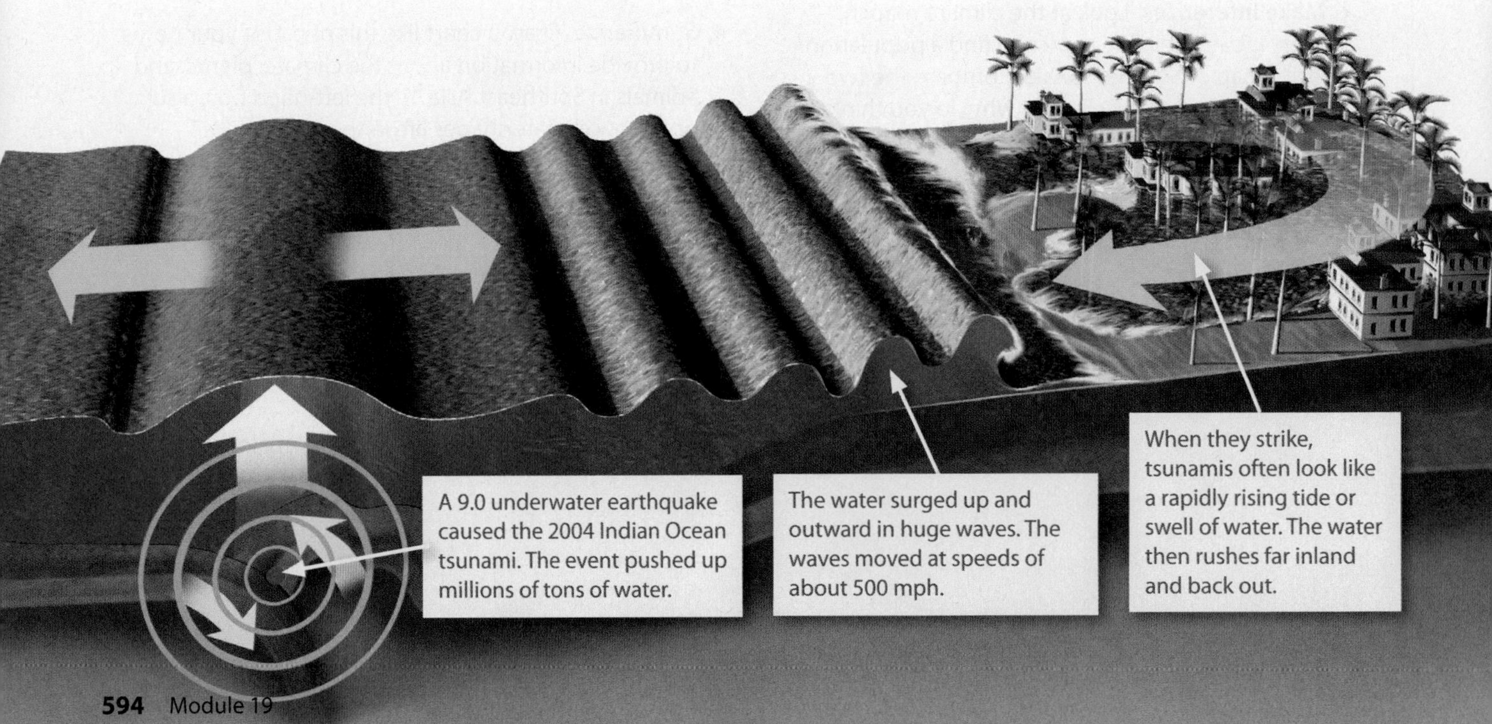

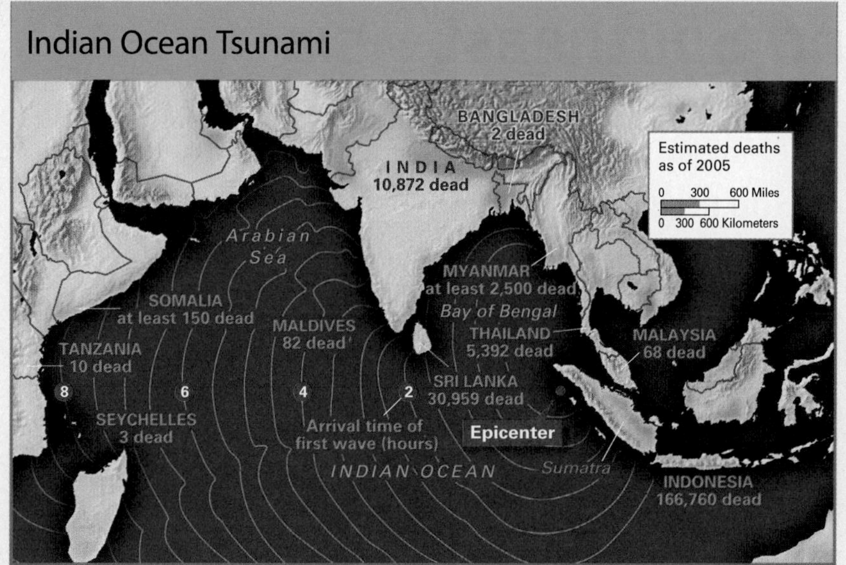

Indian Ocean Tsunami

In 2004 these countries paid a terrible price for their decision. As the map shows, the 2004 tsunami hit countries from South Asia to East Africa. Most people had no warning of the tsunami. In addition, many people did not know how to protect themselves. Instead of heading to high ground, some people went to the beach for a closer look. Many died when later waves hit.

Tilly Smith, a 10-year-old on vacation in Thailand, was one of the few who understood the danger. Two weeks earlier, her geography teacher had discussed tsunamis. As the water began surging, Smith warned her family and other tourists to flee. Her geographic knowledge saved their lives.

What It Means

No one can prevent tsunamis. Yet, by studying geography, we can prepare for these disasters and help protect lives and property. The United Nations is now working to create a global tsunami warning system. People are also trying to plant more mangroves along coastlines. These bushy swamp trees provide a natural barrier against high waves.

A large wave smashes into the beach on Penang Island in Malaysia during the 2004 Indian Ocean tsunami.

Geography for Life Activity

1. **Summarize** What steps are being taken to avoid another disaster such as the Indian Ocean tsunami in 2004?
2. **Make Inferences** About 75 percent of tsunami warnings since 1948 were false alarms. What might be the risks and benefits of early warnings to move people out of harm's way?

Mainland Southeast Asia

The Big Idea

People, ideas, and traditions from China, India, Europe, and elsewhere have shaped Southeast Asia's history and culture. Today, many farming areas of Mainland Southeast Asia are poor but working to improve their economies.

Main Ideas

- Southeast Asia's early history includes empires, colonial rule, and independence.
- The modern history of Southeast Asia involves struggles with war and communism.
- Southeast Asia's culture reflects its Chinese, Indian, and European heritage.
- The area today is largely rural and agricultural, but cities are growing rapidly.
- Myanmar is poor with a harsh military government, while Thailand is a democracy with a strong economy.
- The countries of Indochina are poor and struggling to rebuild after years of war.

Key Terms and Places

Timor
domino theory
wats
Yangon
human rights
Bangkok
klongs
Phnom Penh
Hanoi

If YOU lived there . . .

You live in Vietnam, where your family works on a collective state-run farm. On the side, your family also sells vegetables. Now your older brother wants to start his own business—a bicycle repair shop. The Communist government allows this, but your parents think it is safer for him to keep working on the farm.

What do you think your brother should do?

Early History

Southeast Asia lies south of China and east of India, and both countries have played a strong role in the region's history. Over time, many people from China and India settled in Southeast Asia. As settlements grew, trade developed with China and India.

Early Civilization Recent scientific research suggests that humans lived in the rain forests of Southeast Asia as much as 11,000 years ago, clearing land and cultivating plants for food. The region's most advanced early civilization was the Khmer (kuh-MER). From the AD 800s to the mid-1200s, the Khmer controlled a large empire in what is now Cambodia. The remains of Angkor Wat, a huge temple complex the Khmer built in the 1100s, reflect their advanced civilization and Hindu religion.

In the 1200s the Thai (TY) from southern China settled in the Khmer area. Around the same time, Buddhism, introduced earlier from India and Sri Lanka, began replacing Hinduism in the region.

Colonial Rule and Independence As in many parts of the world, European powers started colonizing Southeast Asia during the 1500s. Led by Portugal, they came to the region in search of spices and other trade goods.

In 1521 explorer Ferdinand Magellan reached the Philippines and claimed the islands for Spain. The Spaniards who followed came to colonize, trade, and spread Roman Catholicism. This religion remains the main faith in the Philippines today.

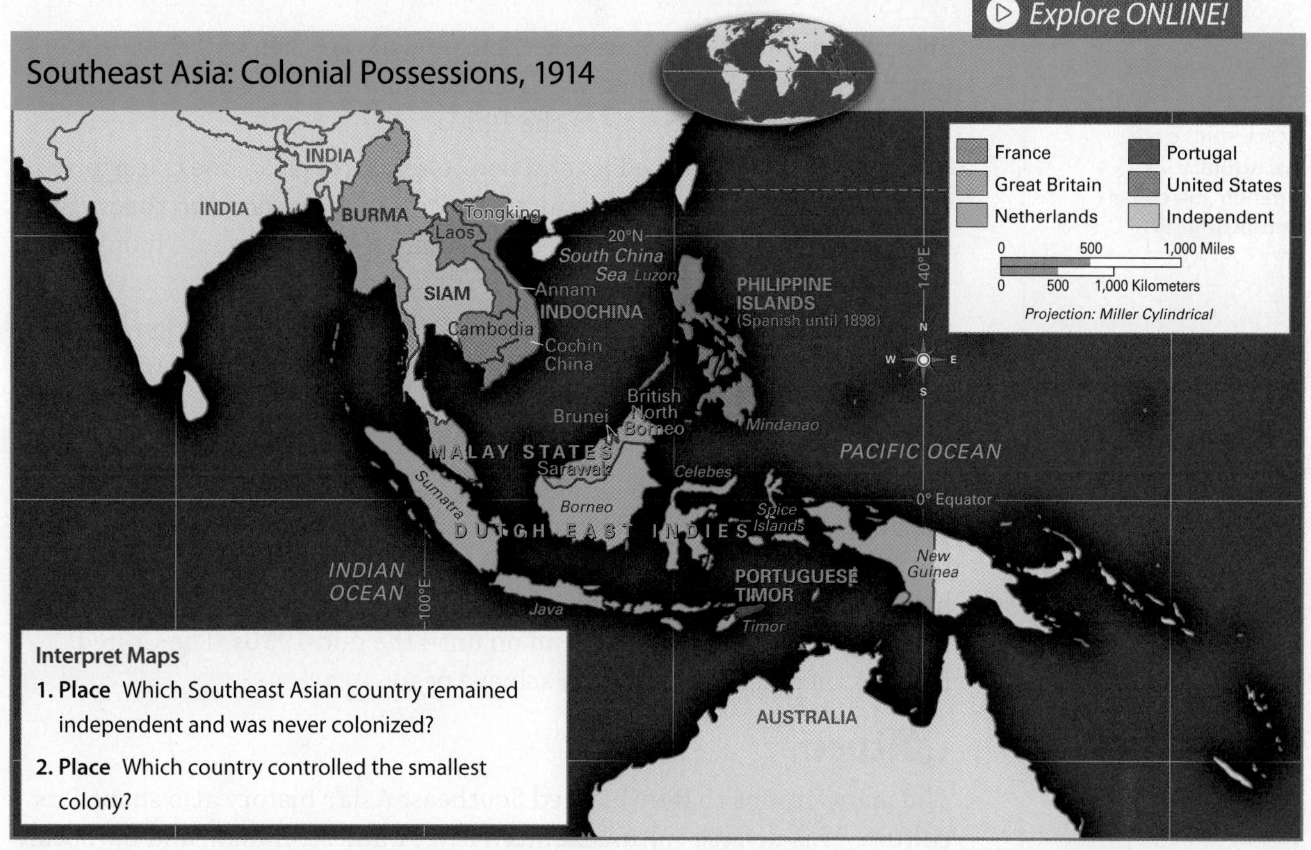

Southeast Asia: Colonial Possessions, 1914

Interpret Maps

1. **Place** Which Southeast Asian country remained independent and was never colonized?
2. **Place** Which country controlled the smallest colony?

In the 1600s and 1700s Dutch traders drove the Portuguese out of much of the region. Portugal kept only the small island of **Timor.** The Dutch gained control of the tea and spice trade on what became the Dutch East Indies, now Indonesia.

In the 1800s the British and French set up colonies with plantations, railroads, and mines. Many people from China and India came to work in the colonies. The British and French spread Christianity as well.

In 1898 the United States entered the region when it won the Philippines from Spain after the Spanish-American War. By the early 1900s, colonial powers ruled most of the region, as the map shows. Only Siam (sy-AM), now Thailand, was never colonized, although it lost land.

In World War II (1939–1945), Japan invaded and occupied most of Southeast Asia. After Japan lost the war, the United States gave the Philippines independence. Soon, other people in the region began to fight for their independence.

One of the bloodiest wars for independence was in French Indochina. In 1954 the French left. Indochina then split into the independent countries of Cambodia, Laos, and Vietnam. By 1970, most of Southeast Asia had thrown off colonial rule.

Reading Check
Identify Cause and Effect
What reasons led other countries to set up colonies across most of Southeast Asia?

Modern History

The move toward independence was not easy. In Vietnam, feelings of nationalism, or pride and loyalty to a country, led people to fight to oust the French who controlled them as a colony. They were led by a man named Ho Chi Minh, who was a Communist. The fighting left the country divided into North and South Vietnam. A civil war then broke out in the south. To defend South Vietnam from Communist forces in that war, the United States sent in troops in the 1960s.

Academic Vocabulary
criterion rule or standard for defining

The United States based its decision to send troops on one **criterion**—the potential spread of communism. According to the **domino theory,** if one country fell to communism, other countries nearby would follow like falling dominoes.

Years of war caused millions of deaths and terrible destruction. In the end, North and South Vietnam reunited as one Communist country. As the Communists took over, about 1 million refugees fled South Vietnam. Many went to the United States.

Civil wars also raged in Cambodia and Laos. In 1975 Communist forces took over both countries. The government in Cambodia was brutal, causing the deaths of more than 1 million people there. Then in 1978 Vietnam helped to overthrow Cambodia's government. This event sparked further fighting, which continued off and on until the mid-1990s. The United Nations then helped Cambodia achieve peace.

Reading Check
Summarize What are some key events in the region's modern history?

Culture

The many groups that influenced Southeast Asia's history also shaped its culture. This diverse culture blends native, Chinese, Indian, and European ways of life.

People and Languages The countries in Southeast Asia have many ethnic groups. As an example, Indonesia has more than 300 ethnic groups. Most of the countries have one main ethnic group plus many smaller ethnic groups.

Not surprisingly, many languages are spoken in Southeast Asia. These languages include native languages and dialects as well as Chinese and European languages.

Focus on Culture

Thai Teenage Buddhist Monks

Would you be willing to serve as a monk for a few months? In a tradition that goes back many centuries in Thailand, many Buddhist boys and young men serve as monks for a short period. This period might last from one week to a few months. These temporary monks follow the lifestyle of actual Buddhist monks, shaving their heads, wearing robes, and maintaining a life of simplicity. During their stay, the teenage monks learn about Buddhism and practice meditation. Some Thai teens decide to become Buddhist monks permanently. This decision is considered a great honor for their families.

Summarize
What are some of the things that Thai boys and young men do while serving as Buddhist monks?

Religions The main religions in Southeast Asia are Buddhism, Christianity, Hinduism, and Islam. Buddhism is the main faith on the mainland. This area features many beautiful **wats,** Buddhist temples that also serve as monasteries.

Islam is the main religion in Malaysia, Brunei, and Indonesia. In fact, Indonesia has more Muslims than any other country. In the Philippines, most people are Roman Catholic. Hinduism is practiced in Indian communities and on the island of Bali.

Reading Check
Generalize How has Southeast Asia's history influenced its culture?

Customs Customs differ widely across the region, but some similarities exist. For example, religion often shapes life, and people celebrate many religious festivals. Some people continue to practice traditional customs, such as dances and music. These customs are especially popular in rural areas. In addition, many people wear traditional clothing, such as sarongs, strips of cloth worn wrapped around the body.

Mainland Southeast Asia Today

Look at the map at the start of the module and identify the countries of Mainland Southeast Asia. These countries include Myanmar, Thailand, Cambodia, Laos, and Vietnam.

War, harsh governments, and other problems have slowed progress in most of Mainland Southeast Asia. However, the area's countries have rich resources and are working to improve their futures. For example, as of 2010 all the countries of Southeast Asia except Timor-Leste had joined the Association of Southeast Asian Nations (ASEAN). This organization promotes political, economic, and social cooperation throughout the region.

Rural Life Mainland Southeast Asia is largely rural. Most people are farmers who live in small villages and work long hours in the fields. Most farm work is done by hand or using traditional methods. Farmers grow rice, the region's main crop, on fertile slopes along rivers and on terraced shelves of land. The wet, tropical climate enables farmers to grow two or three crops each year.

BIOGRAPHY

Aung San Suu Kyi (1945–)

Starting in the 1980s, Aung San Suu Kyi effectively opposed Myanmar's harsh military government. Her party, the National League for Democracy (NLD), won control of the country's parliament in 1990. The military regime, which refused to give up power, placed Aung San Suu Kyi and other NLD members under house arrest. For her efforts to bring democracy to Myanmar, Suu Kyi received the Nobel Peace Prize in 1991. She continued fighting for democratic reforms until finally, in 2016, free elections were held. In addition, the United States and some Asian countries pressed Myanmar's government to change.

In recent years, Aung San Suu Kyi has faced harsh criticism. In 2016 she became State Counselor of Myanmar. Many people believe that Suu Kyi should be doing more to protect the rights of the country's Rohingya Muslims. This ethnic minority group has been persecuted and displaced by Myanmar's military.

Identify Points of View
What did Aung San Suu Kyi hope to achieve through her efforts in Myanmar?

Most rural people live in the area's fertile river valleys and deltas, which have the best farmland. A delta is an area of fertile land around the mouth of a river. A few people live in remote villages in the rugged, forested mountains. These areas have poor soils that make farming difficult. Many of the people who live there belong to small ethnic groups known as hill peoples.

Urban Life Although most people live in rural areas, Mainland Southeast Asia has several large cities. Most are growing rapidly as people move to them for work. Rapid growth has led to crowding and pollution. People, bicycles, scooters, cars, and buses clog city streets. Smog hangs in the still air. Growing cities also mix the old and new. Skyscrapers tower over huts, and cars zip past pedicabs, taxicabs that are pedaled like bikes.

Reading Check **Find Main Ideas** Where do most people in Mainland Southeast Asia live?

Myanmar and Thailand

Myanmar and Thailand form the northwestern part of Mainland Southeast Asia. While Myanmar is poor, Thailand boasts the area's strongest economy.

Myanmar Myanmar lies south of China on the Bay of Bengal. Also known as Burma, the country gained independence from Great Britain in 1948. The largest city is **Yangon,** or Rangoon, and the capital is Naypyidaw.

Most of the people in Myanmar are Burmese. Many live in small farming villages in houses built on stilts. Buddhism is the main religion, and village life often centers around a local Buddhist monastery.

Life is difficult in Myanmar because, for half a century and up until recently, a harsh military government ruled the country. The government abused **human rights,** rights that all people deserve such as rights to equality and justice. A Burmese woman, Aung San Suu Kyi (awng sahn soo chee), led a movement for more democracy and rights. She and others were jailed and harassed for their actions.

Myanmar's poor human rights record isolated the country and hurt its economy. With democratic reforms, Myanmar has normalized trade with some countries. Despite rich natural resources—such as oil, timber, metals, jade, and gems—Myanmar and most of its people remain poor.

Thailand To the southeast of Myanmar is Thailand, once known as Siam. The capital and largest city is **Bangkok.** Modern and crowded, it lies near the mouth of the Chao Phraya (chow PRY-uh) River. Bangkok is known for its many spectacular palaces and Buddhist wats. The city is also famous for its **klongs,** or canals. Klongs are used for transportation and trade and to drain floodwater.

Thailand is a constitutional monarchy. A monarch, or king, serves as a ceremonial head of state. A prime minister and elected legislature hold the real power, however.

A democratically elected government and rich resources have helped Thailand's economy to grow. Industry, farming, fishing, mining, and tourism fuel this growth. Farms produce rice, pineapples, and rubber. Factories produce computers, textiles, and electronics. Magnificent Buddhist wats and unspoiled beaches draw tourists.

Reading Check **Compare and Contrast** What are some similarities and differences between Myanmar and Thailand?

A Bangkok Canal

Sick of crowded roads? In Bangkok, you can use a network of canals, called klongs, to travel through parts of the city. Water taxis and boats transport people and goods. At floating markets, vendors sell fish, fruit, and other foods to locals and tourists.

Analyze Visuals
What advantages do you think klongs provide to both travelers and people selling goods?

The Countries of Indochina

The former countries of French Indochina lie to the east and south of Thailand. They are struggling to overcome decades of war.

Cambodia Cambodia lies to the northeast of the Gulf of Thailand. **Phnom Penh** (puh-NAWM pen) is the capital and chief city. Located in the Mekong River valley, it is a center of trade.

Some 20 years of war, terror, and devastation in Cambodia finally ended in the early 1990s. Today, the country has a stable, elected government similar to Thailand's. Years of conflict left their mark, however. Although farming has improved, the country has little industry. In addition, many land mines remain hidden in the land.

Laos Laos is landlocked with rugged mountains. Poor and undeveloped, it has few roads, no railroads, and limited electricity.

The Communist government of Laos has been increasing economic freedom in hopes of improving the economy. Even so, Laos remains the area's poorest country.

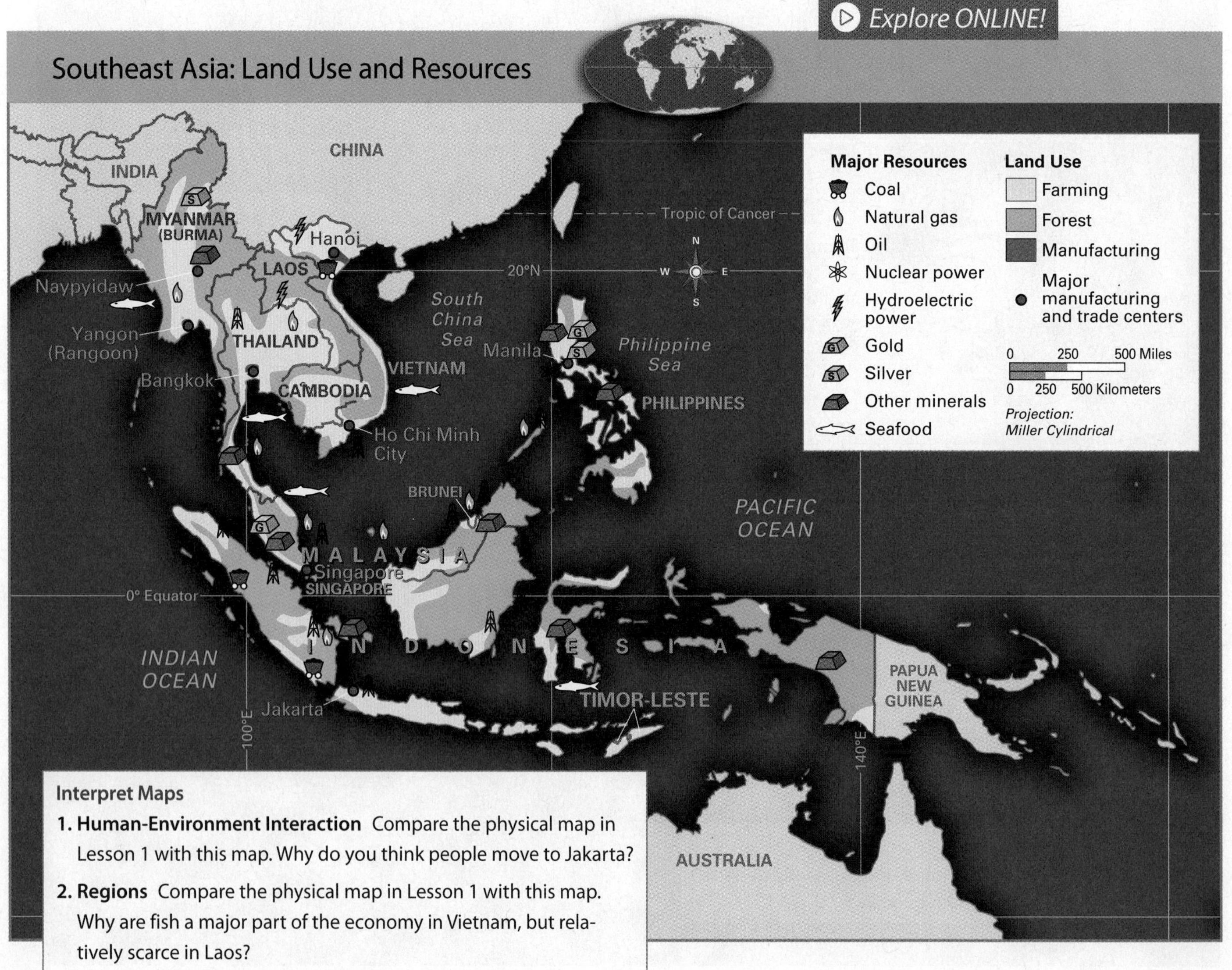

Interpret Maps

1. **Human-Environment Interaction** Compare the physical map in Lesson 1 with this map. Why do you think people move to Jakarta?
2. **Regions** Compare the physical map in Lesson 1 with this map. Why are fish a major part of the economy in Vietnam, but relatively scarce in Laos?

A woman uses traditional methods to carry sea salt across the salt pans in Doc Let Beach in Vietnam.

The economy is based on farming, but good farmland is limited. Most people are subsistence farmers, meaning they grow just enough food for their families.

Vietnam Like Laos, Vietnam is rugged and mountainous. The capital, **Hanoi,** is located in the north in the Hong (Red) River delta. The largest city, Ho Chi Minh City, is in the south in the Mekong delta.

Vietnam's Communist government has been allowing more economic freedom and private business. The changes have helped the economy grow. Most people still farm, but industry and services are expanding. Fishing and mining are also important.

Reading Check
Evaluate How would you rate the economies of these three countries?

Summary and Preview The mainland countries are rural and agricultural with fast-growing cities. Most of the countries are poor despite rich resources. Next, you will read about Island Southeast Asia.

Lesson 2 Assessment

Review Ideas, Terms, and Places

1. a. **Describe** What was the significance of the Khmer Empire?
   b. **Identify Cause and Effect** What was the result of the war for independence in French Indochina?
   c. **Elaborate** How did European colonization shape Southeast Asia's history?
2. a. **Define** What was the domino theory?
   b. **Summarize** What role has communism played in Southeast Asia's modern history?
3. a. **Define** What is a wat?
   b. **Contrast** How does religion in the mainland and island countries differ?
   c. **Elaborate** How has the history of Southeast Asia shaped the region's culture?
4. a. **Recall** In what areas do most people in Mainland Southeast Asia live?
   b. **Identify Cause and Effect** How has rapid growth affected the area's cities?
5. a. **Define** What are klongs, and in what ways are they used?
   b. **Predict** How might Myanmar's economy change if the country's new government respected human rights? Explain your answer.
6. a. **Identify** Use the "Southeast Asia: Land Use and Resources" map and key to make a list of the region's renewable and nonrenewable resources. Then, locate those resources on the map.
   b. **Summarize** What issues and challenges face Cambodia, Laos, and Vietnam?
   c. **Draw Conclusions** Compare the climate map in Lesson 1 with the land use map in Lesson 2. Under which type of climate does the land seem to be used mostly for farming?

Critical Thinking

7. **Categorize** Draw a chart like the one shown. Use your notes to provide information for each category in the chart.

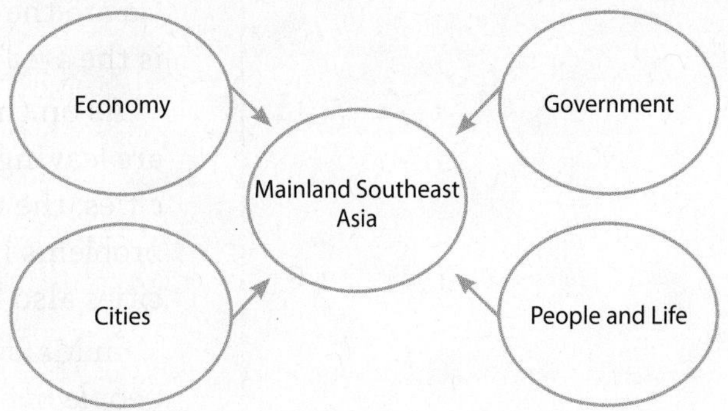

Island Southeast Asia Today

The Big Idea

The countries of Island Southeast Asia range from wealthy and urban to poor and rural.

Main Ideas

- The area today has rich resources and growing cities but faces challenges.
- Malaysia and its neighbors have strong economies but differ in many ways.
- Indonesia and the Philippines are diverse with growing economies, and East Timor is small and poor.

Key Terms and Places

Timor-Leste
kampong
Jakarta
Kuala Lumpur
free ports
sultan
Java
Manila

If YOU lived there . . .

You live in Canada but are visiting your cousins in Singapore. You start to cross the street in the middle of a block, but your cousin quickly stops you. "You have to pay a big fine if you do that!" he says. Singapore has many strict laws and strong punishments, he explains. These laws are meant to make the city safe.

What do you think about Singapore's laws?

The Area Today

Island Southeast Asia lies at a crossroads between major oceans and continents. The area's six countries are Malaysia, Singapore, Brunei (brooh-NY), Indonesia, **Timor-Leste,** and the Philippines.

The future for these countries could be bright. They have the potential for wealth and good standards of living, such as rich resources and a large, skilled labor force. The region's economies are growing, and all but Timor-Leste belong to ASEAN. This organization promotes cooperation in Southeast Asia.

Island Southeast Asia faces challenges, however. First, violent ethnic conflicts have hurt progress in some countries. Second, many people live in poverty, while a few leaders and businesspeople control much of the money. Third, the area has many environmental problems, such as pollution.

Many people in Island Southeast Asia live in rural areas, where they farm or fish. As on the mainland, rice is the main crop. Others include coffee, spices, sugarcane, tea, and tropical fruit. Rubber is a major crop as well, and Indonesia and Malaysia are the world's largest producers of natural rubber. Seafood is the area's main source of protein.

As on the mainland, many people in Island Southeast Asia are leaving rural villages to move to cities for work. The largest cities, the major capitals, are modern and crowded. Common problems in these cities include smog and heavy traffic. Some cities also have large slums.

In Malaysia, Indonesia, and other parts of the area, many people live in kampongs. A **kampong** is a village or city district

Reading Check
Summarize
Why could the future be bright for Island Southeast Asia?

with traditional houses built on stilts. The stilts protect the houses from flooding, which is common in the area. The term *kampong* also refers to the slums around the area's cities such as **Jakarta,** Indonesia's capital.

Malaysia and Its Neighbors

Malaysia and its much smaller neighbors, Singapore and Brunei, were all once British colonies. Today, all three countries are independent and differ in many ways.

Malaysia Malaysia consists of two parts. One is on the southern end of the Malay Peninsula. The other is on northern Borneo. Most of the country's people live on the peninsula. **Kuala Lumpur** (KWAH-luh LOOHM-poohr), Malaysia's capital, is there as well. The capital is a cultural and economic center.

Malaysia is ethnically diverse. The Malays are the main ethnic group, but many Chinese and other groups live in Malaysia as well. As a result, the country has many languages and religions. Bahasa Malay is the main language, and Islam and Buddhism are the main religions.

Malaysia is a constitutional monarchy. The king's duties are largely ceremonial, and local rulers take turns being king. A prime minister and elected legislature hold the real power.

Malaysia's economy is one of the stronger ones in the area. Well-educated workers and rich resources help drive this economy. The country produces and exports natural rubber, palm oil, electronics, oil, and timber.

Singapore A populous country, Singapore is squeezed onto a tiny island at the tip of the Malay Peninsula. The island lies on a major shipping route. This location has helped make Singapore a rich country.

Rubber Tree Plantations

Southeast Asia's tropical climate is well suited to rubber trees. At left, a man taps, or cuts, a rubber tree at a Malaysia plantation. A milky liquid drains from the cut into a cup, as shown above. The liquid dries to form a rubbery material.

Analyze Visuals
What do you think it is like to work on a rubber tree plantation?

Today, Singapore is one of the world's busiest **free ports,** ports that place few if any taxes on goods. It is also an industrial center, and many foreign banks and high-tech firms have located offices there.

Singapore sparkles as the gem of Southeast Asia. The country is modern, wealthy, orderly, and clean. Crime rates are low.

How has Singapore achieved such success? The government has worked hard to clean up slums and improve housing. In addition, laws are extremely strict. To provide **concrete** examples, fines for littering are stiff, and people caught with illegal drugs can be executed. Moreover, the government strictly controls politics and the media. Certain movies are banned, as are satellite dishes. Recently, however, Singapore has loosened up some restrictions.

Academic Vocabulary
concrete specific, real

Brunei The tiny country of Brunei is on the island of Borneo, which it shares with Malaysia and Indonesia. A **sultan,** the supreme ruler of a Muslim country, governs Brunei.

The country has grown wealthy from large oil and gas deposits. Because of this wealth, Brunei's citizens do not pay income tax and receive free health care and other benefits. Brunei's oil will run out around 2020, however. As a result, the government is developing other areas of the economy.

Reading Check
Contrast
How do Malaysia, Singapore, and Brunei differ?

DOCUMENT-BASED INVESTIGATION

Interview: Lee Kuan Yew on Singapore

Lee Kuan Yew was Singapore's prime minister from 1959 to 1990. He remade the tiny country into an economic power. In a 1994 interview, Lee discussed Singapore's strict laws.

"The expansion of the right of the individual to behave or misbehave as he pleases has come at the expense of orderly society. In the East the main object is to have a well-ordered society so that everybody can have maximum enjoyment of his freedoms. This freedom can exist only in an ordered state."

—from "A Conversation with Lee Kuan Yew"

Analyze Sources
Do you agree with Lee that freedom for all can exist only in a society with strict order? Why or why not?

Rice Farming

Terraced rice paddies, such as these in Quezon in the Philippines, are common throughout Southeast Asia.

Indonesia, Timor-Leste, and the Philippines

Indonesia is the largest of the island countries. Timor-Leste is one of the area's smallest countries. The Philippines includes many islands.

Indonesia Indonesia has several claims to fame. It is the world's largest archipelago, with some 13,500 islands. It has the fourth-largest population of any country, as well as the largest Muslim population. Indonesia is extremely diverse as well, as you have read. It has more than 300 ethnic groups who speak more than 250 languages.

Indonesia's main island is **Java.** The capital, Jakarta, is there, as are more than half of Indonesia's people. For this reason, Java is extremely crowded. To reduce the crowding, the government has been moving people to less-populated islands. Many people on those islands dislike that policy.

Indonesia's rich resources have helped its economy to grow. The main resources include rubber, oil and gas, and timber. The country also has good farmland for rice and other crops. Factories turn out clothing and electronics. Islands such as Bali draw thousands of tourists each year.

At the same time, problems have hurt Indonesia's economy. Many of the people are poor, and unemployment is high. In some areas, ethnic and religious conflicts have led to fighting and terrorism.

Timor-Leste Timor-Leste is located on the small island of Timor. In 1999 Timor-Leste declared independence from Indonesia. The island then plunged into violence. Timor-Leste only gained its independence after the United Nations sent in troops to restore peace. Years of fighting have left Timor-Leste one of the region's poorest countries. Most people farm, and coffee is the main export.

The Philippines The Philippines includes more than 7,000 islands. The largest and most populated is Luzon, which includes the capital, **Manila.** These islands are home to ten major ethnic groups and large communities of foreigners, making the Philippines one of the most diverse countries in the region.

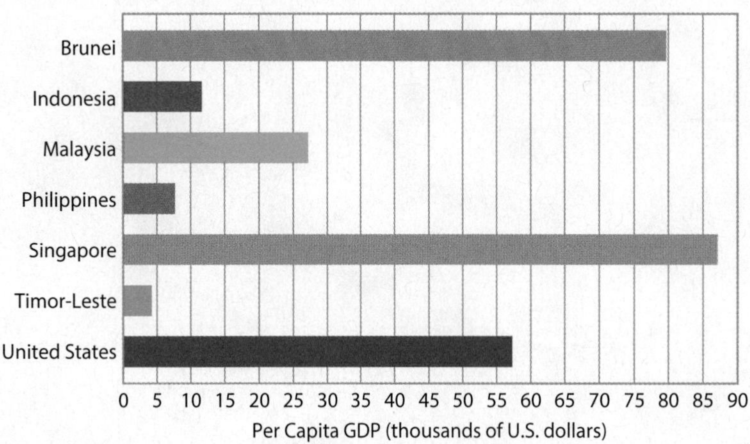

Interpret Graphs
Compare the per capita GDP of Brunei and Timor-Leste. What does it imply about the way the people from these two different countries live?

The Philippines has many resources to fuel economic growth. Natural resources include copper and other metals, oil, and tropical wood. Farmers grow coconuts, sugarcane, rice, and corn. Factories produce and export clothing and electronics.

The Philippine economy has recently improved, but a wide gap exists between the rich and the poor. A few Filipinos are wealthy. Most, however, are poor farmers who do not own the land they work.

Reading Check
Summarize What kinds of challenges do the Filipinos face?

The Philippines has experienced religious conflict as well. Although the country is mainly Roman Catholic, some areas are largely Muslim and want independence.

Summary You have read that Island Southeast Asia has many contrasts. While some countries are wealthy, others are poor. While some countries are modern and urban, others are more traditional and rural.

Lesson 3 Assessment

Review Ideas, Terms, and Places

1. **a. Identify** What problems does the area face?
   b. Compare How does urban life compare between the island and mainland countries?
2. **a. Define** What is a sultan?
   b. Explain How have Singapore and Brunei become rich countries?
3. **a. Recall** What island is Jakarta located on?
   b. Sequence What series of events led to Timor-Leste's independence?
   c. Identify What are the capital city and the main island in the Philippines?
   d. Analyze Why is the Philippines' economic improvement not benefiting many of its people?

Critical Thinking

4. **Categorize** Draw a chart like the one shown. Use your notes to provide information for each category in the chart.

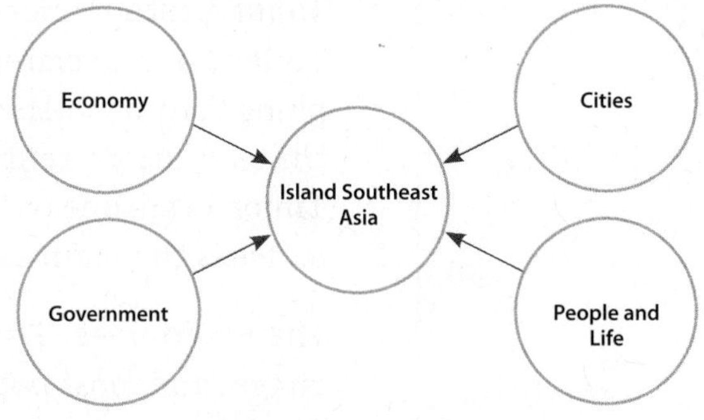

Interpret Visuals

Define the Skill

Geographers get information from many sources. These sources include text and data. They also include visuals, such as photographs, diagrams, charts, timelines, maps, and graphs. Use these tips to interpret information from visuals.

- **Identify the subject.** Read the title and caption, if available. If not, look at the content of the image. What does it show? Where is it located?
- **Analyze the content.** What is the purpose of the image? What information is in the image? What conclusions can you draw from this information? Write your conclusions in your notes.
- **Summarize your analysis.** Write a summary of the information in the visual and of the conclusions you can draw from it.

Learn the Skill

Analyze the photograph. Then answer the following questions.

1. What is the title of the photograph?
2. Where is this scene, and what is happening?
3. What conclusions can you draw from the information in the photograph?

Practice the Skill

Work with a partner to analyze the images of the rubber tree plantation in Lesson 3. Then answer the following questions.

1. What is the purpose of the two photos?
2. What do the photos show about rubber tree farming?
3. Based on the information in the images, write a summary of the steps involved in collecting rubber from trees. Then, with your partner, take turns retelling how a worker collects rubber from trees.

City Life in Southeast Asia

Southeast Asia's cities are growing rapidly. In Hanoi, Vietnam, vehicles and people crowd the streets.

The title tells you that the photo's purpose is to show life in the region's cities.

The photo shows forms of travel, numbers of people, and air quality in Hanoi.

Module 19 Assessment

Review Vocabulary, Terms, and Places

For each group of terms below, write a sentence that shows how all the terms in the group are related.

1. archipelagos
   Indonesia
   Philippines
2. Aung San Suu Kyi
   human rights
   Myanmar
3. Bangkok
   klongs
4. Indochina
   domino theory
5. Jakarta
   kampongs
6. Singapore
   free port
7. Brunei
   sultan

Comprehension and Critical Thinking

Lesson 1

8. a. **Identify** What are the two peninsulas and the two archipelagos that make up the region of Southeast Asia?

   b. **Compare and Contrast** In what ways are the main climate of Mainland Southeast Asia and of Island Southeast Asia similar and different?

   c. **Categorize** What different needs should people weigh when considering how best to protect the region's tropical rain forests?

Lesson 2

9. a. **Recall** What theory led the U.S. military to become involved in Southeast Asia?

   b. **Identify Cause and Effect** Why are so many languages spoken in Southeast Asia?

   c. **Predict** How do you think Southeast Asia might be different today if Europeans had never explored and colonized the area?

   d. **Describe** Where do most people live and work in Mainland Southeast Asia?

   e. **Summarize** What factors have slowed economic progress in Mainland Southeast Asia?

   f. **Evaluate** What actions might Myanmar take to try to improve its economy?

   g. **Analyze Causes** Compare the climate map in Lesson 1 with the land use map in Lesson 2. Why do you suppose more people live on the southern end of the Malay Peninsula rather than in northern Borneo?

Lesson 3

10. a. **Identify** Which two countries in Island Southeast Asia have wealthy economies?

    b. **Compare** What are some ways in which Indonesia and the Philippines are similar?

    c. **Elaborate** How has ethnic diversity affected the countries of Island Southeast Asia?

Module 19 Assessment, continued

Reading Skills

Use Context Clues—Definitions *Use the Reading Skills taught in this module to answer a question about the reading selection below.*

> The humid tropical climate's heat and heavy rainfall support tropical rain forests. These lush forests are home to a huge number of different plants and animals. About 40,000 kinds of flowering plants grow in Indonesia alone. These plants include the rafflesia, the world's largest flower. Measuring up to 3 feet (1 m) across, this flower produces a horrible, rotting stink.

11. What is a rafflesia?

Social Studies Skills

Interpret Visuals *Use the Social Studies Skills taught in this module to answer the questions about the photograph referred to below.*

12. Analyze the photograph of A Bangkok Canal in Lesson 2. What can you learn from the title and captions? What activities are taking place? What conclusions can you draw about the use of canals in Bangkok?

13. Select two different types of visuals from your textbook. For example, you might select a photograph, chart, timeline, map, or graph. Analyze the subject, purpose, and content of each visual. Then organize information from the visuals into a written summary.

Map Activity

14. **Southeast Asia** On a separate sheet of paper, match the letters on the map with their correct labels below.

Bangkok, Thailand	Jakarta, Indonesia
Borneo	Malay Peninsula
Hanoi, Vietnam	Manila, Philippines
Indochina Peninsula	Singapore

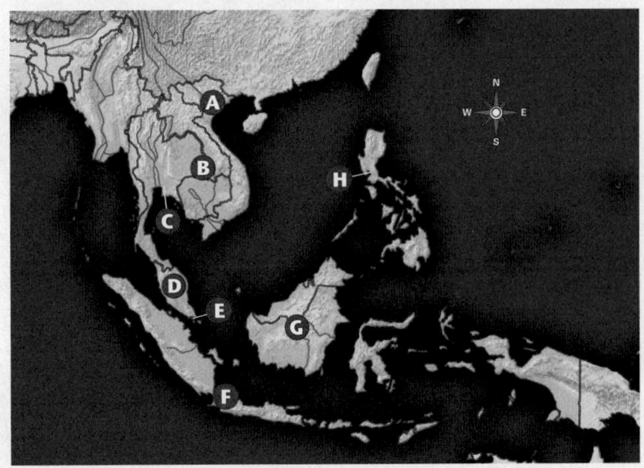

Focus on Reading and Speaking

Use Context Clues—Definitions *Add a phrase or sentence to provide a definition for the underlined word.*

15. In Thailand, many young men serve for short periods in Buddhist <u>monasteries</u>.

16. Much of the <u>cultivated</u> land in Southeast Asia is used to grow rice.

Present an Interview

17. Work with a partner to create a skit in which one of you plays the role of a reporter and the other plays an expert on Southeast Asia. Use the library and print and digital sources, including the Internet, to research good questions and answers for the interview. Choose your five best questions. Try to include questions of varying difficulty. Decide who will play the reporter and who will play the expert. Practice listening to and responding to questions until the interview sounds natural. Then present it to your class.

Module 20

Oceania and Antarctica

Essential Question

Has isolation proven to be helpful or harmful to the region of Oceania and Antarctica?

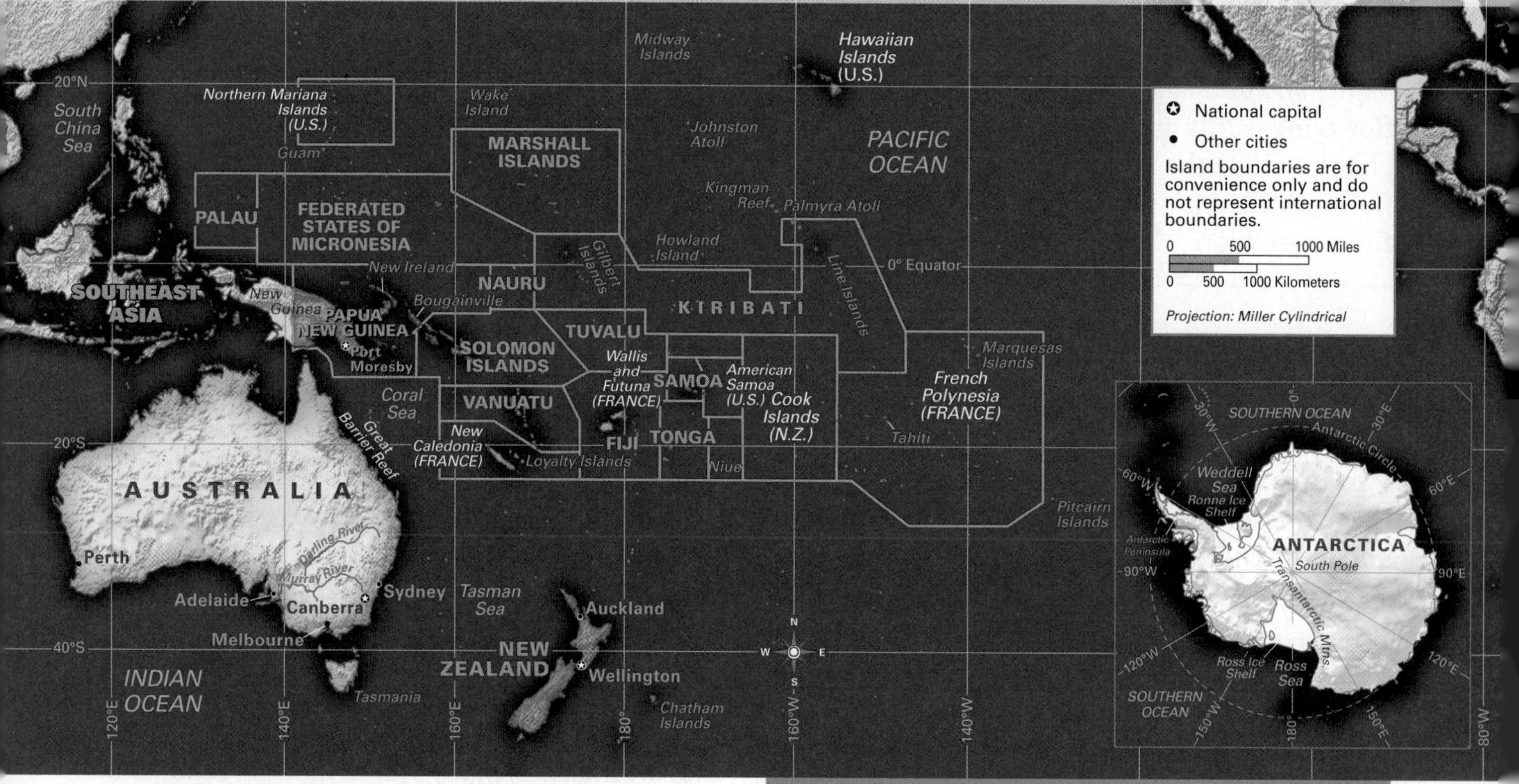

National capital
Other cities
Island boundaries are for convenience only and do not represent international boundaries.
0 500 1000 Miles
0 500 1000 Kilometers
Projection: Miller Cylindrical

In this module, you will learn about the geography and history of Oceania and Antarctica. You will also learn how parts of this region have been shaped by a mixture of native cultures and Western influence.

Explore ONLINE!

VIDEOS, including . . .
- Giants of Easter Island: Settling the Pacific Islands
- *Moai* Stone Heads of Easter Island

- Document-Based Investigations
- Graphic Organizers
- Interactive Games
- Channel One News Video: Great Barrier Reef, Part 1: A Reef in Danger
- Image with Hotspots: Maori Culture
- Process Steps: The Formation of an Atoll
- Channel One News Video: Penguins and Climate Change
- Geographic Feature: Antarctica's Ice Shelves

What You Will Learn

Lesson 1: Australia and New Zealand 615
The Big Idea Australia and New Zealand share a similar history and culture but have unique natural environments.

Lesson 2: The Pacific Islands 622
The Big Idea The Pacific Islands have tropical climates, rich cultures, and unique challenges.

Lesson 3: Antarctica 628
The Big Idea Antarctica's unique environment has made it an important site for research.

Geography From Uluru in the dry Australian Outback to freezing Antarctica, the Pacific realm is a land of great geographic variety.

History The famous *moai* statues on Easter Island reflect the rich history of Oceania.

Culture Sydney's Opera House is one example of the vibrant culture that exists throughout Oceania.

Reading Social Studies

Determine Author's Purpose

READING FOCUS

An author's purpose is the writer's main reason for writing a text. When you read, look for clues that reveal the possible purposes an author might have for writing. For example, is it to inform, entertain, express thoughts or feelings, or persuade? Notice how the paragraph below contains many facts. It starts with a broad view, then, supplies more detailed information. The verbs, nouns, and adjectives are factual and neutral in tone. The author's purpose is to inform.

European explorers first sighted Australia and New Zealand in the 1600s. It wasn't until later, however, that Europeans began to explore the region. In 1769 British explorer James Cook explored the main islands of New Zealand. The following year, Cook landed on the east coast of Australia and claimed the land for Britain.

Word Clues	Tone
European explorers first **sighted Australia** and **New Zealand** in the **1600s.**	neutral, factual
In **1769 British explorer James Cook explored** the **main islands** of **New Zealand.**	neutral, factual
The **following year, Cook landed** on the **east coast** of **Australia** and **claimed** the **land for Britain.**	neutral, factual

YOU TRY IT!

Read the following paragraph. Then, use a graphic organizer like the one on this page to list verbs, nouns, or adjectives that reveal the author's purpose.

The climates of Australia and New Zealand differ greatly. Because much of Australia has desert and steppe climates, temperatures are warm and rainfall is limited. However, along the coasts the climate is more temperate. Unlike Australia, New Zealand is mild and wet. A marine climate brings plentiful rainfall and mild temperatures to much of the country.

As you read this module, look for words that tell about the author's purpose.

Australia and New Zealand

The Big Idea

Australia and New Zealand share a similar history and culture but have unique natural environments.

Main Ideas

- The physical geography of Australia and New Zealand is diverse and unusual.
- Native peoples and British settlers shaped the history of Australia and New Zealand.
- Australia and New Zealand today are wealthy and culturally diverse countries.

Key Terms and Places

Great Barrier Reef
coral reef
Aborigines
Maori
Outback

If YOU lived there . . .

You have just taken a summer job working at a sheep station, or ranch, in Australia's Outback. You knew the Outback would be hot, but you did not realize how hot it could get! During the day, temperatures climb to over 100°F (40°C), and it hardly ever rains. In addition, you have learned that there are no towns nearby. Your only communication with home is by radio.

How will you adapt to living in the Outback?

Physical Geography

Australia and New Zealand are quite unlike most places on Earth. The physical features, variety of climates, unusual wildlife, and plentiful resources make the region truly unique.

Physical Features The physical features of the region differ widely. Australia is home to wide, flat stretches of dry land. On the other hand, New Zealand features beautiful green hills and tall mountains.

Australia Similar to an island, Australia is surrounded by water. However, due to its immense size—almost 3 million square miles (7.8 million square km)—geographers consider Australia a continent.

A huge plateau covers the western half of Australia. Mostly flat and dry, this plateau is home to Uluru, a rock formation also known as Ayers Rock. Uluru is one of Australia's best-known landforms. Low mountains, valleys, and a major river system cover much of eastern Australia. Fertile plains lie along the coasts. Most Australians live in this area because of the more favorable environment. Off Australia's northeastern coast is the **Great Barrier Reef,** the world's largest coral reef. A **coral reef** is a collection of rocky material found in shallow, tropical waters. The Great Barrier Reef is home to an incredible variety of marine animals.

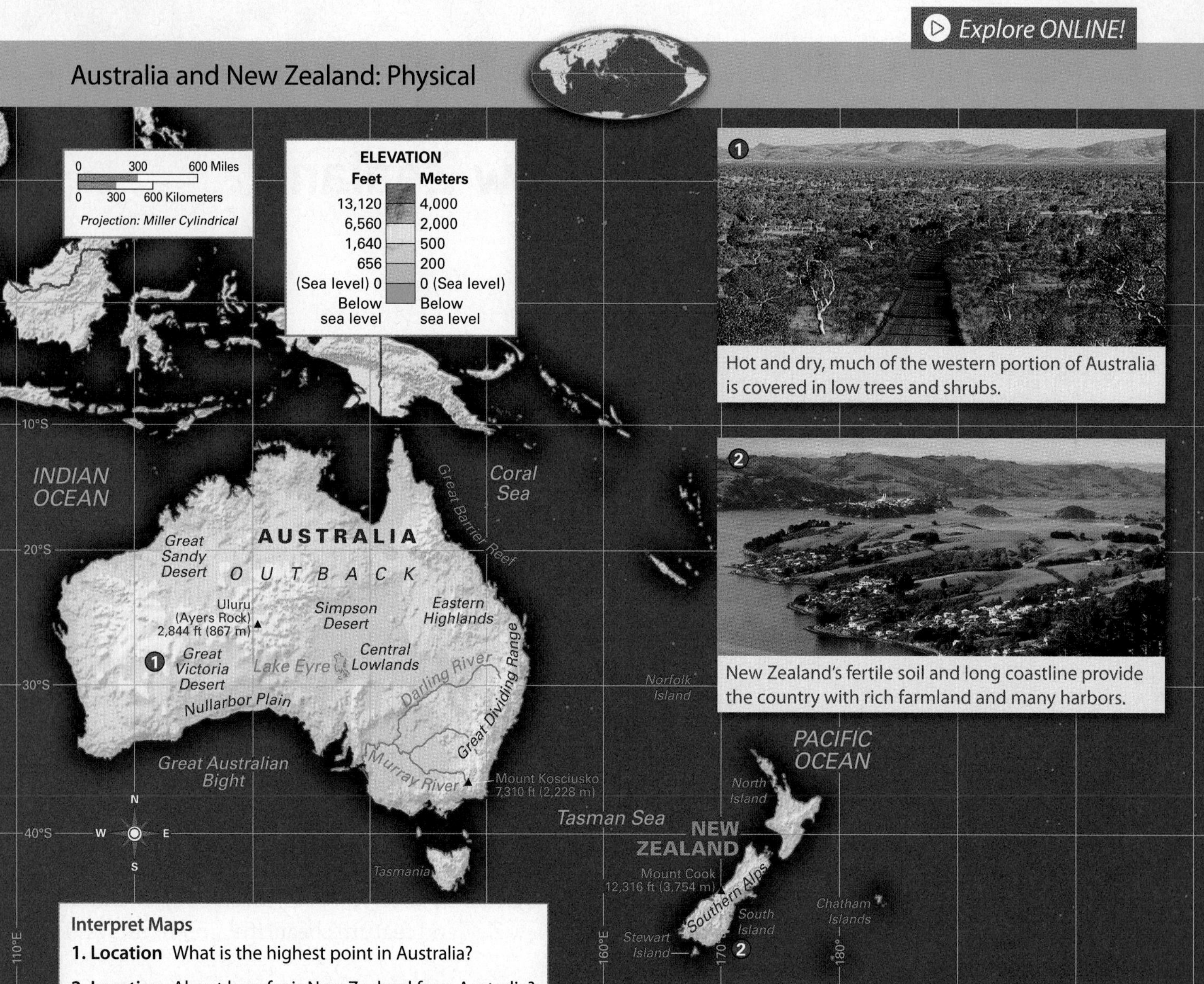

1 Hot and dry, much of the western portion of Australia is covered in low trees and shrubs.

2 New Zealand's fertile soil and long coastline provide the country with rich farmland and many harbors.

New Zealand New Zealand, located about 1,200 miles (1,931 km) southeast of Australia, includes two main islands, North Island and South Island. North Island is covered by hills and coastal plains. It is also home to volcanoes, geysers, and hot springs. One of the key features on South Island is a large mountain range called the Southern Alps. Thick forests, deep lakes, and even glaciers are found in the Southern Alps. The rest of the island is covered by fertile hills and rich plains. Fjords, or narrow inlets of the sea, create many natural harbors along the coasts of both islands.

Climates The climates of Australia and New Zealand differ greatly. Because much of Australia has desert and steppe climates, temperatures are warm and rainfall is limited. However, along the coasts the climate is more temperate. The majority of Australians live here because they have summers that are not too hot and winters that are not too cold. Unlike Australia, New Zealand is mild and wet. A marine climate brings plentiful rainfall and mild temperatures to much of the country.

Wildlife and Resources Both Australia and New Zealand are home to many unique animals. Some of the region's most famous native animals are Australia's kangaroo and koala and New Zealand's kiwi, a flightless bird.

Only 6 percent of Australia's land is arable. The desert environment is too hot and dry for agricultural activities. Despite poor soil across much of the continent, coastal farms and ranches are able to raise wheat, cotton, and sheep.

While the interior of Australia is barren and not ideal for farming, it is rich in resources. This has provided Australia with an opportunity for specialization. Australia is the world's top producer of bauxite and opals and is a leading producer of diamonds and lead. Australia is also home to energy resources like coal, natural gas, and oil. Mining is a valuable industry for the continent. People employed in the mining industry established "mining towns" close to resources. The export of natural resources has been a great contributor to economic growth.

Reading Check
Contrast How does the physical geography of the two countries differ?

Unlike Australia, New Zealand has a great deal of fertile land but few mineral resources. New Zealand's main resources are wool, timber, and gold.

History

Despite their many geographic differences, Australia and New Zealand have both been influenced by similar waves of human migration. Both countries were originally inhabited by settlers who migrated from other parts of the Pacific. Later, both Australia and New Zealand were colonized by the British.

Early Settlers The first settlers in Australia likely migrated there from Southeast Asia at least 40,000 years ago. These settlers, the **Aborigines** (a-buh-RIJ-uh-nees), were the first humans to live in Australia. Early Aborigines were nomads who gathered various plants and hunted animals with boomerangs and spears. Nature played an important role in the religion of the early Aborigines, who believed that it was their duty to preserve the land.

New Zealand's first settlers came from other Pacific islands more recently, about 1,200 years ago. The descendants of these early settlers, the **Maori** (MOWR-ee), settled throughout New Zealand. Like Australia's Aborigines, the Maori were fishers and hunters. Both groups developed distinct ways of life while utilizing the resources of their coastal settlements. Unlike the Aborigines, however, the Maori also used farming to survive.

The Arrival of Europeans European explorers first sighted Australia and New Zealand in the 1600s. It wasn't until later, however, that Europeans began to explore the region. In 1769 British explorer James Cook investigated the main islands of New Zealand. The following year, Cook landed on the east coast of Australia and claimed the land for Britain.

Within 20 years of Cook's claim, the British began settling in Australia. Many of the first to arrive were British prisoners, but other settlers came, too. The British spread the English language and Christianity during their settlement. They took over the Aborigines' lands to build farms and ranches. The use of firearms in their conquest proved to be a major advantage for the settlers. Many Aborigines also died of diseases introduced by the Europeans.

Australian Sports

Outdoor sports are tremendously popular in sunny Australia. Some of Australia's most popular activities include watersports, such as swimming, surfing, and water polo. In recent years, many Australians have dominated the swimming competitions at the summer Olympic Games.

Australia's national sport is cricket, a game played with a bat and ball. Cricket was first introduced to Australia by British settlers. Other popular sports with British roots are rugby and Australian rules football. These two sports allow players to kick, carry, or pass the ball with their hands or feet. Every year, hundreds of thousands of Australians attend professional rugby matches, like the one in the photo.

Draw Conclusions
Why do you think outdoor sports are so popular in Australia?

In New Zealand, large numbers of British settlers started to arrive in the early 1800s. After the British signed a treaty with the Maori in 1840, New Zealand became a part of the British Empire. However, tensions between the Maori and British settlers led to a series of wars over land.

Reading Check
Find Main Ideas
How did early settlers influence the region?

Australia and New Zealand both gained their independence in the early 1900s. Today, the two countries are members of the British Commonwealth of Nations and are close allies of the United Kingdom.

Australia and New Zealand Today

Despite their isolation from other nations, Australia and New Zealand today are rich and well developed. Their governments, economies, and people make them among the world's most successful countries.

Government As former British colonies, the British style of government has influenced both Australia and New Zealand. As a result, both countries have similar governments. For example, the British monarch is the head of state in both Australia and New Zealand. Both countries are parliamentary democracies, a type of government in which citizens elect members to represent them in a parliament. Each country has a prime minister. The prime minister, along with Parliament, runs the government.

The governments of Australia and New Zealand have many features in common with the U.S. government. For example, Australia has a federal system like that of the United States. In this system, a central government shares power with the states. Australia's Parliament, similar to the U.S. Congress, consists of two houses—a House of Representatives and a Senate. A Bill of Rights also protects the individual rights of New Zealand's citizens.

Economy Australia and New Zealand are both rich, economically developed countries. Agriculture is a major part of their economies. The two countries are among the world's top producers of wool. In fact, Australia regularly supplies about one-fourth of the wool used in clothing. Both countries also export meat and dairy products.

Australia and New Zealand also have other important industries. Mining is one of Australia's main industries. Companies mine bauxite, gold, and uranium throughout the **Outback,** Australia's interior. Other industries include steel, heavy machines, and computers. The Australian government has recognized that innovation is key to maintaining economic growth. The National Innovation and Science Agenda is one initiative that has helped support this transformation. For example, the agenda has provided entrepreneurs with funding to start new businesses. New Zealand has also become more industrialized in recent years. Factories turn out processed food, clothing, and paper products. Banking, insurance, and tourism are also important industries.

Australia is considered one of the most open economies in the world. It is a member of the World Trade Organization (WTO). The Australian government works with the WTO to reduce or eliminate tariffs and to allow more foreign products to be sold in Australia. Australia's low or lack of tariffs allows most foreign products to be freely imported and more foreign products to be sold. The Australian government helps Australian businesses compete by using quotas to limit the supply of these foreign products coming into Australia to be sold. This helps Australian businesses remain competitive by keeping prices for foreign products at the same level as those for Australian products.

Australia's location makes it particularly well situated for trading with its Asian neighbors to the north. For example, China is Australia's biggest export market. Australia supplies a good percentage of raw materials for manufacturing to China. Subsequently, nearly a fourth of Australia's manufactured imports come from China.

Even though Australia has many successful trade relationships, the challenge of trade barriers does exist. For political reasons, Australia has embargoes in place for some nations such as North Korea and Syria. In return, nations with certain interests in the embargoed countries have imposed similar restrictions on Australia.

People Today, Australia and New Zealand have diverse populations. Most Australians and New Zealanders are of British ancestry. In recent years, however, peoples from around the world have migrated to the region. For example, since the 1970s Asians and Pacific Islanders have settled in Australia and New Zealand in growing numbers.

Native Maori and Aborigines make up only a small percentage of New Zealand's and Australia's populations. One challenge facing both countries today is improving the economic and political status of those populations. Many of the region's Maori and Aborigines trail the rest of the population in terms of employment, land ownership, and education. In fact, the indigenous people of Australia and New Zealand have much lower literacy rates than non-indigenous people.

Diversity in Populations

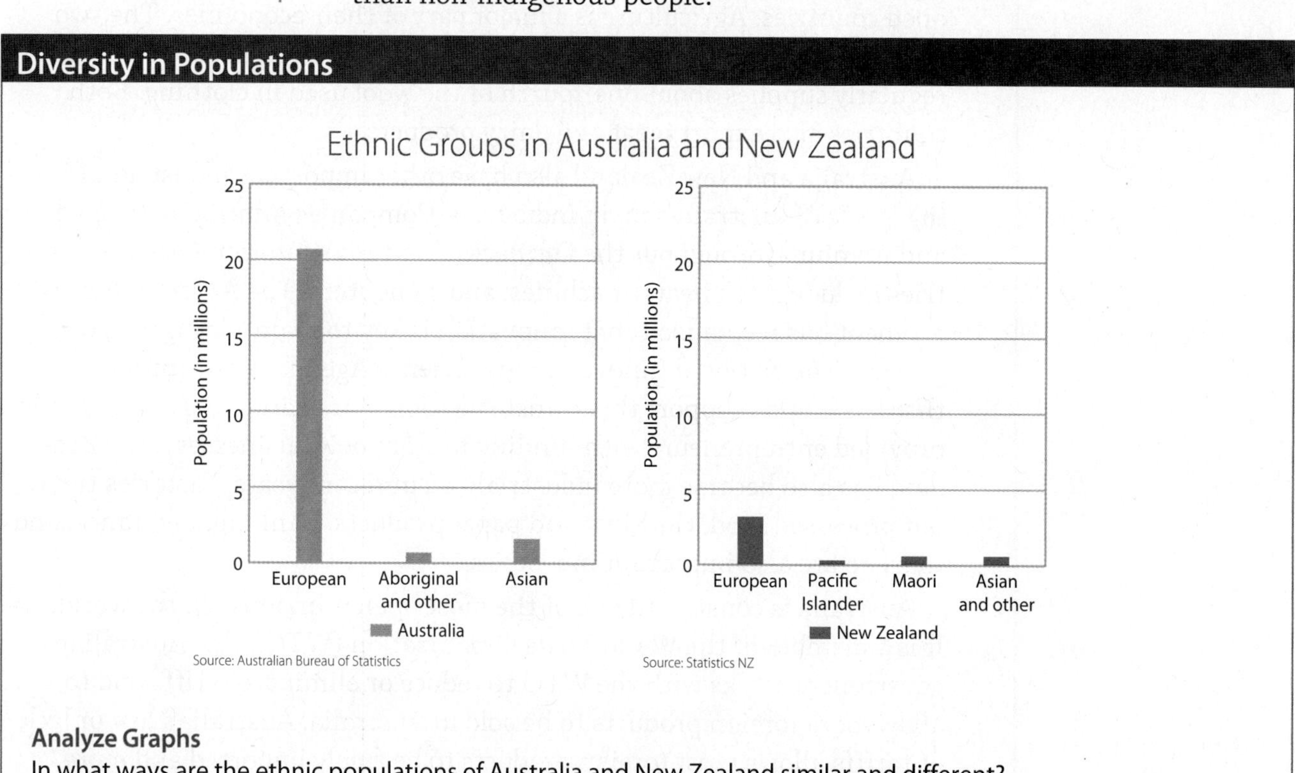

Analyze Graphs
In what ways are the ethnic populations of Australia and New Zealand similar and different?

Auckland is one of New Zealand's large cities on the North Island.

Reading Check **Summarize** What are the economic strengths of these countries?

Most Australians and New Zealanders live in urban areas. About 90 percent of Australia's population lives in large cities along the coasts. Some people are concerned that overpopulation of coastal regions will threaten species preservation and damage the natural environment. Sydney and Melbourne, Australia's two largest cities, are home to just over 8.5 million people. Rural areas like the Outback, on the other hand, comprise only about 10 percent of the population. In New Zealand, a majority of the population lives on the North Island. There, large cities like Auckland are common.

Summary and Preview Despite their geographical differences, Australia and New Zealand have much in common. The two countries share a similar history, culture, and economy. In the next lesson you will learn about another region—the Pacific Islands.

Lesson 1 Assessment

Review Ideas, Terms, and Places

1. a. **Identify** What is the Great Barrier Reef? Where is it located?
   b. **Elaborate** Given its harsh climate, why do you think so many people have settled in Australia?
2. a. **Describe** Who are the Maori? From where did they originate?
   b. **Draw Conclusions** How does religion shape the Aborigines' relationship with nature? How might this differ from other people's?
   c. **Evaluate** How might a lower literacy rate impact the economy of the region's indigenous populations?
3. a. **Explain** How have Australia and New Zealand been influenced by the migration of different people?
   b. **Compare and Contrast** How are the governments of Australia and New Zealand similar to and different from that of the United States?

Critical Thinking

4. **Compare and Contrast** Use your notes and a Venn diagram to compare and contrast the geography, history, and culture of Australia and New Zealand.

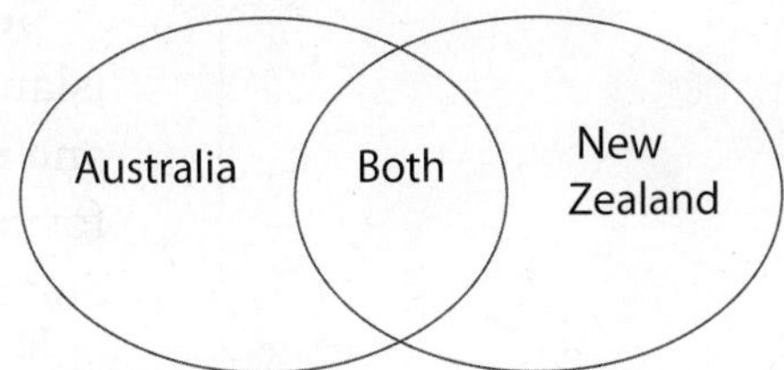

The Pacific Islands

The Big Idea

The Pacific Islands have tropical climates, rich cultures, and unique challenges.

Main Ideas

- Unique physical features, tropical climates, and limited resources shape the physical geography of the Pacific Islands.
- Native customs and contact with the Western world have influenced the history and culture of the Pacific Islands.
- Pacific Islanders today are working to improve their economies and protect the environment.

Key Terms and Places

Micronesia
Melanesia
Polynesia
atoll
territory

If YOU lived there . . .

You live on a small island in the South Pacific. For many years, the people on your island have made their living by fishing. Now, however, a European company has expressed interest in building an airport and a luxury hotel on your island. It hopes that tourists will be drawn by the island's dazzling beaches and tropical climate. The company's leaders want your permission before they build.

Will you give them permission? Why or why not?

Physical Geography

The Pacific Ocean covers more than one-third of Earth's surface. Scattered throughout this ocean are thousands of islands with similar physical features, climates, and resources.

Island Regions We divide the Pacific Islands into three regions—Micronesia, Melanesia, and Polynesia—based on their culture and geography. **Micronesia,** which means "tiny islands," is located just east of the Philippines. Some 2,000 small islands make up this region. South of Micronesia is **Melanesia,** which stretches from New Guinea in the west to Fiji in the east. Melanesia is the most heavily populated Pacific Island region. The largest region is **Polynesia,** which means "many islands." Among Polynesia's many islands are Tonga, Samoa, and the Hawaiian Islands.

Physical Features The Pacific Islands differ greatly. Some islands, like New Guinea (GI-nee), cover thousands of square miles. Other islands are tiny. For example, Nauru covers only 8 square miles (21 square km).

Geographers classify the islands of the Pacific as either high islands or low islands. High islands tend to be mountainous and rocky. Most high islands are volcanic islands. They were formed when volcanic mountains grew from the ocean floor and reached the surface. The islands of Tahiti and Hawaii in

High and Low Islands

Many high islands, like the island of Hawaii, often have mountainous terrain, rich soils, and dense rain forests. Many low islands, like this small island in the Society Islands chain, are formed from coral reefs. Because most low islands have poor soils, agriculture is limited.

Polynesia are examples of high islands. Other high islands, such as New Guinea, are formed from continental rock rather than volcanoes. For example, the country of Papua (PA-pyooh-wuh) New Guinea, located on the eastern half of the island of New Guinea, has rocky mountains that rise above 13,000 feet (3,960 m).

Low islands are typically much smaller than high islands. Most barely rise above sea level. Many low islands are atolls. An **atoll** is a small, ring-shaped coral island that surrounds a lagoon. Wake Island, west of the Hawaiian Islands, is an example of an atoll. Wake Island rises only 21 feet (6.4 m) above sea level and covers only 2.5 square miles (6.5 square km).

Climate and Resources All but two of the Pacific Island countries lie in the tropics. As a result, most islands have a humid tropical climate. Rain falls all year and temperatures are warm. Tropical savanna climates with rainy and dry seasons exist in a few places, such as New Caledonia. The mountains of New Guinea are home to a cool highland climate.

Resources in the Pacific Islands vary widely. Most low islands have thin soils and little vegetation. They have few trees other than the coconut palm. In addition, low islands have few mineral or energy resources. Partly because of these conditions, low islands have small populations.

In contrast to low islands, the Pacific's high islands have many natural resources. Volcanic soils provide fertile farmland and dense forests. Farms produce crops such as coffee, cocoa, bananas, and sugarcane. Some high islands also have many mineral resources. Papua New Guinea, for example, exports gold, copper, and oil.

Reading Check
Contrast
How do the Pacific's low islands differ from its high islands?

Link to Science

The Formation of an Atoll

The Pacific Islands are home to many atolls, or small coral islands that surround shallow lagoons. Coral reefs are formed from the skeletons of many tiny sea animals. When a coral reef forms on the edges of a volcanic island, it often forms a barrier reef around the island.

As the volcanic island sinks, the coral remains. Sand and other debris gradually collect on the reef's surface, raising the land above sea level. Eventually, all that remains is an atoll.

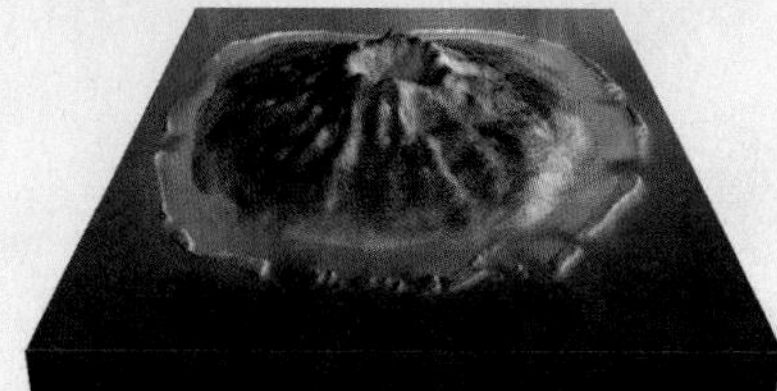

Coral reefs will sometimes form along the edges of a volcanic island, creating a ring around the island.

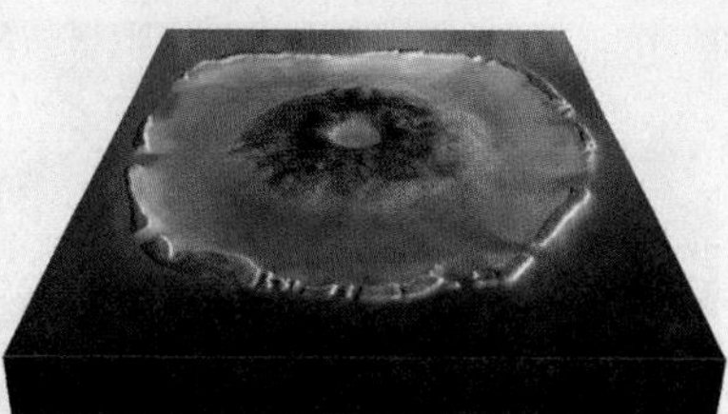

As the island sinks into the ocean floor, the coral reef grows upward and forms an offshore barrier reef.

Over time, sand collects on the surface of the reef, allowing grasses and shrubs to grow. When the island is submerged, the reef forms an atoll, or a ring of coral islands surrounding a lagoon.

Sequence
Describe the process in which atolls form.

History and Culture

The Pacific Islands were one of the last places settled by humans. Because of their isolation from other civilizations, the islands have a unique history and culture.

Early History Scholars believe that people began settling the Pacific Islands at least 35,000 years ago. The large islands of Melanesia were the first to be settled. Over time, people spread to the islands of Micronesia and Polynesia.

Europeans first encountered the Pacific Islands in the 1500s. Two centuries later, British captain James Cook explored all the main Pacific Island regions. By the late 1800s, European powers such as Spain, Great Britain, and France controlled most of the Pacific Islands.

Modern History By the early 1900s, other countries were entering the Pacific as well. In 1898 the United States defeated Spain in the Spanish-American War. As a result, Guam became a U.S. territory. A **territory** is an area that is under the authority of another government. Japan also expanded its empire into the Pacific Ocean in the early 1900s. In World War II, the Pacific Islands were the scene of many tough battles between Allied and Japanese forces. After Japan's defeat in 1945, the United Nations placed some islands under the control of the United States and other Allies.

In the last half of the 1900s, many Pacific islands gained their independence. However, several countries—including the United States, France, and New Zealand—still have territories in the Pacific Islands.

Culture A variety of cultures thrives throughout the Pacific Islands. Some culture traits, such as fishing, are common throughout the entire region. Others are found only on a specific island or island chain.

People More than 10 million people live in the Pacific Islands today. Most Pacific Islanders are descendants of the region's original settlers. However, the population of the Pacific Islands also includes large numbers of ethnic Europeans and Asians, particularly Indians and Chinese. Many ethnic Asians are descended from people brought to the islands to work on colonial plantations. On the Melanesian island of Fiji, for example, Indians make up nearly half of the population.

Before the arrival of Europeans, the people of the Pacific Islands practiced hundreds of different religions. Today, most Pacific Islanders are Christian. In Melanesia, however, some people continue to practice traditional local religions.

Explore ONLINE!

Settling the Pacific

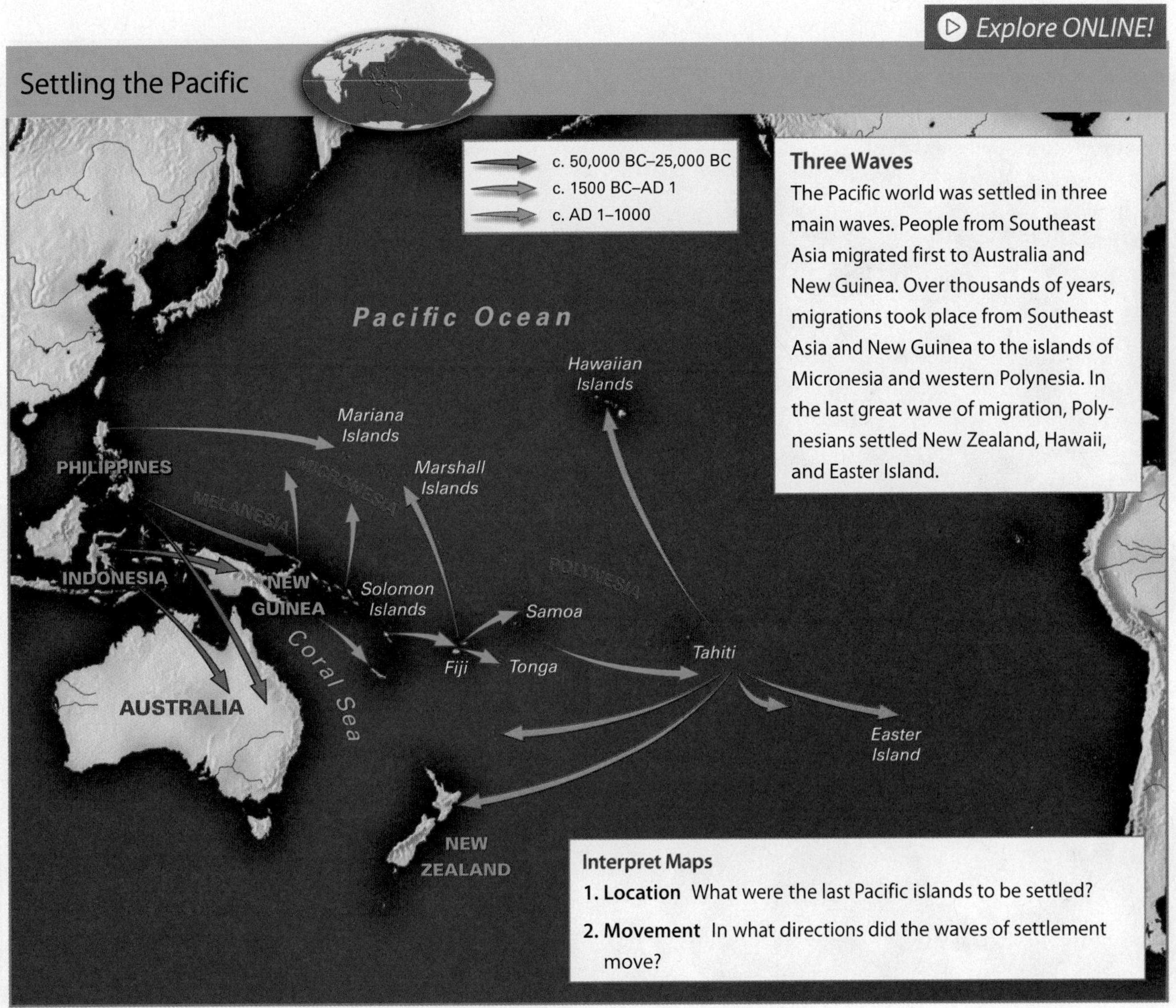

Three Waves

The Pacific world was settled in three main waves. People from Southeast Asia migrated first to Australia and New Guinea. Over thousands of years, migrations took place from Southeast Asia and New Guinea to the islands of Micronesia and western Polynesia. In the last great wave of migration, Polynesians settled New Zealand, Hawaii, and Easter Island.

Interpret Maps

1. **Location** What were the last Pacific islands to be settled?
2. **Movement** In what directions did the waves of settlement move?

Traditions Although modern culture exists throughout the Pacific Islands, many people continue to practice traditional customs. In parts of Polynesia, for example, people still construct their homes from bamboo and palm leaves. Many Pacific Islanders today continue to live in ancient villages, practice customary art styles, and hold ceremonies that feature traditional costumes and dances.

Reading Check
Make Inferences
In what ways have the Pacific Islands been influenced by contact with westerners?

The Pacific Islands Today

Many people imagine sunny beaches and tourists when they think of the Pacific Islands today. Despite the region's healthy tourism industry, however, Pacific Island countries face important challenges.

The countries of the Pacific Islands have developing economies. Fishing, tourism, and agriculture are key industries. Some countries, particularly Papua New Guinea, export minerals and timber. The region's isolation from other countries, however, hinders its ability to trade.

The environment is an important concern in the Pacific Islands. The Pacific Islands were used for nuclear testing grounds from the 1940s to the 1990s. Many people fear that one **effect** of these tests may be health

Academic Vocabulary
effect the results of an action or decision

Explore ONLINE!

The Pacific Islands: Political

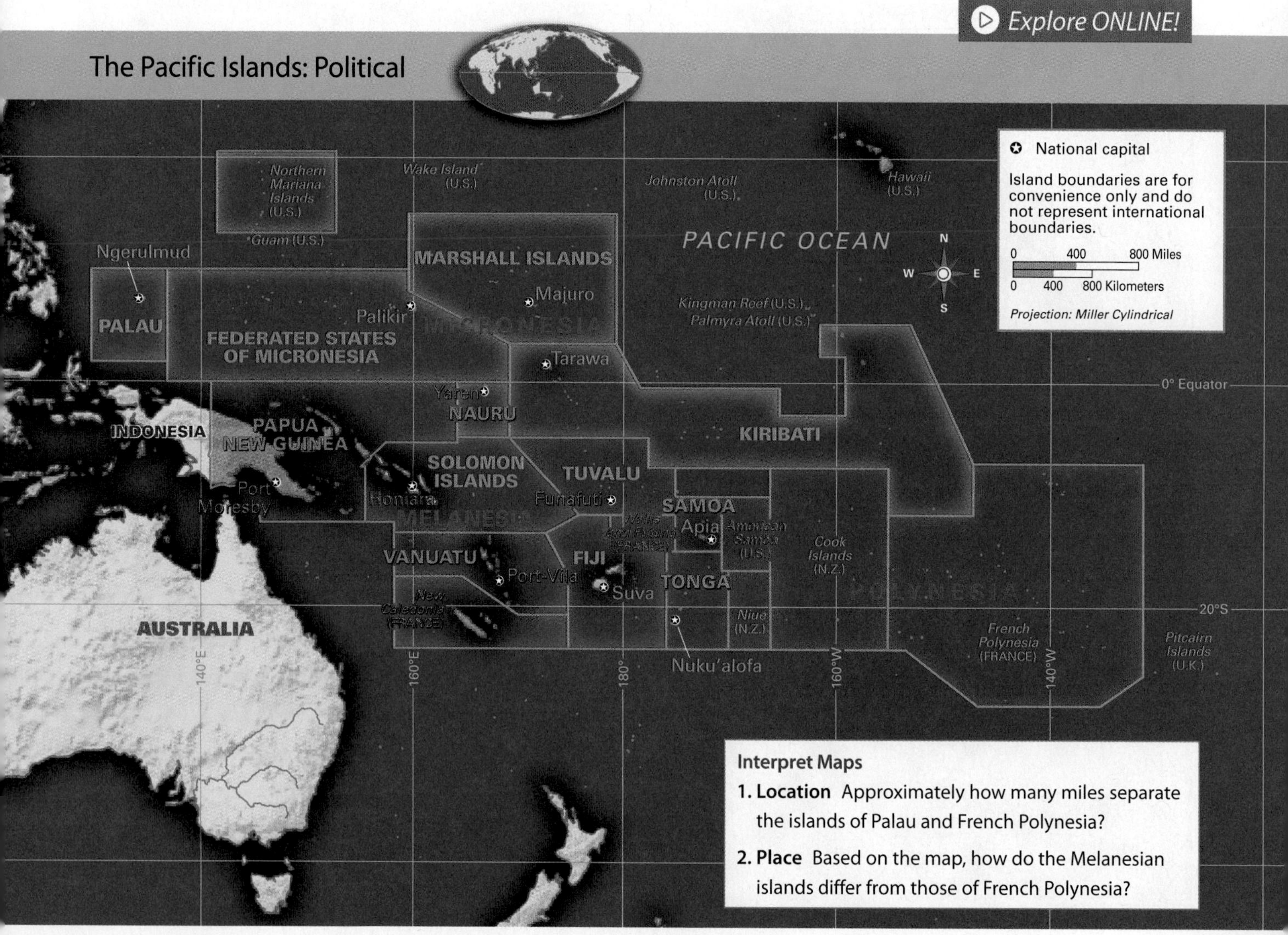

Interpret Maps

1. **Location** Approximately how many miles separate the islands of Palau and French Polynesia?
2. **Place** Based on the map, how do the Melanesian islands differ from those of French Polynesia?

Villagers on Tanna Island in Vanuatu perform a traditional dance.

Reading Check
Summarize What are some challenges Pacific Islanders face today?

problems for people in the region. Global warming also concerns Pacific Islanders. Some researchers believe that rising temperatures may cause polar ice to melt. The rise in ocean levels would threaten low-lying Pacific islands.

Summary and Preview The Pacific Islands are one of the most isolated regions in the world. As a result, unique cultures and challenges exist in the region. In the next lesson you will learn about another isolated part of the globe—Antarctica.

Lesson 2 Assessment

Review Ideas, Terms, and Places

1. a. **Describe** Into what regions are the Pacific Islands divided?
   b. **Draw Conclusions** Why might high islands have larger populations than low islands?
2. a. **Define** What is a territory?
   b. **Make Inferences** Why did other countries seek to control the Pacific Islands?
   c. **Elaborate** Why do you think that many Pacific Islanders continue to practice traditional customs?
3. a. **Recall** What economic resources are available to the Pacific Islands?
   b. **Predict** How might the Pacific Islands be affected by global warming in the future?

Critical Thinking

4. **Find Main Ideas** Look at your notes from this lesson. Draw a chart and record main idea statements about physical geography, history, culture, and today's issues for the region.

Physical Geography	History	Culture	Issues Today

Antarctica

The Big Idea

Antarctica's unique environment has made it an important site for research.

Main Ideas

- Freezing temperatures, ice, and snow dominate Antarctica's physical geography.
- Explorations in the 1800s and 1900s led to Antarctica's use for scientific research.
- Research and protecting the environment are key issues in Antarctica today.

Key Terms and Places

ice shelf
icebergs
Antarctic Peninsula
polar desert
ozone layer

If YOU lived there . . .

You are a scientist working at a research laboratory in Antarctica. One day you receive an email message from a friend. She wants to open a company that will lead public tours through Antarctica so people can see its spectacular icy landscapes and wildlife. Some of your fellow scientists think that tours are a good idea, while others think that they could ruin the local environment.

What will you tell your friend?

Physical Geography

In the southernmost part of the world is the continent of Antarctica. This frozen land is very different from any other place on Earth.

The Land Ice covers about 98 percent of Antarctica's 5.4 million square miles (14 million square km). This ice sheet contains about 90 percent of the world's ice. On average, the ice sheet is more than 1 mile (1.6 km) thick.

The weight of Antarctica's ice sheet causes ice to flow slowly off the continent. As the ice reaches the coast, it forms a ledge over the surrounding seas. This ledge of ice that extends over the water is called an **ice shelf.** Antarctica's ice shelves are huge. In fact, the Ross Ice Shelf, Antarctica's largest, is about the size of Canada's Yukon Territory.

Penguins live in the icy waters around Antarctica, a continent almost completely covered in ice.

Icebergs near Antarctica are monitored using satellite data collected by the U.S. National Ice Center.

Sometimes, parts of the ice shelf break off into the surrounding water. Floating masses of ice that have broken off a glacier are **icebergs.** One iceberg that formed was approximately the size of the country of Luxembourg.

In western Antarctica, the **Antarctic Peninsula** extends north of the Antarctic Circle. As a result, temperatures there are often warmer than in other parts of the continent.

Climate and Resources Most of Antarctica's interior is dominated by a freezing ice-cap climate. Temperatures can drop below –120°F (–84°C), and very little precipitation falls. As a result, much of Antarctica is considered a **polar desert,** a high-latitude region that receives very little precipitation. The precipitation that does fall does not melt due to the cold temperatures. Instead, it remains as ice.

Because of Antarctica's high latitude, the continent is in almost total darkness during winter months. Seas clog with ice as a result of the extreme temperatures. In the summer, the sun shines around the clock and temperatures rise to near freezing.

Plant life survives only in the ice-free tundra areas. Insects are the frozen land's only land animals. Penguins, seals, and whales live in Antarctica's waters. Antarctica has many mineral resources, including iron ore, gold, copper, and coal.

Reading Check
Summarize What are the physical features and resources of Antarctica?

Historical Source

Crossing Antarctica

In 1989 a six-person team set off to cross Antarctica on foot. The 3,700-mile journey took seven months to complete. Team member Will Steger describes his first view of the continent.

"Now, flying over the iceberg-laden Weddell Sea, the biggest adventure of my life was about to begin . . .

To the south I could barely pick out the peaks of mountains, mountains I knew jutted three thousand feet into the air. They lined the peninsula's coast for hundreds of miles. Leading up to them was a two-mile-wide sheet of snow and ice, preceded by the blue of the sea. It was a picture of purity, similar to many I had seen in the picture books . . ."

—from *Crossing Antarctica*, by Will Steger and John Bowermaster

Analyze Sources
What physical features does the author notice on his trip over Antarctica?

Early Explorations

Academic Vocabulary
motive
a reason for doing something

The discovery of Antarctica is a fairly recent one. Although explorers long believed there was a southern continent, it was not until 1775 that James Cook first sighted the Antarctic Peninsula. In the 1800s explorers first investigated Antarctica. One **motive** of many explorers was to discover the South Pole and other new lands. In 1911 a team of Norwegian explorers became the first people to reach the South Pole.

Since then, several countries—including the United States, Australia, and Chile—have claimed parts of Antarctica. In 1959 the international Antarctic Treaty was signed to preserve the continent "for science and peace." This treaty banned military activity in Antarctica and set aside the entire continent for research.

Reading Check
Make Inferences
Why do you think Antarctica is set aside for research?

BIOGRAPHY

Sir Ernest Shackleton (1874–1922)

Irish-born Ernest Shackleton was one of several early explorers of Antarctica. Shackleton led a British expedition from 1907 to 1909 that climbed Mount Erebus, an active volcano; discovered the Beardmore Glacier; and came within 97 miles (156 km) of the South Pole—the farthest south anyone had ever been.

Antarctic Exploration

In the early 1900s several expeditions set out to find the South Pole. The first to reach the pole were members of a Norwegian expedition led by Roald Amundsen. In this photo, a member of the Norwegian expedition poses with his team of dogs near the flag that marks the South Pole.

Analyze Visuals
What words can be used to describe the photo?

Antarctica Today

Today, Antarctica is the only continent without a permanent human population. Scientists use the continent to conduct research and to monitor the environment.

Scientific Research While they are conducting research in Antarctica, researchers live in bases, or stations. Several countries, including the United States, the United Kingdom, and Russia, have bases in Antarctica.

Antarctic research covers a wide range of topics. Some scientists concentrate on the continent's plant and animal life. Others examine weather conditions. One group of researchers is studying Earth's ozone layer. The **ozone layer** is a layer of Earth's atmosphere that protects living things from the harmful effects of the sun's ultraviolet rays. Scientists found a thinning in the ozone layer above Antarctica. Today, scientists continue their research and work in Antarctica.

Environmental Threats Many people today are concerned about Antarctica's environment. Over the years, researchers and tourists have left behind trash and sewage, polluting the environment. Oil spills have damaged surrounding seas. In addition, companies have hoped to exploit Antarctica's valuable resources.

Some people fear that any mining of the resources in Antarctica will result in more environmental problems. To prevent this, a new international agreement was reached in 1991. This agreement forbids most activities that do not have a scientific purpose. It bans mining and drilling and limits tourism.

Antarctica's Ice Shelves

Antarctica is home to many large ice shelves. An ice shelf is a piece of a glacier that extends over the surrounding seas. In recent years, scientists have become concerned that rising temperatures on the planet are causing the rapid disintegration of some of Antarctica's ice shelves. This satellite image shows the breakup of a huge portion of Antarctica's Larsen B Ice Shelf, located on the Antarctic Peninsula. The breakup of this ice shelf released some 720 billion tons (653 billion metric tons) of ice into the Weddell Sea.

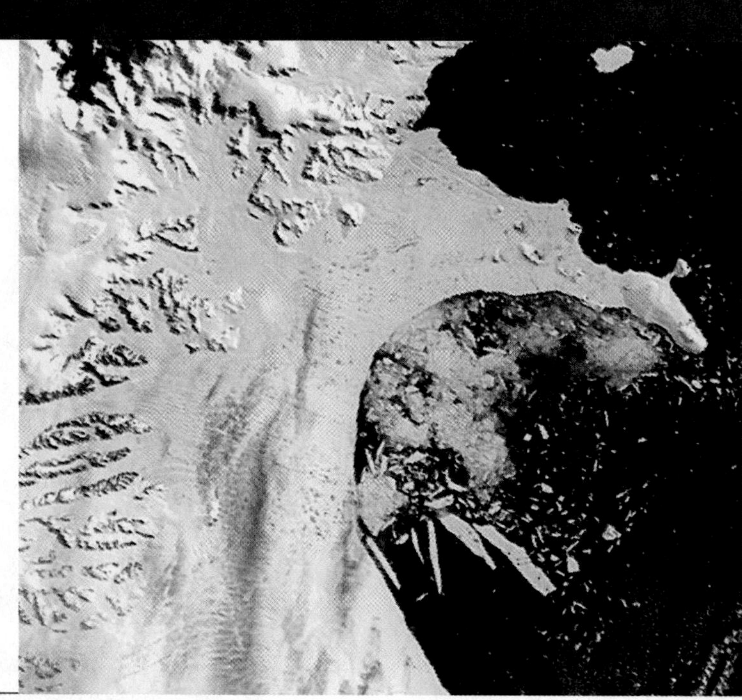

Identify Cause and Effect
What do scientists believe has led to growing disintegration of Antarctica's ice shelves?

Reading Check
Find Main Ideas
What are some issues that affect Antarctica today?

Average global temperatures have been increasing for more than a century. Many scientists fear that if these trends continue, the results will be disastrous. Antarctica's landscape will be threatened. Over time, melting polar ice will raise sea levels and cause flooding in coastal areas. The entire planet will be impacted. Today, many organizations around the world are working to address these challenges.

Summary In this lesson, you have learned about Antarctica's unusual physical geography and harsh climates. Despite the difficulty of living in such harsh conditions, Antarctica remains an important place for scientific research.

Lesson 3 Assessment

Review Ideas, Terms, and Places

1. a. **Define** What are ice shelves and icebergs?
   b. **Contrast** How does Antarctica differ from most other continents?
   c. **Elaborate** What aspects of Antarctica's physical geography would you most like to see? Why?
2. a. **Compare** How do the geographic factors responsible for population patterns in Antarctica compare to those that shape the rest of the region?
   b. **Predict** What might have happened if countries had not agreed to preserve Antarctica for research?
3. a. **Recall** What is Antarctica used for today?
   b. **Analyze** How has Antarctic research benefited science?

Critical Thinking

4. **Summarize** Look at your notes from this lesson. Draw a diagram to list three facts about each aspect of Antarctica's physical geography.

Physical Geography	→	
Early Explorers	→	
Antarctica Today	→	

Social Studies Skills

Make Decisions

Define the Skill

You make decisions every day. Some decisions are very easy to make and take little time. Others are much harder. Regardless of how easy or hard a decision is, it will have consequences, or results. These consequences can be either positive or negative.

Before you make a decision, consider all your possible options. Think about the possible consequences of each option and decide which will be best for you. Thinking about the consequences of your decision beforehand will allow you to make a better, more thoughtful decision.

Learn the Skill

Imagine your parents have given you the option of getting a new pet. Use a graphic organizer like the one on this page to help you decide whether to get one.

1. What are the consequences of getting a pet? Which of these consequences are positive? Which are negative?
2. What are the consequences of not getting a pet? Which of them are positive? Which are negative?
3. Compare your two options. Look at the positive and negative consequences of each option. Based on these consequences, do you think you should get a pet?

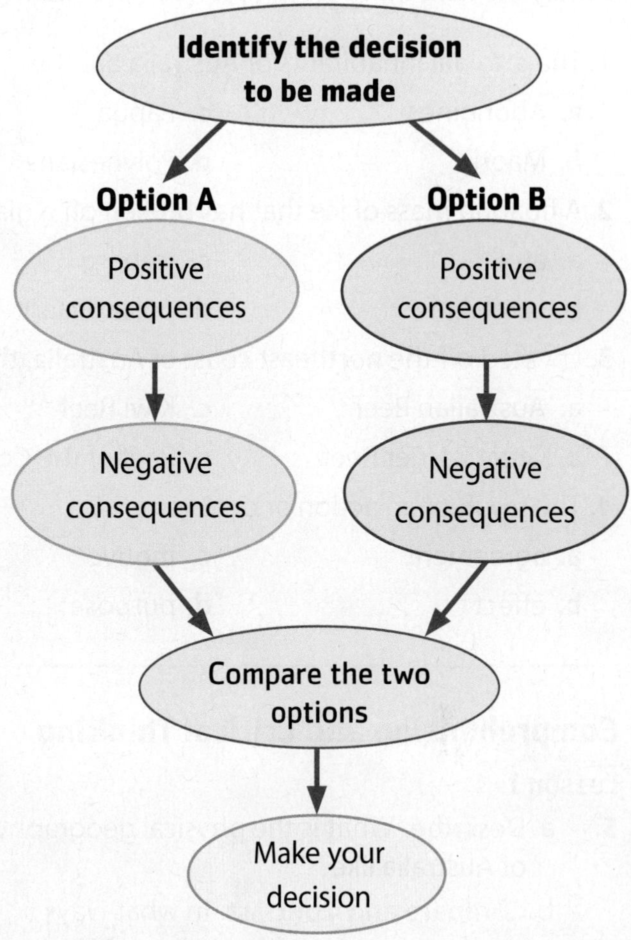

Practice the Skill

Imagine that you have the opportunity to journey into the Outback or join an expedition to the South Pole. You can only choose one of the destinations. Use a graphic organizer like the one on this page to consider the consequences of each option. Compare your lists, and then make your choice. Write a short paragraph to explain your decision.

Module 20 Assessment

Review Vocabulary, Terms, and Places

Identify the term that best completes each statement.

1. The original inhabitants of Australia are the
   a. Aborigines
   b. Maori
   c. Papuans
   d. Polynesians
2. A floating mass of ice that has broken off a glacier is a(n)
   a. atoll
   b. coral reef
   c. iceberg
   d. polar desert
3. Located off the northeast coast of Australia, this is the world's largest coral reef.
   a. Australian Reef
   b. Great Barrier Reef
   c. Kiwi Reef
   d. Reef of the Coral Sea
4. The result of an action or decision is a(n)
   a. agreement
   b. effect
   c. motive
   d. purpose

Comprehension and Critical Thinking

Lesson 1

5. a. **Describe** What is the physical geography of Australia like?
   b. **Compare and Contrast** In what ways are the countries of Australia and New Zealand similar and different?
   c. **Elaborate** Why do you think the economies of Australia and New Zealand are so strong?

Lesson 2

6. a. **Identify** What two types of islands are commonly found in the Pacific Ocean? How are they different?
   b. **Analyze** How were the islands of the Pacific Ocean originally settled? How has migration influenced the character of this region?
   c. **Elaborate** Many Pacific islands are isolated from other societies. Would you want to live in such a place?

Lesson 3

7. a. **Describe** What types of wildlife are found in and around Antarctica?
   b. **Draw Conclusions** Why do you think many of the world's countries supported setting aside Antarctica for scientific research?
   c. **Analyze Effects** What effects might the thinning of the ozone layer have on Antarctica?

Reading Skills

8. **Determine Author's Purpose** *Use the Reading Skills taught in this module to answer a question about the reading selection below. After you read, make a list of verbs, nouns, or adjectives that help you determine the author's purpose.*

> Low islands are typically much smaller than high islands. Most barely rise above sea level. Many low islands are atolls. An atoll is a small, ring-shaped coral island that surrounds a lagoon. Wake Island, west of the Hawaiian Islands, is an example of an atoll. Wake Island rises only 21 feet (6.4 m) above sea level and covers only 2.5 square miles (6.5 square km).

What is the author's purpose for this passage?

Social Studies Skills

9. **Make Decisions** *Use the Social Studies Skills taught in this module to complete the following activity.*

An agreement was reached in 1991 that forbids most activities in Antarctica that do not have a scientific purpose. It bans mining and drilling and limits tourism. The agreement will be open for review in the year 2048. What should happen to the agreement at that time? Think about the decision to be made, your options, and positive and negative consequences. Write a few sentences to share and explain your decision.

Map Activity

10. **Oceania and Antarctica** On a sheet of paper, match the letters on the map with their correct labels.

Great Barrier Reef	Perth, Australia
Outback	Papua New Guinea
Sydney, Australia	North Island
Melbourne, Australia	Pacific Ocean

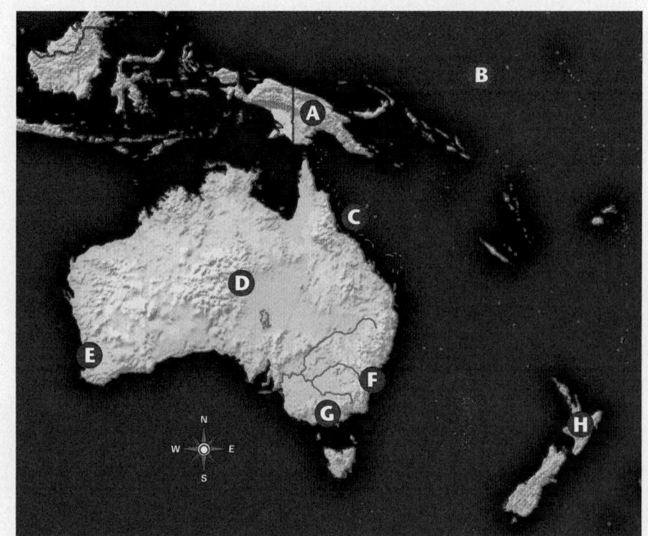

Focus on Writing

11. **Write a Brochure** Use the module, your notes, and other sources to design a brochure. Your brochure should be divided into sections—one on Australia and New Zealand, one on the Pacific Islands, and one on Antarctica. Identify the renewable and nonrenewable resources located in each region. Try to convince the reader to invest in them. You should gather relevant information from multiple print and digital sources. Effectively use search terms on the Internet to look for illustrations to support the points you want to make. The content should be focused and organized. Finally, design a cover page for your brochure. Check for errors in spelling, grammar, capitalization, and punctuation.

References

References

Atlas R2

Regional Atlases and Data Files R22

Gazetteer R60

Writing Workshops R64

English and Spanish Glossary R72

Index R90

Credits and Acknowledgments R111

United States: Physical

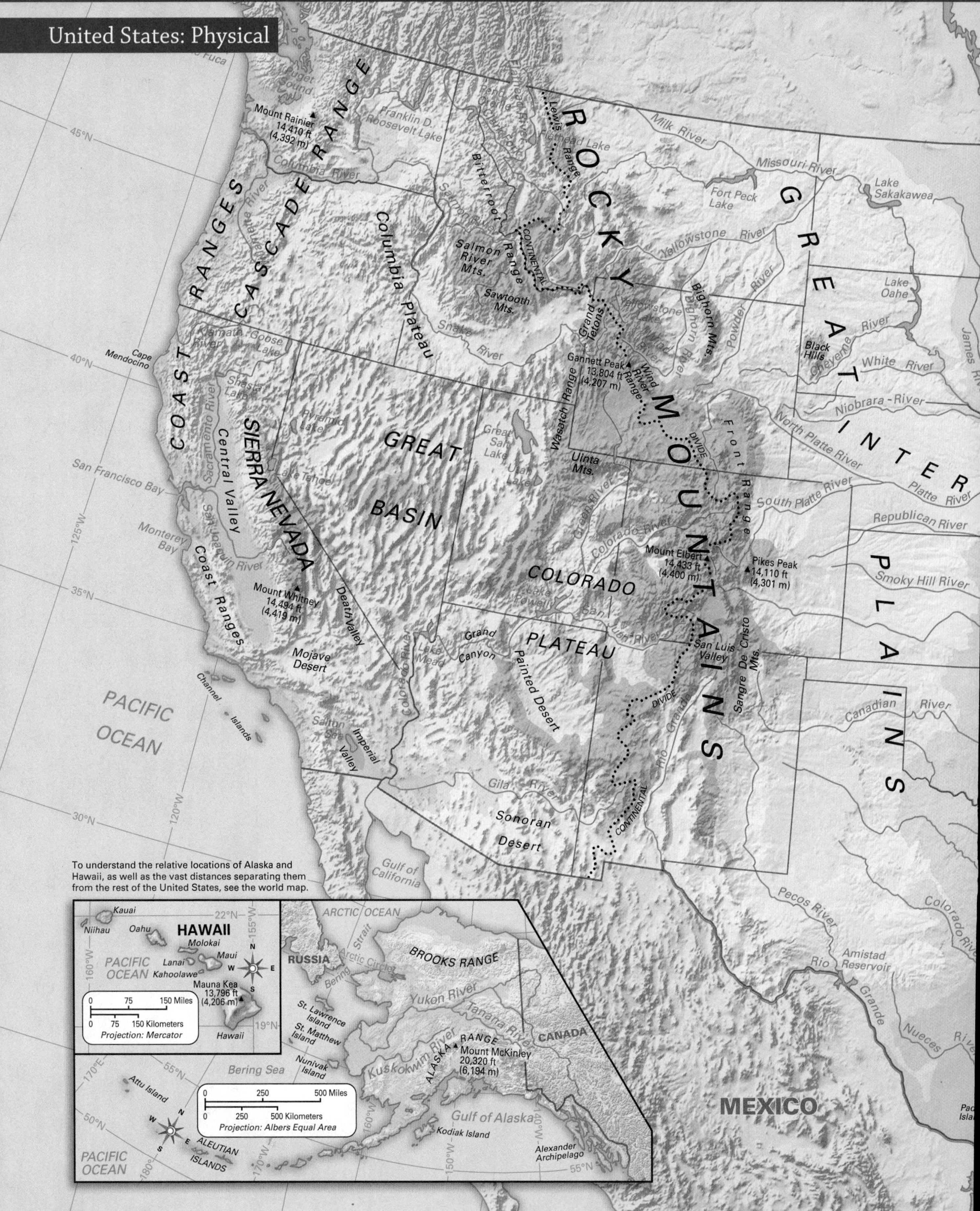

To understand the relative locations of Alaska and Hawaii, as well as the vast distances separating them from the rest of the United States, see the world map.

CANADA
Isle Royale
Lake Superior
Mesabi Range
Red River
Minnesota River
Mississippi River
Wisconsin River
Lake Michigan
Lake Huron
Lake Ontario
Lake Erie
St. Lawrence River
St. Lawrence Seaway
St. John River
Lake Champlain
Adirondack Mts.
Green Mts.
White Mts.
Longfellow Mts.
Penobscot River
Hudson R.
Connecticut River
Catskill Mts.
Cape Cod
Long Island Sound
Long Island
PLATEAU
Allegheny R.
Susquehanna River
Delaware River
APPALACHIAN MOUNTAINS
ALLEGHENY
Monongahela R.
Potomac River
Delaware Bay
Chesapeake Bay
James River
ATLANTIC OCEAN
Missouri River
Des Moines River
Illinois River
Wabash River
Scioto River
Kanawha River
PLAINS
Kansas R.
Ohio River
Roanoke River
Pamlico Sound
Cape Hatteras
Lake of the Ozarks
OZARK PLATEAU
Lake Barkley
Cumberland River
Cumberland Plateau
BLUE RIDGE MOUNTAINS
PIEDMONT
Keystone Lake
Kentucky Lake
Great Smoky Mts.
Arkansas River
White River
Eufaula Lake
Tennessee River
Ouachita Mts.
Lake Texoma
Tombigbee River
Coosa River
Oconee River
Savannah River
Trinity River
Sabine River
Red River
Mississippi River
Pearl River
Alabama R.
Chattahoochee River
Altamaha River
Sea Islands
Toledo Bend Reservoir
COASTAL PLAIN
Okefenokee Swamp
GULF
Chandeleur Islands
Mississippi Delta
FLORIDA PENINSULA
Cape Canaveral
Gulf of Mexico
Lake Okeechobee
The Everglades
Cape Sable
Florida Keys
Straits of Florida
BAHAMAS
N
S
E
W
ELEVATION
Feet
Meters
13,120
6,560
1,640
656
(Sea level) 0
Below sea level
4,000
2,000
500
200
0 (Sea level)
Below sea level
0 100 200 Miles
0 100 200 Kilometers
Projection: Albers Equal Area
40°N
35°N
25°N
70°W
75°W
80°W
85°W
90°W
95°W

United States: Political

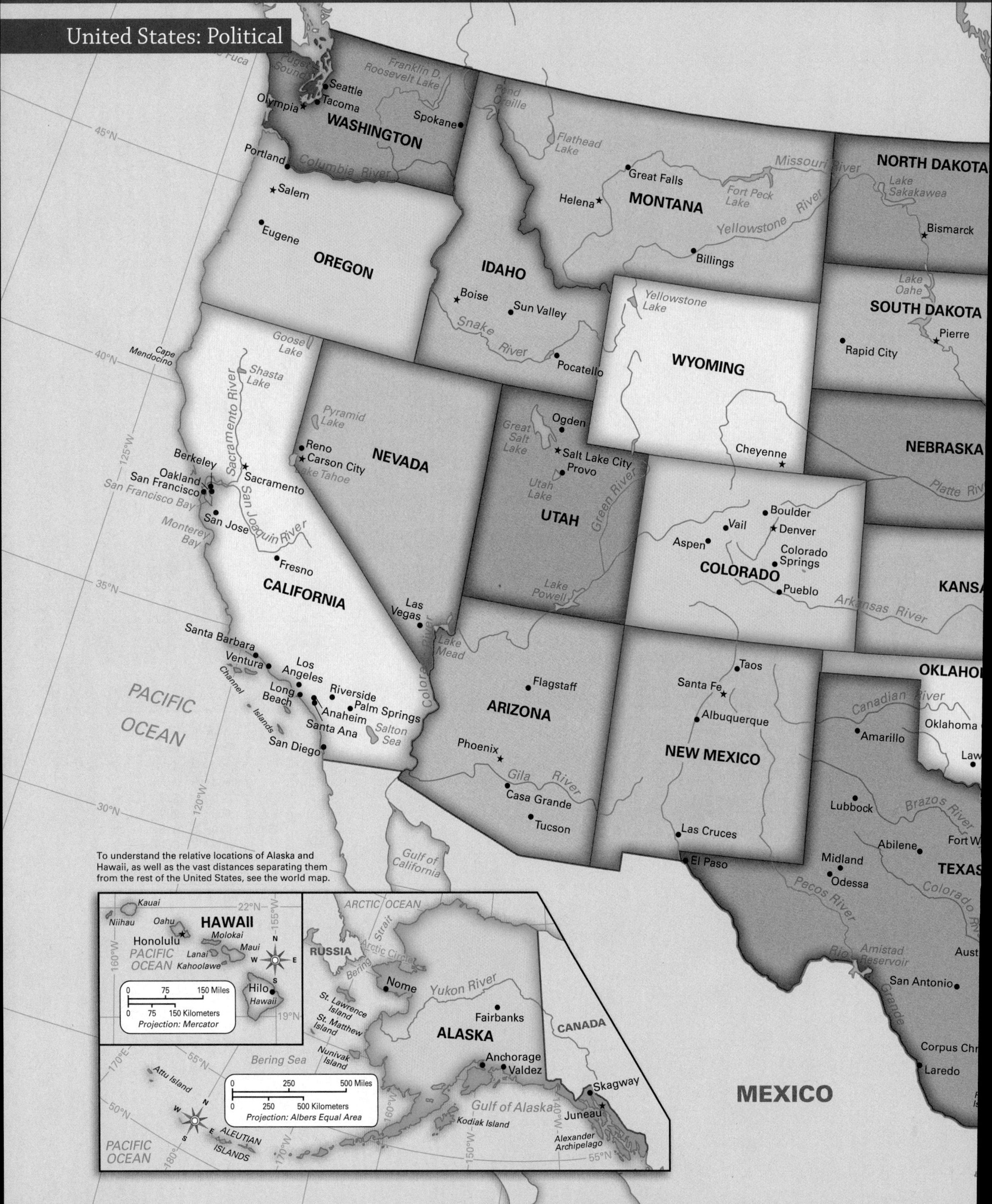

To understand the relative locations of Alaska and Hawaii, as well as the vast distances separating them from the rest of the United States, see the world map.

CANADA
MINNESOTA
WISCONSIN
MICHIGAN
IOWA
MISSOURI
ILLINOIS
INDIANA
OHIO
KENTUCKY
TENNESSEE
ARKANSAS
LOUISIANA
MISSISSIPPI
ALABAMA
GEORGIA
FLORIDA
SOUTH CAROLINA
NORTH CAROLINA
VIRGINIA
WEST VIRGINIA
PENNSYLVANIA
NEW YORK
MAINE
VT
NH
MA
CT
RI
NJ
DE
MD
ATLANTIC OCEAN
Gulf of Mexico
BAHAMAS
Lake Superior
Lake Michigan
Lake Huron
Lake Erie
Lake Ontario
Lake Champlain
St. Lawrence River
Hudson R.
Connecticut R.
Mississippi River
Missouri River
Ohio River
Illinois River
Red River
Minnesota River
Susquehanna River
Savannah River
Chattahoochee R.
Chesapeake Bay
Delaware Bay
Long Island Sound
Long Island
Cape Cod
Cape Hatteras
Cape Canaveral
Cape Sable
Florida Keys
Straits of Florida
Sea Islands
Chandeleur Islands
Lake Okeechobee
Lake of the Ozarks
Lake Barkley
Kentucky Lake
Keystone Lake
Eufaula Lake
Lake Texoma
Toledo Bend Reservoir
Grand Forks
Fargo
Duluth
Superior
Minneapolis
St. Paul
Sioux Falls
Sioux City
Omaha
Lincoln
Topeka
Kansas City
Wichita
Tulsa
Dallas
Waco
Houston
Galveston
Beaumont
Marquette
Sault Ste. Marie
Green Bay
Madison
Milwaukee
Rockford
Chicago
Peoria
Springfield
Cedar Rapids
Davenport
Des Moines
St. Louis
East St. Louis
Jefferson City
Gary
South Bend
Fort Wayne
Indianapolis
Evansville
Louisville
Frankfort
Lexington
Grand Rapids
Lansing
Saginaw
Detroit
Ann Arbor
Toledo
Cleveland
Youngstown
Akron
Columbus
Dayton
Cincinnati
Charleston
Pittsburgh
Erie
Buffalo
Rochester
Syracuse
Albany
Burlington
Montpelier
Augusta
Portland
Concord
Manchester
Boston
Worcester
Springfield
Providence
Hartford
New Haven
Bridgeport
Yonkers
New York City
Jersey City
Newark
Trenton
Camden
Allentown
Harrisburg
Philadelphia
Atlantic City
Dover
Baltimore
Annapolis
Washington, D.C.
Richmond
Newport News
Norfolk
Virginia Beach
Greensboro
Durham
Raleigh
Winston-Salem
Charlotte
Asheville
Knoxville
Nashville
Chattanooga
Memphis
Fayetteville
Little Rock
Pine Bluff
Springfield
Huntsville
Birmingham
Atlanta
Greenville
Columbia
Charleston
Macon
Columbus
Savannah
Meridian
Montgomery
Vicksburg
Jackson
Shreveport
Baton Rouge
New Orleans
Biloxi
Mobile
Pensacola
Tallahassee
Jacksonville
Gainesville
Orlando
Tampa
St. Petersburg
Fort Myers
Fort Lauderdale
Miami
National capital
State capitals
Other cities
0 100 200 Miles
0 100 200 Kilometers
Projection: Albers Equal Area
N
E
S
W
40°N
35°N
25°N
95°W
90°W
85°W
80°W
75°W
70°W

World: Physical

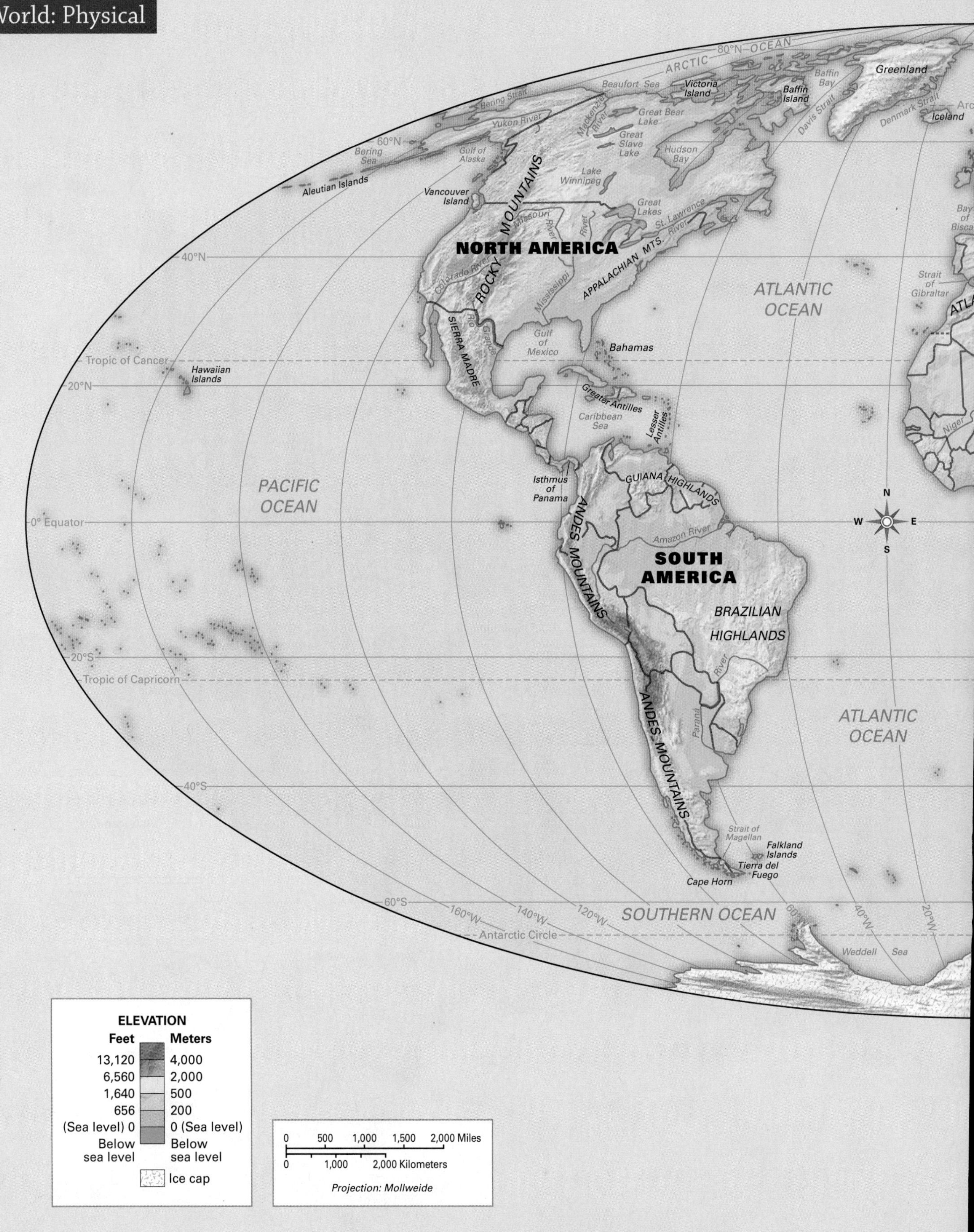

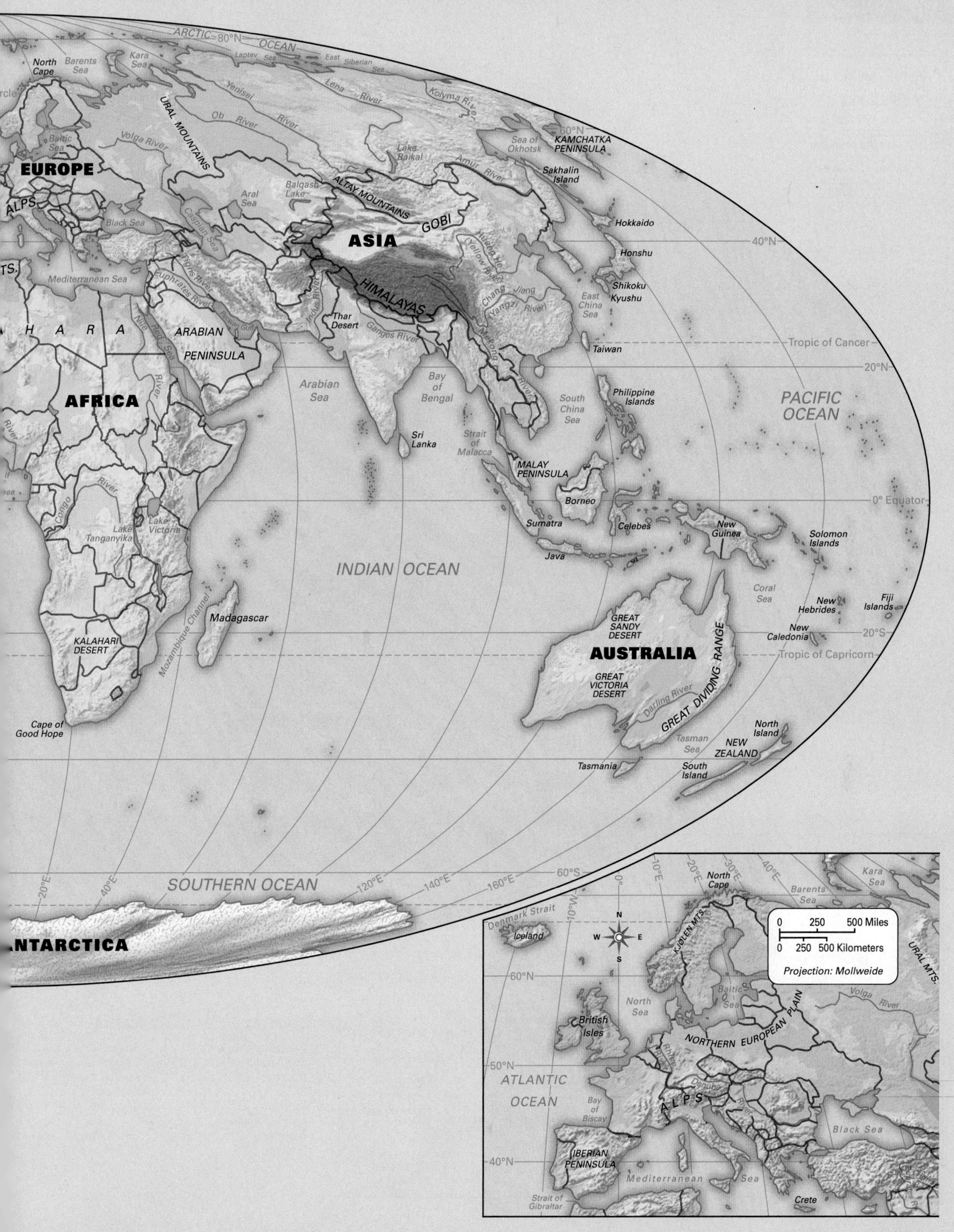

ARCTIC
80°N
OCEAN
North Cape
Barents Sea
Kara Sea
Laptev Sea
East Siberian Sea
Yenisei River
Lena River
Kolyma River
URAL MOUNTAINS
Ob River
Volga River
Baltic Sea
Sea of Okhotsk
KAMCHATKA PENINSULA
60°N
Lake Baikal
Amur River
EUROPE
Sakhalin Island
ALPS
Aral Sea
Balqash Lake
ALTAY MOUNTAINS
Black Sea
Caspian Sea
GOBI
Hokkaido
ASIA
40°N
Honshu
Huang He (Yellow River)
Mediterranean Sea
Tigris River
Euphrates River
Indus River
HIMALAYAS
Shikoku
Kyushu
Chang Jiang (Yangzi River)
East China Sea
Thar Desert
Ganges River
Mekong River
Nile River
Red Sea
ARABIAN PENINSULA
Taiwan
Tropic of Cancer
20°N
Arabian Sea
Bay of Bengal
South China Sea
Philippine Islands
PACIFIC OCEAN
AFRICA
Sri Lanka
Strait of Malacca
MALAY PENINSULA
Borneo
0° Equator
Congo River
Lake Victoria
Lake Tanganyika
Sumatra
Celebes
New Guinea
Solomon Islands
Java
INDIAN OCEAN
Coral Sea
Mozambique Channel
Madagascar
GREAT SANDY DESERT
New Hebrides
Fiji Islands
New Caledonia
20°S
KALAHARI DESERT
AUSTRALIA
Tropic of Capricorn
GREAT VICTORIA DESERT
Darling River
GREAT DIVIDING RANGE
Cape of Good Hope
Tasman Sea
North Island
NEW ZEALAND
Tasmania
South Island
60°S
SOUTHERN OCEAN
20°E
40°E
120°E
140°E
160°E
ANTARCTICA
10°E
20°E
30°E
40°E
North Cape
Barents Sea
Kara Sea
Denmark Strait
10°W
0°
Iceland
KJØLEN MTS.
N
S
E
W
0 250 500 Miles
0 250 500 Kilometers
Projection: Mollweide
URAL MTS.
60°N
Baltic Sea
North Sea
Volga River
British Isles
NORTHERN EUROPEAN PLAIN
Rhine
50°N
ATLANTIC OCEAN
Danube River
ALPS
Bay of Biscay
Black Sea
IBERIAN PENINSULA
40°N
Mediterranean Sea
Strait of Gibraltar
Crete

Atlas

World: Political

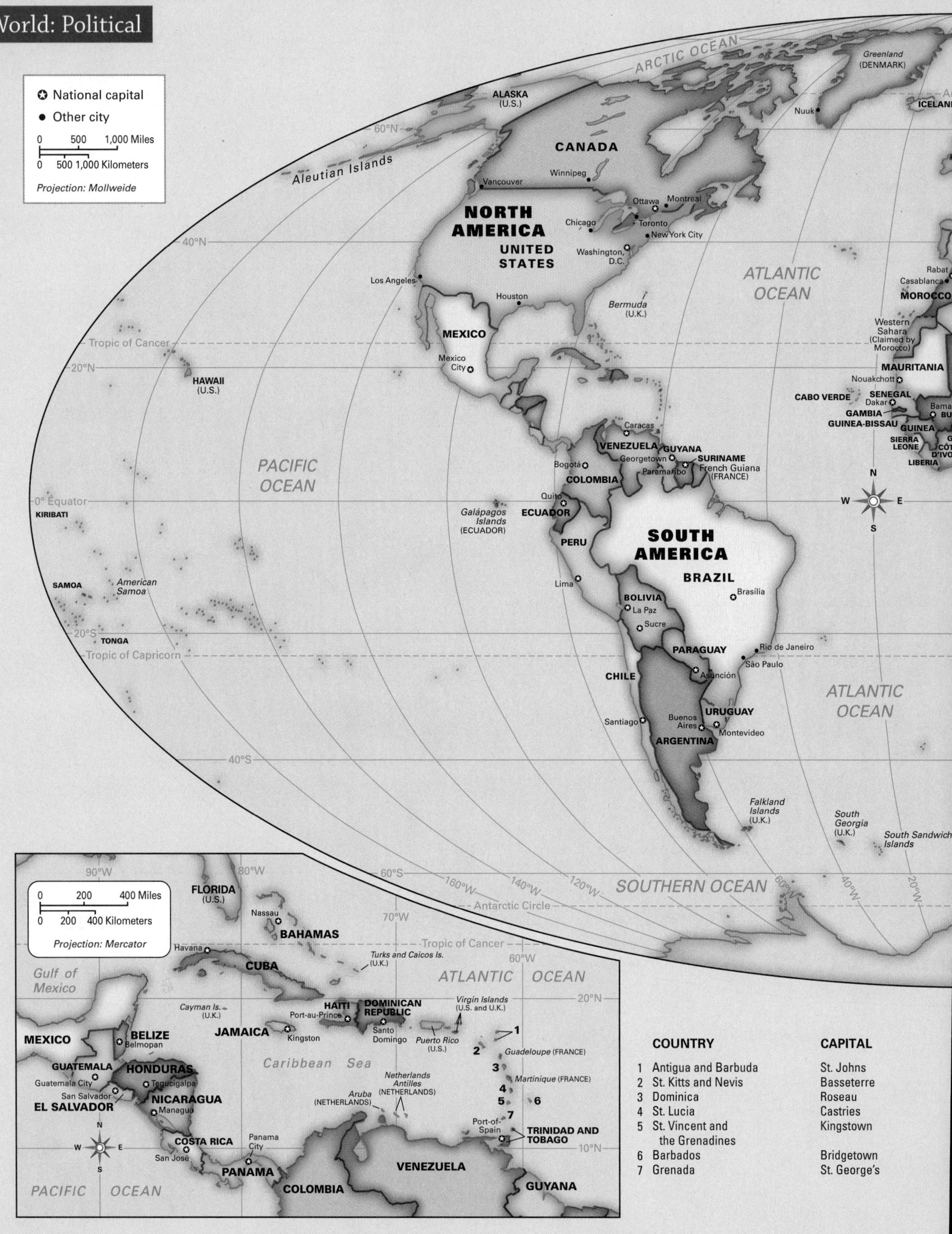

	COUNTRY	CAPITAL
1	Antigua and Barbuda	St. Johns
2	St. Kitts and Nevis	Basseterre
3	Dominica	Roseau
4	St. Lucia	Castries
5	St. Vincent and the Grenadines	Kingstown
6	Barbados	Bridgetown
7	Grenada	St. George's

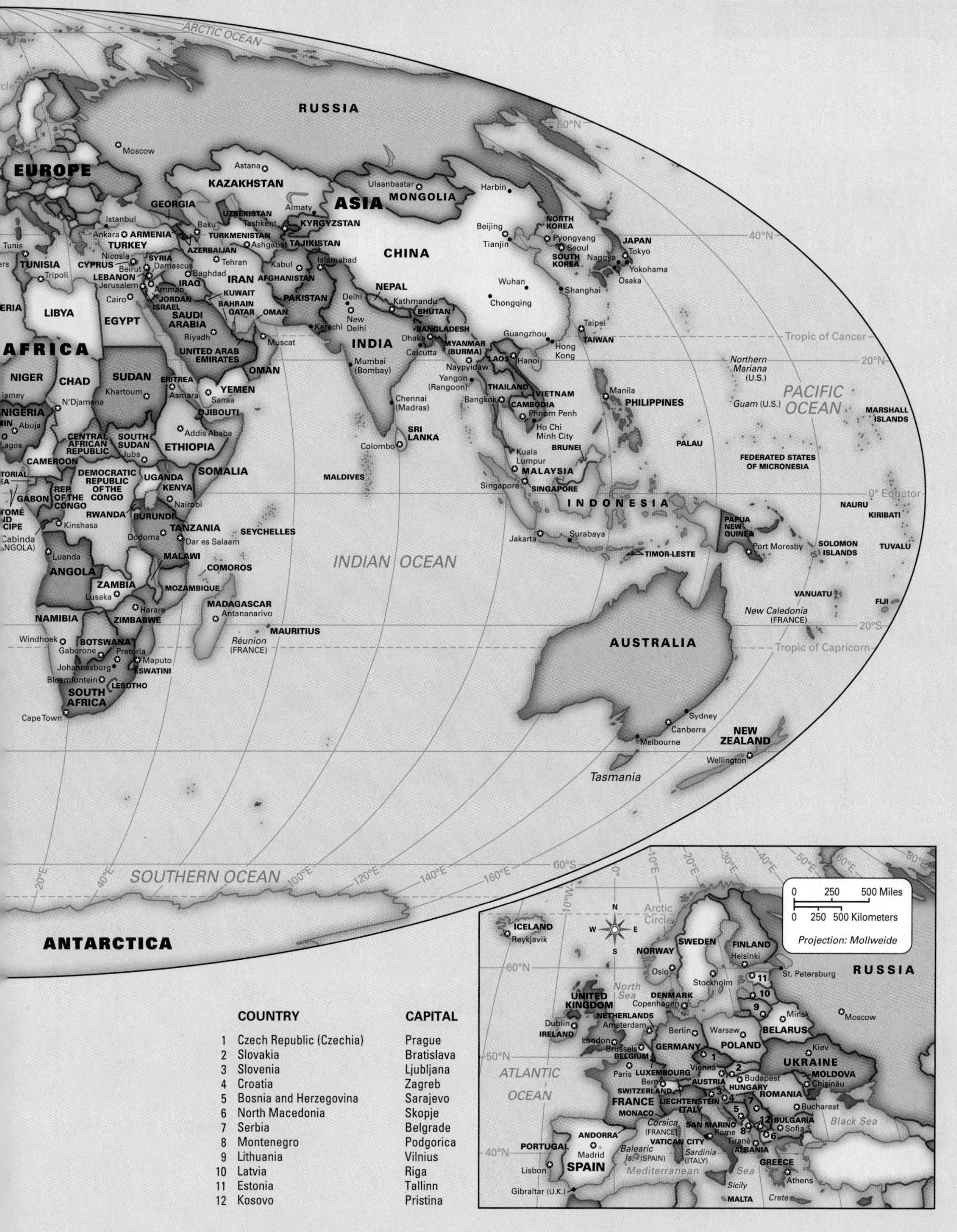

	COUNTRY	CAPITAL
1	Czech Republic (Czechia)	Prague
2	Slovakia	Bratislava
3	Slovenia	Ljubljana
4	Croatia	Zagreb
5	Bosnia and Herzegovina	Sarajevo
6	North Macedonia	Skopje
7	Serbia	Belgrade
8	Montenegro	Podgorica
9	Lithuania	Vilnius
10	Latvia	Riga
11	Estonia	Tallinn
12	Kosovo	Pristina

North America: Physical

North America: Political

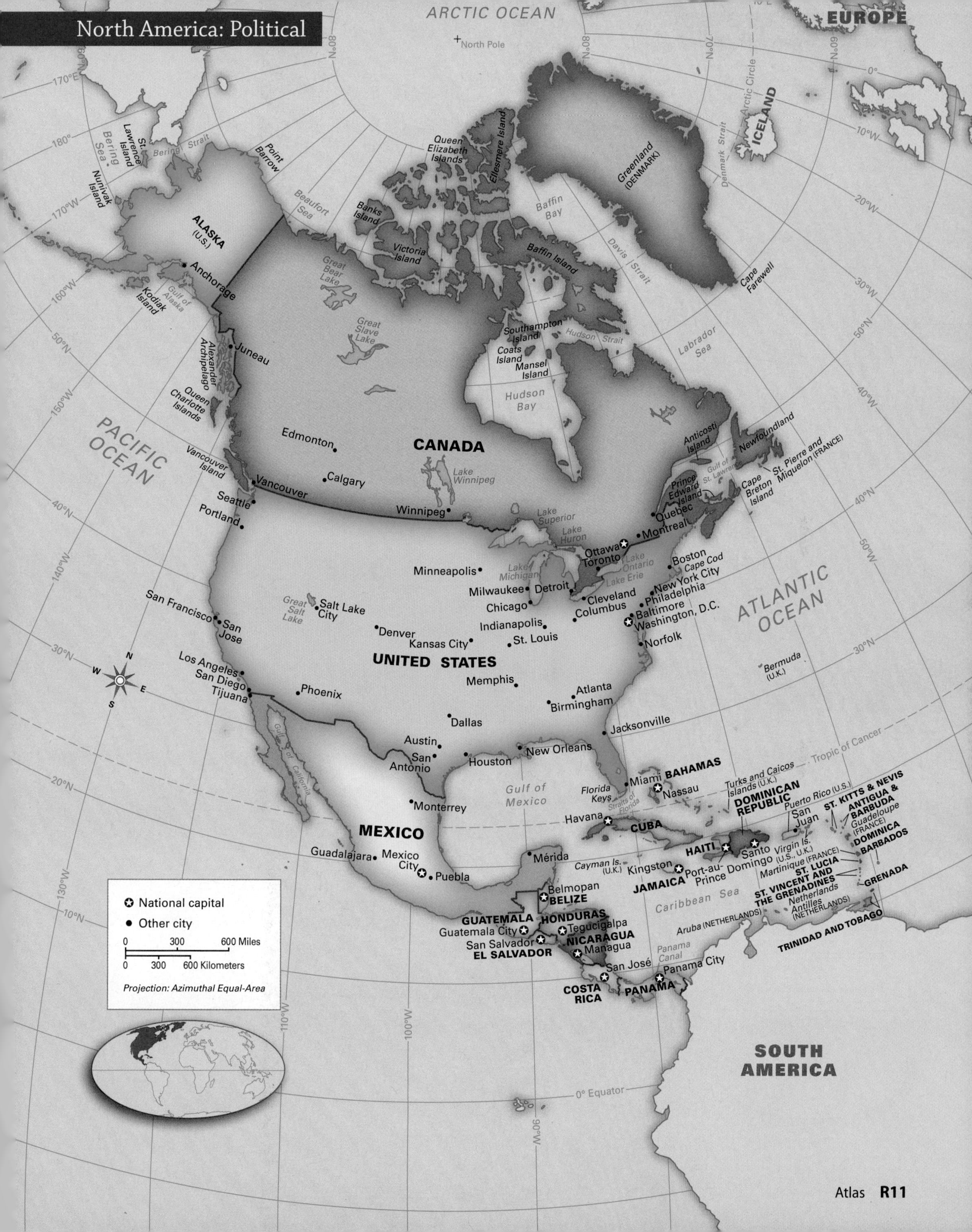

South America: Physical

South America: Political

Europe: Physical

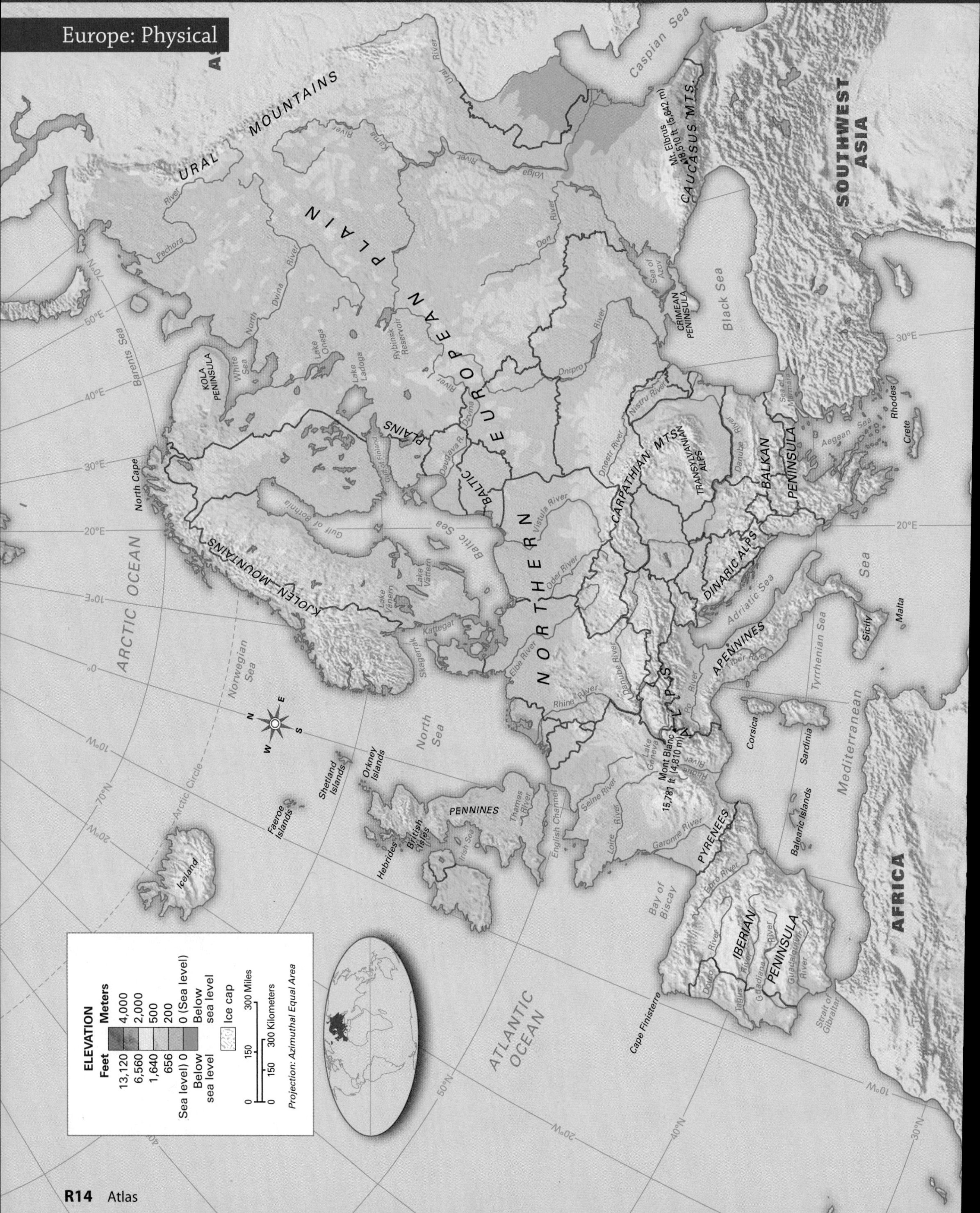

ELEVATION

Feet	Meters
13,120	4,000
6,560	2,000
1,640	500
656	200
Sea level) 0	0 (Sea level)
Below sea level	Below sea level

Ice cap

0 150 300 Miles
0 150 300 Kilometers

Projection: Azimuthal Equal Area

URAL MOUNTAINS
NORTHERN EUROPEAN PLAIN
BALTIC PLAINS
CAUCASUS MTS.
Mt. Elbrus 18,510 ft. (5,642 m)
SOUTHWEST ASIA
Caspian Sea
Black Sea
Sea of Azov
CRIMEAN PENINSULA
Volga River
Kama River
Ural River
Don River
Dnipro River
Dnestr River
Nistru River
Pechora River
North Dvina River
Dvina River
Daugava R.
Rybinsk Reservoir
Lake Onega
Lake Ladoga
White Sea
Barents Sea
KOLA PENINSULA
North Cape
Gulf of Finland
Gulf of Bothnia
Baltic Sea
Lake Vänern
Lake Vättern
Kattegat
Skagerrak
KJOLEN MOUNTAINS
ARCTIC OCEAN
Norwegian Sea
North Sea
Arctic Circle
Vistula River
Oder River
Elbe River
Rhine River
Danube River
CARPATHIAN MTS.
TRANSYLVANIAN ALPS
BALKAN PENINSULA
DINARIC ALPS
Adriatic Sea
Aegean Sea
Sea of Marmara
Rhodes
Crete
APENNINES
Tiber River
Po River
ALPS
Mont Blanc 15,781 ft. (4,810 m)
Lake Geneva
Rhone River
Seine River
Loire River
Garonne River
PYRENEES
Sicily
Malta
Corsica
Sardinia
Tyrrhenian Sea
Mediterranean Sea
Balearic Islands
AFRICA
Shetland Islands
Orkney Islands
Faeroe Islands
Hebrides
British Isles
PENNINES
Thames River
Irish Sea
English Channel
Iceland
Bay of Biscay
Cape Finisterre
Ebro River
IBERIAN PENINSULA
Douro River
Tagus River
Guadiana River
Guadalquivir River
Strait of Gibraltar
ATLANTIC OCEAN
N E S W
70°N 60°N 50°N 40°N 30°N
50°E 40°E 30°E 20°E 10°E 0° 10°W 20°W

ARCTIC OCEAN
Arctic Circle
North Cape
Barents Sea
White Sea
ASIA
URAL MOUNTAINS
RUSSIA
St. Petersburg
Nizhny Novgorod
Moscow
National capital
Other city
0 150 300 Miles
0 150 300 Kilometers
Projection: Azimuthal Equal-Area
ICELAND
Reykjavik
Faeroe Islands (DENMARK)
Shetland Islands
N
E
S
W
NORWAY
Bergen
Oslo
SWEDEN
Stockholm
Göteborg
Gulf of Bothnia
FINLAND
Helsinki
Gulf of Finland
Tallinn
ESTONIA
LATVIA
Riga
LITHUANIA
Vilnius
RUSSIA
BELARUS
Minsk
Baltic Sea
North Sea
DENMARK
Copenhagen
NORTHERN IRELAND
SCOTLAND
UNITED KINGDOM
Edinburgh
Belfast
Dublin
IRELAND
Liverpool
WALES
ENGLAND
London
British Isles
ATLANTIC OCEAN
Channel Islands (U.K.)
English Channel
THE NETHERLANDS
Amsterdam
Brussels
BELGIUM
LUXEMBOURG
Luxembourg
Paris
FRANCE
Lyon
Marseille
Bay of Biscay
Hamburg
Berlin
GERMANY
Cologne
Bonn
Dresden
Munich
POLAND
Warsaw
Krakow
Prague
CZECH REPUBLIC
SLOVAKIA
Bratislava
Vienna
AUSTRIA
SWITZERLAND
Lake Geneva
Bern
Vaduz
LIECHTENSTEIN
ALPS
Milan
Ljubljana
SLOVENIA
Zagreb
CROATIA
Budapest
HUNGARY
UKRAINE
Kiev
MOLDOVA
Chisinau
ROMANIA
Bucharest
Caspian Sea
Black Sea
SAN MARINO
San Marino
BOSNIA AND HERZEGOVINA
Sarajevo
Belgrade
SERBIA
MONTENEGRO
Podgorica
KOSOVO
Pristina
Tirana
ALBANIA
Sofia
BULGARIA
Skopje
NORTH MACEDONIA
GREECE
Athens
Aegean Sea
Rhodes
Crete
SOUTHWEST ASIA
PORTUGAL
Lisbon
Madrid
SPAIN
Valencia
Seville
Gibraltar (U.K.)
Strait of Gibraltar
PYRENEES
Andorra la Vella
ANDORRA
Barcelona
Balearic Islands (SPAIN)
MONACO
Monaco
Corsica (FRANCE)
Sardinia (ITALY)
ITALY
VATICAN CITY
Rome
Naples
Adriatic Sea
Sicily
MALTA
Valletta
Mediterranean Sea
AFRICA
70°N
60°N
50°N
40°N
30°W
20°W
10°W
0°
10°E
20°E
30°E
40°E
50°E

Asia: Physical

ELEVATION

Feet	Meters
13,120	4,000
6,560	2,000
1,640	500
656	200
0 (Sea level)	0 (Sea level)
Below sea level	Below sea level

Ice cap

0 250 500 750 Miles
0 250 500 750 Kilometers

Projection: Two-Point Equidistant

EUROPE
AFRICA
AUSTRALIA
PACIFIC OCEAN
INDIAN OCEAN
North Pole
Arctic Circle
Tropic of Cancer
Equator
URAL MOUNTAINS
WEST SIBERIAN PLAIN
SIBERIA
CENTRAL SIBERIAN PLATEAU
TAYMYR PENINSULA
VERKHOYANSKIY RANGE
CHERSKIY RANGE
KOLYMA MTS.
STANOVOY MOUNTAINS
CENTRAL RANGE
KAMCHATKA PENINSULA
Aleutian Islands
Bering Sea
Sea of Okhotsk
Sakhalin Island
Kuril Islands
Hokkaido
Honshu
Shikoku
Kyushu
Sea of Japan (East Sea)
Korea Strait
Yellow Sea
East China Sea
Ryukyu Islands
Okinawa
Taiwan
Luzon Strait
Luzon
Philippines
Mindanao
Moluccas
Celebes Sea
Celebes
Banda Sea
Arafura Sea
MAOKE MOUNTAINS
New Guinea
South China Sea
Borneo
Java Sea
Java
Bangka
Sumatra
Strait of Malacca
MALAY PENINSULA
Gulf of Thailand
Mentawai Islands
INDOCHINA PENINSULA
Mekong River
Chao Phraya River
Gulf of Tonkin
Hainan
Xi River
BOHEA HILLS
QIN LING
Chang Jiang (Yangzi River)
Huang He (Yellow River)
NORTH CHINA PLAIN
GREATER KHINGAN RANGE
Amur River
YABLONOVY RANGE
Shilka River
Lake Baykal
Aldan River
Lena River
Lower Tunguska River
Angara River
Yenisey River
MONGOLIAN PLATEAU
GOBI
SAYAN MOUNTAINS
ALTAY MOUNTAINS
TARIM BASIN
TAKLIMAKAN DESERT
TIAN SHAN
KUNLUN MOUNTAINS
PLATEAU OF TIBET
Mount Everest 29,029 ft (8,848 m)
HIMALAYAS
Nu River
Brahmaputra River
Irrawaddy River
Hong River
INDO-GANGETIC PLAIN
Ganges River
DECCAN PLATEAU
Godavari River
EASTERN GHATS
WESTERN GHATS
Sri Lanka
Bay of Bengal
Andaman Islands
Andaman Sea
Nicobar Islands
Lakshadweep Islands
Maldives
Arabian Sea
THAR DESERT
Indus River
Sutlej River
HINDU KUSH
KAZAKH UPLANDS
Balqash Lake
Irtysh River
Ob River
Ishim River
Syr Darya
Amu Darya
TURAN LOWLAND
KYZYL KUM
KARA KUM
Aral Sea
USTYURT PLATEAU
Ural River
Caspian Sea
CAUCASUS MTS.
Mount Ararat 16,945 ft (5,165 m)
ANATOLIAN PLATEAU
Bosporus
Black Sea
Cyprus
Mediterranean Sea
SINAI PENINSULA
Red Sea
SYRIAN DESERT
AN-NAFUD
Tigris River
Euphrates River
ZAGROS MTS.
GREAT SALT DESERT
Persian Gulf
Strait of Hormuz
Gulf of Oman
RUB' AL-KHALI
Gulf of Aden
Socotra Island
Barents Sea
Kara Sea
Laptev Sea
Novaya Zemlya
Franz Josef Land
North Land
New Siberian Islands
Wrangel Island

Asia: Political

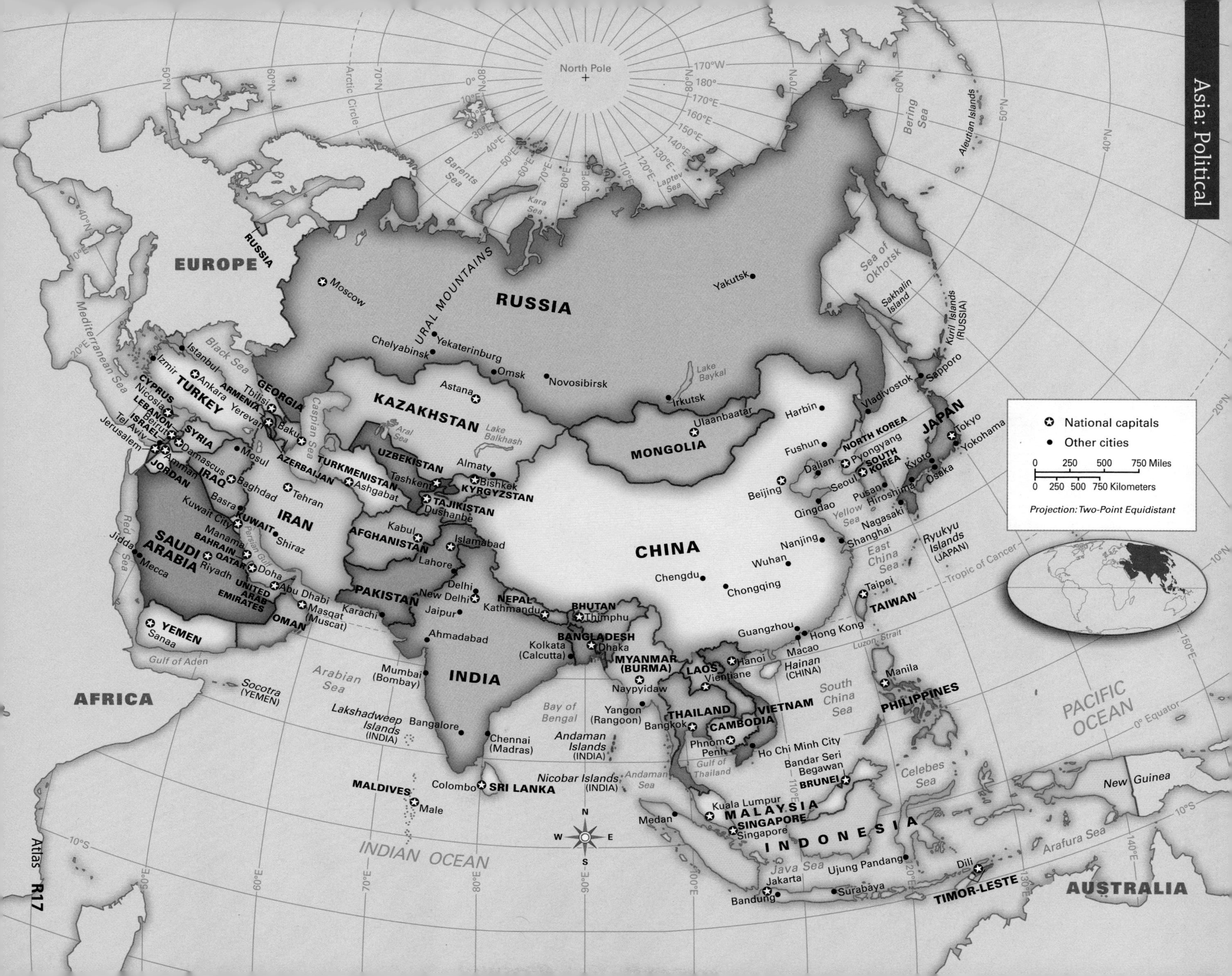

Africa: Physical

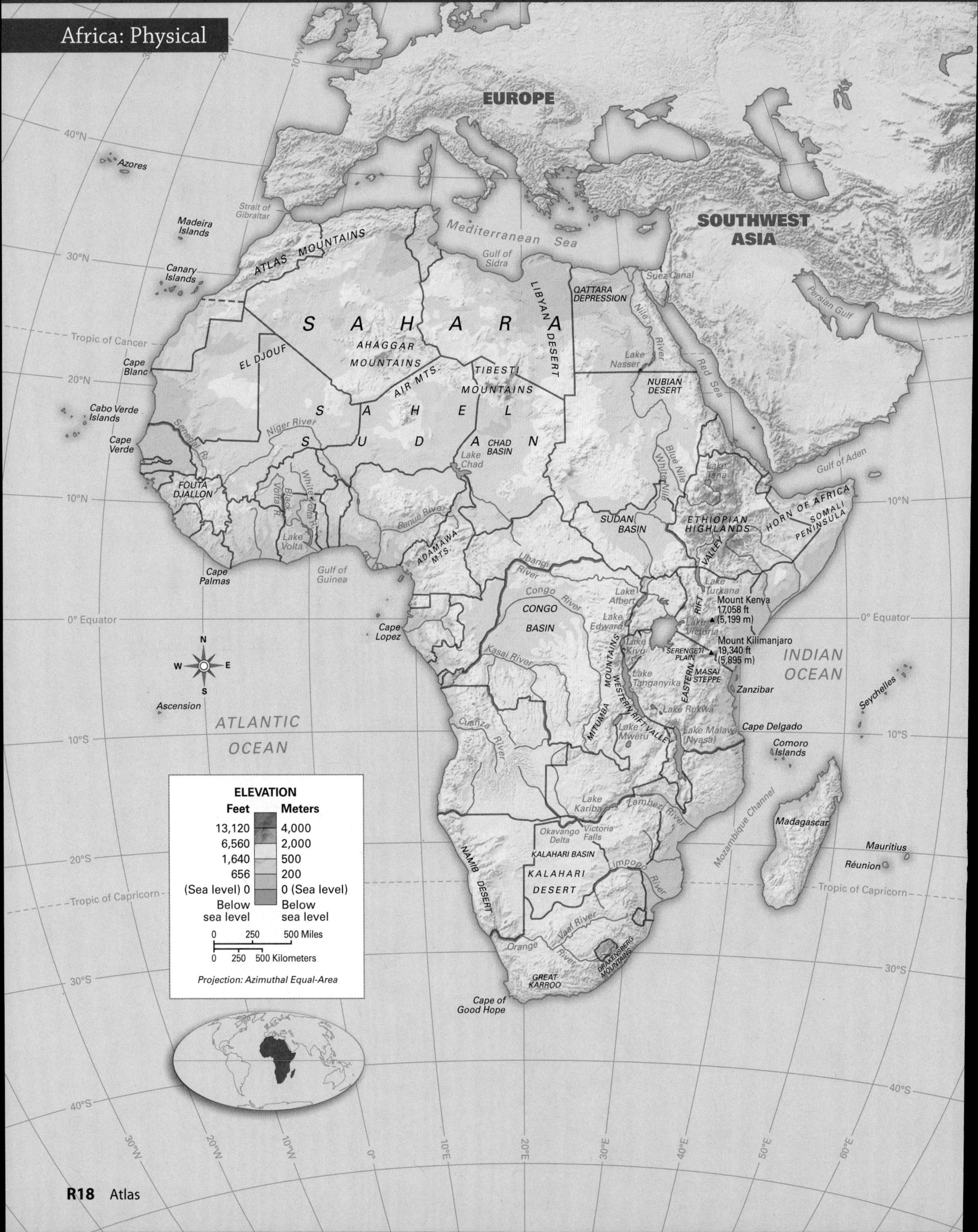

EUROPE
SOUTHWEST ASIA
Azores
Madeira Islands
Canary Islands
Strait of Gibraltar
ATLAS MOUNTAINS
Mediterranean Sea
Gulf of Sidra
Suez Canal
Persian Gulf
QATTARA DEPRESSION
LIBYAN DESERT
SAHARA
AHAGGAR MOUNTAINS
EL DJOUF
AIR MTS.
TIBESTI MOUNTAINS
Nile River
Lake Nasser
Red Sea
NUBIAN DESERT
Cape Blanc
Cabo Verde Islands
Cape Verde
Senegal R.
Niger River
SAHEL
SUDAN
CHAD BASIN
Lake Chad
Blue Nile
White Nile
Lake Tana
Gulf of Aden
FOUTA DJALLON
Volta R.
Black
White Volta R.
Lake Volta
Benue River
ADAMAWA MTS.
SUDAN BASIN
ETHIOPIAN HIGHLANDS
HORN OF AFRICA
SOMALI PENINSULA
Cape Palmas
Gulf of Guinea
Ubangi River
Congo River
CONGO BASIN
Lake Albert
Lake Edward
Lake Turkana
RIFT VALLEY
Mount Kenya 17,058 ft (5,199 m)
Lake Victoria
Mount Kilimanjaro 19,340 ft (5,895 m)
SERENGETI PLAIN
MASAI STEPPE
EASTERN
Lake Kivu
Lake Tanganyika
MITUMBA MOUNTAINS
WESTERN RIFT VALLEY
Lake Rukwa
Lake Mweru
Lake Malawi (Nyasa)
Zanzibar
INDIAN OCEAN
Seychelles
Cape Delgado
Comoro Islands
Cape Lopez
Kasai River
Ascension
ATLANTIC OCEAN
Cuanza River
Lake Kariba
Zambezi River
Okavango Delta
Victoria Falls
Mozambique Channel
Madagascar
Mauritius
Réunion
NAMIB DESERT
KALAHARI BASIN
KALAHARI DESERT
Limpopo River
Vaal River
Orange River
DRAKENSBERG MOUNTAINS
GREAT KARROO
Cape of Good Hope
Tropic of Cancer
Tropic of Capricorn
0° Equator
40°N
30°N
20°N
10°N
10°S
20°S
30°S
40°S
30°W
20°W
10°W
0°
10°E
20°E
30°E
40°E
50°E
60°E
N
S
E
W

ELEVATION

Feet	Meters
13,120	4,000
6,560	2,000
1,640	500
656	200
(Sea level) 0	0 (Sea level)
Below sea level	Below sea level

0 250 500 Miles
0 250 500 Kilometers

Projection: Azimuthal Equal-Area

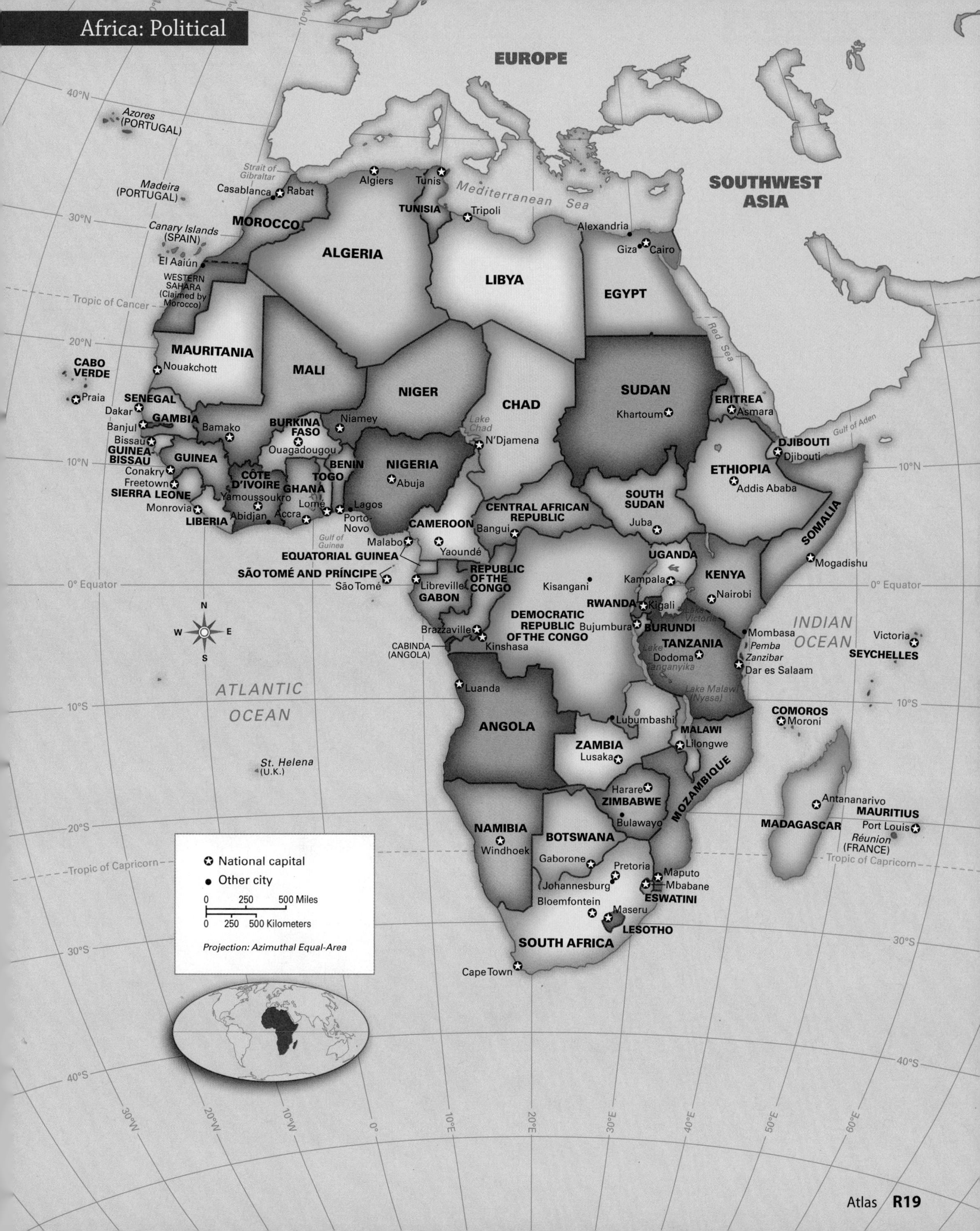
EUROPE
SOUTHWEST ASIA
Azores (PORTUGAL)
Madeira (PORTUGAL)
Canary Islands (SPAIN)
Strait of Gibraltar
Mediterranean Sea
Red Sea
Gulf of Aden
Gulf of Guinea
ATLANTIC OCEAN
INDIAN OCEAN
Lake Chad
Lake Victoria
Lake Tanganyika
Lake Malawi (Nyasa)
Tropic of Cancer
Tropic of Capricorn
0° Equator
MOROCCO
Casablanca
Rabat
El Aaiún
WESTERN SAHARA (Claimed by Morocco)
ALGERIA
Algiers
TUNISIA
Tunis
LIBYA
Tripoli
EGYPT
Alexandria
Giza
Cairo
MAURITANIA
Nouakchott
CABO VERDE
Praia
SENEGAL
Dakar
GAMBIA
Banjul
GUINEA-BISSAU
Bissau
GUINEA
Conakry
SIERRA LEONE
Freetown
LIBERIA
Monrovia
MALI
Bamako
BURKINA FASO
Ouagadougou
NIGER
Niamey
CÔTE D'IVOIRE
Yamoussoukro
Abidjan
GHANA
Accra
TOGO
Lomé
BENIN
Porto-Novo
NIGERIA
Abuja
Lagos
CHAD
N'Djamena
SUDAN
Khartoum
ERITREA
Asmara
DJIBOUTI
Djibouti
ETHIOPIA
Addis Ababa
SOMALIA
Mogadishu
SOUTH SUDAN
Juba
CENTRAL AFRICAN REPUBLIC
Bangui
CAMEROON
Yaoundé
EQUATORIAL GUINEA
Malabo
SÃO TOMÉ AND PRÍNCIPE
São Tomé
GABON
Libreville
REPUBLIC OF THE CONGO
Brazzaville
DEMOCRATIC REPUBLIC OF THE CONGO
Kinshasa
Kisangani
Lubumbashi
CABINDA (ANGOLA)
UGANDA
Kampala
KENYA
Nairobi
Mombasa
RWANDA
Kigali
BURUNDI
Bujumbura
TANZANIA
Dodoma
Dar es Salaam
Pemba
Zanzibar
SEYCHELLES
Victoria
COMOROS
Moroni
ANGOLA
Luanda
ZAMBIA
Lusaka
MALAWI
Lilongwe
MOZAMBIQUE
Maputo
ZIMBABWE
Harare
Bulawayo
NAMIBIA
Windhoek
BOTSWANA
Gaborone
SOUTH AFRICA
Pretoria
Johannesburg
Bloemfontein
Cape Town
ESWATINI
Mbabane
LESOTHO
Maseru
MADAGASCAR
Antananarivo
MAURITIUS
Port Louis
Réunion (FRANCE)
St. Helena (U.K.)
N
S
E
W
40°N
30°N
20°N
10°N
10°S
20°S
30°S
40°S
30°W
20°W
10°W
0°
10°E
20°E
30°E
40°E
50°E
60°E
National capital
Other city
0 250 500 Miles
0 250 500 Kilometers
Projection: Azimuthal Equal-Area

The Pacific: Political

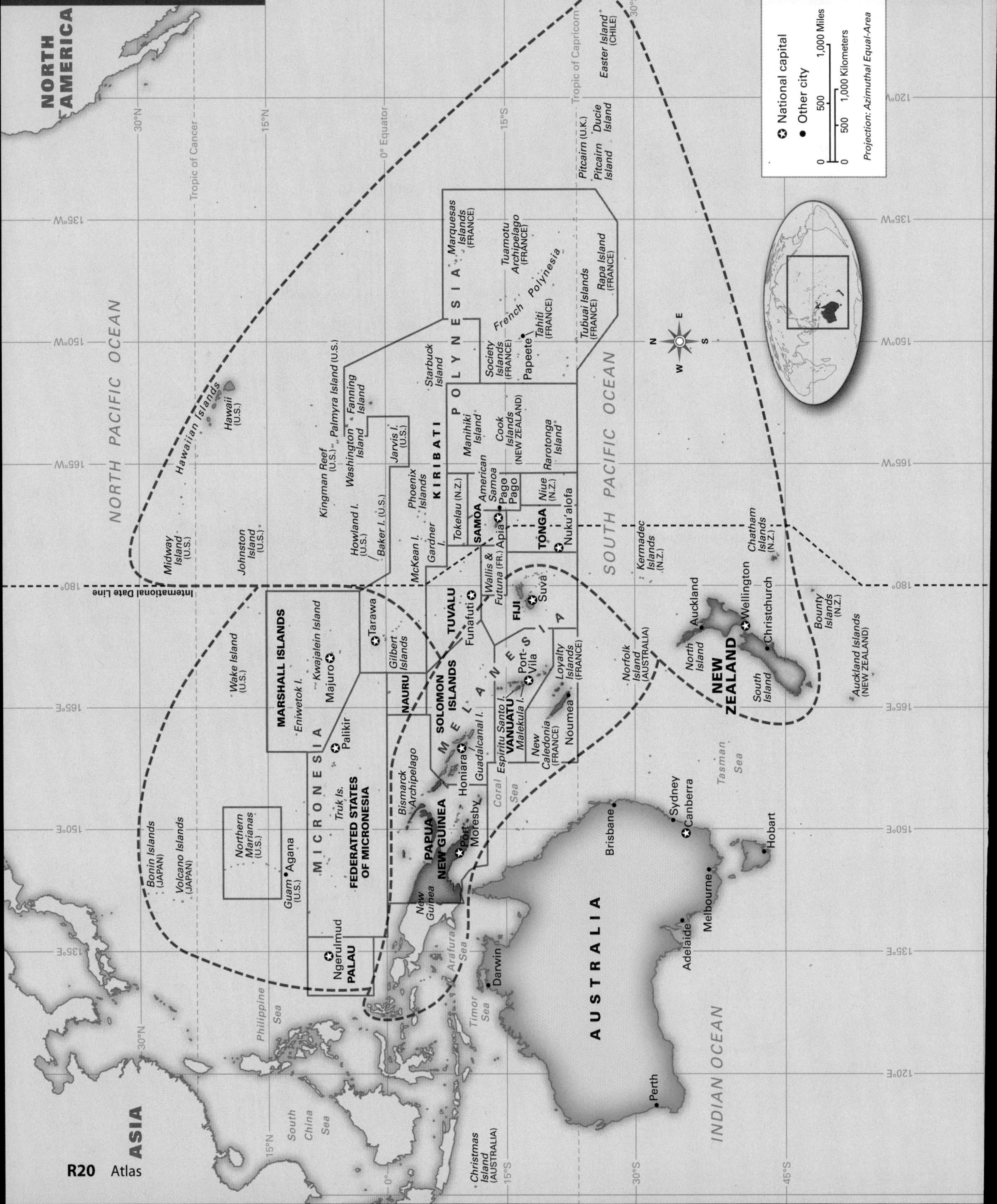

National capital
Other city
0 500 1,000 Miles
0 500 1,000 Kilometers
Projection: Azimuthal Equal-Area

NORTH AMERICA
ASIA
AUSTRALIA
NORTH PACIFIC OCEAN
SOUTH PACIFIC OCEAN
INDIAN OCEAN
Tropic of Cancer
0° Equator
Tropic of Capricorn
International Date Line
30°N
15°N
15°S
30°S
45°S
120°E
135°E
150°E
165°E
180°
165°W
150°W
135°W
120°W

MICRONESIA
MELANESIA
POLYNESIA

Hawaiian Islands
Hawaii (U.S.)
Midway Island (U.S.)
Johnston Island (U.S.)
Kingman Reef (U.S.)
Palmyra Island (U.S.)
Washington Island
Fanning Island
Jarvis I. (U.S.)
Howland I. (U.S.)
Baker I. (U.S.)
Phoenix Islands
McKean I.
Gardner I.
Starbuck Island
KIRIBATI
Manihiki Island
Cook Islands (NEW ZEALAND)
Rarotonga Island
Society Islands (FRANCE)
Papeete
Tahiti (FRANCE)
French Polynesia
Marquesas Islands (FRANCE)
Tuamotu Archipelago (FRANCE)
Tubuai Islands (FRANCE)
Rapa Island (FRANCE)
Pitcairn (U.K.)
Pitcairn Island
Ducie Island
Easter Island (CHILE)
Tokelau (N.Z.)
SAMOA
Apia
American Samoa
Pago Pago
Niue (N.Z.)
TONGA
Nuku'alofa
Wallis & Futuna (FR.)
TUVALU
Funafuti
FIJI
Suva
Kermadec Islands (N.Z.)
Chatham Islands (N.Z.)
Bounty Islands (N.Z.)
Auckland Islands (NEW ZEALAND)
NEW ZEALAND
North Island
South Island
Auckland
Wellington
Christchurch
Norfolk Island (AUSTRALIA)
Loyalty Islands (FRANCE)
New Caledonia (FRANCE)
Noumea
VANUATU
Port-Vila
Espiritu Santo I.
Malekula I.
SOLOMON ISLANDS
Honiara
Guadalcanal I.
Coral Sea
Tasman Sea
NAURU
Gilbert Islands
Tarawa
MARSHALL ISLANDS
Eniwetok I.
Kwajalein Island
Majuro
Wake Island (U.S.)
FEDERATED STATES OF MICRONESIA
Palikir
Truk Is.
Northern Marianas (U.S.)
Guam (U.S.)
Agana
Bonin Islands (JAPAN)
Volcano Islands (JAPAN)
PALAU
Ngerulmud
PAPUA NEW GUINEA
Port Moresby
Bismarck Archipelago
New Guinea
Arafura Sea
Timor Sea
Philippine Sea
South China Sea
Darwin
Brisbane
Sydney
Canberra
Melbourne
Hobart
Adelaide
Perth
Christmas Island (AUSTRALIA)

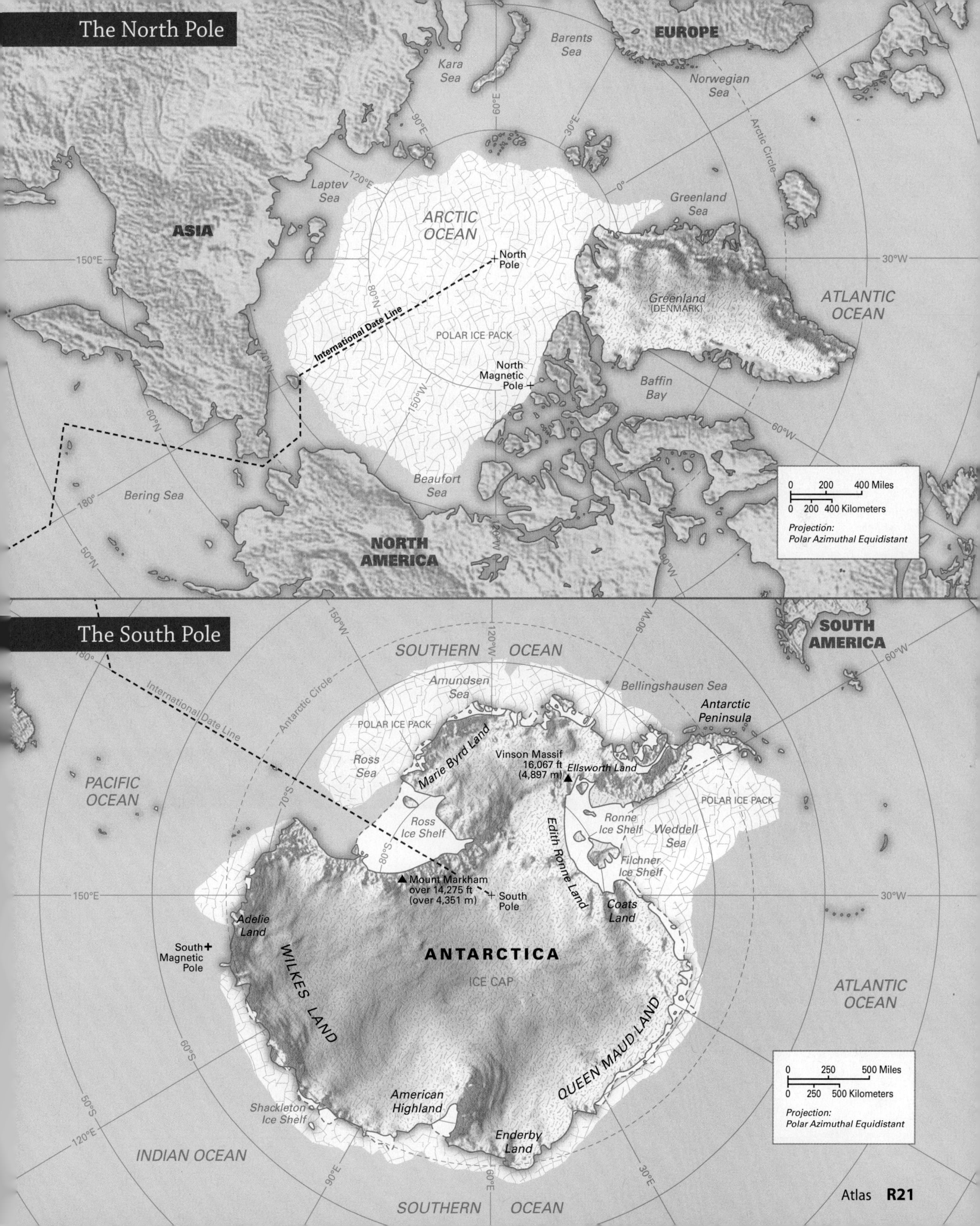

The North Pole
EUROPE
Barents Sea
Kara Sea
Norwegian Sea
Arctic Circle
Laptev Sea
ASIA
ARCTIC OCEAN
Greenland Sea
North Pole
International Date Line
Greenland (DENMARK)
ATLANTIC OCEAN
POLAR ICE PACK
North Magnetic Pole
Baffin Bay
Bering Sea
Beaufort Sea
NORTH AMERICA
0 200 400 Miles
0 200 400 Kilometers
Projection: Polar Azimuthal Equidistant
The South Pole
SOUTH AMERICA
SOUTHERN OCEAN
Amundsen Sea
Bellingshausen Sea
Antarctic Peninsula
International Date Line
Antarctic Circle
POLAR ICE PACK
Marie Byrd Land
Vinson Massif 16,067 ft (4,897 m)
Ellsworth Land
Ross Sea
PACIFIC OCEAN
Ross Ice Shelf
Ronne Ice Shelf
Weddell Sea
Edith Ronne Land
Filchner Ice Shelf
Mount Markham over 14,275 ft (over 4,351 m)
South Pole
Coats Land
Adelie Land
South Magnetic Pole
ANTARCTICA
WILKES LAND
ICE CAP
ATLANTIC OCEAN
QUEEN MAUD LAND
0 250 500 Miles
0 250 500 Kilometers
Projection: Polar Azimuthal Equidistant
American Highland
Shackleton Ice Shelf
Enderby Land
INDIAN OCEAN
SOUTHERN OCEAN

Europe, Russia, and the Eurasian Republics: Physical

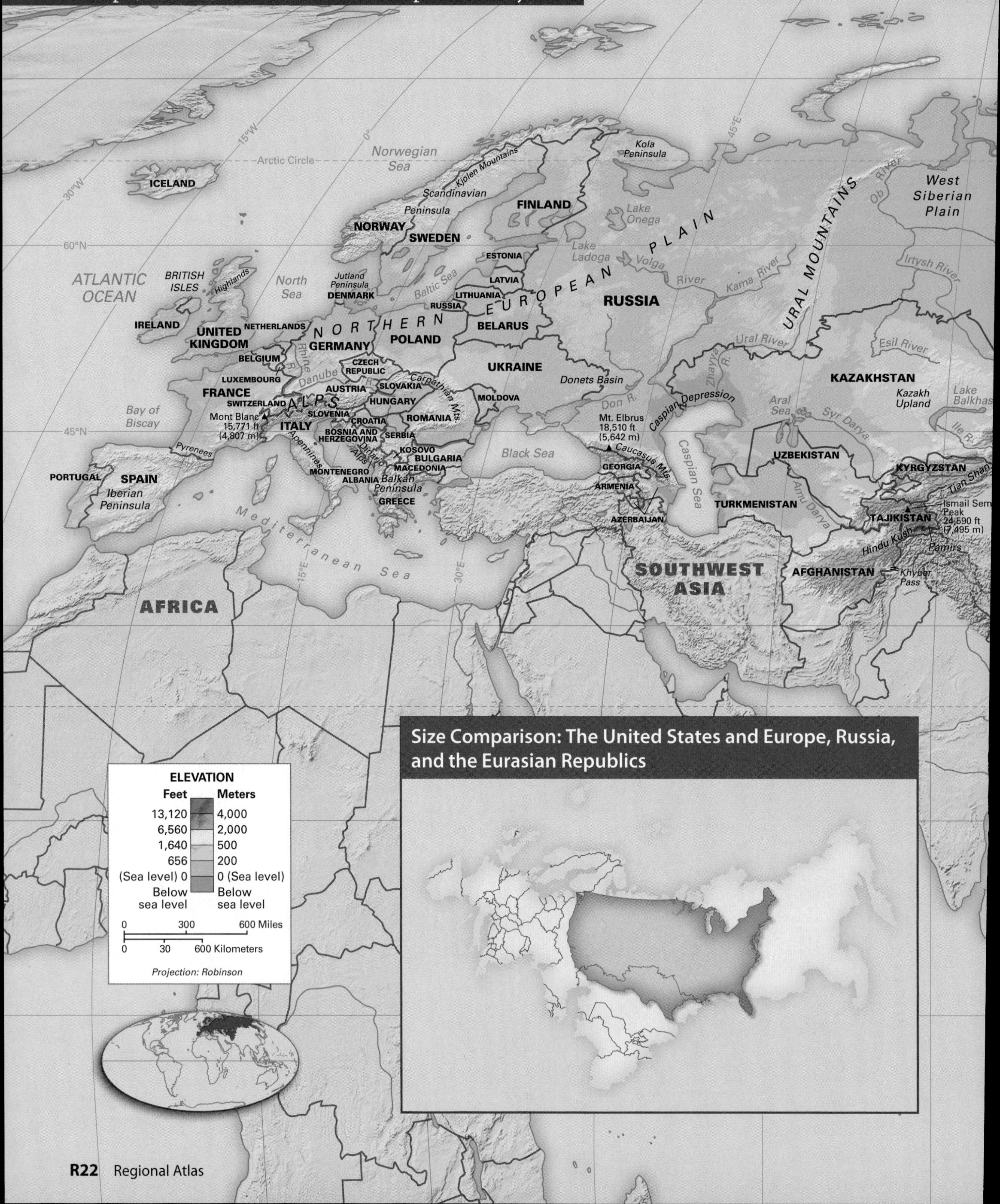

Arctic Circle
60°N
45°N
30°W
15°W
0°
15°E
30°E
45°E
ICELAND
Norwegian Sea
Kjolen Mountains
Kola Peninsula
Scandinavian Peninsula
FINLAND
NORWAY
SWEDEN
Lake Onega
Lake Ladoga
West Siberian Plain
Ob River
URAL MOUNTAINS
EUROPEAN PLAIN
ATLANTIC OCEAN
BRITISH ISLES
Highlands
North Sea
Jutland Peninsula
DENMARK
Baltic Sea
ESTONIA
LATVIA
LITHUANIA
RUSSIA
Volga River
Kama River
Irtysh River
IRELAND
UNITED KINGDOM
NETHERLANDS
NORTHERN
GERMANY
POLAND
BELARUS
BELGIUM
Rhine R.
LUXEMBOURG
CZECH REPUBLIC
Danube R.
AUSTRIA
SLOVAKIA
Carpathian Mts.
UKRAINE
Donets Basin
Ural River
Zhayyq R.
Esil River
KAZAKHSTAN
Kazakh Upland
Lake Balkhash
FRANCE
SWITZERLAND
ALPS
HUNGARY
MOLDOVA
Don R.
Caspian Depression
Aral Sea
Syr Darya
Ile R.
Bay of Biscay
Mont Blanc 15,771 ft (4,807 m)
SLOVENIA
CROATIA
ROMANIA
BOSNIA AND HERZEGOVINA
SERBIA
ITALY
Mt. Elbrus 18,510 ft (5,642 m)
Caspian Sea
Pyrenees
Apennines
Dinaric Alps
KOSOVO
BULGARIA
Black Sea
Caucasus Mts.
UZBEKISTAN
KYRGYZSTAN
Tian Shan
MONTENEGRO
MACEDONIA
GEORGIA
PORTUGAL
SPAIN
Iberian Peninsula
ALBANIA
Balkan Peninsula
GREECE
ARMENIA
AZERBAIJAN
TURKMENISTAN
Amu Darya
Ismail Samani Peak 24,590 ft (7,495 m)
TAJIKISTAN
Hindu Kush
Pamirs
Mediterranean Sea
SOUTHWEST ASIA
AFGHANISTAN
Khyber Pass
AFRICA

ELEVATION

Feet	Meters
13,120	4,000
6,560	2,000
1,640	500
656	200
(Sea level) 0	0 (Sea level)
Below sea level	Below sea level

0 300 600 Miles
0 30 600 Kilometers

Projection: Robinson

Size Comparison: The United States and Europe, Russia, and the Eurasian Republics

Europe, Russia, and the Eurasian Republics

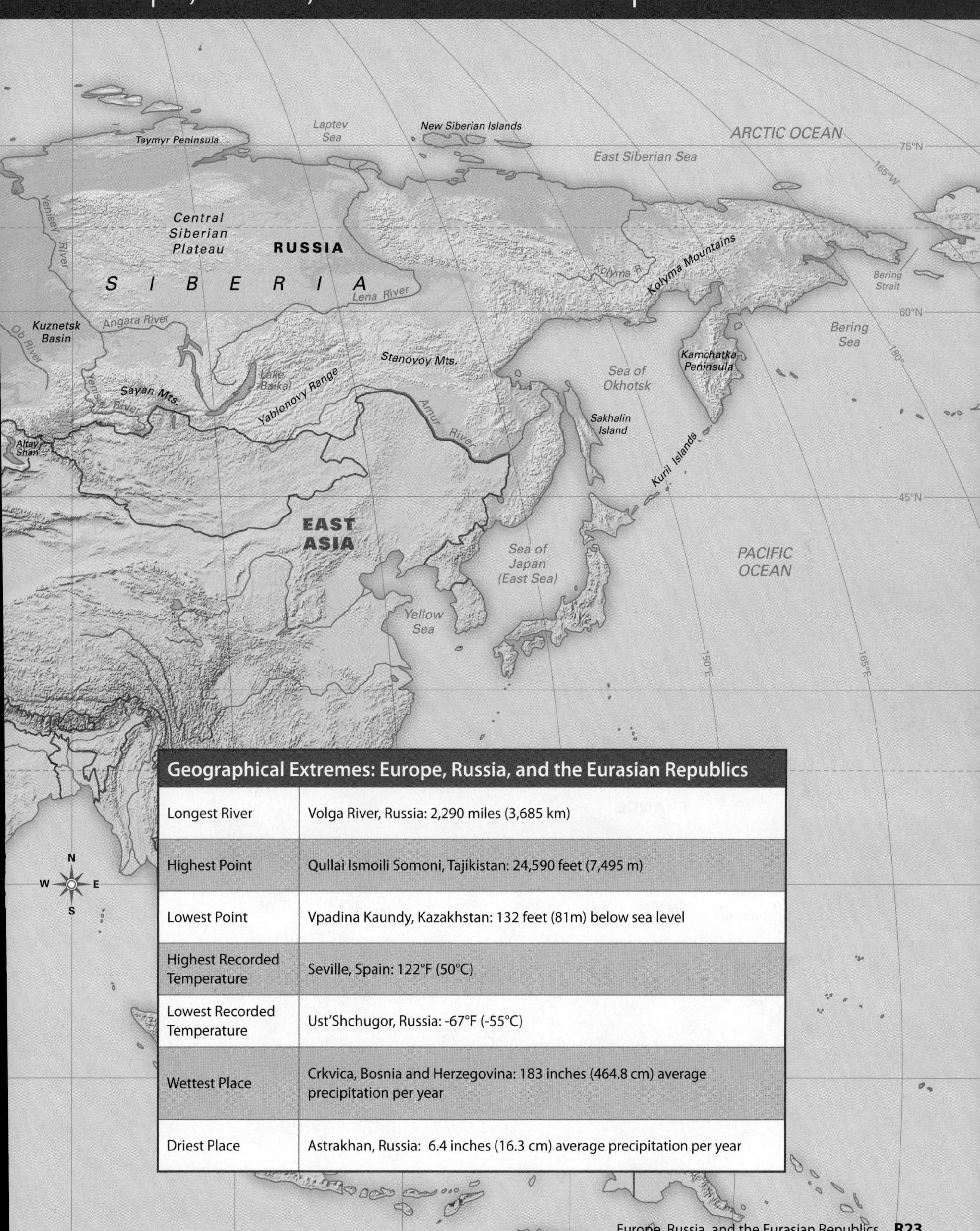

Geographical Extremes: Europe, Russia, and the Eurasian Republics	
Longest River	Volga River, Russia: 2,290 miles (3,685 km)
Highest Point	Qullai Ismoili Somoni, Tajikistan: 24,590 feet (7,495 m)
Lowest Point	Vpadina Kaundy, Kazakhstan: 132 feet (81m) below sea level
Highest Recorded Temperature	Seville, Spain: 122°F (50°C)
Lowest Recorded Temperature	Ust'Shchugor, Russia: -67°F (-55°C)
Wettest Place	Crkvica, Bosnia and Herzegovina: 183 inches (464.8 cm) average precipitation per year
Driest Place	Astrakhan, Russia: 6.4 inches (16.3 cm) average precipitation per year

Europe: Political

National capital
Other city
0 200 400 Miles
0 200 400 Kilometers
Projection: Azimuthal Equal-Area

ARCTIC OCEAN
Norwegian Sea
North Sea
Baltic Sea
ATLANTIC OCEAN
Black Sea
Adriatic Sea
Aegean Sea
Mediterranean Sea
Denmark Strait
Arctic Circle
Strait of Gibraltar
Danube R.
Rhine R.
Dnieper River
70°N
60°N
50°N
40°N
30°W
20°W
10°W
0°
10°E
20°E
30°E
N
S
E
W

ICELAND
Reykjavik
Faeroe Islands (DENMARK)
Shetland Islands (U.K.)
NORWAY
Oslo
SWEDEN
Stockholm
FINLAND
Helsinki
RUSSIA
ESTONIA
Tallinn
LATVIA
Riga
LITHUANIA
Vilnius
Kaliningrad (RUSSIA)
BELARUS
Minsk
DENMARK
Copenhagen
IRELAND
Dublin
UNITED KINGDOM
London
NETHERLANDS
Amsterdam
BELGIUM
Brussels
LUXEMBOURG
Luxembourg
GERMANY
Berlin
POLAND
Warsaw
UKRAINE
Kiev
FRANCE
Paris
CZECH REPUBLIC
Prague
SLOVAKIA
Bratislava
LIECHTENSTEIN
SWITZERLAND
Bern
AUSTRIA
Vienna
HUNGARY
Budapest
MOLDOVA
Chişinau
ROMANIA
Bucharest
SLOVENIA
Ljubljana
CROATIA
Zagreb
BOSNIA AND HERZEGOVINA
Sarajevo
SERBIA
Belgrade
KOSOVO
Pristina
MONTENEGRO
Podgorica
ALBANIA
Tirane
MACEDONIA
Skopje
BULGARIA
Sofia
GREECE
Athens
Crete (GREECE)
ITALY
Rome
SAN MARINO
VATICAN CITY
MONACO
Corsica (FRANCE)
Sardinia (ITALY)
Sicily (ITALY)
MALTA
Valletta
ANDORRA
PORTUGAL
Lisbon
SPAIN
Madrid
Balearic Islands (SPAIN)
Gibraltar (U.K.)
AFRICA
ASIA

Russia and the Eurasian Republics: Political

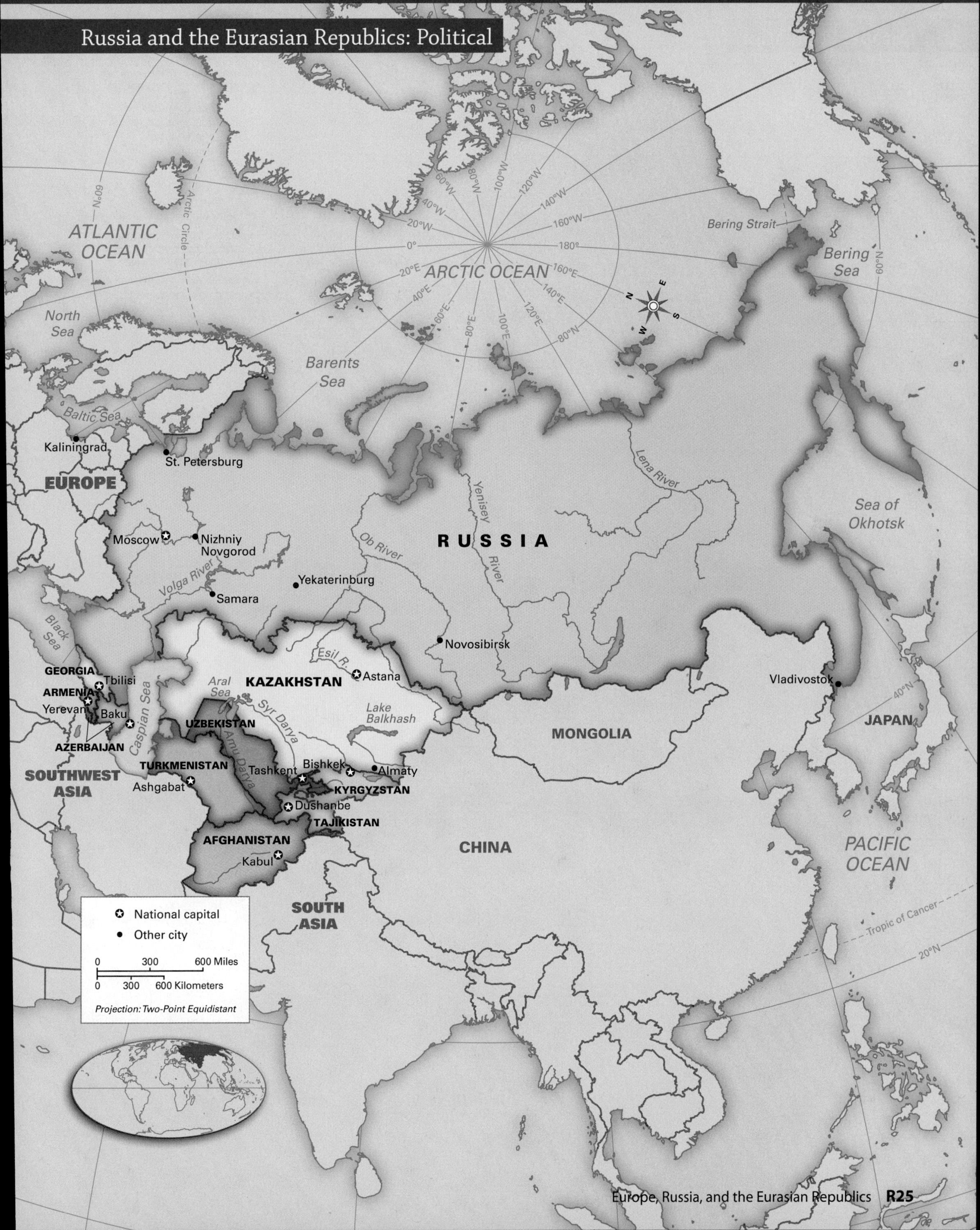

ATLANTIC OCEAN
North Sea
Baltic Sea
Barents Sea
ARCTIC OCEAN
Bering Strait
Bering Sea
Sea of Okhotsk
PACIFIC OCEAN
Black Sea
Caspian Sea
Aral Sea
Lake Balkhash
Arctic Circle
Tropic of Cancer

Kaliningrad
St. Petersburg
EUROPE
Moscow
Nizhniy Novgorod
RUSSIA
Volga River
Samara
Yekaterinburg
Ob River
Yenisey River
Lena River
Novosibirsk
Vladivostok
Esil R.
Astana
KAZAKHSTAN
GEORGIA
Tbilisi
ARMENIA
Yerevan
Baku
AZERBAIJAN
UZBEKISTAN
Syr Darya
Amu Darya
TURKMENISTAN
Ashgabat
Tashkent
Bishkek
Almaty
KYRGYZSTAN
Dushanbe
TAJIKISTAN
AFGHANISTAN
Kabul
SOUTHWEST ASIA
SOUTH ASIA
MONGOLIA
CHINA
JAPAN

0° 20°W 40°W 60°W 80°W 100°W 120°W 140°W 160°W 180° 160°E 140°E 120°E 100°E 80°E 60°E 40°E 20°E 80°N 60°N 40°N 20°N

N E S W

✪ National capital
• Other city

0 300 600 Miles
0 300 600 Kilometers
Projection: Two-Point Equidistant

Europe: Population

Russia and the Eurasian Republics: Climate

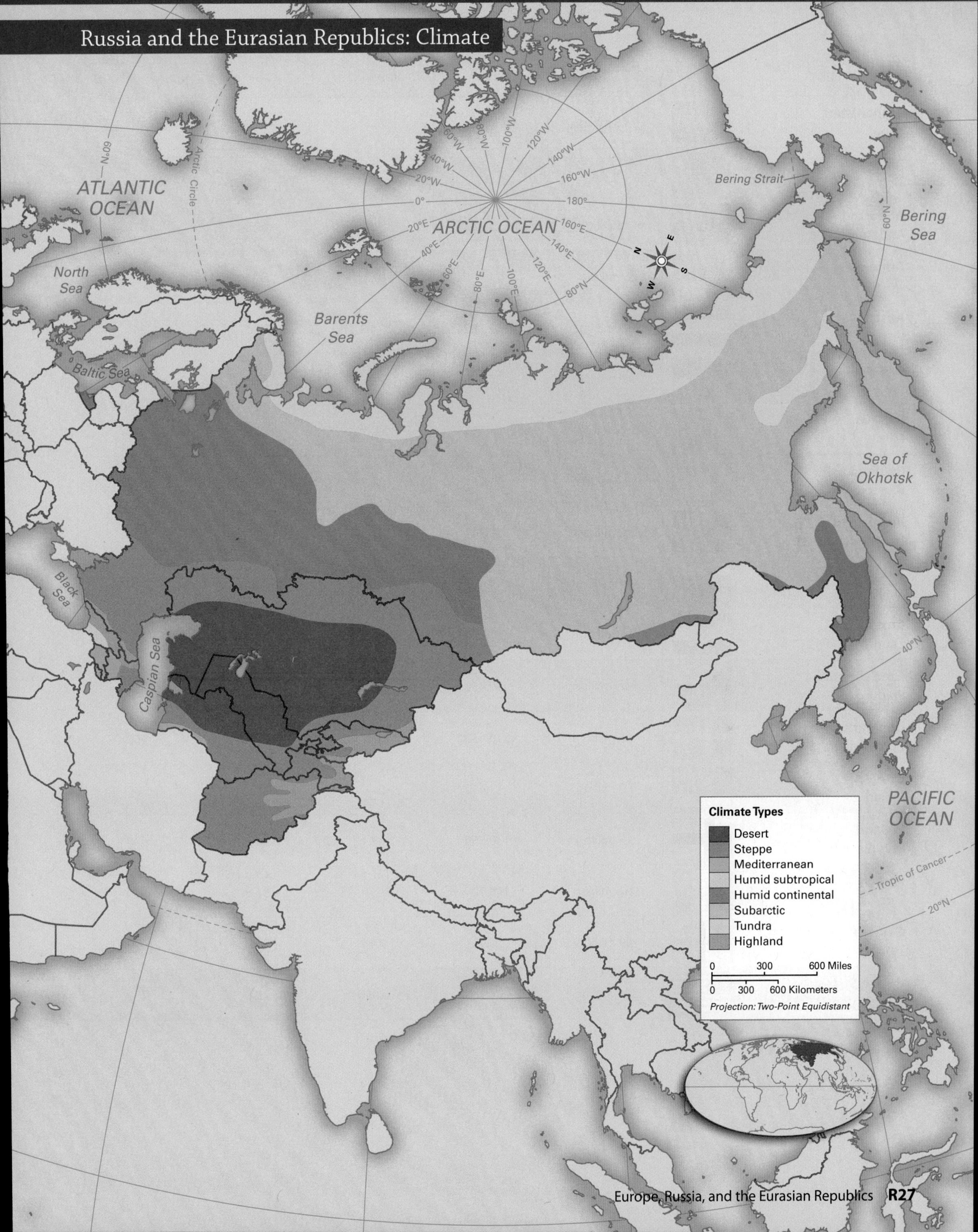

ATLANTIC OCEAN
ARCTIC OCEAN
North Sea
Barents Sea
Baltic Sea
Black Sea
Caspian Sea
Bering Strait
Bering Sea
Sea of Okhotsk
PACIFIC OCEAN
Arctic Circle
Tropic of Cancer
60°N
40°N
20°N
0°
20°W
40°W
60°W
80°W
100°W
120°W
140°W
160°W
180°
160°E
140°E
120°E
100°E
80°E
60°E
40°E
20°E
N
E
S
W
Climate Types
Desert
Steppe
Mediterranean
Humid subtropical
Humid continental
Subarctic
Tundra
Highland
0 300 600 Miles
0 300 600 Kilometers
Projection: Two-Point Equidistant

Regional Data File

Country Capital	Flag	Population	Area (sq mi)	GDP (billions $ U.S.)	Life Expectancy at Birth	Internet Users (per 1,000 pop.)
Afghanistan Kabul		33.3 million	250,001	20.8	51.3	80
Albania Tirana		3 million	11,100	11.4	78.3	630
Andorra Andorra la Vella		85,660	181	4.8	82.8	970
Armenia Yerevan		3 million	11,506	10.5	74.6	580
Austria Vienna		8.7 million	32,382	374.3	81.5	840
Azerbaijan Baku		9.8 million	33,436	54.1	72.5	770
Belarus Minsk		9.6 million	80,155	54.6	72.7	620
Belgium Brussels		11.4 million	11,787	454.3	81	850
Bosnia and Herzegovina; Sarajevo		3.8 million	19,741	16	76.7	650
Bulgaria Sofia		7.1 million	42,823	49	74.5	570
Croatia Zagreb		4.3 million	21,831	48.9	75.9	700
Czech Republic Prague		10.6 million	30,450	185.2	78.6	810
Denmark Copenhagen		5.6 million	16,639	295.1	79.4	960
Estonia Tallinn		1.3 million	17,462	22.7	76.7	880
Finland Helsinki		5.5 million	130,559	232.1	80.9	930
France Paris		66.8 million	248,429	2,420	81.8	850
Georgia T'bilisi		4.9 million	26,911	14	76.2	450
United States Washington, D.C.		324 million	3,794,083	18,040	79.8	750

Europe, Russia, and the Eurasian Republics

Country Capital	Flag	Population	Area (sq mi)	GDP (billions $ U.S.)	Life Expectancy at Birth	Internet Users (per 1,000 pop.)
Germany Berlin		80.7 million	137,847	3,365	80.7	880
Greece Athens		10.7 million	50,942	195.3	80.5	670
Hungary Budapest		9.9 million	35,919	120.6	75.9	730
Iceland Reykjavik		335,878	39,769	16.7	83	980
Ireland Dublin		4.9 million	27,135	283.7	80.8	800
Italy Rome		62 million	116,306	1,816	82.2	660
Kazakhstan Astana		18.3 million	1,049,155	184.4	70.8	730
Kosovo Pristina		1.9 million	4,203	6.4	71.3	Not available
Kyrgyzstan Bishkek		5.7 million	76,641	6.7	70.7	300
Latvia Riga		2 million	24,938	27	69.9	790
Liechtenstein Vaduz		37,937	62	5.1	81.9	970
Lithuania Vilnius		2.9 million	25,174	41.2	74.9	710
Luxembourg Luxembourg		582,291	998	57.8	82.3	970
Macedonia Skopje		2.1 million	9,781	10.1	76.2	700
Malta Valletta		415,196	122	9.8	80.4	760
Moldova Chişinau		3.5 million	13,067	6.5	70.7	500
Monaco Monaco		30,581	1	6.1	89.5	930
United States Washington, D.C.		324 million	3,794,083	18,040	79.8	750

Regional Data File

Country Capital	Flag	Population	Area (sq mi)	GDP (billions $ U.S.)	Life Expectancy at Birth	Internet Users (per 1,000 pop.)
Montenegro Cetinje, Podgorica		644,578	5,415	4	75	650
Netherlands Amsterdam		17 million	16,033	750.7	81.3	930
Norway Oslo		5.2 million	125,021	388.3	81.8	970
Poland Warsaw		38.5 million	120,728	474.8	77.6	680
Portugal Lisbon		10.8 million	35,672	199	79.3	690
Romania Bucharest		21.6 million	91,699	178	75.1	560
Russian Federation Moscow		142.3 million	6,592,772	1,326	70.8	730
San Marino San Marino		33,285	24	1.6	83.3	530
Serbia Belgrade		7.1 million	29,913	36.5	75.5	650
Slovakia Bratislava		5.5 million	18,859	86.6	77.1	850
United States Washington, D.C.		324 million	3,794,083	18,040	79.8	750

Europe, Russia, and the Eurasian Republics

Country Capital	**Flag**	**Population**	**Area** (sq mi)	**GDP** (billions $ U.S.)	**Life Expectancy at Birth**	**Internet Users** (per 1,000 pop.)
Slovenia Ljubljana		2 million	7,827	42.8	78.2	730
Spain Madrid		48.5 million	194,897	1,200	81.7	790
Sweden Stockholm		9.8 million	173,732	493	82.1	910
Switzerland Bern		8.1 million	15,942	664	82.6	880
Tajikistan Dushanbe		8.3 million	55,251	7.8	67.7	190
Turkmenistan Ashgabat		5.3 million	188,456	35.9	70.1	150
Ukraine Kiev		44.2 million	233,090	90.5	71.8	490
United Kingdom London		64.4 million	94,526	2,858	80.7	920
Uzbekistan Tashkent		29.5 million	172,742	65.5	73.8	430
Vatican City Vatican City		1,000	0.2	Not available	Not available	Not available
United States Washington, D.C.		324 million	3,794,083	18,040	79.8	750

Southwest Asia and North Africa: Physical

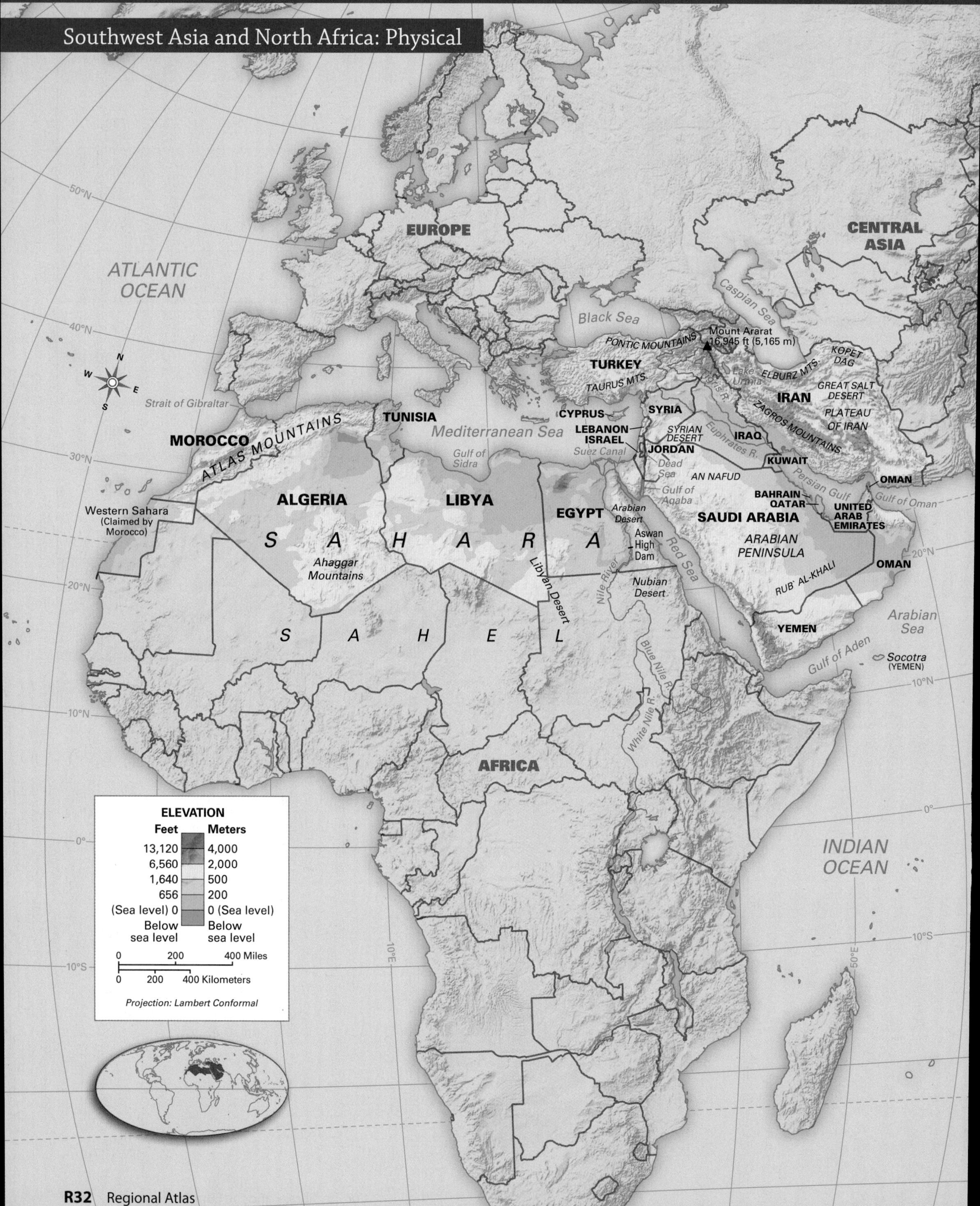

EUROPE
CENTRAL ASIA
ATLANTIC OCEAN
Black Sea
Caspian Sea
Mount Ararat 16,945 ft (5,165 m)
PONTIC MOUNTAINS
TURKEY
TAURUS MTS.
Lake Urmia
ELBURZ MTS.
KOPET DAG
IRAN
GREAT SALT DESERT
PLATEAU OF IRAN
ZAGROS MOUNTAINS
Strait of Gibraltar
TUNISIA
CYPRUS
SYRIA
Mediterranean Sea
LEBANON
ISRAEL
SYRIAN DESERT
IRAQ
Euphrates R.
Suez Canal
JORDAN
Dead Sea
KUWAIT
Persian Gulf
MOROCCO
ATLAS MOUNTAINS
Gulf of Sidra
AN NAFUD
OMAN
Gulf of Aqaba
BAHRAIN
QATAR
Gulf of Oman
ALGERIA
LIBYA
EGYPT
Arabian Desert
SAUDI ARABIA
UNITED ARAB EMIRATES
Western Sahara (Claimed by Morocco)
S A H A R A
Aswan High Dam
ARABIAN PENINSULA
Ahaggar Mountains
Libyan Desert
Nile River
Red Sea
OMAN
RUB' AL-KHALI
Nubian Desert
YEMEN
Arabian Sea
S A H E L
Blue Nile R.
Gulf of Aden
Socotra (YEMEN)
White Nile R.
AFRICA
INDIAN OCEAN
50°N
40°N
30°N
20°N
10°N
0°
10°S
10°E
50°E

ELEVATION

Feet	Meters
13,120	4,000
6,560	2,000
1,640	500
656	200
(Sea level) 0	0 (Sea level)
Below sea level	Below sea level

0 200 400 Miles
0 200 400 Kilometers

Projection: Lambert Conformal

Southwest Asia and North Africa

Geographical Extremes: Southwest Asia and North Africa

Longest River	Nile River, northeastern Africa: 4,132 miles (6,650 kilometers)
Highest Point	Kuh-e Damavand, Iran: 18,606 feet (5,671 m)
Lowest Point	Dead Sea, Israel/Jordan: 1,348 feet (411 m) below sea level
Highest Recorded Temperature	Kebili, Tunisia: 131°F (55°C)
Driest Place	Aden, Yemen: 1.8 inches (4.6 cm) average precipitation per year
Largest Country	Algeria: 919,595 square miles (2,381,741 square km)
Smallest Country	Bahrain: 257 square miles (666 square km)
Saltiest Lake	Dead Sea, Israel/Jordan: 33 percent salt content
Most Powerful Earthquake	Erzincan, Turkey, 1939: 7.8 magnitude

A high salt content keeps people afloat in the Dead Sea.

Size Comparison: The U.S. and Southwest Asia and North Africa

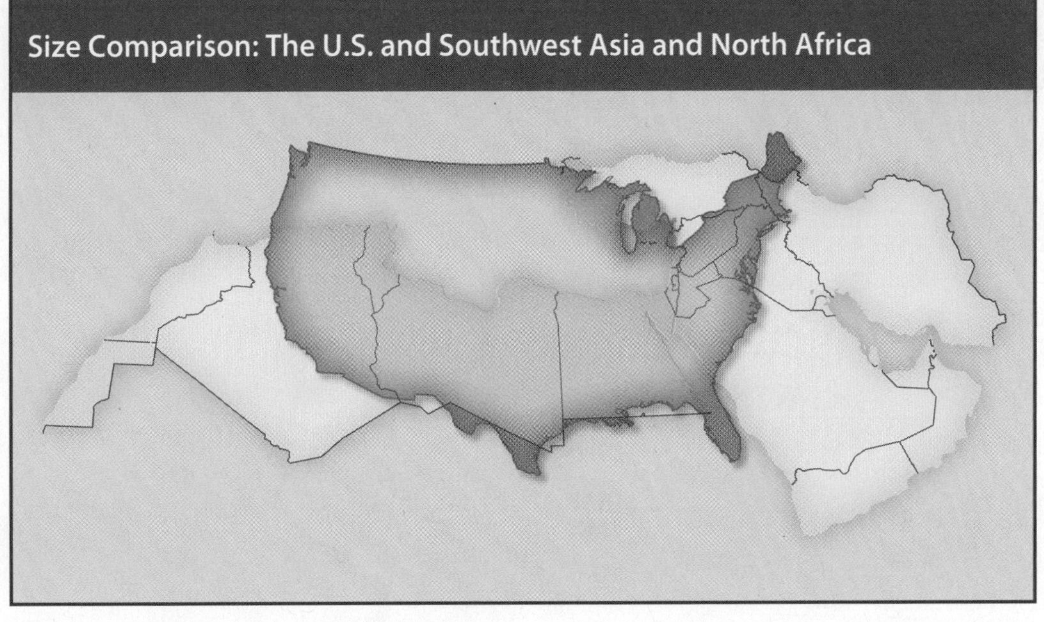

Southwest Asia and North Africa: Political

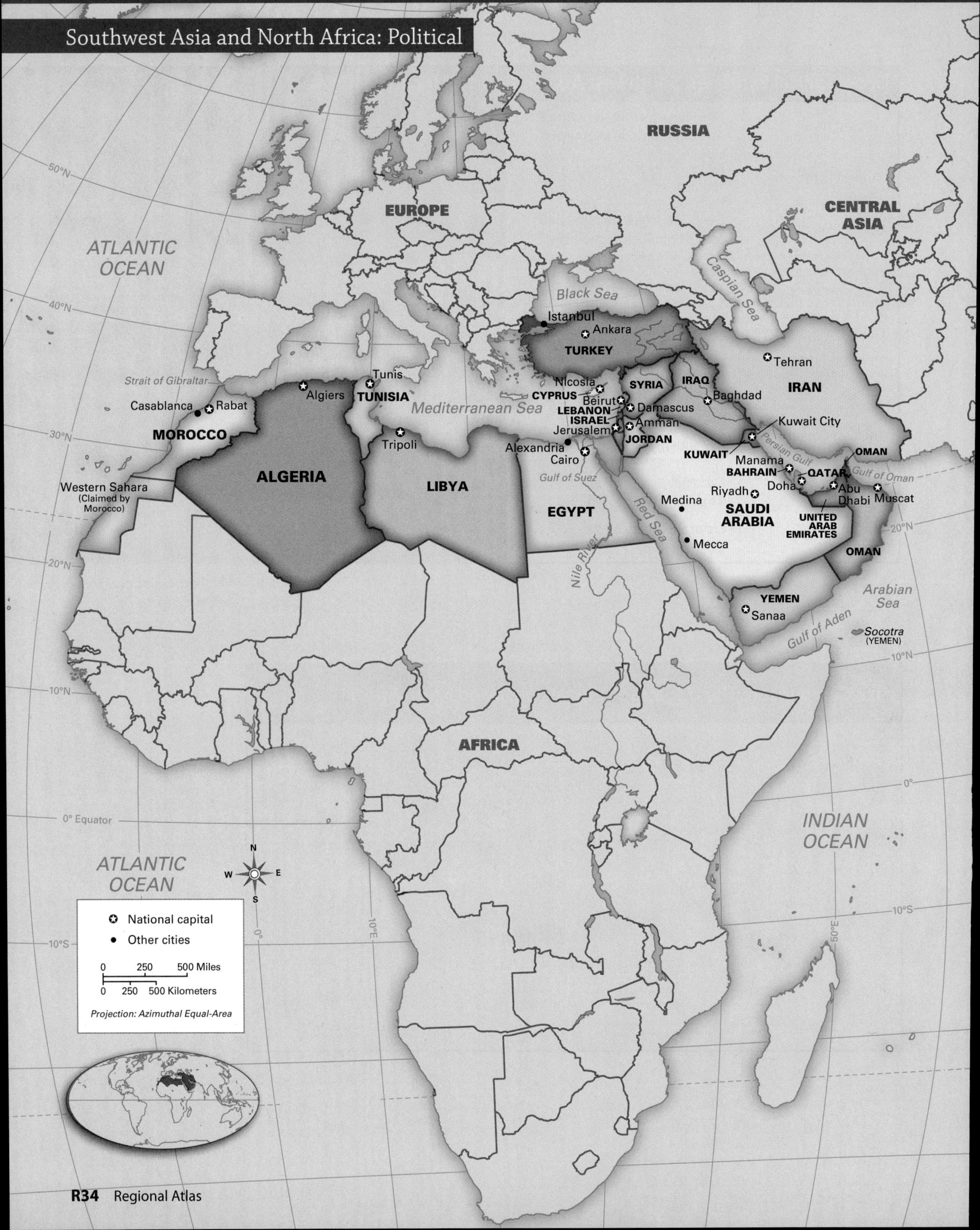

RUSSIA
EUROPE
CENTRAL ASIA
ATLANTIC OCEAN
Black Sea
Caspian Sea
Istanbul
Ankara
TURKEY
Tehran
IRAN
IRAQ
Baghdad
SYRIA
Nicosia
CYPRUS
Beirut
LEBANON
Damascus
ISRAEL
Jerusalem
Amman
JORDAN
Kuwait City
KUWAIT
Persian Gulf
Manama
BAHRAIN
QATAR
Doha
Abu Dhabi
Muscat
OMAN
Gulf of Oman
Riyadh
SAUDI ARABIA
Medina
Mecca
UNITED ARAB EMIRATES
YEMEN
Sanaa
Gulf of Aden
Arabian Sea
Socotra (YEMEN)
Strait of Gibraltar
Casablanca
Rabat
MOROCCO
Algiers
ALGERIA
Tunis
TUNISIA
Mediterranean Sea
Tripoli
LIBYA
Alexandria
Cairo
Gulf of Suez
EGYPT
Red Sea
Nile River
Western Sahara (Claimed by Morocco)
AFRICA
INDIAN OCEAN
ATLANTIC OCEAN
50°N
40°N
30°N
20°N
10°N
0° Equator
10°S
0°
10°E
50°E

N
W
E
S

National capital
Other cities

0 250 500 Miles
0 250 500 Kilometers

Projection: Azimuthal Equal-Area

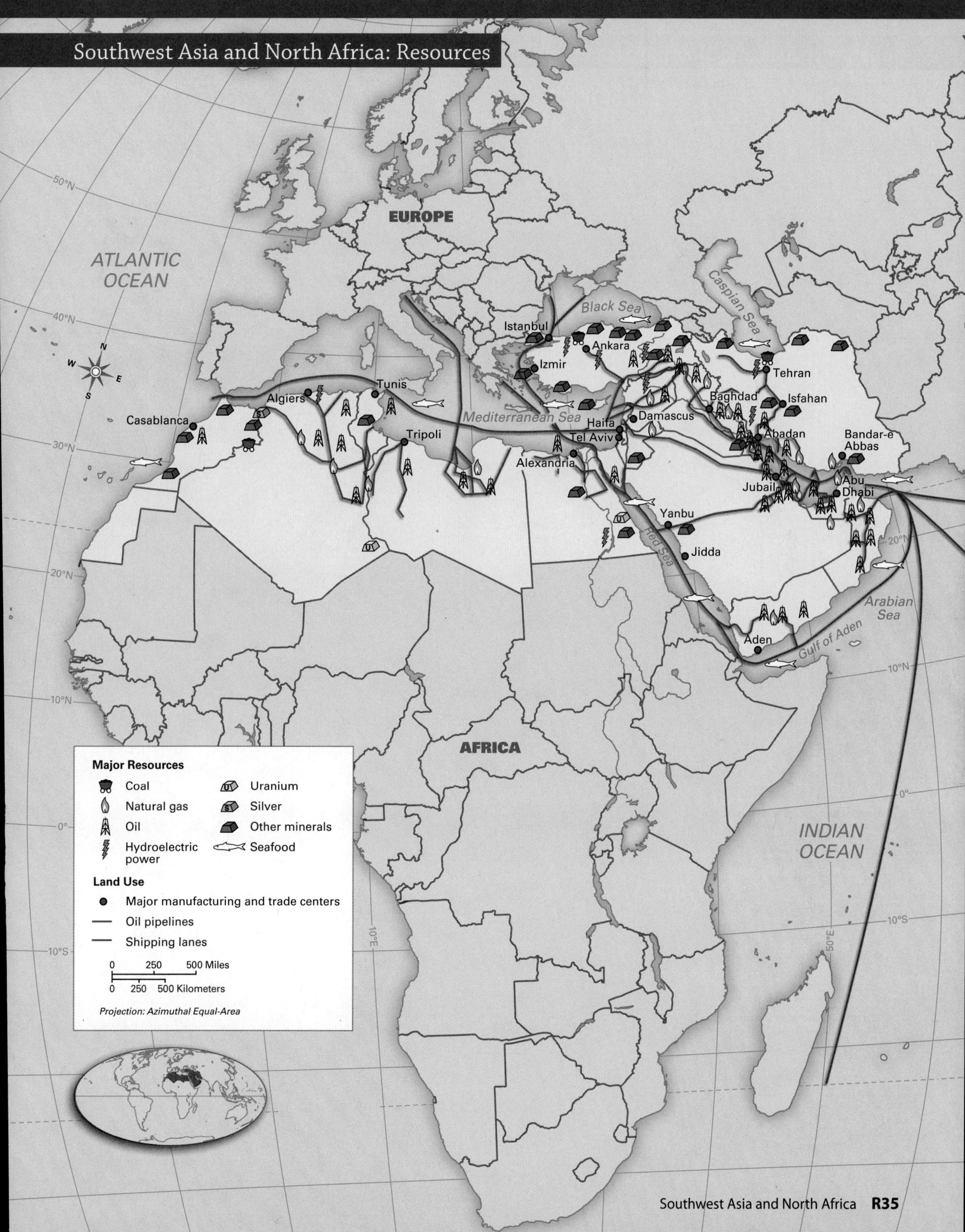
Southwest Asia and North Africa: Resources
EUROPE
ATLANTIC OCEAN
AFRICA
INDIAN OCEAN
Black Sea
Caspian Sea
Mediterranean Sea
Red Sea
Arabian Sea
Gulf of Aden
Istanbul
Ankara
Izmir
Tehran
Isfahan
Baghdad
Abadan
Damascus
Haifa
Tel Aviv
Alexandria
Tunis
Algiers
Casablanca
Tripoli
Bandar-e Abbas
Jubail
Abu Dhabi
Yanbu
Jidda
Aden
50°N
40°N
30°N
20°N
10°N
0°
10°S
10°E
50°E
Major Resources
Coal
Natural gas
Oil
Hydroelectric power
Uranium
Silver
Other minerals
Seafood
Land Use
Major manufacturing and trade centers
Oil pipelines
Shipping lanes
0 250 500 Miles
0 250 500 Kilometers
Projection: Azimuthal Equal-Area

Southwest Asia and North Africa: Population

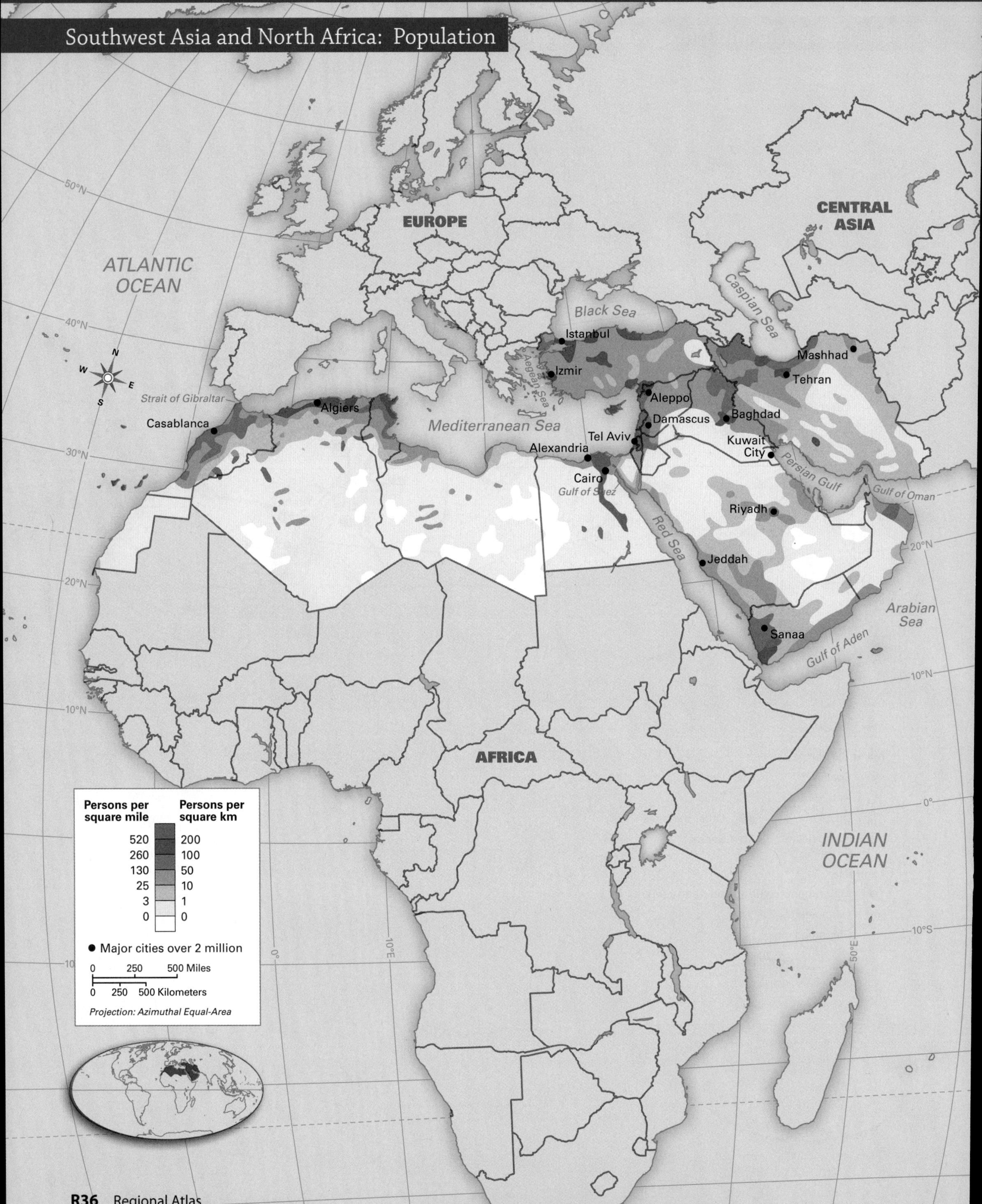

EUROPE
CENTRAL ASIA
ATLANTIC OCEAN
AFRICA
INDIAN OCEAN
Black Sea
Caspian Sea
Aegean Sea
Mediterranean Sea
Strait of Gibraltar
Red Sea
Gulf of Suez
Persian Gulf
Gulf of Oman
Arabian Sea
Gulf of Aden
Istanbul
Izmir
Mashhad
Tehran
Algiers
Casablanca
Aleppo
Damascus
Baghdad
Tel Aviv
Alexandria
Cairo
Kuwait City
Riyadh
Jeddah
Sanaa
50°N
40°N
30°N
20°N
10°N
0°
10°S
0°
10°E
50°E

Persons per square mile	Persons per square km
520	200
260	100
130	50
25	10
3	1
0	0

● Major cities over 2 million

0 250 500 Miles
0 250 500 Kilometers

Projection: Azimuthal Equal-Area

Southwest Asia and North Africa: Climate

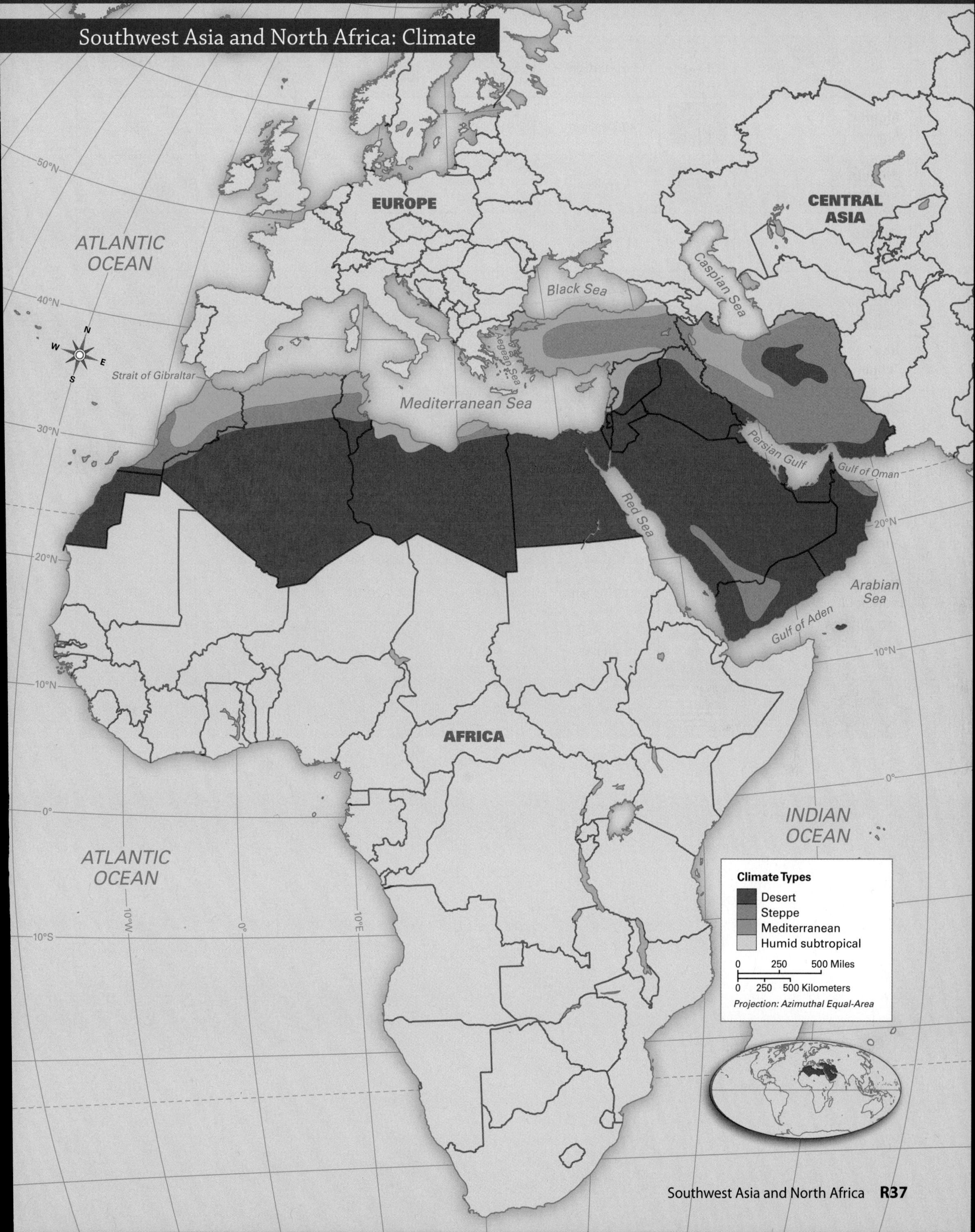

EUROPE
CENTRAL ASIA
ATLANTIC OCEAN
Caspian Sea
Black Sea
Aegean Sea
Strait of Gibraltar
Mediterranean Sea
Persian Gulf
Gulf of Oman
Red Sea
Arabian Sea
Gulf of Aden
AFRICA
INDIAN OCEAN
ATLANTIC OCEAN
50°N
40°N
30°N
20°N
10°N
0°
10°S
10°W
0°
10°E
N
S
E
W

Climate Types

- Desert
- Steppe
- Mediterranean
- Humid subtropical

0 250 500 Miles
0 250 500 Kilometers
Projection: Azimuthal Equal-Area

Regional Data File

Country Capital	Flag	Population	Area (sq mi)	GDP (billions $ U.S.)	Life Expectancy at Birth	Internet Users (per 1,000 pop.)
Algeria Algiers		40.2 million	919,595	166.8	76.8	380
Bahrain Manama		1.3 million	257	30.4	78.9	940
Cyprus Nicosia		1.2 million	3,571	19.3	78.7	720
Egypt Cairo		94.6 million	386,662	330.2	72.7	360
Iran Tehran		82.8 million	636,296	387.6	71.4	440
Iraq Baghdad		38.1 million	168,754	169.5	74.9	170
Israel Jerusalem		8.2 million	8,019	296.1	82.4	790
Jordan Amman		8.1 million	35,637	37.6	74.6	530
Kuwait Kuwait City		2.8 million	6,880	120.7	78	820
Lebanon Beirut		6.2 million	4,015	51.2	77.6	740
United States Washington, D.C.		324 million	3,794,083	18,040	79.8	750

Southwest Asia and North Africa

Country Capital	**Flag**	**Population**	**Area** (sq mi)	**GDP** (billions $ U.S.)	**Life Expectancy at Birth**	**Internet Users** (per 1,000 pop.)
Libya Tripoli		6.5 million	679,362	39.7	76.5	190
Morocco Rabat		33.6 million	172,414	100.6	76.9	570
Oman Muscat		3.4 million	82,031	58.5	75.5	740
Qatar Doha		2.2 million	4,416	185.4	78.7	930
Saudi Arabia Riyadh		28.1 million	830,000	653.2	75.3	700
Syria Damascus		17.1 million	71,498	24.6	74.9	300
Tunisia Tunis		11.1 million	63,170	43.6	76.1	490
Turkey Ankara		80.2 million	301,384	733.6	74.8	540
United Arab Emirates Abu Dhabi		5.9 million	32,278	345.5	77.5	910
Yemen Sanaa		27.4 million	203,850	36.9	65.5	250
United States Washington, D.C.		324 million	3,794,083	18,040	79.8	750

Sub-Saharan Africa: Physical

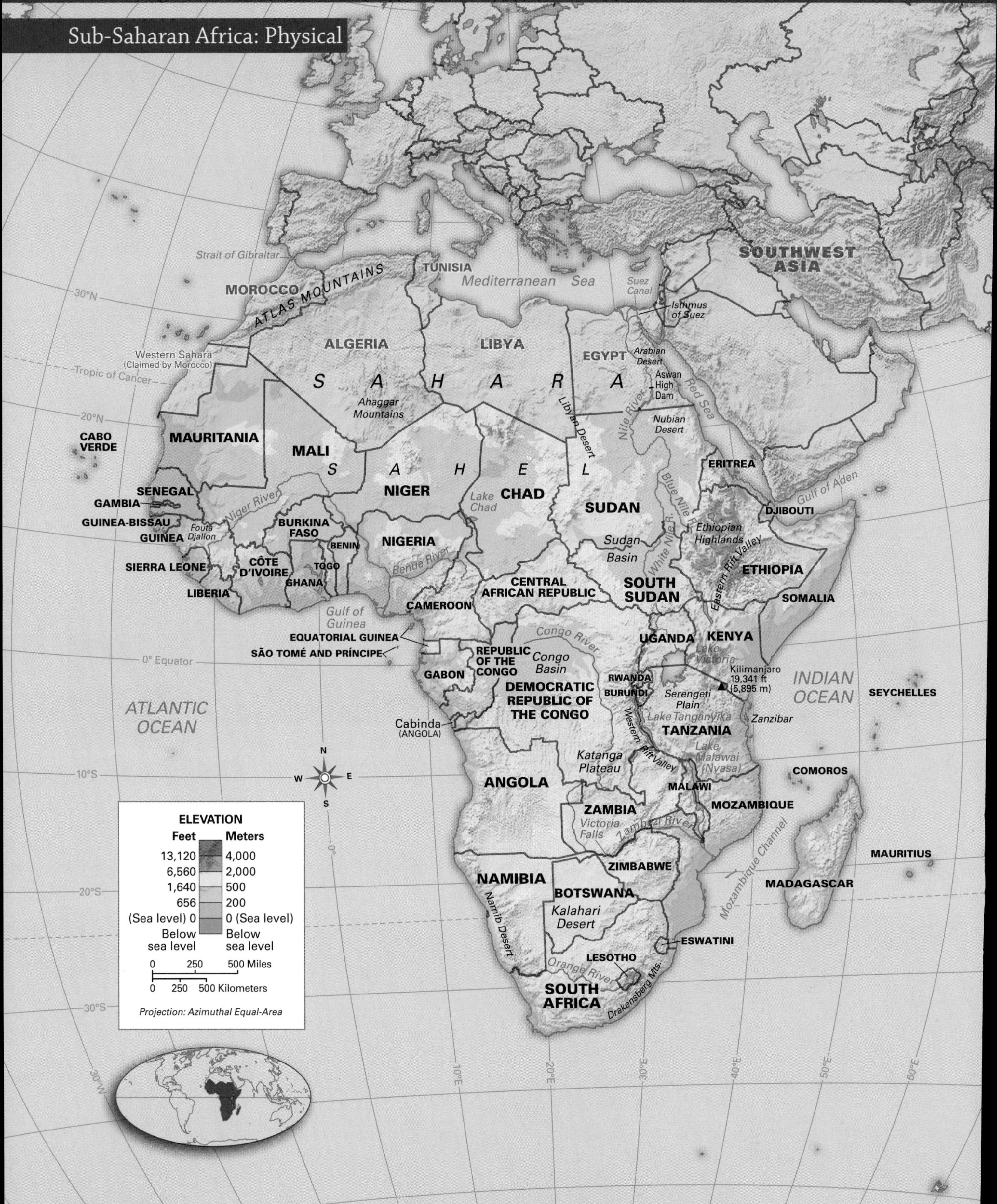

SOUTHWEST ASIA
Strait of Gibraltar
TUNISIA
Mediterranean Sea
Suez Canal
Isthmus of Suez
MOROCCO
ATLAS MOUNTAINS
30°N
ALGERIA
LIBYA
EGYPT
Arabian Desert
Western Sahara (Claimed by Morocco)
Tropic of Cancer
S A H A R A
Aswan High Dam
Red Sea
Libyan Desert
Nile River
Ahaggar Mountains
20°N
Nubian Desert
CABO VERDE
MAURITANIA
MALI
S A H E L
ERITREA
Blue Nile R.
Gulf of Aden
SENEGAL
GAMBIA
NIGER
Lake Chad
CHAD
SUDAN
DJIBOUTI
Niger River
GUINEA-BISSAU
GUINEA
Fouta Djallon
BURKINA FASO
BENIN
NIGERIA
Sudan Basin
White Nile R.
Ethiopian Highlands
Eastern Rift Valley
SIERRA LEONE
CÔTE D'IVOIRE
TOGO
GHANA
Benue River
CENTRAL AFRICAN REPUBLIC
SOUTH SUDAN
ETHIOPIA
LIBERIA
CAMEROON
SOMALIA
Gulf of Guinea
EQUATORIAL GUINEA
SÃO TOMÉ AND PRÍNCIPE
Congo River
UGANDA
KENYA
Lake Victoria
0° Equator
REPUBLIC OF THE CONGO
Congo Basin
GABON
DEMOCRATIC REPUBLIC OF THE CONGO
RWANDA
BURUNDI
Serengeti Plain
Kilimanjaro 19,341 ft (5,895 m)
INDIAN OCEAN
SEYCHELLES
ATLANTIC OCEAN
Cabinda (ANGOLA)
Western Rift Valley
Lake Tanganyika
TANZANIA
Zanzibar
N
W
E
S
Katanga Plateau
Lake Malawi (Nyasa)
COMOROS
10°S
ANGOLA
MALAWI
ZAMBIA
MOZAMBIQUE
Victoria Falls
Zambezi River
Mozambique Channel
0°
MAURITIUS
NAMIBIA
ZIMBABWE
MADAGASCAR
20°S
BOTSWANA
Namib Desert
Kalahari Desert
ESWATINI
LESOTHO
Orange River
SOUTH AFRICA
Drakensberg Mts.
30°S

ELEVATION

Feet	Meters
13,120	4,000
6,560	2,000
1,640	500
656	200
(Sea level) 0	0 (Sea level)
Below sea level	Below sea level

0 250 500 Miles
0 250 500 Kilometers

Projection: Azimuthal Equal-Area

30°W
10°E
20°E
30°E
40°E
50°E
60°E

Geographical Extremes: Sub-Saharan Africa

Longest River	Congo River, Democratic Republic of the Congo: 2,900 miles (4,700 km)
Highest Point	Mount Kilimanjaro, Tanzania: 19,340 feet (5,895 m)
Lowest Point	Lake Assal, Djibouti: 512 feet (156 m) below sea level
Highest Recorded Temperature	Timbuktu, Mali: 130°F (54.4°C)
Lowest Recorded Temperature	Buffelsfontein, South Africa: –4.2°F (–20.1°C)
Wettest Place	Debundscha, Cameroon: 405 inches (1,028.7 cm) average precipitation per year
Driest Place	Wadi Halfa, Sudan: .1 inches (.3 cm) average precipitation per year
Largest Country	Democratic Republic of the Congo: 905,430 square miles (2,344,858 sq km)
Smallest Country	Seychelles: 176 square miles (455 square km)
Largest Desert	Kalahari Desert: 360,000 square miles (930,000 sq km)
Largest Island	Madagascar: 226,658 square miles (587,044 square km)
Highest Waterfall	Tugela, South Africa: 2,800 feet (853 m)

Mount Kilimanjaro, Tanzania

Size Comparison: The U.S. and Sub-Saharan Africa

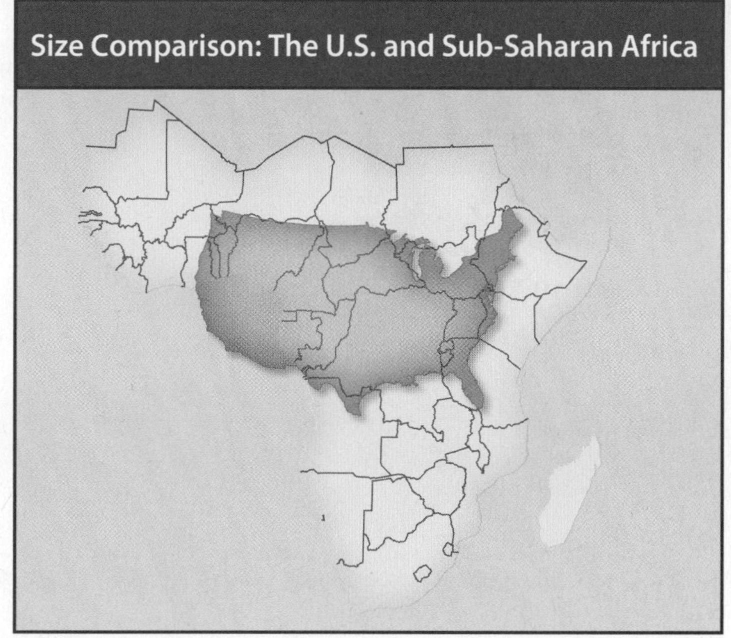

Sub-Saharan Africa: Political

SOUTHWEST ASIA
Strait of Gibraltar
TUNISIA
Mediterranean Sea
30°N
MOROCCO
Western Sahara (Claimed by Morocco)
ALGERIA
LIBYA
EGYPT
Tropic of Cancer
Red Sea
Nile River
20°N
CABO VERDE
Praia
MAURITANIA
Nouakchott
MALI
Timbuktu
NIGER
CHAD
SUDAN
Khartoum
Asmara
ERITREA
Gulf of Aden
SENEGAL
Dakar
Banjul
GAMBIA
Bissau
GUINEA-BISSAU
Bamako
BURKINA FASO
Niamey
Niger R.
Ouagadougou
Kano
Nyala
Blue Nile R.
Djibouti
DJIBOUTI
10°N
GUINEA
Conakry
Freetown
SIERRA LEONE
Monrovia
LIBERIA
CÔTE D'IVOIRE
Yamoussoukro
GHANA
Accra
TOGO
Lomé
BENIN
Porto Novo
Lagos
NIGERIA
Abuja
N'Djamena
SOUTH SUDAN
Juba
White Nile R.
Addis Ababa
ETHIOPIA
SOMALIA
CENTRAL AFRICAN REPUBLIC
Bangui
CAMEROON
Yaoundé
Gulf of Guinea
Malabo
EQUATORIAL GUINEA
SÃO TOMÉ AND PRÍNCIPE
São Tomé
0° Equator
Libreville
GABON
REPUBLIC OF THE CONGO
Congo River
UGANDA
Kampala
KENYA
Nairobi
Mogadishu
SEYCHELLES
Victoria
Kigali
RWANDA
BURUNDI
Bujumbura
DEMOCRATIC REPUBLIC OF THE CONGO
Brazzaville
Kinshasa
Mombasa
Zanzibar
Dar es Salaam
Dodoma
TANZANIA
INDIAN OCEAN
ATLANTIC OCEAN
Cabinda (ANGOLA)
Luanda
N
W
E
S
10°S
ANGOLA
COMOROS
Moroni
MALAWI
Lilongwe
MOZAMBIQUE
ZAMBIA
Lusaka
Harare
ZIMBABWE
Beira
Mozambique Channel
Antananarivo
MADAGASCAR
MAURITIUS
Port Louis
NAMIBIA
Windhoek
Walvis Bay
BOTSWANA
Gaborone
20°S
Pretoria
Johannesburg
Maputo
Mbabane
ESWATINI
Bloemfontein
LESOTHO
Maseru
SOUTH AFRICA
Cape Town
Port Elizabeth
30°S
30°W
0°
10°E
20°E
30°E
40°E
50°E
60°E

National capital
Other cities
0 250 500 Miles
0 250 500 Kilometers
Projection: Azimuthal Equal-Area

Sub-Saharan Africa: Resources

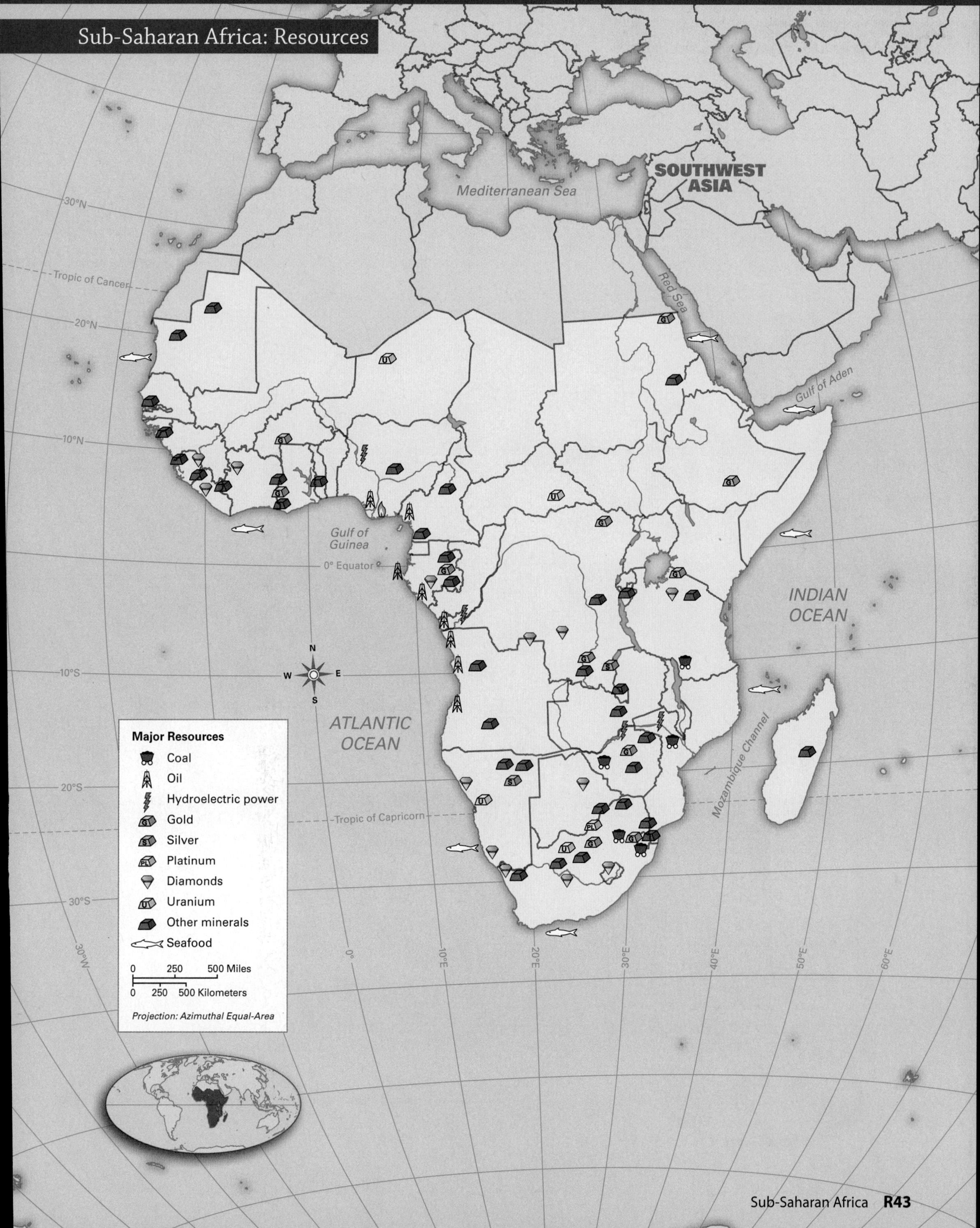

SOUTHWEST ASIA

Mediterranean Sea

Red Sea

Gulf of Aden

Gulf of Guinea

0° Equator

ATLANTIC OCEAN

INDIAN OCEAN

Mozambique Channel

Tropic of Cancer

Tropic of Capricorn

30°N

20°N

10°N

10°S

20°S

30°S

30°W

0°

10°E

20°E

30°E

40°E

50°E

60°E

N S E W

Major Resources

- Coal
- Oil
- Hydroelectric power
- Gold
- Silver
- Platinum
- Diamonds
- Uranium
- Other minerals
- Seafood

0 250 500 Miles

0 250 500 Kilometers

Projection: Azimuthal Equal-Area

Sub-Saharan Africa: Population

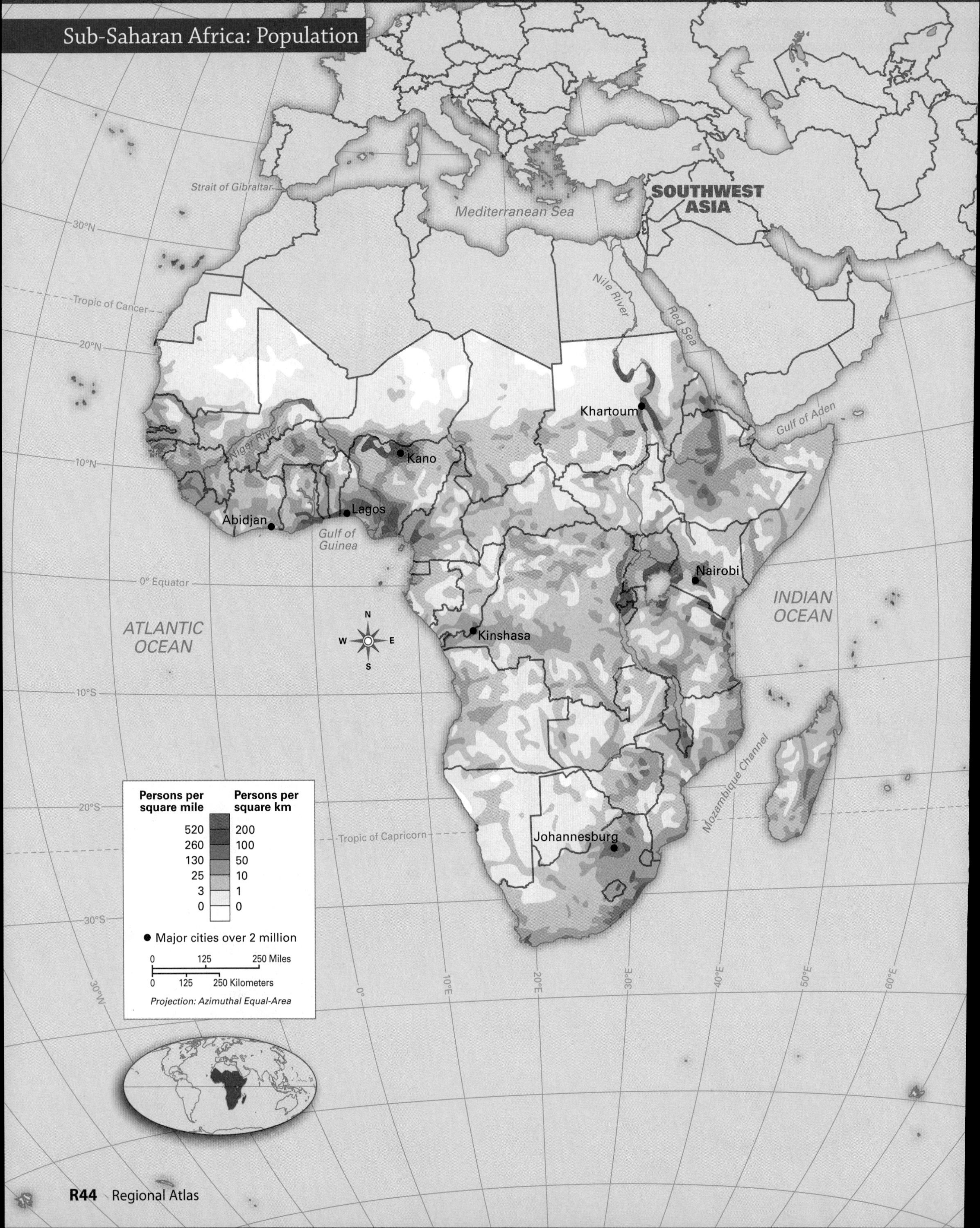

Sub-Saharan Africa: Climate

Regional Data File

Country Capital	Flag	Population	Area (sq mi)	GDP (billions $ U.S.)	Life Expectancy at Birth	Internet Users (per 1,000 pop.)
Angola Luanda		20.1 million	481,354	103	56	120
Benin Porto-Novo		10.7 million	43,483	8.5	61.9	70
Botswana Gaborone		2.2 million	231,804	14.4	54.5	280
Burkina Faso Ouagadougou		19.5 million	105,869	11	55.5	110
Burundi Bujumbura		11 million	10,745	2.9	60.5	50
Cabo Verde Praia		553,432	1,557	1.6	72.1	430
Cameroon Yaoundé		24.3 million	183,568	28.5	58.5	210
Central African Republic Bangui		5.5 million	240,535	1.6	52.3	50
Chad N'Djamena		11.8 million	495,755	10.9	50.2	30
Comoros Moroni		794,678	838	0.6	64.2	80
Congo, Democratic Republic of; Kinshasa		81.3 million	905,568	38.4	57.3	40
Congo, Republic of; Brazzaville		4.8 million	132,047	8.8	59.3	80
Côte d'Ivoire Yamoussoukro		23.7 million	124,503	31.4	58.7	210
Djibouti Djibouti		846,687	8,880	1.7	63.2	120
United States Washington, DC		324 million	3,794,083	18,040	79.8	750

Sub-Saharan Africa

Country Capital	Flag	Population	Area (sq mi)	GDP (billions $ U.S.)	Life Expectancy at Birth	Internet Users (per 1,000 pop.)
Equatorial Guinea Malabo		759,451	10,831	13.8	64.2	210
Eritrea Asmara		5.9 million	46,842	4.7	64.9	10
Eswatini Mbabane		1.4 million	6,704	4	51.6	300
Ethiopia Addis Ababa		102.3 million	435,186	61.6	62.2	120
Gabon Libreville		1.7 million	103,347	14.3	52.1	240
The Gambia Banjul		2 million	4,363	0.9	64.9	170
Ghana Accra		26.9 million	92,456	37.7	66.6	240
Guinea Conakry		12 million	94,926	6.9	60.6	50
Guinea-Bissau Bissau		1.7 million	13,946	1.1	50.6	40
Kenya Nairobi		46.8 million	224,962	63.4	64	460
Lesotho Maseru		1.9 million	11,720	2	53	160
Liberia Monrovia		4.3 million	43,000	2	59	60
Madagascar Antananarivo		24.4 million	226,657	9.7	65.9	40
Malawi Lilongwe		18.5 million	45,745	6.4	61.2	90
United States Washington, DC		324 million	3,794,083	18,040	79.8	750

Regional Data File

Country Capital	Flag	Population	Area (sq mi)	GDP (billions $ U.S.)	Life Expectancy at Birth	Internet Users (per 1,000 pop.)
Mali Bamako		17.4 million	478,767	13.1	55.8	100
Mauritania Nouakchott		3.7 million	397,955	4.9	63	150
Mauritius Port Louis		1.3 million	788	11.5	75.6	500
Mozambique Maputo		25.9 million	309,496	14.8	53.3	90
Namibia Windhoek		2.4 million	318,696	11.5	63.6	220
Niger Niamey		18.6 million	484,191	7.2	55.5	20
Nigeria Abuja		186 million	356,669	493.8	53.4	470
Rwanda Kigali		13 million	10,169	8.1	60.1	180
São Tomé and Príncipe; São Tomé		197,541	386	0.3	64.9	260
Senegal Dakar		14.3 million	75,749	13.7	61.7	220
Seychelles Victoria		93,186	176	1.4	74.7	580
United States Washington, DC		324 million	3,794,083	18,040	79.8	750

Sub-Saharan Africa

Country Capital	Flag	Population	Area (sq mi)	GDP (billions $ U.S.)	Life Expectancy at Birth	Internet Users (per 1,000 pop.)
Sierra Leone Freetown		6 million	27,699	4.4	58.2	30
Somalia Mogadishu		10.8 million	246,201	5.8	52.4	20
South Africa; Pretoria, Cape Town, Bloemfontein		54.3 million	471,011	314.7	63.1	520
South Sudan Juba		12.5 million	248,777	9.3	57	Not available
Sudan Khartoum		36.7 million	718,723	81.4	64.1	270
Tanzania Dar es Salaam, Dodoma		52.5 million	364,900	45.6	62.2	50
Togo Lomé		7.7 million	21,925	4.2	65	70
Uganda Kampala		38.3 million	91,136	24.3	55.4	190
Zambia Lusaka		15.5 million	290,586	21.9	52.5	210
Zimbabwe Harare		14.5 million	150,804	14.17	58	160
United States Washington, DC		324 million	3,794,083	18,040	79.8	750

South and East Asia and the Pacific: Physical

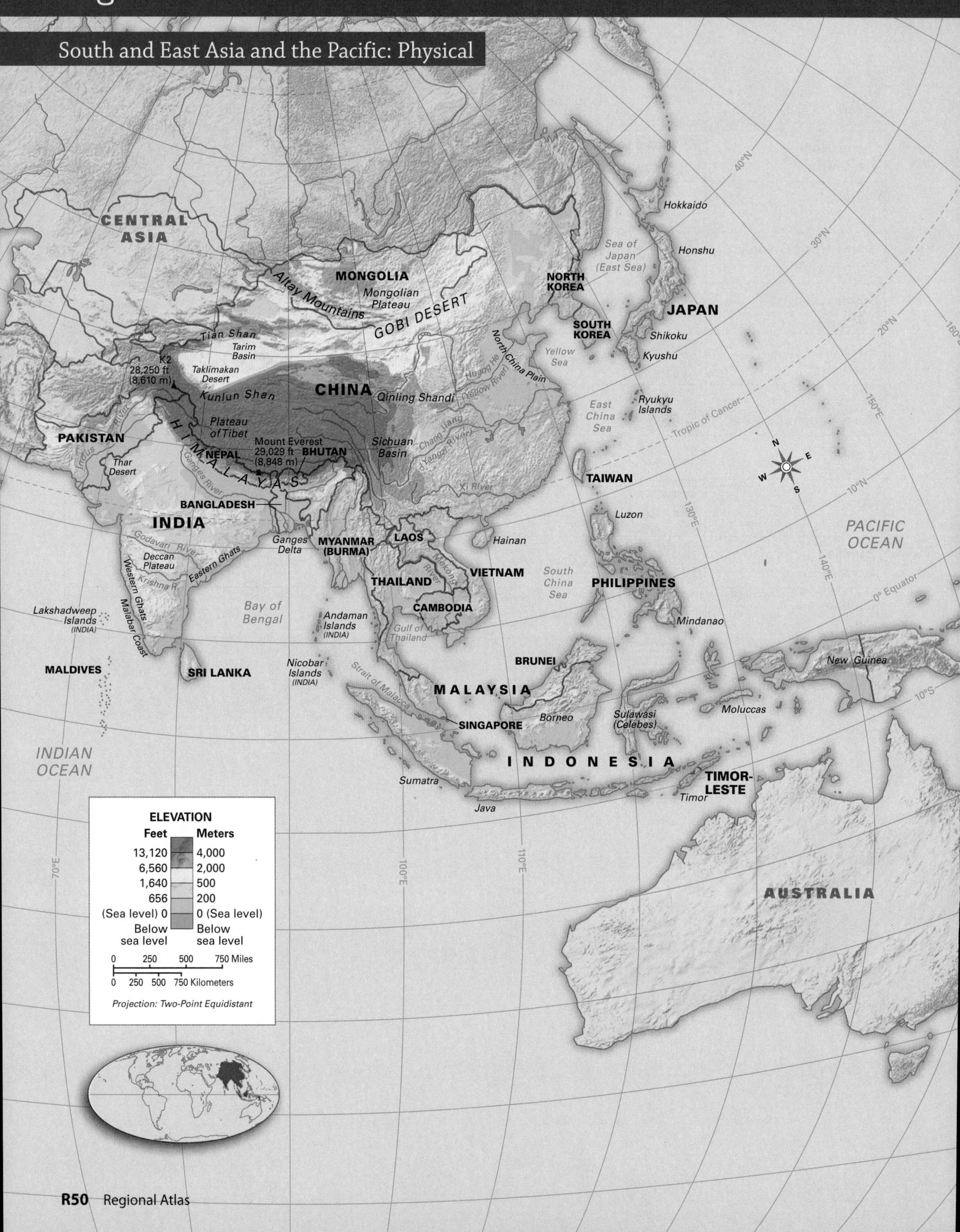

Geographical Extremes: South and East Asia

Longest River	Chang Jiang (Yangzi River), China: 3,450 miles (5,552 km)
Highest Point	Mount Everest, Nepal/China: 29,035 feet (8,850 m)
Lowest Point	Turpan Depression, China: 505 feet (154 m) below sea level
Highest Recorded Temperature	Turpan Depression, China 118°F (48°C)
Wettest Place	Mawsynram, India: 467.4 inches (1,187.2 cm) average precipitation per year
Largest Country	China: 3,705,407 square miles (9,596,960 square km)
Smallest Country	Maldives: 116 square miles (300 square km)
Largest Rain Forest	Indonesia: 386,000 square miles (999,740 square km)
Strongest Earthquake	Off the coast of Sumatra, Indonesia, on December 26, 2004: Magnitude 9.1

Mount Everest

Size Comparison: The United States and South and East Asia

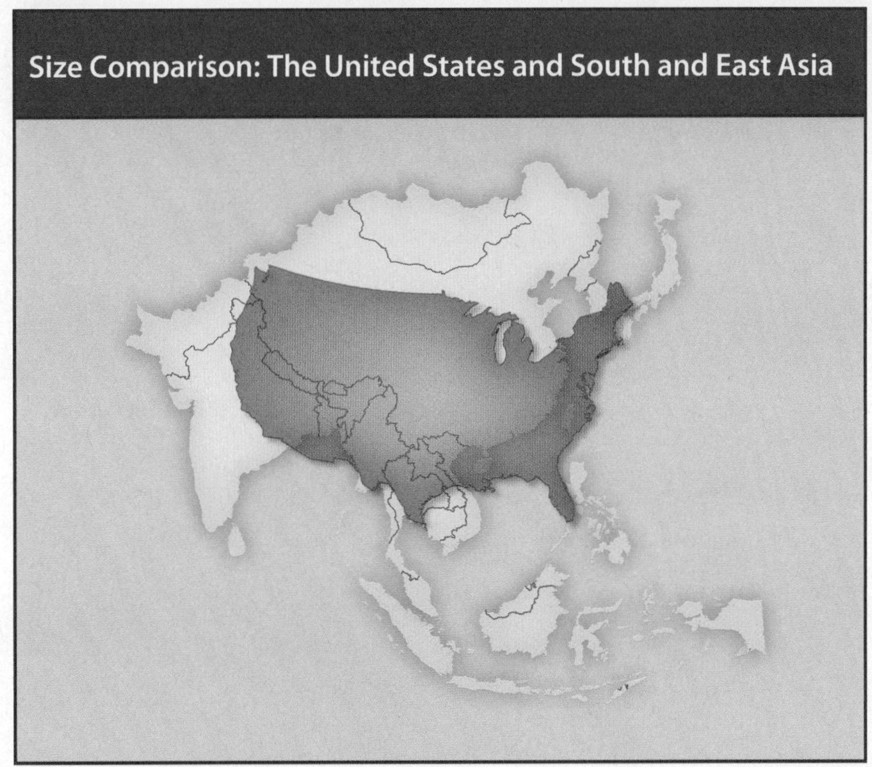

South and East Asia and the Pacific: Political

South and East Asia and the Pacific: Population

South and East Asia and the Pacific: Climate

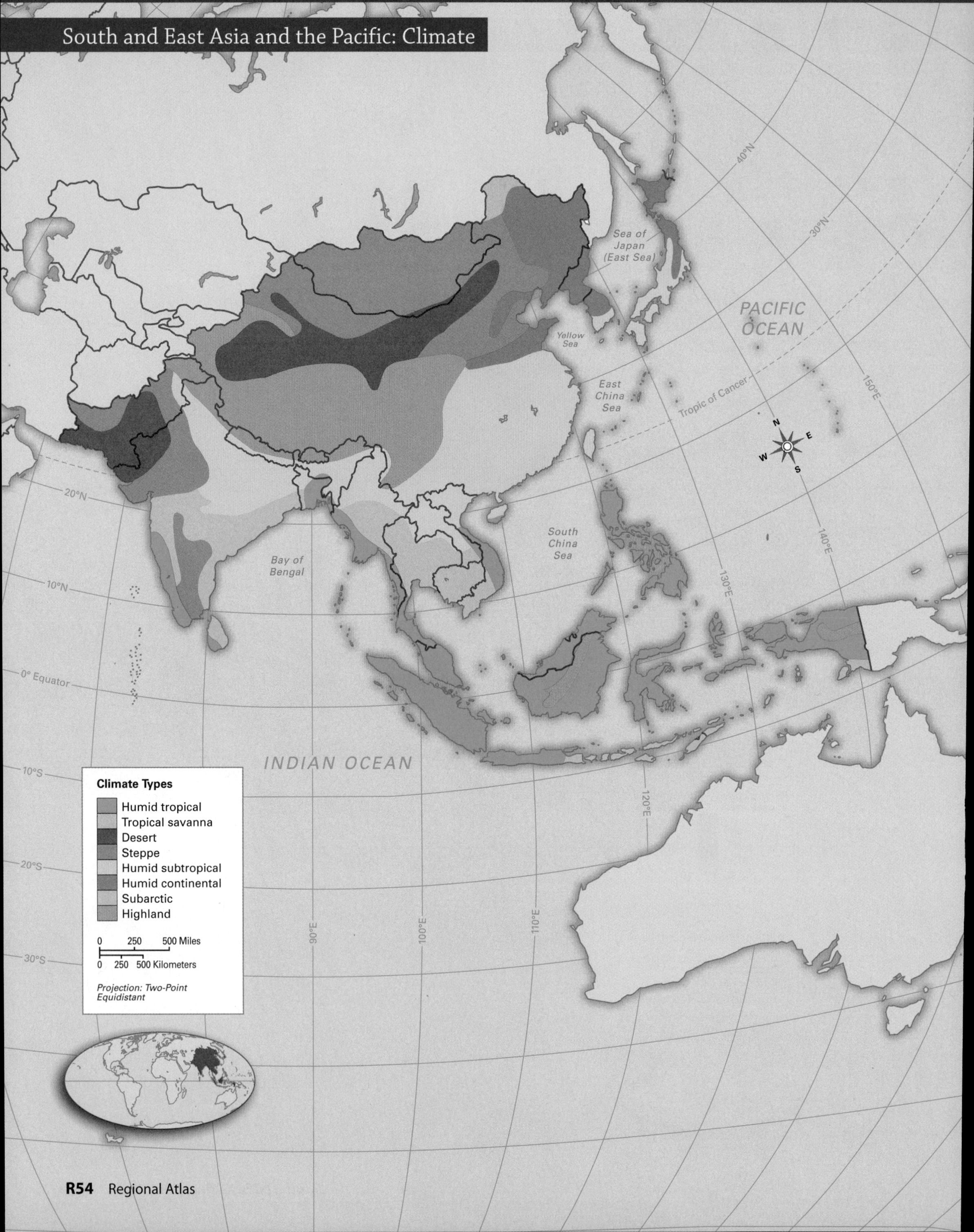

Sea of Japan (East Sea)
PACIFIC OCEAN
Yellow Sea
East China Sea
Tropic of Cancer
South China Sea
Bay of Bengal
INDIAN OCEAN
40°N
30°N
20°N
10°N
0° Equator
10°S
20°S
30°S
90°E
100°E
110°E
120°E
130°E
140°E
150°E
N
E
S
W

Climate Types

- Humid tropical
- Tropical savanna
- Desert
- Steppe
- Humid subtropical
- Humid continental
- Subarctic
- Highland

0 250 500 Miles
0 250 500 Kilometers

Projection: Two-Point Equidistant

South and East Asia and the Pacific: Land Use and Resources

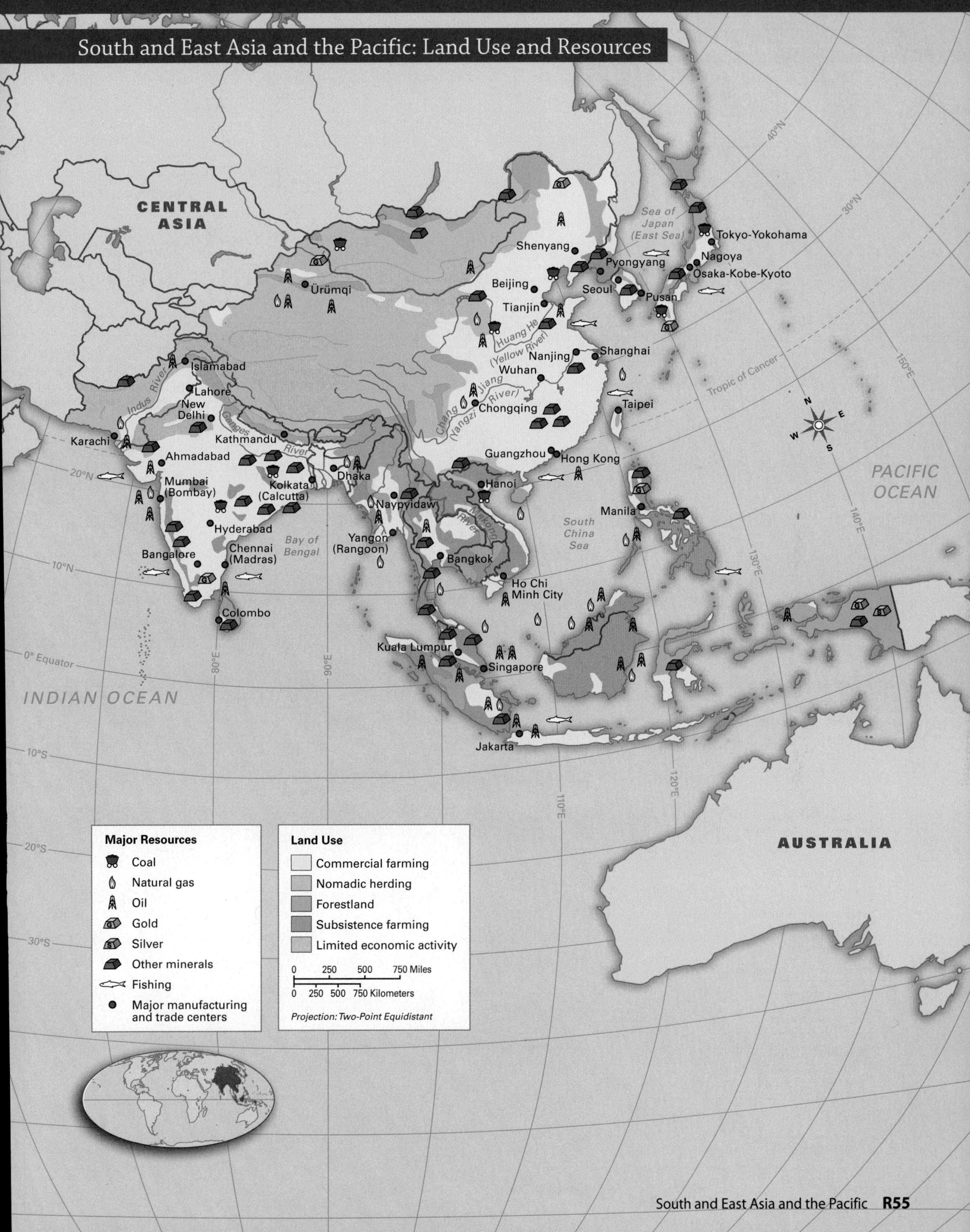

The Pacific Realm: Physical

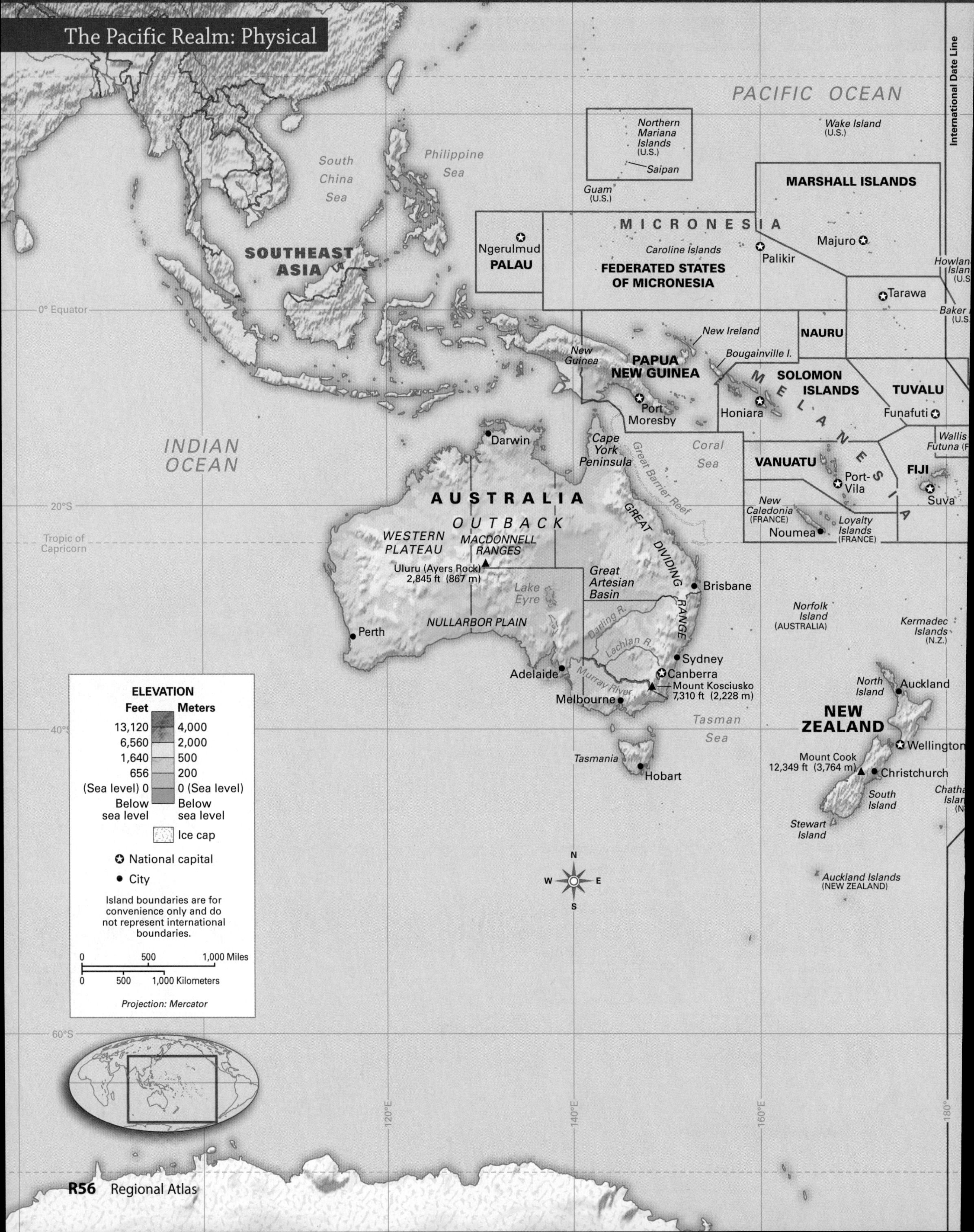

PACIFIC OCEAN
INDIAN OCEAN
South China Sea
Philippine Sea
Coral Sea
Tasman Sea
International Date Line
0° Equator
20°S
Tropic of Capricorn
40°S
60°S
120°E
140°E
160°E
180°

SOUTHEAST ASIA
Northern Mariana Islands (U.S.)
Saipan
Guam (U.S.)
Wake Island (U.S.)
MARSHALL ISLANDS
Majuro
MICRONESIA
Caroline Islands
Palikir
FEDERATED STATES OF MICRONESIA
Ngerulmud
PALAU
Howland Island (U.S.)
Baker Island (U.S.)
Tarawa
NAURU
New Ireland
Bougainville I.
New Guinea
PAPUA NEW GUINEA
Port Moresby
SOLOMON ISLANDS
Honiara
MELANESIA
TUVALU
Funafuti
Wallis and Futuna (France)
VANUATU
Port-Vila
FIJI
Suva
New Caledonia (FRANCE)
Noumea
Loyalty Islands (FRANCE)

AUSTRALIA
OUTBACK
Darwin
Cape York Peninsula
Great Barrier Reef
GREAT DIVIDING RANGE
WESTERN PLATEAU
MACDONNELL RANGES
Uluru (Ayers Rock) 2,845 ft (867 m)
Lake Eyre
Great Artesian Basin
Brisbane
NULLARBOR PLAIN
Darling R.
Lachlan R.
Murray River
Perth
Adelaide
Sydney
Canberra
Mount Kosciusko 7,310 ft (2,228 m)
Melbourne
Tasmania
Hobart
Norfolk Island (AUSTRALIA)
Kermadec Islands (N.Z.)

NEW ZEALAND
North Island
Auckland
Wellington
Mount Cook 12,349 ft (3,764 m)
Christchurch
South Island
Stewart Island
Chatham Islands (N.Z.)
Auckland Islands (NEW ZEALAND)

N
W
E
S

ELEVATION

Feet	Meters
13,120	4,000
6,560	2,000
1,640	500
656	200
(Sea level) 0	0 (Sea level)
Below sea level	Below sea level

Ice cap

National capital

City

Island boundaries are for convenience only and do not represent international boundaries.

0 500 1,000 Miles
0 500 1,000 Kilometers

Projection: Mercator

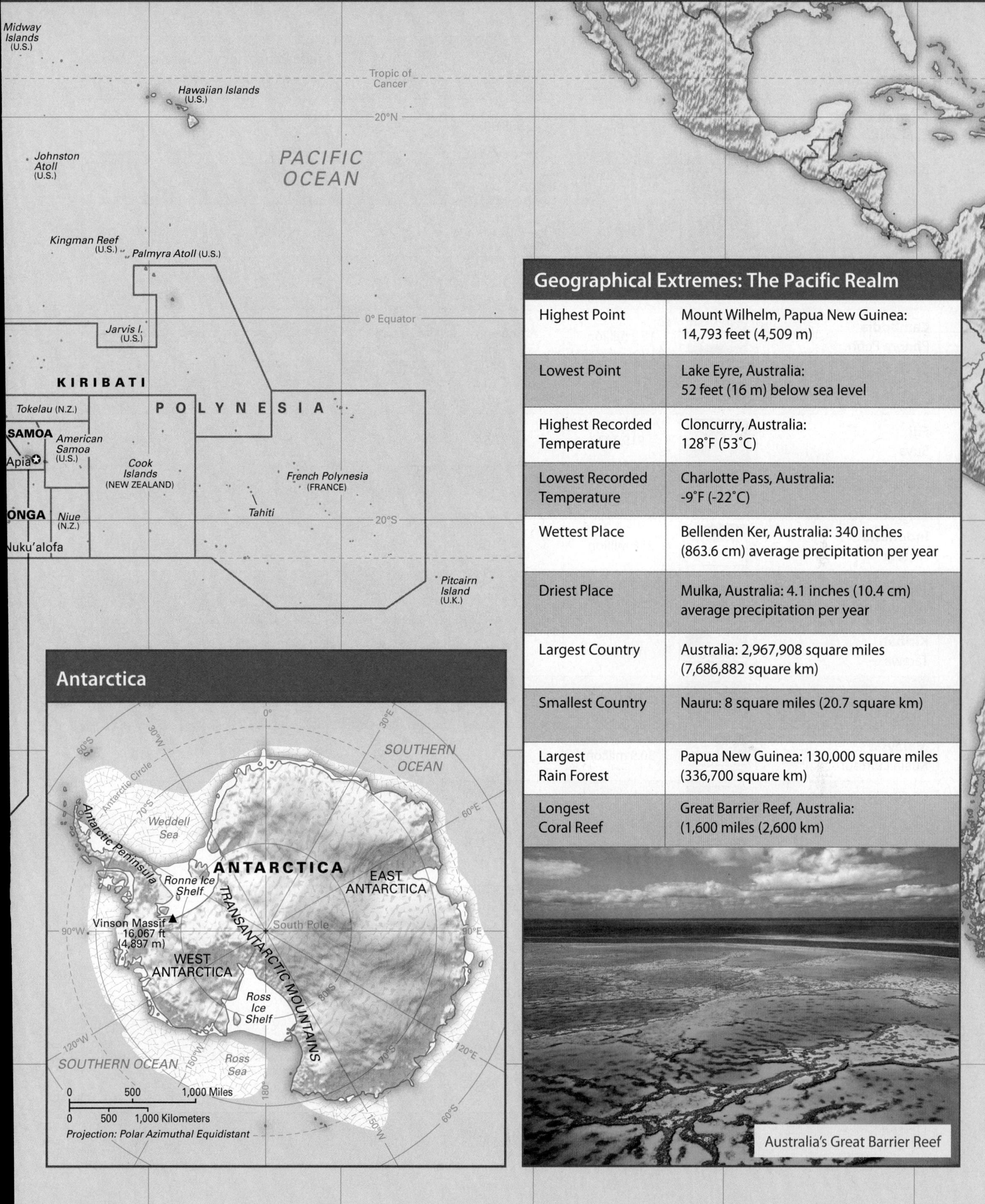

Geographical Extremes: The Pacific Realm

Highest Point	Mount Wilhelm, Papua New Guinea: 14,793 feet (4,509 m)
Lowest Point	Lake Eyre, Australia: 52 feet (16 m) below sea level
Highest Recorded Temperature	Cloncurry, Australia: 128˚F (53˚C)
Lowest Recorded Temperature	Charlotte Pass, Australia: -9˚F (-22˚C)
Wettest Place	Bellenden Ker, Australia: 340 inches (863.6 cm) average precipitation per year
Driest Place	Mulka, Australia: 4.1 inches (10.4 cm) average precipitation per year
Largest Country	Australia: 2,967,908 square miles (7,686,882 square km)
Smallest Country	Nauru: 8 square miles (20.7 square km)
Largest Rain Forest	Papua New Guinea: 130,000 square miles (336,700 square km)
Longest Coral Reef	Great Barrier Reef, Australia: (1,600 miles (2,600 km)

Australia's Great Barrier Reef

Regional Data File

Country Capital	Flag	Population	Area (sq mi)	GDP (billions $ U.S.)	Life Expectancy at Birth	Internet Users (per 1,000 pop.)
Australia Canberra		22.9 million	2,988,902	1,224	82.2	850
Bangladesh Dhaka		156.1 million	55,599	202.3	73.2	140
Bhutan Thimphu		750,125	18,147	2.2	70.1	400
Brunei Bandar Seri Begawan		436,620	2,228	11.8	77.2	710
Cambodia Phnom Penh		15.9 million	69,900	18.2	64.5	190
China Beijing		1,373 million	3,705,407	10,980	75.5	500
Fiji Suva		915,303	7,054	4.8	72.7	460
India New Delhi		1,266 million	1,269,346	2,091	68.5	260
Indonesia Jakarta		258 million	741,100	859	72.7	220
Japan Tokyo		127 million	145,883	4,123	85	930
Kiribati Tarawa		106,925	313	0.2	66.2	130
Laos Vientiane		7 million	91,429	12.5	64.3	180
Malaysia Kuala Lumpur		30.9 million	127,317	296.2	75	710
Maldives Male		392,960	116	3.1	75.6	550
Marshall Islands Majuro		73,376	70	0.2	73.1	190
Micronesia, Federated States of; Palikir		104,719	271	0.3	72.9	320
Mongolia Ulaanbaatar		3 million	603,909	11.7	69.6	210
Myanmar (Burma); Yangon (Rangoon) Naypyidaw		56.8 million	261,970	67	66.6	220
Nauru No official capital		9,591	8	0.15	67.1	540
United States Washington, D.C.		324 million	3,794,083	18,040	79.8	750

South and East Asia and the Pacific

Country Capital	Flag	Population	Area (sq mi)	GDP (billions $ U.S.)	Life Expectancy at Birth	Internet Users (per 1,000 pop.)
Nepal Kathmandu		29 million	58,827	21.4	70.7	180
New Zealand Wellington		4.4 million	103,738	172.2	81.2	880
North Korea Pyongyang		25.1 million	46,541	28	70.4	Not available
Pakistan Islamabad		202 million	310,403	270	67.7	180
Palau Ngerulmud		21,347	177	0.3	73.1	360
Papua New Guinea Port Moresby		6.8 million	178,704	16.1	67.2	80
Philippines Manila		102 million	115,831	292	69.2	410
Samoa Apia		198,926	1,137	0.8	73.7	250
Singapore Singapore		5.7 million	267	292.7	85	820
Solomon Islands Honiara		635,027	10,985	1.1	75.3	100
South Korea Seoul		50.9 million	38,023	1,377	82.4	900
Sri Lanka Colombo		22.2 million	25,332	82.1	76.8	300
Taiwan Taipei		23 million	13,892	523.6	80.1	880
Thailand Bangkok		68.2 million	198,457	395.3	74.7	390
Timor-Leste Dili		1.2 million	5,794	2.6	68.1	130
Tonga Nuku'alofa		106,513	289	0.4	76.2	450
Tuvalu Funafuti		10,959	10	0.03	66.5	430
Vanuatu Port-Vila		277,554	4,710	0.8	73.4	220
Vietnam Hanoi		95.2 million	127,244	191.5	73.4	530
United States Washington, D.C.		324 million	3,794,083	18,040	79.8	750

Gazetteer

A

Alexandria an ancient city in Egypt built by Alexander the Great (p. 340)

Amman (32°N, 36°E) the capital of Jordan (p. 328)

Ankara (40°N, 33°E) the capital and second-largest city of Turkey (p. 316)

Antarctic Peninsula a large peninsula in Antarctica (p. 629)

Arabia or Arabian Peninsula the world's largest peninsula; located in Southwest Asia (p. 275)

Aral Sea an inland sea in Central Asia fed by the Syr Darya and Amu Darya rivers (p. 279)

Atlas Mountains a high mountain range in northwestern Africa (p. 337)

B

Babylon (32°N, 44°E) city located on the Euphrates near what is now Baghdad, Iraq (p. 205)

Baghdad (33°N, 44°E) the capital of Iraq (p. 291)

Bangkok (14°N, 100°E) the capital of Thailand (p. 600)

Beijing (40°N, 116°E) the capital of China (pp. 529, 547)

Beirut (34°N, 36°E) the capital of Lebanon (p. 326)

Bethlehem (BETH-li-hem) a town in Israel where Jesus is said to have been born (p. 253)

Borneo the world's third-largest island; located in Southeast Asia (p. 590)

Bosporus (BAHS-puh-ruhs) a narrow strait in Turkey that connects the Mediterranean Sea with the Black Sea (p. 311)

C

Cairo (30°N, 31°E) the capital of Egypt (p. 340)

Canaan land settled by Abraham on the Mediterranean Sea (p. 245)

Cape of Good Hope a cape at the southern tip of Africa (p. 434)

Cape Town (34°S, 18°E) the legislative capital of South Africa (p. 438)

Chang Jiang (Yangzi River) a major river in China (pp. 513, 543)

Congo Basin a large flat area on the Congo River in Central Africa (p. 393)

Congo River the major river of Central Africa (p. 393)

D

Damascus (34°N, 36°E) the capital of Syria (p. 325)

Dardanelles (dahrd-uhn-ELZ) a strait between the Aegean Sea and the Sea of Marmara; part of a waterway that connects the Black Sea and the Mediterranean Sea (p. 311)

Darfur a region in western Sudan; because of genocide, millions of people have fled from Darfur (p. 430)

Dead Sea one of the saltiest lakes and the lowest point on Earth; located on the border between Israel and Jordan and fed by the Jordan River (p. 312)

Delhi a city in northern India that was the capital of the Mughal Empire (p. 495)

Dhaka (DA-kuh) (24°N, 90°E) the capital of Bangladesh (p. 505)

Djenné a West African city that was a center of learning (p. 369)

E

Esfahan (es-fah-HAHN) (33°N, 52°E) ancient capital of the Safavid Empire; now a city in central Iran (p. 294)

Euphrates River a river in Southwest Asia (p. 275)

F

Fergana Valley a fertile plains region of Uzbekistan in Central Asia (p. 279)

Fertile Crescent a large arc of fertile lands between the Persian Gulf and the Mediterranean Sea; the world's earliest civilizations began in the region (p. 191)

Forbidden City a huge palace complex built by Ming emperors of China (p. 532)

Fuji (FOO-jee) (35°N, 135°E) a volcano and Japan's highest peak (p. 563)

G

Ganges River (GAN-jeez) a major river in northern India (p. 490)

Gao the capital city of the Songhai kingdom in West Africa (p. 368)

Gaza (32°N, 34°E) a city in southwestern Israel on the Mediterranean Sea (p. 323)

Gobi (GOH-bee) a desert in China and Mongolia (p. 542)

Gold Coast British colony in West Africa; was renamed Ghana when it became independent in 1960 (p. 376)

Gazetteer

Grand Canal a canal linking northern and southern China built during the Sui dynasty (p. 521)

Great Barrier Reef a huge coral reef off the northeastern coast of Australia (p. 615)

Great Rift Valley a series of valleys in East Africa caused by the stretching of Earth's crust (p. 421)

Great Zimbabwe an ancient walled town in Southern Africa (p. 433)

H

Hanoi (21°N, 106°E) the capital of Vietnam (p. 603)

Harappa (huh-RA-puh) (30°N, 73°E) ancient city in the Indus Valley (p. 449)

Himalayas the highest mountains in the world; they separate the Indian Subcontinent from China (p. 541)

Hong Kong (22°N, 115°E) a city in southern China (p. 549)

Huang He (Yellow River) a major river in northern China (pp. 513, 543)

I

Indochina Peninsula a large peninsula in Southeast Asia (p. 589)

Indus River a major river in Pakistan (pp. 449, 490)

Istanbul (41°N, 29°E) the largest city in Turkey; formerly known as Constantinople (p. 315)

J

Jakarta (6°S, 107°E) the capital of Indonesia (p. 605)

Java a large island in Indonesia (p. 607)

Jerusalem (32°N, 35°E) the capital of Israel; it contains holy sites of Judaism, Christianity, and Islam (p. 319)

Jordan River a river between Israel and Jordan that empties into the Dead Sea (p. 312)

K

Kabul (35°N, 69°E) the capital of Afghanistan (p. 300)

Kaifeng the capital of China under the Song dynasty (p. 523)

Kao-Hsiung (KOW-SHYOOHNG) a center of heavy industry in Taiwan, and its main seaport (p. 556)

Kara-Kum (kahr-uh-koom) a desert in Central Asia east of the Caspian Sea (p. 280)

Kashmir a disputed region between India and Pakistan (p. 504)

Kathmandu (kat-man-DOO) (28°N, 85°E) the capital of Nepal (p. 505)

Kinshasa (4°S, 15°E) the capital of the Democratic Republic of the Congo (p. 410)

Kolkata (Calcutta) a major city in eastern India (p. 499)

Kongo Kingdom an important Central African kingdom founded in the 1300s near the mouth of the Congo River (p. 407)

Korean Peninsula a peninsula on the east coast of Asia (p. 564)

Kuala Lumpur (3°N, 102°E) the capital of Malaysia (p. 605)

Kush an ancient kingdom south of Egypt (p. 223)

Kyoto (KYOH-toh) (35°N, 136°E) the ancient capital of Japan (p. 567)

Kyzyl Kum (ki-ZIL KOOM) a vast desert region in Uzbekistan and Kazakhstan (p. 280)

L

Lagos (6°N, 3°E) a city in Nigeria; the most populous city in West Africa (p. 402)

Lower Egypt the northern region of Egypt, a country in North Africa on the Mediterranean Sea (p. 211)

M

Maghreb a region in North Africa that includes western Libya, Tunisia, Algeria, and Morocco; it means "west" in Arabic (p. 347)

Malay Archipelago (muh-LAY) a large group of islands in Southeast Asia (p. 589)

Malay Peninsula (muh-LAY) a narrow peninsula in Southeast Asia (p. 589)

Manila (15°N, 121°E) the capital of the Philippines (p. 607)

Mecca (21°N, 40°E) an ancient city in Arabia and the birthplace of Muhammad (p. 262)

Medina a city in Saudi Arabia where Muhammad went when he fled Mecca (p. 264)

Mekong River a major river in Southeast Asia (p. 591)

Melanesia a huge group of Pacific islands that stretches from New Guinea to Fiji (p. 622)

Meroë (MER-oh-wee) (16°N, 33°E) economic center and capital of ancient Kush (p. 235)

Micronesia a large group of Pacific islands located east of the Philippines (p. 622)

Mogadishu (2°N, 45°E) the capital of Somalia (p. 432)

Mohenjo-Daro (27°N, 68°E) one of the largest settlements of the Harappan civilization (p. 449)

Gazetteer

Mount Everest the highest mountain in the world at 29,035 feet (8,850 km); it is located in India and Nepal (p. 490)

Mount Kilimanjaro (ki-luh-muhn-JAHR-oh) (3°S, 37°E) the highest mountain in Africa at 19,341 feet (5,895 m); it is in Tanzania near the Kenya border (p. 422)

Mumbai (Bombay) a major city in western India (p. 499)

N

Namib Desert a desert in southwestern Africa (p. 424)

New Guinea the world's second-largest island; located in Southeast Asia (p. 590)

Niger River the major river of West Africa (p. 391)

Nile River the longest river in the world; located in North Africa (pp. 211, 335)

North China Plain a plains region of northeastern China (p. 543)

Nubia a region in northeast Africa, formerly known as Kush (p. 231)

O

Olduvai Gorge a steep canyon on the Serengeti Plain in northern Tanzania, Africa (p. 357)

Osaka (oh-SAH-kuh) (35°N, 135°E) a city in Japan (p. 571)

Outback the dry interior region of Australia (p. 619)

P

Pamirs a highland region in Central Asia, mainly in Tajikistan (p. 279)

Persian Gulf a body of water located between the Arabian Peninsula and the Zagros Mountains in Iran; it has enormous oil deposits along its shores (p. 275)

Phnom Penh (puh-NAWM pen) (12°N, 105°E) the capital of Cambodia (p. 602)

Plateau of Tibet the world's highest plateau, which lies north of the Himalayas in southwest China (p. 541)

Polynesia the largest group of islands in the Pacific Ocean (p. 622)

Pyongyang (pyuhng-YANG) (39°N, 126°E) the capital of North Korea (p. 581)

S

Sahara the world's largest desert; it dominates much of North Africa (p. 335)

Sahel a semiarid region between the Sahara and wetter areas to the south (p. 392)

Samarqand (40°N, 67°E) an ancient city on the Silk Road in modern Uzbekistan (p. 298)

Sea of Marmara part of a narrow waterway that separates Europe from Asia (p. 311)

Seoul (38°N, 127°E) the capital of South Korea (p. 579)

Serengeti Plain a large plain in East Africa that is famous for its wildlife (p. 423)

Shanghai (31°N, 121°E) a major port city in eastern China (p. 549)

Silk Road a network of trade routes that stretched across Asia from China to the Mediterranean Sea (p. 520)

Suez Canal a canal in Egypt that links the Mediterranean and Red seas (pp. 336, 378)

Sumer another name for Mesopotamia, the region in Southwest Asia between the Tigris and Euphrates rivers (p. 196)

Syrian Desert a desert in Southwest Asia covering much of the Arabian Peninsula between the Mediterranean coast and the Euphrates River (p. 313)

T

Taipei (25°N, 122°E) the capital of Taiwan (p. 556)

Tehran (36°N, 51°E) the capital of Iran (p. 294)

Tibet a China-controlled Buddhist region in southwest China (p. 547)

Tigris River (ty-gruhs) a major river in Southwest Asia; with the Euphrates River it defined the "land between the rivers" known as Mesopotamia (p. 275)

Timbuktu an important trade city of Mali in West Africa (pp. 367, 398)

Timor former colony of Portugal, now part of Timor-Leste in Southeast Asia (p. 597)

Timor-Leste an island country in Southeast Asia (p. 604)

Tokyo (36°N, 140°E) the capital of Japan (p. 569)

Gazetteer

U

Ulaanbaatar (oo-lahn-BAH-tawr) (48°N, 107°E) the capital of Mongolia (p. 554)

Upper Egypt the southern region of Egypt, a country in North Africa on the Mediterranean Sea (p. 211)

W

West Bank a disputed territory in eastern Israel (p. 323)

X

Xi'an the capital of China during the Qin dynasty (p. 516)

Y

Yangon (Rangoon) (17°N, 96°E) the largest city of Myanmar (Burma) (p. 600)

Z

Zambezi River a river in Central Africa that flows into the Indian Ocean (p. 394)

Zanzibar an island in Tanzania; once a major trading center (p. 426)

Writing Workshop 1

Explaining a Process

ASSIGNMENT
Write an expository essay explaining one of these topics:

- how water recycles on Earth
- how agriculture developed

TIP: ORGANIZING INFORMATION
Explanations should be in a logical order. You should arrange the steps in the process in chronological order, the order in which the steps take place.

How does soil renewal work? How do cultures change? Often the first question we ask about something is how it works or what process it follows. One way we can answer these questions is by writing an explanation.

1. Prewrite

Choose a Process

- Choose one of the topics on the left to write about.
- Turn your topic into a big idea, or thesis. For example, your big idea might be "Water continually circulates from Earth's surface to the atmosphere and back."

Gather and Organize Information

- Look for information about your topic in your textbook, in the library, or on the Internet.
- Start a plan to organize support for your big idea. For example, look for the individual steps of the water cycle.

2. Write

Here is a framework that will help you write your first draft.

A WRITER'S FRAMEWORK

Introduction	Body	Conclusion
• Start with an interesting fact or question. • Identify your big idea.	• Create at least one paragraph for each point supporting the big idea. Add facts and details to explain each point. • Use a variety of sentence structures to add interest to your writing. • Use chronological order or order of importance.	• Summarize your main points in your final paragraph.

3. Evaluate and Revise

Review and Improve Your Paper

- Reread your paper and make sure you have followed the framework.
- Make the changes needed to improve your paper.

Evaluation Questions for Your Paper

1. Do you begin with an interesting fact or question?
2. Does your introduction identify your big idea?
3. Do you have at least one paragraph for each point you are using to support the big idea?
4. Do you use a variety of sentence structures?
5. Do you include facts and details to explain and illustrate each point?
6. Do you use chronological order or order of importance to organize your main points?

4. Proofread and Publish

Give Your Explanation the Finishing Touch

- Make sure to use standard grammar, spelling, punctuation, and sentence structure.
- Check for punctuation at the end of every sentence.
- Think of a way to share your explanation.
- Use social studies terminology correctly.

5. Practice and Apply

Use the steps and strategies outlined in this workshop to write your explanation. Present your paper to others and find out whether the explanation makes sense to them.

Compare and Contrast

ASSIGNMENT
Write a paper comparing and contrasting two countries or regions. Consider physical geography, government, and/or culture.

TIP: ORGANIZING INFORMATION
A Venn diagram (two overlapping circles) can help you plan your paper. Write similarities in the overlapping area and differences in the areas that do not overlap.

How are two countries or regions alike? How are they different? Comparing the similarities and contrasting the differences between places can teach us more than by studying each one individually.

1. Prewrite

Choose a Topic

- Choose two countries or regions to write about.
- Create a big idea, or thesis, about the two countries. For example, your big idea might be "Iran and Iraq both have oil-based economies, but they also have many differences."

Gather and Organize Information

- Conduct research and use data from geographic tools, including maps, graphs, charts, databases, and models to identify at least three similarities or differences between the countries.
- Decide how to organize your main ideas and details, for example, by each place or by each similarity or difference.

2. Write

This framework will help you write your first draft.

A WRITER'S FRAMEWORK

Introduction
- Start with a fact or question relating to both countries.
- Identify your big idea.

Body
- Write at least one paragraph for each country or each point of similarity or difference. Include facts and details to help explain each point.
- Use block style or point-by-point style.

Conclusion
- Summarize the process in your final paragraph.

3. Evaluate and Revise

Review and Improve Your Paper

- Reread your draft, then ask yourself the questions below to see if you have followed the framework.
- Make any changes needed to improve your compare-and-contrast paper.

Evaluation Questions for a Compare-and-Contrast Paper

1. Do you begin with an interesting fact or question that relates to both places?
2. Does your first paragraph clearly state your big idea and provide background information?
3. Do you discuss at least three similarities and differences between the places?
4. Do you include main ideas and details from your research?
5. Is your paper clearly organized by country and region or by similarities and differences?

4. Proofread and Publish

Give Your Paper the Finishing Touch

- Make sure you have capitalized the names of countries and cities.
- Reread your paper to check that you have used standard grammar, spelling, sentence structures, and punctuation.
- Share your compare-and-contrast paper by reading it aloud in class or in small groups.

5. Practice and Apply

Use the steps outlined in this workshop to write a compare-and-contrast paper. Compare and contrast your paper to those of your classmates.

Writing Workshop 3

Explaining Cause or Effect

ASSIGNMENT
Write a paper explaining one of the following topics:

- the causes of economic problems in West Africa
- the effects of colonization in Southern Africa

TIP: WHAT RELATIONSHIPS?
Transitional words like *as a result, because, since,* and *so* can help make connections between causes and effects.

"Why did it happen?" "What were the results?" Questions like these help us identify causes and effects. This, in turn, helps us understand the relationships among physical geography, history, and culture.

1. Prewrite

Choose a Topic

- Choose one of the topics on the left to write about.
- Turn that topic into a big idea, or thesis. For example, "Three main factors cause most of the economic problems in West Africa."

Gather and Organize Information

- Depending on the topic you have chosen, identify at least three causes or three effects. Use your textbook, the library, or the Internet.
- Organize causes or effects in their order of importance. To have the most impact on your readers, put the most important cause or effect last.

2. Write

You can use this framework to help you write your first draft.

A WRITER'S FRAMEWORK

Introduction	Body	Conclusion
• Start with an interesting fact or question related to your big idea, or thesis. • State your big idea and provide background information.	• Write at least one paragraph, including supporting facts and examples, for each cause or effect. • Organize your causes or effects by order of importance.	• Summarize the causes or effects. • Restate your big idea.

3. Evaluate and Revise

Review and Improve Your Paper

- Reread your paper and use the questions below to determine how to make your paper better.
- Make changes to improve your paper.

Evaluation Questions for a Cause or Effect Explanation

1. Do you begin with a fact or question related to your big idea, or thesis?
2. Does your introduction identify your big idea and provide any needed background?
3. Do you have at least one paragraph for each cause or effect?
4. Do you include facts and details to support the connections between causes and effects?
5. Do you explain the causes or effects in order of importance?
6. Do you summarize the causes or effects and restate your big idea?

4. Proofread and Publish

Give Your Explanation the Finishing Touch

- Make sure you use social studies terminology correctly and that transitional words clearly connect causes and effects.
- Check for the use of standard grammar, spelling, sentence structure, and punctuation.
- Confirm your understanding by having someone provide feedback on your paper.

5. Practice and Apply

Use the steps and strategies outlined in this workshop to write your cause or effect paper. Share your paper with other students who wrote on the same topic. Compare your lists of causes or effects.

Persuasion

ASSIGNMENT
Write a persuasive paper about an issue faced by the people of Asia and the Pacific. Choose an issue related to the region's environment or culture.

TIP: THAT'S A REASON
Convince your readers by presenting reasons to support your opinion. For example, one reason to create a warning system for tsunamis is to save lives.

Persuasion is about convincing others to act or believe in a certain way. Just as you use persuasion to convince your friends to see a certain movie, people use persuasion to convince others to help them solve the world's problems.

1. Prewrite

Choose an Issue

- Choose an issue to write about. For example, you might choose the danger of tsunamis or the role of governments.
- Create a statement of opinion. For example, you might say, "Countries in this region must create a warning system for tsunamis."

Gather and Organize Information

- Search your textbook, the library, or the Internet for evidence that supports your opinion.
- Identify at least two reasons to support your opinion. Find facts, examples, and expert opinions to support each reason.

2. Write

This framework can help you state your position clearly and present persuasive reasons and evidence.

A WRITER'S FRAMEWORK

Introduction	Body	Conclusion
• Start with a fact or question related to the issue you will discuss. • Clearly state your opinion in a sentence.	• Write one paragraph for each reason. Begin with the least important reason and end with the most important. • Include facts, examples, and expert opinions as support.	• Restate your opinion and summarize your reasons.

3. Evaluate and Revise

Review and Improve Your Paper

- As you review your paper, use the questions below to evaluate it.
- Make changes to improve your paper.

Evaluation Questions for a Persuasive Essay

1. Do you begin with an interesting fact or question related to the issue?
2. Does your introduction clearly state your opinion and provide any necessary background information?
3. Do you discuss your reasons from least to most important?
4. Do you provide facts, examples, or expert opinions to support each of your reasons?
5. Does your conclusion restate your opinion and summarize your reasons?

4. Proofread and Publish

Give Your Paper the Finishing Touch

- Make sure that you have used standard grammar, spelling, sentence structure, and punctuation.
- Check for correct comma usage when presenting a list of reasons or evidence.
- Decide how to share your paper. For example, could you publish it in a school paper or in a classroom collection of essays?

5. Practice and Apply

Use the steps and strategies outlined in this workshop to write your persuasive essay. Share your opinion with others to see whether they find your opinion convincing.

English and Spanish Glossary

Phonetic Respelling and Pronunciation Guide

Many of the key terms in this textbook have been respelled to help you pronounce them. The letter combinations used in the respelling throughout the narrative are explained in the following phonetic respelling and pronunciation guide. The guide is adapted from *Merriam-Webster's Collegiate Dictionary, 11th Edition; Merriam-Webster's Geographical Dictionary; and Merriam-Webster's Biographical Dictionary.*

MARK	AS IN	RESPELLING	EXAMPLE
a	alphabet	a	*AL-fuh-bet
ā	Asia	ay	AY-zhuh
ä	cart, top	ah	KAHRT, TAHP
e	let, ten	e	LET, TEN
ē	even, leaf	ee	EE-vuhn, LEEF
i	it, tip, British	i	IT, TIP, BRIT-ish
ī	site, buy, Ohio	y	SYT, BY, oh-HY-oh
	iris	eye	EYE-ris
k	card	k	KAHRD
ō	over, rainbow	oh	OH-vuhr, RAYN-boh
u̇	book, wood	ooh	BOOHK, WOOHD
ȯ	all, orchid	aw	AWL, AWR-kid
ȯi	foil, coin	oy	FOYL, KOYN
au̇	out	ow	OWT
ə	cup, butter	uh	KUHP, BUHT-uhr
ü	rule, food	oo	ROOL, FOOD
yü	few	yoo	FYOO
zh	vision	zh	VIZH-uhn

*A syllable printed in capital letters receives heavier emphasis than the other syllable(s) in a word.

A

Aborigines (a-buh-rij-uh-nees) the original inhabitants of Australia (p. 618)
aborígenes habitantes originales de Australia

absolute location a specific description of where a place is located; absolute location is often expressed using latitude and longitude (p. 16)
ubicación absoluta descripción específica del lugar donde se ubica un punto; con frecuencia se define en términos de latitud y longitud

acupuncture the practice of inserting fine needles through the skin at specific points to cure disease or relieve pain (p. 519)
acupuntura práctica de insertar agujas finas a través de la piel en puntos específicos para curar enfermedades o aliviar el dolor

Afrikaners (a-fri-kah-nuhrz) Dutch, French, and German settlers and their descendants in South Africa (p. 434)
afrikaners colonizadores holandeses, franceses y alemanes y sus descendientes en Sudáfrica

afterlife life after death, according to some beliefs (p. 217)
la otra vida vida después de la muerte, según algunas creencias

agricultural industries businesses that focus on growing crops and raising livestock (p. 169)
industrias agrícolas empresas dedicadas al cultivo de la tierra y la ganadería

alloy a mixture of two or more metals (p. 481)
aleación mezcla de dos o más metales

alluvial deposition a process in which rivers create floodplains by flooding their banks and depositing sediment along the banks (p. 57)
depósito aluvial proceso en el cual los ríos crean llanuras de inundación inundando sus bancos y depositando sedimentos a lo largo de los bancos

alphabet a set of letters that can be combined to form words (p. 210)
alfabeto conjunto de letras que se pueden combinar para formar palabras

animism the belief that bodies of water, animals, trees, and other natural objects have spirits (p. 401)
animismo creencia de que las masas de agua, los animales, los árboles y otros objetos de la naturaleza tienen espíritu

apartheid South Africa's government policy of separation of races that was abandoned in the 1980s and 1990s; apartheid means "apartness" (p. 435)
apartheid política gubernamental de Sudáfrica de separar las razas, abandonada en las décadas de 1980 y 1990; apartheid significa "separación"

Arab Spring a wave of pro-democracy uprisings that spread throughout Northern Africa and Southwest Asia in 2011 (p. 341)
revolución democrática árabe una serie de levantamientos en favor de la democracia que comenzaron en Túnez en el 2010 y se extendieron hasta el norte de África y el suroeste de Asia en el 2011

arable land that is suitable for growing crops (p. 302)
cultivable tierra buena para el cultivo

archipelago a large group of islands (p. 589)
archipiélago gran grupo de islas

architecture the science of building (p. 202)
arquitectura ciencia de la construcción

assets items of economic value that a person or company owns (p. 176)
activos elementos de valor económico que una persona o empresa posee

atoll a ring-shaped coral island that surrounds a lagoon (p. 623)
atolón isla de coral en forma de anillo que rodea una laguna

B

Bantu migration the movement of 400 ethnic groups who spoke related languages out of West Africa into the southern half of the continent; occurred between 5,000 and 2,000 years ago (p. 370)
migración Bantú el movimiento de 400 grupos étnicos que hablaron lenguas afines de África Occidental en la mitad sur del continente; ocurrió entre 5,000 y 2,000 años atrás

barter the exchange of one good or service for another (p. 173)
trueque intercambio de un bien o servicio por otro

basin a generally flat region surrounded by higher land such as mountains and plateaus (p. 393)
cuenca región generalmente llana rodeada de tierras más altas, como montañas y mesetas

Bedouins Arabic-speaking nomads that live mostly in the deserts of Southwest Asia (p. 328)
beduinos nómadas que hablan árabe y viven principalmente en los desiertos del suroeste de Asia

Berlin Conference meetings of European countries beginning in 1884 during which Africa was divided into European colonies (p. 379)
Conferencia de Berlín reuniones de países europeos que comienzan en 1884 durante el cual África se dividió en colonias europeas

Bible the holy book of Christianity (p. 253)
Biblia libro sagrado del cristianismo

biome a large community of living organisms, both plants and animals, that are adapted to a particular environment; a biome may be made up of several ecosystems (p. 78)
bioma comunidad grande de organismos vivos, tanto plantas como animales, que se adaptan a un entorno particular; un bioma puede estar compuesto de varios ecosistemas

birthrate the annual number of births per 1,000 people (p. 109)
índice de natalidad número de nacimientos por cada 1,000 personas en un año

Boers Afrikaner frontier farmers in South Africa (pp. 381, 434)
bóers agricultores afrikaners de la frontera en Sudáfrica

border a political or geographic boundary that separates one country from another (p. 131)
frontera límite político o geográfico que separa a un país de otro

Buddhism a religion based on the teachings of the Buddha that developed in India in the 500s BC (p. 498)
budismo religión basada en las enseñanzas de Buda, originada en la India en el siglo VI a. C.

bureaucracy a body of unelected government officials (p. 526)
burocracia cuerpo de funcionarios no electos del gobierno

English and Spanish Glossary

C

canals human-made waterways (p. 193)
canales vias navegables creadas por los humanos

cartography the science of making maps (p. 13)
cartografía ciencia de crear mapas

caste system the division of Indian society into groups based on birth or occupation (pp. 456, 499)
sistema de castas división de la sociedad india en grupos basados en el nacimiento o la profesión

cataracts rapids in a river (p. 211)
cataratas rápidos de un río

center-pivot irrigation an irrigation technique that uses a sprinkler in the center of a large circular field; the long arms of the sprinkler circle over the field to water crops (p. 120)
riego por pivote central técnica de riego que usa un rociador en el centro de un gran campo circular; los brazos largos circulan sobre el campo para regar los cultivos

chariot a wheeled, horse-drawn cart used in battle (p. 206)
cuadriga carro tirado por caballos usado en batalla

Christianity a major world religion based on the life and teachings of Jesus of Nazareth (p. 253)
cristianismo una de las pincipales religions del mundo, basada en las enseñanzas de Jesús

city-state a political unit made up of a city and all the surrounding lands (p. 196)
ciudad estado unidad política compuesta de una ciudad y todas las tierras que la rodean

civil service the body of people who work as government officials (p. 526)
servicio civil cuerpo de personas que trabajan como funcionarios del gobierno

civilization an organized society within a specific area (p. 193)
civilización sociedad organizada dentro de un área específica

climate a region's average weather conditions over a long period of time (p. 62)
clima condiciones del tiempo promedio de na región durante un período largo de tiempocloud

cluster settlement a type of settlement that is grouped around or at the center of a resource (p. 115)
núcleo de población tipo de asentamiento que se agrupa alrededor o en el centro de un recurso

colony a territory inhabited and controlled by people from a foreign land (p. 497)
colonia territorio habitado y controlado por personas de otro país

command economy an economic system in which the central government makes all economic decisions (pp. 164, 547)
economía autoritaria sistema económico en el que el gobierno central toma todas las decisiones económicas

commerce the substantial exchange of goods between cities, states, or countries (p. 116)
comercio intercambio sustancial de bienes entre ciudades, estados o países

common good the welfare of a community (p. 139)
bien común bienestar de una comunidad

compass an instrument that uses Earth's magnetic field to show direction (p. 525)
brújula instrumento que utiliza el campo magnético de la Tierra para indicar la dirección

Confucianism a philosophy based on the ideas of Confucius that focuses on morality, family order, social harmony, and government (p. 551)
confucianismo filosofía basada en las ideas de Confucio que se concentra en la moralidad, el orden familiar, la armonía social y el gobierno

constitution a written plan of government (p. 137)
constitución plan escrito del gobierno

continent a large landmass that is part of Earth's crust; geographers identify seven continents (pp. 25, 53)
continente gran masa de tierra que forma parte de la corteza terrestre; los geógrafos identifican siete continentes

contraction a reduction in business activity or growth (p. 162)
contracción reducción de la actividad o crecimiento de negocios

copper belt the area between northern Zambia and southern Democratic Republic of the Congo that has most of Africa's copper (p. 410)
cinturón de cobre área entre el norte de Zambia y el sur de la República Democrática del Congo, que tiene la mayor parte del cobre de África

Coptic Christianity a form of Christianity that blended African customs with Christian teaching (p. 365)
cristianismo cóptico una forma del cristianismo que mexcla costumbres africanas con enseñanas cristianas

coral reef a chain of rocky material found in shallow tropical waters (p. 615)
arrecife de coral cadena de material rocoso que se encuentra en aguas tropicales de poca profundidad

cultural diffusion the spread of culture traits from one region to another (p. 99)
difusión cultural difusión de rasgos culturales de una región a otra

cultural universal a cultural feature found in all societies (p. 101)
rasgo cultural universal rasgo de la cultura que es común a todos los grupos sociales

culture the set of beliefs, values, and practices that a group of people have in common (p. 95)
cultura conjunto de creencias, valores y costumbres compartidas por un grupo de personas

culture region an area in which people have many shared culture traits (p. 97)
región cultural región en la que las personas comparten muchos rasgos culturales

culture trait an activity or behavior in which people often take part (p. 96)
rasgo cultural actividad o conducta frecuente de las persona

cuneiform the world's first system of writing (p. 200)
cuneiforme primer sistema de escritura del mundo

D

Daoism a philosophy that developed in China and stressed the belief that one should live in harmony with the Dao, the guiding force of all reality (p. 551)
taoísmo filosofía que se desarrolló en China y que enfatizaba la creencia de que se debe vivir en armonía con el Tao, la fuerza que guía toda la realidad

deforestation the clearing of trees (p. 83)
deforestación tala de árboles

degree a unit of measurement indicated by parallels circling the globe (p. 24)
grado unidad de medida indicada por paralelos que circundan el globo

delta a landform at the mouth of a river created by sediment deposits (pp. 212, 490)
delta accidente geográfico que se forma en la desembocadura de un río, creado por depósitos de sedimento

demilitarized zone an empty buffer zone created to keep two countries from fighting (p. 580)
zona desmilitarizada zona vacía que se crea como barrera entre dos países para evitar que luchen

democracy a form of government in which the people elect leaders and rule by majority (p. 137)
democracia sistema de gobierno en el que el pueblo elige a sus líderes y gobierna por mayoría

desertification the spread of desert-like conditions (pp. 81, 392)
desertización ampliación de las condiciones desérticas

developed countries countries with strong economies and a high quality of life (p. 171)
países desarrollados países con economías sólidas y una alta calidad de vida

developing countries countries with less productive economies and a lower quality of life (p. 171)
países en vías de desarrollo países con economías menos productivas y una menor calidad de vida

dialect a regional version of a language (pp. 408, 550)
dialecto versión regional de una lengua

Diaspora the dispersal of the Jewish population outside of Israel (p. 319)
Diáspora dispersión de la población judía fuera de Israel

dictator a ruler who has almost absolute power (p. 345)
dictador gobernante que tiene poder casi absolute

Diet the name for Japan's elected legislature (p. 569)
Dieta nombre de la asamblea legislativa electa de Japón

diplomacy the work nations do to keep friendly relations with one another (p. 133)
diplomacia trabajo que hacen las naciones para mantener relaciones amistosas entre sí

direct democracy a form of government in which citizens meet regularly in a popular assembly to discuss issues, pass laws, and vote for leaders (p. 137)
democracia directa forma de gobierno caracterizada por asambleas populares en las que los ciudadanos se reúnen periódicamente para debatir problemas, aprobar leyes y elegir funcionarios públicos

disciples (di-SY-puhls) followers (p. 254)
discípulos seguidores

division of labor an arrangement in which each worker specializes in a particular task or job (p. 194)
división del trabajo organización en la cual cada trabajador se especializa en una tarea o trabajo particular

domino theory the idea that if one country fell to Communism, neighboring countries would follow like falling dominoes (p. 598)
teoría del efecto dominó idea de que si un país cae en manos del comunismo, los países vecinos lo seguirán como fichas de dominó que caen una tras otra

draft law requiring men of certain ages and qualification to serve in the military (p. 146)
servicio militar obligatorio ley que establece que los varones de edades y calificaciones determinadas deben prestar servicio militar

droughts periods when little rain falls and crops are damaged (p. 425)
sequías períodos en los que los cultivos sufren daños por la falta de lluvia

dryland farming farming that relies on rainfall instead of irrigation (p. 302)
cultivo de secano cultivo que depende de la lluvia en vez de la irrigación

dynasty a series of rulers from the same family (p. 214)
dinastía serie de gobernantes de la misma familia

E

earthquake a sudden, violent movement of Earth's crust (p. 55)
terremoto movimiento repentino y violento de la corteza terrestre

ebony a type of dark, heavy wood (p. 233)
ébano tipo de madera oscura y pesada

economic interdependence when producers in one nation depend on others to provide goods and services that they do not produce (p. 163)
interdependencia económica cuando los productores de una nación dependen de otros para proporcionar bienes y servicios que no producen

economy a system of producing, selling, and buying goods and services (p. 159)
economía sistema de producción, venta y compra de bienes y servicios

ecosystem a group of plants and animals that depend on each other for survival, and the environment in which they live (p. 78)
ecosistema grupo de plantas y animales que dependen unos de otros para sobrevivir, y el ambiente en el que estos viven

edicts laws (p. 475)
edictos leyes

embargo a limit on trade (p. 289)
embargo límite impuesto al comercio

empire a land with different territories and peoples under a single ruler (p. 198)
imperio zona que reúne varios territorios y pueblos bajo un solo gobernante

enclave a small territory surrounded by foreign territory (p. 438)
enclave territorio pequeño rodeado de territorio extranjero

engineering the application of scientific knowledge for practical purposes (p. 219)
ingeniería aplicación del conocimiento científico para fines prácticos

entrepreneurs independent business people (p. 378)
empresarios gente de negocios independiente

environment the land, water, climate, plants, and animals of an area; surroundings (pp. 16, 77)
ambiente la tierra, el agua, el clima, las plantas y los animales de una zona; los alrededores

epics long poems that tell the stories of heroes (p. 201)
poemas épicos poemas largos que narran historias de héroes

equator an imaginary line that circles the globe halfway between the North and South Poles (p. 24)
ecuador línea imaginaria que atraviesa el globo terráqueo por la mitad entre el Polo Norte y el Polo Sur

erosion the movement of sediment from one location to another (p. 56)
erosión movimiento de sedimentos de un lugar a otro

escarpment a steep face at the edge of a plateau or other raised area (p. 421)
acantilado cara empinada en el borde de una meseta o de otra área elevada

ethnic group a group of people who share a common culture and ancestry (p. 98)
grupo étnico grupo de personas que comparten una cultura y una ascendencia

ethnocentrism the belief that one's own culture or ethnic group is superior (p. 378)
etnocentrismo creencia de que la propia cultura o grupo étnico es superior

Exodus the journey of the Jews out of Egypt (p. 246)
Éxodo viaje de los judíos fuera de Egipto

expansion the action of becoming larger or more extensive (p. 162)
expansión acción de volverse más grande o más extensa

exports items sent to other regions for trade (p. 235)
exportaciones productos enviados a otras regiones para el intercambio comercial

extended family a family group that includes the father, mother, children, and close relatives (p. 401)
familia extendida grupo familiar que incluye al padre, la madre, los hijos y los parientes cercanos

extinct no longer here; a species that has died out has become extinct (p. 79)
extinto que ya no existe; una especie que ha desaparecido está extinta

F

factors of production the basic economic resources needed to produce goods and services. The four main factors of production are land, labor, capital, and entrepreneurship. (p. 161)
factores de producción los diferentes recursos que se necesitan para la creación de un bien o servicio. Los cuatro factores de producción principales son: la tierra, la mano de obra, el capital y la capacidad empresarial.

famine an extreme shortage of food (p. 405)
hambruna grave escasez de alimentos

fasting going without food (p. 464)
ayunar dejar de comer

fishery a place where lots of fish and other seafood can be caught (p. 566)
pesquería lugar donde suele haber muchos peces y mariscos para pescar

Five Pillars of Islam five acts of worship required of all Muslims (p. 266)
Cinco Pilares del Islam cinco actos de adoración obligatorios para todos los musulmanes

foreign policy a nation's plan for how to act toward other countries (p. 133)
política exterior plan de una nación de cómo actuar hacia otros países

fossil fuels nonrenewable resources that formed from the remains of ancient plants and animals; coal, petroleum, and natural gas are all fossil fuels (p. 84)
combustibles fósiles recursos no renovables formados a partir de restos de plantas y animales antiguos; el carbón, el petróleo y el gas natural son combustibles fósiles

fossil water water underground that is not being replaced by rainfall (p. 278)
aguas fósiles agua subterránea que no es reemplazada por el agua de lluvia

fracking a process that breaks up rock by injecting large amounts of water and chemicals into cracks; forces cracks in the rock to widen, allowing oil and gas to flow out (p. 123)
fractura hidráulica proceso que rompe la roca inyectando grandes cantidades de agua y productos químicos en las grietas; forza las grietas con el objetivo de ampliarlas en la roca, permitiendo que el petróleo y el gas fluyan hacia fuera

free enterprise system an economic system in which businesses can compete freely with one another with little government intervention; capitalism (p. 167)
libre empresa sistema económico basado en la competencia libre entre las empresas con una intervención estatal mínima; también conocida como capitalismo

English and Spanish Glossary

free port a city in which almost no taxes are placed on goods (pp. 349, 606)
puerto libre ciudad donde hay muy pocos impuestos sobre los bienes

free trade the removal of trade barriers between nations (p. 184)
libre comercio eliminación de las barreras comerciales entre las naciones

freshwater water that is not salty; it makes up only about three percent of our total water supply (p. 47)
agua dulce agua que no es salada; representa sólo alrededor del 3 por ciento de nuestro suministro total de agua

front the place where two air masses of different temperatures or moisture content meet (p. 65)
frente lugar en el que se encuentran dos masas de aire con diferente temperatura o humedad

G

genocide the intentional destruction of a people (p. 430)
genocidio destrucción intencional de un grupo de personas

Geographic Information System (GIS) a technology system that combines and provides geographic information from many different sources (p. 22)
Sistema de informacion geografica (SIG) sistema tecnológico que combina y proporciona información geográfica de muchas fuentes diferentes

geography the study of the world, its people, and the landscapes they create (p. 5)
geografía estudio del mundo, de sus habitantes y de los paisajes creados por el ser humano

geothermal energy energy produced from the heat of Earth's interior (p. 429)
energía geotérmica energía producida a partir del calor del interior de la Tierra

ger a large, circular, felt tent used in Mongolia and Central Asia (p. 554)
ger gran tienda circular de fieltro usada en Mongolia y Asia Central

glacier a large area of slow moving ice (p. 47)
glaciar gran bloque de hielo que avanza con lentitud

globalization the process in which countries are increasingly linked to each other through culture and trade (p. 179)
globalización proceso por el cual los países se encuentran cada vez más interconectados a través de la cultura y el comercio

Global Positioning System (GPS) a technology system that transmits information from satellites to Earth, giving the exact location of a given object on our planet (p. 22)
Sistema de posicionamiento global sistema tecnológico que transmite información de los satélites a la Tierra, dando la ubicación exacta de un objeto en nuestro planeta

globe a spherical, or ball-shaped, model of the entire planet (p. 20)
globo terráqueo modelo esférico, o en forma de bola, de todo el planeta

Great Wall a barrier built to protect China from invasion that stood near China's northern border (p. 905)
Gran Muralla barrera construida cerca de la frontera norte de China para proteger a China de las invasiones

green revolution a program that encouraged farmers to adopt modern agricultural methods to produce more food (p. 501)
revolución verde programa que animó a los agricultores a adoptar métodos de agricultura modernos para producir más alimentos

grid a pattern of imaginary lines that circle the globe in east-west and north-south directions (p. 24)
cuadrícula patrón de líneas imaginarias que atraviesan el globo terráqueo en las direcciones este-oeste y norte-sur

grid settlement a type of settlement that is purposefully laid out with a network of transportation routes; the streets form a grid by running at right angles to each other (p. 115)
asentamiento hipodámico tipo de asentamiento que está diseñado de acuerdo a las rutas de transporte; las calles forman una cuadrícula al cruzarse en ángulos rectos entre sí

gross domestic product (GDP) the value of all goods and services produced within a country in a single year (p. 171)
producto interior bruto (PIB) valor de todos los bienes y servicios producidos en un país durante un año

groundwater water found below Earth's surface (p. 48)

agua subterránea agua que se encuentra debajo de la superficie de la Tierra

gunpowder a mixture of powders used in guns and explosives (p. 525)
pólvora mezcla de polvos usados en armas y explosivos

gurdwara a Sikh place of worship (p. 471)
gurdwara lugar de culto en la sociedad sij

H

habitat the place where a plant or animal lives (p. 79)
hábitat lugar en el que vive una planta o animal

Hammurabi's Code a set of 282 laws created by the Babylonian leader Hammurabi (p. 205)
Código de Hammurabi conjunto de 282 leyes creadas por el líder babilonio Hammurabi

hemisphere a half of the globe, divided by lines of latitude and longitude; Earth's hemispheres are the Northern Hemisphere, Southern Hemisphere, Eastern Hemisphere, and Western Hemisphere (p. 25)
hemisferio una mitad del globo, dividida por líneas de latitud y longitud; los hemisferios de la Tierra son el Hemisferio Norte, el Hemisferio Sur, el Hemisferio Oriental y el Hemisferio Occidental

heritage the wealth of cultural elements that has been passed down over generations (p. 103)
patrimonio cultural riqueza cultural que se pasa de una generación a otra

hieroglyphics the ancient Egyptian writing system that uses picture symbols to communicate (p. 226)
jeroglíficos sistema de escritura antiguo de Egipto que usa símbolos ilustrados para comunicarse

Hindu-Arabic numerals the number system we use today (p. 482)
números indoarábigos sistema de números que usamos hoy

Hinduism the main religion of India; it teaches that everything is part of a universal spirit called Brahman (p. 498)
hinduismo religión principal de la India; sus enseñanzas dicen que todo forma parte de un espíritu universal llamado Brahma

hominids early ancestors of humans (p. 357)
homínido primeros antepasados de los seres humanos

human geography the study of the world's human geographic features—people, communities, and landscapes (p. 11)
geografía humana estudio de los habitantes, las comunidades y los paisajes del mundo

humanitarian aid assistance to people in distress (p. 135)
ayuda humanitaria ayuda a personas en peligro

human rights rights that all people deserve, such as rights to equality and justice (pp. 135, 600)
derechos humanos derechos que toda la gente merece como derechos a la igualdad y la justicia

humus (HYOO-muhs) decayed plant or animal matter; it helps soil support abundant plant life (p. 80)
humus materia animal o vegetal descompuesta; contribuye a que crezca una gran cantidad de plantas en el suelo

hunter-gatherers people who hunt animals and gather wild plants, seeds, fruits, and nuts to survive (p. 360)
cazadores y recolectores personas que cazan animales y recolectan plantas silvestres, semillas, frutas y nueces para sobrevivir

hydroelectric power the production of electricity from waterpower, such as from running water (p. 85)
energía hidroeléctrica producción de electricidad generada por la energía del agua, como la del agua corriente

I

ice shelf a ledge of ice that extends over the water (p. 628)
banco de hielo saliente de hielo que se extiende sobre el agua

iceberg a floating mass of ice that has broken off a glacier (p. 629)
iceberg masa de hielo flotante que se ha desprendido de un glaciar

imperialism the practice of building an empire by claiming lands, setting up colonies, and controlling those areas (pp. 378, 427)
imperialismo intento de dominar el gobierno, el comercio y la cultura de un país

imports goods brought in from other regions (p. 235)

English and Spanish Glossary

importaciones productos importados de otras regiones

income the money or wages earned from a job, or money earned by buying and selling goods and services (p. 177)
ingresos dinero o los salarios ganados de un trabajo, o el dinero ganado comprando y vendiendo bienes y servicios

inflation the rise in prices that occurs when currency loses its buying power (p. 411)
inflación aumento de los precios que ocurre cuando la moneda de un país pierde poder adquisitivo

inoculation (i-nah-kyuh-lay-shuhn) the practice of injecting a person with a small dose of a virus to help him or her build a defense to a disease (p. 482)
inoculación acto de inyectar a una persona con una pequeña dosis de un virus para ayudarle a crear defensas contra una enfermedad

interest groups organizations that try to influence government policies (p. 149)
grupos de interés organizaciones que tratan de influir en las políticas gubernamentales

interest rate a percentage of the total amount of money in a customer's account (p. 175)
tasa de interés un porcentaje de la cantidad total de dinero en la cuenta de un cliente

investment the use of money today, such as buying stock in a company, in order to earn future benefits (p. 177)
inversión el uso del dinero hoy en día, como la compra de acciones en una empresa, con el fin de obtener beneficios futuros

irrigation a way of supplying water to an area of land (p. 193)
irrigación método para suministrar agua a un terreno

Islam a religion founded in Arabia by Muhammad based on submitting to God (Allah) and on messages Muslims believe God gave to Muhammad (pp. 263, 282)
Islam una religión fundada por Mahoma en Arabia, basada en la sumisión a Dios (Alá) y en los mensajes que los musulmanes creen Dios le dio a Mahoma

isolationism a policy of avoiding contact with other countries (p. 922)
aislacionismo política de evitar el contacto con otros países

ivory a white material taken from elephant tusks (p. 233)
marfil material blanco procedente de los colmillos de elefante

J

Jainism an ancient religion begun in India that teaches nonviolence as a way of life and that all living things should be valued (p. 499)
Jainismo una religión antigua comenzada en la India que enseña la no violencia como una forma de vida y que todos los seres vivos deben ser valorados

janissaries Christian boys captured by the Ottomans and forced to become soldiers (p. 315)
jenízaros niños cristianos capturados por los otomanos y obligados a convertirse en soldados

jihad the Arabic word for "struggle" or "to make an effort" (p. 266)
yihad palabra árabe para "luchar" o "hacer un esfuerzo"

Judaism (JOO-dee-i-zuhm) the religion of the ancient Israelites (practiced by Jews today); the oldest monotheistic religion (pp. 245, 319)
judaísmo religión de los israelitas (practicada por los judíos hoy en dia); la relgión monoteista más antigua

jury duty obligation to serve as a juror (p. 146)
servicio de jurado obligación que tiene un ciudadano de desempeña la función de jurado

K

karma the effects that good or bad actions have on a person's soul (p. 460)
karma efectos que las acciones buenas o malas producen en el alma de una persona

kibbutz (kih-BOOTS) in Israel, a large farm where people traditionally shared everything in common (p. 322)
kibbutz en Israel, granja grande donde las personas comparten tradicionalmente todo

kimchi a traditional Korean food made from pickled cabbage and spices (p. 577)
kimchi comida tradicional coreana hecha con repollo en vinagre y especias

kimono a traditional robe worn in Japan (p. 569)
kimono bata tradicional usada en Japón

klong a canal in Bangkok (p. 600)
klong canal de Bangkok

kosher a term used to refer to the food allowed under Jewish dietary laws; it means "fit" in Hebrew (p. 322)
kosher término utilizado para referirse a la comida que es permitida bajo las leyes alimenticias judías; significa "ser sano/a" en hebreo

L

landform a shape on the planet's surface, such as a mountain, valley, plain, island, or peninsula (p. 52)
accidente geográfico forma de la superficie terrestre, como una montaña, un valle, una llanura, una isla o una península

landlocked completely surrounded by land with no direct access to the ocean (p. 278)
sin salida al mar que está rodeado completamente por tierra, sin acceso directo al océano

landscape all the human and physical features that make a place unique (p. 5)
paisaje todas las características humanas y físicas que hacen que un lugar sea único

langar a Sikh community kitchen (p. 471)
langar cocina comunitaria sij

latitude the distance north or south of Earth's equator (p. 24)
latitud distancia hacia el norte o el sur desde el ecuador

lava magma that reaches Earth's surface (p. 55)
lava magma que llega a la superficie terrestre

limited government a type of government that has legal limits on its power, usually in the form of a constitution (p. 137)
gobierno limitado forma de gobierno cuyo poder está restringido por la ley, comúnmente la constitución

linear settlement a type of settlement that is grouped along the length of a resource; usually has a long and narrow pattern (p. 115)
asentamiento lineal tipo de asentamiento que se agrupa a lo largo de un recurso; por lo general tiene un patrón largo y estrecho

longitude the distance east or west of Earth's prime meridian (p. 24)
longitud distancia este u oeste del primer meridiano de la Tierra

M

malaria a disease spread by mosquitoes that causes fever and pain (p. 412)
malaria enfermedad transmitida por los mosquitos que causa fiebre y dolor

malnutrition a condition of not getting enough nutrients from food (p. 414)
desnutrición estado producido al no obtener suficientes nutrientes de los alimentos

mandate of heaven the idea that heaven chose China's ruler and gave him or her power (p. 514)
mandato del cielo idea de que el cielo eligió el gobernante de China y le dio su poder

manufacturing industries businesses where people make finished products from raw materials (p. 169)
industria manufacturera actividad económica en la cual las personas transforman materias primas en artículos de consumo

Maori (MOWR-ee) the original inhabitants of New Zealand (p. 618)
maoríes primeros habitantes de Nueva Zelanda

map a flat drawing that shows all or part of Earth's surface (p. 20)
mapa representación plana que muestra total o parcialmente la superficie de la Tierra

map projection a method of showing our round planet on a flat map (p. 26)
proyección de mapas método para mostrar nuestro planeta redondo en un mapa plano

market economy an economic system based on free trade and competition (p. 164)
economía de mercado sistema económico basado en el libre comercio y la competencia

meditation the focusing of the mind on spiritual things (p. 464)
meditación enfoque de la mente en las cosas espirituales

medium of exchange a means through which goods and services can be exchanged (p. 174)
instrumento de cambio un medio para intercambiar bienes y servicios

megalopolis a string of large cities that have grown together (p. 114)
megalópolis serie de ciudades grandes que han crecido hasta unirse

English and Spanish Glossary

mercenaries hired soldiers (p. 474)
mercenarios soldados contratados

merchants buyers and sellers of goods; traders (p. 235)
comerciantes compradores y vendedores de bienes; negociantes

meridian a line of longitude (p. 24)
meridiano línea de longitud

Messiah a leader the ancient Jews predicted would restore the greatness of Israel (p. 253)
Mesías líder que los judíos predecían restauraría la grandeza de Israel

metallurgy (MET-uhl-uhr-jee) the science of working with metals (p. 481)
metalurgia ciencia de trabajar los metales

meteorology the study of weather and what causes it (p. 14)
meteorología estudio de las condiciones del tiempo y sus causas

metropolitan area a city and its surrounding areas (p. 114)
área metropolitana una ciudad y sus alrededores

Middle Kingdom a period of order and stability in ancient Egypt that lasted to about 1750 BC (p. 221)
Reino Medio período de orden y estabilidad en el antiguo Egipto que duró alrededor de 1750 a. C.

Middle Passage the voyages that brought enslaved Africans across the Atlantic Ocean to North America and the West Indies (p. 374)
Paso Central viaje en el que los esclavos africanos atravesaban el océano Atlántico hasta llegar a América del Norte y las Antillas

migration the process of moving from one place to live in another (p. 110)
migración movimiento de personas de un lugar para ir a vivir a otro lugar

minute the unit of measurement of a globe's surface that is part of a degree (p. 24)
minuto la unidad de medida de la superficie de un globo terráqueo que forma parte de un grado

missionaries people who work to spread their religious beliefs (p. 467)
misioneros personas que trabajan para difundir sus creencias religiosas

mixed economy an economy that is a combination of command, market, and traditional economies (p. 165)
economía mixta economía de mercado con características de sistemas tradicionales y dirigidas

money any item, usually coins or paper currency, that is used in payment for goods or services (p. 173)
dinero cualquier artículo, generalmente monedas o billetes, que se utiliza en el pago de bienes o servicios

monotheism a belief in one and only one God (p. 248)
monoteísmo creencia en un solo Dios

monsoon a seasonal wind that brings either dry or moist air (pp. 70, 492)
monzón viento estacional que trae aire seco o húmedo

mosque a building for Muslim worship (pp. 264, 368)
mezquita edificio para el culto musulmán

multicultural society a society that includes a variety of cultures in the same area (p. 98)
sociedad multicultural área de la sociedad en la que convergen culturas diversas

mummies specially treated bodies of the dead wrapped in cloth for preservation purposes (p. 218)
momias cadáver especialmente tratado y envuelto en tela para su conservación

Muslim a person who follows Islam (p. 263)
musulmán seguidor del Islam

N

national interest a country's economic, cultural, or military goals (p. 134)
interés nacional objetivos económicos, culturales o militares de un país

nationalism a devotion and loyalty to one's country (p. 382)
nacionalismo sentimiento de lealtad a unpaís

natural resource any material in nature that people use and value (p. 82)
recurso natural todo material de la naturaleza que las personas utilizan y valoran

New Kingdom the period in which Egypt reached the height of its power and glory (p. 222)
Reino Nuevo período en el cual Egipto alcanzó la cima de su poder y su gloria

nirvana a state of perfect peace (p. 465)
nirvana estado de paz perfecta

nobles people from rich and powerful families (p. 215)
nobles personas de familias ricas y ponderosas

nomads people who move often from place to place (pp. 299, 362)
nómadas personas que se trasladan frecuentemente de un lugar a otro

nonrenewable resource a resource that cannot be replaced naturally; coal and petroleum are examples of nonrenewable resources (p. 83)
recurso no renovable recurso que no puede reemplazarse naturalmente; el carbón y el petróleo son ejemplos de recursos no renovables

nonrepresentative government a system of government where power is unlimited and citizens have few, if any, rights (p. 151)
gobierno sin representación sistema de gobierno con poder ilimitado, en el que los ciudadanos tienen pocos o ningún derecho

nonviolence the avoidance of violent actions (p. 461)
no violencia rechazo de acciones violentas

O

oasis a wet, fertile area in a desert where a spring or well provides water (pp. 261, 336)
oasis zona húmeda y fértil en el desierto con un manantial o pozo que proporciona agua

obelisk a tall, four-sided pillar that is pointed on top (p. 228)
obelisco pilar alto de cuatro caras acabado en punta

ocean currents large streams of surface seawater; they move heat around Earth (p. 64)
corrientes oceánicas grandes corrientes de agua de mar que fluyen en la superficie del océano; transportan calor por toda la Tierra

Old Kingdom a period in Egyptian history that lasted from 2700 to 2200 BC (p. 215)
Reino Antiguo período de la historia egipcia que abarca aproximadamente del 2700 hasta 2200 a. C.

OPEC an international organization whose members work to influence the price of oil on world markets by controlling the supply (p. 283)
OPEP organización internacional cuyos miembros trabajan para influenciar el precio del petróleo en los mercados mundiales controlando la oferta

opportunity cost the value of something you give up in order to get something else (p. 159)
costo de oportunidad el valor de algo que renuncias para obtener otra cosa

ozone layer a layer of Earth's atmosphere that protects living things from the harmful effects of the sun's ultraviolet rays (p. 631)
capa de ozono capa de la atmósfera de la Tierra que protege a los seres vivos de los efectos dañinos de los rayos ultravioleta del sol

P

pagoda a Buddhist temple based on Indian designs (p. 552)
pagoda templo budista basado en diseños de la India

papyrus a long-lasting, paperlike material made from reeds (p. 226)
papiro material duradero hecho de juncos, parecido al papel

parallel a line of latitude (p. 24)
paralelo línea de latitude

partition division (p. 497)
partición división

periodic market an open-air trading market that is set up once or twice a week (p. 409)
mercado periódico mercado al aire libre que funciona una o dos veces a la semana

permafrost permanently frozen layers of soil (p. 74)
permafrost capas de tierra congeladas permanentemente

pharaoh the title used by rulers of ancient Egypt (p. 214)
faraón título usado por los gobernantes del antiguo Egipto

physical geography the study of the world's physical geographic features—its landforms, bodies of water, climates, soils, and plants (p. 10)
geografía física estudio de las características físicas de la Tierra: sus accidentes geográficos, sus masas de agua, sus climas, sus suelos y sus plantas

English and Spanish Glossary

pictographs picture symbols used in early systems of written communication (p. 200)
pictogramas símbolos ilustrados que se usaron en los primeros sistemas de comunicación escrita

plate tectonics a theory suggesting that Earth's surface is divided into a dozen or so slow-moving plates, or pieces of Earth's crust (p. 53)
tectónica de placas teoría que sugiere que la superficie terrestre está dividida en unas doce placas, o fragmentos de corteza terrestre, que se mueven lentamente

polar desert a high-latitude region that receives little precipitation (p. 629)
desierto polar región a una latitud alta que recibe pocas precipitaciones

political party a group of people who organize to gain political power (p. 148)
partido político grupo de personas que se organizan para ganar poder político

polytheism the worship of many gods (p. 199)
politeísmo la adoración de muchos dioses

popular culture culture traits that are well known and widely accepted (p. 179)
cultura popular rasgos culturales conocidos y de gran aceptación

population the total number of people in a given area (p. 106)
población número total de personas en una zona determinada

population density a measure of the number of people living in an area (p. 106)
densidad de población medida del número de personas que viven en una zona

porcelain a thin, beautiful type of pottery (p. 524)
porcelana tipo de cerámica bella y delicada

precipitation water that falls to Earth's surface as rain, snow, sleet, or hail (p. 48)
precipitación agua que cae a la superficie de la Tierra en forma de lluvia, nieve, aguanieve o granizo

prevailing winds winds that blow in the same direction over large areas of Earth (p. 63)
vientos preponderantes vientos que soplan en la misma dirección sobre grandes zonas de la Tierra

priests (Sumer) people who performed or led religious ceremonies (p. 199)
sacerdotes (Sumeria) personas que realizaron o dirigieron ceremonias religiosas

prime meridian an imaginary line that circles the globe and breaks it into an eastern half and a western half (p. 24)
primer meridiano línea imaginaria que atraviesa el globo terráqueo y lo divide en una mitad oriental y una mitad occidental

profit the money left over after the costs of producing a product are subtracted from the income gained by selling that product (p. 160)
ganancia dinero que queda después de que los costos de producción de un producto se restan de los ingresos obtenidos por la venta de ese producto

public goods government goods and services that the public consumes; highways are an example (p. 168)
bienes públicos bienes y servicios públicos que el público consume; las autopistas son un ejemplo

public opinion the way large groups of citizens think about issues and people (p. 149)
opinión pública la manera cómo grupos grandes de ciudadanos piensan sobre temas y personas

pyramids huge stone tombs with four triangle-shaped sides that meet in a point on top (p. 219)
pirámides tumbas gigantescas de piedra con cuatro lados en forma de triángulo que se encuentran en un punto en la parte superior

Q

quota a number or monetary value for the amount of goods that can be imported or exported over a certain time period (p. 283)
cuota número o valor monetario para la cantidad de bienes que pueden ser importados o exportados durante un período de tiempo

Qur'an the holy book of Islam (p. 263)
Corán libro sagrado del Islam

R

rabbi a Jewish religious teacher and leader (p. 248)
rabino líder y maestro religioso judío

reforestation planting trees to replace lost forestland (p. 83)
reforestación siembra de árboles para reemplazar los bosques que han desaparecido

region a part of the world that has one or more common features that distinguish it from surrounding areas (p. 7)
región parte del mundo que tiene una o más características comunes que la distinguen de las áreas que la rodean

reincarnation the process of birth, death, and rebirth of the soul (p. 459)
reencarnación proceso de nacimiento, muerte y renacimiento del alma

relative location a general description of where a place is located; a place's relative location is often expressed in relation to something else (p. 16)
ubicación relativa descripción general de la posición de un lugar; la ubicación relativa de un lugar suele expresarse en relación con otra cosa

renewable resource a resource that Earth replaces naturally, such as water, soil, trees, plants, and animals (p. 82)
recurso renovable recurso que la Tierra reemplaza por procesos naturales, como el agua, el suelo, los árboles, las plantas y los animales

representative democracy an indirect democracy in which people vote for representatives to make and enforce laws (p. 138)
democracia representativa democracia indirecta en la que los ciudadanos votan por los representantes para que creen las leyes y las hagan cumplir

representative government a system of government where people are the ultimate source of government authority (p. 145)
gobierno representativo sistema de gobierno en el que los ciudadanos son la fuente de autoridad absoluta

Resurrection (re-suh- REK-shuhn) the Christian belief that Jesus rose from the dead (p. 254)
resurrección creencia cristiana de que Jesús resucitó de entre los muertos

retail industries businesses that sell directly to final customers (p. 170)
distribuidores minoristas empresas comerciales que venden directamente a los consumidores finales

revolution the 365¼ day trip Earth takes around the sun each year (p. 42)
revolución viaje de 365¼ días que la Tierra hace alrededor del Sol cada año

revolution a drastic change in a country's government and way of life (p. 294)
revolución cambio drástico en el gobierno y la forma de vida de un país

rift valleys places on Earth's surface where the crust stretches until it breaks (p. 421)
valles de fisura puntos de la superficie de la Tierra en los que la corteza se estira hasta romperse

rock art drawings or paintings made on stone by prehistoric peoples (p. 360)
arte roquero dibujos o pinturas realizadas sobre piedra por pueblos prehistóricos

Rosetta Stone a huge stone slab inscribed with hieroglyphics, Greek, and a later form of Egyptian; used by scholars to learn how to read hieroglyphics (p. 227)
piedra de Rosetta gran losa de piedra en la que aparecen inscripciones en jeroglíficos, en griego y en una forma tardía del idioma egipcio; utilizada por los eruditos para aprender a leer jeroglíficos

rotation one complete spin of Earth on its axis; each rotation takes about 24 hours (p. 41)
rotación giro completo de la Tierra sobre su propio eje; cada rotación toma 24 horas

rural describes areas found outside of cities; less densely populated, with primarily agricultural economies (p. 114)
rural describe las áreas que se encuentran fuera de las ciudades; menos densamente pobladas, con economías principalmente agrícolas

S

safari an overland journey to view African wildlife (p. 428)
safari excursión por tierra con el fin de ver animales salvajes en África

saint a person known and admired for his or her holiness (p. 257)
santo persona conocida y admirada por su santidad

English and Spanish Glossary

samurai (SA-muh-ry) a trained professional warrior in feudal Japan (p. 567)
samurai guerrero profesional entrenado del Japón feudal

sanctions economic or political penalties imposed by one country on another to try to force a change in policy (p. 436)
sanciones penalizaciones económicas o políticas que un país impone a otro para obligarlo a cambiar su política

Sanskrit the most important language of ancient India (p. 454)
sánscrito idioma más importante de la antigua India

savanna an area of tall grasses and scattered trees and shrubs (pp. 71, 392)
sabana zona de pastos altos con arbustos y árboles dispersos

savings the income not spent on immediate needs and wants (p. 177)
ahorros ingresos no gastados en necesidades y deseos inmediatos

scarcity conflict that exists because wants are unlimited and resources are limited (p. 159)
escasez conflicto que resulta cuando existe una demanda ilimitada y una oferta limitada de productos

scholar-official an educated member of the government (p. 527)
funcionario erudito miembro culto del gobierno

scribe a person who keeps records or copies documents (p. 201)
escriba persona que mantiene registros o copia escritos ajenos

secular the separation of religion and government; nonreligious (p. 317)
secular separación entre la religión y el gobierno; no religioso

seismograph a device that measures the strength of earthquakes (p. 519)
sismógrafo aparato que mide la fuerza de los terremotos

service industries businesses that provide services rather than goods (p. 170)
empresas de servicios empresas que proveen servicios pero no bienes

settlement any place where a community is established (p. 113)
asentamiento cualquier lugar donde se establezca una comunidad

shah a Persian title that means "king" (p. 294)
sha título persa que significa "rey"

Sherpas an ethnic group from the mountains of Nepal (p. 503)
sherpas grupo étnico de las montañas de Nepal

Shia Muslims who believe that true interpretation of Islamic teaching can only come from certain religious and political leaders called imams; they make up one of the two main branches of Islam (p. 282)
chiítas musulmanes que creen que la interpretación correcta de las enseñanzas islámicas solo puede provenir de ciertos líderes religiosos y políticos llamados imanes; forman una de las dos ramas principales del Islam

shogun a general who ruled Japan in the emperor's name (p. 567)
shogun general que gobernaba a Japón en nombre del emperador

Sikhism a religion native to India that embraces equality for all, belief in one God, service to humanity, and honest labor (p. 499)
sijismo una religión originaria de la India, que abarca la igualdad para todos, la creencia en un solo Dios, el servicio a la humanidad y el trabajo honesto

silent barter a process in which people exchange goods without contacting each other directly (p. 366)
trueque silencioso proceso mediante el cual las personas intercambian bienes sin entrar en contacto directo

Silla one of the Three Kingdoms of ancient Korea (p. 575)
Silla uno de los tres reinos de la antigua Corea

silt finely ground fertile soil that is good for growing crops (pp. 192, 335)
cieno tierra fértil de partículas finas que es buena para el crecimiento de los cultivos

slash-and-burn agriculture the practice of burning forest in order to clear land for planting (p. 119)
agricultura de tala y quema práctica de quemar los bosques para despejar el terreno y sembrar en él

social hierarchy the division of society according to people's rank or class (p. 200)
jerarquía social división de la sociedad según la clase o nivel de las personas

social institution an organized pattern of belief and behavior that focuses on meeting people's basic needs (p. 101)
institución social patrón organizado de creencia y comportamiento que se enfoca en satisfacer las necesidades básicas de la gente

social science a field that focuses on people and the relationships among them (p. 6)
ciencias sociales campo de estudio que se enfoca en las personas y en las relaciones entre

solar energy energy from the sun (p. 41)
energía solar energía del Sol

souk (SOOK) a marketplace or bazaar in the Islamic world (p. 348)
zoco mercado o bazar del mundo islámico

sovereign nation a government with complete authority over a geographic region (p. 132)
nación soberana gobierno con autoridad completa sobre una región geográfica

spatial pattern the placement of people and objects on Earth and the space between them (p. 115)
patrón espacial colocación de personas y objetos en la Tierra y el espacio entre ellos

sphinxes imaginary creatures having the body of a lion and the head of another animal or a human (p. 228)
esfinges criaturas imaginarias que tienen el cuerpo de un león y la cabeza de otro animal o un ser humano

steppe a semidry grassland or prairie; steppes often border deserts (p. 71)
estepa pradera semiárida; las estepas suelen encontrarse en el límite de los desiertos

store of value something that holds its value over time (p. 174)
depósito de valores algo que mantiene su valor con el tiempo

subcontinent a large landmass that is smaller than a continent (p. 489)
subcontinente gran masa de tierra, más pequeña que un continente

suburb an area immediately outside of a city, often a smaller residential community (p. 114)
suburbio área inmediatamente fuera de una ciudad, a menudo una comunidad residencial más pequeña

sultan the supreme ruler of a Muslim country (p. 606)
sultán gobernante supremo de un país musulmán

sundial a device that uses the position of shadows cast by the sun to tell the time of day (p. 519)
reloj de sol dispositivo que utiliza la posición de las sombras que proyecta el sol para indicar las horas del día

Sunnah the way Muhammad lived and a guide for the Muslim way of life (p. 266)
Sunna la vida de Mahoma y una guía para el estilo de vida musulmán

Sunni Muslims who believe in the ability of the majority of the community to interpret Islamic teachings; they make up one of the two main branches of Islam (p. 282)
suníes musulmanes que creen en la capacidad de la mayor parte de la comunidad de interpretar las enseñanzas islámicas; forman una de las dos ramas principales del Islam

surface water water that is found in Earth's streams, rivers, and lakes (p. 48)
agua superficial agua que se encuentra en los arroyos, ríos y lagos de la Tierra

surplus more than what is needed (p. 194)
excedente más de lo que se necesita

Swahili an African society that emerged in the late 1100s along the East African coast and combined elements of African, Asian, and Islamic cultures (p. 373)
Suajili sociedad Africana que surgió a finales del siglo XII a lo largo de la costa africana oriental; combinada elementos de las culturas africana, asiática e islámica

T

Taliban a radical Muslim group that rose to power in Afghanistan in the 1990s (p. 300)
talibanes grupo radical musulmán que llegó al poder en Afganistán de la década de 1990

tariff a fee that a country charges on imports or exports (p. 570)
arancel tarifa que impone un país a las importaciones y exportaciones

technology the use of knowledge, tools, and skills to solve problems (p. 104)
tecnología el uso de herramientas, destrezas y conocimientos necesarios para resolver problemas

English and Spanish Glossary

terraced farming an ancient technique for growing crops by cutting steps into hillsides or mountain slopes (p. 119)
cultivo en andenes técnica antigua para cultivar la tierra en laderas o pendientes de montañas

territory an area that is under the authority of another government (p. 624)
territorio zona que está bajo el control de otro gobierno

theocracy a government ruled by religious leaders (pp. 215, 295)
teocracia gobierno dirigido por líderes religiosos

Torah the most sacred text in Judaism (p. 249)
Torá el texto más sagrado del judaísmo

totalitarian government a type of government that exercises control over all aspects of society (p. 141)
gobierno totalitario forma de gobierno que ejerce control sobre todos los aspectos de una sociedad

townships crowded clusters of small homes in South Africa outside of cities where black South Africans live (p. 436)
distritos segregados grupos de pequeñas viviendas amontonadas ubicadas en las afueras de las ciudades de Sudáfrica, donde vivían los sudafricanos negros

trade barrier any law that limits free trade between nations (p. 184)
barrera comercial cualquier ley que limite el libre comercio entre las naciones

trade network a system of people in different lands who trade goods (p. 235)
red comercial sistema de personas en diferentes lugares que comercian productos

trade route a path used by traders for buying and selling goods (pp. 113, 223)
ruta comercial itinerario utilizado por los comerciantes para la compra y venta de bienes

trade surplus when a country exports more goods than it imports (p. 570)
excedente comercial cuando un país exporta más bienes de los que importa

traditional economy an economy in which production is based on customs and tradition and in which people often grow their own food, make their own goods, and use barter to trade (p. 164)
economía tradicional economía en la que la producción se basa en las costumbres y tradición y en la que la gente suele cultivar su propia comida, hacer sus propios bienes y utilizar el trueque para comerciar

tropics regions close to the equator (p. 45)
trópicos regiones cercanas al ecuador

tsunami (sooh-NAH-mee) a destructive and fast-moving wave (p. 564)
tsunami ola rápida y destructiva

U

unit of account a yardstick of economic value in exchanges, such as money (p. 174)
unidad de cuenta unidad monetaria que se utiliza en las transacciones comerciales, como el dinero

United Nations an organization of countries that promotes peace and security around the world (p. 134)
Naciones Unidas organización de países que promueve la paz y la seguridad en todo el mundo

universal theme a message about life or human nature that is meaningful across time and in all places (p. 103)
tema universal mensaje significativo sobre la vida o la naturaleza humana que se conoce en todo tiempo y lugar

unlimited government a type of government in which there are no legal limits set on its power (p. 141)
gobierno ilimitado forma de gobierno en el que no hay límites legales establecidos en su poder

urban areas that are cities and the surrounding areas; heavily populated and developed (p. 114)
urbano áreas que son ciudades y sus alrededores; densamente pobladas y desarrolladas

urbanization the increase in the percentage of people who live in cities (p. 500)
urbanización aumento del porcentaje de personas que vive en las ciudades

V

veld (VELT) open grassland areas in South Africa (p. 424)
veld praderas descampadas en Sudáfrica

W

wadi a dry streambed (p. 278)
uadi cauce seco de un río o arroyo

wat a Buddhist temple that also serves as a monastery (p. 599)
wat templo budista que sirve también como monasterio

water cycle the movement of water from Earth's surface to the atmosphere and back (p. 48)
ciclo del agua circulación del agua desde la superficie de la Tierra hacia la atmósfera y de regreso a la Tierra

water vapor water occurring in the air as an invisible gas (p. 48)
vapor de agua agua que se encuentra en el aire en estado gaseoso e invisible

weather the short-term changes in the air for a given place and time (p. 62)
tiempo cambios a corto plazo en la atmósfera en un momento y lugar determinados

weathering the process by which rock is broken down into smaller pieces (p. 56)
meteorización proceso de desintegración de las rocas en pedazos pequeños

wholesale industries businesses that sell to businesses (p. 170)
distribuidores mayoristas empresas comerciales que venden productos a otras empresas comerciales

woodblock printing a form of printing in which an entire page is carved into a block of wood (p. 525)
xilografía forma de impresión en la que una página completa se talla en una plancha de madera

work ethic a belief that work in itself is worthwhile (p. 570)
ética de trabajo creencia de que el trabajo tiene valor propio

Y

yurt a movable round house made of wool felt mats hung over a wood frame (p. 300)
yurt tienda redonda y portátil de fieltro de lana que se coloca sobre una armazón de madera

Z

ziggurat a pyramid-shaped temple (p. 202)
zigurat templo en forma de pirámide

Zionism a nationalist movement that began in the late 1800s and called for Jews to reestablish a Jewish state in their original homeland (p. 320)
sionismo movimiento nacionalista que comenzó a finales del siglo XIX y que alentaba a los judíos a reestablecer un estado judío en su tierra natal

zonal organized by zone (p. 392)
zonal organizado por zonas

Index

KEY TO INDEX

c = chart	m = map
f = feature	p = photo

A

Aborigines, 618, 620
Abraham: in Hebrew Bible, 245, 246, 248
absolute location, 16
Abu Simbel: temple at, 228, 228*p*
acid rain, 122, 124
acquired immune deficiency syndrome (AIDS), 136, 413, 441
acupuncture, 519, 519*p*
Adwa, battle of, 382, 382*p*
Afar ethnic group, 431
Afghanistan, 170*c*, 171*f*, 279*m*, 298, 300–301, 303*f*, 303*p*, 494
Africa, 30*m*, 31*m*. *See also* central Africa; east Africa; east and southern Africa; north Africa; southern Africa; west Africa
Africa, human beginnings in: early sites in, 357–360, 357*m*, 359*p*; environmental adaptations of, 361–363, 362*f*, 362*p*; Iron Age, 361; Stone Ages, 360–361, 361*p*
Africa, in global trade: Atlantic slave trade, 374–375, 374*p*, 375*m*; in east Africa, 372–373, 373*p*; European colonies in Africa, 376; European trade with, 374; imperialism and independence in, 378, 383*m*
Africa, kingdoms in: Bantu, 370–371; Christian, 364–365; Ghana, 365–367, 365*m*, 366*p*; Mali, 367–368, 369*m*, 370*f*; Songhai, 368–370, 369*m*
African National Congress (ANC), 435–436
African Union (AU), 442
Afrikaner nationalists, 382–384, 434
afterlife: Egyptian emphasis on, 217–218, 217*f*, 217*p*
agricultural industries, 169, 169*p*
agriculture: Côte d'Ivoire, in west Africa, 404; Ghana, west Africa, 404; Indian subcontinent, 492; Kenya, east Africa, 428; Later Stone Age, 361; Mali kingdom, Africa, 367; north Africa, 348; Sahel region, west Africa, 405*p*; slash-and-burn, 119, 119*p*; Uganda, 430. *See also* farming
ahimsa (nonviolence), 461
Ahmadinejad, Mahmoud, 296–297
Ahmose of Thebes, 222
air pollution, 123*p*; in China, 549
Akbar, 477
Akkadian Empire, 197–198, 198*f*, 198*p*
Aksum kingdom, 238, 364
al-Assad, Bashar, 326
al-Assad, Hafiz, 326
Alawite religion, 326
Alexander the Great: Egypt invaded by, 340
Alexandria, Egypt, 340, 343
Algeria: Algiers, 348, 349*p*; Arab Spring (2011), 345, 346*m*; arts and literature in, 347; France control of, 346; geography of, 6*p*; government and economy of, 348–350; history and culture of, 345–347, 347*f*. *See also* north Africa
Ali, Zine al-Abidine Ben, 151, 350
All India Congress Committee, 496*f*, 496*p*
alloy, 481
alluvial deposition, 57
Almoravids, 367
alphabet, 210
al-Qaeda terrorist group, 135, 301, 429
aluminum, 86*p*, 403
Amharic language, 428
Amman, Jordan, 328
Amu Darya River, 279
Amundsen, Roald, 631*f*
Analects, The (Confucius teachings), 515
Andes Mountains, 55
Angkor Wat, 596
Angola, 409, 411, 412*p*
animism religion, 401, 428
Ankara, Turkey, 316
An Nafud desert, 277
Antarctica, 612*p*; climate, 629; crossing (historical source), 630*f*; early explorations, 630, 631*f*; environmental threats to, 631; icebergs near, 629*p*; ice shelves in, 632*p*; penguins in, 628*p*; physical geography, 628–629; resources, 629; scientific research in, 631
Antarctic Circle, 629
Antarctic Peninsula, 629
Antarctic Treaty, 630
apartheid, 435–436, 436*f*
Apedemek, 237
Apostles, 256, 257*p*
Arab culture region, 97*f*, 97*m*, 98
Arabian Peninsula: Bahrain, 284; Kuwait, 284; Oman, 285; Qatar, 284; Saudi Arabia, 282–284, 284*p*; United Arab Emirates, 285; Yemen, 285, 285*p*. *See also* Middle East (Arabian Peninsula, Iraq, and Iran)
arable land, 302
Arab Spring (2011), 341, 345
Aral Sea, 279, 281, 303
archaeology, 12, 193*f*
archipelago, 589
architecture: Chinese, 552; as cultural expression, 103*p*; in east Africa, 373; of Egypt (ancient), 227–230, 228*p*, 229*p*, 230*p*; in Mughal Empire, 478; Sumerian developments in, 202, 203*p*
Arctic Ocean, 25, 25*c*
arguments, strength of, 185
armed forces service, 146
arquebus guns, 369
art: central Africa, 409; Chinese, 551–552; as cultural expression, 103*p*; Early Stone Age, 360, 361*p*; Egypt, 344; Egypt (ancient), 227–230, 228*p*, 229*p*, 230*p*; Han dynasty, 518–519, 519*p*; Harappan civilization, 452, 452*p*; Indian empires, 478–479, 479*p*;

Islamic, 266*f*, 266*p*; north Africa, 347; southern Africa, 437, 437*p*; Sumerian civilization, 202–204, 203*p*, 204*p*; Tang dynasty, 524–525
arts, link to (feature): African masks, 401*f*, 401*p*
Aryabhata, 481*p*
Aryan civilization, 452–454, 453*m*, 454*p*
ASEAN. *See* Association of Southeast Asian Nations.
Ashanti people, 400
Askia the Great, 369
Asoka, 467, 474*f*, 475
assets, 176
Association of Southeast Asian Nations (ASEAN), 599, 604
Assyrian peoples, 207–208, 207*m*, 208*p*, 234, 235*p*
astronomy: in ancient times, 208, 481*p*
Aswan High Dam, 335, 343*p*
Atatürk, Kemal, 316*p*, 317*f*
Atlantic Ocean, 25, 25*c*
Atlantic slave trade, 374–375, 374*p*, 375*m*
Atlas Mountains, 336*m*, 337
atoll, 623; formation of, 624*f*, 624*p*
Augrabides Falls, 423
Aung San Suu Kyi, 599*f*, 599*p* 600
Aurangzeb, 478
Australia: climate, 616; diverse population in, 620; economy of, 619; elevation map, 616*m*; ethnic groups in, 620*c*; government in, 619; history of, 617–619; Opera House in Sydney, 613*p*; outdoor sports in, 618*f*; physical features, 615; shrubs in western portion, 616*p*; wildlife and resources, 617
***Australopithecus* hominid fossils,** 357, 359, 359*p*
Awaji Island, 583*m*
Ayres Rock, 615

B

Ba'ath Party, in Iraq, 288
Babur, 477, 495
Babylonian peoples, 205–206, 206*f*, 206*p*, 207*m*
Baghdad, Iraq, 291
Bahrain, 284
Bali: traditional dances, 587*p*
Bambuti culture, 362*f*, 362*p*
Bangkok, Thailand, 600
Bangladesh: on Indian subcontinent, 489; overview, 503–505; separation from Pakistan, 498
banking, *See* money and banking
Bantu people: early southern Africa, 433; kingdoms of, 370–371; languages of, 437
barriers to trade, 182*c*, 184
barter, 173
baseball, 100, 100*f*, 100*m*, 100*p*
Battutah, Ibn, 267*f*
bauxite mining, 86*p*, 403
Bedouins, 328
Beijing, China, 511*p*; Forbidden City within, 532, 533*f*, 549; National Day festivities in, 546*f*, 546*p*
Beirut, Lebanon, 326
beliefs: Hinduism, 458, 459*c*, 459*p*; Judaism, 248–249, 249*p*; *ka* (life force) in Egypt, 218; Sikhism, 470–471. *See also entries for specific religions*
Bell, Alexander Graham, 99
Benghazi, Libya, 349
Benin, 404
Berbers, 347*f*, 347*p*
Berlin Conference of 1884: Africa division from, 379–381, 380*m*
Bethlehem, 253
Bhagavad Gita, 480
Bhutan, 489, 503, 505–506
Bible, 253
Biden, Joe, 151*f*, 151*p*
bin Laden, Osama, 301
biography (feature): Asoka (Buddhist ruler of India), 474*f*, 474*p*; Atatürk, Kemal, 316*f*, 316*p*; Aung San Suu Kyi, 599*f*, 599*p*; Battutah, Ibn, 267*f*; Ebadi, Shirin, 297*f*, 297*p*; Gandhi, Mohandas, 497, 497*f*, 497*p*; Hatshepsut, Egyptian queen, 1503–1482 BC, 223*f*, 223*p*; Hirohito, 568*f*, 568*p*; Isabella of Spain, 316*f*, 316*p*; Khan, Kublai, 530*f*, 530*p*; Maathai, Wangari, 83*f*, 83*p*; Mansa Musa (ruler of Mali, 1300s), 370*f*, 370*p*; Mehmed II (Ottoman ruler), 316*f*, 316*p*; Sargon (ruler of Akka-dians), 198*f*, *198p*; Shackleton, Ernest (Sir), 630*f*, *630p*; Shanakhdakheto, queen of Kush, 237*f*, *237p*; Shi Huangdi (Emperor), 515*f*, *515p*
biomes, 77–81, 77*p*, 78*c*, 79*p*, 80*p*, 81*c*
birthrates, 109–110
bishops, spread of Christianity by, 259
Black Sea, 313*p*
blizzards, 65
Block, Herbert, 150*f*
Blue Nile River, 423
Boers, 434
Boer War, in South Africa, 380–381
Bollywood moviemaking industry, 502*f*, 502*p*
Book of the Dead, The (ancient Egyptian text), 227
Borneo, 590; orangutans in, 593*p*
Bosporus, 311, 312*m*, 313*p*
Botswana: art of, 438; Okavango River in, 422*p*; overview, 439; tourism industry in, 423
boundaries and borders of nations, 131–132, 132*p*
Brahma the Creator, 458, 459*p*
Brahmins *varna* (priests), 455
Brazil, government of, 140–141, 140*f*, 140*m*, 140*p*
Brunei, 604. *See also* Islam
Buddha, 567*p*
Buddhism: Buddha statue, 567*p*; in China, 526, 551; in India, 474*f*, 475, 498–499; in Japan, 568–569; in Korea, 575–576; Mahayana branch, 468; Siddhartha's search for wisdom, 463–464, 464*p*; in Southeast Asia, 596, 599; spread of, 467–469, 467*m*, 468*p*, 521;

teachings of, 465–466, 466*f*, 466*p*; Thai teenage Buddhist monks, 598*f*
Bukhara, Uzbekistan, 298, 302
bureaucracy, 526
burial practices, ancient Egyptian, 218, 218*p*
Burkina Faso, 402*p*, 406
Burundi, 430
Bush, George W., 290
Byzantine Empire: Aksum kingdom, in northeast Africa, and, 364

C

Cabo Verde, 791
cacao growing, 404
Cai Lun, 525
Cairo, Egypt, 214, 340, 342–343
calendars: Chaldean, 208
calligraphy, in Islamic art, 266*f*
Cambodia, 602
Cameroon, 411, 412*p*
Canaan, 245–246
canals, 193, 194*p*
Cape of Good Hope, 434
Cape Town, South Africa, 438, 439*p*
Cape Verde. *See* Cabo Verde
capitalist economies, 165–166, 166*c*
Carter, Howard, 230*p*
Carthage, 209, 597*m*
cartogram, 329, 329*m*
cartography, 13–14, 14*f*
Casablanca, Morocco, 349
Casbah, 348
case studies: central Africa forest mapping, 396–397, 396*m*, 397*p*; tsunami, 594–595, 594*c*, 595*m*
Caspian Sea, 279
caste system (India), 455–456, 476, 499
Castro, Raúl, 182*c*, 183*p*, 184
cataracts, on Nile River, 211, 212*m*
Catholicism. *See* Christianity
cause and effect, 356
center-pivot irrigation, 119*p*, 120
Central Africa: climate, vegetation, and animals of, 394–395, 395*p*; culture of, 408–409, 409*f*, 409*p*, 412*p*; features of, 393–394, 394*m;* history of, 407–408, 408*p*; issues and challenges of, 412–414, 413*m*, 414*p*; mapping forests of, 396–397, 396*m*, 397*p*; resources and countries of, 409–800
Central African Republic, 410–411
Central Asia, 278–281; Arab influence in, 298–299, 299*p*; climate and vegetation of, 668; culture of, 299–300; features of, 278–279, 279*m;* history of, 298–299, 299*p*; issues and challenges in, 303–304, 304*p*; Mongol influence in, 299, 299*p*; natural resources of, 280–281, 280*m*, 280*p*; today, 300–303, 301*m*, 303*p*
Central Florida Water Initiative (CFWI), 51
Cetshwayo, 381*p*
CFCs (chlorofluorocarbons), 122–123
Chad, 405–406
Chaldean peoples, 208
Chandra Gupta I, 476
Chandra Gupta II, 476
Chang'an, 523
Chang Jiang River, 543, 549, 550
Chang Jiang Valley, 513
Chao Phraya River, 600
chariots, 206–207, 208*p*
Chiang Kai-shek, 545
China: Australia's trade with, 620; climate in, 543–544; culture in, 550 (*See* Chinese culture); environmental problems in, 549–550, 549*p*, 550*m;* flooding in, 543*f;* landforms in, 541; National Day in, 546*f;* physical features of, 541–543; physical map, 542*m;* population of, 548–549, 548*m;* resources in, 543–544; tension with Taiwan, 555*c*, 555*m;* trade with, 547
China, early civilizations, 510–520; artifacts, 511*p*; dynasties, 514*m*, 522*m;* Five Dynasties and Ten Kingdoms, 522; Grand Canal (China), 523*f;* Han dynasty, 517–520; Ming dynasty, 531–534; Mongol Empire, 528–530, 529*m;* Period of Disunion, 521, 526; Qin dynasty, 516–517; river valley civilization, 513; scholar-officials, 526–527, 526*p*; Shang dynasty, 513–514; Song dynasty, 522–527; Sui dynasty, 521; Tang dynasty, 522–527; Warring States period, 516; Yuan dynasty, 529–530; Zhou dynasty, 514–516. *See also entries for individual dynasties*
China, modern history of, 545-547; Communist system in, 545–546; Qing dynasty, 545; revolution and civil war, 545; since Mao, 545–547
Chinatown: San Francisco (U.S.), 7
Chinese culture: architecture, 552; art, 551–552; ethnic groups, 550, 551*p*; language, 550; literature, 552; martial arts, 552*p*; opera symbolism, 539*p*, 552; popular culture, 552; religion, 550, 551
chlorofluorocarbons (CFCs), 122–123
choice and scarcity (economics), 159
Christianity: acts and teachings of Jesus, 253–256, 255*f*, 255*p*; in African kingdoms, 364–365; in Aksum kingdom, 238; in central Africa, 409, 409*f;* in China, 551; Christian holidays, 255*f*, 255*p*; in east Africa, 426, 428; followers of Jesus, 256–258, 256*f*, 256*p*, 257*p*; Jesus of Nazareth, 253–254, 254*p*; in Kongo kingdom of central Africa, 1300s, 371; Kurdish people practicing, 291; overview,

268*c;* in Southeast Asia, 597, 599; in South Korea, 576; spread of, 258–260, 258*m,* 259*m;* in west Africa, 401
chronological order, 512*f*
cities: in Australia, 621; China's modern, 548–549, 549*p*; Japanese, 571–573; Southeast Asia mainland, 600; South Korea, 577, 579; Tang dynasty, 523
citizenship: duties and roles of, 145–146, 146*p*; media and, 149–150, 150*p*; rights and responsibilities of, 147–149, 147*c,* 148*p*; in societies other than U.S., 151–152, 151*p*
city planning: in Harappan civilization, 451
city-states: of Sumerian civilization, 196–197, 196*p*, 197*m*
civilizations: definition of, 193; food production essential to, 213; of India, 493–494, 494*c,* 494*p*; of Iraq, 288; of Nubia, 231; *See also* Indian civilizations, early
civil service, 526
civil service examinations, 526–527
civil service system, 533–534
climate: Australia and New Zealand, 616; central Africa, 394–395, 395*p*; China, Mongolia, and Taiwan, 543–544; dry, 70–72, 70*p*, 71*p*, 72*p*; east and southern Africa, 423–424; eastern Mediterranean, 313; Indian subcontinent, 491–492, 491*m;* Japan and Korea, 565; Middle East, 277–278, 277*m;* north Africa, 337–338, 338*p*; Pacific Island, 623; Southeast Asia, 591, 605; weather and, 62–67, 62*p*, 63*m*, 64*m*, 65*p*, 66*c*; west Africa, 392–393, 393*m*
climate change, 85
climate types: highland, 74–76, 74*p*, 75*p*; polar, 74–76, 74*p*, 75*p*; polar desert, 629; temperate, 72–73, 73*c*, 73*p*; tropical, 70–72, 70*p*, 71*p*, 72*p*; tropical savanna, 591, 623
climate zones, 68–69, 69*c*, 69*m*
cluster settlements, 115, 115*c*
coal: north Africa, 338
coffee, 404
Cold War, 408
command economy, 164, 165*p*, 563, 547; in North Korea, 581
commerce, 116
common good, 139
communism. *See also* Cuba; Soviet Union
communist economies, 165–167, 166*c*
community of nations, 133–135, 133*f,* 134*p*
Comoros, 441
comparison and contrast, 390
compass, 525
compass rose, 29, 29*c*
computer mapping, 4*f,* 14*f*
conclusions, drawing, 158
condensation, in water cycle, 49*c*
confederations, 138
conflict, 100, 134
Confucianism, 515, 517–518, 526, 551, 575; in Korea, 576–577
Confucius, 515
Congo Basin, 393
Congo River, 393–394
conic map projections, 27, 27*c*
Constantine (emperor of Rome), 260
constitutional monarchy, 138
constitutions, in limited governments, 137
continental drift theory, 54
continents of Earth, 25, 25*c*, 53–54
continuity and change, 385
Cook, James, 618, 624, 630
copper mining, 410, 412
Coptic Christianity, 365
coral reef, 615, 623*p*; atoll formation and, 624*f*
Corn Belt, 115
cotton growing, 280*p*, 281, 341–342
couscous, 344
creative expression, 102–104, 103*p*
Crossing Antarctica (Steger and Bowermaster), 630
crude oil, 84, 87*p*
Cuba: U.S. diplomatic ties with, 133
cultural groups, 97–99, 97*p*, 98*p*. *See also* culture; ethnic groups
Cultural Revolution, in China, 130, 142
culture: Africa, southern, 436–438, 437*p*; Africa, west, 400–401, 400*m*, 401*f,* 402*f;* Bambuti, 362*p*; central Africa, 408–409, 409*f,* 409*p*, 412*p*; Central Asia, 299–300; changes in, 99–100; Chinese, 550–552; Chinese opera, 539*p*; commonalities in, 100–101, 100*m*, 100*p*; creative expressions in, 102–104, 103*p*; description of, 95–97, 96*p*; east Africa, 427–428, 427*p*; Egypt, 343–344, 343*p*, 344*p*; European interference with African, 378; female literacy and, 171*f;* groups in, 97–99, 97*p*, 98*p*; Harappan civilization in contact with, 450; India, 498–499; Iran, 295, 295*p*; Iraq, 290–291, 290*p*; Israel, 322; Kush, 235–236; landform effect on, 58–59, 58*p*; midnight sun, impact of, 44*f,* 44*p*; popular, 179–180, 180*p*; Saudi Arabia, 282–283, 283*f*; science and technology in, 104–105, 104*p*; setting borders of nations by, 132; social institutions in, 101–102, 102*p*; Stone Ages, 361–362, 362*p*; Swahili, 373; Turkey, 317
culture, focus on (feature): baseball, spread of, 100*f,* 100*m*, 100*p*; Berbers, 347*f,* 347*p*; Christian holidays, 255*f*; female literacy, 171*f;* midnight sun, 44, 44*f,* 44*p*;

Muslim art, 266*f*, 266*p*; Seeds of Peace, 323*f*, 323*p*; Thai teenage Buddhist monks, 598*f*, 598*p*; Tuareg people of the Sahara (north Africa), 71*f*, 71*p*
cuneiform writing, 200–201, 200*p*, 201*c*, 201*p*
currents in oceans, 64, 64*m*
cylinder seals, Sumerian art in, 203, 204*p*
cylindrical map projections, 26, 26*c*

D

Dalai Lama, 547
Dalits, as social division in India, 456
Damascus, Syria, 325
dance: Balinese, 587*p*; Korean fan, 576*p*, 577; Tanna Island, 627*p*
Daoism, 515, 551
Dardanelles, 311, 312*m*
Dar es Salaam, Tanzania, 429
Darfur region, Sudan, 430
databases, 305
David (king of Israelites), 246
da Vinci, Leonardo, 257, 257*p*
Dead Sea, 312
De Beers Consolidated Mine Company, 379*f*
Deccan Plateau, 491
deforestation, 124; in China, 549*p*; impacts of, 83; orangutans and, 593*p*
deltas of rivers, 212, 212*m*, 490
demilitarized zone, 580
democratic government: as limited government, 137, 139–140, 145
Democratic Party (U.S. political party), 148, 150
Democratic Republic of the Congo, 409, 410, 410*p*
Deng Xiaoping, 142, 546
density, population, 106–109, 107*m*, 109*c*, 109*f*
Description of the World (Polo), 531
desert climate: in central Africa, 395; in east and southern Africa, 423–424; in north Africa, 337–338; overview, 71, 74*p*; San (traditional culture in modern Africa) in, 362–363, 362*p*
desert ecosystem, 78–79, 78*p*
desertification, 81, 124, 392
development, economic, 169–172, 169*p*, 170*p*, 171*p*
Devil's Millhopper sinkhole (Florida), 50
Dhaka, Bangladesh, 505
dharma guidelines (Hinduism), 460
diagram analysis, 351, 351*p*
dialects of languages, 408–409, 550
diamonds: mining, in Africa, 379*f*, 379*p*; in Sierra Leone, in west Africa, 403; in South Africa, 438; in southern Africa, 435; in Tanzania, 429
diaspora (dispersal of Jewish population), 246, 247*m*, 319
dictators: Arab Spring of 2011 and, 345; Gaddafi, Muammar (Libya), 349; Mobutu, Joseph (Democratic Republic of the Congo), 410; overview, 139*c*
Diet (Japan), 569
diffusion, cultural, 99
diplomacy between nations, 133
direct democracies, 137, 139*c*
disciples, Christian, 254
diversity, 98–99. *See also* culture
division of labor, 194–195
Diwali (Festival of Lights, India), 499, 500*p*
Djenné, Mali, 368–369
Djibouti, 431
DMZ (demilitarized zone), North Korea–South Korea, 133*m*, 133*p*
Doctors Without Borders, 135, 135*p*
document-based investigation, primary source, 606*f*
dodos, 79
domino theory, 598
draft: armed forces service, 146
Drakensberg mountains, 422
drawing conclusions, 158
droughts, 425, 432
Druze religion, 326
dry climates, 70–72, 71*p*, 72*p*
dryland farming, 302
Du Fu, 524
Dutch East India Company, 434
Dutch East Indies, 597
dynasty of pharaohs of unified Egypt, 214

E

Early Stone Age, 360, 361*p*
Earth: climate zones of, 68–69, 69*c*; environments and biomes of, 77–81, 77*p*, 78*c*, 79*p*, 80*p*, 81*c*; forces below surface of, 53–56, 53*c*, 54*c*, 54*p*, 55*c*; landforms of, 52, 52*p*, 58–59, 58*p*; natural resources of, 82–88, 83*p*, 84*p*, 85*p*, 86*p*, 87*p*; physical maps of, 89, 89*m*; polar and highland climates of, 74–76, 74*p*, 75*p*; processes on surface of, 56–57, 56*p*, 57*p*; "ring of fire" earthquakes and volcanoes, 60–61, 60*c*, 61*p*, 590; sun's energy and, 41–45; temperate climates of, 72–73, 73*c*, 73*p*; tropical and dry climates of, 70–72, 70*p*, 71*p*, 72*p*; water on, 46–51, 46*p*, 47*p*, 49*c*, 50*p*, 51*p*; weather and climate of, 62–67, 62*p*, 63*m*, 64*m*, 65*p*, 66*c*
earthquakes: Indian Ocean, 594, 594*c*; Island Southeast Asia, 590; Japan, 565*m*; Korea, 565*m*; "ring of fire," 60–61, 60*c*, 61*p*, 590; tectonic plates sliding to generate, 55–56
east Africa: culture of, 427–428, 427*p*; early hominid discoveries in, 359–360; history of, 426–427; Horn of Africa, 431–432, 432*p*; today, 428–431, 429*p*, 430*m*, 431*p*; trade in, 372–373. *See also* east and southern Africa

East African Plateau, 422
east and southern Africa: southern Africa: climate and vegetation of, 423–424, 424*m;* features of, 421–423, 422*m;* natural resources of, 424–425. *See also* east Africa
East China Sea, 549
Easter Island: *moai* statues on, 613*p*
Eastern Ghats mountains, 489
eastern Mediterranean: climate and vegetation of, 313, 314*m;* Egypt invaded by peoples of, 340; features of, 311–312, 311*p*, 312*m*, 313*p*; natural resources of, 313–314. *See also* Israel; Jordan; Lebanon; Syria; Turkey
East India Company, 497
East Jerusalem, 323–324
Ebadi, Shirin, 297*f*, 297*p*
ebony, 233
economic aid organizations, 182–183
economic choices, 535*f*
economic indicators, 170–171
economics, connect to (feature): Bollywood moviemaking industry in India, 502*f;* diamond mining, in Africa, 379*p;* entrepreneurship, 167*p;* paper money, 525*f*
economies: Australia, 619; Central Asia, 303–304; Chinese command, 547; as cultural institution, 101; developing, 626; development and, 169–172, 169*p*, 170*p*, 171*p*; Egypt, 341–342; free enterprise, 167, 167*p;* free trade, 184; global, 179–184, 180*p*, 181*p*, 182*c*, 183*p;* government and public goods, 168, 168*p;* incentives in, 160; India, 500–502; Indonesia, 607; Iran, 295–297, 296*c*, 296*p*, 297*f;* Iraq, 291–292, 292*p;* Israel, 321; Japan, 570; Japanese, 573; Kush (ancient), 235; Maghreb countries in north Africa, 348; modern, 165–167; money and banking and, 174–176, 175*p;* New Zealand, 619; Nigeria, 402; North Korea, 581; Pacific Islands, 626; resource use in, 161–163, 161*p*, 162*p;* Saudi Arabia, 283–284; scarcity and choice in, 159; South Korea, 578; supply and demand in, 160, 160*c;* systems of, 164, 165*p;* Turkey, 318
ecosystems, 78–79, 78*p*
edicts: Buddhist, 475
Edison, Thomas, 104–105
education: as cultural institution, 102, 102*p;* in east Africa, 431*p;* in Mali kingdom in west Africa, 368
Egypt: achievements of, 226–227, 227*c*, 227*p;* architecture and art of, 227–230, 228*p*, 229*p*, 230*p;* complex society of, 224–226, 225*p;* culture in, 343–344, 343*p*, 344*p;* history of, 339–340, 340*p;* Israelites in, 245; Kush conquered by, 233, 233*p;* Kushite conquest of, 234; Middle Kingdom of (2050–1750 BC), 221–222, 221*c;* New Kingdom of (1550–1050 BC), 222–224, 222*m*, 223*f*, 224*f;* Old Kingdom of (2700–2200 BC), 215–216, 216*p;* pyramids of, 219–220, 219*p;* religion of, 216–218, 217*f*, 217*p*, 218*p;* today, 341–343, 341*p*, 342*m;* two kingdoms of, 212*m*, 213–214, 213*p;* unified, 214–215, 214*p*. *See also* north Africa
Eightfold Path (Buddhism), 465–466, 466*f*
Elburz Mountains, 276
elections: voting in, 147–148
elephants: in central Africa, 394, 397*p*
el-Sisi, Abdel Fattah (Egyptian president), 341
embalming: in ancient Egyptian, 218, 218*p*
embargoes: as trade barriers, 182*c*, 289
Endangered Species Act of 1973, 80
energy: natural resources for, 84–86, 84*p*, 85*p;* pollution from production of, 123*p;* of sun, 41–45; water cycle driven by sun, 48–49, 49*c*
engineering, 219, 219*p*
England. *See* Great Britain; United Kingdom.
Enheduanna (Sumerian priestess), 200
entrepreneurs, 167*f*, 378, 573
environment: Antarctica's, threats to, 631; biomes and, 77–81, 77*p*, 78*c*, 79*p*, 80*p*, 81*c;* in central Africa, 413–414; Central Asian issues in, 303; Chinese problems, 549–550; as geography theme, 16; Pacific Islands and, 626; in southern Africa, 442
environmental adaptations of early humans, 361–363, 362*f*, 362*p*
Environmental Protection Agency (EPA), 124
Epic of Gilgamesh, 201
epics (long poems), 201, 480, 480*p*
equator, 24–25
Equatorial Guinea, 411
Eratosthenes (ancient Greek geographer), 11*f*, 11*p*
Eritrea, 431
Ermes, Ali Omar, 266*f*
erosion, 56–57, 56*p*, 57*p*
escarpments, 421
Esfahan (Safavid Empire), 294
Esma'il (Persian ruler), 294
essential elements of geography, 18*c*, 19
Eswatini (enclave in South Africa), 438–439
Ethiopia: Aksum people retreated to (600–700 AD), 364; Amharic language in, 428; Coptic Christianity in, 365; Ethiopian Highlands of, 422*p*, 423; landlocked, 432; resistance to colonization of, 382, 382*p*
ethnic groups: in central Africa, 408, 412; in Central Asia, 300; in Iraq, 291; overview, 98–99; in southern Africa, 436; in Sri Lanka, 506; in west Africa, 400

Index

ethnocentrism, 378
Euphrates River, 191–192, 275–276
Europe: Africa in global trade with, 374; African colonies of, 376, 427; raw materials search by, 377–378, 377*p*; southern Africa colonized by, 434. *See also* Africa, in global trade: imperialism and independence in; Italy; Portugal; Spain
Exodus from Egypt by Israelites, 245–246
exports, 235. *See also* trade
extended families: in west Africa, 401
extinction, 79, 79*p*
Ezana (king of Aksum, AD 350), 238, 364

F

fact and opinion, 448
Fall Line: linear settlements on, 115
fall season, 43*c*, 44
family: as cultural institution, 101
famine: in west Africa, 405
farming: arable land for, 302; China, 547, 547*p*; dryland, 302; Egypt, 341–343; fertile crescent early civilizations, 193–195, 193*f*, 193*p*, 194*p*; Island Southeast Asia, 604; Japan, 571; Nile River flooding for, 213, 213*p*; North Korea, 581; Southeast Asia, 593; Thailand, 600; types of, 119–120, 119*p*. *See also* agriculture
fasting: in Buddhism, 464; in Islam, 267
Fay, Michael, 396–397, 397*p*
federal governments, 138
fellahin (Egyptian farmers), 343
female literacy, 171*f*
Fergana Valley, 279
Fertile Crescent civilizations: Assyrians, 207–208, 207*m*, 208*p*; Babylonians, 205–206, 206*f*, 207*m;* Chaldeans, 208; farming and cities of, 193–195, 193*f*, 193*p*, 194*p*, 195*p*; Hittites and Kassites, 206–207; Phoenicians, 208–210, 209*m*, 210*p*; rivers support growth of, 191–193, 192*m*
Fès, Morocco, 346, 350*f*
Fieldranger tool, 397
fireworks: as Chinese invention, 511*p*, 524*p*
First Dynasty of Egyptian pharaohs, 215
fishery, 566
Five Dynasties and Ten Kingdoms, 522
Five Pillars of Islam, 266–267
five themes of geography, 16–18, 17*p*, 18*c*
flat-plane map projections, 27, 27*m*
flooding, 50, 65*p*, 212–213, 505
food: of Egypt, 344, 344*p*; Mosaic law, in Judaism, on, 249; of Nile valley kingdoms, 213; surpluses of, 194, 194*p*
Forbidden City, 532, 533*f*, 533*p*, 549
Ford, Henry, 105
foreign policy between nations, 133
forests: Bambuti traditional culture in, 362; in central Africa, 396–397, 396*m*, 397*p*, 410; in Madagascar, 425
Formosa, 554. *See also* Taiwan
fossil fuels, 84–85, 84*p*, 124
fossil water, 278, 278*p*
fracking, 123
France: Morocco controlled by, 346. *See also* Europe
free enterprise, 166*c*, 167, 167*p*
free port, 606; Tangier as, 349
free trade, 184. *See also* trade
freshwater, 47–48, 47*p*
front: air mass, 65–66
Fulani people in west Africa, 400
Fu poets, 518

G

Gabon, 397, 411
Gaddafi, Muammar (dictator of Libya), 349
Gambia, the, 402–403
Gandhi, Mohandas, 480, 496*f*, 496*p*, 497, 497*f*, 497*p*
Ganesha (Hindu god), 458
Ganges Plain, 491
Ganges River, 460, 460*p*, 490
Gao, Mali, 368, 406
Gautama, Siddhartha. *See* Siddhartha Cautama; Buddhism.
Gavi, 136
Gaza, 323–324
GDP (gross domestic product), 171
generalizations, 420
Geneva Conventions (1949), 135
Genghis Khan, 528, 553
genocide: in Rwanda (1990s), 430
Geographic Information System (GIS), 22–23
geography: cartography in, 13–14, 14*m;* description of, 5–6, 6*p*; five themes of, 16–18, 17*p*, 18*c;* Geographic Information System (GIS), 22–23; human, 11–12, 13*p*; hydrology in, 14; landforms, 32–33; latitude and longitude in, 24–25, 24*m*, 25*m;* local, regional, and global views of, 7–9, 8*p*; map features, 28–29, 28*m*, 29*c*; map projections in, 26–27, 26*m*, 27*m;* maps and globes used in, 20–21, 21*m;* meteorology in, 14–15; Phoenician, 209; physical maps, 31, 31*m;* political maps, 30, 30*m;* satellite images in, 22, 22*p*, 35, 35*p*; essential elements of, 18*c*, 19; thematic maps, 31, 31*m*. *See also entries for features of various world areas*
geometric borders of nations, 132
geothermal energy, 85, 429
gers, 554

Ghana, 365–367, 365*m*, 366*p*, 398, 404
Gilgamesh (ruler of Sumerian city-state, Uruk), 197
Giotto, 254*p*
GIS (Geographic Information System), 22–23, 22*p*
glaciers: freshwater in, 47; to erode land, 56–57
Glen Canyon Dam (Arizona), 85*p*
global economics, 179–184, 180*p*, 181*p*, 182*c*, 183*p*
Global Fund to Fight AIDS, Tuberculosis, and Malaria, 136
globalization, 179, 182*f*
Global Positioning System (GPS), 22, 22*p*, 397
global view of geography, 7–9, 8*p*
globes, 20–21, 21*m*
Gobi Desert, 542
Gojoseon kingdom, 575
gold: in Africa, 374; Ghana trade in, 366, 366*p*; in South Africa, 425; in southern Africa, 435; in Tanzania, 429
Gold Coast: as Portuguese colony, 376
Golden Temple, 472, 472*p*
gorillas: in central Africa, 394
Gospels, 257
government: Aryan civilization of India, 453; Australia, 619; as cultural institution, 101; Egypt, 341, 341*p*; European interference with African, 378–379; human rights abuses by, 142–144, 143*m;* India, 500–502; Iran, 295–297, 296*c*, 297*f;* Iraq, 291–292; Israel, 321; Japan, 569; Jordan, 327–328; limited, 137–141, 138*c*, 139*c*, 140*f*, 140*m*, 140*p;* Maghreb countries north Africa, 348; New Zealand, 619; Nigeria, 402; North Korea, 580–581; public goods and, 168, 168*p*; Saudi Arabia, 283–284; South Korea, 578; Syria, 325–326; theocracy as, 215, 295; Turkey, 317; unlimited, 141–142, 142*p*
GPS (Global Positioning System), 22, 22*p*, 397
Grand Canal (China), 521, 523, 523*f*, 523*p*
Grand Canyon, 57
graphs: line, 507, 507*c*
Great Barrier Reef, 615
Great Britain: in Boer War, in South Africa, 380–381; Gold Coast as colony of, 376; in India (starting in 1600s), 495, 495*c*, 495*p*; in Mesopotamia, 288
Great Indian Desert (Thar), 491
Great Pyramid of Egypt, 219, 219*p*, 339
Great Rift Valley, 421
Great Sphinx at Giza, 219*p*, 340*p*
Great Wall of China, 510*p*, 517, 532, 539*p*
Great Zimbabwe kingdom, 370–371, 433, 434*p*
Green Belt Movement (Kenya), 83*p*
Green political party, 148
green revolution, 501
Greenwich, England (prime meridian), 24, 24*m*
grid, of latitude and longitude lines, 24
grid settlements, 115, 115*c*, 116*p*
griots, 403
gross domestic product (GDP), 171
groundwater, 48
Guam, 624
Guinea, 403
Guinea-Bissau, 403
Gulf of Thailand, 602
Gulf Stream currents, 64
gunpowder: as Chinese invention, 524*p*, 525
Gupta Empire (India, AD 300s), 476–477, 476*p*, 477*m*, 494*c*
gurdwaras, 471–472
Guru Gobind Singh, 470
Guru Granth Sahib, 470
Guru Nanak, 470, 499
Gyeongbokgung Palace, 575*p*

H

habitats, 79
Hadar, Ethiopia, 358
Hadith, 266
Hagia Sophia: as mosque, 316
hajj (pilgrimage to Mecca), 267, 374
Halong Bay, Vietnam, 589*p*
Hammurabi's Code (Babylon), 205–206, 206*f*, 206*p*
Han dynasty, 517–520, 517*m;* achievements, 519*p*; art and literature in, 518–519; bronze horse, 519*p*; family in, 518; family shrine, 518*p*; inventions, 519; Korea and, 575; Silk Road trade route, 520; society in, 518
Hanging Gardens of Babylon, 208
Hangzhou: Polo's description of, 531*f*
Hanoi, Vietnam, 603; city life in, 609*p*
Hanukkah (Jewish holiday), 251
Hanuman (Hindu god), 458
Harappa, 449–450
Harappan civilization (2600–1700 BC), 449–452, 450*m*, 451*p*, 452*p*, 493, 494*c*
Hatshepsut (Egyptian queen), 223, 223*f*, 223*p*
Hausa people, 400
Hawaii, 622; mountainous terrain in, 623*p*
Hebrew Bible, 250, 250*p*. *See also* Judaism
hegira (journey, in Islam), 264
hemispheres of Earth, 25, 25*m*
heritage: in creative expression, 103
Herodotus (ancient Greek historian), 211
hieroglyphics, 226, 340
High Holy Days (Judaism), 252
highland climate: in central Africa, 395; description of, 74–76, 74*p*, 75*p*; in east Africa, 423
Himalayas mountain range, 54*p*, 55, 489–490, 541, 542*p*
Hindu-Arabic numerals, 482
Hinduism, 596; beliefs in, 458,

459*c*, 459*f*; in central Africa, 409; Gupta Empire in India and, 476; in India, 498; life and rebirth in, 459; society and, 460; in Southeast Asia, 599; spread of, 461; traditions in, 459*p*, 460–461; Vedic texts as basis of, 454–455; women in, 461

Hindu Kush mountains, 279, 489

Hirohito, 568*f*, 568*p*

historical source (feature): afterlife, Egyptian emphasis on, 217*f*, 217*p*; *Crossing Antarctica*, 630*f*; Dead Sea Scrolls, 320*f*; Gandhi's "quit India" speech (1942), 496*f*; Hammurabi's Code (Babylon), 206*f*, 206*p*; Mesopotamia (ancient), 193*f*, 193*p*; Ramses the Great, Egyptian pharaoh, 1200s BC, 224*f*; Sermon on the Mount, 256*f*, 256*p*

history: Australia, 617–619; central Africa, 407–408, 408*p*; Central Asia, 298–299, 299*p*; China, modern history of, 545–547; east Africa, 426–427; Egypt, 339–340, 340*p*; geography and, 12; Iraq, 288–290, 289*m*; Israel, 319–320, 320*p*; Japan, 567–568; Jordan, 327–328; Judaism, 245–248, 246*c*, 247*m*, 247*p*; Korea, 575–576; Lebanon, 326; Mongolia, 553; New Zealand, 617–619; Pacific Islands, 624–625; Sikhism, 472–473; Southeast Asia, 596–598; southern Africa, 433–436, 434*p*, 435*p*, 436*f*; Syria, 325–326; Taiwan, 555; Turkey, 315–317, 316*f*; west Africa, 398–399, 398*p*, 399*f*, 399*p*

Hittite peoples, 206–207, 223–224

HIV/AIDS: in central Africa, 413; Global Fund to Fight AIDS, Tuberculosis, and Malaria, 136; in southern Africa, 441

Ho Chi Minh, 597

Ho Chi Minh City, Vietnam, 603

Hokkaido, 563

Hokusai, Katsushika, 103, 104*p*

hominids (early human ancestors), 357

Homo erectus, 358, 359*p*, 360

Homo habilis, 358, 359*p*, 360

Homo sapiens, 358, 359*p*, 360

Honshu, 563

Horn of Africa: countries in, 430–431, 431*p*

Horseshoe Bend (Arizona), 57, 57*p*

Huang He river, 513, 543

human beginnings. *See* Africa, human beginnings in

human-environment interaction: changing environment, 121–124, 121*p*, 122*p*, 123*p*; as geography theme, 16–17, 17*p*; responding to environment, 118–121, 118*p*, 119*p*, 120*p*

human geography, 11–12, 13*p*

humanitarian aid, 135

human rights, 135, 142–144, 143*m*, 600

humid continental climate, 73

humid subtropical climate, 72

humid tropical climate, 69, 70, 393, 492

humus: in soils, 80, 80*p*

Huns: invasion of India by, 477

hunter-gatherers: of Early Stone Age, 360; in Mesopotamia, 191

hurricanes: overview, 66

Hussein (king of Jordan), 328

Hussein, Saddam (Iraqi dictator), 142, 288–290

Hutu and Tutsi ethnic groups, 430

hydroelectric power, 85, 85*p*

hydrology, 14

Hyksos peoples, 221–223

I

icebergs, 629, 629*p*

ice cap climate, 75

ice shelf, 628

ICRC (International Committee for the Red Cross), 135–136

Igbo people, 400

IMF (International Monetary Fund), 183

imports, 235. *See also* trade

incentives: economic, 160

income, 177

independence: in central Africa, 408; of India, 497–498, 498*p*; of South Africa, 435; in west Africa, 399. *See also* Africa, imperialism and independence in

India: Buddhism spread in, 467; challenges of, 500–502, 501*m*, 501*p*, 502*f*, 502*p*; culture of, 498–499; daily life in, 499, 500*p*; early civilizations of, 493–494, 494*c*, 494*p*; empires in, 494–497, 495*p*, 496*f*, 496*p*; independence and division of, 497*f*, 497–498, 498*p*; in Indian Subcontinent, 489; Jainism in, 461–462, 462*p*; physical map of, 31*m*. *See also* Hinduism

Indian civilizations, early, 449; Aryan, 452–454, 453*m*, 454*p*; Harappan, 449–452, 450*m*, 451*p*, 452*p*; society divisions, 455–457, 456*p*, 457*p*; Vedic, 454–455

Indian empires: artistic achievements of, 478–479, 479*p*; Gupta, 476–477; literary achievements of, 480, 480*p*; Mauryan, 474–475, 475*m*; Mughal, 477–478, 478*m*; scientific achievements of, 481–482, 481*p*

Indian Ocean, 25, 25*c*; tsunami in, 590, 594–595*f*, 594*c*, 595*m*

Indian Subcontinent: climates of, 491–492, 491*m*; features of, 489–492, 490*m*, 491*p*; natural resources of, 492

Indo-Aryan language, 493

Indochina: countries of, 602–603

Indochina Peninsula, 589

Indonesia, 597, 604. *See also* Islam in, 599; Island Southeast Asia, 607; plantations in, 593

indoor plumbing: in Harappan civilization, 451
Indus River, 449, 490
industry: levels of, 169–170, 169*p*. *See also* economies
inflation, 178, 411
information technology (IT) industry: in India, 501–502
innovation: cultural change from, 99
inoculations: in ancient Indian medicine, 482
intangible assets, 176
interest groups, 149
interest rates, 175–176
International Committee for the Red Cross (ICRC), 135–136
International Monetary Fund (IMF), 183
inventions: Han dynasty, 519; Song dynasty, 524–525; Sumerian civilization, 201–202; Tang dynasty, 524–525
investments: for wealth building, 177–178
Inyanga mountains, 422
Iran: culture of, 295, 295*p*; government and economy of, 295–297, 296*c*, 296*p*, 297*f;* history of, 293–294, 294*m;* Iraq invasion of (1980), 289. *See also* Middle East (Arabian Peninsula, Iraq, and Iran)
Iraq: culture of, 290–291; history of, 289*m*, 290; Iran invaded by (1980), 289; Kuwait invaded by (1990), 284, 289; today, 291–292, 292*p*. *See also* Middle East (Arabian Peninsula, Iraq, and Iran)
Ireland, 110, 110*c*, 110*p*
Iron Age: humans in, 360, 361
iron industry: Assyrian peoples (ancient), 207, 208*p*, 234; Hittite peoples (ancient), 206; Kush (ancient), 235, 236*p*
irrigation, 193–194, 194*p*, 213
Islam: art in, 266*f*, 266*p*; in Brunei, 599; in central Africa, 409; in China, 551; desert lands as concentration of, 262–264, 263*c;* in east Africa, 373, 426, 428; in Egypt, 343; in Indonesia, 599; Kurdish people practicing, 291; in Malaysia, 599; in Mughal Empire, 477–478; Muhammad as prophet of, 262–263, 263*c;* in north Africa, 346– 347; overview, 268*c;* Qur'an in, 264–266, 265*p;* Saudi Arabian culture influenced by, 282; Shariah (Islamic law) in, 267–268; in Southeast Asia, 599; spread of, 264*m;* Sunnah in, 266–267; in west Africa, 367–368, 401. *See also* Muslims
Islamic Revolution: in Iran (1979), 294
Islamic State in Iraq and the Levant (ISIL) terrorist group, 135, 292, 326
Island Southeast Asia, 604–608; Timor-Leste, 607; per capita GDP in, 608*c;* rubber tree plantations, 605*p;* rural and urban life, 604–605. *See also* Brunei; Indonesia; Malaysia; Philippines; Singapore
isolationism, 534
Israel: history of, 319–320, 320*p;* Palestinian territories and, 322–324, 322*m;* today, 321–322. *See also* eastern Mediterranean; Judaism
Issa ethnic group, 431
Istanbul, Turkey, 313*p*, 315, 318*p*
Italy: Libya conquered by, 346; satellite image of, 22*p*, 35*p*. *See also* Europe
Ituri Forest, 395*p*
ivory: trade in, 233, 374, 408*p*

J

Jainism, 461–462, 462*p*, 475, 499
Jakarta, Indonesia, 605, 607
janissaries: in Ottoman army, 315
***Janjaweed* Arab militia,** 430
Japan, 560*m;* cities in, 571–573; climate of, 565; culture in, 568–569; daily life in, 571–572; economic challenges, 573; economy of, 570; government of, 569; history of, 567–568; invasion of Korean Peninsula, 576; invasion of Southeast Asia, 597; issues and challenges, 572–574; kimonos, 569*p;* Mongol invasion, 530; Mount Fuji, 561*p;* natural disasters in, 564–565; physical features, 563–564; physical map, 564*m;* population growth, 573*c*, 573*m;* resources, 570; resources in, 566; rural life in, 571; Tokyo, 569, 571–572; Tokyo fish market, 566*p;* trade and, 570; transportation between cities, 571; tsunami devastation, 574*p;* volcanoes and earthquakes in, 565*m*
***jatis* groups,** 455–456
Java, 607
Jerusalem, Israel, 319, 320*p*, 321
Jesus of Nazareth: acts and teachings of, 254–256, 255*f*, 255*p;* followers of, 256*f*, 256*p*, 257*p;* overview, 253–254, 254*p;* resurrection of, 254. *See also* Christianity
jihad, 266
Johannesburg, South Africa, 438
Johanson, Donald, 358
Jordan, 327–328, 327*m*, 327*p*, 328. *See also* eastern Mediterranean
Jordan River, 312
Joseon kingdom, 575
Judah, 246
Judaism: beliefs in, 248–249, 249*p;* history of, 245–248, 246*c*, 247*m*, 247*p;* Kurdish people practicing, 291; overview, 268*c;* texts of, 249–251, 250*p;* traditions and holy

days, 251–252, 251*p*. *See also* Israel
junks, 531, 532, 589*p*
Jura Mountains, 493
jury duty, 146

K

ka (life force), 218
Kaaba (sacred place in Mecca), 267
Kadesh, Battle of (Egyptians vs. Hittites), 223, 228*p*
Kaifeng, 523
Kalahari Desert, 362, 424
kampong, 604
kanji/kana, 568
Kao-hsiung, Taiwan, 556
Kara-Kum Desert, 280
karma: in Hinduism, 460
karst towers, 542*p*
Kashmir territory, 504
Kashta (ruler of Kush, 700s BC), 234
Kassite peoples, 206–207
Kathmandu, Nepal, 505, 505*p*
Kazakhstan, 301–302
Kemal, Mustafa, 316
Kenya, 384, 428–429
Kerma, 232
Khadijah, 262
Khartoum, Sudan, 423
Khmer civilization, 596
Khoisan languages, 437
Khoisan people, 433
Khufu (pharaoh of ancient Egypt), 215, 219
kibbutz, 322
Kilwa, 372
kimchi, 577
Kim Il Sung (dictator of North Korea), 580; statue of, 561*p*
Kim Jong Il (dictator of North Korea), 580
Kim Jong-un (dictator of North Korea), 141, 580–581
kimonos, 569, 569*p*
Kinshasa, Democratic Republic of the Congo, 410, 410*p*
Klerk, Frederik Willem de, 436*f*
klong (canal), 600, 601*p*
Kolkata (Calcutta), India, 499
Kongo kingdom of central Africa (1300s), 371, 407
Kopet-Dag Mountains, 276
Korea: artifact from Silla kingdom, 561*p*; climate of, 565; culture of, 576–578; history of, 575–576; Korean fan dancers, 576*p*, 577; Korean War, 576, 580; life in South vs. North, 580*p*; natural disasters in, 565; physical features of, 564; physical map, 564*m;* resources in, 566; reunification discussion, 582, 582*p*; volcanoes and earthquakes in, 565*m*. *See also* North Korea; South Korea
Korean Peninsula, 564; Japanese invasion of, 576
Koreas, 560*m*
Koryo, 575
kosher food, 249, 322
Koumbi Saleh (capital of kingdom of Ghana), 366
Kravitz, Lenny, 254*p*
Kshatriyas *varna* (rulers and warriors), 455
Kuala Lumpur, Malaysia, 605
Kublai Khan, 529, 530*f*
Kurdish culture region, 98
Kurdish people, 291, 317
Kush: decline and defeat of, 237–238; early, 231–232, 232*m;* Egypt conquered by, 234; Egyptian conquest of, 223, 233, 233*p;* later, 234–237, 235*p*, 236*m*, 236*p*, 237*f*
Kuwait, 284
Kyoto, Japan, 567
Kyoto Protocol to the United Nations Framework Convention on Climate Change, 85
Kyrgyzstan, 300, 302, 304
Kyushu, 563
Kyzyl-Kum desert, 280

L

labor, division of, 194–195
Laetoli, Tanzania, 359
Lagos, Nigeria, 402, 403*c*, 403*p*
Lake Balkhash, 279
Lake Dongting Hu, 543*f*, 543*p*
Lake Issyk-Kul, 302
Lake Nyasa, 393
Lake Powell, 85*p*
Lake Tanganyika, 393
Lake Victoria, 423
Lakshmi (Hindu goddess), 458
Lalibela (king of Ethiopia, 1200s), 365, 426, 427*p*
landforms, 32–34, 32*m*, 33*c*, 52, 52*p*, 58–59, 58*p*
landlocked countries, 278–279
landscape, 5
langar, 471, 471*p*
languages: Africa, central, 408–409; Africa, east, 427–428, 428*m;* Africa, north, 346; Africa, southern, 437; Africa, west, 400; Aryan civilization, 453–454, 454*p*; Australia, 618; Central Asia, 300, 301*m;* China, 550; Egypt, 343; Indonesia, 607; Israel, 321; Japan, 568; Korea, 576; Malaysia, 605; Meroitic, of Kush, 237; New Zealand, 618; Punjabi, 470; Sanskrit, 493; Southeast Asia, 598; Swahili, 373
Laos, 602–603
Laozi, 515
Last Supper, The (da Vinci), 257*p*
Later Stone Age, 361
latitude and longitude, 24–25, 24*m*, 25*m*, 42, 132
lava, 55
law: citizenship and, 145; in Judaism, 248–249
Leakey, Louis, 357–358
Leakey, Mary, 357–359
Leakey, Richard, 357–358
Lebanon, 326–327, 327*f*, 327*m*, 327*p*. *See also* eastern Mediterranean
Lee Kuan Yew: on Singapore, 606*f*
***Left Behind* books,** 254*f*
legend: on maps, 29, 29*c*, 89, 89
Lesotho, 438
Liberia, 403
Li Bo, 524
Libya: Arab Spring (2011) in, 345, 346*m*, 349; arts and literature in, 347; government and economy of, 348–349; history and culture of,

345–347, 347*f*, 349; Italian capture of, 346. *See also* north Africa
limited governments, 137–141, 138*c*, 139*c*, 140*f*, 140*m*, 140*p*
linear settlements, 115, 115*c*
line graphs, 507, 507*c*
Li Qingzhao, 524
Li River, 542*p*
literacy, 171*f*, 431*p*
literature: Chinese, 552; as cultural expression, 102; Egypt, 344; Han dynasty, 518–519; Indian empires, 480, 480*p*; north Africa, 347; Tang and Song dynasties, 524
Liu Bang, 517
local view of geography, 7–9, 8*p*
location: as geography theme, 16, 17*p*; in settlement patterns, 113–114, 113*p*, 114*p*; sunlight and climate of, 63
locator map, 29, 29*c*
loess, 543
London, United Kingdom, 8*p*
longitude, latitude and, 24–25, 24*c*, 25*c*
Lord of the Rings, The (Tolkein), 104
Lower Egypt, 211, 212*m*
Lucy (*Australopithecus* hominid fossil), 358–359
Luxor: temple at, 228
Luzon, Philippines, 607

M

Maasai culture, 362*f*, 362*p*, 363
Maathai, Wangari, 83*f*, 83*p*
Macao, China, 549
MacArthur, Douglas (U.S. Army general), 562
Madagascar, 424*m*, 425, 441, 441*p*
Magellan, Ferdinand, 596
Maghan (ruler of Mali), 368
Maghreb, 347
magma, 55*f*
Magna Carta (England, 1215), 96
Mahabharata, 480
Mahavira, 461
Mahfouz, Naguib, 344
main ideas: understanding, 94
Malagasy, 436
malaria, 412–413, 413*m*, 414*p*, 441
Malawi, 13*p*, 409, 409*f*, 412
Malay Archipelago, 589, 590*m*
Malay Peninsula, 589, 590*m*, 545; climate of, 591
Malaysia, 604–605; Islam in, 599; plantations in, 593. *See also* Island Southeast Asia
Maldives, 489, 490*m*
Mali, 369*m*; economy of, 406; Mansa Musa of, 370*f*; open-air market in, 406*p*; rise and fall of, 367–368, 398
malnutrition, 414
mandate of heaven, 514
Mandela, Nelson, 436, 436*f*, 480
Manila, Philippines, 607
Manin, Tunka (ruler of Ghana), 366
mansa, 367
Mansa Musa (ruler of Mali, 1300s), 367–368, 370*f*, 374
manufacturing industries, 169, 169*p*
Maori, 617*f*, 618–619
Mao Zedong (Chinese leader), 130, 141–142, 545, 546*p*
maps: cartography, 13–14, 14*m*; climate, 31*m*, 277*m*, 314*m*, 393*m*, 562*m*; comparison of, 483, 483*m*; computer generation of, 4*f*; elevation, 616*m*; features of, 28–29, 28*m*, 29*c*; geographers' use of, 20–21; physical, 31, 31*m*, 89, 89*m*, 276*m*, 279*m*, 312*m*, 336*m*, 391, 392*m*, 394*m*, 422*m*, 483*m*, 490*m*, 542*m*, 564*m*, 590*m*, 616*m*; political, 30, 30*m*, 626*m*; projections of, 26–27, 26*m*, 27*m*; route, 269, 269*m*; thematic, 31, 31*m*; topographic, 583, 583*m*; uses in geography, 21*m*
Mariana Trench, 54
marine west coast climate, 72
market economy, 164, 165*f*
Maronites, 326
masks: African, 401*f*, 401*p*
math, link to (feature): Muslim contributions to, 283*f*; population density, 109*c*, 109*f*
mathematics, 202, 481*p*
Mau Mau movement (Kenya), 384, 427
Mauritania, 405–406
Maurya, Chandragupta (Mauryan ruler), 474, 494, 494*p*
Mauryan Empire, 474–475, 475*m*
Mbanza, 371
Mbema, Nzinga, 371
Mecca, Arabia, 262–263, 262*p*
media: citizenship and, 149–150, 150*p*
medicine: in India, 481–482, 481*p*
Medieval Russia's Epics, Chronicles, and Tales (Zenkovsky), 528
Medina, Arabia, 264, 264*m*
meditation: in Buddhism, 464
Mediterranean climate, 72, 73*c*, 73*p*, 338
Mediterranean coast. *See* eastern Mediterranean
Mediterranean Sea, 336, 336*m*
megalopolis, 114
Mehmed II (Ottoman ruler), 315–316, 316*f*, 316*p*
Mekong River, 591, 591*p*
Melanesia, 622, 624, 625
Melbourne, Australia, 621
Memphis, Egypt, 214–215, 217
Menelik II (ruler of Ethiopia), 382
Menes, 214, 214*p*
Mercator cylindrical map projection, 26
mercenaries: in Mauryan Empire, in India, 474
meridians of longitude, 24, 24*m*, 25
Meroë, 235, 236*p*
Meroitic language, 237
Mesolithic Era (Middle Stone Age), 360
Mesopotamia: Assyrian conquest of, 207–208, 207*m*, 208*p*; Babylonian

conquest of, 205–206, 206*f*, 206*p*; Chaldean conquest of, 208; early civilizations of, 191–195, 192*m*, 193*f*; Great Britain in, 288; Hittite and Kassite conquest of, 206–207. *See also* Sumerian civilization
Messiah, 253
metalworking, 481, 481*p*
meteorology, 14–15
metropolitan areas, 114
Mexico: government of, 140, 140*f*
Micronesia, 622, 624
Mid-Atlantic Ridge mountains, 55
Middle East (Arabian Peninsula, Iraq, and Iran): Central Asian part of, 278–281; climate and vegetation of, 277–278, 277*m*; features of, 275–276, 276*m*; natural resources of, 278. *See also* Arabian Peninsula; Iran; Iraq
Middle Kingdom of Egypt, 221–222, 221*c*
Middle Passage, 374
Middle Stone Age (Mesolithic Era), 360
migrations: of Bantu, 370; from Ireland, 110*c*, 110*p*, 111; push-and-pull factors for, 110–111, 110*c*
minerals: in eastern Mediterranean, 314; on Indian subcontinent, 492; in Namibia, 439; as natural resources, 86–87, 86*p*, 87*p*; in north Africa, 338, 348
Ming dynasty, 531–534; Beijing during, 511*p*; building projects, 532; civil service system, 533–534; isolationism during, 534; sea voyages during, 531–532, 532*f*
minutes of latitude from equator, 24
missionaries, 467–468
Mobutu, Joseph (dictator, Democratic Republic of the Congo), 410
Mogadishu, Somalia, 372, 426, 432
Mohenjo-Daro, 449–450, 451*f*
Mombasa, Kenya, 372, 426, 429
money and banking: economics and, 173–176, 174*f*; management of, 176–178, 176*c*, 177*c*; paper money, 174*f*, 525*f*; purpose of, 173–174
Mongol Empire, 528–530, 529*m*; influence in Central Asia, 299, 299*f*; Mongol warrior, 528*p*; relationship with China, 553
Mongolia: climate in, 543–544; culture, 554; Gobi Desert, 542; history, 553; horses in, 539*p*; location of, 541, 542*m*; nomadic life in, 554*f*; physical map, 542*m*; population, 554; resources in, 543–544
monotheism, 248, 263
monsoons, 65, 69*c*, 70, 491*p*, 492
Moon Jae-in, 579, 579*f*
Morocco: Arab Spring (2011) in, 345, 346*m*; arts and literature in, 347; France control of, 346; government and economy of, 348–349; history and culture of, 345–347, 347*f*; music in, 347; natural resources of, 350; Songhai conquered by (1591), 369; Spain control of, 346. *See also* north Africa
Morsi, Mohamed (Egyptian president), 341
Mosaic law: in Judaism, 249
Moses (in Hebrew Bible), 247
mosques, 264, 368
mountains, 54, 54*f*, 54*p*, 66–67, 66*p*
Mount Ararat, 311*p*
Mount Everest, 490, 541
Mount Fuji, 561*p*, 563–564
Mount Kilimanjaro, 74*p*, 421, 422
Mount Pinatubo, 61
Mount Saint Helens, 60–61, 61*p*
Mount Tambora, 120
movable type, 525
movement: of Earth, 41–42, 42*f*; as geography theme, 17*f*, 18. *See also* earthquakes; plate tectonics
Mozambique, 376, 433, 435, 440–441
Mugabe, Robert (Zimbabwe president), 440
Mughal Empire, 472, 477–478, 478*m*, 494–495, 495*c*
Muhammad (prophet of Islam), 262–263, 263*c*
multicultural society, 98
multimedia connections: China and the Great Wall, 559 MC1–MC2
multinational corporations, 181–182
Mumbai (Bombay), India, 499
mummies: in ancient Egypt, 218, 218*p*
Musharraf, Pervez (Pakistan leader), 504
music: in central Africa, 409; in Sumerian civilization, 203–204, 204*p*
Muslim Brotherhood, 341
Muslims: overview, 263; Shia and Sunni groups of, 282; Songhai people as, 368–369. *See also* Islam
Myanmar (Burma), 600; Shwedagon Pagoda in Yangon, 587*p*

N

NAACP (National Association for the Advancement of Colored People), 149
Nairobi, Kenya, 429
Nalanda: university at, 476
Namib Desert, 424
Namibia, 436, 439
Napata, 234
Napoleon Bonaparte, 340
National Association for the Advancement of Colored People (NAACP), 149
National Innovation and Science Agenda (Australia), 619
national interest, 134
nationalism, 382, 497

national standards of geography, 18*c*, 19
nations: boundaries and borders of, 131–132, 132*p*; community of, 134–136, 134*f*, 135*p*; world, 132–134, 133*m*, 133*p*. *See also individually named nations*
NATO (North Atlantic Treaty Organization), 134
natural gas, 84, 425
natural resources: Antarctica, 629; Australia, 617; central Africa, 409–412, 413–414; changing environment by using, 121–124, 121*p*, 122*p*, 123*p*; China, 544; Côte d'Ivoire, west Africa, 404; east and southern Africa, 424–425; eastern Mediterranean, 313–314, economics and, 161–163, 161*p*, 162*p*; energy, 84–86, 84*p*, 85*p*; Ghana, in west Africa, 404; Indian subcontinent, 492; Japan, 566, 570; Jordan, 328; Korea, 566; Middle East (Arabian Peninsula, Iraq, and Iran), 278; mineral, 86–87, 86*p*, 87*p*; Mongolia, 544; New Zealand, 617; Nigeria, 402; north Africa, 337–338, 338*p*; Pacific Islands, 623; people and, 87–88; renewable vs. nonrenewable, 82–83, 83*p*; Southeast Asia, 593, 602*m;* Taiwan, 544; Turkey, 318; west Africa, 404*m*
Nauru, 622
Naveed, Sana, 266*f*
Ndebele people, 437*p*
Nebuchadnezzar (Chaldean ruler), 208
Nekhen, 214
Neo-Confucianism, 526
Neolithic Era (New Stone Age), 192
Nepal, 489, 491, 503, 505
New Guinea, 59, 590, 622, 623
New Kingdom of Egypt, 222–224, 222*m*, 223*f*, 224*f*
New York Stock Exchange (NYSE), 117*p*
New Zealand: climate, 616; diverse population in, 620; economy of, 619; elevation map, 616*m;* ethnic groups in, 620*c;* fertile soil in, 616*p*; government in, 619; history of, 617–619; Maori culture, 617*f;* physical features, 615, 616; wildlife and resources, 617
Niger, 405–406
Nigeria, 384, 402
Niger River, 391
Nile River, 211, 335, 338*p*, 343*p*, 423
Nile Valley kingdoms: Egypt, old kingdom (2700–2200 BC), 215–216, 216*p*; Egyptian pyramids, 219–220, 219*p*; Egyptian religion, 216–218, 217*f*, 217*p*, 218*p*; Egypt's two kingdoms, 212*m*, 213–214; Egypt unified, 214–215, 214*p*; food production and civilization, 213, 213*p*; location and physical features, 211–213, 212*m*
Nineveh, 207
nirvana (state of peace), 465
Nkrumah, Kwame (leader of Ghana), 399*f*, 399*p*
Nobel Peace Prize, 83*f*, 297*f*, 436*f*
Nobel Prize in Literature, 344
nomads: in Central Asia, 298–299; in desert climates, 261; traditional cultures in modern Africa as, 362–363
nonrenewable natural resources, 83–85, 83*p*, 84*p*
nonrepresentative governments, 151
nonviolence, in Jainism, 461–462
norms, for castes in India, 456
north Africa: climate and resources of, 337–338, 338*p*; features of, 335–337, 336*m*, 337*p*; language in, 346; political map of, 30*m;* religion in, 346–347. *See also* Algeria; Egypt; Libya; Morocco; Tunisia
North Atlantic Treaty Organization (NATO), 134
North China Plain, 543
North Korea: daily life in, 581; government and economy, 580–581; issues and challenges, 581; Kim Il Sung statue, 561*p*; on Korean Peninsula, 564; life in, vs. South Korea, 580*p*; South Korea separated from, 133*m*, 133*p*. *See also* Korea
North Vietnam, 598
Notre Dame Cathedral (Paris, France), 103*p*
Nowruz (Persian New Year), 295
Nubia, 231–232, 232*m*. *See also* Kush (kingdom in Nubia, south of Egypt)
nuclear energy, 86
nuclear weapons: North Korea's possession of, 580–581
numerals: Arabic, 283*f*; Hindu-Arabic, 482

O

oasis, 261, 336, 337*p*
Obama, Barack, 133, 150, 183*p*, 184
obelisks: in Egyptian temples, 228
occupations, fast-growing, 176*c*
Oceania, 612*p*
oceans: currents in, 64, 64*c;* salt water in, 46–47, 46*p*; trenches in, 54–55
oil: Central Asia, 281; east and southern Africa, 425; Gabon, 411; as natural resource, 84, 87*p*; Nigeria, 402; north Africa, 338, 348; Republic of the Congo, 411
okapi, 394, 395*p*
Okavango River, 423
Old Kingdom of Egypt, 215–216
Olduvai Gorge, 357–358, 358*m*
Olympic Games, South Africa banned from, 436
Oman, 285

OPEC. *See* Organization of Petroleum Exporting Countries.
Orange River, 423
orangutans, 593*p*
Organization of Petroleum Exporting Countries (OPEC), 88, 283, 287, 349
organizing information, 125
Osaka, Japan, 571
Ottoman Empire, 316, 316*f*
Outback, 613*p*, 619
ozone layer, 122–123, 631

P

Pacific Islands: climate, 623; culture, 625; economies, 626; history of, 624–625; physical geography, 622–623; political map, 626*m;* population of, 625; resources, 623; settlements, 625*m;* Tanna Island dance, 627*p*; traditions, 626
Pacific Ocean, 25, 25*m*
pagodas, 552
Pakistan, 489, 503–504
Palestinian territories, 322–324, 322*m*
Pali canon: Buddhism teachings in, 465
Palmyra, Syria, 325*p*
Pamirs, 279
Panama Canal, 59
***Panchatantra* stories,** 480
Papua New Guinea, 623
papyrus: Egyptian development of, 226
parallels of latitude, 24–25
paraphrasing, 190
Park Geun-hye (South Korean president), 579
parliament: democracies with, 138*c*
partition of India, 497–498, 498*p*
Pashto language, 300
passenger pigeons: extinction of, 79*p*
Passover (Jewish holiday), 251, 251*p*
Pasteur, Louis, 104
Paul of Tarsus, 257–258, 258*m*
Pe, 214
Pearl Harbor, Hawaii, 568
penguins, 628*p*, 629
People's Republic of China, 545–546, 546*f*
per capita GDP (gross domestic product), 171
performing arts: as cultural expression, 102
Period of Disunion (China), 521
permafrost, 74
Persian Empire, 293
Persian Gulf, 275–276
Persian Gulf War (1990–1991), 289
Peter (Apostle), 256–257
petroleum, 84, 87*p*. *See also* oil
pharaohs of Egypt, 214
Philippines, 604; Roman Catholicism in, 596. *See also* Island Southeast Asia
Phnom Penh, Cambodia, 602
Phoenicians, 208–210, 209*m*, 210*p*
physical borders of nations, 131–132, 132*p*
physical geography, 10–11, 13*p*. *See also features of individually named regions*
physical maps, 31, 31*m*, 89, 89*m*
Piankhi (ruler of Kush, 700s BC), 234, 237
pictograph writing, 200
pilgrimage, 469
pirates: in Somalia, 432
pivot-irrigated fields, 278*p*
place: as geography theme, 16, 17*p*
Plateau of Tibet, 541
plate tectonics of Earth, 53–56, 53*p*, 54*pc*, 55*p*
plow: Sumerian invention of, 201
polar climate, 74–75, 74*p*, 75*p*
political maps, 30, 30*m*
political parties, 148
political symbols, 151*f*, 151*p*
pollution: air, 123*p*, 549*p*; from fossil fuel burning, 84–85; water, 50, 122–123, 122*p*, 404
Polo, Marco, 530; description of Hangzhou, 531*f*
Polynesia, 622–623, 624
polytheism, 199, 216–217
Pontic Mountains, 312
pope (bishop of Rome), 259–260
popular culture, 179–180, 180*p*
population: Africa, slave trade and, 375; Australia, 620; changes in, 109–112, 110*c*, 110*p*, 111*c*, 111*p*; China, 548–549, 548*m;* east Africa, 430*c*, 430*m;* Egypt, 342*c*, 342*m;* India, 500, 501*m*, 501*p*; Israel, 321, 321*c*, 321*p*; Mongolia, 554; New Zealand, 620; Pacific islands, 625; Pakistan, 504; patterns in, 106–109, 107*m*, 108*p*, 109*f;* Taiwan, 555; Turkey, 317*c*, 317*m;* west Africa, 400*c*, 400*m*. *See also* settlement patterns
population pyramid diagram, 415, 415*c*
porcelain, 524, 524*p*
Portugal: Gold Coast as colony of, 376; slave trading by, 374–375; trade with Kongo kingdom of central Africa (1300s), 371. *See also* Europe
potter's wheel, 201
precipitation, 48, 49*c*, 491*m*
prefixes of words, 40
presidential democracies, 138
prevailing winds, 63, 63*c*
priests, 199
primary and secondary sources, 239
primary industries, 169, 169*p*
primary source, 606*f*
prime meridian, 24, 24*c*
problem-solving process, 153
public goods, 168, 168*p*
public opinion, 149–150
Punjabi language, 470
Punjab region of India, 472
purpose setting, 310
Pyongyang, North Korea, 581; compared to Seoul, South Korea, 580*p*
pyramids: Egyptian, 219–220, 219*p*, 339, 351*p*; Kush, 237*f*
Pyramid Texts, 220

Q

Qatar, 284
Qin dynasty, 514*m*, 516–517
quaternary industries, 169*p*, 170
quick facts (feature): Burkina Faso, in west Africa, 402*f*, 402*p*; Eightfold Path, in Buddhism, 466*f;* globalization, 182*f;* hominids, early, 359*f;* Old Kingdom Egypt, 216*f;* South Korea's higher education boom, 578; traditional cultures of modern Africa, 362*f*, 362*p*
quotas: on oil exports, 283; as trade barriers, 182*c*
Qur'an, 263–266, 265*p*

R

rabbis, 248
radiation, 303
rainfall: seasonal impact on, 45
rain shadow effect, 66–67, 66*c*
rajas (Aryan civilization village leaders), 453
Ramadan (Muslim holy month), 267
Ramayana **epic,** 480, 480*p*
Ramses the Great (Egyptian pharaoh), 223, 224*f*
Rangoon (Yangon), Myanmar, 600
raw materials: in Africa, 377–378, 377*p*
Red Sea, 336
reforestation, 83, 83*p*
refugees: in Iraq, 292*p*
regions: cultural, 97–98, 97*m*, 97*p*; as geography theme, 7–9, 8*p*, 17*p*, 18; in settlement patterns, 116–117, 117*p*
reincarnation, 459–460
relative location, 16
religion: art influenced by, in India, 478; Bangladesh, 503; Bhutan, 503; central Africa, 409, 409*f;* Central Asia, 300; China, 550–551; as cultural institution, 102, 103*p*; east Africa, 426, 428; Egypt, 343; Egypt (ancient), 216–218, 217*f*, 217*p*, 218*p*; India, 498–499, 500*p*; Indian Subcontinent, 504*m*; Iraq, 291; Japan, 568–569; Kongo kingdom of central Africa, 1300s, 371; Korea, 576; Lebanon, 326; literacy limited by, 171*f;* Mali kingdom of west Africa, 367; Nepal, 503; north Africa, 346–347; Pakistan, 503; southern Africa, 438; Southeast Asia, 599; southwest Asia, 268*c;* Sri Lanka, 503; Sumerian civilization, 199; Syria, 326; Vedic civilization, 454–455; west Africa, 401. *See also entries for individual religions and philosophies*
renewable natural resources, 82–83, 83*p*, 85, 85*p*
representative democracies, 138, 139*c*, 145
Republican Party (U.S. political party), 148, 150
Republic of the Congo, 411
resources. *See* natural resources.
retail industries, 169*p*, 170
revolution of Earth, 42
Rhodes, Cecil, 378, 379*f*
rice paddies, 547*p*
rift valleys, 312, 421–422
Rigveda **religious writing,** 454
Ring of Fire: earthquakes and volcanoes in, 60–61, 60*c*, 61*p*, 590
Rio de Janeiro, Brazil, 58*p*
risk-return relationship, 177*c*, 178
rock art: of Early Stone Age, 360, 361*p*
rock churches of Lalibela, 427*p*
Roman Catholicism, 596. *See also* Christianity
Rome, ancient: Jews conquered by, 247
Roosevelt, Franklin D., 150*f*
roots of words, 40
Rosetta Stone, 226–227
Rosh Hashanah (Jewish New Year), 252
Ross Ice Shelf, 628
rotation of Earth, 41, 42*c*
Rouhani, Hassan (president of Iran), 297
route maps, 269, 269*m*
Rub' al-Khali desert, 277
rubber tree plantations, 593, 605*p*
runoff: in water cycle, 49*c*
Rwanda, 430

S

safaris: in east Africa, 428
Safavid Empire, 293–294, 294*m*
Sahara desert, 7, 71*f*, 71*p*, 335–336, 337*p*
Sahel region of west Africa, 392, 405–406, 405*p*, 406*p*
salt: Ghana trade in, 366
salt water, 46–47, 46*p*
Samarqand, 298, 302
samskaras **rites of passage,** 460
samurai, 567
San Andreas Fault zone, 56
sanctions: against South Africa, 436
San culture, 362, 362*f*, 362*p*
San Rafael Glacier (Chile), 47*p*
Sanskrit language, 454, 454*p*, 480, 493
São Tomé and Príncipe, 411
Sarasvati River, 449
Sargon (ruler of Akkad), 197–198, 198*f*, 198*p*
satellite images, 22, 22*p*, 35, 35*p*
Saudi Arabia: government and economy of, 283–284; oil in, 286–287, 286*c*, 286*m*, 287*c*, 287*p*; people and customs of, 282–283
savanna climate: in east and southern Africa, 423–424; Maasai (traditional culture in modern Africa) in, 362*p*, 363; in west Africa, 392
savannas, 71
savings: for wealth building, 177–178
scale: on maps, 29, 29*c*
scarcity and choice in economics, 159, 168

Index

scholar-officials, 526–527, 526*p*
school attendance: as citizenship duty, 145
science: geography as, 5–6; in Indian empires, 481–482, 481*p*; Sumerian developments in, 202; technology and, 104–105, 104*p*
science, link to (feature): atoll formation, 624
scribes: in Sumerian civilization, 201
Sea of Marmara, 311, 312*m*, 313*p*
Sea Peoples, 224
seasons of year, 43–45, 43*c*, 44*p*, 73
secondary industries, 169, 169*p*
secondary sources, 239
Second Dynasty of Egyptian pharaohs, 215
secular state, 317
Seeds of Peace, 323*f*, 323*p*
seismograph, 519, 519*p*
Selective Service System, 145–146
Senegal, 402–403
Seoul, South Korea: compared to Pyongyang, North Korea, 580*p*; daily life in, 579; postwar transformation, 577*p*
separation of tectonic plates, 55, 55*c*, 55*p*
September 11, 2001, attacks on World Trade Center (New York), 290, 301
sequencing information, 130
Serengeti National Park (Kenya), 429*m*
Serengeti Plain, 423
Sermon on the Mount (Jesus of Nazareth), 256*f*, 256*p*
service industries, 170
settlement patterns: importance of location in, 113–114, 113*p*, 114*p*; regional interaction in, 116–117, 117*p*; spatial, 115–116, 115*c*, 116*p*; urban and rural, 114, 114*p*. *See also* population
Shabaka (ruler of Kush), 234
Shackleton, Sir Ernest, 630*f*, 630*p*
Shah Jahan (Mughal ruler, 1600s), 478
shahs (Iranian kings), 294
Shaka (Zulu resistance leader), 381
shamanism, 576
Shanakhdakheto (queen of Kush), 237, 237*f*, 237*p*
Shang dynasty, 513–514
Shanghai, China, 549
Shariah (Islamic law), 267–268
Shia Muslims, 282, 291, 295, 326
Shi Huangdi (Chinese emperor), 515–517, 515*f*, 515*p*; tomb of, 516*p*
Shikoku, 563
Shinto religion, 568–569
***shi* poetry,** 518
shoguns, 567
Shona people, 370–371, 433, 434*p*
Shwedagon Pagoda, 587*p*
Siddhartha Gautama, 463–464, 464*p*, 498, 551
Sidon, 210*p*
Sierra Leone, 403
Sikhism: beliefs of, 470–471; history of, 472–473; in India, 499; origins of, 470; practice of, 471–472, 471*c*
silent barter process, 366
Silk Road, 99, 298, 520
Silla, 575; artifact from, 561*p*
silt, 192; in Nile River, 335
Sima Qian, 519
Sinai Peninsula, 336
Singapore, 604, 605–606; Lee Kuan Yew on, 606*f*. *See also* Island Southeast Asia
Singh, Ranjit (ruler of Punjab region of India, 1799), 472–473
Sinhalese ethnic group, 506
sinkholes, 50
Siva the Destroyer (Hindu god), 458, 459*p*
six essential elements of geography, 18*c*, 19
slash-and-burn agriculture, 119, 119*p*
slave trade: Atlantic, 374–375, 374*p*, 375*m*; central Africa, 407; east Africa, 373, 426; Kongo kingdom of central Africa, 1300s, 371; west Africa, 399
social institutions: in cultures, 101–102, 102*p*
socialist economies, 166, 166*c*
social science, geography as, 6
social studies, reading: author's purpose, 614; bias, 562; cause and effect, 356; chronological order, 512; compare and contrast, 390; content clues/definitions, 588; drawing conclusions, 158; fact and opinion, understanding, 448; generalizations, forming, 420; implied main ideas, 540; main ideas, 94; paraphrasing, 190; prior knowledge, 4; purpose setting, 310; rereading, 274; sequencing information, 130; summarizing, 334; synonyms as context clues, 244; visualization, 488; word parts, 40
social studies skills: arguments, strength of, 185; analyzing satellite images, 35, 35*p*; cartogram, 329, 329*m*; computer mapping, 4*f*; continuity and change, 385; databases, 305*c*; diagram analysis, 351; economic choices, 535; line graphs, 507, 507*c*; make decisions, 633; map comparison, 483, 483*m*; organizing information, 125; physical maps, 89, 89*m*; point of view, 557; population pyramid diagram, 415, 415*c*; primary and secondary sources, 239; problem-solving process, 153; route maps, 269, 269*m*; topographic map, 583, 583*m*; visuals, 609; website evaluation, 443
society: Aryan civilization, 453; Egypt (ancient), 224–226, 225*p*; Old Kingdom Egypt, 215–216, 216*p*; Sumerian civilization, 199–200

Society Islands: coral reefs in, 623*p*
Sofala, 372
soil, 80–81, 80*p*, 81*c*
solar energy, 41–45, 42*c*
Solomon (king of Israelites), 246
Somalia, 431–432
Song dynasty, 522–527; invention of fireworks, 511*p*, 524*p*; scholar-officials, 526–527, 526*p*; trade during, 523–524
Songhai kingdom, 368–370, 369*m*, 398
souks, 348
South Africa, 359, 382–384, 438
Southeast Asia, 586–609, 586*m*; city life in, 609*p*; climate of, 591, 592*m*; colonial possessions (1914), 597*m*; natural resources, 593; physical features, 589–591; physical map, 590*m*; plants and animals in, 592. *See also* Island Southeast Asia; Southeast Asia, mainland
Southeast Asia, mainland: culture of, 598–599; early history, 596–597; Indochina, 602–603; land use and resources, 602*m*; modern history, 597–598; rural life, 599–600
southern Africa: culture of, 436–438, 437*p*; history of, 433–436, 434*p*, 435*p*, 436*f*; issues and challenges in, 441–442; today, 438–441, 439*p*, 440*p*, 441*p*. *See also* east and southern Africa
Southern African Development Community (SADC), 438
Southern Ocean, 25, 25*c*
South Korea: daily life in, 579; Geongbokgung Palace, 575*p*; education and employment, 578; government and economy of, 578; higher education boom, 578*c*; on Korean Peninsula, 564; life in, vs. North Korea, 580*p*; North Korea separated from, 133*m*, 133*p*; political upheaval in, 579*f*, 579*p*; postwar transformation, 577*p*. *See also* Korea
South Vietnam, 598
southwest Africa, 362–363
sovereign nations, 132
Soviet Union: Central Asia influenced by, 299, 299*p*; Mongolia and, 553
Spain: Morocco controlled by, 346
Spanish-American War, 597
spatial settlement patterns, 115, 115*c*, 116*p*
sphinxes, 228
spring season, 43*c*, 44
Sri Lanka, 468*p*, 489, 503, 506, 506*p*
Stalin, Joseph, 141
steppe climate: central Africa, 395; description of, 71, 74*p*; north Africa, 338
Stone Ages: humans in, 360–361, 361*p*
Strait of Gibraltar, 349
stratovolcanoes, 61
strength of arguments, 185
stupa (Buddhism temple), 479
subarctic climate, 74
subcontinent, 489. *See also* Indian Subcontinent
suburbs, 114
Sudan, 429–430, 431*p*
Sudras *varna* (laborers and servants), 455
Suez Canal, 336, 340, 342, 378–379
suffixes of words, 40
Sui dynasty, 521
Suleyman I (Ottoman ruler), 316
sultan, 606
Sumatra: orangutans in, 593*p*
Sumer, 196, 289*m*
Sumerian civilization: Akkadian Empire and, 197–198, 198*f*, 198*p*; arts of, 202–204, 203*p*, 204*p*; city-states of, 196–197, 196*p*, 197*m*; inventions and technology of, 201–202; religion of, 199, 199*p*; society of, 200; writing invented by, 200–201, 200*p*, 201*c*, 201*p*. *See also* Mesopotamia
summarizing, 334
summer season, 43–44, 43*c*
sun: energy of, 41–45; water cycle driven by, 48–49, 49*c*. *See also* climate
sundial, 519
Sundiata (ruler of Mali kingdom, 1230s), 367
Sunnah, 266–267
Sunni Ali (ruler of Songhai kingdom), 368–369
Sunni Muslims, 282, 291–292, 295, 326
supply and demand, 160, 160*c*
surface of Earth: features of, 32*m*, 33*c*; forces below, 53–56, 53*c*, 54*c*, 54*p*, 55*c*; processes on, 56–57, 56*p*, 57*p*
surface water, 48
surplus food, 194–195
Susruta (ancient Indian surgeon), 481*p*
Swahili culture, 373
Swahili language, 427–428
Swaziland. *See* Eswatini
Sydney, Australia, 621; Opera House, 613*p*
synonyms as content clues, 244
Syr Darya River, 279
Syria, 325–326, 325*p*, 327, 327*m*, 327*p*. *See also* eastern Mediterranean
Syrian Desert, 313

T

Tahiti, 622
Taipei, Taiwan, 556, 556*p*
Taiwan, 554–556; climate in, 543–544; culture, 555; history, 555; location of, 541; physical map, 542*m*; population, 555; resources in, 544; Taipei, 556, 556*p*; tension with China, 555*c*, 555*m*
Tajikistan, 302
Taj Mahal, 478
Taklimakan Desert, 542
Taliban (radical Muslim group), 300–301, 303*p*
Talmud (commentaries), in Judaism, 250*p*, 251

Tamil ethnic group, 506
Tanakh (Hebrew Bible), 250*p*. *See also* Judaism
Tandja, Mamadou (president of Niger), 405
Tang dynasty, 522–527; art in, 524–525; city life in, 523; Confucianism during, 526; invention of fireworks, 511*p*; inventions, 524–525; porcelain art, 524*p*; trade during, 523–524
tangible assets, 176
Tangier, Morocco, 349
Tanzania, 423, 428–429
Tappan, Eva March, 224*f*
Tarai region, in Nepal, 491
tariff, 570; as trade barrier, 182*c*
Taurus Mountains, 312
taxes: as citizenship duty, 146
technology: regional interaction from, 116–117, 117*p*; science and, 104–105; Sumerian civilization, 201–202
technology, link to (feature): computer mapping, 14*f*
tectonic plates, 54–55, 54*c*, 54*p*, 55*c*, 489
Tehran, Iran, 294
Tel Aviv, Israel, 321
temperate climates, 72–73, 73*c*, 73*p*
Temple of Karnak, 228, 229*p*
Temüjin (Genghis Khan), 528
Ten Commandments, 248–249
terraced hillside farming, 119, 119*p*
territory, 624
terrorism, 135
tertiary industries, 169*p*, 170, 172
Thai people, 596
Thailand, 600; Bangkok, 600, 601*p*; Bangkok klong (canal), 601*f*, 601*p*; Mekong River, 591, 591*p*; Phi Phi Don Island, 587*p*; teenage Buddhist monks in, 598*p*
Thar (Great Indian Desert), 491
thematic maps, 31, 31*m*
themes of geography, 16–18, 17*p*, 18*c*
theocracies, 139*c*, 215, 295
Theravada branch of Buddhism, 468
Third Dynasty of Egyptian pharaohs, 215
Thoreau, Henry David, 480
Three Gorges Dam, 550
Three Kingdoms, 575
thunderstorms, 62*p*, 65–66
Thutmose I (Egyptian pharaoh), 233
Tiananmen Square (Beijing): massacre, 142, 142*p*; National Day festivities, 546*p*; pro-democracy protest (1989), 547
Tibet, 547
Tigris River, 191–192, 275–276
tilt of Earth's axis, 42, 42*c*
Timbuktu, Mali, 367–368, 398, 406
Timor, 597
Timor-Leste, 604. *See also* Island Southeast Asia, 607
Tipitaka: Buddhism teachings in, 465
Togo, 404
Tokyo, Japan: as capital city, 569; life in, 571, 572*f*, 572*p*
tools: Early Stone Age, 360; Later Stone Age, 361; Middle Stone Age, 360
topographic map, 583*f*, 583*m*
Torah, 249, 249*p*, 250*p*
tornadoes, 65–66, 65*p*, 120, 120*p*
totalitarian regimes, 139*c*, 141
tourism industry: Africa, north, 348; Africa, southern, 439*p*, 440*c*, 440*p*; Egypt, 342; Kenya, in east Africa, 428; Kyrgyzstan, 302; Tanzania, in east Africa, 428
townships: in South African apartheid, 436
trade: Africa, east, 426; Africa, north, 348; Aksum kingdom, in northeast Africa, 364; between nations, 133; Central Asia, 298; China, 547; cultural diffusion along routes of, 99–100; Egypt, New Kingdom, 223; Egypt, Old Kingdom, 215–216; Egyptian economy, 342; embargo on, 289; free, 184; free, in Australia, 619–620; Ghana control of, 365–367; global, 180–182, 181*p*, 182*c*; Great Zimbabwe, of early southern Africa, 433; Japan and, 570; Kongo kingdom of central Africa (1300s), 371; Kush, 235, 236*m*, 236*p*; Phoenician, 209–210, 209*m*; settlement patterns based on, 113–114, 113*p*, 114*p*; Silk Road (Han dynasty), 520; Song dynasty, 524; Sumerian civilization, 200; Tang dynasty, 523–524. *See also* Africa in global trade
trade surplus, 570
traditional economy, 164, 165*p*
traits: cultural, 96, 96*p*, 97*p*
transportation: in Japanese cities, 571
Tripitaka. *See* Tipitaka.
Triple Basket. *See* Tipitaka.
Tripoli, Libya, 349
tropical climates, 70–72, 70*p*, 71*p*, 72*p*; Africa, 424; rainfall in, 45
tropical forest, in central Africa, 394
tropical savanna climate: central Africa, 395; description of, 71, 74*p*; India and Sri Lanka, 492; Pacific Island, 623; Southeast Asia, 591
Truman, Harry S., 562
tsunami, 564, 574, 574*p*; Island Southeast Asia, 590; Sri Lanka affected by (2004), 506; Tohoku region of Japan (2011), 121
tsunami, case study, 594–595, 594*c*, 595*m*
Tuareg nomads of the Sahara (north Africa), 71*f*, 71*p*, 368
tuberculosis, 441
tundra climate, 74, 74*p*
Tunis, Tunisia, 349
Tunisia: Arab Spring (2011) in,

345, 346*m*, 348*p*, 350; arts and literature in, 347; France control of, 346; government and economy of, 348–349; history and culture of, 345–347, 350. *See also* north Africa
Turkey: culture of, 317; history of, 315–317, 316*f*; today, 317, 317*m*, 318*p*. *See also* eastern Mediterranean
Turkic ethnic group, 300
Turkmenistan, 302
Turpan Depression, 542
Tutankhamen (king of Egypt), 230, 230*p*
Tutsi and Hutu ethnic groups, 430
Twenty-fifth (Kushite) dynasty of Egypt, 234
typhoons, 66, 565, 591
Tyre, 209, 210*p*

U

Uganda, 429–430
Ulaanbaatar, Mongolia, 554
Uluru, 613*p*, 615
Unas (pharaoh of Egyptian Old Kingdom), 220
UN Convention on the Rights of the Child, 143
unitary states, 138
United Arab Emirates, 285
United Kingdom (UK), 128, 128*p*, 138, 138*c*. *See also* Great Britain
United Nations (UN), 134–135, 134*f*, 289, 320, 432
United Nations Children's Fund (UNICEF), 136
United States: bombing of Hiroshima and Nagasaki, 568; Iranian life versus, 296*c*; trade with China, 547. *See also* United States, physical geography of
United States, physical geograpy of: introduction to, 10–11
United States Agency for International Development (USAID), 135
universals, 101
universal themes, in creative expression, 103–104
unlimited governments, 141–142, 142*p*
Upanishads, 455, 458
Upper Egypt, 211, 212*m*
Ur (Sumerian city-state), 197–198
urban and rural settlement patterns, 114, 114*p*
urbanization, in India, 500
Uruk (Sumerian city-state), 197
Ur-Zababa (ruler of Sumerian city-state, Kish), 198*f*
USAID (United States Agency for International Development), 135
U.S. Air Force Academy, 146
U.S. Department of State, 143
U.S. embassies, as targets of terrorist groups, 429
U.S. Supreme Court, 150*f*
U2 (music group), 254*p*
Uzbekistan, 302–303

V

Vaccine Alliance, 136
Vaisakhi (Sikh holiday), 499
Vaisyas *varna* (farmers, craftspeople, and traders), 455
Vargas, Getúlio, 130
varnas (social divisions, in India), 455–457, 456*p*, 457*p*
Vedas religious writing, 453–455
Vedic civilization, 454–455
Vedic texts, 455
vegetation: central Africa, 394–395, 395*p*; east and southern Africa, 423–424, 424*m*; eastern Mediterranean, 313; Middle East (Arabian Peninsula, Iraq, and Iran), 277–278; southern Africa, 424*m*; west Africa, 392–393
veld, in southern Africa, 424
Victoria Falls, 13*p*, 394
Vietnam, 603; Doc Let Beach, 603*p*; Halong Bay, 589*p*; modern history of, 597–598
Vishnu the Preserver (Hindu god), 458, 459*p*
visual arts, as cultural expression, 102, 103*p*
volcanoes, Ring of Fire, 60–61, 61*c*, 61*p*
voting: as citizenship responsibility, 147–148

W

wadis (dry streambeds), 278
Wake Island, 623
Warring States period (China), 516
water: in Central Asia, 281; climate affected by, 64–66; on Earth, 46–51, 46*p*, 47*p*, 49*c*, 50*p*; in eastern Mediterranean, 313–314; erosion caused by, 57, 57*p*; irrigation to control, 193, 194*p*; oasis for, 337*p*; pollution of, 122–123, 122*p*, 404; uneven distribution of in east and southern Africa, 424–425
water cycle, 48–49, 49*c*
water vapor, 48, 49*c*
wats, 599
wealth building, 177–178
weather, 62–67, 62*p*, 63*m*, 64*m*, 65*p*, 66*c*. *See also* climate
weathering of rock, 56
weather patterns, 14–15
website evaluation, 443
Weddell Sea, 632*p*
Wegener, Alfred, 54
west Africa: climate and vegetation of, 392–393, 393*m*; coastal countries of, 401–404; culture of, 400–401, 400*m*, 401*f*, 401*p*, 402*f*, 402*p*; features of, 391, 392*m*; Ghana as kingdom in, 365–367, 365*m*, 366*p*, 368*p*; history of, 398–399, 398*p*, 399*f*, 399*p*; natural resources of, 404*m*; Sahel region of, 405–406, 405*p*; thematic map of, 31*m*

West Bank (in Palestinian Territories), 323–324
Western Ghats mountains, 489
Western Rift Valley, 393
wheel: Sumerian invention of, 201
White House (Washington, DC), 16
White Nile River, 423
wholesale industries, 169*p*, 170
wild boar, 394
wind erosion, 56, 56*p*
Windhoek, Namibia, 439
winds: global systems of, 63–64, 63*c*
winter season, 43–44, 43*c*
Wolof language, 403
women: in Kushite society, 237; rights in ancient Egypt, 226; role in India, 457
woodblock printing, 525
word parts, 40
work ethic, 570
World Bank's Multi-Country AIDS Programme (MAP), 136
world ocean, 25, 25*c*
world of nations, 132–134, 133*m*, 133*p*
world population density, 106–107, 107*m*
world population growth, 111–112, 111*c*, 111*p*
World's Story, The (Tappan), 224*f*
World Trade Organization (WTO), 184; Australia in, 619
World War II: Egypt involvement in, 340; Japan and, 568; Japan's invasion of Southeast Asia during, 597; Pacific Islands and, 624
writing: in ancient Egypt, 340; early Indian, 450–451; Egyptian hieroglyphics for, 226–227; Phoenician alphabet simplified, 210; Sumerian civilization invention of, 200–201, 200*p*, 201*c*, 201*p*
Writing Workshops, R64–R71; (1) Explaining a Process, R64–R65; (2) Compare and Contrast, R66–R67; (3) Explaining Cause or Effect, R68–R69; (4) Persuasion R70–R71
Wu Daozi, 524
Wudi (Chinese emperor), 517

X

Xi'an, 516, 523

Y

Yang Jian, 521
Yangon, Myanmar, 600
Yangzi River, 543
Yarsan, 291
Yazidism, 291
Yellow River, 543
Yellow Sea, 564
Yemen, 285, 285*p*
Yom Kippur (Jewish High Holy Day), 252
Yoruba people, 400
Yuan dynasty, 529–530; Beijing during, 511*p*
yurt, 300

Z

Zagros Mountains, 276
Zambezi River, 394
Zambia, 409, 412, 412*p*
Zanzibar, 426
Zardari, Asif Ali (Pakistan leader), 504
Zaydan, Ali (Libyan prime minister), 349
Zheng He, 531–532, 532*f*, 534
Zhou dynasty, 514–516
Zhu Yuanzhang, 530–531
ziggurat temples, 202, 203*p*, 204*p*
Zimbabwe: art of, 437–438; Great Kingdom of, 370–371; issues in, 440; religion in, 438; today, 433, 435
Zionism nationalist movement, 320
zonal climates, 392
Zoroastrianism, 291
Zulu people, 381, 434–435

Credits and Acknowledgments

Table of Contents: *North America* ©ESC/Science Source; *Bushmen paintings* ©Hein von Horsten/Gallo Images/Getty Images; *Yunnan rice fields* ©Yann Layma/Stone/Getty Images

Module 1: *Village in Himalayas* ©age fotostock/SuperStock; *Indian girl with goat* ©Anthony Cassidy/The Image Bank/Getty Images; *sandstone formations* ©Digital Vision/Getty Images; *rock climber* ©M. Colonel/Photo Researchers/Science Source; *Sahara Desert, Algeria* ©Frans Lemmens/The Image Bank/Getty Images; *satellite view Europe* ©ESA/K. Horgan/The Image Bank/Getty Images; *Houses of Parliament* ©Sandy Stockwell/Skyscan/Corbis; *Oxford Street, London* ©Kim Sayer/Corbis; *Victoria Falls* ©Torleif Svensson/Corbis; *children dancing* ©Penny Tweedie/The Image Bank/Getty Images; *internet usage map* ©Donna Cox and Robert Patterson/NCSA; *Mojave Desert* ©Kevin Burke/Corbis; *Mount Rainier* ©David R. Frazier/Photo Researchers/Science Source; *Washington, DC* ©Miles Ertman/Masterfile; (bc) *airplane at DFW* ©Paul Buck/AFP/Getty Images; *strawberry picker* ©Morton Beebe/Corbis; *globe* ©D. Hurst/Alamy; *satellite of Italy* ©M-Sat Ltd./Science Source; *satellite of Italy* ©Earth Satellite Corporation/Science Photo Library/Science Source

Module 2: *North America* ©ESC/Science Source; *Monument Valley* ©George H.H. Huey/Corbis; *iceberg* ©Mark Karrass/Corbis; *koala* ©L. Clarke/Corbis; *time lapse sun* ©Paul A. Souders/Corbis; *ocean waves* ©Doug Wilson/Corbis; *hiker in Norway* ©Terje Rakke/The Image Bank/Getty Images; *cruise ship* ©Image Source IS2/Fotolia; *irrigation* ©Alan Sirulnikoff/Photo Researchers/Science Source; *surfer* ©Rick Doyle/Corbis; *hiker* ©Kate Thompson/National Geographic/Getty Images; *Mount Everest Himalayas* ©Marta/Fotolia; *Surtsey Island* ©Yann Arthus-Bertrand/Corbis; *Canyonlands National Park* ©age fotostock/Superstock; *Horseshoe Overlook* ©Owaki - Kulla/Corbis; *cable-car* ©age fotostock/Superstock; *Mount St. Helens* ©David Weintraub/Science Source; *storm cell* ©Minerva Studio/Shutterstock; *tornado on horizon* ©Eric Meola/The Image Bank/Getty Images; *flood rescue* ©William Thomas Cain/Getty Images; *rainforest* ©age fotostock/Superstock; *Tuareg men* ©Ariadne Van Zandbergen/Lonely Planet Images/Getty Images; *Monument Valley* ©Robert Marien/Corbis; *Nice, France* ©Ingram/PictureQuest/Jupiterimages; *zebra by Kilimanjaro* ©Sharna Balfour/Gallo Images/Corbis; *Mount McKinley* ©Robert Glusic/Corbis; *polar bear* ©Paul Souders/Photodisc/Getty Images; *pigeon drawing* Library of Congress; *mushrooms* ©Carl and Ann Purcell/Corbis; *Wangari Maathai* ©Adrian Arbib/Corbis; *children plant trees* ©Peter Arnold, Inc./Alamy; *oil pumps* ©Bill Ross/Corbis; *Glen Canyon Dam* ©Meinzahn/iStock/Getty Images Plus/Getty Images; *mining* ©James L. Amos/Corbis; *airplane* ©Charles Bowman/Photolibrary; *yard sale* ©Sarah Leen/National Geographic Stock

Module 3: *Olympic closing ceremony* ©Gary M. Prior/Getty Images; *Ganges & Yamuna Rivers* ©Richard I'Anson/Lonely Planet Images; *field workers* ©117 Imagery/Getty Images; *Mongolian musician* ©Jerry Kobalenko/Alamy; *Japanese use chopsticks* ©TWPhoto/Corbis; *Kenyan boys* ©Knut Mueller/Das Fotoarchiv/Photolibrary New York; *boy from Oman* ©Photononstop/Superstock; *Jerusalem* ©Peter Armenia; *Korean baseball* ©Reuters/Corbis; *1909 baseball game* Library of Congress Prints & Photographs Division; *Cuban baseball* ©Timothy A. Clary/AFP/Getty Images; *Pledge of Allegiance* ©David Coates/The Detroit News/AP Images; *students in Peru* ©Mike Theiss/National Geographic/Corbis; *Notre Dame Cathedral* ©Corbis; *Buddhist temple* ©MasterLu/Fotolia; *Hokusai's wave* Library of Congress Prints & Photographs Division; *Tokyo* ©Sean Pavone/Shutterstock; *Noosa river estuary* ©Patrick Oberem/iStockPhoto.com; *Ellis Island* The Granger Collection, NYC — All rights reserved; *wheat field & combine* ©Peter Beck/Corbis; *health clinic* ©Jewel Samad/AFP/Getty Images; *Birmingham, Alabama* ©Darryl Vest/Alamy; *harbor* Photodisc/Getty Images; *Times Square* ©holbox/Shutterstock; *farm* ©David Frazier/Corbis Premium RF/Alamy Images; *highway* © PhotoDisc/ Getty Images RF; *stock trader* ©Spencer Platt/Getty Images; *Sami* ©Franz Aberham/Photographer's Choice/Getty Images; *slash and burn farming* ©Paul Franklin/Oxford Scientific/Getty Images; *terraced farming* ©Glen Allison /Getty Images/PhotoDisc; *irrigation* ©David Frazier/Corbis Yellow/Corbis; *indigo sky tornado* ©Photodisc/Don Farrall/Getty Images; *Hoover Dam aerial* ©Getty Images; *pollution in lake* ©Alamy; *smokestacks* ©tomas/Fotolia

Module 4: *Laura Chinchilla* ©Monica Quesada/AP Images; *Houses of Parliament* ©Jose Fuste Raga/Corbis; *Indian voters* ©Narinder Nanu/AFP/Getty Images; *U.N. Headquarters* ©Arnaldo Jr/Shutterstock; *Great Lakes* ©Stocktrek Images/Getty Images; *soldiers patrolling DMZ, Korea* ©Topic Photo Agency; *Doctors Without Borders* Photo by Kate Geraghty/The Sydney Morning Herald/Fairfax Media via Getty Images; *National Congress* ©VISION/easyFotostock/age fotostock; *Mexico City* ©J. D. Heaton/Picture Finders/age fotostock; *Tanks and protester* ©Jeff Widener/AP Images; *Chinese poster* ©Swim Ink/Corbis; *cadets* U.S. Air Force; *voters* ©Blend Images/Hill Street Studios/Getty Images; *planting tree* ©Kidstock/Blend Images/Getty Images; *A 1938 Herblock Cartoon* ©The Herb Block Foundation, Library of Congress Prints & Photographs Division, Washington, D.C. [LC-DIG-ppmsca-17190]; *Joe Biden* ©Reuters/Ronen Zvulnun/Alamy

Module 5: *world map in currencies* ©bcracker/iStockPhoto.com; *Moroccan man* ©Shahn Rowe/Stone/Getty Images; *woman sells pickles* ©Godong/Universal Images Group/Getty Images; *NY Stock Exchange* ©Fotosearch/Getty Images; *dump truck* Vince Streano/Getty Images; *factory worker team* ©Andersen Ross/Getty Images; *baker* ©Monkey Business Images/Shutterstock; *tractor* © Getty Images RF; *tractors harvesting* ©Artville/Getty Images; *Rwandan farming* ©Tony Camacho/Science Source; *Times Square* ©Francisco Diez Photography/Getty Images; *Soviet market* ©Peter Turnley/Corbis; *Inuit fishing* ©White Fox/Tips Images/age fotostock; *Madison Robinson* ©Fish Flops; *firefighter* ©TFoxFoto/Shutterstock; *farmer with cattle* ©Owaki-Kulla/Corbis; *cheese cellar* ©Jack Sullivan/Alamy; *cheese counter* ©Kevin Fleming/Corbis; *cheese inspectors* ©Michelle Garrett/Corbis; *Afghan street market* ©Carl & Ann Purcell/Corbis; *train in Sydney* ©Glen Allison/The Image Bank/Getty Images; *Afghan school girls* Patrick ROBERT/Sygma via Getty Images; *Brazilian real bills* DRGill/Shutterstock; *Japanese yen* ©Takeshi Nishio/Shutterstock; *Mexican peso* ©PhotoSpin, Inc/Alamy Images; *Euro note* ©Westend61 GmbH/Alamy; *rupee* ©Steve Estvanik/Shutterstock; *Chinese yuan* ©bendao/Shutterstock; *bank vault* ©Andrew Sacks/The Image Bank/Getty Images; *Hispanic teen girl* ©asiseeit/iStockPhoto.com; *Seattle port* ©Druid007/Shutterstock; *Trump with Xi Jinping* ©Saul Loeb/AFP/Getty Images

Module 6: *Egyptian Pyramid* ©Dmitry Pichugin/Fotolia*statue from Saqqara* ©De Agostini/S. Vannini/Getty Images; *helmet* ©AKG-Images; *sailboats on the Nile River* ©Anders Blomqvist/Lonely Planet Images; *clay sickles* Kharbine-Tapabor, Paris/Art Resource, NY; *Standard of Ur* ©The Trustees of the British Museum/Art Resource, NY; *cylinder seal* © The Trustees of the British Museum/Art Resource, NY; *lyre* ©The British Museum/Topham-HIP/The Image Works, Inc.; *bull ornament* © Ancient Art & Architecture Collection, Ltd.; *Assyrian Army carving* ©Gianni Dagli Orti/The Picture Desk Limited/Corbis; *tomb painting* ©Erich Lessing/Art Resource, NY; *agriculture in Nile* ©Reza/Webistan/Corbis; *Weighing the Soul* ©Musee du Louvre, Paris/SuperStock; *Anubis* The Bridgeman Art Library International; *Sarcophagus* ©British Museum, London, UK/The Bridgeman Art Library; *Sphinx in front of Pyramid* ©Getty Images; *Egyptian farm worker* ©Gianni Dagli Orti/Corbis; *artifact* © Robert Harding Picture Library; *Abu Simbel* ©Claudia Paulussen/Fotolia; *Archaeologist Howard Carter* ©Time Life Pictures/Getty Images; *King Tut's tomb* ©Scala/Art Resource, NY; *Nile River rapids* ©De Agostini Editore/Photolibrary.com; *Kushites carrying tributes* Kushites carrying tributes of gold, ivory and animal skins, from the Tomb of Rekhmire, vizier of Tuthmosis III and Amenhotep II, New Kingdom (wall painting), Egyptian 18th Dynasty (c.1567–1320 BC) / Valley of the Nobles, Thebes, Egypt / Bridgeman Images; *Assyrian warrior relief* ©Erich Lessing/Art Resource, NY

Module 7: *Dome of the Rock* ©Pavel Bernshtam/Fotolia; *Wailing Wall* ©David Sanger/DanitaDelimont.com; *praying at Taj Mahal* Kamal Kishore/Reuters/Corbis; *Pieta* Scala/Art Resource, NY; *Moses* ©Chiesa della Certosa di San Martino, Naples/SuperStock; *Departure of Abraham* ©SuperStock/SuperStock; *Solomon's Temple* AKG-Images; *Ashkenazi Jews carrying scroll* ©Peter Guttman/Corbis; *girl reading Torah* ©3bugsmom/iStockPhoto.com; *Passover dinner* ©Leland Bobbe/Corbis/Getty Images; *Mary and Jesus Flight into Egypt* Alinari/Art Resource, NY; *living Nativity* D. Hurst/Alamy; *Sermon on the Mount location* Erich Lessing/Art Resource, NY; *The Last Supper* ©Alinari/Art Resource, NY; *studying the Qur'an* © J A Giordano/Corbis; *Esther* ©Ronald Sheridan/Ancient Art and Architecture Collection; *studying the Talmud* © Ted Spiegel/Corbis

Module 8: *Persepolis* ©Corbis; *Islamic women* ©Nader/Sygma/Corbis; *Kazakstan* ©Martin Moos/Lonely Planet Images; *Euphrates River* ©Nik Wheeler/Corbis; *satellite of Saudi Arabia* ©WorldSat International Inc.; *Pech Valley, Afghanistan* ©Francoise de Mulder/Corbis; *Uzbekistan cotton* ©David Beatty/Robert Harding Picture Library Ltd/Alamy; *Turkish astronomers* The Granger Collection, NYC — All rights reserved; *Dubai* ©Ludovic Maisant/Corbis; *Dar al Hajr, Yemen* ©Abbie Enock/Travel Ink/Corbis; *oil pipelines* ©Tom Hanley/Alamy; *Iraqi woman* ©Andrew Parsons/AP Images; *Iranian students* ©Ivan Sekretarev/AP Images; *soldiers in Mosul, Iraq* Staff Sgt. Vanessa Valenti/U.S. Air Force; *Iraqi refugee camp* ©Ari Jalal/Reuters/Alamy; *Imam Mosque* ©JPRichard/Shutterstock; *daily life in Iran* ©Kaveh Kazemi/Corbis; *classroom* ©monkeybusinessimages/iStock/Getty Images; *Shirin Ebadi* ©Scanpix/Tor Richardsen/Pool/Reuters/Corbis; *Islamic tiles* ©Gérard Degeorge/Corbis; *Soviet architecture* ©Christine Osborne/Lonely Planet Images; *Afghan girl* ©Reuters/Corbis; *Kyrgyz protesters* ©David Mdzinarishvili/Reuters/Corbis

Module 9: *Whirling dervish* ©Martin Siepmann/Imagebroker/age fotostock; *The Treasury, Petra* ©Anders Blomqvist/Lonely Planet Images/Getty Images; *Jordan River* ©Jon Arnold Images/Photolibrary; *Mt. Ararat* ©Adam Woolfitt/Robert Harding Picture Library Ltd/Alamy; *Dead Sea* ©Hanan Isachar/Corbis; *satellite of Istanbul* ©WorldSat International Inc.; *Mustafa Kemal Atarurk* The Granger Collection, NYC — All rights reserved; *Mehmed II* The Granger Collection, New York; *Istanbul* ©Danny Lehman/Corbis; *Jerusalem* ©Eric Meola/The Image Bank/Getty Images; *family* ©Russell Mountford/Lonely Planet Images; *Seeds of Peace* Courtesy of www.seedsofpeace.org; *Great Colonnade* ©Alison Wright/Corbis; *Beirut, Lebanon* ©Ayman Trawi/Beirut's Memory; *Jordanian girls* ©Anthony Ham/Lonely Planet Images; *Syrian carpet seller* ©Siegfried Tauqueur/eStock Photo

Module 10: *Moroccan woman* ©Jon Arnold Images/Danita Delimont Stock Photography; *Egyptian necklace* ©Claudia Adams/DanitaDelimont.com; *Hoggar Mountains* ©age fotostock/Superstock; *Nile River* ©Steve Vidler/eStock Photo; *Sphinx* ©age fotostock/Superstock; *Tahrir Square* ©Peter Turnley/Corbis; *Nile River* ©NASA/Science Source; *Couscous dish* ©P. Eoche/Photodisc/Getty Images; *Berber women* ©Patrick Ward/Corbis; *Tunisian rally* ©Fethi Belaid/AFP/Getty Images; *Algiers* ©Andrew Gunners/Photodisc/Getty Images; *Morocco* ©Abbas/Magnum Photos; *Fes, Morocco* ©Karim Selmaoui/EPA/Landov

Module 11: *Women in front of mosque* ©Glen Allison/PhotoDisc/Getty Images; *Lucy vs human skull* ©Sabena Jane Blackbird/Alamy; *salt mounds* ©Nik Wheeler/CORBIS; *Griot* ©ISSOUF SANOGO/AFP/Getty Images; *cro-magnon skull* ©Pascal Goetgheluck/Science Source; *knife* ©Erich Lessing/Art Resource, NY; *Australopithecus africanus* ©Pascal Goetgheluck/Photo Researchers, Inc.; *Homo ergaster skull* ©Pascal Goetgheluck/Photo Researchers, Inc.; *hand ax* ©John Reader/Science Source; *homo habilis skull and tools* ©Pascal Goetgheluck/Science Source; *homo habilis skull and tools* ©Pascal Goetgheluck/Science Source; *African cave painting* ©Photo by Edoardo FORNACIARI/Gamma-Rapho via Getty Images; *Mbenga woman* ©Timothy Allen/Photonica World/Getty Images; *Masai men* ©Royalty Free/ CORBIS; *San hunters* ©WILDLIFE GmbH/Alamy; *Ghana woman jewelry* Carol Beckwith&Angela Fisher/HAGA/The Image Works, Inc.; *herd in the Sahel* ©Steve McCurry/Magnum Photos; *boat sailing in harbor* ©Nik Wheeler/Corbis Documentary/Getty Images; *Elmina Ghana* ©Michael Dwyer/Alamy; *African trade* ©Everett Historical/Shutterstock; *diamond mining* © Mary Evans Picture Library/The Image Works; *Zulu king* ©ART Collection/Alamy; *Battle of Adwa* The Abyssinians routing the Italian troops, scene from the Italian invasion of Abyssinia in 1896 (gouache on paper), Ethiopian School, (20th century)/Private Collection/Archives Charmet/Bridgeman Images

Module 12: *Dakar* ©David Else/Lonely Planet Images; *Ashanti men* ©Owen Franken/Corbis; *Kota reliquary figure* ©Christie's Images/Corbis; *okapi* ©Juniors Bildarchiv/age fotostock; *Michael Fay* ©Michael Nichols/National Geographic Image Collectiion; *elephants* ©Michael Nichols/National Geographic Stock; *camel caravan* ©Michael Lewis/National Geographic/Getty Images; *Kwame Nkrumah* ©Bettmann/Corbis; *Ashanti ceremony* ©Imagestate/Photolibrary New York; *Nankani woman paints* ©Margaret Courtney-Clarke/Corbis; *Lagos, Nigeria* ©Reuters/Corbis; *desert croplands* ©Yann Arthus-Bertrand/Corbis; *Mali market* ©jean claude braun/Fotolia; *Edo ivory armlet* ©The Trustees of the British Museum/Art Resource, NY; *Ivory traders* ©Bojan Brecelj/Corbis Historical/Getty Images; *Malawi* ©Jorgen Schytte/Photolibrary New York; *Kinshasa* ©Robert Caputo/Aurora; *Angola* ©Didier Ruef/Pixsil/Aurora & Quanta Productions Inc.; *Cameroon adobe huts* ©age fotostock/Superstock; *hut in Zambia* ©David Else/Lonely Planet Images; *Burindi Shohmbo* ©Ian Berry/Magnum Photos

Module 13: *Elephants* ©Tim Davis/Corbis; *Kenya* ©Jack Dykinga/The Image Bank/Getty Images; *Bushmen paintings* ©Hein von Horsten/Gallo Images/Getty Images; *Ethiopia* ©Robert Preston/Alamy; *delta* ©Yann Arthus-Bertrand/Corbis; *St. George's Church* ©Dave Bartruff/Corbis; *Sudanese primary school* ©Aurora Photos/Jakub Sliwa/Alamy; *shepherd boys* ©Frances Linzee Gordon/Lonely Planet Images; *Great Enclosure* ©Ariadne Van Zanderbergen/Lonely Planet Images; *Zimbabwe* ©Colin Hoskins/Cordaiy Photo Library Ltd./Corbis; *Jan van Riebeeck* ©The Art Gallery Collection/Alamy; *Nelson Mandela* ©Walter Dhladhla/AFP/Getty Images; *Ndebele woman paints* ©Lindsay Hebberd/Corbis; *N'debele village* ©R. Philips/Arco Images GmbH/Alamy; *South Africa* ©Chris Harvey/The Image Bank/Getty Images; *safari* ©Luke Hunter/Lonely Planet Images; *Avenue of the Baobabs* ©jspix/Imagebroker/Alamy; *website* ©GCIS2016: ALL RIGHTS RESERVED

Module 14: *Religious leaders* ©Rio Helmi/LightRocket/Getty Images; *Priest King bust* ©DEA/A. Dagli Orti/Getty Images; *Ganges bathers* ©Jacob Halaska/Index Stock Imagery, Inc.; *Ajanta cave entrance* ©Richard A. Cooke/CORBIS; *animal seals* ©Borromeo/Art Resource, NY; *Harappan vase* ©The Art Archive; *Sanskrit tablet* ©matiplanas/Fotolia; *Brahma* ©Burstein Collection/Corbis; *Siva* ©Borromeo/Art Resource, NY; *Vishnu* ©V&A Images, London/Art Resource, NY; *woman setting candles in Ganges* ©Chris Cheadle/The Image Bank/Getty Images; *Jain monks* ©MANAN VATSYAYANA/AFP/Getty Images; *Buddha leaving palace* ©HIP/Art Resource, NY; *Golden Buddha statue* ©PhotoLink/Photodisc/L Hobbs/Getty Images; *Buddhism in Sri Lanka* Sena Vidanagama/AFP/Getty Images; *Langar* ©Pardeep Pandit/Hindustan Times/Getty Images; *Golden Temple* ©Luciano Mortula/Shutterstock; *India fresco* ©SEF/Art Resource, NY; *Kesava Temple* ©Sheldan Collins/Corbis; *Temple*

©Lindsay Hebberd/Corbis; *Ramayana Illustration* ©Philadelphia Museum of Art/Corbis; *Indian surgeon Susruta* ©Paris Pierce/Alamy; *Gupta gold coin* ©C. M. Dixon Colour Photo Library/ Ancient Art & Architecture; *Aryabhata statue* Dinodia Photo Library RF/Age Fotostock; *Quadrant* Museum of the History of Science, University of Oxford

Module 15: *Taj Mahal* ©Stefan Huwiler/ Imagebroker/Alamy; *boat on Ganges River* ©Peter Lopeman/Alamy; *Indian boy* ©Anthony Cassidy/The Image Bank/ Getty Images; *Himalayas and Indus River* ©Ronald Naar/ANP Photo/age fotostock; *Indian rice fields summer* ©Steve McCurry/Magnum Photos; *Indian rice fields winter* ©Steve McCurry/Magnum Photos; *Priest King bust* ©DEA/A. Dagli Orti/Getty Images; *Mughal Emperor Babur and his son, Humayan,* Indian miniature from Rajasthan, 16th century (gouache on paper), Chand, Dip (fl. 1760–70). ©Victoria & Albert Museum, London, UK/ The Bridgeman Art Library; *Gandhi and followers* ©Hulton-Deutsch Collection/ Corbis; *Mahatma Gandhi* ©Hulton-Deutsch Collection/Corbis; *Indian refugees* ©Bettmann/Corbis; *Old Delhi* ©Mark Edwards/Photolibrary; *Bollywood posters* ©John Henry C WIlson/Robert Harding World Imagery/Glow Images; *sherpas* ©Sheldan Collins/Corbis; *tea pickers* ©Jeremy Horner/Corbis

Module 16: *Great Wall* ©aphotostory/iStock/Getty Images Plus/Getty Images; *terracotta archer* ©O. Louis Mazzatenta/National Geographic Stock; *fireworks* ©Otto Rogge/ Corbis; *Forbidden City* ©Free Agents Limited/CORBIS; *Terracotta warriors* ©FSG FSG/age fotostock/ Photolibrary; *Han Dynasty painting* ©The Trustees of the British Museum/Art Resource, NY; *Zhang Heng seismoscope* Science Museum/Science and Society Picture Library; *bronze flying horse* ©Erich Lessing/Art Resource, NY; *accupuncture chart* Wellcome Library, London; *barges* © Carl & Ann Purcell/Corbis; *boat* ©Keren Su/China Span/Alamy; *jar* ©Paul Freeman/Private Collection/The Bridgeman Art Library; *Chinese New Year* ©China Photo/Reuters/Corbis; *Emperor of China* ©Private Collection/The Bridgeman Art Library; *Civil Service Exam art* ©Snark/ Art Resource, NY

Module 17: *Chinese Opera* ©Steve Vidler/eStock Photo; *Mongolian men on horses* ©Michel Setboun/Corbis; *Beijing skyline* ©Leonid Andronov/ Fotolia; *Li River, China* ©Panorama Media (Beijing) Ltd./Alamy; *Mt. Everest* ©Pal Teravagimov Photography/Getty Images; *flooding in China* ©CNES, 1998 Distribution Spot Image/Science Photo Library/Science Source; *Chinese flooding* ©CNES, 1998 Distribution Spot Image/ Science Photo/Science Source; *Yunnan rice fields* ©Yann Layma/Stone/Getty Images; *Chinese students* ©Adrian Bradshaw/ Liaison/Getty Images; *Shanghai* ©Mark Henley/Sinopix; *Chinese steelworkers* ©China Photos/Getty Images; *Chinese farmer* ©Keren Su/The Image Bank/ Getty Images; *teen with backpack* ©Jack Hollingsworth/Corbis; *Hui man* ©David Sanger Photography; *monks doing Kung Fu* ©AP Images; *Kazakh yurt village* ©Nik Wheeler/Corbis; *Taipei, Taiwan* ©Wally Santana/AP Images; *Great Wall of China* ©Ilya Terentyev/iStock Exclusive/Getty Images; *Great Wall human cost* ©2010 A&E Television Networks, LLC. All rights reseerved.; *20th century China* ©2010 A&E Television Networks, LLC. All rights reserved.; *Great Wall of China* ©2010 A&E Television Networks, LLC. All rights reserved.

Module 18: *Mt. Fuji* ©Roberto M. Arakaki/International Stock/ ImageState Media; *Silla Crown* ©DEA PICTURE LIBRARY/De Agostini/Getty Images; *Pyongyang, North Korea* ©Tony Waltham/Robert Harding World Imagery/ Getty Images; *Tsukiji fish market* ©AFP/ Getty Images; *Great Buddha* ©age fotostock/Superstock; *Emperor Hirohito* ©Bettmann/Corbis; *Japanese bride & groom* ©R. Creation/amanaimages/ Corbis; *Tokyo subway station* ©Chad Ehlers/Alamy; *capsule hotel in Tokyo* ©Barry Lewis/Alamy; *Sundai tsunami* ©Alamy Images; *Deoksugung Palace* ©Alayne Benson; *South Korean dancers* ©David Gray/Reuters/Corbis; *war damaged Seoul* ©Photo Researchers/Science History Images/Alamy; *traffic Seoul* ©ponsulak/iStockPhoto.com; *President Moon Jae-In* ©Korean Government/Alamy; *pro-Park camp* ©Alayne Benson; *Seoul* ©Jeremy Woodhouse/Digital Vision/ Getty Images; *North Korea* ©David Hume Kennerly/Hulton Archive/Getty Images; *South Korean rally* ©Cho-Yong-soo/Reuters/Corbis; *Samurai* ©Burstein Collection/Corbis; *Death of Samurai* ©2010 A&E Television Networks, LLC. All rights reserved.; *rise of Samurai class* ©2010 A&E Television Networks, LLC. All rights reserved.; *Samurai Warrior* ©2010 A&E Television Networks, LLC. All rights reserved.

Module 19: *Shwedagon Pagoda* ©Christophe Loviny/Corbis; *Thailand* ©Ron Dahlquist/Photodisc/Getty Images; *Balinese dancers* ©Dallas and John Heaton/Free Agents Limited/ Corbis; *Halong Bay* ©Carson Ganci/ Alamy; *Mekong River* ©Kittiphan/ Fotolia; *Rafflesia flower* ©Louise Murray/ Robert Harding Picture Library; *orangutans* ©age fotostock/Superstock; *tsunami* ©AFP/Getty Images; *buddhist monks* ©Kevin R. Morris/Corbis; *Aung San Suu Kyi* ©Alison Wright/Corbis; *Bangkok, Thailand* ©Maxine Cass; *woman carries salt* ©John W. Banagan/Lonely Planet Images; *man taps rubber tree* ©Paul Almasy/Corbis; *rubber tree* ©Neil Rabinowitz/Corbis; *Singapore* ©Shoot PTY/Taxi/Getty Images; *traffic jam* ©Bruno De Hogues/Photographer's Choice/Getty Images

Module 20: *Ayers Rock* ©Catherine Karnow/Corbis; *Sydney Opera House* ©age fotostock/Superstock; *moia statues* ©Kevin Schafer/Corbis; *Australian outback* ©Oliver Strewe/Lonely Planet Images; *New Zealand coast* ©Richard Hamilton Smith/Corbis; *rugby* ©Daniel Berehulak/Reportage/Getty Images; *Auckland Harbor* ©Corbis; *Waipio Valley, Hawaii* ©Digital Vision/Getty Images; *Bora Bora* ©David Alan Parker/ ImageState Media; *dancers in Vanuatu* ©Richard I'Anson/Lonely Planet Images; *emperor penguins* ©David Tipling/Photodisc/Getty Images; *icebergs* ©Digital Vision/Getty Images; *Ernest Shackleton* ©Hulton-Deutsch Collection/ Corbis; *Roald Amundsen* ©Bettmann/ Corbis; *Antarctica* NASA

Regional Atlas Maps: *Dead Sea* ©Steve Vidler/Superstock; *Mount Kilimanjaro* ©Sharna Balfour/Gallo Images/Corbis; *Mount Everest* ©Alison Wright/Science Source; *Great Barrier Reef* ©Daniel Osterkamp/Flickr/Getty Images; *Flags* ©Image Club/Getty Images

Text Credits

Excerpt from "Charter of the United Nations." Text copyright © the United Nations. Reprinted by permission of the United Nations.

Excerpt from "Clots of Blood" from *The Koran,* translated with notes by N. J. Dawood. Text copyright © 1956, 1959, 1966, 1968, 1974, 1990, 1993, 1997, 1999 by N. J. Dawood. Reprinted by permission of Penguin Books, Ltd.

Excerpt from "A Conversation with Lee Kuan Yew" by Fareed Zakaria *from Foreign Affairs Quarterly,* March/April 1994. Copyright © 2004 by Council on Foreign Relations. Reprinted by permission of Council on Foreign Relations.

Excerpt from Matthew 5: 1-16 from *The New Revised Standard Version of the Bible.* Copyright © 1989 by the Division of Christian Education of the National Council of the Churches of Christ in the USA. Reprinted by permission of National Council of the Churches of Christ in the USA. All rights reserved.

Excerpt from "Quit India" Speech by Mohandas Gandhi. Reprinted by permission of the Navajivan Trust India.

"Taiwan: War Bill a Big Provocation" from *CNN.com,* March 14, 2005. Text Copyright © 2005. Reprinted by permission of PARS International.